Collecting
TOYS

IDENTIFICATION AND VALUE GUIDE

EDITION NO.8

Richard O'Brien

Published by

krause publications

700 E. State Street • Iola, WI 54990-0001
Telephone: 715/445-2214

Please call or write for our free catalog. Our toll-free number to place an order or obtain a free catalog is 800-258-0929 or please use our regular business telephone 715-445-2214 for editorial comment and further information.

ISBN: 0-89689-123-2
Printed in the United States of America

CONTENTS

Alphabetical Listings

Sections

COMPANY HISTORIES

COMPANY HISTORIES (CONT.)

List of Cover Photos

Seven Dwarfs, all, Seiberling Rubber, 1938, 5-1/2" high. Photo by Stan Alekna.

Pluto, "Wise Pluto." Photo by Don Hultzman.

HARTLAND No. 804 Sgt. Lance O'Rourke. Photo by Gary J. Linden.

"49-ER." Photo by Charles W. Best.

PEZ. Left to right: Pear, Pineapple, Orange. Courtesy Barry Koester.

PEZ. Left to right: Wolfman, Creature from Black Lagoon, Frankenstein. Courtesy Barry Koester.

WILKINS Aerial Fire Wagon, cast iron, 3 horses, driver, 43" long. Photo by Jeanne Bertoia. Courtesy Bill Bertoia Auctions.

HUBLEY HM28. Photo by Kent M. Comstock.

TOOTSIETOY No. 5105 Kayo Ice Wagon (articulated version) from 1932 Tootsietoy Funnies Series. John Gibson Collection. Photo by John Gibson.

"Gypsy Fortune Teller." Courtesy Don Hultzman.

TPS "Champ On Ice Bear Skater Trio." Photo by Ron Chojnacki. Courtesy Don Hultzman.

CHEIN Handstand Clown (variation). Photo by Scott Smiles.

SCHOENHUT Humpty Dumpty Circus with banners for a side show. Auctioned in overall excellent condition in 1995 for $8250. The tent is 27" high. Photo by Jeanne Bertoia. Courtesy Bill Bertoia Auctions.

KILGORE "TAT," largest Kilgore plane. Photo by Jeanne Bertoia. Courtesy Bill Bertoia Auctions.

Acknowledgments

Once again, a number of knowledgeable collectors have pitched in to make this book a far more expert one than I could have achieved alone. And once again it's been a pleasure dealing with all of them, and once again I'm deeply grateful.

Gramercy, then, to longtime friend Jim Harmon, whose expertise and talent are equally impressive; to Dick Mac-Nary, who may be the fastest man in the world at meeting a deadline; to Barbara and Jonathan Newman for coming through once again; and to Don Hultzman, who is as industrious as he is multifaceted. Kudos, too, to his pal Ron Smith, who is also fast, industrious, and a great photographer.

Jim and Patsy Carlson again weighed in cheerfully, as did Bill Bertoia, the always-willing and ever-energetic Barry Goodman, Dave Leopard, Joe and Sharon Freed (the last three now also authors of their own books), Thomas G. Nefos, David Welch, Mary Brett, Randy Welch, Jim Buskirk, Richard Leach, Mark McManus, Kent Comstock, John Gibson, Aaron Roy, and Raymond V. Brandes.

Photos are a very important part of this book, and thus I'm also grateful to the following, whether they contributed a slew or just a single gem: Jeanne and Bill Bertoia of Bill Bertoia Auctions, Dana Hawkes of Sotheby's, Timothy Luke of Christie's East, John Gibson, Tim Oei, Don Hultzman, Ron Chojnacki, Bob Stevens, Aaron Roy, Randy Welch, Stan Alekna, Bob and Alice Wagner, Bill Conover, Albert W. Lane, James Apthorpe, Charles D. Richards, Joe and Sharon Freed, Ray Haradin, Kent M. Comstock, Barry Goodman, Dave Leopard, Thomas G. Nefos, Scott Smiles, Al Smith, Ann Spivak, and John Monteleone (who also contributed a history of Woodhaven). Thanks too to Jeffrey L. Hubbard, who once again contributed his knowledge of Nylint. No doubt I've forgotten someone. But that doesn't mean I'm not still grateful.

Finally, thanks to my agent Al Zuckerman, who helped me begin all this, and to Dan Alexander for his continuing courtesy, friendliness, and professionalism.

INTRODUCTION

This hobby continues to look very strong. There seem to be more dealers than ever, more customers than ever, and more books, magazines, and other publications than ever. Some recent trends bear a closer examination.

Oddly, at a time when Warner Bros. and Disney are successfully opening store after store dealing in merchandise spawned by their cartoon characters, the categories of comic character, movies, and Disney have all taken striking dips. I'm writing this at a time when rumor has it that both the current comic book industry and the comic book secondary market are in serious trouble. Investors in the toy area might want to keep a careful watch on these categories to see if they're simply momentary aberrations or if a trend is being set. There are some indications, too, that prices of cast-iron toys, aside from banks, may be softening, perhaps because the generation to whom they have the most sentimental value is beginning to decline. On the other hand, though their collectors long ago predicted a falloff by now, dimestore toy soldiers still increase nicely in value. Radio premiums, moribund a few years ago, continue their startling increase, though not as staggeringly as in the last edition. Mechanical banks, to a large extent a province of the wealthy, continue to illustrate that the rich will always be with us and their toys become ever more expensive.

There are some structural differences in this edition. James Theobald's section on German composition civilian figures, planned as a one-time feature in the seventh edition, is no longer in this book. But for any who are disappointed, cheer up—toy soldier collectors enjoyed his contribution so much I've moved it into *Collecting Foreign-Made Toy Soldiers* (a companion book to *Collecting American-Made Toy Soldiers,* Edition 3), which should be in bookstores in the spring of 1997. Also missing is Jim Schleyer's section on Western-style guns. Jim decided to do his own book on the subject and it is out now too, also under the imprint of Books Americana.

If I've made any collectors of cast iron forlorn, take heart. An interesting development in that area occurred at Bill Bertoia's Fall Harvest auction in late 1994. Eight mint cast-iron reproductions that Sears had offered in the 1960s—among them a ladder wagon, a four-door sedan, and an Uncle Sam nodder wagon, the kind of thing that "real" collectors would have sneered at not so long ago—sold for an eye-opening $3500.

Once again, let me remind everyone that when it comes to prices, this book must be thought of as a *guide,* and not as the absolute last word on the price of a toy. Prices may inflate or deflate in the months it takes to publish a book. Even on the same day a toy can vary in price, depending on the dealer, the buyer, the geographical area in which it is being sold, and whether it is being offered in the first expectant rush of a toy show or in its last draggy minutes, when the dealer finds himself confronted with having to pack up all that stuff again. Employed by itself, *Collecting Toys,* Edition 8 should at least prevent serious mistakes from being made. Used with the assistance of a few current prices found in ads, lists, or on dealer tables, it can get the prospective buyer or seller much nearer to the current (always fuzzily defined) market price. Just a reminder: **the numbers listed under the various condition categories (usually C6 - C8 - C10, but not always) are the amounts, in U.S. dollars, the toys are worth**.

Finally, for those who wish to consider this field as an investment (and over the years it has been a very good one), it should be stressed that mint or near-mint conditions provide considerably more financial safety than any of the other conditions, as this is the only category sure to attract all collectors and dealers of any particular toy.

Richard O'Brien
January 1997

CONDITION CODE:

C6   Good; evident overall wear, well played with but acceptable to many collectors
C8   Very Good; minor overall wear, very clean
C10   Mint; like new
Note: Mint in Box commands a higher price. Condition below C6 brings considerably lower prices.

VEHICLES

(Also see Tin Wind-Up)

The average mint price of vehicles in the last edition was $590.17. In this edition it is $610.62, an increase of 3%.

CAST-IRON AUTOMOTIVE TOYS

by C.B.C. Lee

The manufacture of cast-iron toys began shortly after the Civil War and had about reached its zenith by the beginning of the twentieth century. The first toy automobiles began to appear soon after their real-life prototypes began chugging along the horse-carriage roads, by which time some of the great nineteenth century toy makers had already gone out of business. Among those that continued into the automotive era were Hubley, Dent, Wilkins, and Kenton. During the first three decades of this century, others came to the forefront, such as Arcade, Kilgore, A.C. Williams, and Champion. Others also made toy cars and trucks in smaller numbers or for a short period of time, such as Grey Iron, Freidag, and North and Judd. Many of these firms made no identifying marks on their toys, and it has only been in recent years that many very familiar toys have been correctly attributed, as catalogues, patents, and old advertisements have gradually come to light. Probably the greatest American toymaker of all was Ives, but this firm is thought to have made only one toy car, a clockwork-driven horseless carriage runabout with figure, measuring 6-1/2" long and 6" to the top of the jockey-cap on the driver.

Value does not have much relationship to either age or size, however, having more to do with scarcity, complexity and nicety of design, detail, and "desirability." As with anything else in a free market, it is simply the rule of supply and demand.

Demand and "desirability" are affected by a number of factors, one of which is nostalgia. As a guide to other factors affecting desirability, there are a few broad, easy clues. Accuracy of scale and proportion, the use of many different cast parts, cast-in or decal logos and details, hand-painting (by the original maker, but NOT by some later child or collector), etc., all enhance the value. In most cases, a 4-inch roadster with a separate chassis, separate nickel-plated radiator and headlights, and a separate cast figure will be worth much more than a 2-piece one with the halves riveted together.

Values are very volatile, both up and down, and may be badly obsolete even by the time this is printed. The lawyers long ago defined the "fair market value" as the price paid by a (knowledgeable) willing buyer to a (knowledgeable) willing seller.

A word of caution: In recent years several American makers have begun to make cast-iron or brass copies of old toys, and more recently many more have been coming in from Taiwan and perhaps other sources. These are marketed as decorator pieces and sell quite cheaply. Many unscrupulous dealers are using these pieces to cheat unwary

Clint Seeley (8/28/27-3/6/84), a New England doctor, used the pen-name C.B.C. Lee when writing about toys, which he did prolifically. He contributed to books and magazines not only in the U.S. but also in England, France, Italy, New Zealand, Australia, and Japan. Seeley was in touch with collectors on five continents. His extensive research on the subject and his generosity in sharing what he'd learned will keep his name alive as long as interest remains in the hobby he so loved.

new collectors. They usually rust them hurriedly and sometimes make other modifications of tip-off parts (axles or screws) to fool the uninitiated. The makers ("Iron Art," "Utexiqual" and others here and abroad) are running an honest enough business, but the dishonest dealers are using the products to turn a quick profit at the expense of naive buyers.

The fakes are usually easy to spot once one has gained a little experience. They are usually held together by a long screw, which is threaded all the way to the hub, as are standard stove bolts in your local hardware store (only a few genuinely old toys are assembled with a screw rather than a long peaned rivet, and the few screws used often had only about a quarter-inch threaded at the tip (the Hubley Packard is an important exception). Modern axles are usually a hollow rolled piece of sheet metal, much like a long shearpin, though a few are rods with threaded ends and sheet metal acorn nuts. The castings themselves are the most dependable giveaway, but require a little experience: a blind man could tell in an instant. The old castings are thinner, lighter, and smoother, the modern ones being gritty, thick, and coarse of detail.

TOOTSIETOYS, DIE-CAST AND SLUSH

by C.B.C. Lee

Die-casting was an outgrowth of the invention of the Linotype machine, introduced at the Columbian Exposition at Chicago in 1893. Samuel Dowst, a trade-journal publisher in that city, began to adapt the type-casting machine to making small promotional miniatures, collar buttons, and so on related to the *Laundry Journal* he also published. By the turn of the century, however, the die-casting business had become his principal business, and he was producing a myriad of small party favors, candy premiums, political items and penny jewelry. Among these were several charms and miniatures of automobiles, trains, and aircraft. By 1911 he produced a small 47mm limousine with free-turning wheels. By 1914 a 77mm Ford touring car was marketed, and a matching pickup truck was made two years later. All three of these stayed in the catalogue until the late 1920s, and the truck as late as 1932. In 1922 a line of doll furniture was developed and named Tootsietoy after Tootsie Dowst, the daughter of the company's president at the time. The name later was used to identify nearly all of the toys the company sold. However, it continued to make items for other buyers, and still makes the metal marker pieces used in the deluxe Monopoly game. Tootsietoys continue to be made today: the current name of the company is the Strombecker Corporation.

As with other collectibles, the value of obsolete toys is not greatly related to age. The oldest Tootsietoys were made in such large numbers and for so long a period that they are not hard to find today. Others, some of which were unpopular in their day, were not sold in great numbers and are rare today. The 1932 Funnies series of six pieces, drawn from the contemporary comic strips, is an example of this. These were made in a boxed set of six, having cams on the axles that imparted action to the figures as the toy was pushed along the floor, and having details and figures hand-painted in up to seven different colors. This boxed set sold for $1.00. The six pieces were also sold in nonaction versions with simple paint for 10¢ each. For reasons hard to understand today, these toys were not popular. Consequently they are very hard to find and are more valuable. Some of the individual pieces must have been better liked by their owners and were played to death or lost, making them even scarcer. So, though all were made in about equal numbers, some are rarer than others. Uncle Walt Wallet in a roadster is the most valuable; Uncle Willie and Mamie in a boat is at the other end, worth about half as much.

In regular production cars, LaSalles and a sort of pseudo-Lincoln have the greatest value, while other Fords, Yellow Cabs, and early Mack trucks are about one-third of that. A 1925 delivery truck, often called "Federal" by collectors, was made in stock versions with legends on the side panels saying: MILK, MARKET, LAUNDRY, GROCERY, BAKERY, and FLORIST. Their rarity is in about that order, MILK being worth the least. This same line of small trucks was also made in small numbers with custom private liveries, and over a dozen such versions with store names on the sides are presently known to exist. There were probably more. These, too, vary in value according to scarcity, the most common being HORSCHSCHILD KOHN & CO. One that had the J.C. Penney logo is worth twice that, and a few might find a buyer at even higher prices.

Other manufacturers also made die-cast toys, and a few of these are desirable enough to have some value. In the late 1930s Barclay made a small series of separate body/chassis vehicles. A West Coast firm, Tip-Top Toys, made products that are also of fair value. So are a few of the finer die-cast Manoils and Eries. Many others are in little demand, such as Jane Francis, Goodie, Metal Masters and It's a Beaut.

Slush casting was a process simple enough to be done in tiny factories and even in home industries during the Depression. A few large manufacturers made toys in this way: most notably Barclay, Manoil, Savoye, Kansas Toy and Novelty, and others, but many were made by anonymous, small, unidentifiable, local operations, using molds made and marketed by a few firms. Many slush-cast toys are of very little value today, but there are exceptions. Foremost among these were dealer promotional replicas of real cars, made by Banthrico and National Products. Other very accurate and detailed slush models, similar in size and scale to the contemporary Tootsietoys, can be valuable. Most notable among these are certain nicely cast models of the Reo Victoria, Packard, Chrysler Imperial, Cord coupe (late 20s), Buick and Model A Ford. These, and others made with an extra mold part resulting in detailed radiator grilles, were made by the Lincoln White Metal Works. Other small accurate replicas, with the names cast on the door sides, were made by Tommy Toy.

As with other toys, condition is very important. Paint wear can drop the value to half, and broken or missing parts can drop it to nearly nothing. Repairing can occasionally partially rescue an exceptionally rare piece, but more often depresses the value. Reproductions are beginning to appear on the market and will also tend to depress the values of the real thing. As with anything else in a free market, cost is largely a matter of supply and demand, both of which can wax and wane cyclically. Let the buyer beware.

RUBBER TOY VEHICLES

by Dave Leopard

For about 20 years (roughly 1935-1955), American kids enjoyed playing with rubber toys and moms were told that these toys would not mar the furniture or floors. Then, almost as suddenly as they came on the market, they disappeared again but left a rich legacy for toy collectors. The Auburn Rubber Company of Auburn, Indiana, was not the first to introduce rubber toys to the American market, but they were no doubt the largest and had the greatest impact on the toy field. After introducing some toy soldiers in 1935, Auburn brought out its first vehicle in 1936: a beautiful coffin-nosed Cord sedan. Today, the Auburn Cord is one of the most highly prized rubber toys and is seldom seen offered for sale.

Auburn followed the Cord with a wealth of vehicles, including trucks, farm tractors and implements, motorcycles, racers, fire engines, military vehicles, aircraft, ships, and trains. In all, I have catalogued about 90 different varieties of Auburn rubber vehicles and I'm sure there are more than that. To my knowledge, 1952 was Auburn's last year of marketing rubber toys exclusively. The 1953 Auburn catalog contained a vinyl motorcycle, which I believe was their first vinyl toy. By 1955 their toy line was mostly vinyl with a few rubber varieties hanging on. The 1956 catalog is exclusively vinyl, except for two rubber fire engines, which were no doubt the last rubber toys to be marketed by Auburn. Auburn continued in the toy business in Auburn, Indiana, and later in Deming, New Mexico, until they went out of business in 1969.

The Sun Rubber Company of Barberton, Ohio, was the second largest producer of rubber toys. Like Auburn, they produced a full line of toys in addition to vehicles, including dolls, balls, and baby squeak toys. I have catalogs that confirm Sun's line of rubber toy vehicles beginning in 1936 and ending in 1955, which pretty well puts them on the same course with Auburn—about 20 years of rubber toys. The Sun 1936 catalog contains a good selection of cars, trucks, and racers. In later years, they added a few airplanes and military vehicles, but unlike Auburn, never produced any motorcycles, ships, or trains. Among the most famous of the Sun Rubber vehicles are the Walt Disney characters: Mickey Mouse and Donald Duck driving a tractor, firetruck, roadster, or airplane. The Disney tractor and firetruck are the only examples of each produced by Sun. By 1955, Sun's catalog line largely consisted of athletic balls, and the Disney toys were included as the only vehicle toys. Sun existed as a company until 1974, but they did not manufacture rubber toy vehicles past 1955. I have catalogued 32 varieties of Sun Rubber toy vehicles, which I believe accounts for all the toys they made.

Auburn and Sun made the vast majority of rubber toys we see today, but there were a significant number of rubber toys made by other companies mostly prior to World War II. Several companies from the rubber industry produced some rubber toy vehicles, including Firestone, Seiberling, Barr, and Rainbow. All of the Rainbow, Barr, and Seiberling toys appear to have been made in 1935-1936, or at least based on real cars from those years. All of the Seiberling or Barr toys I have seen are 1935 Fords. The Firestone toys include a 1935 Ford, a 1936 Ford, and a 1939 Mercury. Rainbows are mostly based on a 1935 Oldsmobile. Some of these toys were mass-marketed via dimestores, just like Auburn and Sun toys were, but some were sold (or given away?) at expositions and exhibits. All of the Firestone toys seem to be marked with some significant event, like the Texas Centennial in 1936. I have catalogued only 14 varieties of toys produced by these four companies.

Many rubber toys were produced as "promotionals" for the automobile industry and are not marked to indicate

Dave Leopard is a retired Air Force Colonel now employed by the State of South Carolina Budget and Control Board, Division of Human Resource Management. Leopard is a collector of small American-made toy cars and trucks and is an authority on rubber toys. He has written his own book on rubber toy vehicles.

who manufactured them. A number of Chrysler, DeSoto, Dodge, and Plymouth vehicles were produced during the mid-1930s as promotionals and are highly prized as collectibles.

A few rubber vehicles were produced as very inexpensive toys, perhaps sold in sets, and can take the form of either a solid rubber or hollow vehicle. These toys often had the wheels molded in, so they could not turn. Some of these solid rubber toys are two-dimensional and are referred to as "flat" toys. Although they were originally sold as cheap toys, they are actively sought by collectors and constitute a small but important segment of the field.

The following abbreviations are for the details and variations useful in identification of these wheeled toys (may be found in uppercase or lowercase letters). See especially Kansas Toys, page 75.

HG	horizontal grille pattern		SM	sidemounted spare
HL	horizontal hood louvers		SP	string-pull knob in handcrank area
HO	hood cap, Motometer or ornament		T	external trunk
L	lacquer finish		UV	unnumbered version
LI	landau irons on convertibles		VG	vertical grille pattern
MDW	metal disc wheels		VL	vertical hood louvers
MDSW	metal disc solid "spokes"		WS, W/S	windshield
MDWBT	wheels with black painted "tires"		WV	windshield visor
MSW	metal open spoke wheels		WHRT	wooden hubs, rubber tires
MWW	metal simulated "wire" wheels		WRDW	white hard rubber disc wheels
OW	open windows		WRW	white soft rubber wheels (balloon tires)
RM	rearmount spare tire/wheel			

A.C. WILLIAMS (See Williams, A.C.)

Acme (Chicago)

Acme seems to have produced only two toy vehicles, both in clockwork: a 1903 curved-dash Oldsmobile roadster and a delivery truck with a pressed-steel canopied roof. In 1905 Jacob Lauth, the owner of the Chicago firm, turned to production of the real thing, under the name Lauth-Juergens Co.

	C6	C8	C10
Acme Curved Dash Olds, clockwork, circa 1905, 11" long	525	780	1050

ACME Curved Dash Olds, 11" long. Courtesy Wilkinson Collection, Detroit Antique Toy Museum.

Acme (New York)

Many Acme vehicles are exactly like Thomas Toys. The reason is that New York's Ben Shapiro was a financial partner in Thomas Toys, and Thomas Toys' Islyn Thomas made up toys for Shapiro at his request, with the Acme imprint substituted for that of Thomas. Acme was located at 121 East 24th Street in Manhattan.

(End Acme)

	C6	C8	C10
Acme No. 138 Airline Limousine, plastic, 4" long	5.00	7.50	10.00
"Aerocar PT 560 Made in U.S.A. Plas-Tex," 7-1/2", plastic	30	45	60

ALL AMERICAN TOY COMPANY

All American was founded by Clay Steinke in Salem, Oregon, about 1948. It continued until 1955, in its location at the Jorgenson Building on Ferry Street. At its peak it employed 42 people and in its existence sold a total of 26,000 toys. Their most popular toy was the Timber Toter, despite its formidable 1950 price of twenty dollars. Bill Hellie purchased the defunct company: molds, dies, and parts. All American now sells parts and is producing new limited editions (see Leading Collectors and Dealers).

	C6	C8	C10
All American C-5 Cattle Liner, 38" long	500	800	1150
All American CL-8 Cargo Liner, 38" long	470	705	940
All American D-3 Dyna-Dump, 20" long	295	445	590
All American Hay Feed and Grain..................	275	410	550
All American HD-6 Play-Loader, 11" long	No Price Found		
All American HD-7 Play-Dozer, 9" long	338	505	675
All American HH-9 Heavy Hauler, 38" long ..	475	710	950
All American L-2 Timber Toter, with logs, 38" extended length	275	415	555
All American LJ-4 Timber Toter, Jr., with lumber, 20" long	212	318	425
All American MS Midget Skagit, battery-powered, 18" long	300	450	600
All American S-1 Scoop-a-Veyor, 16" long ...	237	355	475
All-Nu "Field Kitchen," slush lead, "Made In USA," approx. 2-1/2" long	No Price Found		
All-Nu Searchlight, "Made In USA," slush lead, approx. 2-3/4" long	No Price Found		
All-Nu Sound Detector, "Made In USA," slush lead, approx. 2-3/4" long	No Price Found		
All-Nu Tank "USA," "Made In USA," slush lead, 3" long	No Price Found		
American Metal Toys Tank, throwing flame, flame touching hull	40	60	80
American Metal Toys Tank, throwing flame, flame not touching hull	45	67	90
American Metal Toys Tank, throwing flame, "No. 25"	60	90	120
American Metal Toys Tank, "22" on side	50	75	100
American National Army Truck, Mack "Giant," 26-1/2" long	800	1400	2000
American National "Juvenile Auto" dump truck pedal car, red and yellow tin, 57" long	2000	3500	5000

A page from an All American Toy Company catalog.

	C6	C8	C10
American National Packard Coupe, 1920s, steerable front wheels, 54" long	3000	5000	7000
American National Velie, child's pedal car, c. 1918	1600	2500	3400
Animate Toy "Baby Tractor," friction, "patented June 20, 1916"	100	150	200

ALL-NU Searchlight, Field Kitchen, Tank, Sound Detector. (Head of soldier missing on Field Kitchen.) Photo by Bill Kaufman. Courtesy Evelyn Besser.

ANIMATE TOY "Baby Tractor," c. 1916. Courtesy Good Old Days Store. Photo by Bill Kaufman.

ARCADE MANUFACTURING COMPANY

by C.B.C. Lee

(Based on information from Dave Davison)

In 1869 a foundry in Freeport, Illinois, was organized as a two-man partnership under the name of Novelty Iron and Brass Foundry. It was dissolved in 1885 when a new, larger factory was incorporated under the name of Arcade Manufacturing Co. Arcade made industrial castings and household items but no toys. After a disastrous fire in 1892 and management changes in 1893, toys began to appear in its catalogue, and by the early 1900s the line had become so extensive that a 50-page catalogue was issued showing a large line of notions and novelties, small stoves, banks and a few trains, including a unique pile-driver. But it was not until an enterprising young lawyer married the daughter of one of the officers and joined the firm in 1919 that the firm rapidly became one of the major makers of cast-iron toys. Struck by the large numbers of Yellow Cabs in the streets of Chicago (my reference doesn't say he was hit or injured by them), the young man approached the Yellow Cab Company with a novel proposition: in return for the sole right to make toy replicas of the cab, the Yellow Cab Company would have the exclusive right to use the toy in its advertising. Success was instantaneous.

Arcade went on to duplicate this pattern with miniature Buicks, Chevrolets, Ford cars, McCormack-Deering and Harvester farm equipment, and several makes of trucks and buses. Arcade's slogan, "They look real," was well justified by its products. In the booming 1920s the company's sales swelled so much that a new and larger plant was built in 1927. Two years later, the stock market crash heralded the Great Depression, and hard times hit the small car business just as it did the large ones.

Cheap competition and dwindling demand for toys costing more than a dime had brought the company to the brink of bankruptcy by 1933. But once again the enterprising management gave the firm new life with an exclusive arrangement to provide souvenir replicas of the fairground buses made by G.M.C. for the Chicago Century of Progress. The Depression caused a cheapening of quality, but WWII gave the firm business in military material.

After the war, the company returned to making industrial and household hardware and a few toys, but cheaper toys of die-cast zamac, plastic, rubber and lithographed tin eclipsed the costlier cast-iron toys. In 1946 the firm was sold to Rockwell Manufacturing Co. of Pittsburgh. Death and retirement soon finished the change of the old firm, and it followed its guiding directors into oblivion when Rockwell moved to Alabama.

Though the source is gone, the toys live on in collections across the land. Arcade is a prestigious name exceeded by none in cast-iron automotive toys and approached by very few of its old competitors. No serious collection of cast-iron toy cars, trucks, buses, or farm and construction equipment can pretend to be representative without its inclusion.

Note: The year noted is the year the toy was introduced.

	C6	C8	C10
(AR1) A.C.F. Bus, 1927, 11-1/2" long	2100	3400	4600
(AR2) Allis-Chalmers Tractor and Trailer, 1936, No. 2650, total length 13" long	175	265	355
(AR3) Allis-Chalmers Tractor and Dump Trailer, 1937, No. 2657, 12-3/4" long with trailer	230	345	460
(AR3A) Allis-Chalmers Tractor and Dump Trailer, 1937, No. 2660, 8-1/4" long	115	175	230
(AR4) Allis-Chalmers Tractor Trailer, 1937, No. 2650, 13" long w/ trailer	112	170	225
(AR5) Allis-Chalmers "WC" Tractor, 1941, 7-3/4" long	250	400	540
(AR6) Ambulance, 1932, No. 187, 7-3/4" long	700	1050	1400

	C6	C8	C10
(AR7) Ambulance, 1932, No. 188, 6" long	370	550	740
(AR8) Ambulance, 1936, (white-painted version of No. 2620X Chevrolet Panel Delivery Truck), 4" long	340	510	680
(AR9) Anthony Dump Truck, 1927, 8-1/8" long	1100	1700	2400
(AR10) Austin Autocrat Road Roller, 1928, No. 291, 7" long	312	468	625
(AR11) Austin Delivery Truck, 1932, No. 173, 3-3/4" long	50	75	100
(AR12) Austin Racer, 1932, No. 175X, 3-3/4" long	65	100	135

ARCADE AR4. Courtesy Dick & Nancy Dice.

ARCADE AR10. Courtesy Mapes Auctioneers & Appraisers.

	C6	C8	C10

(AR13) Austin Roadster, 1932, No. 174,
3-3/4" long 137 205 275

(AR14) Austin "Roll-A-Plane," 8" long 450 675 900

(AR15) Austin Stake Truck, 1932,
No. 176X, 3-3/4" long 150 225 300

(AR16) Austin Wrecker, 1932, No. 177X,
3-3/4" long 150 225 300

(AR17) Avery Tractor, 1923, stack, no hood,
4-1/2" long 30 45 60

ARCADE AR22. Courtesy James S. Maxwell/Virginia Caputo.
Photo by Virginia Caputo.

ARCADE AR17. Photo by Orville C. Britton.

ARCADE AR23.
Courtesy Phillips
New York.

(AR18) Avery Tractor, 1926, has hood,
no stack, 4-1/2" long 200 300 400

(AR19) Borden's Milk Bottle Truck,
1936, No. 2640X, 6-1/4" long 1000 1500 2500

(AR20) Brinks Express Truck, 1932, 11-3/4"
long, auctioned in excellent, 1994, for $20,000

(AR21) Buick Coupe, 1927, 8-1/2" long 2500 4000 5400

ARCADE AR21. Courtesy Phillips New York.

(AR22) Buick Sedan, 1927, 8-1/2" long 2800 4500 6000

(AR23) Bus, Double-Decker, 1929,
No. 316X, 8-1/2" long 525 800 1100

(AR24) Bus, Double-Decker, 1936,
No. 317, "Chicago Motor Coach"
stamp, 8-1/4" long 450 675 900

(AR25) Car Carrier, 1931, No. 238, cargo
has four 25¢ cars or three 50¢ cars,
24-1/2" long 1500 2500 3400

	C6	C8	C10

(AR26) Car Carrier, 1932, No. 296, carries
either 2 No. 114 Ford sedans and one
113X Ford Coupe, or one No. 213 Ford
Stake Truck and one each of the others,
24-1/2" long 1400 2250 3400

(AR27) Car Transport, 1937, No. 3107,
came with 2 No. 1501 sedans, No. 1502
stake truck and No. 1503 wrecker,
18-1/2" long 900 1350 1800

(AR28) Car Transport, 1937, No. 2977,
holds 2 sedans, 2 trucks, 11-1/2" long 427 640 855

(AR29) Carry Car Truck and Trailer Set,
1934, No. 2970, carries three Austins
14-1/4" long 650 1000 1500

(AR30) Caterpillar Tractor, 1930,
No. 271, 7-1/2" long 550 900 1300

(AR31) Caterpillar Tractor, 1931,
No. 269X, 6-7/8" long 650 1100 1550

(AR31A) Caterpillar Tractor, 1931,
No. 268X 5-5/8" long 550 900 1250

(AR32) Caterpillar Tractor, 1931,
No. 267X, 3-7/8" long 250 375 500

(AR33) Caterpillar Tractor, 1931,
No. 266X, 3" long 25 38 50

(AR34) Caterpillar Tractor, 1936,
No. 270Y, later 2700Y, 7-3/4" long 900 1500 2200

(AR35) Century of Progress Bus, 1933,
No. 3200, later No. 3250 (1934),
14-1/2" long 312 470 625

(AR36) Century of Progress Bus, 1933,
No. 3210, 12" long 220 330 440

ARCADE AR37. Courtesy Mapes Auctioneers & Appraisers.

ARCADE Buicks and Chevrolets: on top (left to right) are Chevy 1924 coupe and 1928 sedan and coupe. The latter were later made with double-striping around the waistline, rarer and more valuable. At bottom are the famous Arcade Buicks: sedan and 4-passenger coupe. Photo by C.B.C. Lee.

	C6	C8	C10
(AR37) Century of Progress Bus, 1933, No. 3220, 10-1/2" long	242	365	485
(AR38) Century of Progress Bus, 1933, No. 3230, 7-5/8" long	150	225	300
(AR38A) Century of Progress Bus, 1933, won't pivot or detach, approx. 5-1/2" long	187	280	375
(AR38B) Century of Progress Yellow Cab, 6-1/2" long	500	750	1000
(AR39) Checker Cab, 1923, paint variation of No. 1 Yellow Cab, 9" long	2500	4200	6250
(AR40) Checker Cab, 1932, No. 157, (came with and without "Checker" on visor), 9-1/4" long	5000	8000	12000+
(AR41) Chevrolet Coupe, 1929, No. 121X, 8-1/4" long	1000	1600	2235

ARCADE made other brands of cars and trucks. Top, left to right: 1922 Dodge coupe; 1931 Reo Royal coupe, 9-1/4"; Mack high-lift coal truck, one of a very large range of various trucks. Bottom, left to right: Yellow panel truck; White panel delivery; and International-Harvester panel truck. Each of these vans was issued in various private liveries, the best known being the I-H Hathaway Bakery, which was done in versions using either decal transfers or colored rubber stamping. Photo by C.B.C. Lee.

ARCADE AR41. Courtesy James S. Maxwell/Virginia Caputo. Photo by Virginia Caputo.

	C6	C8	C10
(AR42) Chevrolet Coupe, 1934, rumble seat, No. 1150X, 4-3/8" long	155	232	310
(AR43) Chevrolet Panel Delivery Truck, 1936, No. 2620X, 4" long	125	188	250
(AR44) Chevrolet Sedan, 1929, No. 122X, 8-1/4" long	1000	1600	2200
(AR45) Chevrolet Sedan, 1934, No. 1170X, 4-1/4" long	50	75	100
(AR46) Chevrolet Stake Truck, 1925, 9" long	1050	1700	2300
(AR47) Chevrolet Stake Truck, 1936, No. 2610, 4-1/4" long	No Price Found		
(AR48) Chevrolet Superior Roadster, 1925, 7" long	1100	1800	2500
(AR49) Chevrolet Superior Sedan, 1925, 7" long	415	625	835

	C6	C8	C10
(AR50) Chevrolet Superior Touring Car, 1925, 7" long	700	1100	1600
(AR51) Chevrolet Utility Coupe, 1925, 7" long	395	600	790
(AR52) Chevrolet Wrecker Truck, 1936, No. 2630X, 4-1/4" long	150	225	300
(AR53) "Chief" Fire Chief Coupe, 1934, No. 1230, 6-3/4" long	1500	2500	3400
(AR54) "Chief" Fire Chief Coupe, 1934, No. 1240, 5" long	500	800	1100

ARCADE AR46. Courtesy Lloyd W. Ralston Auctions.

	C6	C8	C10
(AR55) "Coast to Coast GMC" Transcontinental Bus, 1937, No. 4378X, 9" long 212	320	425
(AR56) Corn Harvester, 1939, No. 702, 6-1/2" long 200	300	400
(AR57) Corn Harvester, 1939, No. 4180, 5" long 150	225	300
(AR58) Corn Planter, 1939, 4-1/2" long 62	93	125
(AR59) Coupe, "1922" on spare tire, 9" long 1500	2500	4000
(AR60) Coupe, like above, no 1922 date on spare........................ 850	1275	1700
(AR61) Coupe, 1932, No. 109, no Arcade markings, rumble seat opens, 6" long........ 262	395	525
(AR62) Deluxe Sedan, 1941, No. 1590X, same as Yellow Cab No. 1590Y, but with top lights and sun roof ground off, 8-1/2" long 500	825	1200
(AR63) DeSoto Sedan, 1936, No. 1460X, 4" long 175	265	350
(AR64) Double Decker Bus, 1939, No. 3180, 8" long 312	470	625

ARCADE AR64. Courtesy Ed Hyers Antique Toys.

	C6	C8	C10
(AR65) Dump Truck, 1936, No. 2320, 4-1/2" long 75	112	150
(AR66) Dump Truck, 1941, No. 3910X, 7" long 300	450	600
(AR67) Dump Truck Trailer, 1931, No. 234, 12-7/8" long 700	1150	1700
(AR68) Dump Wagon, 1923, driver, no cab, 7" long........................ 425	638	850

ARCADE AR68. Driver in photo may be wrong. Courtesy Sotheby's New York.

	C6	C8	C10
(AR69) Express Truck, 1929, No. 207X, 8" long .. No Price Found
(AR70) Express Truck, 1929, No. 209X, 6" long .. No Price Found
(AR71) Express Truck, 1929, No. 214X, 5" long .. No Price Found
(AR72) Fageol Bus, 1925, 12" long 375	525	750

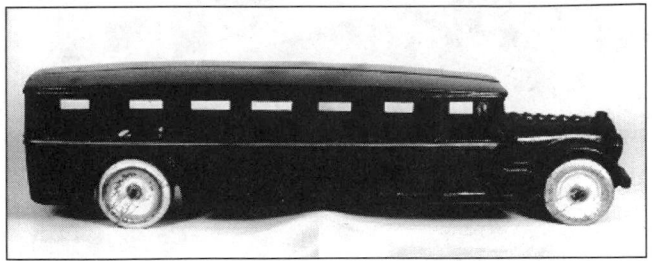

ARCADE AR72. Courtesy Good Old Days Store. Photo by Bill Kaufman.

ARCADE AR73. Courtesy Lloyd W. Ralston Auctions.

	C6	C8	C10
(AR73) Fageol Bus, 12-1/2" long 450	675	900
(AR74) Fageol Bus, 8" long 370	555	740
(AR74A) Fageol Bus, 5" long 162	243	325
(AR75) Farm Mower, 1939, No. 4210X, 4" long.............................. 60	90	120
(AR76) Farmall "A" Tractor, 1941, No. 7050, 7-1/2" long 475	715	950
(AR77) Farmall "M" Tractor, 1941, No. 7070, 7-1/4" long 240	360	480
(AR78) Farmall Tractor, 1929, No. 279, 6" long.................................. 225	338	450
(AR78A) Fire Chief Car, 1941, 5-5/8" long.... 160	240	320
(AR79) Fire Engine, 1923, pumper, 7-1/2" long 250	375	500
(AR80) Fire Engine, 1936, No. 1740, pumper, 9" long 500	785	1150
(AR81) Fire Engine, 1936, No. 1810, 6-1/4" long No Price Found
(AR82) Fire Engine, 1936, No. 2340, 4-1/2" long 90	135	180
(AR83) Fire Engine, 1941, No. 6990, 13-1/2" long 700	1150	1525

ARCADE AR85. Courtesy Mapes Auctioneers & Appraisers.

	C6	C8	C10
(AR84) Fire Ladder Truck, 1936, No. 1820, 7" long 200	300	400
(AR85) Fire Trailer Truck, 1934, No. 1940, ladder truck, 16-1/4" long 600	900	1200
(AR86) Ford Carry Car Truck and Trailer, 1934, No. 2400 .... No Price Found
(AR87) Ford Coupe, 1923, 6" long 175	265	350
(AR88) Ford Coupe, 1924, 6-1/2" long 290	435	580
(AR89) Ford Coupe, 1934, No. 1610X, rumble seat opens, 6-3/4" long 175	262	350
(AR90) Ford Coupe, 1930s, No. 1190X, 4-3/4" long 125	188	250
(AR91) Ford Dump Truck, 1929, No. 219X, 7-1/2" long 285	425	570
(AR92) Ford Express Truck, 1929, No. 210X, 8-1/4" long 700	1100	1550
(AR93) Ford Fordor Sedan, 1924, removable chauffeur, 6-1/2" long 370	555	740
(AR94) Ford Sedan, 1923, 6-1/2" long 325	490	650

ARCADE. Top to bottom: AR96, AR97A. Photo by John M. Ianuzzi.

ARCADE AR94. Courtesy Ed Hyers Antique Toys.

	C6	C8	C10
(AR95) Ford Sedan, 1934, No. 1620X, 6-7/8" long .... No Price Found
(AR96) Ford Sedan, 1934, "Century of Progress," 6-7/8" long 1000	1700	2400
(AR97) Ford Sedan, 1930s, No. 1200, 4-3/4" long 150	225	300
(AR97A) Ford Sedan, 1934, "Century of Progress," 4-3/4" long .... No Price Found
(AR98) Ford Sedan with Trailer, 1937, No. 1970, 12" long (trailer 5-1/2" long) 650	1000	1500

ARCADE AR96. Courtesy Chic Gast.

	C6	C8	C10
(AR99) Ford Stake Truck, 1925, 8-3/4" long 1000	1500	2200
(AR100) Ford Stake Truck, 1927, 9" long 1000	1700	2250
(AR101) Ford Stake Truck, 1934, No. 2010X, 4-3/4" long .... No Price Found
(AR102) Ford Touring Car, 1923, 6-1/2" long 250	375	500
(AR103) Ford Touring Car Bank, 1923, 6-1/2" long 1100	1800	2700
(AR104) Ford Tractor and Plow, 1941, No. 7220, tractor 6-1/2" long, overall length 8-3/4" 550	850	1180
(AR105) Ford Truck, 1923, cab, C-cab, 8-1/2" long 500	750	1000
(AR106) Ford Wrecker, 1929, No. 215, 8-1/4" length to end of hoist 450	680	915
(AR107) Ford Wrecker, 1930, No. 218, 4-1/2" long 125	188	250
(AR108) Fordson Tractor, 1923, 5-3/4" long .. 138	205	275
(AR109) Fordson Tractor, 1928, No. 274, 4-3/4" long 112	168	225

ARCADE AR110. Courtesy Mapes Auctioneers & Appraisers.

	C6	C8	C10
(AR110) Fordson Tractor, 1928, No. 273, 3-7/8" long 55	83	110
(AR111) Fordson Tractor, 1934, rubber shells, No. 2730X, 3-1/2" long 75	112	150

	C6	C8	C10
(AR112) Greyhound Cruiser Coach Bus, 1941, No. 4400, 9-1/8" long 238	238	357	475
(AR113) "Greyhound Lines" Bus, 1937, No. 3850 SP, 7-3/4" long 305	305	455	610
(AR114) "Greyhound Lines Great Lakes Exposition," 1936, No. 437, 11" long 475	475	710	950
(AR115) "Greyhound Lines Great Lakes Exposition," 1936, No. 436, 6-3/4" long ... 420	420	630	840
(AR116) Greyhound Super Coach, 1937, No. 4380, 9" long 250	250	375	500

ARCADE AR116. Courtesy Sotheby's.

	C6	C8	C10
(AR117) "Ice" Truck, circa 1941, No. 1933, 6-3/4" long 270	270	355	540
(AR118) International Delivery Truck, 1932, No. 226, 9-3/4" long 1500	1500	2400	3500
(AR119) International Delivery Truck, 1936, No. 3020, 9-1/2" long 1800	1800	2900	4200
(AR120) International Dump Truck, 1931, No. 236-0, 10-3/4" long 750	750	1200	1750
(AR121) International Dump Truck, 1936, No. 3030, 10-1/2" long 1000	1000	1600	2200
(AR122) International Dump Truck, 1937, No. 3710, 9-1/2" long 475	475	625	950
(AR123) International Dump Truck, 1940, No. 1670, chassis and dump box are steel, 11-5/8" long 700	700	1150	1650
(AR124) International Dump Truck, 1941, No. 7100, 11-1/8" long 600	600	900	1200
(AR125) International Harvester Company Public Utility Truck, 1932, No. 197, 11-1/4" long .... No Price Found			
(AR126) International Pickup Truck, 1941, No. 7000, 9-1/2" long 600	600	950	1280
(AR127) International Stake Truck, 1931, No. 237-0, 12" long 600	600	900	1200
(AR128) International Stake Truck, 1936, No. 3090, 12" long 1000	1000	1500	2000
(AR129) International Stake Truck, 1937, No. 2600, 9-1/2" long 1000	1000	1600	2250
(AR130) International Stake Truck, 1941, No. 7090, 11-1/2" long 1000	1000	1500	2000
(AR131) International Wrecker, 1940, No. 1650, wrecker crane body and crane are steel, 13" long 500	500	800	1100

	C6	C8	C10
(AR132) Ladder Truck, 1936, No. 1700, with ladders 12-1/2" long 475	475	715	950
(AR133) Ladder Truck, 1936, No. 2350, 4-3/4" long 75	75	112	150
(AR134) "Mack" Bus, 1929, No. 318, 13-1/4" long 750	750	1125	1500
(AR135) Mack Cement Mixer, 1931, 6-11/16" long, drum revolves .... No Price Found			
(AR136) Mack Chemical Truck, 1928, fire engine No. 245R, has ladders, 15" long ..2000	2000	3500	5500
(AR137) Mack Chemical Truck, 1929, fire ladder truck, 15" long 800	800	1300	1800
(AR138) Mack Chemical Truck, 1929, fire engine with ladders, 10" long 435	435	655	870
(AR139) Mack Dump Truck, 1925, 12" long 1000	1000	1600	2250
(AR140) Mack Dump Truck, 1929, No. 248X, 8-1/2" long 600	600	950	1350
(AR141) Mack High Dump Truck, 1931, No. 244X, 10" long 1000	1000	1600	2140
(AR142) Mack High Dump Truck, 1931, No. 259X, 8-1/2" long 700	700	1150	1550
(AR143) Mack Fire Apparatus Truck, 1929, No. 242, ladder truck, 21" long 850	850	1350	1840
(AR144) Mack Hoist Truck, 1932, No. 198, body 8" long 900	900	1500	2130
(AR145) Mack Ice Truck, 1930, No. 257, 10-5/8" long 375	375	562	750
(AR146) Mack Ice Truck, 1931, No. 226, 8-1/2" long 450	450	675	900
(AR147) Mack Ice Truck, 1932, No. 257, with driver, glass "ice" and tongs, 10-3/4" long 1700	1700	2800	4000
(AR148) Mack Side Dump Truck, 1932, No. 1960, 9" long 1200	1200	2000	2800
(AR149) Mack Stake Truck, 1929, No. 246X, 12" long 1700	1700	2800	4000
(AR150) Mack Stake Truck, 1929, No. 253, 8-3/4" long 1000	1000	1600	2200
(AR151) Mack Tank Truck, 1925, 13-1/4" long 1000	1000	1600	2200

ARCADE AR151. Courtesy Mapes Auctioneers & Appraisers.

ARCADE AR143. Courtesy Christie's East.

	C6	C8	C10
(AR152) Mack Tank Truck, 1925, "American Gasoline," 13-1/4" long	1200	1850	2500
(AR153) Mack Tank Truck, 1925, "Lubrite," 13-1/4" long	1200	2000	3000

ARCADE AR161. Courtesy Ed Hyers Antique Toys.

ARCADE AR153. Courtesy Sotheby's New York

	C6	C8	C10
(AR154) Mack Tank Truck, 1930, No. 241, sheet metal tank, "Gasoline" "Mack," 13" long	1200	2000	2775
(AR155) Mack Wrecker, 1930 No. 255, 12-1/2" long	1500	2400	3360

ARCADE AR162. Courtesy Ed Hyers Antique Toys.

ARCADE AR155. Courtesy James S. Maxwell/Virginia Caputo. Photo by Virginia Caputo.

	C6	C8	C10
(AR156) McCormick-Deering Farmall Tractor, 1937, 6-1/4" long	250	375	500
(AR157) McCormick-Deering Thresher, 1927, 12" long	500	750	1030
(AR158) McCormick-Deering Thresher, 1930, 9-1/2" long	500	775	1065
(AR159) McCormick-Deering Tractor, 1925, No.10-20, 6-3/4" long	282	425	565
(AR160) Milk Truck, 1931, No. 256, box is wood, 13-5/8" long	No Price Found		
(AR161) Model A Coupe, 1928, No. 116X, rumble seat, 5" long	220	330	440
(AR162) Model A Coupe, 1928, No. 106, rumble seat, 6-3/4" long	500	850	1160
(AR163) Model A Coupe, 1928, No. 113X, 4-1/8" long	125	188	250
(AR164) Model A Fordor, 1928, No. 207, 6-3/4" long	325	488	650
(AR165) Model A Tudor, 1928, No. 108, 6-3/4" long	500	750	1050

	C6	C8	C10
(AR166) Model T Stake Truck, 1927, 9" long	600	925	1250
(AR167) Model T Stake Truck, 1927, 5-3/4" long	130	195	260
(AR168) Model T Wrecker, 1927, 11" long	700	1200	1600
(AR168A) "Mullins Red Cap" auto trailer	225	338	450
(AR169) Nash Wrecker, 1936, 4-1/2" long	250	375	500
(AR170) National Trailways Bus, 1937, No. 3870, 9-1/4" long	750	1300	1700
(AR171) New York World's Fair Bus, 1939, No. 3780, 10-1/2" long	448	675	975
(AR172) New York World's Fair Bus, 1939, No. 3770, 8-1/2" long	332	500	665
(AR173) New York World's Fair Bus, 1939, No. 3750, 7" long	225	338	450
(AR174) New York World's Fair Tractor-Train, 1939, No. 7270, tractor and one car, tractor 3-1/4" long, car 4-1/4" long	245	368	490
(AR175) New York World's Fair Tractor-Train, 1939, No. 7290, same as above with three cars	600	1000	1400
(AR176) Oliver Plow, 1923, 6-1/2" long	250	375	500
(AR177) Oliver Plow, 1941, No. 4230X, 6-1/4" long	138	208	275
(AR178) Oliver Superior Spreader, No. 7140, 1941, 10-1/4" long	No Price Found		
(AR179) Oliver Tractor, 1937, No. 356, 7-1/2" long	338	505	675
(AR180) Oliver Tractor, 1941, No. 3560, 7-1/2" long	90	135	180

ARCADE. Top, left to right: AR171, AR112.
Second row, left to right: AR116, AR37.
Third row, left to right: AR36, AR172.
Bottom row, left to right: AR173, AR38.
Courtesy Sotheby's New York.

ARCADE AR170. Photo by Bob Smith.

ARCADE AR197. Courtesy Phillips New York.

	C6	C8	C10
(AR181) "Plymouth" Coupe, 1934, No. 1340X, 4-1/2" long	300	450	600
(AR182) "Plymouth" Sedan, 1934, No. 1330X, 4-3/4" long	338	510	675
(AR183) "Plymouth" Stake Truck, 1934, No. 1840X, 4-3/4" long	No Price Found		
(AR184) "Plymouth" Wrecker, 1934, No. 1830X, 4-3/4" long	125	188	250
(AR185) Pontiac Sedan, 1934, No. 1350X, 4-1/4" long	162	245	325
(AR186) Pontiac Sedan, 1935, 6-1/2" long	350	525	700
(AR187) Pontiac Stake Truck, 1935, No. 2390X, 6-1/4" long	300	450	600
(AR188) Pontiac Stake Truck, 1936, No. 2780X, 4-1/4" long	No Price Found		
(AR189) Pontiac Wrecker, 1936, No. 2000X, 4-1/4" long	125	188	250
(AR190) Racer, pre-1923, 7-3/4" long	400	600	800
(AR191) Racer, Bullet Racer, 1931, No. 139X, 7-5/8" long	1100	1700	2400
(AR192) Racer, 1931, No. 138X, 6-3/4" long	400	600	800
(AR193) Racer, 1932, No. 140X 10-1/2" long, plastic or celluloid windshield, auctioned in 1994 in excellent condition for $11,500			
(AR194) Racer, 1932, No. 137X, 5-5/8" long	120	180	240
(AR195) Racer, 1937, No. 1440X, 8" long	No Price Found		
(AR196) Racer, 1937, No. 1457, 5-3/4" long	62	93	125
(AR197) Red Baby Dump Truck, 1923, No. 2, 10-3/4" long	600	950	1320

	C6	C8	C10
(AR198) Red Baby Truck, 1923, No. 1, 10-3/4" long	1100	1750	2525
(AR199) Red Baby "Weaver" Wrecker, 1929, 12" long	1000	1600	2230
(AR200) Reo Coupe, 1931, No. 1247, 9-3/8" long	1100	1800	2600
(AR201) Reo Coupe, 1931, smaller size	1000	1700	2300
(AR202) Sand Loading Shovel, 1932, No. 298 (later No. 299)	500	800	1200
(AR203) Scraper, 1929, No. 287, 8-1/4" long	42	63	85
(AR204) Sedan, 1937, No. 1501X, 4-3/4" long	130	195	260

ARCADE AR198. Courtesy James S. Maxwell/Virginia Caputo. Photo by Virginia Caputo.

	C6	C8	C10

(AR205) Sedan and Trailer, 1937,
No. 1497X, car 5-5/8" long, trailer
2-1/2" long 275 415 550

(AR206) Side Dump Trailer, 1932,
No. 290, fastens to trucks or tractors, 7" long No Price Found

(AR207) "Silver Arrow," 1934, 7-1/4" long ... 262 395 535

(AR208) Stake Trailer Truck, 1931,
No. 233, 11-5/16" long 600 950 1250

ARCADE AR208. Courtesy James S. Maxwell/Virginia Caputo. Photo by Virginia Caputo.

(AR209) Stake Truck, 1929,
No. 208X, 6" long...................................... 220 330 440

(AR210) Stake Truck,
1929, No. 213X, 5" long............................. 125 188 250

(AR211) Stake Truck, 1932, No. 208,
no Arcade markings, 6" long 290 435 580

(AR212) Stake Truck,
1937, No. 1502X, 4-1/4" long 108 162 215

(AR213) Steam Shovel, 1932, No. 292
Industrial Derrick, body 6" long 750 1125 1500

(AR214) Tandem Disc Harrow,
1939, No. 704, 6-3/4" long 60 90 120

(AR215) Tank, Army, 1937, No. 400, 8" long 600 950 1325

(AR216) Tank, Army, 1941,
No. 3960, shoots, 4" long 68 105 135

(AR217) Texas Centennial Bus, 1936,
10-3/4" long *(extremely rare)*.................. 1300 2200 3000

(AR218) "Trac-Tractor," International
Harvester, 1937, No. 277, 8-1/4" long 850 1350 1850

ARCADE AR218.

(AR219) Trac Tractor, 1941, No. 7120,
7-1/2" long 1100 1700 2500

(AR220) Unused

(AR221) Unused

(AR222) Tractor, 1941, No. 7200,
6-1/2" long 180 270 360

(AR223) Tractor, 1941, No. 4060X,
black rubber wheels, 6-1/4" long.............. 338 510 675

ARCADE AR219. Courtesy Thomas G. Nefos, National Toy Connection.

	C6	C8	C10

(AR224) Tractor, 1941, No. 7341X,
wood wheels, 6-1/4" long 425 638 850

(AR225) Tractor, 1941, No. 7321X, 4-1/4" long .. No Price Found

(AR226) Tractor, 1941, No. 7260X,
wooden wheels, 3-1/8" long .... No Price Found

(AR227) Tractor, 1941, No. 7240X,
rubber wheels, 3-1/8" long...................... 100 150 200

(AR228) Tractor and Dump Trailer,
1941, No. 7300, 15-1/2" long 600 950 1300

(AR229) Trailer, Farm, 1929, No. 286,
6-3/8" long 40 60 80

(AR230) Trailer, Farm, 1929, No. 288,
4-5/8" long 35 52 70

(AR231) Trailer, Farm, 1929, No. 289,
3-3/4" long 30 45 60

(AR232) Transport Trailer Truck, 1934,
No. 1800, 7-1/2" long 385 580 770

(AR233) W&K Truck Trailer, 1923,
8-1/2" long 80 120 160

(AR234) Two-Wheeled Jack, 1932,
No. 216, 5-1/2" long 30 45 60

(AR235) White Bus, No. 319, 1928,
13-1/4" long 2800 5500 7400

(AR236) White Delivery Truck, 1929,
No. 252X, 8-1/4" long 2000 3000 6000

(AR237) White Moving Van, 1929,
No. 251, 13-1/2" long, auctioned 1994, excellent for $13,200

ARCADE 236. Courtesy James S. Maxwell/Virginia Caputo. Photo by Virginia Caputo.

ARCADE AR237. Courtesy James S. Maxwell/Virginia Caputo.
Photo by Virginia Caputo.

	C6	C8	C10
(AR238) White Dump Truck, 1929, No. 249, 11-1/2" long, auctioned 1994, excellent for $23,000			
(AR239) White Dump Truck, 1931, No. 258X, 13-1/2" long			No Price Found
(AR240) White Tank Truck, 1931, No. 254X, "Gasoline," 14-1/8" long	1000	1500	2000
(AR241) Wrecker, 1929, No. 217, 1928, body 8" long	500	750	1000
(AR242) Wrecker, 1932, No. 225, no Arcade markings	600	950	1350
(AR243) Wrecker, 1934, No. 2020X, 7" long	600	950	1350
(AR244) Wrecker, 1937, No. 1493X, 6-1/2" long	150	225	300
(AR245) Wrecker, 1937, No. 1503X, 4-3/4" long	85	128	170
(AR246) Wrecker, 1941, No. 3900X, 8-1/2" long	170	255	340
(AR246A) Yellow Baby Dump Truck, 1923, 10-1/2" long	1100	2000	3200
(AR247) Yellow Baby Wrecker, 1929, 12" long	650	1100	1600
(AR248) Yellow Cab, 1922, No. 1, 9-1/4" long	600	900	1400
(AR249) Yellow Cab, 1923, No. 2, 8" long	500	800	1200
(AR250) Yellow Cab, 1927, No. 1, 9" long	1100	1800	2400
(AR251) Yellow Cab, 1927, No. 5, 8-1/2" long	425	638	850

ARCADE AR250. Courtesy Wilkinson Collection, Detroit
Antique Toy Museum.

	C6	C8	C10
(AR252) Yellow Cab, 1927, No. 2, 8" long	600	900	1400
(AR253) Yellow Cab, 1927, No. 3, 5-1/4" long	325	485	650
(AR254) Yellow Cab, 1934, Ford Sedan, 6-7/8" long	650	1000	1500
(AR255) Yellow Cab, 1936, No. 1580Y, 8-1/4" long	1800	3000	4100
(AR256) Yellow Cab, 1941, No. 1590Y, 8-1/2" long	500	775	1045
(AR257) Yellow Cab Bank, 1923, 8" long	700	1100	1500
(AR258) Yellow Cab Bank, 1927	850	1400	1850
(AR259) Yellow Cab Panel Delivery Truck, 1925, 8-1/4" long, w/ driver	1100	1800	2500

ARCADE AR259. Courtesy Phillips New York.

ARCADE AR249. Courtesy Sotheby's New York.

ARCADE AR259. Side-mounted tire, original tires
missing. Courtesy James S. Maxwell/Virginia Caputo.
Photo by Virginia Caputo.

ARCADE. "Yellow Cab," 9" long, c. 1928.
Courtesy Mapes Auctioneers & Appraisers.

	C6	C8	C10
(AR260) Yellow Coach Double-Decker Bus, 1925, 14" long	1850	3400	5400
(AR261) Yellow Parlor Coach Bus, 1926, 13" long	800	1400	1900

	C6	C8	C10
(AR262) Yellow Parlor Coach Bus, 1926, 9-1/2" long	325	488	650
Argo Friction Cars, Taxi, Police car each, 3-1/2" long	15	22	30
Argo Friction Cars, Passenger car, Tank each, 3-1/2" long	14	21	28

AUBURN RUBBER

This company also manufactured rubber tires for other companies, including Wyandotte. The following list and its codings were compiled by David Leopard. Vehicles are broken down by types.

AUBURN AA01. Photo by Max Heiss.

AA01 '36 Cord, 4-door coffin-nose sedan, 6" long	65	98	130
AA02 '37 Olds, 4-door sedan, 4-1/2" long	22	33	45
AA03 '38 Olds, 4-door sedan, 5-3/4" long	30	45	60
AA04 '40 Olds, 4-door sedan, open fenders, 6" long	27	41	55
AA05 '40 Olds, 4-door sedan, fender skirts, 6" long	25	38	50
AA06 '48 Buick, 2-door sedanette, fastback, 7-1/4" long	40	60	80
AA07 '39 Buick, Y Job Experimental Roadster, 9-3/4 " long	No Price Found		
AA08 '35 Ford Coupe, 4" long	27	41	55
AA09 '35 Ford 2-door slantback sedan, 4" long	27	41	55
AA10 '50 Cadillac, 4-door sedan, 7-1/4" long	40	60	80
AA11 Unused			
AA12 '39 Plymouth, 2-door trunk back sedan, 4-1/4" long	22	33	45

AA13 '46 Lincoln convertible, 2-door, square headlights, 4-1/2" long	20	30	40
AA14 '46 Lincoln convertible, 2-door round headlights, 4-1/2" long	20	30	40
AA15 Late '40s Futuristic Sedan, fin down back, 5" long	20	30	40
AT01 '37 International Cabover Stake Truck, 5-3/8" long	22	33	45
AT01A '37 Same as above, "US Army" decal, khaki	22	33	45

AUBURN AT01A. Photo by Ed Poole.

AT02 Same as AT01 with rounded bumper, minor variations	22	33	45
AT03 '37 International Cabover Stake Truck, 4-1/4" long	20	30	40
AT03A Same as above, khaki	20	30	40
AT04 Same as above with rounded bumper, minor variations	20	30	40
AT05 '37 International Cabover Stake Truck, 3-3/4 " long	20	30	40
AT06 Unused			
AT07 '37 International Cabover Stake Truck, milk version, 4-1/4" long	60	80	100

AUBURN AA03. Courtesy Dave Leopard, Rubber Toy Vehicles.

AUBURN. Left to right: AA13, AA14. Courtesy Dave Leopard (AA12 and AA13 in his book Rubber Toy Vehicles).

AUBURN. Left to right: AA05, AA04. Courtesy Dave Leopard, Rubber Toy Vehicles.

AUBURN AA15. Courtesy Dave Leopard (AA14 in his book Rubber Toy Vehicles).

AUBURN AA06. Photo by Dave Leopard.

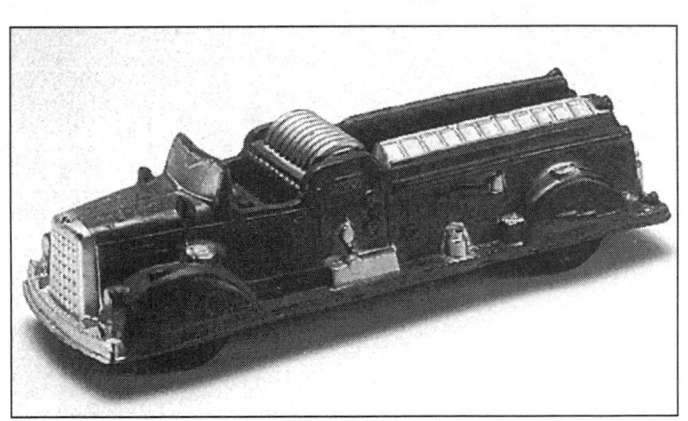

AUBURN AE02. Courtesy Dave Leopard, Rubber Toy Vehicles.

AUBURN AA12. (AA11 in Rubber Toy Vehicles by Dave Leopard.)

AUBURN AF05. Photo by Dave Leopard.

	C6	C8	C10

AT08 '37 International Cabover Stake Truck,
ambulance version .... No Price Found
AT09 Cab-Forward Box Truck,
smooth sides, futuristic, 5-1/2" long............ 22 33 45

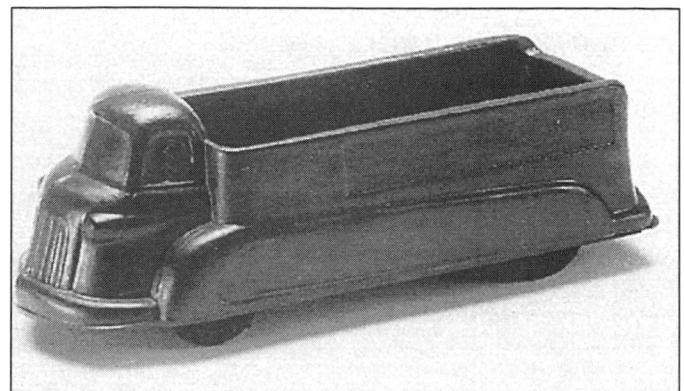

AUBURN AT09. Courtesy Dave Leopard (AT08 in his book Rubber Toy Vehicles*).*

AT10 Cabover Box Truck, smooth sides,
futuristic, 4-1/8" long 20 30 40
AT11 '47 Chevy Cab Forward Box Truck,
5-3/4" long 22 33 45

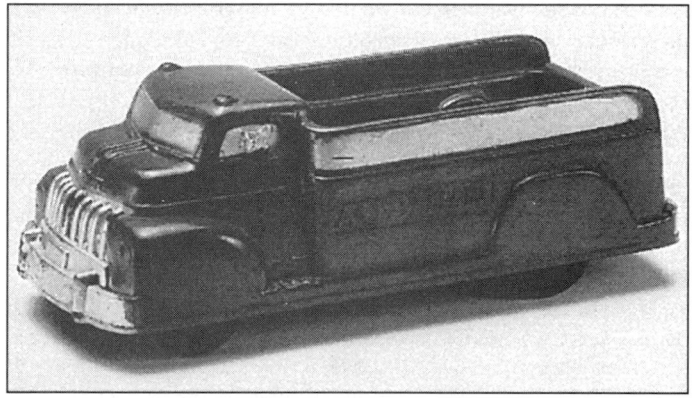

AUBURN AT11. Courtesy Dave Leopard (AT10 in his book Rubber Toy Vehicles*).*

AT12c. '50 Pickup Truck, open fenders,
4-1/2" long 20 30 40
AT13c. '50 Pickup Truck, fender skirts,
4-1/2" long 20 30 40
AT14 '38 GMC "Carry Car" Auto Transport,
11-1/2" long 42 63 85

AUBURN AT14. Photo by Dave Leopard.

	C6	C8	C10

AT15 '38 GMC Cab/Open Squared-off
Trailer, 9" long 42 63 85
AT16 Updated Carry Car Transport,
cab changed, trailer same 11-3/4" long 42 63 85
AT17 Unused
AE01 Ahrens-Fox Fire Engine, 5-1/2" long 75 112 150
AE02 c. 1940s Fire Engine, hose and ladders,
7-3/4" long 27 41 55
AE03 c. 1940s Pumper, Boiler, 7-3/4" long 27 41 55
AE04 c. 1940s Fire Engine, ladders, no hose,
7-3/4" long 27 41 55
AR01 Open Racer, V-6, high fin, 10-1/2" long 55 82 110
AR02 Open Racer, V-6, low fin, 10-1/2" long ... 40 60 80
AR03 Open Racer, short, tapered tail,
large tires, 10-1/2" long 37 56 75

AUBURN AR03. Courtesy Dave Leopard, Rubber Toy Vehicles.

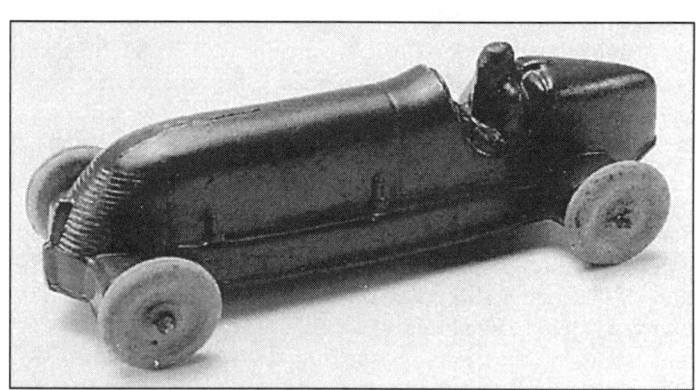

AUBURN AR04. Courtesy Dave Leopard, Rubber Toy Vehicles.

AR04 Open Racer, short, boattail 6-1/2" long ... 27 41 55
AR05 Open Racer, boattail, 4-3/4" long 22 33 45
AR06 Open Racer, small fin, 6-1/4" long 22 33 45
AR07 Open Racer short, boattail, early,
6-1/2" long 35 52 70
AR08 Open Racer, no fenders, low fin,
long back, 5-1/4" long 20 30 40
AR09 Open Racer, boattail, no side pipes,
4-3/4" long 22 33 45
AR10 Open Racer, midget type, early, 5" long...... No Price Found
AF01 Farm Tractor, John Deere "A,"
5" long.. 22 33 45
AF02 Unused
AF03 Farm Tractor, Minneapolis-Moline
"Z," 4" long... 22 33 45

	C6	C8	C10
AF04 Farm Tractor, Minneapolis-Moline "R," early style, 7-1/2" long	37	56	75
AF05 Farm Tractor, Minneapolis-Moline "R," later style, 7-1/4" long	37	56	75
AF06 Farm Tractor, Oliver Row Crop "70," 8" long	37	56	75
AF07 Unused			
AF08 Farm Tractor, McCormick-Deering IH Farmall "M," 4" long	22	33	45
AF09 Farm Tractor, Graham-Bradley, 4-1/2" long	25	38	50
A101 Trailer, 2 wheel, Graham-Bradley, 5-3/4" long	22	33	45
A102 Trailer, 4 wheel, Graham-Bradley, 4-3/4" long	22	33	45
A103 Harvester, open top, 5-1/2" long	27	41	55

	C6	C8	C10
A104 Manure Spreader, David Bradley, 4-3/4" long	20	30	40
A105 Reliable Front-Lift Seeder, 5" long	22	33	45
A106 Plow Seeder, 3-1/2" long	No Price Found		
A107 Side-Cutter Sickle Bar Mower, David Bradley, 3-3/4" long	20	30	40
A108 Two Furrow Plow, David Bradley, 4-3/8" long	20	30	40
A109 Cultipacker (Disc Harrows?), David Bradley, 4-3/8" long	22	33	45
A110 Harrow, 4-1/2" long	20	30	40
A111 Disc Harrows, 4-1/2" long	22	33	45
A112 Unused			
AM01 Tank, Marmon-Harrington, 4-1/2" long	22	33	45
AM02 Tank, Marmon-Harrington, 3-1/4" long	15	22	30
AM03 Tractor and Cannon, olive green, 11-1/2" long	No Price Found		

BANNER

Banner was begun by Emanuel M. Pressner (8/4/1899-1/1/1974) and Bernard Schiller (sp?) in 1945 or 1946 at 150 Bruckner Blvd. in the Bronx, New York. Pressner had been a toy importer before the war. When the war cut off imports, he went to work for Columbia Protektosite, which, among other things, cast Beton's plastic toy soldiers. (Though his family has no recollection of this, in 1942 Pressner was noted in a toy trade magazine as being secretary of Beton.) Schiller was eventually edged out. Banner moved to 80 Beckwith Avenue in Paterson, New Jersey, in 1950, where it remained. The firm's original toys were small plastic cars and trucks, and the leading items for years were tea sets and metalicized plastic forks, knives and spoons. Other items included plastic sand molds. The stamped steel Banner used was made up of "off-falls" -the blanks formed when holes were cut in steel to allow for car windows and television tubes.

The company, which at its peak periods had as many as 200 employees, went into Chapter 11 bankruptcy in 1965, came out of it, and then was sold in 1967 to Tal-Cap, a toy conglomerate in Minnesota. During its heyday, Banner produced at least tens of thousands of toys a week, according to former vice-president Joseph Stern. Banner got its name, according to Stern, because Pressner (his father-in-law) wanted a company with a name "high up in the alphabet."

	C6	C8	C10
Banner American Express Truck, tin, 11" long	90	135	180
Banner American Express Van	50	75	100
Banner "Carnation Milk" Van	163	245	325
Banner Dodge, 1950, plastic, 4" long	5	8	10
Banner Dump Truck, Ford, plastic	17	26	35
Banner Garbage Truck, Ford, plastic, 1954, 4" long	15	22	30
Banner International Harvester Metro 1950 van, plastic, 4" long	12	18	25
Banner Jewel Tea Van	155	232	310
Banner LaFrance Fire Truck, plastic, 1950, 4" long	12	18	25

	C6	C8	C10
Banner North American Van Lines Truck and Trailer, 15" long	110	165	220
Banner Service Station (cardboard) with 3 plastic trucks, c. late '40s-early '50s	25	38	50
Banner Stake Truck, GMC, plastic, 4" long	12	18	25
Banner Station Wagon, 1948, Oldsmobile, plastic, 4" long	12	18	25
Banner Tanker, plastic, 7" long	17	26	35
Banner "Toy Truck" Van, 9" long	59	78	118
Banner Tractor, Wheelhorse, plastic, 3" long	14	21	28
Banner Wonder Bread Truck, c. 1950s, tin litho, 11" long	110	165	220

BARCLAY VEHICLES

Barclay vehicles can be roughly dated by their tires. The earliest are metal. Rubber tires on wooden hubs were introduced about 1934. Around 1936 nail axles began to replace the wooden hubs. Black tires are post-WWII (after 1945).

A number of unmarked vehicles were in the possession of late Barclay-All Nu designer Frank Krupp. Most of these were too early to have been All-Nu and were checked with four early Barclay employees. The number of Xs in parentheses after the toy's description below indicate how many employees thought it had been Barclay. However, it is possible, since these are based on memories of several decades, that not all are Barclay. An X? indicates the employee believed it was Barclay but was not sure. Those not marked with Xs have been identified in other ways.

BARCLAY. Left to right: BV65, BV52. Photo by Bill Kaufman. Courtesy Evelyn Besser.

BARCLAY. Left to right: BV54, BV30, BV81. Photo by Bill Kaufman. Courtesy Evelyn Besser.

	C6	C8	C10
(BV 1) Ambulance, No. 194, small cross, 3-1/2" long	26	39	52
(BV 2) Ambulance, No. 194, large cross, 3-1/2" long	20	30	40
(BV 3) Ambulance, No. 50, 5" long	55	82	110
(BV 4) No. 151 Army Truck with Gun, 2-3/4" long	13	19	27
(BV 5) No. 151 Army Truck with Anti-Aircraft Gun, 2-1/2" long	10	15	21
(BV 6) No. 152 Armored Army Truck, 2-7/8" long	8	13	17
(BV 7) No. 197 Army Tank Truck, c. 1935-36, 3-1/8" long	11	16	22
(BV 8) Army Car with two silver bullhorns, approx. 2-1/2" long (this may be the same as BV 86)	22	33	44

BARCLAY BV8. Photo by Stan Alekna.

	C6	C8	C10
(BV 9) Army Tractor (Minneapolis-Moline "Jeep"), 2-3/4" long	14	21	28
(BV 10) Austin Coupe, c. 1931, No. 43, 2" long	30	45	60
(BV 11) No. 330 Auto Transport Set, 2 '50s cars, 4-1/2" long	36	55	73

BARCLAY. Left to right: BV80, BV10, BV26, BV59. Photo by Bill Kaufman. Courtesy Evelyn Besser.

BARCLAY. Left to right: BV32, BV33, BV41. Photo by Bill Kaufman. Courtesy Evelyn Besser.

	C6	C8	C10
(BV 12) "Beer" Truck, c. 1940, No. 376, wood barrels, 4" long	27	41	55
(BV 13) Beer Truck, No. 377, with barrels	35	52	70
(BV 14) Bus, futuristic, "Made in U.S.A.," 3" long	34	51	68
(BV 15) Cannon Car, gunner low 3-5/16" long	13	21	27
(BV 16) No. 198, Anti-Aircraft Gun Truck, in 1931 Barclay catalog, 3-1/8" long	20	30	40
(BV 17) Cannon Car, slight casting differences from headlight version, 3-1/4" long	19	28	38
(BV 18) Cannon Car, battery-powered headlight, in 1935 catalog, 3-1/2" long	80	130	225
(BV 18A) Same casting as above but with no fitting for bulb	22	33	44
(BV 19) No. 48 Anti-Aircraft Gun Truck, one man, 4" long	22	33	45
(BV 20) No. 48, Anti-Aircraft Gun Truck, two men, 4" long	16	24	32
(BV 21) Cannon Truck, with moveable cannon, 4" long	20	30	40
(BV 22) Unused			
(BV 23) Chrysler Airflow, c. 1936, 4" long	30	45	60
(BV 24) "Coast to Coast" die-cast bus, "Barclay Toy," 2-piece, No. 405, 2-7/8" long	42	63	85
(BV 25) Coupe, 1930s, "Made in U.S.A.," 3" long	12	18	25
(BV 26) Coupe, c. 1935, 2-1/2" long (XXX)	50	75	100
(BV 27) Coupe, 1934, 4-1/4" long (XXX)	40	60	80
(BV 28) Coupe, 2-piece, 1930s, "Barclay Toy," 2-7/8" long	42	63	85
(BV 29) Unused			
(BV 30) Coupe, 1934, 4-1/4" long (XXX)	40	60	80
(BV 31) No. 40 Cord Front Drive Coupe, c. 1931, 3-5/8" long	25	38	50
(BV 32) No. 302 Streamline Car, c. 1936, 3-1/8" long	25	38	50
(BV 33) "Delivery" Truck, No. 309, 2-15/16" long (XXX)	15	23	30
(BV 34) Double Decker Bus, 4" long	60	90	120

BARCLAY. Top, left to right: BV11, BV49, BV14, BV13. Bottom, left to right: BV82, sedan for BV61 set. Photo by Bill Kaufman. Courtesy George Buhler.

BARCLAY BV34 (tires in photo not correct). Photo by James Apthorpe.

BARCLAY. Left to right: BV12, BV13. Photo by Craig A. Clark.

BARCLAY. Top, left to right: Howitzer, 4 wheels, loop hitch horizontal; Howitzer, 4 wheels, loop hitch vertical; BV78 with wire hitch; BV78 with peg hitch. Bottom, left to right: BV7; BV77, peg hitch; BV77, wire hitch; BV76, no hitch. Photo by Ed Poole.

BARCLAY. Top, left to right: BV60, BV63, BV25, BV28, BV71. Bottom, left to right: BV37, BV61, BV55, BV24. Photo by Bill Kaufman. Courtesy George Buhler.

BARCLAY BV45. Courtesy Toy Soldier Review.

BARCLAY BV51. Photo by Craig A. Clark.

BARCLAY. Top, left to right: BV57, BV21 (cannon missing), BV39. Middle, left to right: BV67, BV66, BV70. Bottom, left to right: BV68, BV5, BV69, cannon (4" long, post WWII). Photo by Ed Poole.

BARCLAY BV83. Photo by Ed Poole.

(BV 35) Unused

(BV 36) Unused

(BV 37) "Express" stake truck,
1930s, 2-15/16" long 30   45   60

(BV 38) Fire Engine No. 390?,
moveable ladder, c. 1950s 15   22   30

(BV 39) Field Kitchen, 2-1/4" long 35   52   70

(BV 40) Fire Engine, 2 firemen, black
metal wheels, 1930s, No. 41, 2-3/4" long 17   26   35

(BV 41) Fire Engine, French-looking
(Barclay often copied foreign toys),
4" long (XXX) 17   26   35

(BV 42) Ford, 1931, 2-1/4" long 15   22   30

(BV 43) "Golden Arrow Racer,"
4-1/2" long (X?X) 20   30   40

(BV 44) Mack Pickup Truck, 3-1/2" long 15   22   30

(BV 45) "Milk & Cream" Truck, stamped
No. 377, white rubber tires, 3-5/8" long 81   122   163

(BV 45A) Milk Truck, No. 377, black
rubber tires, 3-5/8" long 22   33   45

(BV 46) Motorcycle with flat rider, full-
dimensional sidecar, No. 55, 2-3/4" long 47   70   95

(BV 47) "Oil-Fuel" Truck,
No. 308, c. 1936, 3-9/16" long 12   18   25

(BV 48) "Parcel Delivery," slush lead,
No. 45, c. 1931, 3-5/8" long 65   98   130

(BV 49) "Police" Car, No. 317,
slush mold, c. 1930s, (Radio Police),
1939 Packard, 3-5/8" long 29   44   58

(BV 49A) Police Car, No. 317,
die-cast, 3-5/8" long 15   22   30

(BV 50) Race Car, 3" long 12   18   24

(BV 51) Racer, closed cockpit, 5-1/2" long 17   26   35

(BV 52) Racer, closed cockpit, c. 1939, 7" long .. 30   45   60

(BV 53) Racer, No. 53, early slush lead,
1920s-30s, approx. 2" long 24   36   48

(BV 54) Racer, two passengers,
4-1/4" long (XXX) 55   82   110

(BV 55) Racer with tail fin,
"Made U.S.A.," 3-1/2" long 17   26   35

(BV 56) Renault Tank, c. 1937, No. 47, 4" long .. 22   33   45

(BV 57) Searchlight Truck, white rubber
tires, c. 1940, 4-1/16" long 87   130   175

(BV 57A) Searchlight Truck, second version 87   130   175

(BV 58) Sedan, 4-door, c. 1936, maybe
Chrysler, 5" long 17   26   35

(BV 59) Sedan, 2-door, c. 1935,
rubber wheels, 3-1/8" long (XX) 37   56   75

(BV 60) Sedan, 2-piece,
No. 401, 2-door, 1930s,
"Barclay Toy" , die-cast, 2-7/8" long 42   63   85

(BV 61) Sedan and "Tourist Trailer,"
"Made in U.S.A.," 1930s, 6-1/2" long 35   52   70

(BV 62) Silver Arrow Race Car, 5-1/2" long 22   33   45

(BV 63) Station Wagon, No. 404,
die-cast, 1930s, 2-piece,
"Barclay Toy," 2-15/16" long 37   56   75

(BV 64) Steam-Roller, traction
type, slush lead with tin roof,
No. 44, c. 1931, 3-1/4" long 30   45   60

(BV 65) Large Streamline Racer, No. 363,
in 1935 catalog, 6-7/8" long 45   68   90

(BV 66) Tank "4562," one man in turret,
3-7/8" long 17   26   35

(BV 67) Tank "4562," two men in turret,
3-7/8" long 21   31   42

(BV 68) Tank T41, 4-1/2" long 15   22   30

(BV 69) Tank, man in turret, die-cast,
black rubber tires, 2-5/8" long 14   21   28

(BV 70) Tank (based on U.S. M2 light tank),
2-1/4" long 20   31   41

(BV 71) Taxi, c. 1940s, slush, 3-1/4" long 14   21   28

(BV 71A) Taxi, No. 318, die-cast, 3-1/4" long .. 50   75   100

(BV 72) Tractor, caterpillar type, slush lead,
approx. 2-5/8" long (XX) 17   26   35

(BV 73) Unused

(BV 74) Trailer Truck variously
"Railway Express," or with Moving
Company name, c. 1950s 5   8   10

(BV 75) Transport Set No. 330, 2 cars, 1960s,
4-1/2" long 25   40   75

(BV 76) U.S. Army Truck, No. 204, no hitch,
red wood hubs, 2-1/2" long 19   28   38

(BV 77) "U.S. Army" Truck, white rubber
wheels, wire or peg hitch, 2-1/2" long 12   18   25

(BV 78) "U.S. Motor Unit" Truck, c. 1940,
white rubber tires, came 3 ways: no hitch,
wire hitch, peg hitch, 3-1/4" long 17   26   35

(BV 79) Wheel-A-Rific speedway track, two
lead racers, black rubber wheels, 10' of
plastic track, sold for $1.00, c. 1970 17   26   35

BARCLAY BV79. Courtesy Toy Soldier Review.

(BV 80) Wrecker, No. 46, c. 1931, 3-1/2" long 22   33   45

(BV 81) Wrecker, c. 1934,
3-15/16" long (XXX) 30   45   60

(BV 82) Wrecker, 2-piece, No. 403,
die-cast, 1930s, "Barclay Toy," 2-7/8" long ... 42   63   85

BARCLAY. Top, left to right: BV15, BV6, BV4, BV9. Middle, left to right: BV56, BV19, BV20. Bottom, left to right: BV16, BV18, BV17. Photo by Ed Poole.

BARCLAY BV88. Photo by Bill Kaufman.

BARCLAY BV90, showing from top to bottom: BV140, BV145, BV144A. Photo by Roger Sanders.

Barclay's chief of maintenance retained 45 plaster castings when he cleaned out the shut-down factory in 1971. In 1984 these were shown to the author in the course of his research. Included were soldiers, Disney figures, vehicles and an autogiro, many never produced. Some of the toys in this photo may now identify previously unmarked vehicles as being made by Barclay.

BARCLAY BV90A. Photo by Perry R. Eichor.

	C6	C8	C10
(BV 83) Cannon Truck, moveable cannon, 4" long ... 37	37	56	75
(BV 84) Milk Truck in shape of bottle, No. 567 ... 162	162	243	325
(BV 85) "Milk" Van Truck, bottle on side, 2-7/8" long ... 20	20	30	41

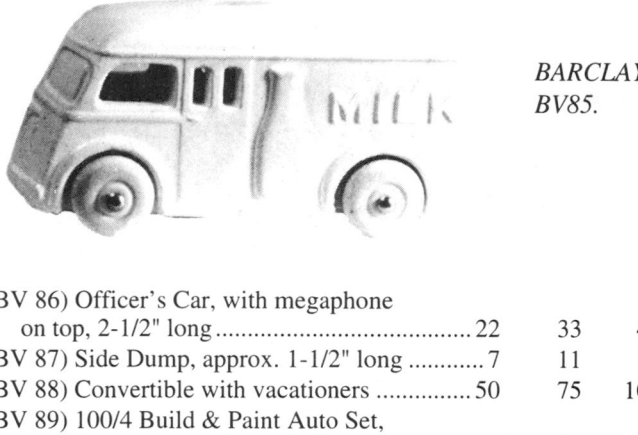

BARCLAY BV84.

BARCLAY BV85.

	C6	C8	C10
(BV 86) Officer's Car, with megaphone on top, 2-1/2" long ... 22	22	33	44
(BV 87) Side Dump, approx. 1-1/2" long ... 7	7	11	15
(BV 88) Convertible with vacationers ... 50	50	75	100
(BV 89) 100/4 Build & Paint Auto Set, 6 vehicles, parts, paints, 1930s ... No Price Found			
(BV 89A) Build and Paint Auto Set, No. 5004, c. 1934 ... No Price Found			
(BV 90) 2004 Build & Paint Set, truck, coupe, sedan, parts, paints, early ... 180	180	270	360
(BV 90A) 2004 Build & Paint Set, same number only 2 vehicles ... No Price Found			
(BV 91) "U.S. Mail" Truck, 1960s, approx. 2" long ... 10	10	17	24
(BV 92) Moving Truck, c. 1960s, approx. 2" long ... 8	8	12	16
(BV 93) Log Truck, c. 1960s, approx. 2" long ... 7	7	11	15
(BV 94) Dump Truck, c. 1960s, approx. 2" long ... 7	7	11	15
(BV 95) Racing Car, c. 1968, approx. 2" long ... 5	5	8	10

BARCLAY. Left to right: BV92, BV93, BV94, BV87. Courtesy Toy Soldier Review.

BARCLAY. Left to right: BV95, BV96, BV97, BV98. Courtesy Toy Soldier Review.

BARCLAY. Left to right: BV99, BV100, BV101, BV102. Courtesy Toy Soldier Review.

	C6	C8	C10
(BV 96) Police Car (like BV86 and BV97), approx. 2" long ... 5	5	8	10
(BV 97) "Chief" Police Car (like BV86 and BV96), approx. 2" long ... 5	5	8	10
(BV 98) Vintage Car, approx. 2" long ... 15	15	22	30
(BV 99) Oil Truck, c. 1960s, approx. 2" long ... 9	9	13	18
(BV 100) Pepsi-Cola Truck, 1960s, approx. 2" long ... 9	9	13	18
(BV 101) Racing Car, c. 1968, no fenders, approx. 2" long ... 5	5	8	10
(BV 102) Volkswagen, 1960s, approx. 2" long ... 12	12	18	24
(BV 103) U.S. Army Truck, c. 1968, approx. 2" long ... 7	7	11	15
(BV 104) Hospital Truck, c. 1968, approx. 2" long ... 9	9	13	18
(BV 105) Army Truck, open bed, c. 1968, approx. 2" long ... 7	7	11	15
(BV 106) Army Oil Truck, c. 1968, approx. 2" long ... 9	9	13	18

BARCLAY BV107. Courtesy Toy Soldier Review.

BARCLAY BV118.

BARCLAY BV117.

BARCLAY BV122.

BARCLAY BV121.

BARCLAY BV123.

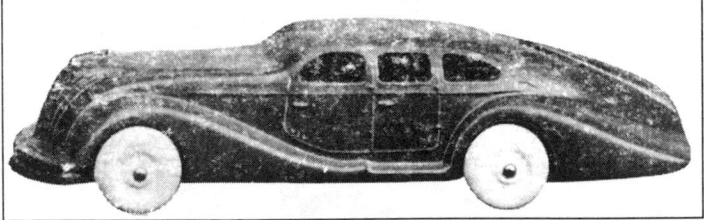

BARCLAY BV124.

BARCLAY BV125.

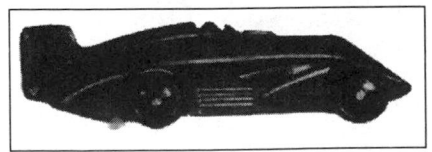

BARCLAY BV126.

BARCLAY BV127.

BARCLAY BV128.

BARCLAY BV129.

BARCLAY BV130.

	C6	C8	C10

(BV 107) Double Transport Set No. 440,
four cars on upper and lower racks, 1960s,
hinged for unloading, 4-1/2" long 72   109   145

(BV 108) 2-door Sedan, 1960s, 1-5/8" long 2   3   5

(BV 109) No. 203 Tractor,
peg hitch, 2-1/8" long 11   16   22

(BV 110) Open Coupe with
driver in cab, early 1930s 15   22   30

(BV 111) "Esso Gas" Truck, 1930s, 5" long 20   30   40

(BV 112) No. 361 Streamline Large Coupe....... 17   26   35

(BV 113) 1935 DeSoto Airflow, 5-3/16" long ... 17   26   35

(BV 114) Car Carrier,
two small cars, early 1930s 25   38   50

(BV 115) No. 371 Racing Car,
large, 1930s, 4-1/4" long 16   24   32

(BV 116) No. 7 Tractor,
c. late 1920s-early 1930s 15   22   30

BARCLAY BV116.

(BV 117) No. 1105 (or 1705)
"Towing Service" Truck, large..................... 82   124   175

(BV 118) 1929 Buick Sedan?, 3" long 27   41   55

(BV 119) No. 312 "Towing" Truck,
in 1936 catalog, 3-3/8" long 17   26   35

(BV 120) No. 306 Racer, in 1936 catalog.......... 15   22   30

(BV 121) No. 303
Streamline Racer, 4-3/8" long 15   22   30

(BV 122) No. 208 Hook and Ladder,
in 1935 catalog, 3" long............................. 16   24   32

(BV 123) No. 301 Coupe Streamline,
3-1/4" long 50   75   100

(BV 124) No. 207 Stake Truck,
in 1935 catalog, 3-1/8" long 39   58   78

(BV 125) No. 362 Streamline
Sedan large, in 1935 catalog...................... 41   61   82

(BV 126) No. 368 Fire Truck, 1930s,
"Fire Dept. No. 99," 5-3/4" long 20   30   40

(BV 127) No. 1703 1935
Chrysler Airflow Sedan, large 17   26   35

(BV 128) No. 42 small Tractor,
in 1931 magazine, 2-3/16" long 12   18   25

(BV 129) No. 39 New Imperial
Chrysler Coupe, c. 1931 15   22   30

(BV 130) No. 5 Racer,
in 1931 magazine, Golden Arrow 15   22   30

(BV 131) No. 206 Delivery Truck "Bakery
Fine Cake Pies," c. 1934, 3-1/8" long 70   105   140

BARCLAY BV131.

BARCLAY BV132.

BARCLAY BV133.

	C6	C8	C10

(BV 132) No. 51 Coupe, c. 1931, 2-3/16" long   17   26   35

(BV 133) No. 210 Fire Truck,
c. 1934, 3-1/8" long 25   38   50

(BV 134) No. 209 Fire Engine,
c. 1934, 3-1/8" long 25   38   50

(BV 135) No. 311 Sedan, c. 1936 21   32   43

BARCLAY BV135.

BARCLAY. Left to right: BV31, BV48, BV43.

*BARCLAY
BV27-
BV110.*

BARCLAY BV136.

BARCLAY BV137.

BARCLAY BV138.

BARCLAY BV139.

BARCLAY BV137A. Photo by Craig A. Clark.

Barclay's trucks in "Bottle" blister packs sell for about $15 in mint. Photo from the Barclay files. Courtesy Toy Soldier Review.

BARCLAY BV141.

BARCLAY. Top, left to right: BV53, BV71, BV49, BV87, BV74. Bottom, left to right: BV46, BV4, BV6, BV68.

BARCLAY BV142.

	C6	C8	C10
(BV 136) No. 309 "Delivery" Truck, c. 1936, 3-1/2" long	12	18	25
(BV 137) No. 50 Fire Truck, c. 1931, 2-3/8" long	22	33	45
(BV 137A) Like BV 137, but with gold hydraulics on both sides, wood hubs, rubber tires, 2-7/16" long	25	38	50
(BV 138) No. 56 Double Decker Bus, c. 1931, 3-1/4" long	22	33	45

	C6	C8	C10
(BV 139) No. 58 Auburn Speedster, c. 1931	17	26	35
(BV 140) Sedan, c. 1934	37	56	75
(BV 141) No. 205 Tow Car, in 1935 catalog, 3-1/16" long	20	30	40
(BV 142) No. 338 Contractor Set, tractor, two hoppers, 1930s, (has hole hitch for wire, unlike BV 109's peg hitch), 6-1/4" long	No Price Found		
(BV 143) Large Streamline Coupe, 1930s	15	22	30

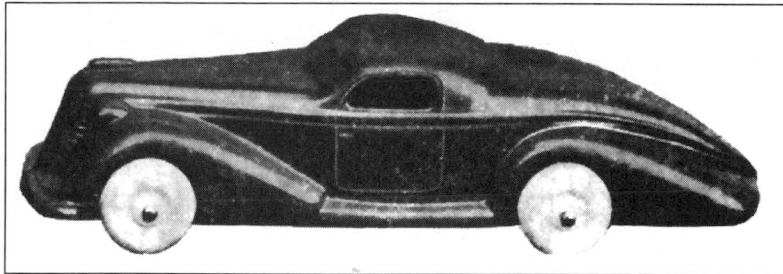

BARCLAY BV143.

BARCLAY BV144.

BARCLAY BV144A.

	C6	C8	C10
(BV 144) "Gasoline" Truck, small, c. 1931, 3 tank top, 2-5/16" long	30	45	60
(BV 144A) Gas Truck, c. 1935, 200 series?, 4 tank top, 3" long	25	38	50
(BV 145) Coupe, cast rear tire, c. 1935, 200 series?, 3-1/8" long	21	31	42
(BV 146) Coupe, removable spare tire, in 1935 catalog, 4-1/2" long	30	45	60
(BV 147) Dump Truck, spring action, ratchet, in 1935 catalog, 4" long	20	30	40
(BV 148) Sport Coupe, removable spare tire, in 1935 catalog, 2-7/8" long	32	48	65
(BV 149) Racing Car, large, raised exhaust pipe, driver, in 1935 catalog	17	26	35
(BV 150) Race Car, open, driver, 4" long	70	105	140
(BV 151) Stake Truck, in 1935 catalog, 4-3/8" long	36	54	72
(BV 152) 2-Car Transport Set, approx. 4-3/4" long	42	63	85

BARCLAY. Left to right: BV148, BV147. Photo by Fred Maxwell.

BARCLAY BV152. Photo by Craig A. Clark.

BARCLAY BV151. Photo by Craig A. Clark.

	C6	C8	C10
(BV 153) 4-Car Transport Set, open-cab Mack Truck, 4 2-1/2" cars, in 1935 catalog, 10-1/4" long	No Price Found		
(BV 154) Roadster, open, driver, dummy spare tire on each side, in 1935 catalog, 4-1/2" long	No Price Found		
(BV 155) Streamline Coupe, in 1937 catalog, 5" long	No Price Found		

BARCLAY BV153. Photo by Dave Leopard.

BARCLAY BV155. Photo by Craig A. Clark.

	C6	C8	C10
(BV 156) "White Horse" Van, (some have sticker reading "Welcome I.C.M.A. compliments the White Motor Co."), approx. 3" long	55	82	110

 # 325 TRAILER TRUCK

 # 339 MINIATURE AUTOS

 # 349 MINIATURE FOREIGN CARS

 # 347 SPORTS CARS

BARCLAY blister pack vehicles, c. 1968. Value is about $25 in mint, except for the No. 339 pack of seven autos, which would go for about $60 in mint. Photo from the Barclay files. Courtesy Toy Soldier Review.

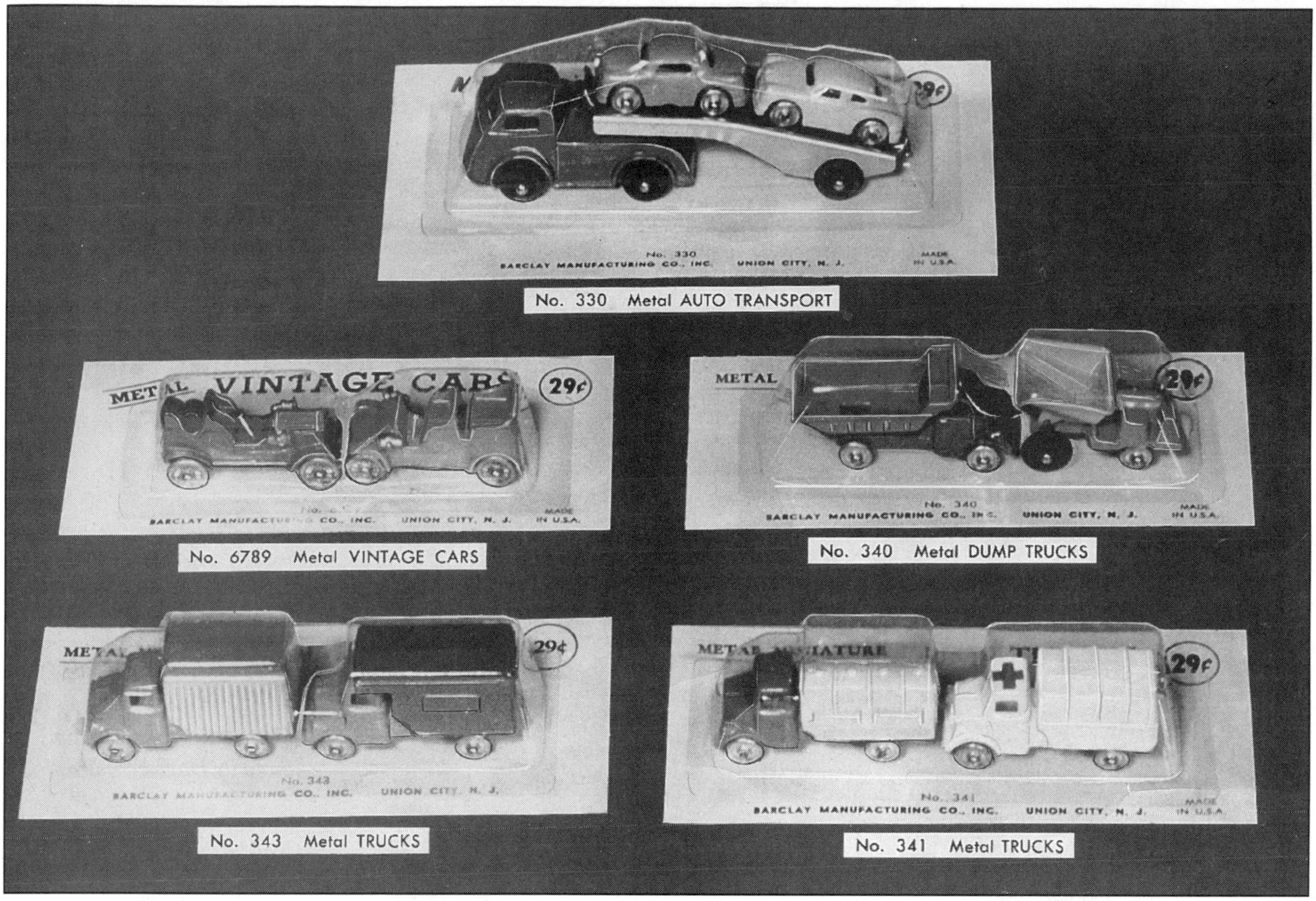

No. 330   Metal AUTO TRANSPORT

No. 6789   Metal VINTAGE CARS

No. 340   Metal DUMP TRUCKS

No. 343   Metal TRUCKS

No. 341   Metal TRUCKS

BARCLAY blister pack sets, c. 1968. The No. 330 Auto Transport (BV75) is worth about $75 in mint. The others are worth about $40 in mint. Courtesy Toy Soldier Review.

BARR RUBBER

Barr Rubber was located in Sandusky, Ohio. The following list, with its codings, was compiled by Dave Leopard.

Vehicles are broken down by type.

BARR. Left to right: BA02, BA01. Photo by Dave Leopard.

	C6	C8	C10
BA01 '35 Ford Coupe, 4" long	27	41	55
BA02 '35 Ford 2-door slantback sedan, 4" long	27	41	55
BT01 '35 Ford Stake Body Truck 4-3/4" long	27	41	55
BT02 '35 Ford Panel Truck/Ambulance, 4-1/4"long	27	41	55
BT03 '35 Ford Army Truck, 4-3/4" long	32	48	65

BARR RUBBER ad from the November 1935 Playthings magazine. Courtesy Playthings.

BARR BT02, both versions. Photo by Dave Leopard.

BARR. Left to right: BT03, BT01. Photo by Dave Leopard.

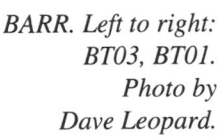

BEAUT MFG. CO.

Beaut Mfg. Co., North Bergen, New Jersey, was founded in 1946 by Eugene Buhler and Irving Reader (former machinist and salesman, respectively) for Barclay Mfg. Co. The company put out five toys: a taxi cab, a police car, a fire engine, a sedan, and a child's wagon. The company was successful at first, employing ten people, and selling to Woolworth's and many overseas buyers. It ceased its toy-making activities (it continued until 1982 as a general machine shop) around 1950 because of competition from plastic toys.

	C6	C8	C10		C6	C8	C10
BEAUT "Fire" car, No. 4, approx. 3-3/4" long	10	15	20	BEAUT "Sedan," approx. 3-3/4" long	10	15	20
BEAUT "Police" car, approx. 3-3/4" long	10	15	20	BEAUT "Taxi," approx. 3-3/4" long	10	15	20

BEAUT "Police" car (left) and "Taxi." Photo by Bill Kaufman. Courtesy George Buhler.

BEST TOY & NOVELTY FACTORY

by Fred Maxwell (Slushmold Contributing Editor) and Margaret Rice with assistance from members of the Best family, Perry Eichor, Kenneth Nudson, and Ferd Zegel

John M. Best, Sr., who founded Best Toy in Manhattan, Kansas, was an entrepreneur who stuck his neck out. Only senior citizens can understand how low our economy was in the 1930s. Starting a new business then, after watching other toy companies fail successively, tells us something about John Best and something about the perennial appeal of good toys. The molding of pot metal toys must have seemed a good risk for a second income to Best, who was a printer and worked with metal alloys. He probably had also been following the ups and downs of "those TOYS with the NUMBERS," because he had lived in Clifton, the home of Kansas Toy Company (p. 75).

Best Toy started as a family hobby for John Best's children, relatives, friends, and neighbors, according to Minnie Nelson, his daughter. Other employees we know of were John Best, Jr. and his family, and Conrad Morsch, a molder. From a hobby it grew into a respectable business, supplying toy distributors and dime stores. The toys are still found in today's toy markets. After several years of operation it was sold in 1939 to Ralstoy, a Ralston, Nebraska, company.

At this point we are not certain when Best started or what "number" in the series was his first molding. Although contradictory, evidence from family members suggests purchase of a Clifton Toy company occurred about 1933. Nor do we know whether he introduced any new patterns, although with his experience it is likely that he did. Regardless, it was an important chapter in the story of those wandering molds.

Of great assistance was a donation from Dee Buchanan, John Best, Sr.'s great-granddaughter, of a faded copy of a Best Toy brochure. It appears to be a pre-publication printer's mockup, and undated; but its 42 illustrations (some shown here) were adequate to identify most of the Best and many of the Kansas Toys in collections. With no paper trail to guide us previously, this was indeed a find. Much of the hearsay, errors, and confusion of this family of toys has now been eliminated. Many thanks to all who helped and continue to help.

Best Toy reproductions can usually be distinguished from those of earlier makes in the "numbers" dynasty if they have white rubber wheels and are embossed "Made in USA." However, some of their toys used the metal wheels (MW) of the Kansas Toy originals, or the later wood hubs with rubber tires (WHRT). It is also possible that Best modified or rebuilt his molds to create variations.

Best molded a great number of designs. In order to reduce redundancy in this book we list them here but will not describe them in detail if they are adequately covered in Kansas Toy or Ralstoy lists. The following numbered toys and some unnumbered duplicates were found: 6, 10, 14, 17, 20, 25, 26, 27, 31, 32, 34, 35, 36, 37, 39, 40, 41, 42, 43, 45, 46, 47, 49, 51, 54, 55, 57, 58, 59, 60, 67, 71, 70, 72, 74, 76, 77, 78, 79, 80, 81, 85, 86, 87, 90, 91, 92, 93, 94, 95, 97, 99, 100, 101, 102.

O'Brien adds this note: Dee Buchanan also contributed a history that may be of interest to readers:

"About 55 years ago, John Milner Best, Sr. and his wife Roseanna purchased a company from Kansas Toy & Novelty Company located in Vining, Kansas—actually a suburb of Clifton. The Bests owned a newspaper, printing plant and book-bindery in Manhatten, Kansas. They moved the toy company to a building in back of their home at 530 Fremont Street, Manhattan. The family, in-laws and friends all worked making the lead cars produced by the toy company and were shipping them all over the world. There were also farm implements, tractors, airplanes, buses and trains as well as all types of cars. One of the Bests' grandchildren, Rosemary, remembers the Toy Factory well, as when she was about three years old and was playing about the factory she fell into one of the lead-melting pots head first. Very fortunately the lead was not hot—so she just had a bad bruise on her head; whereas if the lead had been hot and melted it would indeed have been a tragedy.")

	C6	C8	C10
BEV1 Racer, "85," Record car w/ large square fin, driver, HO, VG, 12 exhaust ports, WHRT, 4" long	10	15	20
BEV2 Sedan, "86," Lincoln ? 2-door fastback, slant grille w/ grid pattern, HL, divided w/s, rear wheel skirts, 4" long			No Price Found
BEV3 Sedan, "87," Brewster ?			No Price Found
BEV4 Sedan, "90," 2-door airflow, hood reaches front bumper w/ no grille, 4 OW, hard rubber wheels, 3-1/2" long			No Price Found
BEV5 Sedan, "91," Cadillac ? 2-door airflow, high style vee grille, faired front fenders, 3-1/2" long			No Price Found
BEV6 Coupe, "92," Dodge ?, chopped top, Brewster-like heart-shaped grille, HO, long streamlined front fenders, 3-3/4" long			No Price Found

BEST (three different wheels). Top, left to right: BEV4, BEV7, BEV9a. Middle, left to right: BEV1, BEV8. Bottom: BEV11, BEV14. Courtesy of Fred Maxwell.

Box from a Best Toys Set. The drawings on the boxtop offer good representations of Best vehicles and cannon. All or most of the toys shown appear to have originated with Kansas Toy & Novelty. Courtesy Margaret Rice & Fred Maxwell.

Box from a Best Toys Farm Set. All the toys illustrated are from molds believed to have originated with Kansas Toys. Photo by Perry Eichor. Courtesy Fred Maxwell.

(BEV 14) No. 100, 4" long

(BEV 13) No. 99, 4" long

(BEV 2) No. 86, 4" long

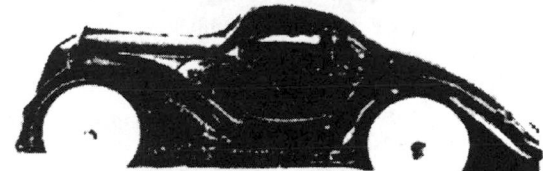

(BEV 10) No. 96, 3-1/2" long

(BEV 5) No. 91, 3-1/2" long

(BEV 9a) No. 95, 3-1/2" long

(BEV 6) No. 92, 3-3/4" long

(BEV 4) No. 90, 3-1/2" long

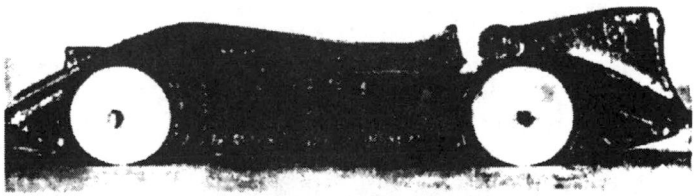

(BEV 11) No. 97, 4-1/2" long

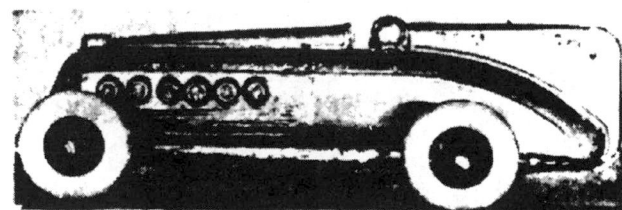

(BEV 1) No. 85, 4" long

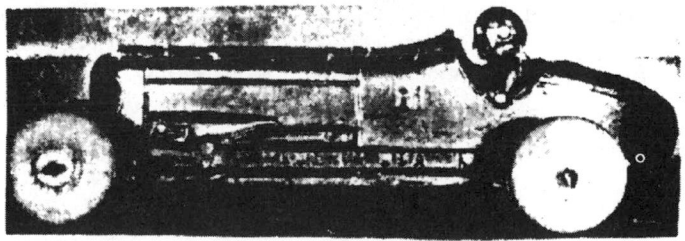

No. 81, 4-1/2" long

No. 26, 4" long

No. 76, 4-1/2" long

No. 10, Medium Racer

	C6	C8	C10
BEV7 Coupe "93," Cadillac ?, Streamlined, hood similar to #91, grid pattern grille, 2 OW, hard rubber wheels (see illustration of #96), 3-5/8" long	16	24	32
BEV8 Large Sedan, "94," 2-door airflow, similar to #90, 4 OW, taxi lamp on roof, 4-1/2" long	No Price Found		
BEV9a Sedan, "95," 2-door airflow similar to #94, w/ 3 headlamps, 4 OW, trunk, hard rubber wheels, Chrysler-Briggs show car?, 3-1/2" long	No Price Found		
BEV9b Sedan, "95," Same as above with "Police Dept." shield on doors. Centered headlamp may be a siren. Other versions have "Police" painted on roof, 3-1/2" long	10	15	20
BEV10 Coupe, "96," Apparently same car as #93, Were both produced? 3-1/2" long	No Price Found		
BEV11 Larger Racer, "97," Bluebird record car, driver, large fin, 12 exhaust ports, hard rubber wheels, faired, 4-1/2" long	10	15	20
BEV12 Coupe, "98"	No Price Found		

	C6	C8	C10
BEV13 Coupe, "99," Pontiac ?, streamlined, HO, rearmount, 4" long	No Price Found		
BEV14 Sedan, "100," Pontiac, streamlined, 2-door, HO, HG, 4 OW, trunk, 4" long	No Price Found		
BEV15 Cab Unit, "101," International? sleeper cab, slanted grille, HO, 2 OW, 3-1/4" long	No Price Found		
BEV16 Oil Transport, "102," Streamlined "Gasoline" semi-trailer to #101, 4 tanks, 4 storage compartments. Total length of cab-trailer 6-3/4", 4" long	47	70	95
BEV17 ?Sedan, no #, DeSoto? Airflow 2-door, HO, VG, HL, 4 OW, divided open windshield, bottom pan, Best? 3-7/8" long	No Price Found		
Big Bang Army Tank No. ST, cast iron, 8-1/8" long	35	50	100
Big Bang Motor Tank No. ST, cast iron, 9-1/2" long	75	250	500
Big Boy: See Kelmet			
Boattail Speedster, cast iron, blue with nickel wheels, driver, c. 1920s 5" long	100	150	200
Brinks Truck Bank, lead alloy, 9" long	175	263	350

BEST TOY Tanker: BEV15, BEV16.
Photo courtesy of Perry Eichor.

BUDDY L

Buddy "L" toys were first manufactured by the Moline Pressed Steel Company of Moline, Illinois, in 1921 and were named after the son of owner Fred Lundahl. Lundahl had started the company about eight years earlier, manufacturing auto and truck parts (fenders, etc.). The toys were originally made as special items for his son, but as Buddy Lundahl's playmates began to clamor for similar toys of their own and their fathers began asking Lundahl senior to make duplicate toys for their sons, Lundahl went into the toy business. Buddy "L" toys were large, typically 21 to 24 inches long or more for trucks and fire engines. Construction was of very heavy steel, strong enough to support a man's weight. These were made until the early 1930s, when the line was modified and lighter weight materials were employed.

Before this time, Fred Lundahl had died, having already lost control of the company. The company has changed names several times, known as the Buddy "L" Corp., Buddy "L" Toy Co., etc., and in recent years has dropped the quotes around the L. The company even put out a few wooden toys during World War II, when its main plant made nothing but war-related items, and continues to make toys today. The early Buddy "L" trains are also popular, and tend to be worth even more than the vehicles. Buddy "L" material from the pre-1932 period is almost indestructible, and as a consequence 50% of the pieces found are either very rusty or have been repainted at some point. The basic metal seems to hold up forever, but repainting and rust drops the price well below "good."

Following is a list of pre-1932 Buddy "L" toys compiled by Thomas W. Sefton.

Large Trucks

	C6	C8	C10
Buddy L 200 Express Truck, 1921-31	1200	2000	2800
Buddy L 201 Dump Truck (Ratchet), 1921-30	500	800	1100
Buddy L 201A Hydraulic Dump Truck, 1926-31	720	1080	1440
Buddy L 202 Coal Truck, 1926-31	2500	4000	6200
Buddy L 202A Sand & Gravel Truck, 1926-31	1500	2500	3500
Buddy L 203 Stake Truck, 1921-24, 1926-28	800	1350	1900
Buddy L 203A Lumber Truck, 1925-30	1500	2500	3500
Buddy L 203B Baggage Truck, 1929-31	1400	2300	3270
Buddy L 204 Moving Van, 1924-30	1100	1800	2500
Buddy L 204A Railway Express, 1926-31	1150	1900	2600
Buddy L 206, 206B Street Sprinkler Truck, 1924-31	1100	1700	2400
Buddy L 206A Oil Truck, 1925-30	900	1450	2175
Buddy L 207 Ice Truck, 1926-31	850	1350	1860
Buddy L 208 Coach, 1928-31 (Lt. Green Motorbus)	2500	4000	5450
Buddy L 209 Auto Wrecker, 1928-31 (Tow Truck)	1800	2900	4000

BUDDY L
No. 204A,
Railway
Express Truck.

BUDDY L No. 205,
Fire Truck.

BUDDY L No. 205, Hook & Ladder. Courtesy Mapes
Auctioneers.

Fire Trucks

	C6	C8	C10
Buddy L 205 Hook & ladder, 1924-31	800	1400	1860
Buddy L 205A Pumper, 1925-30	1200	1800	2500
Buddy L 205AB (Working) Pumper, 1930-31	1100	1800	2540
Buddy L 205B Aerial Ladder, 1926-30	800	1350	1800
Buddy L 205C Insurance Patrol, 1925-30	1400	2300	3300
Buddy L 205D Water Tower Truck (Working), 1930-31	2500	4200	7000

BUDDY L No.
205B, Hydraulic
Aerial Truck.

BUDDY L No.
205AB, Pumping
Fire Engine.

Model T Series

Buddy L 210 Flivver Truck, 1925-30	500	800	1200
Buddy L 210A Flivver Roadster, 1925-27	482	725	965
Buddy L 210B Flivver Coupe, 1925-30	500	800	1200
Buddy L 211 Ford Dump Cart, 1926-30	900	1550	2300

	C6	C8	C10
Buddy L 211A Ford Dump Truck, 1926-30 ...	1100	1700	2650
Buddy L 212 Ford Express Truck, 1929-30 ...	1400	2300	3225
Buddy L 212A One-Ton Ford Delivery Truck, 1929-30	2000	3500	5000

Construction Equipment

Buddy L 220 Steam Shovel, 1921-31	265	400	530
Buddy L 220A Heavy Steam Shovel, 1929-30	400	600	800
Buddy L 220AB Heavy Shovel (on Treads), 1929-30	2500	4000	7000
Buddy L 230 Sand Loader, 1925-31	165	250	330
Buddy L 240 Small Derrick, 1922-31	312	470	625
Buddy L 241 Large Derrick, 1922-31	275	363	550

BUDDY L Model T 210A, Flivver Roadster. Courtesy
Wilkinson Collection, Detroit Antique Toy Museum.

BUDDY L No. 280,
Concrete Mixer.
Courtesy Thomas
G. Nefos, Federal
Shipping Network.

	C6	C8	C10
Buddy L 250 Overhead Crane, 1924-27	700	1100	1600
Buddy L 250A Traveling Crane, 1928-30	1000	1600	2300
Buddy L 260 Pile Driver, 1926-28	700	1100	1500
Buddy L 270 Dredge (Clamshell), 1926-30	1000	2000	3000
Buddy L 270A Tractor Dredge (on Treads), 1929-30	3000	5000	7500
Buddy L 280 Concrete Mixer, 1926-30	500	750	1000
Buddy L 280A Mixer (on Treads), 1929-31	1100	1700	2600
Buddy L 290 Road Roller, 1929-31	2100	3700	5280
Buddy L 300 Sand Screener, 1929-30	700	1100	1700
Buddy L 350 Hoisting Tower, 1929-31	500	900	1250
Buddy L 360 Aerial Tramway, 1929-30	1500	2400	3300
Buddy L 400 Trencher, 1928-31	1800	2700	4200

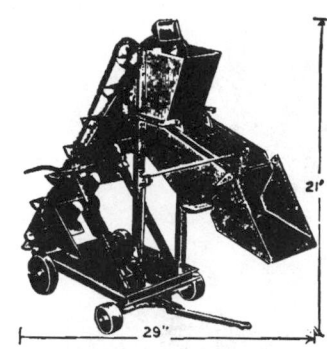

BUDDY L No. 300, Sand Screener.

(End listing by Thomas W. Sefton)

Buddy L post-1932

	C6	C8	C10
Buddy L "Allied Van Lines" Moving Van No. 366, 31" long	338	500	675
Buddy L "Army Signal Corps" Truck, 1941-42, 12" long	140	210	280
Buddy L Army Tank, wood, 1943, 13" long	85	130	175
Buddy L Army Transport, with towed cannon, 6-spoke wheels, 27" long	180	270	360
Buddy L "Army Truck 21," c. 1940, cloth top	120	180	240
Buddy L Army Truck No. 506, 20-1/2" long	125	188	250
Buddy L Army Truck, wood	100	150	200
Buddy L Automatic Tail-Gate Loader with steering handle	230	345	460
Buddy L Baggage Truck No. 11, 1933, 26-1/2" long	250	375	500
Buddy L Baggage Truck No. 41	72	108	145
Buddy L "Big Show Circus" Truck, wood, 1947, No. 484, 25-1/2" long	605	908	1210

BUDDY L No. 484, "Big Show Circus" truck, wood, 1947. Photo by William G. Floyd.

	C6	C8	C10
Buddy L City Baggage Dray No. 439, 1934, 19" long	250	375	500
Buddy L City Baggage Dray No. 839, 1939, 20-3/4" long	125	188	250
Buddy L Coca Cola Truck, wooden, c. WWII, only 3 known, worth $4200 in mint 1984, 19" long			
Buddy L Coca Cola Truck, post-WWII 15" long	135	198	270
Buddy L Concrete Mixer with Truck No. 54, 1937, 34-1/2" long	100	150	200

	C6	C8	C10
Buddy L Concrete Mixer No. 832, 1950-51, with motor sound, 10-3/4" long	275	363	550
Buddy L Country Squire Station Wagon, 15" long	90	135	180
Buddy L Curtiss Candy Truck	232	350	465
Buddy L Dairy Truck No. 2002 (Junior Line) 1930-32, 24" long	1100	1800	2700
Buddy L Dandy Digger No. 33	75	112	150

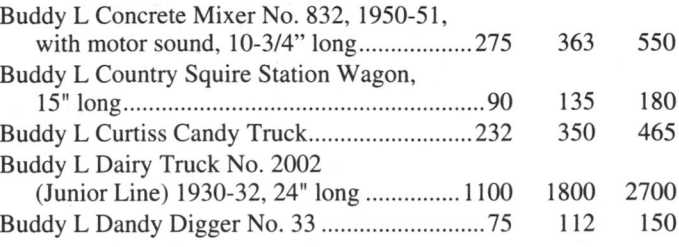

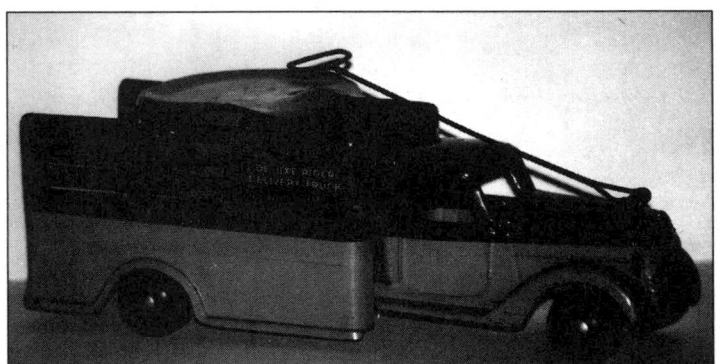

BUDDY L No. 803, Deluxe Rider Delivery Truck. Courtesy Joe and Sharon Freed.

	C6	C8	C10
Buddy L Delivery Truck, Deluxe Rider No. 803, 1945-48, 22-3/4" long	260	390	520
Buddy L Double Hydraulic Self-Loader-N-Dump Truck No. 5892	100	150	200

BUDDY L No. 5892 Double Hydraulic Self-Loader-N-Dump Truck. Courtesy Thomas G. Nefos, Federal Shipping Network.

	C6	C8	C10
Buddy L Dump Truck No. 434, 1936	212	318	425
Buddy L Dump Truck No. 634, 20-1/2" long	140	210	280
Buddy L Emergency Auto Wrecker No. 3317	142	215	285

	C6	C8	C10
Buddy L Engine No. 29, 1933-34, 25-1/2" long 225		338	450
Buddy L Excavator Truck and Shovel Set No. 948, 1940, 27-1/2" long 288		532	575
Buddy L Express Trailer Truck No. 35, 1934.. 475		715	950
Buddy L Fast Delivery Truck No. 3313 75		112	150
Buddy L "Fast Freight," 20" long 165		250	330
Buddy L Fire Chief's Car with Siren No. 483, wood, 1947, 19-1/2" long 475		715	950

BUDDY L No. 483, Fire Chief's Car with siren, wood, 1947. Photo by William G. Floyd.

	C6	C8	C10
Buddy L Fire Ladder Truck, semi, rounded trailer fenders, 1960 100		150	200
Buddy L Greyhound Bus, winds up 16" long .. 208		312	415
Buddy L Greyhound Bus with Bell No. 481, wooden, 18-1/2" long 450		675	900
Buddy L Hose Truck No. 38, 1933, 21-3/4" long 162		243	325
Buddy L Hook and Ladder Truck No. 859, wooden, 21-1/2" long 295		445	590
Buddy L Hydraulic Aerial Truck No. 27, 1933-34, w/ ladders down 40" long 550		850	1200
Buddy L Hydraulic Dump Truck No. 10, 1933-34, 24-3/4" long 600		950	1400
Buddy L Ice Truck No. 12, 1933-34, 26-1/2" long 700		1100	1600
Buddy L International Delivery Truck No. 51, 1935, 24-1/2" long 200		300	400
Buddy L Merry-Go-Round Truck No. 5429 115		172	230

BUDDY L No. 5429, Merry-Go-Round. Courtesy Thomas G. Nefos, Federal Shipping Network.

	C6	C8	C10
Buddy L Mister Buddy Ice Cream Van 105		158	210
Buddy L "Railway Express" Truck No. 480, wooden, 1947, 16-1/4" long 350		525	700
Buddy L Repair-It, 24" long 150		225	300

BUDDY L "Repair-It," 1953. Courtesy Mapes Auctioneers.

	C6	C8	C10
Buddy L Ride-N-Dump Truck 125		188	250
Buddy L "Riding Academy" No. 5455 Truck, with 3 horses 85		128	170
Buddy L Robotoy Dump Truck with driver, operates on remote control 500		750	1050
Buddy L Sand & Gravel Truck, No. 3312 150		225	300
Buddy L Scarab No. 211, no wind-up mechanism 250		375	500
Buddy L Scarab No. 711, winds up 257		385	515

BUDDY L No. 711, "Scarab." Courtesy Heinz Mueller, Continental Hobby House. (Bumpers missing in photo.)

	C6	C8	C10
Buddy L Service Truck, 1953 120		180	240
Buddy L "Shell" Truck, 13-1/2" long 190		285	380
Buddy L Siren Pull-n-Ride 120		180	240
Buddy L Steam Shovel and International Truck No. 16, 1937, 29-1/2" long, 13-1/2" high 112		168	225
Buddy L Steam Shovel, mechanical, No. 30, 1935, 17-1/2" long, 13-1/2" high 225		338	450
Buddy L Steam Shovel on Treads (Junior Line) No. 2005, 1930-32, 24" long 200		300	400
Buddy L Tank Truck No. 438, 1935, 19-1/4" long 450		675	900
Buddy L Tank Truck No. 938, 1941, 21-1/2" long 225		338	450
Buddy L "Texaco Tanker," promo sold at gas stations, 25" long 100		150	200

	C6	C8	C10
Buddy L Traveling Zoo, post-WWII 80	120	160
Buddy L Utility Delivery Truck No. 946, 1941-42, 25" long 90	135	180
Buddy L Victory Jeep and Cannon, wood 100	150	200
Buddy L Water Tower No. 28, 1936............. 1500	2500	3500
Buddy L Wrecker No. 13, 1933, 31" long 1000	1700	3000
Buddy L Wrecker No. 37, 1933, 24" long 200	300	400
Buddy L Wrecker No. W37, 1939, 25-1/4 long.............................. 100	150	200
Buddy L Wrecker No. 437, 1934, 24" long 375	527	750
Buddy L Wrecker No. 503, 1940, 1941-42, 19-1/4" long.................... 112	168	225
Buddy L No. 647, 1949, 26-1/4" long............. 175	262	350
Buddy L Wrecker No. 813, 1938, 32" long ... 1300	2200	2900
Buddy L Wrecker, Emergency Towing Rider No. 903, 1949, 33" long 75	112	150
Buddy L Wrecker No. 903, 1950, Buddy L "Emergency Towing" 33" long 100	150	200
Buddy L Wrecker No. 937, 1939, 25-1/4" long 130	180	285
Buddy L Wrecker No. 937, 1941-42 version, 25" long 87	130	175
Buddy L "Wrigley's Spearmint" Railway Express Truck. No. 835, 1938, 25" long 400	700	1000

	C6	C8	C10
Buddy L "Wrigley's Spearmint" Railway Express Truck, 1935, headlights light up, 23-1/8" long 700	1150	1670
Buddy L "Wrigley's Spearmint Railway Express Agency" Truck No. 953, 1940...... 800	1350	1850
Buffalo Toys Silver Bullet Racer, 26" long 350	525	700
Buick, 1947, plastic, 5-3/8" long 5	8	10
Bus, 1930s, aluminum, 15-1/2" long 1800	3300	5500

BUDDY L "Wrigley's Spearmint" Railway Express Truck, 1935. Courtesy Rodney A. Heesacker.

Bus, 1930s, 15-1/2" long, aluminum. Courtesy James S. Maxwell/Virginia Caputo. Photo by Virginia Caputo.

C.A.W. NOVELTY COMPANY

by Fred Maxwell (Slushmold Contributing Editor) and Ferd Zegel with the assistance of the Clay Center Historical Society, Gary Franson, Arlan and Gerry Conrad

It is remarkable indeed that collectors did not find this fine company until 1990. Charles A. Wood not only ran a substantial operation but made some of the finest replica toys in the slushmold industry. Ironically, Wood had one of the longest histories of the slushmold industry. Founded about 1925, his company was active until about 1940, when lead casting came to a halt with WWII.

All of Wood's output showed artistry, ingenuity and meticulous craftsmanship. All his toys are smooth, crisp, detailed moldings with extra touches such as open windshields and two or three colors per toy. Early products had metal disk wheels with painted black "tires," or metal-spoked wheels. When you find open, V-shaped, divided windshields, drivers inside cabs and trimotored aircraft with the outboard engines mounted on the landing gear struts you wonder how he did it for the 5¢ price. Wood once told a reporter that it sometimes took three or four years to make a mold, which is a machinist's work of art. This tells us about Wood's pride in his work and that toy-making was not his primary occupation at the time.

Charles Wood was born about 1891. He lived and worked in Topeka and in nearby Clifton before moving to Clay Center. He was known for his civic boosterism and good works. After he helped establish the local airport, he built and operated his own aircraft maintenance hangar. A master machinist, he made all his toy molds, production tools, and toy parts, and even plastic wheels.

Although I have researched the slush industry for 20 years, I had only heard rumors of a "small molder in Clay Center, Kansas." Then, a few years ago, I found a small monoplane with initials "CAW" under a tailplane. I put pressure on my Kansas friends, with the happy result that eventually I saw a mint collection owned by a relative of Wood's

and also a few pieces and some paper memorabilia in the Historical Society Museum. What a pleasant surprise!

Although we do not yet have a complete list, we have identified some "orphans" and some never before heard of toys. Wood made airplanes, autos, novelties, and trucks. Some of these have been well known to collectors although unidentified. Clearly this company and its toys deserve to be more fully known.

Note: The C & H Mfg. Co. was formed in 1940 by Rod Hemphill, the last C.A.W. employee, and Howard Clevenger. According to Mrs. Hemphill, they only used original C.A.W. molds. Apparently this brave effort at revival managed to reproduce some toys before folding. These are heavier than C.A.W.'s and have black rubber wheels. Their claim to fame is in publication of the accompanying partial flyer, which allowed us to solve the paternity of those handsome orphans. However, judging from the catalog numbers and our incomplete list below there must be several orphans out there. Can any of you collectors help?

Note: A C.A.W. trademark, seldom found (too costly?), consists of unique, lead blind hubs fitted over a wire axle. They are sometimes found with ordinary nail axles piercing the hubs.

Left to right: C.A.W. CWV4, CWV1. Courtesy Fred Maxwell.

	C6	C8	C10
CWV1 Sport Roadster, no #, Open Packard, driver w/ cap (gilt or silver), no windshield (w/s), horizontal grille (hg), vertical louvers (vl), no headlamps (hl), rear-mount (rm), metal disk wheels (mdw), 3-1/2" long	20	30	40
CWV2 Sport Roadster, no #, similar to above, Buick?, no w/s, plain grille, vl, rm, right sidemount (sm) mdw, also spoked version (msw) 3-1/2" long	22	33	44

C.A.W., CWV3. Courtesy Gary Franson.

C.A.W., CWV2. Courtesy Gary Franson.

CWV3 Overland Bus, no #, Fageol? Yellow Line? tour bus, hg, no headlamps, 12 windows, shallow "observer deck," mdw, left sm, 3-3/4" long .... No Price Found

CWV4 Fuel Tanker, no #, Ford? Truck, cab w/ driver inside, no w/s, hg, 3 tanks, hose compart., msw, 3-3/4" long 20   30   40

	C6	C8	C10
CWV5 Air Drive Coach, #25, Blimp-like bus w/ fin and rear propeller drive. (b. Also a version molded w/o prop.) 12 open windows (ow), white rubber wheels (wrw) with unique fitted hubs and hidden axles (see text note) 3-7/8" long			No Price Found
CWV6 Streamline Coupe, #30, Airflow, V-pattern grille, hood ornament (ho), 4 ow, small rear fin, small winged design on rear-wheel skirts, mdw also wrw. Bottom pan goes over rear axle, not under, 3" long	16	24	32
CWV7 Wonder Special, #33, Airflow coupe, 3-wheeled companion to #30 above, vg, 4 ow, wrw, front wheel skirts, pan goes over front axle, 3-3/8" long	16	24	32

TOYS THAT SELL THEMSELVES

Modern Metal Toys that Sell the Year Around, Realistic in Every
Detail. Finished in Bright Colors with the Best of Lacquers

No. 25 AIR DRIVE COACH
Length 3⅞ in. He'ght 1¾ in. Weight per gro. 33 lbs. Retails for 10c.

Price per doz. ....

No. 32. DE SOTO SEDAN
Length 3⅞ in. Height 1⅜ in. Weight per gro. 32 lbs. Retails for 10c.
Price per doz. ....

No. 30 STREAMLINE COUPE
Length 3 in. Height 1 in. Weight per gro. 19 lbs. Retails at 5c.

Price per doz. ....

No. 33 WONDER SPECIAL
Length 3⅜ in. Height 1 in. Weight per gro. 19 lbs. Retails for 5c.

Price per doz. ....

No. 31. MARVEL RACER
Length 3⅝ in. Height 1 3-16 in. Weight per gro. 20 lbs. Retails at 5c.

Price per doz. ....

No. 38 NEW DESIGN RACER
Length 3⅜ in. Height 1¼ in. Weight per gro. 20 lbs. Retails for 5c.

**No. 39
TRANSPARENT WINDSHIELD RACER**
Length 3 in. Height 1 in. Weight per gro. 15 lbs. Retails for 5c.

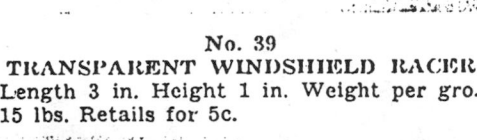

Each number packed one dozen to box.

Colors: On all Airplanes 6 silver 4 red, 2 green, to dozen. On all Autos 6 red, 2 blue, 2 green. 2 silver to dozen.

Rubber Wheels on All Autos
Plastic Wheels on Airplanes Except No. 29

TERMS: 2% Ten Days, Net 30 Days. Prices are f. o. b. St. Louis, Mo.

C & H Mfg. Co.

1610 So. Florissant Rd.
ST. LOUIS, MO.

No. 40 THREE PIECE AUTO SET
Three toys on card. Length 6⅜ in. Height 1 in. Weight per gro. 40 lbs. Retails for 10c per card.

Price per doz. ....

C.A.W. Toys sold between 1940 and early 1942 by C & H. Courtesy Fred Maxwell.

C.A.W., CWV5b (no rear propeller). Courtesy of Gary Franson.

C.A.W., CWV7. Courtesy Gary Franson.

C6   C8   C10

CWV8 Marvel Racer, #31, streamlined FWD Indy
     type, driver, torpedo tail with very small fin,
     V-grille pattern, 8 exhaust ports, alum. wheels.
     Also found in a modern bubblepack, w/ lucent
     hard plastic wheels, "Woodchuck Industries
     Metal Toys, Clay Center, Ks." This name may
     have been a new idea, part of a recent
     market test, 3-5/8" .... No Price Found

CWV9 DeSoto Sedan, #32, Airflow, divided
     windshield, b ow, hl, vg, ho, wrw, 3-7/8" long No Price Found

CWV10 New Design Racer #38, streamlined coupe,
     rounded tail, 2 oval open window shows driver,
     hood ornament loop (stringpull?), wrw w/ hubs,
     3-3/8" long .... No Price Found

Line art of C.A.W. toys. Top to bottom: CWV5, CWV4. Drawings by Deb Eccles.

C.A.W., CWV6. Courtesy Gary Franson.

C.A.W., CWV8. Courtesy Gary Franson.

C.A.W., CWV9. Courtesy Gary Franson.

C.A.W., CWV10. Courtesy Gary Franson.

C.A.W., CWV11b. Courtesy Gary Franson.

C.A.W., CWV12a. Courtesy of Gary Franson.

Vehicles • 51

CWV11 Transparent Windshield Racer, #39, Indy FWD 2 man racer, v-shaped vg, dual exhausts, boattail, unique hub-tires as in #25 (also wrw). [Not complete if divided plastic windshield is missing (fragile)], 3" .... No Price Found

CWV12 Three Piece Auto Set, #40 as follows:
	C6	C8	C10
a. Midget Coupe Racer, no #, hg, hl, divided open w/s, 2 ow, 2 colored body, mdw, headlamps and cowl ventilators!, 2-1/16"	10	15	20
b. Midget Racer, no #, gilt driver, vl, hg, mdw (easily confused w/ Barclay #53), 2-1/8"	10	15	20
c. Austin Bantam, no #, 2-door sedanette, 5 ow, hl, plain grille, rm, mdw (easily confused with other makers' Bantams), 2"	10	15	20

CMV13 Dump Truck, no #, Ford?, hinged dump body, divided open w/s, 2 ow, hg, mdw, 3-1/8" .... No Price Found

CWV14 Tank Truck, no #, Ford?, 3 fuel tanks, otherwise matching above. Unusual 2-piece body connected by rear axle, 3-3/16" .... No Price Found

C.A.W., CWV13. Courtesy Gary Franson.

C.A.W. CWV12b. Courtesy Gary Franson.

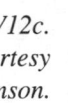

C.A.W., CWV12c. Courtesy Gary Franson.

C.A.W., CWV14. Courtesy Gary Franson.

CHAMPION

The Champion Hardware Co., though in business 1883-1954, produced toys only from 1930-36, as a Depression stopgap. As might be expected from a hardware firm, its toys were cast iron. During its toy years the Geneva, Ohio, outfit was headed by C. I. Chamberlin.

	C6	C8	C10
Champion Coupe, Reo type, 7-1/2" long	212	318	425
Champion Gas and Motor Oil Truck, cast iron, c. 1930s, 8" long	380	570	760
Champion four-casting nickeled radiator car, approx. 4" long	175	262	350
Champion Mack Dump, c. 1930s 7" long	183	275	365
Champion Mack Stake Truck, c. 1930, 4-1/2" long	90	135	180
Champion Mack Stake Truck, 7-1/2" long	175	265	350
"Champion" Motorcycle and Rider, 4-3/4" long	150	225	300
Champion Panel Delivery, 7-3/4" long	495	745	990
Champion Policeman on Motorcycle, rubber tires, 7" long	235	355	470
Champion Race Car, 2 riders, 5-1/2"	125	188	250
Champion Race Car, cast iron, detachable driver, 6" long	150	225	300
Champion Race Car, c. 1930s, 9" long	250	375	500
Champion Sedan, 5-1/4" long	112	188	225
"Champion" Wrecker, cast iron, 7-1/2" long	308	463	615
Chein Army Truck, cannon on back, tin, early, 8-1/2" long	135	202	270
Chein Army Truck, open bed, tin, early, 8-1/2" long	135	202	270
Chein Hercules Mack Dump Truck, tin, 20" long	425	638	850

CHAMPION Mack Dump, 7" long. Courtesy Wilkinson Collection, Detroit Antique Toy Museum.

CHAMPION Policeman on Motorcycle. Courtesy Mapes Auctioneer & Appraisers.

	C6	C8	C10
Chein Hercules Motor Express, tin litho, Mack, 19-1/2" long	530	795	1060
Chein Hercules Roadster	300	450	600

CHEIN Hercules Motor Express. Courtesy Wilkinson Collection, Detroit Antique Toy Museum.

CHEIN Roadster, tin litho, c. 1925, 8-1/2" long. Courtesy Mapes Auctioneers & Appraisers.

CHEIN Mack Tanker Truck, 19" long, c. 1928. Courtesy Phillips New York.

	C6	C8	C10
Chein Hercules Wrecker Truck, 20" long	500	750	1200
Chein "Junior Oil Tank" Truck, 1920s, 8-1/2" long	62	93	125
Chein Mack Tanker Truck, c. 1928, Hercules, 19" long	500	750	1200
Chein Roadster, tin litho, c. 1925, 8-1/2" long	213	320	425
Chein "Royal Blue Line Coast to Coast Service"	640	960	1280
Chein Touring Car, tin litho, 7" long	250	375	500
Chrysler Airflow, heavy sheet metal w/ wind-up motor. Tin grille, headlights and bumper, wooden wheels, 4" long	1200	2200	3000
Chrysler Airflow, cast iron, 1930s, 4-1/2" long	40	60	80
Chrysler Airflow, pressed steel, c. 1937 6" long	50	75	100
Circus Band Wagon, plays record and moves, comic musicians on top, c. 1922, 17" long	1000	1500	2000
"City Fire Dept. Truck," 1930, pressed steel, rubber tires, 26" long	450	675	900

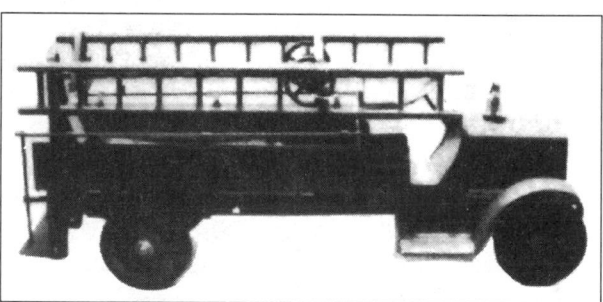

"City Fire Dept. Truck," 1930, 26" long. Courtesy Lloyd W. Ralston Auctions.

	C6	C8	C10
Clark friction auto, c. 1894, wood, iron and tin, 10-1/2" long	315	472	630
Clark friction auto, c. 1901, wood body covered with steel	600	950	1300
Cleveland Toy Racer, aluminum, steel wheels, c. 1935, 13" long	175	262	350
Converse Auto with fringe on top, 3-seat, 1905, painted, pressed steel, clockwork, rubber tires	600	900	1200
Converse Fire Engine Ladder Truck, bell, wooden headlight, 1915, 10" long	1250	1875	2500
Converse Parcel Post Van, 1920s, 15" long	1500	2500	3700

CLEVELAND TOY racer, aluminum, 13" long. Courtesy Mapes Auctioneers & Appraisers.

CLARK Friction Auto, c. 1894, 10-1/2" long, wood, iron and tin. Photo by Joe and Sharon Freed.

CONVERSE Transitional Taxi, 10-1/2" long. Courtesy Sotheby's New York.

	C6	C8	C10
Converse Pick-up Truck, very early, open cab	500	750	1000
Converse Roadster, 1908, wind-up, open cab, 15-1/2" long	1100	1600	3000
Converse Touring Auto, 1910, pressed steel, canvas roof	900	1400	2300
Converse Transitional Taxi, clockwork, 10-1/2" long	525	770	1050

COR-COR

Formed in 1926 in Washington, Indiana, by Louis A. Corcoran. At its peak it employed 590 people. Corcoran retired in 1941 and died in 1945.

					C6	C8	C10
Cor-Cor Airflow windup, electric lights, 16" long	1000	1700	2265	Cor-Cor Graham Paige Sedan, electric, 20" long	900	1450	1950
Cor-Cor Bus, 23" long	425	638	850	Cor-Cor Van, painted metal, c. 1928, 23" long	363	445	725
Cor-Cor Dump Truck, dumps back or side to side, 23" long	225	338	450				

COURTLAND (WALT REACH)

List by Joe and Sharon Freed

Non-Powered Vehicles

600 Courtland Open Van Tractor-Trailer, 1946 retail price 49¢, L 13", W 3", H 3-1/4"	125	200	300
610 Courtland Side Dump Tractor-Trailer, 1946 retail price 49¢, L 13", W 3", H 3-1/4"	100	175	275
620 Courtland Log Truck Tractor-Trailer, 1946 retail price 59¢, L 13", W 3", H 3-1/4"	150	225	350
700 Courtland Side Dump Tractor-Trailer, 1946 retail price 49¢, L 13", W 3", H 3-1/4"	125	200	325
800 Courtland Easter Greetings Rabbit Truck, 9" long	325	525	750
900 Courtland Ice Cream Truck, 1946 retail price 39¢, L 9", W 3", H 2-3/4"	125	200	300
900 Courtland Moving and Storage Truck, 1946 retail price 39¢, L 9", W 3", H 2-3/4"	150	225	350

COURTLAND Non-Powered Vehicle Tractor-Trailer. Same tractor as No. 2000 except marked "Loft-Fresh Candies." Photo courtesy Joe and Sharon Freed.

COURTLAND Non-Powered Vehicle No. 620 Log Truck. Photo courtesy Joe and Sharon Freed.

	C6	C8	C10
900 Courtland Fire Patrol No. 2 Truck, 1946 retail price 39¢, L 9", W 3", H 2-3/4"	100	175	275
900 Courtland Express and Hauling Truck, 1946 retail price 39¢, L 9", W 3", H 2-3/4"	100	175	275
1050 Courtland Logging Camp Train Set, 1946 retail price $1.79, L 26-3/4", W 3", H 3-1/4"	No Price Found		
1060 Courtland Trailer Truck Parade, 1946 retail price $1.79, L 13", W 3", H 3-1/4"	No Price Found		
1070 Courtland Big 4 Truck Parade, 1946 retail price $1.79, The Four 900, L 9-1/2", W 3-1/4", H 3"	No Price Found		
1200 Courtland Side Dump Tractor-Trailer, L 13", W 3", H 3-1/4"	175	250	375
Courtland Tractor-Trailer, same tractor as No. 2000 except marked, "Loft-Fresh Candies"	350	550	850

Friction-Powered Vehicles

	C6	C8	C10
3875 Courtland Mechanical "Gulf" Gasoline Tractor-Trailer, L 13", W 3", H 3-1/4"	225	350	475
4000 Courtland Woody Sedan, red & tan, L 7-1/4", W 3-1/4", H 2-3/4"	65	75	100
4000 Courtland Woody Sedan, blue & tan, L 7-1/4", W 3-1/4", H 2-3/4"	65	75	100

Note: This is one of only four Courtland-styled toys stamped "A Walt Reach Toy by Courtland Toy co. Philadelphia, Pa. Made in U.S.A." The only known Courtland-styled toys marked with Courtland Toy Company, Philadelphia stamping are this No. 4000 sedan, a non-powered "Fire Chief" car, a private garage similar to No. 9075, and a mechanical parking meter bank.

	C6	C8	C10
4000 Courtland "Fire Chief" car, 7-1/4", W 3-1/4", H 2-3/4"	75	125	150
As above, but sparking motor and red plastic bubble on hood	100	125	150

	C6	C8	C10
4050 Courtland FBI Riot Squad Car, similar to 7600 FBI Riot Squad Car, except for color	100	125	150
4060 Courtland Space Rocket Patrol Car, 1952 retail price 98¢, L 7-1/4", W 3-1/4", H 2-3/4"	150	200	250
5450 Courtland "Pop-Up" Ladder Fire Truck, L 13", W 3", H 3-1/4"	250	350	450

COURTLAND Friction-Powered Vehicle No. 3875. Photo courtesy Mapes Auctioneers.

COURTLAND Friction-Powered Vehicle No. 5450, "Pop-up" Ladder Fire Truck. Photo courtesy Joe and Sharon Freed.

COURTLAND Friction-Powered Vehicle No. 4000 Fire Chief Car, red & white, with red plastic bubble on hood. Photo courtesy Joe and Sharon Freed.

COURTLAND Friction-Powered Vehicle No. XXXX, Mechanical Military Gun Car, variation with litho gun shield. Photo courtesy Joe and Sharon Freed.

	C6	C8	C10
7500 Courtland Mechanical State Police Car with siren, L 7-1/4", W 3-1/4", H 2-3/4" 150	200	250
7500 Courtland Mechanical Fire Chief Car with siren, L 7-1/4", W 3-1/4", H 3-1/4" 150	200	250
7600 Courtland FBI Riot Squad Car, L 7-1/4", W 3-1/4", H 2-3/4" 175	200	250
XXXX Courtland Dump Truck w/ dual rear wheels, L 10-1/2", W 3", H 3-3/8" 250	350	475
XXXX Courtland Mechanical Military Gun Car, painted gun shield, L 7-1/2", W 3-1/4", H 2-1/2" 250	350	475
XXXX Variation of above, lithographed gunshield 275	375	500

COURTLAND Friction-Powered Vehicle No. XXXX, Dump Truck with dual rear wheels. Photo courtesy Joe and Sharon Freed.

CRAFTOYS

by Fred Maxwell and Ron Eccles

Craftoy, a small Omaha, Nebraska firm, had a brief career casting slushmold vehicles before the WWII need for lead brought the pot metal era to a long halt. We have discovered little more about the company than a sales sheet. Craftoy acquired some of the molds when Ralstoy was reorganizing in about 1940.

For those readers accustomed to identifying by "those numbers": the #92 sedan has the same number as a Best Toy coupe, but they are not the same car. The #100 racer is obviously not the same as the Best #100 sedan. Older molds were

also used for #78 mixer, #81 racer, #102 gasoline semi-tanker, #101 fire truck, #103 speed car, #104 oil truck. The #105 station wagon possibly came from Ralstoy. The ancestry of Kansas Toy is evident in the #17 tractor and the freight train set. The designs of the railroad coal car, stockcar and tank car are recent or new. Thus we come to the end of the line as "those toys with the numbers" roll into history. These catalog numbers may or may not be found on the toys.

Black rubber wheels are characteristic of this line, but they are not exclusive to Craftoy.

	C6	C8	C10
Craftoy Tractor, "17," "Fordson," "Made in USA," farm tractor, driver, rear wheels larger, visible engine, 2-1/2" 8	12	16
Craftoy Freight Train, "3600," 16-1/2" Locomotive, 0-6-4, 4-1/2", "KT&N RR," cars 3-1/4", caboose 2-3/4", "Made in USA," value of indiv. cars 6	9	12
Craftoy Cement Mixer, "78," 2 open windows, "Made in USA," 3-3/4" 8	12	16
Craftoy Racer, "81," Miller FWD Indy racer, "Made in USA," 4-1/2" 10	15	20
Craftoy Sedan, #92, streamlined 2-door sedan, 4 open windows, screen pattern grille, 4" long ...... No Price Found		
Craftoy Racer #100, Indy type, driver, removable tin hood, rounded nose available in repros., 4-1/4" long ...... No Price Found		
Craftoy ? Racer, no #, Indy type, driver, removable tin hood, slanted nose, available in repros, 3-3/4" long ...... No Price Found		
Craftoy Fire Truck, #101, Hose Truck or Insurance Patrol, 4 open windows, 4-1/2" long ...... No Price Found		
Craftoy Tanker, "102," 1938, International K-Line?, "Gasoline," semi-trailer, 2 open windows, See Ralstoy, 6-3/4" long ...... No Price Found		

	C6	C8	C10
Craftoy Speed Car, #103, streamlined closed racer, body trimmed in fantasy streamlines, 4-1/4" long, available in repros ...... No Price Found		
Craftoy Oil Truck, #104, 1938 International?, COE, "Gas," "Oil" tanker, 2 open windows, 3-3/4" ...... No Price Found		
Craftoy Station Wagon, #105 streamlined, 4 open windows, 3-3/4" ...... No Price Found		

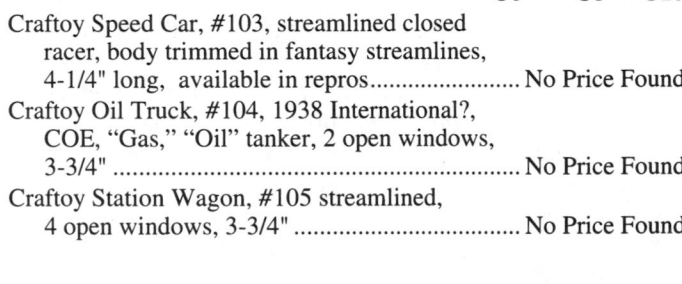

Top: Craftoy #100. Bottom: Craftoy? Racer, Indy type, driver, removable tin hood. Photo by Fred Maxwell.

DAYTON FRICTION WORKS

Dayton was owned by D.P. Clark of Dayton, Ohio. Clark's wood and metal "Hill Climber" friction toys were his best known. Clark was in business from 1898, and his company was one of the first to use a friction motor, which is activated by moving the toy by hand against a surface and then releasing it. William Schieble, who joined the company in the early 1900s, left in 1909 and formed the Schieble Toy and Novelty Company, using the "Hill Climber" name, which he felt was legally his, while Clark continued to use it, despite Schieble's lawsuits. Thus the parentage of some "Hill Climbers" is uncertain.

	C6	C8	C10
Dayton Coal and Ice Truck, tin, friction, c. 1920 200	200	300	400
Dayton Coupe, 1928, pressed steel, 12" 450	450	675	900
Dayton Coupe, c. 1920, 12-1/2" long 600	600	900	1200
Dayton "Dayton Friction," pressed steel, rubber tires, 1920s, 14-1/4" long 250	250	375	500
Dayton Dump Truck 200	200	300	400
Dayton Fire Ladder Truck, 18" long 275	275	365	550
Dayton Fire Pumper, 1920 500	500	750	1000

	C6	C8	C10
Dayton Ladder Truck, 1920s........................... 350	350	525	700
Dayton open Touring Car, dated 1909, friction motor, driver 250	250	375	500
Dayton Touring Car, friction motor, 13-1/2" long 500	500	750	1000
Dayton Touring Car, unpowered, 13-1/2" long 350	350	525	700
Delivery Truck, cast iron, 3-1/2" long.............. 60	60	90	120
Delivery Truck with driver, friction, 10-1/2" long 100	100	150	200
Delivery Truck, Packard, steel, 28" long 400	400	600	800

DENT HARDWARE COMPANY

Dent, of Fullerton, Pennsylvania, was in business from 1895-1973. Henry H. Dent, with four partners, was the owner. Cast-iron toys seem to have first emerged in 1898. Dent is known for particularly fine castings in its vehicles. In the 1920s it was one of the first manufacturers to try aluminum toys (with little success). Toys seem to have been phased out during the hard times of the Depression.

	C6	C8	C10
Dent "American Oil Co.," cast-iron truck, approx. 10-1/2" long 750	750	1125	1500
Dent Bus, cast iron, 6-1/4" long 375	375	563	750
Dent "Bus Line," 9" long 400	400	600	800
Dent Bus, 10-1/2" long 500	500	800	1200
Dent Coast to Coast Bus, 7-1/2" long 125	125	187	250
Dent "Coast to Coast" Bus, 10" long 450	450	675	900
Dent "Coast to Coast" Bus, c. 1925, 15" long 1100	1100	1700	2500
Dent "Contractors" Mack Dump, open cab, 10-1/2" long 1200	1200	1800	2700
Dent Coupe, 5" long 125	125	188	250
Dent "Express J & B" Stakebed Truck, 1915, driver, 14-1/2" long 500	500	800	1100
Dent Fire Truck, cast iron, 7" long................... 150	150	225	300
Dent Fire Ladder Truck with driver, 8-1/2" long 450	450	675	900
Dent Fire Truck with ladder and men, cast iron, 18" long.................................... 900	900	1350	1800
Dent "Freeman's Dairy" Truck, sliding doors, milkman, 6" long 400	400	600	800
Dent Hose Reeler with men, cast iron, large.... 500	500	750	1000
Dent "Interurban" Bus, cast iron, 9" long 417	417	625	835
Dent LaSalle, approx. 4" long 200	200	300	400
Dent Ladder Truck, two drivers, 10" long 250	250	375	500
Dent Mack Dump Truck, c. 1925, iron wheels, 4-1/2" long 55	55	82	110
Dent Model T 2-door sedan, iron wheels, c. 1925 125	125	187	250

	C6	C8	C10
Dent "Patrol," c. 1920s, 6-1/2" long................ 125	125	187	250
Dent "Police Patrol," 8-3/4" long 750	750	1125	1500
Dent "Public Service" Bus, c. 1926, 13-1/2" long 1100	1100	1700	2400
Dent Sedan, spare tire, has stop and go light, full bumpers on front, 7-1/2" 900	900	1350	1800
Dent Steam Roller, cast iron, 6" long................ 45	45	68	90
Dent Touring Car, driver & passenger, 12" long.. 355	355	535	710
Dent "Valley View Dairy," 8" long 700	700	1100	1500
Dent Yellow Cab, approx. 7-3/4" long............. 500	500	750	1150
"Dept. of Street Cleaning" Dump Truck, c. 1935, 10-1/2" long 105	105	158	210

DENT "Police Patrol," approx. 8-3/4" long. Courtesy Phillips New York.

DINKY

Dinky toys were first made in England in 1932 under the name "Modeled Miniatures," later "Meccano Miniatures," and in 1934, "Dinky," which in England means "fetching."

	C6	C8	C10		C6	C8	C10
Dinky 14c Coventry Fork Lift	42	63	85	Dinky 137 Plymouth, 1963	48	72	95
Dinky 23h Ferrari Racer	17	26	35	Dinky 151 Austin Devon	17	26	35
Dinky 25c Flat Truck	83	125	165	Dinky 154 Ford Taurus	17	26	35
Dinky 27f 1948 Plymouth Station Wagon	60	90	120	Dinky 157 Jaguar XK 120	35	53	70
Dinky 29c Double Decker Bus	75	112	150	Dinky 168 Ford Escort	17	26	35
Dinky 30r Fordson Truck	40	60	80	Dinky 170 Ford Sedan, 1950	35	53	70
Dinky 32c/576 Panhard Esso	60	90	120	Dinky 172 Studebaker Land Cruiser	52	78	105
Dinky 33 "Bailly" Van	50	75	100	Dinky 174 Hudson Hornet Sedan	55	83	110
Dinky 34 Royal Mail Van	45	68	90	Dinky 181 Volkswagen MBD	42	63	85
Dinky 36b Bentley	95	143	190	Dinky 197 Morris Mini	32	48	65
Dinky 36c Humber, 1936	100	150	200	Dinky 198 Rolls Royce Phantom V	30	45	60
Dinky 36d Rover	85	127	170	Dinky 200 Matra 630	16	24	32
Dinky 38c Lagonda	93	140	185	Dinky 201 Plymouth Rally, 1976	17	26	35
Dinky 38d Alvis	105	158	210	Dinky 207 Triumph TR7 Leyland	17	26	35
Dinky 39c Lincoln Zephyr	138	205	275	Dinky 227 Beach Buggy	17	26	35
Dinky 40a Riley 4DS	85	127	170	Dinky 241 Austin Taxi	25	38	50
Dinky 45 Vauxhall Victor	15	22	30	Dinky 252 1968 Pontiac	32	48	65
Dinky 97 Euclid Truck	11	16	22	Dinky 254 Taxi	37	56	75
Dinky 106 Thunderbird 2 space	60	90	120	Dinky 261 Telephone Van	62	93	125
Dinky 112 Triumph Purdey	25	38	50	Dinky 267 Dodge Fire Rescue	27	41	55
Dinky 130 Ford Corsair	40	60	80	Dinky 267 Bedford Dump	9	13	18
Dinky 134 Triumph Vitesse	22	33	45	Dinky 308 Leyland Tractor	25	38	50
Dinky 135 Triumph 2000	20	30	40	Dinky 344 Estate Car	35	52	70

DINKY. Left to right: 157 Jaguar KX120 Coupe, 334 Estate Car. Courtesy Phillips New York.

DINKY. Left to right: 174 Hudson Hornet Sedan, 172 Studebaker Land Cruiser. Courtesy Phillips New York.

DOEPKE "MODEL TOYS"

by Ray Funk

(See also Miscellaneous)

Doepke "Model Toys" advertised their toys as outlasting all others 3 to 1. The company's full title was the "Charles Wm. Doepke Mfg. Co., Inc." of Rossmoyne, Ohio. Each toy was an authorized replica of the actual thing, right down to the decals and coloring of the real equipment or trucks. The exception was the manufacturer's own "Model Toys" design.

At the end of WWII, the Doepke Corp. hit the market with five models, the first in a line of heavy-duty metal operating replicas employing metal tread or authentic miniature tires. The tires were either Goodyear or Firestone, with authentic tread and name and tire sizes, exactly as on the real tires. This, to the best of my knowledge, has never since been done as perfectly, even in the model kits of today. They also all had rubber smoke stacks. All these toys received the approval of *Parents* magazine, P.T.A., *Boy's Life* magazine, and all other experts and advocates of good toys at that time.

The first five numbers in the toy series were 2000, 2001, 2002, 2006, 2007. Why not 3, 4, and 5, I cannot say. Perhaps Doepke had toys planned for these numbers that fell through. Following is a list of the Doepke vehicles.

No. 2000. Wooldridge H.D. Earth hauler, bright yellow, four huge tires, 25" long, 10 pounds. The actual manufacturer's address is listed as Sunnyvale, California. I'm sure most of you have seen the John Wayne movie, *The Fighting Seabees,* which used several of these along with caterpillar bulldozers and road graders. These Wooldridge's caught my eye with their maneuvering ability, and could traverse the roughest terrain easily. Two long doors, the length of the bottom of the dirt-hauling area, could be released to deposit a load. Price was $14.75 new in 1945.

No. 2001. The Barber-Greene high-capacity bucket loader, 13" high, 10 pounds, dark green, all steel and rolling on steel tread, was designed as a toy to lead earth haulers. Hand crank operated, operated exactly as the real thing. Price $14.75.

No. 2002. Jaeger Concrete Mixer, bright yellow, 15" long, 8 pounds on four wheels, steerable via draw bar (all these model toys steered exactly like the real thing), though perhaps the best-detailed, was the poorest selling toy. You could really mix concrete in them, although it wasn't advisable, due to the small amount received versus the cleaning time. This toy was priced at $10.75 to $13.75.

No. 2006. The Adams Diesel Roadgrader, dark orange, 26" long, 14 pounds, all six wheels, three axles, and blade adjustable to all angles, exactly like the real thing, steerable via steering wheel, was priced at $14.75.

No. 2007. The Unit Mobile Crane, dark orange, 11-1/2" long, 19-1/2" boom, 8 pounds, 8 ounces, with adjustable side jacks, steered via a drawbar. It boasted a block and tackle and a removable operating clam shell as a standard accessory. Priced at $14.75.

There was no number 2008. The next year No. 2009 was released and No. 2000 dropped.

No. 2009. The Euclid Earth-Hauler Truck with uncoupling 4-wheel tractor to use to tow other toys. It was 27" long, 11 pounds, Euclid green or light roadgrader orange, and the trailer dumped in the same way as the Wooldridge. Priced $14.75.

No. 2010. The American LaFrance Pumper Fire Truck, 18" long, 7 pounds, was bright red with chrome trim, ladder, bell, fire extinguisher, hoses and nozzle, and had a reservoir that held water for hand-operated pressure pump. A beautiful toy at $16.75.

No. 2011. The Heiliner Earth Scraper, 29" long, 13 pounds, bright dark red, loaded and dumped and operated on four wheels as the Wooldridge did. Priced at $16.75.

No. 2012. The Caterpillar D6 Tractor and Bulldozer, caterpillar yellow, 15" long, 7 pounds, with real bulldozer treads for sharp realistic turning (removable only by using punch and hammer to remove connecting pin from between two of the pads) and adjustable bulldozer blade, plus heavy draw bar. Truly a beautiful toy at $13.75. Diesel motor was cast metal.

No. 2013 eliminated and replaced No. 2001. A Barber-Green mobile high-capacity bucket loader, 22" long, 12" high, and 10 pounds, it had buckets on chains and rubber conveyor belt, and was adjustable and steered by steering wheel, priced at $19.75.

No. 2014. The American LaFrance Aerial Ladder Truck, 23" long, 42" extended ladder height, 11 pounds, bright red and chrome, with bell, red light, adjustable side jacks, was a single unit truck steered by steering wheel, priced at $20.75.

Doepke "Model Toys" were doomed to extinction by lower-priced, lightweight imitators of lesser quality, some of which were started in the 1920s. Others came into being in the 1950s, several of which are still around today, but none ever matched the heavy-duty construction and realistic operating qualities of the one and only "Model Toys."

Of the Doepke "Model Toys" that were mass produced, several had variations in their basic construction from time to time. Usually these changes were an elimination of the more intricate operating procedures and had little or no effect on the toy's overall appearance.

In *Antique Toy World*, Philip Sayer wrote a two-part article on the Doepke Co. and featured pictures of nearly all the toys manufactured by the firm. The toys that were produced in limited numbers were mentioned and often described. Also listed were nearly all of the slight changes in the mass-produced toys, though I could not find mention of the change in the D6 Caterpillar. The first models to hit the market had front axles held tightly forward by springs, so that when pushed forward and over a solid object there was something to absorb the shock and protect the tract pads. Later models eliminated this and opted for simple axle wells, as in the rear wheels. Had I not had both types, this slight change could have escaped my notice.

It seems that the Doepke Co. accepted orders to make models of the real thing for various companies, and the toys with the most allure, playability, feasible mass production design, and greatest entertainment value would be mass produced. The others, those that would not withstand rough handling by young hands or were too expensive or time-intensive to produce, were only manufactured in low numbers, sometimes only one. This is no doubt the explanation for the number gaps between the marketed items.

Among the most scarce articles produced were a few automobiles, now avidly sought after by collectors who have delved deeply into this company's past history. These may have been featured in catalogs or brochures, but I have seen only catalogs dealing with the mass-produced toys I have listed.

Ray Funk is a leading collector and authority on trains and other toys, as well as a collector and authority on comic books and western literature.

An ad for DOEPKE Model Toys. Photo by Bill Kaufman. Courtesy Ray Funk.

	C6	C8	C10
Doepke No. 2000 Wooldridge H.D. Earth Hauler, 25" long	100	150	200
Doepke No. 2001 Barber-Greene high-capacity bucket loader, tracks, 13" high	190	285	380
Doepke No. 2002 Jaeger Concrete Mixer, 15" long	140	210	280
Doepke No. 2006 Adams Diesel Road Grader, 26" long	118	177	235
Doepke No. 2007 Unit Mobile Crane, 11-1/2" long	155	232	310
Doepke No. 2008 American LaFrance Aerial Ladder Truck	200	300	400
Doepke No. 2009 Euclid Earth Hauler Truck, 27" long	150	225	300
Doepke No. 2020 American LaFrance Pumper Fire Truck, 18" long	185	278	370
Doepke No. 2011 Heiliner Earth Scraper, 29" long	190	285	380

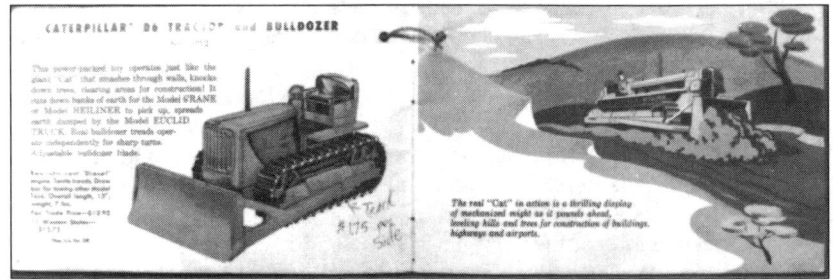

DOEPKE Catalog illustration of Model No. 2012. Photo by Bill Kaufman. Courtesy Ray Funk.

DOEPKE No. 2000 Wooldridge. Courtesy Ray Funk.

DOEPKE No. 2001 Barber-Greene high-capacity bucket loader. Courtesy Ray Funk.

DOEPKE No. 2007 Unit Mobile Crane. Courtesy Ray Funk.

DOEPKE No. 2012 Caterpillar D6's. Courtesy Ray Funk.

Dump Truck, steel wind-up, 4-1/2" long, Courtesy James S. Maxwell/Virginia Caputo. Photo by Virginia Caputo.

	C6	C8	C10
Doepke No. 2012 Caterpillar D6 Tractor and Bulldozer, 15" long	287	430	575

	C6	C8	C10
Doepke No. 2013 Barber-Greene Mobile high-capacity bucket loader, wheels, 22" long	145	218	290
Doepke No. 2014 American LaFrance Aerial Ladder Fire Truck, 23" long	205	308	410
Doepke No. 2015 Clark Airport Tractor and Baggage Trailers	300	450	600
Doepke No. 2015 MG, 1954, 15" long	205	308	410
Doepke No. 2018 Jaguar, 1955	295	442	590
Doepke No. 2023 Searchlight Truck 1955	400	600	800
Druge Bros. "Hyster" lumber carrier	162	243	325
Dump Truck, cast iron, "2205," 4-1/2" long	90	135	180
Dump Truck, tin, wooden wheels, 5-3/4" long	20	30	40
Dump Truck, pressed steel, c. 1939, 6" long	50	75	100
Dump Truck, cast iron, driver, 7" long	90	135	180
Dump Truck (Beck), steers via horn on top of cab, late 1940s, large	60	90	120
Dump Truck, steel windup, 4-1/2" long	20	30	40

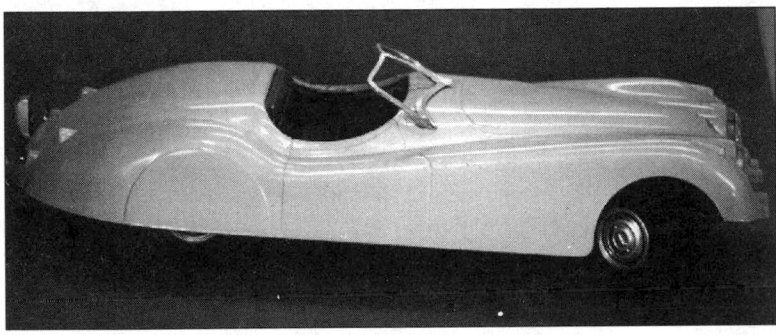

DOEPKE No. 2018 Jaguar. Courtesy Ray Funk.

DUNWELL

Dunwell was the trade name given to its toys by Metal Products Co. of Clifton, New Jersey. Its trucks seem to have been sold c. 1953-1958. Their line closely resembles Tonka's and is rare.

	C6	C8	C10		C6	C8	C10
Dunwell Auto Transport	162	243	325	Dunwell "Red Star Express Lines" Truck	300	450	600
Dunwell Cattle Semi	90	135	180	Dunwell "Snowcrop" Refrigerator Semi	350	525	700
Dunwell Dump Truck	100	150	200	Dunwell "Steel Carrier Co." Semi	170	255	340
Dunwell "Grain Hauler"	50	75	100	Dunwell Wrecker	168	254	335
Dunwell Log Truck	110	165	220				

DYNA-MODEL PRODUCTS COMPANY

"Dyna-Mo"

by Fred Maxwell

Dyna-Model Products Co., 93 South Street, Oyster Bay, Long Island, New York, may have pioneered the scale model industry of today's markets with their "Dyna-Mo" brand of HO toys. They are rather high-quality pot metal toys, identified by their method of assembling body parts (clamping axles between small posts) and by the standardized appearance of the undersides of the whole line.

Probably produced in the 1930s, and perhaps in the post-war era, the toys were made by a coarse die-casting process. The earlier vintage cars were made in two to five parts, exclusive of wheels and axles, to be pinned, clamped or glued together: body, frame, steering wheel, top, and windshield. Some were packaged as kits with instructions printed on the box: "Pinch ends of axel (sic) after installing wheels" (R-26). The toys were factory painted in as many as four colors per toy.

*DYNA-MODEL. Top, left to right: D1; Ford T Roadster, 1-7/8";
D7; D3; Franklin Steam Touring, 2-1/8". Middle, left to right: D5;
D6; D9; D10; D8. Bottom, left to right: D11; Cadillac Sedan, 2";
D23; D16. Photo by Fred Maxwell.*

	C6	C8	C10
D1 Dyna "R-26 HO Surrey, 35c." Horseless carriage, tiller steering, 3 colors, 3-piece body, kit, 1-3/4"	4	6	8
D2 Dyna Touring Car. Antique Stanley Steamer, open tonneau, rt. hand steering, 4 colors, 4-piece, 2"	4	6	8
D3 Dyna Speedster. Antique Mercer, rt. hand steering, 4 colors, 3-piece, 2"	4	6	8
D4 Dyna Roadster. Antique Buick?, open, rt. hand steering, 4-piece, 3 colors, 1-7/8"	4	6	8
D5 Dyna Touring Car. Antique, realistic folded top attachable w/ hinge pins, left hand steering, 5-piece, 2 colors, 1-7/8"	4	6	8
D6 Dyna "R-61 HO Model T Ford 1914 touring with top 60c." 1-piece body, top up, 3 colors, "cut plastic windshield to fit, darken edges with ink or paint and glue top and windshield in place, in slots provided," 1-5/8"	4	6	8
D7 Dyna Touring Car. 1914 Ford, top down cast in 1-piece body, glued windshield, 3 colors, 1-3/4"	4	6	8
D8 Dyna Roadster. 1920s Packard convertible, top down, rumble seat, 1-piece body, glued windshield, spoked wheels, 3 colors, 2"	6	9	12
D9 Dyna Roadster. Packard, same as above, top up, 3 colors, 2"	6	9	12
D10 Dyna Touring. Packard, same as above, top down, 3 colors, 2"	6	9	12
D11 Dyna Roadster. Model A Ford? top down, open rumble seat, disc wheels, 1-piece body, unpainted, 2"	2	3	4
D12 Dyna Sedan. Buick Sedan, 1930s, open windshield and windows, 2 colors, 2"	4	6	8
D13 Dyna "R-68 HO Buick Convertible 55c." Late 1930s, open, 2-door sedan, top down, 1-piece body, solid cast windshield, disc wheels, 2-3/8"	6	9	12
D14 Dyna Sedan. Buick 2-door airflow, open windshield and windows, 2-3/8"	6	9	12
D15 Dyna Taxi. Buick Sedan, late 1930s, open windshield and windows, 2 colors, 2-3/8"	6	9	12
D16 Dyna Convertible, Cadillac 2-door Sedan, late 1930s, 2-3/8"	6	9	12
D17 Dyna Sedan. Cadillac 2-door Sedan, open windshield and windows, incl. rear, late 1930s, 2-3/8"	6	9	12
D18 Dyna Taxi. Cadillac Sedan, late 1930s, open windshield and windows including rear, 2 colors, 2-3/8"	6	9	12
D19 Dyna Sedan. Pontiac 4-door airflow, open windshield and windows incl. rear, 2-3/8"	6	9	12
D20 Dyna Limousine. Cadillac, late 1930s, open windows as above, 2-1/2"	6	9	12
D21 Dyna Delivery Van. Pontiac, late 1930s, open windshield and door windows, 2-3/8"	4	6	8
D22 Dyna Pickup Truck. GMC?, late 1930s, open windows, spoked wheels, 2-piece, 3 colors, 2-1/2"	4	6	8
D23 Dyna Wrecker. GMC?, late 1930s, open windows, 3-piece, 4 colors, 2-3/4"	6	9	12
D24 Dyna Dump Truck. Open windows, hinged body with realistic load of coal, 3-piece, 2 colors, dual rear wheels, 2-3/4"	8	12	16
D25 Dyna Pickup Truck. GMC?, 1930s, 1-piece, open windows, one color, 2"	4	6	9
D26 Dyna Pickup Truck. Mack?, "US Army," Air Corps star decals, late 1930s, 2-piece body, 2 colors, 2"	4	6	8
D27 Dyna Truck. Mack? same chassis as above, but tarpaulin-covered, 2-piece body, 2"	4	6	8
Eldon Corvette, 14" long	37	56	75
Eldon Road Race slot car set, 1965	32	48	65
Eldon Rocket-Firing Tank, 8" long	19	28	38
Eldon Tow Truck, plastic, 18" long	50	75	100

*DYNA-MODEL. Top, left to right: D14; D20?; D12; Cadillac
2-door sedan, 2-3/8". Middle, left to right: D15; D18; D21.
Bottom, left to right: D22; D23; D24. Photo by Fred Maxwell.*

ERIE

(Parker White Metal)

Listing by Dave Leopard

According to James Apthorpe, Erie toys were made by Parker White Metal Company, which apparently began in Erie, Pennsylvania, but moved to Fairview (West of Erie), Pennsylvania in the early 1960s. However, according to company officials he contacted, the firm made toys only prior to WWII. It printed no catalogs.

ERIE Sedan, 2-door. Photo by James Apthorpe.

	C6	C8	C10
EV01 Lincoln Zephyr Sedan, 1936, painted, 5-1/2" long	40	50	60
EV02 Lincoln Zephyr Sedan, 1936, plated, 5-1/2" long	45	55	65
EV03 Lincoln Zephyr Sedan, 1936, painted, 3-1/2" long	25	30	35
EV04 Lincoln Zephyr Sedan, 1936, plated, 3-1/2" long	30	35	40
EV05 Packard Roadster, 1936, painted, 6" long	40	50	60
EV06 Packard Roadster, 1936, plated, 6" long	45	55	65
EV07 Packard Roadster, 1936, painted, 3-1/2" long	25	30	35
EV08 Packard Roadster, 1936, plated, 3-1/2" long	30	35	40

	C6	C8	C10
EV09 Ford Pickup Truck, 1935, low sides, painted, 5" long	40	50	60
EV10 Ford Pickup Truck, 1935, low sides, plated, 5" long	45	55	65
EV11 Ford Pickup Truck, 1935, high sides, large rear window, 5" long	40	50	60
EV12 Ford Pickup Truck, 1935, high sides, small rear window, 5" long	40	50	60
EV13 Ford Ice Truck, 1935, "Pure Ice Co.," 5" long	50	60	70
EV14 Ford Tow Truck, 1935, "Servel Body," 5" long	50	60	70
EV15 Cabover Truck, c. 1937, no tailgate, 3-1/4"	20	25	30
EV16 Cabover Truck, c. 1937, tailgate, updated, 3-1/4" long	20	25	30
EV17 Tow Truck, c. 1939, no chassis, 4-1/4" long	30	35	40
EV18 Sedan, c. 1939, futuristic, fin on trunk, no chassis, 4-1/4" long	30	35	40
EV19 Coupe, c. 1939, futuristic, no chassis, 4-1/4" long	30	35	40
EV20 Sedan, c. 1939, sharknose, no chassis, 4-1/4" long	30	35	40

ERTL

Ertl was started by Fred Ertl Sr. in 1945, working out of his Dubuque, Iowa, home. As business expanded, the firm moved to Dyersville. Ertl had learned to use sand molds in his native Germany, and very early in the company's history he began working directly from the original blueprints to make his toy tractors, trucks, and other wheeled toys. Ertl's specialty is farm toys, with rights obtained from such manufacturers as International Harvester and John Deere. Today Ertl is the largest manufacturer of toy farm equipment in the world and in addition makes a number of other toys, such as cars, trucks and airplanes.

Ertl Case "L" Tractor	42	63	85
Ertl Caterpillar D-6	93	140	195
Ertl Fleetstar 10-wheel Dump Truck, red	85	128	170
Ertl Ford 7500 Backhoe	37	56	75
Ertl GMC Dump	100	150	200
Ertl Grader	225	338	450
Ertl Hydraulic Dump Truck No. 1645	20	30	40
Ertl International Backhoe	50	75	100
Ertl International Dump	100	150	200
Ertl Iron Horse Van	35	52	70
Ertl John Deere 440 Bulldozer	20	30	40
Ertl John Deere 500 Bulldozer w/ blade	50	75	100
Ertl John Deere 6600 Combine	70	105	140
Ertl John Deere Tilt Bed	92	138	185
Ertl Loadstar Dump Truck	132	198	265
Ertl Loadstar Grain/Cattle Stake Truck	60	90	120
Ertl Loadstar Tilt Bed, green/gray	85	128	170
Ertl Loadstar Tow Truck, white/red	100	150	200
Ertl Mary Kay Cosmetics Trailer Truck	75	112	150
Ertl Mobile Tanker	42	63	85
Ertl Picker	30	45	60
Ertl Tractor and Wagon 8600	44	66	88
Ertl Transtar Rowe Furniture Truck	27	41	55
Ertl Transtar Texaco Tanker	45	68	90
Ertl Velveeta Semi	25	38	50

	C6	C8	C10
Fallows Toys, Frederick & Henry Horseless Carriage with driver, cast iron and tin, c. 1905, 8"	1500	2500	3900
Fire Pumper, cast iron, c. 1935 5" long	85	128	170
Fire Pumper, cast iron, approx. 6-1/2" long	100	150	200
Fire Pumper, cast iron, 11" long	125	187	250

FALLOWS TOYS. Frederick & Henry, Horseless Carriage with driver, 8" long. Courtesy Wilkinson Collection, Detroit Antique Toy Museum.

Fire Pumper, cast iron, 5" long, c. 1935. Courtesy Mapes Auctioneers & Appraisers.

Fire Pumper, cast iron, 11" long. Photo by Bill Kaufman. Courtesy Good Old Days Store.

FIRESTONE

The following list, with its codings, was compiled by Dave Leopard.

FIRESTONE FA03 (both) with original box. Photo by Ron Smith.

	C6	C8	C10
FA01 '39 Mercury fastback 4-door sedan, 4-3/4" long	80	100	150
FA02 '35 Ford 2-door humpback sedan, 4-7/8" long	70	105	140
FA03 '36 Ford 2-door humpback sedan, 4-7/8" long	75	112	150
Ford coupe, 1924, 4" long	80	120	160
Ford coupe, blue, chrome wheels, 5" long	80	120	160
Ford coupe, cast iron, black, chrome wheels, c. 1920s, 5" long	80	120	160
"Fordson" Tractor w/ driver, cast iron, 5-3/4" long	140	210	280
Fordson Tractor with hay rake, cast iron, 1930s	150	225	300

FREIDAG

Pronounced "Friday," c. 1920-22, Freeport, Illinois.

	C6	C8	C10
Freidag Bus, cast iron, 6-3/4" long	225	338	450
Freidag Coupe, cast iron, 5-3/4" long	290	435	580
Freidag Racer, driver & passenger, 6-1/2" long	550	900	1300
Gibbs "Gibbs No. 701" Truck	150	250	350
Giftcraft (possibly only the distributor) TA01 Fastback Sedan, c. 1946, Nash, solid rubber, 4" long	15	22	30
Girard Coupe, battery operated headlights, 14" long	290	435	580
Girard Fire Chief Car, 15" long	175	262	350
Girard "Fire Chief Siren Coupe," 14-1/2" long	350	525	700
Girard Fire Truck, 1920s, 12" long	125	188	250
Girard Pump Truck, battery-operated, headlights, 10" long	100	150	200

	C6	C8	C10
Girard Roadster, electrified, 14-1/2" long	195	292	390
Girard Side Dump, 11-1/2" long	97	145	195
Girard Stake Truck, electric, headlights, 10" long	200	300	400
Girard Tank Truck, wood wheels, 11-1/2" long	70	105	140
Girard Touring Bus, painted tin, c. 1920, 12" long	125	188	250
Girard Truck with Trailer, 1930s, 17" long	107	160	215
Grey Iron, Convertible Midget, 1-1/2"	20	30	40
Grey Iron, Coupe Midget, 1-1/2" long	20	30	40
Grey Iron, Delivery Truck, Midget, 1-1/2" long	20	30	40
Grey Iron, Ford Coupe, 8-3/8" long	475	715	950
Grey Iron, Racer, Midget, 1-1/2" long	20	30	40

GIRARD Fire Chief Siren Coupe. Photo by Bill Kaufman.

GIFTCRAFT TA01. Photo by Dave Leopard.

GIRARD Touring Bus. Courtesy Mapes Auctioneers & Appraisers.

GREY IRON "Midget" Vehicles, approx. 1-1/2" long. Photo by Stan Alekna.

	C6	C8	C10
Grey Iron, Sedan, Airflow Type, Midget, 1-1/2" long	20	30	40
Grey Iron, Sedan, older, Midget, 1-1/2" long	20	30	40
Grey Iron, Sedan, 1927, 9" long	1000	1500	2000

	C6	C8	C10
"Guided Missile Unit No. 10" Truck, tin litho, c. 1960	60	90	120
Hafner "Auto Express Co." Truck, steel clockwork, 8-1/2" long	450	675	900
Hafner Curved Dash Olds, c. 1903, pressed steel, clockwork, 10" long	500	750	1000
Hafner Roundabout with upholstered drivers seat, steel clockwork, 7"	450	675	900
Hafner Touring Car, pressed steel, clockwork, 10" long	1200	2000	2800
Happy Sam driving wood truck, c. 1920s, 8" long	80	120	160

Grey Iron made this Ford Coupe. It came in two sizes, 8-3/8" long and 5-5/8" long. It appears in a No. 24 Grey Iron catalog, suggesting it may have been sold in 1924. It came with a driver, as shown.

HAFNER. Left to right: "Auto Express Co.," roundabout with upholstered driver's seat. Courtesy Sotheby's New York.

HAFNER Curved Dash Olds, c. 1903. Courtesy Sotheby's New York.

HAFNER Touring Car, 10" long. Photo by Jeanne Bertoia. Courtesy Bill Bertoia Auctions.

HESS

by Thomas G. Nefos

Plastic promotional vehicles are turned out annually for Hess Service Stations in limited editions available to the public through the Christmas season. Hess headquarters are in Woodbridge, New Jersey, under the name Amerada Hess. Virtually all collector sales are mint in the box, thus the pricing here.

	MIB
1964 B-Model Mack Tanker	1900
1967 Split Window, Velvet Bottom Box	2400
1968 Tanker Truck	675
1969 Amerada Hess Truck	2500
1970 Pumper Fire Truck	695

HESS 1970 Red Pumper Fire Truck. Courtesy Thomas G. Nefos, Federal Shipping Network.

1972 Split Window Tanker	395
1975 Box Trailer	395
1976 Box Trailer w/ Barrels	395

HESS 1976 Box Trailer. Courtesy Thomas G. Nefos, Federal Shipping Network.

1977 Tank Truck - Large Label	175
1978 Tank Truck - Small Label	185
1980 Training Van	395
1982-1983 "First Hess Truck"	95
1984 Tank Truck Bank	95
1985 "First Hess Truck," Bank	125
1986 Ladder, Fire Truck, red	100
1987 "19 Wheeler" Truck w/ Barrels	75
1988 Race Car Transporter	70
1989 Ladder Fire Truck w/ Siren, white	65
1990 Tanker Truck w/ Horn	45

HESS 1982 "First Hess Truck." Courtesy Thomas G. Nefos, Federal Shipping Network.

HESS 1989 Ladder Fire Truck. Courtesy Thomas G. Nefos, Federal Shipping Network.

	MIB
1991 Semi Tanker Truck	35
1992 Like 1991 but remote control	40
1993 Hess Patrol Car	28
1994 Hess Rescue Car	25
1995 Hess Truck and Helicopter	20

	C6	C8	C10
Hillclimber "Ambulance," very early, 10-1/2" long	500	800	1100
Hillclimber Armored Truck, pressed steel, friction, 11" long	500	800	1100
Hillclimber Auto, woman driver, friction, very early, 6" long	500	750	1000
Hillclimber Hook and Ladder Wagon, painted pressed steel, friction, driver, 20" long	300	450	600
Hillclimber Horseless Carriage, woman driver, cast iron and wood, very early, 7" long	350	525	700
Hillclimber Racer with track, 7-1/2" long	375	562	750
Hillclimber Touring Car, 11" long	475	715	950
Hiller Comet Race Car, "3," fuel-powered, c. 1940-42	1200	2000	2800
Hoge Fire Chief Car, 15" long	335	500	670

HILLCLIMBER Horseless Carriage, woman driver, 7" long. Courtesy Mapes Auctioneers & Appraisers.

HILLER Comet Race Car "3." Photo by William G. Floyd.

	C6	C8	C10
Hook and Ladder, aluminum, with driver, 13" long	100	150	200
Hook and Ladder, tin friction, 21" long	100	150	200
Hose Wagon, 1897, two riders, friction toy	125	187	250

	C6	C8	C10
"Holmes Coal Co." pressed steel delivery truck, 17-1/2" long	400	600	800

"Holmes Coal Co." Courtesy Sotheby's New York.

HUBLEY

The Hubley manufacturing company was founded at least as early as 1892 by John Hubley and made iron toys from the start at its plant in Lancaster, Pennsylvania. At the beginning all toys were cast iron. Early toys included coal ranges, circus wagons, and mechanical banks. Hubley's cast-iron toys were popular almost from the start and have long been collector's items, as they were well made and attractive. By 1940, however, the cast-iron toy, due to the increased cost of freight and foreign competition, was becoming a thing of the past. At this time, when Hubley was the largest producer of cast-iron toys and cap pistols in the world, it began to introduce die-cast zinc alloy toys. During WWII Hubley was 98% engaged in war production, turning out over five million M-74 bomb fuses, which the Hubley engineers had played a large part in developing. Since the war, Hubley has manufactured die-cast toys and plastic toys exclusively. In 1952 Hubley manufactured 9,763,610 toys and 11,184,878 cap pistols, about ten times the amount of toys and pistols they produced in 1930 but with a line of toys 80% smaller than in 1930. Hubley was acquired by Gabriel Industries in late 1965, and puts out holster sets, cap pistols, vehicles, hobby kits, and a number of other toys.

	C6	C8	C10
Hubley Air Compress Truck, c. 1950s, 7" long	50	75	100
Hubley Army Motor Truck No. 807 with driver, 15" long	1100	1700	2500
Hubley Auto, 6-1/2" long	80	120	160
Hubley Auto, 1922, Chevy?, 9" long	400	600	800
Hubley Auto Carrier, w/ three cars and one pickup truck, c. 1939, 10" long	262	395	525
Hubley Auto Express, cast iron, 9"	900	1400	1900
Hubley Auto, c. 1950s, black plastic wheels, die-cast	12	18	25

	C6	C8	C10
Hubley Avery Tractor, very early, 4-3/4" long	112	168	225
Hubley Bell Telephone Truck, 3-3/4" long	150	225	300
Hubley Bell Telephone, 5-1/4" long	175	262	350
Hubley Bell Telephone, 7" long	600	950	1300
Hubley Bell Telephone, tools and ladders, 8-1/4" long	425	638	850
Hubley Bell Telephone, with tools, 12" long	500	800	1100
Hubley Bell Telephone Truck, 1940s, 12-1/2" long	75	112	150

HUBLEY Bell Telephone, 24" long, postwar. Courtesy Thomas G. Nefos, Federal Shipping Network.

HUBLEY Caterpillar, 3-1/4" long. Courtesy Mapes Auctioneers & Appraisers.

HUBLEY Dump Truck, Mack, 1930s, 6 tires, 10-3/4" long. Driver missing in photo. Courtesy James S. Maxwell/Virginia Caputo. Photo by Virginia Caputo.

HUBLEY "Elgin, The" Street Sweeper, 8" long. Courtesy Chic Gast.

HUBLEY 5 Ton Truck. Courtesy Sotheby's New York.

Left to right: HUBLEY "Merchants Delivery." ARCADE ambulance, "City Ambulance," 6" long. Courtesy Chic Gast.

	C6	C8	C10
Hubley Bell Telephone Truck, 1931, with derrick and windlass, auger, trailer with 10" pole, three digging tools, and two loose ladders, 10"	500	750	1040
Hubley Bell Telephone, just ladders as equipment, 13" long	250	375	500
Hubley Bell Telephone Truck, implements, 9" long	600	1000	1350
Hubley Bell Telephone, post-WWII, 24" long	87	130	175
Hubley Black & White Cab, 1920s	1200	2000	3000
Hubley "Borden's Milk Cream," deluxe version, rubber tires, clicker, 7-1/2"	2000	3500	5500
Hubley "Borden's Milk Cream," standard version, 6" long	475	715	950
Hubley Bulldozer, die-cast, front scoop, c. 1950, rubber treads, 10-1/4"	62	93	125
Hubley Bus, (futuristic type), c. 1935, 3-1/2" long	50	75	100
Hubley Bus, c. 1938, rubber wheels, 5-1/2" long	50	75	100
Hubley Bus, 1930s, 8" long	60	90	120
Hubley, die-cast, c. 1950s, 9" long	20	30	40
Hubley Cadillac, die-cast, 7" long	40	60	80
Hubley 2278 Car and 2279 House Trailer, c. 1939	150	225	300
Hubley Caterpillar Tractor, driver in cab, 3-1/4" long	92	138	185
Hubley Caterpillar Tractor, 9" long	62	93	125
Hubley Cattle Truck, post-war	85	128	170
Hubley Cement Mixer, 18" long	400	600	800
Hubley Champion Stake Truck, 1930s, white rubber tires, 8-1/2" long	140	210	280
Hubley Chemical Truck with ladders 13" long	200	300	400
Hubley Chevrolet 1932 Coupe, kit	25	38	50
Hubley Chevrolet 1932 Phaeton kit, 1960s	40	60	80
Hubley Chevrolet 1932 Roadster kit, 1960s	25	38	50
Hubley Chrysler Airflow, take-apart body, 4-1/2" long	117	175	235
Hubley Chrysler Airflow, take-apart body, 6-3/4" long	425	638	850
Hubley Chrysler Airflow, electrified, white rubber tires on wood hubs, 8" long	1200	2000	3240
Hubley Chrysler Airflow Racing Car, c. 1938	100	150	200
Hubley "Coal" Truck, c. 1922, cast iron, 9-1/2" long	438	655	875
Hubley Coal Truck, cast iron, with driver 16-3/4" long	1200	1800	2500
Hubley "Coast to Coast" Bus, cast iron, 1927, 13" long	1000	1600	2200
Hubley Corvette, 13-1/2" long	255	380	510
Hubley Coupe, 1933 Ford	140	210	280
Hubley Coupe Roadster, rumble seat, rubber tires, 11" long	212	318	425
Hubley Crash Car, 3-wheel motorcycle, chrome wheels, 11-1/2" long	2400	4200	6365
Hubley Crash Car, c. 1937, white rubber tires, 4-3/4" long	100	150	200
Hubley Digger, Mack, General, 10" long	450	700	1000

	C6	C8	C10
Hubley Duesenberg Town Car, build-it model, 9" long	30	45	60
Hubley Dump Truck, 5-1/2" long	87	130	175
Hubley Dump Truck, c. 1938, 7-1/2" long	295	442	590
Hubley Dump Truck, Mack, 1930s, 6 tires, 10-3/4" long	650	1000	1500
Hubley "Elgin, The" Street Sweeper, cast iron, 1931, 8" long	1550	2800	4350
Hubley Fire Engine Pumper, c. 1920, cast iron, black rubber tires, driver, boiler-tender, 12-1/2" long	350	525	700
Hubley Fire Engine Pumper, early, No. 504	350	525	700
Hubley Fire Engine No. 526, c. 1936, 10-1/2" long	175	263	350
Hubley Fire Engine, die-cast, white rubber tires with wooden rims, c. 1941	112	168	225
Hubley Fire Ladder Truck, early, 8-1/2"	350	525	700
Hubley Fire Ladder Truck, c. 1920, 2 wood ladders, 15-1/2" long	300	450	600
Hubley Fire Ladder Truck, 19-1/2" long	600	950	1450
Hubley Fire Truck w/ searchlight, white rubber tires with wooden rims	55	82	110
Hubley Fire Truck, 5" long	120	180	240
Hubley "5 Ton Truck," 8 wooden barrels, c. 1920, 17" long	700	1150	1760
Hubley Ford Coupe, 1936	40	60	80
Hubley Ford Model A Coupe Kit, 1960s	27	41	55
Hubley Ford Model A Phaeton Kit, 1960s	32	48	65
Hubley Ford Model A Pickup Kit, 1960s	32	48	65
Hubley Ford Model A Station Wagon Kit, 1960s	37	56	75
Hubley Ford Model A Town Car Kit, 1960s	32	48	65
Hubley Ford Model A Victoria Kit, 1960s	40	60	80
Hubley Fordson Front-End Loader, cast iron, c. early 1930s, 9" long	800	1400	2000
Hubley Hook & Ladder No. 463	28	42	56
Hubley Hook & Ladder Truck, cast iron, 19-1/2" long	200	300	400
Hubley Huber Road Roller, 4-1/2" long	110	165	220
Hubley Huber Road Roller, 8" long	382	575	765

HUBLEY Huber Road Roller, 8" long. Courtesy Mapes Auctioneers & Appraisers.

	C6	C8	C10
Hubley Huber Road Roller, tractor-like, 7-3/4" long	257	385	515
Hubley Huber Road Roller, 13" long	2200	3300	5000
Hubley Huber Road Roller, 15" long	2500	3700	6000

	C6	C8	C10
Hubley "Jaeger" Cement Mixer 185	278	370
Hubley Jaguar Roadster, 1950s, 9" 55	82	110
Hubley Kiddietoy No. 432 MGTD Roadster, 6" long 110	165	220
Hubley Kiddietoy No. 510 series Dump Truck 125	188	250
Hubley Kiddietoy No. 457 Racer, die-cast, rubber tires, 6-1/2" long 27	41	55
Hubley Kiddietoy "Patrol" Stake Truck, c. 1937 27	41	55
Hubley Ladder Truck c. late 1930s, 5" long 45	68	90
Hubley Ladder Truck, Terraplane front, 1930s, 6" long 312	468	625
Hubley Ladder Truck, 1930s, 10" long 110	165	225
Hubley Ladder Truck, c. 1940, 13-1/2" long ... 350	525	700
Hubley Life Saver Truck, c. 1930, hole in rear is large enough to hold pack of Life Savers, 4-1/4" long 675	1100	1650
Hubley Life Saver Truck, small hole in rear, can't hold Life Savers 400	600	800
Hubley Limousine, 6-door, 1920s, 7" long 138	205	275
Hubley Lincoln Zephyr, 7-1/4" long 240	360	480
Hubley Lincoln Zephyr and House Trailer, cast iron, 14" overall 375	563	750
Hubley Log Truck No. 469 55	83	110
Hubley Log Truck with five chained logs, black rubber tires, die-cast, approx. 19" long 138	205	275
Hubley Low Boy Truck, trailer, tractor 200	300	400
Hubley Mack Dump Truck, with driver, 11-1/2" long 650	1100	1600
Hubley Mack Truck Steam Shovel-Digger, c. 1920, nickel wheels and scoop, 7" long 1300	2200	3200
Hubley "Merchants Delivery," 1920s, approx. 6" long 400	600	800
Hubley MG, 8-3/4" long 112	168	225
Hubley MG, 5-3/4" long 55	82	110
Hubley "Milk Cream" Truck, 1930s, cast iron, white rubber tires, 3-1/2" 400	600	800
Hubley Model T Coupe, 4" long 100	150	200
Hubley Monarch Tractor, 5-1/2" long 600	900	1200
Hubley Motor Express Tractor and Trailer, black rubber tires, 500 series, approx. 19" long 95	143	190
Hubley 2287 "Motor Express" Truck and Trailer, 8" long 162	243	325
Hubley Motorcycle, Armored, w/ sidecar and removable riders, 9" long 1200	2000	2750
Hubley Motorcycle, has light in front and place for battery, 6" long 300	450	600
Hubley Motorcycle and rider, 4" long 110	165	220
Hubley Motorcycle, "Harley-Davidson," civilian rider, 6-1/4" long 382	575	775
Hubley Motorcycle, Harley-Davidson, w/ policeman, 1930s, swivel head, small wheels near feet, 7-1/4" long 700	1200	1600
Hubley Motorcycle, Harley-Davidson, w/ policeman, white rubber wheels, 5-1/2" long 275	363	550
Hubley Motorcycle, Harley-Davidson, Police, w/ sidecar and rider, 5-1/4" long 250	350	500

HUBLEY Motorcycle, Harley-Davidson with policeman, 1930s, approx. 7-1/4" long, swivel head, wheels and color variation. Courtesy Wilkinson Collection, Detroit Antique Toy Museum.

HUBLEY Motorcycle, 6" long, has light in front and place for battery. Courtesy Sotheby's New York.

HUBLEY Motorcycle with sidecar. Courtesy Sotheby's New York.

	C6	C8	C10
Hubley Motorcycle Hill Climber, 1936, No. 649, 6-3/4" long 400	600	800
Hubley Motorcycle, Indian, policeman rider, nickel-plated cylinder, 9-1/4" long 800	1300	1800
Hubley Motorcycle, Kiddietoy, plastic, 5" long 15	22	30

HUBLEY Motorcycle with sidecar, battery-operated headlight, cop driver, passenger. Courtesy Sotheby's New York.

HUBLEY Motorcycle, Harley-Davidson with sidecar and rider (wrong driver on motorcycle). Courtesy Sotheby's New York.

	C6	C8	C10
Hubley Motorcycle, policeman, "Cop," 1920s, 4" long	50	75	100
Hubley Motorcycle with detachable cop, cast iron, "Made USA," c. mid-1930s, 4-1/4" long	60	90	120
Hubley Motorcycle w/ sidecar, battery-operated headlight, cop driver, passenger, 8" long	1150	1900	2650
Hubley Motorcycle with sidecar, No. 46-F, two demountable policemen, 8-1/2" long	700	1200	1600

	C6	C8	C10
Hubley Motorcycle, 2-cylinder Indian, w/ sidecar, two cops, 9" long	600	900	1200
Hubley Motorcycle "Traffic Car," four cylinder Indian w/ stake sides on 2-wheel cart, 11-1/2" long	1500	2500	3500
Hubley Motorcycle, Parcel Post Delivery, w/ 2-wheel cart, 9-1/4" long	1300	2200	2900
Hubley Motorcycle, "U.S. Air Mail," 9-1/2" long	1100	2000	2700
Hubley Motorized Steam Pumper, c. 1930s, 4" long	50	75	100
Hubley Nite Coach, metal wheels, went on "Nu-Car" carrier, 1930s, 3-1/2" long	30	45	60

HUBLEY Motorcycle, Parcel Post Delivery. Courtesy Sotheby's New York.

HUBLEY Nite Coach, 3-1/2" long, metal wheels, went on "Nu-Car" carrier, 1930s. Courtesy Chic Gast.

HUBLEY Motorcycle, "U.S. Air Mail." Courtesy Sotheby's New York.

HUBLEY "Panama" Digger, 13" long. Courtesy Joe and Sharon Freed.

	C6	C8	C10
Hubley "Nucar Transport" w/ trailer, 4 cars, 17" long	490	735	980
Hubley Packard, 15 parts, 1929, 11" long, straight eight, auctioned 1994, excellent, minor repairs, for $16,000			
Hubley Packard, 1930 "Phaeton" kit	50	75	100
Hubley Packard Roadster Kit	50	75	100
Hubley "Panama" Digger, (hard to find), approx. 3-1/2" long	162	243	325
Hubley "Panama" Digger, 9-1/2" long	800	1300	1800
Hubley "Panama" Digger, Mack, 13" long	800	1400	2100
Hubley Parcel Post Motorcycle and sidecar, Harley-Davidson, 9-1/2"	1600	2800	4000
Hubley "Patrol," driver, policeman, 15-1/2" long	1400	2100	2800
Hubley Pipe Truck No. 803, c. 1950s, 9-1/2" long	35	52	70
Hubley Power Shovel, 14"	105	158	210
Hubley Pumper, c. late 1930s	115	172	230
Hubley Pumper, Terraplane front, 1930s, 6-1/4" long	150	225	300
Hubley Racer, "1790," approx. 5"	100	150	200

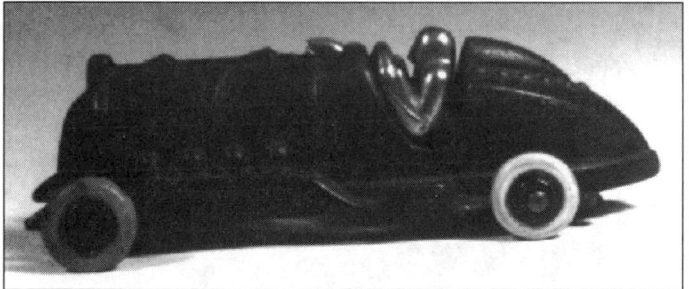

HUBLEY Racer "1790." Photo by Bill Kaufman.

	C6	C8	C10
Hubley Racer, 1930s, 2 passengers, 5-1/2" long	130	195	260
Hubley Racer, plastic, 6-1/2" long	48	72	95
Hubley Racer, driver, large tail fin, 7" long	165	248	330
Hubley Racer, 2241, 1930s, 7-1/2" long	55	83	110
Hubley Racer No. 5, early wheels	1200	2000	2700
Hubley Racer No. 5, painted and nickeled iron and aluminum, raise hood-see motor, 9-1/2" long	900	1600	2290

	C6	C8	C10
Hubley Racer 629, 1936, 6-3/4" long	142	215	285
Hubley Racer "No. 1," 8" long	250	375	500
Hubley Racer, driver, rubber tires, 8"	250	375	500
Hubley Racer, die-cast, black rubber tires, 4" long	80	120	160
Hubley Racer, animated exhaust stacks, driver, 8" long	600	1000	1400
Hubley "Railway Express" Truck, rubber tires, 5" long	150	225	300
Hubley Road Grader, 12" long	60	90	120
Hubley Road Roller, late 1920s, driver, 8" long	300	450	600
Hubley Road Scraper No. 481	60	90	120
Hubley "Say it with Flowers" 10-1/2" long, auctioned 1994, excellent, for $18,000			
Hubley Sedan, 1920, cast iron, 7" long	100	150	200

HUBLEY "Railway Express" Truck, 5" long. Courtesy Mapes Auctioneers & Appraisers.

	C6	C8	C10
Hubley Sedan, 1928, cast iron, 7" long	150	225	300
Hubley Sedan, c. 1938, 2-door, looks like Ford, rubber wheels, 3-1/2"	70	105	140
Hubley Service Car, 4-1/4" long	60	90	120

HUBLEY Stake Bed Truck, 7" long. Courtesy Mapes Auctioneers & Appraisers.

	C6	C8	C10
Hubley Service Car, cast iron, including wheels, 5" long	200	300	400
Hubley Sport Car No. 485	70	105	140
Hubley Stake Truck, c. late 1930s	165	248	330
Hubley No. 614 Stake Truck, c. 1930s	75	112	150
Hubley Stake Bed Truck, cast iron, 3-1/2" long	25	38	50
Hubley Stake Bed Truck, 7" long	100	150	200
Hubley Stake Truck w/ trailer, No. 927, two-piece, 21" long	100	150	200
Hubley No. 452 Stake-type Truck, black rubber tires, c. post-WWII	55	82	110
Hubley Station Wagon, c. 1940s, 1950s, 8-1/2" long	75	112	150
Hubley Steam Roller, 5" long	100	150	200
Hubley Steam Shovel, "General," 7" long	238	357	575
Hubley Steam Shovel, "General," rubber tires on hubs, 9" long	375	563	750
Hubley Steam Shovel, "General," 15" long	450	700	1000
Hubley Studebaker Roadster, frame and body separate	300	450	600
Hubley Studebaker Touring Car, cast iron	325	518	650
Hubley Telephone Truck, plastic	25	38	50
Hubley Touring Auto, 1915, cast iron, chauffeur and rider, 9-1/2" long	700	1300	1750
Hubley Tow Truck, cast iron, c. 1930s, 8-3/4" long	180	270	360
Hubley T-Bird	120	180	240
Hubley Tractor No. 472	30	45	60
Hubley Tractor, Ford 6000	150	225	300
Hubley Tractor, steam boiler in front, c. early 1920s, 4-3/4" long	125	188	250
Hubley Tractor, 1930s, 5" long	362	545	725
Hubley Tractor Loader No. 501, 1950s, 11" long	77	115	155
Hubley Tractor Trailer and Road Scraper No. 506	100	150	200
Hubley Trailer Truck, c. 1936-38	100	150	200
Hubley Transitional Fire Patrol, cast iron, driver, firemen, 1920, 12"	800	1300	2000

	C6	C8	C10
"Hubley U.S.A." Airflow type, c. 1937, approx. 3-1/2" long	20	30	40
Hubley Wrecker, chrome wheels, service car	45	68	90
Hubley Wrecker, 3-1/2"	32	48	65
Hubley Wrecker, rubber wheels, 1930, 4-1/2" long	65	98	130
Hubley Wrecker, 4-3/4" long	115	172	230
Hubley Wrecker, c. 1940, white wheels on large hubs, 6" long	65	98	130
Hubley Wrecking Truck, 1930, cast iron, rubber tires, 7-1/2" long	150	225	300
Hubley Yellow Cab, c. 1939, 8" long	650	1150	1600
Ideal American LaFrance Fire Truck	72	108	145
Ideal Barracuda Coupe, 1964, plastic, 4" long	15	22	30
Ideal Cadillac, 4-door, 1948, plastic, 4" long	25	38	50
Ideal Car Trailer, c. 1945, plastic, 3" long	20	30	40
Ideal Car Trailer, 4 cars, plastic, 27" long	40	60	80
Ideal Corvette	50	75	100
Ideal Fix-it Convertible	65	98	130
Ideal Mercedes Sedan, plastic, 9" long	35	52	70
Ideal Pickup Truck, American, 1948, plastic, 4" long	7	10	14
Ideal Pickup Truck, Ford, 1940, plastic, 4" long	20	30	40
Ideal Semi, 12" long	35	52	70
Ideal "Television Repair" Truck	50	75	100
Ideal Tow Truck, plastic and metal, 17" long	48	72	95
Ideal Tractor, 1948, plastic, 4" long	20	30	40
Irwin Dream Car Convertible, metal, 16" long	200	300	400
Irwin Ford Sunliner, plastic friction, 9"	88	132	175
Irwin Ice Cream Truck, plastic, 15" long	42	63	85
Irwin Jaguar Roadster, 6" long	35	52	70
Ives horseless carriage runabout, 6-1/2" long, 6" high to the top of jockey cap on driver	2500	3750	5000
Ives steamer, cast iron, two drivers, 19-1/2" long	500	750	1000
Jaeger Cement Mixer, cast iron	475	712	950

JAEGER Cement Mixer. Courtesy Mapes Auctioneers & Appraisers.

JANE FRANCIS TOYS

Information and listing from Dave Leopard

These toys seem to have been made in Pittsburgh, Pennsylvania, during the early post-WWII period. All of their vehicles were die-cast.

	C6	C8	C10
JF01 Pickup Truck, 6-1/2" long	30	40	50
JF02 Pickup Truck, No. 347, 5" long	20	25	30
JF03 Pickup Truck, No. 447, 5" long	20	25	30
JF04 Tow Truck, No. 447, 5" long	30	35	40
JF05 Gulf Truck, tin cover, No. 447, 5" long	35	52	70
JF06 Sedan, fastback, futuristic, 6-1/2" long	42	63	85
JF07 Sedan, fastback, futuristic, with wind-up motor, 6-1/2" long	70	105	140
Jane Francis "Gulf" Service Station, 8 pieces	375	562	750
Jeep, glass candy container, 4" long	20	30	40
"Jeepster," rubber tires, 14-1/4" long	20	30	40
Jones & Bixler "Express J & B" Truck 15-1/2" long	800	1300	1900

JONES & BIXLER, "Express J&B" Truck. Courtesy Sotheby's New York.

THE JUDY COMPANY

History and listing by Dave Leopard

The Judy Company of Minneapolis, Minnesota, made educational toys, including a farm set called Happy's Farm Family (patented in 1945), which included a solid rubber car, pickup truck, and tractor, along with human and animal figures.

	C6	C8	C10
JA01 Sedan, 2 dimensional, (part of set), solid rubber, 5-1/4" long	15	20	25
JT01 Pickup Truck, 2 dimensional, (part of set), solid rubber, 5-1/4" long	15	20	25
JF01 Farm Tractor, 2 dimensional (part of set), solid rubber, 3-1/2" long	15	20	25

KANSAS TOY & NOVELTY COMPANY

by Fred Maxwell (Slushmold Contributing Editor) and Bob Condray with the assistance of Lorene Sorell, L.D. Morgison & the Clifton Historical Society

Although neither the first nor the last Kansas Toy has been firmly identified, we have made enough progress to have confidence in this listing. We found that those "toys with numbers" was more collector gossip than a good rule. Some slushmolds with numbers are not Kansas Toy & Novelty Company (KT&N) and many KT&N were not numbered. Numbers on racers and railroad cars seem appropriate, but on some others they are so disfiguring as to suggest a commercial need. Being unlabeled, unboxed bin-toys, the number may have been a convenience to certain wholesale buyers.

Arthur L. Haynes, an auto mechanic, started molding toys in his Clifton, Kansas, shed for local stores in 1923. With clever hands and an artist's eye, he charmed his friends and local townspeople with his bright-colored toys. He made his patterns from advertising pictures, from local vehicles and probably from other makes of toys such as Tootsietoy. He made his own production tools. His range was diverse.

This was a town enterprise from the beginning. Jess Foster, the News editor, helped with alloy mixtures; Mr. Hadsell, the Union Pacific agent (see #38, an early promotional?), suggested they send samples to Woolworths in New York. Clayton D. Young, a traveling salesman, saw the toys, joined the company, and built a profitable business with the chain stores, including Kress, Kresge, and Sears-Roebuck. He also became a partner. At its peak of international sales in the late 1920s the company employed as many as 65 in two shifts during the Christmas order season.

They were young people who had grown up together, a happy gang who joked and sang at their work. This informality was reflected in the local name, "the Hoopie Factory." Two or three of their early toys, and #26 and #33, were strip-downs—hoopies—probably raced locally. Whether "Whoopee," tractor toy #48, was a local spelling of this or whether it celebrated a fat cheering order is not known. Certainly a lot of happy "Whoopee-e-e-s" must have floated from hoopie-land.

Teamwork there must have been, for a molder, according to Ernes Istas, could produce 2000 toys a day. Helen Istas was the secretary and Bill Haynes was another molder, evidence of the family nature of the work force with its clippers (trimmers), painters, clampers (axles), and boxers. "Butch" Morgison, one of our sources, was each of these during his long career with the company. Haynes believed that he invented hollow-casting of metal toys, so he must have started with solid toys. One day he dropped his full mold, spilling its hot metal. To his delight he had a perfect, hollow auto toy, with promise of savings of metal and shipping costs.

Because KT&N founded a dynasty of several reproducers using original molds, many of which are in use today, collectors and dealers may be confused. To reduce this confusion I am including pertinent design details.

Metal wheels of several sizes and styles (disc, simulated wire, and spoked), were characteristic of early KT&N. Rubber tires on wood hubs (popularized by Tootsietoy Grahams) were introduced on #75 in 1932. These were followed by white soft-rubber wheels (simulating balloon tires) and realistic white hard-rubber disc wheels sometimes painted with black "tires." Rubber wheels were used industry-wide, so are not good clues. Several Kansas Toys were made in 2 or 3 sizes (5¢, 10¢, 15¢). Bottom-pans were not cast until high numbers (#76). Many were made with string-pull loops or knobs in the handcrank position. All colors were used, including gold, silver, and pink; a few found with two-colored bodies may have been sales samples. Many early toys were finished in Egyptian lacquer, a japanning applied thinly so the bright metal showed through with a glittery look. A mint toy with this finish has a modern look. Later toys were enameled. "Made in USA" embossed on the bodies is a sure clue to reproductions (this copyright law went into effect in the late 1930s) as are black rubber wheels.

We found that Clayton Stevenson, a toymaker in his own right (see Lincoln White Metal Works and Midwest Toy), had been furnishing some molds and some patterns as a subcontractor since the mid-1920s. He must have originated those handsome designs from 3-piece molds, such as #8, #58, #60, #80, and #91, with their intricate, realistic front ends. Some higher numbers have Stevenson-type patterned pans. These features slowed production and added to costs while blurring the difference between Kansas and Lincoln toys, but they made for rarity.

During its good years KT&N produced more toys than any in the industry save Barclay. Mr. Young left the company in the late 1920s: whether it was the loss of his talents and assets or the onset of the Great Depression, the company was in trouble by 1930. George Hoeffer reorganized the company and moved it across town, but this effort lasted only a few months. Although KT&N continued until 1935 a happy era was coming to an end for Clifton.

Among its many designs we were not surprised to find toys reflecting familiar vehicles (hoopies, stripdowns, midget racers, trucks, tractors, and farm implements), but KT&N also made miniatures of record-setting aircraft and land-speed record cars (#6, #32, #46 and #97). All in all, a remarkable output from a shed in a small farming center!

Fred Maxwell, collector and occasional author, has been collecting antique aircraft and vehicle toys for 25 years. This retirement hobby was started from scratch, for his lead soldiers were missing when he returned home from college. He founded Capital Miniature Auto Collectors Club 20 years ago to promote interest in the Central Atlantic states. He felt challenged by the lack of public knowledge and the ambiguity of the orphan category known as pot metal or slushmold toys.

Note: For additional photos and different views refer to Best Toy and Novelty Co., Craftoy, and Ralstoy, all of whom reproduced from original KT&N molds up to #102.

Note: See list of abbreviations, page 13.

	C6	C8	C10
KTV0 Large Coupe, no #, crude, high-bodied "Ford," HO, HG, no headlamps, SP, VL, 5 windows, door handles, wheel type unknown because only a reproduction has been found, 3-1/4"			No Price Found
KTV1 Midget Racer, no #, no driver, torpedo tail, HO, SP, VL, HG, 5/8" MDW w/ simulated lug nuts, lacquer finish. Some say this was their first toy; some say first had non-moveable wheels or was a large racer, 3" long	20	30	40
KTV2 Midget Racer, no #, same as above, w/ driver, plain MDW, lacquer. Easily confused with another maker's copy. See #31 and #67, 3" long	70	105	140
KTV3 Large Indy Racer, no #, driver, boattail, HO, MDW, lacquer, 6" long			No Price Found

	C6	C8	C10
KTV4 Coupe, no #, crude, slant roof, shallow rear body, no fenders, hood similar to first racer above, lacquer. First "hoopie" or stripdown made?, 3-1/8" long	32	48	65
KTV5 Sedan, no #, crude limousine or stretch taxi, 6 windows, louvered rear quarters, HO, VL, HG, T, SP, large MDW, lacquer, 3-3/8" long			No Price Found
KTV6 Coupe, no #, Convertible, LI, VL, HG, WV, SP, MDSW, lacquer, 2-7/8	30	45	60
KTV7 Coupe, "8," Convertible, LI, VL, HG, WV, SP, RM, MWW, no HO, no headlamps, enamel finish, also UVs with "Chrysler," headlamps and HO; or with MDSW, 3-1/8" long	20	30	40

KTV8 Coupe, "8," trunk convertible, T, HO, VG, SM, MDW, 3-1/8" .... No Price Found

Note: #8 is the lowest-numbered vehicle found. Its realistic high quality signals the ending of a novice toymaker's experimental phase. The five coupes above have the same 1924 Chrysler hood and nice details like landau irons and kickplates, but not all had headlamps. The basic body expanded into this series of coupes, #14 roadsters, and sedans (all(?) unnumbered), lacquered or enameled, with three types of wheels: MDW, MD-SW, and MWW. They were unnamed or named Chrysler, Cadillac, or Chevrolet. Any Fords out there? The large coupe, KTV9, is a scale-up of #8. Only three of these large pieces are known: the racer KTV3, John Deere tractor KTV19, and a mail-plane.

KANSAS TOY Autos. Top, left to right: KTV4, KTV5. Middle, left to right: KTV7, KTV7. Bottom, left to right: KTV26, KTV26, KTV43. Photo courtesy Fred Maxwell.

	C6	C8	C10

KTV9 Large Coupe, no #, Chrysler convertible, MWW and 2 golf club doors, larger version of #8, 5" .... No Price Found

KTV10 Sedan, no #, "Chevrolet," 6 windows, LI, WV, VL, SP, RM, MWW, 2-7/8" long .. 16   24   32

KTV11 Sedan, no #, "Chevrolet," as above, HG, HO, MSW, 3-1/4" .... No Price Found

KTV12 Overland Bus, "9," "Fageol," solid windows, 3-1/2" long 42   63   85

KANSAS TOY Bus, KTV12. Photo courtesy Fred Maxwell.

	C6	C8	C10

KTV13 Overland Bus, no #, "Fageol," 9 male passengers, driver and "baggage" cast on windows, HG, RM, MDW, also an UV w/ various family passengers on windows, also w/ comic characters (Kansas Toy?) 3-1/2" 26   39   52

KTV14 Indy Racer, "10," driver, boattail, exhaust right, VL, HG, HO, SP, MSW or MWW, also UV, 3-1/8" 6   9   12

KTV15 Roadster, "14" open "Chrysler," solid W/S, plain grille, HO, VL, SP, RM, MDSW, 3-1/8" long 18   27   36

KANSAS TOY Commercial Vehicles. Top, left to right: KTV20, KTV33. Middle, left to right: KTV34, KTV36. Bottom, left to right: KTV38, KTV41. Photo courtesy Fred Maxwell.

KANSAS TOY Racers. Top, left to right: KTV1, KTV2. Middle, left to right: KTV14, KTV24, KTV52. Bottom, left to right: KTV35, KTV25. Photo courtesy Fred Maxwell.

KANSAS TOY Farm Vehicles. Top, left to right: KTV17, KTV17. Middle, left to right: KTV23, KTV21. Bottom, left to right: KTV23, KTV17. Photo courtesy Fred Maxwell.

KANSAS TOY Vehicles. Top, left to right: KTV16, KTV15. Second row: KTV14, KTV25. Third row: KTV33, KTV35. Bottom row: KTV36, KTV58. Photo courtesy Fred Maxwell.

	C6	C8	C10
KTV16 Roadster, no #, same as above, HG, 2 golf club doors, 3-1/8"	No Price Found		
KTV17 Farm Tractor, "17," "Fordson," driver, HG, crank, no tow hook, large 1-1/4" and 3/4" MDW with 4 holes in discs, also found with same size 6 spoke wheels, 2-7/8" long, see #57	35	52	70
KTV18 Farm Tractor, no #, same basic body as above, "Fordson" on radiator and crankcase, VG and tow hook, with smaller, plain MDW, 2-5/8"	No Price Found		

	C6	C8	C10
KTV19 Large Farm Tractor, no #, Deere Model D, a finely crafted replica in 2 colors, steering shaft, fly wheel, belt drive wheel, rear fenders, large 2" and 1" 12-spoke wheels, 4-7/8"	No Price Found		
KTV20 Truck, "20," Ford?, solid w/s, 2 OW, 3 tanks, VL, HG, rear faucet, MWW, versions w/ and w/o driver, also an UV, 3-1/8" long	16	24	32

KANSAS TOY. Left to right: KTV22, mid 1930s; KTV25, 1920s. Photo by Perry Eichor.

KANSAS TOY AND NOVELTY. Left to right: KTV17, KTV 47, KTV 46. Photo by Chic Gast.

	C6	C8	C10

KTV21 Steam Tractor, "25," "Case," crew of 2, tow loop, large front, small rear MSW and flywheel, 3" (See #71, also an UV w/ no name) 35 52 70

KTV22 Racer, "26," "Bearcat," stripdown, long hood, motometer, 3 intakes, driver, open frame, left exhaust, 4" long (See #33) .... No Price Found

KTV23 Separator-Thresher, "27," tow hook, auto-type MSW (not tractor rims), lacquer or enamel, also UV, see #72, 3" long 35 52 70

KTV24 Midget Racer, "31," driver, torpedo tail, VL, HG, HO, MWW, lacquer, also UV, 2-1/8" (See #67)..................12 15 18

KTV25 Racer, "33," "Bearcat," stripdown, smaller version of #26 above, 3" long..............No Price Found

KTV26 Coupe, "35," Convertible, LI, VL, HG, HO, RM, MWW, also an UV, 2-1/4" long.......No Price Found

KTV27 Locomotive-Tender, "36," "KT & N RR," 6 MSW, 4 MDW, 0-6-4, 4-3/8" long 7 10 14

KTV28 "Pullman" Car, "37," "KT & N RR," 4 MDW, 3-1/2".....................No Price Found

KTV29 Box Car "38," Union Pacific shield (an early promotional?), "KT & N RR," 4 MDW, 3-1/4"..................No Price Found

KTV30 Tank Car, "39," ladder, filler, "KT & N RR," MDW, 3-1/8" long ....No Price Found

KTV31 Caboose, "40," "KT & N RR," stack, brakeman's cab, MDS, 2-3/4" ....No Price Found

KTV32 Stock Car, "41," "KT & N RR," MDW.... No Price Found

KTV33 Dump Truck, "42," Ford?, driver, no cab, diamond emblem on hinged body, LV, HG, SP, MWW, 3-1/2".................35 52 70

KTV34 Steam Road Roller, "43," driver, SP, boiler, wooden rollers, 3-1/4"...................... 10 15 20

KTV35 Racer, "46," 1929 Golden Arrow record car, driver, large tail fin, MWW, 2-7/8" long 12 18 24

KTV36 Warehouse Tractor, "48," "Caterpillar," "Whoopee," driver, VL, HG, HO, SP, tow loop, MWW, also an UV, 3" long 18 27 36

KTV37 Tour Bus, "49," 1928 Pickwick COE "Nite Coach," HG, SP, MDW duals, also an UV, 2-3/8" (See #59)..........No Price Found

KTV38 Pickup Truck, "51," Ford w/ cab, VL, HG, tow loop, MDW, lacquer, also an UV, 2-3/4" long ....No Price Found

KTV39 Roadster, "54," Buick, driver w/ cap, rumble seat, T, plain hood and grille, no headlamps, SM, MWW, also an UV, 2-3/8" long (See #77)....................10 15 20

KTV40 Roadster, "54," same as above, no trunk, 2-1/4" long....................No Price Found

KTV41 Truck-Semi, "55," Ford, stake trailer, VL, HG, MDW, 4" long ....No Price Found

KTV42 Farm Tractor, "57," Fordson, driver, SP, MDW rear, MSW front. Smaller version of #17, also an UV, 1-3/4" long..........No Price Found

KTV43 Sedanette, "58," Austin Bantam, unique fighting cock on door panels, 4 OW, HL, VG, RM, MWW, 2-1/4" ....No Price Found

KTV44 Tour Bus, "59," 1928 Pickwick COE double-deck night-coach, screen grille, larger version of #49 above, also an UV with dual wheels, 3-3/8" long..........No Price Found

KTV45 Sedan, "60," 1930 Reo Royale? or Chrysler 2-door Brougham, plain hood, vee-VG, square rear deck, MDW, MDWSM, also an UV with MWW and MWWSM, 3-1/2"....................24 36 48

KANSAS TOY AND NOVELTY, KTV34. Photo by R.F. Sapita.

KANSAS TOY Towed Implements. Top, left to right: KTV46, KTV49. Bottom, left to right: KTV47, KTV50. Photo courtesy Fred Maxwell.

Note: *The following is a unique towed farm set with several hinged or moving parts, each a different color and large 1-1/4" spoked tractor wheels.*

KTV46 Planter, "KTN No. 61," V-blade plough with seed hopper, 4 pieces incl. wheels and 3 colors, 4" long....................40 60 80

KTV47 Disc Harrow, "62," 8 discs on same 1-5/8" wide frame as #61, 13 pieces, incl. discs and wheels, 4 colors, 4" long..............35 52 70

KTV48 Plough, "63," single blade on same shaft as #61, 4" long....................35 52 70

KTV49 Dirt Tumble, "64," adjustable dumping scoop, 1-1/2" wide on same frame as #62, 6 pieces, 4 colors, 4" long............20 30 40

KTV50 Dirt Scraper, "65," blade 1-7/8, adjustable, on same frame as #62, 3-5/8" long ....No Price Found

KTV51 Coupe, "66," streamlined 3-wheeler, 6 OW, MWW, lacquer, 3-1/2" long.................No Price Found

KTV52 Midget Racer, "67," driver, torpedo-tail, VL, HG, HO, MDW, smaller version of #31, also an UV, 1-1/2" long 44   66   88

KTV53 Fire Engine, "70," Seagrave? pumper, driver, VL, HG, MDW, 2-1/4" long .... No Price Found

KTV54 Steam Tractor, "71," crew of 2, tow-loop, small version of #25, 2-1/2" long 10   15   20

KTV55 Separator-Thresher, "72," tow hook for #71, 2+" .... No Price Found

KTV56 Army Tank, "74," "US Army," WWI-type, high turret, large front, small rear wheels, OD color, 2-1/4" long .... No Price Found

KTV57 Racer, no #, miniature solid-cast version of #10, moving wheels, charm loop on nose, 1" long .... No Price Found

Kansas Toy Transitional Vehicles

KTTV58 Tractor, "48," "Caterpillar," "Whoopee" same as KTV36 except -3/4" grooved metal wheels with rubber track, 3" long 35   52   70

KTTV59 Tour Bus, no #, Pickwick COE, a more streamlined version of #59 above, with 8 open windows, 3-3/8" long............................ No Price Found

KTTV60? Fire Engine, no #, pumper, 2 firemen w/ old-style helmets, hose reel, HG, MDW, Kansas?, 3-1/4" long 12   18   24

KTTV61 Army Tank, "74," "US Army," 2 gun turret, OD color, a different tank than #74 above, 2-1/4" long .... No Price Found

KTTV62 Coupe, "75," Graham-like (Tootsietoy), VG, SM, T, WHRT, 1933 issue, 4-1/4" long ... No Price Found

KTTV63 Racer, "76," Auburn speedster, low driver, headrest fairing, SP, HG, slanted louvers, large oval fin, kickplates, HWRW or WHRT, 4-1/4" 20   30   40

KTTV64 Roadster, "77," open sport Duesenberg, W/S down, driver, VG, slanted louvers, SM, T, WHRT, 4" long 16   24   32

KTTV66 Sedan, "79," 2-door, Graham-like, 4 OW, VG, HL, RM, WHRT w/ 5 removable tires, found both with and w/o bottom pan, 4-1/4" .... No Price Found

KTTV67 Coupe, "80," convertible, top up, LI, 2 OW, VG, T, MWW w/ MWW SM, 3-1/2" long 20   30   40

KTTV68 Coupe, "80," same as above except HRDW w/ MDW SM (a different casting re sidemounts), 3-1/2" long .... No Price Found

KTTV69 Racer, "81," Miller, FWD, driver, 8 cyl., right exhaust, HG, WHRT, 1933 issue, 4-3/8" long .... No Price Found

KTTV70 Sedan, "82" Pierce Arrow Silver Arrow fastback, 6 OW, HRDW, also an UV, 4" long No Price Found

KTTV71 Indy Racer, "83," FWD type driver, VG, HL, right exhaust, WHRT, 4-5/8" long .... No Price Found

KTTV72 Sedan "84," DeSoto?, airflow, 4 OW, HO, HG, HL, HRDW, 1934 issue, 3-5/8" long 20   30   40

KANSAS TOY autos with hard rubber wheels. Top, left to right: KTTV59, KTV45. Middle, left to right: KTTV63. Bottom, left to right: KTTV67, KTTV72. Photo courtesy Fred Maxwell.

KANSAS TOY KTV64. Photo by Craig A. Clark.

KTTV65 Concrete Mixer, "78," Truck w/ water tank & mixing barrel, VG, HL, WHRT, found both with and w/o a bottom pan, sometimes called a fuel tanker, 3-3/4" long .... No Price Found

(Note: Although it is not yet certain when the hobo molds changed hands, the higher numbers are described and illustrated under Best Toy and Ralstoy.)

KANSAS TOY vehicles with wood hubs. Top, left to right: KTTV64, KTTV65. Bottom, left to right: KTTV66, KT & N? #85. Photo courtesy Fred Maxwell.

	C6	C8	C10
Kelmet Aerial Ladder Truck, 30" long	605	908	1210
Kelmet No. 501, White Dump Truck, 25" long	900	1500	2200

KENTON Boat-tail, cut-down speedster, 1910, 7" long. Courtesy Lloyd W. Ralston Auctions.

KELMET No. 501, White Dump Truck, "Big Boy." Courtesy Joe and Sharon Freed.

	C6	C8	C10
Kelmet Tanker, 27" long	1800	3000	4100
Kelmet White Fire Truck (ladder)..................	1000	1650	2400
Kenton Ambulance, cast iron, 7" long	750	1300	1700

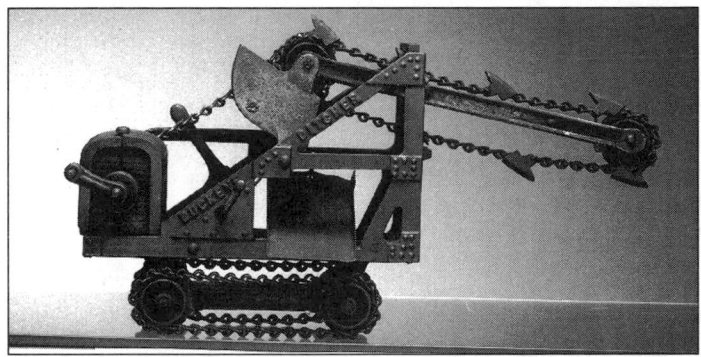

KENTON Buckeye Ditcher, 12-1/2" long. Courtesy Sotheby's New York.

	C6	C8	C10
Kenton Buckeye Ditcher, 9" long	470	705	940
Kenton Bus, Double-Decker, 1920s 6" long	312	470	625
Kenton Bus, Double-Decker, 1920, 7-1/4" long	1100	1650	2200
Kenton Bus, Double-Decker, 9-1/2"	650	1050	1550

KENTON Ambulance, 7" long, cast iron, driver incorrect. Courtesy Sotheby's New York.

	C6	C8	C10
Kenton "Army Motortruck 807," cast iron, 14" long	600	950	1300
Kenton Auto, cast iron, early, 6" long..............	250	375	500
Kenton Boattail Cut-Down Speedster, 1910, 7" long	120	180	240

KENTON Bus, Double-Decker, 1920s, 7-1/4" long. Courtesy Lloyd W. Ralston Auctions.

KENTON "Army Motor Truck 807," incorrect driver in photo. Courtesy Sotheby's New York.

KENTON Bus, Double-Decker, 1920s, 7-1/4" long. Courtesy Lloyd W. Ralston Auctions.

	C6	C8	C10
Kenton Bus, cast iron, 8" long	175	262	350
Kenton Bus, 1920s, 10-3/4" long	375	525	750
Kenton Cattle Truck, cast iron, c. 1938, 8" long	150	225	300
Kenton Cement Mixer, 7" long	423	635	845
Kenton Circus Truck, 10" long	1500	2500	3900
Kenton "Coal" Dump Truck, 8-1/2" long	300	450	600
Kenton "Coast-to-Coast" Bus	350	525	700
Kenton "Contractors" Dump Wagon, cast iron, 9-3/4" long	500	750	1000
Kenton Coupe, 5" long	230	345	460
Kenton Coupe, 6-1/2" long	425	638	850
Kenton Coupe, 8" long	700	1100	1600
Kenton Coupe, 1926, 10" long	3000	5500	9500
Kenton Dump Truck, 6" long	170	255	340
Kenton Emergency Truck, c. 1930s, black rubber tires, takes batteries for headlights and spotlight	180	270	360
Kenton Fire Apparatus Truck	400	600	800
Kenton Fire Pump Truck, early with driver, approx. 10" long	220	330	440
Kenton Fire Pumper, 1920s, 14-1/2" long	500	850	1260
Kenton Fire Pumper, c. 1920s, has gong, 18" long	350	525	700

KENTON Fire Pumper, 18" long, has gong. Courtesy Mapes Auctioneers & Appraisers.

	C6	C8	C10
Kenton Fire Truck, w/ pumper, 15" long	1200	2000	2800
Kenton Franklin, air-cooled, 8-1/2"	1300	1950	2600
Kenton "Hose" Truck, open cab, c. 1920s, green, driver, rider, hose, ladders, approx. 6-3/4" long	285	430	570
Kenton "Hose" Truck, 9" long	500	750	1050
Kenton Ice Truck, tongs and glass ice, 7-1/2" long	400	600	800

KENTON "Jaeger" Cement Mixer Truck, 8" long. Courtesy HAKE'S Americana & Collectibles.

	C6	C8	C10
Kenton Jaeger Cement Mixer, 6-1/2" long	365	545	730
Kenton Jaeger Cement Mixer, 8" long	1100	1700	2500
Kenton Jaeger "Mixer," cast iron cement truck, 9" long	1100	1900	2600
Kenton Ladder Truck, cast iron, approx. 7-1/2" long	310	465	620
Kenton Ladder Truck, pressed steel ladders, 16" long	325	488	650

KENTON Ladder Truck, pressed steel ladders, 16" long. Courtesy Lloyd W. Ralston Auctions.

	C6	C8	C10
Kenton Ladder Truck, 17-1/4" long	750	1200	1700
Kenton "Merchant Delivery"	450	675	900
Kenton Overland Circus Cage Truck w/ driver, 7-1/2" long	800	1300	2000
Kenton Overland Circus w/ lion, 9" long	800	1300	2000
Kenton Patrol Wagon, marked "Patrol" on side, c. 1920s-30s, 9" long	500	750	1030
Kenton Phaeton Touring Car, 12" long	350	562	700
Kenton "Pickwick Nite Coach," cast iron, 14" long	1500	2500	3800
Kenton Pontiac, approx. 4" long	150	225	300
Kenton Racer, early, 7-1/2" long	175	262	350
Kenton Racer, early, cast iron, 9" long	600	1000	1400
Kenton Red Devil w/ driver, 6" long	200	300	400
Kenton Road Grader, cast iron, rubber tires, nickel-plated moveable blade, 7-1/2" long	212	318	425
Kenton Roadster, driver, c. 1908, 6" long	300	450	600
Kenton Runabout Auto, 1900, 5" long	170	255	340
Kenton Runabout Auto, cast iron, resembles a 1910 Franklin, has driver, 7" long	175	262	350
Kenton Sedan, 4" long	110	165	225
Kenton Sedan, late 1930s, rubber tires, take-apart body, 7" long	1200	2000	2800

KENTON Sedan, 7" long, late 1930s. Courtesy Lloyd W. Ralston Auctions.

	C6	C8	C10
Kenton "Speed" Stake Truck, c. 1927, 5-1/2" long	408	612	815
Kenton Sprinkler Truck, early, 8"	425	638	850
Kenton Stake Truck, 6" long	235	352	470
Kenton Steam Roller, "Galion Master" 6-1/2" long	225	338	450
Kenton Steam Shovel, Marion, 7-1/4"	600	900	1200

KENTON Steam Shovel. Courtesy Mapes Auctioneers & Appraisers.

KENTON Touring Car, open, driver and passenger, 8-1/2" long (air-cooled Franklin). Courtesy Sotheby's New York.

	C6	C8	C10
Kenton Tank, cast iron 2-1/2" long	80	120	160
Kenton Touring Car, open, driver and passenger, 8-1/2" long	650	975	1300

	C6	C8	C10
Kenton Tow Auto, 1920s, 9-1/2" long	1100	1800	2700
Kenton Yellow Cab, 1950s, 6-3/8" long	470	705	940

KENTON Tow Auto, 1920s, 9-1/2" long. Courtesy Lloyd W. Ralston Auctions.

KEYSTONE

Keystone of Boston, Massachusetts, had an odd assortment of products: movie projectors, steel trucks, wooden boats and pressed wood forts and garages. Founded in June of 1922 or 1923 by Chester Rimmer and Arthur Jackson, it was first located in a small shop in Malden, Massachusetts, under the name Jacrim, using parts of the partners' last names. Rimmer retired in 1958 and sold out to various companies. The address in Boston was 288 A Street. All numbers and descriptions in bold type are Keystone's own.

KEYSTONE No. 43, American Railway Express.

	C6	C8	C10
Keystone **No. 41 Dump Truck**, 26-1/2" long	500	750	1050
Keystone **No. 43 American Railway Express**, 26" long	700	1200	1690
Keystone **No. 44 Truck Loader**, 17-3/4" high	175	263	350
Keystone **No. 45 U.S. Mail Truck**, 26" long	900	1450	2100
Keystone **No. 46 Steam Shovel**, when arm is extended 26" long	243	365	485
Keystone **No. 47 Steam Shovel**, when arm is extended 34-1/2" long	195	295	390
Keystone **No. 48 U.S. Army Truck**, 26" long	500	800	1200
Keystone **No. 49 Fire Truck**, 27-1/2" long	1100	1800	2700
Keystone **No. 51 Police Patrol**, 27-1/2" long	800	1400	1900
Keystone **No. 52 Fire Truck**, 27-1/2" long	645	968	1290
Keystone **No. 53 Sprinkler Truck**, tank 12" long	1000	1600	2400
Keystone **No. 54 Koaster Truck**, with skids, hoist cable, windlass, 26" long when skids retracted	800	1300	1800

KEYSTONE No. 49 Fire Truck. Photo by Calvin L. Chaussee.

	C6	C8	C10
Keystone **No. 55 Koaster Truck**, without skids and windlass	478	720	955
Keystone **No. 56 Water Pump Tower**, 29" long	700	1100	1600
Keystone **No. 57 Chemical Pump Engine**, 27-1/2" long	1000	1550	2100
Keystone **No. 58 Moving Van**, 26" long	700	1200	1650
Keystone **No. 60 Riding Steam Roller**	300	450	600
Keystone **No. 62 Hydraulic Dump Truck**, 26" long	500	800	1100
Keystone **No. 73 Ambulance**, military, 27" long	800	1300	1800
Keystone **No. 78 Wrecking Car**, 27" long	850	1350	1880
Keystone **79 Aerial Ladder**, 30-1/2" long	700	1100	1550
Keystone No. ? "Dugan Brothers" "ride'm" Truck	1200	2000	2800
Keystone No. ?? Greyhound Bus wind-up	400	600	800
Keystone No. ?? Ladder Truck, 24" long	475	700	950
Keystone No. ?? Plastic Sedan, c. 1950, hood lifts, gas tank fills & drains 4-1/2" long	18	27	36
Keystone No. ?? Steam Roller, red and black, air pressure whistle, brass bell, 20" long	350	525	700
Keystone No. ?? "World's Greatest Circus" Truck, c. 1930s, 26" long	1500	2700	4000

KEYSTONE No. 51 Police Patrol. Photo by Calvin L. Chaussee.

KEYSTONE No. 55. Courtesy Joe and Sharon Freed.

KEYSTONE "Moving Van Long Distance Hauling." Courtesy Mapes Auctioneers & Appraisers.

KEYSTONE Packard Dump Truck, 26" long. Courtesy PB Eight-Four, New York.

KEYSTONE No. ??, "Dugan Brothers" "ride'm" truck. Courtesy Joe and Sharon Freed.

KEYSTONE No. 58 Moving Van.
Courtesy Joe and Sharon Freed.

KILGORE

Kilgore of Westerville, Ohio, appears to have begun toy-making in the 1920s. Its toys were cast iron and low-priced, with cap pistols its most popular line. But it also did well with a number of attractive trucks, fire engines and cars, as well as scattered aircraft and ships. Some subsidiary manufacturing was done in Lancaster, Pennsylvania, and Canada.

In 1937 Kilgore began making plastic cars, trucks, planes and buses, and later added plastic cap pistols, placing it among the first (if not the first) companies to produce plastic toys. Kilgore remained in business until at least 1978. The first owner, a Mr. Kilgore, sold out in 1921.

	C6	C8	C10
Kilgore Arctic Ice Cream Truck, 8" long	800	1300	1800
Kilgore "Arctic Ice Cream" Truck, 9"	500	750	1000

KILGORE Arctic Ice Cream Truck.

	C6	C8	C10
Kilgore Auto, "LF 1300A," w/ driver	180	270	360
Kilgore Bus, plastic, advertised in 1937, 4" long	20	25	30
Kilgore Convertible w/ rumble seat, early 1930s, w/ driver, 7" long	160	240	320

	C6	C8	C10
Kilgore Coupe, streamlined, plastic, advertised in 1937, 4" long	20	25	30
Kilgore Double-Decker Bus, c. 1930, 6" long	450	675	900
Kilgore Dump Truck, cast iron, c. 1934, 5-3/4" long	160	240	320
Kilgore Dump Truck, 1930s, 7" long	175	262	350
Kilgore Dump Truck, cast iron, c. 1934, 8-1/2" long	450	675	900
Kilgore "Express" Truck, plastic, advertised in 1937, 4" long	20	25	30
Kilgore "Fire Chief" Sedan, plastic, advertised in 1937, 4" long	20	25	30

KILGORE "Fire Chief" Sedan, plastic. Photo by Dave Leopard.

	C6	C8	C10
Kilgore Fire Truck w/ ladders, 1929, 6-3/4" long	188	282	375
Kilgore Livestock Truck, 1930s, 7" long	275	365	550
Kilgore Livestock Truck, 9" long	500	800	1200
Kilgore Motorcycle, single rider, 4"	112	168	225
Kilgore Packard Luxury Sedan, take-apart body, 8-1/4" long	700	1300	1600
Kilgore Pierce-Arrow Roadster, take-apart body, 6-1/8" long	250	375	500
Kilgore Police Car, plastic, 1937, 4"	20	25	30
Kilgore Pontiac, cast iron, 1930, 10"	1200	1800	2700

KILGORE Coupe, streamlined, plastic. Photo by Dave Leopard.

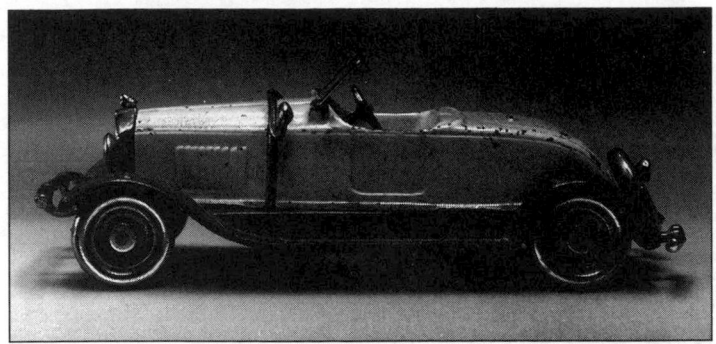

KILGORE Pontiac, 10" long.
Courtesy Sotheby's New York.

	C6	C8	C10
Kilgore Roadster, driver, rumble seat, 6" long	250	375	500
Kilgore Sedan, 3-1/4" long	65	98	130
Kilgore "Special Delivery" Motorcycle, 4-1/4" long	150	225	350

	C6	C8	C10
Kilgore Stutz Roadster, 13 parts	1100	1500	2500
Kilgore "Taxi," plastic, advertised in 1937, 4" long	20	25	30
Kilgore "Toy Town Delivery" Truck, 6-1/8" long	445	668	890

KINGSBURY

Kingsbury had its origins in 1886 in Keene, New Hampshire. Its owner was Harry T. Kingsbury, who bought the Wilkins Toy Company, and apparently didn't change that firm's name until after WWI. Steel and spring motors characterize Kingsbury's toys. Cars, fire engines, farm equipment, and racing cars comprised its primary output. Kingsbury is still in business but apparently ended toy production in 1942.

	C6	C8	C10
Kingsbury Aerial Ladder Truck, pressed steel wind-up, c. 1941, ladder rises automatically to height of 38" when the truck runs into any obstruction, fireman on ladder climbs up and down by turning crank at base of ladder, early version new in 1905, 24" long	180	270	360
Kingsbury earlier version of Aerial Ladder Truck	425	638	850
Kingsbury Airflow, c. 1934, pressed steel, rubber tires, 14" long	310	465	620
Kingsbury Airflow, clockwork, 14" long	500	750	1060
Kingsbury Auto, very early, steel wind-up, 9-3/4" long	250	375	500
Kingsbury Bluebird Racer, 18" long	1000	1500	2100
Kingsbury Brougham Sedan, pressed steel wind-up, 13" long	1100	1700	2425
Kingsbury Bus, pressed steel, 18" long	390	585	780
Kingsbury Cannon Truck, very early, clockwork, 11" long	210	315	420

	C6	C8	C10
Kingsbury Cannon Truck, c. 1939, wind-up, 15" long	125	188	250
Kingsbury Caterpillar, wind-up, 8-1/2"	225	338	450
Kingsbury Cattle Truck, 1930s, 19" long	212	318	425
Kingsbury DeSoto, pressed steel wind-up, c. 1938, 14-1/2" long	218	327	435
Kingsbury Dump Truck, tin, driver, 10" long	450	675	900
Kingsbury Dump Truck, early 1930s, clockwork, 16" long	350	525	700
Kingsbury "Fire Chief" Coupe, 1930s, 14" long	325	438	650
Kingsbury Fire Pumper, very early, clockwork iron and steel, 11" long	363	545	725
Kingsbury Fire Pumper, 1920s, 23" long	225	338	450
Kingsbury Fire Truck, 18" long	250	375	500
Kingsbury Ford Sedan & House Trailer, 1937, pressed steel, 23" long	450	675	900
Kingsbury Golden Arrow Racer, pressed steel wind-up, 20" long	600	1000	1375

KINGSBURY Golden Arrow Racer, 20" long.
Courtesy Wilkinson Collection, Detroit
Antique Toy Museum.

	C6	C8	C10
Kingsbury Greyhound Bus, wind-up, 18" long	262	395	525
Kingsbury Ladder Truck, steel, driver, 22" long	187	280	375
Kingsbury Ladder Truck, c. 1930, 35" long	1200	2100	3100

KINGSBURY Ladder Truck, 35" long. Courtesy Christie's East.

KINGSBURY Phaeton Auto, 1900, 9-1/2" long. Courtesy Lloyd W. Ralston Auctions.

	C6	C8	C10
Kingsbury Ladder Wagon Fire Truck, tin, rubber tires, 23-1/2" long	165	250	330
Kingsbury Phaeton Auto, 1900, rubber slip tires, 9-1/2" long	1400	2700	3500
Kingsbury Rack Truck, pressed steel wind-up, 16" long	350	525	700
Kingsbury Roadster, No. 242, electric headlights, spring motor, luggage rack, 13" long	375	563	750

	C6	C8	C10
Kingsbury Sunbeam Racer, sheetmetal, red w/ rubber tires on steel wheels, clockwork motor, 19" long	800	1300	1725
Kingsbury Tractor, mechanical w/ driver, 8" long	250	375	500
Kingsbury Tractor and Cart, tin, w/ iron driver, white rubber wheels, c. 1930s, 11-1/2" long	195	292	390
Kingsbury Transit Truck, 1930s, 19" long	100	150	200
Kingsbury Truck w/ C Cap, tin, 10" long	175	262	350
Kingsbury Wind-up Car, curved dash, driver, 9" long	225	338	450
Kingsbury Wrecker, pressed steel wind-up, 13" long	1000	1600	2300
Kingston Producers, Kokomo, Indiana, Electricar, the Red Arrow, 1930s, 15" long	150	225	300
Kingston Producers, Kokomo, Duesenberg, electric with transformer and steel track, 12" long	1200	2500	3700
Knapp "Electric Automobile," c. 1903, pressed steel, battery-activated, 11" long	1100	1750	2600
Ladder Truck, driver front and rear, cast iron, 5" long	45	68	90
Laketoy "John Wanamaker" Delivery Van, wooden, 10-1/2" long	180	270	360

KNAPP "Electric Automobile," c. 1903. Courtesy Sotheby's New York.

LANSING SLIK-TOYS

Listing and history by Dave Leopard

Lansing Slik-Toys were made in Lansing, Iowa, and sometimes bear the name "Kipp," in addition to the "Lansing" and "Slik-Toy" trademarks. Most Slik-Toys are made of aluminum in a single casting but some were made of hard plastic. The company made many farm and construction toys but the list below is confined to cars and trucks. All Slik-Toys I have seen bear a four-digit number beginning with "9." If a toy bears such a number, even if it has no other markings, it is almost surely a Slik-Toy.

	C6	C8	C10
Stakebody Truck, No. 9500, 11" long	40	50	60
Sedan, Fastback, No. 9600, 7" long	25	30	40
Sedan, Fastback, No. 9600, taxi version, 7" long	30	40	45
Pickup Truck, No. 9601, 7" long	25	30	40
Open Stake Truck, No. 9602, 7" long	25	30	40
Tank Truck, No. 9603, 7" long	25	30	40

	C6	C8	C10
Sedan, 4-door, No. 9604, 6" long	20	25	35
Pickup Truck, No. 9605, 6" long	25	30	40
Fire Truck, No. 9606, 6" long	20	25	35
Tank Truck, No. 9607, 6" long	20	25	35
Tractor/Trailer rig (milk tanker), No. 9610, 8" long	30	35	45

	C6	C8	C10
Tractor/Trailer rig (grain trailer), No. 9611, 8" long	25	30	40
Tractor/Trailer rig (flatbed trailer), No. 9613, 8" long	25	30	40
Tractor/Trailer rig (log trailer), No. unknown, 8" long	25	30	40
Fire Truck, No. 9700, 3-1/2" long	20	25	35
Roadster, No. 9701, 3-1/2" long	20	25	35
Pickup Truck, plastic, No. 9703, 4" long	20	25	35
Lapin Cadillac, 1948, 4-door, 6" long	10	15	20
Lapin Coupe, plastic, 1939 Hudson?	15	20	30

LAPIN Coupe, plastic, 1939, Hudson? Photo by Dave Leopard.

LAPIN Sedan, 6 side windows. Photo by Dave Leopard.

	C6	C8	C10
Lapin Sedan, six side windows, plastic, 1939 Hudson?	15	20	30
Lapin Stake Truck, Chevrolet, plastic, 1947, 4" long	10	15	20
Lincoln Toys (Windsor, Ontario, Canada) Dump Truck, 7" long	55	82	110
Lincoln Toys "Dunlop Tires Tow Truck" wrecker	150	225	300
Lincoln Toys "Sand Truck," dump, 14" long	55	82	110

LINCOLN WHITE METAL WORKS

by Fred Maxwell, Slushmold Contributing Editor, Perry Eichor and Ferd Zegel

This Lincoln, Nebraska, firm is now recognized as the maker of many of those high-quality pre-war slushmold "orphan toys." This long obscurity is all the more surprising because Clayton E. Stevenson, the founder, was a many-talented personage in the dime store toy industry: an artist, a skilled craftsman, and a salesman with worldwide contacts. He had made toys at home since the early 1920s (see Mid-West Metal Novelty Co.). As a salesman for Western Diecasting Co. he furnished some molds to Kansas Toy Co. and may have furnished some to Tip Top Toy Co. and others. He may also have invented 3-piece molds, which were his specialty. The third piece was used to cast those uniquely realistic re-entrant front-ends (grille, headlamps, fenders) but had to be pulled away in order to open the mold and dump the hot toy. These molds and the even more complex molds for those beautiful tri-motored aircraft (Lincoln's Fokker and C.A.W.'s Fords) were surprising in this competitive industry because it slowed production and added to costs. For collectors, though, it created rarity.

Stevenson's was a remarkably long toy-making career, about 15 years, through the Great Depression. What we know came from a Christmas story in the *Nebraska State Journal* (November 20, 1931), a fine article in *Antique Toy World* (January 1984), and from biographical information, photos and toys saved by his daughter, Marian.

Stevenson, an auto mechanic, was born in 1896 and raised in Axtell, Kansas. He and his wife, Esther, moved to Lincoln in 1931 and started marketing toys in his name at 1250 Dakota St. His new business grew rapidly. In his first season he made "800,000 toys in three months." He was manager, purchaser, worker, and salesman.

As his business grew - "30,000 toys a day and 27 to 30 laborers" at one time - he moved to a larger facility at 2204 Y Street. In 1935 he was listed at 3433 J Street. The toys were sold to Woolworth, Kress, Kresge, and Schwartz Paper Co. stores, as well as all over the country (especially California and New York) and even abroad.

The factory was sold in 1940, after 9 (?) years of production, due to shortages of lead and rubber and the rising costs of labor: all due to expansion of war production. (We were not told who bought what, although a few clues point to nearby Ralstoy. Although 1940 is the date given by a family member, I did not find the business listed in Lincoln directories after 1937.)

A variety of toys were made: "tiny airplanes, midget racers, larger speed cars - about 6" long - brilliant sedans, small coupes, tri-motor plane models and miniature sawmills. They range in size from 3 to 7" (?) in length." "Mr. Stevenson, who does the modeling, uses pictures of planes and cars shown in magazines. For his midget racer he used a picture of a Miller special. His sedan is a replica of the front-drive Cord. His coupe is a Nash model. His trimotor plane is taken from a photo of a Ford product." This in 1931; other patterns were issued later. Early toys used metal wheels and tin propellers and had neat patterned bottom-pans collectors use as clues to identification. Later toys had rubber wheels. The list is incomplete; we were dependent on the few toys we have found. Can any of you collectors of rare Slush add to this history? Have you seen a Cord sedan? Could Stevenson have patterned or produced the "Cord" sold by Tommy Toy Co.? Have you seen a Nash coupe or others from three-piece molds?

LINCOLN WHITE METAL. Left: LWV1, mid 1930s. Right: LWV28, mid 1930s. Photo by Perry Eichor.

LINCOLN WHITE METAL. Top: LWV2. Bottom: LWV3. Photo by Perry Eichor.

	C6	C8	C10

LWV1 Indy Racer, Miller FWD Special, driver, rounded grille, horizontal cooling fins alongside hood, torpedo tail, 5-1/8" long .... No Price Found

LWV2 Speed Car, Bluebird record car, driver, V-8 engine with intake ports, triangular fin with wing design embossed, 6" long .... No Price Found

LWV3 Speed Car, Bluebird, smaller version of above, 4" long .... No Price Found

LWV4? Speed Car, A V-12 version of Bluebird with triangular fin, Lincoln?, 4-5/8" long......... No Price Found

LWV5 Sedan, Pierce-Arrow Silver Arrow, vertical vee-grille, headlamps and front fenders faired, 6 open windows (OW), divided windshield (W/S), plain pan, 3-1/2" long .... No Price Found

LWV6 Sedan, 2-door Chrysler or DeSoto airflow, hood ornament (HO), divided open W/S, horizontal louvers (HL), plain pan, 3-3/4" .... No Price Found

LWV7 Sedan, 2-door Pontiac, HO, grid pattern grille, HL, 4 OW, trunk, 3-7/8" long .... No Price Found

LWV8 "Wrecker," high style with chopped top, Graham-like grille, 2 OW, fenders faired bumper to bumper, solid crane with grid pattern and hook, patterned pan "Made in USA," 3-1/2" long .... No Price Found

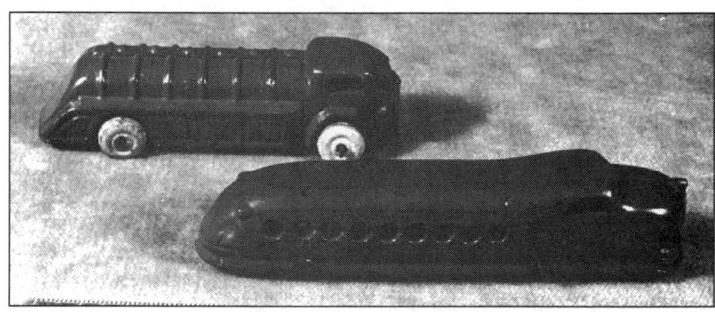

LINCOLN WHITE METAL. Top: LWV10. Bottom: LWV11. Photo by Perry Eichor.

LINCOLN WHITE METAL LWV8. Photo by Perry Eichor.

LWV9 Fire Engine Pumper with fireman on rear step. Graham-like grille, fenders faired bumper to bumper, patterned pan "Made in USA," 3-3/4" long .... No Price Found

LWV10 Tanker Truck, COE, 2 OW, 6 tanks, 8 compartments, patterned pan, "Made in USA," 3-3/4" .... No Price Found

LWV11 Railcar, Streamlined "UNION PACIFIC" and shield symbol, 2 OW in cab, 18 OW in passenger section, hidden rubber wheels, patterned pan, "Made in USA," 4-1/2" long .... No Price Found

	C6	C8	C10

LWV12 Fire Engine, steam pumper, 2-man crew, hose reel compartment, HO, HG, 3-1/4" long .... No Price Found

LWV13 Speed Car, Bluebird, w/ crossed flags on fin, V12, horizontal trim, patterned pan, 4-1/8" long .... No Price Found

LWV14 Coupe, streamlined Pontiac, HO, VG, HL, 2 OW, H trim on front fenders, embossed folded "trunk rack," patterned pan, 3-3/8" .... No Price Found

LWV15 Coupe, Graham? slanted vee-grille, divided WS, 2 OW, SM, T, from 3-piece mold, 3-3/8" long .... No Price Found

LWV16 Coupe, Oldsmobile, streamlined, slanted vee-grille, HO, HL, divided WS, 2 OW, RM, patterned pan, 4" long .... No Price Found

LWV17 Coupe, streamlined Lincoln?, slanted vee-grille, divided WS, 2 OW, patterned pan, 3-1/2" long .... No Price Found

LWV18 Coupe, Graham?, VG, SM, 2 OW, LI, T, from 3-piece mold 3-1/2" .... No Price Found

LWV19 Coupe, slanted hood, rear-mount hub for rubber tire, (see Tootsie Graham).................... No Price Found

LWV20 Coupe, vertical hood, wraparound?, rear window, T.. No Price Found

LWV21 Brougham, Graham?, vertical vee-grille, SM, 4 OW, T, from 3-piece mold, 3-1/2" long No Price Found

LWV22 Stake Truck, slanted HG, divided WS, 2 OW, open stakes, rounded pan, 3-1/2" long .. No Price Found

LWV23 Limousine, Graham? VG, MDWSM, 4 OW, LI, T, from 3-piece mold, 3-1/4" long .. No Price Found

LINCOLN WHITE METAL. Top to bottom: LWV14, LWV18, LWV21. Photo by Fred Maxwell.

LINCOLN WHITE METAL. Top to bottom: LWV24, LWV23, LWV15. Photo by Fred Maxwell.

	C6	C8	C10
LWV24 Limousine, Nash?, VG, VL, MWWSM, 4 OW, T, from 3-piece mold, 2-1/2" long .... No Price Found			
LWV25 Indy Racer, small, 2-man, FWD, rounded hood, 4 cyl., exhaust left side .... No Price Found			
LWV26 Tractor, small Fordson .... No Price Found			
LWV27 Bus, Overland, HO, HG, VL, 10 OW, 3-1/2" long .... No Price Found			
LWV28 Indy Racer, large, driver, slanted vee-grille, horizontal cooling fins, torpedo tail .... No Price Found			
LWV29 Indy Racer, large, driver, unusual grille design .... No Price Found			
LWV30 Indy Racer, large, different version of above .... No Price Found			
LWV31 Sedan, Lincoln Auto Co.? .... No Price Found			
LWV32 Sedan, Ford V-8 .... No Price Found			

LINCOLN WHITE METAL LWV31. Photo by Fred Maxwell.

Note: Some of the above are so rare that they may not have been put into production. Lincoln used several types of wheels: metal disc and metal "wire" with black painted "tires"; white rubber "balloon tires" then standard in the industry. Abbreviations used above same as used for Kansas Toy Co. Many of the above list came from private collections or photographs. I have not seen realized prices for several years. The asking prices seen have been so volatile as to be unhelpful as guides. Collectors of rare, quality slushmold toys should expect to pay above-average prices.

LINDSTROM

The Lindstrom Tool & Toy Company made wind-ups of light pressed steel as well as tin. It was located in Bridgeport, Connecticut, and began making toy cars about 1913. It seems to have ceased production sometime in the 1940s.

	C6	C8	C10
Lindstrom Lumber Truck no. 160, steerable front wheels, tin, with driver, 10" long	125	187	250
Lindstrom Steam Roller no. 181, mechanical, 12" long	50	75	100
Lionel Electric Racing Automobile set	1000	1700	2400
Log Truck (Beck), steers via horn on top of cab, late 1940s, large .... No Price Found			

	C6	C8	C10
Lumar: See Marx			
Lupor Ambulance	52	77	105
Lupor Fire Chief Car, friction, siren, 7" long	50	75	100
Lupor Police Car, 1949 Ford	90	135	180

LIONEL Electric Racing Automobile set. Courtesy Sotheby's New York.

M&L Toy Co. Inc.

M&L was incorporated October 21, 1947. It was located on Paterson Plank Road in Union City, New Jersey, and got its name from the father & son who owned it, Morris and Louis (last name unknown). The company may have begun in 1946, and lasted until at least 1948. It made vehicles, trains, "jeweled swords, water guns, mechanical toys, and plastic horns." Most or all of its vehicles seem to have been sold unpainted and with plastic wheels. The alloy used in the vehicles was more than 99% zinc, with a smidgen of aluminum added. Most or all of their toys were copies. There were about 30 employees. By 1947 it was located at 123-33rd Street, Union City, New Jersey.

	C6	C8	C10
M&L (1) Racer, 2-3/4" long	10	15	20
M&L (2) Cabin Racer	12	18	25
Mack Dump Truck, cast iron, 12" long	650	1100	1600

M&L (1) Racer. Photo by Craig A. Clark.

MACK Dump Truck, cast iron, 1930s. Courtesy Mapes Auctioneers & Appraisers.

M&L (2). Top: Cabin Racer, cast headlamps. Bottom: Barclay prototype, rhinestone headlamps missing. Photo by Perry Eichor.

	C6	C8	C10
Mack Dump Truck, cast iron, 1930s, 8-1/2" long	275	362	550
"Mack" Ladder Truck, cast iron, 18" long	300	450	600
Mack Stake Truck, cast iron, 7" long	70	105	140

MACK Stake Truck, cast iron, 7" long.
Courtesy Mapes Auctioneers & Appraisers.

MANOIL

List compiled by Terry Sells

Numbers and words in bold are Manoil's own description. 701-706 began production in 1934.

	C6	C8	C10
Manoil **700 Sedan**, futuristic	57	85	115
Manoil **701 Sedan**, futuristic	50	75	100
Manoil **702 Coupe**, futuristic	67	100	135
Manoil **703 Wrecker**, futuristic	75	112	150
Manoil **704 Roadster**, futuristic, Pat. No. 95791	54	81	108
Manoil **705 Sedan**, futuristic, Pat. No. 95792	40	60	80
Manoil **706 Rocket**, futuristic bus-like vehicle, Pat. No. 95793	50	75	100
Manoil **70 Soup Kitchen**, large number	7	11	15
Manoil **70A Soup Kitchen**, small number	9	13	18
Manoil **71 Shell Carrier with Soldier on Shell Box**, has loop	12	18	24
Manoil **71A** same as above, no loop	8	12	17
Manoil **72 Water Wagon**, large number	11	16	22
Manoil **72A** same as above, small number	9	13	18
Manoil **72B** No number	10	15	20
Manoil **73 Tractor**, loop front	12	18	25
Manoil **73A Tractor**, plain front	12	18	25
Manoil **74 Armored Car with Anti-Tank Gun**	20	30	41
Manoil **75 Armored Car with Anti-Aircraft Gun**	27	41	55
Manoil **75A Armored Car with Siren**, siren cast separately	25	38	50
Manoil **75A Armored Car with Siren**, siren cast with vehicle	34	51	68
Manoil **95 Tank**	11	16	22
Manoil **96 Large Shell on Truck**	11	16	22
Manoil **97 Pontoon on Wheels**	17	26	35
Manoil **98 Torpedo on Wheels**	9	14	19
Manoil **103 Gasoline Truck**	11	16	22
Manoil **104 Chemical Truck**	11	16	23
Manoil **105** Five Barrel Gun on Wheels	12	18	24
Manoil **(MC5) Tank**, composition	22	33	45

Manoil Post-War Vehicles

	C6	C8	C10
Manoil **707 Sedan**	31	46	62
Manoil **708 Roadster**, horizontal radiator	27	41	54
Manoil **708A Roadster**, vertical radiator	32	48	64
Manoil **709 Fire Engine**	16	24	33

	C6	C8	C10
Manoil **710 Oil Tanker**	13	20	27
Manoil **711 Aerial Ladder**	200	300	400
Manoil **712 Pumper**	200	300	400
Manoil **713 Bus**	12	18	24
Manoil **714 Towing Truck**	10	15	20
Manoil **715 Commercial Truck**	10	15	20
Manoil **716 Sedan**	10	15	20

MANOIL. Top, left to right: 713, 716, P-7. Bottom, left to right: 714, P-10, P-11, P-9. Courtesy Marjorie and Peter Ruben.

MANOIL. Top, left to right: 705, 708 early, 708 later. Bottom: 707, 710, 709. Courtesy Marjorie and Peter Ruben. Photo by Norbert Schachter.

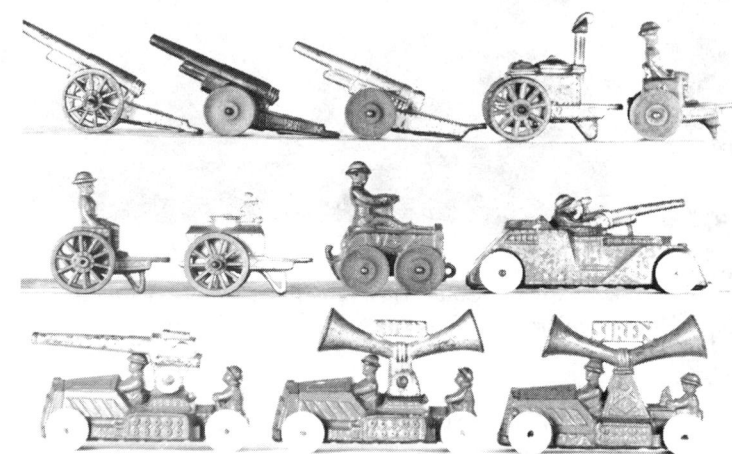

MANOIL. Top, left to right: 69 Cannon, metal wheels; 69 Cannon, wood wheels; 69 Cannon, wood wheels variant; Vehicle 70; Vehicle 71. Middle, left to right: 71 with variant on wheel support; 72; 73 with front tow loop; 74. Bottom: 75; 75A with siren cast separately; 75A siren cast integrally. Photo by Ed Poole.

MANOIL Vehicles. Top, left to right: 95, 96, 97, 98. Bottom: 103, 104, 105, MANOIL "Metal Action Cannon" No. 200. Photo by Ed Poole.

MANOIL. Top: 712 Pumper. Bottom: 711 Aerial Ladder. Courtesy Marjorie and Peter Ruben. Photo by Norbert Schachter.

	C6	C8	C10
Manoil **717 Hard Top convertible**	25	38	50
Manoil **718 Convertible**	10	15	20
Manoil **719 Sport Car**	10	15	20
Manoil **720 Ranch Wagon**	10	15	20

Manoil Plastic Vehicles

	C6	C8	C10
Manoil **P-7 Roadster**	7	11	14
Manoil **P-8 Sedan**	7	11	14
Manoil **P-9 Pick-Up**	7	11	14
Manoil **P-10 Towing Truck**	7	11	14
Manoil **P-11 Road Scraper**	7	11	14
Manoil **P-12 Tractor**	7	11	14
Manoil **P-13 Dump Cart**	7	11	14
Marx Air Force Truck, "Air Defense Group," ride'm toy, No. 3290, 32"	125	188	250
Marx Air Force Truck, canvas top, 20"	105	158	210
Marx Ambulance, No. 8500, 1930s, approx. 14" long	250	375	500
Marx Ambulance, No. 8600, 1930s, approx. 14" long	240	360	480
Marx "American Railroad Express Agency Inc.," early 1930s, open cab, 7" long	120	180	240
Marx American Truck Co. No. 65 moving truck, friction	65	98	130
Marx Army Corps of Engineers, canvas top, 20" long	87	130	175
Marx Army Jeep w/ Searchlight Trailer, steel	87	130	175
Marx Army Staff Car, plastic friction, 9"	12	18	25
Marx Auto Transport, 1950s, w/ tin litho cars (2 of them), 34" long	175	205	350
Marx "Auto Transwalk" No. T-50447B, 1930s truck w/ three cars	200	300	400
Marx Big Boss Car Carrier, 42" long	90	135	180
Marx "Big Shot" Cannon Truck, plastic, fires cap-loaded missile, 22" long	75	112	150
Marx "Chief-Fire Dept. No. 1," "Friction Drive," c. 1948	75	112	150
Marx "Cities Service" Wrecker, 4-1/2", Linemar	65	98	130
Marx "City Sanitation Dept. Help Keep Your City Clean," c. 1940, 12-3/4" long	115	172	230
Marx Coal Truck, electric motor & lights, early	280	420	564
Marx "Cloverdale Farms" Milk Truck	135	202	270
Marx Coca Cola Truck, Linemar, tin, friction, 3" long	50	75	100
Marx Coca Cola Truck, Sprite decal, stamped steel, late 1940s to early 1950s, 20" long	182	275	365
Marx Convertible Roadster, 1930s, nickel-plated tin, 11" long	200	300	400
Marx Cord Convertible, 11" long	250	375	500

*MARX "City Sanitation Dept. Help Keep Your City Clean."
Photo by Calvin L. Chaussee.*

	C6	C8	C10
Marx Corvette Coupe, plastic, friction, 8"	30	45	60
Marx "Deluxe Delivery" Truck	75	112	150

*MARX "Deluxe Delivery" Truck. Courtesy Thomas G. Nefos,
Federal Shipping Network.*

	C6	C8	C10
Marx Corvette Coupe, plastic friction, 8"	30	45	60
Marx "Deluxe Delivery" Truck	75	112	150
Marx Dump Truck, No. 695B, 17" long	120	180	240
Marx Dump Truck, 2-color, No. T751, c. 1930s	85	128	170
Marx No. 1084 Dump Truck	30	45	60
Marx Easter Stake Truck, 1938, 10-1/2" long	190	275	380
Marx "Electrically Lighted Truck and Trailer Set," No. T-5715, c. 1930s, 15"	150	225	300
Marx Falcon w/ plastic bubble top, black rubber tires	145	218	290
Marx "Fanny Farmer" Candy Truck, plastic	100	150	200
Marx Fire Truck, friction, 25" long	225	338	450
Marx Fix-All Convertible & Wrecker (set)	125	188	250
Marx Fix-It Jaguar, plastic, 12" long	65	98	130
Marx G-man Pursuit Car, No. 7000, 1930s, 15" long	250	375	500
Marx Gang Buster Car, No. 7200, 1930s, approx. 14" long	550	825	1100
Marx "Gravel" Truck, 13" long	112	168	225
Marx "Gravel" Truck, 9" long	68	102	135
Marx Grocery Truck, 1950s, 14-1/2"	62	93	125
Marx Guided Missile Truck No. 4488	220	330	440
Marx "Heavy Gauge Tractor" No. 926	100	150	200
Marx "High-Boy Climbing Tractor," No. 950, 10-1/2" long	75	112	150

*MARX Coca-Cola Truck, 20" long. Courtesy Richard
MacNary.*

	C6	C8	C10
Marx Hi-Way Express Truck	123	185	245
Marx Hydraulic Dump	55	83	110
Marx Ice Truck w/ Tongs & Ice	235	352	470
Marx Jeep, 11" long	37	56	75
Marx Lazy-Dazy Dairy Farm Pick-Up Truck and Trailer, 22" long	95	142	190
Marx Livestock Truck	85	128	170
Marx Lonesome Pine Trailer and Convertible Sedan, 1930s, 19" long	462	695	925
Marx "Lumar Contractors" No. 962 Dump Truck	480	720	960
Marx "Lumar Contractors" Steam Shovel	132	198	265
Marx "Lumar Contractors" Crane	120	180	240
Marx Lumar Power Grader	35	52	70
Marx Lumar Scoop-A-Dump	100	150	200
Marx M.D. War Dept. Ambulance, 1930s	650	975	1300
Marx No. 1016 Machinery Moving Truck	262	395	525
Marx "Mammoth Truck Train," No. T-50-12345, c. 1930s, truck w/ 5 trailers	175	262	350
Marx Marcrest Dairy Stake Truck	163	245	325
Marx "Motor Market"	135	205	270
Marx Mystery Taxi, c. 1930s, press down to operate	80	120	165
Marx Navy Jeep No. 1078	65	98	130
Marx Navy Jeep w/ Searchlight Trailer	100	150	200
Marx Nutty Mad Cars, friction, c. 1965, each, 4" long	135	205	270
Marx Panel Wagon	40	60	80
Marx Pepsi-Cola Truck, 1950s, 11" long	35	52	70
Marx "Pet Shop Delivery," 1950s, 10"	80	120	160
Marx Pickup Truck, 11" long, electric lights	100	150	200
Marx "Power Grader" No. 1759, black or white wheels, 17-1/2" long	40	60	80
Marx Pure Milk Dairy Truck w/ glass bottles, pressed steel, tin wheels, c. 1940	100	150	200
Marx REA Express Truck No. 1021	220	330	440
Marx Road Grader, Heavy-duty	48	72	95
Marx Rocker Dump No. 1752, 17-1/2"	60	90	120
Marx "Sand & Gravel" Dump Truck, 1940s, 10" long	60	90	120
Marx Searchlight Truck	150	225	300
Marx "Sinclair" Fuel Truck, steel	175	263	350
Marx Side Dump Truck, 4-color, No. T-475, c. 1940	105	158	210
Marx Side Dump Truck and Trailer, No. T-4045, c. 1930s	100	150	200
Marx "Siren Fire Chief," c. 1930, "F.D. 1st. Batt.," 15" long	330	495	660

	C6	C8	C10
Marx Siren Police Car, No. 8300, 1930s, approx. 14" long 200	300	400
Marx "Sparkling Hot Rod Racer," 1950s plastic wind-up, 8" long.....................37	52	75
Marx Sports Coupe, 1930s, 15" long 200	300	400
Marx Stake-type Truck, 3-color, No. E-271, c. 1941 95	145	190
Marx Stake Truck, c. 1941, 15" long 83	125	165
Marx "Tricky Taxi," friction, 4-1/2" 50	75	100
Marx "U.S. Army Truck w/ Searchlight Trailer," 1950s, 27" total length 130	195	260
Marx "U.S. Mail" Truck, 14" long...................125	188	250
Marx "USA 41573147" Army Truck, c. 1952, 13-3/4" long 100	150	200
Marx "U.S. Navy Jeep w/ Searchlight Trailer," 1950s, 21" total length 125	188	250
Marx Willys Jeep, steel, c. 1938, hood opens, windshield folds down, 12"......90	135	180
Marx Willys Jeep and Trailer, c. 1940s 133	200	265
Marx Willys Jeepster, plastic, wind-up..............75	112	150
Marx Wrecker Truck No. T-16, c. 1930s.........150	225	300
Marx Wrecker Truck, 1920s, 10" long.............100	150	200
Mattel Hot Wheels Breakup Bucket, blue..........25	38	50

MARX Tricky Taxi. Photo by William G. Floyd.

	C6	C8	C10
Mattel Hot Wheels Custom Eldorado, rose pink.....................25	38	50
Mattel Hot Wheels Flat Out 442, green 38	56	75
Mattel Hot Wheels Daredevil Loop Pak, 1968 4	6	8
Mattel Hot Wheels Large Charger, chrome 7	10	14
Mattel Hot Wheels Mighty Maverick, hot pink 48	72	96
Mattel Hot Wheels Python, red 4	6	9
Mattel Hot Wheels Seasider, red.......................11	16	23
Mattel Hot Wheels Ruby Red Passion 10	15	20

METAL CAST PRODUCTS COMPANY

by Fred Maxwell, Slushmold Contributing Editor

Metal Cast Products, a reorganization (c. 1925) of a venerable toy soldier and novelty company (S. Sachs) made hand-operated slushcasting molds for small businesses and hobbyists—what some have called the home-casting industry. Since identical molds were sold to many franchisees we cannot identify the actual makers unless they engraved their names on their products. One who did was Fred Green Toys. Metal Cast offered full support services to its franchisees, including marketing, printing, publishing, and parts.

A variety of wheels may be found on Metal Cast vehicles: metal disk wheels, metal spoke wheels, wood wheels w/ rubber tires, and white or black rubber wheels.

We see many home-cast lead soldiers and novelties, but the production of toy vehicles has not left much of a mark. Perhaps it was the Great Depression or perhaps it was the lack of identity: demand today seems weak. However, collectors of the unusual should find much to like: most of those I have seen were well designed and professionally finished.

Metal Cast Van Truck, #01-02, COE, cab, semi-trailer moving van. Trailer also found in a "FRED GREEN" version, 6" .... No Price Found

Metal Cast Tank Truck, #01-03, same COE cab, semi-fuel tanker. My version is 5-3/4", "FRED GREEN TOYS," "Made in U.S.A.," 6".............4   6   8

Metal Cast Open Rack Truck, #01-04, COE cab, stake semi-trailer, 6" 8   12   16

Metal Cast War Tank, #08, early heavy Sherman Tank, 4" 33   49   66

Metal Cast Cadillac Sedan, #40, 2-door, 5-1/4" long .... No Price Found

Metal Cast Packard Convertible, #41, 2-door, top down, 5-1/4" 10   15   20

Metal Cast Dump Truck, #43, COE chassis, dump body w/ activating mechanism, 5-1/4" ... No Price Found

Metal Cast Streamline Sedan, #60, DeSoto? Airflow, 8 open windows, spoke wheels, rubber tires, 4" 10   15   20

Metal Cast Fire Engine, #61, hook and ladder truck, crew of 2, 4-1/2" 6   10   14

Metal Cast Racer, #62, Bluebird type record car, driver, 4-1/2" .... No Price Found

Metal Cast Coupe #63, convertible, 2 open windows, sidemounts, trunk .... No Price Found

Metal Cast Truck, #64, Dodge?, stake-body, 1920s, 2 OW, 4-1/4" .... No Price Found

METAL CAST PRODUCTS Tank #08. Photo by Ed Poole.

METAL CAST PRODUCTS. Top: Greyhound Bus, MCP #62. Middle: Limousine, MCP #40, MCP #60. Bottom: MCP #64. Photo by Perry Eichor.

	C6	C8	C10
Metal Cast Fire Engine, #65, Steam pumper w/ watercannon, driver, 4"			No Price Found
Metal Cast Fire Engine, no #, similar to #65 w/o watercannon, 3-3/8"	6	10	14
Metal Cast Racer, #92, large, no driver			No Price Found
Metal Cast Greyhound bus			No Price Found

METAL CAST PRODUCTS. Top: MCP #01-02. Middle: MCP #01-03. Bottom: MCP #40. Photo by Perry Eichor.

METAL MASTERS

Listing by Dave Leopard

	C6	C8	C10
MM01 Roadster, c. 1938, 7" long	20	30	40
MM02 Bus, c. 1938, 7-1/4" long	23	35	47
MM03 Pickup Truck, c. 1938, 7" long	20	30	40
MM04 Fire Truck version of pickup, c. 1938, 7" long	30	40	50
MM05 Tow Truck version of pickup, c. 1938, 7" long	30	40	50
MM06 Jeep, c. 1947, 5-1/2" long	9	13	18
MM07 Station Wagon, c. 1940, 8-1/2"	40	55	65
MM08 Station Wagon, c. 1940, wind-up motor, 8-1/2"	45	55	70
MM09 Station Wagon, c. 1940, ambulance version, 8-1/2" long	75	112	150
MM10 Tow Truck, c. 1940, "ABC Towing Service," 10" long	40	50	65
MM11 Tow Truck, c. 1940, wind-up motor, 10" long	19	28	38
MM12 Fire Truck, c. 1940, removable ladders, 10" long	30	45	60
MM13 Fire Truck, c. 1940, ladders, wind-up motors, 10" long	50	65	80

METALCRAFT

Metalcraft of St. Louis, Missouri, began producing its pressed steel trucks in 1931. About a million were sold, most as advertising toys. In 1937, defeated by the Depression, Metalcraft shuttered.

	C6	C8	C10
Metalcraft "Bordens Milk" Truck	225	338	450
Metalcraft "Bunte Candies" Truck, 12" long	175	262	350
Metalcraft Coca-Cola Truck, pressed steel, rubber tires, c. late 1920s-early 1930s, 10 bottles in rack, "Every Bottle Sterilized," 11" long	500	800	1140
Metalcraft Coca-Cola Truck, 10 bottles, 1930s, 10-1/2" long	430	645	860
Metalcraft Coca-Cola Truck, 10 bottles, late 1930s, long nose, stamped metal, 12" long	450	675	900
Metalcraft Coca-Cola Truck, c. 1928, w/ bottles in racks	500	800	1100
Metalcraft CW Coffee Dump Truck, 10-3/4" long	335	500	670
Metalcraft CW Coffee Wrecker	335	400	675

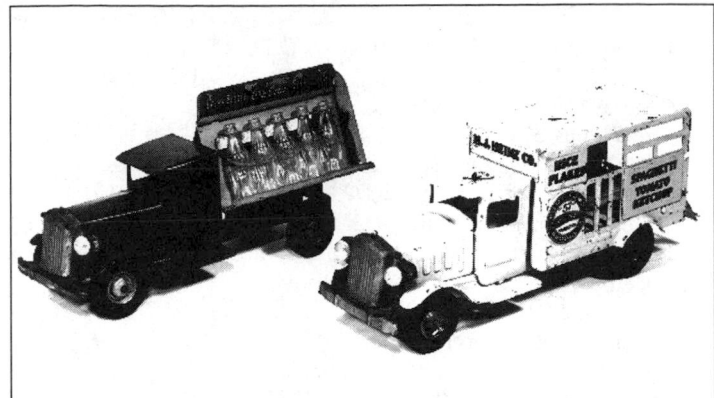

METALCRAFT. Left to right: Coca-Cola Truck, "Heinz" Truck. Courtesy Phillips New York.

METALCRAFT Coca-Cola Truck, 11" long. Courtesy Wilkinson Collection, Detroit Antique Toy Museum.

	C6	C8	C10
Metalcraft Delivery Truck Van, steel, 11" long	215	322	430
Metalcraft "Goodrich Silvertone Tires" wrecker, w/ 3 spare tires	240	360	480
Metalcraft "Heinz" Truck, c. 1932, "Baked Beans," "Bottled Vinegar," "Rice Flakes," 12" long	300	450	600
Metalcraft "Kroger Food Express," 11" long	325	488	650
Metalcraft "Krug Bakery" Truck	450	675	935
Metalcraft "Machinery Hauling"	500	850	1200
Metalcraft "Meadow Gold Butter" Truck, battery lights, 13" long	275	362	550
Metalcraft "Plee-Zing Quality Products"	275	362	550
Metalcraft "Pure" Oil Truck	600	900	1225
Metalcraft "Shell Motor Oil" Truck	375	565	750
Metalcraft "St. Louis" Truck, c. 1930, 11" long	250	375	500
Metalcraft Steam Shovel	85	128	170
Metalcraft "Sunshine Biscuits" Truck	207	310	415

METALCRAFT Coca-Cola Truck, late 1930s, 12" long. Courtesy Richard L. MacNary.

	C6	C8	C10
Metalcraft "Towing & Repairs"	250	375	500
Metalcraft "Toy Town Grocery"	275	410	550
Metalcraft "Werks Tag Soap" Truck	200	300	400
Metalcraft "Weston's Biscuits"	215	322	430
Metalcraft "White King Delivery" Truck, 12" long	223	335	445

MIDGETOY

(A & E Tool & Gage Co., Inc.)

by Thomas G. Nefos

The original owners of the Midgetoy factory in Rockford, Illinois, were engaged in precision instrument production during WWII. In 1946 they decided to branch out into the die-cast toy business, and Midgetoy was born. Their toys included everything from military vehicles to sports cars, jeeps, and racers. In only 20 years (by 1966) they became the second largest producers of die-cast toys in the nation (Tootsietoy was first). At their peak, Midgetoy produced over 20,000 toys per day.

Some of the ideas that were implemented by Midgetoy (making several toys off the same mold at one time instead of only one, and blister packaging of toys for point of sale) were quickly copied by the competition.

Each toy was given four coats of lead-free paint, and all materials were purchased locally (no foreign materials were ever used). It was not uncommon for the owners to employ elderly folks (some from nursing homes) to do some of the toy painting. Midgetoy would actually take the unfinished product to the elderly for final painting and decaling, thus giving them the opportunity to make some money and pass the time.

Midgetoy produced die-cast toys from 1946 to 1981, when the original owners became too old and the factory was shut down.

MIDGETOY 6" Oil Tank Truck, 1957. Photo by Thomas G. Nefos, National Toy Connection.

MIDGETOY 9" Semi-Auto Transporter (unlisted) with MG & Mustang, 1962. Value in mint $60. Photo by Thomas G. Nefos, National Toy Connection.

MIDGETOY Scenic Cruiser Bus-Midgetoy Bus Lines, 1955. Photo by Thomas G. Nefos, National Toy Connection.

MIDGETOY Truck Set, Chevrolet chassis with 3 interchangeable bodies, 1946. Value in mint $45. Photo by Thomas G. Nefos, National Toy Connection.

MIDGETOY 6" Self-Propelled Artillery. Photo by Thomas G. Nefos, National Toy Connection.

MIDGETOY 9" Semi-Tanker (unlisted), 1963. Value in mint $30. Photo by Thomas G. Nefos, National Toy Connection.

MIDGETOY 6" American LaFrance Fire Truck, 1957. Mint value $32. Photo by Thomas G. Nefos, National Toy Connection.

	G	V6	M		G	V6	M
Midgetoy Ford Torino, 1971, green, 2-1/2"	7	10	14	Midgetoy Self-Propelled Artillery, late 1940s, 4"	12	18	25
Midgetoy Ford Mustang w/ tow hook, 1970, orange, 2-1/2"	7	11	15	Midgetoy Half Track, late 1940s, 4-3/4"	12	18	25
Midgetoy Sunbeam Racer-Utah Salt Flats, 1950, 3-1/2"	10	15	20	Midgetoy Self-Propelled Artillery, 1957, 6"	14	21	28
Midgetoy Cadillac Convertible, 1949, green, 3-1/2"	10	15	20	Midgetoy Fuel Tank Truck, 1954, 4-1/2"	11	16	22
Midgetoy Ford Mark IV, 1971, blue, 2-1/2"	7	11	15	Midgetoy U.S.A. Jeep, 1950, 2-3/4"	7	11	15
				Midgetoy U.S.A. Jeep, 1950, 1-1/2"	5	8	10
				Midgetoy Howitzer, late 1940s, 3"	7	11	15
				Midgetoy Staff Car, 1950s, 4-1/2"	12	18	25
				Midgetoy Utility Trailer, 1940s, 1-1/2"	6	9	12
				Midgetoy Army Bus, 1950s, 3-1/2"	10	15	20

Army Vehicles - O.D.

	G	V6	M
Midgetoy Sherman Tank, late 1940s, 4"	14	21	28

MID-WEST METAL NOVELTY MANUFACTURING COMPANY

by Fred Maxwell, Slushmold Contributing Editor, assisted by Ferd Zegel and John West

In the late 1920s the U.S. auto industry, led by Ford, was not only booming but dominating global production, and auto toys were keeping up with their prototypes. Here we focus on three companies that had developed a thriving slush-mold toy business: C.A.W. Novelty Co., Mid-West Metal Novelty Co., and Kansas Toy and Novelty Co. These were in small northern Kansas towns, Clay Center and Clifton, only a few miles apart. These toy makers had other things in common: they loved racers, they all used metal disc wheels with black-painted "tires," they tended to follow the lead of Tootsietoy, and they left almost no paper trail. This last accounts for the difficulty toy historians have had identifying some excellent models and toys.

The above clues suggest that Mid-West was C.E. Stevenson's business title. Stevenson, an active business man, was at the center of all this. In 1923 he started casting toys at home. In 1925 he joined Western Diecasting Co., of Clay Center, probably as an outside salesman. Shortly after Kansas Toy Co. opened he contracted to furnish molds to them.

He may also have sold master patterns and those prepainted wheels to C.A.W. and Kansas Toy: all these were probably made in the foundry of Western Diecasting. Our sole surviving newsclip on Mid-West, from a 1929 *Toys and Novelties* magazine, shows a deluxe (5-window) coupe, a fairly exact copy of the Tootsie Buick but with those Kansas black-painted "tires."

But what else did Mid-West make? Over the years we have found a group of auto toys with a family resemblance: Tootsie copies or look-a-likes; Tootsie wheels, including those distinctive lug boltheads; metal disc wheels with a suggested rim between wheel and tire (see photos MV3, MV4); and most important, several versions of that Buick coupe seen in *Toys and Novelties*. The most likely maker was Stevenson, before he moved on to a larger city in 1931 and founded Lincoln (Nebraska) White Metal Works, with which he thrived for years in spite of the Great Depression.

These Mid-West(?) toys are rarely seen today. If found, they should be low priced.

	C6	C8	C10
MW1 Large Coupe, no lamps, large die-cast?, 5 "grooved" solid windows, disc wheels w/ "lug bolts," HG, HO, VL, 3-1/2"			No Price Found
MW2 Yellow Taxicab, no lamps, door handles, 7 "grooved" solid windows, MDW w/ rims but no bolts, HG, HO, VL, 2-3/4" long			No Price Found

MIDWEST. Left to right: MW2, MW1. Photo by Fred Maxwell.

MIDWEST MW2, two versions. Photo by Fred Maxwell.

The only known mention of Mid-West, as shown in the August 1929 issue of Toys & Novelties magazine.

MIDWEST. Two versions of MW3. Photo by Fred Maxwell.

              C6   C8   C10

MW3 Buick Coupe, no lamps, disc wheels, 5 "grooved" solid windows, HG, HO, VL, sidemounts, 3 variations: 4 open windows, 5 smooth windows, MDW w/ "lug bolts," 3"... No Price Found

MW4 Midget Racer, driver crouched & hunched over steering wheel, torpedo tail, small disc wheels w/ "lug bolts," HG, HO, VL, variation: narrower body and large wheels (the post-war "M & L" reproduction is more often found), 2-3/4" .... No Price Found

MW5 Large Racer, basically similar to above but boattailed w/ medium-sized disc wheels, 3-5/8" .... No Price Found

MW6 Truck, closed body, AC Mack, gas tank ahead of windshield, VG, screen louvers, stake-side body. Unique slushmold design w/ solid pan and body open in rear (for pouring alloy), 3-1/4" .... No Price Found

MW7 Large Roadster, Buick or Packard, long hood, top up, HG, HO, VL, door handles & hinges, RM, rear bumper. Variation: 2 colors, 3 solid windows, different, painted disc wheels, 3-5/8" .... No Price Found

              C6   C8   C10

MIDWEST. Top: MW7. Bottom, left to right: MW7, MW11. Photo by Fred Maxwell.

MW8 Touring Car, Ford T, driver & lady passenger w/ muff, top down, no lamps, plain grille, HO, VL, door handles, disc wheels, 3-1/8" ...... No Price Found

MW9 Touring Car, top up, no seats, HG, HO, VL, RM, side lamps, door handles, disc wheels, 3-1/8" .... No Price Found

MIDWEST. Top: two versions of MW4. Bottom: MW5. Photo by Fred Maxwell.

MIDWEST. Left to right: MW9, MW8. Photo by Fred Maxwell.

MIDWEST. Left to right: Unlisted, MW13. Photo by Fred Maxwell.

	C6	C8	C10

MW10 Bus, Yellow Coach?, high, school-bus
   body, no doors, 13 solid grooved windows,
   HG, RM, painted disc wheels, 3-3/4" .... No Price Found

MW11 Town Car, chauffeur, long hood, HG, HO,
   VL, L/I, 3 colors, 5 solid windows, grooved,
   door handles & hinges, disc wheels, 3-5/8" ..... No Price Found

MW12 Bus, overland/safety, no lamps, no doors,
   no spares, HG, HO, 10 open windows, disc
   wheels (same bus later reissued by Stevenson
   at Lincoln Metal Works), 3-1/2" .... No Price Found

	C6	C8	C10

MW13 Sedan, 2-door, Ford A, finely detailed screen
   grille, headlamps and fenders, (made with a
   3-piece mold, a Stevenson specialty), VL,
   WSV, 4 open windows, door handles & hinges,
   painted disc wheels, 2-3/4" .... No Price Found

MW14 Sedan ?, Buick, same finely detailed front-end
   as above, "B" cast on grille, HO, VL, side lamps,
   WSV, 6 open windows, door hinges, RM,
   painted wheels (a similar car has been attributed
   to Barclay Mfg.), 3-1/16" .... No Price Found

MINIATURE VEHICLE CASTINGS INC.

Though these appear to be toys from the 1930s, they were first produced in 1985. The models were carved and cast by owner Robert E. Wagner. Made of die-cast lead from silicone molds, they were sold for $21 apiece, and at least 3500 have been sold. Some are beginning to appear at toy shops and on dealer lists. Twenty-one different types were made, among them a 1937 Ford Sedan, a 1937 Studebaker coupe, and a 1936 Plymouth sedan. The average length is about 4-1/2", and the New Jersey firm's name is visible (sometimes dimly) on a piece of tin soldered to the bottom. The toys today seem to sell at about double their original price.

"Moxie" Horse Car (based on the actual
   promotional vehicle) tin litho, 8" long 350   525   700

"Moxie" Horse Car. Courtesy Sotheby's New York.

MINIATURE VEHICLE CASTINGS, INC. cars. Courtesy Robert E. Wagner.

NEFF-MOON TOY COMPANY

Neff-Moon, of Sandusky, Ohio, was owned by William Moon and Charles Neff. Production of their pressed steel toys began in 1923. The firm, which seems to have been located above a grocery, was apparently an early victim of the Depression.

	C6	C8	C10
Neff-Moon Groceries Van	300	450	600
Neff-Moon Taxi, 12" long	350	525	700
Neff-Moon Tow Truck, c. 1925, 16" long	200	300	400

	C6	C8	C10
Nonpareil Ambulance	30	45	60
Nonpareil Dry Goods	30	45	60
Nonpareil Police Patrol	30	45	60
Nonpareil Toyville Express	30	45	60

NORTH & JUDD

Research by collector C.B.C. Lee suggests that this company, located at the time in New Britain, Connecticut, made cast-iron toys for only one year, probably 1930, for S.H. Kress. Their original designs appear to have been marked with the company's name, but their copies for the most part are unmarked. The company is still in business, making quality hardware.

	C6	C8	C10
Austin Convertible, open top, marked "North & Judd"	No Price Found		
Austin Sedan, 2-door, marked "North & Judd"	No Price Found		
Bus, looks like Dent, 4.667" long	No Price Found		
Ford Model A Coupe, looks like Arcade, length of left cab 1.528", has driver in window, trunk at rear	No Price Found		
Ford Model T Stake Truck, like Arcade but marked "Anchor Truck Co." (an anchor is North & Judd's trademark)	1500	2500	4200
Motorcycle Cop, like Hubley's "Cop," separate nickeled driver is held by mushrooms at front of handlebars and on driver's feet	No Price Found		
Semi-Trailer Stake Truck, marked "North & Judd," 5-5/8" long	500	800	1100
Tractor, looks like Arcade but has nickeled driver, 2.988" long	No Price Found		

NYLINT

The Nylint Tool and Manufacturing Company was formed in 1937 by Bernard C. Klint and David Nyberg (thus its name) in Rockford, Illinois. Toy production began in the spring of 1946. Since 1951, the firm has concentrated on the production of heavy-duty scale reproductions, in steel, of earth-moving equipment and over-the-road trucks. Part of the following list was provided by Jeffrey L. Hubbard.

Nylint No. 600 Amazing Car, 1946-49, windup, 13-3/4" long	100	150	200
Nylint No. 700 Lift Truck (fork lift), 1947-49, windup	75	112	150
Nylint No. 800 Scootcycle, 1948-50, windup, 7-1/4" long	200	300	400
Nylint No. 1000 Deliverall, 1948-51, windup, 10" long	300	450	600

NYLINT No. 1300 Tournarocker.
Courtesy Continental Hobby House.

NYLINT No. 1600 Payloader. Courtesy Thomas G. Nefos, Federal Shipping Network.

NYLINT No. 2200 Michigan Shovel. Courtesy Continental Hobby House.

	C6	C8	C10
Nylint No. 1100 Elgin Street Sweeper, 1950-52, windup, 8-1/4" long	250	375	500
Nylint No. 1200 Pumpmobile, 1950-52, windup, 8-5/8" long	125	188	250
Nylint No. 1300 Tournarocker, 1951-52, open tractor w/ driver, 18" long	62	93	125
Nylint No. 1300 Tournarocker, 1953-57, closed cab, no driver, 18" long	105	158	210
Nylint No. 1400 Road Grader, 1951, small wheels, 19-1/4" long	65	98	130
Nylint No. 1400 Road Grader, 1952-58, larger wheels	70	105	140
Nylint No. 1500 Tournahopper, 1951-56, 22-1/2" long	175	263	350
Nylint No. 1600 Payloader, 1951-54, red, 18" long	75	112	150
Nylint No. 1600 Payloader, 1955, tan	125	188	250
Nylint No. 1600 Payloader, 1956-57, light green	100	150	200
Nylint No. 1600 Payloader, 1958, dark green and before year was out yellow (add 20% to yellow price)	100	150	200
Nylint No. 1700 Tournahauler, 1953-56, 30-1/4" long	70	105	140
Nylint No. 1800 Traveloader, 1953-55, 30" long	113	170	225
Nylint No. 1900 Tournatractor, 1954-55, 14-3/4" long	150	225	300

	C6	C8	C10
Nylint No. 2000 Speed Swing, 1955-58, 19" long	100	150	200
Nylint No. 2100 Tournadozer, 1956-59, 20" long	110	165	220
Nylint No. 2200 Michigan Shovel, 1955-65, 31-1/2" long	78	117	155
Nylint No. 2300 Elgin Street Sweeper, 1956-57, battery-operated version, closed cab	120	180	240
Nylint No. 2400 Electronic Cannon, 1956, has no radar antenna	100	150	200
As above with radar antenna, 22-1/2" long	88	132	175
Nylint No. 2500 Telescoping Crane, 1957-60, 27" long	128	188	250
Nylint No. 2600 Missile Launcher, 1957-60, 31-1/2" long	125	188	250
Nylint No. 2700 Uranium Hauler, 1958-59, 22-1/2" long	125	188	250
Nylint No. 2800 Guided Missile Carrier, first version (1958), nose cone of missile doesn't fire, 15-1/2" long	150	225	300
Nylint No. 2800 Guided Missile Carrier, later (through 1960), cone of missile fires	75	112	150
Nylint No. 2900 Jack Hammer, 1958-60, 19-1/2" long, with box	150	225	300
Nylint No. 3000 Grader-Loader, 1959-61, 23-3/4" long	92	138	185

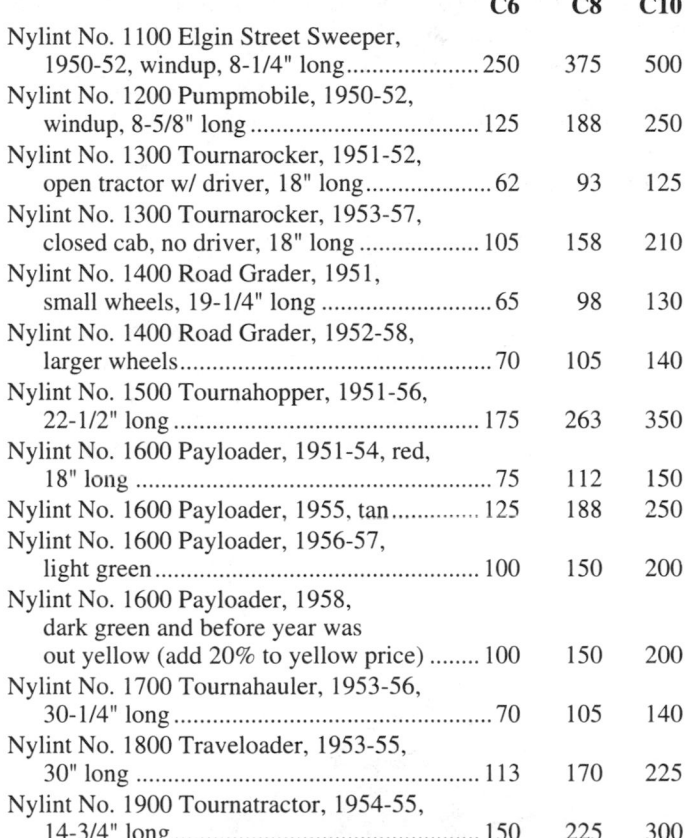

NYLINT No. 8411, 1975, U-Haul Truck. Courtesy Thomas G. Nefos, Federal Shipping Network.

	C6	C8	C10
Nylint No. 3100 Payloader Tractor-Shovel, 1959-61, 17-5/8" long	100	150	200
Nylint No. 3200 Power & Light Lineman Truck, 1959-61, 35-3/4" long	150	225	300
Nylint No. 3300 Power & Light Posthole Digger, 1959-61, 35-3/4" long	150	225	300
Nylint No. 3400 Highway Emergency Unit, 1959-63, 18-5/8" long	72	108	145
Nylint No. 3500 Countdown Rocket Launcher, 1959-61, 21" long	125	188	250
Nylint No. 3600 Ford Rapid Delivery, 18-1/4" long	163	245	325
Nylint No. 3700 Street Sprinkler Truck, 18" long	140	210	280
Nylint No. 3800 Ford Sales & Service, 13-5/8" long	140	210	280
Nylint No. 3900 Ford Platform Tilt Truck, 15-3/4" long	125	188	250
Nylint No. 4000 Ford Speedway Truck w/ Racer, 24-3/4" long	122	185	245
Nylint No. 4100 Ford Pickup & U-Haul Box Trailer	110	165	220
Nylint No. 4200 Bulldozer, 14" long	65	98	130
Nylint No. 4300 Ford U-Haul Rental Fleet, 3 pieces	175	263	350
Nylint No. 4400 Camper on Pickup, 13-1/2" long	70	105	140
Nylint No. 4500 Ranch Truck, 14" long	75	112	150
Nylint No. 4600 Construction 4-Wheel Platform Dump, 15-3/4" long	88	132	175
Nylint No. 4700 Happy Acres Truck w/ horses, 14" long	65	98	130
Nylint No. 4800 U-Haul Trailer, 8" long	50	75	100
Nylint No. 4900 U-Haul Trailer, 9" long	50	75	100
Nylint No. 5000 Dump Truck w/ Cement Mixer, 20-1/2" long	125	188	250
Nylint No. 5100 Dump Truck, 13-1/2"	75	112	150
Nylint No. 5200 Pickup Truck (Econoline), 11-1/4" long	80	120	160
Nylint No. 5300 Custom Camper on above, 12-1/2" long	75	112	150
Nylint No. 5400 Custom Camper on above w/ boat, 23-1/2" long	120	180	240
Nylint No. 5500 Pepsi Truck, 16-1/2"	125	188	250
Nylint No. 5800 Ford Econoline Van, 12" long	72	105	145

	C6	C8	C10
Nylint No. 6000 American Oil Emergency Truck, 11-1/4" long	100	150	200
Nylint No. 6200 Kennel Truck w/ dogs, 11-1/2" long	88	132	175
Nylint No. 6300 Horse Van, 23-1/2"	78	117	155
Nylint No. 6600 Mobile Home, Semi type, 30" long, 1964	125	188	250
Nylint No. 6700 Ambulance, 12" long	100	150	200
Nylint No. 6800 Jalopy, 9-5/8" long	30	45	60
Nylint No. 6900 Airport Courtesy Van, "Holiday Inn," 12" long	275	332	550
Nylint No. 7100 Fun on Farm Econoline Truck, 29 pieces, 11-1/4" long	87	130	175
Nylint No. 7300 Army Ambulance, 12" long	60	90	120
Nylint No. 7900 Road Grader, 15" long	62	93	125
Nylint No. 8000 Pony Farm Van, 7-piece set, 11-1/4" long	135	198	270
Nylint No. 8100 Suburban Fire Pumper, 12-1/2" long	100	150	200
Nylint No. 8200 Bronco, 12-1/2" long	75	112	150
Nylint No. 8300 Texaco Service van, 12" long	150	225	300
Nylint No. 8400 U-Haul Cube Van, 1965, 22" long	87	130	175
Nylint No. 8410 U-Haul Truck & Trailer, 1974, 22" long	75	112	150
Nylint No. 8411 U-Haul Truck, Chevy	75	112	150
Ohio Armored Car, c. WWI, friction, 7-1/4" long	225	337	450
Ohio Coupe, 2-door, pressed steel, 17" long	150	225	300
Ohio Delivery Truck, 1920s, painted pressed steel, friction, 12" long	300	450	600
Ohio Fire Ladder Truck, 1920s, 13-1/2" long	200	300	400
Ohio Fire Patrol, pressed steel, cast iron, wood, very early, 9-3/4"	500	750	1000

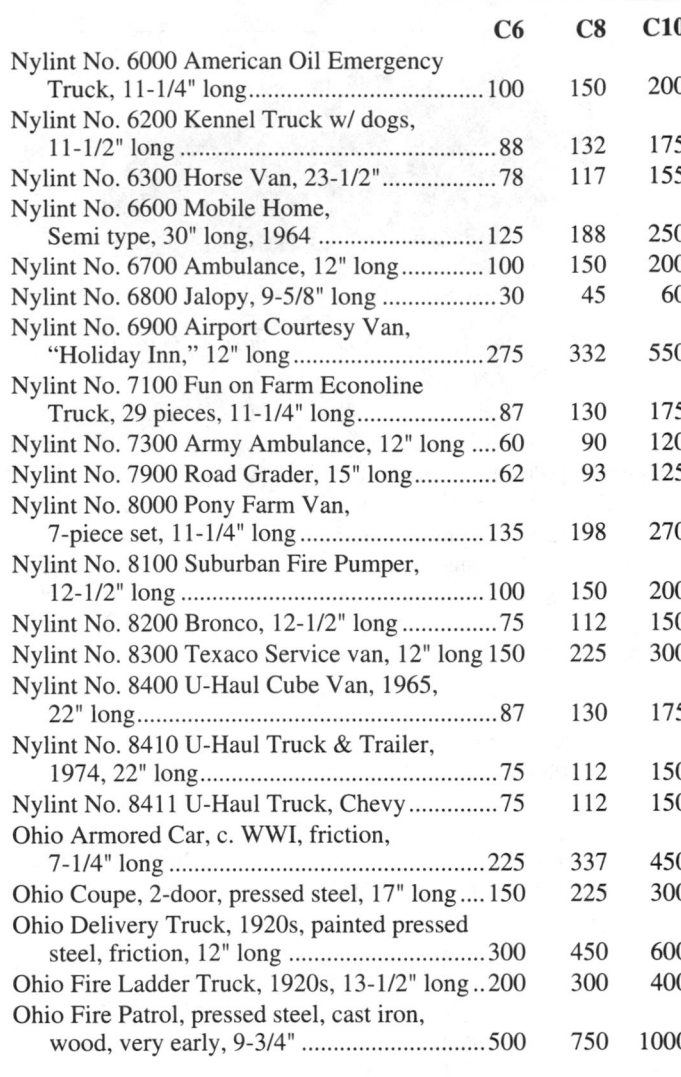

OHIO Armored Car, c. WWI, 7-1/4" long. Courtesy Lloyd W. Ralston Auctions.

OHIO Delivery Truck, 1920s, 12" long. Courtesy Lloyd W. Ralston Auctions.

OHIO Fire Truck, 19-1/2" long, 1910. Courtesy Lloyd W. Ralston Auctions.

Pedal Car, Cadillac, early, 40-1/4" long. Courtesy James S. Maxwell/Virginia Caputo. Photo by Virginia Caputo.

	C6	C8	C10
Ohio Fire Truck, pressed steel, cast iron, wood, very early, 10-1/2"	1200	1800	2400
Ohio Fire Truck, friction, 19-1/2"	250	375	500
Ohio Pickup Truck, 1920s, friction, 13" long	238	358	475
Ohio Roadster, cast iron and wood, friction, very early, 7-1/2" long	350	525	700
Ohio Roadster, 1920s, 13" long	175	262	350
Ohio Roadster, 1920s, friction, pressed steel, 18" long	312	468	625
Ohio Touring Auto, friction	100	150	200
Ohio Truck, "1909," friction, 10-1/2" long	450	675	900
Ohlsson & Rice, midget race car, aluminum body, rubber tires, c. 1940s	325	488	650
Oil and Gas Truck, cast iron, 8"	200	300	400
Oil Truck, c. 1936, pressed steel, 10-3/4" long	100	150	200
"Patrol" Motorcycle and rider, c. 1940, cast iron, 6-1/4" long	160	240	320

"Patrol" Motorcycle and rider, c. 1940, 6-1/4" long, cast iron.

	C6	C8	C10
"Patrol" Stake Truck, Wyandotte?, pressed steel, 4-7/8" long	40	60	80
Pedal Car, American National "Big Boy" Dump Truck	6000	10,000	22,000
Pedal Car, "American National Company Toledo Ohio, USA," sheet metal and wooden, dashboard with dials, rubber tread on wheels, 46" long	1000	1500	2000

OHIO Roadster, 18" long, 1920s. Courtesy Lloyd W. Ralston Auctions.

	C6	C8	C10
Pedal Car, "AMF," Hook and Ladder, late 1970s	200	300	400
Pedal Car, Boycraft, 1925, open coupe	2000	3500	6000
Pedal Car, c. 1905, chain driver, wooden spoke wheels	1250	1875	2500
Pedal Car, Cadillac, c. 1915, Toledo Metal Wheel Co. lithographed dashboard	500	750	1000
Pedal Car, Cadillac, early, 40-1/2"	800	1200	1600
Pedal Car, Chrysler Airflow, 1937	1400	2500	3200
Pedal Car, DeSoto, 1939	1250	1875	2500
Pedal Car, Essex, 1927	1100	1650	2200
Pedal Car, Fire Truck, Mack, Steel-Craft	2500	4000	7000
Pedal Car, "Ford, 1896," tubular frame w/ wire wheels, sheet metal seat w/ wooden back rest and steering lever, plate under seat has diagram of motor, 9" long	1000	1500	2000
Pedal Car, "Ford," 1937, painted steel	750	1125	1500
Pedal Car, Garton "Hot Rod"	410	615	825
Pedal Car, Gendron Lincoln	1500	2500	4000
Pedal Car, Gendron "Skippy," 1940	1200	2200	3500
Pedal Car, Hudson, wood and steel, folding windshield, tilt-up steering wheel	400	600	800
Pedal Car, Kidillac, c. 1950s	800	1400	2000
Pedal Car, Lincoln 1921, Toledo	2500	5000	7500
Pedal Car, Lincoln, 1937	1500	2400	3500
Pedal Car, Mercer Raceabout, 1920	2000	3000	4000
Pedal Car, Murray "Earth Mover"	600	950	1300
Pedal Car, Murray "Champion," 1955	500	800	1100

Pedal Car, "Ford." Courtesy Mapes Auctioneers & Appraisers.

	C6	C8	C10
Pedal Car, Nash Sideway, 1920s, 34" long	1000	1500	2000
Pedal Car, open coupe, 1920s or early 1930s, Gendron, 36" long	1200	1800	2400
Pedal Car, Packard Dual Cowl Phaeton, American National, 6' long	3000	4500	6000
Pedal Car, Packard Roadster, 1920s, American National, 45" long	3000	5500	8000
Pedal Car, "Packard," early, wire wheels	300	450	600
Pedal Car, "Pioneer" Race Car, metal and wood	700	1050	1400
Pedal Car, "Pioneer Lines," Gendron 36" long	1800	3000	5000
Pedal Car, Steelcraft Auburn streamliner	3000	5500	8000

	C6	C8	C10
Pedal Car, Steelcraft Buick, late 1920s, 36" long	4000	7000	12,000
Pedal Car, Steelcraft Chrysler Airflow	1500	2500	4000
Pedal Car, Steelcraft Jewett open coupe, 55" long	2500	5000	7500
Pedal Car, Steelcraft 1939 Lincoln Zephyr	1700	2600	4000
Pedal Car, Terraplane, 1934	1500	2250	3000
Pedal Car, Winner, c. 1906	1000	1500	2000
Perfect Rubber Co. '35 Pontiac Slantback Sedan, 3-3/4" long	35	52	70
Playboy Dump Truck, tan, 22" long	150	225	300
Playboy "Intercity Bus," cream color, 23-1/2" long	300	450	600

PYRO

Pyro began in 1939 in Pyro Park, Union City, New Jersey. The owner was William Lester. At its height, the company had 400 employees.

Racing Car, cast iron, with figure, 5-1/2" long. Courtesy Wilkinson Collection, Detroit Antique Toy Museum.

	C6	C8	C10
Pyro Race Car, 4" long	17	26	35
Pyro Range Patrol Truck	10	15	20
Pyro Road Roller	12	18	25
Pyro "U.S. Army" Truck	5	8	10
Pyro "U.S.M.C." Truck	10	15	20
Pyro "U.S. Navy" Truck	10	15	20
Race Car, cast iron, 9" long	235	352	470
Racer "Parker Special," simple body of heavy steel with steel wheels, 11"	75	112	150
Race Car, friction, w/ driver, c. 1925	150	225	300
Race Car, c. 1918, 8" long	150	225	300
Racer, pressed steel w/ driver, white rubber tires, rubberband and gear powered, 7-1/2" long	17	26	35
Racing Car, cast iron, w/ figure, 5-1/2"	150	225	300
Racing Car, cast iron, w/ driver, full figure, spiked wheels, early 1920s	75	112	150
Racing Car, cast iron, 7-1/4" long	260	390	520
Racing Set, 1930s, 3 tin racing cars, small tin garage	125	187	250
"Railway Express" Truck, cast iron, early 1930s, 5" long	110	165	220

RAINBOW

The following list, with its codings, was compiled by Dave Leopard. Vehicles are broken down by types.

	C6	C8	C10
RA01 '35 Oldsmobile Coupe, 3-3/4"	30	45	60
RA02 '35 Oldsmobile 4-door Sedan, 3-1/4" long	29	45	58
RA03 '35 Oldsmobile 4-door Sedan, 5" long	41	62	82

	C6	C8	C10
RT01 '35 Studebaker (?) stake side pickup, 5-1/4" long	41	62	82
RR01 Open Racer, tapered tail, 4" long	25	38	50
RR02 Open Racer, tapered tail, 5" long	No Price Found		

RALSTOY

(Ralston Toy and Novelty Company)

by Fred Maxwell (Slushmold Contributing Editor) and Ferd Zegel with the assistance of Alice Shooter and the Ralston Archives

Ralston Toy & Novelty Co. was founded in July 1939 to manufacture slushmold toys and novelties. It was formed by Dr. Felix Despecher, former Mayor of Ralston, Nebraska, A.M. Erickson, and Henry C. Nestor to acquire the assets of Best Toy Co. of Manhattan, Kansas, and the surviving molds of Kansas Toy Co. of Clifton, Kansas. These assets included the temporary services of John M. Best, his molder Conrad Morsch, and about 140 molds from these pioneering slushmold vehicle toy companies. The new enterprise was located in a building formerly occupied by the American Legion, at 7632 Burlington St. In this way Ralston continued a low-cost toy line that had been familiar to collectors since Kansas Toy was founded in 1923.

With the death of founder Dr. Despecher about a year later, the young company was forced into reorganization. Paul Massey, a lawyer, reorganized the company but had to give up production of pot metals soon thereafter due to the war's need for lead. To survive he turned to making wooden toys, including a replica of the famous Army Jeep which sold about 2 million copies through the dime stores (mainly Woolworth and Kresge). Other wooden toys included an Army tank, a Navy PT boat and a (rumored) DUKW amphibious landing craft. These toys were completely made in Ralston except for Jeep wheels, which were made in Omaha by blind workers, who were hired during the wartime labor shortage.

After the war the company turned to die-casting toys and novelties. As the business expanded it moved to 5707 So. 77th St., where it is today producing a well-known line of promotional trucks under Art Massey.

By now the history of those migrating molds "with the numbers" is getting confusing. Although market values will depend on other factors than the actual makers, we will mention some clues to assist collectors. Ralstoy did label a few of its toys. They liked bottom pans, introduced by Best to increase rigidity of these fragile toys: the pan also provided a surface to emboss "Ralstoy" and "Made in USA." Military olive drab colors reflected the growing war consciousness. Wheels are not a good clue: even the trendy black rubber wheels are not an unmistakable identifier.

Ralstoy probably reproduced many pieces from their acquired molds, but there is no practical way to know who made them if they are not labeled. (See Best Toy Co. and Kansas Toy Co.) The toys described below are mostly new issues.

	C6	C8	C10
RAV1 Dump Truck, "42," International ? COE, 2 open windows (OW), hinged tin dump body, different casting than Kansas Toy dump truck #42, 3-3/8"			No Price Found
RAV2 Tractor, "48," "Caterpillar" tractor, "Whoopee," driver in different color, grooved wood -3/4" wheels w/ rubber tracks on Kansas Toy body, 3"			No Price Found
RAV3 Army tank, "74," "US Army," 2-gun turret, entirely different tank than Kansas Toy #74, 2-1/4"	13	20	26

	C6	C8	C10
RAV4 Tanker Truck, "No. 102," "Ralstoy" International? sleeper cab, 3-3/8", 2 OW, vertical grille w/ "Gasoline" semi-trailer, "No. 102," 4 tanks, storage compartments, 6-3/4"	30	45	60
RAV5 Large Transporter, "Ralstoy" cab unit in RAV4 above, steel semi-trailer w/ #74 tank, #34 muzzle loading cannon and #32 aircraft, olive drab color, not known if Ralstoy issued them as a set. (some stamped No. 108, some No. 101), 9"	40	60	80
RAV6 Large Gun Truck, "US Army Anti-Aircraft Unit," 3 axle carrier, AA gun, searchlight and crew of 3, 5-5/8"	28	42	56
RAV7 Army Tank, "107," "US Army," wood grooved -3/4" track-laying wheels, 2 gun turret, larger version of #74 above, also version w/ black rubber wheels, 3-1/8"	13	20	26

RALSTOY. Top, left to right: RAV4. Middle: RAV2a, RAV2b, metal wheels. Bottom: Ralstoy Field Gun. Photo courtesy of Perry Eichor.

RALSTOY RAV11. Photo by Ed Poole.

RALSTOY. Top, left to right: RAV5 Transporter with tank #74, Cannon #34, Aircraft #32?. Middle: RAV6 Anti-Aircraft Unit, RAV8 Railway? Cannon. Bottom: RAV7 Tank #107, Cannon. Photo by Ed Poole.

	C6	C8	C10
RAV8 Railway ? Gun, "108," version of #23 muzzle-loading cannon on wheeled platform w/ hook and loop connectors, perhaps addition to #3600 toy train, 3-1/4" ... 12	18	25
RAV10 Army Jeep, wooden, WWII issue ... 20	30	40
RAV11 Army Tank, wooden, "USA W356," "Ralstoy" on bottom, WWII issue ... 30	45	60
RAV12 Large Sedan, "2R," die-cast, Cadillac?, "Ralstoy," "Made in USA," 4 open vent windows, divided open windshield, 3 open rear windows, long fenders, rear-wheel skirts, bumper guard, black rubber wheels, early postwar issue?, 5-5/8" ... 37	56	75
Ralstoy Ford Tractor, 1948, w/ trailer, overall 9" long ... 30	45	60
Ralstoy Mayflower Moving Van ... 20	30	40
Rehrberger "David" Moving Van, c. 1924, 7-1/4" long ... 1800	3000	4800

	C6	C8	C10
Remco Bulldog Tank ... 50	75	100
Remco Flying Dutchman Antique Car ... 65	98	130

RALSTOY Sedan RAV12. Photo by Fred Maxwell.

RENWAL

The Renwal Manufacturing Company, founded in 1939 by either Irving Rosenblum or Irving Lawner (accounts vary), seems to have begun as the manufacturer of a glass knife. A plastic knife replaced it, and probably led to the manufacture of plastic toys. Toy production began about 1945. When the firm went out of business c. the 1970s, the tooling was sold to Chein, which in turn sold it to Revell.

Renwal Cadillac Hardtop Convertible, 5-1/2" ... 40	60	80
Renwal Cement Truck, 1940s, 6-1/2" ... 50	75	100
Renwal Fire Ladder Truck plastic ... 40	60	80
Renwal Gasoline Truck No. 49, plastic ... 32	48	65
Renwal Hardtop Convertible, 1940s, 6-1/2" ... 22	33	45
Renwal Pickup Truck, die-cast, black rubber tires, approx. 7" long ... 12	18	25
Renwal Racer No. 173, w/ driver, 9-1/2" ... 85	128	170
Renwal Speed King Racer, 6-1/2" long ... 32	48	65
Renwal TV Truck No. 260, w/ camera, mike, working spotlight, 18" long ... 75	112	150

Renwal Visible Auto Chassis ... 225	338	450
Republic Roadster, 1920s, 10" long ... 140	210	280
Republic Taxi Cab w/ driver, sheet-metal, friction motor, c. 1926 ... 287	430	575
Reuhl Caterpillar D-7 ... 312	468	625
Reuhl Cedar Rapids Rock Crusher ... 600	900	1230
Revell Plumber's Truck, plastic 10" long ... 50	75	100
Richmond Dump Truck ... 62	93	125
"Rocket Launcher" Truck, "U.S.A.F.," friction, pressed steel and plastic, c. 1960 ... 60	90	120

RUBBER VEHICLES

(Unknown Manufacturers)

The following list, with its codings, some since identified and placed elsewhere, was compiled by Dave Leopard.

Vehicles are broken down by types.

	C6	C8	C10
UA06 '35 DeSoto 4-door Airflow Sedan, 5" long	50	75	100
UA07 Chrysler 4-door Airflow Sedan, rear spare, ad on roof, 4-3/4" long	No Price Found		
UA08 '35 Chrysler 2-door Airflow Sedan, 5-1/8" long	50	75	100
UA09 '36 Plymouth 4-door Trunkback Sedan, 4-7/8" long	75	112	150
UA10 '37 Plymouth 4-door Trunkback Sedan, 4-7/8" long	75	112	150
UA11 '46 Nash, 2-door Fastback Sedan, hollow, molded tires, 4" long	12	18	25
UT04 '34 Dodge Rack Truck, 4-7/8"	No Price Found		
UR01 Open Racer, left side header pipes, solid rubber, 3-1/2" long	20	35	50
UR02 Open Racer, V-8, solid, large tires on wood hubs, 4" long	25	40	60

RUBBER VEHICLES UA11. Photo by Dave Leopard.

	C6	C8	C10
UR03 Open Racer, solid, rubber tires on wood hubs, 6" long	No Price Found		
Saunders Fire Truck, siren, 13" long	50	75	100
Saunders Police Car	27	41	55
Saunders Sedan	32	48	65

SAVOYE PEWTER TOY COMPANY

Savoye was incorporated August 1930. In 1931 Savoye Pewter Toy Co., manufacturer of "pewter toys" (pewter was often the word used for lead alloy or pot metal) was listed in a directory at 69 Paterson Plank Road in North Bergen, New Jersey, with six male and three female employees. The names of the owners may have been Selma and Joseph Wigh. In 1934 at the same address the workforce was seven males and two females. Slushmold toys were probably their only product. Savoye was in the 1936 phone book but not the February 1937 directory.

Collectors identify vehicle toys as Savoye if they have a somewhat coarse appearance, heavy slushmold body, and white rubber tires on oversized red wooden hubs that are smooth on the outside surface (no axle showing): but this may be simply collectors' lore. The son of one of the owners of Tommy Toy Co. thinks some Savoye-looking vehicles were made by Tommy Toy. If so, it's possible Savoye sold its molds to nearby Tommy Toy. The following was contributed by Fred Maxwell, one of our principal slushmold researchers:

Those big red hubs and rubber tires are consistent with industry styles of the early 1930s, but the style of some of the vehicles is from an earlier era (see SA17 & SA19, whose metal wheels suggest an earlier beginning of the Savoye-Tommy Toy-Barclay dynasty).

	C6	C8	C10
SA1 Roadster, driver, open rumble seat, silver vertical grille, (VG, reminiscent of Tootsietoy Graham), vertical louvers (VL), 3-1/2" long	20	35	50
SA2 Roadster, similar to above, different casting, 3-1/2" long	No Price Found		
SA3 Coupe, 2 open windows (OW), silver VG, (Graham like), VL, 3-3/8" long	20	35	50
SA4? Coupe, similar to above (Savoye or copy?), slanted louvers, fantasy grille and large black rubber wheels (original?), 3-3/8" long	14	21	28
SA5 Van, "Milk Grade A," 2 OW, sidemounts (SM), 3-1/4" long	30	50	75
SA6 Van, "Police Patrol," policeman on rear step, 6 OW, gilt trim, SM, 4" long	30	50	75
SA7 Bus, Heavy 5th Ave. Sight-Seeing bus, open overhanging upper deck, 12 OW, gilt or silver trim, 4-3/4"	92	138	185
SA8 Bus, Cross-Country Bus, partial upper deck, 12 OW, rearmount spare, 3-3/8"	30	50	65
SA9 Bus, Tour Bus; Mack cab, 3-1/2", 2 OW, "Motor Coach," 5-1/4", dual-axle semi-trailer, 12 OW, gilt trim, 7-1/2" long	No Price Found		
SA10 Truck, Heavy "Beer Truck," 6 wood barrels set in cast depressions, 4-3/8" long	40	60	80
SA11 Truck, stake body, 4-1/2" long	12	18	24
SA12 Truck, stake body, hinged tailgate w/ chains, 5-3/4" long	No Price Found		
SA13 Truck, Tow Truck, SA3-like coupe cab, chain & hook on crane, 4" long	No Price Found		
SA14 Truck, Heavy Tow Truck, over-sized crane, wire hook, 5-3/4"	No Price Found		

	C6	C8	C10
SA20 Tank Car Set, tow cab shorter version of SA13, 3-1/4"; 2 tank cars 3-1/2", "Oil" "Cap. 80000" (RR type), not known whether Savoye sold these as a set; no known Savoye train, either, 10-1/4"	40	60	80
SA21 Gun Truck, Army, driver & gunner, (angular rear deck distinguishes it from similar gun trucks), 3-1/4"	No Price Found		
SA22 Pickup Truck	30	50	65

SAVOYE, SA22. Photo by Perry R. Eichor.

SAVOYE. Top, left to right: SA10, SA15. Middle: SA7, SA6. Bottom: SA14, SA12. Photo by Fred Maxwell.

	C6	C8	C10
SA15 Fire Truck, driver and steersman w/ high style gilt helmets, bell on hood, 2 ladders (glued on), oversized wheel wells, oversized tires, 4-1/4" long	30	50	70
SA16 Fire Truck, driver & fireman w/ high style gilt helmets, 2 detachable ladders on high rack, oversized wheel wells, oversized tires, 3-3/4" long	No Price Found		
SA17? Fire Engine, steam pumper, driver & fireman w/ high style gilt helmets, large 10-spoke metal wheels, an early Savoye? in the style of the fire trucks above; large wheels would explain over-sized wheel wells in SA15 & SA16 above, 3-3/4"	No Price Found		
SA18 Tractor, Caterpillar? tractor w/ stack, 2-3/4" long	10	15	20
SA19? Tractor, same as above w/ large 10-spoke metal wheels, an early Savoye? (same casting as Tommy Toy but longer wheelbase than Barclay #7), 3" long	No Price Found		

SAVOYE. Top, left to right: SA1, SA2. Middle: SA7, SA3. Bottom: SA9. Photo by Fred Maxwell.

See the Aircraft Section for a blimp and a monoplane. Since we are still finding additions to our 7th Edition list, this list is probably still incomplete. Any help will be appreciated.

SCHIEBLE TOY AND NOVELTY

Schieble, located in Dayton, Ohio, was formed in 1909 when William Schieble, former partner with D.P. Clark in the firm of that name, bought it out. Clark then formed the Dayton Friction Works, continuing to use Schieble's patents as well as the Hillclimber name, and protracted lawsuits followed.

	C6	C8	C10
Schieble Racer, team, c. 1910, steel windup, 12" long	450	675	900
Schieble Roadster, spare tire on back, 18-1/4" long	362	543	725
Schieble Sedan, 17" long	305	458	610
Schieble Touring Car, c. 1909, 14" long	300	450	600
Schoenhut "Every Boy Auto Build 5 in 1 toy" wood set to build, boxed	45	67	90

SCHIEBLE Racer team, 12" long. Courtesy Wilkinson Collection, Detroit Antique Toy Museum.

SCHIEBLE Roadster, 18-1/4" long. Courtesy Joe and Sharon Freed.

SEIBERLING RUBBER

Compiled by Dave Leopard

	C6	C8	C10
GA01 '35 Ford 2-door slantback sedan, 5" long	32	48	65
GA02 '35 Ford 2-door slantback sedan, 4" long	27	41	55

SLIK-TOYS: See Lansing

SEIBERLING GA01. Photo by Dave Leopard.

SMITTY TOYS

by Ray Funk

A line of large cast metal and aluminum toy trucks hit the market in 1945: the Smith-Miller (Smitty Toys) "Famous Trucks in Miniature," produced in Santa Monica, California. These trucks were doomed from the beginning because they were entering a highly competitive market. Toy trucks had been manufactured since the 1930s and earlier by such companies as Buddy "L," Structo, Marx, and Hubley, and in 1946 by Ny-Lint, by Tonka in the early 1950s, and in the mid-1950s by Eldon plastics. Despite the heavy competition, Smitty Toys stayed on the market for a full ten years (into 1955) outclassing virtually all toy trucks before and after, although the last year they changed their profile from Mack Trucks to Auto-Car diesels with opening doors and steering wheels that actually steered like the real thing. Their first trucks had two different classes: expensive replicas, or a smaller type of truck of no name that looked to be a half-breed Ford.

The cheaper line consisted of No. 401 Tow Truck, 15" long; No. 402 Dump Truck 11-1/2" long; No. 403 Scoop Dump, 14" long (same dump with scoop). All were complete cast with cast wheels and rubber tires.

The larger scale models were cast and aluminum, such as No. 404 Lumber Truck (six wheels), 19" long, $10.75; No. 404T Lumber Trailer, 17" long, $6.95; No. 405 Silver Streak, 28" long (14 wheels), six-wheel tractor and eight-wheel bogey'd heavy duty grain trailer, $15.95; No. 406 Bekins Van, 29" long, six-wheel tractor and four-wheel trailer (single axle); No. 407 Searchlight Truck, long based (six-wheel) frame, 18-1/2" long with platform that has diesel motor (to hold batteries) and huge searchlight, at $16.95; No. 408 Blue Diamond ten-wheel huge dump truck, last double set of duals bogey'd, 18-1/2" long, $17.95; No. 409 Pacific Intermountain Express (P.I.E.) six-wheel tractor semi with eight-wheel bogey'd aluminum trailer, 29" long, $19.75; No. 410 Aerial Ladder semi, six-wheel tractor and four-wheel single axle trailer, 36" long, ladder extends to 48" high, $27.95. By 1950 some midwest stores had the Aerial Ladder priced at $37.50, and various others were higher priced.

Later various modifications were produced. One was a straight Box Bed Truck, using the Searchlight Truck with metal box and rear double doors. Another variation was the Box Truck employing the eight-wheel bogey set-up, and the log trailer base with a same box to make a ten-wheel straight truck and eight-wheel trailer, the kind that covered the California highways. A third variation was the long base tractor (ten-wheeler) with bogey or rear eight wheels, hooked to Silver Streak and P.I.E. trailers. Other variations included the P.I.E. eight-wheel trailer minus top and raising rear door, as a high-side grain hauler, and finally a long refrigeration trailer with small side door, all using ten-wheel tractors.

At the same time the company was putting the smaller wheels on the P.I.E. and Silver Streak trailers, and using the small six-wheeled cast "Half Breeds" tractors, which were priced at lower competitive prices.

Their first Mack trucks were the older 1940s types with running boards, old-type fenders and raised separate headlights. All had fuel tanks. The later Mack trucks (1954) had an air horn on top. (These were produced for just one year.)

The final year saw a complete change. Smith dropped out and Ironson came in, and the name was changed to M.I.C. Toys (Miller-Ironson Corporation). To the best of my knowledge they produced only four cast trucks, definitely Auto-Car diesels. One was a heavy-duty tow truck (the kind that tows large semis). One was a flat bed with removable side racks and turndown hydraulically lowering tailgate (up and down), door handles that worked to open doors, and a steering wheel and front wheel that were steered like on the "model toy" fire trucks and others of the "model toy" line. The fire truck #410 with a Mack tractor, I cannot describe, as I only have the cab and no catalog or advertisement of this toy.

Mention must be made of one company in Minnesota, owned by Teamster's President Beck's son (in the late 1940s). This company put out huge cast metal trucks, mostly loggers and dumpers, which steered via a horn on top of the cab. In 1950 Wyandotte put out a very realistic cab over semi six-wheel tractor of cast and eight-wheel bogey'd long aluminum trailer, with beautifully realistic cast center replica wheels and rubber tires. The fifth wheel on the tractor was operational to couple and uncouple from the trailer, and the cast tractor was finely detailed, fuel tanks and all. The Wyandotte sold at $10. The aforementioned unnamed and very short-lived trucks sold at $20 each—much too high a price for the 1940s. All are now gone, but live on in memories. There were a few minor variations of the Smith-Miller that I did not mention. Any information collectors can add would be appreciated.

Photographic evidence has unearthed the fact that there are more items in this toy truck line than I have listed.

An early Smitty truck is all pot metal, usually painted as an armored bank truck with square box and locking doors.

I received a picture of a tanker using the small bastard six-wheel tractor and a trailer having the dual-tandem setup. There did not seem to be any spare room in the wheel wells, so I must assume that this was only produced with the small wheels and tractor. It is bright yellow, and has "SHELL" on the trailer.

Still another early toy was a cattle hauling truck. This one was as large as the largest S.M. and had the large early Mack with long frame. I have found this truck, minus wheels: I can assume it was produced, like many others with similar tractor frames, as an 18-wheeler and also 14-wheeler. The enclosed trailer features double doors on the rear with a latch, and slotted vented sides. The truck was the same yellow as the tanker. The frame and fenders (all actually one piece on the early 'Macks') were gloss black, making an eye-catching toy.

How many different trucks or variations Smitty produced, I have no idea. I begin to suspect that, like Doepke, at times they made one or only a few of a particular toy.

Note: New versions of SMITTY vehicles, using original and new parts, are currently being produced. See "Leading Collectors and Dealers."

	C6	C8	C10
Smitty (Smith-Miller) No. 201-L Lumber Truck, 60 boards, 6 wheels, 14" long 500	800	1140
Smitty No. 202-M Material Truck, 3 barrels, 3 cases, 18 boards, 4 wheels, 14" long 450	675	900
Smitty No. 203-H Heinz Grocery Truck, 6 wheels, 14" long 317	475	635
Smitty No. 204-A Arden Milk Truck, 12 milk cans, 4 cases, 4 wheels, 14" long 300	450	600
Smitty No. 205-P Oil Truck, 4 drums, 6 wheels, 14" long 225	338	450

SMITTY No. 206-C GMC Coca-Cola Truck. Courtesy R.L. MacNary.

SMITTY catalog illustrations of models 402 and 401. Photo by Bill Kaufman. Courtesy Ray Funk.

	C6	C8	C10
Smitty No. 206-C Coca-Cola Truck, 16 Coca-Cola cases, 4 wheels, 14" long 600	1000	1400
Smitty No. 208-B Bekins Vanliner, 14 wheels, 22-1/2" long 650	1050	1600
Smitty No. 209-T Timber Giant, 3 logs, 14 wheels, 23-1/2" long 250	375	500
Smitty No. 210-S Stake Truck, 14 wheels, 23-1/2" long 250	375	500
Smitty No. 211-L Sunkist Special, 14 wheels, 23-1/2" long 150	250	375

	C6	C8	C10
Smitty No. 212-R Red Ball, 14 wheels, 23-1/2" long	150	250	375
Smitty No. 301-W GMC Wrecker, 4-wheeler	175	262	350
Smitty No. 302-M GMC Materials Truck, 4 barrels, 3 timbers	200	300	400
Smitty No. 303-R GMC Rack Truck, 6 wheels	140	210	280
Smitty No. 304-K GMC Kraft Foods, 4 wheels	425	638	850
Smitty No. 305-T GMC Triton Oil, 3 drums	175	263	350
Smitty No. 306-C GMC Coca-Cola, 4 wheels, 16 Coke cases	275	362	550
Smitty No. 307-L GMC Redwood Logger Tractor-Trailer, 3 logs	225	338	450
Smitty No. 308-V GMC Lyon Van Tractor-Trailer, 14 wheels	275	410	550
Smitty No. 309-S GMC Super Cargo Tractor-Trailer, 14 wheels, 10 barrels	250	375	500
Smitty No. 310-H GMC Hi-Way Freighter Tractor-Trailer, 14 wheels	150	225	310
Smitty No. 311-E GMC Silver Streak Express Tractor-Trailer, 14 wheels	243	365	485
Smitty No. 312-P GMC Pacific Inter-Mountain Express ("P.I.E.") Tractor-Trailer	250	375	500
Smitty No. 401 Tow Truck, 15" long	125	188	250
Smitty No. 402 Dump Truck, 11-1/2"	185	278	370
Smitty No. 403 Scoop Dump, 14" long	275	410	550
Smitty No. 404 Lumber Truck, 19"	300	450	600
Smitty No. 404T Lumber Trailer, 17"	500	750	1000
Smitty No. 405 Silver Streak, 6-wheel tractor, 28" long	110	165	220
Smitty No. 406 Bekins Van, 6-wheel tractor and 4-wheel trailer, 29" long	338	528	675
Smitty No. 407 Searchlight Truck, "Hollywood Filmad" 18-1/2" long	450	675	900
Smitty No. 408 Blue Diamond, 10-wheel dump truck, 18-1/2" long	1225	1840	2450
Smitty No. 409 Pacific Intermountain Express (P.I.E.), 6-wheel tractor semi w/ 8-wheel aluminum trailer, 29" long	475	715	950

SMITTY catalog illustrations of models 406 and 405. Photo by Bill Kaufman. Courtesy Ray Funk.

	C6	C8	C10
Smitty No. 410 Aerial Ladder Semi, 6-wheel tractor and 4-wheel trailer, "SMFD," 36" long	415	622	830
Smitty No. 401-W GMC Wrecker, 6 wheels	85	128	170
Smitty No. 402-M GMC Material Truck, 4 barrels, 2 timbers	210	315	420
Smitty No. 403-R GMC Rack Truck, 6 wheels	175	262	350
Smitty No. 404-B GMC Bank of America, lock and key, 4 wheels	180	270	360

SMITTY No. 404-B GMC "Bank of America" Armored Truck. Courtesy Good Old Days Store.

	C6	C8	C10
Smitty No. 405-T GMC Triton Oil, 6 wheels, 3 drums	175	262	350
Smitty No. 406-L GMC Lumber Tractor-Trailer, 14 wheels, 8 timbers	212	318	425
Smitty No. 407-V GMC Lyon Van Tractor-Trailer, 10 wheels	200	300	400
Smitty No. 408-H GMC Machinery Hauler, 13 wheels	212	318	425
Smitty No. 409-G GMC Mobilgas Tanker, 14 wheels, 2 hoses	250	375	500
Smitty No. 410-F GMC Transcontinental Tractor-Trailer, 14 wheels	165	255	370
Smitty No. 411-E GMC Silver Streak Tractor-Trailer, 14 wheels	219	328	438
Smitty No. 412-P GMC P.I.E., 14 wheels	300	450	600
Smitty "B" Mack "Associated Truck Lines," 14 wheels	No Price Found		
Smitty "B" Mack Jr. Fire Truck, warning light, battery-operated, 4 wheels	495	742	990
Smitty "B" Mack Orange Dump, 10 wheels	400	600	800
Smitty "B" Mack P.I.E., 18 wheels	500	750	1000
Smitty Chevy Bekins Van, 14 wheels, plain tires, hubcaps, '45-46	200	300	400
Smitty Chevy Coca-Cola, 4 wheels, plain tires, early, '45-46	450	675	900
Smitty Chevy Flatbed Tractor-Trailer, 14 wheels, unpainted wood trailer, plain tires, hub caps, early, '45	280	420	560
Smitty Chevy Milk Truck, 4 wheels, plain tires, hub caps, early, '45-46	200	300	400
Smitty Ford Bekins Van, 14-wheeler, plain tires, hub, earliest Smitty?, '44	200	300	400

SMITTY Box Truck with Box Trailer, 10-wheeler. Courtesy Ray Funk.

	C6	C8	C10
Smitty Ford Coca-Cola, 4 wheels, wood soda cases, early, '44	300	450	600
Smitty GMC Be Mac 14 wheel T-Trailer, 1949	185	278	370
Smitty Coca-Cola Truck, 24 plastic bottles in 6 cases, 4 wheels 1954-55	262	393	525
Smitty GMC "Drive-O" Steerable Dump, 6 wheels, cable w/ hand control, 1946	212	318	425

SMITTY catalog illustrations of models 407, 403 and 409. Photo by Bill Kaufman. Courtesy Ray Funk.

	C6	C8	C10
Smitty GMC "Furniture Mart" Pickup, 4 wheels	155	232	310
Smitty GMC Heinz Grocery Truck	200	300	400
Smitty GMC Machinery Hauler, 10 wheels	388	582	775

SMITTY catalog illustration of model 410. Photo by Bill Kaufman. Courtesy Ray Funk.

SMITTY GMC Searchlight Truck, "Hollywood Film-Ad." Photo by Bob Smith.

SMITTY "L" Mack Army Materials Truck, 7-piece cargo load, 10 wheels. Photo by Bob Smith.

SMITTY "L" Mack Army Personnel Carrier, 10 wheels. Photo by Bob Smith.

	C6	C8	C10
Smitty GMC Marshall Field & Company Tractor-Trailer, 10-wheel T-Trailer	500	750	1000
Smitty GMC Peoples First National Bank and Trust Company armored Truck, lock and key, 1951	262	393	525
Smitty GMC Rexall Drug, 4 wheels	350	525	700
Smitty GMC Searchlight Truck, "Hollywood Film Ad" w/ trailer, 1953	600	1000	1400
Smitty GMC U.S. Treasury Truck, armored truck, w/ lock and key, 1952	250	375	500
Smitty "L" Mack Aerial Ladder, "SMFD," 8 wheels	390	585	780
Smitty "L" Mack Army Materials Truck, 3 barrels, 2 boards, 1 large crate, 1 small crate, 10 wheels	383	575	765
Smitty "L" Mack Army Personnel Carrier, 10 wheels	312	468	625
Smitty "L" Mack Bekins Van, all white, 10 wheels	800	1350	1950
Smitty "L" Mack Blue Diamond Dump, 10 wheels	788	1180	1575
Smitty "L" Mack International Paper Co., 10 wheels	1000	1500	2000
Smitty "L" Mack Lyon Van, 6 wheels	1000	1500	2080

	C6	C8	C10
Smitty "L" Mack Material Truck, 2 barrels, 6 timbers, 6 wheels	500	750	1000
Smitty "L" Mack Merchandise Van, 6 wheels	375	562	750
Smitty "L" Mack Merchandise Van & Trailer, 12 wheels	1050	1550	2200
Smitty "L" Mack Mobil Tandem Tanker, 12 wheels	1000	1500	2000

SMITTY "L" Mack Merchandise Van & Trailer, 12 wheels. Photo by Bob Smith.

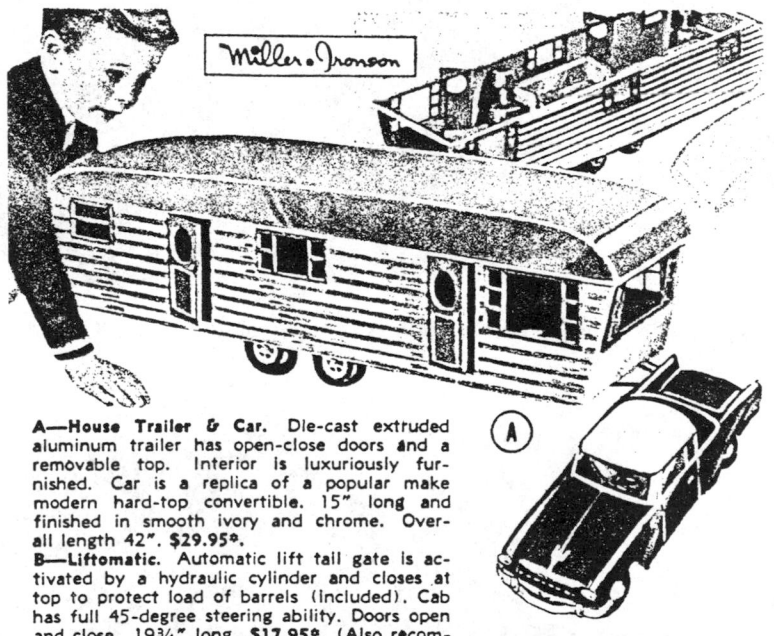

A—House Trailer & Car. Die-cast extruded aluminum trailer has open-close doors and a removable top. Interior is luxuriously furnished. Car is a replica of a popular make modern hard-top convertible. 15" long and finished in smooth ivory and chrome. Overall length 42". **$29.95*.**

B—Liftomatic. Automatic lift tail gate is activated by a hydraulic cylinder and closes at top to protect load of barrels (included). Cab has full 45-degree steering ability. Doors open and close. 19¾" long. **$17.95*.** (Also recommended: Tow Truck, $14.95; Hydraulic Dump, $17.95*; Freuhauf, $19.95*.)

* Prices Approximate—See Page Six

MILLER-IRONSON TOYS are designed and built to exemplify perfection. Their unusual play features give them distinction which is positively unique.

SMITTY. Top: MIC House Trailer and MIC Lincoln Capri. Bottom: MIC Lift Gate Truck (Liftomatic). From The Toy Yearbook, 1953-54.

SMITTY MIC Aerial Ladder. Courtesy Ray Funk.

SMITTY MIC Lift Gate Truck, 6 wheels. Photo by Bob Smith.

SMITTY MIC Tow Truck, "Official Tow Car." Photo by Tim Oei.

SONNY "US 1120" Artillery Truck, 26" long. Courtesy Joe Freed.

SONNY "USA 1120" Anti-Aircraft Truck, 24" long. Courtesy Joe and Sharon Freed.

"Star Brand Shoes Are Better" racing car. Courtesy Sotheby's New York.

STEELCRAFT Fire Truck, approx. 25" long.

	C6	C8	C10
Smitty "L" Mack Orange Hydraulic Dump, 10 wheels	900	1400	1900
Smitty "L" Mack Orange Material Truck, 3 barrels, 2 boards, 1 large crate, 1 small, 10 wheels	500	750	1000
Smitty "L" Mack P.I.E., 14 wheels	600	900	1260
Smitty "L" Mack "Sibley's" Van, 6 wheels (rare)	450	675	900
Smitty "L" Mack Tandem Timber, 18 or 24 timbers (varies), 6 wheels	600	950	1300
Smitty "L" Mack Telephone Truck, 6 wheels	700	1150	1500
Smitty "L" Mack West Coast Transport, 6 wheels	900	1400	1900
Smitty MIC Aerial Ladder	383	575	765
Smitty MIC "Fruehauf Road Star" Tractor-Trailer, 14 wheels	500	800	1200
Smitty MIC House Trailer	400	600	800
Smitty MIC Hydraulic Dump, 10 wheels	700	1100	1675
Smitty MIC Lift-O-Matic, 2 barrels, 6 wheels	500	800	1100
Smitty MIC Lincoln Capri (for MIC House Trailer), steerable	450	675	900
Smitty MIC Lumber Truck, 9 timbers, 6 wheels	338	505	675
Smitty MIC P.I.E. Tractor-Trailer, 14 wheels	500	800	1100
Smitty MIC "Teamsters" Hydraulic Dump, 10 wheels	650	1000	1500
Smitty MIC "Teamsters" Tow Truck, 6 wheels.....	No Price Found		
Smitty MIC "Teamsters" Tractor-Trailer, 14 wheels	462	695	925
Smitty MIC Tow Truck, "Official Tow Car," 6 wheels	700	1100	1600
Smitty MIC Tow Truck, unpainted, polished, 6 wheels	475	700	950
Smitty MIC Tractor-Trailer, polished aluminum trailer, no decals, 14 wheels	450	675	900
Sonny Army Truck "U.S.A. 1120"	350	525	700
Sonny Dump Truck, 26" long	400	600	800
Sonny Moving Van	550	825	1100
Sonny Parcel Post Van	600	900	1300
Sonny "USA 1120" Anti-Aircraft Truck..........	600	900	1200
Sonny "US 1120" Artillery Truck, 26" long	350	525	700
"Star Brand Shoes Are Better," racing car, "The Winner," tin litho, 8-1/2" long	1200	1900	2800
Steam Pumper, "Boston," with lamp, cast-iron wheels, 15-1/2" long	2500	3750	5000
Steam Pumper Fire Truck, cast iron, 5"	45	68	90
Steam Pumper Truck, cast iron, hard rubber wheels, driver, 12" long	150	225	300
Steam Pumper, tin and wooden chain, friction drive w/ driver, "National," 10" long	200	300	400
Steam Pumper, tin and wooden friction drive, 11" long	70	105	140
Steam Roller, steam-engine powered..........	200	300	450
Steam Roller, cast iron, c. early 1930s, 4-3/4" long	75	112	150
Steam Shovel, "Sand Digger," 28"	150	225	300
Steelcraft Army Truck, Mack, c. 1930, 22" long	420	630	840
Steelcraft "City Delivery" Truck	270	405	540
Steelcraft "City Milk Co.," 18" long	283	425	575

	C6	C8	C10
Steelcraft Coca-Cola Truck, 12 bottles on side	400	600	800
Steelcraft "Cream Crest" Truck	450	675	900
Steelcraft Dump Truck, Airflow	2000	3500	5000
Steelcraft Dump Truck, Mack	600	900	1300
Steelcraft Fire Truck, 25" long	600	900	1300
Steelcraft "Fro-Joy" Ice Cream Truck, c. 1930s	350	525	700
Steelcraft GMC Scissor Dump Truck	500	800	1250
Steelcraft Inter City Bus, 24" long	330	495	660
Steelcraft Little Jim Fire Truck	500	850	1200
Steelcraft "Marion" Steam Shovel	143	215	285
Steelcraft Model T Roadster pedal car, Lic. #65-287, 50" long	325	488	650
Steelcraft Railway Express Truck, 26" long ..	1100	1600	2600
Steelcraft Road Roller, 16" long	200	300	400
Steelcraft "Sheffield Farms" Truck, 1930s, 21" long	600	900	1300
Steelcraft Shell Motor Oil Truck w/ oil barrels	300	450	600
Steelcraft Steam Shovel..........	143	215	285
Steelcraft Tank Truck, sheet metal, 25-1/2" long	600	1000	1430
Steelcraft "U.S. Mail" c. 1928, 27-1/4" long ...	800	1300	1800

*STEELCRAFT
Steam Shovel.*

STEELCRAFT "U.S." Mail. Photo by Calvin L. Chaussee.

STRUCTO

Structo of Freeport, Illinois, was founded in 1908 by three men: brothers Louis and Edward Strohacker, and C.C. Thompson. They initially manufactured Erector Construction Kits, and about 1919 they started making toy vehicles.

In 1935, J.G. Cokey bought a majority of the business, and when he died in 1975, the toy patents and designs were taken over by the Ertl Company. (Numbered Structos are found at the end of this listing.)

	C6	C8	C10
Structo Aerial Fire Truck, c. 1950s	100	150	200
Structo Army Ambulance No. 416, 17" long	175	263	350
Structo Army Truck w/ canvas top, 21" long	250	375	500
Structo Army Van, pressed steel and canvas, No. 415, 17-1/2" long	170	255	340
Structo Bearcat Racer, clockwork, 12-1/4" long	325	490	650
Structo Camper w/ cloth top, 12" long	25	38	50
Structo Cement Mixer, c. 1950s, 20" long	112	168	225
Structo Coupe, convertible, c. 1920s	550	850	1200
Structo Caterpillar Tractor w/ trailer, heavy spring clockwork motor, steel treads, No. 46	225	338	450
Structo Communications Center Truck, 21" long	70	105	140
Structo Delivery Truck, tin, electric lights	150	225	300
Structo Dump Truck, early, Mack type	200	300	400
Structo Fire Dept. Emergency Patrol Truck, red bubble light, 1950s, 12" long	90	135	180
Structo Garbage Truck, 21" long	123	185	245
Structo Gasoline Truck, No. 912, 1950s, 13" long	75	112	150

	C6	C8	C10
Structo Guided Missile Launcher, No. 906 w/ plastic launcher, missiles of wood and vinyl, 13" long	70	105	140
Structo Guided Missile Launching Truck, truck metal, missiles, etc., plastic, rubber tires	50	75	100
Structo Ladder Truck, 1950s	145	220	290
Structo Machinery Hauler	120	180	240
Structo Moving Van, open cab, c. 1920, No. 427, 16" long	238	358	475
Structo Packard Dump Truck, No. 405, c. 1930, 18" long	600	950	1400
Structo Pickup Truck, 13" long	90	135	180
Structo Pile Driver, 13" high	175	262	350
Structo Police Patrol Truck, No. 426, 17" long	500	800	1100
Structo Renault Tank, clockwork, green w/ red turret	225	338	450
Structo Roadster, 1920s, clockwork, 16" long	450	675	900
Structo Sand Loader, c. 1928, 12" high	44	66	88
Structo "Sanitation Dept." Garbage Truck	112	168	225

STRUCTO Tank, 11" long, No. 48. Courtesy Mapes Auctioneers & Appraisers.

STRUCTO Dump Truck, early, Mack type. Courtesy Joe and Sharon Freed.

	C6	C8	C10
Structo Searchlight Truck, metal, light and generator plastic, uses batteries, has rubber tires	132	198	265
Structo Stake Truck, lights work, 1930s, 21" long	212	318	425
Structo Steam Shovel, 14" x 11"	200	300	400
Structo Steam Shovel, 16"	57	87	115
Structo Steam Shovel, 21" x 18"	50	75	100
Structo "Structo Telephone Co.," c. 1948, 12" long	38	56	75
Structo Tank, #48, 11" long	225	338	450
Structo Tank, olive drab w/ orange turret, 10 metal wheels, 12-1/2"	150	225	300
Structo "Toyland Garage" Wrecker	50	75	100
Structo Toyland Oil Co.	115	172	230
Structo Tractor w/ cast-iron driver, early, caterpillar type, 8-1/2" long	200	300	400
Structo Truck Assortment No. 317: Dump Truck, blue, Stake Truck, Lumber Truck, each 9" long, 3-1/2" wide, 3-1/2" tall, heavy gauge metal, rubber wheels, original box folds to form garage, 1920s, price per set	75	112	150
Structo U.S. Mail Delivery Truck, No. 428, 17" long	187	280	375
Structo Whippet Tank, heavy spring clockwork motor enameled green, red and black, may read "Patented 1920," on sale in 1929, No. 48, 12"	300	450	600

	C6	C8	C10
Structo No. 601 Motor Express Stake Truck, early 1950s	55	83	110
Structo No. 603 Package Delivery, early 1950s	73	110	145
Structo No. 605 Shovel Dump, early 1950s	100	150	200
Structo No. 607 Machinery Truck, early 1950s	170	255	340
Structo No. 609 Barrel Truck, early 1950s	115	173	230
Structo No. 700 Transport Trailer, early 1950s	90	135	180
Structo No. 702 Steel Cargo Trailer, early to mid-1950s	187	280	375
Structo No. 704 Overland Freight Trailer, early 1950s	60	90	120
Structo No. 704 Grain Trailer, early and mid-1950s (replaced Freight Trailer)	100	150	200
Structo No. 706 Auto Transport Trailer, sold 1953-54, w/ cars	90	138	180
Structo No. 708 Cattle Trailer	75	112	150
Structo No. 811 Barrel Truck, windup, early to mid-1950s	65	98	130
Structo No. 822 Wrecker Truck, windup, early to mid-1950s	90	135	180
Structo No. 844 Hi-Lift Dump, windup, early 1950s	110	165	220
Structo No. 866 Gasoline Truck, windup, early 1950s	130	195	260
Sturdi Built Logging Truck	325	510	650
Sturditoy Ambulance, open cab, c. 1929, 26" long	2000	3500	5000
Sturditoy American Railway Express Truck, c. 1920s, 26" long	800	1300	1800
Sturditoy Coal Dump Truck, 1920s, 25" long	1300	2100	2900
Sturditoy Dump Truck, 1920s, 25" long	800	1300	1900
Sturditoy Dump Truck, 1920s, 26-1/2"	600	950	1300
Sturditoy Pumper, c. 1930, 26" long	800	1350	2000
Sturditoy "Sturditoy Oil Company" Truck, c. 1929, 27" long	800	1350	2000
Sturditoy Traveling Store	2000	3500	5200
Sturditoy "U.S. Mail" Truck	No Price Found		
Sturditoy U.S. Mail Screenside Truck	800	1300	2000
Sturditoy Water Tower	850	1350	2150
Sturditoy "Wells Fargo" Armored Truck, c. 1927, 24" long	1000	1600	2700
Sturditoy Wrecker, 30" long	1000	1650	2750

SUN RUBBER

Sun Rubber of Barberton, Ohio, was founded in 1923. Toymaking started in 1924 and autos were introduced in April 1935. The owner was Tom W. Smith, Jr.

	C6	C8	C10
SA01 Coupe, external exhaust pipes, from 1936, No. 515, 4" long	20	30	40
SA02 '34 DeSoto Airflow, 4-door sedan, No. 500, 4" long	20	30	40
SA03 '40 Dodge, 4-door sedan, No. 12001, 4-1/2" long	20	30	40
SA04 "Teardrop" Sedan, c. 1936 No. 1010 (1936), 5-1/2" long	25	35	55
SA05 Art Deco Housetrailer, fits SA04, No. 1025, 4-3/8" long	50	75	100
SA06 Town Car, Brewster type limo, exposed driver, No. 1015, 5-3/8"	25	45	65
SA07 Station Wagon, Woody, mid-30s, No. 12007, 3-3/4" long	20	30	40
ST01 Pickup Truck, stake sides, streamlined, No. 510, 4-1/2" long	22	33	45
ST02 Open Truck, stake sides, streamlined (White?), No. 1005, 5-1/4"	25	38	50
ST03 Tractor/Trailer, 1 piece, 3 axles, futuristic, No. 12013, 5-1/8" long	20	30	40

SUN SA04. Photo by Dave Leopard.

SUN SA07. Photo by Dave Leopard.

	C6	C8	C10
ST04 Open Truck, futuristic, No. 12003, 4-1/2" long	20	30	40
ST05 Open "Master" Truck, futuristic, No. 12111, 5-5/8" long	22	33	45
ST07 '36 White Bus, streamlined, No. 520 (1936), 4-1/4" long	20	30	40
ST08 Ambulance, c. late 1930s, No. 12006, 3-3/4" long	20	30	40

	C6	C8	C10
SR01 Open Racer, 2 drivers, No. 505 (1936), 4-3/8" long	20	30	40
SR02 Open Racer, full fenders on rear, No. 1000 (1936), 6-1/2" long	30	45	60
SR03 Open Racer, boattail, "Super" racer, No. 12012, 6-3/4" long	25	40	55
SM01 Tank, revolving turret and gunner, No. 12015 (1946), 6" long	52	78	105
SM02 Scout Car, 4 gunners, No. 12014 (1946), 6" long	40	60	80
Ted Toys Racer, wood, 2 riders, pull toy	125	188	250
Texaco Tank Truck, 24" long	35	52	70
Thimble Drome Racer, pusher, 1950s	130	190	260

SUN ST01. Courtesy Dave Leopard, Rubber Toy Vehicles.

SUN ST02. Courtesy Dave Leopard, Rubber Toy Vehicles.

SUN ST03. Photo by Dave Leopard.

SUN ST07. Photo by Dave Leopard.

SUN ST04 and ST05. Photo by Dave Leopard.

SUN ST08. Photo by Dave Leopard.

SUN. Both SR01. Photo by Dave Leopard.

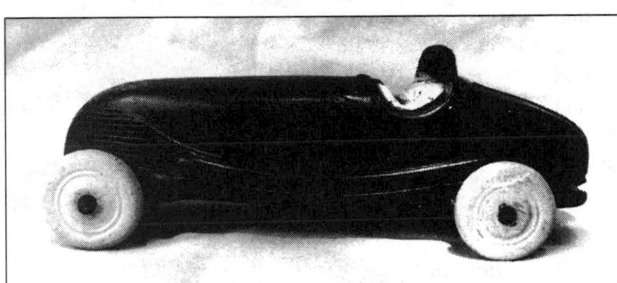

SUN SR03. Photo by Dave Leopard.

THOMAS TOYS

Thomas Toys was founded by Islyn Thomas in 1944. Located from first to last at 80 Clinton Street, Newark, New Jersey, at its peak it had 350 employees. The company's first toys were plastic jeeps, planes, and vinyl dolls. In 1960 Thomas sold the firm to Banner.

THOMAS TOYS No. 457 Jet Car. Courtesy Islyn Thomas.

	C6	C8	C10
Thomas Toys No. 133 Buick Torpedo Sedan, plastic, 11" long	20	30	40
Thomas Toys Harley-Davidson with removable rider, 3" long	75	112	150
Thomas Toys Jet Car, No. 457	No Price Found		
Thomas Toys No. 140 Loudspeaker Van, plastic, 4" long	20	25	30
Thomas Toys Wrecker, 4-1/2" long	12	18	24

TIP TOP TOY CO.

List by C.B.C. Lee and Craig A. Clark

The Tip Top Toy Co. was located in San Francisco, and produced die-cast and slush cast vehicles through most of the 1920s and 30s. The firm embossed its name inside some, but not all, of its toys. All Tip Top vehicles are *extremely* scarce.

	C6	C8	C10
Tip Top Coupe, 1923 Dodge, 3-1/8"................ 16		24	32
Tip Top Tanker, marked "Gasoline," 3-1/2" long.. No Price Found			
Tip Top Tow Truck, 3-5/16" long..................... 16		24	32
with trailer, 5-1/4" overall .... No Price Found			
Tip Top Pickup Truck w/ tailgate, 3-3/16" long .... No Price Found			
Tip Top Bus, 3-3/8" long .... No Price Found			
Tip Top Coupe, 3-3/16" long .... No Price Found			
Tip Top Coupe, 1935 Hupmobile 3-1/4" long .... No Price Found			
with trailer .... No Price Found			
Tip Top Small Tanker, 2-11/16" long .... No Price Found			
Tip Top Small Tanker w/ bumpers .... No Price Found			
Tip Top "Parcel Delivery" Panel Truck,			
2-1/8" long .... No Price Found			
Tip Top Small Coupe, 2-1/8" long .... No Price Found			
Tip Top Studebaker Sedan, 1935, 2-9/16" long ..... No Price Found			
Tip Top Stake Truck, 4 or 6 wheels, 5-5/16" long No Price Found			
Tip Top Airflow, smaller .... No Price Found			
Tip Top Airflow, larger..................................... No Price Found			

These are a rare make of toys, evidently manufactured through most of the twenties and thirties in San Francisco by the Tip Top Toy Co. Photo by C.B.C. Lee.

TOLEDO METAL WHEEL COMPANY

The Toledo Metal Wheel Company was located in Toledo, Ohio, during at least the early and late 1920s. It manufactured a large range of pedal cars as well as toy trucks. The trade name for its products was "Blue Streak."

	C6	C8	C10
Toledo No. 45 "Bull Dog" Truck, open cab,			
26" long 500	1000	1500	
Toledo No. 46 "Bull Dog" Dump Truck,			
26-1/2" long 600	1000	1475	
Toledo No. 47 "Bull Dog" Sprinkler Truck,			
27-1/2" long 600	1100	1510	

	C6	C8	C10
Toledo No. 48 "Bull Dog" Moving Van,			
26" long.....................................550	1050	1550	
Toledo No. 50 "Bull Dog" Coal Truck,			
25" long.....................................800	1350	1875	
Toledo Fire Pumper Pedal Car,			
red painted, 59" long..................1250	1875	2500	

TOMMY TOY

Tommy Toy was in business in Union City, New Jersey, from November 13, 1935, to about 1938 or mid-1939. The following vehicles have been identified by Charles E. Weldon, Jr., son of one of the owners of Tommy Toy. He is sure these are Tommy Toy, but admits there is always a chance he could be mistaken. Certainly the Cannon Truck, aside from the hubs, looks just like Barclay's, which was produced in the same years. Some others resemble Metal Cast, Savoye and other companies' vehicles. Since slush molds did tend to change hands, production of a vehicle by one company would not preclude later manufacture of the same toy by another company. American Alloy is known to have produced copies of Tommy Toy's soldiers using new molds. The only vehicle known to bear the Tommy Toy trademark is the 810 Cord.

	C6	C8	C10
TTV1 Aerial Ladder Truck (like Savoye),			
late 1920s type......................20	30	40	
TTV2 Airflow-type Auto (like Kansas Toy),			
c. 1935 32	48	65	
TTV3 "Ambulance," late 1920s-early			
1930s type............................16	24	32	

	C6	C8	C10
TTV4 "Beer Truck" w/ wooden barrels,			
late 1930s................................14	21	28	
TTV5 Cannon Truck, mid-1930s (like			
Barclay; Barclay's had wooden hubs) 17	25	34	
TTV6 Convertible, no driver, mid to late 1930s..8	12	16	

TOMMY TOY TTV8. Courtesy C.B.C. Lee.

	C6	C8	C10
TTV15 Ladder Truck, mid-1930s	20	30	40
TTV16 "Milk" Truck, late 1930s	20	30	40
TTV17 "Milk Truck," grilled window, c. late 1930s	20	30	40
TTV18 "Milk Truck," smooth window, c. late 1930s	20	30	40
TTV19 "Motorcoach," mid-1930s (like Savoye)	No Price Found		
TTV20 "Oil" Tanker, "Cap 80000" (like Metal Cast, which has different capacity number), 1930s, attaches to Tommy Toy Towing Car Coupe	8	12	16
TTV21 "Packard," Coupe, mid-1930s	17	26	35

TOMMY TOY. Top, left to right: TTV18, TTV17, TTV14, TTV16. Bottom: TTV10, TTV11, TTV12. Photo by Bill Kaufman. Courtesy Charles E. Weldon Jr.

	C6	C8	C10
TTV7 Convertible w/ driver, mid to late 1930s, 1935 Oldsmobile	20	30	40
TTV8 Cord, 810 (1935)	40	60	80
TTV9 "Delivery Deluxe" Delivery Truck (like Savoye), late 1930s	18	27	36
TTV10 Double-Decker Bus, closed top, early 1930s	16	24	32
TTV11 Double-Decker Bus, open top, extended hood (like Savoye), late 1920s	35	52	70
TTV12 Double-Decker Bus, open top, no hood (like Barclay), late 1930s	16	24	32
TTV13 Dump Truck, late 1930s, (resembles Kansas Toy, Best Toy, Manhattan Toys)	16	24	32
TTV14 "General Trucking," late 1930s	12	18	25

TOMMY TOY. Top, left to right: TTV20, TTV5, TTV7, TTV21. Bottom: TTV4, TTV18, TTV6. Photo by Bill Kaufman. Courtesy Charles E. Weldon Jr.

	C6	C8	C10
TTV22 "Police Patrol," open windows, late 1920s-early 1930s type	40	60	80
TTV23 "Police Patrol," solid windows, late 1920s-early 1930s type	35	52	70
TTV24 Pumper, mid-1930s	12	18	25
TTV25 Pumper, large, red hubs, late 1930s	11	16	22
TTV26 Pumper, small, late 1930s	8	12	16
TTV27 Racing Car, large, c. mid-1930s	16	24	32
TTV28 Racing Car, small, c. mid-1930s	12	18	25
TTV29 Sedan, 4-door, c. 1935	17	26	35
TTV30 Sedan towing "Tourist" trailer, c. 1936-37	60	90	120
TTV31 Towing Car Coupe (like Savoye), early 1930s type	16	24	32
TTV32 Tractor	12	18	25
TTV33 Wrecker, late 1930s	10	15	20

TOMMY TOY. Top, left to right: TTV27, TTV28. Bottom: TTV2, TTV30, TTV32. Photo by Bill Kaufman. Courtesy Charles E. Weldon Jr.

TOMMY TOY. Top, left to right: TTV31, TTV33, TTV13. Bottom: TTV9, TTV29, TTV30. Photo by Bill Kaufman. Courtesy Charles E. Weldon Jr.

TONKA

Tonka was incorporated in Mound, Minnesota, in September 1946. The firm had secured the tooling for a steam shovel and crane and clam from Streator Industries, which had unsuccessfully introduced these toys at the Toy Fair in February 1946. Tonka, which means "great" in Sioux-French, was located on the banks of Lake Minnetonka (and is now situated in Minnetonka itself). In 1948, Tonka introduced a forklift with trailer, and in 1949 premiered its line of trucks, including a dump and wrecker. The firm had originally been incorporated as Mound Metal Crafts, with a line of tie racks and garden tools.

1947

	C6	C8	C10
Tonka No. 50 Steam Shovel, 20-3/4" long	115	172	230
Tonka No. 150 Crane and Clam, 24" long	88	132	175

1948

	C6	C8	C10
Tonka No. 200 Lift Truck and Cart	350	525	750

1949

	C6	C8	C10
Tonka No. 100 Steam Shovel Deluxe, 22" long	83	125	165
Tonka No. 120 Tractor and Carry-All Trailer w/ No. 50 Steam Shovel	175	262	350
Tonka No. 125 Tractor and Carry-All Trailer w/ No. 100 Steam Shovel	175	262	350
Tonka No. 130 Tractor and Carry-All Trailer, 30-1/2" long	125	188	250
Tonka No. 140 "Tonka Toy Transport Van," 22-1/4" long	185	275	370
Tonka No. 170 Tractor and Carry-All Trailer w/ No. 150 Crane and Clam	200	300	400
Tonka No. 180 Dump Truck, 12" long	150	225	300
Tonka No. 190 Loading Tractor, 10-1/2" long	No Price Found		
Tonka No. 250 Wrecker Truck, 12-1/2" long	100	150	250

1950

	C6	C8	C10
Tonka No. 145 Steel Carrier Semi, 22" long	175	262	350
Tonka No. 175 Utility Hauler, 12" long	100	150	200
Tonka No. 185 "Express" Truck, 13-1/2" long	No Price Found		

1951

	C6	C8	C10
Tonka No. 400 Allied Van Lines Semi, 23-1/2" long	150	225	300

1952

	C6	C8	C10
Tonka No. 500 Livestock Hauler Semi, 22-1/4" long	140	210	280
Tonka No. 550 Grain Hauler Semi, 22-1/4" long	138	205	275

1953

	C6	C8	C10
Tonka No. 575 Logger Semi, 22-1/4"	150	225	300
Tonka No. 575 Logger Semi, wood flat bed	125	188	250
Tonka No. 600 Road Grader, 17" long	80	120	160
Tonka No. 650 Green Giant Transport Semi, 22-1/4" long	155	235	310
Tonka Wrecker	125	188	250
Tonka No. 675 Trailer Fleet Set, 2 tractors (5 interchangeable trailers), per set	350	580	775

1954

(Newer style trucks - rounded fenders)

	C6	C8	C10
Tonka No. 580 Pickup Truck	125	188	250
Tonka No. 700 Aerial Ladder Semi Fire Truck, 32-1/2" long	187	280	375
Tonka No. 725 Minute Maid Delivery Van, 14-1/2" long	275	362	550
Tonka No. 725 Star Kist Van, 14-1/2"	150	225	300
Tonka No. 750 Carnation Milk Step Van, 11-3/4" long	168	290	335

TONKA 1954 No. 750. Photo by Mark McManus.

	C6	C8	C10
Tonka No. 750 Parcel Delivery Van, 11-3/4" long	180	270	360
Tonka Steel Carrier Truck	115	172	230

TONKA 1954 Steel Carrier Truck. Courtesy Continental Hobby House.

	C6	C8	C10
Tonka Wrecker	140	210	280
Tonka Utility Truck	112	168	225
Tonka No. 775 Road Builder Set - 5-piece set - Road Grader (semi T&T crane and dump truck)	350	525	700

1955

	C6	C8	C10
Tonka No. 725 Minute Maid Orange Juice Van	275	415	550
Tonka No. 750 Carnation Milk Delivery Van	163	245	325
Tonka No. 880 Pickup Truck	132	200	265
Tonka No. 0850 Lumber Truck, 6 wheels	225	338	450
Tonka No. 0860 Stake Truck, 6 wheels	210	315	420
Tonka Allied Van Lines	188	280	375
Tonka Dump	108	162	215
Tonka Freighter	138	210	275
Tonka Hook & Ladder	165	250	330
Tonka Livestock Truck	120	180	240
Tonka Loboy & Shovel	213	320	425
Tonka Rescue Van	180	270	360
Tonka Wrecker	100	150	200
Tonka No. 65 Trailer, stake side	30	45	60
Tonka No. 600 Grader	75	112	150

1956

	C6	C8	C10
Tonka No. 120 Shovel & Carry-All (Loboy), 33" long total	125	188	250
Tonka No. 180 Dump Truck, 13" long	113	170	225

TONKA 1956 No. 950 Pumper. Photo by Calvin L. Chaussee.

	C6	C8	C10
Tonka No. 600 Road Grader, 17" long	50	75	100
Tonka No. 700 Aerial Ladder, 32-1/2" long	210	315	420
Tonka No. 880 Pickup Truck, 13-3/4"	155	235	310
Tonka No. 950 Pumper, 17" long	128	185	255
Tonka No. 980 Hi-Way Dump Truck, 13" long	120	180	240
Tonka No. 990 Suburban Pumper, 17"	175	262	350
Tonka No. 991 Farm Stake Truck, 13" long	138	210	275
Tonka No. 992 Aerial Sand Loader Set, Loader and Dump Truck	225	338	450
Tonka No. 994 Sand Loader Set, Loader and Dump Truck	90	135	180

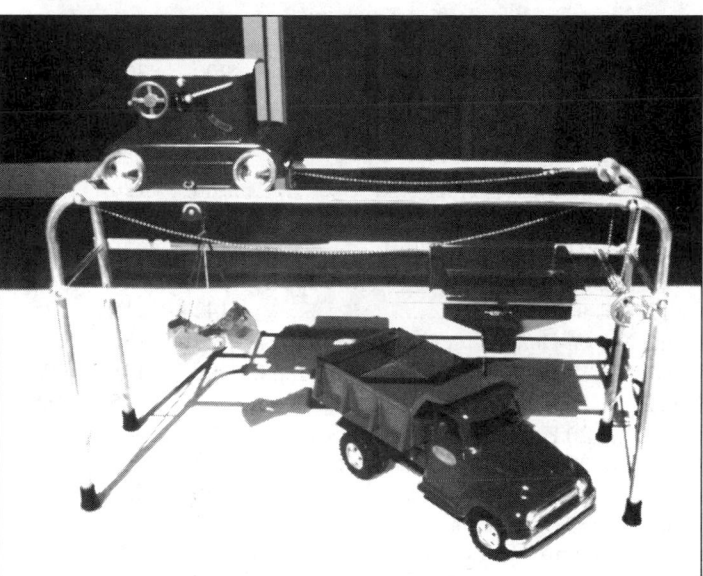

TONKA 1956 No. 992 Aerial Sand Loader Set. Courtesy Thomas G. Nefos, Federal Shipping Network.

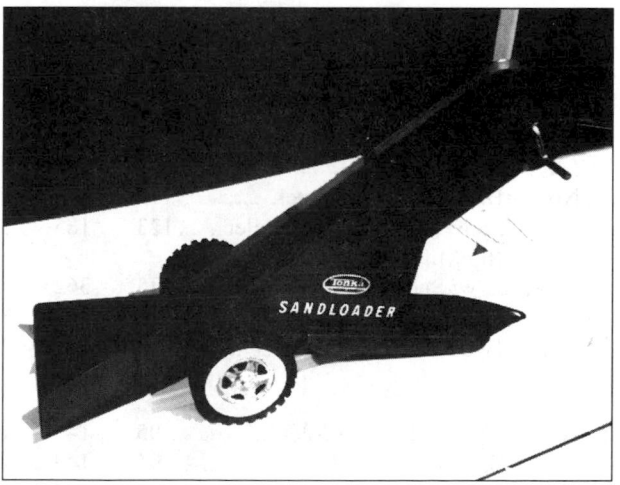

TONKA 1956 No. 994 Sand Loader. Courtesy Thomas G. Nefos, Federal Shipping Network.

	C6	C8	C10
Tonka No. 996 Wrecker (white color), (AAA), 12" long	125	188	250
Tonka No. 998 Lumber Truck, 18-3/4" long	80	120	160
Tonka Rescue Squad Van, 11-3/4"	175	263	350
Tonka Green Giant Semi Reefer	200	300	400

1957

	C6	C8	C10
Tonka Aerial Ladder Truck	158	235	315
Tonka Big Mike Dual Hydraulic Dump Truck, 14" long	380	570	760
Tonka Farms Stake Truck	195	292	390
Tonka Gasoline Truck, 15" long	450	675	900
Tonka Hook & Ladder	150	225	300
Tonka Parcel Delivery Van, 12" long	130	195	260
Tonka Pickup w/ Stake Trailer, 20-1/2" long	150	225	300
Stake Trailer alone	27	41	55
Tonka Stock Rack Truck w/ Animals, 16-1/4" long	225	338	450
Tonka 3 in 1 Hi-Way Service Truck, w/ 2 snowblades, 13" long	190	285	380
Tonka Thunderbird Express Semi, 24" long	200	300	400
Tonka Wrecker	125	188	250

1958 Next Generation Cars

	C6	C8	C10
Tonka No. 02 Pickup Truck	80	120	160
Tonka No. 03 Utility Truck	150	225	300
Tonka No. 04 Farm Stake Truck	193	275	385
Tonka No. 05 Sportsman Pickup w/ Topper, 12-3/4" long	142	215	285
Tonka No. 06 Dump Truck	123	185	245
Tonka No. 12 Road Grader	98	148	195
Tonka No. 18 Wrecker Truck	143	215	285
Tonka No. 20 Hydraulic Dump Truck	200	300	400
Tonka No. 28 Pickup w/ Stake Trailer & Animal	150	225	300
Tonka No. 29 Sportsman Truck w/ Box Trailer	150	225	300
Tonka No. 32 Stock Rack Truck	150	225	300
Tonka No. 33 "Gasoline" Truck, hinged back door, hose & nozzle	323	485	645
Tonka No. 34 Deluxe Sportsman w/ Boat Trailer, 22-3/4" long	150	225	300
Tonka No. 35 Farm Stake w/ 2-Horse Trailer, 21-3/4" long	90	135	180
Tonka No. 36 Livestock Van	163	245	325
Tonka No. 37 Thunderbird Express	170	255	340
Tonka No. 39 Nationwide Moving Van, 24-1/2" long	185	280	370
Tonka No. 41 Hi-Way Service Truck	115	175	230
Tonka No. 43 Shovel & Carry-All Trailer	123	185	245
Tonka No. 45 Big Mike Dual Hydraulic Dump Truck w/ Snow Plow	275	362	550
Tonka No. 46 Suburban Pumper	150	225	300
Tonka No. 48 Hydraulic Aerial Ladder	135	203	270

1959

	C6	C8	C10
Tonka No. 01 Service Truck, 12-3/4"	95	143	190
Tonka No. 05 Sportsman	95	143	190
Tonka No. 14 Dragline, 20" long	90	135	180
Tonka No. 16 Air Express	150	225	300
Tonka No. 22 Deluxe Sportsman	150	225	300
Tonka No. 30 Tandem Platform Stake, 28-1/4" long	218	327	435
Tonka No. 36 Tandem Air Express, w/ Trailer, 24-3/4" long	225	338	450
Tonka No. 40 Car Carrier	85	128	170
Tonka No. 41 Boat Transport, 38"	175	263	350

	C6	C8	C10
Tonka No. 42 Hydraulic Land Rover, 15" long	350	525	700
Tonka No. 44 Dragline & Trailer, 26-1/4" long	165	250	330
Tonka Sanitary Truck (square back)	250	375	500

1960

(Two center ribs on truck cabs replaced by one rib)

	C6	C8	C10
Tonka No. 01 Service Truck	118	175	235
Tonka No. 02 Pickup	68	105	135
Tonka No. 04 Farm Stake Truck	90	135	180
Tonka No. 05 Sportsman	75	112	150
Tonka No. 06 Dump Truck	100	150	200

TONKA 1960 No. 06 Dump Truck. Courtesy Thomas G. Nefos, Federal Shipping Network.

	C6	C8	C10
Tonka No. 08 Logger	110	165	220
Tonka No. 18 Wrecker, white sidewalls	75	112	150
Tonka No. 20 Hydraulic Dump	70	105	140
Tonka No. 22 Deluxe Sportsman	70	105	140
Tonka No. 28 Pickup & Trailer	145	220	290
Tonka No. 35 Farm Stake & Horse Trailer	100	150	200
Tonka No. 37 Thunderbird Express	175	263	350
Tonka No. 40 Car Carrier	75	112	150
Tonka No. 41 Boat Transport, 38" long	128	190	255
Tonka No. 46 Surburban Pumper	115	170	230
Tonka No. 48 Aerial Ladder	120	180	240
Tonka No. 100 Bulldozer, (plated roller wheels only in 1960), 8-7/8"	37	56	75
Tonka No. 105 Rescue Squad, 13-3/4"	140	210	280
Tonka No. 110 Fisherman Pickup w/ Sportsman cover, 14" long	83	125	165
Tonka No. 115 Power Boom Loader (1960 only), 18-1/2" long	275	363	550
Tonka No. 120 Cement Mixer, 15-1/2"	105	158	210
Tonka No. 125 Loboy & Bulldozer, 26-1/4" long	190	275	380
Tonka No. 130 Deluxe Fisherman (also new boat & trailer)	175	263	350
Tonka No. 135 Mobile Dragline	85	128	170
Tonka No. 140 Sanitary Truck	300	450	600
Tonka No. 145 Tanker (first Tonka w/ major use of plastic), 28" long	185	280	370
Tonka Ford Falcon (from set)	50	75	100

	C6	C8	C10
Tonka "Jolly Green Giant" Special, white, green stake racks	150	225	300
Tonka "Standard" Oil Company Wrecker Special	250	375	500

1961

("T" eliminated in grille's center)

	C6	C8	C10
Tonka No. 02 Pickup	110	165	220
Tonka No. 04 Farm Stake	65	98	130
Tonka No. 05 Sportsman	80	120	160
Tonka No. 06 Dump	93	140	185
Tonka No. 12 Road Grader, yellow	50	75	100
Tonka No. 14 Dragline, yellow	62	93	125
Tonka No. 18 Wrecker	125	188	250
Tonka No. 20 Hydraulic Dump	60	90	120
Tonka No. 22 Deluxe Sportsman	125	188	250
Tonka No. 35 Farm Stake Truck & Horse Trailer	95	143	190
Tonka No. 39 Allied Van	80	120	160
Tonka No. 40 Car Carrier	120	180	240
Tonka No. 41 Boat Transport Truck	275	363	550
Tonka No. 48 Aerial Ladder	138	185	275
Tonka No. 116 Dump Truck w/ Sandloader, 23-1/4" long total	105	158	210
Tonka No. 117 Boat Service Truck (1961 only)	125	188	250
Tonka No. 118 Giant Dozer, 12-1/2" long	50	75	100
Tonka No. 120 Cement Mixer	50	75	100
Tonka No. 130 Deluxe Fisherman	150	225	300
Tonka No. 134 Grading Service Truck, Trailer & Bulldozer, 25-1/2" long	163	245	325
Tonka No. 135 Mobile Dragline	133	200	265
Tonka No. 136 Houseboat Set, 29" long total	250	375	500
Tonka No. 140 Sanitary Truck	(Extremely Rare)		
Tonka No. 142 Mobile Clam, 27-1/4" long	110	165	220
Tonka No. 145 Tanker	200	300	400

1962

(New Tonka logo; "Tonka" above wavy line, "Mound, Minnesota," below)

	C6	C8	C10
Tonka No. 200 Jeep Dispatcher, 9-3/4"	40	60	80
Tonka No. 201 "Serv-I-Car" 9-1/8"	60	90	120
Tonka No. 249 Jeep Universal	37	56	75
Tonka No. 250 Tractor, 8-5/8" long	50	75	100
Tonka No. 300 Bulldozer	73	110	145
Tonka No. 301 Utility Dump, (revised Golf Club Tractor, 1961 only) 12-1/2"	108	162	215
Tonka No. 302 Pickup	35	50	100
Tonka No. 308 Stake Pickup, 12-5/8"	75	112	150
Tonka No. 350 Jeep Surrey, fringe top, 10-1/2" long	55	83	110
Tonka No. 402 "Loader," yellow & green	40	60	80
Tonka No. 404 Farm Stake Truck	150	225	300
Tonka No. 405 Sportsman	55	82	110
Tonka No. 406 Dump Truck	50	75	100
Tonka No. 410 "Jet Delivery" Truck, (1962 only), 14" long	100	150	200
Tonka No. 420 Airlines Luggage Service, 16-5/8" long	108	160	215
Tonka No. 512 Road Grader	45	68	90

	C6	C8	C10
Tonka No. 514 Dragline	85	128	170
Tonka No. 516 Jeep Runabout, Trailer, Boat, 25-5/8" long total	80	120	160
Tonka No. 518 Wrecker	63	95	125
Tonka No. 520 Hydraulic Dump	60	90	120
Tonka No. 524 Dozer Packer, Packer has 11 tires, sold only in 1962, total 18-1/4" long	100	150	200
Tonka No. 528 Pickup & Trailer	125	188	250
Tonka No. 530 Camper, 14" long	93	140	185
Tonka No. 616 Dump Truck & Sand Loader	70	105	140
Tonka No. 618 Giant Dozer	100	150	200
Tonka No. 620 Cement Mixer	130	195	260
Tonka No. 735 Farm Stake & Horse Trailer	102	153	205
Tonka No. 739 Allied Van	95	140	190
Tonka No. 834 Grading Service Truck	70	105	140
Tonka No. 840 Car Carrier	100	150	200
Tonka No. 926 Pumper Truck	83	125	165
Tonka No. 942 Mobile Clam	88	132	175
Tonka No. 1348 Aerial Ladder	125	188	250

1963

(Faceted headlights introduced)

	C6	C8	C10
Tonka No. 50 Mini-Tonka Jeep Pickup, 9-1/4" long	35	52	70
Tonka No. 56 Mini-Tonka Stake Truck, 9-1/4" long	35	52	70
Tonka No. 60 Mini-Tonka Dump 9-3/4" long	75	112	150
Tonka No. 68 Mini-Tonka Wrecker, 9-1/2" long	17	26	35
Tonka No. 70 Mini-Tonka Camper, 9-5/8" long	75	112	150
Tonka No. 200 Jeep Dispatcher	No Price Found		
Tonka No. 201 "Servi-I-Car"	75	112	150
Tonka No. 250 Tractor, yellow w/ red seat	75	112	150
Tonka No. 251 Military Jeep Universal, 10-1/2" long	50	75	100
Tonka No. 300 Bulldozer	55	82	110
Tonka No. 302 Pickup	50	75	100
Tonka No. 308 Stake Pickup	60	90	120
Tonka No. 350 Jeep Surrey	60	90	120
Tonka No. 352 Loader	40	60	80
Tonka No. 354 Style-Side Pickup, 14" long	40	60	80
Tonka No. 404 Farm Stake Truck	60	90	120
Tonka No. 406 Dump Truck	45	68	90
Tonka No. 422 Back Hoe, 17-1/8"	80	120	160
Tonka No. 425 Jeep Pumper 10-3/4"	105	158	210
Tonka No. 512 Road Grader, red clearance lights	No Price Found		
Tonka No. 514 Dragline	60	90	120
Tonka No. 516 Jeep Runabout, Trailer & Boat	73	108	145
Tonka No. 518 Wrecker	75	112	150
Tonka No. 520 Hydraulic Dump Truck	105	158	210
Tonka No. 522 Style-Side Pickup & Stake Trailer, 22-3/4" long total	No Price Found		
Tonka No. 524 Dozer Packer, yellow	200	300	400
Tonka No. 530 Camper	82	125	165
Tonka No. 534 Trencher, 18-1/4"	55	83	110
Tonka No. 536 Giant Dozer	112	168	225
Tonka No. 616 Dump Truck & Sand Loader, yellow	90	135	180

	C6	C8	C10
Tonka No. 620 Cement Mixer	85	130	170
Tonka No. 625 Stake Pickup & Horse Trailer, 21-3/4" long overall	110	165	220
Tonka No. 640 Ramp Hoist, red & white, 19-1/4" long	200	300	400
Tonka No. 720 Terminal Train, 15 suitcases, 33-5/8" long total	105	158	210
Tonka No. 739 Allied Van	118	175	235
Tonka No. 840 Car Carrier	35	52	70
Tonka No. 926 Pumper	130	195	260
Tonka No. 942 Mobile Clam	95	140	190
Tonka No. 1001 Trencher & Loboy, 28-1/2" long total	140	210	280
Tonka No. 1348 Aerial Ladder Truck	100	150	200
Tonka No. 2100 Airport Service Set	138	210	275

1964

(Futuristic cab introduced)

	C6	C8	C10
Tonka No. 77 Mini-Tonka Mixer, 9"	50	75	100
Tonka No. 86 Mini-Tonka Van, 16"	35	52	70
Tonka No. 90 Mini-Tonka Livestock Van, 16" long	50	75	100
Tonka No. 96 Mini-Tonka Car Carrier, 2 cars, 18-1/2" long	75	112	150
Tonka No. 250 Military Tractor, black seat	73	110	145
Tonka No. 251 Military Jeep Universal	37	56	75

	C6	C8	C10
Tonka No. 304 Jeep Commander, canvas top, 10-1/2" long	30	45	60
Tonka No. 315 Dump Truck, 13-1/2"	63	95	125
Tonka No. 375 Jeep Wrecker, 11"	75	112	150
Tonka No. 380 Troop Carrier, 14"	87	130	175
Tonka No. 384 Military Jeep & Box Trailer, 19-3/8" overall	75	112	150
Tonka No. 404 Stake Truck, red	85	128	170
Tonka No. 425 Jeep Pumper, black steering wheel	87	130	175
Tonka No. 504 Stake Pickup & Trailer, 21-5/8" long	75	112	150
Tonka No. 525 Jeep & Horse Trailer, 2 horses, 19-1/4" long total	62	93	125
Tonka No. 526 Shovel, 20" long	No Price Found		
Tonka No. 616 Dump Truck & Sandloader, orange & yellow	87	130	175
Tonka No. 640 Ramp Hoist, park green & white, very rare	300	450	600
Tonka No. 739 Allied Van Lines, black knob on door	87	130	175
Tonka No. 900 Mighty Tonka Dump Truck (most popular Tonka of all: 9,655,000 sold between 1964-1983)	65	98	130
Tonka No. 942 Mobile Clam, yellow	50	75	100
Tonka No. 998 Aerial Ladder, 2 auxiliary ladders	50	75	100

TOOTSIETOY

Compiled by John Gibson

Pre-war

	C6	C8	C10
Tootsietoy 4528 Limousine	24	32	40
Tootsietoy 4570 Ford Model T, Open Tourer	33	50	65
Tootsietoy 4610 Ford Model T, Pickup Truck	30	50	70
Tootsietoy 4629 Yellow Cab Sedan	15	23	30
Tootsietoy 4630 Federal "Grocery" Delivery Van	38	57	75
Tootsietoy 4631 Federal "Bakery" Delivery Van	50	80	105
Tootsietoy 4632 Federal "Market" Delivery Van	35	60	75
Tootsietoy 4633 Federal "Laundry" Delivery Van	51	68	85
Tootsietoy 4634 Federal "Milk" Delivery Van	28	41	55
Tootsietoy 4635 Federal "Florist" Delivery Van	141	188	235

TOOTSIETOY No. 4630 "Store Name" Federal Delivery Van (1924). Emil Kraus, State at 18th, an Erie, Pennsylvania, store. Collection and photo John Gibson.

TOOTSIETOY No. 4635 "Florist" Delivery Van, issued 1924. Collection and photo John Gibson.

	C6	C8	C10
Tootsietoy 4636 Buick Coupe	23	34	45
Tootsietoy 4638 Mack Stake Truck	23	34	45

TOOTSIETOY No. 4638. Courtesy Phillips New York.

TOOTSIETOY No. 4657 Tin Plate Garage with No. 103 Buick Sedan. Collection and photo John Gibson.

	C6	C8	C10
Tootsietoy 4639 Mack Coal Truck	23	34	45
Tootsietoy 4640 Mack Tank Truck	23	34	45
Tootsietoy 4641 Buick Touring Car	28	42	55
Tootsietoy 4642 Long Range Cannon	13	18	25
Tootsietoy 4643 Mack Anti-Aircraft Gun	25	38	50
Tootsietoy 4644 Mack Searchlight Truck	27	41	55
Tootsietoy 4645 Mack "US Airmail Service" Truck	38	57	75
Tootsietoy 4646 Caterpillar Tractor, original treads only	27	41	55
Tootsietoy 4647 Renault Tank, original treads only	23	34	45
Tootsietoy 4648 Steamroller	65	95	125
Tootsietoy 4651 Fageol Safety Coach	30	40	50
Tootsietoy 4652 Fire Engine, Hook & Ladder	39	52	65
Tootsietoy 4653 Fire Engine, Water Tower	38	56	75
Tootsietoy 4654 Farm Tractor	35	53	70
Tootsietoy 4655 Ford Model A Coupe	20	30	40
Tootsietoy 4656 Buick Coupe in tin plate garage	60	90	150
Tootsietoy 4657 Buick Sedan in tin plate garage	60	90	150
Tootsietoy 4658 Mack Insurance Patrol in tin plate garage	100	150	200
Tootsietoy 4665 Ford Model A Sedan	20	30	40
Tootsietoy 4666 Bluebird I Dayton Record Car	33	44	55

	C6	C8	C10
Tootsietoy 4670 Mack Tractor & 2 Semi-Trailers: "A&P" & "American Express"	115	170	225

TOOTSIETOY No. 4670 Mack A&P Trailer Truck, 1929. Collection and photo John Gibson.

TOOTSIETOY Funnies No. 5101, 5106. Courtesy Christie's East.

TOOTSIETOY. Left to right: 4670, 4680, 4651, 4634. Courtesy Phillips New York.

TOOTSIETOY No. 4680 "Overland Bus," issued 1929 (later Diesteel wheels). Collection and photo John Gibson.

	C6	C8	C10
Tootsietoy 4680 Overland Bus Lines	45	65	85
Tootsietoy 23 Racer w/ Driver intact	48	64	80
Tootsietoy 190 Mack Auto Transport w/ 3 Buicks	105	140	175
Tootsietoy 190 Mack Auto Transport w/ 4 Buicks	115	170	225
Tootsietoy 191 Contractors' Tipper Set	90	130	175
Tootsietoy 5101 Andy Gump Roadster, standard	175	265	350
Tootsietoy 5101 Andy Gump Roadster, articulated	225	340	450
Tootsietoy 5102 Uncle Walt Roadster, standard	175	265	350
Tootsietoy 5102 Uncle Walt Roadster, articulated	225	340	450
Tootsietoy 5103 Smitty Motorcycle, standard	175	265	350
Tootsietoy 5103 Smitty Motorcycle, articulated	225	340	450

TOOTSIETOY No. 5104 Moon Mullins Police Wagon (non-articulated) from the 1932 Funnies series. Collection and photo John Gibson.

	C6	C8	C10
Tootsietoy 5104 Moon Mullins Police Wagon, standard	175	265	350
Tootsietoy 5104 Moon Mullins Police Wagon, articulated	225	340	450
Tootsietoy 5105 Kayo Ice Wagon, standard	150	225	300
Tootsietoy 5105 Kayo Ice Wagon, articulated	185	285	375

TOOTSIETOY No. 5105 Kayo Ice Wagon (articulated version) from 1932 Tootsietoy Funnies Series. Collection and photo John Gibson.

	C6	C8	C10
Tootsietoy 5106 Uncle Willie Rowboat, standard	135	210	275
Tootsietoy 5106 Uncle Willie Rowboat, articulated	175	265	350
Tootsietoy 6001 Buick Roadster, GM series	30	45	60
Tootsietoy 6002 Buick Coupe, GM series	28	41	55
Tootsietoy 6003 Buick Brougham, GM series	28	41	55
Tootsietoy 6004 Buick Sedan, GM series	28	41	55
Tootsietoy 6005 Buick Touring Car, GM series	50	75	100
Tootsietoy 6006 Buick Screenside Delivery Truck, GM series	35	53	70
Tootsietoy 6101 Cadillac Roadster, GM series	40	60	80
Tootsietoy 6102 Cadillac Coupe, GM series	40	60	80
Tootsietoy 6103 Cadillac Brougham, GM series	40	60	80
Tootsietoy 6104 Cadillac Sedan, GM series	40	60	80
Tootsietoy 6105 Cadillac Touring Car, GM series	60	90	120
Tootsietoy 6106 Cadillac Screenside Delivery Truck, GM series	48	71	95
Tootsietoy 6201 Chevrolet Roadster, GM series	38	55	75

TOOTSIETOY No. 6105 Cadillac Touring Car from Tootsietoy GM series (1927). Collection and photo John Gibson.

	C6	C8	C10
Tootsietoy 6202 Chevrolet Coupe, GM series	33	50	65
Tootsietoy 6203 Chevrolet Brougham, GM series	33	50	65
Tootsietoy 6204 Chevrolet Sedan, GM series	33	50	65
Tootsietoy 6205 Chevrolet Touring Car, GM series	55	83	110
Tootsietoy 6206 Chevrolet Screenside Delivery Truck, GM series	35	53	70
Tootsietoy 6301 Oldsmobile Roadster, GM series	38	55	75
Tootsietoy 6302 Oldsmobile Coupe GM series	35	53	70
Tootsietoy 6303 Oldsmobile Brougham, GM series	35	53	70
Tootsietoy 6304 Oldsmobile Sedan, GM series	35	53	70
Tootsietoy 6305 Oldsmobile Touring Car, GM series	55	83	110
Tootsietoy 6306 Oldsmobile Screenside Delivery Truck, GM series	45	68	90
Tootsietoy 6-01 "No Name" Roadster GM series	55	83	110

	C6	C8	C10
Tootsietoy 6-02 "No Name" Coupe, GM series	55	83	110
Tootsietoy 6-03 "No Name" Brougham, GM series	55	83	110
Tootsietoy 6-04 "No Name" Sedan, GM series	55	83	110
Tootsietoy 6-05 "No Name" Touring Car, GM series	75	113	150
Tootsietoy 6-06 "No Name" Screenside Delivery Truck, GM series	65	95	125
Tootsietoy -- Ford Model A Van, "US Mail," sold in sets only	38	56	75
Tootsietoy 4654 Farm Tractor for Army Field Battery Set #5071	58	86	115
Tootsietoy -- Box Trailer & Roadscraper Raker, sold only in boxed set, Farm Tractor No. 7003	135	205	275

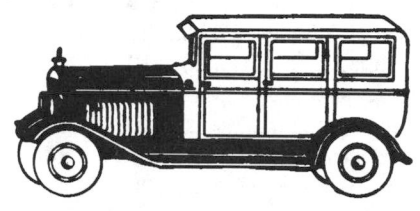

TOOTSIETOY. 6-04 Sedan.

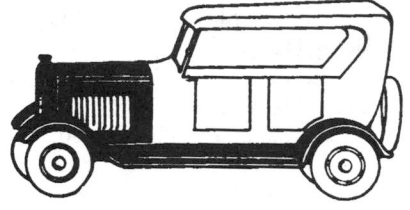

TOOTSIETOY. 6-05 Touring Car.

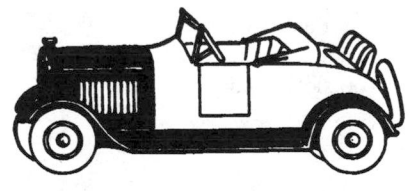 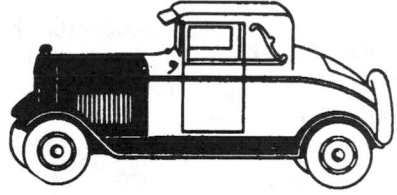 

TOOTSIETOY. Left to right: 6-01 Roadster, 6-02 Coupe, 6-03 Brougham.

  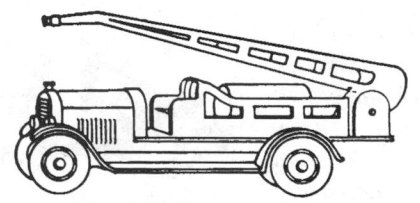

TOOTSIETOY. Left to right: 6-06 Delivery Truck, No. 4652 Hook & Ladder, No. 4652 Water Tower.

TOOTSIETOY No. 6-05 "No Name" Touring Car (1933), GM series. Collection and photo John Gibson.

TOOTSIETOY No. 6-06 "No Name" Delivery Truck (1933), often called "Screenside" (GM series). Collection and photo John Gibson.

	C6	C8	C10
Tootsietoy 6665 Ford Model A Sedan	25	38	50
Tootsietoy 101 Buick Coupe	10	15	20
Tootsietoy 102 Buick Roadster	13	19	25
Tootsietoy 103 Buick Sedan	10	15	20
Tootsietoy 104 Mack Insurance Patrol	23	34	45
Tootsietoy 105 Mack Tank Truck	28	41	55
Tootsietoy 108 Caterpillar Tractor, original treads only	23	34	45
Tootsietoy 109 Ford Pickup Truck	20	30	40
Tootsietoy 110 Bluebird I Daytona Record Car	28	41	55
Tootsietoy 0192 Mack Tootsietoy Dairy, 1-piece cab, 3 trailers	75	113	150
Tootsietoy 0192 Mack Tootsietoy Dairy, 2-piece cab, 3 trailers	117	156	195

	C6	C8	C10
Tootsietoy 0198 Mack Auto Transport, 1-piece cab, 3 '35 Fords	150	225	300
Tootsietoy 0198 Mack Auto Transport, 2-piece cab, 3 '34 Fords	215	320	425
Tootsietoy 0801 Mack "Express" Stake Semi-Trailer, 1-piece cab	55	80	105
Tootsietoy 0801 Mack "Express" Stake Semi-Trailer, 2-piece cab	81	108	135
Tootsietoy 0802 Mack "Domaco" Tank Semi-Trailer, 1-piece cab	60	90	120
Tootsietoy 0802 Mack "Domaco" Tank Semi-Trailer, 2-piece cab	90	120	150
Tootsietoy 0803 Mack "Long Distance Hauling" Semi-Trailer	87	130	175
Tootsietoy 0804 Mack "City Fuel" Coal Truck, 10 wheels	100	132	165

TOOTSIETOY 0192. Courtesy Phillips New York.

	C6	C8	C10
Tootsietoy 0804 Mack "City Fuel" Coal Truck, 4 wheels	125	187	250
Tootsietoy 0805 Mack "Tootsietoy Dairy" Semi-Trailer Truck	70	105	140
Tootsietoy 0806 Graham Wrecker	75	113	150

TOOTSIETOY No. 801 Mack Stake Truck, 1933. Collection and photo John Gibson.

TOOTSIETOY No. 802 Mack "Domaco" Oil Trailer (1933). Collection and photo John Gibson.

TOOTSIETOY 0802. Photo by Bill Kaufman. Courtesy Good Old Days Store.

TOOTSIETOY No. 804 Mack "City Fuel Company" Truck, 10-wheel version issued 1933. Collection and photo John Gibson.

TOOTSIETOY 0805. Photo by Bill Kaufman. Courtesy Good Old Days Store.

TOOTSIETOY 0806. Courtesy Phillips New York.

TOOTSIETOY No. 804 Mack City Fuel Truck, rarer 4-wheel version made 1936-38. Collection and photo John Gibson.

TOOTSIETOY No. 805 Dairy Trailer, 1933. Collection and photo John Gibson.

	C6	C8	C10
Tootsietoy 0807 Delivery Motorcycle adapted from 5103	175	260	350
Tootsietoy 0808 Graham "Tootsietoy Dairy"	75	113	150
Tootsietoy 0809 Graham Ambulance	75	113	150
Tootsietoy -- Graham "Commercial Tire & Supply"	112	168	225
Tootsietoy 0810 Mack "Railway Express Co." Truck w/ Wrigleys Gum ad (1-piece cab)	70	105	140
Tootsietoy 0810 Mack "Railway Express Co." Truck w/ Wrigleys Gum ad (2-piece cab)	75	115	150
Tootsietoy 0511 Graham Roadster, 5 wheels	83	125	165
Tootsietoy 0512 Graham Coupe, 5 wheels	72	110	145

	C6	C8	C10
Tootsietoy 0513 Graham Sedan, 5 wheels	72	110	145
Tootsietoy 0514 Graham Convertible Coupe, 5 wheels	80	120	160
Tootsietoy 0515 Graham Convertible Sedan, 5 wheels	80	120	160
Tootsietoy 0516 Graham Towncar, 5 wheels	88	130	175
Tootsietoy 0611 Graham Roadster, 6 wheels	83	125	165
Tootsietoy 0612 Graham Coupe, 6 wheels	72	110	145
Tootsietoy 0613 Graham Sedan, 6 wheels	72	110	145
Tootsietoy 0614 Graham Convertible Coupe, 6 wheels	80	120	160
Tootsietoy 0615 Graham Convertible Sedan, 6 wheels	80	120	160
Tootsietoy 0616 Graham Towncar, 6 wheels	75	113	150
Tootsietoy -- Graham Roadster, 4 wheels, Bild-A-Car	88	130	175
Tootsietoy -- Graham Coupe, 4 wheels, Bild-A-Car	65	98	130
Tootsietoy -- Graham Sedan, 4 wheels, Bild-A-Car	65	98	130
Tootsietoy 0712 LaSalle Coupe	133	200	265
Tootsietoy 0713 LaSalle Sedan	133	200	265
Tootsietoy 0714 LaSalle Convertible Coupe	143	214	285
Tootsietoy 0715 LaSalle Convertible Sedan	143	214	285
Tootsietoy 0716 Briggs Lincoln prototype, "Doodlebug"	90	120	150
Tootsietoy 6015 Lincoln Zephyr (plain version)	165	245	325
Tootsietoy 6015 Lincoln Zephyr (wind-up)	240	365	485

TOOTSIETOY unnumbered Graham "Commercial Tire & Supply Co." Van, issued 1935. Collection and photo John Gibson.

TOOTSIETOY No. 716 Doodlebug, issued 1935 and patterned after Briggs prototype sedan. Collection and photo John Gibson.

TOOTSIETOY No. 6015 Lincoln Zephyr (1937). This was a revised version of the #716 Doodlebug, and issued with or without a windup motor. Collection and photo John Gibson.

	C6	C8	C10
Tootsietoy 6016 Lincoln Wrecker (plain version)............275		415	550
Tootsietoy 6016 Lincoln Wrecker (wind-up) ..350		525	700
Tootsietoy 0111 1934 Ford V8 Sedan 30		45	60
Tootsietoy 0111 1935 Ford V8 Sedan 15		23	30
Tootsietoy 0112 1934 Ford V8 Coupe 33		49	65
Tootsietoy 0112 1935 Ford V8 Coupe 18		26	35
Tootsietoy 0113 1934 Ford V8 Wrecker 38		56	75
Tootsietoy 0113 1935 Ford V8 Wrecker 33		49	65

	C6	C8	C10
Tootsietoy -- 1935 Ford V8 Roadster Firechief s Car.............50		75	100
Tootsietoy 0117 Zephyr Railcar...........38		56	75
Tootsietoy 0118 DeSoto Airflow Sedan 23		34	45
Tootsietoy 120 Oil Tank Truck............23		34	45
Tootsietoy 0121 Ford Pickup Truck............18		26	35
Tootsietoy 0123 Ford "Special Delivery," "Camelback Van" 25		38	50
Tootsietoy 0123 Ford "Wieboldt's" Camelback Van............145		215	285
Tootsietoy 0123 Ford "Lewis's" Camelback Van............135		205	275

TOOTSIETOY No. 113 Ford Wrecker (1935). Collection and photo John Gibson.

Tootsietoy 0114 1934 Ford V8			
Convertible Coupe......................40		60	80
Tootsietoy 0114 1935 Ford V8			
Convertible Coupe......................30		45	60
Tootsietoy 0115 1934 Ford V8			
Convertible Sedan 40		60	80
Tootsietoy 0115 1935 Ford V8			
Convertible Sedan 30		45	60
Tootsietoy 0116 1935 Ford V8 Roadster 23		34	45

TOOTSIETOY No. 0123 "Lewis's" Light Delivery Truck, store promotional version issued 1937. Frequently called "Camelback Van" by collectors. Collection and photo John Gibson.

Tootsietoy 0123 Ford "Miller & Rhoads"			
Camelback Van.............................145		215	285
Tootsietoy 0123 Ford "McLeans"			
Camelback Van.............................145		215	285
Tootsietoy 0123 Ford "Shepards"			
Camelback Van.............................145		215	285
Tootsietoy 180 Lincoln Zephyr & Roamer			
House Trailer w/o wind-up motor 555		740	925

TOOTSIETOY Dodge D100 Panel Truck from 1956 and a No. 1008 Texaco Oil Truck (1939-41). Courtesy Mapes Auctioneers.

TOOTSIETOY No. 1009 "Shell" Oil Tanker, issued 1938. Collection and photo John Gibson.

	C6	C8	C10
Tootsietoy 180 Lincoln Zephyr & Roamer House Trailer w/ wind-up motor	660	880	1100
Tootsietoy 187 Mack Auto Transport w/ uptilted trailer & 3 vehicles	275	415	550
Tootsietoy 4634 Army Supply Truck	33	49	65
Tootsietoy 4635 Armored Car	33	49	65
Tootsietoy 1006 "Standard" Oil Truck	55	80	110
Tootsietoy 1007 "Sinclair" Oil Truck	55	80	110
Tootsietoy 1008 "Texaco" Oil Truck	55	80	110
Tootsietoy 1009 "Shell" Oil Truck	60	90	120
Tootsietoy 1010 "Wrigley" Box Van	55	80	110
Tootsietoy 1011 "Massey-Ferguson" Farm Tractor	200	300	400
Tootsietoy 1016 Auburn Roadster, jumbo torpedo-single color	23	34	45
Tootsietoy 1016 Auburn Roadster, jumbo torpedo-two tone	25	38	50
Tootsietoy 1017 Coupe, jumbo torpedo-single color	20	30	40
Tootsietoy 1017 Coupe, jumbo torpedo-two tone	23	34	45
Tootsietoy 1018 Sedan, jumbo torpedo-single color	20	30	40
Tootsietoy 1019 Pickup Truck, jumbo torpedo-single color	20	30	40
Tootsietoy 1019 Pickup Truck, jumbo torpedo-two tone	23	34	45

	C6	C8	C10
Tootsietoy 1026 Cross Country Bus, jumbo torpedo-fully skirted	30	45	60
Tootsietoy 1027 Wrecker, jumbo torpedo-single color	23	34	45
Tootsietoy 1027 Wrecker, jumbo torpedo-two tone	25	38	50
Tootsietoy 1040 Fire Engine, Hook & Ladder	35	50	70
Tootsietoy 1041 Fire Engine, Hose Car	35	55	75
Tootsietoy 1042 Fire Engine, Insurance Patrol, open end	30	45	60

TOOTSIETOY No. 1040 Hook & Ladder. Courtesy The Graham Werkes.

TOOTSIETOY No. 1044 Roamer Trailer (1937). Collection and photo John Gibson.

	C6	C8	C10
Tootsietoy 1042 Fire Engine, Insurance Patrol w/ single ladder & rear fireman	38	56	75
Tootsietoy 1043 No. 111 Ford Sedan & small House Trailer	35	53	70
Tootsietoy 1044 Roamer House Trailer w/ door & tin bottom	275	415	550
Tootsietoy 1045 Greyhound Deluxe Bus, open front fenders & tin bottom	55	83	110
Tootsietoy 1045 Greyhound Deluxe Bus, open front fenders	35	50	70
Tootsietoy -- TransAmerica Bus (sold only in sets)	90	130	175
Tootsietoy 1046 Station Wagon	43	64	85
Tootsietoy 230 LaSalle Sedan	15	20	30
Tootsietoy 231 Coupe	15	20	30
Tootsietoy 232 Open Touring Coupe	15	20	30
Tootsietoy 233 Boattail Roadster	15	20	30
Tootsietoy 234 Box Van	15	20	30
Tootsietoy 235 Oil Tank Truck	13	18	25
Tootsietoy 236 Fire Engine, Hook & Ladder	20	30	40
Tootsietoy 237 Fire Engine, Insurance Patrol	15	25	35
Tootsietoy 238 Fire Engine, Hose Wagon	20	30	40
Tootsietoy 239 Station Wagon	20	30	40

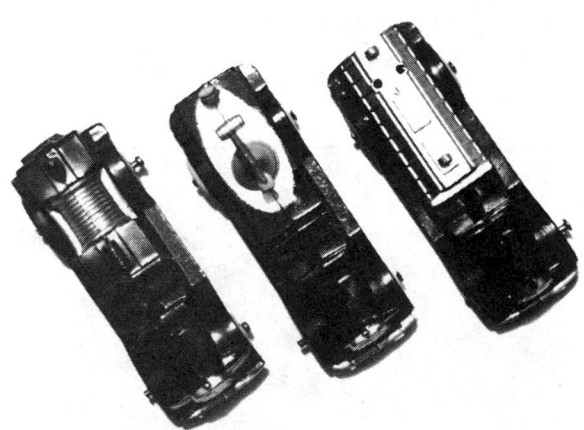

TOOTSIETOY Firetrucks resembling Macks. Left to right: No. 237 Insurance Patrol, No. 238 Hose Car, No. 236 Hook & Ladder (all issued 1940 and reissued postwar with black tires). Collection and photo John Gibson.

Miniature Vehicles

	C6	C8	C10
Tootsietoy 510 Midget Assortment Boxed Set (8-piece)	75	100	150
Tootsietoy 510 Midget Assortment Boxed Set (10-piece)	90	130	175
Tootsietoy 610 Midget Assortment Boxed Set (12-piece)	100	150	200
Tootsietoy 1628 Bus	6	9	12
Tootsietoy 1629 Wrecker	7	10	14
Tootsietoy 1630 Racer	5	7	10
Tootsietoy 1631 DeSoto Airflow Sedan	5	7	10
Tootsietoy 1632 Zephyr Railcar	7	10	14
Tootsietoy 1634 Firetruck	7	10	14
Tootsietoy 1635 Delivery Van	6	9	12
Tootsietoy 1635 Delivery Van (Ambulance)	7	10	14
Tootsietoy 1666 Army Tank	4	6	8
Tootsietoy 1667 Armored Car	5	7	10

Post-war

	C6	C8	C10
Tootsietoy 1954 American LaFrance Pumper, 3" long	10	15	20
Tootsietoy -- Atomic Cannon/155mm Howitzer, 5-1/4" long	100	150	200
Tootsietoy 1956 Austin Healy 100-6, 4-passenger roadster, 6" long	20	30	40
Tootsietoy 1955 Austin Healy 100-6, unassembled kit, 6" long	150	225	300
Tootsietoy 1954 Buick Century Estate Wagon, 6" long	18	26	35

TOOTSIETOY 1948 Buick Super Estate Wagon, open grille (postwar). Collection and photo John Gibson.

	C6	C8	C10
Tootsietoy 1951 Buick LeSabre Experimental Roadster, 6" long	23	34	45
Tootsietoy 1949 Buick Roadmaster 4-door sedan, 6" long	25	38	50
Tootsietoy 1956 Caterpillar Roadscraper, 6" long	18	26	35
Tootsietoy 1950 Chevrolet Ambulance, 4" long	13	19	25
Tootsietoy 1955 Chevrolet BelAir, 4-door sedan, 3" long	10	15	20
Tootsietoy 1956 Chevrolet Cameo Pickup, 4" long	13	19	25
Tootsietoy 1947 Chevrolet Coupe, 4" long	13	19	25

Tootsietoy 1950 Chevrolet Deluxe Panel Truck, 4" long 13 19 25

Tootsietoy 1950 Chevrolet Deluxe Panel Truck, 3" long 10 15 20

Tootsietoy 1960 Chevrolet El Camino w/ camper/boat, 6" long 50 75 100

Tootsietoy 1960 Chevrolet El Camino, 6" long 18 26 35

Tootsietoy 1950 Chevrolet Fleetline 2-door Fastback Sedan, 3" long 10 15 20

Tootsietoy 1959 Chevrolet Semi Cab only 63 94 125
- w/ "Mobile" Trailer 80 120 160
- w/ Hook & Ladder 93 139 185
- w/ Log Trailer 75 113 150
- w/ 3 Boat Trailer 78 116 155
- w/ 3 Car Transport 78 116 155
- w/ Army Flatbed 80 120 160
- w/ "Dean Van Lines" 75 113 150

Tootsietoy 1953 Chrysler New Yorker, 4-door sedan, 6" long 18 26 35

Tootsietoy 1942 Chrysler Thunderbolt Experimental Roadster, 6" long 23 34 45

Tootsietoy 1941 Chrysler Windsor Convertible, 4" long 14 21 28

Tootsietoy 1950 Chrysler Windsor Convertible, 6" long, windshield intact 72 96 120

Tootsietoy 1960 Chrysler Windsor Convertible, 4" long 13 19 25

Tootsietoy 1954-55 Corvette Roadster, 4" long 13 19 25

Tootsietoy 1956 Dodge D100 Panel Truck, 6" long 20 30 40

Tootsietoy 1950 Dodge Pickup Truck, 4" long 13 19 25

Tootsietoy 1956 Ferrari Racer, 6" long 28 41 55

Tootsietoy 1931 Ford B Hot Rod, 3" 8 11 15

Tootsietoy 1956 Ford C600 Oil Tanker, 3" long .9 14 18

Tootsietoy 1962 Ford C600 Truck, 6" 18 26 35

Tootsietoy 1959 Ford Country Sedan Station Wagon, 6" long 18 26 35

Tootsietoy 1962 Ford Country Sedan Station Wagon, 6" long 13 19 25

Tootsietoy 1949 Ford Custom Convertible, 3" long 11 16 22

Tootsietoy 1949 Ford Custom 4-door sedan, 3" long 11 16 22

Tootsietoy 1955 Ford Customline V8, 2-door sedan, 3" long 11 16 22

Tootsietoy 1962 Ford Econoline Pickup, 6" long 15 23 30

Tootsietoy 1949 Ford F1 Pickup, 3" 8 11 15

Tootsietoy 1949 Ford F6 Oil Tanker, 6" long 30 45 60

Tootsietoy 1949 Ford F6 Oil Tanker, 4" long 10 15 20

Tootsietoy 1949 Ford F6 Stake Truck (Pickup), 4" long 13 19 25

Tootsietoy 1957 Ford F100 Styleside Pickup w/ rear window, 3" long 8 11 15

Tootsietoy 1957 Ford F100 Styleside Pickup w/o rear window, 3" long 8 11 15

Tootsietoy 1956 Ford F600 Army Gun Truck, 6" long 18 26 35

Tootsietoy 1955 Ford F600 Stake Truck w/ tin cover, 6" long 60 90 120

Tootsietoy 1957 Ford Fairlane 500 Convertible, 3" long 8 11 15

Tootsietoy 1960 Ford Falcon 2-door sedan, 3" long 8 11 15

Tootsietoy 1956 Ford Farm Tractor, 6" 25 38 50

Tootsietoy 1960 Ford LTD 2-door hardtop, 4" long 13 19 25

Tootsietoy 1952 Ford Mainline 4-door Sedan, 3" long 8 11 15

Tootsietoy 1954 Ford Ranch Wagon, 4" 13 19 25

Tootsietoy 1954 Ford Ranch Wagon, 3" 8 11 15

Tootsietoy 1940 Ford Special Deluxe Convertible, 6" long 28 41 55

Tootsietoy 1940 Ford V8 Hot Rod, 6" 18 26 35

Tootsietoy 1948 GMC 3751 Greyhound Bus, 6" long 23 34 45

Tootsietoy 1957 Greyhound Sceni-Cruiser Bus, 6" long 23 34 45

Tootsietoy 1040 Hook & Ladder, 4" 18 26 35

Tootsietoy 1041 Hose Car, 4" long 18 26 35

Tootsietoy 1941 International K1 Panel Truck, 4" long 20 30 40

Tootsietoy 1946 International K11 Oil Tanker, 6" long 18 26 35

Tootsietoy 1960 International Metro Step Van, 6" long 88 131 175

Tootsietoy 1955 International RC180, 6" long
- w/ Rocket Launcher, Army version 60 90 120
- w/ Grain Trailer 30 50 65
- w/ Oil Tanker, no decals 30 50 65
- w/ Moving Van 30 50 65
- w/ Boat Transport 30 45 60
- w/ Car Transport 30 45 60
- w/ Gooseneck Trailer 25 38 50

Tootsietoy 1957 Jaguar type D, 3" 8 11 15

Tootsietoy 1954 Jaguar XK120 Roadster, 3" long 10 15 20

Tootsietoy 1956 Jaguar XK140 Coupe, 6" long 18 26 35

Tootsietoy 1950 Jeep CJ3, Army version, 3" long 8 11 15

Tootsietoy 1950 Jeep CJ3, Civilian version, 3" long 8 11 15

TOOTSIETOY Jeep CJ3, 3", 1950. Photo by Ed Poole.

	C6	C8	C10
Tootsietoy 1950 Jeep CJ3, Army version, 4" long	13	19	25
Tootsietoy 1950 Jeep CJ3, Civilian version, 4" long	13	19	25
Tootsietoy 1960 Jeep CJ5, Civilian version, 6" long	18	26	35
Tootsietoy 1960 Jeep CJ5, Army version, 6" long	18	26	35
Tootsietoy 1960 Jeep CJ5, snowplow version, 6" long	38	56	75
Tootsietoy 1947 Jeepster, 3" long	9	14	18
Tootsietoy 1947 Kaiser Sedan, 6" long	20	30	40
Tootsietoy 1956 Lancia Racer, 6" long	38	56	75
Tootsietoy 1952 Lincoln Capri 2-door hardtop, 6" long	18	26	35
Tootsietoy 1955 Mack B Line Cement Mixer, 6" long	20	30	40
Tootsietoy 1955 Mack B Line Hook & Ladder, 6" long	38	56	75
Tootsietoy 1955 Mack B Line Moving Van (w/o doors), 6" long	43	64	85
Tootsietoy 1955 Mack B Line Moving Van (w/ doors), 6" long	60	90	120
Tootsietoy 1955 Mack B Line Log Trailer, 6" long	43	64	85
Tootsietoy 1955 Mack B Line Oil Tanker, 6" long	23	34	45
Tootsietoy 1955 Mack B Line Open Stake Truck, 6" long	63	94	125
Tootsietoy 1947 Mack L Line Dump Truck, 6" long	18	26	35
Tootsietoy 1947 Mack L Line Fire Pumper, 6" long	43	64	85
Tootsietoy 1947 Mack L Line Fire (ladder) Trailer, 6" long	43	64	85
Tootsietoy 1947 Mack L Line Log Truck, 6" long	43	64	85
Tootsietoy 1947 Mack L Line Moving Van, 6" long	25	38	50
Tootsietoy 1947 Mack L Line Closed Side Stake, 6" long	20	30	40
Tootsietoy 1947 Mack L Line Stake Trailer, 6" long	63	94	125
Tootsietoy 1947 Mack L Line "Tootsietoys Coast to Coast," 6"	43	64	85
Tootsietoy 1947 Mack L Line Tow Truck, 6" long	20	30	40
Tootsietoy 1956 Mercedes 190SL, 6"	18	26	35
Tootsietoy 1955 Mercedes 300SL Gullwing (doors intact), 9" long	150	225	300
Tootsietoy 1952 Mercury Custom Sedan, 4-door, 4" long	13	19	25
Tootsietoy 1949 Mercury Fire Chief Car, 4" long	14	21	28
Tootsietoy 1949 Mercury Sedan 4-door, 4" long	13	19	25
Tootsietoy -- Metro Van, HO Series	8	11	15
Tootsietoy 1954 MG TF Roadster, 6"	21	32	42
Tootsietoy 1954 MG TF Roadster, 3"	10	15	20
Tootsietoy 1954 Nash Metropolitan Convertible, 3" long	30	45	60

	C6	C8	C10
Tootsietoy 1947 Offenhauser Hill Climber Racer, 3" long	9	13	18
Tootsietoy 1949 Oldsmobile 88 Convertible, 4" long	15	23	30
Tootsietoy 1959 Oldsmobile Dynamic 88 Convertible, 6" long	13	19	25
Tootsietoy 1955 Oldsmobile 98 Holiday, 2-door hardtop, 4" long	13	19	25
Tootsietoy 1955 Oldsmobile 98 Holiday, 4-door hardtop, Army version, 4"	13	19	25
Tootsietoy 1956 Packard Patrician, 4-door sedan, 6" long	18	26	35
Tootsietoy 1957 Plymouth Belvedere, 2-door hardtop, 3" long	8	11	15
Tootsietoy 1950 Plymouth Special Deluxe 4-door Sedan, 3" long	8	11	15
Tootsietoy 1950 Pontiac Chieftan Deluxe Coupe Sedan, 4" long	13	19	25
Tootsietoy 1950 Pontiac Chieftan Fire Chief Coupe Sedan, 4" long	18	26	35
Tootsietoy 1955 Pontiac Safari Station Wagon, (#895), 9" long	100	150	200
Tootsietoy 1959 Pontiac Star Chief 4-door Sedan, 4" long	13	19	25
Tootsietoy 1956 Porsche Spyder Roadster, 6" long	18	26	35
Tootsietoy 1960 Rambler Super Cross Country Station Wagon, 4" long	15	23	30
Tootsietoy -- School Bus, HO series	10	15	20
Tootsietoy 1947 Studebaker Champion 5-window coupe, 3" long	25	38	50
Tootsietoy 1960 Studebaker Lark Convertible, 3" long	8	11	15
Tootsietoy 1955 Thunderbird Coupe, 4" long	11	17	22
Tootsietoy 1955 Thunderbird Coupe, 3" long	8	11	15
Tootsietoy 1956 Triumph TR3 Roadster, 3" long	9	14	18
Tootsietoy 1950 Twin Coach Bus, 3"	23	34	45
Tootsietoy 1960 Volkswagen Beetle, 6" long	18	26	35
Tootsietoy 1960 Volkswagen Beetle, 3" long	5	8	10
Tootsietoy 1941 White Army Half Track, 4" long	18	26	35
Tow Truck, cast iron, 6" long	300	450	600

Tow Truck, cast iron, 6" long. Courtesy Mapes Auctioneers & Appraisers.

	C6	C8	C10
Tow Truck, cast iron, rubber wheels, 7-1/2" long	125	187	250
Traveleer Land Coach Traveler, Trailer Co., L.A., 1927	180	270	360
Turner Bulldog Mack, closed cab dump truck, red and green steel, 23" long	263	395	525
Turner Car Hauler	175	262	350
Turner Dump Truck, friction, c. early 1930s, 15-1/2" long	1000	1700	2500
Turner Dump Truck, C-cab, 22" long	335	500	670
Turner Dump Truck, 26" long	575	860	1150
Turner Fire Engine Pumper, 15" long	600	950	1400
Turner Hook and Ladder, c. 1930s, 15" long	170	255	340
Turner Lincoln Sedan, 26" long	1500	2800	4300
Turner "Overland Bus," pressed steel	No Price Found		
Turner Packard Roadster, 1920s, 16-1/2" long	800	1300	1900
Turner Packard (?) Roadster, friction, 26" long	700	1200	1700

	C6	C8	C10
Turner Speedster, c. late 1920s, early 1930s, 17" long	500	750	1000
Turner Steam Shovel	105	158	210
Turner Tow Truck	250	375	500
Turner Water Truck w/ Copper Tank	150	225	300
"U.S. Army Shooting Tank," wood, pre WWII, metal action, 6" long	22	33	45
U.S.A.W. No. 60118 Half-Track, black wooden wheels, die-cast, approx. 4-3/4"	10	15	20
Vindex Coast to Coast Bus, cast iron, c. 1929, Salesman's sample, 12" long, mint, auctioned 1994 for $18,000			
Vindex Hay Loader, Case, 9" long	2000	3500	5600
Vindex "John Deere" Thresher, 15" long	1400	2300	3900
Vindex "P&H" power shovel, cast iron, wheels in caterpillar base, handle revolves rig, 12" (17" extended)	2700	4100	8000
Vindex Pickup Truck, cast iron, 7-1/2"	300	450	600
Vindex Racer, cast iron, "2," c. 1920s, 11-1/2" long	1000	1600	2500

VINDEX MOTORCYCLES

List by Kent M. Comstock

	C6	C8	C10
(VM1) Motorcycle w/ detachable cop, "Henderson," red or green, 9", auctioned in 1994 in excellent condition for $3500			
Wannatoy Delivery Truck, 4" long	3	4	6
Wannatoy Tank Truck, 5" long	7	11	14
Weeden Auto, live steam, early, 8-3/4"	1500	3000	4500

VINDEX VM1. Photo by Kent M. Comstock.

WEEDEN Auto, live steam, early. Courtesy Sotheby's New York.

	C6	C8	C10
(VM2) Motorcycle w/ sidecar, 2 detachable cops, "Henderson," red or green, 9" long, auctioned in 1994 in near mint condition for $7500			
(VM3) Motorcycle w/ package truck, "Henderson PDQ Delivery," w/ detachable blue rider, red or green, 9" long	1800	2500	3500
Wannatoy Cadillac, plastic, 9" long	7	11	15
Wannatoy Convertible, 6" long	7	11	14
Weeden Steam Fire Pumper	1300	2200	3500
Weeden Steam Road Roller, 1920s, brass, tin, cast iron, steam toy fired by alcohol, 7" long	250	375	500
Weeden Steam Tractor, 9" long	250	375	500
Wilkins Aerial Ladder Truck, 1910, wind-up, 18" long	325	488	650
Wilkins Dray, driver, barrels, tiller	400	600	800
Wilkins Fire Engine, c. 1900 w/ driver, steam boiler, 9" long	210	315	420
Wilkins Hook and Ladder open truck, steel, wind-up motor, 9-1/4" long	238	360	475

WILKINS Hook & Ladder open truck, steel, windup motor, 9-3/4" long. Courtesy Phillips New York.

	C6	C8	C10
Wilkins, Olds, 1904, curved dash, wind-up, 10"	400	600	800
Wilkins Truck, open cab, very early, clockwork, 11" long	450	675	900

A.C. WILLIAMS

A.C. Williams was founded in 1886 when Adam Clark Williams (1/22/1848-6/15/1932) bought the J.W. Williams Company from his father. After a fire the firm was moved in 1893 from Chagrin Falls, Ohio, to Ravenna. Toy production began about this time. Small cast-iron toys were Williams' specialty. Banks, cars and aircraft were predominant. A.C.

Williams retired in 1919, but the firm continued to make toys until 1938, after which it continued in business in a non-toys capacity. Williams marked few, if any, of its toys. Two clues to an A.C. Williams toy are turned steel hubs and starred axle peens.

	C6	C8	C10
Williams "C to C Co." Stake Truck, 2 pieces, 7" long	200	300	400
Williams Car Carrier, w/ 3 Austins, 1920, 12-1/2" long	450	675	900
Williams "Coast to Coast Cartage Co.," 8-1/2" long	250	375	500
Williams Coupe, 2-piece body, 1936, 3" long ...	95	145	190
Williams Coupe, rumble seat, side mounts, 1930, cast iron, rubber tires, 6-3/4" long	155	225	310
Williams Delivery Van, 8" long	350	525	700
Williams Dump Truck, 6--1/4" long	195	292	390
Williams 4-casting nickeled radiator car, approx. 4" long	75	112	150
Williams Laundry Truck, 8" long	400	600	800
Williams Lincoln Touring Car, 7" long	312	470	625
Williams Mack Gas Tank Truck, 3-3/4" long ..	122	185	245
Williams Mack Gas Tank Truck, 5-1/8" long ..	100	150	200
Williams Mack Gas Tank Truck, 7--1/4" long	350	525	700
Williams Mack Stake Truck, 3-1/2"	45	68	90
Williams Mack Stake Truck, 4-1/4"	80	120	160
Williams Mack Stake Truck, 5-1/8	112	170	225
Williams Mack Stake Truck, 7" long	150	225	300
Williams Mack Stake Truck, 8-1/2"	200	300	400
Williams Mack Truck, 3-1/2" long	45	68	90
Williams Mack Truck, 4-3/4" long	95	140	190
Williams Mack Truck, 6-3/4" long	100	150	200
Williams Model T Coupe, 6" long	180	270	360
Williams "Moving & Storage Truck," 3-1/2" long	112	168	225
Williams Racer, boattailed, 6-1/2" long	262	395	525
Williams Sedan, 5" long	75	112	150
Williams Sedan, c. 1930, cast iron, streamlined rear fender, 6-1/2" long	175	265	355
Williams Sedan, c. 1931, cast iron, interchangeable body, 6-3/4" long	350	525	700
Williams Steam Roller, 1930s, 5-1/2"	95	145	190
Williams Studebaker, c. 1933-34, 2-tone sedan, approx. 4" long	110	165	220
Williams Tank, 4" long	73	110	145
Williams Taxi, 5-3/4" long	182	275	365

WILLIAMS Sedan, 6-1/2" long. Courtesy Phillips New York.

Choice small cast-iron pieces. Top, left to right: A.C. Williams 1934 Ford (series included coupe and sedan); A.C.W. 1936 Ford (series included coupe, sedan, roadster and panel truck and in a simpler single-piece casting only three, omitting the roadster); A.C.W. generic take-apart (series included coupe, sedan and stake truck). Bottom, left to right: Arcade 1933 Nash (coupe and sedan); Arcade 1935 Ford (sedan and stake truck); Dent 1935 LaSalle (sedan, coupe, roadster, pickup truck, wrecker and panel truck). Photo by C.B.C. Lee.

	C6	C8	C10
Williams Touring Car, cast iron, 9-1/2" long...475	712	950
Williams Touring Car w/ driver, 5" 100	150	200
Williams Wrecker, 6-1/2" long 250	375	500
Willys Knight, cast iron, 1920s, w/ driver, 8" long 120	180	240
Wolverine Car & Trailer, press down to operate, 27" long 200	300	400

	C6	C8	C10
Wolverine "Mystery Car," press down to make car move, c. 1938, 13" long 150	225	300
Wolverine Speeding Bus "5 Via Main St.," tin litho, driver and occupants, "19302," press down on rear to move, 14" long 100	150	200
Wolverine Taxi, tin, 13" long 225	338	450
Wolverine "White Mustang" dump truck, 14" long........70	105	140
Wood Commodities Corp., Army Jeep and Cannon, 23" long 62	93	125

WYANDOTTE

(All Metal Products Company)

Wyandotte was formed in the fall of 1921. Toy pistols and rifles were at first its main product, but by 1935 the Wyandotte, Michigan, firm became best known for its simply built, streamlined, art deco steel cars and trucks, almost all of them employing wooden wheels. During WWII Wyandotte made clips for the M-1 rifle and after the war moved to Piqua, Ohio. In an attempt to diversify, it bought the Hafner trains line, but went out of business in 1956. Wyandotte's heavy gauge steel toys with baked enamel finish also included aircraft, doll buggies, musical toys, wagons, and games.

	C6	C8	C10
Wyandotte Ambulance, swinging rear door, No. 340, 11-1/4" long 112	168	225
Wyandotte Army Truck, steel w/ wood wheels, 10" long 75	112	150
Wyandotte Army Truck, 22" long....................100	150	200
Wyandotte Auto Transport, c. 1950s 75	112	150
Wyandotte Bank Truck, 6-1/2" long 37	56	75
Wyandotte Boattail Racer, steel, red w/ white rubber tires, electric headlamps, 8-1/2" long 100	150	200
Wyandotte Car Carrier, early 1930s................125	188	250
Wyandotte Car Carrier, late, 22" long.............150	225	300
Wyandotte Circus Truck, 10-3/4" long 250	375	500

WYANDOTTE Cord, Fire Dept. version, red, windup motor. Photo by Time Oei.

	C6	C8	C10
Wyandotte Coupe, 2-door, about 1930, 6" long 45	68	90
Wyandotte Coupe, c. 1940, 6" long 75	112	150
Wyandotte Coupe, c. 1930s, 7-1/2"................107	160	215
Wyandotte Coupe w/ rumble seat, early 1930s, 8" long 125	188	250
Wyandotte Coupe, c. 1935, red w/ white rubber tires, electric headlight, 8-1/2" long 100	150	200
Wyandotte Dairy Truck, 1930s, 12"...................95	142	190
Wyandotte "Deluxe Delivery" Truck, c. 1936, 11" long.........50	75	100
Wyandotte Dump Truck No. 122 45	68	90
Wyandotte Dump Truck No. 124 50	75	100
Wyandotte Dump Truck No. 326, 1931 178	225	345
Wyandotte Dump Truck, 1930s, 6"...................65	100	130
Wyandotte Dump Truck, pressed steel, c. 1940, approx. 6-1/2" long 100	150	200
Wyandotte Dump Truck, steel, c. 1937, 7" long........45	68	90
Wyandotte Dump Truck, 12" long 52	78	105
Wyandotte Dump Truck, c. mid-1930s, white rubber tires, 15" long 67	100	135
Wyandotte Dump Truck, 1930s, 12-1/2" 57	85	115

WYANDOTTE Circus Truck, 10-3/4".

	C6	C8	C10
Wyandotte Circus Truck, No. 503, 11" long....250	375	500
Wyandotte Circus Truck w/ Trailer, 19" long..438	655	875
Wyandotte City Delivery Truck, c. 1940 225	338	450
Wyandotte Convertible (open) Roadster, 1930s, 10" long 143	215	285
Wyandotte Cord, pressed steel, rubber tires, 13" long 283	425	565
Wyandotte Cord, Fire Dept. version, red, wind-up motor 365	548	730

	C6	C8	C10
Wyandotte Dump w/ Sand Loader, c. 1941	300	450	600
Wyandotte Dump w/ Scoop, post-war	55	83	110
Wyandotte "Express" Trailer Truck, tin wheels	102	153	205
Wyandotte Fire Truck w/ ladder, ringing bell, 1939, 12" long	300	450	600
Wyandotte "Grey Van," late, 24" long	173	215	355
Wyandotte Hydraulic Dump Truck, rear and side tip, 20" long	150	225	300
Wyandotte Ice Truck, marked "ICE" in sides, c. 1940, No. 348	250	375	500
Wyandotte LaSalle Sedan, 1930s	188	293	375
Wyandotte LaSalle Sedan w/ trailer, 1930s, 25-1/2" long	420	630	840

WYANDOTTE LaSalle Sedan with trailer. Photo by Bob Smith.

	C6	C8	C10
Wyandotte "Medical Corps" open truck, c. 1939, 12" long	100	150	200
Wyandotte Motor Express Trailer Truck, c. 1950s	67	100	135
Wyandotte "Official AAA Service Car," 1930s, 12" long	238	305	475
Wyandotte Oil Tanker, 1930s	185	250	370

WYANDOTTE Oil Tanker, 1930s. Photo by Calvin L. Chaussee.

	C6	C8	C10
Wyandotte Pickup Truck, c. late 1930s, 6" long	30	45	60
Wyandotte "Pickway Pastures" Livestock Truck	105	158	210
Wyandotte Race Car, pressed steel, rubber tires, c. 1937, 8-1/2" long	132	200	265
Wyandotte Railway Express Truck, c. 1939, 12" long	60	90	120
Wyandotte School Bus, 1930s, 24"	100	150	200
Wyandotte Sedan, c. 1940, 4" long	42	63	85
Wyandotte Sedan, c. 1940, 6" long	50	75	100
Wyandotte Semi, Grey Lines, cast wheels	200	300	400

	C6	C8	C10
Wyandotte Semi-Trailer Stake Truck "Valley Farms Livestock Produce," 2-piece, 1940s, 8-1/2" long	52	78	105
Wyandotte Side Dump, 1930s, 20"	125	188	250

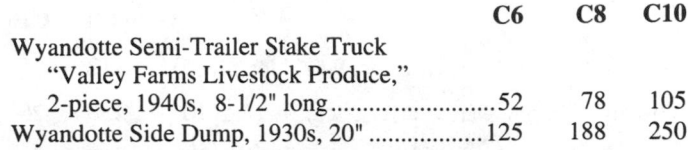

WYANDOTTE Side Dump, 1930s, 20" long. Photo by Calvin L. Chaussee.

	C6	C8	C10
Wyandotte Soap Box Derby Racer	200	300	400
Wyandotte Stake Truck, rubber wheels, 5-1/2" long	42	63	85
Wyandotte Stake Truck about 1930, 6-3/4" long	60	90	120
Wyandotte Stake Truck 1930s, white rubber wheels, 7-1/2" long	115	170	230
Wyandotte Stake Truck, 1931, No. 325, 9-3/4" long	134	200	268
Wyandotte Stake Truck, battery-operated headlights, 10" long	150	225	300
Wyandotte Stake Truck, c. 1930s, 12" long	88	132	175

WYANDOTTE Stake Truck, 10" long, battery-operated headlights. Courtesy Mapes Auctioneers & Appraisers.

	C6	C8	C10
Wyandotte Stake Truck, 1930s, 15"	300	450	600
Wyandotte Stake Truck, 20" long	90	135	180
Wyandotte Station Wagon, Cadillac, 1941, Woody model, No. 1007, metal, 21" long	188	280	375
Wyandotte Steam Shovel, 16" long	138	205	275
Wyandotte Sunshine Dairy Truck, 12"	60	90	120
Wyandotte Tow Truck, late	100	150	200
Wyandotte Town & Country Chrysler Convertible, 1940s, 12" long	105	158	210

	C6	C8	C10
Wyandotte "Toytown Delivery," 1941, 21" long	200	300	400
Wyandotte "Toytown Estate" Station Wagon	125	188	250
Wyandotte "Toytown Ice Co.," c. 1941	100	150	200
Wyandotte Trailer Truck, plastic cab	65	98	130
Wyandotte Trailer Truck, 1950, extruded aluminum trailer	100	150	200
Wyandotte "Valley Farms," 8-1/2"	85	128	170
Wyandotte Woody Convertible, top converts, 12" long	162	243	325

	C6	C8	C10
Wyandotte Wrecker, 1930s, wooden wheels, 10" long	75	112	150
Wyandotte "Wyandotte Truck Lines" Stake Van	95	143	190
Wyandotte "Wyandottey," pressed steel, 2-door sedan, sweeping long fenders, c. WWII, black plastic wheels	30	45	60

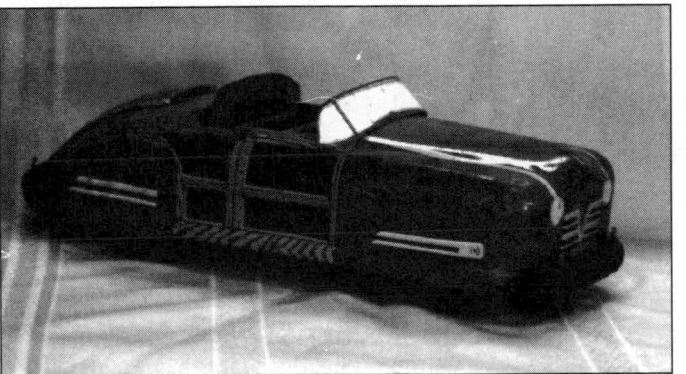

WYANDOTTE Woody Convertible, top goes up and down. Photo by Calvin L. Chaussee.

WYANDOTTE "Wyandotte Truck Lines" Stake Van. Photo by Calvin L. Chaussee.

A Wyandotte ad from December 1931, in Toys and Novelties magazine.

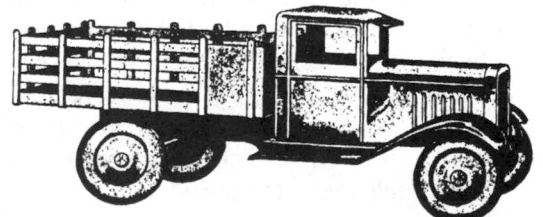

MATCHBOX

The average mint price of these toys was $29.93 in the last edition. In this edition it is $33.46, an increase of 12%.

THE MAKING OF A HOUSEHOLD NAME

by Mark McManus

Matchbox Toys grew out of a company begun in 1947 by two Navy friends, Leslie Smith and Rodney Smith (no relation). Manufacturing toys was not even in the plan at the beginning. On June 19, 1947, the two partners combined portions of their first names, and the name Lesney was born. In 1948 Lesney Products produced their first toy, a 4-1/2-inch Aveling Barford Road Roller. Encouraged by the brisk sales, they produced three other toys that year: a 4-1/2-inch Caterpillar Bulldozer, a 3-3/4-inch Caterpillar Tractor, and a 3-3/4-inch Cement Mixer. Value on these rare early Lesney toys today ranges up to $1000. It was decided to package the toys in a matchbox-type box, and thereafter the toys would be known as "Matchbox."

These small vehicles quickly became very popular, and all other toy lines were discontinued. These first small vehicles had metal wheels, but these were quickly changed to plastic. These type of wheels are now known to collectors as "Regular" wheels, not to be confused with the "Superfast" wheels that were introduced in 1969.

Mark B. McManus lives in Boonville, New York, with his wife Suzanne and son Turner. Mark and Suzanne own and operate an AmeriSpec Home Inspection Service franchise in northern New York. Mark is an avid miniature vehicle collector specializing in Matchbox vehicles. He currently owns several hundred Matchbox vehicles. He also owns numerous Tonka vehicles and several GI Joes and their accessories, as well as many miscellaneous items. Photo courtesy Mark McManus.

It is not uncommon to find slight color and style variations for the same vehicle. These variations were often due to paint or part shortages and are highly sought after by collectors.

The "Models of Yesteryear" line was introduced in 1956. The king-size line was first developed and marketed in 1957 and was known as Major Packs. Matchbox toys were first marketed in the United States in 1958, and by the early 1960s had become a household standard. The year 1993 marked the 40th anniversary of Matchbox toys. These small vehicles are rapidly gaining popularity and value among collectors. Listed in the following pages are all of the basic models and some important variations. The C10 prices are for *unboxed* Matchboxes.

Photos in this section courtesy of Gary Linden, unless otherwise noted.

	C6	C8	C10
No. 1 Diesel Road Roller, 1953	17	20	39
No. 1 Aveling Barford Road Roller, 1964	16	23	34
No. 1 Mercedes Benz Lorry, 1968	6	10	15
No. 1 Mod Rod, 1971	7	11	17
No. 1 Dodge Challenger, 1976	4	6	8
No. 2 Dumper, 1953	22	37	45
No. 2 Muir-Hill Dumper, 1962	9	15	24
No. 2 Mercedes Trailer, 1968	5	7	12
No. 2 Hot Rod Jeep, 1971	5	7	12
No. 2 Hovercraft, 1976	5	7	12
No. 3 Cement Mixer, 1953	22	33	44
No. 3 Bedford Ton Tipper, 1961	6	12	17
No. 3 Mercedes Benz Ambulance, 1968	5	10	15
No. 3 Monteverdi Hai, 1973	5	8	12
No. 3 Porsche Turbo, 1978	4	7	10
No. 4 Tractor, 1954	34	45	60
No. 4 Triumph Motorcycle & sidecar, 1959	22	35	47
No. 4 Stake Truck, 1967	4	7	12
No. 4 Gruesome Twosome, 1971	3	6	10

Different versions of MATCHBOX boxes.

	C6	C8	C10
No. 4 Pontiac Firebird, 1976 3	6	10
No. 4 '57 Chevy, 1981 3	5	8
No. 5 London Bus, 1954 23	35	45
No. 5 Lotus Europea Sports Car, 1969 10	20	28
No. 5 Seafire, 1976 3	7	10
No. 5 U.S. Mail Truck, 1981 4	6	10
No. 6 Quarry Truck, 1955 17	24	35
No. 6 Euclid 10 Wheel Quarry, 1964 17	25	35
No. 6 Ford Pickup, 1969 8	13	20
No. 6 Mercedes Tourer, 1974 5	8	12
No. 7 Horse Drawn Milk Cart, 1955 45	66	90
No. 7 Ford Anglia, 1961 14	24	34
No. 7 Ford Refuse Truck, 1967 7	10	15
No. 7 Hairy Hustler, 1971 5	8	12
No. 7 VW Golf, 1976 4	6	9
No. 8 Caterpillar Tractor, 1955 25	40	57
No. 8 Ford Mustang Fastback, 1966 9	13	19
No. 8 Wildcat Dragster, 1971 7	12	16
No. 8 De Tomaso Pantera, 1975 15	22	38

	C6	C8	C10
No. 9 Dennis Fire Engine, 1955 33	50	67
No. 9 Merryweather Marquis Fire Engine, 1959 16	23	30
No. 9 Boat & Trailer, 1967 6	9	11
No. 9 Javelin, 1972 5	9	11
No. 9 Ford Escort RS2000, 1978 3	5	7
No. 10 Mechanical Horse & Trailer, 1955 35	52	67
No. 10 Sugar Container Truck, 1961 27	40	55
No. 10 Pipe Truck, 1967 10	17	22
No. 10 Piston Popper, 1973 5	8	14
No. 10 Plymouth "Gran Fury" Police Car, 1980 3	4	5
No. 11 Petrol Tanker (Esso decal), 1955 22	35	48
No. 11 Petrol Tanker, green body, no number on bottom 135	200	325
No. 11 Jumbo Crane (Taylor), 1964 7	12	17
No. 11 Scaffolding Truck (Mercedes), 1969 5	9	14
No. 11 Flying Bug, 1972 5	8	13
No. 11 Car Transporter, 1977 5	8	10
No. 12 Land Rover, 1953 17	23	35

MATCHBOX No. 12 Land Rover.

	C6	C8	C10
No. 12 Safari Land Rover, 1965 11	18	30
No. 12 Setra Coach, 1971 8	14	18
No. 12 Big Bull, 1975 5	8	11
No. 12 Citroen CX, 1981 5	7	12
No. 13 Bedford Wreck Truck, 1955 22	39	57
No. 13 Thames Wreck Truck (MB Garages), 1959 22	35	47
No. 13 Dodge Wreck Truck (BP Label), 1961, yellow cab, green body 18	23	30
No. 13 Dodge Wreck Truck, green cab, yellow body (rare) 300	490	675
No. 13 Baja Buggy, 1971 4	6	12
No. 13 Snorkel Fire Engine, 1977 4	5	6
No. 14 Daimler Ambulance, 1955 17	25	41

MATCHBOX No. 9 Merryweather Marquis Fire Truck.

MATCHBOX No. 14 Bedford Lomas Ambulance.

MATCHBOX No. 19 MGA Sports Car.

	C6	C8	C10
No. 14 Bedford Lomas Ambulance	22	33	47
No. 14 Iso Grifo Sports Car, 1968	5	9	15
No. 14 Mini Ha Ha, 1975	6	9	15
No. 15 Prime Mover, 1955	27	38	52
No. 15 Dennis Refuse Truck, 1963	14	20	29
No. 15 Volkswagen 1500 Saloon, 1968	8	17	27
No. 15 Fork Lift Truck, 1972	5	7	11
No. 16 Low-Loading Trailer, 6 wheels, 1955	18	26	36
No. 16 Low-Loading Trailer, 8 wheels, 1955	18	26	36
No. 16 Scammel Mountaineer Dump w/ plow, 1961	10	17	24
No. 16 Case Tractor Bulldozer, 1969	6	11	18
No. 16 Badger, 1974	5	8	13
No. 16 Pontiac, 1981	2	4	6
No. 17 Bedford Removal Van, 1955	33	60	90
No. 17 Austin Taxi, 1960	27	44	61
No. 17 8 Wheel Tipper "Hoveringham," 1964	7	13	18
No. 17 Horse Box "Ergomatic Cab," 1969	5	8	13
No. 17 Londoner, 1973	8	12	18
No. 18 Caterpillar Bulldozer, 1955	17	28	36
No. 18 Field Car, 1969	7	10	15
No. 18 Field Car, green plastic tires (rare)	55	133	165
No. 18 Hondarora, 1975	5	9	14
No. 19 MG Midget Sports Car, 1955	26	37	48
No. 19 MGA Sports Car, 1959	27	44	69
No. 19 Aston-Martin F.I., 1961	21	33	46
No. 19 Lotus Racing Car, 1965	6	8	11
No. 19 Road Dragster, 1971	4	6	10
No. 19 Cement Truck, 1976	5	7	9
No. 20 E.R.F. Lorry Truck, 1955	30	48	66
No. 20 Taxi Cab (Chevrolet Impala), 1965	15	25	34
No. 20 Lamborghini Marzel, 1969	9	13	16
No. 20 Police Patrol, 1975	4	6	10
No. 21 Long Distance Coach "London to Glasgow," 1955	24	39	54
No. 21 Commer Milk Truck, 1961	24	38	53

	C6	C8	C10
No. 21 Foden Concrete Truck, 1969	8	12	18
No. 21 Road Roller, 1973	6	8	14
No. 22 Vauxhall Cresta, 1955	30	36	48
No. 22 Pontiac "Grand Prix" Sports Coupe, 1964	10	14	18
No. 22 Freeman Inter City Commuter, 1970	6	9	14
No. 22 Blaze Buster, 1975	4	6	10
No. 23 Caravan Trailer, 1956	6	9	12
No. 23 House Trailer Caravan, 1967	14	25	35
No. 23 Volkswagen Camper, 1970	6	8	11
No. 23 Atlas, 1975	5	7	12
No. 24 Excavator, 1956	17	24	33

MATCHBOX No. 25 Bedford "Dunlop" Van.

	C6	C8	C10
No. 24 Rolls Royce Silver Shadow, 1967	8	10	13
No. 24 Team "Matchbox," 1973	8	13	19
No. 24 Diesel Shunter, 1979	3	5	7
No. 25 Bedford "Dunlop" Van, 1956	30	48	64
No. 25 Volkswagen 1200 Sedan, 1958	30	48	64
No. 25 B.P. Tanker, 1960	19	29	42
No. 25 Ford Cortina G.T., 1968	6	8	10
No. 25 Mod Tractor, 1972	9	12	19
No. 25 Flat Car & Container, 1979	3	5	7
No. 26 Ready Mix Concrete Truck, 1956	18	26	36
No. 26 GMC Tipper Truck, 1968	7	10	12
No. 26 Big Banger, 1972	4	6	9
No. 26 Site Dumper, 1976	3	5	8
No. 27 Bedford Low-Loader, 1956	30	42	60
No. 27 Bedford Low-Loader, metal wheels (rare)	180	265	360
No. 27 Cadillac Sedan, 1960	38	55	77
No. 27 Mercedes Benz, 230SL, 1965	6	8	12
No. 27 Lamborghini Countach, 1974	5	7	10
No. 28 Bedford Compressor Truck, 1956	24	36	48

	C6	C8	C10
No. 30 Swamp Rat, 1977	4	6	8
No. 30 Articulated Truck, 1981	4	6	8
No. 31 Ford Customline Station Wagon, 1956	26	40	49
No. 31 Ford Fairlane Station Wagon, 1959	24	41	60
No. 31 Lincoln Continental, 1964	7	12	17
No. 31 Volks Dragon, 1971	5	7	10
No. 31 Caravan, 1977	4	6	8
No. 32 Jaguar XK 140 Coupe, 1956	30	41	54
No. 32 Leyland Tanker, 1968	16	24	34
No. 32 Excavator, 1981	10	18	24
No. 33 Ford Zodiac MKII, 1956	24	38	54
No. 33 Ford Zephyr 6 MKIII, 1963	19	27	38
No. 33 Lamborghini Muira P400, 1969	9	15	22
No. 33 Datsun 126X, 1973	5	8	12
No. 33 Police Motorcyclist, 1977	4	6	8
No. 34 Volkswagen Microvan "Matchbox" Express, 1956	30	44	60
No. 34 Volkswagen Camper, 1961	14	21	28
No. 34 Formula 1 Racing Car, 1971	7	11	14
No. 34 Vantastic, 1976	4	7	12
No. 34 Chevy Pro Stocker, 1981	2	4	6
No. 35 Marschall Horse Box, 1956	41	66	82
No. 35 Sno-Trac Tractor, 1961	13	20	29
No. 35 Merryweather Marquis Fire Engine, 1970	5	10	14
No. 35 Fandango, 1975	5	7	10
No. 36 Austin A50 w/ towbar, 1956	18	30	40
No. 36 Lambretta & Sidecar, 1960	36	54	71

MATCHBOX No. 28 Bedford Compressor Truck.

	C6	C8	C10
No. 28 Thames Compressor Truck, 1959	18	24	30
No. 28 Mack Ten Jaguar, 1964	33	49	66
No. 28 Mack Dump Truck, 1968	6	10	15
No. 28 Stoat, 1974	7	12	19
No. 28 Lincoln Continental, 1980	8	12	15
No. 29 Bedford Milk Delivery Van, 1956	18	27	36
No. 29 Austin A55 Cambridge, 1961	16	27	36
No. 29 Fire Pumper Truck, 1965	9	11	16
No. 29 Racing Mini, 1971	4	7	9
No. 29 Shovel Nose Tractor, 1976	5	8	12
No. 30 Ford Prefect w/ towbar, 1956	30	42	55
No. 30 German Crane Truck, 1961	22	33	44
No. 30 Favin Crane, 8-wheel, 1965	11	16	22
No. 30 Beach Buggy, 1971	4	6	9

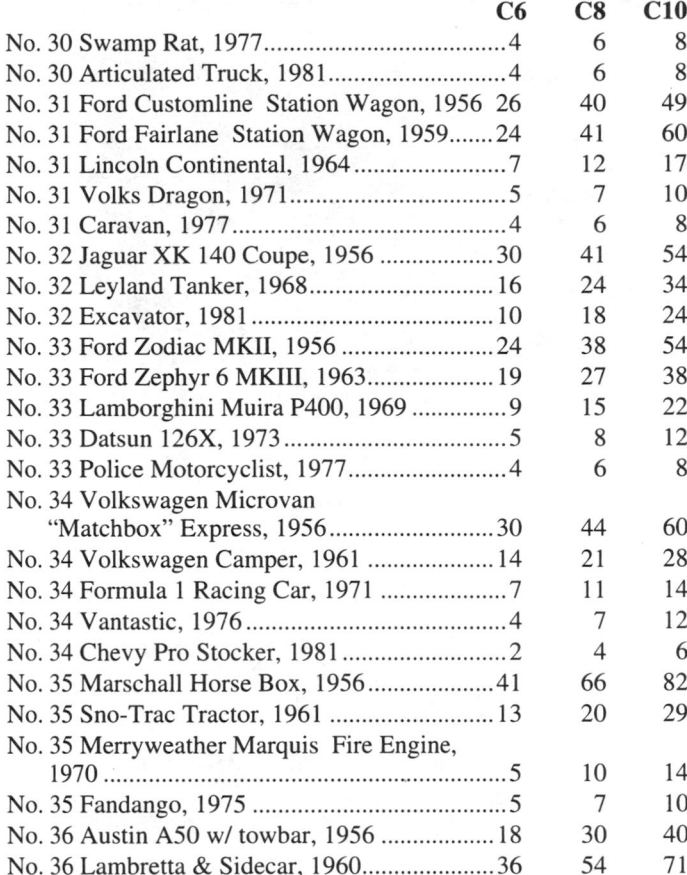

MATCHBOX No. 36 Lambretta Motorcycle w/ sidecar.

	C6	C8	C10
No. 36 Opel Diplomant, 1966	8	13	19
No. 36 Hot Rod Draguar, 1971	5	8	19
No. 36 Formula 5000, 1975	4	6	8
No. 36 Refuse Truck, 1981	3	5	8
No. 37 Coca-Cola Truck, 1956	39	54	71
No. 37 Cattle Truck (Dodge), 1967	7	9	11
No. 37 Soopa Coopa, 1973	5	7	11
No. 37 Skip Truck, 1976	4	6	8

MATCHBOX No. 37 Coca-Cola Truck.

MATCHBOX No. 38 Darrier Refuse Collector.

	C6	C8	C10
No. 38 Darrier Refuse Collector	20	29	38
No. 38 Vauxhall Estate, 1963	11	20	27
No. 38 Honda Motorcycle w/ Trailer, 1968	11	16	22
No. 38 Stingeroo, 1973	6	8	11
No. 38 Armored Jeep, 1976	5	9	13
No. 38 Camper, 1981	3	5	7
No. 39 Ford Zodiac Convertible, 1956	28	41	56
No. 39 Pontiac Convertible, 1962	35	51	65
No. 39 Ford Tractor, 1967	6	10	16
No. 39 Clipper, 1973	6	8	12
No. 39 Rolls-Royce Silver Shadow MKII	4	6	8
No. 40 Bedford 7-Ton Tipper, 1956	24	34	47
No. 40 Hay Trailer, 1967	4	8	12
No. 40 Leyland "Royal Tiger" Coach/Long Distance, 1961	11	18	26
No. 40 Guildsman, 1971	5	8	12
No. 40 Horse Box, 1977	4	6	8
No. 41 "D" Type Jaguar Racing Car, 1956	80	115	150
No. 41 Ford G.T. 40 (Sports Racer), 1965	14	21	30

	C6	C8	C10
No. 41 Siva Spyder, 1972	6	9	13
No. 41 Ambulance, 1978	4	6	8
No. 42 Bedford "Evening News" Van, 1956	30	42	57

MATCHBOX No. 42 "Bedford Evening News" Van.

	C6	C8	C10
No. 42 Studebaker Lark Wagonaire, 1965	12	19	27
No. 42 Iron Fairy Crane, 1969	7	11	18
No. 42 Iron Fairy Crane, 1970 (spoke wheels)	30	42	54
No. 42 Tyre Fryer, 1972	4	8	12
No. 42 Container Truck, 1977	4	6	8
No. 43 Hillman Minx, 1957	30	46	54
No. 43 Aveling-Barford Shovel, 1962	11	19	27
No. 43 Pony Trailer, 1968	9	13	19
No. 43 Dragon Wheels, 1972	5	7	10
No. 43 Steam Loco, 1978	4	6	8
No. 44 Rolls-Royce Silver Cloud, 1957	19	26	37
No. 44 Refrigerator Truck, GMC, 1967	8	12	18

MATCHBOX No. 46 Morris Minor 1000.

	C6	C8	C10
No. 44 Boss Mustang, 1972	3	5	8
No. 44 Passenger Coach, 1978	3	5	7
No. 45 Vauxhall Victor, 1957	14	24	33
No. 45 Ford Corsair w/ green boat, 1959	11	15	20
No. 45 Ford Group Six, 1970	6	9	11
No. 45 BMW, 1976	5	8	11
No. 46 Morris Minor 1000, 1957	30	48	60
No. 46 Pickfords Removal Van, 1960	18	31	45
No. 46 Mercedes-Benz 300SE, 1968	6	11	16
No. 46 Stretcha Fetcha, 1972	5	9	15
No. 46 Ford Tractor, 1978	5	7	9
No. 47 Trojan "Brooke Bond" Van, 1957	30	46	60

MATCHBOX No. 49 Army Half Track MKIII.

MATCHBOX No. 47 Trojan "Brooke Bond Tea" Van.

	C6	C8	C10
No. 52 Maserati 4 CLT, 1958	34	44	61
No. 52 BRM Racing Car, 1965	9	13	18
No. 52 Dodge Charger MKIII, 1970	4	8	11
No. 52 Police Launch, 1976	3	5	7
No. 53 Aston-Martin DB2/4, 1959	19	26	35
No. 53 Mercedes-Benz 220SE, 1968	16	24	34
No. 53 Ford Zodiac MKIV, 1968	10	13	18
No. 53 Tanzara, 1972	3	7	10
No. 53 C.J. 6 Jeep, 1977	4	6	8
No. 54 Army Saracen Personnel Carrier, 1959	14	20	30
No. 54 Cadillac Ambulance, 1965	16	25	34
No. 54 Ford Capri, 1971	4	7	9

	C6	C8	C10
No. 47 Neilson Ice Cream Van, 1963	30	46	60
No. 47 Daf Tipper Container Truck, 1968	8	12	16
No. 47 Beach Hopper, 1973	5	7	10
No. 47 Pannier Loco, 1980	3	5	7
No. 48 Sports Boat & Trailer, 1957	28	39	53
No. 48 Dodge Dumper Truck, 1967	11	16	22
No. 48 Pi-Eyed Piper, 1973	4	6	10
No. 48 Sambron Jack Lift, 1977	4	6	8
No. 49 Army Half Track MKIII, 1958	19	30	41
No. 49 Mercedes Unimog Truck, 1967	11	18	24
No. 49 Chop Suey, 1973	5	7	10
No. 49 Crane Truck, 1976	3	5	8
No. 50 Commer Pickup Truck, 1958	22	34	45
No. 50 John Deere-Lanz Tractor, 1963	14	22	32
No. 50 Ford Kennel Truck, 1969	10	15	20
No. 50 Articulated Truck, 1973	6	11	16
No. 50 Harley Davidson Motorcycle, 1981	2	3	5
No. 51 Albion Truck "Portland Cement," 1958	16	24	33
No. 51 Tipping Farm Trailer, 1963	8	10	12
No. 51 8 Wheel Tipper Truck, 1969	7	10	13
No. 51 Citroen SM, 1972	5	7	10
No. 51 Combine Harvester, 1979	4	6	8

MATCHBOX No. 54 Army Saracen Personnel Carrier.

	C6	C8	C10
No. 54 Personnel Carrier, 1976	5	7	10
No. 54 Mobile Home, 1981	3	5	7
No. 55 D.U.K.W. (Army Amphibian), 1959	25	34	47
No. 55 Ford Police Car, 1963	52	77	105

MATCHBOX No. 55 Ford Police Car.

	C6	C8	C10
No. 55 Mercury Parkland Police Car, 1969	13	20	26
No. 55 Mercury Police Car (Station Wagon), 1970	5	10	14
No. 55 Hell Raiser, 1975	4	6	8
No. 55 Ford Cortina, 1980	5	9	11
No. 56 London Trolley Bus, 1959	34	51	72
No. 56 Fiat 1500, 1965	9	12	17
No. 56 BMC 1800 Pininfarina, 1970	7	10	13
No. 56 Hi Trailer, 1975	4	6	9
No. 56 Mercedes 450SEL, 1980	4	6	8

MATCHBOX No. 56 Fiat 1500.

	C6	C8	C10
No. 57 Wolseley 1500, 1959	19	26	34
No. 57 Chevrolet Impala, 1966	21	30	39
No. 57 Eccles Caravan, 1970	5	9	14
No. 57 Wild Life Truck, 1973	7	9	11
No. 58 British European Airways Coach, 1959	16	24	32
No. 58 Drott Excavator, 1963	25	28	51
No. 58 Daf Girder Truck, 1968	9	12	16
No. 58 Woosh-N-Push, 1972	6	10	13
No. 58 Faun Dumper, 1976	5	9	15
No. 59 Ford "Singer," Van, 1959	44	61	83

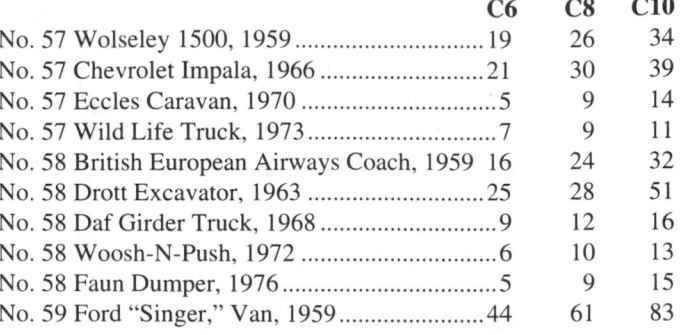

MATCHBOX No. 59 Ford "Singer" Van.

MATCHBOX No. 60 Morris Omnitruck J-2 Pick-up.

	C6	C8	C10
No. 59 Ford Fairlane Fire Car, 1964	27	42	68
No. 59 Fire Chief Car, 1966	73	99	137
No. 59 Planet Scout, 1975	13	18	27
No. 59 Porsche 928, 1981	5	7	9
No. 60 Morris Omnitruck J2 Pickup	17	26	35
No. 60 Truck w/ Site Office, 1967	8	11	15
No. 60 Lotus Super Seven, 1971	6	9	12
No. 60 Holden Pickup, 1977	8	11	15
No. 61 Military Scout Car (Ferret), 1959	16	23	32
No. 61 Alvis Stalwart, 1967	20	30	44
No. 61 Blue Shark, 1971	4	6	10
No. 61 Wreck Truck, 1978	3	5	7
No. 62 General Army Lorry, 1959	17	22	28
No. 62 TV Service Van, 1964	20	33	44
No. 62 Mercury Cougar, 1969	8	10	14
No. 62 Rat Rod Dragster, 1971	4	7	11
No. 62 Renault 17 TL, 1974	5	7	10
No. 62 Chevrolet Corvette, 1980	2	4	6
No. 63 Army Ambulance, 1959	24	37	48
No. 63 Airport Fire Fighting Crash Tender, 1964	16	23	32
No. 63 Dodge Crane Truck, 1968	10	14	20
No. 63 Freeway Gas Tanker, 1973	9	14	19
No. 64 Scammell Army Wreck Truck, 1959	17	30	38
No. 64 MG 1100, 1966	8	12	16
No. 64 Slingshot Dragster, 1971	5	9	15
No. 64 Fire Chief Car, 1976	3	5	8
No. 64 Caterpillar Tractor, 1981	3	5	7
No. 65 Jaguar 3.4 Litre Saloon, 1959	11	16	19
No. 65 Claas Combine Harvester, 1968	8	11	15
No. 65 Saab Sonnet, 1973	5	8	10
No. 65 Airport Coach, 1977	6	9	14
No. 66 Citroen DS19, 1959	18	22	30
No. 66 Harley Davidson Motorcycle & Sidecar, 1963	41	63	80

MATCHBOX No. 64 Scammell Army Wreck Truck.

	C6	C8	C10
No. 66 Greyhound Bus, 1967	22	28	37
No. 66 Mazda RX500, 1972	5	8	10
No. 66 Ford Transit, 1977	5	9	16
No. 67 "Saladin" Armored Car, 1959	20	30	39
No. 67 Volkswagen 1600 T.L., 1968	7	10	12
No. 67 Hot Rocker, 1973	4	6	9
No. 67 Datsun 260Z, 1978	4	6	8
No. 68 Army Austin MKII Radio Truck, 1959	12	17	22

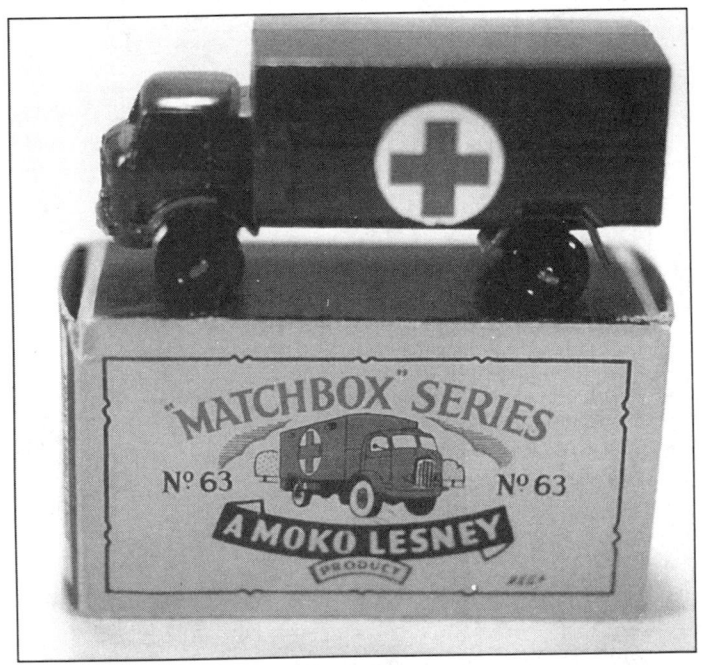

MATCHBOX No. 63 Army Ambulance.

MATCHBOX No. 68 Army Austin MK II Radio Truck.

	C6	C8	C10
No. 68 Mercedes Coach, 1965	19	27	36
No. 68 Porsche 910, 1970	7	10	12
No. 68 Cosmobile, 1975	14	21	30
No. 69 Chevrolet Van, 1980	12	18	26

MATCHBOX No. 69 Commer 30 Cwt., "Nestle's" Van.

	C6	C8	C10
No. 69 Commer 30 Cwt. Van "Nestle's," 1959	27	38	49
No. 69 Hatra Tractor Shovel, 1965	13	17	24
No. 69 Rolls-Royce Silver Shadow, 1970	10	19	26
No. 69 Turbo Fury, 1973	6	8	12
No. 69 Wells Fargo security, 1978	5	9	14
No. 70 Ford Thames Estate Car, 1959	20	28	36
No. 70 Atkinson Grit-Spreading Truck, 1965	7	11	16
No. 70 Dodge Dragster, 1971	7	11	16
No. 70 S.P. Gun, 1977	3	6	10
No. 70 Ferrari, 1981	2	3	6
No. 71 Army Water Truck, 1959	15	24	33
No. 71 Jeep Pickup Truck, 1964	15	24	36
No. 71 Ford Heavy Wreck Truck, 1968	8	15	21

MATCHBOX No. 73 R.A.F. 10-Ton Pressure Refueler Tanker.

	C6	C8	C10
No. 71 Ford Heavy Wreck Truck, amber windows, light and white bumper	55	83	110
No. 71 Jumbo Jet, 1973	3	5	8
No. 71 Cattle Truck, 1976	4	6	8
No. 72 Fordson Tractor (Power Major), 1959	22	32	45
No. 72 Standard Jeep, 1967	8	13	18
No. 72 Hovercraft SRN6, 1972	7	11	19
No. 72 Bomag Road Roller, 1980	4	6	8
No. 73 RAF 10 Ton Pressure Refueler Tanker, 1959	22	32	45
No. 73 Ferrari Racing Car, 1963	15	27	36
No. 73 Mercury Station Wagon (Commuter), 1969	8	13	17
No. 73 Weasel, 1974	2	4	7
No. 73 Model "A" Ford, 1981	2	4	6
No. 74 Mobile Refreshment Bar (Canteen), 1959	24	37	51
No. 74 Daimler Bus, 1966	13	19	27
No. 74 Toe Joe, 1972	4	6	10
No. 74 Cougar Villager, 1978	4	6	8
No. 75 Ford Thunderbird, 1959	48	71	96
No. 75 Ferrari Berlinetta, 1965	11	16	22
No. 75 Alfa Carabo, 1971	6	9	13
No. 75 Helicopter, 1976	4	6	9

Matchbox "Models of Yesteryear"

(With year of introduction)

	C6	C8	C10
Y-1 1925 Allchin 7 N.H.P. Traction Engine, 1955	38	55	77
Y-1 1911 Model "T" Ford, 1964	14	22	30
Y-1 1936 Jaguar SS100, 1977	14	22	32
Y-2 1911 "B" Type London Bus, 1955	49	75	104
Y-2 1911 Renault 2-seater, 1963	11	19	31
Y-2 Prince Henry Vauxhall, 1970	10	16	22
Y-3 1907 London "E" Class Tramcar, 1955	55	87	115
Y-3 1910 Benz Limousine, 1965	13	22	29
Y-3 1934 Riley MPH, 1972	11	15	21
Y-4 Sentinel Steam Wagon, 1955	53	73	99
Y-4 1905 Shank-Mason Horse-Drawn Fire Engine, 1960	104	148	203
Y-4 1909 Opel Coupe, 1966	15	27	44
Y-4 1930 Dusenberg Model J, 1976	15	25	35
Y-5 1929 LeMans Bentley, 1955	48	64	87
Y-5 1929 Supercharged 4-1/2 Litre Bentley, 1960	16	25	33
Y-5 1907 Peugeot, 1968	17	29	36
Y-5 1927 Talbot Van, 1978	20	28	39
Y-6 1916 A.E.C. "Y" type Lorry Truck, 1955	32	43	55
Y-6 1926 Type "35" Bugatti, 1961	22	33	44
Y-6 1913 Cadillac, 1967	27	42	58
Y-6 1920 Rolls-Royce Fire Engine, 1978	18	29	44
Y-7 1914 4-Ton Leyland, 1955	37	54	74
Y-7 1913 Mercer Raceabout Sportcar, 1961	28	44	57
Y-7 1912 Rolls-Royce, 1967	25	39	48
Y-8 1926 Morris Cowley "Bullnose," 1955	66	93	121
Y-8 1914 Sunbeam Motorcycle w/ sidecar, 1962	23	37	53
Y-8 1914 Stutz Roadster, 1968	12	19	33
Y-8 1945 MC TC Sports Car, 1978	7	11	15

MATCHBOX Y-5 Talbot Van.

MATCHBOX Y-6 1913 Cadillac.

MATCHBOX Y-12 1912 Model T Ford.

	C6	C8	C10
Y-9 1924 Fowler "Big Lion" Showman Engine, 1955	58	78	100
Y-9 1912 Simplex, 1967	25	41	56
Y-10 1908 Grand Prix Mercedes Racing Car, 1957	40	60	80
Y-10 1928 Mercedes-Benz 36/220, 1963	24	38	50
Y-10 1906 Rolls-Royce Silver Cloud, 1968	12	17	25
Y-11 1920 Aveling & Porter Steam Roller, 1957	39	57	76
Y-11 1912 Packard Landaulet, 1963	19	29	37
Y-11 1938 Lagonda Drophead Coupe, 1972	15	22	32
Y-12 1899 Horse-Bus (London), 1957	81	113	150
Y-12 1909 Thomas Flyabout, 1967	22	33	44
Y-12 1912 Model "T" Ford, 1979	12	19	25
Y-13 1862 American 4-4-0 Locomotive	33	49	66
Y-13 1911 Daimler, 1965	17	26	32
Y-13 1918 Crossley Truck, 1972	20	33	42
Y-14 1903 "Duke of Connaught" Locomotive, 1957	85	122	159
Y-14 1911 Maxwell Roadster, 1965	25	38	54
Y-14 1931 Stutz Bearcat, 1972	10	15	20
Y-15 1907 Rolls-Royce "Silver Ghost," 1960	20	32	44
Y-15 1930 Packard Victoria, 1969	10	16	22
Y-16 1904 Spyker Veteran Auto, 1961	29	43	58
Y-16 1928 Mercedes SS, 1971	10	16	22
Y-17 1938 Hispano Suiza, 1972	11	17	26
Y-18 1937 Cord 812, 1979	8	10	12
Y-19 1935 Auburn 851, 1980	5	8	11
Y-20 1938 Mercedes 540K, 1981	6	8	10
Y-21 1929 Woody Wagon, 1981	7	11	17

MATCHBOX Y-14 1931 Stutz Bearcat.

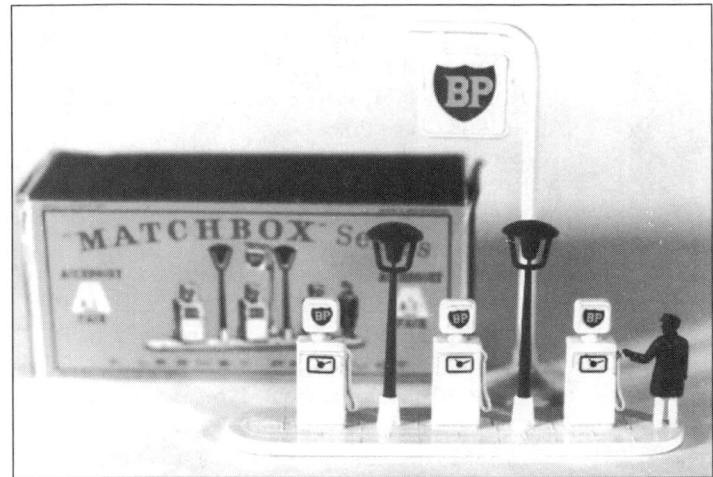

MATCHBOX Accessory Pack A-1 BP Gas Pump and BP sign, w/ box.

Box Cover for MATCHBOX Service Station.

Japanese Tin Cars

The average mint price of these toys was $359.12 in the last edition. In this edition it is $363.55, an increase of 4%.

Tin Cars and Their Values: A Diverse Range

by Ron Smith

Tin toy cars have been manufactured since the first horseless carriages roamed the streets of the United States and Europe. They ranged in size and price from the tiny one-inch penny toy to the 28-inch Eldorado that sold for ten dollars. Although there are German, Spanish, and French toy cars listed here, our concentration will be the 1950s' Golden Era of Japanese tin toy cars. These examples enjoy much popularity today and prices have been raised by the limitlessness of some people's insanity. Keep one thing foremost in your mind when trying to sell a toy at the mint listed price: the person who paid that price already has one.

Ron Smith has always loved toy cars and planes. He can still show you his first DinkyToy, bought for him in 1940 by his aunt in Fred Harvey's Toy Store inside Cleveland's Terminal Tower Building. Born and raised in Shaker Heights, Ohio, Ron served in the United States Navy and attended John Carroll University. He has collected die-cast cars, trucks and planes, cast-iron toys, and plastic promotional cars. For the last 10 years he has specialized in tin plate cars and planes. Ron lives in Solon, Ohio, with his wife Joan and their two cats, Trouble and Bogart.

Photos in this section courtesy of Ron Smith, unless otherwise noted.

No.	Year	Model	Manufacturer	Power	Size	C6	C8	C10
J1	1960s	Aston-Martin DB5 (James Bond)	Gilbert	Friction	11-1/2"	75	150	300
J2	1960s	Aston-Martin DB6	Asahi Toy Co.	Friction	11"	100	430	600
J2A	1959	Austin Healey 100 Six Coupe	Bandai	Friction	8"	60	100	180
J2B	1959	Austin Healey 100 Six Convertible	Bandai	Friction	8"	60	100	180
J3	1953	Buick	Marusan	Friction	7"	50	100	200
J4	1954	Buick Station Wagon	Unknown	Battery	8"	75	150	200
J5	1955	Buick Roadmaster	Yoshiya	Friction	11"	125	175	400
J6	1958	Buick Century	Yonezawa	Friction	12"	400	600	1000+
J7	1958	Buick Century	Bandai	Friction	8"	80	110	130
J8	1959	Buick	T.N.	Friction	11"	90	150	300

J1

J2

J5

J6

J7

J8

No.	Year	Model	Manufacturer	Power	Size	C6	C8	C10
J9	1959	Buick	Ichiko	Batt/Fric	12"	100	275	350
J10	1960	Buick	Ichiko	Friction	17-1/2"	150	250	600
J11	1961	Buick	T.N.	Friction	11"	100	200	300
J12	1961	Buick Emergency Car	T.N.	Friction	14"	50	95	125
J13	1963	Buick Wildcat	Ichiko	Friction	15"	200	400	800
J14	1966	Buick LeSabre	Asahi Toy Co.	Friction	19"	100	150	275
J15	1968	Buick Sportswagon	Asakusa	Friction	15"	150	180	250
J16	1950	BMW 600 Isetta	Bandai	Friction	9"	150	200	250
J17	1950	BMW Isetta (three wheels)	Bandai	Friction	6-1/2"	75	125	150
J18	1950	Cadillac	Marusan	Friction	11"	400	600	800
J19	1950	Cadillac	Marusan	Battery	11"	400	800	1100
J20	1952	Cadillac	Alps	Friction	11-1/2"	250	500	800
J21	1952	Cadillac	T.N.	Battery	13"	100	200	400
J22	1954	Cadillac	Gama	Friction	12"	200	300	500
J23	1954	Cadillac	Joustra	Battery	12"	200	300	500
J24	1959	Cadillac Sedan	Bandai	Friction	12"	50	100	200
J25	1959	Cadillac Convertible	Bandai	Friction	12"	50	100	200

J13

J18

J20

J24

J25

J29

J31

J34

J37

No.	Year	Model	Manufacturer	Power	Size	C6	C8	C10
J26	1960s	Cadillac	Bandai	Friction	17"	125	175	375
J27	1960	Cadillac	Yonezawa	Friction	18"	100	150	300
J28	1961	Cadillac 60	Unknown	Friction	9"	95	125	150
J29	1961	Cadillac Fleetwood	SSS	Friction	17-1/2"	150	300	500
J30	1962	Cadillac	Yonezawa	Friction	22"	100	250	350
J31	1963	Cadillac	Bandai	Friction	17"	125	200	350
J32	1965	Cadillac	Asahi Toy Co.	Friction	17"	125	250	400
J33	1965	Cadillac	Ichiko	Friction	22"	300	400	600
J34	1967	Cadillac	K.O.	Friction	10-1/2"	100	150	300
J35	1967	Cadillac	Unknown	Friction	10-3/4"	75	100	125
J36	1967	Cadillac El Dorado	Ichiko	Friction	28"	200	400	800
J37	1953	Chevrolet Corvette	Bandai	Friction	7"	100	150	200
J38	1958	Chevrolet Corvette	Yonezawa	Friction	9-1/2"	200	300	600
J39	1962	Chevrolet Corvette	Bandai	Friction	8"	50	75	100
J40	1965	Chevrolet Corvette	Bandai	Friction	8"	50	75	100
J41	1964	Chevrolet Corvette	Ichida	Battery	12"	150	225	350
J42	1968	Chevrolet Corvette	Taiyo	Battery	9-1/2"	20	40	60
J43	1960s	Chevrolet Corvair	Bandai	Friction	8"	30	50	70
J44	1963	Chevrolet Corvair	Ichiko	Friction	9"	50	65	95
J45	1967	Chevrolet Camaro	Taiyo	Friction	9-1/2"	10	20	30
J46	1967	Chevrolet Camaro	T.N.	Friction	14"	150	250	400
J47	1967	Chevrolet Camaro	Modern Toys	Friction	11"	25	50	75
J48	1971	Chevrolet Camaro Rusher	Taiyo	Battery	9-1/2"	10	20	30
J49	1954	Chevrolet	Marusan	Friction	11"	300	400	800

J38

J41

J46

J42

No.	Year	Model	Manufacturer	Power	Size	C6	C8	C10
J50	1955	Chevrolet	Marusan	Battery	10-3/4"	300	600	1000
J51	1956	Chevrolet Station Wagon	Bandai	Friction	9-1/2"	60	120	160
J52	1956	Chevrolet Pickup	Bandai	Friction	9-1/2"	75	125	175
J53	1956	Chevrolet Convertible	Bandai	Friction	9-1/2"	100	150	225
J54	1958	Chevrolet Red Cross Ambulance	Bandai	Friction	8"	20	30	50
J55	1958	Chevrolet Pickup Truck	Bandai	Friction	8"	50	65	90
J56	1958	Chevrolet Convertible	Bandai	Friction	8"	60	90	125
J57	1958	Chevrolet Station Wagon	Bandai	Friction	8"	50	60	85
J58	1958	Chevrolet Sedan	Bandai	Friction	8"	75	100	125
J59	1959	Chevrolet Sedan/Convertible/Wagon	SY	Friction	11-1/2"	200	300	600
J60	1960	Chevrolet	Marusan	Friction	11-1/2"	200	300	600
J61	Unused							
J62	1961	Chevrolet Impala Sedan	Bandai	Friction	11"	100	200	400
J63	1961	Chevrolet Impala Convertible	Bandai	Friction	11"	100	200	400
J64	1962	Chevrolet Secret Agent	Unknown	Battery	14"	50	75	125
J65	1962	Chevrolet	Unknown	Friction	11"	125	250	350
J66	1963	Chevrolet Impala	Unknown	Friction	18"	200	300	400
J67	1960	Citroen DS 19 Convertible	Bandai	Friction	12"	300	600	900
J68	1960	Citroen DS 19 Sedan	Bandai	Friction	12"	300	600	900
J69	1960	Citroen DS 19 Station Wagon	Bandai	Friction	12"	300	600	900

J48

J49

J50. Photo courtesy Abensur.

J57

J59

J60

J62

J63   J64   J65

No.	Year	Model	Manufacturer	Power	Size	C6	C8	C10
J70	1950	Chrysler	Guntherman	Friction	11"	100	200	500
J71	1955	Chrysler	Yonezawa	Friction	8"	100	200	300
J72	1957	Chrysler New Yorker	Alps	Friction	14"	500	700	1000+
J73	1958	Chrysler	Unknown	Battery	13"	300	400	800
J74	1959	Chrysler Imperial Convertible	Bandai	Friction	8"	50	100	200
J75	1959	Chrysler Imperial Sedan	Bandai	Friction	8"	50	100	200
J76	1960	Chrysler Valiant	Bandai	Friction	8"	20	30	50
J77	1962	Chrysler Imperial	Asahi Toy Co.	Friction	16"	500	700	1000+
J78	1960	DKW 1000 Convertible	Bandai	Friction	8"	90	125	200
J79	1960s	Datsun Bluebird 1200	Bandai	Friction	8"	60	75	125
J80	1950s	Divco Dugans Bakery Truck	Unknown, Japan	Friction	7-1/2"	200	400	500
J81	1930s	DeSoto	Masudaya	Friction	8"	300	400	800
J82	1958	Dodge Sedan	T.N.	Friction	11"	300	400	800
J83	1959	Dodge Truck	Unknown	Friction	24"	350	500	800
J84	1959	Dodge Pickup	Unknown	Friction	18-1/2"	350	500	800
J85	1968	Dodge Yellow Cab	T.N.	Friction	12"	100	200	400
J86	1958	Edsel Convertible/Sedan	Haji	Friction	10-1/2"	300	400	800
J87	1958	Edsel Wagon	Haji	Friction	10-1/2"	200	300	400
J88	1958	Edsel Ambulance	Haji	Friction	11"	200	250	300
J89	1958	Edsel Station Wagon	T.N.	Friction	11"	150	200	300
J90	1958	Edsel H.T.	Asahi	Friction	10-3/4"	300	400	600
J91	1958	Edsel H.T.	Toy Nomura	Friction	8-1/2"	100	150	250
J92	1958	Edsel	Yonezawa	Friction	10-1/2"	300	400	600
J93	1949	Ford Sedan	Guntherman	Wind-Up	11"	150	300	400
J94	1951	Ford Sedan	Guntherman	Wind-Up	11"	150	300	400
J95	1950	Ford Good Humor Ice Cream Truck	KTS, Japan	Friction	10-3/4"	100	200	400
J96	1955	Ford Pickup	Bandai	Friction	12"	150	250	300
J97	1955	Ford Station Wagon	Bandai	Friction	12"	150	250	300
J98	1955	Ford Ambulance	Bandai	Friction	12"	150	250	300
J99	1955	Ford Panel Truck, "Flowers"	Bandai	Friction	12"	200	400	600
J100	1955	Ford Convertible	Bandai	Friction	12"	200	400	600
J101	1956	Ford H.T.	Yonezawa	Friction	12"	300	500	800
J102	1956	Ford Convertible	Haji	Friction	11-1/2"	400	600	1000+
J103	1956	Ford Sedan	Marusan	Friction	13"	500	800	1000+
J104	1956	Ford Wagon	Nomura	Friction	10-1/2"	100	150	300
J105	1957	Ford Fairlane Sedan	Ichiko	Friction	10"	100	200	300
J106	1957	Ford H.T.	T.N.	Friction	12"	100	200	300
J107	1957	Ford Sedan/Conv./Wagon/Pickup	Joustra	Friction	12"	200	250	300
J108	1957	Ford Sedan/Conv./Wagon/Pickup	Bandai	Friction	12"	200	250	300
J109	1957	Ford Station Wagon	Nomura	Friction	7-1/2"	60	80	100
J110	1958	Ford Retractable Top	K. Japan	Friction	10"	80	100	165
J111	1958	Ford Retractable Top	T.N.	Battery	11"	80	100	165
J112	1958	Ford Country Squire Station Wagon	Bandai	Friction	8"	60	80	100
J113	1958	Ford Fairlane H.T./Conv.	Bandai	Friction	8"	60	80	100
J114	1958	Ford Fairlane H.T./Conv.	Sankei Gangu	Friction	9"	90	115	125
J115	1959	Ford Fairlane Skyliner	Sankei Gangu	Friction	9"	90	115	125
J116	1950	Ford Station Wagon	T.N.	Friction	12"	100	150	200
J117	1959	Ford Retractable	T.N.	Friction	11"	80	100	165
J118	1960s	Ford Falcon	Bandai	Friction	8"	20	30	50

J72. Photo courtesy Bruce Sterling.

J71

J73

J77

J86

J86

J87

J93

J96

J99

J100

J103 Photo courtesy Bruce Sterling.

No.	Year	Model	Manufacturer	Power	Size	C6	C8	C10
J119	1960	Ford	Haji	Friction	11"	125	150	300
J120	1961	Ford Country Sedan	Bandai	Friction	10-1/2"	125	150	250
J121	1962	Ford Country Sedan	Asahi	Friction	12"	200	300	600
J122	1964	Ford H.T.	Ichiko	Friction	13"	200	400	600
J123	1964	Ford H.T.	Rico	Friction	17"	200	400	600
J124	1964	Ford Convertible	Rico	Friction	17"	200	400	600
J125	1965	Ford Galaxie H.T.	MT	Friction	11"	125	150	250
J126	1968	Ford Torino	S.T.	Friction	16"	200	300	500
J127	1956	Ford Thunderbird	T.N.	Friction	11"	200	300	400
J128	1956	Ford Thunderbird H.T. Clear Top	T.N.	Friction	11"	200	300	400
J129	1956	Ford Thunderbird	T.N.	Battery	11"	200	300	400
J130	1959	Ford Thunderbird Sedan	Bandai	Friction	8"	50	60	80
J131	1959	Ford Thunderbird Convertible	Bandai	Friction	8"	50	60	80
J132	1961	Ford Thunderbird Retractable	Yonezawa	Battery	11"	80	120	175
J133	1962	Ford Thunderbird Retractable	Yonezawa	Battery	11"	80	120	175
J134	1963	Ford Thunderbird Retractable	Yonezawa	Battery	11"	80	120	175
J135	1964	Ford Thunderbird Convertible	Asahi	Friction	12-1/2"	150	200	400
J136	1964	Ford Thunderbird H.T.	Asahi	Friction	12"	150	200	400
J137	1964	Ford Thunderbird	Ichiko	Friction	16"	100	200	400
J138	1965	Ford Thunderbird H.T.	Bandai	Friction	10-3/4"	60	85	125
J139	1965	Ford Mustang F.B.	Bandai	Friction	11"	45	65	90
J140	1965	Ford Mustang H.T./Conv.	Bandai	Fric/Bat	11"	75	125	150
J141	1965	Ford Mustang (FBI)	Bandai	Friction	11"	75	100	125
J142	1965	Ford Mustang Convertible	Yonezawa	Battery	13-1/2"	90	125	200
J143	1966	Ford Mustang F.B.	T.N.	Friction	17"	120	200	325
J144	1967	Ford Mustang	Bandai	Battery	13"	45	65	100
J145	1960s	Ford Taunus 17M Convertible	Bandai	Friction	8"	30	40	60
J146	1960s	Ford GT	Bandai	Battery	10"	65	85	125
J147	1957	Ferrari 250 G. Convertible	A.T.C.	Friction	9-1/2"	150	300	700
J148	1958	Ferrari	Bandai	Battery	11"	90	150	300
J149	1960	Ferrari Super America Coupe	Bandai	Friction	12"	100	200	300
J150	1960s	Ferrari Super America Convertible	Bandai	Friction	12"	100	200	300
J151	1960s	Fiat 600 Sedan	Bandai	Friction	8"	50	65	95
J152	1950s	International Cement Mixer	SSS	Friction	19"	300	600	800
J153	1950s	International Grain Hauler	SSS	Friction	23"	300	600	800
J154	1960	Jaguar XK150 H.T. Conv.	Bandai	Friction	9-1/2"	75	125	200
J155	1960s	Jaguar XKE Convertible	T.T.	Friction	10-1/2"	95	125	175
J156	1960s	Jaguar XKE Coupe	Lendolet Auto	Friction	10-1/2"	75	100	125
J157	1960s	Jaguar XK 140	Bandai	Friction	9-1/2"	40	60	90
J158	1960s	Jaguar XKE	Bandai	Battery	10"	90	125	200
J159	1960s	Jaguar 3.4 Sedan	Bandai	Friction	8"	50	60	100
J160	1960s	Jaguar 3.4 Convertible	Bandai	Friction	8"	50	60	100
J161	1965	Jaguar XKE120	Alps	Friction	6-1/2"	90	150	350
J162	1954	Lincoln	Unknown	Friction	12"	175	275	375
J163	1955	Lincoln Sedan	Yonezawa	Friction	12"	250	325	500
J164	1956	Lincoln Continental Mark II	Linemar	Friction	12"	400	600	1000+
J165	1956	Lincoln	Ichiko	Friction	16-1/2"	150	250	375
J166	1959	Lincoln Continental Mark III Conv.	Bandai	Friction	12"	90	125	175

J102

J106

J107

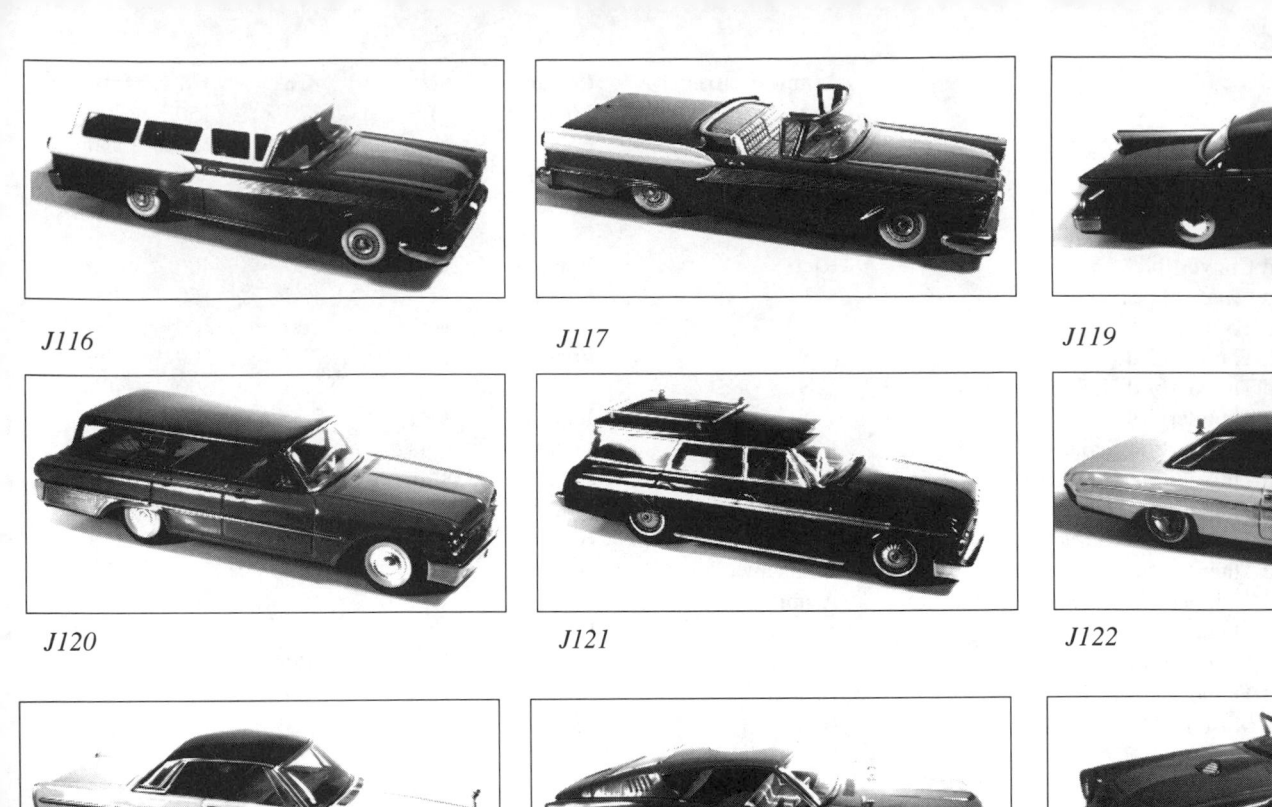

J116

J117

J119

J120

J121

J122

J125

J126

J129

J134

J136

J137

J138

J140

J164

J166

J168

J177

J193

J195

J197

J208

J209

J210

No.	Year	Model	Manufacturer	Power	Size	C6	C8	C10
J167	1959	Lincoln Continental Mark III Sedan	Banzai	Friction	12"	90	125	175
J168	1960	Lincoln H.T./Convertible	Yonezawa	Friction	11"	100	150	300
J169	1964	Lincoln	Unknown	Friction	10-1/2"	90	175	275
J170	1950s	Lotus Elite	Bandai	Friction	8-1/2"	25	35	45
J171	1960s	Land Rover "88" Station Wagon	Bandai	Friction	8"	30	40	60
J172	1950s	Mercedes Limousine	Tipp & Co.	Friction	14"	500	800	1000
J173	1950s	Mercedes Benz Racer	Line Mar	Friction	9-1/2"	95	150	185
J174	1950s	Mercedes Benz Racer W196	Marusan	Battery	10"	150	200	250
J175	1960s	Mercedes	Ichiko	Friction	12-1/2"	115	155	185
J176	1960s	Mercedes Benz 219 Sedan	Bandai	Friction	8"	50	80	100
J177	1960s	Mercedes Benz 219 Convertible	Bandai	Friction	8"	50	80	100
J178	1960s	Mercedes Benz 230 SL	Modern Toys	Battery	15"	175	210	250
J179	1960s	Mercedes Benz 230 SL	Alps	Battery	10"	65	75	95
J180	1960s	Mercedes Benz 230 SL	Yanoman	Battery	14-1/2"	125	155	185
J181	1960s	Mercedes Benz 250 SE	Ichiko	Battery	13"	110	140	185
J182	1960s	Mercedes Benz 250 S	Daiya	Friction	14"	110	155	175
J183	1950s	Mercedes Benz 300 SL	T.N.	Battery	11"	125	150	200
J184	1950s	Mercedes Benz 300 SL	KS	Battery	7"	45	65	85
J185	1950s	Mercedes Benz 300 SL	Dist. Cragstan	Battery	9"	65	95	125
J186	1950s	Mercedes Benz 300 SL	Bandai	Friction	8"	65	95	125

J207A

J218A

J215

J219

J222

J223

J224

J225

J227

J232

J235

J236

J237

J240

J242

J243

J252

J260

J265

J276

No.	Year	Model	Manufacturer	Power	Size	C6	C8	C10
J187	1957	Mercedes Benz 300 SL	Marusan	Friction	8-1/2"	200	300	400
J188	1960s	Mercedes Benz 600	Unknown	Friction	10"	95	125	175
J189	1960s	Mercedes Benz Taxi	Bandai	Battery	10"	75	100	125
J190	1962	Mercedes Benz	SSS	Battery	12"	200	250	350
J191	1970	Mercedes Benz	Ichiko	Friction	24"	125	150	200
J192	1954	Mercury H.T.	Rock Valley Toys	Battery	9-1/2"	100	150	250
J193	1956	Mercury H.T.	Alps	Friction	9-1/2"	600	800	1000+
J194	1958	Mercury Station Wagon	Bandai	Friction	8"	60	80	100
J195	1958	Mercury H.T.	Yonezawa	Friction	11-1/2"	250	325	400
J196	1967	Mercury Cougar H.T.	Taiyo	Battery	10"	25	45	65
J197	1967	Mercury Cougar H.T.	Asakusa Toys	Friction	15"	200	400	600
J198	1952	MG TF	Unknown	Friction	8-1/2"	50	75	95
J199	1954	MG TD	SSS	Friction	6-1/2"	35	65	85
J200	1955	MG TF	Bandai	Friction	8"	95	125	150
J201	1957	MGA	A.T.C.	Friction	10"	175	250	400
J202	1960s	MG Magnette Mark III Sedan	Bandai	Friction	8"	95	125	150
J203	1960s	MG Magnette Mark III Convertible	Bandai	Friction	8"	95	125	150
J204	1960s	Messerschmitt 4 Wheels Convertible	Bandai	Friction	8"	200	250	300
J205	1960s	Messerschmitt 4 Wheels Sedan	Bandai	Friction	8"	200	250	300
J206	1950s	Nash	MSK	Battery	8"	40	70	90
J207	1956	Nash Ambassador	Sankei Gangu	Friction	8"	100	125	150
J207A	1952	Oldsmobile	Y	Friction	11"	150	350	500
J208	1956	Oldsmobile Sedan	Ichiko/Kanto	Friction	10-1/2"	200	400	600
J209	1956	Oldsmobile Super 88 Sedan	Masudaya	Friction	16"	300	400	600
J210	1958	Oldsmobile Sedan	A.T.C.	Friction	12"	200	300	400
J211	1958	Oldsmobile Super 88 Sedan	A.T.C.	Friction	13"	250	325	425
J212	1958	Oldsmobile Sedan	Y	Friction	16"	300	400	700
J213	1959	Oldsmobile Sedan	Ichiko	Friction	12-1/2"	75	125	175
J214	1961	Oldsmobile Convertible	Yonezawa	Friction	12"	75	125	175
J215	1966	Oldsmobile Toronado	Bandai	Battery	11"	65	110	150
J216	1968	Oldsmobile Toronado	Ichiko	Friction	17-1/2"	300	400	500
J217	1950s	Opel Sedan	Yonezawa	Battery	11-1/2"	70	90	125
J218	1954	Pontiac Star Chief	Asahi	Friction	11"	250	350	600
J218A	1954	Pontiac	Minister	Friction	11"	New Issue		20
J219	1967	Pontiac Firebird	Akasura	Friction	15-1/2"	90	150	275
J220	1967	Pontiac Firebird	Bandai	Friction	10"	30	55	75
J221	1967	Pontiac Firebird (w/ wipers)	Bandai	Battery	9-1/2"	40	55	75
J222	1953	Packard Convertible/Sedan	Alps	Friction	16"	500	800	1500
J223	1957	Packard Hawk Convertible	Schuco	Battery	10-3/4"	300	400	800
J224	1956	Plymouth H.T.	Unknown	Friction	8-1/2"	200	400	600
J225	1956	Plymouth H.T.	Alps	Battery	12"	300	400	600
J226	1957	Plymouth Fury H.T.	Y	Friction	11-1/2"	300	400	600

J265A

J278A

No.	Year	Model	Manufacturer	Power	Size	C6	C8	C10
J227	1958	Plymouth Fury	Bandai	Friction	8"	75	90	150
J228	1959	Plymouth Hardtop	A.T.C.	Friction	10-1/2"	200	400	600
J229	1959	Plymouth Convertible	A.T.C.	Friction	10-1/2"	250	400	600
J230	1961	Plymouth Sedan	Ichiko	Friction	12"	125	250	350
J231	1961	Plymouth Station Wagon	Ichiko	Friction	12"	125	165	195
J232	1961	Plymouth T.V. Car	Ichiko	Battery	12"	125	175	250
J233	1964	Plymouth Fury H.T.	Kusama	Friction	10"	60	80	100
J234	1960	Porsche 911	Bandai	Battery	10"	65	95	125
J235	1950s	Porsche Speedster	Distler	Battery	10-1/2"	200	300	500
J236	1960	Rolls Royce "Silver Coupe" Conv.	Bandai	Friction	12"	100	150	300
J237	1960s	Rolls Royce "Silver Coupe" Sedan	Bandai	Friction	12"	100	150	250
J238	1960s	Rolls Royce (with electric lights)	Bandai	Battery	12"	150	300	600
J239	1960	Rolls Royce	T.N.	Friction	10-1/2"	200	300	500
J240	1960s	Rambler Rebel Station Wagon	Bandai	Friction	12"	50	85	125
J241	1960	Renault	Bandai	Friction	7-1/2"	95	150	200
J242	1960s	Studebaker Avanti	Bandai	Friction	8"	125	175	300
J243	1954	Studebaker	Yoshiva	Friction	9"	150	200	300
J244	1960s	Saab 93B	Bandai	Friction	7"	50	70	90
J245	1960s	Subaru 360	Bandai	Friction	7"	75	100	125
J246	1960s	Triumph TR-3 Convertible	Bandai	Friction	8"	50	75	150
J247	1960s	Triumph TR-3 Coupe	Bandai	Friction	8"	50	75	150
J248	1960s	Toyopet Crown	Bandai	Friction	9"	40	50	75
J249	1960s	Toyota	Ichiko	Friction	16"	150	275	325

J284

J286

J289

J287

No.	Year	Model	Manufacturer	Power	Size	C6	C8	C10
J250	1967	Toyota 2000 GT	A.T.C.	Friction	15"	150	275	325
J251	1960s	Vespa	Bandai	Friction	9"	50	75	125
J252	1960	VW Karmanna-Ghia	Bandai	Friction	7"	100	150	250
J253	1960s	Volkswagen Bus	A.T.C.	Friction	12"	125	175	350
J254	1960s	Volkswagen Pickup Truck	Bandai	Friction	8"	50	60	75
J255	1960s	Volkswagen Bus	Bandai	Friction	8"	50	60	75
J256	1960s	Volkswagen Bus	Bandai	Bat/Fric	9-1/2"	75	125	175
J257	1950s	Volkswagen Bus	Tipp & Co	Battery	9"	250	375	450
J258	1950s	Volkswagen Convertible	T.N.	Friction	9-1/2"	100	150	225
J259	1960s	Volkswagen Convertible	Bandai	Battery	7-1/2"	50	70	90
J260	1960s	Volkswagen Convertible	Bandai	Battery	11"	110	145	185
J261	1960s	Volkswagen Convertible	Taiyo	Battery	10-1/2"	25	45	90
J262	1960s	Volkswagen	Bandai	Friction	8"	25	45	60
J263	1960s	Volkswagen	Bandai	Battery	10-1/2"	25	50	75
J264	1960s	Volkswagen	Bandai	Battery	11"	25	50	75
J265	1960s	Volkswagen w/ or w/o Sun Roof	Bandai	Friction	15"	60	90	125
J265A	1950s	Volvo	Sweden	Windup	11"	600	700	1800
J266	1960s	Willys Jeep FC-150 Pickup	T.N. Toy Nomura	Friction	11"	50	75	95
J267	1950s	Zuendapp Janus	Bandai	Friction	8"	125	150	200
J268	1950s	Mazda Auto Tricycle K360	Bandai	Friction	6"	75	100	200
J269	1950	Daihatsu Midget	Kokyu Shokai	Friction	5"	75	100	200
J270	1950s	Daihatsu Midget	Yonezawa	Friction	7"	75	100	200
J271	1950s	Mitsubishi Auto Tricycle Leo	Bandai	Friction	5"	75	100	200
J272	1950s	Mitsubishi Auto Tricycle	Bandai	Friction	11"	100	150	300
J273	1950s	Orient Auto Tricycle	Yonezawa	Friction	9"	75	100	200
J274	1950s	Mazda Auto Tricycle	Bandai	Friction	8"	75	100	200
J275	1950s	Daihatsu Auto Tricycle	Nomura	Friction	11"	100	150	300
J276	1950s	Buick Futuristic LeSabre	Yonezawa	Friction	7-1/2"	200	300	600
J277	1963	Corvair Bertone	Bandai	Battery	12"	75	150	200
J278	1950s	Dream Car Buick Phantom	Tipp & Co.	Friction	12"	300	400	800
J278A	--	Dream Car	Y	Friction	17"	600	800	1500
J279	1960s	Dream Car Firebird III	Alps	Friction	11"	100	200	400
J280	1960	Ford Gyron	Ichida	Battery	11"	75	100	150
J281	1956	GM's Gas Turbine Powered Firebird II	Ashahi	Friction	8-1/2"	100	200	500
J282	1950s	Pontiac Dream Car	Mitsubishi	Friction	10"	100	200	500
J283	1950s	Atom Jet Car	Y	Friction	30"	300	500	1000
J284	1950s	Atom Car	Yonezawa	Friction	17"	200	400	800
J285	1950s	Record Racer NSU	Bandai	Friction	18"	100	150	200

J290

J291

No.	Year	Model	Manufacturer	Power	Size	C6	C8	C10
J286	1950s	Agajanian Racer No. 98	Y	Friction	18"	500	800	2000+
J287	1950s	Champion Racer No. 98	Y	Friction	18"	500	800	1200
J288	1950	Champion Racer No. 42	Gem	Friction	18"	500	750	1200
J289	1950	Champion Racer No. 15	German	Friction	18"	500	750	1200
J290	--	Electrospecial #21	Y	Battery	10"	300	500	800
J291	--	Midget Special #6	Y	Friction	7"	300	500	800

J288

JAPANESE TIN AIRPLANES

The average mint price of these toys was $497.50 in the last edition.
In this edition it is $498.86, showing no significant change.

by Ron Smith

Photos in this section courtesy of Ron Smith, unless otherwise noted.

No.	Type	Manufacturer	Power	Wingspan	C6	C8	C10
A1	Cessna	T.N.	Friction	25"	100	200	400
A2	Jenny Biplane	S&E	Friction	14-1/2"	75	125	150
A3	Jenny Biplane	S&E	Friction	14-1/2"	75	125	150
A4	Bristol Bulldog	S&E	Friction	14-1/2"	80	150	225

A1

A2

A3

A4

A5

A6

A7

A8

A9

A10

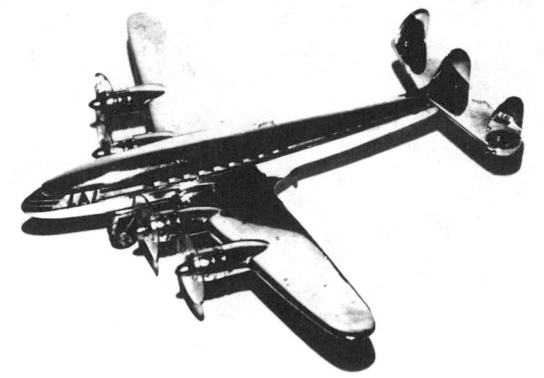

Left: A11

A12

A13

A14

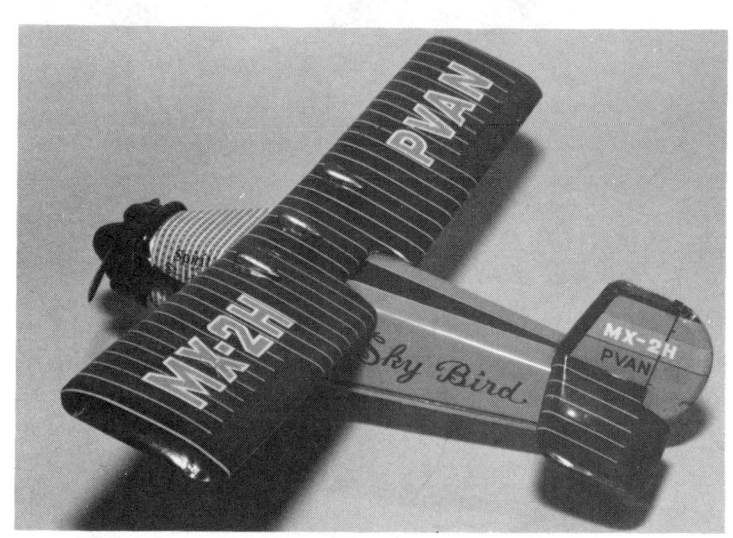

A15

A17

A18

A20

A21

A23

A22

A24

A25

A26

A27

No.	Type	Manufacturer	Power	Wingspan	C6	C8	C10
A5	Cessna	W. German	Friction	12"	50	80	150
A6	Ford	T.N.	Friction	15"	60	90	175
A7	Jenny Biplane	Haji	Friction	11-1/2"	30	50	100
A8	Ryan Spirit of St. Louis	HTC	Friction	12"	100	300	500
A9	U.N. Hospital Plane	HTC	Friction	12"	70	120	210
A10	WWII Fighter	Japan	Friction	14-1/2"	80	150	250
A11	Constellation	Ingap	Friction	15"	100	200	400
A12	F3F Biplane	Cragstan	Battery	11-1/2"	150	300	600
A13	Bluebird Seaplane	S&E	Friction	13"	50	80	150
A14	B50	Bandai	Friction	7-1/2"	40	60	90
A15	Sky Bird "Spirit of St. Louis"	Bandai	Friction	9"	50	80	120
A16	Spitfire	HTC	Friction	10"	80	150	200
A17	P-51 Mustang	HTC	Friction	10"	100	200	300
A18	P-47 Thunderbolt	HTC	Friction	10"	100	200	300
A19	Zero	Japan	Friction	15-1/2"	New Issue		150
A20	De Havilland Comet	Rico	Wind-up	13"	100	150	350
A21	WWII Fighter	Spain	Wind-up	8-1/2"	100	200	300
A22	F-80	Bandai	Friction	7-1/2"	40	70	100
A23	Disney Comic Plane	Linemar	Friction	10"	100	150	400
A24	WWII Fighter	Spain	Wind-up	9"	100	150	300
A25	WWII Tri-Motor	Spain	Wind-up	9"	100	150	300
A26	Hospital Plane	Tekno	—	14"	300	600	1000

A28

A29

A32. Photo courtesy of Tanaka.

A33. Photo courtesy of Tanaka.

No.	Type	Manufacturer	Power	Wingspan	C6	C8	C10
A27	German Biplane	Tipp	Bar/WU	20"	500	1000	3000
A28	Construction	England	—	22"	125	175	400
A29	30s German	Tipp	Wind-up	16"	700	1500	3200
A30	Fiat CR-42	Ingap	Wind-up	10"	500	700	1500
A31	Stuka	Dux	—	12"	200	400	800
A32	Hein	Banda	Friction	14"	200	350	500
A33	Zero	Nomura	Friction	14"	150	275	350
A34	Zero	Nomura	Friction	14"	150	275	350
A35	Lockheed Sirus	Japan	Friction	13"	400	800	1000
A36	Farman	Japan	Friction	10"	400	600	1000
A37	American Airlines DC-7	Japan	Battery	24"	200	300	500
A38	American Airlines Electra	Linemar	Battery	20"	200	400	500
A39	American Airlines Boeing 727	Y	Battery	16"	125	175	225
A40	Boeing 707	Japan	Battery	18"	200	300	400
A41	Boeing Stratocruiser	T.N.	Friction	20"	300	400	600
A42	Comet Jetliner	Y	Friction	19"	100	200	300
A43	Eastern Constellation	MSK	Friction	7-1/2"	100	150	200
A44	Eastern Constellation	Hadson	Friction	12"	200	350	450
A45	Eastern DC-7	Bandai	Friction	17-1/2"	300	400	600
A46	Presidents Plane	Japan	Battery	20"	275	350	500
A47	Pan Am DC-7	T.N.	Friction	17"	300	600	800
A48	Pan Am Stato Clipper	Japan	Friction	14"	225	300	450
A49	Pan Am Jet Clipper	Linemar	Battery	18"	200	300	425

A34. Photo courtesy of Tanaka.

A35. Photo courtesy of Tanaka.

No.	Type	Manufacturer	Power	Wingspan	C6	C8	C10
A50	Northwest DC-7	Y	Friction	10"	100	150	225
A51	Northwest Orient	Y	Battery	24"	300	500	650
A52	Northwest DC-7	Asahi	Friction	19"	300	600	900
A53	TWA Constellation	Y	Friction	12"	200	300	400
A54	TWA DC-4	Linemar	Friction	19"	150	350	475
A55	TWA DC-2	Japan	Wind-up	10"	175	300	425
A56	United DC-7 Mainliner	T.N.	Battery	19"	150	275	350
A57	United DC-7	Japan	Friction	23"	125	250	400
A58	B-29	Y	Friction	19"	150	300	475
A59	B-36	Y	Friction	26"	300	600	1000+
A60	B-45 Tornado	Bandai	Friction	16"	100	150	250
A61	B-47 USAF	Daiya	Friction	12"	150	225	325
A62	B-50 USAF	Y	Battery	19"	200	300	400
A63	B-50 Superfortress	TCP	Friction	15"	200	300	400
A64	C-120 Pack Plane	Japan	Friction	16"	250	500	800
A65	C-124 Globemaster	Y	Friction	20"	250	600	800
A66	F-84 Airforce	Linemar	Battery	13"	100	150	200
A67	F-86 Airforce	J	Friction	10"	75	125	175
A68	F-94C Starfire	Y	Friction	18"	150	300	450
A69	F-102 USAF	HTS	Friction	11"	125	150	225
A70	F-104 Lockheed	Y	Friction	16"	125	150	175

A36. Photo courtesy of Sotheby's.

ANIMAL-DRAWN

The average mint price in this section in the last edition was $1498.78. The average mint price in this edition is $1520.52, an increase of 1%. (Left out of this averaging is the price paid for the George Brown "Charles.")

THE APPEAL OF ANIMAL-DRAWN VEHICLES

In this category, the toys generally commanding the highest prices are horse-drawn cast-iron pieces. One reason for the eye-opening prices is that horse-drawn cast-iron toys have considerable value apart from their lure as toys. There is an air of genuine Americana about them and they are likely to attract the interest of many who otherwise pay no attention to toys (decorators figure largely in this area).

Since prices are often so high, reproductions, whether honest or dishonest, can be a problem. Things to look for when a reproduction is suspected include a rougher surface than an old toy would have (recastings are invariably rougher), uneven fit of pieces, a blurring of details, and "aging" that doesn't have the patina of age. Since at least one company, John Wright (formerly Grey Iron), is still manufacturing turn-of-the-century horse-drawn vehicles—some of them from the original molds—it is wise to become familiar with the field before investing heavily.

	C6	C8	C10
All-Nu Trotter, lead alloy, 1941, approx. 4" long	29	44	58

ALL-NU Trotter. Photo by Bill Kaufman. Courtesy Evelyn Besser.

ALTHOF, BERGMANN

Althof, Bergmann began in 1867, when L. Althof teamed with the brothers Bergmann to form a jobbing firm (the brothers were already jobbers). In 1874 the New York company received two patents, one for a bell toy with three soldiers. In addition to bell and animal-drawn toys, they made (or jobbed out) toy furniture, banks, and hoop and clockwork toys.

	C6	C8	C10
Althof, Bergmann "Express" Wagon pull toy, tin w/ iron wheels, 26"	3000	5000	8000
Althof, Bergmann "Fruits and Vegetables," 17-1/2" long	5000	7500	10,000
Althof, Bergmann Milk Cart, "Pure Milk," c. 1880, 14" long	500	750	1000
Althof, Bergmann "Milk Wagon," tin, 13" long	600	900	1200

ALTHOF, BERGMANN "Express" Wagon, 26" long. Courtesy Sotheby's New York. Courtesy Ed Hyers Antique Toys.

ALTHOF, BERGMANN "Milk Wagon," 13" long, tin. Courtesy Sotheby's New York.

ALTHOF, BERGMANN "Fruits and Vegetables." Courtesy Ed Hyers Antique Toys.

ARCADE

(All Arcade toys are cast iron)

	C6	C8	C10
Arcade Bakery Wagon, 13" long	300	450	600
Arcade "Big Six Circus & Wild West" Wagon, (see Movies: Tom Mix Big Six Circus, appears to be the same except for name), 14-1/2" long	425	638	850

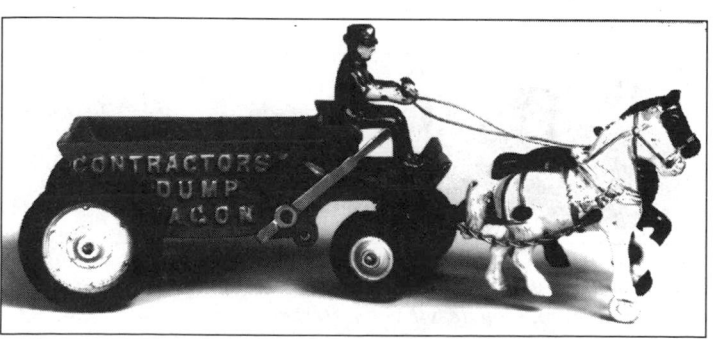

ARCADE "Contractors Dump Wagon." Courtesy Mapes} Auctioneers & Appraisers.

	C6	C8	C10
Arcade Circus Wagon, c. 1917	400	600	800
Arcade Cart, wicker, horse, driver, cast iron	100	150	200
Arcade Coal Car w/ Horse	150	225	300
Arcade Contractors Dump wagon, horse team, driver, 14" long	250	375	500
Arcade "Contractors Dump Wagon," 2 horses, driver, 1930s, 13-1/4"	230	345	460
Arcade Farm Wagon, 2 horses, driver, 10-3/4" long	463	695	925
Arcade McCormick Deering Plow	175	263	350
Arcade McCormick Deering Farm Wagon, 2 horses	400	600	800
Arcade McCormick Deering Manure Spreader, w/ team of horses, 14" long	375	562	750
Arcade Sulky Plow, 1 horse, 10-1/2"	150	250	350
Auburn Rubber Farm Wagon & Team	48	72	95
Bakery Wagon, 1 horse, cast iron, 13" long	100	200	300
Barclay "Animal Cage" Circus Wagon, c. 1930s, lead and tin, slush lead, approx. 9-7/8"	30	45	60
Barclay Coach and Four, slush lead, c. 1930s, approx. 10-1/4"	30	45	60

Toy Hansom Cab

A very good idea of the design of this toy can be formed from the illustration, but the decoration which we use is one of its strong selling points.

The cab itself is finished in brightly colored enamels. The driver wears a snappy uniform.

Altogether this is one of the most attractive toys that we have.
Extreme length 13½ inches. Extreme height 6½ inches.

PACKING

Each in a paper box, ¼ gross in a case.
Case weight, net 82 pounds, gross 109 pounds.
Case measurements, 32x22x12 inches.

Toy Ice Wagon

Every toy dealer should carry a large stock of these toy ice wagons as they are one of the largest sellers that we have.

It seems that an ice wagon is particularly attractive to children and this toy is correspondingly so.

We have made this of very heavy castings to stand rough handling and have decorated it with bright enamels.
Extreme length 12 inches. Extreme height 5½ inches.

PACKING

Each in a paper box, ¼ gross in a case.
Case weight, net 121 pounds, gross 153 pounds.
Case measurements, 26x22x17 inches.

167

A page from Arcade Catalog No. 26, with the date "1917" hand-stamped on it.

Circus Wagon

Every day is Circus Day for the child who has one of these toys. It is one of the most attractive items in our line. It fulfills the requirement of "a lot for the money."

The horses are black. The wagon is decorated in three brilliant colors. The driver wears the regulation circus uniform.

The extreme length of the toy including the horses is 14 inches.

The height, including driver is 9¾ inches.

No. 1 Circus Wagon includes the Animal.

No. 2 Circus Wagon is without the Animal.

Nos. 1 and 2 can also be supplied with four or six horse teams at a small additional cost.

PACKING

Packed each in a paper box, 3 dozen in a case.

No. 1.   Case weight, net 145 pounds, gross 170 pounds.
Case measurements, 56x20½x17 inches.

No. 2.   Case weight, net 125 pounds, gross 150 pounds.
Case measurements, 56x20½x17 inches.

A page from Arcade Catalog No. 26, with the hand-stamp "Received March 19, 1917" on it.

Toy Transfer Wagon

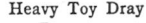

This is one of our most popular toys.
The body of the wagon is made of stamped steel, the other parts of cast iron.
The color scheme used adds greatly to the selling qualities of the toy.
No. 1.   Without seat and figure.
No. 2.   Complete as illustrated.

PACKING

No. 1.   ½ dozen in a paper box, ¼ gross in a case.
Case weight, net 54 pounds, gross 70 pounds.
Case measurements, 26x13x12 inches.
No. 2.   Each in a paper box, ¼ gross in a case.
Case weight, net 63 pounds, gross 84 pounds.
Case measurements, 25x16x13 inches.

Heavy Toy Dray

This is a strong, substantial toy made of the best grade of cast iron. It will stand very hard use.

The dray is finished in attractive enamels and helps to make it sell.
Extreme length 13½ inches. Extreme height 7½ inches.

PACKING

Each one packed in a paper box. 3 dozen in a case.
Case weight, net 126 pounds, gross 154 pounds.
Case measurements, 26x19x17 inches.

168

A page from Arcade Catalog No. 26, with the hand-stamp "Received March 19, 1917" on it.

ARCADE McCormick Deering Spreader.

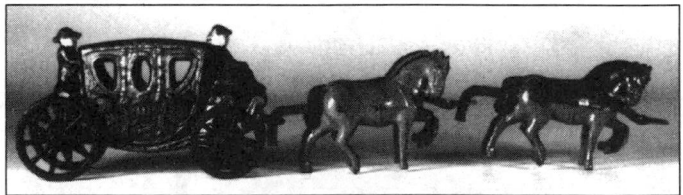

BARCLAY Coach and Four, approx. 10-1/4" long. Photo by Bill Kaufman. Courtesy Evelyn Besser.

	C6	C8	C10
Barclay Coach and Two, driver, no outrider	30	45	60
Barclay Covered Wagon w/ Oxen, 1930s, "1849," 7" long	27	38	55

	C6	C8	C10
"Barnum and Bailey" Circus Cage, elephant-drawn, 1930, painted, stained and litho wood, 35" long	400	600	800

BARCLAY Coach and Two, driver, no outrider. Photo by K. Warren Mitchell.

"Barnum and Bailey" Circus Cage, 35" long. Courtesy Lloyd W. Ralston Auctions.

BLISS

Bliss was founded about 1832 by Rufus Bliss. Toymaking may not have begun until the late 1860s or early 1870s in its Rehoboth, Massachusetts, plant, but we know that by 1871 its toys were being advertised. Most were made of wood. The range was wide: from doll houses to trains, Noah's arks, and ships. In 1883 Bliss made what might have been the first toy telephone set. The brilliant color lithography of Bliss's toys has made many of them prime collectibles.

	C6	C8	C10
Bliss Cinderella coach, 1890, paper litho on wood, 2 horses, 4 coachmen, lift off roof, blocks inside tell Cinderella story, 26" long	1000	3500	5500

BLISS Cinderella Coach, 1890. Courtesy Lloyd W. Ralston Auctions.

	C6	C8	C10
Bliss Fire Hook and Ladder, 2 firemen, 2 horses, 29" long	2000	3000	4000
Bliss Fire Hook and Ladder, paper litho on wood, 31" long	1500	2500	4000
Bliss Pansy 4-Horse Stagecoach, 1890, paper litho on wood, 31"	1000	1500	2500
Bliss "Rough and Ready" Fire Engine, 2 horses, 30" long	1600	2700	4000

BLISS Fire Hook & Ladder, 2 horses, approx. 30" long. Courtesy Wilkinson Collection, Detroit Antique Toy Museum.

BLISS Pansy 4-Horse Stagecoach, 1890. Courtesy Lloyd W. Ralston Auctions.

BLISS "Rough and Ready" Fire Engine (missing rear fireman). Courtesy Christie's East.

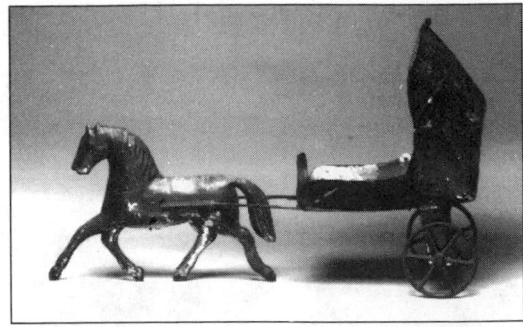

Buggy and Horse, tin. Courtesy Sotheby's New York.

	C6	C8	C10
"Borden's Farm Products," wood, horse-drawn wagon pull-toy with articulated legs	313	470	625
Bread Wagon "Bread and Cakes" w/ driver, tin horse, 12-1/2" long	350	525	700
Brewery Wagon, cast iron and pressed steel, 2 horses w/ driver, 20-1/2"	350	525	700

	C6	C8	C10
Brownie on Elephant-Drawn Cart, cast iron	400	700	1000
Buckboard, cast iron, 1 horse and driver, 14" long	200	300	400
Buggy and Horse, tin, 7" long	175	263	350
Buggy, pressed steel, cast-iron wheels and horse	40	60	80
Buggy w/ driver, cast iron, 6-1/2"	70	105	140

CARPENTER

Carpenter (Francis W.) of Harrison and Port Chester, New York, was in business from 1844 to 1925. Malleable iron was its trademark, malleable iron being a type that has a bit of give, making it less fragile. Its two predominant lines were horse-drawn toys and trains.

	C6	C8	C10
Carpenter Cart, animated, c. 1902, cast iron, 10-1/2" long	450	675	900
Carpenter Cart, 2 horses, 12" long	635	950	1270
Carpenter Cart, 2-wheel, 1 horse, no driver, pat. 1882	250	400	500
Carpenter Coal Cart, iron	2000	3000	4000
Carpenter Delivery Wagon, pat. 1881, 12" long	200	300	400
Carpenter Doctor's Cart	400	600	800
Carpenter Dump Cart, 1 horse, 12"	400	600	800
Carpenter Dump Cart, 2 horses	350	600	800
Carpenter Fire Patrol, cast iron, 2 horses, driver and 3 figures, 1885, 16-1/2" long	900	1400	1900
Carpenter Fire Wagon, 1 horse, 1 fireman	350	500	750

CARPENTER Fire Patrol, cast iron, 2 horses (one figure in photo missing). Courtesy Sotheby's New York.

	C6	C8	C10
Carpenter Hook and Ladder, 2 horses, 2 firemen in standard helmets, early	800	1200	1600
Carpenter Hook and Ladder, cast iron, 2 horses w/ driver and rear man, ladders c. 1883-1890, 26-1/2"	700	1050	1400
Carpenter Horse and Carriage, 1880, painted, cast iron, 14" long	750	1000	1500
Carpenter Horse Cart, cast iron, c. 1880, 1 horse, 2 men, 14-1/2" long	800	1200	1600
Carpenter Ox Cart, 2 oxen, cast iron, c. 1880-1903, 11" long	400	600	800
Carpenter Pumper, 2 horses, No. 33, 18" long	1100	1850	2800
Carpenter Tally-Ho, 4 horses, cast iron, 7 festive riders in coach, 27-1/2"	4000	9500	12,000
Carpenter Wagon, 2 horses, 10" long	550	850	1300
Carriage, metal and wood, 1 horse, malleable iron horse w/ articulated legs and tail, carriage made of wood	300	450	600

CARPENTER Doctor's Cart. Courtesy Ed Hyers Antique Toys.

CARPENTER. Left to right: Cart, 2 horses, 12" long. Dump Cart, 1 horse, 12" long (driver not correct in photo). Courtesy Sotheby's New York.

Cart, 1 horse, tin, 15" long. Courtesy Lloyd W. Ralston Auctions.

Chariot with Clown, Camel-Drawn. Courtesy James S. Maxwell/Virginia Caputo. Photo by Virginia Caputo.

CARPENTER "Tally-Ho," approx. 27-1/2" long. Courtesy Sotheby's New York.

CARPENTER Wagon, 2 horses, 16" long (driver in photo replaced). Courtesy Sotheby's New York.

DENT Hook and Ladder, 1915, 14" long. Courtesy Lloyd W. Ralston Auctions.

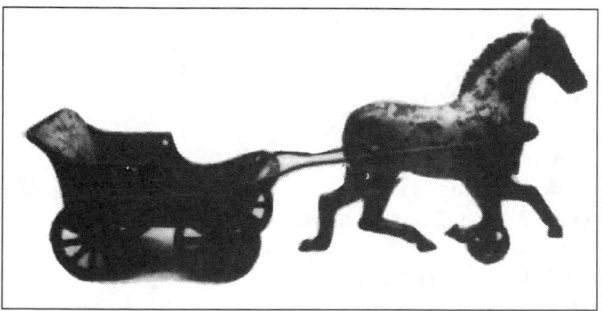

CARPENTER Horse and Carriage, 1880, 14" long. Courtesy Lloyd W. Ralston Auctions.

DENT Hose Reel, 3 horses. Courtesy Sotheby's New York.

	C6	C8	C10
Cart, bull-pulled, cast iron, 2-wheeled cart	100	150	200
Cart, cast-iron lion, 2 wheels, 8" long	125	188	250
Cart, 1 horse, cast iron, 9" long	75	112	150
Cart, 1 horse, early tin, 8" long	200	300	400
Cart, 1 horse, painted tin, 1890, 15" long	250	500	750
Cart w/ driver and buffalo, cast iron, 7-1/2" long	400	600	800
Cart w/ woman and prancing horse, cast iron, 10-1/4" long	500	750	1200
Cart w/ elephant, cast iron, 7" long	125	188	250
Cart, stake sides, 1 horse, early cast iron, 7" long	150	225	300
Chariot drawn by tin horse, highly decorated, 13-1/2" long	125	187	250
Chariot w/ clown, camel-drawn, cast iron	1000	1600	2400
Chein "Dispatch" Wagon, 1 horse, 11-1/2" long	90	135	180
Chief's Wagon, cast-iron "Chief," 1 horse, c. 1915-1920, 12" long	150	225	300
"Chief" Fire Chief Wagon, cast iron, 1 horse, 15-1/2" long	350	525	700
Circus Wagon, iron and tin, 2 horses, lion cage, 9" long	200	300	400
Circus Wagon, cast iron and wood, containing carved wood bear, 13" long	250	337	500
"City Sprinkler" cast iron, 8-1/4"	No Price Found		
Coal Wagon, cast iron, small	50	75	100
"Coal" Wagon, cast iron w/ driver and coal shovel, 9-1/4"	137	202	275
Conestoga Wagon, cast iron, w/ cloth cover and 2 horses, 12-1/2" long	50	75	100
Conestoga Wagon, litho walking horses, iron wheels, 18" long	140	210	280
Confectionary Wagon, early, 1 horse	500	750	1000
Converse "Delivery" Wagon, wood seat, 1 horse, c. 1915	350	525	700
Converse "Milk 16" Wagon	70	1100	1700
Converse "U.S. Mail 17" Wagon	700	1100	1700
Covered Wagon, cast iron, cloth top, 1 horse, driver, 13" long	170	255	340
Covered Wagon, tin, driver and horse, Indian head litho on side	40	60	80
Dent Buckboard, rider, 1 horse, very early, primitive looking	125	188	250
Dent Cart, horse and driver, 10" long	125	188	250
Dent Cart, lady driver, horse, 11" long	150	225	300
Dent Cart, mule, driver	250	375	500
Dent Contractors Dump Wagon, 2 horses, 15" long	150	225	300
Dent Coupe, 1 horse, driver, 9-3/4"	125	188	250
Dent Dray, 2 horses, driver	550	980	1300
Dent Dump Cart, black man, mule	300	450	600
Dent Fire Engine Pumper, silver w/ white horses, 2 horses, 21" long	400	750	1000
Dent Fire Engine Steam Pumper, 3 horses, 21" long	1000	1700	2400
Dent Fire Hook & Ladder, 27" long	1000	1700	2400
Dent Fire Patrol, 3 horses, firemen figures, 15-1/2" long	400	1000	2000
Dent Fire "Patrol," c. 1905, 3 horses, cast iron, driver, 6 riders, 22" long	1200	2000	2800
Dent Fire Pumper, c. 1908, 3 horses, driver, paint and nickel plate, 15-1/2"	500	800	1100
Dent Fire Snorkle Wagon, 3 horses, driver	500	750	1000
Dent Hansom Cab, cast iron, c. 1905, lady passenger, driver, 14" long	700	1150	1600
Dent No. 57 Hansom Cab, 2-wheeled, 1 horse	175	262	350
Dent Hook and Ladder, 3 horses, extra large	500	1000	1500
Dent Hook and Ladder, painted cast iron, 1915, mechanized horses, 14" long	250	400	800
Dent Hose Reel, 3 horses, figures, 24" long, 10" horse	1200	2000	2900
Dent Horse and Cart, cart is tin	150	225	300
Dent Horse and Cart, low sides, all cast iron	125	188	250
Dent "Ice" Wagon, 2 horses, 12" long	100	200	300
Dent "Ice" Wagon, 1 horse, 14" long	300	500	750
Dent "Ice" Wagon, cast iron, black horse pulling yellow and orange ice wagon, w/ driver, c. 1910, 15-1/2"	675	1000	1350
Dent Ladder Wagon, 1890, 4 horses, may be longest cast-iron toy made, 43-1/2"	3000	4500	6500
Dent Ox Wagon, 2 oxen, driver, cast iron, 16" long	250	500	600
Dent Ox Cart, stake sides, 1 ox	125	188	250
Dent Police Patrol, 3 horses, driver and 4 patrolmen, 21" long	800	1350	1875
Dent Pony Cart No. 20, has driver, team of horses, stake sides on cart	125	187	250
Dent Pumper, painted cast iron, 1915, moving horses, 14-1/2" long	650	1000	1500

DENT Pumper, 1915, 14-1/2" long. Courtesy Lloyd W. Ralston Auctions.

	C6	C8	C10
Dent Road Car, 1 horse, driver in top hat, 2 seats, 16" long	450	675	900
Dent Sleigh, 1 horse, c. 1905, 16-1/4"	900	1500	2200
Dent Small Truck Wagon, stake sides	200	300	400
Dent 1-horse Truck Wagon, stake sides, w/ driver, 16" long	200	300	400
Dent Sulky w/ Jockey	150	225	300
Dent Surrey, horse has wheel attached to one leg	200	300	400
Dent "Transfer" Wagon, 2 horses, 21" long	450	750	1150
Dent Transfer Wagon, 2 horses, driver, 26" long	500	850	1200
Dent Water Tower, c. 1910, 2 horses, 31" long	900	1500	2200
Doctors Cart, cast iron, 11" long	850	1450	2000
Dog Cart (baby carriage), black cloth top, tin, 5-1/2" long	75	112	150

DENT Fire Hook & Ladder, 27" long. Courtesy Christie's East.

Doctor's Cart, cast iron, 11" long. Courtesy Sotheby's New York.

DENT Water Tower, c. 1910 (driver missing). Courtesy Christie's East.

	C6	C8	C10
Dog Cart, c. 1875, tin, 10" long	400	600	800
Donkey and Cart, cast iron, w/ driver	200	300	400
Donkey and Cart, tin, iron star wheels, 8" long	300	450	600
Donkey and Cart, tin, 8-1/2" long	250	375	500
Dray, cast iron, 1 horse, black horse pulling dray, 14" long	150	225	300
Dray Wagon, cast iron, driver and 2 horses, 18" long	250	375	500
"Dry Goods" cloth and wood 2-horse drawn wagon pull-toy, c. 1860, 26" long	400	600	800

Dump Cart, "Hard and Soft Coal - Coke and Kindlings." Courtesy Lloyd W. Ralston Auctions.

	C6	C8	C10
Dump Cart, "Hard and Soft Coal-Coke and Kindlings," tin, 19" long	500	750	1000
"Dump Cart," horse pulling cart pull toy, 7-3/4" long	80	120	160
Dump Truck, cast iron and tin, 1 horse	200	300	400

JAMES FALLOWS

James Fallows was a foreman at the very early American tin toy company Francis, Field and Francis. In 1874 he formed James Fallows & Company in Philadelphia. His toys were often marked "IXL," which may have stood for "I excel." Most of Fallows's toys were tin, though often with cast-iron wheels. Papier mache was another primary material in a toy line that consisted of over 200 items.

	C6	C8	C10
Fallows Cart, tin, 12" long	500	750	1000
Fallows Cart and Horse, painted tin, 1870, 8-1/2" long	100	200	400

FALLOWS Covered Wagon, 12" long. Courtesy Lloyd W. Ralston Auctions.

FALLOWS Horse and Carriage, 1890, 12-1/2" long. Courtesy Lloyd W. Ralston Auctions.

	C6	C8	C10
Fallows Covered Wagon, painted tin, litho paper scenes on sides, 12"	800	1000	1500
Fallows "Dump Cart," 1 horse, tin, c. 1890, 16" long	600	1000	1200
Fallows "Fancy Goods and Toys," 21" long	1750	2625	3500
Fallows "Fine Groceries" Delivery Wagon, 7-1/2" long	1250	1875	2500
Fallows Fire Pumper, 2 horses, very early, 18" long	5000	8500	10,000
Fallows Fire Pumper, tin, very early, 24" long	5000	10,000	15,000
Fallows Horse and Carriage, 1890, American painted and stenciled tin, 12-1/2" long	500	750	1000
Fallows "Pure Milk" Wagon, 1895, painted and stenciled tin, 12-1/2"	800	1200	2000

FALLOWS "Pure Milk" Wagon, 12-1/2" long. Courtesy Lloyd W. Ralston Auctions.

	C6	C8	C10
Fallows Streetcar, "4th Avenue," 1 horse, tin	500	800	1200
Fallows Streetcar, 9" long	400	600	900
Fallows Streetcar, 2 horses, 10" long	350	500	800
Fallows Wagon and Donkey, cast iron, 10-1/2" long	175	263	350
Farm Wagon, cast iron, 2 horses, 10"	200	300	400
Farm Wagon, cast iron, 2 unusual horses, w/ driver, 14" long	250	375	500
Farm Wagon, cast iron, large heavy horses, body wood, 25-1/2" long	300	450	600
Farm Wagon, tin, w/ horse, 10-1/2"	40	60	80
"Fine Groceries," tin wagon, 2 horses, 14" long	400	600	800

FALLOWS Streetcar, "4th Avenue." Courtesy Ed Hyers Antique Toys.

	C6	C8	C10
Fire Hose Reel, cast iron, horse-drawn, 6" long	150	225	300
"Fire Patrol," cast iron, 3 horses, wagon contains 2 firemen and driver, 17" long	900	1350	1800
"Fire Patrol," 3 horses, driver, riders, 18-3/4" long	1000	1500	2000
"Fire Patrol" cast iron, 2 horses, 3 firemen, driver, c. 1910, 19"	1250	1875	2500
"Fire Patrol," cast iron, 2 horses, 3 firemen, 1 driver, c. 1890, 20-1/2" long	600	950	1300
Fire Pumper, cast iron, 3 horses, 11-1/4"	500	750	1000
Fire Pumper, cast iron, 2 horses w/ driver, 13" long	600	900	1200
Fire Pumper, cast iron, 3 horses, 14-1/2"	650	1050	1500
Fire Pumper, cast iron, 2 horses, driver, 19-3/4" long	500	750	1000
Fire Pumper, c. 1910, cast iron, 3 horses, 17-1/2" long	500	750	1000
Fire Pumper, cast iron, 3 horses w/ driver, fireman, c. 1910, 18-1/4" long	425	638	850

"Fire Patrol," cast iron, 2 horses, 3 firemen and driver, 20-1/2" long, c. 1890. Courtesy Phillips New York.

	C6	C8	C10
Francis, Field and Francis Doctor's Buggy, 1 horse, tin, c. 1860, 14"			No Price Found
"Friendship 1774" Fire Pumper, cast iron, rubber hose, 16" long	375	563	750

"Friendship 1774" Fire Pumper, 16" long. Courtesy Christie's East.

GEORGE BROWN

In 1856 George W. Brown, with Chauncey Goodrich, founded George W. Brown and Company, toymakers. Brown, an innovator, introduced the American clockwork toy (he'd spent 11 years in the clockmaking business). He invented many of his toys' mechanisms and may also have designed all or most of his toys. Brown worked primarily in tin, jobbing some of the work out to companies like Union Manufacturing Company in Clinton, Connecticut. Necessarily simple because of the material and manufacturing techniques employed, Brown's toys made up for it with brilliant hand-painted color and stenciling. Tops, rattles, flutes, wagons, fire engines, swords, trains, and toy buckets were among the many items put out by the firm. The company merged with Stevens in 1868 and was dissolved in 1880.

	C6	C8	C10
George Brown Cab, driver, 1 horse, 8-1/2" long	560	840	1120
George Brown Cart and Horse, 1880, painted and stenciled tin, 7-1/2" long	200	300	500

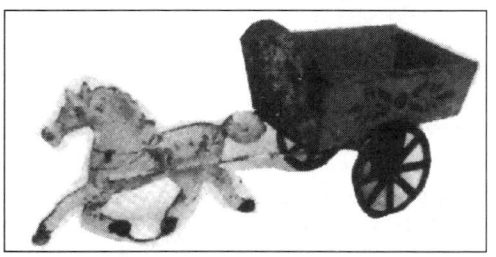

GEORGE BROWN Cart and Horse, 1880, 7-1/2" long. Courtesy Lloyd W. Ralston Auctions.

	C6	C8	C10
George Brown "Charles" Hose Reel, c. 1870, tin, 15" long, auctioned in 1991 for $231,000			
George Brown Delivery Cart, 12"	1100	1800	2600
George Brown Doctor's Buggy, tin, cast iron, 14" long	650	975	1300
George Brown Dog Cart, c. 1870	400	700	1000
George Brown Dump Cart, painted tin, 1885, 8-1/4" long	100	150	200

GEORGE BROWN Dump Cart, 1885, 8-1/4" long. Courtesy Lloyd W. Ralston Auctions.

	C6	C8	C10
George Brown Dump Cart, 1880, tin, back gate lifts out for dumping, 13"	200	300	400
George Brown "Eagle Chariot," painted tin, 1870, 11" long	500	1000	2500

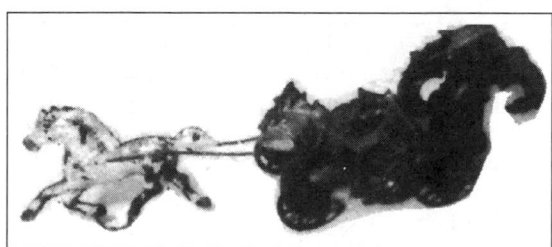

GEORGE BROWN Eagle Chariot. Courtesy Lloyd W. Ralston Auctions.

GEORGE BROWN "Express" Wagon, 10-1/2" long. Courtesy Sotheby's New York.

	C6	C8	C10
George Brown "Express" Wagon, tin w/ iron wheels, 10-1/2" long	300	450	600
George Brown "Fine Groceries" Cart and horse	1250	1875	2500
George Brown Gig, tin, 9" long	300	450	600
George Brown Gig, tin, 1 horse, 10" long	150	225	300
George Brown Goat Cart, 7" long	300	450	600
George Brown "Grand Central Depot" tin trolley, 2 horses, 13-1/2" long	600	950	1350
George Brown Horse Cart, 1870, tin, 11-1/2" long	125	188	250
George Brown Ox Cart, 1880, painted tin, 9" long	500	1000	2000

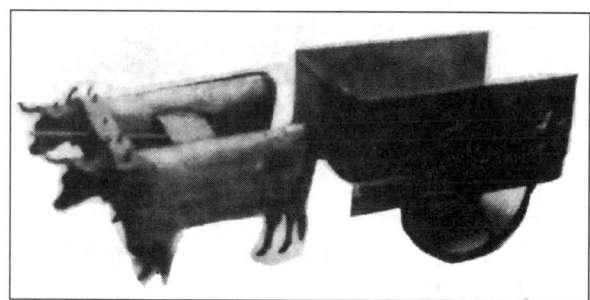

GEORGE BROWN Ox Cart, 9" long. Courtesy Lloyd W. Ralston Auctions.

	C6	C8	C10
George Brown Peddle Wagon, tin, c. 1880, 2 wheeled horses, driver, awning, 20" long	1000	2500	5000
George Brown Rockaway Passenger Cart, 2 horses, 13" long	1850	2500	4500
George Brown Sulky, 8-3/4" long	250	375	500
George Brown Sulky, clockwork, 13" long	3000	5500	9000
George Brown Yankee Notions Peddler Wagon, 16-1/2" long	3000	7000	10000

GIBBS

Gibbs Manufacturing Company of Canton, Ohio, began turning out toys in 1896 (after manufacturing wooden barrels and tubs and metal plows since about 1830). The company's first toy was a political giveaway for William McKinley, who was from Canton. The first toy was a spring-operated top, and variations of it remained in the firm's catalogs until 1969, when it stopped making toys. Most Gibbs toys were wood or tin, with much use made of lithographed paper for decoration. Many of Gibbs's playthings were of the push and pull variety. Lewis Gibbs was the original owner.

	C6	C8	C10
Gibbs No. 6 Pony Chariot	165	250	350
Gibbs No. 14 "Delivery 14"	150	225	300
Gibbs No. 15 Pony Pacer, 7" long	115	172	230
Gibbs No. 27 "U.S. Mail" Cart	300	450	600

GIBBS "U.S. Mail" No. 27, 12" long. Courtesy Wilkinson Collection, Detroit Antique Toy Museum.

Gibbs No. 32 Pioneer Wagon	66	99	132
Gibbs No. 35 "Pacing Joe"	175	263	350
Gibbs No. 40 English Pony Cart	110	165	220
Gibbs No. 50 "Gray Beauty Pacers"	150	225	300

GIBBS No. 50 "Gray Beauty Pacers." Courtesy Lloyd W. Ralston Auctions.

Gibbs No. 53 "Pony Circus" Wagon	200	300	400
Gibbs No. 56 "Yankee" Dump Cart	225	338	450
Gibbs No. 57 "Gypsy Wagon"	250	375	500
Gibbs Cart and Horse, paper litho on wood, 13" long	150	225	300
Gibbs Dog Cart, boy driver	375	562	750
Gibbs "Groceries The Great Atlantic and Pacific Tea Co." mule-drawn cart, 12" long	350	500	1000
Gibbs Hay Wagon, 2 horses, 19" long	100	150	200
Gibbs Tea Co. Mule Cart	350	500	1000

No. 830.

Little, if anything, is known about Grey Iron's animal-drawn toys. This "Ice" wagon appears in a 1920s catalog. Probably the toy originated earlier. It seems to have come in three sizes: No. 825 at 10-1/4" long; No. 830 at 12-1/2" long; and No. 845 at 14-5/8" long.

	C6	C8	C10
Girard Wagon, 2 tin horses, stake sides	125	188	250
Goat Cart, iron goat and wheels, tin cart, 7-1/2" long	100	150	200
Goat Cart, tin, early, 10-1/2" long	150	225	300

"Golden Pasture Farm Products, Milk and Cream." Courtesy Lloyd W. Ralston Auctions.

"Golden Pasture Farm Products, Milk & Cream," 1915, horse-drawn milk wagon, steering mechanism for child to ride, painted and stenciled wood, 30" long	500	750	100
Grass Cutter, 2 horses, driver, 2-wheeled cart, cast iron	1000	1500	2000
Hansom Cab, cast iron, no horse or figures	1500	2250	3000
Hansom Cab, 8" long	150	225	300
Hansom Cab w/ driver, cast iron, 9-1/2"	120	188	250
Hansom Cab w/ driver, cast iron, 9-3/4"	250	375	500
Hansom Cab, 1 horse, driver, cast iron, 10" long	285	426	570
Hansom Cab, tin, movable legs on horse, 15-1/2" long	175	263	350

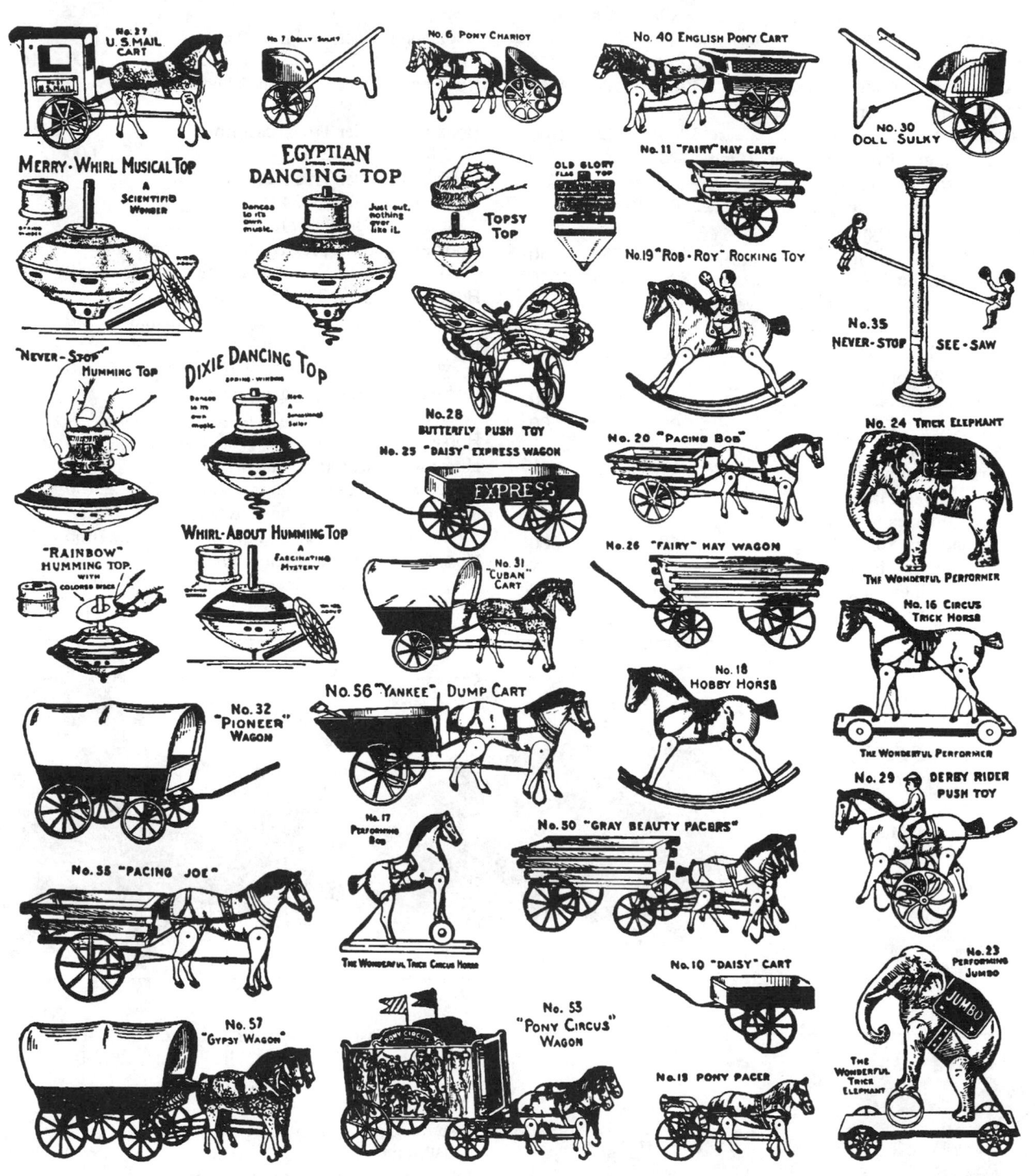

GIBBS TOYS

The best selling and most attractive toys on the market. Children cannot resist them. You have only to put Gibbs Toys on your counters and they sell themselves. All jobbers carry Gibbs Toys.

TO RETAIL AT 5c., 10c., 25c., 50c.

Gibbs Toys are always on display at our New York Agents

THE GIBBS MFG. CO. CANTON OHIO

NEW YORK AGENTS

The Owens-Kreiser Co.
The Strobel & Wilken Co.

Geo. Borgfeldt & Co.
Baker & Bennett Co.

An April 1914 Gibbs ad.

HARRIS

Harris Toy Company of Toledo, Ohio, seems to have begun production of cast-iron toys during the late 1880s. The firm, which also jobbed for Dent, Hubley and Wilkins, stopped making toys in 1913.

	C6	C8	C10
Harris Brownie Shell Cart, 1903, cast iron	225	338	450
Harris Cart, mule driver, 10" long	250	500	750
Harris "City Truck," 1 horse, driver	1300	2000	3150
Harris "City Truck," 2 horses, driver, 15" long	1200	1900	2700
Harris Dog Cart, girl driver, cast iron, 7" long	275	363	550
Harris "Fire Patrol" wagon, driver, 3 riders, 2 horses, 19" long	800	1400	1900
Harris Goat Cart, shell-type, cast iron, driver, 5" long	100	250	350
Harris Goat Cart, rider, 9-1/2" long	800	1425	1950
Harris Goat Cart, 2 goats, cast iron, driver	1000	2500	3000
Harris Hook and Ladder, 3 horses, cast iron, 19" long	140	210	280
Harris Transfer Wagon, 1903, 3 horses, 18-1/2" long	400	650	850
Harris Wagon, mule, 12" long	300	450	600
"Hood's Milk," Rich Toys, wood and tin, horse-drawn wagon pull-toy	37	56	75
Hook and Ladder, cast iron, tin and wood, 2 horses w/ driver and three ladders, 16-1/2" long	150	225	300
Hook and Ladder, cast iron and tin, 3 horses, 2 firemen, ladders, 21"	175	263	350

	C6	C8	C10
Hook and Ladder, cast iron, 2 horses, 22-3/4" long	1000	1650	2000
Hook and Ladder, cast iron, 3 horses w/ driver, 25" long	500	750	1000
Hook and Ladder Truck, cast iron, 3 horses, 25-1/2" long	600	900	1200
Hook and Ladder Truck, cast iron, 3 horses, 2 drivers, 4 ladders, c. 1910-1914, 31-1/4" long	1000	1500	2000
Hook and Ladder, pressed steel and iron, figures, ladders, unusual hanging horses	250	375	500
Hook and Ladder, 3 horses, driver, 27-1/2" long	750	1125	1500
Hook and Ladder, wood ladder w/ figurines, 3 horses, 29-1/2" long	750	1125	1500
Horse and Cart, litho paper on wooden horse, tin cart	150	225	300
Horse pulling 2-wheel cart, tin	450	675	900
Horse w/ open carriage and driver in top hat, tin, 5-1/2" long	150	225	300
Hose Reel, cast iron, 1 horse w/ driver, 11" long	1000	1650	2500
Hose Reel, cast iron, 1 horse w/ driver, 12" long	1000	1650	2500

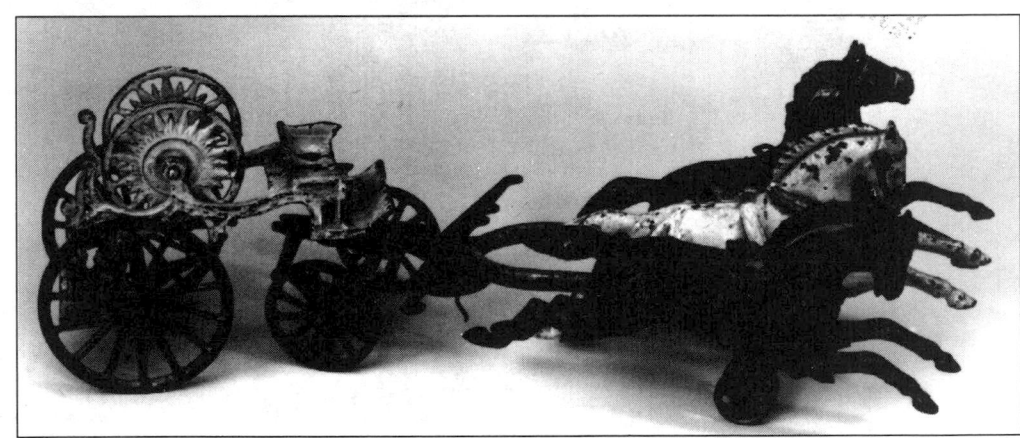

HOSE REEL, cast iron, 3 horses, 19" long. Courtesy Mapes Auctioneers & Appraisers.

HUBLEY Brake, 4-seat, 4 horses, 8 articulated passengers. Courtesy Sotheby's New York.

	C6	C8	C10
Hose Reel, cast iron w/ driver and cord fire hose, 1 horse, 12-1/2" long	500	750	1000
Hose Reel, early, 2 horses, cast iron, w/ figure, 14-1/2" long	500	750	1000
Hose Reel, cast iron, 3 horses, c. 1910, 19" long	600	900	1200
Hose Reel, Wagon, cast iron, driver, 2 horses, man standing on rear bumper, 21" long	750	1125	1500
Hose Reel, cast iron, c. 1910-1914, 3 horses w/ driver and fireman, 21"	1000	1500	2000
Hose Reel, early, cast iron, unusual horse	500	750	1000
Hose Wagon, cast iron, 2 firemen, 3 horses and bell, 21-1/2" long	750	1125	1500

HUBLEY Brakes. Left to right: 2-seat and 3-seat. Courtesy Sotheby's New York.

HUBLEY Chariot with clown, early, cast iron, 3 horses, 12-1/2" long. Courtesy Ed Hyers Antique Toys.

HUBLEY Coal Wagon, 16" long, 2 horses. Courtesy Sotheby's New York.

HUBLEY Fire Pumper, 3 horses, cast iron, 22" long. Photo by Jeanne Bertoia. Courtesy Bill Bertoia Auctions.

HUBLEY "Dray," 22" long (driver and horses in photo wrong). Courtesy Sotheby's New York.

HUBLEY Hook & Ladder Wagon, "126." Photo by Jeanne Bertoia. Courtesy Bill Bertoia Auctions.

HUBLEY Hose Reel, 1 horse, 3 figures, 13" long (figures in photo replacements). Photo by Jeanne Bertoia. Courtesy Bill Bertoia Auctions.

HUBLEY Brake, 2-seat, 16" long. Courtesy Sotheby's New York.

	C6	C8	C10
Hubley Brake, 4-seated, 4 horses, 8 articulated passengers, 28"	2000	3500	5625
Hubley Brake, 3-seated, 2 horses, cast iron, 18" long	4000	7000	12,500
Hubley Brake, 3-seated, 4 horses, cast iron, 18" long	4200	7300	13,000
Hubley Brake, 2-seated, driver, 3 women passengers, 16-1/2" long	2500	5000	7500
Hubley Brake, 2-seated, 16" long	1600	2700	4000
Hubley Brougham, cast iron and nickeled, horse and driver, 16" long	300	1000	1500
Hubley Brougham, top-hatted driver, 1 horse, 17" long	550	850	1300
Hubley Cab, 14" long	300	500	700

HUBLEY Cab, 14" long. Courtesy Sotheby's New York.

	C6	C8	C10
Hubley Cane Wagon, 15" long	600	900	1200
Hubley Cart, driver, 5-1/2" long	150	225	300
Hubley Cart, horse and driver, 8" long	155	232	310
Hubley Cart, wood, iron wheels, iron horse, 1910, 10-1/2" long	175	263	350
Hubley Chariot, cast iron, 8-3/4" long	500	750	1000
Hubley Chariot, 2 horses, driver, 9-1/2"	600	900	1200
Hubley Chariot w/ clown, early, cast iron, 3 horses, 12-1/2" long	800	1200	1600
Hubley Chariot Bank, elephant-drawn, 13" long	650	1100	1600
...ley Chariot, Roman, w/ driver, ...ses, 16" long	200	300	400

nimal-Drawn

	C6	C8	C10
Hubley Coal Wagon, 2 horses, 16"	500	750	1000
Hubley Coal Wagon, mule, 9" long	300	450	600
Hubley Conestoga Wagon, tin & cloth canopy, 2 horses, 15" long	550	825	1350
Hubley "Dray," 22" long	375	562	750
Hubley "Dray" Barrel Wagon w/ barrels, barrel ramp, driver, 2 horses, 23" long	1100	1750	2500
Hubley "Eagle Milk & Cream" Wagon, 12" long	500	750	1000
Hubley Essex Trap, 1890, cast iron, driver and horse, 13" long	500	1500	2500
Hubley Expandable Wagon w/ wood bed, cast iron, 2 horses, driver, 26"	750	1125	1500
Hubley Farm Wagon, 1 horse, c. 1915, cast iron, 12-1/2" long	400	600	800
Hubley Fire Patrol, driver, 4 riders, all in standard helmets, 13" long	750	1200	1750
Hubley Fire Patrol, driver, 4 firemen, prancing horse team, 21" long	700	1100	1500
Hubley Fire Pumper, cast iron, 2 horses w/ driver, c. 1910, 14" long	200	400	600
Hubley Fire Pumper, cast iron, 2 horses, white-painted, c. 1906-1910, 19" long	500	775	1100
Hubley Fire Pumper, 2 horses, cast iron, w/ driver and 2 firemen, 20" long	750	1125	1500
Hubley Fire Pumper, 3 horses, w/ driver, c. 1906-1910, 20-1/2" long	800	1200	1600
Hubley Fire Pumper, 2 horses, cast iron, w/ American Eagle, c. 1905-1910, 21" long	500	1000	1500
Hubley Fire Pumper, 3 horses, cast iron, 22" long	800	1400	2090
Hubley Gig, lady driver, horse-drawn, 15" long	350	650	950
Hubley Hansom Cab, driver cast in window, horse	300	500	750
Hubley Hook and Ladder, 3 horses, 2 firemen, 2 wooden ladders, c. 1906-1910, 27-3/4" long	550	850	1300
Hubley Hook and Ladder, 2 horses, cast iron, 28" long	700	1200	1650
Hubley Hook and Ladder Wagon, 3 horses, w/ eagle on shield on side, 33" long	1000	1700	2450
Hubley Hook and Ladder Wagon "126," 3 horses, 33-1/2" long	438	657	875
Hubley Hose Reel, cast iron, 3 horses w/ driver, c. 1906, 19" long	750	1200	1700
Hubley Hose Reel, 1 horse, 3 figures, 13" long	500	750	1000
Hubley Hose Tower Wagon, c. 1915, 28" long	800	1300	1800
Hubley Ice Wagon, 8" long	100	150	200
Hubley "Ice Wagon," 1920s, 9-1/2"	175	263	350
Hubley "Ice Wagon," 1910, cast iron, driver, horse, paint and nickel plate, 14"	400	850	1200
Hubley "Ice" Wagon, 1 horse, 15"	800	1300	2000
Hubley "Ice" Wagon, 2 horses, cast iron, 15" long	500	800	1200
Hubley "Ice" Wagon, 2 horses, cast iron, black horses pulling green wagon, w/ driver, c. 1906, 15-1/2" long	800	1300	2000

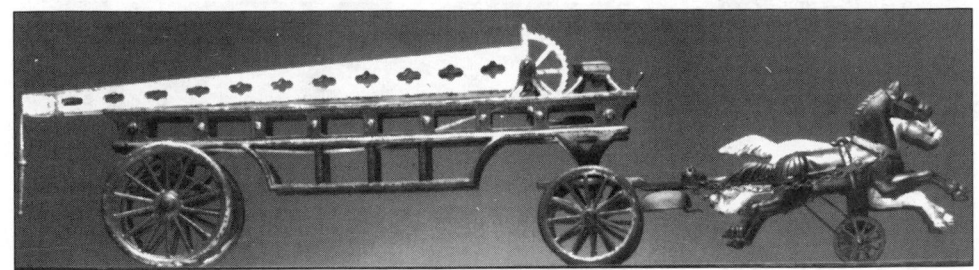

HUBLEY Hose Tower Wagon, c. 1915, 28" long. Courtesy Sotheby's New York.

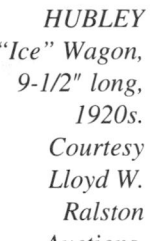

HUBLEY "Ice" Wagon, 9-1/2" long, 1920s. Courtesy Lloyd W. Ralston Auctions.

HUBLEY "Ice" Wagon, 1 horse, 15" long. Courtesy Sotheby's New York.

HUBLEY Landau Carriage, 1905, 16-1/2" long. Courtesy Lloyd W. Ralston Auctions.

HUBLEY Log Wagon, 15" long, 2 oxen, driver. Courtesy Ed Hyers Antique Toys.

HUBLEY "Police Patrol," 21" long. Courtesy Sotheby's New York.

HUBLEY "Royal Circus" Farmer Van. Photo by Jeanne Bertoia. Courtesy Bill Bertoia Auctions.

HUBLEY "Royal Circus" Lion Cage. Photo by Jeanne Bertoia. Courtesy Bill Bertoia Auctions.

	C6	C8	C10
Hubley "Ice" Wagon, driver, 2 horses, 16-1/2" long	1000	1650	2200
Hubley Landau Carriage, 1905, painted cast iron, 16-1/2" long	1400	2100	2800
Hubley Log Wagon, 2 oxen, driver, c. 1905, 15" long	500	750	1100
Hubley Log Wagon, horse, 19" long	400	600	800
Hubley Milk Cart, 12-1/2" long	425	638	850
Hubley Milk Wagon, 5" long	140	210	280
Hubley Monkey Trapeze Circus Mirror Van, 12-1/2" long	500	800	1300

HUBLEY "Royal Circus" Calliope, 12-3/4" (medium).
Courtesy Ed Hyers Antique Toys.

HUBLEY Monkey Trapeze Circus Van, 12-1/2"
long. Courtesy Christie's East.

	C6	C8	C10
Hubley Phaeton, 1 horse	1200	2000	3000
Hubley "Police Patrol," driver, early, 3 riders, 13" long	500	750	1000
Hubley "Police Patrol," driver, riders, 17-1/2" long	600	950	1430
Hubley "Police Patrol," driver, 6 cops, 21" long	1000	1600	2200
Hubley Revolving Monkey Cage auctioned for $30,000 in 1988			
Hubley Roman Chariot, 3 small horses	425	637	850
Hubley Roman Chariot, 3 large horses	600	900	1200
Hubley Royal Circus, animals, driver, 2 horses, 15" long	500	1000	1200
Hubley Royal Circus Band Wagon, cast iron, 4 horses, 7 riders, 22"	1000	2000	3000
Hubley Royal Circus Band Wagon, c. 1920, cast iron, 2 horses, 7 riders, 22-1/2"	1800	2900	4000
Hubley "Royal Circus" Bandwagon, 8 musicians and driver, 1920, 30"	1500	2250	3000

HUBLEY "Royal Circus" Lion Wagon, 15-3/4" long with rare
grey horses and wagon. Courtesy Ed Hyers Antique Toys.

	C6	C8	C10
Hubley Royal Circus Bear Wagon, cast iron, 15" long	1500	2250	3000
Hubley "Royal Circus" Calliope, 12-3/4" long (medium)	1400	2400	3400
Hubley "Royal Circus" Clown on Trapeze Van, 1920, oval-mirrored sides, 16-1/2"	1600	2700	4000
Hubley "Royal Circus" Farmer Van, 1920, head revolves and disappears in top of wagon as toy pulled, 16" long	1700	1850	4250
Hubley "Royal Circus" Giraffe Cage w/ large and small giraffes, driver, 1920, 27" long	3000	5500	9200
Hubley Royal Circus Lion Cage, 9"	375	563	750
Hubley "Royal Circus" Lion Wagon, w/ rare grey horses and wagon, 15-3/4"	700	1100	1650
Hubley Royal Circus Polar Bear Cage, 1920s, 11-3/4" long	600	1000	1375

HUBLEY Royal Circus Bear Wagon, 15" long. Courtesy
Sotheby's New York.

Animal-Drawn

HUBLEY "Royal Circus" Polar Bear Cage. Photo by Jeanne Bertoia. Courtesy Bill Bertoia Auctions.

	C6	C8	C10
Hubley Royal Circus Rhino Wagon, 16" long	850	1700	2500
Hubley "Royal Circus" Tiger Wagon Cage, 1920, driver, 2 tigers, 16" long	500	750	1000
Hubley Santa Claus Sleigh, early, 1 reindeer, 15" long	1500	2500	4000
Hubley Santa Claus Sleigh, 1910, cast iron, 2 reindeer, 16" long	600	1000	1500
Hubley Santa Claus Sleigh, early, 17" long	800	1300	2000
Hubley Shell Cart and Horse, 1905, 7" long	250	375	500
Hubley Sleigh, 1 horse, painted, cast iron, 1910, 14-1/2" long	500	800	1200
Hubley Sleigh, 1 horse, woman w/ movable arms, early, 14-3/4" long	700	1200	1700
Hubley Sleigh, 1 horse, 1900, painted cast iron, nickel plated, 15" long	250	375	500

HUBLEY "Royal Circus" Band Wagon, 22" long, 4 horses, 7 riders (driver in photo incorrect). Courtesy Sotheby's New York.

	C6	C8	C10
Hubley Sleigh, 2 horses, 1910, painted, nickel plated, cast iron, 15" long	800	1300	2000
Hubley Spring Wagon, horse, driver, cast iron	200	300	400
Hubley Stanhope Gig, cast iron, 11-1/2"	200	300	400
Hubley Sulky, 8-1/2" long	187	280	375
Hubley Surrey, clockwork, 1894, cast iron, brass works, 5 colors, 9" long	500	1000	1500
Hubley Surrey, 1 horse, lady driver, 13-3/4" long	318	475	635

HUBLEY Santa Claus Sleigh, 16" long. Courtesy Sotheby's New York.

HUBLEY. Left to right: Royal Circus Band Wagon, 30" long. Revolving Monkey Cage (extremely rare). Courtesy Sotheby's New York.

HUBLEY "Royal Circus." Left to right: Rhino Wagon, Tiger Wagon. Courtesy Sotheby's New York.

	C6	C8	C10
Hubley Surrey, 2 horses, driver, rider, c. 1900, 12" long......240		360	480
Hubley Surrey, 2 horses, woman driver, 13-3/4" long......750		1125	1500
Hubley Surrey, 2 horses, driver, 18"......400		600	800
Hubley Surrey, tin and cast iron, 2-seat w/ driver and woman passenger, 2 horses..600		900	1200
Hubley Surrey, 2-seat, driver, woman passenger, 2 horses, 13-3/4" long......600		900	1200
Hubley Trotter, 1900, cast iron, horse and driver, 8-3/4" long......200		300	400
Hubley Trotter Gig, lady driver, 11"......150		225	300
Hubley Wagon, horse, cast iron, 12"......150		225	300
Hull & Stafford Dump Cart......700		1000	1600
Hull & Stafford Express Wagon......350		550	750
Hull & Stafford Gig, China doll, c. 1885, 12" long......650		1150	1500

	C6	C8	C10
Hull & Stafford Liberty Hose Reel, c. 1870, 15-3/8", auctioned in touched-up condition in 1993 for $22,000			
Hull & Stafford "Prospect Park" Omnibus, c. 1880, 2 horses, driver, 16-1/2"......5000		10,000	15,000
Hull & Stafford Wagon, 9" long......800		1400	2000
Ice Cart, tin, horse-drawn......200		300	400
"Ice" Wagon, 1 horse, cast iron, 12"......500		750	1000
Ice Wagon, cast iron, 2 horses, 12"......600		900	1200
Ideal Fire Pumper, 2 horses, cast iron, 2 riders, 20-1/2" long......250		500	750
"Ideal Fire Department," 3 horses, cast iron, 30" long......500		1000	1500
Ideal "Patrol" cast-iron fire patrol, 21" long......1000		1700	2500

HUBLEY Sleigh, 1 horse, 14-1/4" long. Courtesy Lloyd W. Ralston Auctions.

HUBLEY Stanhope Gig. Courtesy Sotheby's New York.

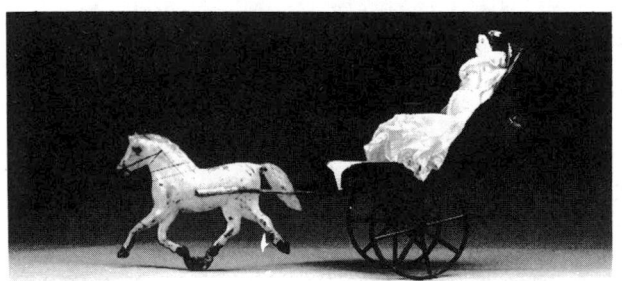

HULL & STAFFORD Gig, China Doll. Courtesy Christie's East.

IDEAL "Patrol," cast-iron Fire Patrol, 21" long. Courtesy Sotheby's New York.

IVES

Ives is one of the fabled companies in American toy history. It was founded by Riley Ives as a metal stamping shop by at least the late 1850s. About 1865 the company made tin whistles for New York Rubber's squeak toys. This seems to have led to Ives' first true toys: hot air playthings that were put in motion by the hot air from stoves, lanterns, etc. These were first sold in 1868. Son Edward Ives joined about 1860.

Edward's son, Harry, took over the reins in 1895. He was ousted in 1929 and the firm was dissolved in 1932. During its heyday, which lasted about 40 years, the firm put out a deluge of toys of every type, and quality was its watchword. Toymaking was carried on in Bridgeport, Connecticut, from about 1870 until the end.

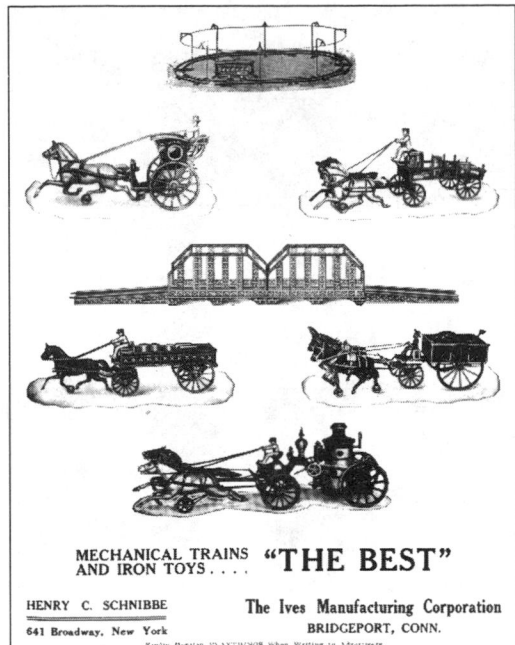

IVES toys from November, 1908. Courtesy Playthings magazine.

IVES Bandwagon, 31-1/2" long, 5 figures missing in photo. Courtesy James S. Maxwell/Virginia Caputo. Photo by Virginia Caputo.

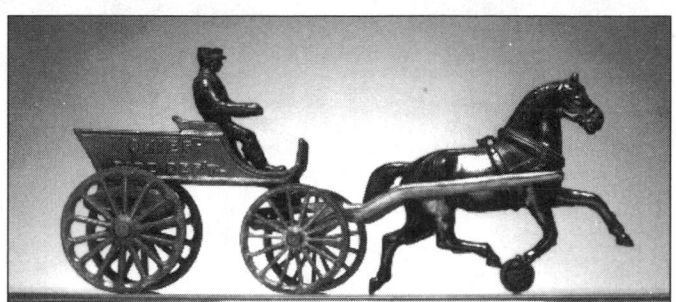

IVES "Chief Fire Dept.," 14-1/2" long (driver in photo incorrect). Courtesy Sotheby's New York.

	C6	C8	C10
Ives "Adams Express," 2 horses, 21"	750	1300	1800
Ives Bandwagon, 9 passengers, cast iron, 31-1/2" long	2500	4000	6000
Ives "Brewery Wagon," 2 horses, 18-1/2" long	1000	1700	2500
Ives Caisson, driver, cannon, rider, 2 horses, 21" long	1700	3000	4000
Ives "Chief Fire Dept.," 14-1/2" long	400	700	1000
Ives Coal Dump Cart, donkey, black driver	363	545	725
Ives Coal Dump Wagon, donkey, black driver	375	562	750

	C6	C8	C10
Ives Doctor's Cart, 2 wheels, 10-1/4"	400	600	1000
Ives Dog Pulling Stake Cart	200	300	400
Ives Donkey Cart, 1 of 4 walking animal toys by Ives, c. 1890, cast iron, 15" long	1300	2300	3300
Ives Dray Wagon, stake sides, 1 horse, 15" long	1100	2100	3000
Ives "Fast Mail" Wagon, cast iron, walking horses, 17" long	750	2000	3500
Ives "Fire Patrol," c. 1890, 1 horse, 5 riders, driver, 19" long	1200	1900	2700
Ives "Fire Patrol," 2 horses, driver, cast iron, 6 firemen, c. 1880-1910, 20-1/2"	900	1400	2200

IVES Coal Dump Wagon, Courtesy Sotheby's New York.

IVES "Fire Patrol," 20-1/2" long. Courtesy Sotheby's New York.

	C6	C8	C10
Ives Fire Pumper, 2 horses, 13" long	400	650	900
Ives Gig, 1890s, driver w/ top hat, 5-1/2" long	500	750	1000
Ives Hansom Cab w/ walking horse, oversized, 18" long	1500	2500	4000

IVES Dray Wagon, stake sides, 17" long. Courtesy Sotheby's New York.

IVES Hook and Ladder No. 45. Courtesy Christie's East.

IVES Hook and Ladder, c. 1890, cast iron, 2 horses, 2 riders, 29" long. Photo by Jeanne Bertoia. Courtesy Bill Bertoia Auctions.

IVES Hook and Ladder, 34" long. Courtesy Sotheby's New York.

IVES Hook and Ladder, c. 1890, 29" long. Courtesy Sotheby's New York.

IVES Hook and Ladder, Phoenix. Courtesy Sotheby's New York.

IVES Hose Reel Wagon, 1 horse, driver, 16" long. Courtesy Sotheby's New York.

IVES "Patrol" Fire Wagon, 22" long. Courtesy Sotheby's New York.

IVES Phoenix Pumper (clockwork). Courtesy Sotheby's New York.

IVES Phoenix Pumper, driver, 2 horses, cast iron, 17-1/2" long. Photo by Jeanne Bertoia. Courtesy Bill Bertoia Auctions.

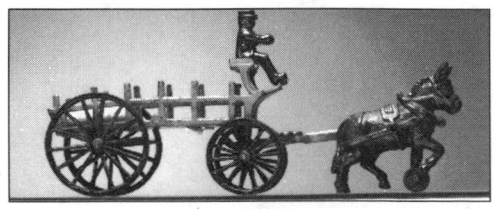

IVES Stake Wagon, 2 donkeys, 15-1/2" long. Courtesy Sotheby's New York.

	C6	C8	C10

Ives Hook and Ladder, Phoenix,
c. 1890, 28" long 1500 2400 3600

Ives Hook and Ladder, No. 45, c. 1885,
ladders, pails, 28" long 900 1500 2100

Ives Hook and Ladder, c. 1890,
cast iron, 2 horses, 2 riders, 29" long 900 1400 2200

Ives Hook and Ladder, cast iron,
driver, 2 horses, 34" long 1500 2400 3700

Ives Horse Cart, 1870, tin, 10" long 600 950 1400

Ives Horse Cart, 1883, 2 horses, 17-1/2" 750 1200 2500

Ives Hose Reel, very low back platform,
driver, rider, 1 horse 2000 4000 7000

Ives Hose Reel, cast iron, 1 horse,
driver, "Phoenix,"
c. 1880-1910, 15" long 1600 2400 3200

Ives Hose Reel Wagon, 1 horse,
driver, 16" long 600 950 1300

Ives Ice Wagon w/ mules, 1896 ...... 600 950 1400

Ives Ox Cart, 2 oxen 400 750 1150

Ives "Patrol" Fire Wagon, 22" long 800 1350 2050

Ives Phoenix Pumper, driver,
2 horses, cast iron, 17-1/2" long 950 1600 2300

Ives Phoenix Pumper, c. 1890, cast iron,
rarest of Ives pumpers
(clockwork), 19" long 900 1500 2200

Ives Police Patrol Wagon, 1890s,
6 patrolmen, driver, 20-1/2" long 1000 2000 3000

Ives Pumper, 23" long 2000 3200 4500

Ives Stake Wagon, 2 donkeys, 15-1/2" 400 600 800

Ives Steam Pumper, 2 horses, 20-1/2" 4000 6000 8000

Ives Walking Horse, pull toy, late
19th century, horse that walks
by means of wheel mechanism
under it, pulling a 2-wheeled cart 1800 2800 4000

Ives and Blakeslee Fire Pumper, 1893,
cast iron, largest cast-iron pumper
made by Ives, 25" long 1500 3000 5500

Jacrim "American Ice Company,"
2 horses, wooden, 30-1/2" long 450 725 1100

Jones & Bixler Uncle Sam Chariot,
cast iron, 11-1/2" long 750 1200 1800

JONES & BIXLER Uncle Sam Chariot. Courtesy Sotheby's New York.

KENTON

Kenton Lock Manufacturing Co. was incorporated in May 1890, in Kenton, Ohio. In November of 1894 it became the Kenton Hardware Manufacturing Company, and around this period the company began producing toys. It ceased production of horse-drawn toys in the early 1920s (except for a 1930s beer wagon), but in 1939 introduced a completely new line of horse-drawn pieces. This line continued through 1954.

Kenton Aerial Fire Tower, 3 horses,
driver, 30" long 800 1400 1900

Kenton "Ambulance - 2nd Regiment,"
driver, 1 horse, 15" long 1200 2400 3600

Kenton Back to Back Trap, driver,
woman rider, 12-1/2" long 1100 1900 2750

Kenton Bakery Wagon, marked
"Bakery," 1941 ...... 325 500 650

Kenton Band Wagon, musicians,
driver, rider on horse 150 225 300

Kenton "Beer" Wagon, cast iron, driver,
2 horses, 15" long 500 800 1200

Kenton Boar Cart, c. 1910, cast iron,
Egyptian driver, 8" long 350 500 750

Kenton Cabriolet, painted cast iron,
2nd series made into 1950s, 15" 162 243 325

Kenton Cement Mixer, driver, horse, 14" long 350 750 1000

Kenton Chariot, camel-drawn,
clown driver, 11" long 700 1200 1600

Kenton Chariot, cast iron, 6" long 150 225 300

Kenton Chariot, w/ comic driver, 1910,
cast iron, 7-1/2" long 250 375 500

Kenton Chariot, 3 horses, cast iron 600 900 1200

Kenton "Chief" Wagon, 1 horse, driver,
12-1/4" long 500 800 1500

Kenton Circus Cage Wagon, 2 horses,
2 riders, driver, animal in cage 350 700 1000

Kenton "City Express" Wagon, driver,
1 horse, 17" long 500 750 1045

Kenton "Coal" Cart, donkey pulling,
black driver 365 550 725

Kenton "Contractor's" Wagon,
w/ black driver, 2 horses, 15-1/2" long 500 800 1200

Kenton Covered Wagon, cast iron, 2 horses 130 195 260

Kenton "Cupid in Slipper," 1-horse cart,
cast iron, 8-1/2" long 450 800 1100

Kenton "Cupid" in horse-drawn slipper,
1 horse, 10-1/2" long 550 950 1400

Kenton Delivery Cart, donkey, cast iron 150 225 300

Kenton Delivery Wagon No. 5 w/ driver
and 2 horses, 15" long 250 375 500

Kenton Dog Cart, greyhound pulling
dog riding, 7" long 250 375 500

Kenton Dray, 13-1/4" long 100 150 200

Kenton Dray, cast iron, 2 horses,
black and white horses pulling green
dray, w/ driver, 13-1/2" 300 450 600

KENTON Dray No. 5, 14-1/2" long. Courtesy Lloyd W. Ralston Auctions.

	C6	C8	C10
Kenton Dray No. 5, painted cast iron, 1930, 14-1/2" long	175	263	350
Kenton Dray Wagon w/ horse and driver, cast iron, 14-3/4"	437	655	875
Kenton Dray, cast iron, 2 horses, pulling a green cart w/ driver, late 1940s, 14-3/4" long	95	140	190
Kenton Dump Cart, mule	125	187	250
Kenton Dump Wagon, early 1900s, 10-1/4" long	150	225	300
Kenton Dump Wagon, 2 horses, lever releases bottom wagon	250	375	500
Kenton Egyptian Cart, "Cairo Express," elephant-drawn, 10" long	500	800	1100
Kenton Egyptian Cart, elephant drawn	300	450	600
Kenton English Trap, 2 horses, woman, dog, c. 1895, 14" long	1600	2700	4000
Kenton Express Wagon, horse, driver, cast iron, 12" long	200	300	400
Kenton Express Wagon, 11" long	225	337	450
Kenton Farm Cart, mule, black driver, 10-1/2" long	375	562	750
Kenton Farm Wagon, driver, 1 horse, 14" long	500	750	1100
Kenton Farm Wagon, 2 horses, cast iron, w/ figure, 14-1/2" long	500	750	1100
Kenton Farm Wagon, driver, early, 1 horse, 15" long	300	450	600
Kenton Farm Wagon, 2 horses w/ driver, 15" long	325	490	650
Kenton Fire Ladder Wagon, front driver only, 12" long	150	225	300
Kenton Fire Ladder Wagon, horse drawn, drivers front/rear, 17" long	135	202	270
Kenton "Fire Patrol" Wagon, driver, 3 riders, 12" long	357	535	714
Kenton Fire Pumper, 2 horses, driver, 20" long	175	262	350
Kenton Fire Pumper, cast iron, 26-1/2" long, horses 11" long	600	1000	1400
Kenton Fire Wagon, 2 horses, driver, equipment, bell, wagon nickel-plated, 23" long	200	300	400
Kenton Goat Cart, figure w/ large cars, 7" long	250	375	500
Kenton Gravel Wagon, with 2 horses, 13" long	150	225	300
Kenton Hansom Cab, lady rider, driver in top hat, cast iron	700	1050	1400

	C6	C8	C10
Kenton Hansom Cab, top-hatted driver, 8" long	150	225	300
Kenton Hansom Cab, 1 horse, top-hatted driver, 10" long	1000	1500	2000
Kenton Hansom Cab, 12" long	500	750	1000
Kenton Hansom Cab, figures, horse, 15-1/2" long	300	500	700
Kenton Hook and Ladder Wagon, 2 horses, driver, 20" long	250	375	500
Kenton Hook and Ladder Wagon, nickel-plated, 2 horses, driver, 20" long	200	300	400
Kenton Hook and Ladder, 3 horses, cast iron, 16" long	300	450	650
Kenton Hook and Ladder, wagon, 3 horses, 17" long	250	375	500
Kenton Hook and Ladder, cast iron, 3 horses, c. 1910, 19" long	150	225	300
Kenton Hook and Ladder, 1915, painted cast iron, ladders, 26" long	600	1000	1400

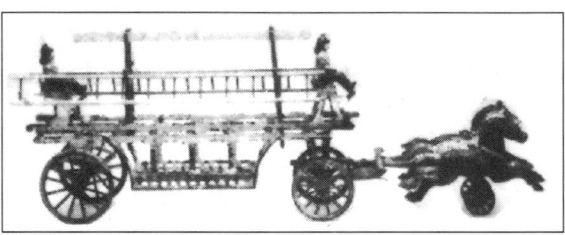

KENTON Hook & Ladder, 1915, 26" long. Courtesy Lloyd W. Ralston Auctions.

	C6	C8	C10
Kenton Hook and Ladder, 30" long	1400	2200	3200
Kenton Hose Reel, 1920, painted cast iron, 13-1/2" long	500	750	1000
Kenton Hose Reel, cast iron, c. 1905, 2 horses, 14-1/2" long	600	900	1200

KENTON Hook and Ladder, 30" long. Courtesy Sotheby's New York.

KENTON Hose Reel, 1920, 13-1/2" long. Courtesy Lloyd W. Ralston Auctions.

KENTON Log Wagon, 15" long. Courtesy Sotheby's New York.

KENTON "Milk" Wagon. Courtesy Sotheby's New York.

	C6	C8	C10
Kenton "Ice" Wagon, 2 horses, driver, 1920s, cast iron, 15" long	250	375	500
Kenton Landau, cast iron, white horse pulling green carriage w/ driver, c. 1910, 15" long	600	900	1200
Kenton Log Wagon, 1 horse w/ driver, 14-1/2" long	425	638	850
Kenton Log Wagon, black man, 2 oxen, early 1900s, cast iron, 15" long	500	800	1100
Kenton "Milk" Wagon, w/ horse and driver, 12-1/2" long	280	420	540
Kenton Overland Circus Band Wagon, 6 musicians and driver, 15-3/4"	500	800	1210
Kenton "Overland Circus" Bear Wagon, cast iron, 2 horses w/ driver, cage containing cast-iron bears, 1940s, 13"	235	352	470
Kenton "Overland Circus" Calliope Wagon, 14-1/2" long	300	500	700
Kenton "Overland Circus," cast iron, 2 horses w/ driver, cage containing cloth bear, 14" long	500	800	1200

	C6	C8	C10
Kenton Ox Cart, cast iron, 5" long	100	150	200
Kenton Ox Cart, 7" long	110	165	220
Kenton Ox Cart, 12-1/2" long	385	575	770
Kenton Ox Wagon, 2 oxen, 18" long	400	600	800
Kenton "Patrol" Wagon, driver, rider, 12" long	275	415	550
Kenton "Patrol" No. 526, 2 horses, driver, riders, 17" long	650	1100	1500
Kenton Plantation Cart, 1910, black driver, mule, 10" long	500	800	1210
Kenton "Polar Ice" Wagon, 2, donkeys	700	1300	1800
Kenton Police Patrol w/ mule team, 16"	500	750	1000
Kenton Pumper, 3 horses, 18" long	400	600	800
Kenton Rabbit, pulling cart w/ 2 wheels and seat, cast iron, 5" long	200	300	500
Kenton Rhino Cart, 8" long	100	200	300

KENTON Plantation Cart, 1910. Courtesy Mapes Auctioneers & Appraisers.

KENTON "Overland Circus" Calliope Wagon. Courtesy Sotheby's New York.

KENTON Overland Circus. Left to right: Band Wagon, Bear Wagon. Courtesy Sotheby's New York.

KENTON Spider Phaeton, 11-1/2" long. Courtesy Sotheby's New York.

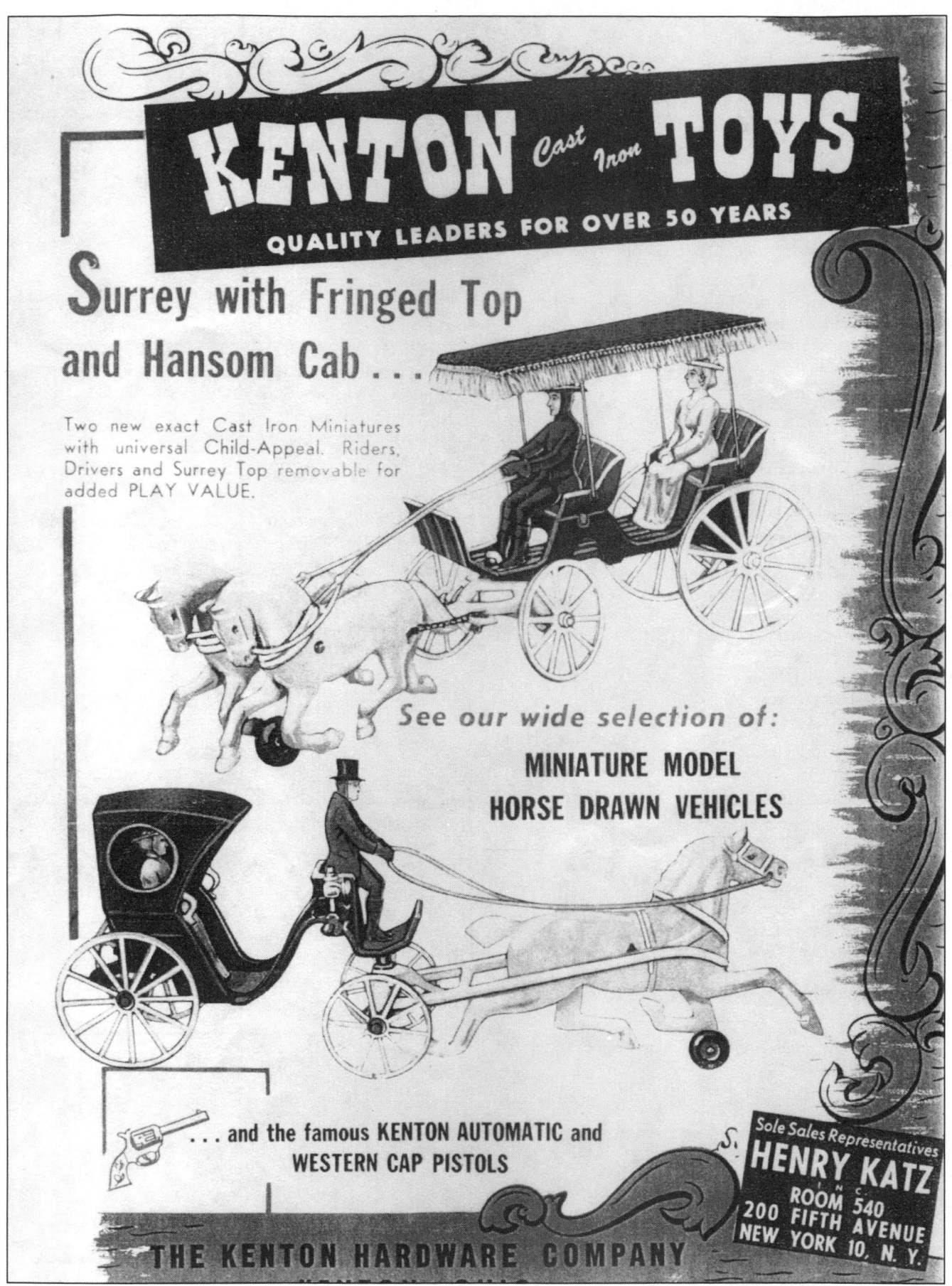

Late-date animal-drawn toys from Kenton, as shown in the March 1952 issue of Playthings magazine.

	C6	C8	C10
Kenton "Sand and Gravel" Dump Wagon, driver, 2 horses, 15" long	175	263	350
Kenton "Sand and Gravel" Dump Wagon, driver, 2 horses, 10" long	180	270	360
Kenton Spider Phaeton, cast iron, 11-1/2" long	850	1350	2000
Kenton Stake Wagon, 2 horses, driver w/ reins, 15" long	83	125	165
Kenton Sulky, driver cast to sulky, 6" long	75	112	150
Kenton Sulky, 2-wheel race cart w/ jockey and horse, 6" long	75	112	150
Kenton Sulky and driver, cast iron, 7" long	250	375	500
Kenton Surrey, 2 horses, cast iron, w/ driver and passenger, 12-1/2"	263	395	525
Kenton Surrey w/ fringe top, driver and passenger, 2 horses, 1952, 13" long	145	218	290
Kenton Surrey, 1 horse, approx. 1940, 16" long	150	225	300
Kenton Team of Horses w/ log and black driver	500	750	1000
Kenton Transfer Wagon, 2 horses, driver	650	975	1300
Kenton 3.2 Beer Delivery Wagon, cast iron, 1930s, 2 horses, driver, 10 wooden kegs, 14-1/2" long	350	525	700
Kenton Victoria Cab and horse, cast iron, w/ driver and woman, 15-1/2" long	150	225	300
Kenton No. 3, 1-horse wagon, w/ driver, 15" long	125	187	250
Kenton No. 5 Wagon, 1 horse, 15"	125	187	250
Kenton Wagon, 2 horses, 15" long	90	135	180
Kenton Wagon w/ driver, 2 horses, 10-1/4"	100	150	200
Kenton Water Tower Wagon, c. 1915, driver, 2 horses, 32" long	440	660	880
Kingsbury Dray, 2 horses, cast iron, 20-1/4" long	300	450	600
Kingsbury Hook and Ladder, 3 horses, 2 riders, rubber covers on wheels, cast iron and pressed steel, 25-1/2"	400	600	800
Kingsbury Hook and Ladder, 2 horses, driver, 3 ladders, 27" long	600	900	1200
Kingsbury Ladder Truck, 1900, cast iron, tin and wood, 13" long	300	450	600
"The Klondike Ice Co., New York," tin ice wagon, 2 horses, 17-1/2"	350	525	700
Kyser & Rex Hay Wagon, driver, 1 steer, cast iron, 11-1/2" long	550	850	1300
Kyser & Rex Hay Wagon, driver, 2 steers, cast iron, 13" long	700	1200	1700
Kyser & Rex Santa Claus in sleigh, cast iron and steel, auctioned in 1990 for $2,970			
Ladder Wagon, cast iron, 2 ladders and 3 galloping horses, 13-1/2"	150	225	300
Ladder Wagon, cast iron, w/ 2 horses, 3 sections of ladder, bell, 25-1/2"	250	375	500
Ladder Wagon, cast iron, w/ 2 drivers, 4 sections of ladder and 3 horses, Dart type, 30-1/2" long	800	1400	2100
Lancaster Hook and Ladder, 2 horses, cast iron, 25" long	150	225	300
Lancaster Hook and Ladder, 2 horses, 2 drivers, cast iron, 28" long	200	300	400
Lancaster Hook and Ladder, cast iron, 3 horses, 2 drivers, 28" long	250	375	500

	C6	C8	C10
Lancaster Hubley No. 58 Surrey, no driver	75	112	150
Lancaster Hubley No. 174 Surrey, w/ 1 seat, driver, horse	150	225	300
Landau, 4 horses w/ driver, 24" long	300	450	600
Lehmann "Africa" tin friction toy, ostrich pulling cart	363	545	725

LEHMANN "Africa." Courtesy Sotheby's New York.

	C6	C8	C10
Lehmann "Duo" Rooster pulling egg cart w/ a rabbit perched on top, tin friction	462	695	925
Lincoln Logs No. 30 Covered Wagon Set	62	93	125
Log Wagon, cast iron, w/ driver and 2 oxen, 15-1/4" long	450	675	900
Mail Cart, tin, horse-drawn	140	210	280
Marx Cart and Horse	90	135	180
Marx Covered Wagon, tin litho, friction, 9" long	60	90	120
Marx Parcel Wagon w/ 2-horse team	55	83	110
Mason & Parker, Buckboard, 1 horse, 1910, pressed painted steel, 31"	500	750	1000

MASON & PARKER Buckboard, 1 horse, 31" long. Courtesy Lloyd W. Ralston Auctions.

	C6	C8	C10
Mason & Parker Cart & Horse, 1910, painted pressed steel, mechanical action from axle, 13" long	500	750	1000
Mason & Parker Sleigh, 1 horse, 31"	600	1000	1400
McCormick Deering Farm Wagon, 2 horses, cast iron, 12-1/2" long	125	187	250
Merriam, Cab and Horse, 1880, painted and stenciled tin, 8-1/2" long	1300	2700	4000
Merriam Wagon and Horse, American painted & stenciled tin, 1890, 19-1/2" long	2500	3375	5000

	C6	C8	C10
Mess Cart, WWI-type, tin, 2 horses, painted ...	100	150	200
Milk Wagon, goat-drawn, possibly George Brown, painted tin, 6" ...	150	225	300
"Milk" Wagon, driver and 1 horse, 12-3/4" long ...	200	300	400
Milk Wagon, tin, Merriam?, 13" long ...	500	800	1200
Mower, 2 horses and driver, cast iron, 10" long ...	150	225	300
"National Express" Wagon, tin litho, horse, 15" long ...	250	375	500
Omnibus, "People's" tin, w/ 2 horses, driver, c. 1880s-1890s ...	4000	6000	8000
Ox Cart, cast iron, w/ ox, 5" long ...	120	180	240
Ox Cart, cast iron, 11-1/2" long ...	300	450	600

	C6	C8	C10
"Pansy" Stage Coach, Reed, 4 horses, driver, litho alphabet blocks, 28" ...	1000	1500	2000
Phaeton, 1 horse w/ driver, 16" long ...	450	700	1000
Plow, 1 horse, cast iron, 10-3/4" long ...	150	225	300
Police Patrol Wagon, cast iron, figures and driver, 1 horse, 11-1/2" long ...	100	150	200
"Police Patrol," cast iron, 1 horse, 12" ...	150	225	300
"Police Patrol" Wagon, cast iron, w/ driver and 5 policemen and 2 horses, 15" ...	1700	2800	4000

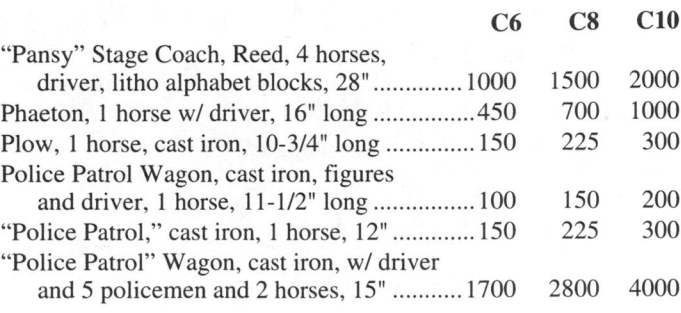

MERRIAM Cab and Horse, 1880, 8-1/2" long. Courtesy Lloyd W. Ralston Auctions.

MASON & PARKER Cart and Horse, 13" long. Courtesy Lloyd W. Ralston Auctions.

MERRIAM Wagon & Horse, 1890, 19-1/2" long. Courtesy Lloyd W. Ralston Auctions.

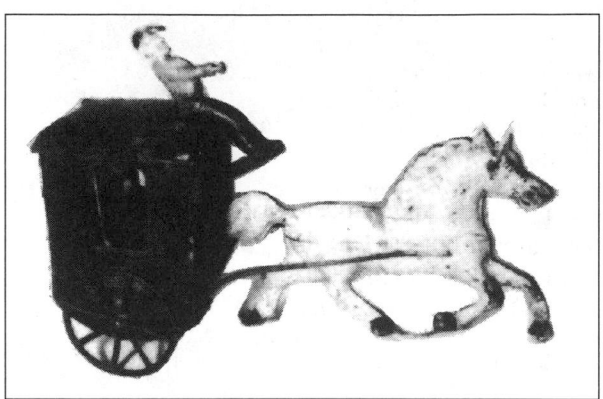

Milk Wagon, tin, 13" long (Merriam?). Courtesy Sotheby's New York.

PRATT & LETCHWORTH

Pratt and Letchworth was in business from about 1880 into the 1890s. The Buffalo, New York, firm sold its toys under the name Buffalo Toy Works. Iron and steel were its main materials, and all of its most prominent toys seem to have been horse-drawn.

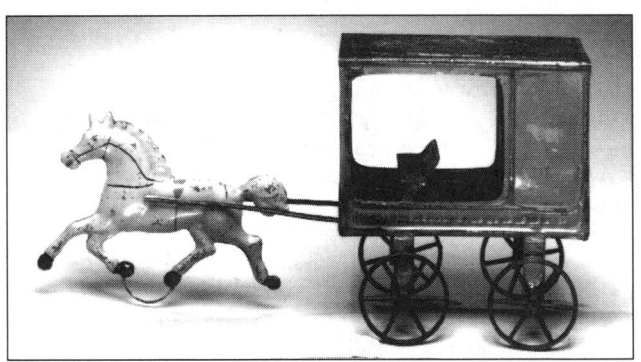

PRATT & LETCHWORTH Artillery. Courtesy Sotheby's New York.

PRATT & LETCHWORTH 4-seat Brake, 28" long. Courtesy Sotheby's New York.

	C6	C8	C10
Pratt & Letchworth Artillery, c. 1890, cast iron, hand-painted, 4-horse caisson, cannon, 4 riders, 34", one auctioned in late 1990 for $19,250			
Pratt & Letchworth Barouche, driver, 2 horses, 17" long	750	1400	2000
"Pratt & Letchworth" Cart, 10" long	150	225	300
Pratt & Letchworth Chemical Wagon, 3 horses, driver	3000	6000	9000
Pratt & Letchworth Chief's Wagon	1100	1650	2200
Pratt & Letchworth City Delivery Wagon, c. 1885, driver, barrels, horse	1100	1700	2500
Pratt & Letchworth Doctor's Cart, 1 horse, driver, 11" long	650	1100	1550
Pratt & Letchworth Double Surrey, 15" long	450	750	1100
Pratt & Letchworth Dray, 1 horse, cast iron and wood, 1890, 12" long	800	1450	2200
Pratt & Letchworth Fire Chief's Wagon, c. 1885, figure, 1 horse, 12" long	700	1100	1500
Pratt & Letchworth 4-seat Brake, 4 horses, driver, 7 passengers, 28" long	4000	7000	11,000
Pratt & Letchworth Gig, cast iron and pressed steel, 7 colors, 1 horse, 1 rider, 10-1/2" long	400	600	800
Pratt & Letchworth Hansom Cab, c. 1892, cast iron, 13" long	700	1200	1800
Pratt & Letchworth Hay Cart, 10-1/2"	500	750	1000
Pratt & Letchworth Hose Reel, small, 1 horse, driver in standard helmet	900	1350	1800
Pratt & Letchworth Hose Reel, 1 horse, 14-1/4" long	900	1350	1800
Pratt & Letchworth Pony Cart, 11" long	413	620	825
Pratt & Letchworth Pony Phaeton, c. 1892, driver, 1 horse, 15-1/4" long	600	1000	1500
Pratt & Letchworth Pumper, driver, rider, 2 horses, 17" long	750	1400	2000

PRATT & LETCHWORTH Pumper, driver, rider, 2 horses, 17" long. Photo by Jeanne Bertoia. Courtesy Bill Bertoia Auctions.

	C6	C8	C10
Pratt & Letchworth Sulky, 8-1/2" long	700	1200	1815
Pratt & Letchworth Sulky, 15" long	550	850	1300
Pratt & Letchworth Surrey, rear seat, c. 1890, 1 horse, 15-1/2" long	500	850	1100

PRATT & LETCHWORTH Surrey, rear seat, c. 1890, 1 horse, 15-1/2" long. Photo by Jeanne Bertoia. Courtesy Bill Bertoia Auctions.

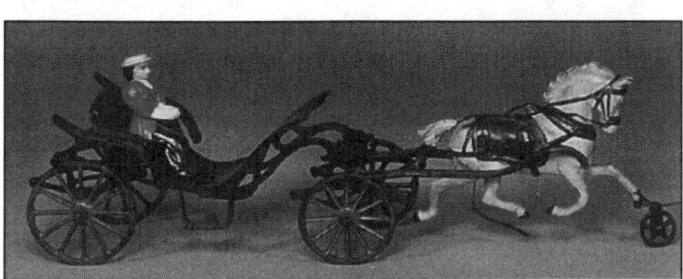

PRATT & LETCHWORTH Pony Phaeton, c. 1892. Photo by Jeanne Bertoia. Courtesy Bill Bertoia Auctions.

PRATT & LETCHWORTH Surrey, 15" long. Courtesy Sotheby's New York.

PRATT & LETCHWORTH. *Top to Bottom: Hansom Cab, c. 1892; Double Surrey, 15" long. Courtesy Sotheby's New York.*

Produce Wagon, painted tin, 1 horse (George Brown?). Courtesy Sotheby's New York.

REED "Band Chariot." Courtesy Christie's East.

REED "Cinderella Coach." Courtesy Christie's East.

	C6	C8	C10
Pratt & Letchworth-Welker & Crosby Dray, 1 horse, driver, 14-1/2" long	500	850	1500
Produce Wagon, painted tin, 1 horse, George Brown?, 12-1/2" long	350	525	700
Pull Toy, tin, horse and cart, iron wheels, 11" long	250	375	500
Pull Toy, horse and covered Delivery Wagon, tin, 5-1/4" long	150	225	300
Pull Toy, horse and wagon, 2 wheels, tin, 9-1/4" long	125	187	250
Pull Toy, horse-drawn carriage, tin, 12"	150	225	300
Pull Toy, horse pulling water wagon, tin, iron wheels, 6-3/4" long	350	525	700
Pull Toy, horse pulling water wagon, tin, iron wheels, 7-1/4" long	125	187	250
Pumper, driver part of casting, 2 horses, early, 15-1/2" long	200	300	400
Pumper, cast iron w/ driver and 2 horses	125	188	250
Pumper, cast iron, 3 horses w/ figure, 13" long	300	450	600
Reed "Band Chariot," 14 bandsmen, 28-1/2" long	800	1200	2000

REED "Polar Bear." Courtesy Christie's East.

	C6	C8	C10
Reed "Cinderella Coach" 26" long, auctioned in 1994 for $2,760			
Reed "Mammoth Show Circus Wagon," 3 animals, 2 trainers, c. 1890, paper on wood, 14" long	1100	1700	2500

	C6	C8	C10
Reed "Polar Bear," auctioned in 1994 for $7,475			
Reed Trolley, "Bowery & Central Park," paper on wood, 2 horses, 28" long	1500	2300	3500

RICH TOYS

Rich Toys was founded in 1921 by E.M. and M.E. Rich. Its toy line was added about 1923. Its toys were first manufactured in Morrison, Illinois, and later in Clinton, Illinois. Rich moved to Tupelo, Mississippi, in 1953. About 1962 a flood put an end to the business.

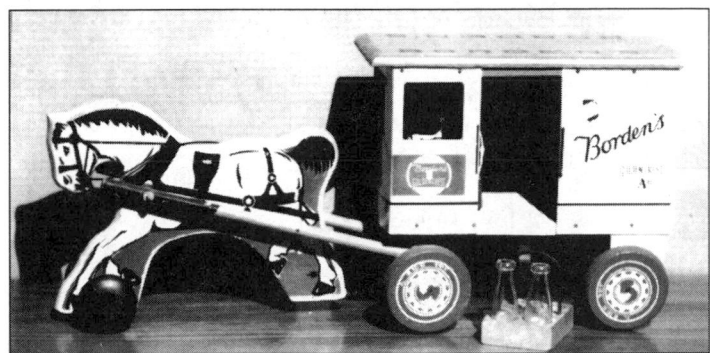

RICH TOYS "Borden's Golden Crest" wooden dairy cart. Courtesy Joe and Sharon Freed.

	C6	C8	C10
Rich Toys "Borden's Golden Crest," wooden dairy cart, 18" long	240	360	480
Rich Toys "Budweiser" Beer Wagon	300	500	800
Rich Toys "National Biscuit Company" Wagon, 1 horse	400	600	800
Rich Toys "Rich's City Dairy"	125	188	250
Rich Toys Streetcar No. 59, 2 horses, c. 1925, 20" long	600	900	1200

RICH TOYS No. 59 Streetcar, 2 horses, 20" long. Courtesy Wilkinson Collection, Detroit Antique Toy Museum.

	C6	C8	C10
"Sand and Gravel" wagon w/ driver, cast iron, 9-1/2" long	150	225	300
Sand and Gravel Wagon, cast iron, 2 horses, 10" long	150	225	300
Sand and Gravel Wagon, 1 horse w/ driver, cast iron, 10-1/2" long	175	262	350

	C6	C8	C10
"Sand and Gravel" Wagon, cast iron, driver, 2 horses, 14-3/4" long	100	150	200
"Sand and Gravel" Wagon w/ driver and 2 horses, cast iron, 15" long	150	225	300
Santa and Sleigh, cast iron, 16" x 7"	500	750	1000
Santa Claus in wooden sleigh pulled by reindeer, Santa composition, reindeer plush w/ cast-pewter antlers, early, 25" long	1500	2250	3000

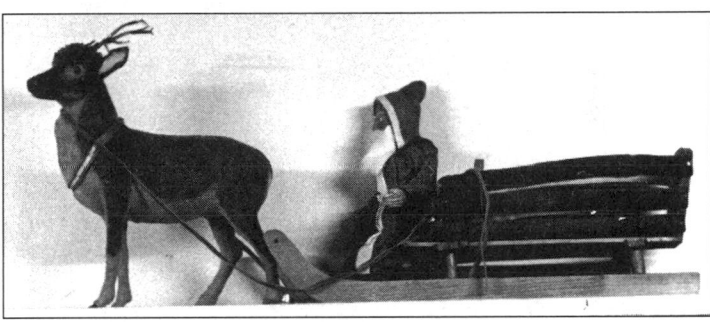

Santa Claus in wooden sleigh pulled by reindeer, 25" long. Photo courtesy Garth's Auction Inc.

	C6	C8	C10
Santa Claus, reindeer pulling sled, 2 reindeer pulling white sled containing black-painted Santa Claus	500	800	1200
Schoenhut "Alderney Dairy," wooden, driver, 1 horse	1300	2300	3200
Sheep, cast iron, pulling 2-wheeled tin wagon, 8" long	125	200	300

SHIMER "Choice Family Groceries Tea, Coffee & Spices." Courtesy Sotheby's New York.

SHIMER "Patrol," animated, black prisoner. Courtesy James S. Maxwell/ Virginia Caputo. Photo by Virginia Caputo.

	C6	C8	C10
"Sheffield Farms Company," wooden horse-drawn milk wagon, horse has articulated legs, 21" long	250	400	650
Shimer "Choice Family Groceries Tea, Coffee & Spices," 12-1/2" long	500	800	1200
Shimer "Ice" Wagon, cast iron, driver, 2 horses, 13" long	375	562	750
Shimer Lumber Wagon, 2 horses, cast iron, 26" long	358	535	715
Shimer "Patrol," animated, cast iron, black prisoner, 5 cops, 21" long	3500	6500	9000
Shimer Surrey, woman driver	375	562	750
Smith, S.A., wood wagon, horse, c. 1910, 23" long	500	750	1000
Spring Wagon, cast iron w/ driver, horse, 11" long	150	225	300
Spring Wagon, cast iron, driver, 1 horse, 14-1/2" long	150	250	350
Spring Wagon, driver and 2 horses, cast iron, 14-1/2" long	150	275	400
Spring Wagon, driver and 2 horses, miniature pick, shovel, sledgehammer, cast iron, 14-1/4" long	600	900	1200
Spring Wagon, cast iron, 2 horses, 15"	150	225	300
Stagecoach w/ cowboy driver and 2 horses, cast iron, 11" long	130	195	260
Stagecoach, 6 horses, cast iron, 27" long	60	90	120
Stake Bed Wagon, cast iron, 1 horse, 14-3/4" long	400	700	1000
Stanley Hay Wagon, 11" long	125	188	250
Stanley Pumper, 3 horses, driver	55	83	110
"Stanley" Surrey w/ driver, lady passenger, 2 horses, 14-3/4" long	100	150	200
Steam Pumper w/ stationary driver, 2 horses, cast iron, 9-1/4" long	100	150	250
Steam Pumper w/ stationary driver, 3 horses, cast iron, 10-1/2" long	150	225	300
Steam Pumper w/ stationary driver, 2 horses, cast iron, 15" long	500	750	1000
Steam Pumper w/ stationary driver, 2 horses, cast iron, 15-1/4" long	800	1350	2000
Steam Pumper, cast iron, driver, 3 horses, bell, 17-1/2" long	600	900	1200
Steam Pumper, 2 horses, cast iron w/ driver, 18" long	600	1000	1500
Steam Pumper, cast iron, driver and 2 horses, 20-1/2" long	800	1300	2000

	C6	C8	C10
Steam Pumper, cast iron, 3 horses and bell, 21-1/2" high	500	750	1000
Steamer w/ driver, 2 horses, 17" long	600	900	1500
Stevens Black Man in cart whipping mule, painted cast iron, mechanical, 1890, 9" long	400	600	900
Stevens Donkey Cart, cast iron, 8"	375	562	750

STEVENS Black Man in cart whipping mule, 9" long. Courtesy Lloyd W. Ralston Auctions.

STEVENS Donkey Cart. Courtesy Sotheby's New York.

	C6	C8	C10
Sulky, cast iron, horse and rider, cart mounted w/ 4 bells, 6-1/2" long	200	300	400
Sulky, cast iron, w/ driver, 7-1/4" long	150	225	300
Sulky, cast iron w/ driver, c. 1890s, 8-1/2" long	250	400	550
Sulky Rig, horse and driver pull toy, comic style, 10" long, 8" high, 1-1/4" thick	100	150	200
Surrey, cast iron, 2 horses, 13" long	150	225	300
"Teddy Bear" enclosed cart, painted litho tin, 1915, 9" long	600	900	1200
"Transfer" Wagon, cast iron, 2 horses, driver, 18" long	300	450	600
"Transfer Wagon," 3 horses and driver, cast iron, wagon bolted to team, 19"	325	488	650
"Transfer" Wagon, cast iron, driver and 2 horses, 19-1/2" long	400	600	800
"Trotter, Jockey and Horse," cast iron, 6" long	150	225	300
Uncle Sam Eagle Head Chariot, 2 horses, cast iron, Jones & Bixler?	3000	5000	8000
"United States Transfer Co. No. 7," wood wagon w/ cast-iron wheels, 2 stuffed horses, 31" long	300	450	600
U.S. Mail Wagon, tin, 2 horses, 17"	175	262	350
Vindex John Deere Farm Wagon, 2 horses, 7-1/2" long	800	1300	1900
Vindex "Whitewater" Farm Wagon, 2 horses	1400	2400	3700
Wagon, 2-wheeled, w/ driver, cast iron, 7-1/4" long	100	150	200

	C6	C8	C10
Wagon, cast iron, mule, driver, 2-wheeled wagon, 9-1/2" long	300	450	600
Wagon, 2-seater, cast iron, 1 horse	150	225	300
Walking Horse and Sulky Cart, horse of wood, moving legs and cart of tin, wheels cast iron, 7" long	250	375	500
Water Tower w/ 3 horses, cast iron and pressed steel, 43" long, horse 11" long	1000	1500	2000
Welker & Crosby Hose Reel 13-1/2"	800	1400	1900
Welker & Crosby Ox Cart, 2 oxen, black driver	600	900	1200

Uncle Sam Eagle Head Chariot, 2 horses. Courtesy James S. Maxwell/Virginia Caputo. Photo by Virginia Caputo.

WILKINS TOY COMPANY

Wilkins Toy Company of Keene, New Hampshire, was begun as the Triumph Wringer Company by James S. Wilkins. The tiny model Wilkins produced to promote his product proved so intriguing to prospective customers and their children that requests for them poured in. Wilkins quickly forgot his original product and turned to toymaking. Wilkins's toys were generally cast iron and steel. The firm was acquired in 1894 by Kingsbury, which is still in business as a tool and die maker.

	C6	C8	C10
Wilkins Aerial Fire Wagon, cast iron, 3 horses, driver, 43" long	2000	3500	5150
Wilkins Artillery, c. 1895, 2 horses, rider on caisson, seat top lifts off, cannon, 10" long	1000	1500	2000

	C6	C8	C10
Wilkins "Boys Express Co." Wagon, cast iron, 2 horses, 16-1/2" long	700	1200	1600
Wilkins Buckboard, cast iron	120	180	240
Wilkins Caisson, horse-drawn, 18"	650	1000	1500
Wilkins Cane Wagon, mule, driver, 11" long	300	450	600

WILKINS Aerial Fire Wagon, cast iron, 43" long. Made c. 1895, believed to be the largest cast-iron toy made during the 19th century. Courtesy Phillips New York.

	C6	C8	C10
Wilkins Carriage, driver in derby, 1 horse, passenger	1000	1500	2000
Wilkins Cart, animated, 6" long	250	375	500
Wilkins Cart and Horse, 10" long	450	700	1000
Wilkins Car and Horse, driver, 12"	750	1200	1600
Wilkins Chariot, 4 horses, 7" long	180	270	360
Wilkins (?) Chariot, woman driver, 3 horses, cast iron, 10-1/2" long	400	600	800

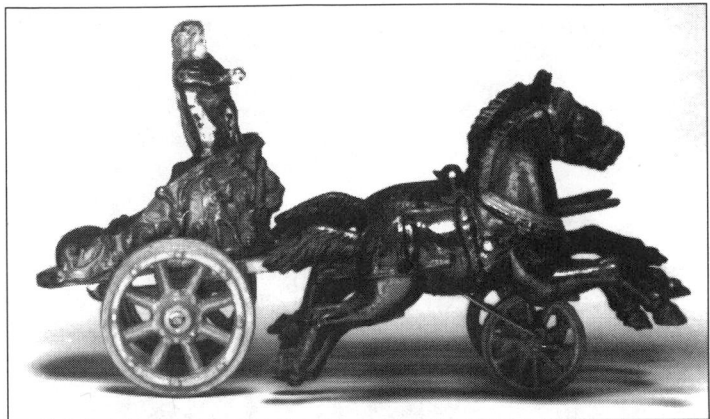

WILKINS (?) Chariot, woman driver. Courtesy Sotheby's New York.

	C6	C8	C10
Wilkins "City Truck" cast iron, 2 horses w/ driver	1000	1500	2000
Wilkins "Coal and Wood" Wagon	750	1125	1500
Wilkins Delivery Wagon, driver, prancing horse team, 21" long	600	900	1200
Wilkins Doctor's Cart, c. 1900, 10-1/2" long	500	750	1100

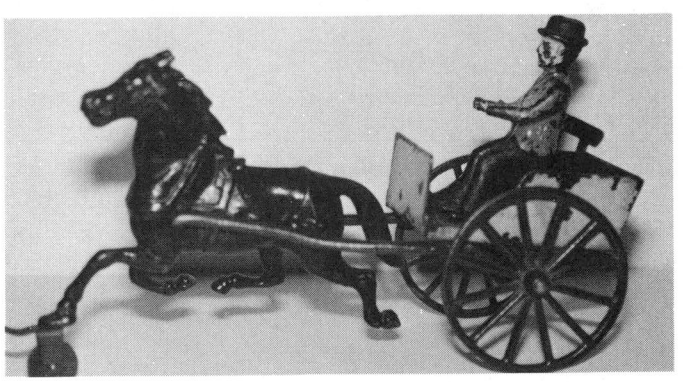

WILKINS Doctor's Cart, 10-1/2" long. Courtesy Christie's East.

	C6	C8	C10
Wilkins Dog Cart, 1890, cast iron, 7-1/2" long	150	225	300
Wilkins Dog Cart, c. 1890, cast iron, large St. Bernard-type dog, rider in cap, 10-1/2" long	600	950	1400
Wilkins Donkey Cart, 11" long	237	355	475
Wilkins Donkey Cart, 13-1/4" long	350	525	700
Wilkins Dray, cast iron, black driver, 1 horse, 12" long	500	750	1100
Wilkins Dray, cast iron, 15" long	300	450	600

	C6	C8	C10
Wilkins Dray, 2 horses, cast iron, 16" long	325	500	700
Wilkins Dray, 2 mules, driver, 17-1/2" long	600	900	1250
Wilkins Dray, cast iron and tin barrel, drawn by 2 horses, driver in derby hat, c. 1910, 20-1/2" long	900	1350	2200
Wilkins Fire Chief Buggy, 1 horse w/ rider, 12" long	650	1050	1500
Wilkins Fire Chief Engine Pumper, 2 horses, 19" long	500	750	1000
Wilkins Fire Hose Reel, 10-1/2" long	350	550	750
Wilkins Fire Ladder Truck, cast iron, 3 horses, c. 1910, 2 firemen, 20"	415	622	830
Wilkins "Fire Patrol," 6 firemen, 3 horses, 20" long	500	750	1050
Wilkins Fire Patrol Wagon, 4 firemen in wagon, 12" long	450	675	900
Wilkins Fire Patrol, 2 horses, 2 men, cast iron, 20-1/2" long	550	825	1200
Wilkins Fire Pumper, 2 horses, 18"	1700	2800	4000
Wilkins Fire Pumper, horizontal chemical tank, 2 horses, 19-1/2" long	1700	2800	4000
Wilkins Fire Pumper, 2 horses, driver, 20" long	600	900	1200
Wilkins Fire Pumper, 3 horses, driver, 25" long	1800	3200	5000

WILKINS Fire Pumper, 3 horses, driver, 25" long. Photo by Jeanne Bertoia. Courtesy Bill Bertoia Auctions.

	C6	C8	C10
Wilkins Gentleman's Cart, 1900, gentleman driver, white horse, 10"	300	450	600
Wilkins Gig, fancy, and driver, 10"	150	225	300
Wilkins Goat Cart, driver, c. 1900, 9-1/2" long	900	1350	2200
Wilkins "Groceries" Wagon, 1 horse, c. 1900, 13-1/2" long	200	300	400
Wilkins Hansom Cab, cast iron, 15" long	600	950	1400
Wilkins Hook and Ladder, 24" long	700	1100	1700
Wilkins Hook and Ladder, prancing team, cast iron, 27" long	600	925	1350

WILKINS Hook & Ladder, 2 horses, 2 firemen, 19-1/2" long. Photo by Jeanne Bertoia. Courtesy Bill Bertoia Auctions.

WILKINS Dray, cast-iron and tin barrel. Courtesy Sotheby's New York.

WILKINS Fire Ladder Truck, cast iron, 3 horses, 20" long, c. 1910. Courtesy Mapes Auctioneers & Appraisers.

Top: WILKINS Fire Pumper, 19-1/2" long, horizontal chemical tank. Bottom, L to R: WILKINS Fire Pumper, 18" long, 2 horses; WILKINS Hose Reel, 16" long, 2 horses, 2 firemen. Courtesy Christie's East.

WILKINS Ox Cart, cast iron. Courtesy Sotheby's New York.

WILKINS Phaeton, woman driver. Courtesy Christie's East.

WILKINS Hose Reel, 2 horses, 2 firemen in standard helmets. Courtesy Ed Hyers Antique Toys.

WILKINS Hook and Ladder, 2 horses, 2 firemen. Courtesy Ed Hyers Antique Toys.

	C6	C8	C10
Wilkins Hook and Ladder, 2 horses, horses sit on pegs, has ladders, figures	1000	1500	2000
Wilkins Hook and Ladder, 2 horses, 2 firemen, 19-1/2" long	385	575	770
Wilkins Hose Reel, 2 horses, 2 firemen in standard helmets, 16" long	1500	2500	3500
Wilkins Hose Reel, c. 1890, cast iron, 1 horse, 18" long	800	1300	1900
Wilkins Huckster's Wagon, 2 horses, driver	800	1450	1950
Wilkins Ice Wagon, horse, tin and cast iron, 10" long	150	225	300
Wilkins Landau, cast iron, articulated horses, door opens, 2 coachmen, 15-1/4" long	1200	2000	3100
Wilkins "Panama" Earth Mover, driver, 2 horses, 1903, 20" long	400	600	800
Wilkins Ox Cart, cast iron	300	500	700
Wilkins Phaeton, driver in top hat, gray pony	450	750	1100
Wilkins Phaeton, woman driver, late 1800s, 16" long	1000	2500	4000
Wilkins Plantation Cart, 1910, cast iron and pressed steel, tilt dump, 11"	460	690	920
Wilkins Plow, 1 horse, driver, 10-1/2"	1200	1900	2800
Wilkins Police Patrol, driver, 2 horses, 6 policemen, 1911, 20" long	1700	2700	3700

	C6	C8	C10
Wilkins Pony Cart, 1 horse, driver, 7-1/2" long	400	600	800
Wilkins Pony Cart, 1 horse, driver, 9-1/2" long	500	750	1075
Wilkins Pumper, 2 horses, 2 firemen	1100	1650	2200
Wilkins Spring Wagon, driver, horses	300	450	600
Wilkins Stake Wagon, 1907	500	675	1000
Wilkins Steam Engine, 2 horses w/ driver, 17" long	600	900	1300
Wilkins Street Sweeper, "D.P.W.," 1 horse, brush, driver, 13" long	2000	3200	5700
Wilkins Streetcar, "Broadway Car Line 75," horse-drawn	900	1600	2400
Wilkins Streetcar, "Consolidated Street RR712," cast iron, 14" long	1200	1900	2800
Wilkins Transfer Wagon, tin and cast iron, 15" long	500	850	1200
Wilkins Wagon, driver, mule, 9" long	300	450	600
Wilkins "Worlds Fair Street RR 372," 1 horse, 6 passengers, cast iron, 15"	900	1600	2400
Williams Sulky, c. 1920, cast iron, 8" long	150	225	300
Wolverine Sulky Racer, plastic wind-up	55	82	110

WILKINS Pumper, 2 horses, 2 firemen. Courtesy Ed Hyers Antique Toys.

WILKINS Streetcar, "Broadway Car Line 75," horse-drawn. Courtesy Mapes Auctioneers & Appraisers.

WILKINS Streetcar, "Consolidated Street R.R. 712." Courtesy Wilkinson Collection, Detroit Antique Toy Museum.

WILKINS. Top to Bottom: "World's Fair Street R.R. 372"; Transfer Wagon, tin and cast iron. Both 15" long. Courtesy Sotheby's New York.

Mechanical Banks

The average mint price in this category in the last edition was $8813.03. In this edition it is $9658.78, an increase of 10%.

A Popular Early Collectible

by Bill S. Bertoia

After trains, mechanical banks are perhaps the most avidly pursued of all the toys cataloged in this book. The most collectible remain those that were produced in cast iron from around 1870 to 1908. Over three hundred different types were produced during that period. One factor that adds to their interest is that many were manufactured with an eye toward adults as well as children (the "Tammany" bank, for instance). As a result, prices are high—and they were high long before any of the other toys in this book were thought of as collector's items. With such valuable items the problem of counterfeiting arises, and care is urged in the purchase of any high-priced bank. Counterfeits tend to be rougher, to fit together less smoothly, and to lack the patina or "look" of age.

Bill S. Bertoia is a recognized authority in the field of antique toys and banks. As an avid toy and bank collector, he is a member of the Antique Toy Club of America, the Mechanical Bank Collectors of America and the Still Bank Collectors of America. As an active antiques dealer specialist, he has handled and appraised some of the largest collections that have been offered for sale, including those from the Perelman Antique Toy Museum and The Atlanta Toy Museum, as well as the Hegarty Mechanical Bank Collection, The Barenholtz Toy Collection and, most recently, the largest toy collection ever sold: The Acevedo Toy Collection. He is married to author Jeanne Bertoia and they have two young children who are starting to share their interest in collecting. The family resides in Vineland, New Jersey.

Acrobat. Courtesy PB Eighty-Four, New York.

Alligator In Trough. Courtesy Sotheby's New York.

	C6	C8	C10
Acrobat Bank, 5" high	3000	6000	8800
Alligator in Trough, patented 1867	10,000	20,000	35,000
Always Did Despise A Mule, black jockey on mule, 1879, 10" long	600	1200	1800
Always Did Despise A Mule, black on bench being kicked by mule, 1897	550	1100	1700
American Bank sewing machine	3000	6000	10,000
Artillery Bank, Union Officer w/ mortar, firing at fort, 1877	500	900	1400
Astronaut's Bank-gold moon w/ rocket on stand, has rings showing orbit of space capsule, ring has astronauts' names: "Shepard, Grissom, Glenn, Carpenter, Schirra, Cooper," little plane up side of rocket shoots money into moon, pot metal, 11" high	25	38	50

Always Did Despise A Mule. Courtesy PB Eighty-Four, New York.

Always Did Despise A Mule. Courtesy Christie's East.

Artillery. Courtesy Christie's East.

Boy On Trapeze. Courtesy Sotheby's New York.

Bad Accident. Courtesy Christie's East.

Bird On Roof. Courtesy Sotheby's New York.

Boy Scout. Courtesy Sotheby's New York.

Boys Stealing Watermelons. Courtesy Christie's East.

Bread Winner. Courtesy Sotheby's New York.

Buffalo, bucking. Courtesy Sotheby's New York.

	C6	C8	C10
Atlas Bank	1000	1750	3000
Bad Accident, mule and black on 2-wheeled cart, 1887	1100	1900	3300
Bear Hugging Tree	450	675	900
Bill E. Grin	500	1300	2100
Bird on Roof	1200	2400	3600
Book of Knowledge Reproduction of Original Banks, c. 1950; Artillery Bank; Bulldog Bank; Creedmore; Eagle and Eagles; Jonah & Whale; Magician; Man and Pig; Man milking Cow; Teddy and the Bear; Trick Dog; Trick Pony, Tree Trunk and Buffalo. Price per each	195	295	390

Note: The original markings are sometimes filed away from the bottom in an attempt to sell one of these items as an original.

	C6	C8	C10
Boy on Trapeze, J. Barton & Smith	1450	2900	4300
Boy Robbing Nest	850	2500	4000
Boy Scout	3100	4700	8250
Boys Stealing Watermelons	750	1500	2500
Bread Winner	7500	15,000	22,000
Bull & Bear, brass model	1000	1750	2500
Bulldog Savings Bank, Ives, Blakeslee & Wms	1400	2800	4200

Bulldog Savings. Courtesy PB Eighty-Four, New York.

	C6	C8	C10
Bulldog, c. 1887, Judd	600	1200	1800
Bulldog, Stevens	350	525	700
"Butting" Buffalo	2600	5200	7800
Butting Goat In Tree Stump, c. 1887, Judd	262	393	525
Calamity, pat. August 29, 1905, J&E Stevens Co., 3 football players	5000	10,000	15,750

Called Out, 3 known, auctioned in 1993 for $14,300

Chief Big Moon. Courtesy PB Eighty-Four, New York.

	C6	C8	C10
Cat and Mouse Bank, Stevens	750	2000	3500
Charlie McCarthy, sitting w/ legs crossed on top of trunk, drop coin in back and mouth moves, pot metal, copyright 1938, 5-3/4" high	75	125	200
Chein Monkey, seated, tips hat when coin dropped in, tin litho, 5" high	70	105	140
Chief Big Moon, Indian in teepee, 1899	1000	2000	3000
Chimpanzee	1500	2200	3500
Chinese Reclining, 1882	2900	4300	8800

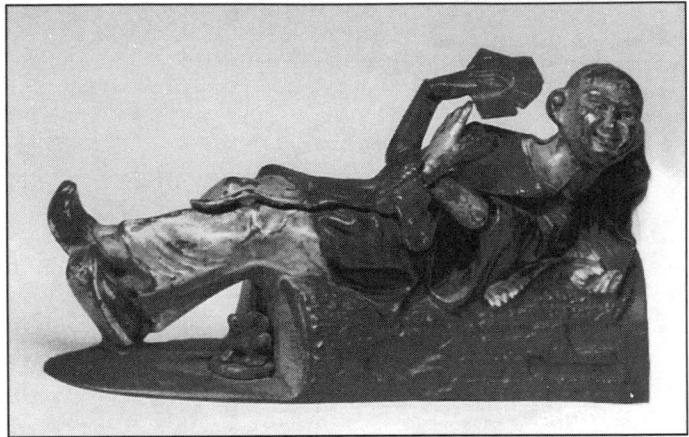

Chinese Reclining. Courtesy Christie's East.

Circus Bank, auctioned in 1994 for $14,950

	C6	C8	C10
Circus Ticket Taker	500	1000	1500

Clown & Harlequin, auctioned in 1988 for $90,000

Clown on Bar, auctioned in 1993 for $70,000

	C6	C8	C10
Clown on Globe, 1873	1150	2400	3500
Columbus	300	450	600
Confectionary	3500	7000	12,000
Cow Kicking, cow kicks over boy	7500	15,000	25,000

Cow Kicking. Courtesy Sotheby's New York.

	C6	C8	C10
Creedmore Bank, man firing into tree, 1877, 10" long, Stevens	390	585	785
Crowing Rooster	500	750	1000
Dapper Dan	200	400	600
Darktown Battery, black pitcher and catcher, 1888	1750	3500	5200

Darky Football, auctioned in 1988 for $245,000

	C6	C8	C10
Darky and Cabin, 1885	500	750	1000
Dentist Bank, white dentist working on black patient, 1880	4500	9500	14,000
Dinah, bust of black woman, 6-1/2"	450	675	900
Dog Charges Boy, bronze finish	400	700	1000
Dog on Turntable, Judd Mfg. Co.	480	720	960
Dog Standing	150	350	500

Bulldog, dog swallows coin. Courtesy Sotheby's New York.

Creedmore. Courtesy Sotheby's New York.

Clown On Globe. Courtesy PB Eighty-Four, New York.

Cat And Mouse, cat balancing. Courtesy Phillips New York.

Dentist. Courtesy PB Eighty-Four, New York.

Fortune Teller. Courtesy PB Eighty-Four, New York.

Darky And Cabin. Courtesy Sotheby's New York.

Frog On Lattice. Courtesy PB Eighty-Four, New York.

Darktown Battery. Courtesy PB Eighty-Four, New York.

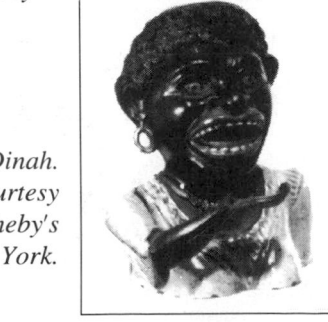

Dinah. Courtesy Sotheby's New York.

Dog On Turntable. Courtesy PB Eighty-Four, New York.

Elephant And Clowns. Courtesy Sotheby's New York.

	C6	C8	C10
Eagle and Eaglets, 1883	500	1000	1500
Elephant, late-cast iron, Hubley	100	175	250
Elephant, Three Star, cast iron, trunk flips up to catch coin, 5" high	50	75	100
Elephant and Clowns	900	1800	2700
Elephant Howdah, 1920	250	500	750
Elephant Howdah, c. 1934, Hubley	375	563	750
Ferris Wheel, Hubley/Bauer	1000	2000	3000
Fortune Teller, pat. February 19, 1901, safe, complete w/ roll of fortunes	400	600	800
Forty-Niner, The, donkey moves ear and tail	100	225	400
Fowler, sportsman shoots bird, Stevens	6500	14,000	20,000
Freedman, auctioned in 1988 for $250,000			
Frog and Snake In Pond, litho tin mechanical bank in the form of a snake striking at a frog which opens its mouth to receive the coin	3000	4500	6500
Frog, Goat and Old Man	1500	3500	6000
Frog on Arched Track, auctioned in 1988 for $35,000			
Frog on Lattice, Stevens, 1870s	450	675	900
Frog on Rock, Kilgore Mfg. Co.	500	750	1000
Frog on Stump, 1872	435	650	870
Frogs, two, J&E Stevens	1200	2400	4000

Frogs, Two. Courtesy Sotheby's New York.

Gem. Courtesy Sotheby's New York.

	C6	C8	C10
Gem, Dog and Building	250	375	500
Giant, holding a club	10,000	15,000	20,000
Girl Skipping Rope, w/ key	10,000	20,000	31,000
Globe Savings Fund Bank	250	375	500

Girl Skipping Rope. Courtesy PB Eighty-Four, New York.

	C6	C8	C10
Guessing Bank	1500	2500	3500
Hall's Excelsior Bank, monkey cashier	500	800	1100
Hall's Lilliput, 1875	500	750	1000
Hen and Chick, c. 1901, Stevens	1300	2600	3850
Hindu, 1882, Kyser & Rex	1000	1500	2000
Hold the Fort, 5-hole, c. 1877	1200	2500	3500
Home building w/ 2 pillars, teller at window, tin	230	345	460
Horse Race	6000	9000	15,000

Horse Race. Courtesy Christie's East.

	C6	C8	C10
Humpty Dumpty	800	1600	2400
Independence Hall	300	450	600
Indian Shooting Bear, 1888	1150	1725	2300

Indian Shooting Bear. Courtesy Sotheby's New York.

	C6	C8	C10
Initiating Bank First Degree	3500	6500	10,000
Jolly Nigger, bust	270	405	540
Jolly Nigger, high hat, 8" high	225	338	450
Jolly Nigger, moves ears	75	112	150
Jonah and the Whale, cast iron (Jonah in boat)	1350	2700	4000
Jonah and Whale (Jonah emerges)	20,000	30,000	45,000
Jumbo on Platform	850	1700	2500
"Keeping 'Em Flying" dime register, tin	25	37	50

Jonah And The Whale. Courtesy Garth's Auction Inc.

Giant. Courtesy
Sotheby's New York.

Home. Courtesy
Sotheby's New York.

Humpty Dumpty. Courtesy PB Eighty-
Four, New York.

Magician. Courtesy
Sotheby's New York.

Magic. Courtesy
Sotheby's
New York.

Mammy Feeding
Child. Courtesy
Sotheby's New
York.

Mule Bucking. Courtesy
Sotheby's New York.

Organ Bank,
monkey only.
Courtesy
Sotheby's New York.

Mason And Hod-Carrier. Courtesy PB
Eighty-Four, New York.

Novelty. Courtesy
Sotheby's New York.

Monkey And
Coconut.
Courtesy
Sotheby's
New York.

Pegleg
Beggar.
Courtesy
Sotheby's
New York.

New Bank.
Courtesy
Sotheby's
New York.

Organ Grinder And Monkey. Courtesy
Sotheby's New York.

Kick Inn. Courtesy Christie's East.

Lion And Monkeys. Courtesy Sotheby's New York.

Kick Inn. Courtesy Sotheby's New York.

Lion Hunter. Courtesy PB Eighty-Four, New York.

	C6	C8	C10
Kick Inn, litho paper and wood mechanical bank, Presto, a mule standing in front of a small building	250	375	500
King Aqua, auctioned in 1988 for $95,000			
Leap Frog Bank, 2 boys, tree, 1891	1300	2600	3900
Liberty Bell	200	300	500
Lighthouse Bank, 1891	750	1600	2300
Lion and Monkeys	650	1300	1950
Lion Hunter	2000	4000	6000
Little Jocko	500	1000	1500
Little Joe	122	185	245
Locomotive	300	600	900

	C6	C8	C10
Magic	540	1100	1625
Magician Bank, 1882	1750	3500	5250
Mama Katzenjammer and the Kids, 5-3/4"	3200	5000	6500
Mammy Feeding Child	3200	5000	6500
Mason and Hod Carrier, 1887	2300	4700	7000
Merry-Go-Round, Kyser & Rex	5300	11,000	16,000
Meyers No. 84, Jumbo Elephant	100	250	350
Money Box Bank, hand-carved on wood base, 10-1/4"	800	1200	1600
Monkey and Coconut	850	1700	2500
Mosque	550	1200	1750
Mule Bucking, black man riding a mule	500	750	1000
Mule Entering Barn	500	800	1200

Leap-Frog Bank. Courtesy Sotheby's New York.

Mule Entering Barn. Courtesy Sotheby's New York.

	C6	C8	C10
National Bank	2500	5000	8000
Naughty Girl Bank, modern	25	50	75
New Creedmore Meyer No. 54	600	1200	2000
New Bank, cast iron, c. 1875, brass policeman in building, 4-1/2" long	170	255	340
North Pole, J&E Stevens Co., Eskimos and dog sled	10,000	15,000	25,000

Owl, turns head.
Courtesy PB
Eighty-Four,
New York.

Piano. Courtesy Sotheby's New York.

Punch And Judy. Courtesy PB
Eighty-Four, New York.

Presto. Courtesy
Sotheby's
New York.

Picture Gallery. Courtesy Sotheby's
New York.

"Professor Pug Frog's Great Bicycle Feat".
Courtesy Sotheby's New York.

Pig In High Chair. Courtesy
Sotheby's New York.

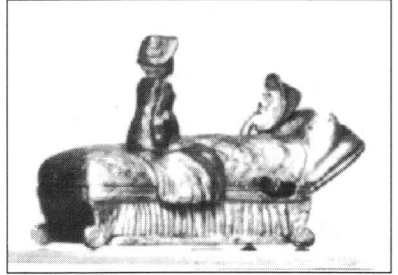

Red Riding Hood. Courtesy
Sotheby's New York.

Roller
Skating.
Courtesy
Sotheby's
New
York.

Santa Claus At
The Chimney.
Courtesy PB
Eighty-Four,
New York.

Speaking Dog.
Courtesy PB
Eighty-Four,
New York.

Stump Speaker.
Courtesy PB Eighty-
Four, New York.

	C6	C8	C10
Novelty Bank, house-like bank, 1873	450	900	1500
Organ Bank, monkey and revolving cat and dog, 7-1/4" high	500	750	1050
Organ Bank, monkey only	500	775	1070
Organ Boy and Girl, pat. June 13, 1882, monkey flanked by boy and girl holding tambourine	450	675	900
Organ Grinder And Bear	1400	2800	4200
Organ Grinder And Monkey, 1929	330	485	600
Owl, slot in book, cast iron	290	400	585
Owl, slot in head	150	300	500
Owl, turns head, cast iron	425	635	850
Paddy and His Pig	900	1800	3000

Paddy And His Pig. Courtesy Garth's Auctions Inc.

	C6	C8	C10
Panorama, building	3000	6000	10,000
Patronize the Blind Man and His Dog, pat. Feb. 19, 1878, J&E Stevens Co.	2000	4500	7000
Pegleg Beggar	565	1200	1700
Pelican, cast iron, "Boy thumbs nose"	775	1550	2310
Perfection Registering	4500	7000	10,000
Piano, c. 1900, E.M. Roche	250	500	750
Picture Gallery	6000	10,000	16,000
Pig, Bismarck	1500	3000	4500
Pig in High Chair	400	600	800
Preacher in Pulpit	30,000	40,000	50,000
Presto, shape of building	165	250	330
Presto-Mouse on Roof, litho paper on wood	7500	12,000	17,500
Professor Pug Frog's Great Bicycle Feat	3300	6600	11,000
Pump, Bucket	300	700	1000
Punch & Judy, Shepherd Hardware, Buffalo, NY, c. 1890	1050	2100	3500
Rabbit, tall	600	1200	2000
Rabbit, small, circular base	275	415	550
Rabbit in Cabbage Patch	100	150	200
Red Riding Hood	15,000	20,000	35,000
Roller Skating	20,000	30,000	45,000
Rooster	445	670	890
Santa Claus at Chimney	675	1350	2260
See Him Frisk, auctioned in 1988 for $55,000			
Shoot the Chute	12,500	17,500	25,000

	C6	C8	C10
Speaking Dog Bank, J&E Stevens, pat. 1885	630	945	2100
Springing Cat, lead alloy, sold in 1991 for $23,100			
Squirrel and Tree Stump	1200	2400	3600
Standing Bear	100	165	220
Strato Bank, pot metal, rocket and planet, 1950s, 8" long	10	15	25
Stump Speaker, cast iron	1400	2800	4200
Tabby	150	350	600
Tammany Bank, 1875, 5-3/4" high	325	490	650
Tank and Cannon, 1916	325	490	650
Teddy and The Bear, man firing at bear in tree, 1907	900	1800	3000

Teddy And The Bear. Courtesy PB Eighty-Four, New York.

	C6	C8	C10
Telephone	150	300	450
3-Star Elephant, brass	150	300	450
Trick Dog, clown w/ hoop, dog and barrel, 1888 version, has 6-part base	750	1500	2500
Trick Dog, clown w/ hoop, dark dog and dark barrel, 1929	365	550	730
Trick Pony	535	1070	1600

Trick Dog. Courtesy Sotheby's New York.

Trick Pony. Courtesy PB Eighty-Four, New York.

	C6	C8	C10
Turtle Bank, auctioned in 1988 for $30,000			
Two Frogs (see Frogs, Two)			
U.S. Building, c. 1878,			
boy and dog in windows, Stevens?	3100	4650	6200
U.S. and Spain	3000	4000	5000
Uncle Remus	2500	3500	5500
Uncle Sam, bust	300	450	600
Uncle Sam, has umbrella in left hand, 1886	935	1900	2800
Uncle Tom, w/ lapels and 1 star	325	485	650

	C6	C8	C10
Uncle Tom, w/ lapels, 1 star, brass base	600	900	1200
United States Bank, Stevens	650	975	1300
Watchdog Safe	270	405	540
Weeden's Plantation, tin	600	1250	1850
William Tell, 1896	500	750	1000
Wireless Bank, 1913	125	190	250
Woodpecker	1500	2800	4000
World's Fair	600	1200	1800
Zoo	450	900	1400

William Tell. Courtesy PB Eighty-Four, New York.

Uncle Remus. Courtesy Sotheby's New York.

Zoo. Courtesy Sotheby's New York.

A full-color ad card for the bank listed here as "Eagle And Eaglets." This was sold at auction in late 1990 for $200. Courtesy James S. Maxwell/ Virginia Caputo. Photo by Virginia Caputo.

AMERICAN PAPER TOYS

The average mint price of paper toys in the last edition was $61.00. In this edition it is $63.29, an increase of 4%.

THE PROLIFIC WORLD OF PAPER

by Barbara and Jonathan Newman

The price of paper toys has barely fluctuated since the last edition. Although the economy seems to be gaining strength, paper toys haven't taken off. Celebrity paper dolls of the 1940s and WWII military-theme materials continue to show more of an increase than other paper toys. There is a constant stream of new models from around the world and an increased availability of some interesting East European paper toys.

Paper toys are so numerous that individual types continue to receive only superficial treatment, even in books devoted solely to paper toys. Nevertheless, a brief introduction will be attempted here.

They have been called cut-outs, punch-outs and press-outs. Forts, planes, trains, paper dolls and much, much, more have been produced in paper. What adult does not have some memories of crisp uncut booklets, shiny boxes, or cardboard toys?

From the end of the last century to the period after WWII, paper was, if not king, certainly close to the throne. It was, in many ways, the plastic of its day. Almost every type of toy can be found in a paper or cardboard version.

No collector of military toys or toy soldiers can be unfamiliar with the world of paper soldiers. Born in Europe about 200 years ago, paper soldiers were never quite as popular in the U.S. until American companies began turning out paper toys by the thousands around 1900. The most popular manufacturer was easily the McLoughlin Bros. Company, which started out with paper toys in 1857 in New York City. It was eventually bought out by Milton Bradley and moved to Springfield, Massachusetts, in 1920. McLoughlin/Milton Bradley products included beautifully lithographed covered boxed sets of cardboard figures on wooden stands, and, for the child with less resources, over a hundred different sheets of American and foreign armies to be cut out and mounted on little wooden stands.

During the years 1895-1905, almost every major newspaper in the country (at least the big-city papers with large Sunday editions) had Sunday "Art Supplements," which varied their "give away" fare from armies or navies of the world to historical panoramas, from political figures and personalities of the day to cut-out dolls of celebrities with vast wardrobes. The "Globe Quadruple Perfecting Press" in complete diorama cut-out form was the *Boston Sunday Globe*'s offering on August 6, 1896.

Paper houses and villages, favorites with little girls of the day, were sold by several companies. The earlier ones included the ubiquitous McLoughlin Bros. and Milton Bradley (yes, they're still around), and WWII-era giants in the field were Built-Rite and Megow.

There was no shortage of paper toys in the 1920s and 1930s, but the WWII-era was really the Golden Age of paper toys in the U.S. The lack of traditional material caused even the king of toy companies, Lionel, to produce as its only wartime offering a complete train set in die-cut cardboard. Who would have thought such a poor substitute in 1943 would be a sought-after rarity today? If you have one of these toys in mint condition, you have a real gem in the world of toy trains and the world of paper toys.

During the war years every conceivable type of toy was available, usually with a patriotic wartime theme. Punch-out cardboard sets of "Rap-A-Jap," "Sink the Axis," and "Camouflage Defense Force"; books of punch-out Naval Craft by Rigby; these were the birthday and Christmas presents of the 1940s and early 1950s. A whole range of Built-Rite forts, trenches, troops and doll houses are among the authors' own memories. Celebrity paper dolls were at their zenith, and except for the enemy called school, the days of little Barbara and Jonathan were filled with paper toys.

Someday perhaps the definitive book on paper toys will be written. In the meantime, we offer these listings and pictures to jog your memory or perhaps kindle a life-time passion for paper toys.

For those of you who already have that passion, there are now quite a few books on paper dolls and a good general book on paper toys. At least two exceptional books are out; one on paper soldiers by Edward Ryan and one on WWII-era paper toys by John Matthews.

Barbara and Jonathan Newman have been toy collectors for over 30 years. For most of that time they have run a mail-order paper toy business from Clifton Park in historic Saratoga County, New York. Barbara has successfully managed a business, two children (who are grown and have children of their own), and Jonathan. Jonathan is a retired Army officer and retired New York State government employee. Their major disappointments in life are that they carelessly shot the heads off of hundreds of Britains soldiers in the 1940s and that they bought toys instead of McDonald's stock in the 1960s.

Photos in this section by Jonathan Newman, and courtesy of Barbara and Jonathan Newman, unless otherwise noted.

	C6	C8	C10
Air-Hostess, 1947, Saalfield 2546	30	40	50
Alice Faye, 1941, Merrill 4800	95	200	235

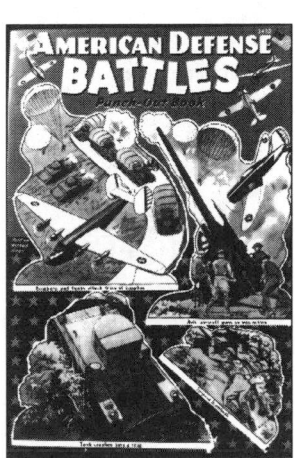

Top: "Alice Faye"; Right: "American Defense Battles Punch-Out Book."

	C6	C8	C10
All-Nu decal sheet of soldiers, meant to be attached to heavy cardboard backing, c. 1942, by Frank Krupp	60	75	100
All-Nu soldiers, c. 1942-3, 5" high on heavy cardboard			
100 Officer marching w/ sabre	3.50	5	7
101 Marching, slope arms, WWI helmet	3.50	5	7
102 Bugler, campaign cap	3.50	5	7
103 Signalman, WWI helmet	3.50	5	7
104 Officer kneeling w/ binoculars	3.50	5	7
105 Kneeling firing rifle w/ WWI helmet	3.50	5	7
106 Throwing grenade, WWI helmet	3.50	5	7
107 Fixed bayonet, WWI helmet	3.50	5	7
108 Charging w/ gas mask, WWI helmet	3.50	5	7

ALL-NU Cardboard Soldiers, No. 111, 109, 106, 108.

	C6	C8	C10
All-Nu soldiers, c. 1942-3, 5" high on heavy cardboard			
109 Charging w/ rifle, port arms, WWI helmet	3.50	5	7
110 Seated machine gunner, WWI helmet	3.50	5	7
111 Flag-bearer, WWI helmet	3.50	5	7
112 General McArthur	12	14	16
113 Nurse	3.50	5	7
114 2 Men carrying wounded soldier on stretcher, WWII helmets	3.50	5	7
115 2 Men firing rifles from prone position, WWII helmets	3.50	5	7
116 Soldier on wireless radio	3.50	5	7
117 3 Soldiers w/ rifles leaving boat, WWII helmets	3.50	5	7
118 2 Paratroopers, 1-w/ tommy gun, WWII helmets	3.50	5	7
119 Ski Trooper	3.50	5	7
120 Soldier advancing w/ rifle, WWII helmet	3.50	5	7
150 3 Men in jeep, WWI helmets	3.50	5	7
151 5 Man team w/ cannon, WWI helmets	3.50	5	7
152 2 Men manning wheeled AA gun, WWI helmets	3.50	5	7
153 Tank w/ 3 men	3.50	5	7
154 Ambulance	3.50	5	7
155 Truck w/ soldiers in rear, WWII helmets	3.50	5	7
All-Nu boxed set of 24 of the above soldiers	No Price Found		
American Beauties, Paper Dolls, c. 1942, Reuben Lilja & Co., No. 917	18	24	28
American Beauty Paper Dolls w/ dresses worn by White House First Ladies 1789-1951, Merrill No. 154815, 1951	27	37	48
American Defense Battles Punch-out Book by George Trimmer, Merrill No. 3430, 1940	75	95	105
American Family Paper-Doll Book "Costumes for all the family from 1610 to now," Grinnel No. C1002	50	65	80
Amos & Andy Cut-out cardboard of just Andy, 8-1/2" high, stand-up	4.50	6.50	8.50
Animal Paper Dolls to Dress, 1950, Saalfield 2598, Bear, Monkey, Pig, Kitten	15	18	24
Animals to Paint, 1910, Saalfield	12	18	24
Ann Blythe, 1952, Merrill No. 2250-25	55	85	100
Army Air Forces Aircraft Identification Silhouette Model-Feb. 1943, 1/72 scale of Japanese fighter Najajima T-97, A.N.F. 7" x 11" envelope	16	20	27
Army Ambulance, c. 1942, Handi-Kraft	30	40	48

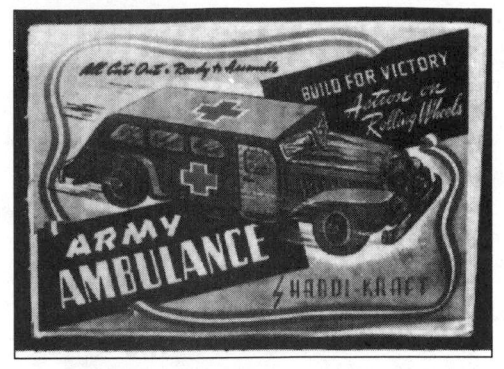

"Army Ambulance Build For Victory Action On Rolling Wheels."

	C6	C8	C10
Army Cut-outs, 1937, Saalfield No. 245	55	65	80
Army Nurse and Doctor Paper Dolls, 1942, Merrill 3425	45	55	80

"Army Nurse And Doctor Paper Dolls."

	C6	C8	C10
Around the World w/ Bob and Barbara, 1946, Children's Press No. 3000	12	18	22
Assemble 9 Model Warplanes, 4 Model Tanks, 1941, Fawcett Publications, Lowe	55	75	85
Ava Gardner, 1949, 1952, Whitman No. 119215	75	85	100
Baby Brother by Queen Holden, 1929, Whitman 920	90	120	130
Baby First Step, 1965 (Mattel), Whitman No. 1997	10	15	18
Babyland 1955, Merrill No. 3642	45	55	70
Baby Pat, 1963, Whitman No. 2072	9	12	14
Babysitter Paper Dolls, Lowe No. 945	32	40	45
Barbara Britton Paper Dolls w/ Magic Stay-on costumes, 1954, Saalfield No. 5190, boxed set	55	65	70
Barbie and Ken, 1962, Whitman No. 4797, 7" x 12" boxed set	25	40	50
Barbie and Skipper, 1964, Whitman No. 1957, Yachting outfits	22	32	45
Barbie Boutique, 1973, Whitman No. 1954	14	22	27
Beautiful Paper Dolls by Betty Campbell, 1941, Saalfield No. 242, has some of same paper dolls as Little Miss America Paper Dolls	50	60	75

	C6	C8	C10
Belle of the Ball Paper Dolls, 1948, Saalfield No. 2702	25	32	40
Betsy McCall, 1971, Whitman No. 4744	15	20	25
Betsy McCall Around the World Paper dolls, c. 1962	17	30	35
Betsy McCall Dress 'N Play Paper Dolls, 1963, Standard/Toycraft/McCall No. 802, 12" x 18" boxed set	18	30	35
Betsy Ross and Her Friends-1963, Platt and Munk No. 224B, 7" x 11" boxed set	18	28	32
Betty and Joan, 1941, 1945, Whitman No. 1015, Joan also appears in Mary and Joan, Lois and Joan	30	45	55
Betty Bonnet Her Family and Friends by Sheila Young, George W. Jacobs & Co., Phila., 1915. Each series w/ 6 sheets & folder.			
First series	125	150	180
Second series	100	145	175
Third series	100	145	175

"Betty Bonnet Her Family And Friends" (second series).

	C6	C8	C10
Betty Grable, 1951, Merrill No. 1558	65	90	110
Betty Sue A Cut Out Doll, c. 1940, No. 1010	18	25	30
The Beverly Hillbillies: Jed, Jethro, Granny and Elly May, Whitman No. 1955, 1964	27	38	42
Big-Girl Paper Dolls, 1940, McLoughlin Bros., No. 707, actually Milton Bradley	20	28	38

"Bild-A-Set Constructor Kit."

	C6	C8	C10
Big Invasion Punch-Out Book, 1964, Whitman No. 1936, punch-out of beach landing	25	35	40
Bild-A-Set Construction Kit No. 85 boxed, Erector-type set of cardboard	22	30	35
Binson-Freeman Pre Flight Trainer, cockpit and how to fly course	75	113	150
Birthday Party Stand-Up Cut-Out Dolls, 1944, National Syndicate Displays, Inc., 20 boys and girls	35	45	55

"Birthday Party Stand-Up Cut-Out Dolls."

	C6	C8	C10
Blue Bonnet Paper Dolls by Florence Salter, Merrill No. 3444, 1942	32	42	48
Blue Feather and Silver Cloud, 1940s, Abbott No. 1356, Indian dolls	40	50	60
Boarding School Dolls and Clothes, 1942, Merrill No. 3492	40	55	60
Bob Hope and Dorothy Lamour, 1942, Whitman No. 976	190	225	240
Bobby Socks Cut Out Dolls designed by Doris Lane Butler, 1945, Whitman, No. 988	45	55	65
Bombers by Schomburg, Whitman No. 961, 1943, B-17, B-25, B-24, Douglas A-20A, short "Stirling"	60	75	100

	C6	C8	C10
Book of Airplanes, A. Whitman No. 923, 1930	20	25	30
Book of Paper Doll cut-outs, 1927, Saalfield No. 2051	40	60	75
The Brady Bunch, 1973, Whitman No. 1976	15	25	30
Brenda Lee, 1964, No. 4360 De Journette, 6-1/2" x 10" boxed set, includes toy phonograph and records	50	65	75
Brenda Lee Teenage Celebrity, 1961, Lowe No. 2785	20	35	42
Bridal Party, 1950, Whitman No. 1187, five dolls	22	30	35
Bride and Groom, 1949, Merrill No. 3443	50	65	75
Bride and Groom, 1949, Merrill No. 1555	50	65	75
Bride and Groom Military Wedding Party, 1941, Merrill No. 3411, 16 dolls	80	90	100
Bride Doll Cut-Out Book, 1940s, Samuel Lowe No. 1043	25	45	55
Brother and Sister Statuette Dolls, 1950, Whitman No. 1182-15, 2 heavy cardboard 7-1/2" dolls	20	35	40
Buffy Paper Dolls ("Family Affair"), 1968, Whitman No. 1955	20	30	35
Buffy and Jody, 1970, ("Family Affair"), Whitman No. 4764, two magic dolls w/ stay-on wardrobes	20	30	35

"Bob Hope Dorothy Lamour Cut-Out Book."

BUILT-RITE

Built-Rite began in 1922 as a manufacturer of cardboard boxes. Somewhere along the line, at least as early as 1934, it began to produce cardboard construction toys. Judging by catalogs, Built-Rite sold its last fort (25A) in 1954 and its last few construction sets (three train accessories sets) in 1956 (until 1963-64, when the No. 1033 Doll House and No. 1027 Stock Farm appeared).

All construction sets were out from 1967-68 on. In 1978 Built-Rite added plastic playsets No. 6002 Fort Laredo and No. 6001 Starship Counterforce Action Playset. It dropped the Built-Rite name for Warren in 1976, and continues to make card games, games and puzzles under that name. Its greatest period of success was probably enjoyed prior to and during WWII.

	C6	C8	C10
No. 1 Toy Soldiers, WWI helmets, per each	2	3	4
No. 2 Toy Trench	25	45	60
No. 7 Private Garage, brick	35	45	55
No. 7 Army Plane Hangar	48	60	70
No. 8 House, brick	65	80	90
No. 9 House, stucco and brick	65	80	90
No. 10 House, 2-story, brick and shingle	65	80	90

	C6	C8	C10
No. 14 "Front Line" Trench and Soldier set, w/ trench, 6 WWII soldiers	40	55	60
No. 15 Commercial Garage	65	80	90
No. 16 Fort, no ramp	70	90	125
No. 17 Service Station	65	80	90
No. 18 Airport	65	80	85
No. 19 Railroad Station	60	70	80
No. 20 Railroad Tunnel	12	22	27

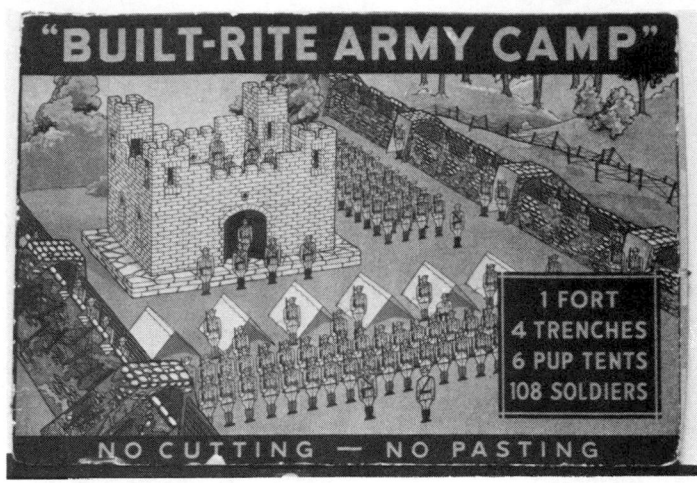

BUILT-RITE, Fort No. 16. Courtesy John D. (Jack) Matthews.

BUILT-RITE, Fort No. 25 w/ Barclay soldiers. Photo by Ed Poole.

BUILT-RITE, No. 20, Army Battery Set. Photo by Ed Poole.

	C6	C8	C10
No. 20 Army Battery Set	90	125	145
No. 22 Army Outpost	45	65	75

BUILT-RITE, No. 22, "Army Outpost." Courtesy John D. (Jack) Matthews.

	C6	C8	C10
No. 25 Fort, one ramp	90	120	130
No. 25A 26-piece Fort and Soldier Set, same fort as No. 25, WWII soldiers, 2 sandbag foxholes and fiberboard pistol, sold through 1954	120	150	175

BUILT-RITE, Airport No. 26.

	C6	C8	C10
No. 26 United Airlines Airport Hangar	60	75	85
No. 27 Barn w/ animals	30	45	55
No. 28 Garage and Super Service Station	70	85	95
No. 29 Three Cart Set	25	40	45
No. 33 Lokdwood Dolls, late 1940s, paper dolls	25	35	45
No. 33 House, Tudor type	65	80	90
No. 34 House, two-story	65	80	90
No. 35 Modern Doll House	65	80	90
No. 36 House	65	80	90
No. 36F 3-Room Furnished Doll House	85	95	105
No. 37 Farm Machinery Set	35	50	60
No. 45 Living Room Furniture	45	55	65
No. 46 Dining Room Furniture	45	55	65
No. 47 Bedroom Furniture	45	55	65
No. 48 Bathroom Furniture	45	55	65
No. 49 Kitchen Furniture	45	55	65
No. 50 Army Raiders' Victory Unit, 28 pieces, truck, tank, AA gun, jeep, semi-track truck, 20 soldiers, WWII	75	90	100
No. 55 5 Miniature cardboard houses	35	55	65
No. 56 5 Miniature buildings, church, school, RR station, firehouse, drugstore	35	55	65
No. 57M 8-piece Farm Set	40	50	65
No. 60 Navy Battle Fleet and Coast Artillery Gun	35	60	75
No. 66 3-piece Kitchen	30	45	55
No. 75 Living Room Furniture	45	55	65
No. 76 Dining Room Furniture	45	55	65

	C6	C8	C10
No. 77 Bedroom Furniture 45	55	65
No. 77 American Ranger Fighters, 8 vehicles, WWII soldiers 80	90	100
No. 78 Kitchen Furniture 45	55	65
No. 83 Weapons Carrier..............15	20	30
No. 84 Armored Car..............15	20	30
No. 100A Fortress, c. 1938, 2 ramps..............120	155	180
No. 105 Farm Set w/ 20 plastic animals 35	45	55
No. 111 Railroad Accessory Set 25	30	40

No. 112 American Fighters-includes 100A fortress w/ soldiers, cannons, etc., 55 pieces, no flag on tower 120 155 180

No. 115 Doll House, Garage Set (w/ car) 65 80 90
No. 119 Farm Set 45 65 75
No. 120 5-room Suburban Doll House 65 85 90
No. 127 Large Barn w/ animals 30 40 50
No. 128 Miniature Village and Scenery Set.......35 48 60
No. 148 Train Accessory Set 30 40 50
No. 156 Miniature Houses and Buildings 55 65 70
No. 178 Train Accessory Set 30 40 50

No. 201 26-piece Guardsman Set, 2 trenches, artillery base, cannon, pistol, WWII soldiers..............70 90 120

No. 202 Train Scenery (28 pieces, Terminal, Scenery, etc.)..............45 65 75
No. 204F Furnished Country Estate..............60 80 90
No. 205 Medlee game, w/ ships, cannon, etc......... No Price Found
No. 210 Railroad Station and Accessories..........30 40 50
No. 212 Station and Railroad Accessories..........35 45 55
No. 245 Miniature Village 35 50 60

No. 252 Fort Set, 26 pieces, No. 25 Fort, post-war..............110 150 180

No. 257 Fort Set, No. 25 Fort, 25 soldiers .... No Price Found
No. 298 Train Accessory Set 30 40 50
No. 300 Stock and Grain Elevator 30 35 45
No. 375 Station and Railroad Set 30 40 50

No. 415 House, c. 1943, 13" x 20" boxed set w/ 19" house and garage, 27 pieces of furniture, sedan, baby buggy, shrubbery, etc...........85 110 135

No. 459 5 Rooms of Toy Furniture..............45 55 65

No. 460 Pocket Size Series of Miniatures Paperdoll Set 15 20 24

No. 498 Train Accessory Set 25 35 45
No. 556 Miniature Village .... No Price Found
No. 566 Village 40 55 65
No. 1001 Modern Stock Farm..............50 60 80
No. 1027 Stock Farm 50 60 80
No. 1033 Doll House..............50 65 75

No. 1422 Fort and Soldiers (94 pieces, 2-ramp fort) 110 145 175

No. 1621 Army Camp: No. 16 Fort, trenches, tents, 108 soldiers.............. No Price Found

No. 2011 Doll House, 88 pieces........... No Price Found

No. 2050 Country Estate, house, bushes, dog, cat, baby buggy..............70 90 100

No. 2075 Colonial Cottage, 57 pieces.................... No Price Found

Built-Rite Ranch, over 180 pieces 150 185 200

"Camouflage Defense Force."

	C6	C8	C10

Camouflage Defense Force, airplanes, soldiers, anti-aircraft guns all hidden within farm buildings. Heavy cardboard. Jay Line Mfg. Co., 431, boxed, c. 1943........55 75 90

Career Girls w/ Cloth-Like Clothes, 1944, Whitman No. 937, by Doris Lane Butler......25 45 50

Charmin' Chatty, 1964, Whitman No. 1959 ......12 18 20

Charming Paper Dolls, c. 1960, Saalfield No. 1357 ......10 15 18

Cheerleader-Teenage Doll, 1950?, Stephens Publishing Co., No. 182, Mary & Elaine and 4 pages of clothes..........10 15 18

Children From Other Lands, 1961, Whitman No. 2089, 8 cut-out dolls and native costumes..............12 18 20

Children In The Shoe, 1949, Merrill No. 1562 ..38 48 58

Cinderella Steps Out, Lowe No. 1242..............25 45 55

Circus Day, 1946, by Art Tanchon, Stephens Printing No. 135, animals, clown, circus cages and wagons 18 22 28

"Circus Day Cut-Out Book."

Circus Paper Dolls, 1952, Saalfield No. 2610....10 15 18

Claire McCardell-designer of the American look, 1956, Whitman No. 2067....50 60 68

Claudette Colbert, 1943, Saalfield No. 2451....165 195 235

Cloth-Like Clothes for 3 Cute Girls, 1949, Whitman No. 1178:15, flocked clothes 25 35 45

Clothes Make A Lady, 1941, Lowe No. 1029....25 35 45

"Claudette Colbert Paper Dolls."

	C6	C8	C10
Cowboy and Cowgirl Cut-Outs, 1950, Merrill No. 3449 30		40	50
Cowboy Cutouts, c. 1930s, Platt and Munk 28		35	42
Cowboys and Indians Cut-outs, 1937, Saalfield 50		55	60
Cowgirl Jill and Cowboy Joe, Merrill No. 3459 28		40	48
Cradle Crowd, The, 1948, 4 doll babies w/ cloth-like clothes, Whitman No. 1173 45		55	65
Cut and Stick, Our Army and Navy in Action, Merrill No. 4835, 1942 35		45	50

	C6	C8	C10
Coke Crowd, The, 1946, Merrill No. 3445, 8 teens, costumes 50		65	75
College Style Paper Dolls, 1941, Merrill No. 3400 50		65	75

"College Style Paper Dolls."

"Cut And Stick."

	C6	C8	C10
Colorgraphic Statue-ettes, 1943, 3-dimensional and stand-up paper dolls of Marine, Soldier, Sailor, Nurse, WAAC, WAVE, boxed 30		40	50
Comet Model Airplane Co. Die Cut Glider, 5-1/2" x 8" sheet containing die-cut U.S. Army fighter, printed in 1942 by the Comet Model Airplane Co. 10		15	18
Commando Machine Gun, 1940s, thin cardboard cut-out makes model over 25" long 18		22	28
Connie Francis, 1963, Whitman No. 1956 45		55	65
Coronation Cut-Out Model Book 55		65	70
Coronation Glitter Model Book 35		45	48
Coronation Paper Dolls and Coloring Book, 1953, Saalfield No. 4450, 10-1/2" x 15" book. Queen Elizabeth, Prince Philip, young Prince Charles, and Princess Ann 65		75	90

	C6	C8	C10
Cut-Me-Out Paper Dolls, 1940s, Abbott No. 1358 18		25	30
Cut-Out Dolls, Puppies and Kittens, Whitman No. 931, 1939 75		90	125
Cut-Out Dolls w/ Paints and Clothes to Color, by Avis Mac, Whitman No. 983, c. 1930s, 11" x 18" book w/ four 17" children and 16 pages of clothing and sheet of paints 55		70	75
Cyd Charisse, 1956, Whitman No. 2084 55		75	95
Dancing Dolls w/ famous costumes, Merrill No. 3448, 1954, ballet dancers 40		50	60
Davy Crockett Punch Out Book, 1955, No. 1943 55		75	90
Deanna Durbin, 1940, Merrill No. 3480 180		200	235
Debs and Sub Debs Paper Doll Book, 1941, Saalfield No. 2361, 20 punch-outs 30		40	50

"Cut-Out Dolls Puppies And Kittens."

"Double Wedding 15 Paper Dolls."

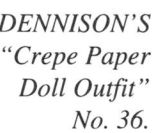

DENNISON'S "Crepe Paper Doll Outfit" No. 36.

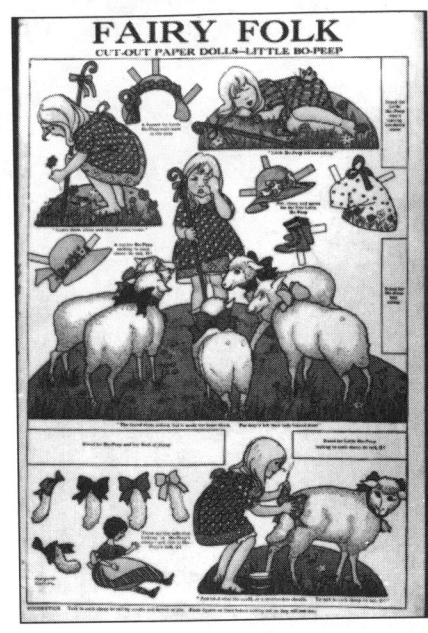

FAIRY FOLK
CUT-OUT PAPER DOLLS—LITTLE BO-PEEP

*"Fairy Folk
Cut-Out
Paper Dolls -
Little Bo-Peep."*

	C6	C8	C10
Farm Cut-outs by Milo Winter, 1938, Whitman No. 1054, 6-1/2" x 10-1/2", 6 pages of heavy paper cut-outs	30	38	48
The Fashion Book of the Round About Dolls, 1936, McLoughlin Bros., over 1" thick, 8 stand-up dolls plus scissors and pack of paper dolls clothes in package by Betty Campbell	55	75	85
Fashion Cut Outs w/ Sturdibilt Dolls, 1940s, Lowe No. 1243	20	25	35
Fifteen ABC Blocks to Play and Learn, 1933, Whitman No. 976, book containing 15 die-cut blocks to put together. Illustrations of nursery rhymes, alphabet letters, animals and numbers on each block	20	30	40
Fire Fighters in Action, Saalfield, 1938	22	48	52
Fire House P-18 by Megow, 1945, brick firehouse, boxed set	35	48	58
Five Little Peppers, Little Women and Annie Lauries, 1941, Lowe L1030, 3-book set	50	65	78
The Flying Nun, 1968, 1969, Artcraft No. 4417	25	35	40
Four Sisters Paper Dolls, 1943, Saalfield No. 269	20	27	32
Fourteen Dogs To Cut Out and Stand Up, copyright 1930, Whitman No. 935, 12 pages of dogs, cardboard punch-outs	25	35	48
French Infantry-Milton Bradley?, c. 1915, approx. 6" high, single figure, each cardboard	3	5	6
Frontier Fort, 1952, Merrill No. 257225	15	25	30
Fun Farm, Reed and Associates	8	15	18
Gene Autry Melody Ranch Cut-Out Dolls, 1950, Whitman No. 990-10	60	80	90
Gene Autry Ranch cut-out book, 1940, Merrill	65	80	90
Gene Autry Ranch cut-out book, 1953	50	70	80
Gigi Perreau Paper Dolls, 1951, Saalfield No. 1542	35	50	55
Gigi Perreau, 1951, Saalfield No. 2605	35	50	55

	C6	C8	C10
Girl Friend-Boy Friend Paper Dolls, 1955, Saalfield No. 1605	18	22	24
Girl Friends paper dolls, 1944, Whitman No. 974	28	38	48
Girl Pilots of the Ferry Command, 1943, Merrill No. 4852	80	95	115
Girls in Uniform Paper Dolls Book, c. 1942, No. L1048	60	80	90
Glamour Parade Cut-out Dolls, Stephens Publishing Co., No. 184, 1950s?, 4 models and 4 pages of clothes	12	18	22
Glenn Miller, Marion Hutton Turnabout Doll Book, 1942, Lowe No. 21041	140	160	200

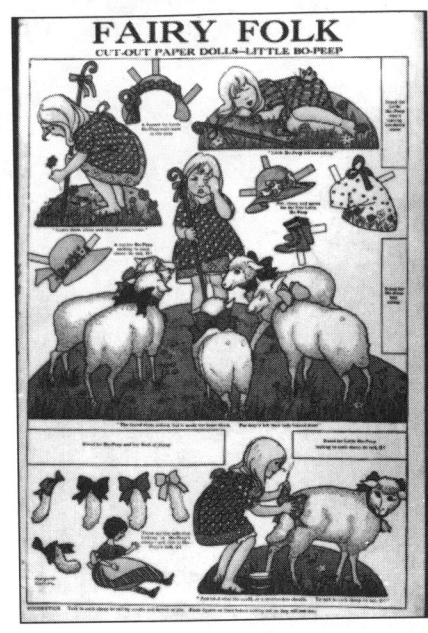

GLENN MILLER MARION HUTTON
Turnabout DOLL BOOK

*"Glenn Miller
Marion Hutton
Turnabout
Doll Book."*

	C6	C8	C10
Gloria Jean Paper Doll Cut-outs, 1940, Saalfield No. 1661	75	90	110
Gone With The Wind, 1940, Merrill No. 3404, 18 dolls	325	350	400
Gone With The Wind, 1940, Merrill No. 3405, 5 dolls	300	350	400
Good Neighbor Paper dolls, 1944, Saalfield No. 2487	15	22	27
Grace Kelly 2 Cut Out Dolls and Clothes Whitman No. 2049, 1955	65	85	95
Grace Kelly, 1956, Whitman No. 2069	65	85	95
Gulliver's Travels cut-outs, 1939, Saalfield No. 1261	60	70	80
Hair-Do Dolls by Queen Holden, 1948, Whitman No. 991	60	80	100
Harry the Soldier, 1941, Samuel Lowe, No. L1074	45	65	75
Hayley Mills, "The Moonspinners," 1964, Whitman No. 1960	40	45	50
Heavy Cruiser, "This is the Navy," c. 1943, Skyline Mfg. Co.	20	30	40
Hedy Lamarr Paper Dolls, Saalfield No. 1555	100	120	150
Hee Haw, 1971, Artcraft No. 5139	25	40	45
Heidi and Peter, c. 1970, Saalfield No. 1355	12	15	20
Here Comes the Bride, 1952, Whitman No. 118915	25	45	55
Here's the Bride, 1953, Whitman No. 2109	25	45	55

"Grace Kelly 2 Cut-Out Dolls And Clothes."

	C6	C8	C10
Howdy Doody Sticker Fun, copyright 1953, Whitman No. 215825	25	35	40
Howdy Doody Sticker Fun Circus, copyright 1955, Whitman No. 2165	25	35	40
I Love Lucy, Lucille Ball and Desi Arnaz, 1953, Whitman No. 2101	60	80	90
Jack and Jill, 1962, Merrill No. 1561, 6 dolls and clothes from storyland	25	30	35
Jane Russell, 1955, Saalfield No. 2611	45	75	85
Janet Leigh Cut-outs and Coloring Books, 1953, Merrill No. 2554	55	70	80
Janet Leigh, 1958, Abbott No. 1805	48	60	68
Jaunty Juniors, 1946, No. 903	25	35	40

	C6	C8	C10
High School Girls, 1948, Merrill No. 1551	50	60	65
Historical Dolls To Cut Out and Dress, 1961, Platt & Munk No. 226B, 7" x 11" boxed set. Mother, father, and 2 children of heavy cardboard, plus outfits	20	30	35
Holiday Paper dolls, 1950s, Saalfield No. 1742	15	18	22
Hollywood Fashion Dolls, 1939, Saalfield No. 397, 12 male and female dolls, clothes	35	45	55
Hollywood Fashions, 1949, Saalfield No. 1535	25	35	50
Hour of Charm Paper Dolls, 1943, women musicians, Saalfield No. 2481	80	95	120
House For Sale, 1962, Lowe No. 9042	35	45	50

"Jaunty Juniors."

"House For Sale."

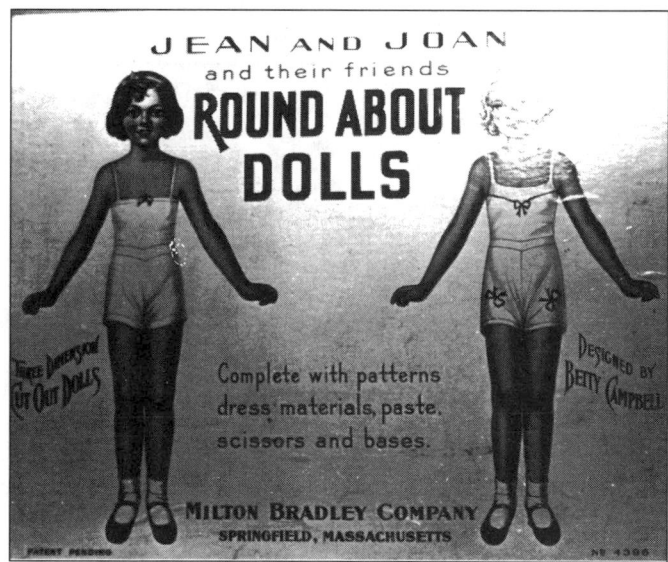

"Jean And Joan And Their Friends Round About Dolls."

	C6	C8	C10
House That Jack Built, c. 1895, Bliss, R.I. paper litho, house and story's characters w/ stands	400	500	600
Howdy Doody Puppet Show Punchout Book, copyright 1952, Whitman No. 211129, punch-out cardboard puppets may be controlled by strings. Includes Howdy, Bluster, Inspector, Dilly Dally, Clarabell, and Flubadub	55	65	70
Howdy Doody Sticker Fun, copyright 1951, Whitman No. 219525	25	35	40

	C6	C8	C10
Jean and Joan and their Friends, Roundabout Dolls designed by Betty Campbell, 1934, boxed set, Milton Bradley No. 4396	75	90	110
Jeanette MacDonald, 1941, Merrill No. 3640	175	200	225
Jimmy & Jane Visit Gene Autry at Melody Ranch, 1951, Whitman No. 118415	55	68	75
Joan's Wedding by Florence Sarah Winship, clothes designed by Ruth M. Ruhman, 1942, Whitman No. 990	45	55	65

"Kiddieland Village."

	C6	C8	C10
Judy and Jack, Peg & Bill Cut-out Dolls by Pelagie Doane, 1940, Lowe No. L1024	45	65	80
"Julia," Diahann Carroll, Julia, Corey, Marie and Earl J. Waggedorn, 1968, Artcraft No. 5140	30	40	45
Julia w/ Julia, Earl J. Waggedorn and Corey, 1969, Saalfield	30	40	45
June Allyson, 1950, 1952, Whitman No. 119015	50	80	95
June Allyson, 1953, Whitman No. 1173:15	60	80	95
June Bride by Art Tanchon, 1946, Stephens No. 136	22	32	42

"June Bride."

	C6	C8	C10
Junior Bombardier, 1953, Einson & Freeman Co. No. 202	25	40	45
Junior Prom by Newman, 1942, Lowe 1042	35	45	50

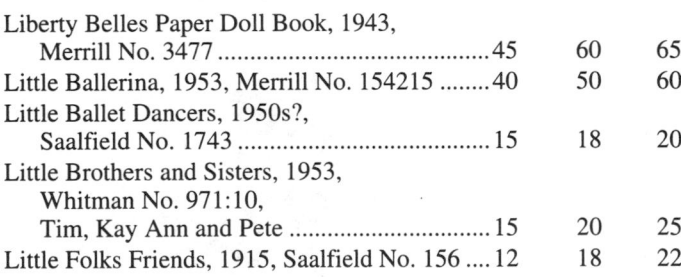

"Kellogg's Pep" Warplane, cardboard, c. 1944. Courtesy HAKE'S Americana & Collectibles.

	C6	C8	C10
Karen Goes to College!, 1955, Merrill No. 1564	25	40	45
Kiddieland Village, c. 1935, Whitman No. 2004, 11-1/2" x 15" boxed set, 9 buildings and 65 cut-out figures	65	80	95
Kitty goes to Kindergarten, 1956, Merrill No. 1548	25	35	45
Lennon Sisters, 1957, Whitman No. 1979	35	50	60

	C6	C8	C10
Lennon Sisters, 1961, Whitman No. 1983	35	50	60
Lettie Lane Paper Family, Third Series, 1909, George W. Jacobs & Co., original house folder and 6 sheets	130	155	180

"The Lettie Lane Paper Family."

	C6	C8	C10
Liberty Belles Paper Doll Book, 1943, Merrill No. 3477	45	60	65
Little Ballerina, 1953, Merrill No. 154215	40	50	60
Little Ballet Dancers, 1950s?, Saalfield No. 1743	15	18	20
Little Brothers and Sisters, 1953, Whitman No. 971:10, Tim, Kay Ann and Pete	15	20	25
Little Folks Friends, 1915, Saalfield No. 156	12	18	22

"Little Folk's Friends."

	C6	C8	C10
Little Friends from History by Muriel Wilhoite, Rand McNally No. 186, 1936	55	65	70

"Little Friends From History."

"Lots Of Little Paper Dolls."

"Little Mary Mixup And Her Friend Peggy." (See Comic Characters)

	C6	C8	C10
Lots of Little Paper Dolls by Angela Tuite Price, 1949, Saalfield No. 1537	25	35	40
Lucille Ball, Desi Arnaz Cut-Out Dolls w/ Little Ricky, 1953, Whitman No. 2116:25	70	80	90
Lucille Ball Paper Dolls, 1944, Saalfield No. 2475	70	80	90

"Lucille Ball Desi Arnaz Cut-Out Dolls With Little Ricky."

	C6	C8	C10
Little Friends Paper Dolls, 1950s, Saalfield No. 1746	12	18	20
Little Miss America Paper Doll Book, 1941, Saalfield No. 2358, 15 punch-outs by Campbell	35	45	50
Little Nurse Cut-Out Book, early 1940s, Reuben H. Lilja and Co., Inc., No. 909	20	30	35
Little Red School House Kindergarten, The, by Margo Voight, McLoughlin Bros., 1940, 2 teachers, 23 children	45	55	60
Little Women, c. 1970, Artcraft No. 5127	15	20	25
Lois and Joan Cut-out Dolls, 1941, 1945, Whitman No. 1015 (Joan also appears in Betty & Joan and Mary and Joan)	30	45	50
The Lone Ranger Rides Again Punchout Set, DeJournette Mfg. Co., makes fences, figures of LR and Tonto, horses, campfire	35	45	55
Look-a-Like Cut-Out Dolls, 1952, Whitman No. 97210, 2 mother and daughter pairs of dolls	20	25	30
Look Who I Am! 1952, Hart Publishing Co. by Doris Stelberg, 18" doll w/ 15 costumes, spiral bound	15	20	25
Lori Martin in National Velvet, 1962, Whitman No. 4612, 6" x 11-1/2" boxed set, paper dolls	25	35	40
Lost Horizon, 1973, Artcraft No. 5112	15	20	25

	C6	C8	C10
Madame Hattie Fashions, 1940s, Reuben Lilja No. 908	35	45	48
Magic Mary, 1955, Milton Bradley No. 4010-1, 10-1/2" x 10-1/2" boxed set, complete w/ magnetic doll and strips to put on clothes	15	18	22
Make Your Own Battle Set Mechanized Force, 1942, Electric Corporation of America	45	50	55

"Make Your Own Battle Set Mechanized Force."

	C6	C8	C10
Margaret O'Brien Paper Dolls, Whitman No. 96410	100	120	150
Marge and Gower Champion, 1959, Whitman	60	80	100
Martha Hyer Paper Dolls, 1958, Saalfield No. 4423	45	55	60
Mary and Joan, 1941, 1945, Whitman No. 1015 (Joan also appears in Lois & Joan and Betty & Joan)	35	45	50

	C6	C8	C10
Mary Belle Cut-Out Doll by Fern Bisel Peat, Saalfield No. 2100, 4 separate sheets, 17" doll w/ 3 sheets of clothes, 1934	55	65	75
Mary Jane, A Cut-Out Doll, by Florence Winship, 1939, 1941, Whitman No. 1010 w/ suitcase for accessories	40	45	50
Mary Lee, A Cut-Out Doll, Whitman No. 1010, c. 1939	40	45	50
Mary Martin, 1942, Saalfield No. 2427	160	180	200
Mary of the WACS, A Young American, by Hilda Miloche and Wilma Kane, Whitman No. 1012, 1943	45	55	65
Mary Poppins, 1973, Whitman No. 1977	25	35	40
Marybelle Mercer's Front and Back Dolls w/ Wrap-Around Dresses by Queen Holden No. 978	85	95	110

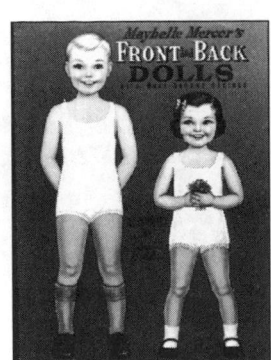

"Maybelle Mercer's Front And Back Dolls."

McLOUGHLIN BROS.

McLoughlin Brothers was the largest American producer of paper soldiers and one of the earliest in the paper doll field. The Brooklyn, New York, firm, founded in 1828, began producing paper dolls at least as early as 1857. Among the other paper toys it sold were dollhouse furniture, toy theaters with actors and scenery, and blocks. The company was sold in 1920 to Milton Bradley.

McLoughlin Bros., c. 1884, mounted U.S. Cavalry, Hussar type, charging, several different poses. Price per figure 2.75   3   3.50

McLoughlin Bros. Infantry Soldiers, printed 1857, price per each $5, complete set $200-250

McLoughlin Bros. Infantry, c. 1875, price per each 3   4   5

McLoughlin Bros., Zouaves, 1884, price per each 2.75   3.50   4.50

McLoughlin Bros. Brass Band, 1890, price per each 3.50   4.50   5.50

McLoughlin Bros. Grenadiers, 1890, price per each 3   3.50   4

McLoughlin Bros. Paper Dolls, 1860-1890, price per cut set $50 and up; uncut $100 and up, depending on title, date, etc.

McLoughlin Bros. 100 Soldiers on Parade, c. 1898 300   350   400

	C6	C8	C10
McLoughlin Bros. 100 Soldiers on Parade, second set, c. 1898	300	350	400
McLoughlin Bros. 260 Series, c. 1889-1895			
c. U.S. Regulars, spiked helmet, each	2.25	3	4
d. U.S. Infantry	2.25	3	4
f. West Point Cadets	2.25	3	4
g. U.S. Regulars	2.25	3	4
h. U.S. Infantry	2.25	3	4
i. Bandsmen, various instruments, each	2.75	3.50	4.50
j. Navy - USS Boston	2.25	3	4
k. Grenadier Guards, each	2.25	3	4
l. Annapolis Cadets, each	2.25	3	4
McLoughlin Bros. c. 1890, uncut horizontal sheet of 10 figures	35	50	75
McLoughlin Bros., printed 1898, sailor 5-1/4" high, landing party for USS Texas	4	5	6
McLoughlin Bros., U.S. Infantry from Spanish-American War, c. 1898, approx. 6" high on wooden blocks, price per figure	4	5	6
McLoughlin Bros., c. 1898, small glossy series, 4-1/2" high, West Point Cadets, price per figure	4	5	6
McLoughlin Bros., c. 1898, glossy series, U.S. Regulars, full dress, 5" high	4	5	6
McLoughlin Bros., c. 1898, British Infantry Red Coats, spiked helmets, 6" high on small wooden blocks, price per figure	4	5	6
McLoughlin Bros., c. 1898, U.S. Zouaves, Civil War era, blue coats, red baggy trousers, 6" high on small wooden blocks	4	5	6
McLoughlin Bros. "02" Series, c. 1904-1910, price per figure	2	2.50	3
a. British Highlanders			
b. U.S. Zouaves			
c. U.S. Continentals			

McLOUGHLIN BROS. "100 Soldiers On Parade."

	C6	C8	C10

McLoughlin Bros. "02" Series, (cont.)
  d. U.S. Navy
  e. U.S. Infantry in Campaign
    Uniforms (Spanish-American War)
  h. American Indians, kneeling and standing
  i. West Point Cadets
McLoughlin Bros., same as above
  g. West Point Cadets (round base),
    c. 1915 ....2.50   3   3.50
McLoughlin Bros. No. 0103 Dutch Paper
  doll, boy of the Village of Vollendam,
  c. 1910, 10-1/2" x 10-1/2" sheet 18   25   30
McLoughlin Bros., c. 1915, Boy Scouts
  holding rifles across chests 5   6   7
McLoughlin Bros., Series No. 4026
  10-1/2" x 10-1/2" paper soldiers on
  sheet, 7 soldiers plus officer
  (5-1/2" high) in field uniform,
  c. 1916, price per sheet 20   30   40
    1. Belgium   3. Italy
    2. France   4. Britain

McLoughlin Bros., New Folding
  Doll House, 1897, boxed set,
  cardboard w/ litho paper 400   500   575
McLoughlin Bros., New Pretty
  Village Church Set, 1897......................90   125   145
McLoughlin Bros., New Pretty
  Village School Set, 1897 90   125   145
McLoughlin Bros., New Pretty
  Village, individual bldgs..............................12   15   18

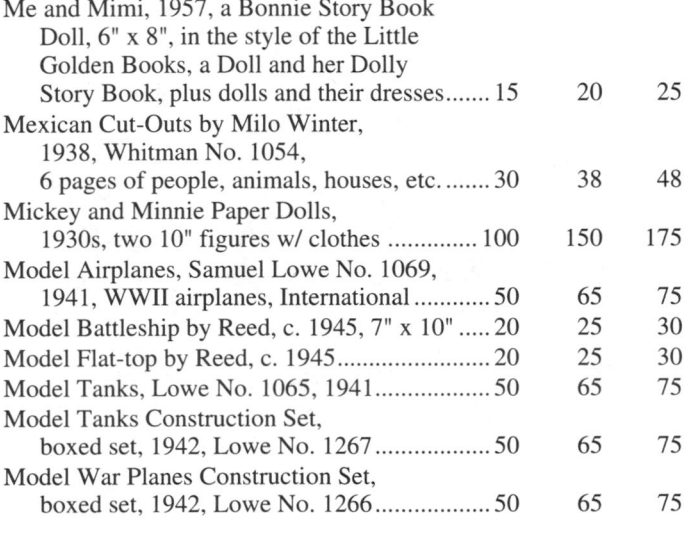

McLOUGHLIN BROS. "The New Pretty Village."

McLOUGHLIN BROS., Building from New Pretty Village.

Me and Mimi, 1957, a Bonnie Story Book
  Doll, 6" x 8", in the style of the Little
  Golden Books, a Doll and her Dolly
  Story Book, plus dolls and their dresses.......15   20   25
Mexican Cut-Outs by Milo Winter,
  1938, Whitman No. 1054,
  6 pages of people, animals, houses, etc. 30   38   48
Mickey and Minnie Paper Dolls,
  1930s, two 10" figures w/ clothes 100   150   175
Model Airplanes, Samuel Lowe No. 1069,
  1941, WWII airplanes, International 50   65   75
Model Battleship by Reed, c. 1945, 7" x 10" 20   25   30
Model Flat-top by Reed, c. 1945.....................20   25   30
Model Tanks, Lowe No. 1065, 1941.................50   65   75
Model Tanks Construction Set,
  boxed set, 1942, Lowe No. 1267..................50   65   75
Model War Planes Construction Set,
  boxed set, 1942, Lowe No. 1266.................50   65   75

"Model Tanks Construction Kit."

"Model War Planes Construction Kit."

	C6	C8	C10
Modern Miss in Paper Dolls, 1942, by Van Swearingen, Saalfield No. 2397	30	40	45
Molly Bee, 1962, Whitman No. 2091	20	35	45
Mommy and Me, 1954, Whitman No. 977:10	18	25	30
Mother and Daughter by Patrie Winston, Grinnel Lithographic No. C-1005, 15" mother, 11" daughter, 2 Scotties, 1940	30	45	50
Mouseketeer Cut-Outs, 1957, Whitman No. 1974	45	55	60
Movie Starlets, 1946, Whitman No. 960, Gail Russell, Diana Lynn, Olga San Juan, Marjorie Reynolds, Joan Caulfield	70	80	100
Movie Starlets Paper Dolls, c. 1949, Stephens Publishing Co. No. 178, 4 dolls (Miss Premier, Miss Stardust, Miss Hollywood, Miss Preview) and 4 pages of costumes	25	30	35
Mrs. Beasley Paper doll Book, 1970, ("Family Affair" TV show), Whitman No. 1973	15	20	25
My Fair Lady, 1965, Ottenheimer Publishers No. 2960-2, by Evon Hartman	35	40	45
My Paper Doll's Sewing Kit, 1940, by Margot Voight, Grinnell C-1018	22	45	48
My Twin Babies With Older Brother and Sister, 1940, Whitman No. 970	40	55	65
My Very First Paper Doll Book, 1957, a Bonnie Book No. 4732, Samuel Lowe	12	18	20
Nancy and Her Dolls w/ 7 Busy Days of Fun, 1944, Saalfield No. 2478	25	40	45
Natalie Wood Paper Dolls, 1958, Whitman	70	85	100

	C6	C8	C10
National Velvet, 1961, Whitman No. 1958	30	40	48
Navy Scouts Paper Doll Book, 1942, Merrill No. 3428	70	80	95
New Shirley Temple In Paper Dolls, The, 1942, Saalfield No. 2425	100	125	150
New York World's Fair Make A Model, 1963, by Ottenheimer, Spertus No. 600-50, includes Unisphere, Swiss Ride, N.Y. Port Authority, Heliport, etc.	25	30	35
Night Before Christmas w/ Cut-Outs, Whitman No. 948	20	25	30
19 Farmyard Animals To Cut Out and Stand Up, Copyright 1930, Whitman No. 935, 12 pages	35	40	45
Oklahoma w/ Shirley Jones and Gordon MacRae, 1956, Whitman No. 1954	55	75	85
On Guard, 1942, Lowe No. L535	40	45	50
One Hundred Soldiers Punch-Out Book, 1943, Whitman No. 999	55	60	65
Our Happy Family Cut-Out Sheets, 1928, Sam'l Gabriel Sons Co. No. D141	65	75	90

"On Guard A Punchout Book."

"The New Shirley Temple In Paper Dolls."

"100 Soldiers Punch-Out Book," 1943, Whitman 999. Courtesy John D. (Jack) Matthews.

"Our Happy Family Cut-Out Sheets."

"Paper Doll Family And Their Trailer."

"Our Soldiers Cut Out Army Uniforms."

	C6	C8	C10
Our New Home, 1930, story by Susan S. Popper, pictures by Helen E. Ohrenschall, Sam'l Gabriel Sons, hardcover book, 6 pages of rooms 6 gummed pages of people, furniture, etc. ...	80	100	125
Our Nurse Nancy, A Young American, by Hilda Miloche and Wilma Kane, 1943, cut-outs, Whitman No. 1012	50	55	60
Our Sailor Bob, 10" doll w/ uniforms, Whitman, c. 1943	45	50	55
Our Soldier Jim, 1943, Whitman No. 3980, designed by Hilda Miloche and Wilma Kane, 10-1/2" standup doll w/ uniforms	45	50	55
Our Soldiers Cut-Out Army Uniforms by Nat Falk, Dell, 1941, 4 cut-out dolls and several uniforms..........................	55	60	75
Our Wave Joan, A Young American by Hilda Miloche and Wilma Kane, 1943, Whitman No. 1012	45	50	55
Outdoor Paper Dolls, 1941, Saalfield No. 1958, 14 dolls and 4 pages of clothes....	12	18	20
Over 80 Turn-About, Standup Sailors, 1943, Lowe No. 141	45	55	60
Over 80 Turn-About, Standup Sailors, 1943, Lowe No. 140	45	55	60
Paper Doll Family And Their House by Florence and Margaret Hoopes, 1934, Saalfield No. 4125	60	70	75
Paper Doll Family And Their Trailer, Merrill No. 3436, 1938.................................	70	80	90
Paper Doll "Joan" and Paper Doll "Bobby" by Queen Holden, 1928, Whitman No. 907	80	90	100
Paper Doll Outfit, American Toy Works No. 102, boxed set	50	65	80
Paper Doll Playmates, 1940, Saalfield No. 154, Nurse, 19 children, costumes, toys	45	50	55

"Paper Doll Outfit Dresses And Hats."

	C6	C8	C10
Paper Dolls from Mother Goose, 1957, Saalfield No. 2758, Mary, Bo-Peep, Boy Blue, Bobbie Shaftoe, Miss Muffet, Jack Horner	18	22	27
Paper Dolls Julia and Marie by Angela Tuite Price, 1958, Saalfield No. 1530...........	20	22	25

"Paper Dolls Julia Marie."

"Paper Dolls Of All Nations New York World's Fair 1939."

	C6	C8	C10
Paper Dolls Of All Nations, New York World's Fair, 1939, Saalfield No. 227	50	55	65
Paper Dolls of Eve Arden, 1956, Saalfield No. 1706	55	70	80
Paper Dolls Peter and Peggy, 1935, Whitman No. 965, 64 pages by Dixon, very large punch-outs on front and back	45	55	60
Paper Dolls To Cut Out and Paint, 1920s, Saalfield No. 1180	55	65	75

Paper Dolls To Cut Out And Paint.

	C6	C8	C10
Paper Dolls United We Stand by Margot Voight, Saalfield No. 113, 6 children w/ uniforms	50	65	75
The Partridge Family, 1971, Artcraft No. 5137	20	30	35
Partridge Family, 1972, Artcraft No. 5143	20	30	35
Pat Boone, 1959, Whitman No. 1968	45	50	60
Pat Crowley, 1955, Whitman No. 2050	50	60	68
Patience and Prudence, 1958, Lowe No. 2736 (Popular singers of the 1950s)	20	25	30
Patsy, 1946, Children's Press, No. 30002, Patsy, dog, doghouse, etc.	30	35	40
Patsy A Wooden Doll W/ Dresses (actually a 10" standup cardboard doll with wood backing), c. 1938, Whitman No. 3037	40	45	50
Patsy Ann and Her Trunk full of Clothes by Queen Holden, 1939, Whitman No. 992	85	95	105
Patti Page, 1958 book of paper dolls	45	60	75
Patty's Party Paper Dolls, c. 1950, Stephens Publishing Co. No. 175	15	20	22
Pert and Pretty, 1948, Merrill No. 1552	42	48	52

	C6	C8	C10
Peter and Peggy, 1950, Whitman No. 99210	15	22	27
Peter and Peggy, Jerry and Joan Paper Dolls by Rachel Taft Dixon, 1935, Whitman No. 985	55	65	75
Photo Fashions, 1953, Whitman No. 973	20	25	30
Pig Tails, 1949, Merrill No. 344410	35	45	50
Pilot and Stewardess Paper Doll Book, 1941, Merrill No. 3423	42	47	52

"Pilot And Stewardess Airliner Paper Dolls."

	C6	C8	C10
The Pink Wedding, 1952, Merrill No. 1559	50	58	65
Piper Laurie, 1953, Merrill No. 2551	45	58	70
Playhouse Dolls, 1949, Stephens Publishing Co. No. 1965, 4 dolls and 4 pages of clothes	15	20	22
Playhouse Paper Dolls designed by Doris and Marion Henderson, Lowe No. 1028, 1941	27	38	42
Playhouse Paper Dolls, 1947, Saalfield No. 381	18	26	32

"Playhouse Paper Dolls ... designed by Doris and Marion Henderson."

"Playhouse Paper Dolls."

	C6	C8	C10
Playmates, 1952, Whitman No. 99510	15	20	25
Playthings To Cut Out and Stand Up, c. 1935, Whitman No. 934, contains ventriloquist's dummy, floating ships, general's hat, lantern, animals, other moving toys	32	36	45
Play Time, 1952, Whitman No. 210525	12	15	18

	C6	C8	C10
Playtime Pals, 1946, Lowe No. 1045	15	20	24
Polly Patchwork and Her Friends by Pelagie Doane, 1941, Lowe No. 1024	35	42	46
Polyanna Cut-Out Dolls, 1941, Whitman No. 995	50	55	65
Popular Paper Dolls, 1942, Saalfield No. 1973	25	30	35
Portrait Girls W/ Cloth-Like Clothes, 1947, designed by Hilda Miloche and Wilma Kane, Whitman No. 1170	35	45	48
Power Models Cut-Out Dolls Book, 1942, 6 dolls, Whitman No. 981	65	90	110
Pressed Board Dolls and Their Dresses, boxed set, Lowe No. 1942	30	40	48
Pre-Teen Paper Dolls, c. 1960s, Saalfield No. 1366	10	14	18
Prince and Princess Paper Dolls, 1949, Saalfield No. 2706	20	30	35
Prom Time, 1962, Whitman No. 2084, 2 dolls and party clothes	15	20	25
Queen Holden! Betty and Bob, 1952, 12-1/2" children, Whitman No. 99110	55	60	65
Queen Holden! Hair-Do Dolls, 1948, 3 dolls, clothes and 31 different hair-dos, Whitman No. 99110	50	60	80
Quiz Kids Paper Dolls, 1942, Saalfield No. 2430	95	105	135
Raggedy Ann and Andy, 1953, by Ethel Hays, Saalfield No. 2719	25	32	36
Raggedy Ann and Andy Paper Dolls, 1944, Saalfield No. 2719-15	45	50	55
Raggedy Ann and Andy Paper Dolls, 1944, Saalfield No. 2741, by Ethel Hays	45	50	55
Raggedy Ann and Andy, 1968, Whitman No. 4740	15	20	25
"Rap-A-Jap," c. 1943, Woodburn Mfg. No. C1	55	65	72

"Rap-A-Jap." Courtesy Jack Matthews.

	C6	C8	C10
Ready Cut Village, 1930s, no mfg. listed	55	70	80
Ricky Nelson paper dolls, 1959	40	46	52
Riders of the West Paper Dolls, 1950, Saalfield No. 2716-15	15	20	25

RIGBY'S "Book of Model Ships." Courtesy Mapes Auctioneers & Appraisers.

	C6	C8	C10
Rigby's Book of Model Ships, 1953	75	85	90
Rigby's Easy to Build Models of Fighting Planes	85	95	115
Rigby's Easier to Build Models of Naval Craft, 24 models of warships, 27 pages, 11-1/2" x 14", designed by Wallace Rigby, 1944, includes Battleship North Carolina, aircraft carrier, cruiser, destroyer, etc.	95	120	135
Rigby Flying Models of Jet and Rocket Planes, 10 planes, 1949, Garden City Books	70	80	90
Rigby's Model Book of Flying Clippers, 11"x14" book designed by Wallace Rigby, 2 scale models of Douglas DC-Jet Clipper and Douglas DC-7C, 1947	60	70	80
Rigby's Model Sports Cars of the World, 1954, includes 18" "Sportsracer," Chevette, Jaguar, Mercedes-Benz, etc.	60	70	80
Robin Hood and Maid Marian, 1950s, Saalfield No. 1761, paper dolls	25	40	45
Rock Hudson Paper Dolls, 1957, Whitman No. 2087	38	48	58
Rosemary Clooney, Samuel Lowe No. 1256	42	48	58
Rosemary Clooney, 1958, Samuel Lowe No. 2487	45	60	70
Rowan & Martin's Laugh-In Punch-Out Paper Doll Book, 1969, Saalfield No. 1325, Rowan, Martin, Jo Ann Worley, Arte Johnson, Judy Carne and Goldie Hawn	27	38	42
Roy Rogers and Dale Evans, 1950, Whitman No. 1186	55	70	85
Roy Rogers and Dale Evans, 1954, Whitman No. 1950	55	70	85
Roy Rogers Cut-Out Dolls, 1948, Whitman No. 995	60	90	125
Roy Rogers Sticker Fun Book, 1953, No. 2161	22	30	36

Royalty Cut-Out Books: A Procession
of the Knights of the Garter 55 65 70

Royalty Cut-Out Books: Trooping The Colour 55 65 70

Ruth Newton's Cut-out Dolls and Animals
"w/ over 80 pieces to cut out and
play with," 1934, 11" x 17" 55 65 75

Sally Ann A Cut-Out Doll, c. 1940,
Whitman No. 1010 .... 30 40 45

Sally's Silver Skates, 1956 Merrill No. 1549 .... 42 47 56

Sally the Standing Doll,
1940s, Lowe No. 1042 .... 35 45 48

"Sally
The Standing Doll."

Sandra and Sue Statuette Dolls and
Their Clothes, by Lee Lunzer,
1948, Whitman No. 1180 .... 32 40 45

Sandra Dee, 1959, boxed, 2 dolls and
34 costume pieces, Saalfield No. 5511 .... 45 55 60

Sandy and Sue, 1963, Whitman No. 1956 .... 15 20 25

School Girl Paper Dolls, 1942,
Saalfield No. 2400 .... 35 45 48

Scissors Bird Paper Dolls, 1946,
Stephens No. 137 .... 15 20 25

Service Kit of America's Armed
Forces-On Land-On Sea-In the Air,
1942, Lowe No. 265 .... 45 55 60

6 Good Little Dolls, no date,
Stephens Publishing Co. No. 183 .... 15 20 25

"Service Kit Of America's Armed Forces On Land On Sea In The Air."

6 Movie Starlets, 1942, Anne Nagel,
Peggy Moran, Jane Frazee, Anne
Gwynne, Helen Parrish, Ann Gillis 135 150 175

Sharp Shooters, c. 1915, Milton Bradley
No. 4103, boxed set w/ 2 sets of 5
cardboard soldiers and 1 officer on stands ... 85 100 135

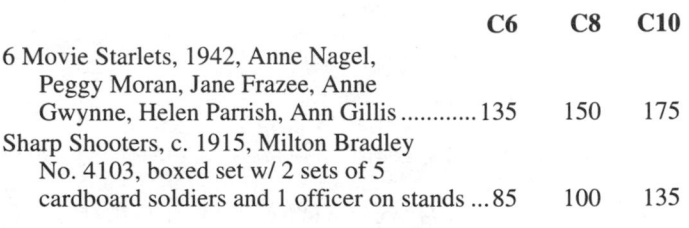

"Sharpshooters," box and contents.

Skating Party Paper Doll Book, 1941,
Saalfield No. 2328, 17 punch-outs 32 40 45

Skating Stars, 1954, Whitman No. 2105 .... 20 30 40

Smart Paper Dolls, 1940, Saalfield No. 1935 ..... 30 45 50

Smash the Axis, 1943,
Electric Corp. of America 40 55 60

Snow White and the Seven Dwarfs
Paper Dolls, 1938, 12" x 17",
Whitman No. 970 .... 100 125 150

Snow White and the Seven Dwarfs,
c. 1970, Whitman No. 1998 .... 18 30 35

Soldiers, c. 1940, Concord Toy Co.,
boxed set contains 9 press-out
soldiers, 3-1/2" each,
wooden cannon and ammunition 50 60 75

Soldiers Set by J. Pressman and Co., Inc.,
New York, No. 1551, c. 1940,
contains 5 cardboard soldiers,
4-1/2" high and marbles 35 50 60

Soldiers, cardboard, approx. 6" high on
wooden blocks, Navy, both officer
and sailors, c. 1920, price per single figure 3 4 4.50

Soldiers, cardboard, approx. 6" high on
wooden blocks, Sailor, U.S. 3 4 4.50

Soldiers, cardboard, approx. 6" high on
wooden blocks, U.S. Infantry in campaign
hats, mounted. Price per single figure 3 4 4.50

Soldiers, cardboard approx. 6" high on
wooden blocks, West Point Cadets 4 5 6

"Stand-Up Dolls Honey And Bunny."

Top: "Soldiers" by Concord; Right: "Streamline Flyer."

"Soldiers Five With Pistol."

"Statuette Dolls And Their Clothes."

	C6	C8	C10
Soldiers Five, c. 1920, boxed set, Milton Bradley No. 4395, 5 cardboard soldiers, pistol	80	100	125
Soldiers on Parade, early, Milton Bradley No. 4518, set of 10	55	80	90
Spaceport, U.S.A., 1953, Whitman	15	20	22
Sports Time, 1952, Whitman No. 210525	10	15	18
Square Dance Paper Dolls, 1950, Saalfield No. 2717	20	25	28
Square Dance Paper Dolls, By J. Voelz, Lowe No. 968-10	20	25	28
Stage Door Canteen, 1943, Saalfield No. 2468	65	80	95
Stand-Up Dolls, Honey and Bunny, Merrill No. 3403, 1936	60	75	90
Statuette Dolls, 1943, Whitman No. 992, 2 women	30	35	40
Statuette Dolls And Their Clothes, 1942, Whitman No. 998	30	40	50
Statuette Dolls And Their Clothes, 1946, Whitman No. 986, 2 girls and a boy	25	35	40

	C6	C8	C10
Stencils Large and Small by Roy Best, c. 1935, No. 954 (Whitman?) folder of 30 animals to punch out and use as stencils. Comes w/ tiny box of crayons	15	22	28
Stock Farm Set, c. 1944, Concern No. 123, boxed 1200 die-cut pieces including house, barn, silo, chicken house, tractor, etc.	45	55	60
The Story of Cinderella, A Fold-A-Way Toy Book designed by Will Pente, c. 1925, Reilly & Britton Co.	30	45	48
Streamline Flyer, 10-3/4"x13-1/2" boxed set, Concord Toy Co., No. 122, c. 1940, contains engine, station, crossing gates, crossing signal, baggage truck, baggage and people	45	55	62
Style Shop Paper Dolls, 1943, Saalfield No. 1516	25	35	40
Sub-Deb Paper Dolls by Irving Nurick, 1941, Merrill No. 3408, 12 teenage boy and girl dolls, clothes	30	45	48
Sue and Tom Cut-Out Dolls Book, The, 1946, Lowe No. 149	20	28	38
Sunbonnet Sue, 1951, Whitman No. 2062-29	20	25	30
Sunshine Cut-Outs, Sports Series, Spring, by M&F Hoopes, 1926, 4-part foldout, Stroll & Edwards Co.	70	80	90
Susan Dey as Laurie ("Partridge Family" TV show), 1972, Artcraft, Fashions by Kate Greenaway	20	30	32
Sweetheart Paper Dolls, 1943, Saalfield No. 2458	30	40	45

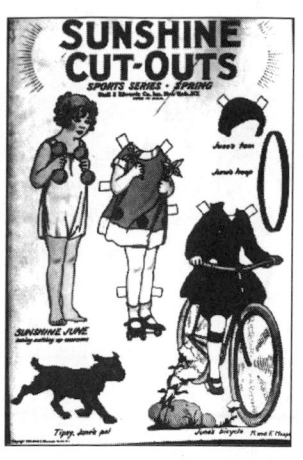

"Sunshine Cut-Outs Sports Series Spring."

	C6	C8	C10
Sweetie Pie Twins, 1949, Stephens Publishing Co. No. 166, Jane and Jean	18	22	25
Swing-A-Plane by J.L. Schilling Co., Model of a Flying Tiger, 1944, flies on string	12	18	20
Tammy, 1963, A Little Golden Story Book w/ paper dolls to cut out and dress, illustrated by Ada Salvi	15	20	25
Tarzan of the Apes, 1933 figure set	40	50	55
Teen Gal Cut-Out Dolls, 1943, by Hilda Miloche and William Kane, Whitman No. 980	40	50	55
Teen Town, 1949, Merrill No. 3443	35	45	50
That Girl Marlo Thomas, 1967, Saalfield No. 1351	30	40	50
That Girl Marlo Thomas, 1967, Saalfield No. 1379	30	40	50
They Stand Up by Avis Mac, 1939, Whitman No. 932, 13" x 18" w/ 5 children	65	75	90
30 Toy Soldiers, c. 1943, Whitman No. 2950	40	50	60
This is Bunny One Of The Five Cut-Out Dolly Sisters, Whitman, 1939	35	45	50
This is Dotty One Of The Five Cut-Out Dolly Sisters, Whitman, 1939	35	45	50
This is Magic One Of The Five Cut-Out Dolly Sisters, Whitman, 1939	35	45	50
This is Patsy, One Of The Five Cut-Out Dolly Sisters, Whitman, 1939	35	45	50

	C6	C8	C10
This is Peggy One Of The Five Cut-Out Dolly Sisters, Whitman No. 1002, 1939	35	45	50
This Is The Navy No. 500A Skyline Mfg., Destroyer and PT Boat, c. 1942	25	35	40
This Is The Navy No. 501, c. 1942, Skyline Mfg., Heavy Cruiser	25	35	40
Three Bears Cut-Out Book, Copyright 1939, Whitman No. 1020, Goldilocks and 3 Bears	45	55	60
Three Flying Models of Famous Allied Fighting Planes by Judd Reed, 9"x12", contains Hell Cat, Spitfire and Stormovik planes, included is "American Ace Spotter," w/ turning dial of 48 3-view silhouettes of 16 planes in little windows, 1944	30	40	50
Three Little Girls Who Grew And Grew And This Is How They Grew, 1945, Whitman No. 99410	40	45	50
Three Little Girls Who Grew And Grew And This Is How They Grew, w/ clothlike clothes, flocked, 1945, Whitman No. 1176	35	45	50
Three Little Pigs Cut-Out Book, Copyright 1939, Whitman No. 1020, Pigs and Big Bad Wolf	40	55	60
Three Sweet Baby Dolls To Cut Out And Dress, 1954, Whitman No. 975	15	20	25
Thrilltown Railroad, 1943, Reed, Pullman Passenger Set	65	80	90
Tiny Chatty Twins Paper Dolls, 1963, Whitman No. 1985	20	25	30
Toby Tyler Circus Playbook Punch-Out, 1959, No. 1936	30	40	45
Tom Corbett Space Cadet Punch-Out Book, 1952, Saalfield No. 4304, 14" long, 10-1/2" wide	40	48	52
Tom the Aviator, c. 1942, Samuel Lowe No. L1074	25	35	45
Toni Hair-Do Cut-Out Dolls, Lowe No. 1284, 1950	40	50	55

Left: *"This Is Bunny One Of The Five Cut-Out Dolly Sisters."*
Right: *"This Is Patsy, One Of The Five Cut-Out Dolly Sisters."*

"Toni Hair-Do Cut-Out Dolls."

	C6	C8	C10
Top Notch Paper Dolls, 1948, Saalfield No. 1504	20	28	35
Toy Models: Warplane and Tank Punch-out, 1941, Fawcett Publications, Lowe	45	50	65
Toy Town, 1916, series of 50 different buildings by American Color Type Co., boxed set	75	100	125
Transfer Pictures, Copyright 1939, Whitman No. 1085, 100 decalcomanias	10	15	18
Treasure Hour Puppet Book, No. 4, 1968, Murray Sales and Service, The Rustlers of Rocky Ranch, a play of cowboys and Indians in 5 scenes, cut-out section makes model theater	20	30	35
Tricia, 1969, Artcraft No. 4248	25	35	40
Tricia Paper Dolls, 1970, Saalfield No. 1248, White House tour game, White House stand-up doll of Tricia Nixon and costumes	25	35	40
Trudy Phillips and Her Crowd, 1954, Whitman No. 2104	25	35	40
Tuesday Weld Paper dolls, 1960, Saalfield No. 5112, boxed, 2 dolls and 58 costume pieces	45	55	60
Turnabouts Dolls Book, The, 1940s, Lowe No. 1048, dolls printed front view on each side	35	45	48
TV Star Time Paper Dolls, c. 1950s, Abbott No. 1367	18	22	25
TV Tap Stars Paper Dolls, Lowe No. 99010	18	20	22
22 Animals To Cut Out and Stand Up, Copyright 1930, Whitman No. 935, rabbits, bears, owls, squirrels, etc.	35	45	50
Twiggy Paper Doll, 1967, Whitman No. 1999, w/ "plastilon" Twiggy dress for small girls	30	35	40
Tyrone Power & Linda Darnell, 1941, Merrill No. 3438	155	180	200
Umbrella Girls, 1956, Merrill No. 2562, wrap-around dresses	45	50	55
Uncle Sam's Little Helpers Paper Dolls by Ann Kovach, 1943, Saalfield No. 2450	38	48	52
United States Soldiers, 1942, Samuel Lowe No. L1063	50	55	60
U.S. Commandos Book, 1943, Lowe No. 1089	45	55	60
U.S. Infantry-Spanish/American War, approx. 6" high soldier on small wooden block	3.50	4.50	5
Victory Girls Arlene the Airline Hostess, c. 1940s, Lowe	50	60	65
Victory Punch-Out Tanks, Soldiers, Sailors, Planes, c. 1943, Lowe No. 848	50	55	60
Victory Volunteers, 1942 dolls w/ uniforms by Merlin, Merrill No. 3424	60	75	90
Virginia Mayo, 1957, Saalfield No. 4422	50	60	70
WACS and WAVES, 1943, Whitman No. 985	60	75	85
Walking Paper Doll Family, Saalfield No. 1074, 1934	65	75	80
Walt Disney's Babes in Toyland, 1961, Golden Punch-Out Book No. 10363	30	45	48
Walt Disney's Jane and Michael from Mary Poppins, 1963, Watkins/Strathmore 1892-6	25	35	40
Walt Disney's Let's Build Disneyland, 1957, Whitman No. 1986, forms sets for Adventureland, Frontierland, Tomorrowland and Fantasyland	25	35	40
Walt Disney's Mary Poppins, 1964, Whitman No. 1982	30	35	40
Walt Disney Match and Patch Sticker Fun, 1953, Whitman, Mickey Mouse, Donald Duck, Pluto, Goofy, etc.	15	18	20
Walt Disney Presents Hayley Mills in "That Darn Cat," 1965, Whitman No. 1955	30	35	45
Walt Disney Sticker Fun Book, 1951, Whitman	10	12	15
Walt Disney Sticker Fun With Peter Pan, 1952, Whitman	12	15	18
War Between The States, 1959, Golden Press No. GF152	55	65	75
War Plane Cut-Outs, 1943, heavy-stock, 8 different scale models, 10" x 14"	35	40	45
Wedding Paper Dolls, 1970, Whitman No. 1970	15	18	22
We're A Family Cut-Out Dolls, 1954, Whitman No. 1181	30	40	45
White House Party Dresses, 1961, Merrill No. 1550	30	35	40
Whitman No. 1146, little paper doll books, 3-1/2" x 7-1/2", copyright 1939	45	60	65
a. Nancy and Tommy			
b. Ann and Arthur			
c. Kitty and Billy			
d. Muriel and David			
e. Cynthia and Bobby			
f. Judy and Dick			
Whitman Paper Doll Book, 1933, No. 3059, 4 dolls, 10 sheets of clothes in folder	45	55	65
Winnie's New Wardrobe by Geraldine Cline, 1939, McLoughlin Bros., No. 555	30	32	36
Young Patriot Invasion Set, c. 1944, Colorgraphic No. 500, contains destroyer, amphibian tractor, tank, jeep, anti-tank gun, bomber and diver bomber, 10-1/2" x 13" boxed set	75	80	95
Young Patriot Learn To Know Your Army, 1943, Colorgraphic No. 350, tank, howitzer, jeep, anti-tank gun, bomber, fighter and soldiers. Guns shoot, bombs drop, etc.	75	80	95
Young Patriot Learn To Know Your Navy, 1943, Colorgraphic construction set No. 360, 10" x 14" boxed set includes battleship, destroyer, aircraft carrier, mosquito boat, submarine, planes, depth charges, etc., w/ moveable parts	75	80	95
Ziegield Girl Paper Dolls, No. "1," 1941, Merrill No. 3466	170	190	225
Zoo Cut-Outs by Milo Winter, 1938, Whitman No. 1054, 6 pages of heavy cut-out animals	30	38	48

TIN WIND-UPS

(See also Movies, Comic Characters, Disney)

The average mint price for tin wind-ups in the last edition was $521.73. In this edition it is $532.54, an increase of 2%.

MOVING INTO COLLECTORS' HEARTS

Unlike most toys in this book, tin wind-ups do not "feel" particularly good in the hand, and depend more on the lure of motion and colorful lithography. Aesthetically the most appealing, perhaps, are those of Lehmann, a German company that patented a number of its toys in the United States. These toys hold a strong attraction for a large number of collectors.

	C6	C8	C10
A.C. Gilbert Delivery Truck, open, c. 1915	210	320	425
A.C. Gilbert Racer, early	500	750	1050
A.C. Gilbert "U.S. Mail Parcel Post" Truck, c. 1915	425	638	950
Aircraft Carrier, c. post-WWII, tin litho, Japan, approx. 15" long	90	135	180
"Aircraft Carrier X53," w/ 5 jet planes, tin litho, c. 1950s	75	112	150

A.C. GILBERT "U.S. Mail Parcel Post" Truck. Courtesy Christie's East.

ANIMATE TOY CO.

In 1918 this firm was located at East 17th Street in New York City, and its president was L.T. Savage. By 1931 it had moved to 30 North 15th Street in East Orange, New Jersey, and employed ten men and forty women. In 1934 the president-vice president was George V. Turnbull and the secretary-treasurer was George H. Webb. Five men and eleven women made up the work force.

ARNOLD Motorcycle "Mac 700," getting on. Photo by Scott Smiles.

ARNOLD Motorcycle "Mac 700," riding. Photo by Scott Smiles.

244

	C6	C8	C10
Animate Toy "U.S. Baby Tank," pat. 6/20/16, new in 1918, 2-1/2" long	40	60	80
Animate Toy "Climbing Tractor," 1929, 9" long	100	150	200
Arnold Motorcycle, "Mac 700," black version	400	600	800
Arnold Motorcycle, "Mac 700," red version	750	1125	1500
Automatic Toy Co., 77 Alaska Street, Staten Island, N.Y.			
Automatic Toy Co. "Alpine Express"	75	112	150

AUTOMATIC TOY COMPANY Auto Speedway. Photo by Don Hultzman.

	C6	C8	C10
Automatic Toy Co. "Auto Speedway," c. 1930	100	150	200
Automatic Toy Co. Cross-Over Trolley Set	90	135	180
Automatic Toy Co. "Dizzy Liz," No. 180, 1940s, 5" long	100	150	200
Automatic Toy Co. "Jungle Pete," No. 175, 15" long	90	135	180
Automatic Toy Co. "Mystery Alpine Express," 1940s, 20" long, 14" wide, 2" high	82	123	165
Automatic Toy Co. "Operation Airlift," 1950s, 2 plastic planes	80	120	160
Automatic Toy Co. "Rocket Space Ship" No. 305, sparks, 1940s, 8-1/2" long	87	130	175
Automatic Toy Co. "Space Shooting Range," 1950s, 15" long	150	225	300
Automatic Toy Co. "Magic Crossroads" Track, 2 wind-up cars, c. 1950	130	195	260

	C6	C8	C10
Automatic Toy Co. Speedway, 1930s, w/ 2 race cars, garage	175	262	350
Baby L Racing Boat, 1930, Lindstrom, 11" long	110	165	220

BABY L Racing Boat, 11" long. Courtesy Lloyd W. Ralston Auctions.

	C6	C8	C10
"Barnum & Bailey," c. 1935, elephant pulling a 4-wheeled cart loaded with a collapsible cage containing a camel, a monkey, a lion and a giraffe, each mounted on 4 wheels	150	225	300
Biplane, very early, Wright Bros.-like paper propeller blades, 6" long	400	600	800
Bird in Cage, German, 3-1/2" high	225	338	450
Bird w/ flapping wings, 1930s, German, 6-1/2" long	100	150	200
Black Boy eating watermelon w/ dog biting his backside, 1920s, German	580	870	1160
Boy on St. Bernard on rocker, 6-3/4"	600	900	1200
Bueschel, Fritz (Hackettstown, NJ), "George Washington Bridge"	650	975	1300
Buffalo Bill, hand-painted, hand-soldered, German, 1910	400	600	800
Buffalo Toys, "Aero Speeders," 1920s, carousel w/ 3 planes, screw-rod spring drive, 10" tall	125	188	250
Buffalo Toys, "Aero-Zeps," 3 zeppelins fly on carousel, 9" high	150	225	300
Buffalo Toys, "Bumper Ride," 1930s, 10" long	100	150	200
Buffalo Toys, Dodgem Car, 1930s, 10" long	125	188	250

BUESCHEL, FRITZ (Hackettstown, NJ) "George Washington Bridge." Courtesy Christie's East.

BUFFALO TOYS Aerospeeders. Courtesy Don Hultzman. Photo by Ron Chojnacki.

CATERPILLAR Tractor, "1916." Photo by Bill Kaufman. Courtesy Good Old Days Store.

	C6	C8	C10
Buffalo Toys, "T-zer," 1925, (screw drive), 6" high	180	240	360
"The Cackling Hen of Paradise," turn side handle and hen cackles; patented, 8" long	80	120	160

	C6	C8	C10
"Cakewalk Dancers," short black man dancing w/ tall, heavy black woman	400	600	800
"Candy" Cart driven by monkey in cap, also marked "Candy," c. 1950s	100	150	200
Carousel w/ 4 biplanes and pilots, paper vanes, flag finial, 1920s, German, 17" high	1200	1800	2400+
Carousel w/ 4 double horse and riders that alternate w/ 4 women in cars, velvet top w/ ball fringe, flag finial, 17" high	1600	2400	3200+
Carousel w/ 4 men in canoes, propellers w/ paper vanes, 11" high	1400	2100	2800+
Carter, Chinese pushes Cart, 1920s	130	195	260
Carter, "Pan-Gee the Funny Dancer," 1920, 10" high	350	525	700
Cat pushing Cage w/ 2 mice, 8-1/4"	300	450	600
Caterpillar Tractor, "1916," rubber treads, tin wind-up, probably by Woodhaven Metal Stamping Co., Brooklyn, NY	142	214	285

CHEIN

Chein (pronounced "Chain") was founded in 1903 by Julius Chein. The New Jersey company specialized in lithographed metal toys, the majority of them mechanical. In 1918 it was located at 310 Passaic Avenue, Harrison, New Jersey, with 250 employees. In 1934 it had 55 male and 92 female workers. In a 1946-47 directory it listed 148 males and 132 female employees. Chein made toys until 1979 and is still in business in Burlington, New Jersey.

	C6	C8	C10
Chein Alligator w/ native on its back	155	232	310
Chein "Army Drummer," 1930s, plunger-activated, 7" high	130	195	260
Chein Barnacle Bill, looks like Popeye, 1930s	225	338	450
Chein "Barnacle Bill in a Barrel," 1930s, 7" high	250	375	500
Chein "Barnacle Bill the Sailor," punching a bag, 7-1/2"	212	319	425
Chein Bass Drummer (like Chein Drummer Boy, but drum vertical)	150	225	300
Chein Bear w/ hat, pants, shirt, bow tie, c. 1938	55	83	110
Chein Cabin Cruiser, 1940s, 9" long	65	98	130

CHEIN "Barnacle Bill in a Barrel." Courtesy PB Eighty-Four, New York.

CHEIN Barnacle Bill. Courtesy PB Eighty-Four, New York.

*CHEIN Bear with Hat.
Courtesy Scott Smiles.*

*CHEIN
Drummer Boy.
Courtesy
Scott Smiles.
Photo by
Mike Adams.*

	C6	C8	C10
Chein Chick, brightly colored clothes and polka dot bow tie, 4" high	50	75	100
Chein Chicken pulling wheelbarrow, 1930s, 6" x 3-1/2"	50	75	100
Chein "Clown in Barrel," 1930s, 8" high	275	362	550
Chein Clown Puncher	375	562	750
Chein Clown w/ umbrella	120	180	240
Chein "Dan-Dee Dump Truck"	200	300	400
Chein "Doughboy," 1920s, 6" high	175	262	350
Chein Drum Major, 8-1/2" high	210	315	420

*CHEIN Duck.
Courtesy
Scott Smiles.*

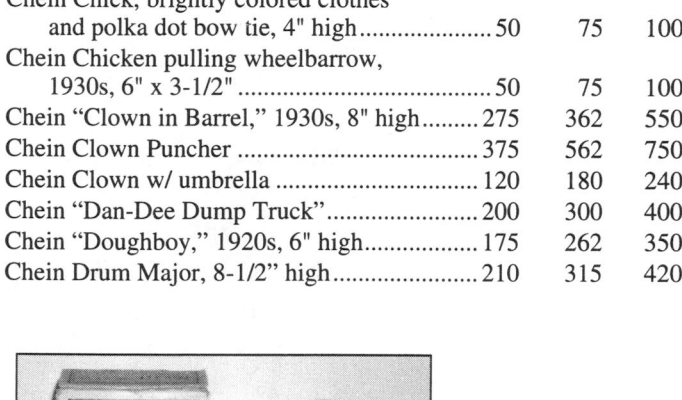

*CHEIN Drum
Major with
original box.
Photo by
Ron Chojnacki.
Courtesy
Don Hultzman.*

	C6	C8	C10
Chein "Drummer Boy," w/ shako, c. 1930s, 9" high	100	150	200
Chein Duck, waddles, 1930, 4" high	50	75	100
Chein Duck, long-beaked, in orange sailor suit, not Donald Duck, but similar, waddles, 6" high	100	150	200
Chein "Ferris Wheel," 6 compartments, ringing bell, 1930s, 16-1/2" high	240	360	480
Chein "Greyhound" Bus, 9" long	85	130	175
Chein Handstand Clown, 1940s, 6" high	58	88	115
Chein "Indian In Headdress," 1930s, 5-1/2" high	100	150	200

	C6	C8	C10
Chein "Jumping Rabbit," 1925, 5" long	120	180	240
Chein Marine, hand on belt, 1950s, 6" high	120	180	240
Chein "Mark I" Cabin Cruiser, 1957, 8-1/2" long	33	50	65
Chein "Mechanical Aquaplane," No. 39, boat-like pontoons, 1932, no insignia, 8-1/2" long, 7-1/2" wingspan	200	300	400
Chein "Mechanical Aquaplane," post-WWII insignia	188	280	375
Chein "Mechanical Aquaplane," pre-WWII insignia	113	170	225
Chein "Mechanical Fish," 1940s, 11"	40	60	80
Chein "Mechanical Frog Man," 1950s, 11" long	92	138	185
Chein "Mechanical Rocket Ride," No. 400, 1950s, 18" high	600	900	1200
Chein "Melody Player," No. 135, 1930s, 4 rolls, 6-3/4" high	100	150	200
Chein "Musical Aero Swing," 1940s, 10" high	283	425	565
Chein "Navy Frog Man," No. 122, 1950s, 12" long	100	150	200

CHEIN "Ferris Wheel," 1930s. Courtesy Scott Smiles.

CHEIN Handstand Clown. Courtesy Scott Smiles.

	C6	C8	C10
Chein Pan-Am Clipper, 1930s, pontoons, 11" wingspan	388	582	775
Chein Peggy Jane Boat, 13" long	62	93	125
Chein Penguin in tuxedo type jacket, c. 1940	55	83	110

CHEIN Handstand Clown (variation). Photo by Scott Smiles.

CHEIN Indian In Headdress. Photo by Scott Smiles.

	C6	C8	C10
Chein Pig, 1940s, 4-1/2" high	45	68	90
Chein "Playland Merry-Go-Round," 1930s, 9-1/2" high	365	550	730
Chein "Playland Whip," No. 340, 4 bump cars, driver's head wobbles	450	675	900
Chein Rabbit in shirt and pants, c. 1938	53	78	105
Chein Rabbit pulling cart	48	72	95
Chein Rabbit w/ wheelbarrow	75	112	150
Chein "Race Car No. 52," 1930s, 6-1/2" long	80	120	160
Chein "Racer #3," 1920s, 6-1/2" long	150	225	300
Chein "Ride-A-Rocket"	300	450	600
Chein "Rocket Ride" No. 400, 4 rockets, 18" high, base 11" diameter	455	685	910
Chein "Roller Coaster," c. 1938, includes 2 cars	230	345	460
Chein "Roller Coaster," 1950s, includes 2 cars	195	293	390
Chein "Santa Elf," 1920s, 6" high	220	330	440

CHEIN Marine, hand on belt. Courtesy Scott Smiles. Photo by Mike Adams.

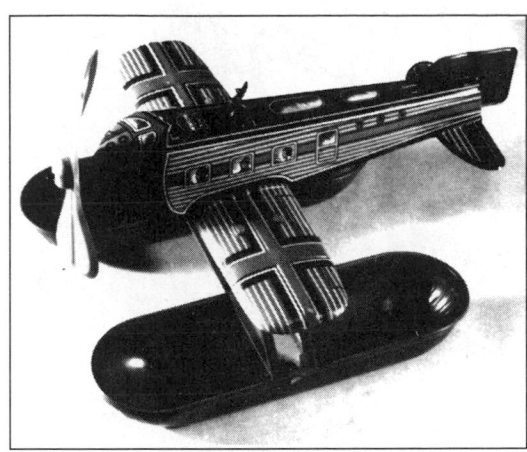

CHEIN Mechanical Aquaplane, 7-1/2" wingspan. Courtesy Perry R. Eichor.

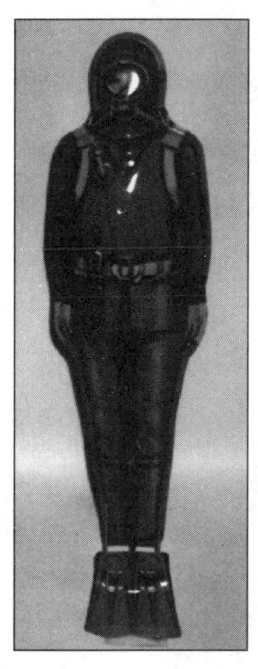

CHEIN Mechanical Frog Man. Photo by Don Hultzman.

CHEIN Penguin. Courtesy Scott Smiles. Photo by Mike Adams.

	C6	C8	C10
Chein "Ski Boy" No. 157, 1940s, 7-3/4" long, 5-1/4" tall	138	205	275
Chein "Ski-Ride" No. 320, 19" long	213	320	425
Chein "Skin Driver No. 122," 1950s, 12" long	55	83	110
Chein "Space Ride" No. 205, 1950s, 10" high	500	750	1000
Chein "Space Ride," 1940s, lever action, 9" high	425	638	850
Chein "Spirit of St. Louis" Airplane, 1930s, 8" long, 8" wingspan	250	375	500

CHEIN Pig. Photo by Scott Smiles.

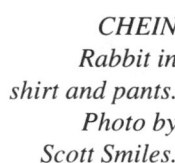

CHEIN Rabbit in shirt and pants. Photo by Scott Smiles.

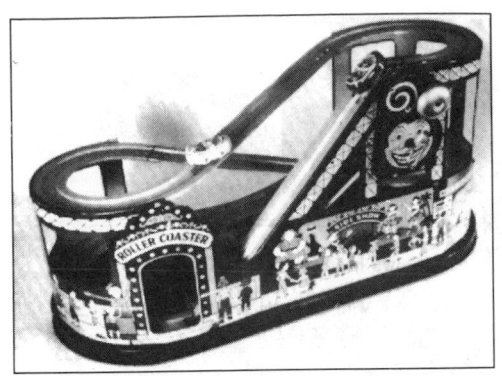

CHEIN "Roller Coaster," 1930s. Courtesy Don Hultzman. Photo by Ron Chojnacki.

CHEIN "Roller Coaster," 1950s. Courtesy Don Hultzman. Photo by Ron Chojnacki.

	C6	C8	C10
Chein Taxi, 1920s, 7" long	200	300	400
Chein Toy Town Helicopter, 1950s, 13" long	65	98	130
Chein Turtle w/ native on back	225	338	450
Chein "U.S. Army Sergeant" No. 153, 1950s, 5-1/2" high	105	158	210
Chein "Walking Pelican," 1930s, 5" high	100	150	200

	C6	C8	C10
Circus-type Trainer, baton in hand, revolves, w/ rooster on each side, musical, German, 3-1/2" long	200	300	400
Clown in Donkey Cart, 7-1/2" long	60	90	120
Clown in Hoop, Japan, 6-1/2" high	150	225	300
Clown Musicians, 4, on a pedestal, musical, 8" high	300	450	600
"Clown on Scooter," 1915, Tipp Co., 6" tall	200	300	400

COURTLAND MFG. CO.

(History based on information from Joe and Sharon Freed)

Walter Reach, owner of Courtland, had a burning desire to be known as the second Louis Marx. He began production in 1944 with two die-cut cardboard toys (a rabbit and cart and horse and cart) of his own design. Reach turned to tin litho toys after the war, a number of them non-wind-ups. At his height, Courtland, located first in Camden, New Jersey, and later in Philadelphia, had 600 workers, and in 1947 its sales exceeded 1.5 million dollars. But success was short-lived: the firm lasted just seven years.

Courtland Toys listing by Joe and Sharon Freed

Joe and Sharon Freed.

	C6	C8	C10
No. 15 Mechanical Lawn Mower, 1950 retail price 79¢, 1951 retail 98¢, 8-1/4" wide, 24" high, 3" wheels	50	75	100

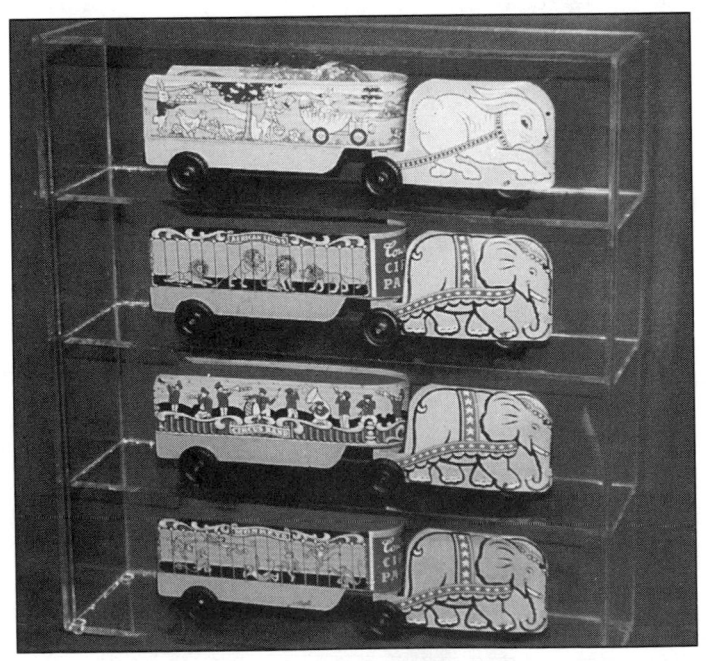

COURTLAND. Top to Bottom: No. 200 Easter Rabbit pulling van; Circus Parade No. 400, "African Lions"; Circus Parade No. 500, "Circus Band"; Circus Parade No. 300, "Monkeys."

	C6	C8	C10
No. 20 Mechanical Lawn Mower, 1950 retail $1.29; 1951 retail $1.49, 11-1/4" wide, 29" high, 5" wheels	50	75	100
No. 21 Mechanical Lawn Mower, 1951 retail $2.98, 12" wide, 29" high, 5" wheels	50	75	100
No. 25 Mechanical Power Lawn Mower, 1951 retail $2.98, 12" wide, 29" high, 5-3/4" wheels	75	100	125
No. 200 Easter Rabbit and Trailer, 1946 retail 49¢, 11-5/8" long, 3" wide, 3-1/2" high	75	125	200
No. 300 Circus Elephant & "Monkeys" Cart, 1946 retail 49¢, 11-5/8" long, 3" wide, 3-1/2" high	250	450	700

COURTLAND No. 300. Courtesy Joe and Sharon Freed.

	C6	C8	C10
No. 400 Circus Elephant & "African Lions" Cart, 1946 retail 49¢, 11-5/8" long, 3" wide, 3-1/2" high	250	450	700
No. 500 Circus Elephant & "Circus Band" Cart, 1946 retail 49¢, 11-5/8" long, 3" wide, 3-1/2" high	350	550	850
No. 1070 Mechanical Big 4 Truck Parade, 1947 retail $3.39, 9" long, 3" wide, 2-3/4" high	No Price Found		
No. 1200 Mechanical Trailer-Truck, 1947 retail $1.00, 13" long, 3" wide, 3-1/4" high	200	250	375
No. 1300 Mechanical Ice Cream Truck, retail 79¢, 9" long, 3" wide, 2-3/4" high	150	200	250
No. 1300 Mechanical Moving & Storage Truck, 1947 retail 79¢, 9" long, 3" wide, 2-3/4" high	175	250	375
Same as above, w/ No. 130 litho on the sides of the truck bed	175	250	375
No. 1300 Mechanical Fire Patrol No. 2 Truck, 1947 retail 79¢, 9" long, 3" wide, 2-3/4" high	125	200	275
No. 1300 Mechanical Express and Hauling Truck, 1947 retail 79¢ 9" long, 3" wide, 2-3/4" high	125	200	275
No. 1400 Mechanical "Automatic Ladder" Fire Truck, 1947 retail $1.00, 9" long, 3" wide, 2-3/4" high	175	250	350
No. 1500 Mechanical Road Roller Truck, 9" long, 3" wide, 3-1/4" high	250	350	450
No. 1600 Mechanical Dump Truck, 7" long, 3" wide, 2-3/4" high	100	150	200

	C6	C8	C10
No. 2000 Mechanical "ESSO" Gasoline Tractor-Trailer, 13" long, 3" wide, 3-1/4" high	250	350	450
No. 2000 Mechanical Gasoline Tractor-Trailer, 13" long, 3" wide, 3-1/4" high	250	350	450

COURTLAND No. 2000 Mechanical Gasoline Tractor-Trailer (Motor Guaranteed for Life). Packed in individual boxes, all with motor guarantee certificate. Courtesy Joe and Sharon Freed.

	C6	C8	C10
No. 2050 Mechanical Milk Tractor-Trailer, "American Dairies," 13" long, 3" wide, 3-1/4" high	350	575	800

Note: 1951 catalog shows Milk Trailer markings that read the same as above except "Approved" is used in the place of the words "Vitamin D." This variation is not known to have been produced.

COURTLAND No. 2050 Mechanical Milk Tractor-Trailer (Motor Guaranteed for Life). Courtesy Joe and Sharon Freed.

	C6	C8	C10
No. 2100 Mechanical Hook and Ladder Tractor-Trailer, 13" long, 3" wide, 3-1/4" high	100	150	200
No. 2150 Mechanical Emergency Rescue Squad Tractor-Trailer, 13" long, 3" wide, 3-1/4" high	150	200	250

COURTLAND No. 2100 Mechanical Hook & Ladder Tractor-Trailer (Motor Guaranteed for Life). Courtesy Joe and Sharon Freed.

COURTLAND No. 2200 Mechanical Logging Tractor-Trailer (Motor Guaranteed for Life). Courtesy Joe and Sharon Freed.

COURTLAND No. 2150 Mechanical Emergency Rescue Squad (Motor Guaranteed for Life). Courtesy Joe and Sharon Freed.

	C6	C8	C10
2 No. 2350 Open Van Trucks, 2 No. 2600 Freight Hauler Trucks and 2 No. 2700 Side Tipper Trucks. Wholesale assortment only, in mint.................................			3,000
No. 3000 Mechanical Road Roller Truck, 9" long, 3" wide, 3-1/4" high	250	350	450
No. 3100 Mechanical Dump Truck,			

COURTLAND No. 3000 Mechanical Road Roller Truck. Courtesy Joe and Sharon Freed.

	C6	C8	C10
No. 2200 Mechanical Logging Tractor-Trailer, 13" long, 3" wide, 3-1/4" high...................................	150	200	250
No. 2300 Mechanical Open Van Tractor-Trailer, 13" long, 3" wide, 3-1/4" high...................................	125	175	225
No. 2350 Mechanical Open Van Tractor-Trailer, 13" long, 3" wide, 3-1/4" high...................................	150	200	250
No. 2375 Mechanical Heavy Duty Sand and Gravel Tractor-Trailer, 13" long, 3" wide, 3-1/4" high	175	225	275
No. 2400 Mechanical Trailer Tow Truck, 13" long, 3" wide, 3-1/4" high	225	325	400
No. 2600 Mechanical Freight Haulers Tractor-Trailer, 13" long, 3" high, 3-1/4" wide...................................	200	300	375
No. 2700 Mechanical Side Tipper Tractor-Trailer, 13" long, 3" high, 3-1/4" wide	200	300	375
No. 2800 Assortment consists of No. 2000 Gasoline Trucks, 2 2 No. 2050 Milk Trucks, 2 No. 2200 Log Trucks,			

	C6	C8	C10
7" long, 3" wide, 3-1/4" high	100	125	150
No. 3200 Mechanical Stake Bed Truck, 7" long, 3" wide, 3-1/4" high	125	150	175
No. 3800 Assortment consists of 6 No. 3200 Stake Bed Trucks and 6 No. 3100 Dump Trucks. Wholesale Assortment Only			No Price Found
No. 3900 Courtland Mechanical Side Tipper Tractor-Trailer, "Black Diamond Coal Company-340," 13" long, 3" high, 3-1/4" wide	250	350	450

COURTLAND No. 4000 Checker Cab Car. Courtesy Joe and Sharon Freed.

COURTLAND No. 4000 City Meat Market Delivery Sedan. Courtesy Joe and Sharon Freed.

	C6	C8	C10
No. 4000 City Meat Market Delivery Sedan, 7-1/4" long, 3-1/4" wide, 2-3/4" high	75	125	150
No. 4000 Modern Bakery Delivery Sedan, 7-1/4" long, 3-1/4" wide, 2-3/4" high	100	150	175
No. 4000 Fire Chief Car, red & white, 7-1/4" long, 3-1/4" wide, 2-3/4" high	75	100	125
Same as above, all red	100	125	150
No. 4000 Checker Cab Car, green & yellow, 7-1/4" long, 3-1/4" wide, 2-3/4" high	175	200	325
Same as above, green and white	200	225	350

COURTLAND No. 3900. Mechanical Side Tipper Tractor-Trailer, "Black Diamond Coal Company 340." Courtesy Joe and Sharon Freed.

COURTLAND No. 5100 "Black Diamond" Coal Truck (Motor Guaranteed For Life). Courtesy Joe and Sharon Freed.

	C6	C8	C10
No. 4500 Express Service Pickup, 7-1/4" long, 3-1/4" wide, 2-3/4" high	75	100	125
No. 4500 Country Produce Pickup, 7-1/4" long, 3-1/4" wide, 2-3/4" high	75	100	125
No. 4500 Modern Decorators Pickup, 7-1/4" long, 3-1/4" wide, 2-3/4" high	100	125	150
No. 5000 Mechanical Operation No. 51 Crane Truck, 13" long, 3-5/8" wide, 5" high	225	325	400
No. 5100 Mechanical "Black Diamond" Coal Truck, 10-1/2" wide, 3" wide, 3-3/8" wide	150	225	300
No. 5200 Mechanical No. 51 Steam Shovel, 15-1/2" long, 3-3/4" wide, 9-1/2" high	135	185	235
No. 5300 Mechanical Combination Steam Shovel carried by low-boy tractor-trailer, 15-1/2" long, 3-7/8" wide, 10-1/2" high	350	550	775

COURTLAND 5300. Photo by Joe Freed.

	C6	C8	C10
No. 5800 Assortment consists of 3 No. 2300 Aluminum Open Van Trucks, 3 No. 2150 Emergency Rescue Squad Trucks, 3 No. 2375 Sand & Gravel Trucks & 3 No. 2400 Towing Service Trucks Wholesale Assortment Only			No Price Found
No. 6000 Mechanical Farm Tractor w/ scraper, rear tires are large rubber and front are small rubber tires, 8-3/4" long, 4-3/4" wide, 4-1/2" high	100	150	200

	C6	C8	C10

COURTLAND No. 6050 Mechanical Farm Tractor. Courtesy Continental Hobby House.

No. 6050 Mechanical Farm Tractor
w/o scraper, rear tires are large rubber
and front are small rubber tires, 7-1/2"
long, 4-3/4" wide, 4-1/2" high 75 100 150

No. 6075 Mechanical Farm Tractor
w/o scraper, rear tires are large tin litho
while the front are small rubber tires,
7-1/2" long, 4-3/4" wide, 4-1/2" high 250 350 450

No. 6100 Mechanical Caterpillar
Tractor w/ rubber treads, 6" long,
3" wide, 4-1/2" high...................................250 350 450

No. 6500 Mechanical Ice Cream Scooter,
6-1/2" long, 3" wide, 4-1/2" high 200 300 400

No. 7000 Mechanical Fire Chief Car
w/ siren, 7-1/4" long,
3-1/4" wide, 2-3/4" high 125 175 225

No. 7500 Mechanical State Police Car
w/ siren, 7-1/4" long,
3-1/4" wide, 2-3/4" high 150 200 250

No. 7500 Mechanical Parking Meter
and Bank, base 6" x 6", 24-1/2" high. 150 225 300

Note: This is one of only four Courtland
toys stamped "A Walt Reach Toy by
Courtland Toy Co., Phila. Pa. Made in
U.S.A." The only other known Courtland-styled toys marked with the Courtland Toy Company, Philadelphia,
stamping are a No. 4000 sedan, a non-
power "Fire Chief" car, a private and a
garage similar to No. 9075.

No. 8000 Mechanical "Rocking R Ranch"
See-Saw, 17-3/4" long,
2-1/8" wide, 6" high...................................125 175 225

No. 8500 Mechanical Chromed Trimmed
Tow Truck, tow boom shows detail,
8" long, 3-1/4" wide, 3-1/2" high 125 200 275

No. 8500 Mechanical Chromed Trimmed
Tow Truck, tow boom is solid color,
8" long, 3-1/4" wide, 3-1/2" high 225 350 450

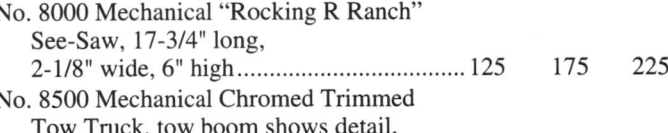

COURTLAND No. 6500 Mechanical Ice Cream Scooter (Motor Guaranteed For Life). Courtesy Joe and Sharon Freed.

End Courtland

Dancing dogs, 2, and a boy w/ whip 200 300 400

Dancing horse, 2 small bells on top
of bridle, 7-1/2" high 100 150 200

Ferris Wheel carrying eight gondolas,
the gondolas containing a total
of 16 small bisque dolls, 33-1/2" high......1200 1800 2400

Ferris Wheel, carved
w/ figures and music box, 17" 400 600 800

Freight Cart pulled by man in cap,
w/ luggage on cart, c. 1940...........................60 90 120

Gama "Komical Walking Cat," c. 1929, 7" high 150 225 300

GIRARD

C.G. Wood founded Girard Model Works in Girard, Pennsylvania, in 1906. Originally the company made patterns, models, and special machinery. Wood's son Frank joined the firm a few years after its inception. In 1918 they began making toys for "a large firm in New York" (otherwise unidentified), and in 1920 began making them under their own name, originally as "Wood's Mechanical Toys."

By 1931 the firm had 1000 employees, and Louis Marx was by then associated with Girard. During the Depression Marx took over the firm. The last Girard toys seem to have been produced in 1975, though the firm remained in business until 1980. Many of Marx's and Girard's toys are interchangeable.

Girard Air Mail Biplane, 3-engine 600 900 1200

Girard "Airways Express" plane,
13" wingspan 175 263 350

	C6	C8	C10
Girard "Bi-Wing Monoplane," 1918, 12" long, 14" wingspan (Wood's)	150	225	300
Girard Bus w/ driver, 12-1/2" long	187	280	375
Girard Coolie & Pushcart	140	210	280
Girard "Farm Boy Walking," 1920, (w/ shovel and rake) (Wood's), 6"	450	675	900
Girard "Fire Chief" Siren Coupe, 1930s, 14" long	288	430	575
Girard "Flasho the Mechanical Grinder," 1920s	212	318	425

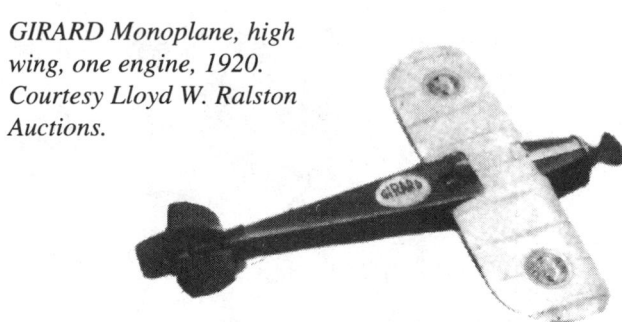

GIRARD Monoplane, high wing, one engine, 1920. Courtesy Lloyd W. Ralston Auctions.

GIRARD "Flasho the Mechanical Grinder." Courtesy Scott Smiles. Photo by Mike Adams.

	C6	C8	C10
Girard Monoplane, high wing, 1-engine, 1921-22, 13" long	350	525	700
Girard Pierce-Arrow Coupe, c. 1932, green, orange & cream, 14" long	225	338	450
Girard Race Car No. 2, 8" long	300	450	600
Girard Railroad Handcar	200	300	400
Girard "Spirit of St. Louis," 9" long	400	600	800
Girard "Tri-Motor Air Lines," 1920s	175	263	350
Girard "U.S. Marines" Monoplane	No Price Found		
Girard "Whiz Sky Fighter" biplane, 7" wingspan	313	470	625
"Ham and Sam," 1950s, Linemar, 4" x 5" base, 6" high	750	1125	1500
"Ham and Sam," maker unknown, piano player and dancer	450	675	900

	C6	C8	C10
Girard "Goble, the Gobbling Goose"	120	180	240
Girard Man pushing wheelbarrow, 5-1/2"	200	300	400
Girard Monoplane, high wing, 1-engine, pilot, 9" long	262	395	525

"Ham and Sam" piano player and dancer, maker unknown. Courtesy Ed Hyers Antique Toys.

GIRARD Railroad Handcar. Courtesy Mapes Auctioneers & Appraisers.

	C6	C8	C10
Hansom Cab, horse moves backward and forward as wheels rotate, driver atop cab, 5-3/4" long	100	150	200
Hy Line Car, Ultra-Streamlined 2-door coupe type, c. 1938	100	150	200

INGAP Mouse Car.
Courtesy Christie's East.

	C6	C8	C10
Hy-Lo, Buffalo Toys Ferris Wheel, 14-1/2" high	150	225	300
Indian (like cigar store Indian), c. 1937	70	105	140
Ingap Mouse Car, Italian, eccentric wheels, arms extend, 6" long	1650	2475	3300
Ives "Destroyer 3009," 1923, painted, 9" long	400	600	800

IVES Destroyer, "3009." Courtesy PB Eighty-Four, New York.

	C6	C8	C10
Ives Submarine, 10-1/2" long	300	450	600
Ives Tugboat "King"	150	225	300

IVES Tugboat "King." Courtesy PB Eighty-Four, New York.

	C6	C8	C10
Jantzen Bathing Suit Girl Scooter	400	600	800
Jep Seaplane (France), 13-1/2" long	1500	3000	5200

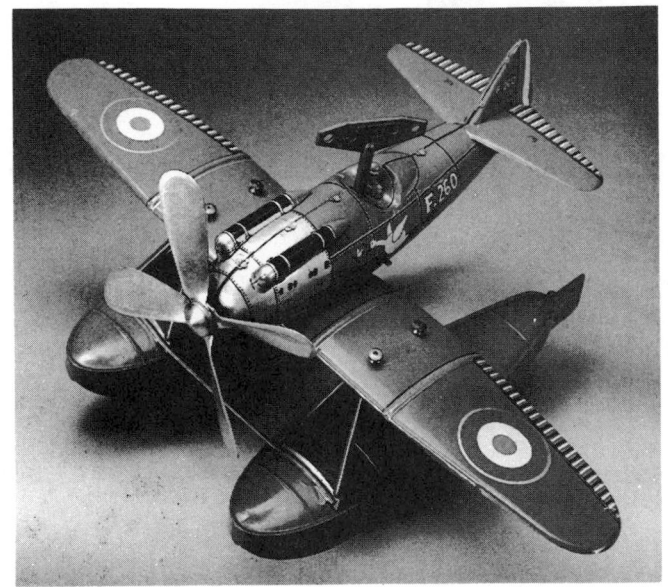

JEP Seaplane (France). Courtesy Christie's East.

	C6	C8	C10
Katz Toys, "Coney Island," 1930s, 18" long-roller coaster w/ 8-passenger car and 4 monoplanes on pylon	400	600	800
Katz Toys NY, "The Question Mark" airplane, 18" wingspan, high-wing, 2-motors	250	375	500
Kellerman "Armored Vehicle," 1930s, 4" long	55	88	110
Kingsbury Ambulance, 7" long	500	750	1000
Kingsbury Artillery Launcher	75	112	150
Kingsbury Biplane, c. 1925, single engine, rubber wheels, 16" long	437	655	875
Kingsbury "Bi-Wing Airplane," 1918, 16" long, 17" wingspan (w/ cast-iron pilot)	400	600	800
Kingsbury Borden's Milk Truck	250	375	500
Kingsbury Convertible w/ rumble seat, electric headlamps, hard rubber wheels, 12-1/2" long	180	270	360
Kingsbury Fireman's Ladder Truck, hard rubber wheels, driver, 23-1/2" long	200	300	400

	C6	C8	C10
Kingsbury Monoplane, high wing, single engine, windup wheels and spins prop via rubber band, 1930s, 11" long	300	450	600
Kingsbury Roadster, electric headlamps, 12-1/2" long	250	375	500
Kingsbury Station Wagon, 1920s	150	225	300
Kingsbury "Streetcar," 1930s, No. 782, 9" long	200	300	400
Kingsbury "Transatlantic Air-Go-Round"	250	375	500
Lehmann "Adam the Porter," 1920s, 9" high	880	1320	1760
Lehmann "Aha" Delivery Van, 1920s, 5-1/2" long	500	750	1000
Lehmann "Ajax" Warrior w/ 2 clubs	650	1000	1425
Lehmann "Alabama Coon Jigger"	300	450	600

LEHMANN Alabama Coon Jigger.

LEHMANN Dancing Sailor. Courtesy Christie's East.

	C6	C8	C10
Lehmann "Also"	285	430	570
Lehmann "Am Pol," Amundsen driving, figure behind w/ umbrella, map of North Pole	1800	2700	3750
Lehmann "Anxious Bride," chauffeur on tricycle, woman in car	800	1300	1965
Lehmann "Autin"	95	143	190
Lehmann Autobus	700	1300	2000
Lehmann "Autohutte" Garage No. 771, 6" long	450	675	900

	C6	C8	C10
Lehmann Baker & Sweep	1500	2600	4260
Lehmann Baldur Limousine, 10" long	700	1100	1800
Lehmann Balky Mule, 1930s, 7-1/2" long	200	300	400
Lehmann Berolina Car	1500	2400	3500
Lehmann "Bucking Bronco, Wild West," 6-1/2" long	415	622	830
Lehmann "Climbing Miller," cardboard blades	340	510	680
Lehmann "Crawling Beetle, The," 1900s, 4" long	140	210	280
Lehmann Crocodile, c. 1905	200	300	400
Lehmann "Dancing Sailor," 1920s, 7-1/2" high	358	540	715
Lehmann "Daredevil" Zebra Cart	400	600	800
Lehmann "Duo," rooster pulling rabbit	750	1100	1540
Lehmann "Echo Motorcycle" No. 725, 1907, 8-3/4" long	1000	1500	2500
Lehmann "EHE & Co.," open bed	320	480	640
Lehmann EPL I dirigible	390	585	780
Lehmann EPL II dirigible	463	695	925
Lehmann "Express," porter pulling cart, c. 1927, 6" long	243	365	485
Lehmann Galop Racer No. 1 w/ garage	800	1200	1600
Lehmann "Galop" Zebra Cart	150	225	300
Lehmann "Going to the Fair"	800	1300	1800
Lehmann Heavy Swell, dude-it-up man	850	1400	1975

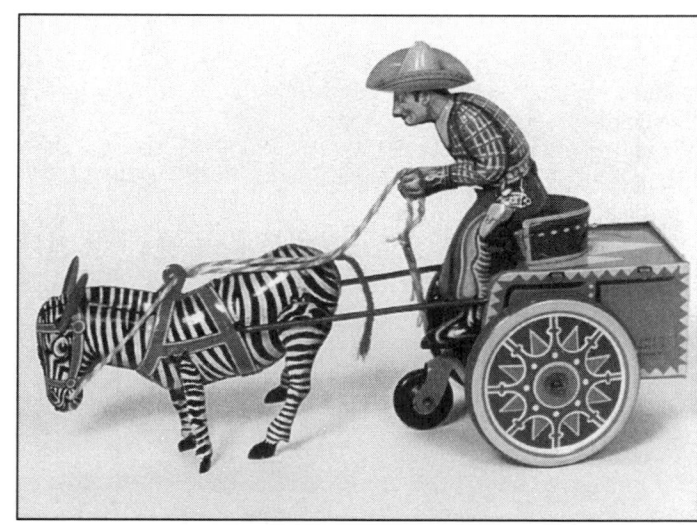

LEHMANN "Galop." Photo by Scott Smiles.

LEHMANN. Left to Right: "Express," "Paddy Pig." Courtesy Sotheby's New York.

LEHMANN "Ito." Courtesy Christie's East.

LEHMANN "Kadi." Courtesy Sotheby's New York.

LEHMANN Masuyama. Courtesy Mapes Auctioneers & Appraisers.

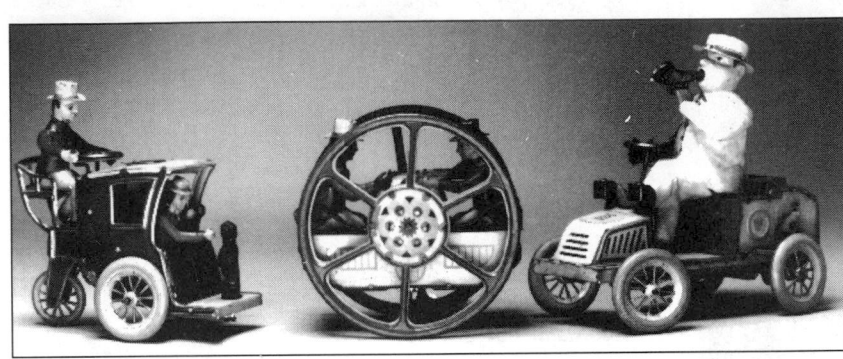

LEHMANN. Left to Right: "Li La," "Zig Zag," "Tut Tut." Courtesy Sotheby's New York.

	C6	C8	C10
Lehmann "Ito" Sedan, 1920s, 6-1/2"	468	700	935
Lehmann "Kadi," 2 Chinese carrying chest	600	950	1400
Lehmann Lana Auto	1200	2000	2800
Lehmann "Lehmann's Autobus 590"	1000	1800	2400
Lehmann "Li La," early car w/ 2 excited women passengers, driver in top hat and dog w/ turning head, 5-1/2"	1000	1850	2500
Lehmann "Lo Li," clown and ring master	5000	8000	12,000
Lehmann "Lo Lo," early car, driver	500	750	1100

	C6	C8	C10
Lehmann "Lu-Lu" bird.....................................	100	150	200
Lehmann "Lu-Lu" delivery truck, 7-1/4" long	1500	2500	4000
Lehmann "Mandarin," 2 coolies carrying Chinese in sedan chair	1400	2300	3540
Lehmann Mars Cycle	450	675	900
Lehmann "Masuyama," coolie pulling rickshaw	800	1400	2000
Lehmann Mensa Delivery Van......................	1400	2300	3500

LEHMANN. Left to Right: Stubborn Donkey, EPL-II Dirigible, "Motor Coach," "Bucking Bronco, Wild West." Courtesy Sotheby's New York.

LEHMANN. Left to Right: "Naughty Boy," "Quack-Quack," "Onkel." Courtesy Sotheby's New York.

	C6	C8	C10
Lehmann "Mikado Family," 1920s, 6-1/2" long	650	1100	1500
Lehmann Mixtum	800	1350	1960
Lehmann "Motor Car Kutsche," 1897, 5-1/2" long	270	405	540
Lehmann "Motor Coach," 1920s, 5-1/2" long	339	510	675
Lehmann "Naughty Boy"	800	1300	1870
Lehmann "Na-Ob," man driving horse cart, wheels marked w/ elf, 6" long	178	270	355
Lehmann "New Century Cycle," 1907, 5" long	370	555	740
Lehmann "Nu-Nu" No. 733, rickshaw w/ puller and rider, c. 1913, 4-1/2" long	600	950	1400
Lehmann "Oh My," 10" high	350	525	700
Lehmann "OHO" patented 1903	270	405	540
Lehmann "Onkel"	375	562	750
Lehmann "Paak-Paak," ducklings in cart pulled by duck	315	472	630
Lehmann "Paddy Pig," c. 1912, 6" long	600	950	1360
Lehmann "Pao Pao" peacock, 10" long	250	375	500
Lehmann "Performing Sea Lion, The," 1900s, 7" long	75	112	150
Lehmann "Peter," 3-wheeled car	1200	1900	2700
Lehmann "Power Carriage"	360	540	720
Lehmann "Quack-Quack," mother duck pulling cart w/ 3 small ducks	300	450	600
Lehmann "Rad-Cycle," c. 1927, 5" long	650	1180	1575
Lehmann "Rollo Chair"	1000	1700	2400
Lehmann "Sedan" No. 765, 5-1/2" long	275	403	550
Lehmann Skirolf, skier	1300	2300	3050
Lehmann Stubborn Donkey, clown in donkey cart, 7-1/2" long	313	470	625

LEHMANN. Top to Bottom: "Uhu," "Lehmann's Autobus 590." Courtesy Sotheby's New York.

	C6	C8	C10
Lehmann "Zulu," black man in cart pulled by ostrich	500	780	1130
Lewco "See-Saw Circus," 1940s, 6-1/2"	95	143	190

LEWCO See-Saw Circus with box. Courtesy Scott Smiles. Photo by Mike Adams.

	C6	C8	C10
Lehmann "Taka" Battleship	450	675	900
Lehmann Tap Tap, man pushing wheelbarrow	150	225	300
Lehmann "Terra"	550	950	1385
Lehmann "Tom" climbing monkey, 8" long	40	60	80
Lehmann "Tut-Tut," man in car w/ horn, 6-3/4" long	500	900	1300
Lehmann Tyras Walking Dog, 6" long	350	525	700
Lehmann "Uhu" amphibious car	800	1400	2050
Lehmann "Walking down Broadway," strolling couple	2000	3000	4200
Lehmann Walking Sailor, 7-1/2" high	525	775	1050
Lehmann Wild West	350	525	700
Lehmann "Zig Zag" patented 1903, 5" long	750	1125	1500
Lehmann "Zikra" No. 752, 1920s, 7" long	800	1300	1800

	C6	C8	C10
Limousine, license plate "N.Y. 1918" litho, approx. 6" long	200	300	400
Lindstrom "American Railway Express" Truck & Trailer, 16" long	363	545	725
Lindstrom "Baby Wee" speedboat, 10-1/2" long	38	56	75
Lindstrom Bird	95	140	190
Lindstrom "Betty," 1930s, shako walker, 8" tall	175	263	350
Lindstrom Bumper Car, 6-1/2" long	112	168	225
Lindstrom Dancing Dutch Boy, 1930s, 8" high	125	188	250
Lindstrom "Dancing Lassie," shako, 1930s, 8" tall	100	150	200
Lindstrom "Delfine 7" Motorboat, c. 1930	175	263	350

LINDSTROM. Toys from the 1930s: Sweeping Mammy, Betty, Mammy (Shakos). Courtesy Don Hultzman.

	C6	C8	C10
Lindstrom "Johnny the Dancing Clown," No. 122, 1930s, 8" tall 200		300	400
Lindstrom "Katrinka," 1930s, 8" tall 100		150	200
Lindstrom "Lindstrom's Ferry Boat," litho, approx. 8-1/4" 100		150	200
Lindstrom "Lindstrom Flyer," 14" 100		150	200
Lindstrom "Mammy," 1930s, shako walker, 8" tall 300		450	600
Lindstrom "Miss America" speedboat 120		180	240
Lindstrom "Parcel Post No. 2" Truck 200		300	400
Lindstrom Racing Car, 1930s, 6" 175		263	350
Lindstrom "Skeeter Bug," 1930s, (bumper car), 9" long 100		150	200
Lindstrom Speedboat, 7" long 46		69	92
Lindstrom Speedboat, c. 1950, 18-1/2" long 163		245	325
Lindstrom "Sweeping Betty" 120		180	240
Lindstrom "Sweeping Mammy," No. 1750, 1930s, shako walker while sweeping, 8" tall 212		318	425
Lupor "City Cab" 67		100	135
Lupor Metal Products N.Y. Racer No. 8, 1930s 105		158	210

LOUIS MARX

By the 1950s Louis Marx was the largest manufacturer of toys in the world: his empire included six large factories in the U.S. and ownership of interest in factories in seven other countries. Marx, born in Brooklyn in 1896, worked for "Toy King" Ferdinand Strauss when he was in his teens, and by the age of twenty his energy and enterprise had made him a director of that company. A falling out with Strauss persuaded him to go into business for himself, and in 1921 he and his brother began making their own toys, including some adaptations of items by the now-defunct Strauss. Marx's watchword seems to have been quality at the lowest possible price, and he was such a favorite with toy buyers that he had virtually no need for salesmen or advertising. Although Marx made almost every type of toy (with the exception of dolls), his tin wind-up toys are probably the most favored by toy collectors. In April 1972 Marx sold his company to the Quaker Oats Company, who in 1976 sold it to Europe's largest toy manufacturer, Dunbee-Combex-Marx. The company went into bankruptcy in 1980. Louis Marx died in 1982 at the age of 85. In 1982 American Plastics bought much of the Marx assets and in 1990 began producing toys from the original molds. In the first Marx break-up, certain rights and molds were retained in Mexico, and these continue.

	C6	C8	C10
"Acrobatic Marvel," 1930s, monkey on 13" spring and 7-1/2" rocking base 118		175	235
Air Mail Biplane, 1930, 4-engine 300		450	600
Air Mail Monoplane, 1930, 2-engine 165		248	330
Airplane, U.S. Army No. 6, 2-engine, no guns, 18" wingspan 163		245	325
Airplane No. 90, light fuselage 100		150	200
Airplane No. 90, medium fuselage 100		150	200
Alligator 65		98	130
"Ambulance" w/ siren, 1930s, 14-1/2" 350		525	700

	C6	C8	C10
Ambulance, "M.D. War Dept.," 1930s 450		675	900
"American Tractor" w/ implements, 1920s, 10" long 200		300	400
"Amored Trucking Co." 150		225	300
"Army Dive Bomber" No. 482 137		205	275
Army Staff Car, 1930s, litho steel 250		375	500
"Army Staff Car," W-601158, with flasher and siren, 1940s, 11" long 115		172	230
Army Truck, cloth cover, 1930s, 10" 290		435	580
Automatic Car Wash, wind-up car, 6" 200		300	400
"Automatic Fire House," 1950s, Fire Chief Car, 7-1/2" long, Volunteer Fire Dept. Garage, 19" long 200		300	400
"Automatic Reversing Road Roller," 1925, 9" long 200		300	400
Balky Mule, pre-war 113		140	225
"Balky Mule," 1950s, 8" long 85		128	170
"Bear Cyclist," 1930s, 6" long 163		245	325
"Beat It" The Komikal Kop, 1930s 460		690	920
"Be Bop-The Jivin' Jigger," 1948, 10" 188		290	375
"Bi-Wing Airplane," 1930s, 18" wingspan 250		375	500

MARX "Ambulance" with siren. Courtesy Mapes Auctioneers & Appraisers.

MARX Acrobatic Marvel. Photo by Don Hultzman.

MARX Balky Mule, post-war, with box. Courtesy Scott Smiles. Photo by Mike Adams.

	C6	C8	C10
"Big Parade," moving vehicles, soldiers, tin airplane, etc., 1929, 24" long ..	313	470	625
"Big Silver," Mack Dump Truck	250	375	500

	C6	C8	C10
Big Three Aerial Acrobats, 1920	200	300	400
Big Lizzie Car, early 1930s, 7-1/4"	150	225	300
Bomber, 4-engine, c. 1941, 18" wingspan	195	290	390
Bomber, 4-engine, c. 1941, copper color, tricycle landing gear	225	338	450
Bomber, 4-engine, c. 1940, camouflaged, 18" wingspan......................	163	245	325
Bomber, 2-engine, camouflaged	112	168	225
Boy on Trapeze	100	150	200
Bulldozer Climbing Tractor, caterpillar type, c. 1950s, 10-1/2" long	150	225	300
Bumper Auto, streamlined, c. 1939, large bumpers, front and rear	150	225	300

MARX "Big Silver" Mack Dump Truck. Courtesy Ed Hyers Antique Toys.

MARX Bomber, 4-engine, c. 1941, copper color, tricycle landing gear. MacNary Collection. Photo: RLM

MARX Bomber, 2-engine, camouflaged. MacNary Collection. Photo: RLM.

	C6	C8	C10
"Busy Bridge," vehicles on bridge, 1935	330	495	660
"Busy Delivery" (black Pinocchio), 1930s, 9" long, 8" high	675	1015	1350
"Busy Miners," 1930s, includes 2-1/4" tin litho miner's car, 16-1/2" long	150	225	300
"Busy Parking Station," 1930s, 17" long w/ 2" tin race car	200	300	400
"Butter & Egg Man," 1930s, 8" high	495	745	990
Cadillac Coupe, 1931	500	750	1150
Cadillac Roadster, trunk w/ tools on luggage carrier, 1930, 13" long	250	375	500
Car Carrier, 3 racers, 22-3/4" long	1000	1600	2200

MARX Bulldozer Climbing Tractor. Courtesy Continental Hobby House.

MARX "Busy Bridge." Courtesy PB Eighty-Four, New York.

	C6	C8	C10
"Careful Johnnie," 1950s, 5-1/2" long	100	150	200
Cat w/ ball in front, 2 wheels in back, c. 1938: see "Roll Over Cat"			
Caterpillar Climbing Tractor, c. 1950s, 10" long	100	150	200

	C6	C8	C10
"Charleston Trio," 1 black adult, dog, black kid dancer, 1921	500	750	1000
Chicken Snatcher, black holding chicken, dog biting at the seat of his pants, c. 1927	595	895	1190

MARX "Butter & Egg Man." Courtesy Scott Smiles. Photo by Mike Adams.

MARX Charleston Trio, 1 adult, child, dog. Courtesy Ed Hyers Antique Toys.

	C6	C8	C10
"Climbing, Fighting Tank"	125	188	250
Climbing Tractor, sparkling, 1960s, 8-1/2" long	112	168	225
"Coast Defense," circular, w/ 3 cannon, revolving airplane, 1929	450	685	925
"Coast to Coast" Greyhound Bus, 1930s	500	850	1200
"Coke Coal City Coal Co." Truck	500	800	1150
"Construction" Tractor	300	450	600
"Coo Coo Car," 1920s, 7-1/2" long	255	383	510

MARX Coo-Coo Car. Photo by Don Hultzman.

	C6	C8	C10
"Cowboy Rider," c. 1941, cowboy w/ lariat on dapple or black horse	157	235	315

MARX "Cowboy Rider." Courtesy Scott Smiles.

	C6	C8	C10
Crazy Dora nodder head (also "Dan")	100	150	200
"Cross-Country Flyer," Zeppelin and Airplane, 1920, fly around 18" hangar tower	400	600	800
"Dan Dipsy Car," 1950s, (plastic nodder), 5-1/2" long	170	255	340
"Dapper Dan Coon Jigger," 1910	500	800	1155

	C6	C8	C10
Dare Devil Flyer, new in 1928	400	600	800
"Daredevil Motor Drome," 1930s, 2" wind-up car, 5-1/2" high, 9" diameter	100	150	200
"Deluxe Delivery Truck," 1950s, 11"	100	150	200
Deluxe Tractor, 6 wheels, four in treads	250	375	500
"Dipsy Doodle Bug" Dodgem cars (Dan or Dora), 6" high (pair)	262	395	525
Donkey pulling cart, w/ rider, 1950s, 10" long	110	165	220
"Dora Dipsy Car," 1950s, (plastic nodder), 5-1/2" long	100	150	200
"Dottie the Driver," 1950s, 6-1/2"	100	150	200
Doughboy Tank, no side turrets	118	175	235
Doughboy Tank, 2 side turrets, w/ top turret, 1930, soldier w/ gun pops out, 9-1/4" long	155	233	310
"Driver Training Car," 1950s, 6" long	70	105	140
"Drive-UR-Self Car," 1950s, 11" long	325	488	650
Dump Truck, 13" long	425	638	850
"Fire Dept. Chief," c. 1950s, 11" long	123	185	245
"Firemen Joe," ladder 24" high, 1930s, 8" tall	125	188	250

MARX Fireman on Ladder. Courtesy Scott Smiles.

	C6	C8	C10
"1st Batt. F.D. Chief's Car," siren, battery headlights, 16"	300	450	600
"Firewater Boat," 1920, 9" long	350	525	700
"Flipo the Jumping Dog, See Me Jump," on hind legs, c. 1940, 3-1/2" x 4"	105	158	210
"Flying Fortress 2095" sparkling aeroplane, 1940s	225	338	450
"Funny Face," new in 1928	500	750	1000
"Funny Flivver," c. 1925	325	490	650
G-Man Pursuit Car, 1930s	355	525	710
"George the Drummer Boy," 1930s, 9" tall w/ moving eyes	138	210	275

*MARX
"Flipo the
Jumping Dog."
Courtesy Mapes
Auctioneers.*

MARX "Flying Fortress 2095." MacNary Collection. Photo: RLM.

MARX G-Man Pursuit Car. Courtesy Gary Linden.

	C6	C8	C10
"George the Drummer Boy," 1930s, 9" tall w/ stationary eyes, No. 881	100	150	200

	C6	C8	C10
"Ghee Whiz" Auto Racer, 1930s, 4 2" long tin cars, 13" diameter	450	700	1000
"Giant King Racer," c. 1930s, "711"	150	225	300
Giant Reversing Tractor Truck w/ tools, "Hauling," c. 1950s, 14" long	140	210	280
Golden Pecking Goose, dated July 8, 1924, hops along pecking at ground, 9-1/2" long	83	125	165
"Hauling" 6-wheel Tractor Truck	200	300	400
"Hee-Haw" balky mule, 1929, 6-color litho, goes backward, forward and rears, farmer and his dog on seat and 5 milk cans in cart, 10-3/4" long	200	300	400

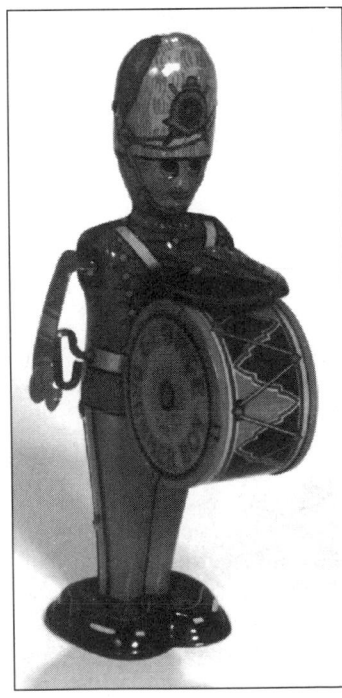

*MARX
George the
Drummer Boy
with moving eyes.
Courtesy
Scott Smiles.
Photo by
Mike Adams.*

*MARX
Highboy
Climbing
Tractor.
Photo by
Don Hultzman.*

	C6	C8	C10
"Helicopter Skyport," 1950s, 2 plastic copters, 9" x 11"	100	150	200
Highboy Climbing Tractor, c. 1950s, 10-1/2" long	75	112	150
Highboy Tractor, sparkles, c. 1950s, 10" long	100	150	200
"Honeymoon Cottage" RR	125	188	250
"Honeymoon Express," old-fashioned train on circular track, 1927	140	210	280
"Honeymoon Express," c. late 1930s	95	143	180

MARX "Honeymoon Express," c. late 1930s. Courtesy Phillips New York.

	C6	C8	C10
"Honeymoon Express," c. 1940, circling train and plane, 9-3/8" diameter	120	180	240
"Honeymoon Express," streamlined train on circular track, 1947, 9-3/8"	72	108	145

MARX "Honeymoon Express," streamlined train. Courtesy Continental Hobby House.

	C6	C8	C10
"Hoppo the Waltzing Monkey w/ Cymbals," 1930s, 9-1/2" high	200	300	400
"Ice Man"	300	450	600
Jalopy Pickup Truck, 7"	80	120	160
"Jazzbo Jim," 1920s, 9" high	255	385	510

	C6	C8	C10
"Jolly Joe" Jeep, 1940s, plastic helmet, 6" long	188	293	375
"Joy-Rider" 1929, College Boy driver w/ bag, wording on car "goes backward, forward, circles and rears" head moves, 8" long	293	450	585
Jumpin' Jeep, c. WWII, 6"	120	180	240
"King Racer," 1930s, 8-1/2" long	325	490	650
"Let the Drummer Boy Play," 1930s, 8-1/2" high	438	658	875
Light Duty Climbing Tractor, 1930s	162	243	325
"Limping Lizzie" Car	200	300	400
"Looping Plane," No. 182	200	300	400
"Looping Plane," No. 382	200	300	400
Lucky Stunt Flyer	200	300	400
"Mack Dump Truck," 1930s, (City Coal Co.), 13" long	350	525	700
"Main Street," moving vehicles, traffic cop, etc., 1929	328	490	655
"Mammy's Boy," 1930s, 11" tall	500	750	1000
"Mechanical Airplane," new in 1928	200	300	400
"Mechanical Roadster," 1950s, 11"	100	150	200
Mechanical Speed Racer, 9" long, 1930s	100	150	200

MARX Mechanical Speed Racer, 9" long. Photo by Ron Chojnacki. Courtesy Don Hultzman.

	C6	C8	C10
"Mechanical Speedway Racer"	65	98	130
Mechanical Station Wagon	125	188	250
"Mechanical Taxi Cab," 1950s, 11"	80	120	160
"Mechanical Tractor," c. 1930s, 6"	110	165	220
"Mechanical Tractor w/ Earth Grader," c. 1950s, 21-1/2" long	107	160	215
Merrymakers, 4 mice, 3 in band, 1 a dancer, 1929, w/ marquee	750	1250	1725

MARX "Merrymakers" with marquee. Photo by Jeanne Bertoia. Courtesy Bill Bertoia Auctions.

MARX "Merrymakers" without marquee. Courtesy Phillips New York.

	C6	C8	C10
Same as above w/o marquee, has conductor with baton	500	825	1175
Same as above w/o marquee, has violinist	600	950	1300
"Midget Climbing Fighting Tank," c. 1935, Pat. No. 1,334,539, approx. 5-1/2" long	65	98	130
Midget Climbing Tractor, c. 1950, 5-1/2" long	70	105	140
"Midget Racer," 1950s, plastic, 6"	50	75	100

MARX "Midget Climbing, Fighting Tank." Courtesy K. Warren Mitchell.

MARX "Midget Special." Courtesy Scott Smiles.

	C6	C8	C10
"Midget Special," race car driver in old headgear and goggles, No. 2 racer, 1930s, 5" long	65	98	130
"Midget Special," race car driver in old headgear and goggles, No. 7 racer, 1930s, 5" long	72	108	145
"Monkey Cyclist," 1930s	100	150	200
"Moon Creature," 1950s, (Japan) 5-1/2" high	90	135	180
"Motor Squad," sidecar	240	360	480
"Motorcycle Trooper," 1935	212	318	425
"Mountain Climber," 1960s (Japan), 32" long, 4" car	80	120	160
"Mysterious Kitty Kat," 1950s, 8"	90	135	180
"Mystery Police Cycle," 1930s, 4-1/2"	110	165	220
Mystery Tunnel	60	90	120
"Mystic Motorcycle," c. 1930s	130	195	260

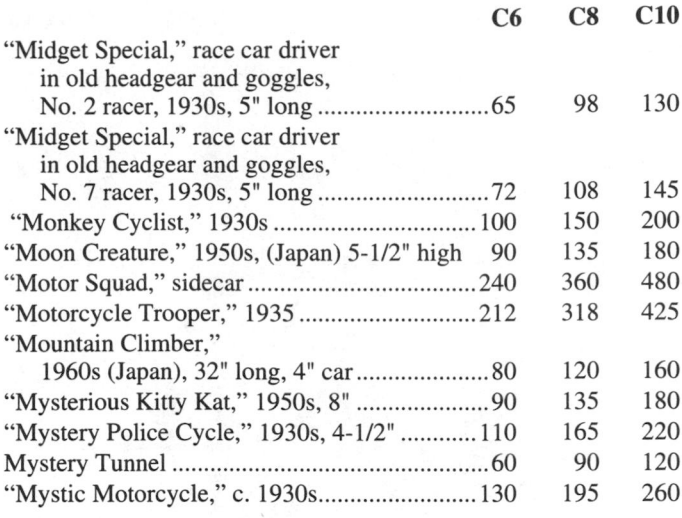

MARX Mystic Motorcycle. Courtesy Scott Smiles. Photo by Mike Adams.

MARX Mystic Motorcycle (variation). Photo by Scott Smiles.

	C6	C8	C10
"New Flivver," 1920s, 7" long	200	300	400
"New Rocket Racer," 1930s, 16"	200	300	400
"New York," circular, w/ train, new in 1928, tin airplane, 9-1/2" diameter	600	900	1200
Nodding Goose	70	105	140
"North American Van Lines Inc. Long Distance Moving" Truck	125	188	250
"Old Jalopy"	150	225	300
"Old Jalopy," small, 1950s, Linemar	130	195	260
"Old Jalopy," college boys, post-WWII	150	225	300

MARX "Old Jalopy," 1950s. Courtesy Harvey K. Rainess.

MARX "Old Jalopy," college boys, post-WWII. Courtesy Scott Smiles.

	C6	C8	C10
Peter Rabbit, eccentric car	300	450	600
"Piggy," 4" high	50	75	100

MARX "Old Jalopy" large and small. Courtesy Ed Hyers Antique Toys.

MARX Piggy. Courtesy Scott Smiles. Photo by Mike Adams.

	C6	C8	C10
"P.D." Motorcyclist, Pat. No. 2001625, approx. 4" long	150	225	300
"P.D." Police motorcycle w/ sidecar, wood wheels, on-off lever, 1930s, 3-1/2" long	150	225	300

MARX "P.D." Police motorcycle with sidecar. Courtesy Gary Linden.

	C6	C8	C10
"Parade Drummer," 1930s, "Let the Drummer Boy Play While You Swing and Sway"	400	600	800
"Parcel Post U.S. Mail," early, 8-1/2" long	225	338	450

"Pike's Peak Mountain Climber," 1930s, 3-1/2" tin car, 30" long	300	450	600
"Pinched" Roadster, motorcycle cop in circular track, c. 1927, 9-1/2" x 9-1/2"	325	488	650
"Play-Away-Piano," 1930s, w/ songbook, 9" x 9"	60	90	120
"Police Patrol," motorcycle w/ sidecar, 1935	262	395	525
Police Precinct Police Patrol armored truck, c. early 1930s, 10-1/2"	1800	2800	3800
"Police Siren Motorcycle," 1930s, 8" long	175	263	350
"Police Squad," motorcycle cop w/ sidecar, 8-1/2" long	250	375	500
"Power Snap Caterpillar Climbing Tractor," 1950s, 8" long	112	168	225
"Prone WW I Soldier," 1925, 8" long	100	150	200
Racer No. 2, 1930s, 5" long	70	105	140
Racer No. 3, 1930s, 5" long	110	165	220
Racer No. 4, 5" long	75	112	150
Racer No. 5, 1930s, 5" long	75	112	150
Racer No. 7, 1930s, 5" long	80	120	160
Racing Car, c. 1940, 2-man team, litho, 12"	110	165	220
Racing Car, "12," c. 1950, plastic driver, litho, 16" long	125	188	250
Racing Car, "27," plastic driver, litho, c. 1950	95	143	190

	C6	C8	C10
"Range Rider," 1940s, 8-1/2" high	150	225	300
"Range Rider," 1940s, 10-1/2" high on rocker base	200	300	400
"Red Cap" Porter	338	508	675
"Red Devil Stunt Auto," 1930s, 12" long ramp w/ 2-1/2" tin racer	150	225	300
"Reversible Coupe," "The Marvel Car," c. 1938, 16-3/4" long	248	372	495

MARX Ride 'Em Cowboy. Photo by Don Hultzman.

MARX "Reversible Coupe, The Marvel Car." Courtesy Mapes Auctioneers & Appraisers.

	C6	C8	C10
Reversing Road Roller	135	202	270
Reversing Tank, 1930s	65	98	130
"Reversing Tractor"	275	412	550
"Rex" Race Car, 1920s	162	243	325

MARX "Rex Race Car." Courtesy Thomas G. Nefos, Federal Shipping Network.

MARX Ring-A-Ling Circus. Photo by Scott Smiles.

	C6	C8	C10
"Rollover Tank"	55	83	110
"Rookie Cop" w/ siren, 1930s, 8-1/2"	233	350	465

	C6	C8	C10
"Rex Mars Planet Patrol," 1950s, pastel colors, 9-1/2" long	250	375	500
"Ride 'Em Cowboy"	120	180	240
"Ring-A-Ling Circus," early ringmaster and circus animals, green base	550	825	1280
Same as above, pink base	550	850	1300
Road Roller, c. 1930, has driver, 8-1/2" long	375	562	750
"Rocket Fighter," c. 1950s, complete w/ tail fin and sparking mechanism	215	322	430
Rocket Racer, 1930, 16-1/2" long	205	308	410
"Rodeo Joe," 1933	175	263	350
"Roll Over Cat"	65	98	130
"Roll Over Plane," c. 1920s	138	205	275
"Rollover Plane," c. 1940	112	168	225

MARX "Rocket Fighter." Courtesy Continental Hobby House.

MARX Roll Over Cat. Courtesy Scott Smiles.
Photo by Mike Adams.

MARX Rookie Pilot. Photo by Scott Smiles.

	C6	C8	C10
Rookie Pilot, No. 77, c. 1940, 7" long	295	445	590
Rooster Pulling Wagon, 1930s	60	90	120
Royal Bus Line, 10" long	275	410	550
"Royal Coupe," 1920s, 9" long	350	525	700
"Royal Van Co."			
"We Haul Anywhere," 9" long	375	562	750
"Running Scottie," 1940s, 5-1/2" long	115	172	230
"Safe Driving School": See Driver Training Car			

MARX "Royal Van Co." Courtesy Mapes Auctioneers & Appraisers.

	C6	C8	C10
"Sam, the Gardner," 1950s, 8" tall, (includes 6 plastic tools)	108	162	215
"Sand and Gravel Truck-Builders Supply Co.," 1920	100	150	200
Scenic Express Train Set, c. 1950s	90	135	180
"Sheriff Sam & His Whoopee Car," 1960s, 6" long	187	280	375
"Single Track Speedway," 1938, 8 track sections, 4" long wind-up car	70	105	140
"Sky Hawk" Airport Tower, No. 333, 2 planes, tower 7-1/2" high	175	263	350
Skybird Flyer, new c. 1927	187	280	375
"Skyscraper Go-Round," 1930s, monoplane, Zeppelin, 13-1/2" high	400	600	800
Smoky Joe, The Climbing Fireman, 1930s	178	270	355
Smoky Sam, The Wild Fireman	138	210	275
Snoopy & Gus Hook & Ladder, 8" x 7-1/4"	700	1100	1550
"Soap Box Derby Racer," marked #3, 5-1/2" long	100	150	200
Soldier, prone, firing rifle, WWI helmet	90	135	180
"Space Mobile," 1960s (Japan), 32" long, 3 sections, 4" long car	120	180	240
"Space Satellite w/ Launching Station," 1950s, 9" x 12" base and plastic accessories	70	105	140
Sparkling Climbing Bulldozer Tractor, later	187	280	375
"Sparkling Climbing Fighting Tank," cannon recoils	125	188	250

MARX "Sparkling Climbing Fighting Tank," cannon recoils. Courtesy Charles D. Richards.

	C6	C8	C10
"Sparkling Climbing Tank," 1939	85	128	170
Sparkling Climbing Tractor, 1940s	93	140	185
Sparkling Climbing Tractor, c. 1950s, 8-1/2" long	88	135	175
"Sparkling Climbing Tractor and Trailer," c. 1950s, 16" long	130	195	260
Sparkling Heavy Duty Bulldog Tractor w/ Road Scraper, c. 1950s, 11"	115	162	230
"Sparkling Luxury Liner," 1950s, 14" long	85	128	170
"Sparkling Mountain Climber Train Set," 1950s, tin loco & car, 9" long	100	150	200
Sparkling Soldier, crawls, 7-3/4" long	150	225	300
Sparkling Soldier Motorcycle, c. 1940	310	465	620
Sparkling Rocket Fighter Ship	425	638	850
Sparkling Space Tank	187	280	375
Sparkling Super Power Tank, c. 1950s, 9-1/2" long	115	172	230
Sparkling Tank, 4" long	95	142	190
"Sparkling Tractor," tractor w/ plow blade, 1939	140	210	280

MARX Sparkling Soldier. Photo by Joe Freed.

MARX "Speed Boy Delivery." Courtesy Don Hultzman. Photo by Ron Chojnacki.

MARX Sparkling Soldier Motorcycle (Tin Wind-Up). Courtesy Don Hultzman. Photo by Ron Chojnacki.

	C6	C8	C10
"Spic and Span, the Hams What Am," drummer and dancer, 1924	1000	1600	2250
"Spic Coon Drummer," 1924, 8-1/2" high	900	1400	2000
"Streamline Speedway," 1938 (tin figure-8 track, 2 wind-up cars), 31" long	118	175	235
Streamlined Coupe	225	338	450
"Subway Express" w/ plastic tunnel 1950s, 9-3/8" diameter	90	135	180

MARX Sparkling Tank, 4" long. Courtesy Continental Hobby House.

MARX "Subway Express," CHEIN "Boy Skier." Courtesy Don Hultzman. Photo by Ron Chojnacki.

	C6	C8	C10
Sparkling Tractor and Trailer Set "Marbrook Farms," c. 1950s, 21" long	100	150	200
Sparkling Turn Over Tank	50	75	100
Sparkling Warship (same as U.S.S. Washington), 14" long	90	135	180
"Speed Boy Delivery" (motorcycle delivery), 1930s, battery-operated lights, 9-3/4" long	280	420	560
Same as above, no lights	230	345	460
"Speed King" Racer, 1930s, 16" long	425	638	850
Speedway Coupe, battery to be inserted for headlights, 8" long	312	468	625

	C6	C8	C10
"Super Streamline Racer," 1950s, 17" long	138	207	275
"Tidy Tim" Streetcleaner, pushing wagon, 1933, 7-1/2" high, 8-1/2" long	325	490	650
"Tom Tom Jungle Boy"	100	150	200
"Toto Acrobat"	100	150	200
"Tower Aeroplane," 1940s, two 3" tin airplanes, 7-1/2" high	200	300	400
"Toyland Farm Products," 1930s, milk wagon, 10-1/2" long	295	450	590

MARX "Tom Tom Jungle Boy." Photo by Ed Hyers Antique Toys.

MARX Toyland's Farm Products.

	C6	C8	C10
Trolley, headlight, bell, 9" long	170	255	340
"Tumbling Monkey," 1930s, on two chairs, 5" high	110	165	220
"Tumbling Monkey on Trapeze," 1920s, 6" high	100	150	200

MARX Tumbling Monkey on two chairs. Photo by Scott Smiles.

	C6	C8	C10
"Toy Town Dairy," horsedrawn cart, 1930s, 10-1/2" long	150	225	300
Tractor, early 1940s	105	158	210
Tractor and Trailer Set, 1930s, similar to climbing tractor set but w/ rounded and radiator front and copper finish metal. Tin plow attaches to front, silver metal trailer attaches to rear; has tin, copper finish and "balloon" tires	135	200	270
Tractor and Trailer, c. 1950s, 16-1/2" long	150	225	300
"Trans-Atlantic Zeppelin," 1930s, rear propeller, 10" long	250	375	500
"Tricky Fire Chief," 1925, 4" car on 6" x 10" base	200	300	400
"Tricky Motorcycle," 1930s, non-fail action, 4-1/4" long	150	225	300
"Tricky Taxi," 1940s, 4-1/2" long	85	128	170
Tricky Taxi On A Busy Street	175	262	350

	C6	C8	C10
Turn Over Tank No. 3	105	158	210
"TWA-U.S. Mail-990," c. 1941, 5"	120	180	240
"U.S. Army" bomber, post-war, 1940s, 2-engine	162	243	325
"U.S. Army Fighter Plane," 1940, 8" wingspan	185	280	370
"U.S. Mail" Truck, 9-1/2" long	450	680	975
"U.S. Mail-TWA Biplane," 1930s, 15" long, 18" wingspan	400	600	800
"U.S.S. Washington" Battleship	65	98	130
"Uncle Wiggily, He Goes A Ridin'," 1935: See Comic Character chapter			
Vacationland Express	62	93	125
Wacky Taxi	110	165	220
Walking Clancy	400	600	800

MARX Turnover Tank No. 3. Photo by Max Heiss.

MARX "TWA U.S. Mail 990-5." MacNary Collection. Photo: RLM.

MARX "U.S. Army" bomber, post-war, 1940s, 2-engine. MacNary Collection. Photo: RLM.

MARX "U.S. Mail" Truck, 9-1/2" long. Courtesy Phillips New York.

	C6	C8	C10
Walking Drummer Boy, "Let The Drummer Boy Play While You Swing and Sway," c. 1939	350	525	700
Wee Scottie, 5" long	88	130	175

MARX. Five versions of "Wee Scottie," also identified on its boxes as "Running Scottie." Photo by Scott Smiles.

Whoopee Car, laughing cows on wheels, driver looks like cowboy, 1929	190	285	380
Whoopee Car, "Yale-Princeton" pennants on wheels	350	525	700
"Whoopee Car w/ Flappers," 7-1/2" long	250	375	500

MARX Whoopee Car. Laughing cows on wheels. Photo by Mark Adams. Courtesy Scott Smiles.

"Wonder Cyclist," 1930s, 9" high	170	255	340
Xylophonist, 5"	100	150	200
"Yellow Cab-LMN 52," 1940s, 6-1/2" long	150	225	300
Zeppelin, 10" long	162	243	325

MARX "Whoopee Car." Yale, Princeton pennants on wheels. Courtesy Mapes Auctioneers & Appraisers.

	C6	C8	C10
"Zeppelin," 1925, (propeller on front), 11" long	175	263	350
Zeppelin, 1930s, 27" long	200	300	400
Zeppelin TransAtlantic, 10" long	162	243	325
"Zippo, The Climbing Monkey," 1930s, 9-1/2" long	80	120	160

	C6	C8	C10
Mohawk Toys Yellow Taxi, c. 1920s, 6-3/8" long	188	290	375
"Movie Man" Touring Car, rare	2000	3000	4000
Newsboy "Extra" w/ cab and bell, c. 1940s, Japan	150	225	300
"Nifty Bus"	800	1300	1800
Nifty "N.Y. to Paris" PNX211 plane, 7" wingspan	400	600	800
Ohio Art "Automatic Airport," 1940s, 9" high	90	135	180

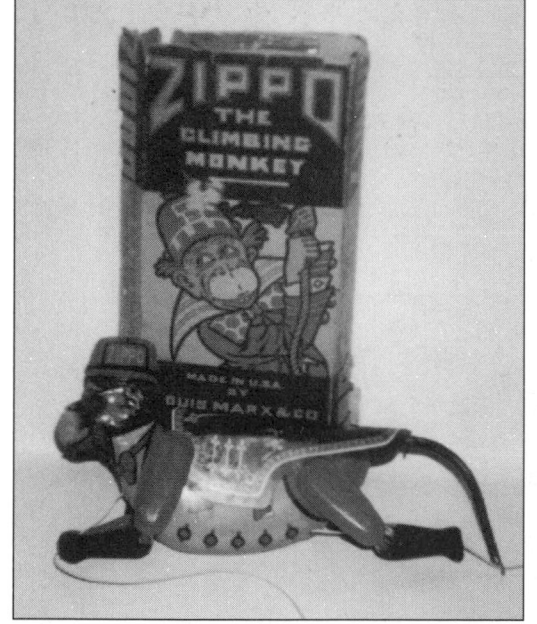

MARX Zippo the Climbing Monkey. Photo by Ron Chojnacki. Courtesy Don Hultzman.

OHIO ART Automatic Airport. Photo by Ron Chojnacki. Courtesy Don Hultzman.

	C6	C8	C10
"Mike Mallard The Climbing Fireman," 1950s, Linemar Co., 13-3/4" high (ladder), w/ 4-1/2" long tin duck	200	300	400
Mohawk Toys Checker Cab, c. 1920s, 6-3/8" long	188	290	375

	C6	C8	C10
Ohio Art Boat, 14" long	80	120	160
Ohio Art Cabin Cruiser, 15" long	58	88	115
Ohio Art "Circus Shooting Gallery," 1950s, 12" high, 17" long	60	90	120
Ohio Art "Coast Guard Seaplane," 1950s, 10" wingspan	72	108	145
Ohio Art "Commando Joe," 1950s, 8" long	118	175	235
Ohio Art "Giant Ride Ferris Wheel," 1950s, 16" high	225	338	450
Ohio Art Hot Job Floatplane	92	138	185

	C6	C8	C10
Ohio Art "Injun Chief," 1950s, 8" long	80	120	160
Ohio Art "Jungle Eyes Shooting Gallery," 1950s, 18" long, 14" high	90	135	180
Ohio Art "Mechanical Sea Plane"	100	150	200
Ohio Art "Musical Sail Away" ride	200	300	400
Ohio Art "Sea Patrol" Seaplane, 10" wingspan	90	135	180
Ohio Art "Switch and Dump Train," 1950s, 28" long	100	150	200
Ohio Art "Traffic Control," 1950s, tin wind-up cars, 3-1/2" long, base 19" x 13"	60	90	120
Ori-O Tailspin 4" puppy	10	15	20
Orkin Coast Guard Cutter, 25" long	350	525	700
Pecking Bird, 1927, 5-1/2" long	45	68	90
Pecking Chicken, 1927, 5-1/2" high	40	60	80
"PT 10," tin litho PT boat, c. 1941	60	90	120
Ranger Steel Products (Roslyn Heights, NY), Billiard Table, 2 players, No. 850, 1950s, 14" long	135	200	270
Ranger Steel Products Cross Country Turnpike, 26" x 14"	85	128	170
Roadster, orange and green	120	180	240
Santa Claus in red cloth suit and holding Christmas tree, 5-1/2" high, (Occupied Japan)	200	300	400

OHIO ART Giant Ride Ferris Wheel. Photo by Don Hultzman.

	C6	C8	C10
Santa Claus w/ green sleigh, Christmas tree, presents and white celluloid reindeer, bell, sleigh on 3 wheels, (Occupied Japan), 8-1/2" long	100	150	200

SCHUCO

by Don Hultzman

Schuco was founded in 1912 by Heinrich Muller and Herr Schreyer. It was later called Schreyer and Co. and adopted the name "Schuco" as its trademark. Schuco toys are noted for their ingenious mechanisms. They were produced from the 1930s to the 1950s and were marked either "Germany" or "U.S. Zone-Germany." Other markings are reissues.

	C6	C8	C10
"Akustico 2002," 1940s, 5-1/2" long	87	130	175
"Anno 2000," 1940s, 5-1/2" long	80	120	160
Beer Drinker, 1950s, 5-1/2" high	100	150	200
"Buick" No. 5311, 9" long	200	300	400
"Cadillac DeVille Convertible 5505," 1960s, plastic, 11" long	90	135	180
"Charly 1005," 1950s, motorcycle w/ driver, 3-1/2" long	300	450	600
"Clown Juggler" No. 965, 1950s, 5" high	300	450	600
"Combinatio 4003," 1950s, w/ wind-up horn, 7-1/2" long	175	263	350
"Commando Auto" No. 2000, 1950s, 5-3/4" long, responds to whistle	150	225	300
"Curvo 1000," 1950s, 5" long	138	200	275
"Dalli 1011," 1950s, tin car & plastic driver, 6-1/2" long	162	243	325
"Disneyland Alweg Monorail," 1950s, playset	300	450	600
"Electro Ingenico" No. 5311/61, 1950s, 8-1/2" long car, playset	600	900	1200
"Electro Radiant 5600," 1950s, battery operated, 16" long, 19" wingspan	400	600	800
"Electro Submarine" No. 5552, 1950s, 13" long	90	135	180

	C6	C8	C10
"Elektro Ingenico 5311," 1950s, remote control, 8-1/2" long	180	270	360
"Examico 4001," 1950s, 5-speed BMW, 6" long	67	100	135

SCHUCO Examico 4001. Photo by Ron Chojnacki. Courtesy Don Hultzman.

	C6	C8	C10
Fernlenk Auto No. 3000, 1950s, 4-1/4" long, part of playset	160	240	320
"Fex 1111," 1950s, 6" long	100	150	200
Fire Engine, 1950s, 11-1/8" long, with remote control	1000	1500	2000+
"Fox and Goose" No. 969, 1950s, 4-1/4" high	800	1200	1600

	C6	C8	C10
"Gas Station 3054," 1950s, 8" long	60	90	120
"Grand Prix Racer 1070," 1950s, 6"	100	150	200
"Hegi-Fipsi 110," 1950, airplane kit (glider)	70	105	140
"Hopsa," 1950s, 4" high	120	180	240
"Ingenico" 5311/56-MK, 1950, 8-1/4" long car, part of playset	500	750	1000+
"Ingenico" 5335 MK, 1950s, 8" long car, playset	700	1050	1400
"Jaguar 1250," 1940s, 5-1/2" long	160	240	320
"Kommando Anno 2000," 1940s, 5-1/2" long	100	150	200
"Latso 3042," 1950s, truck, 4-1/2"	60	90	120
"Magico Alpha Romeo" No. 2010, 1950s, 9-1/2" long, responds to blowing	600	900	1200
"Magico Auto 2008," 1950s, responds to blowing, 5-1/2" long	300	450	600

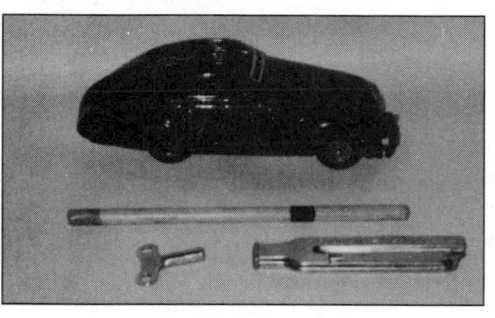

SCHUCO Magico Auto 2008. Photo by Don Hultzman.

"Magico Car and Garage," 1950s, 6"	120	180	240
"Mercedes 190SL, 2095," 1950s, 8"	225	338	450
"Mercedes TYP SSK 1928," 1950s, 4" long	100	150	200
"Mercer Auto 1225," 1950s, 7-1/2"	85	128	170
"Micro-Jet 1030" Thunderjet, 1950s, 5" wingspan, 5-1/2" long	80	120	160
"Micro-Jet 1031" Magister 170R, 1950s, 5" wingspan, 5-1/2" long	80	120	160
"Micro-Jet 1032" Super Sabre F 100, 1950s, 5" wingspan, 5-1/2" long	90	135	180
"Micro-Jet 1033" Douglas F4 D-1, 1950s, 5" wingspan, 5-1/2" long	80	120	160
"Micro Racer 101," 1950s, Porsche style, 3-1/2" long	90	135	180
"Micro Racer 102," 1950s, Indy style, 3-1/2" long	90	135	180
"Micro Racer 104," 1950s, Indy style, 3-1/2" long	90	135	180
"Micro Racer 1036," 1950s, 4-1/2"	100	150	200
"Micro Racer 1040," 1950s, 4" long	75	112	150
"Micro Racer 1041," 1950s, 4" long	60	90	120

SCHUCO Micro Racer 1040. Photo by Don Hultzman.

SCHUCO Motodrill Clown 1007. Photo by Don Hultzman.

	C6	C8	C10
"Micro Racer 1042," 1950s, 4" long	100	150	200
"Micro Racer 1043," 1950s, 4" long	100	150	200
"Micro Racer '57 Ford 1045," 1950s, 4" long	100	150	200
"Micro Racer Apha Romeo 1048," 1950s, 4" long	90	135	180
"Micro Racer Go Kart 1035," 1950s, 4" long	100	150	200
"Micro Racer Hot Rod 1036," 1950s, 4" long	90	135	180
"Micro Racer Mercedes-Benz 1038," 1950s, 4" long	100	150	200
"Micro Racer Mercedes Benz 1044," 1950s, 4" long	110	165	220
"Micro Racer Mercer 1036/1," 1950s, 4" long	100	150	200
"Micro Racer Porsche 1047," 1950s, 4" long	110	165	220
"Micro Racer Rally 1034," 1950s, 10'6" long, eight 3-lane tracks	60	90	120
"Micro Racer Stake Truck 1049," 1950s, 4" long	90	135	180
"Micro Racer Volkswagen 1046," 1950s, 4" long	90	135	180
"Micro Racer Volkswagen Polizei 1039," 1950s, 4" long	100	150	200
"Mikifex 922," 1950s, non-fall action mouse, 3-1/2" long	40	60	80
"Mirako-Peter" No. 1013, 1950s, 5" long, rare	1000	1500	2000+
"Mirakocar 1001," 1950s, non-fall action, 4-1/2" long	72	108	145
"Mirakomot 1012," 1950s, non-fall action, 5-1/4" long	300	450	600
"Monkey Car," 1930s, orange-black, smiling monkey, 6" long	1400	2100	2800
"Motodrill 1006," 1950s, circular action, 5" long	300	450	600
"Motodrill Clown 1007," 1950s, motorcycle, composition head, 5" long, rare	1000	1500	2000+
"Mystery Car 1010," 1950s, non-fall action, 5-1/2" long	90	135	180
"PanAm Clipper," 533S, 19" wingspan	300	450	600
"Patent Motorcar" 1950s, 4-1/2" long	100	150	200
"Pick-Pick" No. 905, 1950s, birds, 4-1/2" long	100	150	200
"Porsche Formel II-1037," 1950s, 4-1/2" long	80	120	160
"Racing Boat 1015," 1950s, non-fall action, 5" long	90	135	180
"Radio 4012," 1950s, musical car, 6"	200	300	400
"Solisto," Clown Drummer, 1950s, 4-1/4" tall	100	150	200
"Solisto," Clown Fiddler, 1950s, 4-1/4" tall	90	135	180

SCHUCO. Left to Right: Solisto Clown Drummer, Clown Juggler, Clown Fiddler. Photo by Don Hultzman.

SCHUCO. Left to Right: Solisto Monkey Drummer, Monkey Lifter, Monkey Fiddler. Photo by Don Hultzman.

	C6	C8	C10
"Solisto," Clown Flutist, 1950s, 4-1/4" tall	130	195	260
"Solisto," Clown Juggler, 1950s, 4-1/2" tall	200	300	400
"Solisto," Monkey Drummer, 1950s, 4-1/2" tall	140	210	280
"Solisto," Monkey Fiddler, 1950s, 4-1/2" tall	125	188	250
"Solisto," Monkey Flutist, 1950s, 4-1/2" tall	120	180	240
"Solisto," Monkey Lifter, 1950s, lifts pig or bear, 4-1/2" tall	150	225	300
"Sonny 2005," 1950s, mouse w/ balloon in BMW, 5-1/4" long	300	450	600
"Spirit of St. Louis" plane, 4" long, 1920s, Lindbergh figure, rare	800	1200	1600
"Station Car 3118," 1950s, 4-1/2" long	60	90	120

SCHUCO Studio Racer 1050. Photo by Don Hultzman.

	C6	C8	C10
"Studio Racer 1050," 1950s, includes tools, 5-1/2" long	125	188	250
"Submarine 3007," 1950s, tin and plastic, 12" long	113	170	225
"Synchromatic 5700," 1950s, resembles Packard Hawk, 11" long	500	750	1000
"Telesteering 3000 Limo," 1950s, 4" long	50	75	100
"Tippy" No. 990, Scotty, 1950s, 4" long	80	120	160
"Trip-Trap," 1950s, dog, 7" long	400	600	800
"Turn Miki Clown," 1950s, 3-3/4" high	200	300	400
"Varianto 3010," 1950s, tin cars are 4-1/2" long, 2-car playset	100	150	200
"Varianto 3010 Super," 1950s, service station w/ two 4-1/2" tin cars	170	225	340
"Varianto 3010/0," 1950s, truck and garage, 4-1/2" long	50	75	100
"Varianto 3041 Limo," 1950s, 4" long	80	120	160
"Varianto 3064," 1950s, all plastic, 8" long	30	45	60
"Varianto Box 3010/30," (tin garage and 3041 Limo), 1950s, 4-1/2" long	110	165	220
"Varianto Bus 3044," 1950s, 4" long	70	105	140
"Varianto Electro 3112," 1950s, truck, 4" long	60	90	120
"Varianto Electro 3112u," 1950s, truck, 4-1/2" long	60	90	120
"Varianto Lasto" No. 3042, 1950s, 4-1/4" long truck	80	120	160

End Schuco

	C6	C8	C10
Selrite, "Home Run King," 1930s, 4" x 6" base w/ 5" tall hitter	437	655	875
"Skidoodle," Nifty, c. 1920, family in odd-looking car	1300	2100	3100

SELRITE "Home Run King." Photo by Scott Smiles.

"Skidoodle," Nifty. Photo courtesy PB Eighty-Four, New York.

	C6	C8	C10		C6	C8	C10
Speedboat, "G.E. 200," tin litho, c. 1930	80	120	160	"Spirit of America" Airplane PNX211, NY to Paris, litho on wings	200	300	400
Spinning Globe, tin litho, 2 tin planes circling it, c. 1930	200	300	400	Steam Roller, c. 1925	100	150	200

STRAUSS

Ferdinand Strauss emigrated to the U.S. from Alsace, France. He worked as a toy importer in the early 1900s and by 1914 had four New York toy shops. When the war disrupted imports, he began to manufacture toys himself. In 1918 his company was located in East Rutherford, New Jersey, and was staffed by fifty employees. Eventually Strauss was known as "The Founder of the Mechanical Toy Industry in America." Evidently Strauss was wholly or partially out of business in the late 1920s, but later resumed production of wind-ups and other toys until at least 1941-42. He is also famous for having employed the very young Louis Marx.

	C6	C8	C10
"Air Devil" monoplane	300	450	600
"Alabama Coon Jigger," 9-3/4"	350	525	700
"Alabama Coon Jigger-Tombo," 1918, 10-1/2" high, 3" x 5" base	370	555	740

	C6	C8	C10
"Aluminum Flying Airship" LA 1017, 1930s, 9" long	275	362	550
"Big Show Circus Truck," 9-1/2" long	600	950	1400
"Big Trixo," climbing monkey, 10" long	150	225	300
Billiards Player	300	450	600
Black Porter pulling wheelbarrow, 6-1/4"	150	225	300
"Bus Deluxe," 1920s, 12" long	550	825	1250
"Check-A-Cab," 8-1/2" long	500	750	1025
"Chicago Zeppelin," 1930s, 9" long	400	600	800
Circus Wagon, containing lion and tamer, no engine compartment, 8-1/2" long	420	630	840
Circus Wagon, has engine compartment, 10" long	1100	1700	2500
"Dandy Jim," copyright 1921	500	750	1100
"Dizzie Lizzie"	250	375	500
Flying Airship dirigible	188	275	375
"Ham and Sam The Minstrel Team," piano player and banjoist, 1921, 6-1/2" long	500	800	1200

STRAUSS "Alabama Coon Jigger." Courtesy Mapes Auctioneers & Appraisers.

STRAUSS "Ham And Sam The Minstrel Team." Photo by Jeanne Bertoia. Courtesy Bill Bertoia Auctions.

STRAUSS Circus Wagon, containing lion and tamer. Courtesy Sotheby's New York.

	C6	C8	C10
"Haul Away Truck," No. 22, dump body	240	360	480
Hooligans Hack	300	450	600
Interstate Double Decker Bus, 1920, 10-1/2" long	478	715	955
"Jackee The Hornpipe Dancer," No. 51, 8-1/2" long	500	800	1150

STRAUSS Hooligan's Hack. Courtesy Mapes Auctioneers & Appraisers.

STRAUSS Interstate Double-Decker Bus, 10-1/2" long. Courtesy Lloyd W. Ralston Auctions.

	C6	C8	C10
"Jazzbo Jim The Dancer on the Roof," 1910, 10" high	345	520	690
"Jenny the Balky Mule," 6-color litho, goes backward, forward and rears, farmer holding extended tin grain pail from his seat in front of mule's face to keep him moving, vegetables in cart, No. 55, 10" long	188	285	375
"Jitney Bus," 9-1/4" long	213	320	425
"Jocko the Golfer"	218	327	435
Knock-Out Prize Fighters, c. 1910, No. 52, 7" high	250	375	500
"Kraka Jack Car," 1920s, 5-1/2" long	150	225	300
"Leaping Lena"	295	445	590
"Long Haulage Truck"	350	525	700
"Lux-A-Cab," 8-1/2" long	500	800	1200
"Mailplane"	225	338	450

STRAUSS Jenny the Balky Mule. Photo by Scott Smiles.

STRAUSS. Top Left: Jackee the Hornpipe. Top Right: Leaping Lena. Middle Right: Knockout Prize Fighters. Bottom: Billiards Player. Courtesy PB Eighty-Four, New York.

	C6	C8	C10
"Miami Sea Sled," 1920s, w/ 4" dinghy attached, 10" long	238	360	475
Monkey driving 3-wheel cart pulled by bulldog, 1930s, 4-1/2" high	280	420	560
"Old Jalopy, The," 4 college kids	100	150	200
"Play Golf," 1920s, 7" x 12" base w/ 5" high golfer	275	412	550

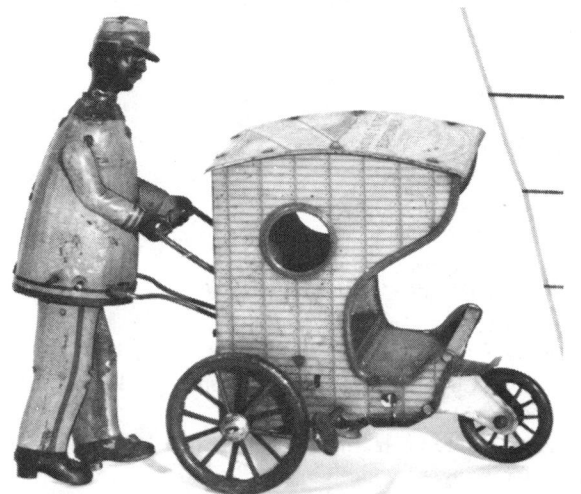

STRAUSS Rollo Chair.

	C6	C8	C10
"Red-Cap Porter," porter pushing a large trunk	300	450	600
"Red Star Van"	400	600	800
Rollo Chair, black man pushing boardwalk chair, "Stock, DRGM, December 6, 1921"	500	800	1100
"Santee Claus," 1921, in sleigh, 2 reindeer, 6" high	950	1425	1900
"Speedwagon"	200	300	400
"Standard Oil," Truck, "73"	325	488	650
"Tip Top" man w/ wheelbarrow	80	120	160
"Tip Top Dump Truck"	500	750	1050
"Tip Top Porter," No. 40, 1920s, 6" long	245	370	490
Tippy Canoe	167	250	335
"Tom Twist," 1920s, 8-1/2" tall	450	675	900
"Travel Chiks," chickens on railroad car	362	543	725
"Trikauto," No. 53	185	278	370
"Water Sprinkle" Truck	450	675	900
"What's It?" Car, No. 53, 1925, 9-1/2" long	600	900	1200
"Yell-O Taxi," 8-1/2" long	405	610	810

End Strauss

	C6	C8	C10
"Super Rocket Racer," tin litho, 1940s?	200	300	400
Sweetie Pie Boat, Lindstrom, 1920s	100	150	200

STRAUSS "Santee Claus."
Courtesy Sotheby's,
New York.

TECHNOFIX

by Don Hultzman

The Technofix Co., founded in Nuremberg, Germany, by Gebruder Einfalt, was engaged in German military technology during WWII. After the war Technofix diverted its expertise to toy manufacturing. It was noted for its quality, detailed, mechanical toys. Among these were impressively large, 3-dimensional, platform toys. These colorful toys were made from stamped tin blanks and highlighted with delicate relief features that duplicated realistic outdoor-recreational themes. In the late 1950s vacuform plastic took the place of tin. As a result, quality declined, the toys were less durable, and sales dropped. Soon after, many Technofix toys began to carry the Ohio Arts trademark.

	C6	C8	C10
"Alpine Express #300," 1950s, (Ohio Art #614), 6-1/2" x 32" long extended, two 3" tin cars	120	180	240
"Cable Car #303," 1950s, 7-3/4" x 18-1/2" long, two 1-3/4" long tin cars	220	330	440

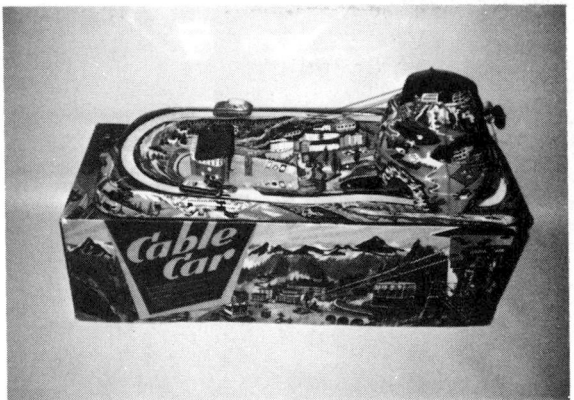

TECHNOFIX "Cable Car" on box. Photo by Don Hultzman.

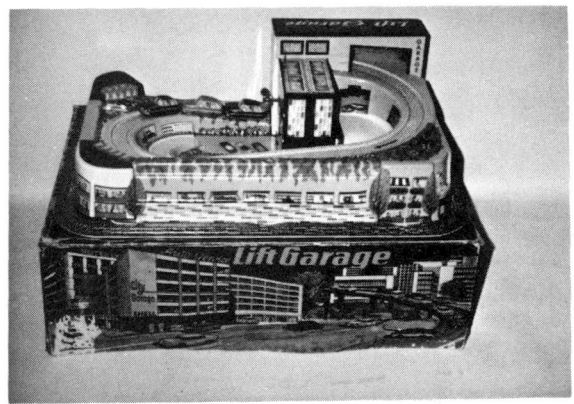

TECHNOFIX "Lift Garage" on box. Photo by Don Hultzman.

	C6	C8	C10
"Coney Island #290," 1950s, 14" x 21" long, two 3" long tin cars	115	172	230
"Grand Prix," 1950s, 14" x 21" long, three 3" tin cars	140	210	280
"Holiday Camp #304," 1950s, 9" x 28-1/2" long, two 3-1/2" cars	400	600	800
"International Airways #309," 1950s, 9" x 28" base, 5" long plastic jet airplane	300	450	600
"Lift Garage #308," 1950s, 10-1/2" x 15" long base, three 1-3/4" tin cars	88	133	175
"Motorcycle & Sidecar #225," 1950s, 7" long, 4-3/4" high	165	250	330
"Mystic Station #306," 1950s, 17" x 8" base, tin car	70	105	140
"Rallye," 1950s, 15" x 18", plastic base and 4 tin cars	300	450	600
"Rocket Express," 1950s, 14-3/4" long, includes 2 tin cars	220	330	440
"Silver Mine Express," 1950s, 23" x 6" base, w/ 3" long tin car	90	135	180
"Toboggan #290," 1950s, 14" x 21" long base, two 3-1/2" tin cars	150	225	300
"Touchdown Chimp," 1950s, 3-1/2" high	140	210	280
"Traffic Control," 1950s, 13" x 19" long base, three 3-1/2" tin cars	50	75	100
"Traffic Crossing w/ Police Control," 1950s, two 3" tin cars	100	150	200
"Trick Motorcycle," 1950s, 7" long	300	450	60

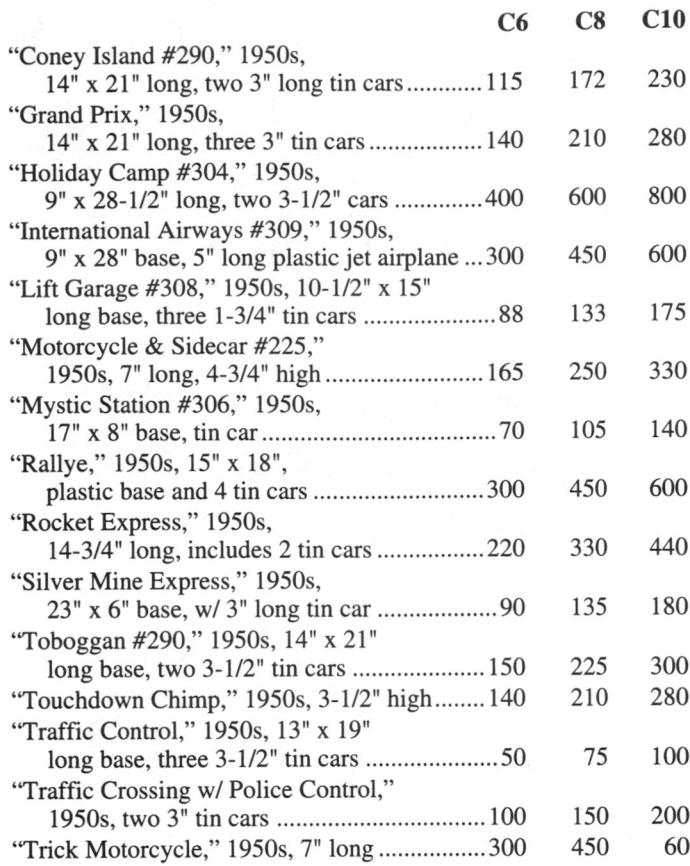

TECHNOFIX "Trick Motorcycle." Photo by Ron Chojnacki. Courtesy Don Hultzman.

End Technofix

	C6	C8	C10
"Tip Top Toy Airplane" high wing single engine, "Giant Flyer No. 200," 1930s, 23" long, 19-1/2" wingspan	500	750	1000
Tom Turkey, "B&S," turkey struts, tail spreads, then moves up and down, German, 6" long	180	270	360

T.P.S.

by Don Hultzman

T.P.S. is the trademark of Toplay, Ltd., founded in 1956 and noted for its most unusual and unique mechanical toys. A Japanese company. (More T.P.S. toys in "Battery Operated" section.)

	C6	C8	C10
"Animal Barber Shop," 1950s, 5" high	200	300	400
"Animals Playland," 1950s, 9-1/4"	120	180	240
"Ball Playing Giraffe," 1950s, 8-1/2" tall	100	150	200
"Bear Golfer," 1950s, assembled 7-1/2" long	150	225	300
"Bear Playing Ball," 1950s, 19" long, 4" high	200	300	400

TPS "Bear Playing Ball" with box. Photo by Don Hultzman.

"Big League Hockey Player," 1950s, 6" tall	150	225	300
"Bobo The Mechanical Juggling Clown," 1950s, 6" tall, (flips ball)	300	450	600

TPS "Bobo The Mechanical Juggling Clown." Photo by Ron Chojnacki. Courtesy Don Hultzman.

"Bo Bo the Strongman," 1950s, 6"	200	350	600
"Bouncing Ball Dolly," 1950s, 5-1/4" tall	100	150	200
"Bunny Family Parade," 1950s, 13"	50	75	100
"Busy Choo Choo," 1950s, 5-1/2" x 9-1/4" base, w/ 2-1/4" tin locomotive	90	135	180
"Busy Mouse," 1950s, 6" x 9" base, w/ 3-1/4" tin mouse	90	135	180
"Calypso Joe," 1950s, 6" tall......................	300	450	600
"Candy Loving Canine," 1950s, 5-1/2" high	90	135	180
"Champ On Ice-Bear Skater Trio," rare, 9" long	400	600	800
"Circus Acrobatic Seal and Ball," 5" high	80	120	160
"Circus Bugler," 1950s, (w/ trombone), 7" tall	300	450	600
"Circus Clown and Monkey," 1950s, 5" high ..	150	225	300

TPS "Champ On Ice Bear Skater Trio." Photo by Ron Chojnacki. Courtesy Don Hultzman.

	C6	C8	C10
"Circus Clown on Ball" (?), 1950s, 5-1/2" high......................	150	225	300
"Circus Cyclist," 1950s, 6-1/2" tall	150	225	300
"Circus Parade," 1950s, 11-1/2" long	200	300	400
"Circus Parade-Juggling Duck and Friends," 1950s, 9" long	150	225	300

TPS Circus Parade. Photo by Scott Smiles.

"Circus Seal," 1950s, (w/ plastic ball on nose), 6-1/2" high............	70	105	140
"Cleo Clown-The Dogs," 1950s, 4-1/2" high ..	200	300	400
"Climbing Panda," 1970s, all plastic, 6" high	40	60	80
"Climbing Pirate," 1950s, (string climber), 6" long.............................	120	180	240
"Climbo the Climbing Clown," 1950s, (string climber), 6" long	150	225	300
"Clown Jalopy Cycle," 1950s, friction, 9" long...	200	300	400
"Clown Juggler," 1950s, 6" tall........................	200	300	400
"Clown Juggler w/ Monkey," 1950s, 9-1/2" tall..	600	900	1200
"Clown Making The Lion Jump Thru The Flaming Hoop," 1950s, 4-1/2"	180	270	360
"Clown on Rollerskates," 1950s, 5-3/4" tall	200	300	400
"Clown Trainer and His Acrobatic Dog," 1950s, 4-1/2" high.......................................	150	225	300
"Cock-A-Doodle," 1960s, 8" long	50	75	100
"Combat Tank On Battle Front," 1950s, 6-1/4" x 15" base, w/ 2-1/4" tin wind-up tank	120	180	240

	C6	C8	C10
"Comical Clara," 1950s, 5-1/2" tall 350	525	700	
"Coney Island Scooter," 1950s, 10" square w/ 2-1/2" tin bumper car 100	150	200	
"Dancing Couple," 1950s, 5-1/2" tall 90	135	180	
"Dreamland Airport," 1950s, 6-1/2" x 12" base w/ 3-1/2" tin helicopter 90	135	180	
"Drive Tester," 1950s, 7" x 10-1/2" base and two 2" tin cars 80	120	160	
"Duck Amphibious Taxi," 1950s, 6-1/2" long, 4-3/8" high 140	210	280	
"Duck Family Parade," 1950s, 12" long 70	110	140	
"Duck the Mailman," 1950s, (Turn-N-Go action), 4-1/2" high 300	450	600	
"Educational Pet Pooch," 1950s, 4" high 100	150	200	
"Elephant Circus Parade," 1950s, 11-1/2" long, (similar to "Circus Parade") 200	300	400	
"Fairyland Taxi," 1950s, 11" long, (similar to "Wagon Fantasyland") 140	210	280	
"Family Giraffe Loco," 1950s, 11" long, (locomotive and three cars called "Kiddy," "Mammy," and "Pappy") 150	225	300	
"Fishing Bear," 1950s, 7-1/2" high 100	150	200	
"Fishing Monkey on Whale," 1950s, 9" long .. 400	600	800	
"Flying Birds w/ voice," 1950s, (includes 2 tin birds), 4" diameter base 200	300	400	
"Gay 90s Cyclist," 1950s, 7" high 150	225	300	

TPS "Happy Skaters" (Rabbit). Photo by Ron Chojnacki. Courtesy Don Hultzman.

TPS Happy the Violinist. Photo by Ron Chojnacki. Courtesy Don Hultzman.

TPS Gay '90s Cyclist. Photo by Scott Smiles.

	C6	C8	C10
"Hockey Player," 1950s, 6" tall 150	225	300	
"Hungry Whale," 1950s, w/ 3" long small whale or fish, 5" long 40	60	80	
"Joe The Acrobat," 1950s, 6" tall 300	450	600	
"Joe The Acrobat," (clown), 1950s, 5-1/2" high 150	225	300	
"Joe The Xylophone Player," 1950s, 5" tall 200	300	400	

TPS Hockey Player with box. Photo by Don Hultzman.

	C6	C8	C10
"Girl Skipping Rope," 1950s, 12" long, 6" high 150	225	300	
"Girl w/ Chickens," 1950s, 6" tall, 5" long 100	150	200	
"Happy Caterpillar," 1950s, 13" long 80	120	160	
"Happy Hippo," 1950s, 5-1/2" long 350	525	700	
"Happy Skaters" (bears), 1950s, 6-1/2" tall 250	375	500	
"Happy Skaters" (monkey), 1950s, 5-1/2" tall 250	375	500	
"Happy Skaters" (rabbit), 1950s, 5-1/2" tall 250	375	500	
"Happy the Violinist," 1950s, 9" tall 150	225	300	

TPS Jolly Wiggling Snake. Photo by Ron Chojnacki. Courtesy Don Hultzman.

	C6	C8	C10
"Jolly Wiggling Snake," 1950s, 7-1/2" long	90	135	180
"Juggling Clown," 1950s, 8-1/2" tall	200	300	400

TPS Juggling Clown. Photo by Ron Chojnacki. Courtesy Don Hultzman.

"Juggling Popeye and Olive Oyl," 1950s, 9-1/2" high (marked "Linemar")	1000	1500	2000
"Ladder Truck," 1950s, 2" tin fire engine, 5-1/2" x 9-1/4" base	80	120	160
"Lady Bug Family Parade," 1950s, 12" long	80	120	160
"Lady Bug & Tortoise With Babies, 1950s, 7" long, (flips over)	60	90	120
"Lucky Monkey Playing Billiards," 1950s, (includes plastic balls), 6" long	150	225	300
"Magic Choo Choo," 1950s, 5-1/2" x 9-1/4" base w/ 2-1/4" tin locomotive	90	135	180
"Magic Circus," 1960s, (includes tin seal and monkey), 6" high	80	120	160
"Magic Cross Road," 1950s, 5-1/2" x 9-1/4" base w/ 2-1/4" tin locomotive	90	135	180
"Magic Tunnel," 1950s, 6" x 9" base w/ 2" tin "Dreamland Bus"	90	135	180

TPS Lady Bug & Tortoise With Babies. Photo by Ron Chojnacki. Courtesy Don Hultzman.

TPS Lucky Monkey Playing Billiards. Photo by Ron Chojnacki. Courtesy Don Hultzman.

	C6	C8	C10
"Mailman with Geese," 1950s, 6" tall	150	225	300
"Mama Kangaroo w/ Playful Baby In Her Pouch," 1950s, 6" tall	100	150	200
"Midget Lady Bug," 1950s, 7-1/2" tall	60	90	120
"Missile Robot," 1960s, 6" high	80	120	160
"Mr. Caterpillar," 1950s, 12" long	50	75	100
"Monkey Basketball Player," 1950s, 7" high	150	225	300
"Monkey Golfer," 1950s, assembled 7-1/2" long	150	225	300
"Monkey on Whale," 1950s, 4" long, 3-3/4" high	300	450	600
"Mountain Climber," 1950s, (string climber), 6-1/2" long	120	180	240

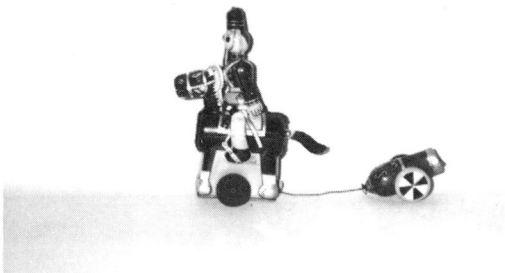

TPS Mounted Cavalryman with Cannon. Photo by Don Hultzman.

	C6	C8	C10
"Mounted Cavalryman w/ Cannon," 1960s, 5-1/2" high, w/ 2-1/2" long tin cannon	300	450	600
"Mouse Race Cat," 1950s, 10" x 10"	90	135	180
"Oscar the Seal," 1950s, 6-1/2" high, (with 4-bladed plastic propeller on nose)	80	120	160
"Pango Pango," 1950s, 6" tall	120	180	240

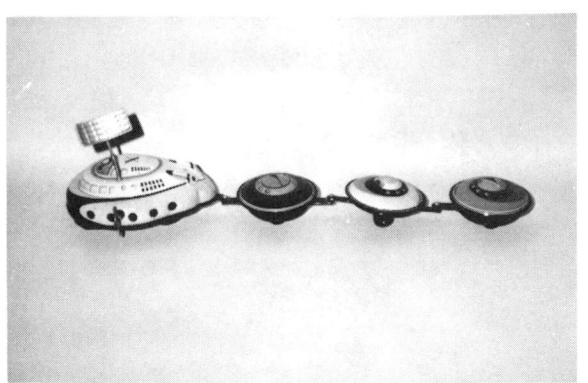

TPS Satellite Fleet. Photo by Don Hultzman.

TPS Pango-Pango with box. Photo by Scott Smiles.

	C6	C8	C10
"Performing Seal and Monkey w/ Fish," 1950s, 4-1/2" tall	300	450	600
"Plane The Loop Pilot," (with remote control), 1950s, 6" high	150	225	300
"Playland Scooter," 1950s, 6" x 9" base w/ 2" tin car	90	135	180
"Police Patrol," 1950s, 5-1/2" x 9-1/2" base and 2" tin police car	80	120	160
"Pop Eye Pete," 1950s, 5-1/2" tall	350	525	700

	C6	C8	C10
"Shuttle Zoo Train," 1950s, 5-1/2" x 9-1/4" base and 2-piece tin train	80	120	160
"Skating Chef," 1950s, 6" tall	150	225	300
"Skating Chef' (black), 1950s, 6"	250	375	500
"Skip Rope Animals," 1950s, 8" long	110	165	220
"Skippy the Tricky Cyclist," 1950s, 6" tall	150	225	300
"Slim the Seal and Friends," 1950s, 10" long (with 4-bladed propeller on nose)	300	450	600
"Sports Car Race," 1960s, 8" x 14" base and 4 plastic racers	100	150	200
"Susie the Ostrich," 1950s, rare, 5-1/2" high	300	450	600
"Suzy Bouncing Ball," 1950s, 5-1/2" tall	90	135	180
"Take-off Airport," 1950s, 5-1/2" x 9-1/2" base w/ 3" tin airplane (fighter)	80	120	160
"Tippy Toy Train," 1960s, gravity action, 6" diameter, 4" high	60	90	120
"Touchdown Pete," 1950s, 5" tall	170	235	340

TPS Pop Eye Pete and Comical Clara. Photo by Don Hultzman.

TPS "Touchdown Pete." Photo by Scott Smiles.

	C6	C8	C10
"Popeye and Olive Oyl," 1950s, 9-1/2"	1000	1500	2000+
"Popeye Cyclist," 1950s, 6-1/2" high	400	600	800
"Popeyc Skater," 1950s, (Linemar), 6-1/2" tall	500	750	1000+
"Pussy Cat Chasing Butterfly," 1950s, 4-1/2" high	110	165	220
"Rabbit and Bear Playing Ball," 1950s, 19" long, 5" high	200	300	400
"Samson the Strongman," 1950s, 6" tall	250	375	500
"Satellite Fleet," 1960s, 12" long	150	225	300
"Seal and Monkey w/ Fish," 1950s, rare, 5" high, 4" long	250	375	500

	C6	C8	C10
"Tricycle Tot," 1960s, 5-1/2" long	70	105	140
"Trombone Player," 1950s, 5-1/4" tall	150	225	300
"Tumbling Chimp," 1950s, 4-1/2"	150	225	300
"Two Gun Tex," 1960s, 11" long	110	165	220
"Violin Player," 1950s, 5-1/4" tall	200	300	400
"Wagon Fantasyland," 1950s, 11" long	150	225	300
"World Champion Auto Racer," 1950s, 5-1/2" x 9-1/2" base, 2-1/4" tin car	70	105	140

TPS Two Gun Tex. Photo by Ron Chojnacki. Courtesy Don Hultzman.

	C6	C8	C10
Trolley, horse-drawn, German	150	225	300
Two rotating blimps and two cars, w/ passengers, that spin and rotate, German, 11-1/2" high	600	900	1200
"2001 Circus," 1930, 8" long	450	675	900
Train Set, 1930s, 3 pieces, wooden wheels, 20" long	150	225	300
"U.S.A. Army," D-105 Truck, 10-1/2" long	100	150	200

UNIQUE ART MFG. CO.

Unique Art Mfg. Co. was in business from 1916, when it introduced its Merry Juggler and Charlie Chaplin. In 1931 it was located at Waverly and Peshine Avenues in Newark, New Jersey. Its president was Wm. Marbe, and there were 28 male employees (no females listed). In 1934 employees numbered 110 male and 165 female (same address). In a 1946-47 directory the address was 200 Waverly Avenue in Newark, and the president was Smuel Burger (this last name may be incorrect: the handwriting in my notes is hard to read). Employees were equally divided: 125 male and 125 female. Unique was still manufacturing toys, mainly wind-ups, in 1952. Little else is known about the company, except that at some date Louis Marx bought it.

	C6	C8	C10
Unique Artie the Clown in his Crazy Car	300	450	600
Unique "Bombo the Monk," 2-piece, tree 9-1/2" high, monkey 5-1/2" long, 1930s	100	150	200
Unique "Capitol Hill Racer," 1930s, 17-1/2" long, w/ 2" tin racing car	100	150	200
Unique "Casey the Cop," early	500	800	1200
Unique "Dandy Jim" Dancer, 1921	475	712	950
Unique "Daredevil Motor Cop," 1940s, 8-1/2" long	255	380	510

UNIQUE Artie the Clown in his Crazy Car. Courtesy Don Hultzman. Photo by Ron Chojnacki.

UNIQUE Daredevil Motor Cop, tin windup. Photo by Kent M. Comstock.

	C6	C8	C10
Unique "Finnegan," 1930s, w/ cardboard luggage, 14" long	160	240	320
Unique Flying Circus, elephant supports flying plane and flying clown	450	675	900

UNIQUE Flying Circus. Photo by Don Hultzman.

	C6	C8	C10
Unique "G.I. Joe and His Jouncing Jeep," post-WWII, 7"	158	235	315
Unique "G.I. Joe and the K-9 Pups," c. 1941, 9" high	130	195	260
Unique "Gertie the Galloping Goose," 1930s, 9-1/2" long	145	220	290
Unique "Hee Haw" donkey pulling milk cart, 10" long	140	210	280
Unique "Hillbilly Express," 1930s, 3 pieces and 3-1/4" tin locomotive, 18" long	90	135	180
Unique "Hobo Train," 1920s, dog biting pants of hobo atop train, 8-1/2"	300	450	600
Unique "Hott an' Tott" musical band, 1920s	500	800	1200
Unique "Jazzbo Jim" dancer, new in 1921	375	562	750
Unique "Jazzbo Jim-The Dancer on the Roof," 1920s, 10" high, base 5" x 3" x 3"	250	375	500

UNIQUE " Jazzbo Jim-The Dancer on the Roof." Courtesy Sotheby's New York.

UNIQUE G.I. Joe And His Jouncing Jeep. Courtesy Scott Smiles. Photo by Mike Adams.

	C6	C8	C10
Unique "Kid-Go-Round" plastic horsemen and boat	150	225	300
Unique "Kiddy Cyclist," 1930s, steers figure-8 pattern and rings bell, 8-3/4" tall	173	260	345

UNIQUE "Kiddy Cyclist." Courtesy Scott Smiles.

	C6	C8	C10
Unique Krazy Kar, new in 1921	300	450	600
Unique "Lincoln Tunnel," moving vehicles, cop, 1935, 24" long	190	285	380
Unique "Motorcycle Cop," 1930s, 9" long	220	330	440
Unique Musical Sail-Way Carousel w/ 3 kids in spinning plastic boats, 9" tall	170	255	340
Unique "Pecking Goose," Witch and Cat	350	525	700
Unique "Rap & Tap," boxers in ring, 1921	500	750	1000
Unique "Rodeo Joe" Crazy Car	138	205	275
Unique "Rollover Motorcycle Cop," 1935	200	300	400
Unique "Sky Rangers" plane and Zeppelin revolving from tower, 1933	180	270	360

End Unique

	C6	C8	C10
Walking Man, carrying red top hat over his head. Head revolves to reveal 3 different faces (Unique?)	1000	1700	2500
Wilkins Roadster, early w/ driver, 9" long	300	450	600
Wilkins Auto, early, woman driver, 9" long	290	425	580
Wolverine Acrobat	110	165	220

UNIQUE "Lincoln Tunnel." Courtesy Christie's East.

UNIQUE Rodeo Joe Crazy Car. Courtesy Mapes Auctioneers & Appraisers.

Top: "2001" Circus. Bottom: UNIQUE Krazy Kar, 1940. Courtesy Lloyd W. Ralston Auctions.

Left to Right: UNIQUE Sky Rangers, MARX Skybird Flyer. Courtesy Phillips New York.

	C6	C8	C10
Wolverine "Acrobatic Monkeys," No. 810, 1930s, 10" diameter base	200	300	400
Wolverine "Autolift," 1930s, includes 2-1/2" tin car and 4 sections of track, 10-1/4" high	205	308	410
Wolverine "Drummer Boy," 14" high	140	210	280
Wolverine "Drum Major," No. 27, patent 1892546, 1930s, 13-1/4" tall on circular 4-1/4" base	163	245	325
Wolverine "Drum Major," No. 27, pat. 1892546, 1930s, 13-5/8" tall on rectangular 4-1/2" x 6-1/2" base	200	300	400
Wolverine Farm Wagon, 1950s, plastic, 10" long	25	38	50

	C6	C8	C10
Wolverine Jet Roller Coaster and small car, 21" long extended	155	233	310
Wolverine "Loop-A-Loop," 1930s, includes small car No. 30, 19"	175	262	350
Wolverine Luxury Liner	100	150	200
Wolverine "Mechanical Man on the Flying Trapeze," 1930s, 8-1/2" high	120	180	240
Wolverine "Merry-Go-Round," 1930s, includes 4 tin-litho flags, No. 31, 11" diameter, 12" high	238	355	475
Wolverine, "Neck & Neck,"			

Walking Man, carrying red top hat over his head, head revolves to reveal three different faces. Photo courtesy PB Eighty-Four, New York.

WOLVERINE S.S. Wolverine Oceanliner. Courtesy Don Hultzman.

	C6	C8	C10
1940s, horse-racing game, 36" long	70	105	140
Wolverine Pontiac Mystery Car	100	150	200
Wolverine "S.S. Wolverine," 14-1/2" long	100	150	200

	C6	C8	C10
Wolverine Sandy Andy Caterpillar Tractor, Trailer, 21" long	500	750	1000
Wolverine "Sandy Andy Circus," dancing toy	150	225	300
Wolverine "Sandy Andy" Tank, 14" long	90	135	180
Wolverine "Zilotone," w/ 6 interchangeable records, 1930s	323	490	645

WOODHAVEN

Research by John Monteleone has established that in the 1930s Herman Joerger bought Animate Toy, and about the same time, Ranger Toys. He sold the business to his son, Herman Jr., who in turn sold it to his son, Kurt, the present owner. The firm made toys until at least 1939. It was located in Woodhaven, New York, and is now called Woodhaven Telesis Corporation, making sheet metal parts to order.

WOODHAVEN Tractor, "1916," with original box. (Actually produced and sold much later.) Photo by John Monteleone.

	C6	C8	C10
Woodhaven "Robot Bus w/ the Mechanical Brain," 1940s, 13-1/2" long	78	115	155
Woodhaven Tractor, "1916"	65	100	130

WYANDOTTE "Ducky Ducklings." Photo by Ron Chojnacki. Courtesy Don Hultzman.

	C6	C8	C10
World on base, wind-up plane circles it, German	100	150	200
Wyandotte "Acrobatic" Monkeys	200	300	400
Wyandotte Carnival, 16" x 11"	425	638	850
Wyandotte Carousel, 5-1/4" high	150	225	300
Wyandotte Chicken pulling Chick in Cart, 7-1/2" long	60	90	120
Wyandotte Duck pulling tin Easter cart, litho, wooden wheels, 15" long	50	75	100
Wyandotte "Ducky Ducklings"	90	135	180
Wyandotte "Hoky-Poky," handcar w/ 2 clowns	123	185	245
Wyandotte "Man On The Flying Trapeze," 1930s, 9" high	100	150	200
Wyandotte "Mechanical Handcar," 1935, 6-1/2" long	200	300	400
Wyandotte "Red Ranger Ride 'Em Cowboy," No. 515, 6-1/2" high	140	210	280

WYANDOTTE "Hoky Poky" Handcar. Photo by Scott Smiles.

YONE

Yone was a Japanese manufacturer of tin wind-up and friction toys, c. early to mid-1960s.

	C6	C8	C10
Yone Bears Seesaw	130	195	260
Yone Chef, Japanese, c. 1960s	90	135	180
Yone Soldier, Japanese, c. 1960s	90	135	180
Yone Pirate, Japanese, c. 1960s	115	172	230

YONE. Left to right: Soldier, Chef, Pirate. Photo by Scott Smiles.

BATTERY-OPERATED TOYS

The average mint price of these toys was $392.76 in the last edition. In this edition it is virtually unchanged.

HISTORY, VALUE AND CARE

by Don Hultzman

"Made in Japan" are the words toy collectors look for in their pursuit of high-quality mechanical tin toys.

Before WWII, these same words were synonymous with cheap, poor-quality, drab-looking toys made from recycled materials and ideas. Most of the toys were people-animal-oriented with less emphasis on vehicle, nautical, or aircraft-type toys. They were powered either by a spring or a flywheel and didn't last very long or do very much as far as play-value goes. These inexpensive, poor-quality toys kept Japan a third-rate toy manufacturing nation until after WWII, when Japan's surrender resulted in economic chaos for this industrial nation.

In their quest for economic recovery and to compete in a toy market already dominated by Germany and America, the Japanese knew they had to come up with a new, different, and exciting type of toy that would be more desirable than those produced by their competitors.

The Japanese toy designers concentrated their technology on a different type of toy operation. Not satisfied with the limited action and short duration of spring-driven or flywheel-propelled toys, the toy engineers developed a small electric motor powered by flashlight batteries. This mini-motor took up less room than other mechanisms, had a longer-running duration, and enabled the toy to perform more functions. This development opened up an entirely new dimension in toy design: it introduced the concept of the battery-operated toy.

The toy designers integrated this new concept into hundreds of automaton-like toys, capable of as many as eight different types of actions in one cycle. These unique toys were an instant hit with the foreign market, especially the U.S. These clever, unusual, and high-quality toys made Japan the dominant toy producer and exporter for the next 20-30 years.

It should be noted that Japan flooded the market with these ingenious, well-made toys while quality control remained a high priority. These merits were not only apparent in their figural toys, but also in their vehicle line. The Japanese toy makers concentrated on very fine detail and quality, especially in their scale-model passenger cars. Their ultimate goal was to produce toys that looked like the real thing, and they succeeded. Their workmanship carried over into their other vehicle lines, such as motorcycles, emergency and construction vehicles, and novelty (silly) and comic character cars, trucks, and space toys.

No other nation was able to equal (much less surpass) the impetus and determination of the Japanese toy makers until Japan relinquished its domination by redirecting its economy.

Now that they are approaching middle age, it is no wonder that these fine toys remain in great demand today and often command a very high price.

Don Hultzman confesses he has always been a collector of toys, but about ten years ago he really got serious about the hobby. Now he not only collects but also repairs toys. Born and raised in Cleveland, Ohio, he received a master's degree in guidance and administration at Kent State, and is currently employed by the Panama City school system as a school counselor. He does freelance writing as a science consultant to the encyclopedia department of World Publishing Co. and lives in Brunswick Hills, Ohio. Many of his tin wind-up toys can be seen in the 1983 MGM movie A Christmas Story, and 1994's It Runs In The Family.

The value of a battery-operated toy depends not only on its desirability, rarity, and complexity, but very much on its condition. A toy in "mint" condition is generally worth twice as much as a toy in "good" condition. A toy in "very good" condition will be priced about halfway between good and mint.

C-10: Mint. A mint toy is in the condition in which it was originally issued (perfect) regardless of age. It will also be in perfect mechanical condition, complete with all accessory parts when applicable, and will look brand new. The cloth or fur (plush) covering on some battery toys may reveal some discoloration (yellowing) due to age, but this should not affect its value as a mint toy as long as it is clean. All toys in this category must be in perfect working condition. The original box in mint condition will significantly enhance the value of any mint toy.

C-8: Very Good. A battery toy that has seen some use and is starting to show its age is described as very good. It will still be in perfect working order and have all its accessory parts when applicable. It will have some age-soiling, but will have no rust or corrosion. Overall, it will have an appearance of freshness and still be highly desirable to the fussy collector.

C-6: Good. The term good applies to a battery toy that has seen considerable use, wear, and tear, and some age-soiling, but is still in perfect working condition with no missing parts or accessories. The "wet" toys may show some slight surface rust that can be easily removed. A toy in good condition is still a welcome addition to any toy collection, but will be targeted for upgrading by a piece in better condition.

Any battery toy below the condition of good will reflect a drastic reduction in value. Toys in good shape, but missing accessory parts, will not lose as much value as those that are severely rusted, corroded, painted over, have parts broken off, or are totally inoperable. These "poor" toys are usually collected for their scrap value by the toy repairer and seldom are they worth more than $10.00.

The key to grading is to use common sense and avoid wishful thinking. Grading the condition of a toy may be difficult at times, and consulting with an expert in the field can help dispel doubts about your judgment or your purchase. (See the back section of this book for a guide to toy collectors and dealers.)

To keep it in excellent condition, your prized battery toy needs T.L.C. If it stops working, you could have frustration, if not a disaster, on your hands. The following suggestions should be of some help in avoiding this.

Battery toys, like other mechanical toys, should be operated periodically to keep them loosened up. A lightweight spray lubrication now and then will help considerably if the mechanism is accessible. Do not overlubricate as the excess may stain any cloth or fur covering on the toy.

A quality car wax or polish will keep the lithographed and bare metal parts looking like new, especially on the "wet" toys. Always test an obscure lithographed area to make sure the polish doesn't soften or dissolve the paint. Care should be exercised when polishing metal parts adjoining any cloth or plush covering, as the cleaning substance may stain the coverings. Light surface rust usually disappears with a careful polishing. Nothing can be done for deep rust or corrosion without further ruining the value of the toy. Repainting will only further reduce the value and is not recommended.

Should your battery toy fail to operate, the following steps might be helpful:

1. Make sure it is not gunked-up and that no moving parts are binding.
2. Make sure the battery contacts are not dirty or corroded. If they are, clean them with crocus cloth. **Always use fresh batteries!**
3. Lightly tap the toy with your finger or **lightly** nudge one of the moving parts while the switch is "on."

If none of the above steps work, then your toy needs major surgery. This means the toy must be completely torn down, repaired, and reassembled. Most battery toys are repairable as long as they have not been destructively tampered with and no parts are missing or corroded beyond repair. This job is best left to an expert in toy repair and should never be attempted by one who doesn't know what he or she is doing. Expert repairs will not affect the value of a battery toy as long as the repair is undetectable and the toy looks and functions exactly as it did before the repair. Such repairs are acceptable in toy collecting circles. Expert repairs are expensive but well worth the investment if it means the difference between a highly-prized mint toy and one below the grade of good. An inoperable toy is practically worthless, regardless of condition.

Photos in this section by Don Hultzman and Ron Chojnacki, and courtesy of Don Hultzman, unless otherwise noted.

	C6	C8	C10
"A-B-C Fairy Train," 1950s, M-T Co., 14-1/2" long, one piece, four actions	80	120	160
"Accordion Bear," 1950s, "Y" Co., 10-1/2" tall, six actions	220	330	440
"Accordion Bear," 1950s, MST Co. (Flare Toy), 9-1/4" high, five actions	140	210	280
"Accordion Player Bunny," 1950s, Alps Co., 12" tall, 9" long, six actions	200	300	400

	C6	C8	C10
"Accordion Player Hobo With Baby Monkey Playing Cymbals," 1950s, Alps Co., six actions	250	375	500
"Acrobat Clown," 1960s, 9" tall, Y-M Co., minor toy	60	90	120
"Acro Chimp Porter," 1960s, Y-M Co., 8-1/2" tall, minor toy	50	75	100
"Acrobat Robot," 1970s, S-H Co., 4-1/2" tall, three actions	225	338	450

Accordion Bear.

Accordion Player Hobo,
Baby Monkey Playing
Cymbals.

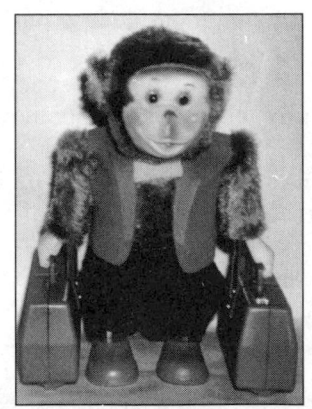

Acro Chimp Porter.

Acrobat
Robot.

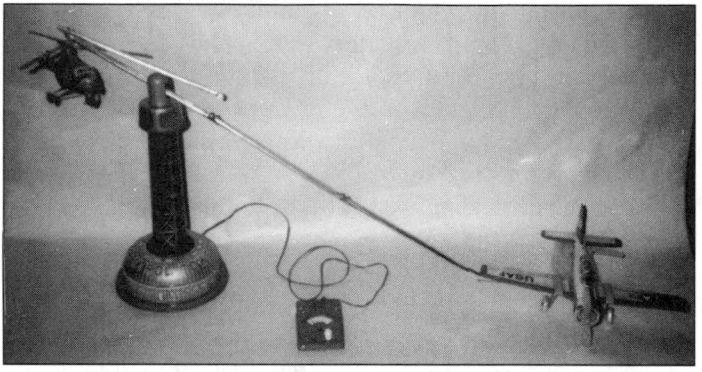

Air Control Tower.

	C6	C8	C10
"Air Cargo Prop-Jet Airplane, Seaboard World Airlines," 1960s, Marx Co., 12" long, 14-1/2" wingspan, five actions	200	300	400
"Air Control Tower," 1960s, Bandai Co., 11" high, 37" span (extended), four actions (includes detachable airplane and helicopter)	200	300	400
"Air Defense Pom-Pom Gun," 1950s, Linemar Co., 14" long, five actions	130	195	260
"Air Taxi Helicopter," 1960s, Haji Co., three actions	50	75	100

	C6	C8	C10
"Aircraft Carrier," 1950s, Marx Co., six actions, 20" long	300	450	600
"Aircraft Carrier Forrestal," 1950s, Linemar, 13-3/4" long, three actions (includes detachable plastic airplane)	200	300	400
"Aircraft Carrier," 1950s, Marx Co., 20" long, eight actions	200	300	400
"Airport Saucer," 1960s, MT Co., 8" diameter, four actions	90	135	180
"Airport Saucer," 1960s, S-T Co., four actions, 9" diameter	100	150	200
"All Stars Mr. Baseball Jr.," 1950s, K Co., three actions, rare (includes 8 plastic balls)	500	750	1000
"Alley, The Exciting New Roaring Stalking Alligator," 1960s, Marx Co., 17-1/2" long, five actions	150	225	300

Air Defense
Pom-Pom Gun.

Aircraft Carrier.

Aircraft Carrier Forrestal.

	C6	C8	C10
"American Airlines Electra," 1950s, Linemar Co., 18" long, 19-1/2" wingspan	200	300	400
"American Airlines Flagship Caroline" 1950s, Linemar Co., 18" long, 19-1/2" wingspan, three actions	190	285	380
"American Circus Television Truck" 1950s, Exelo Co., 9-1/4" long, six actions, rare (includes detachable metal antenna)	600	900	1200
"Amphibian Navy Patrol Plane" with flashing lights, 1950s, Alps Co., 13" long, 15" wingspan, five actions, rare	900	1350	1800
"Amtrak Locomotive," 1960s, ST Co., 16" long, minor toy	60	90	120
"Andy Gard Brink's Armored Car-Bank," 1950s, General Molds & Plastics Corp., 6-3/4" long, minor toy	40	60	80

Alley ... Alligator.

	C6	C8	C10
"American Airlines 4 Prop Airliner," 1960s, Waco Co., 12" long, 16-1/2" wingspan, four actions	120	180	240
"American Airlines DC-7" (with automatic turnover propellers), c.1950s, Linemar, seven actions, 19" wingspan	200	300	400
"American Airlines Airliner DC-7 Multiaction," 1960s, Yonezawa Co., 21" long, 23-1/2" wingspan, seven actions	195	285	380
"American Airlines Airliner DC-7," 1960s, Linemar Co., 17-1/2" long, 19" wingspan, seven actions	200	300	400
"Andy Gard Combat Knight No. 143," 1960s, General Molds & Plastics Corp., 10-1/4" high, three actions (includes lance, stanchion, 3 plastic rings, and helmet plume)	50	75	100
"Animated Santa on Rotating Globe," 1950s, HTC Co., 15" high, five actions	400	600	800
"Animated Squirrel," 1950s, S&E Co., 8-1/2" tall, eight actions, rare	100	150	200
"Answer Game Machine" robot, 1960s, Ichida Co., 14-1/2" tall, educational toy, eight actions	400	600	800
"Anti-Aircraft Jeep," 1950s, "K" Co., 9-1/2" long, five actions	100	150	200

American Airlines Electra.

American Circus Television Truck.

	C6	C8	C10
"Anti-Aircraft Jeep," 1950s, T-N Co., 11" long, six actions (includes detachable tin radar antenna)	250	375	500
"Anti-Aircraft Unit No. 1," 1950s, Linemar Co., 12-1/2" long, three electrical actions and three manual actions	150	225	300
"Antique Gooney Car," 1960s, Alps Co., 9" long, four actions	70	105	140

	C6	C8	C10
"Apollo II-American Eagle Lunar Module," 1960s, DSK Co., 10" high, seven actions, (includes detachable plastic antenna)	200	300	400
"Apollo Lunar Module," 1970s, DSK Co., 6" high, four actions, mostly plastic	170	205	240
"Apollo Spacecraft," 1960s, M-T Co., 10" long, four actions (includes detachable astronaut)	200	300	400
"Apollo Space Ship USA NASA," 1960s, M-T Co., 9" long, four actions	70	105	140

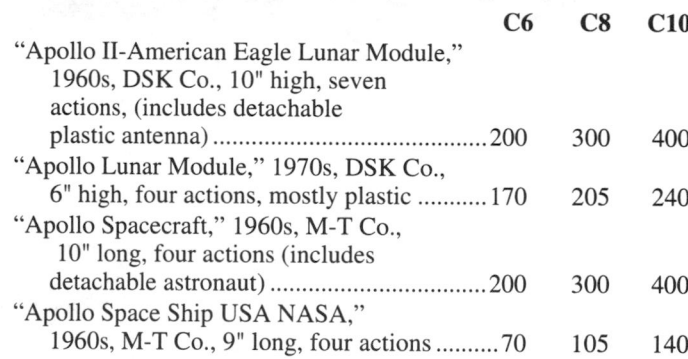

Amphibian Navy Patrol Plane.

Animated Squirrel, Cock-A-Doodle-Doo Rooster, Josie-the-Cow, Sparky-the-Seal.

Anti-Aircraft Jeep.

Antique Gooney Car.

Armored Attack Set.

	C6	C8	C10
"Army Radio Jeep J1490," 1950s, Linemar Co, 7-1/4" long, four actions	100	150	200
"Army Helicopter," Huey by Bell, 1960s, T-N Co., six actions, 10-1/2" long	90	135	180
"Arthur A-Go-Go," 1960s, Alps Co., 10" high, six actions (includes detachable cymbals and drum set)	200	300	400
"Astro Captain," 1960s, Daiya Co., 6-1/2" tall, three actions, rare	300	450	600
"Astro Dog," 1960s, "Y" Co., 11" high, two cycles, five actions (looks like Snoopy)	100	150	200
"Astro Dog," 1960s, Y-M Co., 11" tall, three actions	90	135	180

Astro Dog.

	C6	C8	C10
"Apollo Super Space Capsule," 1960s, S-H Co., 9" high, five actions	100	150	200
"Apollo-X Moon challenger," rocket, 1960s, T-N Co., 16" long, six actions	120	180	240
"Armored Attack Set," 1960s, Marx Co., jeep 6-1/4" long and tank 5-1/4" long, (plus 15 2" plastic figures)	150	225	300

Arthur A-Go-Go.

	C6	C8	C10
"Astrobase" (motorized), 1960s, Ideal Co., 20" high, six actions	140	210	280
"Atom Motorcycle," 1950s, M-T Co., five actions, 11-3/4" long	450	675	900
"Atom Rocket 7," vehicle with fins, 1950s, M-T Co., 9-1/2" long, four actions	120	180	240
"Atomic Boat," 1950s, Famus Co., minor toy, 15" long	150	225	300
"Atomic Fighter" robot, 1950s, S-H Co., 11" tall, five actions	100	150	200
"Atomic Rocket X-1800," 1960s, M-T Co., three actions, 9" long	150	225	300
"Attacking Martian Robot," 1950s, S-H Co., 11-1/2" tall, seven actions, two cycles	120	180	240
"Auto-Top Ferrari Convertible," 1960s, Bandai Co., three actions, 11" long	450	675	900

Atom Motorcycle.

Atomic Boat.

Ball Blowing Clown, Sammy Wong-the Tea Totaler, Nutty Nibs.

	C6	C8	C10
"Automated Santa," c. 1960s, Santa Creations Co., three actions, 10-1/4" tall....	100	150	200
"Automatic Toll Gate," 1955, Sears, 16" x 17" base, six actions (includes 8" tin Valiant)	150	225	300

Automated Santa.

Ball Playing Dog.

Balloon Vendor, Miss Friday, Sam the Shaving Man, Gino the Neapolitan Balloon Blower.

	C6	C8	C10
"B-58 Hustler Jet," 1950s, Marx Co., four actions, 21" long, 12" wingspan	450	675	900
"Baby Carriage," 1950s, T-N Co., 11-3/4" long, 7" high, minor toy (includes plastic baby bottle to activate switch)	60	90	120
"Ball Blowing Clown," 1950s, T-N Co., 11" tall, three actions (with ball)	180	270	360
"Ball Playing Bear," 1940s, no marking, 10-1/2" tall, six actions (includes five celluloid balls and one umbrella), rare	200	300	400
"Ball Playing Dog," 1950s, Linemar Co., 9" high, three actions	120	180	240
"Balloon Blowing Monkey," 1950s, Alps Co., 11-1/8" tall, five actions with balloon	100	150	200
"Balloon Blowing Teddy Bear," 1950s, Alps Co., 11-1/8" tall, six actions with balloon	100	150	200
"Balloon Vendor," 1960s, "Y" Co., 12" tall, four actions (includes four plastic balloons and tin tray)	130	195	260
"Baragon (Godzilla)," 1960s, Bullmark Co., three actions, 10" tall	290	435	580
"Barber Bear," 1950s, T-N Co. (Linemar), 9-1/2" tall, five actions	300	450	600
"Barking Boxer Dog," 1950s, Marx, 7" long, minor toy	50	75	100
"Barking Dog," 1950s, STS Co., 7" long, 7" high, four actions, two cycles	50	75	100
"Barking Spaniel Dog," 1950s, Marx, 7" long, minor toy	50	75	100
"Barney Bear Drummer," 1950s, Alps Co., 11" tall, five actions, resembles "Steiff" bear	130	195	260
"Barnyard Rooster," 1950s, Marx, 10" high, five actions	100	150	200

Baragon (Godzilla).

Barber Bear.

Barking Spaniel Dog, Sleeping Baby Bear, Barking Boxer Dog, Pap Bear Smoking.

Bartender. Photo by Bill Kaufman. Courtesy Good Old Days.

Bear Target Game.

	C6	C8	C10
"Bartender," 1960s, T-N Co., 11-1/2" tall, six actions	40	60	80
"Batmobile," 1972 National Periodical Publications, ASC Co., 12" long, three actions	180	270	360
"Battery Locomotive No. 123," 1950s, T-N Co., 10" long, three actions	30	45	60
"Bear Chef" (Cutey Cook), 1960s, "Y" Co., 9-1/2" tall, five actions (includes chef hat and tin litho egg)	150	225	300

	C6	C8	C10
"Bear Target Game," 1950s, M-T Co., 8-3/4" high and 4" x 5" base (includes gun, rubber-tipped darts, detachable drum), four actions	200	300	400
"Bear the Cashier," 1950s, M-T Co., 7-1/2" high, five actions	190	285	380
"Bear the Magician," 1950s, MTS Co., nine actions, 12-1/2" tall, rare	1000	1500	2000
"Beauty Parlor Bear," 1950s, S&E Co., 9-1/2" high, seven actions, rare	600	900	1200
"Begging Puppy," 1960s, "Y" Co., 9" long, six actions	40	60	80

Beauty Parlor Bear.

Big John The Indian Chief.

	C6	C8	C10
"Bengali The Exciting New Growling, Prowling Tiger," 1961, Marx Co., Linemar Div., 18-1/2" long from nose to end of tail, 2 cycles, three actions	100	150	200
"Betty Bruin Cashier," 1950s, Linemar, 9" tall, six actions: See Super Susie			
"Big Dipper," 1960s, Technofix Co., minor toy, 21" long, 11" high (includes three tin cars)	100	150	200
"Big Hunter Automatic Gun," 1950s, Tada Co., 21" long extended, three actions	50	75	100
"Big John," 1960s, Alps Co., 12" high, three actions	60	90	120
"Big John The Indian Chief," c. 1960s, T-N Co., five actions, 12-1/2" tall	90	135	180
"Big Loo Your Friend From The Moon," 1960s, Marx Co., 38" tall, twelve actions (includes ball, darts, compass, etc.)	1000	1500	2000

	C6	C8	C10
"Big Max Robot," 1958, Remco Co., 8" long, 7" tall, four actions	100	150	200
"Big Ring Circus Truck," 1950s, M-T Co., 13" long, three actions	140	210	280
"Big Shot Cadillac," 1950s, T-N Co., 10" long, four actions, rare	200	300	400
"Big Wheel Coca Cola Truck," 1970s, Taiyo Co., three actions	80	120	160

Big Wheel Coca-Cola Truck.

	C6	C8	C10
"Big Wheel Family Camper," 1970s, 10" long, three actions	60	90	120
"Big Wheel Ice Cream Truck," 1970s, 10" long, three actions	60	90	120
"Biller Train No. 573," 1950s, T-N Co., 13" long (includes rubber cable track and two hopper cars), a minor toy, rare	70	105	140
"Billy Blastoff Space Scout," Eldon Co., 1960s, four actions, 16" long	90	135	180
"Billy the Kid Sheriff," 1950s, "Y" Co., 10-1/2" tall, two cycles, four actions	180	270	360
"Bimbo the Clown," 1950s, Alps Co., 9-1/4" tall, three actions (includes detachable hat)	300	450	600
"Bingo Clown," 1950s, T-N Co., 13" tall, three actions	200	300	400
"Blacksmith Bear," 1950s, A-1 Co., 9-1/2" tall, six actions	180	270	360
"Black Smithy Bear," 1950s, T-N Co., 9" high, four actions, rare	125	185	250

Big Loo. Courtesy Christie's East.

Black Smithy Bear.

Blushing Frankenstein, Hootin' Haunted House, Frankenstein Monster.

Bongo Monkey, Chef Cook, Cola Drinking Bear.

	C6	C8	C10
"Blink-A-Gear-Robot," 1960s, S-H Co., 14-1/2" tall, five actions	400	600	800
"Blinky-the-Clown," 1950s, no marking, 10-1/2" tall, five actions (includes multicolor paper hat)	300	450	600
"Blow-Up-Ball Locomotive," 1950s, M-T Co., 9-1/2" long, minor toy (includes celluloid ball)	80	120	160
"Blushing Willie," 1960s, "Y" Co., 10" tall, four actions	60	90	120
"Bobby Drinking Bear," 1950s, "Y" Co., 10" tall, six actions	200	300	400
"Bobby the Drumming Bear," 1950s, Alps Co., 10" tall, four actions	210	315	420
"Boeing 727 Jet Liner," 1960s, "Y" Co., 17-1/2" long, 16-1/4" wingspan, three actions	140	210	280
"Boeing 727 Jet Plane," 1960s, M-T Co., 12-1/2" long, 10-3/8" wingspan, three actions	150	225	300
"Bomber Pilot," 1960s, K-O Co., 10-1/2" long, 9" wingspan, six actions	190	285	380
"Bongo, Drumming Monkey," 1960s, Alps Co., 9-1/2" high, three actions, includes plastic hat	80	120	160

	C6	C8	C10
"Bongo Player," 1960s, Alps Co., 10" tall, four actions	80	120	160
"Bowling Bank," 1960s, M.B. Daniel & Co., 10" long, three actions	90	135	180
"Brave Eagle," 1950s, T-N Co., five actions, 11" tall	90	135	180
"Breakfast Chef," 1960s, K Co., 8-1/4" tall, minor toy (includes plastic egg and coffee maker)	70	105	140
"Brewster the Rooster," 1950s, Marx Co., 9-1/2" high, five actions	120	180	240
"Bristol Bulldog Airplane," T-360, S&E Co., four actions (lights, prop spins, stop & go, noise), 12" long, 14-1/2" wingspan	160	240	320

Bongo Player.

Bowling Bank.

Brewster the Rooster.

Broadway Trolley, Battery Locomotive No. 123, A-B-C Fairy Train, Smoking Pop Locomotive The General.

Bubble Blowing Kangaroo.

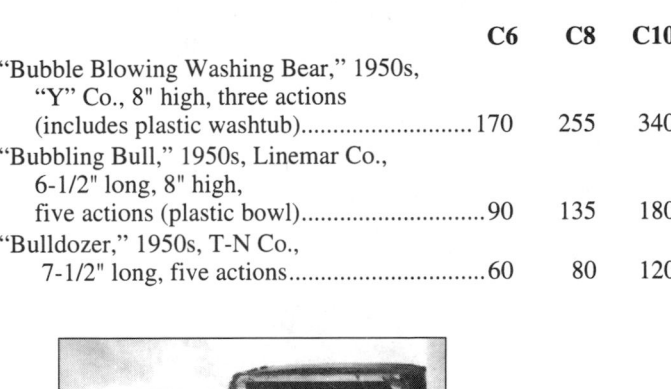

Bubble Blowing Musician.

	C6	C8	C10
"Broadway Trolley," 1950s, M-T Co., 10-1/2" long, four actions, two cycles: See "Tinkling Trolley"			
"Bruno the Accordion Bear," 1950s, "Y" Co., 10-1/2" tall, five actions	140	210	280
"Bubble Blowing Bear," 1950s, M-T Co., 9-1/2" high, 4" x 5" base, four actions	140	210	280
"Bubble Blowing Boil Over Car," 1950s, M-T Co., three actions, 10" long	90	135	180
"Bubble Blowing Boy," 1950s, "Y" Co., 7" high, four actions	100	200	300
"Bubble Blowing Bunny," 1950s, "Y" Co., 7" high, four actions	100	150	200
"Bubble Blowing Dog," 1950s, "Y" Co., 8" high, three actions	100	150	200
"Bubble Blowing Kangaroo," 1950s, M-T Co., 9" high (base to tip of ears), three actions, rare	200	300	400
"Bubble Blowing Lion," 1950s, M-T Co., 7-1/2" high, 3-1/2" x 7" base, four actions	100	150	200
"Bubble Blowing Musician," 1950s, "Y" Co., 11" tall, three actions	200	300	400
"Bubble Blowing Monkey," 1950s, Alps Co., 10" tall, four actions, includes plastic bowl for bubble solution	100	150	200
"Bubble Blowing Popeye," 1950s, Linemar Co., 11-3/4" tall, five actions	1000	1500	2000

	C6	C8	C10
"Bubble Blowing Washing Bear," 1950s, "Y" Co., 8" high, three actions (includes plastic washtub)	170	255	340
"Bubbling Bull," 1950s, Linemar Co., 6-1/2" long, 8" high, five actions (plastic bowl)	90	135	180
"Bulldozer," 1950s, T-N Co., 7-1/2" long, five actions	60	80	120

Bubble Blowing Popeye.

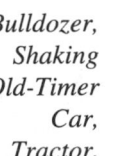

Bulldozer, Shaking Old-Timer Car, Tractor.

Bubble Lion, Wild West Rodeo, CRAGSTAN Bullfighter.

	C6	C8	C10
"Bulldozer," 1950s, M-T Co., 11" long, six actions	70	105	140
"Bunny The Cashier," 1950s, M-T Co., five actions, 7-1/2" high	150	225	300
"Bunny The Magician," 1950s, Alps Co., 14-1/2" tall, five actions (includes card-ribbon apparatus for card trick)	200	300	400

Busy Secretary.

Bunny The Magician.

	C6	C8	C10
"Butt Stompin' Ashtray," 1977, Poynter Prod., 7-1/4" high, four actions (includes tin manhole cover, ashtray insert and 4-1/2" high plastic shoe)	40	60	80
"Buttons, Puppy With A Brain," also called "Buttons The Push Button Pup," 1960s, Marx, 12" high, eight actions	200	300	400
"B-Z Porter" Baggage truck, 1950s, M-T Co., 7-1/2" long, 6-1/2" high, minor toy, includes three pieces of luggage (tin)	140	210	280
"B-Z Rabbit," c. 1950s, M-T Co., four actions, 7" long	60	90	120
"B-Z Vendor," ice cream cart, 1950s, M-T Co., three actions, 7-1/2" along, rare	450	675	900

	C6	C8	C10
"Burger Chef," 1950s, "Y" Co., 9" tall, eight actions (includes chef's hat and tin-litho hamburger)	100	150	200
"Busy Bizzy Friendly Bug," 1950s, M-T Co., 6-1/4" long, three actions	60	90	120
"Busy Housekeeper, The," 1950s, Alps Co., 8-1/2" tall, four actions	160	240	320
"Busy Housekeeper, The" (bunny), 1950s, Alps Co., 10" tall, four actions	150	225	300
"Busy Cart Robot," c. 1960s, S-H Co., four actions, 11" high (includes plastic wheelbarrow)	200	300	400
"Busy Secretary," 1950s, Linemar Co., 7-1/2" high, 7-1/4" long, seven actions	150	225	300
"Busy Shoe Shining Bear," 1950s, Alps Co., 10" high, five actions	140	210	280

B-Z Porter, CRAGSTAN Tugboat, Goodtime Charlie, Picnic Bunny.

	C6	C8	C10

"Cabin Cruiser," c. 1950s, SGK Co.,
three actions, 21-1/2" long........................ 150 225 300
"Cabin Cruiser With Outboard Motor,"
1950s, Linemar Co., 12" long, minor toy ... 100 150 200

Cabin Cruiser with Outboard Motor.

"Cable Train," 1940s, T-N Co.,
12" long, four-piece set, minor toy 80 120 160
"Cadillac" car, 1949, Ashai Toy Co.,
10" long, three actions 140 210 280
"Calypso Joe," 1950s, Linemar,
11" tall, four actions, rare 300 450 600
"Camera Shooting Bear," 1950s,
Linemar Co., 11" tall, five actions
(includes plastic worms),
also called Cine-Bear................................ 450 675 900
"Candy Vending Machine Bank,"
1950s, Wonderful Toy Co., 9" high,
five actions, rare 600 900 1200
"Capitol Airlines Viscount 321," 1950s,
Linemar, 11" long, 14" wingspan,
four actions 160 240 320
"Cappy the Baggage Porter Dog," 1960s,
Alps Co., 12" high, 11" long, four actions 100 150 200
"Captain Blushwell," 1960s, "Y" Co.,
11" tall, six actions 80 120 160
"Captain Hook," 1950s, Marusan Co.,
10-3/4" high, three actions, (includes
tin sword and felt hat), rare........................ 800 1200 1600

Captain Blushwell.

	C6	C8	C10

"Caterpillar," 1950s, Alps Co.,
16" long, three actions 90 135 180
"Caterpillar Tank M-1," 1950s, M-T Co.,
five actions, 8-1/2" long, 11" long
with barrel extended 150 225 300

Caterpillar Tank M-1.

"Central Choo Choo," 1960s, M-T Co.,
15" long, three actions 40 60 80
"Champion Weight Lifter," 1960s,
Y-M Co., 10" tall, five actions................... 100 150 200

Champion Weight Lifter.

*Charlie Weaver. Photo by
Bill Kaufman. Courtesy
Good Old Days.*

"Chaparral 2F," car, 1960s, Alps Co.,
11" long, five actions 80 120 160
"Charlie the Drumming Clown," 1950s,
Alps Co., six actions (includes
detachable drum and cymbals), 9-1/2" tall 150 225 300
"Charlie Weaver," 1962, T-N Co.,
12" tall, six actions.. 40 60 80

"Change Man Robot," astronaut, 1960s,
S-H Co., four actions, 13-1/4" tall, rare....4000 / 6000 / 8000

"Charm the Cobra," 1960s, Alps Co.,
6" high, three actions .... 150 / 225 / 300

"Chee Chee Chihuahua," 1960s, Mego Co.,
8" high, five actions .... 30 / 45 / 60

"Chef Cook," 1960s, "Y" Co., 11-1/2" tall
with hat on, five actions (includes tin
litho egg and hat) .... 150 / 225 / 300

"Chemical Fire Engine," 1950s, HTC Co.,
10" long, four actions .... 100 / 150 / 200

"Chief Robotman," 1950s, K.O. Co.,
12" tall, four actions .... 450 / 675 / 900

"Chimp and Pup Rail Car,"
1950s, T-N Co., 8" high, four actions .... 90 / 135 / 180

"Chimp With Xylophone," 1970s,
"Y" Co., 12" long, 8" high, minor toy
(includes 4 records and hammer) .... 100 / 150 / 200

"Chimpee the One-Man Drummer,"
1950s, Alps Co., 9" high, six actions,
includes detachable drum and cymbals .... 70 / 105 / 140

*Chimpy, Drumming Monkey, Happy Santa One-Man
Band, Fred Flintstone's Bedrock Band, Dalmatian
One-Man Band.*

"Chippy the Chipmunk," 1950s, Alps Co.,
12" long (nosetip to tail tip), four actions .... 90 / 135 / 180

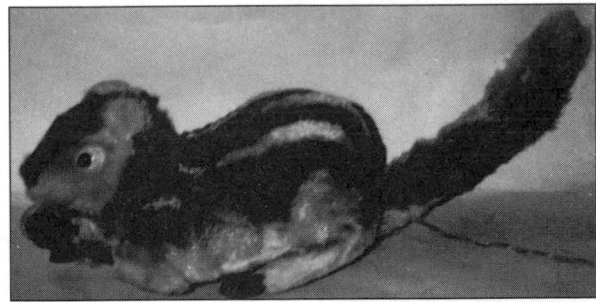

Chippy the Chipmunk.

"Christmas Time," 1950s, Marusan Co., 10"
high, 7" base diameter, three actions, rare .. 400 / 600 / 800

"Cindy the Meowing Cat," 1950s,
Tomiyama Co., 12" high (nosetip to tail
tip), two cycles, four actions .... 50 / 75 / 100

"Cine Bear": See "Camera Shooting Bear"

"Circus Elephant With Blowing Ball and
Parasol," 1950s, T-N Co., 9-3/4" high,
three actions (includes celluloid ball
and tin litho umbrella), rare .... 150 / 225 / 300

"Circus Fire Engine," 1960s, M-T Co.,
11" long, four actions.................................. 130 / 195 / 260

"Circus Jet," 1950s, T-N Co., three actions,
9" high assembled, jet 6-1/4" long .... 90 / 135 / 180

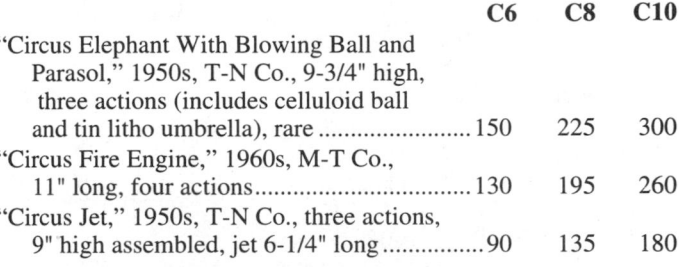

*Circus
Jet.*

*Circus
Lion.*

"Circus Lion," 1950s, Rock Valley Toy Co.
(Via), 11" high, four actions, includes
whip and flannel carpet with levers
(two cycles)... 300 / 450 / 600

"Clancy The Great," 1960s, Ideal Toy Co.,
three actions, 19-1/2" tall without hat
(includes plastic hat and test coin).............. 100 / 150 / 200

*Clancy
the Great,
Ideal.*

	C6	C8	C10
"Climbing Donald Duck On His Friction Fire Engine," 1950s, Linemar Co., four actions, 12" long	450	675	900
"Climbing Fireman," 1950s, T.P.S. Co., 24" high assembled, five actions (includes three tin ladder sections)	200	300	400
"Climbing Linesman," 1950s, T.P.S. Co., 24" high when assembled, three actions, (includes three tin pole sections), rare	250	375	500
"Clown Circus Car," 1960s, M-T Co., 8-1/2" long, 9" high, five actions	140	210	280
"Clown and Lion," 1960s, M-T Co., four actions, 11-3/4" high from base to top of tree	240	360	480
"Clown on Unicycle," 1960s, M-T Co., 10-1/2" high, three actions	210	315	420
"Clown with Lion," 1950s, T-N Co., 12" high, four actions (includes spiral apparatus)	200	300	400

Clown & Lion.

	C6	C8	C10
"Clowns Bank, The," 1940s, unmarked, 10" high, minor toy (all plastic)	80	120	160
"Clown The Magician No. 40244," 1950s, Alps Co., 12" tall, six actions includes card-ribbon apparatus for card trick	200	300	400
"Coca-Cola Dispenser Bank," 1950s, Linemar Co., minor toy, 9-1/2" tall (includes four plastic Coke glasses and rubber stopper)	450	675	900

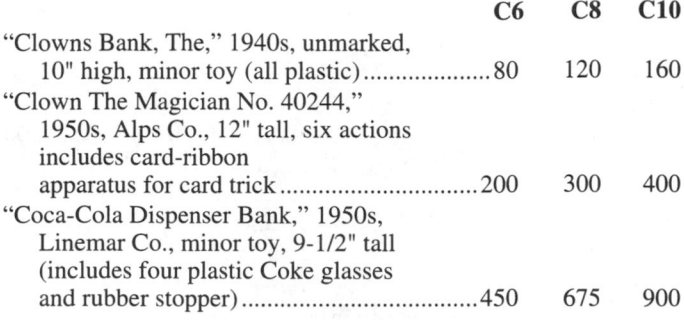

Coca-Cola Dispenser Bank.

	C6	C8	C10
"Cock-A-Doodle-Doo Rooster," 1950s, Mikuni Co., 8" high, four actions	80	120	160
"Colonel Hap Hazard" Robot, 1968, Marx Co., 11-1/4" tall, four actions	350	525	700
"Combi-O-Mixer," 1950s, Excelo Co., mixer-blender, 9" long, 9" high, minor toy	30	45	60
"Comic Hungry Bug," VW auto, 1970s, Tora (S-T) Co., 7-3/4" long, five actions	40	60	80
"Comic Musical Car," 1960s, T-N Co., four actions, 6" long, 8-1/2" tall	70	105	140
"Comic Road Grader," 1950s, Bandai Co., 9" long, four actions	70	105	140
"Comic Road Roller," 1960s, Bandai Co., four actions, 9" long	70	105	140
"Coney Island Penny Machine," 1950s, Remco Co., 13" high, minor toy (includes plastic prizes)	120	180	240

Clown & Monkey Car.

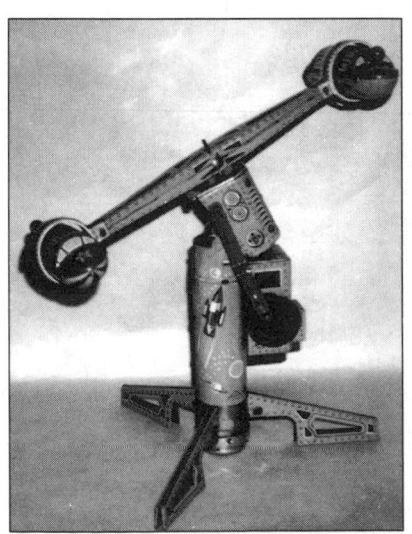

Coney Island Rocket Ride.

	C6	C8	C10
"Coney Island Rocket Ride," 1950s, Alps Co., 13-1/2" high, four actions	400	600	800
"Continental Blue Locomotive," 1960s, M-T Co., 12-1/2" long, four actions	30	45	60
"Corvair Bertone," 1970s, Bandai Co., four actions, 12" long	50	75	100
"Cowboy Riding Horse," 1950s, T-N Co., 7" high, three actions	70	105	140
"Cragstan Astronaut," 1950s, Daiya Co., 14" tall, four actions	400	600	800

CRAGSTAN Crapshooter, Tumbles the Bear, Overland Stage Coach.

CRAGSTAN Astronaut.

	C6	C8	C10
"Cragstan Crapshooting Monkey," 1950s, Alps Co., 9" tall, three actions, includes pair of small dice	70	105	140
"Cragstan Dishwasher Automatic," 1960s, Alps Co., 9" high, (includes 24-piece dish set, two dish baskets and metal tray), minor toy	50	75	100

	C6	C8	C10
"Cragstan Beep Beep Greyhound Bus," 1950s, Cragstan Co., 20" long, three actions	110	165	220
"Cragstan Biplane," 7F7, U.S. Navy, 1950s, T-N Co., 9-1/2" long, 11-1/2" wingspan, four actions	200	300	400
"Cragstan Biplane 7F18," 1950s, T-N Co., 12" long, 14-3/8" wingspan, five actions	220	330	440
"Cragstan Crapshooter," 1950s, "Y" Co., 9-1/2" tall, four actions, includes pair of small dice	100	150	200

CRAGSTAN Automatic Dishwasher, Bengali Tiger, Holiday Sink/Stove Combination.

CRAGSTAN Biplane 7F18.

	C6	C8	C10
"Cragstan Firebird III," 1950s, Alps Co., three actions, 11-1/2" long	400	600	800
"Cragstan Flying Plane With Pylon Tower," 1950s, minor toy, plane 8" long, 9-1/2" wingspan, tower 26" high	120	180	240
"Cragstan Great Astronaut, 1960s, Alps Co., 14" tall, five actions	500	750	1000
"Cragstan's Mr. Robot," 1960s, "Y" Co., 10-1/2" tall, four actions	350	525	700
"Cragstan Mother Goose," 1960s, "Y" Co., 8-1/4" high, six actions	90	135	180
"Cragstan One-Arm Bandit," 1960s, "Y" Co., 6-1/4" high, three actions, includes 3" x 3-1/4" sign	100	150	200
"Cragstan Peanut Vendor," 1950s, T-N Co., 8" tall, five actions (includes felt hat)	180	270	360
"Cragstan Playboy," 1960s, Cragstan Co., 13" high, five actions	100	150	200

CRAGSTAN
Roulette
A Gambling
Man.

	C6	C8	C10
"Cragstan Roulette, A Gambling Man," 1960s, "Y" Co., 9" tall, five actions (includes steel ball, chips, tin table, game sheet)	140	210	280
"Cragstan Satellite," 1950s, Cragstan Co., 8" diameter, 5-1/2" high	90	135	180

CRAGSTAN Schoolbus, CRAGSTAN Western Locomotive, New Bell Ringer Choo-Choo.

"Cragstan Smoking Jet Plane - U.S.A.F." 1950s, T-N Co., 11-1/2" long, 7-1/2" wingspan, four actions	120	180	240
"Cragstan Talking Robot," 1960s, "Y" Co., 10-1/2" tall, three actions	320	480	720

CRAGSTAN Tootin'-Chuggin' Locomotive, Greyhound Bus Scenicruiser.

	C6	C8	C10
"Cragstan Telly Bear," 1950s, S&E Co., 8" high, six actions	240	360	480
"Cragstan Tootin'-Chugging Locomotive," 1950s, Cragstan Co., 24" long, three actions (longest single-piece battery toy made)	70	105	140
"Cragstan Tugboat," 1950s, San Co., 12-3/4" long, three actions	140	210	280
"Cragstan Vertol 1107 Helicopter," 1950s, T-N Co., 13-1/2" long, four actions, includes rotors	120	180	240
"Cragstan Western Locomotive," 1950s, Cragstan Co., 12" long, four actions	60	90	120
"Cragstan's Two Gun Sheriff," 1950s, "Y" Co., 9-1/2" tall, five actions (includes tin hat)	130	195	260
"Crane Tractor," 1950s, SKK Co., 7-1/2" long, 11-1/2" high extended	70	105	140
"Crawling Baby," 1940s, Linemar Co., 11" long, 8-1/2" high, minor toy	50	75	100

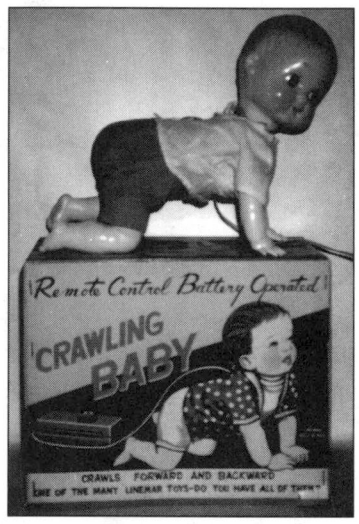

Crawling
Baby.

	C6	C8	C10
"Crazy Car," 1950s, Marusan Co., five actions, 9" long	60	90	120
"Cycling Daddy," 1960s, Bandai Co., 10" high, four actions	100	150	200
"Cyclist Clown," 1950s, K Co., seven actions, 7" high	200	300	400

Crazy Car.

"Cyclist Clown," 1950s, M-T Co.,
6-1/2" high, six actions .... 200 — 300 — 400

"Cyclist Clown," 1950s, Alps Co.,
9" high, five actions .... 200 — 300 — 400

"Cymbal Playing Turnover Monkey,"
1960s, T-N Co., 8" tall, three actions .... 50 — 75 — 100

"Daisy The Jolly Drumming Duck,"
1950s, Alps Co., 9" high, seven
actions, rare (includes detachable
drum and cymbals) .... 140 — 210 — 280

"Dalmatian One-Man Band No. 90262,"
1950s, Alps Co., 9" high, six actions,
includes cymbals and stand .... 120 — 180 — 240

"Dancing Merry Chimp," 1960s, Kuramochi
Co. (C-K), 11" tall, five actions .... 100 — 150 — 200

"Dancing Sweethearts," 1950s, T-N Co.,
7" tall, minor toy .... 90 — 135 — 180

"Dandy The Happy Drumming Pup,"
1950s, Alps Co., 8-1/2" high, six actions
(includes detachable drum and cymbals) ... 100 — 150 — 200

"Dapper Jigger Dancer," 1950s, Haji Co.,
12" tall, minor toy .... 140 — 210 — 280

"Dennis The Menace" (Playing London
Bridge), 1950s, Rosko, 9" high,
three actions, includes xylophone .... 100 — 150 — 200

"Dentist Bear," 1950s, S&E Co., 9-1/2" tall,
6-3/4"x4-1/4" base, seven actions,
includes detachable head .... 300 — 450 — 600

"Desert Patrol Jeep," 1960s, M-T Co.,
11" long, four actions,
includes turret gunner .... 90 — 135 — 180

"Destroyer 206" boat, 1950s, "Y" Co.,
14" long, six actions, includes
detachable antenna and five depth charges 110 — 165 — 220

"Diesel Locomotive," 1950s,
Cragstan Co., minor toy, 16-1/2" long .... 30 — 45 — 60

"Dino Robot," 1960s, S-H Co., 11" tall,
five actions .... 500 — 750 — 1000

"Disney Acrobats" (Mickey, Donald
& Pluto), 1950s, Linemar Co.,
9" high, minor toys .... 400 — 600 — 800

"Disney Fire Engine," 1950s, Linemar Co.,
11" long, four actions .... 440 — 660 — 880

"Disneyland Fire Engine," 1950s,
Linemar Co., 18" long, five actions .... 350 — 525 — 700

"Docking Rocket," 1960s, Daiya Co.,
16" long, 24" extended, six actions
(includes plastic radar antenna) .... 100 — 150 — 200

"Dog Family," 1960s, Alps Co.,
11" long, four actions .... 30 — 45 — 60

"Dog Sled," T-N Co., 14" long,
four actions, rare, 1950s .... 300 — 450 — 600

"Dolly Dressmaker," 1950s, T-N Co., 7"
high, ten actions, includes cloth sample
("Dolly Seamstress" on box), rare .... 150 — 225 — 300

"Donald Duck," 1960s,
Linemar Co., 8" tall, four actions .... 200 — 300 — 400

"Donald Duck Locomotive," 1970s,
M-T Co., three actions, 9" long .... 150 — 225 — 300

"Donald Duck Trolley," 1960s,
M-T Co., 11" high, three actions .... 160 — 240 — 320

"Douglas C-124 Globe Master," c. 1950s,
Yonezawa Co., eight actions,
20-1/2" wingspan, 18" long .... 300 — 450 — 600

"Douglas DC-9TWA Jet Plane," 1960s,
T-N Co., four actions,
14" long, 17" wingspan .... 100 — 150 — 200

"Doxie The Dog," 1950s, Linemar Co.,
9" long, five actions .... 30 — 45 — 60

"Dozo The Steaming Clown,"
1960s, T-N Co., Rosko toys,
10" tall, five actions .... 200 — 300 — 400

"Dream Boat Hot Rod," c. 1950s,
T-N Co., four actions, 7" long .... 140 — 210 — 280

"Drill," 1950s, Linemar Co., 6" long,
includes attachments, minor toy .... 20 — 30 — 40

"Drinker's Savings Bank," 1960s,
Illfelder Co., 9" high, minor toy .... 90 — 135 — 180

"Drinking Bear," c. 1970s, 12" high,
Alps Co., six actions .... 60 — 90 — 120

"Drinking Captain," 1960s, S&E Co.,
12" tall, six actions .... 100 — 150 — 200

*Drinking Captain, Hi Jinks of the Circus,
CRAGSTAN Playboy.*

"Drinking Dog," 1950s, "Y" Co.,
four actions .... 90 — 135 — 180

"Drinking Licking Cat," 1950s, T-N Co.,
10" high, 4" x 4" base, six actions .... 120 — 180 — 240

Drinking Dog.

	C6	C8	C10
"Drum Bear," c. 1950s, Alps Co., five actions (walks, lights, beats drum, noise), 7-3/4" tall	150	225	300
"Drum Monkey," 1970s, Yada Co., 8" high, three actions	40	60	80

Drum Monkey.

	C6	C8	C10
"Drummer Bear," 1950s, Alps Co., 10" tall, six actions	140	210	280
"Drumming Mickey Mouse," 1950s, Linemar, 10" tall, four actions, rare	700	1050	1400
"Drumming Polar Bear," 1960s, Alps Co., 12" tall, three actions	100	150	200
"Ducky Duckling," 1960s, Alps Co., 8" high, four actions	50	75	100
"Dump Truck No. 7343," 1960s, T-N Co., 10-1/4" long, seven actions	60	90	120
"Dynamic Fighter Robot," 1960s, Junior Toy Co., 10" tall, five actions	70	105	140

Dynamic Fighter Robot.

	C6	C8	C10
"Earthman-Astronaut," 1950s, T-N Co., five actions, 9-1/2" tall, rare	900	1300	1800
"El Toro-Cragstan Bullfighter," 1950s, T-N Co., 9-1/2" long, four actions, includes detachable tin matador	100	150	200
"Electric Powered TV and Radio Station," 1950s, Marx, 30" long, three actions	80	120	160
"Electric Remote Control Robot," 1950s, M-T Co., 7-1/2" tall, four actions, rare	500	750	1000
"Electric Robot," 1950s, Marx, 14-1/2" tall, five actions	300	450	600
"Electric School Bus," 1950s, M-T Co., 9-1/2" long, minor toy	70	105	140
"Electric Vibraphone," 1950s, T-N Co., 7-1/2" long, 5-1/2" high, three actions	70	105	140

Electric Vibraphone.

	C6	C8	C10
"Electro Special Racer," 1950s, Yonezawa Co., 10" long, three actions	500	750	1000
"Electro Train Transcontinental," 1950s, "M" Co., 20-1/2" long, three pieces, three actions	90	135	180

Electro Train Transcontinental.

	C6	C8	C10
"Electronic Countdown," 1959, Ideal Toy Co., 24" long, six actions	60	90	120
"Electronic Fighter Jet 4800," 1950s, 19" long, eleven actions	120	180	240
"Electronic Fire House," 1940s, Banner Co., 7" square, minor toy (includes plastic fire engine)	70	105	140
"Electronic Periscope (Nautilus) Firing Range," 1950s, Cragstan, 11" high on tripod, three actions	100	150	200
"Electronic Twin Train Set #372," 1950s, Woodhaven Metal Stamping Co., minor toy, 28" long, 11" wide (includes two 3-piece trains)	100	150	200
"Engine Robot," 1960s, S-H Co., 9-1/2" tall, four actions	100	150	200
"Excavator Robot," 1960s, S-H Co., 10" tall, four actions	200	300	400

Electronic Periscope (Nautilus) Firing Range.

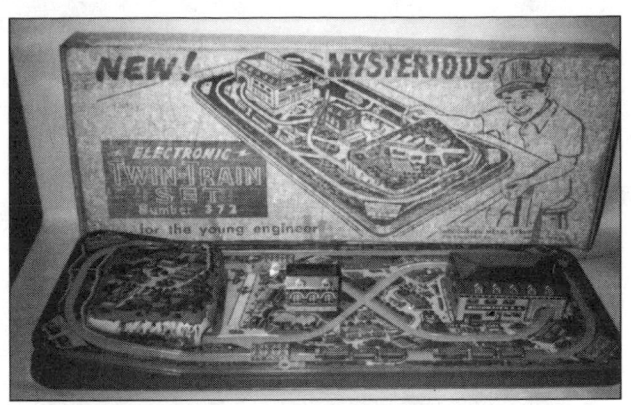

Electronic Twin Train Set, Woodhaven Co.

Excavator Robot.

Farm Truck.

	C6	C8	C10
"Expert Motor Cyclist," 1950s, MT Co., 12" long, five actions, rare	600	900	1200
"F-14-A Navy Jet Fighter," 1960s, T-N Co., six actions, 13" long, 13" wingspan	200	300	400
"F-101A Voodoo Fighter," 1960s, K-O Co., minor toy, 15" long, 14" wingspan	100	150	200
"FS-059 Fighter Plane," jet with prop, 1950s, T-N Co., five actions, 11" long, 13" wingspan	170	255	340

	C6	C8	C10
"Fairyland Loco," locomotive, 1950s, Daiya Co., 9" long, four actions	60	90	120
"Farm Truck," 1960s, Alps Co., 11" long, three actions	120	180	240
"Farm Truck," 1950s, T-N Co., five actions, 9" long	120	180	240
"F.D. Fire Engine," 1960s, Y-M Co., 10" long, 12" high when ladder is extended, four actions	110	165	220
"Feeding Bird Watcher," 1950s, Linemar, 9" high, five action, includes detachable tin branch and bird, rare	300	450	600

Farm Truck.

F.D. Fire Engine, Fire Engine, Fire Chief Mystery Action Car, Police Motorcycle Cop.

	C6	C8	C10
"Ferris Wheel Truck," c. 1950s, Linemar Co. (?), four actions, 11" long	400	600	800
"Fido The Xylophone Player," c. 1950s, Alps Co., six actions (incl. body sways, head turns, arms activate lights, sound), 8-3/4" high, includes detachable xylophone	125	188	250

Fighter.

	C6	C8	C10
"Fighter," (airplane), 1960s, K-O Co., 10-1/2" long, 9" wingspan, six actions	160	240	320
"Fighter Airplane," c. 1960s, Marx Co., four actions, 7" wingspan	60	90	120

Fighter Airplane.

	C6	C8	C10
"Fighter Jet" c. 1960s, Marx Co., four actions, 7" wingspan	60	90	120
"Fighting Bull," 1960s, Alps Co., 9-1/2" long, five actions	70	105	140

Fighter Jet.

	C6	C8	C10
"Fighting Bull," 1970s, Rock Valley Tech Co., 12" long nose to tail tip, four actions, two cycles	100	150	200
"Fighting Robot," 1970s, S-H Co., four actions, 10" tall (all plastic)	70	105	140
"Fighting Spaceman," 1960s, S-H Co., 12" tall, five actions	150	225	300

Fighting Spaceman.

	C6	C8	C10
"Fire Boat," 1950s, M-T Co., 15" long, five actions	150	225	300
"Fire Chief No. 8 Car," 1960s, "Y" Co., 11-1/4" long, three actions	90	135	180
"Fire Chief Mystery Action Car," 1960s, T-N Co., 9-3/4" long, four actions	130	195	260
"Fire Command Car," 1950s, T-N Co., five actions	170	255	340

Fire Command Car.

	C6	C8	C10
"Fire Engine," 1950s, Marusan Co., four actions, 9" long	120	180	240
"Fire Engine," 1950s, T-N Co. (Electro Toy), three actions, 9" long, ladder extends 13"	150	225	300
"Fire Engine," 1950s, "Y" Co., 12" long, ladder extends 16", six actions	100	150	200
"Fire Engine," c. 1950s, S-H Co., three actions, 8" long	100	150	200
"Fire Patrol Boat," 1950s, KKS Co., 12" long, three actions	110	165	220
"Firebird Racer," 1950s, Tomiyama Co., four actions, 14-1/4" long	300	450	600
"Fire Tricycle," 1950s, T-N Co., 9-1/2" long, four actions	180	270	360

Fishing Bear, three variations.

	C6	C8	C10
"Fishing Bear," (also Fishing Panda Bear, Polar Bear, Forest Bear), 1950s, Alps Co., 10" high, six actions (includes detachable pond, tin fish)	160	240	320
"Fishing Bears Bank," 1950s, Wonderful Toy Co., 9-1/2" tall, six actions, rare	500	750	1000
"Flashing Jet-FC-657 Airplane-U.S.A.F. 7452," 1950s, Marx Co., 7" long, 6" wingspan, four actions	100	150	200
"Flashy Jim," 1950s, S.N.K. Co. (Ace), minor toy, 7-3/4" tall, rare	1100	1650	2200
"Flashy Ray Space Gun," 1950s, T-N Co., 18-1/2" long, minor toy	50	75	100

Flashy Jim Robot.

Flintstone Yacht.

	C6	C8	C10
"Flintstone Yacht," 1961, Remco Co., 17" long	100	150	200
"Floating Satellite Target Game, The," 1960s, 8-1/2" high (includes tin gun, rubber-tipped darts & celluloid ball)	100	150	200

The Floating Satellite Target Game.

Flower Watering Pup, Rock 'N Roll Monkey, Barney Bear Drummer.

	C6	C8	C10
"Flutter Birds," 1950s, Alps Co., 26-1/2" high when assembled, six actions, includes detachable pulley assembly, rare	300	450	600
"Flying Dutchman-PH-KLM Airliner," 1950s, T-N co., 11" long, 14" wingspan, five actions	100	150	200
"Flying Jet Plane-Boeing 747P," 1960s, J Toy Co., 13" long, 12" wingspan, five actions	90	135	180
"Flying Platform," 1950s, Cragstan Co., four actions, 5-1/2" diameter, 9" high, includes detachable tin soldier, rare	200	300	400
"Flying Tiger Airplane," 1960s, Marx Co., 7" long, 7" wingspan, four actions (remote control)	60	90	120
"Ford Model T," 1950s, Nihonkogei Co., 10-1/4" long, four actions (includes detachable tin roof)	60	90	120
"Ford Mustang 2" x 2"," 1960s, Wenmac-AMF Co., four actions, 16" long	60	90	120
"Ford Skyliner," 1950s, T-N Co., four actions, 9" long	100	150	200
"4 Prop Airplane," 1960s, Waco Co., 17" long, 16-1/4" wingspan, four actions	140	210	280

Fork Lift Truck.

	C6	C8	C10
"Fork Lift Truck," 1960s, M-T Co., 10-1/4" high, minor toy	80	120	160
"Foto Finish," racehorse, 1950s, M-T Co., minor toy, 12" long	120	180	240

Foto Finish.

	C6	C8	C10
"Frankenstein" (tin), 1950s, Marx Co. (Japan), 12" tall, five actions (remote control)	600	900	1200
"Frankenstein Monster," 1960s, T-N Co., 14" tall, six actions	140	210	280
"Frankie The Rollerskating Monkey," 1950s, Alps Co., 12" tall	130	195	260

Frankie the Rollerskating Monkey, Buttons Puppy with a Brain, Jocko the Drinking Monkey, Blushing Willie.

	C6	C8	C10
"Fred Flintstone on Dino," 1961, Marx Co. (Japan), eight actions, 22" long	350	525	700
"Fred Flintstone Bedrock Band," 1962, Alps Co., 9-1/2" high, four actions	400	600	800

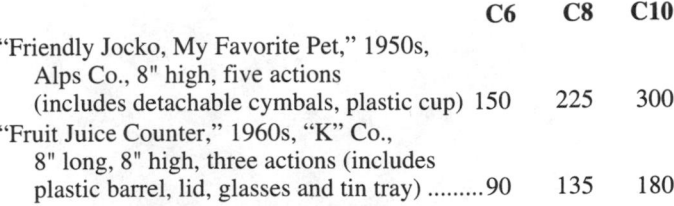

	C6	C8	C10
"Friendly Jocko, My Favorite Pet," 1950s, Alps Co., 8" high, five actions (includes detachable cymbals, plastic cup)	150	225	300
"Fruit Juice Counter," 1960s, "K" Co., 8" long, 8" high, three actions (includes plastic barrel, lid, glasses and tin tray)	90	135	180

Fruit Juice Counter.

	C6	C8	C10
"Funland Cup Ride," 1960s, Sonsco Co., 7" tall, 6"x6" base, three actions, includes 6" umbrella	100	150	200

Funland Cup Ride, Big Shot Cadillac.

	C6	C8	C10
Galloping Cowboy Savings Bank," 1950s, "Y" Co. (Cragstan), 8" high, 6-1/2" long, minor toy, rare	450	675	900
"Gama Mercedes-Benz 220 SE Sedan," 1960s, Mignon Co., 9" long, three actions	140	210	280
"Gear Robot," 1960s, "Y" Co., 10" tall, four actions	250	375	500
"Gino The Neapolitan Balloon Blower," 1960s, Tomiyama Co. (Rosko), 10" tall, five actions, includes bubble solution plastic tray	110	165	220
"Girl With Baby Carriage," 1960s, T-N Co., 8" high, three actions	90	135	180
"Go-Go Girl," (bar toy), 1969 Poynter Prod. Co., 15-1/4" tall, minor toy (risqué toy, PG-rated)	40	60	80

Gear Robot.

Grandpa Bear.

Go-Kart, M-T Co.

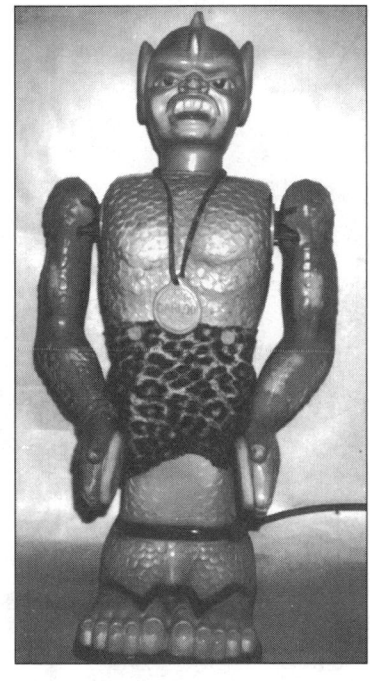

The Great Garloo.

	C6	C8	C10
"Go-Kart," 1960s, M-T Co., 6-1/2" long, minor toy (includes control wire with steering key)	90	135	180
"Go-Kart," 1950s, Rosko Co., 10" long, three actions, includes detachable head	90	135	180
"Godzilla," 1960s, Bullmark Co., five actions, 10-1/2" tall	300	450	600
"Godzilla Monster," 1970s, Marusan Co., 11-1/2" tall, three actions	200	300	400
"Golden Locomotive," 1950s, Nihonkogei Co., 10-1/2" long, minor toy	40	60	80
"Golden Gear Robot," 1960s, S-H Co., five actions, 9" tall	300	450	600
"Golden Roto Robot," 1960s, S-H Co., 8-1/2" tall, five actions	100	150	200
"Gomora Monster," 1960s, Bullmark Co., four actions, 8" tall (includes plastic missiles)	150	225	300
"Gorilla," 1950s, T-N Co., five actions, 9-1/4" tall (white or brown)	200	300	400
"Go-Stop Benz Racer," 1950s, Marusan Co., three actions, 11" long	150	225	300
"Good Time Charlie," 1960s M-T Co., 12" tall, seven actions	100	150	200
"Grace Ocean Liner," 1950s, M-T Co., three actions, 15" long	250	375	500
"Grandpa Bear," (incl. rocking chair), 1950s, Alps Co., 9" tall, five actions	150	225	300
"Grand-Pa Car," 1950s, "Y" Co., 9" long, four actions	50	75	100
"Grandpa Panda Bear," 1950s, M-T Co., five actions, 9" tall	140	210	280
"Great Garloo, The," 1960s, Marx Co., 23" tall, seven actions (includes chain and medallion)	235	350	475

	C6	C8	C10
"Green Caterpillar," 1950s, Daiva Co. three actions, 19-1/2" long	150	225	300
"Greyhound Bus," 1950s, KKK. Co., minor toy, 7-1/4" long	90	135	180
"Greyhound Bus Scenicruiser," 1950s, I.Y. Metal Toy Co., 16" long, three actions	90	135	180
"Greyhound Bus with Headlights," 1950s, Linemar Co., 10-1/4" long, three actions	100	150	200

Green Caterpillar.

Greyhound Bus.

Hamburger Chef.

	C6	C8	C10
"Grumman F9F Navy Jet," Cougar, 1950s, K Co., three actions, 11-1/2" long, 10-1/4" wingspan	150	225	300
"Guided Missile Launcher," 1950s, Irco Co., 8" long, 3" tall, 5" wide, three actions, (includes plastic missiles)	110	165	220
"Gypsy Fortune Teller," 1950s, Ichida Co., five actions, 12" high with hat, 5-3/4" x 7" base, (includes 20 fortune cards), rare	700	1050	1400+

	C6	C8	C10
"Happy Fiddler Clown, The," 1950s, Alps Co., 9-1/2" high, four actions, includes tin litho violin	230	345	460

Gypsy Fortune Teller.

Happy Fiddler Clown, Roarin' Jungle Lion, Mama Dog Feeding Hungry Baby Dog.

	C6	C8	C10
"Happy Miner," 1960s, Bandai Co., 11" tall, three actions	110	165	220
"Happy Naughty Chimp," 1960s, Daishin Co., 9-1/2" high, assembled, four actions	50	75	100
"Happy 'N' Sad Face Cymbal Clown," 1960s, "Y" Co., 10" tall, five actions	200	300	400

	C6	C8	C10
"H-O Gauge Electric Train set with Real Smoke," 1960s, Amico Co., 23" long, 17-piece set	70	105	140
"Hamburger Chef," 1960s, K Co., 8" long, 8" high, three actions (includes tin frying pan, hamburger, plastic bottles)	110	165	220
"Handy Hank Mystery Tractor," 1950s, T-N Co., 9" long, four actions	50	75	100
"Happy Band Trios," 1970s, M-T Co., 12" high, seven actions, rare	400	600	800
"Happy Clown Car," 1960s, "Y" Co., 6-1/2" long, three actions	100	150	200
"Happy Clown Theater" (with Pinocchio-like puppet), 1950s, "Y" Co., 10" tall, three actions	190	285	380

Happy Naughty Chimp.

Happy 'N Sad Magic Face Clown.

Happy Plane, TPS Co., 3 actions.

Happy Singing Bird in Cage, CRAGSTAN One-Arm Bandit, Comic Hungry Bug, Magoo.

Happy the Clown Puppet Show, Drummer Mickey Mouse, Clown the Magician.

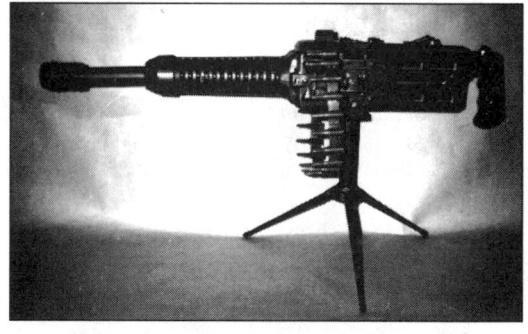

Heavy Machine Gun.

Highway Drive.

Hiller Hornet Helicopter.

Highway Skill Driving.

Hoop Zing Girl.

	C6	C8	C10
"Highway Skill Driving," 1960s, K Co., 13" long, three actions	70	105	140
"Hiller Hornet Helicopter," 1950s, Alps Co., 12-1/4" long, 15" 2-piece metal rotor, four actions	120	180	240
"Hippo Chef" (Cuty Cook) 1960s, "Y" Co., 10" tall, five actions (includes chef hat and tin litho egg)	150	225	300
"Hobo Clown With Accordion" (with cymbal-playing monkey), 1950s, Alps Co., six actions, 10-1/2" high	200	300	400
"Hole-In-One Bank," 1960s, no marking, 8-1/2" long x 3-1/2" wide, minor toy, includes marked test coin and golfer	70	105	140
"Holiday Sink-Stove Combination," 1950s, T-N Co., 9" high, minor toy (includes 3-piece pan set)	40	60	80
"Hoop Zing Girl," 1950s, Linemar Co., 11-1/2" tall, minor toy	150	225	300
"Hoopy the Fishing Duck," 1950s, Alps Co., 10" high, seven actions (includes magnetic fish and detachable pond)	180	270	360
"Hootin' Hollow Haunted House," 1960s, Marx, 11" high, eight actions	500	750	1000
"Hooty the Happy Owl," 1960s, Alps Co., 9" tall, six actions	90	135	180
"Hot Rod" car, 1950s, T-N Co., 10" long, minor toy	160	240	320
"Hot Rod Custom 'T' Ford," 1960s, Alps Co., four actions, 10-1/2" long	180	270	360
"Hot Rod Limousine," 1960s Alps Co., four actions, 10-1/2" long	180	270	360

Hy-Que Monkey.

	C6	C8	C10
"Hungry Baby Bear," 1950s, "Y" Co., 9-1/2" tall, six actions	180	270	360
"Hungry Cat," 1960s, Linemar Co., 9" high, seven actions (includes tin tray and plastic fish)	300	450	600
"Hungry Hound Dog," 1950s, "Y" Co., 9-1/2" high, six actions	190	285	380
"Hungry Sheep," 1950s, M-T Co., 9" long, three actions, two cycles	100	150	200

	C6	C8	C10
"Hy Que Monkey," 1960s, T-N Co., 17" tall, six actions	150	225	300
"Hysterical Robot, The," (a.k.a. Hysterical Harry and Happy Harry), 1960s, S-H Co., 13-1/2" tall, seven actions	150	225	300
"Ice Cream Baby Bear," 1950s, M-T Co., 9-1/2" high, three actions, rare	200	300	400
"Ice Cream Truck," 1960s, Bandai Co., 10-1/2" long, five actions	100	150	200
"Indian Joe," 1960s, Alps Co., 12" tall, four actions	80	120	160
"Indian Signal Choo Choo," 1960s, Kanto Toys Co., 9-1/2" long, four actions	80	120	160
"Interceptor," target game, 1950s, S&E Co., 13" high, 16" wingspan, four actions	150	225	300
"Interplanetary Rocket," 1960s, "Y" Co., 14-3/4" tall, five actions	120	180	240
"JDN 7673 Sedan-4-door," 1920s, Distler Co., minor toy and one of the earliest battery-operated toys, 14" long, rare	400	600	800

"James Bond's Aston-Martin": See "007 Aston-Martin"

James Bond's Aston-Martin.

"James Bond 007 Car M101," 1960s, Daiya Co., 11" long, seven actions, includes ejectable driver: See "M101 Aston Martin"

	C6	C8	C10
"Jeep USA," 1950s, TKK Co., 12-1/2" long, minor toy	70	105	140
"Jeep No. 10560," 1950s, Cragstan, 5-1/2" long, minor toy	70	105	140
"Jet Airport with 4 Jet Airplanes, 1960s, Turnpike Lines (Sears), 12-1/2" long, seven actions	150	225	300
"Jet Plane Base," 1950s, "Y" Co., 7-1/4" x 11" base, plane 9" long, 7" wingspan, seven actions (includes crank), rare	450	675	900

Jet Plane Base.

	C6	C8	C10
"Jig-Saw-Matic," 1950s, Z Co., 7-1/4" high, 4-1/2" x 8-1/2", minor toy	40	60	80
"Jo-Jo the Flipping Monkey," 1970s, T-N Co. (Illfelder), 10" high, minor toy	50	75	100
"Jocko the Drinking Monkey," 1950s, Linemar, 11" tall, four actions, includes top hat	90	135	180
"John's Farm Truck," 1950s, T-N Co., 9" long, seven actions	100	150	200
"Jolly Bambino," 1950s, Alps Co., 9" high, five actions, includes candy pieces	300	450	600

Jolly Bambino.

	C6	C8	C10
"Jolly Bear Peanut Vendor, The" 1950s, T-N Co., five actions, 8" high (includes felt hat)	200	300	400
"Jolly Bear the Drummer Boy," 1950s, K Co., 7" tall, five actions	100	150	200

Jolly Bear the Drummer Boy.

Jolly Daddy.

	C6	C8	C10
"Jolly Bear With Robin," 1950s, M-T Co., 10" high, three actions, rare	400	600	800
"Jolly Daddy," 1950s, Marusan Co., four actions, 8-3/4" tall	160	240	320
"Jolly Drummer Chimpy," 1950s, Alps Co., 9" high, six actions, includes cymbals and stand	80	120	160

	C6	C8	C10

"Jolly Drumming Bear," 1950s,
  T-N Co., 7" tall, four actions 70 105 140

Jolly Penguin, 1950s, T-N Co.,
  7" tall, five actions 100 150 200

"Jolly Pianist," 1950s, Marusan Co.,
  8" high, five actions 100 150 200

Jolly Pianist.

"Jolly Santa on Snow," 1950s, Alps Co.,
  12-1/2" tall, four actions,
  two cycles (includes tin skis) 150 225 300

Jolly Santa on Snow.

"Josie The Walking Cow," 1950s,
  Daiya Co., 14" long, 8-1/2" high,
  seven actions, two cycles 120 180 240

Jumbo The Bubble Blowing Elephant.

	C6	C8	C10

"Journey Pup," c. 1950s, S&E Co.,
  four actions, remote control, 7-1/2" long 50 75 100

"Jumbo The Bubble-Blowing Elephant,"
  1950s, "Y" Co., 7-1/4" high,
  three actions, includes plastic
  bowl for bubble solution 80 120 160

"Jungle Jumbo," 1950s, B.C. Co.,
  10" high, six actions, two cycles,
  hunter resembles Teddy Roosevelt 200 300 400

Jungle Jumbo.

Jungle Trio.

"Jungle Trio," 1950s, Linemar, 8" high,
  eight actions, includes tin litho whistle 450 675 900

"Jupiter Robot," 1950s,
  Yonezawa Co., 12-3/4" tall, four actions 150 225 300

"Jupiter Rocket Launching Pad,"
  1960s, T-N Co., 8-1/2" long, 7" high 190 285 380

"K-55 Electric Tractor," c. 1950s,
  M-T Co., three actions, 7" long 70 105 140

"King Flying Saucer," 1960s,
  K.O. Co., 7-1/2" diameter, three actions 70 105 140

"King Size Fire Engine," 1960s,
  Bandai Co., three actions, 12-1/2" long 150 225 300

"Kissing Couple," 1950s, Ichida Co.,
  10-3/4" long, five actions 150 225 300

*King Size
Fire Engine.*

Kissing Couple.

Lambo.

	C6	C8	C10
"Kitchen-ette Stove and Sink," 1940s, no marking, 6-1/2" long x 6-3/4" high, minor toy, includes kitchen utensils and side tray and stoppers	50	75	100
"Knight In Armor," 1950s, M-T Co., five actions, 10" tall, rare	1100	1650	2200

*Knight In Armor
Target game.*

	C6	C8	C10
"Laughing Clown, The," 1960s, S-H Co., 14" tall, seven actions	160	240	320
"Lectric Revolver," 1950s, Daisy Mfg. Co., 11-1/2" long, three actions	40	60	80
"Leo The Growling Pet Lion With Magic Face Change," 1970s, Toyiyama Co., 9" long, 2 cycles, three actions	100	150	200
"Light House," 1950s, Alps Co., 8-1/2" high, 6-3/4" x 6-3/4" base, five actions (includes detachable spin-ball tower), rare	600	900	1200

	C6	C8	C10
"Knight in Armor Target Game," 1950s, M-T Co., 12" tall, three actions (includes crossbow and rubber tipped darts)	200	300	400
"Knitting Grandma," 1950s, T-N Co., 8-1/2" tall, three actions	140	210	280
"Kooky-Spooky Whistling Tree," 1950s, Marx Co., 14-1/4" tall, six actions (two color schemes)	600	900	1200
"Ladder Fire Engine," 1950s, Linemar Co., five actions, 13" long	170	255	340
"Lady Pup Tending Her Garden," 1950s, Cragstan Co., 8" high, five actions	170	255	340
"Lambo" With Magnetic Trunk and Light, 1950s, Alps Co., seven actions, 16" long with trailer (includes two tin logs and trailer), rare	250	375	500

*Leo
The Growling
Pet Lion with
Magic Face
Change.*

Light House.

Lion.

Loop the Loop Clown.

	C6	C8	C10
"Lighted Freight Train," 1950s, "Y" Co., four actions, 25-1/2" long, five pieces, 8-section track	70	105	140
"Lighted Space Vehicle with Floating Satellite," 1960s, M-T Co., 8-1/2" long, three actions (includes celluloid ball)	150	225	300
"Linda Lee Laundromat," washing machine, 1940s, T-N Co., 6-1/2" high, minor toy	30	45	60
"Linemar Music Hall," 1950s, Linemar Co., four actions, 8" high, 7-3/4" x 5-1/2" base	150	225	300

	C6	C8	C10
"Los Walky-Son" 1960s, Geyper Co., 11-1/2" high, 15" wide, includes detachable rifles and baton	120	180	240
"Lost in Space Robot," 1966, Remco Co., 13" tall, three actions	200	300	400

Linemar Music Hall.

Lost in Space Robot.

	C6	C8	C10
"Lion," 1950s, Linemar, 9" long, four actions	70	105	140
"Lion Target Game," 1950s, M-T Co., 7-1/2" high, four actions (includes dart gun and darts)	120	180	240
"Locomotive Continental Blue," 1970s, 13" long, four actions, M-T Co.	40	60	80
"Loop The Loop Clown," 1960s, T-N Co., minor toy, 10" high	80	120	160
"Looping Airplane," c. 1960s, "Y" Co., Sears (distributor), minor toy, 14-1/2" high, airplane 5" long	40	60	80
"Looping Space Tank," 1960s, Daiya Co., five actions, 8" long	300	450	600

	C6	C8	C10
"Love-Beetle-Volks," 1960s, K.O. Co., 10" long, three actions	60	90	120
"Lucky Crane," 1950s, M-T Co., 8-1/2" high, five actions (includes tin prizes), rare	400	600	800

Lucky Crane with Box.

	C6	C8	C10
"M-101 Aston-Martin Secret Ejector Car," 1960s, Daiya Co., 11" long, six actions, (includes ejectable passenger)	200	300	400
"Mac the Turtle," 1960s, "Y" Co., 8" high, five actions	100	150	200
"Magic Action Bulldozer," 1950s, T-N Co., 9-1/2" long, three actions	100	150	200
"Magic Color Moon Express," 1960s, S-H Co., 13" long, four actions	90	135	180
"Magic Man Clown," 1950s, Marusan Co., five actions, 11" tall	260	390	520

Magic Man Clown.

	C6	C8	C10
"Lucky Locomotive," 1950s, Marusan Co., four actions, 8" long	40	60	80
"Lucky Seven Dice-Throwing Monkey," 1960s, Alps Co., 11-1/2" tall, five actions (includes plastic straw hat, five dice, two game sheets, twenty chips)	35	52	70

Lucky Seven Dice Throwing Monkey.

	C6	C8	C10
"Lufthansa Jet Airplane," 1960s, GAMA Co., 19-1/2" long, 18-1/2" wingspan, three actions	110	165	220
"Lunar Captain," 1960s, T-N Co., 13-1/2" long extended, five actions	110	165	220
"Lunar Loop/Swing and Orbiting Action," 1960s, Daiya Co., 14" high, 12" diameter hoop, three actions	100	150	200

"Magic Snowman," 1950s, M-T Co. (Santa Creations), 11-1/4" tall, four actions (includes detachable tin broom, plastic pipe, and styro ball) 150 225 300

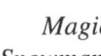

Magic Snowman.

M-101 Aston-Martin Secret Ejector Car.

	C6	C8	C10
"Magnet Rail Moon Orbiter," 1960s, "Y" Co., 14" high, 12" diameter, minor toy	70	105	140
"Main Street," 1950s, Linemar Co., three actions, 19-1/2" long, rare	250	375	500
"Major Tooty," 1960s, Alps Co. (R.F.), 14" tall, three actions, includes drum and hat	100	150	200

Main Street.

Marvelous Fire Engine.

	C6	C8	C10
"Make Up Bear," 1960s, M-T Co., four actions, 9" high, rare	500	750	1000
"Mambo the Jolly Drumming Elephant," 1950s, Alps Co., 9-1/2" high, six actions, includes cymbals and stand	100	150	200
"Man in Space Astronaut," 1960s, Alps Co., 6" tall, minor toy	100	150	200
"Mars Explorer," robot, 1950s, S-H Co., 9-1/2" tall, seven actions	200	300	400
"Mars Explorer," astronaut, 1960s, S-H Co., six actions, 10" tall	250	375	500
"Mars King Robot No. 12101," 1960s, S-H Co., 9-1/2" tall, four actions	210	315	420
"Marshal Wild Bill," 1950s, "Y" Co., 10-1/2" tall, four actions, two cycles, includes tin cowboy hat	180	270	360

	C6	C8	C10
"Marvelous Fire Engine, 1960s, "Y" Co., 11" long, four actions	100	150	200
"Marvelous Mike," 1950s, Saunders Co., 17" long, four actions	150	225	300
"Maxwell Coffee-Loving Bear," 1960s, T-N Co., 10" tall, five actions	120	180	240
"McGregor," 1960s, T-N Co., 12" tall when standing, six actions	100	150	200

Marshal Wild Bill.

Maxwell Coffee-Loving Bear, Bird Watching Bear, CRAGSTAN Peanut Vendor.

	C6	C8	C10
"Martian Robot," 1970s, SJM Co., 12" tall, four actions	60	90	120
"Marvelous Car," T-Bird, 1956, T-N Co., three actions, 11" long	250	375	500

Mechanized Robot (Robbie).

Marvelous Mike.

Mechanized Robot. Courtesy Christie's East.

Mickey Mouse Locomotive.

	C6	C8	C10
"Mechanic Robot," 1960s, S-T Co., 12" tall, five actions	150	225	300
"Mechanized Robot, The," ("Robby"), 1950s, T-N Co., 13-1/2" tall, four actions, rare	600	900	1200

Mechanized Robot (Robby). This toy was auctioned, with box, in late 1990 in near-mint condition for $27,830. Courtesy James S. Maxwell/ Virginia Caputo. Photo by Virginia Caputo.

	C6	C8	C10
"Mickey Mouse and Donald Duck Fire Engine," 1960s, M-T Co., 16" long, three actions	300	450	600
"Mickey Mouse Locomotive," 1960s, M-T Co., six actions, 9" long	200	300	400
"Mickey Mouse Melody Railroad," 1960s, Frankonia Co., minor toy, 6-3/4" long (handcar), (includes 4 circular rails with xylophone bars), rare	800	1200	1600
"Mickey Mouse on Handcar," 1960s, M-T Co., 9-3/4" long, 7-3/4" high, three actions	300	450	600

Mickey Mouse on Handcar.

	C6	C8	C10
"Mercury Explorer," 1960s, T.P.S. Co., 8" long, five actions	120	180	240
"Mercury X-1 Space Saucer," 1960s, "Y" Co., 8" diameter, four actions	70	105	140
"Merry Christmas" Santa In His Rockin' Chair, 1950s, Alps Co., three actions, 21" tall assembled, (includes detachable tree and stocking), rare	500	750	1000
"Merry Ice Cream Truck," 1960s, Bandai Co., 10-1/2" long, five actions	90	135	180
"Mexicali Pete-Drum Player," 1960s, Alps Co., 10-1/2" high, three actions	60	90	120

Mickey The Magician.

	C6	C8	C10
"Mickey Mouse Sand Buggy," 1960s, M-T Co., 11" long, four actions	150	225	300
"Mickey Mouse Trolley," 1960s, M-T Co., 11" high, three actions	150	225	300
"Mickey the Magician," 1960s, Linemar, 10" tall, four actions, includes tin rabbit	900	1350	1800
"Mighty Mike the Barbell Lifter Bear," 1950s, "K" Co., 10-1/2" tall, four actions	150	225	300

Military Police Car, Desert Patrol Jeep.

Mighty Mike The Barbell Lifter Bear.

	C6	C8	C10
"Mighty Kong," 1950s, Marx, 11" tall, five actions	250	375	500
"Mighty Robot," 1960s, K-O Co., 11-1/2" tall, four actions	900	1350	1800
"Military Air Defense Truck," 1950s, Linemar Co., four actions, 15-1/4" long	100	150	200
"Military Command Car," 1950s, T-N Co., five actions, 11" long	150	225	300

Military Command Car.

	C6	C8	C10
"Military Jet Plane," 1960s, Marx Co., 16" long, 14" wingspan, three actions	100	150	200
"Military Police Car," 1950s, Linemar, 8-1/2" long, six actions	100	150	200
"Million Bus," 1950s, KKK Co., three actions, 12" long, rare	1250	1875	2500

	C6	C8	C10
"Mimi Poodle with Bone," 1950s, T-N Co., 11" long, 10" high, five actions, two cycles (includes plastic bone)	50	75	100
"Mischievous Monkey," 1950s, M-T Co., 18" tall, six actions, includes tree and monkey	300	450	600
Mischievous Monkey with Bulldog, 1950s, T-N Co., 12" high, four actions	220	330	440

Mischievous Monkey.

Mr. Atom, robot.

	C6	C8	C10
"Miss Friday The Typist," 1950s, T-N Co., 8" tall, six actions, removable head	150	225	300
"Missile Robot Mr. 45," M-T Co., 17-1/2" tall, five actions	100	150	200
"Mr. Atom The Electronic Walking Robot," 1950s, Advance Doll & Toy Co., 17" tall, six actions	400	600	800

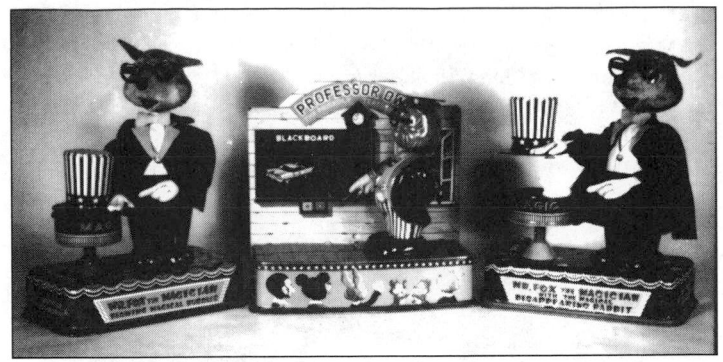

Mr. Fox The Magician Blowing Magical Bubbles, Professor Owl, Mr. Fox The Magician With The Magical Disappearing Rabbit.

	C6	C8	C10
"Mr. Atomic," robot, 1950s, Cragstan, 11" tall, three actions, rare	2500	3750	5000
"Mr. Baseball Jr.," 1950s, T-N Co., 7" high, three actions (with game box)	450	675	900
"Mr. Chief" Robot, 1950s, K-O Co., 12" tall, four actions	450	675	900
"Mr. Fox, the Magician With the Magical Disappearing Rabbit," 1960s, "Y" Co., 9" tall, five actions, includes plastic rabbit	400	600	800
"Mr. Hustler Robot," 1960s, Taiyo Co., 11" tall, six actions	200	300	400
"Mr. MacPooch" Taking A Walk And Smoking His Pipe, 1950s, SAN Co., four actions, 8" tall	130	195	260
"Mr. Magoo Car," 1961, Hubley Co., 9" long, five actions, includes cloth roof top	175	260	350
"Mr. Mercury" Type I (all tin), 1960s, Marx Co., 13" tall, seven actions	400	600	800
"Mr. Mercury" Type II (lighted), 1960s, Marx Co., seven actions	400	600	800
"Mr. Robot" The Mechanical Brain, 1950s, Alps Co., three actions, 8" tall, rare	600	900	1200

	C6	C8	C10
"Mr. Strong Pup Weight-Lifting Dog," 1950s, "K" Co., 9" tall, five actions	130	195	260
"Mr. Traffic Policeman," 1950s, A-I Co., 14" tall, 6"x6" base, four actions	250	375	500
"Mr. Zerox," 1960s, S-H Co., 9-1/2" tall, four actions	150	225	300
"Mix-ette Mixer," 1940s, KDP Co., 9" high when assembled, minor toy, includes mixer stand and bowl	30	45	60
"Mobile Satellite Tracking Station," 1960s, "Y" Co., six actions, 9" long (includes detachable antenna)	400	600	800
"Mobile Space TV Unit With Trailer," 1960s T-N Co., six actions, rare	500	750	1000
"Mod Monster Blushing Frankenstein," 1960s, T-N Co., 13-1/4" tall, five actions	150	225	300
"Modern Robot," 1950s, Yoshiya Co., four actions, 12" tall, rare	450	675	900
"Monkee Mobile," 1967, ASC Co. (Aoshin Co.), minor toy, 12" long	300	450	600

Mix-ette Mixer, Wash-O-Matic Washing Machine, Jig-Saw-Matic Jigsaw, Kitchen Stove & Sink.

Mr. Robot.

Mobile Satellite Tracking Station.

Monkee-Mobile.

	C6	C8	C10
"Monkey Handcar," 1950s, T-N Co., 7" high, three actions	70	105	140
"Monkey On A Picnic," 1950s, Alps Co., 9-1/2" high, seven actions	150	225	300
"Monorail Rocket Ship," 1950s, Linemar Co., 10" long with supports and rail rods, minor toy	140	210	280
"Monster Robot," 1970s, S-H Co., three actions, 10" tall	70	105	140
"Moon Astronaut," 1950s, Daiya Co., 9" tall, four actions	500	750	1000
"Moon Explorer" Robot, 1960s, Bandai Co., 17-1/2" tall (feet to antenna top), five actions, rare	600	900	1200
"Moon Explorer" Vehicle, 1960s, Gakken Co., five actions, 11" long	150	225	300
"Moon Express," Magic Color, 1950s, TPS Co., 12" long, three actions	120	180	240
"Moon Globe Orbiter," c. 1960s, "Y" Co. (Mego), three actions (rocket orbits globe, noise, lights), 10-1/2" high	100	150	200

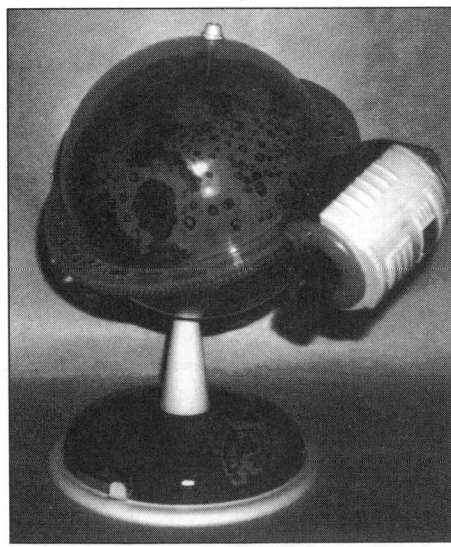

Moon Globe Orbiter.

	C6	C8	C10
"Moon Orbiter," 1960s, "Y" Co., minor toy, 4" long, includes 6 sections of track and trestles	120	180	240
"Moon Patrol Space Rover," 1960s, Gakken Toy Co., 11-1/2" long, five actions	140	210	280

Moon Patrol Space Rover.

	C6	C8	C10
"Moon Rocket," 1950s, "Y" Co., 15-1/4" long, three actions, rare	400	600	800
"Moon Traveler Apollo Z," 1960s, T-N Co., 12" long, 15" extended, five actions	120	180	240
"Mother Bear Sitting and Knitting In Her Old Rocking Chair," 1950s, M-T Co., 9-1/2" high, four actions	170	255	340
"Motorcycle Cop," 1950s, Daiya Co., 10-1/2" long, 8-1/4" high, five actions	300	450	600
"Mountain Cable Car," 1950s, Cragstan Co., 9" long, minor toy, includes cable	60	90	120
"Movieland Drive-In Theater," 1959, Remco Co., 14" long, minor toy (includes 6 small cars, ad cards, filmstrips)	60	90	120
"Multi Action Electra Jet KLM Royal Dutch Airlines PH-DSF," 1960s, T-N Co., 14" long, 17" wingspan, three actions	110	165	220
"Mumbo Jumbo," Hawaiian drummer, 1960s, Alps Co., 9-3/4" high, three actions	100	150	200
"Musical Bank Organ Grinder & Monkey," 1950s, HTC Co., 8" tall, four actions, includes test coin and detachable celluloid monkey, rare	500	750	1000
"Musical Bear" (Drum and cymbals), 1950s, Linemar Co., 10" tall, six actions (includes detachable tin horn)	200	300	400

Musical Bulldog.

	C6	C8	C10
"Musical Bulldog Playing Piano," 1950s, SAN Co., 8-1/2" tall, 6" x 9" base, four actions	600	900	1200
"Musical Cadillac Car," 1950s, Irco Co., 9" long, minor toy	200	300	400
"Musical Clown" (New Adventures of Clown), 1960s, T-N Co., 9" tall, three actions	150	225	300
"Musical Comic Jumping Jeep," 1970s, Alps Co., 12" long, six actions	70	105	140
"Musical Drummer Robot," 1950s, T-N Co., 8-1/4" tall, three actions, rare	4000	6000	8000
"Musical Jackal," 1950s, Linemar Co., 10" tall, six actions, rare	250	375	500
"Musical Jolly Chimp," 1960s, C-K Co., 10-1/2" high, five actions, two cycles	50	75	100

Musical Jolly Chimp, Grand-Pa Car, Circus Fire Engine.

"Musical Marching Bear," 1950s, Alps Co., four actions, 11" tall (includes detachable tin horn)	200	300	400

Musical Showboat.

	C6	C8	C10
"Musical Showboat," 1960s, Gakken Toy Co., 13" long, minor toy (includes two detachable smokestacks)	100	150	200
"My Fair Dancer," 1950s, Haji Co., 10-1/2" tall, minor toy	100	150	200
"Mystery Fire Chief Car No. 81," 1950s, Sanshin Co., 9-1/4" long, three actions	100	150	200
"Mystery Plane," 1950s, T-N Co., four actions, 10" long, 10-1/2" wingspan	120	180	240
"Mystery Police Car," 1960s, T-N Co., 9-3/4" long, 6" wide, 4" high, three actions	100	150	200

Mystery Police Car.

"NAR Television Truck," 1950s, Linemar Co., 12" long, four actions (includes six strip film inserts)	300	450	600
"NBC Television Truck," 1950s, Linemar Co., five actions, 9" long	300	450	600
"Neptune Tugboat," 1950s, M-T Co., 15" long, 7" high, four actions	90	135	180
"New Astronaut" Robot, 1970s, S-H Co., 9-1/2" tall, six actions	80	120	160
"New Bell Ringer Choo Choo," locomotive, 1960s, M-T Co., 10" long, three actions	50	75	100
"New Space Capsule," 1960s, S-H Co., six actions, 9" long	120	180	240
"News Service Car," 1960s, T.P.S. Co., 10" long, four actions	150	225	300
"Non-Stop Robot," 1960s, M-T Co., 15" tall, three actions, rare	600	900	1200
"Nutty Mad Indian," 1960s, Marx, 12" tall, four actions	90	135	180
"Nutty Mads Car" (Drincar), 1960s, Marx Co., 9-1/4" long, three actions	140	210	280

Nautilus SSN 571 Submarine.

*New
Astronaut.*

*New
Space
Capsule.*

*Nutty
Mads
Car.*

*Ol' Sleepy
Head Rip,
1950s.*

	C6	C8	C10
"Ol' Sleepy Head Rip," 1950s, "Y" Co., 9" long, seven actions	150	225	300
"Old Fashioned Fire Engine," 1950s, M-T Co., four actions, 12-1/2" long	120	180	240

	C6	C8	C10
"Nutty Nibs," 1950s, Linemar, 11-1/2" tall, minor toy, includes litho bowl of nuts and steel ball, rare	550	825	1100
"007 Aston-Martin," 1966, Gilbert Co., 11-1/2" long, eight actions (includes ejectable passenger)	210	315	420
"007 Secret Agent's Car," (Impala), 1960s, Spesco Co. (Joy Toy), 15" long, five actions	170	255	340
"Ol' MacDonald's Farm Truck," 1960s, Frankonia, four actions (includes plastic pig, cow and chicken)	100	150	200

*Old
Fashioned
Fire Engine.*

*Ol'
MacDonald's
Farm Truck.
Courtesy
Mapes
Auctioneers
& Appraisers.*

	C6	C8	C10
"Old Fashioned Car," 1950s, S-H Co., 10" long, four actions	50	75	100
"Old Fashioned Telephone Bear" (?), 1950s, M-T Co., 9-1/2" high, four actions	100	150	200

Old-Fashioned Telephone Bear, CRAGSTAN Telly Bear, V.I.P. the Busy Boss, Telephone Bear.

	C6	C8	C10
"Old Ford Touring Car," 1950s, Z Co., 10" long, four actions	40	60	80
"Old Time Automobile," 1950s, "Y" Co., 8-3/4" long, three actions (includes detachable tin litho driver and steering wheel)	80	120	160
"Old Timer," Car, 1950s, Cragstan Co., 9" long, three actions	90	135	180

Old Timer Car, Cragstan. Courtesy Mapes Auctioneers & Appraisers.

	C6	C8	C10
"Oldtimer Automoball," 1950s, M-T Co., 10" long, three actions, includes celluloid ball	90	135	180
"Oldtimer Sunday Driver," 1960s, Daiya Co., 9" long, four actions	70	105	140
"Overland Choo Choo Express" locomotive, 1950s, M-T Co., 14" long, minor toy	30	45	60
"Overland Stage Coach," 1960s, Ichida Co., 18" long, four actions	100	150	200
"P-51 Mustang Shooting Fighter Plane," 1950s, T-N Co., minor toy, 9" long, 9" wingspan	90	135	180
"Pacific Piping Express Locomotive," 1960s, Kanto Toy Co., 14" long, four actions	40	60	80
"Pan Am Sky Taxi Helicopter," 1960s, Haji Co., three actions, 11" long	70	105	140
"Pan American World Airways 'Seven Seas' DC-7," 1950s, T-N Co., 15" long, 19" wingspan, five actions	140	210	280

	C6	C8	C10
"Panda Bear," 1970s, M-T Co. (Masudaya Co.), 10" long, four actions, mostly plastic	30	45	60

Papa Bear Reading & Drinking In His Old Rocking Chair.

	C6	C8	C10
"Papa Bear Reading & Drinking in His Old Rocking Chair," 1950s, M-T Co., four actions, 10" high	150	225	300
"Passenger Bus," 1950s, "Y" Co., 16" long, four actions	230	345	460
"Pat O'Neill," 1960s, T-N Co., 12" tall, standing, six actions	150	225	300

Pat O'Neill.

	C6	C8	C10
"Pat The Dog," 1950s, NGS Co., 9-1/2" long, five actions, two cycles	30	45	60
"Pat the Roaring Elephant," 1950s, "Y" Co., 9" long with attached baby elephant, four actions	150	225	300
"Patrol Auto Tricycle," 1960s, T-N Co., 19" long, 7-1/2" high, four actions	200	300	400
"Patrol Helicopter No. 7," 1960s, Bandai Co., 11" long, four actions	70	105	140
"P.D. No. 5 Police Patrol Car," (Buick), 1960s, Asakusa Toy Co., 11-1/2" long, three actions	80	120	160

Patrol Helicopter, CRAGSTAN Biplane, T360 Monoplane.

	C6	C8	C10
"Penguin on Tricycle," 1950s, T-N Co., 6-1/2" high, three actions	100	150	200
"Pepi Tumbling Monkey," 1960s, Yanoman Toy Co., 9-1/2" high, minor toy	40	60	80
"Peppermint Twist Doll," 1950s, Haji Co., 12" tall, minor toy	150	225	300

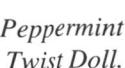

Peppermint Twist Doll.

	C6	C8	C10
"Peppy Puppy," 1950s, "Y" Co., 8" long, 6-1/2" high, seven actions, two cycles (includes tin litho bone)	50	75	100
"Pet Turtle," 1960s, Alps Co., 7" long, four actions, two cycles	70	105	140
"Pete the Space Man," 1960s, Bandai Co., 5" tall, minor action (Walking Mate Series)	60	90	120
"Peter The Drumming Rabbit," 1950s, Alps Co. (VIA-Cragstan), 13" tall, five actions	150	225	300

Peter the Drummer Rabbit, Picnic Bear, Bunny the Magician.

	C6	C8	C10
"Phillips '66' Power Yacht," 1950s, unmarked, minor toy, 18" long (includes plastic parts for yacht and dock)	70	105	140
"Pick-Up Truck," T-N Co., 10" long, four actions	100	150	200
"Picnic Bear," 1950s, (with Coke, Pepsi and generic logo), Alps Co., 10" high, five actions	90	135	180
"Picnic Bunny," 1950s, Alps Co., 10" tall, four actions	100	150	200
"Picnic Monkey," 1950s, Alps Co., four actions, 10" high	70	105	140
"Picnic Poodle," 1950s, STS Co., 7" long, 7" high, four actions, two cycles	30	45	60
"Pierrot Monkey Cycle," 1950s, M-T Co., 8" long, 10-1/2" high, five actions	300	450	600
"Piggy Barbecue," 1950s, "Y" Co., 9-1/2" tall, five actions, includes chef's hat and tin litho fried egg	150	225	300
"Piggy Cook," 1950s, "Y" Co., 9-1/2" tall, 4" x 6" base, five actions, includes chef's hat and tin litho fried egg	140	210	280
"Pinkee the Farmer," 1950s, M-T Co., 9-1/2" long, seven actions	100	150	200
"Pinky The Clown," 1950s, Rock Valley Toy Co. (Via), 10-1/4" tall, five actions, includes tin litho propeller, ball on nose, rare	200	300	400

Pinky The Clown, Circus Elephant, Tom & Jerry Handcar (Tom).

	C6	C8	C10
"Pinocchio Playing London Bridge," 1962, T-N Co. (Rosko), 10" tall, three actions, includes xylophone	150	225	300
"Pioneer Covered Wagon," 1960s, Ichida Co., 14-1/2" long, four actions (includes detachable canopy and driver)	120	180	240

Pioneer Covered Wagon.

	C6	C8	C10
"Pipie the Whale," 1950s, Alps Co., 12" long, minor toy	70	105	140
"Pistol Pete," 1950s, Marusan Co., five actions, 10-1/4" high, includes tin hat	200	300	400

Pistol Pete.

Piston Action Robot (Robbie).

Piston Robot.

	C6	C8	C10
"Piston Action Bulldozer," 1960s, Linemar Co., 7-1/2" long, two cycles	90	135	180
"Piston Action Robot," 1950s, T-N Co., three actions, 8-1/4" tall, resembles "Robbie"	900	1350	1800
"Piston Head Robot," 1960s, S-H Co., three actions, 10" tall	150	225	300
"Piston Robot," 1960s, S-H Co., 10-1/2" tall, four actions	110	165	220
"Planet Explorer," 1950s, S-H Co., four actions, 9" long	150	225	300
"Planet Rover," wheeled tank, 1960s, J Co., 9" long, 6-1/2" high, six actions	140	210	280
"Planet 'Y' Space Station," 1960s, T-N Co., three actions, 9" diameter	140	210	280
"Playful Pup in Shoe," 1960s, "Y" Co., 10" long, three actions	40	60	80
"Playful Puppy," 1950s, M-T Co., 7-3/8" long, 5" high, four actions	100	150	200

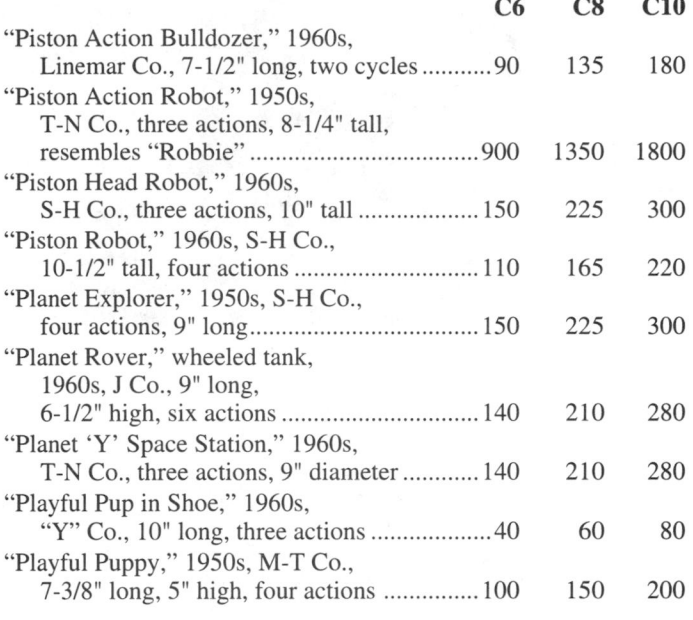

Playful Puppy.

	C6	C8	C10
"Pluto," 1960s, Linemar Co., 10" long, five actions	300	450	600
"Polar Bear," 1970s, Alps Co., 8" long, three actions	50	75	100
"Police Auto Cycle," 1960s, motorcycle and plastic driver, Bandai Co., five actions, remote control	150	225	300
"Police Motorcycle," 1950s, M-T Co., 11-3/4" long, seven actions	180	270	360
"Police No. 5" Police Car, 1950s, T-N Co., four actions, 9-1/2" long	90	135	180

Police Auto Cycle.

Police Motorcycle.

Pretty Peggy Parrot.

Police No. 5.

	C6	C8	C10
"Pretty Peggy Parrot," 1950s, T-N Co., 11" long, six actions	250	375	500
"Princess the French Poodle," 1950s, no markings, 9" long, 8" high, five actions	40	60	80
"Professor Owl," 1950s, E-T Co., 8" high, five actions, includes two discs	200	300	400
"Project Yankee Doodle," 1959, Remco Co., 15" long, six actions (includes plastic missiles, rockets & accessories)	60	90	120
"Puffy Morris," 1960s, "Y" Co., 10" tall, five actions, uses real cigarette	100	150	200

	C6	C8	C10
"Police Patrol Jeep," 1960s, T-N Co., four actions (lights, bump & go, noise, smoke), 9-1/4" long	100	150	200
"Pom Pom Tank," 1950s, S&E Co., 12" long, five actions	160	240	320
"Popcorn Eating Bear," 1950s, M-T Co., 9" high, five actions	100	150	200
"Popcorn Vendor," No. 4035, 1960s, S&E Co., 8" high, 7" long, six actions, includes litho umbrella	200	300	400
"Popcorn Vendor Truck," 1960s, T-N Co., 9" long, three actions	150	225	300
"Popeye and Rowboat With Moving Oars," 1950s, Linemar Co., three actions, 10" long rare	5000	7500	10,000+
"Porsche With Visible Engine," 1964, Bandai Co., 10" long, three actions	90	135	180
"Poverty Pup," bank, 1966, Poynter Products Co., 6" long, 4-1/4" high, three actions	60	90	120
"Power Shovel," 1950s, Alps Co., 15" long, extended, six actions	90	135	180

Puffy Morris, Piggy Cook, CRAGSTAN Crapshooting Monkey.

	C6	C8	C10
"Puzzled Puppy," 1950s, M-T Co., 7-1/2" long, 5" high, five actions	100	150	200

Power Shovel.

Puzzled Puppy, Shutter Bug, Popcorn Vendor.

Queen of the Sea.

	C6	C8	C10
"Queen of the Sea," 1950s, M-T Co., four actions, 21-1/2" long (includes detachable antenna and flag)	300	450	600
"RCA NBC Mobile Color TV Truck," 1950s, Yonezawa Co., 9" long, four actions	300	450	600
"R.R. Line Locomotive," 1950s, Marx, 6-1/2" long, four actions	40	60	80
"R-35 Robot," 1950s, M-T Co., 7-1/2" tall, five actions	300	450	600

R-35 Robot.

Rabbits And The Carriage.

	C6	C8	C10
"Racecar #25," 1950s, Alps Co., three actions, 9" long, rare	800	1200	1600
"Radar Jeep," 1950s, T-N Co., 11" long, four actions	150	225	300
"Radar Robot," 1960s, T-N Co., 9" tall, three actions, remote robot, face control box	600	900	1200

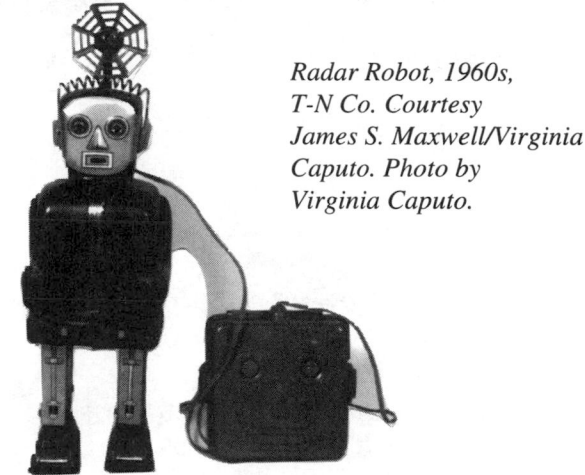

Radar Robot, 1960s, T-N Co. Courtesy James S. Maxwell/Virginia Caputo. Photo by Virginia Caputo.

	C6	C8	C10
"Radar Robot," 1970s, S-H Co., 12" tall, five actions	70	105	140
"Radar Scope Space Scout," 1960s, S-H Co., three actions, 9-1/4" tall	140	210	280

Radar Scope Space Scout.

	C6	C8	C10
"Radio Rex," 1920s, Elmwood Button Co., 5" x 7" dog house, minor toy (includes celluloid dog)	100	150	200
"Railroad Hand Car," 1950s, KDP Co., 8" long, minor toy, includes rubber track	90	135	180
"Railway Yard Shuttle Train," 1950s, ATC Co., 8" long, track 28" long, three actions, includes locomotive boxcar and track	100	150	200
"Ranger Robot," 1950s Daiya Co., six actions, 11" tall	400	600	800
"Ray Gun," machine gun, 1950s, T-N Co., 17-1/2" long, three actions, includes tripod	50	75	100

Radio Rex. Unlike the listing, this toy was made by John Hugo Co. of New Haven, Conn., with a last patent date of 1922. Auctioned with box in generally fine condition in late 1990 for $198. Courtesy James S. Maxwell/Virginia Caputo. Photo by Virginia Caputo.

Railroad Handcar, Winner-25-Rocket, Biller Train No. 573.

	C6	C8	C10
"Reading Bear," 1950s, Alps Co., 9" tall, five actions	100	150	200
Rembrandt Monkey Artist, 1950s, Alps Co., 8" high, five actions	200	300	400
"Reversible Diesel Electric Tractor," 1950s, Marx Co., minor toy	50	75	100
"Ricki The Begging Poodle," 1950s, Rock Valley Toys (VIA), 9" long, 8" high, five actions	30	45	60
"Riverboat," 1950s, Marusan Co., 12-3/4" long, three actions (includes detachable tin smokestack)	130	195	260

River Boat.

	C6	C8	C10
"River Queen Sidewheeler," 1950s, M-T Co., 13-1/2" long, three actions	140	210	280
"Road Construction Roller," 1950s, Daiya Co., 8-1/2" long, four actions	60	90	120

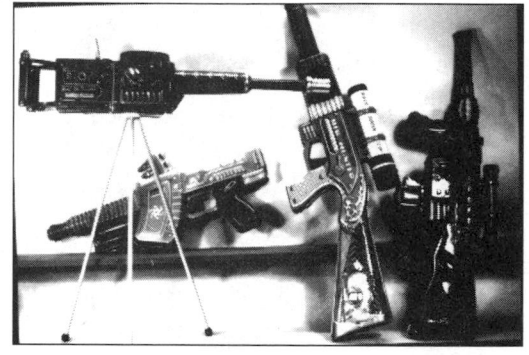

Ray Gun, Universal Machine Gun, Big Hunter Automatic Gun, Flashy Ray Gun.

	C6	C8	C10
"Road Grader," 1960s, T-N Co., 12" long, three actions	50	75	100
"Road Roller," 1950s, M-T Co., 9" long, four actions	60	90	120
"Roaring Gorilla" (white gorilla), 1950s, T-N Co., 9-1/4" tall, five actions: See "Gorilla"			
"Roaring Gorilla Shooting Gallery," 1950s, M-T Co., 9-1/2" tall, three actions (includes fold-out target box, tin gun, plastic darts)	200	300	400
"Roarin' Jungle Lion," (?) 1950s, Marx Co., 16" long, nose to tail tip, four actions, two cycles	140	210	280

Roaring Gorilla, Mighty Kong, Dancing Merry Chimp.

Roaring Gorilla Shooting Gallery.

	C6	C8	C10
"Robbie Robot," 1950s, Yonezawa Co., 13" tall, five actions: See "Mechanized Robot"			
"Robby Space Patrol," 1950s, T-N Co., 12-1/2" long, five actions, rare	2000	3000	4000+
"Robert the Robot," 1950s, Ideal Toy Co., 14" tall, three actions	120	180	240
"Robert the Robot Mechanical Bulldozer," 1950s, Ideal Toy Co., 9" long, four actions, rare	300	450	600

Robert The Robot Mechanical Bulldozer, rare, value $400 in mint.

"Robot," 1950s, "Y" Co., minor toy, 6" tall, rare	600	900	1200
"Robot," 1960s, "Y" Co., 10-1/2" tall, three actions	400	600	800
"Robot 2500," 1970s, Durham Industries, 10-1/2" tall, four actions	60	90	120
"Robotank TR-2," 1960s, T-N Co., four actions, 5" high	140	210	280
"Robotank Z Space Robot," 1960s, T-N Co., 10-1/4" high, five actions	300	450	600
"Rock 'N' Roll Hotrod," (Dreamboat), 1950s, T-N Co., three actions, 7" long	140	210	280
"Rock 'N' Roll Monkey," 1950s, Rosko Co., 13" tall, five actions, includes plastic hat (3 variations)	100	150	200

Rocket Express, monorail.

	C6	C8	C10
"Rocket Express" Rocket Ship Monorail, 1950s, Linemar Co., three actions, 10" long (20-piece rail & girder set)	100	150	200
"Rocket Launching Pad," 1950s, "Y" Co., 8-1/2" high, five actions (includes tin litho satellite and rocket)	160	240	320
"Rocking Chair Bear," (?) 1950s, M-T Co., 10" high, five actions	100	150	200
"Rocking Santa," 1950s, Alps Co., 10" high, four actions, rare	300	450	600
"Roller Skater," 1950s, Alps Co., minor toy, 12" tall	90	135	180
"Rollerskating Clown," 1950s, T.P.S. Co., 6" tall, minor toy, rare	500	750	1000
"Romance Car M-841," 1950s, "M" Co., 8" long, three actions	90	135	180
"Rootbeer Counter," 1960s, "K" Co., 8" long, 8" high, three actions (includes plastic barrel, glasses, and tin tray)	100	150	200

Root Beer Counter.

"Rosko Robot," 1950s, Rosko Co., five actions, 13" tall	500	750	1000
"Rotate-O-Matic Super Astronaut," 1960s, S-H Co., 11-1/2" tall, six actions, two cycles	100	150	200

Rotate-O-Matic Super Astronaut, with box.
Courtesy James S. Maxwell/Virginia Caputo.
Photo by Virginia Caputo.

Santa Claus, bellringer.

	C6	C8	C10
"Rover The Poodle Bell Ringer," 1960s, Alps Co., three actions, two cycles, 10-1/2" tall 60		90	120
"Roy Rogers Western Telephone," Ideal Co., 1950s, three actions, 9" high 90		135	180
"Royal Cub In Buggy," pushed by Mama Bear, 1940s, S&E Co., 8" long, 8" high, six actions 140		210	280

	C6	C8	C10
"Santa Claus Bellringer," 1950s, Santa Creations Co., 13" tall, five actions 90		135	180
"Santa Claus," No. M-750 (Sitting on House), 1950s, H.T.C. Co., 8" high, four actions 100		150	200
"Santa Claus on Handcar," 1960s, M-T Co., 10" high, three actions 120		180	240
"Santa Claus on Scooter," 1960s, M-T Co., 10" high, four actions 120		180	240

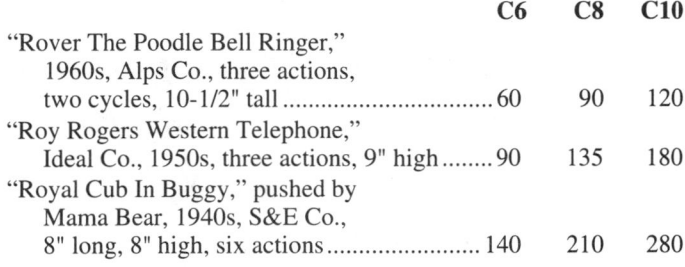

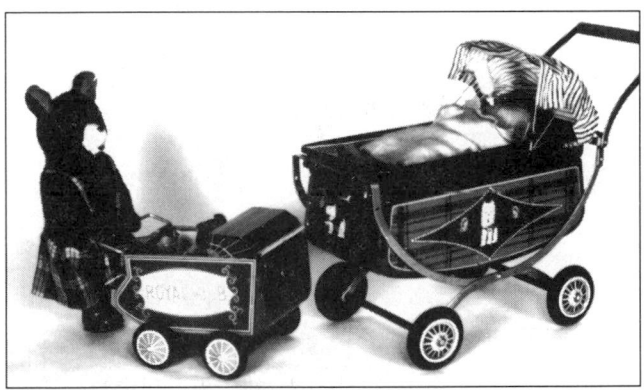

Royal Cub in Buggy, Cry-Baby-In-Buggy.

Santa Claus on scooter.

	C6	C8	C10
"Rudy the Robot," 1968, Remco Co., 16-1/4" tall, four actions 110		165	220
"SSN-571 Submarine" Nautilus, 1950s, Marusan Co., minor toy, 16" long (rudder extended)...................................... 120		180	240
"SSN-571 Submarine," Skate, 1950s, Marusan Co., minor toy, 16" long (rudder extended)...................................... 120		180	240
"Sam the Shaving Man," 1960s, Plaything Toy Co., 11-1/2" tall, seven actions, includes metal mirror 150		225	300
"Sammy Wong The Tea Totaler," 1950s, T-N Co., 10" tall, four actions 85		135	175
"Santa Bank," 1960, HTC Co. (Trim a Tree), 11" high, four actions.......... 150		225	300

	C6	C8	C10
"Santa Claus Stands & Sits," 1960s, T-N Co., 10" tall, six actions 150		225	300
"Santa Copter," 1960s, M-T Co., 8-1/2" long, three actions 70		105	140
"Santa in Rocker," 1950s, Alps Co., 21" high, from base to tree top, four actions (includes detachable tree and stocking), rare: See "Merry Christmas"			
"Santa Claus Phone Bank," 1950s, S&E Co., seven actions, 8" high, includes remote 4-3/4" high pay phone 400		600	800
"Santa Sled," 1950s, T-N Co., 14" long, four actions, rare 300		450	600
"Santa the Bellringer," 1950s, Chase Import Co., 7" high, minor toy (electromagnet activated & Blinker bulb) ..100		150	200

Santa Pay-Phone Bank.

Santa Fe Diesel.

	C6	C8	C10
"Santa Fe Diesel" Battery Cable Train With Headlight, 1950s, T-N Co., minor toy, 13-1/2" long, (2-piece hookup)	80	120	160
"Satellite Interceptor," target set, 1950s, Linemar Co., minor toy (2-piece set with 6-1/2" long gun-telescope, 5" high blower and two plastic darts and styro ball)	200	300	400

Satellite Interceptor.

	C6	C8	C10
"Satellite Target Game," 1960s, S-H Co., 8" high, 10-1/2" wide, minor toy (includes celluloid ball and special gun)	100	150	200

	C6	C8	C10
"Saxophone Playing Monkey," 1950s, Alps Co., 9-1/2" high, four actions	200	300	400
"School Bus," 1950s, Cragstan, 20-1/2" long, minor toy	70	105	140
"Sea Bear #7 Racing Boat," 1950s, Bandai Co., minor toy 10" long	60	90	120
"Seascape Tugboat," 1950s, Marx Co., three actions, 6-1/2" long	50	75	100
"Secret Service Action Car," (Green Hornet motif), 1960s, ASC Co., 11" long, four actions, rare	400	600	800
"Serpent Charmer," 1950s, Linemar Co., 7" high, four actions	250	375	500
"Shaggy The Friendly Pup," 1960s, Alps Co., 8" long, three actions	40	60	80
"Shaking Classic Car," 1960s, T-N Co., 7" long, four actions	50	75	100
"Shaking Old-Timer Car No. 2511-1," 1960s, T-N Co., 9" long, four actions, includes plastic driver	60	90	120
"Shark-U-Control Racing Car," 1961, Remco Ind. Inc., 19" long, all plastic, minor toy	80	120	160
"Sheriff Car," 1950s, T-N Co., four actions, 10" long	80	120	160
"Shoe Maker Bear," 1960s, T-N Co., 8-1/2" high, three actions	140	210	280
"Shoe-Shaking Dog," 1950s, M-T Co., 8" long, 6" tall, five actions	40	60	80
"Shoe Shine Bear," 1950s, T-N Co., 9" tall, five actions	130	195	260
"Shoe Shine Joe," 1950s, Alps Co., 11" high, six actions	140	210	280

Shoe Shine Joe.

	C6	C8	C10
"Shoe Shine Monkey," 1950s, T-N Co., 9" high, five actions	140	210	280
"Shooting Bear," 1950s, SAN Co., 10" tall, six actions	160	240	320
"Shooting Gorilla," 1950s, M-T Co., 12" high, four actions (includes tin gun and darts)	160	240	320
"Shutterbug," photographer, 1950s, T-N Co., 9" tall, five actions	400	600	800

Shooting Bear.

Silver Mountain Express, Spirit of 1776.

	C6	C8	C10
"Shuttling Freight Train," 1950s, Cragstan Co., six actions, 51" long assembled (includes locomotive, lumber car, four pieces of track, platform, logs)	110	165	220
"Shuttling Train and Freight Yard," 1950s, Alps Co., 11" long, track 51" long, four actions, includes locomotive, baggage car, two platforms, litho luggage	120	180	240
"Sight Seeing Bus," 1960s, Bandai Co., 14-1/2" long, four actions	100	150	200
"Sight Seeing Bus," 1950s, Yonezawa Co., minor toy, 9" long	140	210	280
"Sikorsky Rescue Army Helicopter," 1950s, Alps Co., four actions, 11" long	90	135	180

Sikorsky Rescue Army Helicopter.

	C6	C8	C10
"Silver Bell Choo Choo," 1950s, Kanto Co., 12" long, three actions	40	60	80
"Silver Mountain Express Locomotive," 1960s, M-T Co., four actions, 15-3/4" long	40	60	80
"Silver Mountain Locomotive," 1950s, M-T Co., 16" long, three actions	40	60	80
"Silver Ray Secret Weapon Space Scout," 1960s, S-H Co., six actions, 9" tall, rare	750	1075	1500+

	C6	C8	C10
"Silver Streak Locomotive No. 6682," 1950s, M-T Co., 16" long, four actions	40	60	80
"Singing Bird In Cage," 1950s, T-N Co., 9" high, 4" x 6" rectangular base, four actions	100	150	200
"Siren Fire Car," 1950s, M-T Co., 9" long, four actions	130	195	260
"Siren Patrol Car," 1960s, M-T Co., four actions, 12-1/2" long	90	135	180
"Siren Patrol Motorcycle," 1960s, M-T Co., three actions, 12" long	200	300	400
"Skating Circus Clown," 1950s, T.P.S. Co., minor toy, 6" tall, rare	500	750	1000
"Skiing Santa," 1960s, M-T Co., 12" tall, four actions (includes tin skis)	150	225	300
"Skipping Monkey," 1960s, T-N Co., 9-1/2" tall, minor toy	40	60	80
"Sky Patrol Flying Saucer," 1950s, K-O Co., 7-1/2" diameter, seven actions, includes detachable antenna	100	150	200
"Sky Patrol" Space Cruiser, 1950s, T-N Co., five actions, 13" long	150	225	300

Sky Patrol.

	C6	C8	C10
"Sky Taxi-Panam-Boeing Vertol 107," 1970s, Haji Co., 12-3/4" long, three actions, includes two detachable rotors	120	180	240
"Slalom Game," 1960s, T-N Co., minor toy, 15-1/4" long (includes plastic skier)	100	150	200
"Sleeping Baby Bear," 1950s, Linemar, 9" long, six actions, includes detachable alarm clock	240	360	480
"Sleeping Pup," 1960s, Alps Co., 9" long, five actions	60	90	120
"Slurpy Pup," 1960s, T-N Co., 6-1/2" long, 4" high, four actions	50	75	100

Slalom Game.

	C6	C8	C10
"Smilex Deluxe Coffee Set," 1950s, "Y" Co., 12" high assembled, minor toy, includes four sets of cups, saucers and spoons, plastic	60	90	120
"Smoky Bear," 1950s, SAN Co., four actions, 9" tall (includes detachable tin hat-Pioneer)	220	330	440

Smoking Grandpa in Rocking Chair, Rocking Chair Bear, Mama Bear & Hungry Baby Bear, Pop Drinking Bear.

	C6	C8	C10
"Smoky Bill on Old-Fashioned Car," 1960s, T-N Co., 9" long, four actions	120	180	240

Smoking Popeye.

	C6	C8	C10
"Smokey the Bear Jeep," 1950s, M-T Co., 10" long, four actions	220	330	440
"Smoking Bulldozer," 1960s, WKC Co., 9" long, four actions	90	135	180
"Smoking Bunny," 1950s, SAN Co., 10-1/2" tall, four actions	100	150	200
"Smoking Elephant," 1950s, Marusan Co., 8-3/4" tall, four actions	130	195	260
"Smoking Grandpa," (in Rocking Chair), 1950s, SAN Co., 8" tall, four actions (Type I: eyes open)	150	225	300
"Smoking Grandpa," (in Rocking Chair), 1950s, SAN Co., 8" tall, four actions (Type II: eyes closed)	160	240	320
"Smoking Jet Plane," 1950s, T-N Co., 12" long, 11" wingspan, four actions	150	225	300
"Smoking Pop Locomotive: The General," 1950s, SAN Co., 10-1/4" long, four actions	70	105	140
"Smoking Popeye," 1950s, Linemar, 9" tall, five actions, rare	800	1200	1600
"Smoking Robot," 1960s, M-T Co., 10" tall, four actions (all plastic)	90	135	180

Smoking Robot.

	C6	C8	C10
"Smoking Spaceman," 1950s, Linemar Co., 12" tall, six actions	800	1200	1600
"Smoking U.S.A.F Jet," 1950s, T-N Co., 13" long, 12" wingspan, four actions	150	225	300
"Smoking Volkswagen," 1960s, Aoshin Co., 10-1/2" long, four actions	60	90	120
"Smoking PaPa Bear," 1950s, SAN Co., 8" tall, four actions	110	165	220
"Smoky Joe Fancy Mobile," 1960s, T-N Co., four actions (smokes, lights, bump & go, noise), 9" long	100	150	200
"Snake Charmer (And Casey the Trained Cobra)," 1950s, Linemar Co., 8" high, four actions	250	375	500

Smoky Bear.

	C6	C8	C10
"Snappy the Dragon," 1960s, T-N Co., 30" long, six actions, rare	2000	3000	4000+
"Sneezing Bear," 1950s, Linemar Co., 9" high, five actions	125	185	250

Sneezing Bear.

	C6	C8	C10
"Snoopie the Non-Fall Dog," 1960s, Amico Co., 8" long, three actions	50	75	100
"Snoopy Sniffer," 1960s, M-T Co., four actions, 8" long	50	75	100
"Somersaulting Pup With Bark," 1960s, T-N Co., four actions, two cycles, 9" long	50	75	100

Somersaulting Pup.

	C6	C8	C10
"Sonicon Space Rocket," 1960s, M-T Co., minor toy, 13" long	250	375	500
"Space Capsule," 1960s, M-T Co., 10" long, four actions, includes styrofoam saucer and astronaut	100	150	200
"Space Capsule-5," 1960s, M-T Co., four actions, 10-1/2" long	150	225	300

Space Capsule 5.

	C6	C8	C10
"Space Commando Spaceman," 1960s, M-T Co., 7-3/4" tall, four actions	500	750	1000
"Space Commando" Space Station, 1960s, T-N Co., 10" diameter, four actions	150	225	300
"Space Explorer #1041, 1960s, Yonezawa Co., 7-3/4" high, extends to 11-1/2" high, six actions, rare	600	900	1200
"Space Explorer Ship," 1950s, M-T Co., six actions, 11" diameter (saucer)	80	120	160

Space Explorer Ship X-7.

	C6	C8	C10
"Space Fighter," Robot, 1970s, S-H Co., 9" tall, six actions	70	105	140
"Space Frontier Saturn 5 Rocket," 1960s, K-Y Co. (Yoskino Toy Co.), 18" long, six actions	100	150	200
"Space Patrol Car," 1950s, T-N Co., four actions, 9-1/2" long	300	450	600
"Space Patrol Car," with lighting guns, 1950s, Linemar Co., 9" long, three actions	450	675	900
"Space Patrol Robot," 1950s, S-H Co., 11" tall, six actions	140	210	280
"Space Patrol Rocket," 1970s, M-T Co., 11" long, three actions	70	105	140
"Space Patrol Snoopy," 1960s, M-T Co., 11" long, four actions	100	150	200
"Space Patrol Tank," 1950s, Cragstan Co., five actions, 9" long (includes detachable tin jet plane)	150	225	300

Space Patrol 3 Saucer.

	C6	C8	C10
"Space Patrol 3 Saucer," 1950s, K-O Co., 7-1/2" diameter, five actions	100	150	200
"Space Patrol Vehicle," 1950s, K Co., 9" long, four actions	130	195	260
"Space Patrol Vehicle," 1960s, M-T Co., 9-1/2" long, three actions	100	150	200
"Space Pioneer" Vehicle, 1960s, M-T Co., three actions, 12" long	100	200	300

Space Pioneer.

	C6	C8	C10
"Space Robot Trooper," 1950s, K-O Co., 7-1/2" tall, three actions, rare	500	750	1000
"Space Robot (X-70)," 1960s, T-N Co., 12" tall, five actions	500	750	1000
"Space Robot Car," 1950s, Yonezawa Co., six actions, 9-1/4" long, rare	1000	1500	2000
"Space Rocket Blue Eagle," 1950s, Masuya Toy Co., 15" long (tail to probe tip)	120	180	240
"Space Rocket Solar X," 1960s, T-N Co., 15-1/2" tall, five actions	150	225	300
"Space Scooter," 1960s, M-T Co., 10-1/2" high, 8" long, three actions	100	150	200
"Space Scooter," Snoopy or Astro-Dog, 1960s, M-T Co., three actions, 8" long	80	120	160
"Space Ship," 1950s, I.Y. Co., 9-1/2" diameter, four actions	180	270	360
"Space Ship," 1970s, M-T Co., 9" long, three actions	90	135	180
"Space Ship X-5," 1970s, M-T Co., 8" diameter, four actions	60	90	120
"Space Ship X-8," 1960s, Tada Co., 8" long, four actions	100	150	200
"Space Station," 1950s, T-N Co., 9" diameter, four actions	100	150	200
"Space Station," 1950s, S-H Co., 11-3/4" diameter, five actions	500	750	1000

	C6	C8	C10
"Space Tank," 1960s, K-O Co., 6" long, four actions, "Robbie Type"	2000	3000	4000+
"Space Tank," 1950s, Daiya Co., 8" long, four actions	120	180	240
"Space Tank-M41," 1950s, M-T Co., 9" long, four actions (includes detachable plastic antenna)	100	150	200
"Spaceman," Robot, 1950s, Linemar, 7-1/2" tall, three actions	350	525	700
"Spaceman," Robot, 1950s, T-N Co., 9-1/4" tall, four actions	400	600	800
"Spad XIII S-7 Stunt Biplane," 1960s, T.P.S. Co., 9" long, 10-3/8" wingspan, three actions	130	195	260
"Spanking Bear," 1950s, Linemar Co., 9" high, six actions	150	225	300
"Sparking Burp Gun," 1950s, Mark Co., three actions, 24" long	40	60	80
"Sparkling Mike The Robot," 1950s, Ace Co., 7-1/2" tall, three actions, rare	1000	1500	2000
"Sparky Savings Bank," 1930s, Byron Co., 4" long, 4-1/2" high doghouse, minor toy (electromagnet action, includes 4" long compo dog)	60	90	120
"Sparky the Seal," 1950s, M-T Co., 6" high, 7" long, four actions, two cycles, includes celluloid ball	80	120	160
"Spirit of 1776," locomotive No. 4406, 1976, M-T Co., 15-3/4" long, five actions	40	60	80
"Sports Car Race Set," 1960s, T.P.S. Co., minor toy, 8" x 14" base, includes four plastic race cars	80	120	160
"Star Strider" Robot, 1980s, S-H Co., six actions, 12" tall	110	165	220

Star Strider.

	C6	C8	C10
"Steam Roller (Road Roller)," 1950s, T-N Co. (Rosko), 12" long with trailer, four actions	90	135	180
"Steam Roller," 1950s, "Y" Co., 8" long, four actions (includes tin trailer)	100	150	200
"Steerable Tank," 1950s, Linemar Co., 9" long, five actions	60	90	120
"Strange Explorer," 1960s, DSK Co., 7-1/2" long, four actions	300	450	600
"Strato Jet U.S.A.F.," 1950s, T-N Co., 13" long, 14" wingspan, three actions	120	180	240

	C6	C8	C10

"Strutting My Fair Dancer,"
   (Dancing Sailor Girl), 1950s,
   Haji Co., 12" tall, two pieces, minor toy 100   150   200

"Struttin' Sam," 1950s, Haji Co.,
   10-1/2" tall, minor toy 200   300   400

Strutting Sam.

"Sunbeam Jeep No. 1," 1940s,
   10" long, Marusan Co., three actions 100   150   200

"Sunday Driver," 1950s, M-T Co.,
   10" long, four actions, includes
   detachable driver 70   105   140

Sunday Driver.

"Super Astronaut," Robot, 1960s, S-H Co.,
   11-1/2" tall, five actions, two cycles 110   165   220

"Super Astronaut Robot," 1960s,
   SJM Co., 12" tall, four actions 150   225   300

"Super Giant Robot, 1960s, S-H Co.,
   15-1/2" tall, six actions 200   300   400

	C6	C8	C10

"Super Jet," 1950s, T-N Co., three actions,
   12" long, 8" wingspan 250   375   500

"Super Space Capsule," 1960s, S-H Co.,
   9" high, four actions 100   150   200

"Super Space Commander," 1960s,
   S-H Co., 10" tall, three actions 70   105   140

"Super Susie," 1950s, Linemar Co.,
   9" high, six actions 350   625   700

"Superman Tank," 1950s, Linemar Co.,
   10-1/4" long, three actions, rare 600   900   1200+

"Surrey Jeep," 1960s, T-N Co.,
   11" long, three actions 90   135   180

Super Susie.

"Suzy-Q Automatic Ironer," 1950s,
   GW Co., 7" high, four actions 90   135   180

"Suzette the Eating Monkey," 1950s,
   Linemar Co., 8-3/4" high, 7"x5" base,
   five actions, (includes tin litho steak), rare 300   450   600

"Swingtail Airplane Flying Tigers,"
   1960s, Marx Co., 19-1/2" long,
   21" wingspan, seven actions 300   450   600

"Swing Tail Cargo Plane Flying Tiger,"
   1960s, T-N Co., five actions,
   14" long, 14" wingspan 300   450   600

"Switchboard Operator," 1950s,
   Linemar, 7-1/2" high, four actions, rare 350   525   700

"Swivel-O-Matic Astronaut" robot,
   1960s, S-H Co., 11-1/2" tall,
   five actions, 2 cycles 80   120   160

"T 360 Monoplane," 1950s, S&E Co., 12" long,
   14-1/2" wingspan, four actions: See "Bristol Bulldog Airplane"

Superman Tank,
Linemar. Courtesy
Christie's East.

Talking Parrot ("Pete").

	C6	C8	C10
"Talking Parrot," 1950s, T-N Co., 18" high, six actions (called "Pete")	200	300	400
"Talking Police Car Mystery Action," 1960s, "Y" Co., 14" long, three actions	70	105	140
"Talking Robot," 1960s, Yonezawa Co., three actions, 10-3/4" tall, rare	600	900	1200

Talking Robot.

	C6	C8	C10
"Tank M-4 Combat Tank," 1960s, Taiyo Co., 11-1/2" long, 13" with gun barrel extended, five actions	80	120	160
"Tank M-35," 1950s, HTC Co., 8" long, three actions	100	150	200
"Tank M-41," 1970s, J Co., 8-1/4" long, four actions	100	150	200
"Tank M-48-T," 1960s, T-N Co., 8-1/4" long, four actions	90	135	180
"Tank M-56," 1940s, M-T Co., 7-1/2" long, wheel drive, seven actions	100	150	200
"Tank M-81," 1960s, M-T Co., 8-1/2" long, seven actions	100	150	200
"Tank M-103," 1950s, M-T Co., 7" long, three actions	90	135	180

Tank (M-4), Tank (X-3), Tank (M-103).

Tank (M-81), Tank (M-35), Tank (M-56), Tank (M-197).

	C6	C8	C10
"Tank M-107 U.S. Army," 1950s, "Y" Co., 6" long, four actions (includes four missiles)	120	180	240
"Tank M-X," 1950s, T-N Co., 8-1/2" long, five actions	70	105	140
"Tank T-5," 1950s, T-N Co., 8-1/2" long, three actions (includes detachable radar antenna)	110	165	220
"Tank 392 U.S. Tank Division," 1950s, Marx Co., three actions, 9-1/2" long	70	105	140
"Tank X-3" (explorer defense), 1950s, Cragstan Co., 7-3/4" long, five actions (includes six cartridge shells)	130	195	260
"Tank X-75," 1950s, M-T Co., 9" long, three actions (includes tin gun and darts)	110	165	220
"Tank Daisymatic No 64 Rapid Fire Tank," 1960s, Daisy Mfg. Co., 8" long, four actions	120	180	240
"Tank Daisy-Matic No. 80," 1965, Daisy Mfg. Co., 8-1/2" long, five actions (includes darts)	100	150	200
"Tank Robot," 1960s, S-H Co., five actions, 10" tall	300	450	600
"Tarzan," 1966, Marusan Co. (Banner), four actions, 13" tall	500	750	1000
"Taxi," yellow cab, 1950s, Linemar Co., 7-1/2" long, five actions	100	150	200
"Taxi Cab," 1950s, "Y" Co., 8-1/2" long, five actions	90	135	180

	C6	C8	C10

"Taxi Cab," 1960s, "Y" Co.,
four actions, 9" long 90 135 180

"Teddy Bear Circus Acrobat," 1950s,
Tomiyana Co., three actions, 15" high,
includes detachable bear flyer, rare 500 750 1000

"Teddy Bear Swing," 1950s, T-N Co.,
three actions, two cycles, 17" high
(includes four wire supports and tin sign) .. 250 375 500

	C6	C8	C10

"Teddy-Go-Kart," 1960s, Alps Co.,
10-1/2" long, four actions 100 150 200

"Teddy the Artist," 1950s, "Y" Co.,
8-1/2" high, 5-1/4" x 7" base,
three actions, includes removable
tray and nine patterns 300 450 600

"Teddy the Boxing Bear," 1950s,
"Y" Co., 9" tall, five actions 150 225 300

"Teddy the Rhythmical Drummer,"
1960s, Alps Co., 11" tall, three actions 100 150 200

"Telephone Bear," 1950s, Linemar,
7-1/2" high, six actions 160 240 320

"Telephone Bear Ringing and Talking
In His Old Rocking Chair," 1950s,
M-T Co., 10" high, four actions 200 300 400

Teddy Bear Swing.

Telephone Bear Ringing And Talking In His Old Rocking Chair.

Teddy-Go-Cart, Mambo The Jolly Drumming Elephant.

"Telephone Bunny Ringing and Talking
In His Old Rocking Chair," 1950s,
M-T Co., 10" high, four actions 170 255 340

"Television Spaceman," 1960s, Alps Co.,
14-1/2" high to tip of antenna, six actions .. 400 600 800

Telephone Bunny Ringing And Talking In His Old Rocking Chair.

Teddy The Rhythmical Drummer, Major Tooty, McGregor, Cycling Daddy.

Television Spaceman.

	C6	C8	C10
"Television Truck," 1950s, Linemar Co., 11" long, three actions	250	375	500

The Big Parade.

The Loser.

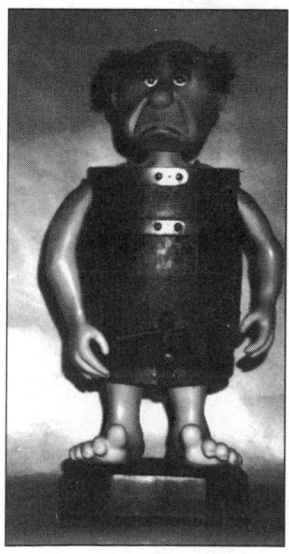

	C6	C8	C10
"The Big Parade," 1963, Marx Co., 11-1/2" tall, 15" wide, four actions (includes detachable gun and baton)	120	180	240
"The Loser," (Bar Toy), c. 1971, Poynter Prod. Co., three actions, 13" high	40	60	80
"The Rabbits and Carriage," 1950s, S&E Co., four actions, 10" tall (should have tin butterfly)	150	225	300
"The Playing Monkey," 1950s, S&E Co. (Ahi Brand), six actions, 10" tall, includes detachable hat and tin yo-yo	200	300	400

The Playing Monkey.

Thunder Jet Boat.

	C6	C8	C10
"Thunder Jet Boat," 1950s, Bandai Co., 9-3/4" long, three actions	130	195	260
"Tin Man" Robot, 1960s, Remco Industries, Inc., 21" tall, all plastic, four actions	100	150	200
"Tinkling Trolley," 1950s, M-T Co., four actions, two cycles, 10-1/2" long, includes two plastic cowcatchers	110	165	220
"Tiny Jeep," 1950s, WACO Co., 4-1/4" long, minor action	30	45	60
"Tiny Tank," 1950s WACO Co., 4-1/4" long, minor action	30	45	60
"Tom and Jerry Car," 1960s, Rico Co. (Spain), 13" long, three actions, rare	400	600	800
"Tom and Jerry Choo Choo," 1960s, M-T Co., 10-1/4" long, five actions	120	180	240
"Tom and Jerry Handcar," Jerry, 1960s, M-T Co., 7-3/4" high, 7-3/4" long, three actions	130	195	260
"Tom and Jerry Handcar," Tom, 1960s, M-T Co., 9-3/4" high, 7-3/4" long, three actions	130	195	260

Tom and Jerry Car.

Tom & Jerry Choo-Choo, Old Timer Automoball.

Tom and Jerry Handcars.

	C6	C8	C10
"Torpedo Boat-PT 107," 1950s, Linemar, 11-1/2" long, three actions	110	165	220
"Tractor," 1950s, Showa Co., 7-1/2" long, four actions (includes litho tin driver)	60	90	120
"Tractor," 1960s, "Y" Co., 6" long, three actions	50	75	100
"Tractor On Platform," 1950s, T-N Co., tractor 9" long, trailer 7" long, minor toy	80	120	160
"Train Robot," 1950s, M-T Co., four actions, 15-1/2" tall, rare	1500	2250	3000+
"Traveler Bear," 1950s, Linemar Co., 8" high, three actions	80	120	160
"Treasure Chest" Bank, 1960s, Illfelder Co., 11" tall, five actions, two cycles, risqué toy, PG-rated	90	135	180

	C6	C8	C10
"Tom and Jerry Helicopter," 1960s, M-T Co., 9-1/2" long, three actions	110	165	220
"Tom and Jerry Highway Patrol," 1960s, M-T Co., 8" long, three actions	120	180	240
"Tom and Jerry Jumping Jeep," 1960s, M-T Co., 9" long, three actions	120	180	240
"Tom-Tom Indian," 1961, "Y" Co., 10-1/2" tall, four actions	80	120	160
"Topo Gigio Playing the Xylophone," 1960s, T-N Co., three actions	300	450	600

Treasure Chest Bank, Santa Bank, Hole-In-One Bank, Poverty Pup Bank.

Tom Tom Indian.

	C6	C8	C10
"Tric-cycling Clown," 1960s, M-T Co., five actions, 12" high	300	450	600
"Tricky Dog House," No. 673, 1960s, "Y" Co., 6-3/4" high, 7-1/4" long, 6-3/4" wide, four actions	60	90	120
"Trumpet Playing Bunny," 1950s, Alps Co., 10" high, four actions	150	225	300
"Trumpet Playing Monkey," 1950s, Alps Co., 9" high, four actions, includes tin horn	170	255	340
"Tubby the Turtle," 1950s, "Y" Co., 7" long, three actions	50	75	100
"Tugboat," 1950s, Marx, 6-1/2" long, minor toy	50	75	100

Tric-Cycling Clown.

Trumpet Playing Bunny.

Trumpet Playing Monkey, Monkey On A Picnic, Busy Housekeeper.

	C6	C8	C10
"Turntable Xylophone Melody Train," 1960s, Cragstan Co., 29-1/2" long assembled, three actions	50	75	100
"TWA Multiaction DC-7C Airliner," 1960s, Yonezawa Co., 22-1/2" long, 23-1/4" wingspan, seven actions	200	300	400
"Twin Coupled Tram Cars," 1950s, K Co., minor toy, 11-1/2" long (two cars)	100	150	200

Twin Coupled Tramcars.

	C6	C8	C10
"Tugboat," 1950s, Marusan Co., three actions, 13-1/2" long	110	165	220
"Tumbles the Bear," 1960s, Y-M Co. (Yanoman), 8-1/2" tall, minor toy, includes porter's hat	80	120	160
"Turn Signal Robot," 1960s, T-N Co., 11" tall, five actions (Auto Accessory)	160	240	320
"Turn-O-Matic Gun Jeep," 1960s, T-N Co., 10" long, five actions	100	150	200
"Twin Racing Cars," 1950s, Alps Co., three actions, 7" long, 10" long with coupling rod	400	600	800

Turn-O-Matic Gun Jeep.

Twin Racing Cars.

	C6	C8	C10

"Twirly Whirly," 1950s, Alps Co.,
four actions, 13-1/2" high 350   525   700

"Twist Dancer" (Let's Twist), 1960s,
no mfr. mark, minor toy, 15" high 100   150   200

"Two Stage Rocket Launching Pad,"
1950s, T-N Co., 7" long, 4" wide,
8" high, three actions (includes
two plastic-rubber rockets) 250   375   500

Two Stage Rocket Launching Pad.

U.S. Army Machine Gunner. Photo by Don Hultzman. Collection of Beau Cassity.

	C6	C8	C10

"U.S. Air Force Military Airlift
Command Jet," 1960s, T-N Co.,
14" wingspan, four actions 130   195   260

"U.S. Air Force Smoking Jet No. 75029,"
1950s, T-N Co., 12" wingspan,
three actions (smokes, engine noise,
bump & go), rare 200   300   400

U.S. Air Force Smoking Jet.

"UFO-X05," 1970s, M-T Co.,
7-1/2" diameter, three actions 50   75   100

"Union Mountain Cable Lines,"
Monorail set, 1950s, T-N Co.,
car 8" long, 16-piece oval track,
22" x 32", minor toy 80   120   160

"United DC7 Mainliner," 1950s, Yonezawa
Co., 14" wingspan, five actions 200   300   400

"United Mainliner Stratocruiser,"
1950s, Linemar, 19-1/2" long,
13" wingspan, four actions 190   285   380

"United States Ocean Liner," 1950s,
Linemar Co., 14" long, three actions 200   300   400

"United States Ocean Liner," 1950s,
"Y" Co., three actions, 18-1/2" long 300   450   600

"Universal Machine Gun," 1950s,
T-N Co., 14-3/4" long, three actions 70   105   140

"USA NASA Apollo Space Ship,"
1960s, M-T Co., 9" long, four actions 150   225   300

"USA NASA Gemini Space Capsule,"
1960s, M-T Co., 9" long, four actions
(includes detachable astronaut) 120   180   240

"U.S. Army Machine Gunner,"
1960s, unmarked, 10" long, four actions 100   150   200

"U.S. Navy Pom Pom Gun," 1950s,
Remco Co., 20" long, four actions 80   120   160

"U.S. Royal Tire Mechanical Toy"
(Ferris wheel), souvenir for 1964-65
N.Y. World's Fair (now permanently
located at Uniroyal Co. on Rt. 94,
west of Detroit), includes plastic
figures, minor toy, 10" high, Ideal 100   150   200

"Video Robot," 1960s, S-H Co.,
10" tall, three actions 110   165   225

"V.I.P. the Busy Boss," 1950s,
S&E Co., 8" high, six actions 185   280   375

"Visible Ford Mustang," 1960s,
Bandai Co., 10" long, four actions 80   120   160

"Vision Robot," 1960s, S-H Co.,
11-3/4" tall, five actions 150   225   300

"Voice Control Astronaut Base,"
1969, Remco Co., 19" long, four
actions (includes plastic missiles
and phonograph records) 90   135   180

"Volkswagen Convertible," 1950s,
T-N Co., three actions, 9-3/4" long 250   375   500

"Volkswagen-Elektrik," 1950s,
Mignon Co., 8-1/2" long, three actions 70   105   140

	C6	C8	C10
"Volkswagen No. 7653," 1960s, Bandai Co., 10" long, three actions	90	135	180
"Volkswagen With Visible Engine," 1960s, K.O. Co., 7" long, three actions	80	120	160
"Volkswagen with Visible Engine No. 4049," 1960s, Bandai Co., 8" long, three actions	90	135	180
"Wagon Master," 1960s, M-T Co., 18" long, four actions	120	180	240
"Walking Bear with Xylophone," 1950s, Linemar Co., 10" high, seven actions	200	300	400

Walking Bear with Xylophone.

	C6	C8	C10
"Walking Elephant," 1950s, Linemar Co., 8-1/2" long, three actions	90	135	180
"Walking 'Esso' Tiger," 1950s, Marx Co., 11-1/2" tall, four actions	250	375	500
"Walking Itchy Dog," 1950s, Alps Co., 9" long, five actions	60	90	120
"Walky-Son" (Los), 1960s, rare, Geyper Co., four actions, 11-1/2" high, includes detachable guns and baton: See "Los Walky-Son"			
"Warpath Indian," 1950s, Alps Co., 12" tall, three actions	80	120	160

Warpath Indian, Nutty Mad Indian, Indian Joe.

	C6	C8	C10
"Wash-O-Matic" washing machine, 1940s, T-N Co., 5-3/4" high, 4-1/4" diameter, minor toy, includes lid	30	45	60
"Water Spouting Whale with Flopping Tail," 1950s, KKS Co., 13" long, minor toy	100	150	200
"Western Badman" Red Gulch Bar, 1960s, M-T Co., 9-3/4" high, eight actions, includes three plastic bottles and two plastic glasses	300	450	600

Western Badman Red Gulch Bar, Drinker's Savings Bank.

	C6	C8	C10
"Western Express," Locomotive, 1960s, Kanto Toy Co., 14" long, four actions	50	75	100
"Western Locomotive," 1950s, M-T Co., 10-1/2" long, four actions	50	75	100
"Western Special Locomotive," 1950s, M-T Co., 12" long, five actions	50	75	100
"Wheel-A-Gear" Robot, 1960s, Taiyo Co., 14" tall, five actions	250	375	500
"WHOH Skyway Patrol Helicopter," 1950s, M-T Co., 18" long, four actions	100	150	200
"Whirlybird Helicopter," 1960s, Remco Co., 25" long, three actions	80	120	160
"Whistling Showboat," 1950s, M-T Co., 14" long, three actions	120	180	240
"Wild West Rodeo," 1950s, Linemar, 6-1/2" long, 8" high, five actions, includes plastic bowl for bubble solution	100	150	200
"Windy the Elephant," 1950s, T-N Co., 9-3/4" high, three actions, includes celluloid ball and tin litho umbrella	140	210	280
"Winner 23," Rocket, 1950s, KDP Co. (Excelo), 5-1/2" long, minor action, includes rubber track	150	225	300
"Winner of the West" Overland Stagecoach with Four Galloping Horses, 1950s, Alps Co., four actions, 18" long	200	300	400
"Winston the Barking Bulldog," 1950s, Tomiyama Co., three actions, two cycles, 10" long	70	105	140
"Worried Mother Duck and Baby," 1950s, T-N Co., 11" long, 7" high, three actions	100	150	200
"X-7 Space Explorer Ship," 1960s, M-T Co., 7" diameter, four actions	90	135	180

Winner of the West.

	C6	C8	C10
"X-70 Robot," 1960s, T-N Co., 12-1/4" tall, five actions, rare	500	750	1000+
"X-1800 Space Vehicle," 1960s, M-T Co., 9" long, five actions (includes detachable plastic antenna)	140	210	280
"X-F 160 Jet Airplane," 1960s, K-O Co., 8" wingspan	80	120	160
"Yeti the Abominable Snowman," 1960s, Marx, 12" tall, four actions	300	450	600
"Yo-Yo Clown," 1960s, Alps Co., 9" high, three actions (includes plastic yo-yo)	170	255	340
"Yo-Yo Monkey," 1960s, Alps Co., 9" tall, three actions (includes plastic yo-yo)	140	210	280
"Yo-Yo Monkey," 1960s, Y-M Co., 12" tall, spring extension to 32", minor toy	100	150	200
"Yummy Yum Kitty," 1950s, Alps Co., 9-1/2" high, five actions	200	300	400
"Zero Fighter Plane," 1950s, Bandai Co., 12-1/2" long, 15" wingspan, three actions	160	240	320
"Zoom Motorboat," 1950s, K Co., 12" long, three actions	90	135	180
"Zoomer the Robot," 1950s, T-N Co., 8" tall, three actions	250	375	500

Worried Mother Duck & Baby.

SOLDIERS

The average price of American dime-store soldiers in the last edition was $50.74. In this edition it is $54.77, an increase of 8%.

RANKING A TOY SOLDIER

The price of a toy soldier depends not only on its desirability, but on its condition. "Mint" means the item is in the condition in which it was originally issued: perfect, regardless of age, not the slightest blemish. Needless to say this is a fairly rare state of affairs, but enough soldiers exist in mint condition to make it an employable term. Many people, hoping to dispose of toys, are tempted to term them "mint" when they are really "near mint," "very good," or sometimes even just "good." Inevitably this can result in unhappiness all around and, not infrequently, in a canceled sale.

"Very Good" indicates a soldier that has obviously seen use. It has signs of wear and aging, but most of its paint remains and in general it has a freshness to its appearance that makes it seem attractive and collectible to all but the most discriminating.

"Good" signals a soldier that has seen considerable wear, but has at least one-half to one-third of its original paint, and is basically sound. Collectors will collect it, but will often not be wholly satisfied with it as an example of their collection, and thus the price is well below that of the same item in mint.

A condition below good results in another drastic drop in price. Figures with missing parts, although otherwise in excellent condition, will usually fall into this lower-priced category. At present, a Barclay soldier minus its tin helmet (signaled by a large round hole in the top of its head) is worth about half of what it would otherwise bring. On the cast-iron soldiers, even small spots of rust can seriously lower their price, as can repainting of any of the soldiers. "Near mint," "fine," "very fine," and similar terms denote conditions between mint and very good, and are priced accordingly.

The key to grading is to avoid wishful thinking. Grading can sometimes be a problem for the uninitiated, but common sense will usually prevail, and when possible a consultation with an expert in the field can often clear up lingering doubts. A toy in its original box is worth up to 10 to 20 percent more if the box is in mint condition, with the price dropping as condition lessens.

BARCLAY

(See Vehicles, Animal-Drawn, Aircraft, and Miscellaneous)

Barclay Mfg. Co. was the largest manufacturer of toy soldiers in the U.S. prior to WWII, selling millions of figures annually. The company, named after Barclay Street in West Hoboken, New Jersey (now 10th Street in Union City), began in 1924 or late 1923, and was owned by an elderly Frenchman, Leon Donze (1865 or 1866-1950) and by Michael Levy (c. 1895-10/9/64), who became affiliated by buying a partnership. Levy eventually took over the company (around 1929) and it was he who turned it into a major manufacturer. From five employees in 1924, the company expanded to a pre-war peak of 400 workers and moved several times to increasingly larger quarters.

Barclay's soldiers came in four styles prior to WWII. Soldiers from the first group, probably produced almost from Barclay's beginning, were small, with moving arms on the mounted figures. The second group, approximately 3-1/4" high, seems to have debuted in 1935. These were designed and sculpted by Barclay employee Frank Krupp and had a separate tin helmet, which was subcontracted. These figures are rather stiff and are known by collectors as "short stride" because the marching figures' feet are close together. The third style, again by Krupp, also had a separate tin helmet, was more realistic, and is known as "long stride." These were on sale as early as 1936. In 1937 or 1938, a clip was designed to hold on the tin helmets, as the formerly glued-on helmets frequently came off, drawing complaints from the chain stores, such as Woolworth's, that sold Barclay toys. The fourth style was introduced about 1939-1940, when Barclay moved from slush-casting to die-casting its soldiers. It was by freelance artist Olive Kooken (1904-1964) and is known as "cast helmet," as the soldiers featured helmets that were an integral part of the figure.

Barclay's soldiers were made of antimonial lead, consisting of about 13% antimony and the rest lead. When slush-molding was done, only one mold was made of each figure. The lead would be poured into the mold, rocked, and immediately poured out, providing a hollow figure. Later, the die-cast molds produced a number of the same figure at the same time.

During WWII Barclay laid off all but four of its employees and did subcontract work. The company was never as successful after the war, and finally closed down in 1971, by this time employing only 50-75 people. Although Barclay assigned numbers to its figures from the beginning for its own records, many of the soldiers themselves bore no numbers. Figures listed with a question mark after the number are based on the memory of longtime Barclay employee George Fall, whose memory, judged against known Barclay numbers, is accurate, but not infallible.

Pre-1934

(All bold words and numbers are Barclay's own description)

	C6	C8	C10
(Ba) 87? Mounted Officer, moving arm holding sword, on rearing horse	26	39	52

Top, left to right: Ba, Baa, Bb, Bba, Bc
Bottom, left to right: Be, Bfa, Bg, Bh

	C6	C8	C10
(Baa) 87? Same as above on cantering horse	27	41	55
(Bb) 87? Mounted Officer, moving arm holding bugle, on rearing horse	27	41	55
(Bba) 87? Same as above, on cantering horse	26	39	52
(Bc) 87? Mounted Officer, moving arm holding pistol, on cantering horse	32	48	65
(Bd) 88? Mounted Cowboy with lasso	No Price Found		
(Be) 89? Mounted Indian, moving arm holding rifle	40	60	80
(BeA) Same as above, holding pistol	40	60	80
(Bf) 90? Mounted Cowboy with pistol	40	60	80
(BfA) 90? Mounted Cowboy with moving arm, holding rifle (horse's tail missing in photo)	35	53	70
(Bfa) Indian Chief on foot, 54mm high, blue and red-striped headdress, may look like Christies' I-14	No Price Found		
(Bfb) Indian Brave on foot, 54mm high, carrying rifle across stomach	No Price Found		

	C6	C8	C10
(Bg) 186? Cavalryman mounted, 2-3/4" high, no moving parts, modeled on French toy soldier, c. late 1920s-early 1930s	12	18	25
(Bh) **486 Cavalryman**, approx. 2-1/4" high, c. early 1930s, no moving parts	10	15	21
(Bi) Baseball fielder, approx. 1-7/8" high, c. 1920s	42	63	85

Left to right: Bi, Bj, Bk

	C6	C8	C10
(Bj) Baseball pitcher, c. 1920s	42	63	85
(Bk) Baseball batter, c. 1920s	42	63	85
(Bl) Mounted Indian on rearing horse	18	27	36
(Bm) **200 Jockey on Horse**	17	25	35
(Bn) **No. 87 Officer on Horse**, smaller size, c. 1931 (8 known)	125	188	250

Left to right: Bl, Bm

Bn
Courtesy Bill O'Brien

1934 and After

	C6	C8	C10
(BA) Paint Your Own Army Set No. 2003, c. 1934, boxed	120	180	240
(BAa) Paint Your Own Army Set No. 2003, larger size than above, same toys, with compartment for one more toy. Only 1 known		No Price Found	
(BAC) **89 Indian on Horse** (on catalog sheet with Ethiopians)	23	35	46

Top, left to right: BAC, BAD, B1, B1a
Bottom, left to right: B2, B2A, B2AA

	C6	C8	C10
(BAD) **90 Cowboy on Horse** (on catalog sheet with Ethiopians)	22	33	45
(B1) **89 Indian on Horse**	14	21	28
(B1-A) As above, Indian's head turned to his right	22	33	44
(B1a) **89 Indian on Horse**, two feathers (earlier)	26	39	52
(B2) **90 Cowboy on Horse**	15	22	30
(B2A) **90 Cowboy on Horse**, variation, thinner bullets in gunbelt, saddle not as long	12	18	24

	C6	C8	C10
(B2AA) **90 Cowboy on Horse**, variation, no bullets in gunbelt	50	75	100
(B2AAA) **100 Masked Rider on Horse**, only 1 known	350	525	700
(B2B) 100? "Masked Rider with Lasso," horse's tail down	25	38	50
(B2C) 100? "Masked Rider with Lasso," horse's tail up	18	27	36
(B3) 87? Mounted, in grey cap, intermediate size	35	52	70

Left to right: B2C, B3

Left to right: B3A, B4

Top, left to right: B5, B6, B7, B9, B10, B11
Bottom, left to right: B12, B13, B14, B15, B16

Left to right: B12, B12A
Photo by K. Warren Mitchell

	C6	C8	C10
(B3A) 87 Officer on Horse, in cap, khaki or grey, larger black, grey or brown horse	15	22	30
(B4) 87? Mounted in colored jacket and cap, may be Chinese or Japanese (horse's tail missing in photo)	24	36	48
(B5) 701 Flagbearer, tin helmet, short stride	13	19	26
(B6) 701 Flagbearer, tin helmet, long stride	11	16	22
(B7) 701 Flagbearer, cast helmet	11	16	22
(B8) 701 Flagbearer, Cuban flag variation painted for 10 Woolworth's in Cuba, cast helmet or pot helmet	No Price Found		
(B9) 701 Machine-Gunner, kneeling, short stride	8	12	16
(B10) 702 Machine-Gunner, kneeling, long stride	10	15	21
(B11) 702 Machine-Gunner, kneeling, cast helmet	11	16	23
(B12) 703 Sniper, kneeling, firing, short stride	10	15	21
(B12A) 703 Sniper, kneeling, firing, short stride, shorter rifle, in front of fingers fat portion of gun and thin portion of barrel about equal length	10	15	20
(B13) 703 Sniper, kneeling, firing, long stride, tin helmet	11	16	23
(B14) 704 Soldier on Parade, shoulder arms, short stride	9	14	19
(B15) 704 Soldier on Parade, shoulder arms, long stride, tin helmet	9	14	19

	C6	C8	C10
(B16) 705 Soldier at Attention (actually port arms)	11	16	22
(B17) 705 Soldier at Attention (actually port arms), cast helmet	11	16	22
(B18) 706 Soldier, charging, short stride	11	16	23
(B18a) Same as above, with shorter rifle, sling around hand, two known	425	638	850
(B19) 706 Tall, tin helmet, solid puttees	300	450	600
(B20) 706 Soldier, charging, tin helmet, long stride	55	82	110
(B21) 706 Soldier, charging, cast helmet	14	21	28
(B22) 707 At Attention, cast helmet	11	16	22
(B23) 708 Officer with sword, short stride	12	18	24
(B24) 723 Marine Officer, same as above, in blue	16	24	32

Top, left to right: B17, B18, B18a, B19, B20, B21
Bottom, left to right: B22, B23, B24, B25, B25a, B25b, B26, B27, B28
(B18a Courtesy Don Pielin)

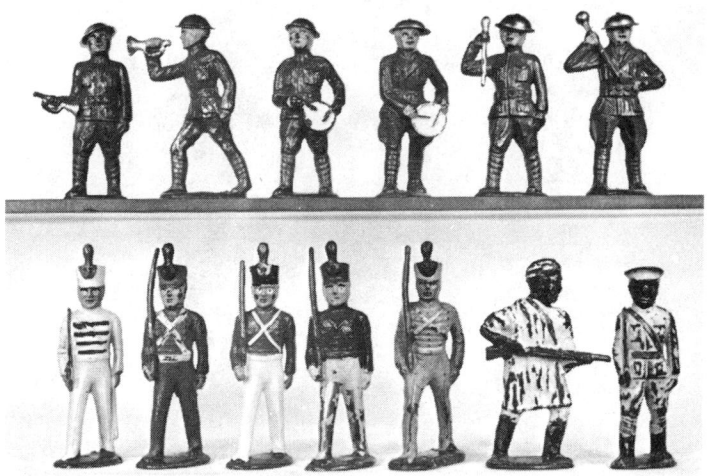

Top, left to right: B29, B30, B31, B32, B33, B34
Bottom, left to right: B35, B36, B37, B37a, B38, B39, B40

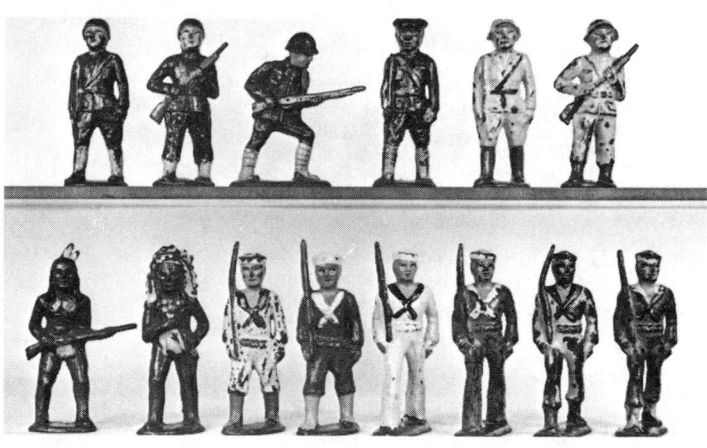

Top, left to right: B41, B42, B43, B44, B45, B46
Bottom, left to right: B47, B48, B49, B50, B51, B51a, B52, B52a

	C6	C8	C10
(B25) **708 Officer**, with sword, tin helmet, long stride	9	13	18
(B25a) 708 Officer with sword, tin helmet, long stride, no chest strap	60	90	120
(B25b) 723 Marine Officer with sword, tin helmet, long stride, no chest strap, in blue	60	90	120
(B26) **723 Marine Officer**, with sword, tin helmet, long stride	19	28	38
(B27) **708** Officer with sword, cast helmet	30	45	60
(B28) **708** Marine Officer with sword, cast helmet	35	52	70
(B29) **709 Bugler**, short stride	12	18	24
(B30) **709 Bugler**, long stride, tin helmet	10	15	21
(B31) **710 Drummer**, short stride	12	18	24
(B32) **710 Drummer**, long stride, tin helmet	13	19	26
(B33) **711 Drum Major**, short stride	12	18	25
(B34) **711** Drum Major, long stride, tin helmet	11	16	23
(B35) **743 West Point Officer**, short stride	8	12	17
(B36) **718 West Point Cadet**, with rifle, short stride	10	15	20
(B37) Same as above but painted as wooden soldier, only 4 known	300	450	600
(B37a) Same as B36, with line-and-dot eyes, white pants, white gloves	10	15	20
(B38) **718 West Point Cadet**, long stride	8	12	16
(B39) **724 Ethiopian Soldier**, c. 1935-36	100	150	205
(B40) **725 Ethiopian Officer**, c. 1935-36	125	188	250
(B41) **727 Italian Officer**, c. 1935-36	75	112	150
(B42) **726 Italian Soldier**, c. 1935-36	100	150	200
(B43) **724** Japanese, charging with rifle, c. 1937	60	90	120
(B44) Japanese Officer, c. 1937 (this is the original Ethiopian officer, painted as a Japanese)	82	123	165
(B45) Chinese or Mongolian Officer in steel helmet, c. 1937	125	188	250
(B46) Chinese or Mongolian Rifleman, c. 1937, pronounced right breast pocket	80	120	160
(B46a) Same as above, narrower face, faint right breast pocket	82	123	165

	C6	C8	C10
(B47) **717 Indian Brave**, rifle across waist	8	12	16
(B48) **716 Indian Chief**	7	11	15
(B49) **719 Sailor White Uniform**, marching, short stride	8	12	17
(B50) **720 Sailor Blue Uniform**, like above	10	15	21
(B51) **719** Sailor White Uniform, long stride, bell bottoms	9	13	19
(B51a) 720 Sailor in Blue Uniform, long stride, bell bottoms	11	16	23
(B52) **719 Sailor in White Uniform**, in puttees	8	12	16
(B52a) **720 Sailor Blue Uniform**, in puttees	10	15	20
(B53) **756 Sailor Flagbearer**, long stride	15	22	30
(B54) **721 Naval Officer**, short stride, tin top to cap	45	68	90
(B54a) Same as above, in blue	50	75	100
(B55) **721 Naval Officer**, short stride	12	18	24

Top, left to right: B53, B54, B55, B55a, B56, B57, B58
Bottom, left to right: B59, B59a, B60, B61

	C6	C8	C10
(B55a) **721 Naval Officer,** same as above, in blue 100	150	200
(B56) **721 Naval Officer,** long stride 11	16	23
(B57) **722 Marine,** short stride, tin top to cap 50	75	100
(B58) **722 Marine,** short stride 10	15	20
(B59) **722 Marine,** long stride 12	18	25
(B59a) **722 Marine,** long stride, white cap (probably post-war) 22	33	45
(B60) **757 Sailor with Signal Flags** 13	19	26
(B60a) **757 Sailor with Signal Flags,** flat underbase, minor variations in cap 13	19	27
(B61) **728 Machine Gunner Lying Flat** 9	14	19
(B62) **728 Machine Gunner Lying Flat,** cast helmet 10	15	20

Top, left to right: B72, B73, B74, B75, B76, B77
Bottom, left to right: B78, B79, B79a, B80, B81, B81a, B82, B83

Top, left to right: B62, B63, B64, B65
Bottom, left to right: B66, B67, B68, B69, B70, B71

(B63) **728 Machine Gunner Lying Flat,** cast helmet, lip of base extends under gun barrel 11	16	22
(B64) **750 Soldier Crawling** 11	16	22
(B65) **730 Soldier Signal Man with Flag** 13	19	26
(B66) **731 Soldier Pigeon Dispatcher** 15	22	30
(B67) **732 Soldier Telephone Operator** 9	14	19
(B68) **733 Soldier Bullet Feeder** (actually a shell) 9	13	18
(B69) **734 Soldier Ammunition Carrier** 11	16	22
(B70) **735 Soldier Range Finder** 10	15	21
(B71) **736 Soldier Sentry** 11	16	23
(B72) **737 Soldier Charging Machine Gunner,** tin helmet 9	14	18
(B73) **737 Soldier Charging Machine Gunner,** cast helmet 17	26	35
(B74) **738 Soldier Bomb Thrower** 11	16	23
(B75) **738 Soldier Bomb Thrower,** tall, tin helmet, solid puttees 300	450	600
(B76) **738 Soldier Bomb Thrower,** rifle off ground, tin helmet 15	22	31
(B77) **738 Soldier Bomb Thrower,** rifle off ground, cast helmet 18	27	36
(B78) **739 Soldier Fifer** 12	18	25
(B79) **740 Soldier French Horn** 11	16	23

	C6	C8	C10
(B79a) **Machine Gunner,** seated, cast helmet, bandage-type puttees 17	25	34
(B80) **741 Aviator** 9	14	19
(B81) **745 Navy Doctor,** in white, flat underbase 11	16	23
(B81a) **746 Army Doctor,** in brown, flat underbase 11	16	23
(B81A&B) **746 Doctor,** as above, inverted base 8	12	17
(B82) **767 Nurse,** kneeling 13	19	26
(B83) **744 Nurse,** hand on hip 10	15	21
(B83a) Same as above in blue 50	75	100
(B84) **751 Soldier Sharpshooter,** prone position 11	16	22
(B85) **762 Wounded,** sitting, arm in sling 12	18	24
(B86) **707 Sharpshooter,** standing, firing, short stride 10	15	21
(B87) **747 Sharpshooter,** standing, firing, long stride 10	15	20
(B88) **747 Sharpshooter,** standing, firing cast helmet 10	15	20
(B89) **748 Soldier Running,** with rifle, tin helmet 11	16	22
(B90) **748 Soldier Running,** with rifle, cast helmet 13	20	27

Top, left to right: B84, B85, B86, B87, B88
Bottom, left to right: B89, B90, B91, B92

Top, left to right: B93, B93b, B93c
Bottom, left to right: B93d, B93A, B93B

	C6	C8	C10
(B91) 749 Soldier Gas Mask, charging with rifle	10	15	20
(B92) 749 Soldier Gas Mask, charging with rifle cast helmet	13	20	27
(B93) 310 Army Motorcyclist	18	27	36
(B93a) 310 Cop on Motorcycle	25	38	50
(B93b) 310 Motorcyclist, head higher	25	38	50
(B93c) 310 Cop on Motorcycle, head lower	20	30	40
(B93d) 310 Motorcyclist, larger, markings on cycle, like B93A and B93B but cruder	25	38	50
(B93A) 310 Army Motorcyclist, post-war, dot eyes or none at all, larger, motor variation	25	38	50
(B93B) 310 Cop on Motorcycle, post-war, dot eyes or none at all, larger, motor variation	22	33	45
(B94) 715 Cowboy, with tin hat brim	10	15	20
(B94A) Same as above, badge, stripes, painted on vest	No Price Found		
(B95) 752 Cowboy with Lasso	9	14	19
(B95A) 752 Masked Cowboy with Lasso	8	12	16
(B95a) 752 Cowboy with Lasso, post-WWII version, lasso goes directly through hands	9	14	18

Top, left to right: B94, B95, B95A, B95a, B96
Bottom, left to right: B97, B97a, B98, B99, B100

	C6	C8	C10
(B96) 753 Cowboy with Two Guns, pointing one	8	12	16
(B97) 754 Indian Chief, tomahawk and shield	7	11	14

	C6	C8	C10
(B97a) Same as above, flat base, some with fatter legs	8	12	17
(B98) **755 Indian Bow and Arrow**	9	13	18
(B99) **756 Indian Chief**, long headdress, may only have been produced post-WWII	40	60	81
(B100) **757 Indian Brave**, standing with bow and arrow, may only have been produced post-WWII	15	22	31
(B101) **758 Camera Man**, kneeling, tin helmet	17	25	34

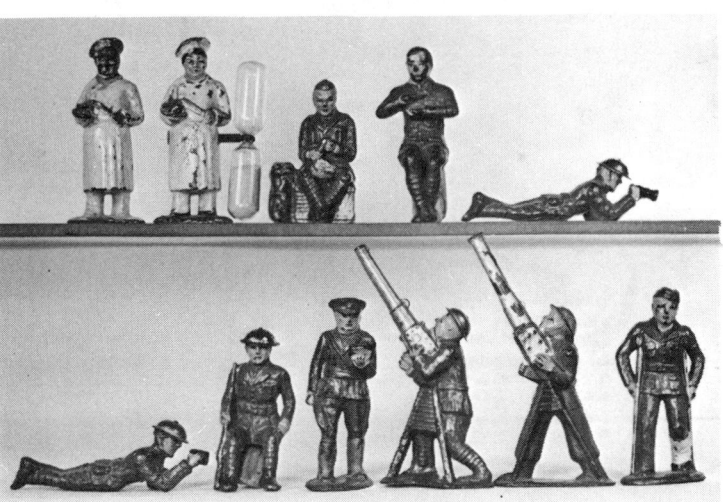

Top, left to right: B101, B102, B102a, B103, B104
Bottom, left to right: B105, B106, B107, B107a, B108, B109

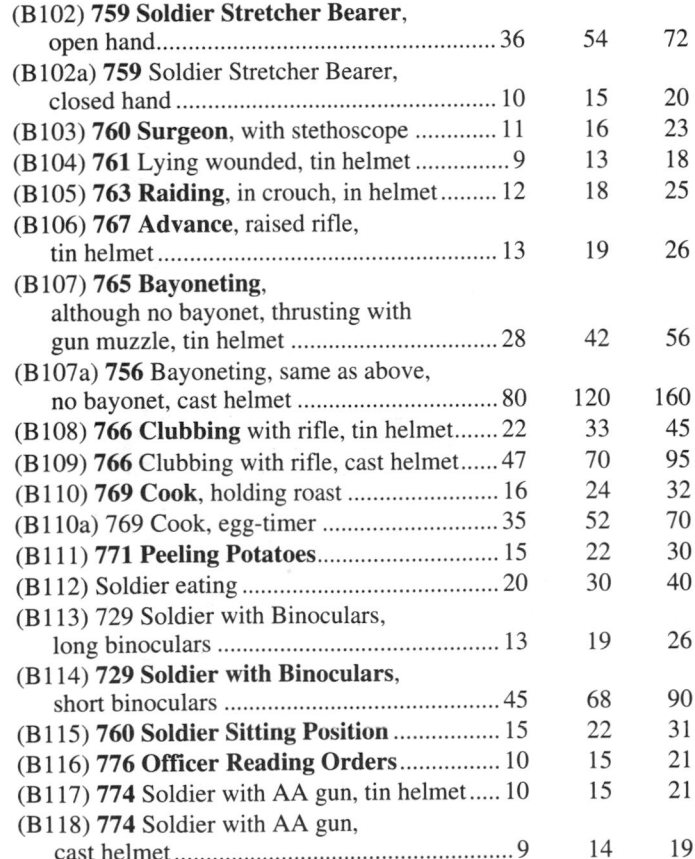

(B102) **759 Soldier Stretcher Bearer**, open hand	36	54	72
(B102a) **759** Soldier Stretcher Bearer, closed hand	10	15	20
(B103) **760 Surgeon**, with stethoscope	11	16	23
(B104) **761 Lying wounded**, tin helmet	9	13	18
(B105) **763 Raiding**, in crouch, in helmet	12	18	25
(B106) **767 Advance**, raised rifle, tin helmet	13	19	26
(B107) **765 Bayoneting**, although no bayonet, thrusting with gun muzzle, tin helmet	28	42	56
(B107a) **756 Bayoneting**, same as above, no bayonet, cast helmet	80	120	160
(B108) **766 Clubbing** with rifle, tin helmet	22	33	45
(B109) **766 Clubbing** with rifle, cast helmet	47	70	95
(B110) **769 Cook**, holding roast	16	24	32
(B110a) **769 Cook**, egg-timer	35	52	70
(B111) **771 Peeling Potatoes**	15	22	30
(B112) **Soldier eating**	20	30	40
(B113) **729 Soldier with Binoculars**, long binoculars	13	19	26
(B114) **729 Soldier with Binoculars**, short binoculars	45	68	90
(B115) **760 Soldier Sitting Position**	15	22	31
(B116) **776 Officer Reading Orders**	10	15	21
(B117) **774 Soldier with AA gun**, tin helmet	10	15	21
(B118) **774 Soldier with AA gun**, cast helmet	9	14	19

Top, left to right: B110, B110a, B111, B112, B113
Bottom, left to right: B114, B115, B116, B117, B118, B119

	C6	C8	C10
(B119) **775 Wounded on crutches**	13	20	27
(B120) **776 Standing at searchlight**, smooth lens, elevation wheel	50	75	100
(B120a) **776 Standing at searchlight**, smooth lens, no elevation wheel	55	82	110
(B121) **776 Standing at searchlight**, ridges along base (this and following have ridged lenses)	16	24	32

Left to right: B120, B120a, B121

(B122) **776 Standing at searchlight**, smooth base connected to searchlight, no elevation wheel	16	24	32

Left to right: B122, B123, B124, B125

	C6	C8	C10
(B123) **776** Standing at searchlight, low seat, not connected to searchlight 14	21	29	
(B124) **776** Standing at searchlight, high seat, two rivets in front of left foot 18	27	37	
(B125) **776** Standing at searchlight, high seat, no rivets in front of left foot 16	24	32	
(B126) **777** Marching with pack, tin helmet 13	19	26	

Left to right: B136, B137, B139, B140, B141

Left to right: B126, B127, B128, B129, B130

	C6	C8	C10
(B141) **789 Soldier Shooting Triple-Barreled Gun,** cast helmet, sitting 12	18	25	
(B142) **793 Soldiers In Boat,** cast helmet 32	48	65	

Left to right: B142, B143, B144, B145

(B127) **777** Marching with pack, cast helmet 10	15	21
(B128) **778** Officer with gas mask, cast helmet 13	19	26
(B129) **779** Firing from behind wall, cast helmet 33	50	67
(B130) **780** Falling with rifle, cast helmet 19	29	39
(B131) **781** Digging, cast helmet 26	39	53

	C6	C8	C10
(B143) **791 Soldiers with Mortar** 14	21	29	
(B144) **792 Airplane Mechanic,** prop spins, brace on back of engine bulges 24	36	49	
(B144a) Same as above, brace on back of engine doesn't bulge) 22	33	44	
(B145) **790 Soldier Shooting Anti-Tank Gun,** cast helmet 12	18	25	

Left to right: B131, B132, B133, B134, B135

(B132) **782** Leaning out, with field phone, antenna, cast helmet 33	50	66
(B133) **783** Crouching with binoculars, cast helmet 18	27	37
(B134) **784** Parachutist landing 12	18	25
(B135) **785** Skier in white, cast helmet, 1940, with separate metal skis, meant to be Finn, no left breast pocket 23	35	47
(B135a) As above, has left breast pocket, same value as above		
(B136) **785** Skier in white, no skis 13	19	26
(B137) **785** Skier in brown, no skis 26	39	52
(B138) 785 Skier in red, meant to be Russian, may not have been produced (listing based on memory) .... No Price Found		
(B139) **787** Diver with axe 350	525	700
(B140) **788 Soldier Marching with Gun Slung Behind Back,** cast helmet 10	15	21

Left to right: B146, B147, B148, B149, B150

(B146) **960 Surgeon and Soldier** 46	69	92
(B147) **951 Soldier Wireless Operator** 18	27	36
(B148) **952 Soldier Dispatcher with Dog** 25	38	50
(B149) **953** American Legionnaire in overseas cap, tall, made for 1937 Legion convention in New York, 12 known color combinations 145	218	290
(B150) 954? American Legionnaire flagbearer, tall, cloth flag, made in 1937, as above, five known 300	450	600

Left to right: B151, B151A, B152, B153

	C6	C8	C10
(B151) **961 At Typewriter**, with typewriter and table	38	58	77
(B151A) **770 At Mess**, typist alone, apparently meant to sit at mess table	7	11	15
(B152) **374 Army Motorcycle**, with sidecar	32	48	65
(B153) **45** "Machine Gunner and Driver"	28	42	56
(B154) **714 Pirate**	7	11	14

Left to right: B154, B155, B156, B157, B158, B159

	C6	C8	C10
(B155) **713 Knight**, with pennant	9	14	19
(B156) **712 Knight**, with shield	7	11	15
(B157) **610 Woman Passenger**, with dog	8	12	16
(B158) **611 Man Passenger**, overcoat over arm	7	11	15
(B159) **614 Red Cap**, with bags	9	14	19
(B160) **613 Porter**, with whisk broom	8	12	16

Left to right: B160, B161, B162, B163, B164, B165, B166

	C6	C8	C10
(B161) **612 Conductor**	8	12	16
(B162) **615 Engineer**	8	12	16
(B163) **616 Boy**	7	11	14
(B164) **617 Girl**	7	11	14
(B165) **618 Elderly Woman**	7	11	14
(B166) **619 Old Man**	8	12	16
(B167) **620** Minister walking	27	41	55
(B168) **621** Minister holding hat	9	14	18

Left to right: B167, B168, B169, B170, B171, B171a, B172

	C6	C8	C10
(B169) **621 Newsboy**	7	11	15
(B170) **622 Shoeshine boy**	15	22	30
(B171) **623 Detective with pistol**	65	98	130
(B172) **624 Burglar**	60	90	120
(B173) **625 Bride**	8	12	17

Left to right: B173, B174, B175, B176, B177, B178, B179

	C6	C8	C10
(B174) **626 Groom**	10	15	20
(B175) **627 Girl in Rocker**	10	15	20
(B176) **628 Boy Skater**	6	9	12
(B177) **629 Girl Skater**	6	9	12
(B178) **630-1/2 Man and Woman on Park Bench**	15	22	30
(B179) Seated man and woman in winter coats	15	22	31
(B180) **635 Man Speed Skater**	8	12	16
(B181) **636 Girl Figure Skater**	7	11	15

Top, left to right: B180, B181, B182, B183, B184, B185
Bottom, left to right: B186, B186a, B187, B187a, B188, B189

	C6	C8	C10
(B182) **801 Boy Scout Hiking** 20	30	40
(B183) **802 Boy Scout Saluting** 14	21	28
(B184) **803 Boy Scout Signaling** 17	26	35
(B185) **804 Boy Scout Cooking** 26	39	52
(B186) **850 Policeman**, arm raised 9	14	18
(B186a) 850 Policeman, figure eight base 9	14	19
(B187) **851 Fireman**, with axe 12	18	25
(B187a) Fireman, with axe, flat underbase 13	20	27
(B188) **852 Fireman**, with hose 14	21	28
(B189) **853 "Postman"** 8	12	16
(B190) **495 Man on Skis** 12	18	24

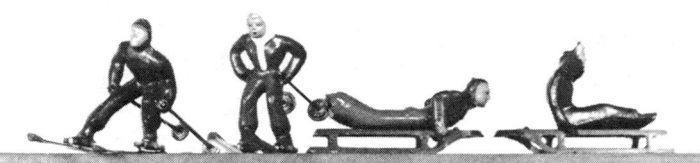

Left to right: B190, B191, B192, B193

	C6	C8	C10
(B191) **496 Girl on Skis** 12	18	24
(B192) **497 Man on Sled** 9	13	19
(B193) **498 Girl on Sled** 9	13	18
(B194) **499 Santa Claus on Sled** 20	30	40

Left to right: B194, B195, B196, B197

	C6	C8	C10
(B195) **500 Santa Claus on Skis** 26	39	52
(B195a) **500 Santa Claus on Skis**, no skis or poles and no holes for them 27	41	55
(B196) Santa Claus with holly sprig 35	52	70
(B197) Santa Claus seated, bag of toys at side, made to ride in sleigh 100	150	200
(B198) **510 One Horse Open Sleigh** (Sleigh, horse, seated man and woman) 44	66	88

B198

Left to right: B199, B200

	C6	C8	C10
(B199) **530 Man Pulling Children on Sled** 23	35	47
(B200) **535 Young Man Putting Skates on Girl Sitting on Bench** ... 50	75	100

Post-WWII

	C6	C8	C10
(B201) **701** Flagbearer, pot helmet 12	18	24
(B202) 703? Kneeling, firing rifle 26	39	52

Top, left to right: B201, B202, B203, B204, B205
Bottom, left to right: B206, B207, B208, B209

	C6	C8	C10
(B203) **705** Port Arms 12	18	25
(B204) **707** Order Arms 11	16	23
(B205) 708 Officer with Sword 11	16	22
(B206) **728** Prone Machine Gunner 10	15	20
(B207) 737 Tommy Gunner 11	16	22
(B208) **747** Standing Firing Rifle 10	15	21
(B209) 774 AA Gunner 13	19	26

Left to right: B210, B211, B212, B212a, B213

	C6	C8	C10
(B210) 777 Marching at Slope	10	15	21
(B211) **788** Marching, rifle slung	10	15	21
(B212) **789** AA gunner	12	18	25
(B212a) Cowboy, two pistols, one in air	22	33	45
(B213) Drum Major	32	48	64
(B214) Drummer	27	41	54

Top, left to right: B219, B220, B221
Bottom, left to right: B222, B223

Left to right: B214, B215, B216, B217, B218, B218a

	C6	C8	C10
(B221) **83 Two Soldier Crew at Searchlight**	14	21	29
(B222) **84 Two Soldier Crew at Mobile Cannon**	13	19	26
(B223) **85 Two Soldier Crew at AA Gun**	13	20	27
(B224) **187 Officer on Horse,** with pot helmet	42	63	85
(B225) **188 Cowboy on Horse,** with lasso	14	21	29
(B226) **189 Indian on Horse**	12	18	25
(B227) **190 Cowboy with Pistol on Horse**	15	22	30
(B228) **800 Black Knight w/ Sword & Shield**	12	18	24
(B229) **801 Knight w/ Red & Blue Shield & Sword**	14	21	28
(B230) **802 Knight w/ Orange & Black Shield & Sword**	8	12	17

Left to right: B215, B215a
Courtesy Charles Breslow

	C6	C8	C10
(B215) Bugler	27	41	54
(B215A) Bugler, buttons run down front of uniform	28	42	56
(B216) Clarinetist	28	42	57
(B217) Tubist	28	42	56
(B218) Sailor, white	20	30	41
(B218a) **720 Blue Sailor**	22	33	45

Barclay Podfoot Series

C. 1950s to 1971; most podfoot soldiers came in khaki and later, green. Add 50% to the price for green.

	C6	C8	C10
(B219) **81 Two Soldier Crew at Radar Equipment**	15	22	30
(B220) **82 Three Soldier Crew at Range Finder**	17	25	34

Top, left to right: B224, B225, B226
Bottom, left to right: B227, B228, B229, B230, B231

	C6	C8	C10
(B231) **803 Knight** w/ Red & Green Shield & Sword	8	12	17
(B232) **901 Soldier Flag Bearer**	7	11	14
(B232A) Same as above, in red (probably never made)			
(B233) **903 Soldier Sniper,** kneeling	5	8	11
(B233A) 903 same as above, in red (not shown)	45	68	90
(B234) **906 Soldier Charging**	6	9	13
(B234A) Same as above, in red (not shown)	52	78	105
(B235) **908 Soldier Officer**	6	9	12
(B235A) Same as above, in blue	32	48	64
(B235B) Same as above, in red	60	90	120

Top, left to right: B239, B240, B240a, B241
Bottom, left to right: B242, B242a, B243, B243a, B244, B244a

	C6	C8	C10
(B246) **948 Soldier Running**	6	9	13
(B246A) Same as above, in red	52	78	105
(B247) **950 Cowboy** w/ Pistol Shooting	18	27	36
(B248) **951 Cowboy w/ Rifle**	8	12	16
(B249) **952 Cowboy w/ Lasso**	8	12	16
(B250) **953 Cowboy w/ Pistol** (upraised)	8	12	16
(B251) **954 Indian** w/ Shield & Tomahawk	6	9	13
(B252) **955 Indian w/ Rifle**	7	11	14
(B253) **956 Indian** w/ Knife & Spear	6	9	13
(B254) **957 Indian w/ Bow & Arrow**	7	11	14
(B255) **960 Soldier, Wounded** w/ Crutches	15	22	31
(B255A) Same as above, in red	62	93	125

Top, left to right: B232, B233, B233a, B234
Bottom, left to right: B235, B235A, B235B, B236, B237, B238

	C6	C8	C10
(B236) **909 Soldier Bugler**	7	11	15
(B236A) Same as above, in red (not shown)	52	78	105
(B237) **919 Sailor White Uniform**	7	11	15
(B238) **920 Sailor Blue Uniform**	9	13	18
(B239) **922 Marine**	8	12	16
(B240) **928 Soldier Machine Gunner Lying Flat**	7	11	14
(B240A) Same as above, in red	45	68	90
(B241) **929 Soldier w/ Pistol Crawling**	14	21	28
B(241A) Same as above, in red	55	82	110
(B242) **937 Soldier, Charging Machine Gunner** (holding tommy gun)	7	10	14
(B242A) Same as above, in red	50	75	100
(B243) **938 Soldier Bomb Thrower**	7	11	15
(B243A) Same as above, in red	62	93	125
(B244) **941 Aviator**	7	11	14
(B244A) Same as above, in red	62	93	125
(B245) **947 Soldier Marksman**	6	9	12
(B245A) Same as above, in red	52	78	105

Top, left to right: B245, B246, B247, B248, B249
Bottom, left to right: B250, B251, B252, B253, B254

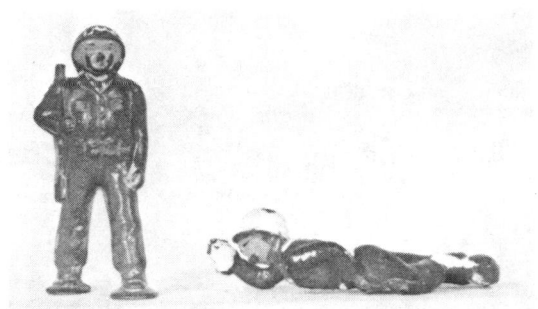

Left to right: B260a, B241a

	C6	C8	C10
(B256) **961 Soldier, Wounded Head & Arm**	14	21	28
(B256A) Same as above, in red (not shown)	62	93	125
(B257) **962 Nurse**	17	25	34
(B258) **974 Soldier, Anti-Aircraft Gunner**	7	10	14

	C6	C8	C10
(B258A) Same as above, in red	52	78	105
(B259) **977 Soldier Under Marching Orders**, marching	5	8	11
(B259A) Same as above, in red (not shown)	45	68	90
(B260) **988 Soldier, Marching w/ Gun on Back**, gun slung over shoulder	6	9	12
(B260A) Same as above, in red	50	75	100
(B261) **990 Soldier w/ Bazooka**	7	11	15
(B261A) Same as above, in red	52	78	105
(B262) **991 Soldier Flame Thrower**	7	11	14
(B262A) 991, same as above, in red	50	75	100

"Midi" Size (Smaller Than Podfoot)

	C6	C8	C10
(B263) **200** Flame Thrower	47	70	95
(B264) Bugler	32	48	65
(B265) Officer with binoculars	40	60	80
(B266) Talking on Field Phone	31	46	62
(B267) Advancing with Rifle	30	45	60
(B268) Marching, slung rifle	37	56	75
(B269) Firing Bazooka	30	4560	
(B270) Firing Tommy Gun	30	4560	
(B270A) Walking Forward, rifle at side, pointing down	30	4560	
(B271) Cowboy with Rifle	25	3850	
(B272) Cowboy with Pistol	25	3850	
(B273) Indian with Hatchet	25	3850	

Top, left to right: B255, B256, B257, B258, B258a, B259
Bottom, left to right: B260, B261, B261a, B262, B262a

Left to right: B271, B272, B273, B274
Photo by Don Pielin

Top, left to right: B270, B269, B267, B268, B265
Bottom, left to right: B270a, B263, B264, B266
Courtesy John Schmidt

Top, left to right: 350, 351, B295, 353, 354, 355, 356, 357, 358, 359
Bottom, left to right: 360, 361, 362, 363, 366, 369, 370, 371, 372, 373

	C6	C8	C10		C6	C8	C10
(B274) Indian with Rifle	25	38	50	(B285) **360 Hobo**	5	8	11
(B275) **350 Policeman**	5	8	11	(B286) **361 Newsboy**	5	8	11
(B276) **351 Man**	5	8	11	(B287) **362 Mailman**	5	8	11
(B277) **352 Woman**	5	8	11	(B288) **363 Fireman**	5	8	11
(B278) **353 Conductor**	5	8	11	(B289) **366 Peg Legged Gateman**	6	9	13
(B279) **354 Redcap**	5	8	11	(B290) **369 Woman Carrying Baby**	5	8	11
(B280) **355 Oiler**	5	8	11	(B291) **370 Little Boy**	5	8	11
(B281) **356 Brakeman**	5	8	11	(B292) **371 Little Girl**	5	8	11
(B282) **357 Engineer**	5	8	11	(B293) **372 Bride**	10	15	20
(B283) **358 Porter**	5	8	11	(B294) **373 Groom**	8	12	17
(B284) **359 Dining Steward**	5	8	11	(B295) Woman with dog	Extremely Rare		

MANOIL

(See also Vehicles, Aircraft, Ships and Miscellaneous)

Manoil began production of toy soldiers in 1935. It was in business as early as 1927 under the name Jack Manoil, turning out metal lamps and novelties at 34 West Houston Street in New York City. The company changed its name to Man-O-Lamp Corporation on July 11, 1928, and was owned by Maurice Manoil (12/4/1893-9/15/1974) and Jack Manoil (1/29/02-9/1/1955), two brothers who had emigrated from Rumania in the early 1900s. The final name change to Manoil Manufacturing Co., Inc. took place on July 7, 1934.

The two brothers were essentially partners. Maurice handled the business end of the operation and Jack oversaw the creative area, working closely with Walter Baetz (1894-1978), who sculpted all the company's toys.

Manoil advanced firmly into toy making in 1934, manufacturing seven vehicles. The company moved to other addresses as it grew, leaving Manhattan in 1937 for Brooklyn, and moving to Waverly, New York (which afforded excellent shipping by rail) in June 1940, employing 225 people at its peak.

With the onset of WWII, Manoil shut down, but resumed production of soldiers in a fine-grained composition form (employing sulfur) in January 1944. The pieces were brittle and ultimately unsuccessful, and their manufacture ended by the end of the year.

After WWII the company introduced several new lines of soldiers (also containing some of its pre-war soldiers and its appealing Happy Farm series), but they were no longer distributed as widely.

Manoil's soldiers have a distinctive jauntiness to them, at times veering on caricature, the latter trait becoming more pronounced as the years wore on. In 1953 the firm moved to a smaller location in Waverly, changing its name to Jack Manoil Specialty Company, but went out of business shortly after Jack's death. Baetz and Jack Manoil were both keenly interested in the company's soldiers and would work late into the night as they collaborated on ideas for them. One of Baetz's continuing concerns was to design the molds so that there was no structural weakness in the soldiers as a result of air bubbles. For this reason, many of Manoil's soldiers were redesigned a number of times with sometimes subtle, and sometimes broad, variations.

Unlike Barclay, Manoil also produced plastic toys, selling millions of vehicles and airplanes in its later years. Models of Manoil and Barclay soldiers are being reproduced (see Leading Collectors and Dealers), hollow-cast from the original molds.

All bold words and numbers are Manoil's own description.

	C6	C8	C10
(M1) **7 Flag Bearer,** hollow base version	45	68	90
(M2) **7 Flag Bearer,** second version	13	19	26
(M3) **7 Flag Bearer**	13	19	26
(M4) **8 Parade,** hollow base version	21	31	42
(M5) **8 Parade,** stocky version	10	15	20
(M6) **8 Parade,** campaign cap straight on head	21	31	43
(M7) **8 Parade,** number on back	32	48	64
(M8) **8 Parade,** fifth version	10	15	20
(M9) **9 Officer,** hollow base version	38	57	76
(M10) **9 Officer,** second version	11	16	22
(M11) **10 Bugler,** hollow base version	40	60	80
(M12) **10 Bugler,** second version	11	16	22
(M13) **11 Drummer,** hollow base version	38	57	75
(M14) **11 Drummer,** stocky version	13	20	27
(M15) **11 Drummer,** vertical drum	23	35	46

	C6	C8	C10
(M16) **12 Machine Gunner (Prone),** grass on base	13	20	26
(M17) **12 Machine Gunner (Prone),** flat base, no grass	14	21	28
(M18) **12 Machine Gunner (Prone),** spaces under body	30	45	60
(M19) **12 Machine Gunner (Prone),** no aperture between hands and gun	11	16	23
(M20) **12 Machine Gunner (Prone),** no aperture, pack on back	12	18	25
(M21) **13 Cadet,** hollow base, no buckle on belt	26	39	52
(M22) **13 Cadet,** second version	12	18	25
(M23) **14 Sailor,** hollow base	27	41	55
(M23a) Same as above, in blue	30	45	60
(M24) **Sailor,** second version	11	16	22
(M25) **15 Marine,** hollow base	33	50	66

Top, left to right: M1, M2, M3, M4, M5, M6, M7, M8
Bottom, left to right: M9, M10, M11, M12, M13, M14, M15

Left to right: M16, M17, M18

Top, left to right: M19, M20
Bottom, left to right: M21, M22, M23, M23a, M24, M25, M26

	C6	C8	C10
(M26) **15 Marine**, second version	10	15	21
(M27) **16 Ensign**	12	18	24
(M27a) **16 Ensign**, hollow base	30	45	60

Left to right: M27a, M27, M28, M29

	C6	C8	C10
(M28) **17 Signal Man**, hollow base version	23	35	46
(M29) **17 Signal Man**, second version	21	32	43
(M30) **18 Cowboy**, hollow base version	21	32	42
(M31) **18 Cowboy**, second version	10	15	21
(M32) **18A Cowboy with Hands Up**	12	18	24
(M33) **18A Cowboy with Hands Up**, subtle variation	12	18	24
(M34) **20 Doctor**, same as 20K, but in white	12	18	25

Left to right: M30, M31, M32, M34, M35, M36, M36a

	C6	C8	C10
(M35) **20K Doctor**, khaki	18	27	36
(M36) **21 Nurse**	10	15	21
(M36a) **21 Nurse**, no hem in skirt, shorter, etc.	14	21	28
(M37) **Indian**, with hatchet	75	112	150

Left to right: M37, M38, M38aa, M38a, M38b, M39

	C6	C8	C10
(M38) **22 Indian**, with knives	11	16	22
(M38aa) **22 Indian**, with knives, same as above, minor difference in hairline may be casting flaw	No Price Found		
(M38a) **22 Indian**, with knives, right toes off base	10	15	21
(M38b) **22 Indian**, with knives, sarong-like garment, only three known	No Price Found		
(M39) **23 Machine Gunner Sitting**, seated on four pillows, bullets feed from ammo box	13	20	27
(M40) **23 Machine Gunner Sitting**, markings under base	13	19	26

Left to right: M40, M41, M42

	C6	C8	C10
(M41) **Machine Gunner Sitting**, squarer-looking, markings near right leg	12	18	25
(M42) **24 Cannon Loader**	9	14	19
(M43) **25 Sniper (kneeling)**, hollow base, not Manoil, probably Paul Paragine	40	60	80
(M44) **25 Sniper (kneeling)**, folding rifle	165	248	330
(M45) **25 Sniper (kneeling)**, short thin rifle	16	25	33
(M46) **25 Sniper (kneeling)**, longer, thicker rifle	11	16	23
(M47) **26 Sniper**, folding rifle	188	282	375
(M48) **26 Sniper**	10	15	21
(M48a) **26 Sniper**, shorter rifle, angle different on underside of rifle	11	16	22

Top, left to right: M43, M44, M45, M46
Bottom, left to right: M47, M48, M48a, M49, M50

	C6	C8	C10
(M49) **27 Tommy Gunner**, bloated version	21	31	42
(M50) **27 Tommy Gunner**, second version	10	15	21
(M51) **28 Observer**	12	18	24

Top, left to right: M51, M52, M53, M54
Bottom, left to right: M55, M56, M57, M58, M58a

(M52) **29 Wounded Soldier (Walking)** 12	18	25
(M53) **30 Wounded Soldier (Lying)** 10	15	21
(M54) **30 Wounded Soldier (Lying)**, number on back, shorter head 11	16	22
(M55) **31 Bomb Thrower**, three grenades in pouch 14	21	28
(M56) **31 Bomb Thrower**, two grenades in pouch 14	21	28
(M57) **32 Stretcher Carrier**, no medical kit 11	16	23
(M58) **32 Stretcher Carrier**, medical kit.......... 12	18	25
(M58a) **32 Stretcher Carrier**, medical kit, number on back, buttons on uniform, different pockets and collar from above 50	75	100
(M59) **33 Sitting Soldier** 20	30	40
(M60) **34 Aviator** 16	24	32

Top, left to right: M59, M60, M61, M61, M61a, M62
Bottom, left to right: M63, M64, M65, M66

	C6	C8	C10
(M61) **35 Hostess**, in white	55	83	110
As above, in green	32	48	65
(M61a) **35 Hostess in Khaki**	150	225	300
(M62) **36 Soldier with Bayonet Charging**	21	31	42
(M63) **37 Soldier with Gun Charging**	24	36	38
(M64) **38 Soldier with Gun Butting**	27	41	55
(M65) **39 Soldier with Bayonet Jabbing**	26	39	53
(M66) **40 Soldier (Kneeling with Bayonet)**	30	45	60
(M67) **41 Soldier (Crouching with Hand Grenade)**	27	41	54

Left to right: M67, M68, M69

(M68) **42 Field Doctor (Crawling)** 30	45	60
(M69) **43 Officer (Lying Down-Shooting Revolver)** 27	41	55
(M70) **44 Crawling Scout with Gun**, left leg high when right leg on ground, only 3 known 90	135	180
(M71) **44 Crawling Scout with Gun**, left leg lower 26	39	52
(M72) **45 Observer (with Periscope)** 17	26	35
(M73) **46 Anti-Aircraft Gunner**, barrel of gun drops below arm..................... 11	16	23
(M74) **46 Anti-Aircraft Gunner**, barrel of gun ends at arm 12	18	24

Left to right: M70, M71, M72

	C6	C8	C10
(M75) **47 Anti-Aircraft Searchlight** 13	13	19	26
(M75a) **47** like above, with tin lens 55	55	83	110
(M75b) **47** like M75, number on back, helmet looks as if it was adapted to look like WWII helmet 19	19	28	39

	C6	C8	C10
(M79) **50 Bicycle Dispatch Rider** 17	17	25	34
(M80) **51 Motorized Machine Gunner** 33	33	50	66
(M81) **52 Motorcycle Rider,** number over rear wheel, grass base 21	21	31	42
(M81a) **52** Same as above, motor variation .... No Price Found			
(M82) **52 Motorcycle Rider** 20	20	30	40
(M83) **53 Sitting Soldier without Gun** 20	20	30	40
(M84) **54 Sitting Soldier Eating** 25	25	38	50
(M85) **55 Sitting Soldier at Table with Phone & Map** 16	16	24	32
(M86) **56 Paymaster** 85	85	128	170
(M87) **57 Camouflage Sharpshooter Lying Down** 14	14	21	29

Top, left to right: M73, M74, M75, M75a, M75b
Bottom, left to right: M76, M77, M78, M79

	C6	C8	C10
(M76) **48 Navy Gunner** 13	13	20	27
(M77) **49 Policeman** 10	10	15	21
(M78) **49 Policeman**, slightly larger 9	9	13	19

Top, left to right: M87, M88, M89, M89a
Bottom, left to right: M90, M91, M92, M92a, M93, M94

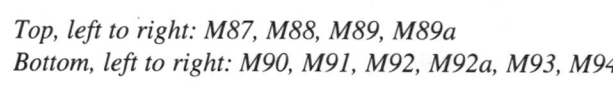

Top, left to right: M80, M81, M81a
Bottom, left to right: M82, M83, M84, M85, M86

	C6	C8	C10
(M88) **58 Parachute Jumper** 15	15	22	31
(M89) **59 Soldier Writing Letter** 35	35	52	70
(M89a) Same as M89, foot not curled up, pencil is flat, helmet rounder, fuller 37	37	56	75
(M90) **60 Cook's Helper with Ladle,** normal helmet 23	23	35	46
(M91) **60 Cook's Helper with Ladle,** helmet looks as if it was adapted to look like WWII helmet 60	60	90	120
(M92) **61 Soldier with Camera** 36	36	54	73
(M92a) **Soldier with Camera**, thinner arm 33	33	49	66
(M93) **62 Soldier with Gas Mask & Gun** 13	13	20	27
(M94) **63 Soldier with Gas Mask with Flare Pistol** 13	13	20	27

Top, left to right: M95, M96, M97, M98, M99, M100, M101
Bottom, left to right: M102, M103, M104, M105, M106

Top, left to right: M107, M108, M109, M110, M111
Bottom, left to right: M112, M112a, M113, M114, M115, M115a

	C6	C8	C10
(M95) **64 Soldier Playing Banjo**	55	82	110
(M96) **65 Deep Sea Diver**	12	18	25
(M96a) As above, painted gray	13	19	26
(M97) **65 Deep Sea Diver** with "65" on chest	12	18	25
(M98) **66 Soldier with Gun on Parade with Overseas Cap**	32	48	65
(M99) **67 Soldier with Gun and Pack Marching**	10	15	20
(M100) **68 Soldier Boxing**	42	63	85
(M101) **77 Lineman & Telephone Pole,** pole comes with two different-shaped bases, oval or diagonal	50	75	100
(M102) **78 Anti-Tank Gun,** round shield, 4 variations based on Vickers 2.95 mountain gun	16	24	33
(M103) **78 Anti-Tank Gun,** squared shield	18	27	36
(M103a) **78 Anti-Tank Gun,** angled shield	No Price Found		
(M104) **78 Anti-Tank Gun,** wooden wheels	27	41	55
(M105) **79 Soldier marching** with gun slung at angle	87	130	175
(M106) **80 Anti-Aircraft Machine Gunner**	11	16	23
(M107) **81 Machine Gunner and Helper,** aperture between hand and machine gun	17	25	34
(M108) **81 Machine Gunner and Helper,** no aperture	16	24	32
(M109) **82 Anti-Aircraft with Range Finder**	14	21	28
(M110) **83 Soldier Trench Mortar**	15	22	31
(M111) **84 Soldier with Shell**	17	26	35
(M112) **85 Aviator Holding Bomb**	14	21	29
(M112a) **Aviator Holding Bomb,** hand variation	15	22	30
(M113) **86 Aviator Mechanic with Propeller,** away from head	250	375	500
(M114) **86 Aviator Mechanic with Propeller,** orange prop, flat lower hand	52	78	105
(M114a) **86** Silver prop	60	90	120
(M114b) **86** Orange prop, curved lower hand	44	66	88

	C6	C8	C10
(M115) 87 Aviator carrying bomb sight	22	33	45
(M115a) 87 Aviator carrying bomb sight, smaller base	No Price Found		
(M116) **88 Radio Operator Standing**	35	52	70
(M117) **89 Radio Operator (Lying Down)**	17	26	35
(M118) **90 Soldier Digging Trench**	34	51	68
(M119) **91 Soldier with Barbed Wire,** wide-faced version	21	31	42

Top, left to right: M116, M117, M118, M119, M120
Bottom, left to right: M121, M121a, M122, M123, M124

Left to right: M123a, M123

	C6	C8	C10
(M120) **91 Soldier with Barbed Wire** 18	27	37
(M121) **92 Fire Fighter**, in white.....................50	75	100
(M121a) **92 Fire Fighter**, in gray.....................90	135	180
(M122) **93 Soldier on Guard Duty** 42	63	85
(M123) **94 Soldier Running with Cannon**, marked "Manoil USA," "1," cannon slants to right when looked at from above....23	35	46
(M123a) **94 Soldier Running with Cannon**, no markings, cannon straight from above, face narrower 19	28	38
(M124) **94 Soldier Running with Cannon**, wooden wheels, thin face 31	46	62
(M125) **99 Finn with Skis**.................35	52	71
(M126) **100 Finn Machine Gunner** 27	41	55
(M127) **101 Soldier Jumping with Chute** 52	77	105
(M127a) **101 Soldier Jumping with Chute**, foot variation, number in different place ....No Price Found		
(M128) **102 Soldier Jumping with Machine Gun** 46	69	92

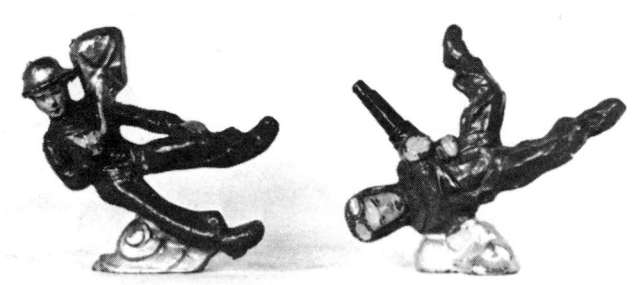

Top, left to right: M125, M126
Bottom, left to right: M127, M128

Happy Farm Series

According to the late Peter Ruben, a great number of color varieties and shades in this series exist, many of which can be related to the women who did the detail painting, and the season, as represented by 41/2 with long and short sleeve dresses. A number of Happy Farm figures were produced c. 1960 for the Smithsonian Museum, solid-cast with a patina or black finish.

	C6	C8	C10
(M129) **41/1 Bench**..............5	8	10
(M130) **41/2 Girl** 5	8	10
(M131) **41/3 Young Man** 5	8	10
(M132) **41/4 Man Carrying Sack on Back** 13	19	26
(M133) **41/5 Farmer Pitching Sheaves**...........13	19	26

Top, left to right: M129-M131, M132, M133, M134, M135
Bottom, left to right: M136, M137, M138, M139, M140

	C6	C8	C10
(M134) **41/6 Farmer Sharpening Scythe** 11	16	23
(M135) **41/7 Blacksmith Making Horseshoes**.....................13	20	27
(M136) **41/8 Farmer Cutting with Scythe** 13	19	26
(M137) **41/9 Farmer Cutting Corn**.................13	19	26
(M138) **41/10 Farmer Sowing Grain** 11	16	23
(M139) **41/11 Man Carrying Sheaves Under Arm** 12	18	24
(M140) **41/12 Scarecrow with Top Hat**...........13	20	27
(M141) **41/13 Farmer Carrying Pumpkin** 13	19	26

Top, left to right: M141, M142, M143, M144, M145, M146
Bottom, left to right: M147, M148, M149, M150, M151

	C6	C8	C10
(M142) **41/12 Darky Eating Watermelon** 82	63	84
(M143) **41/15 Scarecrow with Straw Hat** 12	18	24
(M144) **41/16 Watchman Blowing Out Lantern**.....................12	18	25

	C6	C8	C10
(M145) **41/17 Hod Carrier with Bricks** 16	24	33
(M146) **41/18 Man Chopping Wood** 12	18	25
(M147) **41/19 Mason Laying Bricks** 20	30	41
(M148) **41/20 Man Dumping Wheel Barrow** 14	21	28
(M149) **41/21 Old Man Fixing Shoe** 16	24	32
(M150) **41/22 Blacksmith with Wheel** 13	20	27
(M151) **41/23 Carpenter Carrying Door** 20	30	40
(M152) **41/24 Hound** 12	18	24

M156

M157

M152

M158

M159

(M153) **41/25 Carpenter Sawing Lumber** 13   20   27

M153

	C6	C8	C10
(M156) **41/28 Lady with Pie** 15	22	30
(M157) **41/29 Lady with Child** 16	24	32
(M158) **41/30 School Teacher** 22	33	45
(M159) **41/31 Girl Watering Flowers** 12	18	25
(M160) **41/32 Woman Lifting Hen From Nest** 14	21	29
(M161) **41/33 Woman with Butter Churn** 13	19	26

(M154) **41/26 Carpenter with Square** 32   48   64
(M155) **41/27 Shepherd with Flute** 31   46   62

M154

M155

M160

M161

Top, left to right: M162, M163, M164, M164a, M165
Bottom, left to right: M166, M167, M168, M169

	C6	C8	C10
(M162) **41/34 Woman Laying Out Wash on Grass**	14	21	28
(M163) **41/35 Woman Sweeping with Broom**	13	20	27
(M164) **41/36 Man Juggling Barrel**	27	41	55
(M164a) As above, in khaki	24	36	48
(M165) **41/37 Man Planting Tree**	20	30	40
(M166) **41/38 Girl Picking Berries**	23	35	47
(M167) **41/39 Farmer at Water Pump**	13	20	26
(M168) **41/40 Boy Carrying Wood**	14	21	28
(M169) **41/41 Stacks of Sheaves**	11	16	22
(M169) **41/41/ Haystack,** a rare variant, easily distinguished by the bottle and jug by its side	No Price Found		
(M169a) Boxed Happy Farm Set (10 pieces) mint with box, no standard contents	188	282	375

Manoil Composition

	C6	C8	C10
(MC1) Prone machine-gunner	26	39	53

Top, left to right: MC1, MC2.
Bottom, left to right: MC3, MC3a, MC4.
Courtesy Marjorie Ruben and the late Peter Ruben.

	C6	C8	C10
(MC2) Seated machine-gunner	24	36	48
(MC3) Motorcyclist	26	39	53
(MC3A) Motorcyclist, minor variation of above	26	39	53
(MC4) Firing camouflaged AA gun	24	36	48

Post-War

M170 through M176 were the first new post-WWII series, and were produced only for a limited time. On a trial basis, early production was also sold unpainted.

	C6	C8	C10
(M170) Flag Bearer, thin, c. late 1945	14	21	29
(M171) **46-A Parade**, thin, c. late 1945	18	27	36
(M172) Tommy Gunner, thin, c. late 1945	16	24	32
(M173) Machine Gunner Sitting, thin, c. late 1945	36	54	72

Top, left to right: M170, M171, M172, M173
Bottom, left to right: M174, M175, M176

	C6	C8	C10
(M174) Machine Gunner Lying, thin, c. late 1945	50	75	100
(M175) Sniper, thin, c. late 1945	27	41	55
(M176) **45/6 Parade**, thin, c. late 1945	14	21	28
(M177) **45/7 Flag Bearer**	20	30	40
(M178) **45/8 Parade**	10	15	21
(M179) **45/9 Combat**	14	21	29
(M180) **45/10 At Attention**, present arms	16	24	32
(M181) **45/11 Sniper**	19	28	38
(M182) **45/12 Tommy Gunner**	15	22	30
(M183) **45/13 Soldier with Bazooka Cannon,** some marked "45/18"	18	27	37
(M184) **45/14 Soldier with Shell for Bazooka,** some marked "46/14"	17	25	35
(M185) **45/15 General**, some "46/15"	78	117	155

Top, left to right: M177, M178, M179, M180, M181, M182
Bottom, left to right: M183, M184, M185, M186

	C6	C8	C10
(M186) **45/16 Mine Detector,** some "46/16" 22		33	45
(M187) **521** Flag Bearer, all 500s, c. 1950 19		29	39
(M188) **522** Parade 14		21	28
(M189) **523** Soldier in poncho 19		28	38
(M190) **524** Combat 15		23	31
(M191) **525** Aviator Holding Bomb 17		25	34
(M192) **526** Observer 19		28	38
(M193) **527** Aircraft Spotter 19		28	38
(M194) **528** Soldier with bazooka 14		21	28
(M195) **529** Motorcycle rider 28		42	56
(M196) **530** Machine gunner, lying 17		26	35
(M197) **531** Machine gunner, sitting 17		26	35
(M198) **532** Sniper, kneeling 18		27	36
(M199) **533** Soldier with gas mask with flare pistol 19		29	38
(M200) **534** Sniper 19		29	38

Left to right: M187, M188, M189, M190, M191, M192, M193

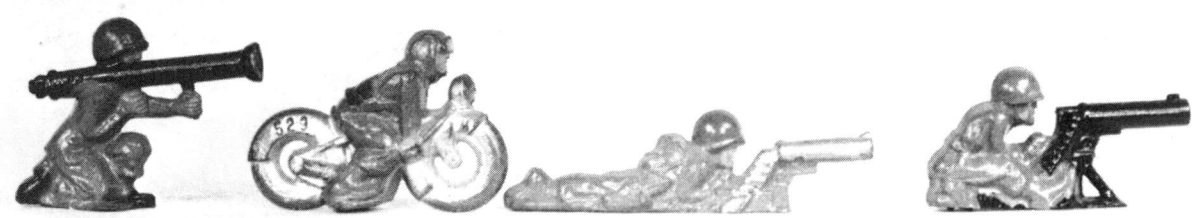

Left to right: M194, M195, M196, M197

Left to right: M198, M199, M200, M201, M202

Left to right: M203, M204, M205, M206

	C6	C8	C10
(M201) **535** Soldier throwing hand grenade	24	36	48
(M202) **536** Anti-Aircraft gunner	19	29	39
(M203) **537** Soldier with tommy gun	20	30	41
(M204) **538** Soldier firing up	19	29	39
(M205) **539** Stretcher bearer	55	83	110
(M206) **540** Wounded Soldier, lying	57	86	115

My Ranch Corral Series

	C6	C8	C10
(M207) **C-23** Cowboy Rider	7	11	15
(M208) **C-24** Cowgirl Rider	7	11	15

Left to right: M212, M213, M214

	C6	C8	C10
(M216) C28 Short Cactus	9	14	18
(M217) C14 Brahma Bull	9	14	19
(M218) C26 Large Cactus	13	20	26
(M219) C1 Fence	6	9	10
(M220) C25 Small Horse	11	16	23
(M221) C22 Horse for Mounted Cowboy	15	22	30
(M222) C22 Horse for Mounted Cowgirl	15	22	30
(M223) Small Gate	15	22	30
(M224) Large Gate	14	21	28

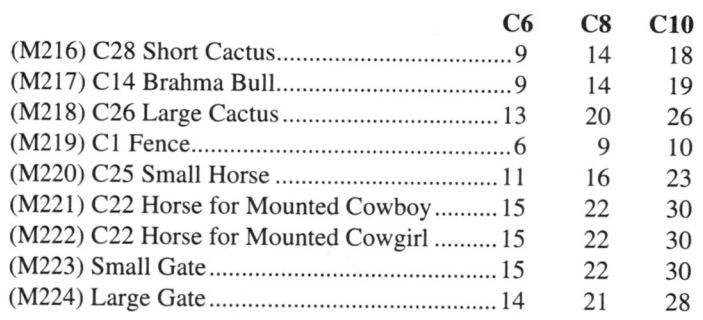

Left to right: M207, M208, M209, M210

	C6	C8	C10
(M209) **C-29 Mounted Cowboy**	28	42	57
(M210) **C-30 Mounted Cowboy Shooting**	27	41	55
(M211) C2 Ranch fence, gate	33	50	67
(M212) C12 Blanket over Fence Section	24	36	48
(M213) C18 Small Calf	7	11	15
(M214) C20 Bull, head turned	9	14	18
(M215) C19 Cow feeding	8	12	16

M211

Top, left to right: M215, M216, M217, M218
Bottom, left to right: M219, M220, M221, M222

GREY IRON

Grey Iron made the only 3-1/4" cast-iron soldiers. The company began in 1840 as the Brady Machine Shop in Mount Joy, Pennsylvania, where it has remained to this day. In 1881 the company was organized as the Grey Iron Casting Company, Limited. As early as 1903 it was manufacturing toy banks and stoves, cap pistols, wheeled toys and trains, as well as a number of non-toy items. On August 14, 1917, the company was granted two patents for their 40mm solid cast-iron Grey Klip Armies, which they manufactured through 1941, the last of the series emerging in 1938 as "Uncle Sam's Defenders," which were painted khaki rather than nickel-plated as the earlier versions had been. The soldiers were not successful at first, but with the advent of a new distributor the company was swamped with orders, and in January 1933, introduced a new line of thirty-five different cast-iron soldiers that were approximately 3" tall. Four Revolutionary War soldiers (an infantryman, a foot officer, a flag-bearer, and a mounted officer) may have been introduced earlier, as they are numbered lower, but were not part of the 1933 announcement.

The figures tended to be slight and, while apparently successful, were superseded in July 1936 by Grey's "Iron Men" series, slightly larger, more robust models that continued to be sold until WWII ended all toy production. There were at least two designers for the soldiers: Edward Musser and Samuel S. Schmidt. The soldiers were hand-poured and then painted on an assembly-line basis, and at least initially were sold for a dime, while their competitors charged a nickel.

Grey is still in business today as the John Wright division of Donsco, and has recently been producing, on an erratic basis, some unpainted soldiers from its old molds. Some years ago the author saw, at a Pennsylvania flea market, some crude, cast-iron Continental Soldiers, about 2-1/2" high, which he believes may be early Grey Iron. None have surfaced since and there is no evidence that Grey made them; however, they would be valuable to serious collectors, and in mint would probably bring about $40 apiece.

All bold words and numbers are Grey Iron's own description.

Greyklip Armies

	C6	C8	C10
(GA) Set 1/Company A, at attention, consists of bugler, officer, flagbearer, drummer, rifleman, price per each 2		3	4

GREY IRON (GB) Set 2, Company B. Courtesy Karl Zipple.

GREY IRON (GA) Set 1, Company A. Courtesy Karl Zipple.

	C6	C8	C10
(GB) Set 2/Company B, marching, consists of bugler, officer, flagbearer, drummer, rifleman, price per each 2.25		3.38	4.50
(GC) Set 3/Company C, charging, consists of bugler, officer, flagbearer, drummer, rifleman, price per each 2.25		3.38	4.50
(GD) Set 4/Troop D, consists of four mounted troopers, one mounted officer, troopers all look alike, price per each 3.50		5.25	7

GREY IRON (GC) Set 3, Company C. Courtesy Karl Zipple.

GREY IRON (GD) Set 4, Troop D. Courtesy Karl Zipple.

GREY IRON (GE) Set 5, Battery E. Courtesy Don Pielin.

GREY IRON (GF) Set 6, Battery F. Courtesy Don Pielin.

	C6	C8	C10
(GE) Set 5/Battery E, 2-piece set, led by officer from Troop D, second piece is a gun limber with four horses, several attached soldiers, price for second piece	7	11	14
(GF) Set 6/Battery F, consists of shell stack, loader bending, loader standing, gunner, cannon, price per each, shells double	4.50	6.75	9
(GG) Set 5/Aviator Corps, consists of pilot (two of the same figure in set) and plane with detachable wing, price for set	70	105	142
(GH) Uncle Sam's Defenders, consists of charging rifleman, machine gunner, charging officer, rifleman at attention, flagbearer, officer saluting, price per each (double the price on saluting officer and flagbearer)	3	4.50	6

GREY IRON (GG) Set 5, Aviation Corps (above two photos). Courtesy the late Karl Zipple.

End Greyklip Armies

GREY IRON (GH) Uncle Sam's Defenders.

	C6	C8	C10
(G1) **1 Colonial Soldier**	14	21	28
(G2) **1A Colonial Foot Officer**	14	21	28
(G3) **1B Colonial Color-Bearer**	175	263	350
(G3a) 1B Colonial Color-Bearer, 1950s version, with rifle barrel drilled out for flag	25	38	50
(G4) **1MA Colonial Mounted Officer**	24	36	48
(G5) **2 Cadet**, early version	10	15	21

*Left to right:
G10, G10A*

Left to right: G1, G2, G3, G3a, G4
Photo by Ed Poole.

	C6	C8	C10
(G6) **2 Cadet**	14	21	28
(G7) **2A Cadet Officer**, early	11	16	22
(G8) **2A Cadet Officer**	14	21	29
(G9) **3 U.S. Infantry, Shoulder Arms,** early	9	14	19
(G10) **3 U.S. Infantry, Shoulder Arms**	7	11	15
(G10a) Same as above, no tie		No Price Found	
(G11) **3/1 U.S. Infantry, Port Arms**	10	15	21
(G12) **3A U.S. Infantry Officer**, early	9	13	18
(G13) **3A U.S. Infantry Officer**	9	13	18

	C6	C8	C10
(G14) **3AP Traffic Officer,** same as above, in blue	12	18	24
(G15) **3AR Red Cross Officer,** same as above, with armband	23	35	46
(G16) **4 U.S. Infantry, Port Arms,** early	10	15	20
(G17) **4A U.S. Doughboy Officer with Field Glasses**	15	22	30
(G18) **4/1 U.S. Doughboy Signaling**	15	22	30
(G19) **4/2 U.S. Doughboy Combat Trooper**	13	20	27
(G20) **4/3 U.S. Doughboy with Range Finder**	38	57	76

Top, left to right: G19, G20, G21, G22, G23
Bottom, left to right: G24, G25, G26, G27, G28, G29, G30

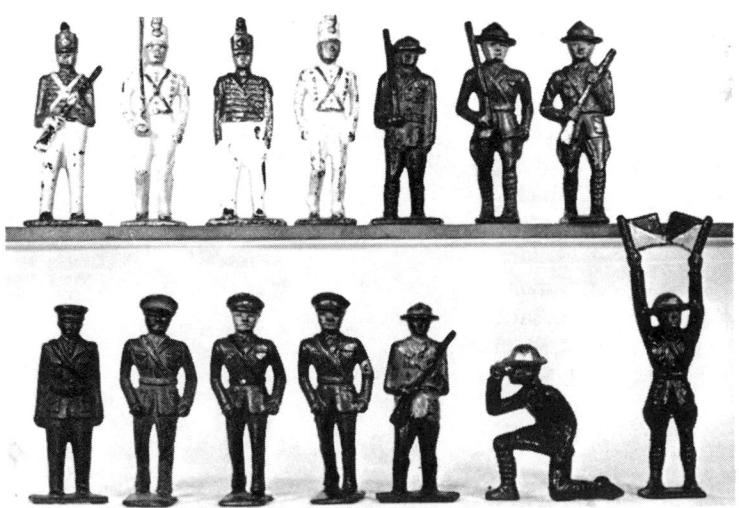

Top, left to right: G5, G6, G7, G8, G9, G10, G11
Bottom, left to right: G12, G13, G14, G15, G16, G17, G18

	C6	C8	C10
(G21) **4/4 U.S. Doughboy Ammunition Carrier**	42	63	85
(G22) **4/5 U.S. Doughboy Sharpshooter**	13	20	27
(G23) **4/6 U.S. Doughboy with Bayonet**	13	19	26
(G24) **5 U.S. Infantry Charging**, early	7	11	15
(G25) **6 U.S. Doughboy, Port Arms,** early	9	14	19
(G26) **6 U.S. Doughboy, Shoulder Arms**	8	12	16

	C6	C8	C10
(G27) **6A U.S. Doughboy Officer**, early 10	15	21
(G28) **6A U.S. Doughboy Officer** 9	14	19
(G29) **6/1 U.S. Doughboy Charging** 9	14	18
(G30) **6/2 U.S. Doughboy Sentry** 11	16	23
(G31) **6/3 U.S. Doughboy Bomber**, crawling 12	18	24

Top, left to right: G31, G32, G33, G34
Bottom, left to right: G35, G37, G38

	C6	C8	C10
(G32) **6/4 U.S. Doughboy Grenade Thrower** 17	26	35
(G33) **7 U.S. Doughboy Charging**, early 10	15	21
(G34) **8M U.S. Cavalryman**, early 18	27	36
(G35) **8M U.S. Cavalryman** 18	27	36
(G36) **8M U.S. Cavalry Color Bearer with Silk Flag** (not shown, same as G34) .... No Price Found		
(G37) **8MA U.S. Cavalry Officer**, early 20	30	40
(G38) **8MA U.S. Cavalry Officer** 21	31	42
(G39) **9 U.S. Marine**, early 9	14	19

Top, left to right: G39, G40, G41, G42, G43, G44
Bottom, left to right: G45, G46, G47, G48, G49

	C6	C8	C10
(G40) **9 U.S. Marine** 13	20	26
(G41) **10 Royal Canadian Police**, early 12	18	24
(G42) **10 Royal Canadian Police** 16	24	33
(G43) **10M Royal Canadian Mounted Police** (same as G34) 21	32	43
(G44) **10M Royal Canadian Mounted Police** (same as G35) 26	39	52
(G45) **11 Indian**, with hatchet, early 8	12	16
(G46) **11 Indian Chief**, with knife 9	14	19
(G47) **11/1 Indian Brave**, shielding eyes 14	21	28
(G48) **11/2 Chief Attacking**, upraised tomahawk 50	75	100
(G49) **11M Indian Mounted**, early 18	27	37
(G50) **11M Indian Mounted**, lying on horse 37	56	75

Top, left to right: G50, G51, G52, G53, G54
Bottom, left to right: G55, G56, G57, G58, G59

	C6	C8	C10
(G51) **11/1M Indian Scout Mounted**, firing pistol rearward 112	168	225
(G52) **12 Cowboy**, early 10	15	20
(G53) **12 Cowboy** 9	14	18
(G54) **12/1/Hold-Up Man** 11	16	23
(G55) **12/2 Cowboy with Lasso**, with lasso price is 55.00 in mint 23	36	47
(G56) **12/3 Bandit**, surrendering 54	81	108
(G57) **12M Cowboy Mounted**, early 20	30	41
(G58) **12M Cowboy Mounted** 28	42	56
(G59) **12/1M Masked Cowboy Mounted** 162	243	325
(G60) **13 U.S. Machine Gunner**, early 10	15	21
(G61) **13 U.S. Machine Gunner** 8	12	17
(G62) **13/1 U.S. Machine Gunner** 9	14	19
(G63) **14 U.S. Sailor**, in blue, early 10	15	20
(G64) **14 U.S. Sailor**, in white, early 10	15	20
(G65) **14 U.S. Sailor**, in blue 9	14	19
(G66) **14W U.S. Sailor**, in white 9	14	19
(G67) **14A U.S. Naval Officer**, early, in blue 9	14	19
(G68) **14AW U.S. Naval Officer**, early, in white 10	15	20
(G69) **14A U.S. Naval Officer**, in blue 10	15	21
(G70) **14AW U.S. Naval Officer**, in white 9	14	19
(G71) **14/1W U.S. Sailor Signalman** 15	22	31
(G72) **15/1 Boy Scout Saluting**, early 11	16	23

Top, *left to right: G60, G61, G62, G63, G64*
Bottom, *left to right: G65, G66, G67, G68, G69, G70, G71*

Top, *left to right: G86, G87, G88, G89, G90, G91, G92*
Bottom, *left to right: G93, G94, G95, G96, G97*

	C6	C8	C10
(G73) **15/2 Boy Scout Walking,** early 11	16	22
(G74) **16/1 Pirate Boy** 14	21	28
All pirates c. 1935, were also sold as a Treasure Island set, with either a tent or treasure chest included. The pirates were meant to represent Jim, Captain Flint, Long John, Blind Pew, and Billie Bones.			
(G75) **16/2 Pirate Chief** 12	18	25
(G76) **16/3 Pirate with Dagger** 12	18	24
(G77) **16/4 Pirate with Hook** 11	16	23
(G78) **16/5 Pirate with Sword** 12	18	24
(G79) **17/1 Legion Drum Major,** early 25	38	50
(G80) **17/1 Legion Drum Major** 11	16	22
(G81) **17/2 Legion Bugler,** early 11	16	22
(G82) **17/2 Legion Bugler** 9	14	19
(G83) **17/3 Legion Drummer,** early 11	16	23
(G84) **17/3 Legion Drummer** 10	15	21
(G85) **17/4 Legion Color Bearer** 10	15	20
(G86) **18/1 Ethiopian Tribesman,** c. 1936 27	41	54
(G87) **18/2 Ethiopian Chief** 37	55	74

	C6	C8	C10
(G88) **18/3 Ethiopian Soldier, Shoulder Arms** 32	48	64
(G89) **18/3A Ethiopian Officer** 35	52	69
(G90) **18/5 Ethiopian Soldier Charging** 36	54	72
(G91) Italian or English Desert Infantryman 115	172	230
(G92) Italian or English Desert Officer 75	112	150
(G93) **19 Knight in Armor** 10	15	20
(G94) **20 Red Cross Doctor** 16	24	32
(G95) **21 Stretcher Bearer** 20	30	40
(G96) **22 Stretcher with Patient** 15	22	30
(G97) **22/1/Wounded Sitting** 45	68	90
(G98) **22/2 Wounded on Crutches** 23	35	47

Top, *left to right: G98, G99, G100, G101, G102*
Bottom, *left to right: G103, G104, G105*

	C6	C8	C10
(G99) **23 Red Cross Nurse** 10	15	20
(G100) **25 Aviator** (24 is non-soldier) 22	33	44
(G101) Ski Trooper, c. 1940, with skis four times the noted price 12	18	25
(G102) Greek Evzone 55	82	110

Top, *left to right: G72, G73, G74, G75, G76, G77, G78*
Bottom, *left to right: G79, G80, G81, G82, G83, G84, G85*

	C6	C8	C10
(G103) **75 Radio Set, Operator and Aerial** ... 155	232	310
(G103A) **75 Radio Set, Operator Only** ... 49	74	98
(G104) **D26 Nurse and Wounded Soldier** ... 100	150	200
(G105) **D27 Doughboy Supporting Wounded Soldier** ... 130	195	260
(G106) **U.S. Cavalryman, earliest version** ... 70	105	140
(G107) **U.S. Cavalry Officer, earliest version** ... 70	105	140

Left to right: G107, G106
Photo by K. Warren Mitchell.

	C6	C8	C10
(G108) **6AF Foreign Legion Officer** ... 19	29	38
(G109) **6F Foreign Legion-Shoulder Arms** ... 17	25	34
(G110) **6/1F Foreign Legion Charging** ... 17	25	34
(G111) **6/3 Foreign Legion Bomber** ... 40	60	80
(G112) **13F Foreign Legion Machine Gunner** ... 17	26	35
(G113) **8A/F Foreign Legion Cavalry Officer** ... 31	46	63

Top, left to right: G108, G109, G110, G111
Bottom, left to right: G112, G113, G114

	C6	C8	C10
(G114) **8/F Foreign Legion Cavalryman** ... 34	51	68
(G115) Foreign Legion Stretcher Bearer, only one known ... No Price Found		

American Family Series
(Approximately 2-1/4" high)

The American Family Travels

	C6	C8	C10
T-1 **Man in traveling suit** ... 6	9	12
T-2 **Woman in traveling costume** ... 6	9	12
T-3 **Boy in traveling suit** ... 6	9	12
T-4 **Girl in traveling suit** ... 7	10	14
T-5 **Conductor** ... 6	9	12
T-6 **Engineer** ... 7	10	14
T-7 **Porter** ... 8	12	16
T-8 **Policeman** ... 7	11	15
T-9 **Postman** ... 6	9	13
T-10 **Newsboy** ... 9	14	18
T-11 **Preacher** ... 8	12	16
T-12 **Old Colored Man-sitting** ... 10	15	20
T-13 **Seat** ... 5	8	10

Top, left to right: T1, T2, T3, T4, T5, T6, T7
Bottom, left to right: T8, T9, T10, T11, T12-T13

Top, left to right: F1, F2, F3, F4, F5
Bottom, left to right: F6, F7, F8, F9

The American Family on the Farm

	C6	C8	C10
F-1 Farmer	5	8	11
F-2 Farmer's Wife	6	9	13
F-3 Girl	7	10	14
F-4 Hired Man digging	6	9	12
F-5 Horse	4	6	9
F-6 Cow	5	8	10
F-7 Calf	5	8	10
F-8 Pig	4	6	9
F-9 Sheep	4	6	9

Top, left to right: F10, F11, F12
Bottom, left to right: F13, F14

F-10 Goat	4	6	9
F-11 Goose	4	6	9
F-12 Dog	4	6	9
F-13 Gate with Post	10	15	20
F-14 Fence	8	12	16

Top, left to right: H1, H2, H3, H4, H5, H6 on H13
Bottom, left to right: H7, H8, H9, H10, H11, H12

The American Family at Home

	C6	C8	C10
H-1 Man with watering can	7	11	14
H-2 Woman with basket	8	12	16
H-3 Boy flying kite	10	15	20
H-4 Girl skipping rope	12	18	24
H-5 Old man sitting	5	8	10
H-6 Old woman sitting	5	8	10
H-7 Colored cook	11	16	22
H-8 Colored man digging	18	27	37
H-9 Garageman	8	12	16
H-10 Delivery Boy	7	11	15
H-11 Milkman	7	11	15
H-12 Dog	4	6	9
H-13 Lawn Seat	5	8	10

The American Family on the Beach

	C6	C8	C10
B-1 Man in bathing suit	13	19	26
B-2 Woman in bathing suit	13	19	26
B-3 Boy in summer suit	6	9	12
B-4 Girl in slacks	9	14	18

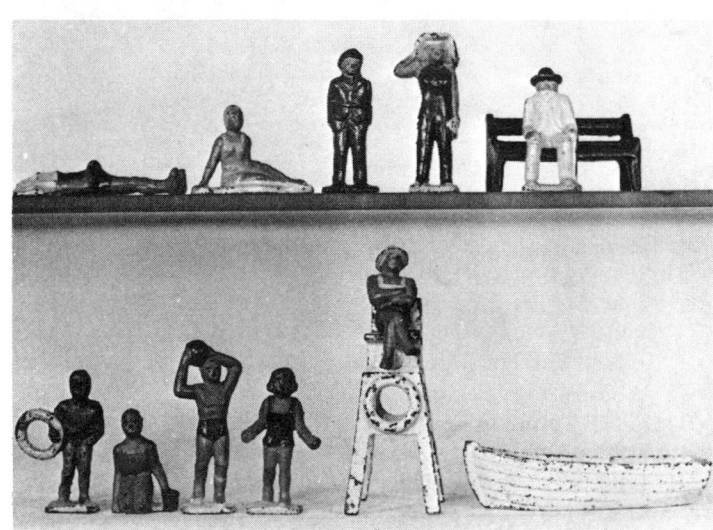

Top, left to right: B1, B2, B3, B4, B5 on B13
Bottom, left to right: B6, B7, B8, B9, B10, B11, B12

B-5 Old Man Sitting	3	5	7
B-6 Boy with Life Preserver	10	15	21
B-7 Girl with Sand Pail	10	15	21
B-8 Boy with Ball	10	15	21
B-9 Girl Catching Ball	10	15	21
B-10 Life Guard	13	19	26
B-11 Life Guard's Chair	14	21	28
B-12 Life Boat	14	21	28
B-13 Bench	4	6	8
B-14 Cabana			No Price Found

The American Family on the Ranch

R-1 Cowboy with lasso	12	18	24
R-2 Cowboy Rider	19	28	38
R-3 Cowboy squatting	8	12	17
R-4 Boy in Cowboy Suit	8	12	16
R-5 Girl in Riding Suit	9	14	18

	C6	C8	C10
R-6 Cowgirl Rider	11	16	22
R-7 Stallion	8	12	17
R-8 Bucking Bronco	10	15	20
R-9 Colt	6	9	12
R-10 Burro	7	11	15
R-11 Calf	5	8	11
R-15 Rooster and Chickens	4	6	8
R-16 Three Ducks	5	8	10

The Champions on the Diamond

	C6	C8	C10
M69 Fielder in Position, approx. 1-1/2" high	17	26	35

Top, left to right: R1, R2-R8, R3, R4, R5, R6-R9
Bottom, left to right: R10, R11, R15, R16

AUBURN RUBBER

Auburn (also Aub-Rub'r) was founded in 1913 in Auburn, Indiana, as the Double Fabric Tire Corporation, making auto tubes and tires for Model T Fords, etc. It produced its first toy in 1935, when it manufactured five soldiers. The prototype was a Palace Guard that Auburn president and chief stockholder A.L. Murray had obtained in England. The model was taken to a local pattern-maker and then the company made original molds from lead and molded sample toys. These samples were taken to an artist and decorated per Murray's instructions. They immediately caught on when presented to buyers.

The soldiers were molded in 24" rubber presses, each containing forty to sixty soldiers. Cure time was approximately 6-12 minutes. Once trimmed, the soldiers were dipped in a base lacquer (advertised as "pure vegetable dyes") and sent down a decorating conveyor where as many as 24 women using small camel hair brushes added finishing touches: painting the faces, shoes, belts, buttons, medals, and finally eyes. After drying, each toy was wrapped individually in waxed paper and packed three dozen to a chipboard carton and twelve dozen to a corrugated carton for shipment. Design of the soldiers was credited to Edward McCandlish, a freelance artist.

The soldiers sold well from the beginning. Approximately 200 of the 400 Auburn employees (Auburn consistently made non-toy products as well) were involved in them and other toys on a two-shift basis. Shortly after the first soldiers were introduced, animals and wheeled vehicles (the first a Cord automobile) were marketed, all successfully. Auburn produced no soldiers during the war and few after it, though it continued to make toys in great quantity (70,000 wheeled items a day in 1962, for example). In 1960 the toys portion of Auburn was purchased by the town of Deming, New Mexico, where it remained until it went out of business in 1969.

Auburn's soldiers, all approximately the standard 3-1/4" length, went through three stages. The first were frail-looking with long, thin bodies; the second, which emerged as early as September 1938, were stockier and larger-headed; and the third, introduced in 1941, were more well-proportioned and realistic. Unlike its competitors, Auburn produced no cowboys, Indians, sailors, or civilians, except for baseball and football players and two farm workers. Auburn's infantry came in colors other than brown. The blue were meant to represent U.S. Marines. The white also were sold as Marines. It is thought that some Auburn Ethiopians remain to be discovered. Still elusive is the A35 running pilot, known to have been sold, but with none currently known to be in any collection.

All bold words and numbers are Auburn's own description.

	C6	C8	C10
(A1) **1200 Infantry Private**	8	12	17
(A2) **200 U.S. Infantry Private**	7	11	14
(A3) **1202 Infantry Bugler**	10	15	20
(A4) **202 Bugler, U.S. Infantry**	9	14	19
(A5) **Foreign Legion**, also **White Guard** officer, **No. 220**	12	18	24
(A6) **214 & 218 Foreign Legion Private**	12	18	24
(A7) Ethiopian with shield and rifle	60	90	120
(A7a) Ethiopian bugler, only 1 known	No Price Found		
(A7b) Ethiopian with rifle and shield, in robes, only 1 known	75	112	150
(A8) Officer, early	10	15	20
(A9) 204 U.S. Infantry Officer	9	14	18
(A10) **1238 Charging Soldier**	23	35	47
(A11) **238 Charging Soldier**, with tommy gun	8	12	17
(A12) **232 Officer on Horse**	17	25	34
(A13) **230 Machine Gunner**	10	15	21
(A14) **224 Red Cross Doctor**	17	25	34
(A14a) Army Doctor, Khaki uniform	No Price Found		
(A15) **226 Red Cross Nurse**, white or khaki uniform	19	29	39
(A16) **206 Stretcher Bearer**	18	27	36
(A17) **208 Wounded Soldier**	19	29	39
(A18) **216 Observer with Binoculars**	8	12	17

Top, left to right: A1, A2, A3, A4, A5, A6, A6a
Bottom, left to right: A7, A7a, A7b, A8, A9, A10, A11

A14a

	C6	C8	C10
(A19) **236 Signalman**	30	45	60
(A19a) **Signalman**, early smaller size, only 3 known	100	150	200
(A20) **222 Sniper**, crawling, rifle over shoulder	25	38	50
(A21) **234 Bomb Thrower**	15	22	30
(A22) **242 Anti-Aircraft Gun**	17	25	34

	C6	C8	C10
(A23) **1546 Motorcycle Cop**, blue or khaki as soldier	30	45	60
(A24) **240 Motorcycle Soldiers**, with sidecar	25	38	50
(A25) **Aircraft Defender**	15	22	30
(A26) **Color Bearer**	22	33	44
(A27) **Marching Soldier**	12	18	25
(A28) **Firing Soldier**	22	33	44
(A29) **272 Plane Shooter**	18	27	36

Top, left to right: A12, A13, A14, A15, A16
Bottom, left to right: A17, A18, A19, A20

Top, left to right: A21, A22, A23, A24
Bottom, left to right: A25, A26, A27, A28, A29

BUDDY L No. 2007 Monoplane and Catapult Hangar. Photo by Jeanne Bertoia. Courtesy Bill Bertoia Auctions.

SCHOENHUT "Humpty Dumpty Circus," c. 1925. Courtesy Christie's East.

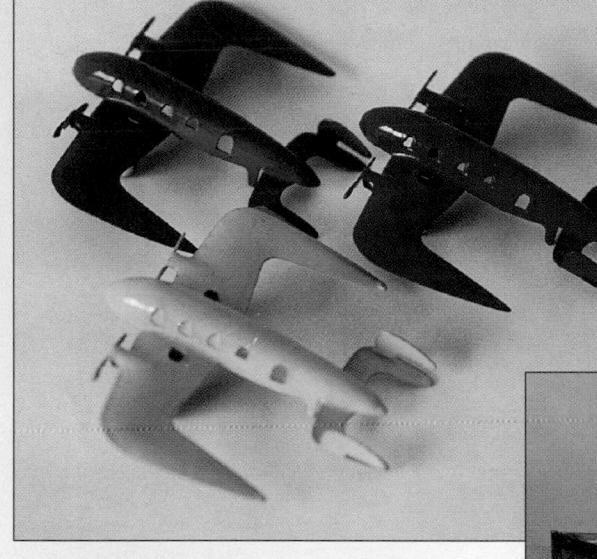

BUDDY L No. 3000 Tugboat, 28" long. Photo by Jeanne Bertoia. Courtesy Bill Bertoia Auctions.

WYANDOTTE Mystery Planes (No. 101). Photo by John Gibson.

MARKLIN "Priscilla" Riverboat, 30" long. Photo by Jeanne Bertoia. Courtesy Bill Bertoia Auctions.

BING Gunboat, painted tin, 29" long. Photo by Jeanne Bertoia. Courtesy Bill Bertoia Auctions.

SCHOENHUT Circus Animals with their original boxes.
Photo by Jeanne Bertoia. Courtesy Bill Bertoia Auctions.

Top, left to right: Hubley H16; Hubley H37; Hubley H10. Bottom, left to right: Kilgore "TAT," largest Kilgore plane; Hubley H1; Dent Ford Trimotor. Photo by Jeanne Bertoia. Courtesy Bill Bertoia Auctions.

BARCLAY (BA6) No. 611 Rocket Ship.
Photo by Stan Alekna. (Aircraft.)

C.A.W. (Charles A. Wood) CWA13 Monoplane.
Photo by Perry Eichor.

An extremely rare twin-engine tin litho plane. It's marked "General Metal Toys Ltd., Toronto, Canada" but otherwise gives every evidence of being a Marx product. No price found. MacNary Collection. Photo: RLM.

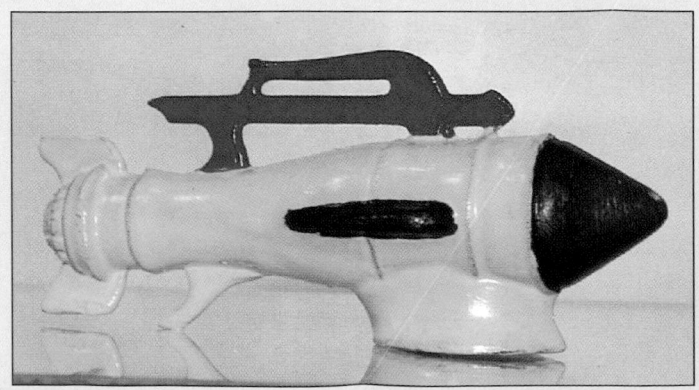

BARCLAY (BA5) No. 610 Rocket Ship.
Photo by Stan Alekna. (Aircraft.)

	C6	C8	C10
(A34) **Tank Soldier**, running with box............	19	29	39
(A35) Pilot running, looking skyward, in pilot helmet and goggles............................	No Price Found		
(A36) **Motor Scout**..	24	36	48
(A37) **258 Baserunner**	24	36	48
(A38) **252 Batter**..	20	30	41
(A39) **256 Fielder or Baseman**	21	31	42
(A40) **250 Pitcher**	26	39	52
(A41) **254 Catcher**	27	41	55
(A42) **268 Carrier**, football player	17	25	34
(A43) **264 Center**, football player	16	24	32
(A44) **262 Backfieldman**, football player	20	30	40
(A45) **260 Lineman**, football player................	19	28	38
(A46) **266 Passer**, football player	19	28	38
(A47) Motorcycle Cop, large 5" high................	25	38	50
(A48) Cowboy, large, on wheeled horse	42	63	85

Top, left to right: A30, A31, A32, A33
Bottom, left to right: A34, A36, A37, A38, A39

	C6	C8	C10
(A30) **Sound Detector**	15	22	31
(A31) **Searchlight**..	20	30	40
(A32) **296 Trench Mortar**	16	24	33
(A33) **Tank Defender**	24	36	48

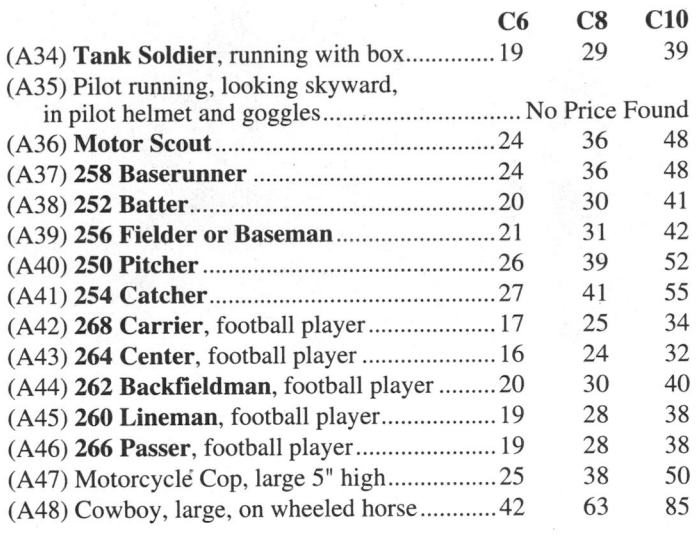

A35. Rough sketch from memory going back 40 years. Note no box in hand, head tilted up toward left, left hand forward. None known.

Top, left to right: A40, A41, A42, A43
Bottom, left to right: A44, A45, A46

AMERICAN METAL TOYS

Until recently, these 3-1/4" dime-store soldiers were attributed to Chicago toy soldier maker J. Edward Jones. Though Jones did make many other figures, research by the author has established that the following group were produced by American Metal Toys, Inc., also of Chicago. The president of the firm was Royce Reyff (1898-1986) and his equal partner was C. Raymond Pierson. (Pierson was born December 27, 1904, and is still alive at the time of this writing.) The address was 215 No. Racine. Although the company formally incorporated on October 24, 1939, it began in 1937 and went out of business in April 1942, when its supply of metal was cut off by the demands of WWII. The sculpting and diemaking were done by Henry Kasselowski, who had also worked for Jones. Four of the soldiers sold by American Metal Toys (AM1, AM2, AM26, AM43) were originally produced by Jones (all four are in a range below 3-1/4"), who sold the molds to American Metal Toys.

Left to right: AM1, AM1a
Courtesy K. Warren Mitchell.

For American Metal soldiers in gray, increase the price by 40%.

	C6	C8	C10
(AM1) German, kneeling with rifle	95	142	190
(AM1a) Same as above, short rifle	110	165	220
(AM2) German, charging with rifle	107	160	215
(AM3) German, prone machine gunner	71	106	143
((AM4) Observer w/ binoculars and rifle..........	41	61	82
(AM5) Wire-cutter, prone	225	338	450
(AM6) Soldier with rifle, gassed or shot in neck	170	255	340
(AM7) Stretcher-bearer	50	75	100
(AM8) Kneeling with AA Gun	45	68	91
(AM9) Charging, port arms..............................	125	188	250
(AM10) Firing machine gun on stump..............	40	60	80
(AM10a) Same as above, No. 1 on pocket.......	100	150	200
(AM11) Grenade thrower, no weapons.............	67	100	135
(AM12) Seated with rifle	40	60	80
(AM13) Officer in greatcoat, pointing, holding pistol	110	165	220
(AM14) Prone with rifle, trunk upraised...........	70	105	140
(AM15) Prone, firing double-barreled machine gun	78	117	155
(AM16) Kneeling, firing anti-tank gun..............	52	78	105
(AM16a) Same as above with barrel brace, "23" on wheel..................	50	75	100

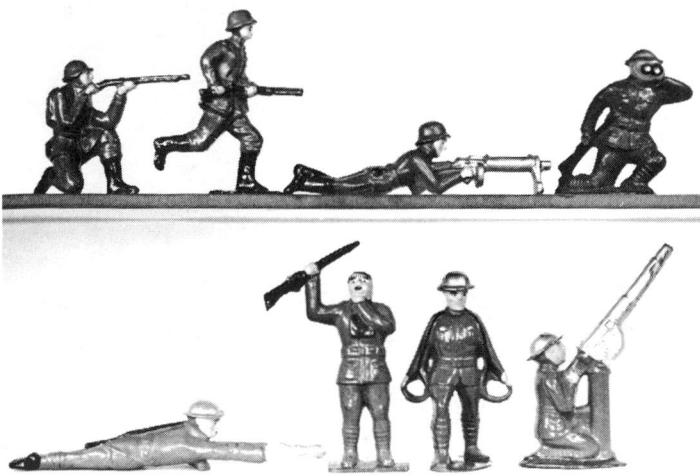

Top, left to right: AM9, AM10, AM10a, AM11,
Bottom, left to right: AM12, AM13, AM14, AM15

Top, left to right: AM1, AM2, AM3, AM4
Bottom, left to right: AM5, AM6, AM7, AM8

	C6	C8	C10
(AM17) Cook w/ chef's hat, frying pan	75	112	150
(MA18) Ammunition Carrier	200	300	400
(AM19) Motorcyclist with machine gun mounted on motorcycle	70	105	140
(AM20) Flagbearer (similar to Barclay B7)	120	180	240
(AM21) Kneeling with searchlight....................	62	93	125
(AM21a) Kneeling with searchlight, "27," "Made in USA" on sides of stanchion..........	55	82	110
(AM22) Seated with phone	55	83	110
(AM23) Kneeling, firing rifle, no stand	60	90	120
(AM23a) Same as above, shorter rifle...............	75	112	150
(AM24) Prone, body arched, firing machine fun....................................	60	90	120
(AM25) Bugler	78	117	155
(AM26) Soldier with gas mask, plunging rifle down, slightly smaller in size	107	160	215

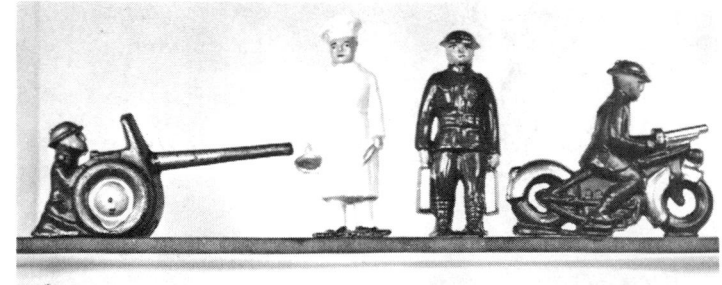

Top, left to right: AM16, AM17, AM18, AM19
Bottom, left to right: AM20, AM21, AM22, AM23, AM23a

Top, left to right: AM24, AM25, AM26, AM27
Bottom, left to right: AM28, AM28a, AM29, AM30, AM31

	C6	C8	C10
(AM27) Nurse w/ bag, like Barclay B82	45	68	90
(AM28) Doctor with bag, like Barclay B81 (in khaki, add $45 in mint)	40	60	80
(AM29) Standing, firing rifle	49	73	98
(AM30) Wounded supine, like Manoil M53	42	63	85
(AM31) Cowboy on rearing horse, firing backward	130	195	260
(AM32) Marching with rifle	57	85	115
(AM33) Cowboy kneeling	30	45	60
(AM33a) Cowboy kneeling, with base, rare	No Price Found		
(AM34) Indian on rearing horse	50	75	100
(AM35) Indian with bow (copy of Beton's)	No Price Found		
(AM35a) Indian kneeling, shooting	27	42	55
(AM36) Tramp	7	11	15
(AM37) Farmer	6	9	13
(AM38) Farmer's Wife	7	10	14
(AM39) Cowboy on Prancing Horse, similar to Barclay B2	No Price Found		

Top, left to right: AM32, AM33, AM34
Bottom, left to right: AM36, AM37, AM38

	C6	C8	C10
(AM40) Knight w/ shield, flat underbase	No Price Found		
(AM41) Knight with pennant, flat underbase	64	95	128
(AM42) Kneeling Nurse, *probably* American Metal, copy of Barclay's but shorter, squatter	No Price Found		
(AM43) Cowboy shooting (on foot)	15	22	30

AM35a

Left to right: AM40, AM41 Courtesy Don Pielin.

AM39 Courtesy Don Pielin.

AM43 Courtesy Don Pielin, Old Toy Soldier.

Barclay kneeling nurse at left, AM42 at right. Photo by Barry S. Josephs.

Marx Playsets

by Barry Goodman

One of the most successful toy lines in the history of plastic toys was the playset. Although the history of the playset spans from the late 1940s to the present, its heyday was from the mid-1950s to the late 1960s. A playset is a toy containing figures and varied accessories designed to be played with. The most common themes are those involving military campaigns throughout the ages. These include Prehistoric Scenes, Vikings and Romans, The Civil War, Western Adventures and World War II. Those containing either an important historical figure (Johnny Ringo) or an event (i.e. Custer's Last Stand) are the most desirable. Prices have steadily increased in the past few years. Literally hundreds of sets were made by the Marx company. The sets come in different sizes, and variations upon the same theme are common. The only constant was the child's imagination in creating a new adventure each and every time the playset was set up and played with!

Alamo Play Set. Mint in box value $850. Photo by Barry Goodman.

Arctic Explorer, Series 2000. Mint in box value $600. Photo by Barry Goodman.

Atomic Cape Canaveral Missile Base. Value mint in box $275. Photo by Barry Goodman.

Battle of the Blue & Gray. Mint in box value $750.

Battleground Play Set. Mint in box value $400.
Photo by Barry Goodman.

Beachhead Assault Set. Mint in box value $150.
Photo by Barry Goodman.

Beach-Head Landing Set. Mint in box value $500.
Photo by Barry Goodman.

Ben-Hur. Mint in box value $900.
Photo by Barry Goodman.

Blue and Gray Armies. Value in mint $300.
Photo by Barry Goodman.

Blue and Gray, Sears Heritage Play Set. Value mint in box $250.
Photo by Barry Goodman.

Construction Camp. Value mint in box $300.
Photo by Barry Goodman.

Cape Canaveral. Value mint in box $400.
Photo by Barry Goodman.

Daniel Boone Frontier Play Set. Value mint in box $275.
Photo by Barry Goodman.

Desert Fox. Value mint in box $450.
Photo by Barry Goodman.

Fort Apache Set, Series 1000. Value mint in box $300.
Photo by Barry Goodman.

Fort Apache, Sears Heritage. Value mint in box $250.
Photo by Barry Goodman.

Fort Dearborn. Value mint in box $400.
Photo by Barry Goodman.

Gunsmoke Dodge City. Value mint in box $1300.
Photo by Barry Goodman.

Gallant Men Army Play Set. Value mint in box $600.
Photo by Barry Goodman.

Jungle Animal Playset. Value mint in box $700.

Knights & Castle Miniature Playset. Value mint in box $175.
Photo by Barry Goodman.

Knights & Vikings. Value mint in box $250.
Photo by Barry Goodman.

Military Academy. Value mint in box $350.
Photo by Barry Goodman.

Modern Colonial Doll House, series 750. Value mint in box $200.
Photo by Barry Goodman.

Modern Farm Set. Value mint in box $250.
Photo by Barry Goodman.

Modern Farm Set. Value mint in box $200.
Photo by Barry Goodman.

Modern Service Station. Value mint in box $350.
Photo by Barry Goodman.

Prehistoric Times, Series 1000. Value mint in box $300.
Photo by Barry Goodman.

Rhine River Battle. Value mint in box $200.
Photo by Barry Goodman.

Robin Hood Castle Set. Value mint in box $350.
Photo by Barry Goodman.

Service Station. Value mint in box $300.
Photo by Barry Goodman.

Sons of Liberty, Sears Heritage. Value mint in box $250.
Photo by Barry Goodman.

Tales of Wells Fargo. Value mint in box $600.
Photo by Barry Goodman.

Troll Village, Miniature Play Set. Value mint in box $175.
Photo by Barry Goodman.

Untouchables. Value mint in box $1400.
Photo by Barry Goodman.

U.S. Armed Forces Training Center, Series 1000. Value mint in box $350.
Photo by Barry Goodman.

U.S. Army Training Center. Value mint in box $250.
Photo by Barry Goodman.

Western Town. Value mint in box $600.
Photo by Barry Goodman.

ACTION FIGURES

THE DAWN OF THE ACTION FIGURE

Although previously there had been similar toys, it was Hasbro's G.I. Joe that truly created the category of the action figure.

Don Levine, the director of development for Hasbro, conceived the idea of G.I. Joe while standing outside a Manhattan art supply shop in February 1963. A licensing agent had suggested a military toy based on a TV series, *The Lieutenant*. Levine had discarded the idea of a tie-in because the series was for adults, but the thought was in his mind as he looked at an artist's mannequin in the shop window. The idea of a boy's soldier with movable parts came to him.

Sam Speers, who worked under Levine, engineered G. I. Joe. He designed both the mechanical and esthetic facets (for which he received many patents), including a way for the toy to stand on its own (unlike artists' mannequins) in various positions while holding weapons or bearing equipment. Speers also thought of the added touch of a facial scar. The height was made 11-1/2" because the Barbie doll was that tall and a great success.

Noted artist Phil Kraczkowski sculpted the head, which was *not* a composite of 23 Medal of Honor winners, despite ad claims to that effect. Speers designed the parts of the body and how they should go together, and Walter Hansen and Norman Jacques did the sculpting of the body. It wasn't an easy sell to the Hasbro executives for Levine and Speers, but after the first year's enormous success, Levine was upped to vice president and Speers moved up to Levine's job as director of development.

Photos for Hasbro (GI Joe) and Marx by Barry J. Goodman, unless otherwise noted. Photos for Hartland by Gary J. Linden, unless otherwise noted. Photos for Star Wars courtesy of Whit Alexander and Neal Bates, unless otherwise noted.

Note: After the Hasbro/G.I. Joe listing, all action figures are listed alphabetically by company.

HASBRO (G.I. JOE)

The average mint price for G.I. Joe toys in the last edition was $102.64. In this edition it is $115.02, an increase of 12%.

by Barry Goodman

G.I. Joe first entered the U.S. market in 1964. The 11-1/2" doll would undergo several changes during its eleven-year life span (1964-75). The first dolls (1964-69) had painted hair and were based primarily upon military uniforms of WWII. In 1965 Hasbro added six foreigners to the series (Japanese, German, French, Australian, Russian, British). These were distinctly different in appearance. An easy way of knowing if you have a foreigner is that the scar found on the U.S. G.I. is not present.

In 1965 Hasbro introduced a black G.I. Joe, which today is one of the most sought-after models.

In 1967 Hasbro introduced its "Vietnam series" outfits, which were pulled off the market very quickly due to the negative response to the Vietnam war raging in southeast Asia. Thus these uniforms (green and tan Airborne M.P., Air Security set, and Marine Jungle Fighter) are the most sought after and scarcest. This was also the year that produced the extremely scarce nurse doll.

Protests about the war continued, so in 1969 Hasbro dropped the military line and substituted the "adventurer series." G.I. Joe was transformed from a military doll to an adventure doll. In 1970 G.I. Joe received flocked hair and then a flocked moustache and beard. Furthermore, the "adventurer" line was dropped and the "Adventure Team" line substituted. The theme of this line was that G.I. Joe would fight nature and the elements, rather than other men.

Barry James Goodman is a leading collector and authority on Hasbro's G.I. Joe dolls and 1960s character figures. As an active toy dealer he has amassed one of the largest collections of G.I. Joes.

In 1972 G.I Joe was given a "kung-fu" grip. The same year, the oil embargo created havoc by making oil-based plastic prohibitively expensive. Because of this, in 1973 Hasbro changed the basic composition of the plastic. This created a much more fragile doll, and by 1975 children had totally lost interest in G.I. Joe.

Most collectors concentrate on the 1964-69 dolls. Hasbro consulted military manuals to create the most realistic and authentic boys' doll ever made.

Action Soldier

Revised listings by Barry Goodman. Prices in parentheses indicate mint in box or mint on card with cello.

	C6	C8	C10
7000 G.I. Joe 5-Star Jeep, 106mm rocket launcher, 1/4-ton trailer, tripod mounted searchlight, four 106mm shells (250)	100	150	200
7100 "Let's Go Joe" board game (100)	40	60	80
7500 G.I. Joe Action Soldier (150)	40	60	80
7501 Combat Set A, field jacket, M-1 rifle, bayonet, cartridge belt, six hand grenades (150), individually	5	10	15
7502 Combat Set B, back pack, canteen and cover, entrenching tool and cover, mess kit, utensils, single pouch cartridge belt, individually	5	10	15
Price for 7502 set	35	50	60

	C6	C8	C10
7503 Combat Fatigue Shirt (45)	5	8	12
7504 Combat Fatigue Pants (45)	5	8	12
7505 Combat Field Jacket (45)	8	15	20
7506 Combat Field Pack, entrenching tool and cover (45)	10	20	30
7507 Combat Helmet, camouflage netting and foliage (35)	10	20	25
7508 Army Sandbags Set (25)	5	10	12.50
1709 Canteen, cover and mess kit, utensils (40)	5	10	15
7510 M-1 Rifle, bayonet and cartridge belt with six grenades (50)	20	40	50
7511 Camouflage Netting, with poles and foliage (50)	5	10	15

1965 catalog illustrations.

7512 Bivouac Set A, zipped sleeping bag,
M-1 Rifle, bayonet, cartridge belt,
canteen with cover, mess kit
with utensils, individually 5 10 15

7513 Bivouac Set B, tent, stakes, poles,
foliage, camouflage netting, entrenching
tools with cover (125 for set)....................10 20 35

7514 30 cal. tripod
mounted machine gun, ammo box (45)........10 15 25

7515 Zippered Sleeping Bag (35) 10 15 25

7517 Command Post Set, rain poncho,
.45 pistol w/ belt and holster,
field radio, field phone, wire roll,
map and map case, individually 5 10 15

7518 .45 Pistol with holster and belt, ammo
pouch, six grenades, cloth hat, individually ...5 10 15
Price for 7518 Set 25 45 80

7519 Rain Poncho (35)..5 10 15

7520 Field Phone, field radio,
wire spool, map case and map,
individually (50 for set) 5 10 15

7521 Military Police Set, "Ike" Jacket,
trousers, ascot, white belt, nightstick,
.45 pistol, holster, armband, duffel bag,
stem gun (250) 35 55 65

7522 Jungle Fighter Set, belt,
entrenching tool, mess kit, utensils,
canteen, cover, machete, sheath,
jungle knife (250) 35 50 70

7523 Duffel bag (35) 5 10 15

7524 MP Uniform (1000)................................250 350 500

7524 "Ike" Jacket, ascot
and MP armband (250) 15 25 35

7525 "Ike" Trousers (35) 5 10 15

7526 MP Helmet, black......................................50 100 150

7526 MP Helmet, white belt, .45 pistol,
holster, nightstick (75)................................20 30 40

7527 Ski patrol helmet, winter white
cartridge belt, winter white M-1 rifle,
six grenades (125) 20 30 40

7528 Bazooka and two shells (90) 10 20 30

7529 Snow Shoes, pick axe, climbing rope,
and sun goggles (125) 15 20 35

7530 Mountain Troops Set, snow shoes,
winter white belt, winter white
field pack, pick axe, climbing rope,
four grenades (125) 25 35 50

7531 Ski Patrol Set, 2-piece white parka,
gloves, boots, skis, poles,
sun goggles (125) 20 50 75

7532 Special Forces Set, uniform, beret,
bazooka, two shells, four grenades (375) 25 75 125

7533 Beret, M-16 rifle and field radio (250)......25 30 75

7536 Green Beret Set, G.I. Joe action
soldier dressed in special forces
uniform, M-16 rifle, .45 pistol, belt,
holster, six grenades, field radio (1500) 100 225 300

7537 West Point Cadet Set, parade
uniform, cap, feather, sword, scabbard,
M-1 rifle, dress shoes (450) 75 200 275

	C6	C8	C10

7538 Heavy Weapons Set, 81mm mortar,
three shells, M-60 machine gun, tripod,
ammo belt, bulletproof vest, bullet belt,
two grenades (500) 40 100 125

7590 G.I. Joe Talking Action Soldier (250).......75 125 150

8000 Official G.I. Joe footlocker......................10 15 30

8030 G.I. Joe Desert Patrol Jeep, .50 cal.
tripod mounted machine gun, radio
antenna, G.I. Joe desert trooper (1200).......300 600 900

G.I. Joe 8030 Desert Patrol Jeep box.

Action Sailor

7600 G.I. Joe Action Sailor (250) 50 75 100

7601 Sea Rescue Set A, inflatable raft,
oar, sea anchor, tow line, flare gun, knife,
scabbard, first aid kit, individually (90)..........5 10 15

G.I. Joe Action Sailor.

7602 Frogman Set, 3-piece black scuba set, swims fins, face mask, oxygen tanks, depth gauge, knife, scabbard, depth charges (350) 50   125   185

7603 Black scuba suit jacket and hood (150) 15   50   100

7604 Black scuba suit pants (40) 7.50   25   35

7605 Swim fins, face mask, knife, scabbard, depth gauge (40) 15   20   30

7606 Oxygen tanks (35) 5   10   15

7607 Navy Attack Set, life jacket, semaphore flags, hand held searchlight, binoculars, individually (95) 15   20   25

7610 Navy attack helmet, handheld searchlight and binoculars (95) 15   30   40

7611 Life Jacket (45) 5   10   15

7612 Shore Patrol, jumper, neckerchief, trousers, white belt, .45 pistol, holster, nightstick, armband, sailors cap, duffel bag (250) 35   75   90

7613 Shore Patrol Jumper Set (35) ... 15   30   40

7614 Shore Patrol Pants (35)............... 5   10   15

7615 USN Duffel Bag (45) 5   10   15

7616 Shore Patrol w/ stripe (1000 - gift set) 100   200   350

7616 Shore Patrol helmet, white belt, .45 pistol, holster, nightstick (75) 10   25   30

7618 .30 ca. tripod mounted machine gun and ammo box (45) 20   30   45

7619 Dress Parade, M-1 rifle, bayonet, white cartridge belt, white billyclub (250) 15   45   60

7620 Deep Sea Diver Set, diver's suit, gloves, helmet, breastplate, air pump, hoses, weighted belt, weighted shoes, signal float, line, knife, scabbard, sledge hammer (500) 30   55   90

7621 Landing Signal Officer Set, safety striped jumpsuit, cloth helmet with headphones, goggles, binoculars, signal paddles, clip board, pad, pencil, flare gun (250) 30   50   100

7622 Sea Rescue Set B, same as Sea Rescue Set A, also includes life jackets (150) 10   30   40

7623 Deep Freeze Set, fur parka, pants, boots, snow sled, flare gun, ice pick (400) 35   75   105

7624 Annapolis Cadet Set, dress parade jacket, cap, pants, belt, shoes, sword, scabbard, white M-1 rifle (400) 100   225   325

7625 Breeches Buoy Set, buoy, pulley, slicker jacket, pants, flare gun, handheld searchlight (275) 75   150   225

7626 LSO helmet w/ headphones, signal paddles, flare gun, clip board, pad, pencil (350) 25   50   75

7627 USN Life Ring (45)..................... 10   25   30

7628 White sailor's cap, boots, G.I. Joe dog tags (45) 15   25   35

7690 G.I. Joe Talking Action Sailor (350) 100   175   225

8050 Official G.I. Joe Sea Sled, w/ G.I. Joe frogman (450)........................... 100   225   275

G.I. Joe Action Sailor No. 8050. Official Sea Sled and Frogman (box).

Sears' G.I. Joe Forward Observer Set.

G.I. Joe Astronaut. (C6: 30. C8: 50. C10: 70.) Mint in box add 70%.

Action Marine

7700 G.I. Joe Action Marine (300) 60   110   195

7701 Communications Set, M-1 carbine, camouflage poncho, field phone, field radio, wire spool, binoculars, map and map case (50), individually 5   10   15

7702 Camouflage poncho (35) 5   10   15

7703 Field radio, field phone, wire spool, map and map case (50) 5   10   15

7704 Flag Set, Old Glory, Army flag, Navy flag, Marine Corps flag, Air Force flag (200) 30   60   100

7705 Paratrooper Set, parachute pack, M-1 carbine, six grenades, knife, scabbard, belt, ammo pouch, canteen and cover (200), individually 5   15   25

G.I. Joe Action Marine.

	C6	C8	C10
7706 M-1 carbine, six grenades, knife, scabbard, belt, ammo pouch, canteen and cover (45), individually 5	10	15
7707 Camouflage helmet, foliage, helmet cover (35)........................10	25	30
7708 Camouflage netting, foliage, poles, securing line (45)............5	10	15
7709 Parachute Pack (40)...................15	20	25
7710 Dress Parade Set, traditional Marine "dress blues," cap, white M-1 rifle (200)........................20	40	50
7711 Beachhead Set A, flame thrower, camouflage tent, poles, stakes, belt, ammo pouch, mess kit, utensils (50), individually...........................5	10	15

G.I. Joe Action Marine equipment box.

	C6	C8	C10
7712 Beachhead Set B, M-1 rifle, cartridge belt, six grenades, field pack, bayonet, entrenching tool, cover, canteen and cover (150), individually 5	10	15
7713 Field Pack, entrenching tool and cover (50)........................10	30	40
7714 Camouflage fatigue shirt (30)......................5	8	12
7715 Camouflage fatigue pants (30) 5	8	12
7716 Mess Kit, utensils, canteen and cover (40)........................5	10	15
7717 M-1 rifle, bayonet, cartridge belt, six grenades (80)........................20	30	40
7718 Flame Thrower (35)........................10	15	20
7719 Medic Set, stretcher, crutch, satchel, stethoscope, plasma bottle, IV tube, splints, bandage rolls, armbands, hospital flag, cloth bag (250)........................50	100	125
7720 Crutch, stethoscope, plasma bottle, I.V. tube, splints, bandage rolls (250)...........10	25	35
7721 Medic's helmet, satchel, two armbands (125)........................15	30	50
7722 Fatigue cap, boots, G.I. Joe dog tags (55)........................20	25	35
7723 G.I. Bunk Bed (200) 25	40	55
7727 Weapons Rack Set, rack, M-1 rifle, M-1 carbine, M-16 rifle, 40mm grenade launcher (150)........................30	50	60
7731 Tank Commander Set, leather jacket, tanker's helmet, belt, .30 cal. M-60 machine gun, tripod, ammo box, radio, tripod (500)........................75	100	150

G.I. Joe Vietnam Marine Jungle Fighter.

	C6	C8	C10
7732 Jungle Fighter Set, green fatigue shirt, pants, campaign hat, AR-15 rifle, belt, knife, machete, sheath, canteen, cover, flame thrower, field phone (850).....250	400	600
7790 G.I. Joe Talking Action Marine (350).......95	150	200

Action Pilot

	C6	C8	C10
7800 G.I. Joe Action Pilot (400) 50	85	130

	C6	C8	C10

7801 Survival Set, inflatable raft, sea anchor, tow line, oar, knife, scabbard, flare gun, first aid kit, inflatable USAF life vest (250)......50 75 100

7802 Inflatable raft, sea anchor, tow line, oar (150) 15 30 40

7803 Dress Uniform, jacket, shirt, tie, pants, garrison cap, wings, captain's bars (400)......40 80 140

7804 Dress Jacket (50) 10 15 20

7805 Dress Pants (50) 10 15 20

7806 Dress Shirt and Cap (50) 10 15 20

7807 Scramble Set, gray flight suit, inflatable life vest, .45 pistol, holster, belt, clipboard, pad, pencil (175)......25 40 75

7808 Gray flight suit (40)......15 25 35

7809 Inflatable life vest, flare gun, knife, scabbard, first aid kit (75)......10 20 30

7810 Crash helmet w/ oxygen mask (75) 20 40 50

7811 Parachute pack (50)......10 15 25

7812 Communications Set, field radio binoculars, map, map case, clipboard, pad, pencil (95)......20 30 60

7813 A.P. Helmet Set (150) 10 30 40

7820 Crash Crew Set, metallic heat suit, hood, gloves, boots, tool belt, CO_2 fire extinguisher (250)......35 65 90

7822 Colorado Air Cadet Set, uniform, sash, cap, dress shoes, M-1 rifle, sword, scabbard (600) 100 175 275

7823 Fighter Pilot Set, G-suit, boots, "Mae West" life jacket, helmet, oxygen mask, flashlight, working parachute (900)......75 200 375

7824 Air Sea Rescue Set, 3-piece orange scuba suit, mask, swim fins, air tanks, flare gun, first aid kit, rescue life ring, marker buoy (250) 25 60 100

7890 G.I. Joe Talking Action Pilot (400)......75 200 275

7900 G.I. Joe Action Soldier Colored [sic] (800) 150 250 400

8020 Official G.I. Joe Space Capsule, space suit, boots, gloves, helmet, recording of Mercury Control Communications (250) 50 75 100

8040 Deluxe Crash Crew Set, fire truck, working water pump, working siren, blinking red light, fire axe, metallic heat suit, boots, gloves, hood, white stretcher (750)......200 350 450

G.I. Jane (1965) Army Nurse (1700) 500 800 1000

Action Soldiers of the World

8100 German Storm Trooper, cartridge belt, Luger pistol, holster, field pack, "Potato Masher" grenades, 9mm Schmeisser machine gun, iron cross medal (850) 150 300 350

8101 Japanese Imperial Soldier, field pack, Nambu pistol, holster, cartridge belt, Arisaka rifle, bayonet, Order of the Kite medal (850)......200 450 575

G.I. Joe German.

G.I. Joe Japanese.

	C6	C8	C10

8102 Russian Infantry Man, D.P. light machine gun, bi-pod, field glasses, case, anti-tank grenades, ammo box, order of Lenin medal (850)......200 350 475

G.I. Joe Russian.

G.I. Joe Nurse.

8103 French Resistance Fighter, Lebel revolver, shoulder holster, knife, grenades, radio set, 7.65mm Mas submachine gun, Croix de Guerre medal (850)......175 265 325

	C6	C8	C10
8104 British Commando, gas mask, case, canteen, cover, sten mark 25 submachine gun, Victoria Cross medal (850)	160	325	360
8105 Australian Jungle Fighter, grenades, flame thrower, jungle knife, entrenching tool, bush machete, sheath, Victoria Cross medal (850)	175	275	350

	C6	C8	C10
8200 German Storm Trooper (500)	150	250	325
8201 Imperial Japanese Soldier (500)	180	255	350
8202 Russian Infantry Man (500)	150	250	325
8203 French Resistance Fighter (500)	130	230	300
8204 British Commando (500)	150	250	325
8205 Australian Jungle Fighter (500)	130	230	300
8300 Equipment for German Storm Trooper, field pack, Luger pistol, holster, cartridge belt, 9mm Schmeisser machine gun, "Potato Masher" hand grenades, Iron Cross medal (200)	30	75	100

G.I. Joe Australian.

G.I. Joe Polar Explorer. (C6: 100. C8: 200. C10: 250.) Mint in box add 70%.

Left to right: G.I. Joes 8200, 8201, 8202, 8203, 8204, and 8205. (The figures in this photo are not those actually sold in foreign uniforms.) Courtesy Sam Speers.

G.I. Joe 5 Star Jeep.
(C6: 50. C8: 80. C10: 150.)
Mint in box add 70%.

	C6	C8	C10
8301 Equipment for Japanese Imperial Soldier, cartridge belt, field pack, Arisaka rifle, bayonet, Nambu pistol, holster, order of Kite medal (200)	30	90	150
8302 Equipment for Russian Infantry Man, field glasses, case, D.P. light machine gun, bi-pod, belt, ammo box, anti-tank grenades, order of Lenin medal (175)	30	75	125
8303 Equipment for French Resistance Fighter, shoulder holster, Lebel revolver, 7.65 Mas submachine gun, grenades, radio, knife, Croix de Guerre medal (150)	15	30	45
8304 British Commando Equipment, canteen, case, cartridge belt, gas mask, case, sten mark 2-S submachine gun, Victoria Cross medal (200)	45	110	150
8305 Australian Jungle Fighter Equipment, flame thrower, jungle knife, grenades, bush machete, sheath, entrenching tool and Victoria Cross medal (200)	15	20	30

G.I. Joe Cadet Photo Boxes, each worth $500 in mint.

G.I. Joe Photo Boxes, worth $400 each in mint.

G.I. Joe Tan Airborne M.P.,
1967

G.I. Joe Irwin German Staff Car.

G.I. Joe Irwin Amphibious Duck.

	C6	C8	C10
The Irwin Company made the following vehicles and planes for G.I. Joe under license from Hasbro: an Armored Car, a Half Track, two motorcycles, a Duck, three airplanes, a German staff car, a Mine Sweeper, and a Racing Car. The boxes are very desirable and add 70% to the price of each toy.			
All sell in the following range (850)	200	350	500
Crash Crew Fire Truck, Mego	100	250	350
Photo Boxes run $400-$500 in Mint			
Miscellaneous: Racing Car (950)	200	400	600

G.I. Joe Adventurers

	C6	C8	C10
7782 Air Adventurer (150)	40	65	85
7280 Land Adventurer (150)	25	50	60
7281 Sea Adventurer (150)	30	55	65
7283 Talking Man of Action (150)	50	75	100
7284 Man of Action, lifelike hair (200)	50	75	100
7290 Talking Adventure Team Commander (200)	40	70	90
7291 Talking Adventure Team Commander Black (350)	80	150	225
7292 Talking Adventure Team Commander, lifelike hair, beard (300)	60	125	140
Astronaut and Space Capsule Set, equipment (350)	100	170	250
Secret of the Mummy's Tomb Set, figure, vehicle, equipment (250)	60	120	180
Adventure Team Helicopter (125)	20	50	75
Adventure Team Training Tower (150)	20	45	65
Adventure Team Headquarters (75)	25	40	60
Adventure Team Outfit, pants, flare gun (40)	8	12	16
Adventure Team Outfit, trenchcoat, walkie-talkie (30)	8	12	16
Adventure Team Outfit, camouflage clothes, gun, holster (30)	8	12	16

4200 - 4255

	C6	C8	C10
4200 Mess Kit & Canteen Set (45)	15	20	30
4205 Machete & Scabbard Set (55)	20	30	40
4210 Pistol & Helmet Set (45)	15	20	30
4211 Pistol Belt & Holster (45)	15	20	30
4215 Walkie Talkie (35)	10	15	25

GI Joe Adventurers: Talking Adventure Team Commander, life-like hair, beard.

GI Joe Adventurers: Sea Adventurer box.

	C6	C8	C10
4219 Morse Code Set (40)	15	20	30
4221 Flame Thrower Water Gun (50)	20	30	40
4226 Flare Gun Flashlight (45)	20	25	30
4230 Combat Boots (90)	15	20	30

	C6	C8	C10
4245 Poncho (35)	10	20	25
4250 Pup Tent (55)	20	30	40
4255 Combat Jacket Set (65)	15	30	45
4256 M.P. Set (60)	20	30	40

End G.I. Joe

	C6	C8	C10
Hasbro Charlie's Angels, Cheryl Ladd, 8" high (35)	6	12	18
Hasbro Charlie's Angels, Farrah Fawcett-Majors, 8" high (35)	6	12	18

	C6	C8	C10
Hasbro Charlie's Angels, Jaclyn Smith, 8" high (35)	6	12	18
Hasbro Charlie's Angels, Kate Jackson, 8" high (35)	6	12	18
Hasbro Charlie's Angels Outfits, each	4	8	12

COLORFORMS

List by Jim Main

Prices in parentheses are mint on card or in box.

Outer Space Men

	C6	C8	C10
Colossus Rex (250)	60	100	200
Cmdr. Comet (450)	50	90	180
Astro-Nautilus (750)	75	125	250

	C6	C8	C10
Xodiac (250)	35	50	90
Orbitron (750)	50	90	180
Electron (250)	35	50	90
Alpha (525)	40	60	100

End Colorforms

	C6	C8	C10
Gabriel The Lone Ranger No.23620, 9-1/2" high, fully-jointed, cloth clothes (55)	10	30	45
Gabriel Tonto No. 23621, 9-1/2" high, fully-jointed, cloth clothes (75)	15	35	55
Gabriel Scout No. 23626, jointed (75)	9	20	25
Gabriel Silver plus 8-Way Action Saddle No. 27625, jointed (70)	9	20	25
Gabriel Tonto and Scout No.28691, cloth clothes	20	40	60
Gabriel The Lone Ranger and Silver No. 28675, with 8-way trick Action Saddle, cloth clothes	20	40	60
Gabriel Silver No.31635, with removable saddle, bridle (35)	7	12	20
Gabriel Scout No. 31636 for 3-3/4" Tonto, removable saddle and bridle (35)	7	12	20
Gabriel Butch Cavendish No. 31632, 3-3/4" high, jointed, new in 1981, with pistol (20)	6	9	15
Gabriel Smoke No. 31637 (Butch Cavendish stallion), removable saddle and bridle (20)	6	9	15
Gabriel The Lone Ranger No. 31630 (Legend of the Lone Ranger), 3-3/4" high, jointed, new in 1981 (20)	5	8	12
Gabriel Tonto No. 31631, 3-3/4" high, pistol and knife, new in 1981 (20)	4	6	8
Gabriel General George Custer No. 31633, 3-3/4" high, pistol (20)	5	8	12
Gabriel Buffalo Bill Cody No.31634, 3-3/4" high, jointed, comes with carbine (20)	4	6	8

	C6	C8	C10
Gabriel Figure Assortment No. 31601, 3-3/4" high, Lone Ranger, Tonto, Butch Cavendish, General Custer, Buffalo Bill, each individually	7	12	20
Gabriel House Assortment No. 31602, includes Silver, Scout, Smoke (for 3-3/4" figures), each individually	7	12	20

GABRIEL. Foreground: The Lone Ranger riding Silver. Background: Tonto riding Scout.

Prices in parentheses are mint on card or in box.

Defenders of the Earth (5-1/2" Tall)

	C6	C8	C10
Flash Gordon (20)	7	11	15
Garax (18)	7	11	15
The Phantom (22)	7	11	15

	C6	C8	C10
Ming (20)	7	11	15
Mongor (95)	10	15	20
Mandrake (20)	7	11	15
Lothar (20)	7	11	15
Flash's Swordship (30)	10	15	20
Garax's Swordship (40)	10	15	20

End Galoob

	C6	C8	C10
Gilbert Honey West, 12" high, 1965 (300)	70	120	160
Gilbert James Bond, 12" high (400)	60	90	120
Gilbert (James Bond) Odd Job, 1960s (400)	100	150	200
Gilbert James Bond Action Toy Set No.1, 1965, figures of 007 as scuba diver, Domino and Largo with Disco Volante's yacht, display box	40	95	130
Gilbert James Bond Action Playset No.2, Bond, Goldfinger, Odd Job, spin-top pool table, display box	35	55	75
Gilbert James Bond Action Toy Set No. 3 in display box, 1965, figures of 007 on Laser Table, Goldfinger, Odd Job, Dr. No	35	55	75
Gilbert James Bond Action Playset No. 4, Dr. No, Bond, Domino, firespitting Dragon Tank, display box	35	55	75
Gilbert James Bond Action Playset No.5, Bond with Beretta, Money Penny, M, M's secret desk, display box	35	55	75
Gilbert James Bond No. 1, 3-1/2" high, Beretta pistol (22)	4	7	9
Gilbert James Bond No. 2 with rifle, 3-1/2" tall, 1965 (20)	4	7	9
Gilbert James Bond No. 3 in Scuba Suit with Spear Gun, 3-1/2" tall, 1965 (18)	4	7	9
Gilbert James Bond No. 4 Odd Job, 3-1/2" tall, 1965 (18)	5	8	10

	C6	C8	C10
Gilbert James Bond No. 5 M, Bond's boss (15)	4	7	9
Gilbert James Bond No. 6 Goldfinger (12)	4	6	8
Gilbert James Bond No. 7 Miss Moneypenny (20)	5	8	10
Gilbert James Bond No. 8 Largo, 3-1/2" tall, 1965 (15)	5	8	10
Gilbert James Bond No. 9 Domino, 3-1/2" tall, 1965 (10)	3	5	7
Gilbert James Bond No. 10 Dr. No with poison vial (15)	4	7	9
Gilbert Man From U.N.C.L.E. Illya Kuryakin, 12" high (150)	50	75	100
Gilbert Man From U.N.C.L.E. Napoleon Solo (150)	45	70	90

Gilbert Moon McDare

Listing by Jim Main

	C6	C8	C10
Moon McDare 12" figure (150)	50	75	95
Space Suit outfit (100)	25	40	50
Space Mutt Set (140)	35	50	70
Space Gun Set (35)	10	15	20
Moon Explorer Set (60)	15	20	25
Action Communication Set (60)	15	20	25
Space Accessory Pack (65)	15	20	35

GILBERT James Bond figures 1-10 (3-1/2"). Courtesy Bill Nutting.

HARTLAND PLASTIC ACTION FIGURES

by Gary J. Linden

Hartland Plastics, Inc. is located in southern Wisconsin and has been producing plastic figures and other plastic products since the 1950s. In 1953 The Lone Ranger, Tonto, Roy Rogers, Dale Evans and Bullet were produced. The production of these and other western figures lasted for about 10 years. The figures were molded in acetate plastic and then painted. Most of these figures came with removable accessories, including hats, hand guns, rifles, saddles, and reins. Some of the figures had unique accessory items. Josh Randle's mares leg (rifle), Custer's saber, and Wyatt Earp's Bunt line special (long barrel revolver) are a few examples.

The reason for the vast price range in these western figures is that most of the common ones (C10 price of $150) had over 200,000 cast. The rarer figures (Col. Mackenzie for example) were cast in smaller numbers, usually around 5,000.

The figures were molded in two halves, front and back for people, left and right for the animals (horses and Bullet). A few things to keep in mind: first, there were two different Lone Ranger figures. The older one wears chaps and is more of a generic figure, and the newer figure looks more like Clayton Moore. Also, there were three different Lone Ranger horses (Silver). The generic Lone Ranger's horse has a chain for reins. The newer Lone Ranger (Clayton Moore type) has both a standing horse and a rearing horse. The #804 Sgt. Preston and the #804 Sgt. Lance O'Rourke appear to be the same figure with a different name on the box. The #817 Jim Bowie and his horse Blaze are the same horse and figure used for Davy Crockett and his horse Streak, the only difference being the hats. Crockett has a coonskin cap and Bowie has a cowboy-type hat. The boxes that all these figures came in were one of three types. The box was either plain cardboard with some printing or some colored artwork on it, or it had a full color photo on the outside. The gunfighters who had moveable arms came in either an artwork box or a box with a see-through front. The 8" western wranglers came in a window box and the 5-1/2" western horse and riders came on a blister card. Some of the accessory parts (hats, guns, and saddles) are being reproduced today.

Hartland also produced sport figures. There were 30 different football figures: an offensive and a defensive player from each of the 14 different teams of the time and two different personage figures, Johnny Unitas being the most sought after. The figures of the Redskins and the Cowboys are the most wanted out of the 28 non-personage players. There were 18 different personage baseball players produced, along with a bat boy. The rarest of the baseball figures is Dick Groat. To celebrate the baseball figures' 25th Anniversary in 1989, the Hartland Company reissued all 18 players and the bat boy. These figures have a "25" in a circle on their back just below the belt.

CONDITION CODE:

C10 A figure that is mint in the box with all paperwork and paper tag

C8 A mint figure that does not have the box or paperwork or paper tag

C6 A figure that has been played with and shows some wear; a few accessory parts are missing and there is no box, paperwork, or paper tag

Hartland Western and Historical Figures

List by Gary J. Linden, with additional information by Barry Goodman

9-1/2" Tall Figures

	C6	C8	C10
801 Lone Ranger (old/chaps) (300)	40	80	120
801 The Lone Ranger (newer) (300)	40	80	120
801P Western Champ (300)	50	90	150
801P Western Champ (extra large) (300)	50	90	200
802 Dale Evans (300)	40	70	100
804 Sgt. Preston (300)	75	140	250
804 Sgt. Lance O'Rourke (400)	75	140	250
805 Tonto (300)	30	60	90
806 Roy Rogers (450)	50	90	135
808 General Robert E. Lee (300)	50	90	135
809 Wyatt Earp (300)	50	90	135
812 Brave Eagle (600)	75	140	300
813 Chief Thunder Cloud (500)	65	125	275

HARTLAND No. 801 Lone Ranger (old chaps).

HARTLAND No. 802 Dale Evans.

HARTLAND No. 806 Roy Rogers.

HARTLAND No. 805 and No. 801 Lone Ranger (newer). Courtesy Rex and Richard Gray.

HARTLAND No. 804 Sgt. Lance O'Rourke.

HARTLAND No. 808 General Robert E. Lee (flag not shown in photo).

	C6	C8	C10
814 General Custer (450)	40	70	100
815 General George Washington (300)	50	90	150
816 Cochise (300)	30	60	90
817 Jim Bowie (500)	75	140	250
818 Cheyenne (350)	45	85	125
819 Buffalo Bill (500)	75	140	250
821 Tom Jeffords (600)	70	110	180
822 Matt Dillon (300)	45	85	130
823 Annie Oakley (450)	50	90	200
824 Major Seth Adams (400)	50	90	200
825 Hoby Gilman (600)	85	135	270

	C6	C8	C10
826 Lucas McCain (500)	70	110	180
827 Bill Longly (700)	100	240	400
828 Josh Randle (700)	120	290	480
829 Colonel Randal Mackenzie (1200)	150	400	800
864 Jim Hardie (300)	70	110	180
866 Paladin (300)	50	90	150
? Davy Crockett (450)	100	185	350
? Gil Favor (700)	135	250	450
? Bret Maverick (350)	60	100	175
? Johnny Yuma (950)	120	325	600
? Turfking & Jockey (350)	60	100	175
700 Bullet (125)	25	40	65

HARTLAND No. 809 Wyatt Earp.

HARTLAND No. 814 General Custer (flag not shown).

HARTLAND No. 816 Cochise.

HARTLAND No. 817 Jim Bowie.

HARTLAND No. 819 Buffalo Bill.

HARTLAND No. 821 Tom Jeffords.

HARTLAND No. 822 Matt Dillon.

HARTLAND No. 826 Lucas McCain.

HARTLAND No. 828 Josh Randle.

HARTLAND No.700 Bullet.

HARTLAND No. 864 Jim Hardie.

Famous Gunfighter Series

	C6	C8	C10
709 Marshall Wyatt Earp (300)	50	90	150
761 Chris Colt (400)	50	90	150
762 Bret Maverick (300)	50	90	150
763 Clay Holister (400)	75	125	190
764 Jim Hardie (400)	75	125	200
765 Vint Bonner (550)	85	180	325
766 Paladin (400)	100	175	375
767 Dan Troop (600)	75	140	300
768 Johnny McKay (750)	100	240	400
769 Bat Masterson (450)	120	270	450

8" Western Wranglers (Riders are Removable)

611 Alkali Ike (250)	35	75	125
612 Cactus Pete (250)	35	75	125
613 Comanche Kid (250)	35	75	125

HARTLAND No. 761.

HARTLAND No. 769 Bat Masterson.

5-1/2" Western Horse and Riders
(Hats and Riders are Removable)

	C6	C8	C10
C10 Mint on blister card 115			
C8 Mint, complete, off card 80			
C6 Played with, off card, missing hat 35			

Cheyenne, Gill Favor, Johnny Yuma, Wyatt Earp, Matt Dillon, The Lone Ranger, Tonto, Bret Maverick, Roy Rogers, Jim Hardie, Lucas McCain, Paladin

Note: Captain Action 2nd Edition boxes (*) contain rings and are worth 50% more than MIB prices.

	C6	C8	C10
Ideal Captain Action No. 3400-9, costumed figure, lightning sword, scabbard, gun, gun belt, 12" high (400) 100		150	300

IDEAL Captain Action and Action Boy.

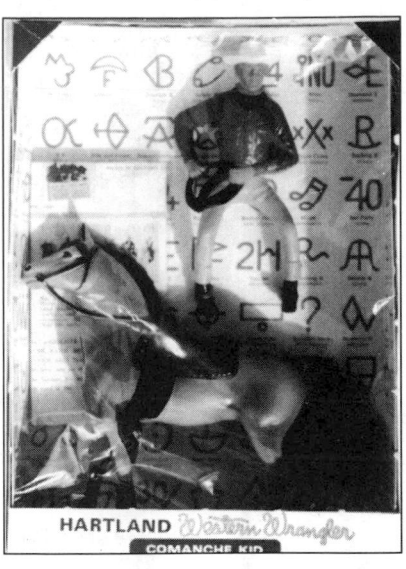

HARTLAND No. 613 Comanche Kid.

	C6	C8	C10
Ideal Action Boy 3420-7, new in 1967, 9" high, costumed, panther, space helmet, utility belt, ray gun, knife (500) 175	250	325
Ideal Dr. Evil No. 3465-2, new in 1968, 12" high, costumed, laser gun (500) 150	250	400
Ideal Batgirl, 12" high, 1967 (800) 250	375	550
Ideal Mera (Aquaman's wife), 1967, 12" high (800) 250	350	400
Ideal Supergirl, 12" high, 1967 (800) 250	350	400
Ideal Wonder Woman, 1967, 12" high (800) 250	350	400
Ideal Aqua Lad Outfit No. 3423-1, costume, octopus, boots, belt with sea horse knife, sea shell axe, no figure included with outfits (800) 250	375	675
* Ideal Aquaman Outfit No. 3408-2, costume, swordfish sword, conch horns, fins, trident spear, knife with sheath, Aquaman face mask (600) 250	350	400
Ideal Bat Girl, helmet, cape, Batarang, boots, Bat gloves, halter dress for alter ego Barbara Gordon (800) 250	375	575
* Ideal Batman Outfit No. 3402-5, costume, emblem, cape, boots, utility belt with 2-way radio buckle, flashlight, Batarang, laser beam, Batrope, reel with grappling hook, hood, Batman face mask (600) 100	175	225
* Ideal Buck Rogers Outfit No.3416-5, face mask, space belt, twin jet packs, space helmet, space gun, space light, space boots, canteen (700) 170	270	380
* Ideal Captain America Outfit No. 3409-0, uniform, belt with holster, ultrasonic pistol, laser-beam gun, boots, shield, Captain America face mask (450) 180	250	300
* Ideal Flash Gordon Outfit No. 3403-3, silver astro-suit, space helmet, silver boots, space belt with holster and ray pistol, oxygen guidance "Zot" gun, Flash Gordon face mask (400) 120	150	200

	C6	C8	C10
* Ideal Green Hornet Outfit No. 3413-2, face mask, watch message receiver, gas pistol, hornet sting, TV scanner with phone, shoulder holster, gas mask, shoes, costume (1200)	300	450	725
* Ideal Lone Ranger Outfit No.3406-6, Wild West cowboy outfit, gun belt, two holsters, two pistols, boots with spurs, Winchester rifle, cowboy hat, Lone Ranger face mask, blue shirt version (600)	225	325	400
Red shirt version (700)	250	375	450
* Ideal The Phantom Outfit No. 3407-4, costume, rifle with scope, belt, holster, pistol, knife, boots, Phantom face mask (350)	70	120	150
Ideal Robin Outfit No. 3421-5, two suction grips, Bat-a-rang Launcher, Bat-a-rang, two Bat grenades (500)	160	225	300
* Ideal Sgt. Fury Outfit (500)	80	135	185
* Ideal Spider-Man Outfit No. 3414-0, spray tank with hose, utility belt, Spider-hook with rope and handle, mask, light, boots (750)	225	275	375
* Ideal Steve Canyon Outfit No. 3405-8, uniform, 50 mission hat, parachute pack, garrison belt, holster, .45 automatic, helmet with oxygen mask, knife, boots, Steve Canyon face mask (500)	70	120	150

	C6	C8	C10
Ideal Super Girl, cape, costume, boots, Krypto dog, halter dress for alter ego Linda Lee Danvers (900)	250	350	450
Ideal Superboy Outfit No. 3422-3, uniform, belt, boots, cape, telepathic scrambler, interspace language translator, chem lab (600)	200	275	350
* Ideal Superman Outfit No. 3401-7, costume, super shield, belt, flying cape, boots, arm shackles, block of Kryptonite, Superman face mask, Krypto the dog (450)	140	190	220
Ideal Tonto Outfit No. 3415-7, face mask, gun belt, head band, pistol, knife, bow, quiver, 4 arrows, moccasins, eagle (450)	150	225	300
Ideal Communicator Kit No. 3454-6, solar power pack, rotating antenna dome, beam projectors, secret sound horn (650)	150	275	350
Ideal Directional Communicator Set No. 3454-6, solar power pack, rotating antenna dome, power plugs, beam projectors, secret sound horn (650)	150	250	300
Ideal Dr. Evil Gift Set No. 3466-0, Dr. Evil, lab coat, two disguise masks, reducer, hypnotic eye, ionized hypo, laser ray gun, thought control helmet (1200)	250	450	850
Ideal Dr. Evil Sanctuary No. 8701-5, "space age" carry case, storage bins, Dr. Evil figure (1400)	350	600	800

Top, left to right: Flash Gordon Outfit, Spider-Man Outfit, Steve Canyon Outfit, Green Hornet Outfit, Lone Ranger Outfit, Tonto Outfit. Bottom, Left to Right: The Phantom Outfit, Batman Outfit, Captain America Outfit, Aquaman Outfit, Buck Rogers Outfit, Superman Outfit.

*IDEAL
Directional
Communicator
Set No. 3454-6.
Solar Power
Pack, Rotating
Antenna Dome,
Power Plugs,
Beam
Projectors,
Secret
Sound Horn*

*IDEAL
Parachute
Pack No.
3453-B.
Parachute
with Body
Harness and
Back Pack,
Crash Helmet,
Jump Boots.*

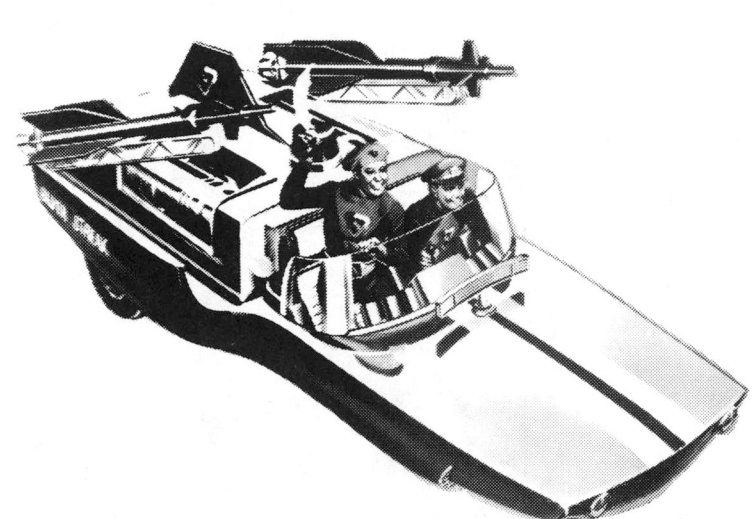

*IDEAL
Silver Streak
Amphibian.*

	C6	C8	C10
Ideal Jet Mortar No. 3452-0, mortar with blaster tripod, radar scanner, ammo carrier, two mortar missiles (500)	70	150	210
Ideal Parachute Pack No. 3453-B, parachute with body harness and back pack, crash helmet, jump boots (450)	100	150	250
Ideal Power Pack No. 3455-3, thrust ejector, cosmic boots, cosmic gloves, flight helmet (350)	90	135	175
Ideal Silver Streak Amphibian No. 3449-6, 21-1/4" long (1300)	200	600	900

	C6	C8	C10
Ideal Survival Vest No. 3450-4, utility vest with fishing kit, mirror, first aid kit, folding spade, 3-piece extension claw hook, machete, utility belt with flare pistol and holster, flares, dagger, ammo, hatchet (650)	175	300	400
Ideal Weapons Arsenal No. 3451-2, electronic rifle, two revolvers, carbine, automatic, two grenades, combat knife, all-purpose knife, ray gun, storage rack (500)	100	150	225

KENNER

Kenner was formed in 1947 on Kenner Street in Cincinnati by three brothers: Al, Phil and Joe Steiner. In 1967 General Mills took it over. The Star Wars toys have probably been its most notable success, and follow Kenner's other action figures and toys in this listing.

Because figures that are mint on the card or in the box are so important in this category, their prices are shown in parentheses immediately following the listing.

	C6	C8	C10
Alien, 18" high, new in 1980, *Alien* movie. Fully articulated jaws, tail moves, head glows in dark (350)	75	150	200

Raiders of the Lost Ark

Listing by Jim Main

3-3/4" Figures

	C6	C8	C10
Indiana Jones (120)	18	25	35
Marion Ravenwood (225)	55	85	100
Toht (15)	4	5	6
German Mechanic (25)	6	8	10
Indiana Jones in German Uniform (60)	10	15	20
Belloq (30)	10	20	30
Belloq (mail in figure) (25)	6	8	10
Cairo Swordsman (20)	6	9	12
Arabian Horse (85)	5	10	15
Sallah (50)	12	16	20
Streets of Cairo playset (50)	13	16	20
Well of Souls playset (75)	20	30	45
Map Room playset (45)	10	15	20
Desert Convoy Truck (60)	8	12	15
Indiana Jones 12" figure (250)	60	100	130

Six Million Dollar Man

Listing by Jim Main

12" Figures

	C6	C8	C10
Steve Austin (80)	15	20	25
Bionic Woman, Jamie Summers (65)	12	16	20
Oscar Goldman (55)	9	12	15
Fembot (150)	20	25	30
Maskatron (100)	20	25	30
Bionic Bigfoot (165)	20	25	30
Bionic Beauty Salon (55)	20	25	30
Bionic Mission Vehicle (80)	15	18	21
Mission Control Playset (65)	25	35	45
Venus Space Probe (75)	20	30	40
Transport Repair (45)	8	12	16
O.S.I. Headquarters (55)	20	30	40
Test Flight at 75,000 Ft. (10)	3	5	7
O.S.I. Undercover (10)	3	5	7
Mission to Mars (35)	9	13	17
Critical Assignment Arms (25)	7	10	12

Super Powers Figures

Listing by Jim Main

	C6	C8	C10
Aquaman (35)	8	12	16

	C6	C8	C10
Flash (18)	4	6	8
Batman (55)	12	18	25
Superman (35)	7	11	15
Green Lantern (50)	15	22	30
Hawkman (60)	15	22	30
DeSaad (25)	5	8	11
Robin (45)	7	11	15
Braniac (25)	5	8	11
Luthor (15)	3	5	7
Penguin (30)	5	8	10
Joker (25)	5	8	10
Wonder Woman (25)	4	6	8
Mr. Freeze (60)	13	19	26
Tyr (65)	20	30	40
Plastic Man (120)	27	41	55
Golden Pharoah (135)	25	38	50
Orion (45)	10	15	20
Steppenwolf (70)	7	11	15
Clark Kent (60)	25	38	50
Parademon (30)	5	8	11
Cyborg (325)	50	75	100
Mantis (35)	6	9	12
Kalibak (20)	5	8	10
Samurai (100)	20	30	40
Mr. Miracle (155)	32	48	65
Captain Marvel (Shazam) (55)	15	22	30
Firestorm (30)	10	15	20
Darkseid (15)	5	8	10
Red Tornado (70)	17	26	35
Green Arrow (55)	5	8	10
Martian Manhunter (40)	9	13	18
Dr. Fate (70)	17	26	35
Cyclotron (65)	12	18	25

Vehicles/accessories

Listing by Jim Main

	C6	C8	C10
Batmobile (100)	12	18	25
Supermobile (40)	7	10	15
Batcopter (90)	15	22	30
Delta Probe One (60)	7	10	14
Justice Jogger (30)	7	10	14
Lex-Soar 7 (25)	6	10	13
Kalibak Boulder Bomber (30)	6	10	13
Darkseid Destroyer (60)	10	15	20
Hall of Justice playset (160)	30	45	60
All Terrain Trapper (85)	20	40	60

Steve Scout

	C6	C8	C10
Steve Scout figure (40)	10	15	20

Star Wars

By Whit Alexander and Neal Bates

The first set of 12 figures was introduced in 1977 and by 1984 over 80 different action figures were offered. Over the seven-year marketing period the attention to detail and variation of accessories increased.

The first set of action figures all read 1977 on their legs and included SW-A1, SW-A3, SW-A4, SW-A5, SW-A6, SW-A10, SW-A11, SW-A12, SW-A15, SW-A17, SW-A18, and SW-A20. The next set read 1978 and included the five cantina figures (SW-A8, SW-A9, SW-A19A, SW-A19B, SW-A21), plus four more (SW-A13, SW-A14, SW-A15, SW-A16, SW-A7). Boba Fett (SW-A2) was the only figure issued in 1979.

Prices are for single loose figures; prices in parentheses are for figures in perfect mint containers.

Star Wars Action Figures (SW-A)

Loose

SW-A1 Ben (Obi-Wan) Kenobi:
3-1/4" high, rust with removable brown cape,
retractable blue lightsaber, 1977 (125) 16
SW-A2 Boba Fett: 3-3/4" high, blue-gray
with backpack, laser pistol (Weapon No. 1).
Originally offered only through special
mail order and was the only Empire
Strikes Back character to be offered a year
prior to the movie's release date. 1979 (330) 10
SW-A3 Chewbacca: 4-1/4" high, brown with silver
bandolier, laser rifle (Weapon No. 6), 1977 (125) 10
SW-A4 C-3PO: 3-3/4" high, metallic gold,

Left to right: SW-A3, SW-A17, SW-A4, SW-A10.

no accessories, 1977 (130) 9
SW-A5 Darth Vader: 4-1/4" high, black with removable
black cape, retractable red lightsaber, 1977 (110) 15
SW-A6 Death Squad Commander (Star Destroyer
Commander): 3-1/4" high, gray with black helmet,
laser pistol (Weapon No. 1), 1977 (100) 9
SW-A7 Death Star Droid: 3-3/4" high,
metallic silver, no accessories, 1978 (120) 9

Left to right: SW-A7, SW-A16, SW-A14, SW-A2, SW-A13.

430 • Action Figures

Loose

SW-A8 Greedo: 3-3/4" high, green with
laser pistol (Weapon No. 2), 1978 (100) 10
SW-A9 Hammerhead: 4" high, brown with blue
suit, laser pistol (Weapon No. 1), 1978 (100)...........................8

Left to right: SW-A9, SW-A19B, SW-A19A, SW-A21, SW-A8.

SW-A10 Han Solo: 3-3/4" high, white shirt
with black vest and pants, laser pistol
(Weapon No. 2), 1977 (450) 18
SW-A11 Jawa: 2-1/4" high, brown with brown
cloth cape, laser rifle (Weapon No. 4), 1977 (105) 11
SW-A12 Luke Skywalker: 3-3/4" high;
white shirt with beige pants,
retractable lightsaber, 1977 (330) 25
SW-A13 Luke Skywalker X-Wing Pilot:
3-1/4" high, orange with white helmet,
laser pistol (Weapon No. 2), 1978 (125) 16
SW-A14 Power Droid: 2-1/4" high, blue TV set
shape with clicking legs, no accessories, 1978 (85) 12
SW-A15 Princess Leia Organa: 3-1/2" high,
white with removable white cape,
laser pistol (Weapon No. 3), 1977 (215) 25

Left to right: SW-A15, SW-A12, SW-A1, SW-A5.

SW-A16 R5-D4: 2-1/2" high, white trash-can
shape with red detail, no accessories, 1978 (85) 16
SW-A17 R2-D2: 2-1/4" high, white with blue
detail and chrome-dome head that clicks
when turned, no accessories, 1978 (125) 12
SW-A18 Sand People: 3-3/4" high, tan with removable
tan cape, Gaffie Stick (Weapon No. 5), 1977 (145) 11

SW-A19A Snaggletooth: 3-3/4" high, blue with
  silver boots, laser pistol (Weapon No.1),
  offered only with Cardboard Cantina, 1978 (65) 8
SW-A19B Snaggletooth: 2-7/8" high, red,
  laser pistol (Weapon No. 1), 1978 (75) 8
SW-A20A Stormtrooper: 3-3/4" high, white with
  white helmet, laser pistol (Weapon No. 1), 1977 (80) 15
SW-A21 Walrus Man: 3-3/4" high, blue with
  orange suit and green head, laser pistol
  (Weapon No. 1), 1978 (115) 8

Left to right: SW-A20, SW-A11, SW-A18, SW-A6.

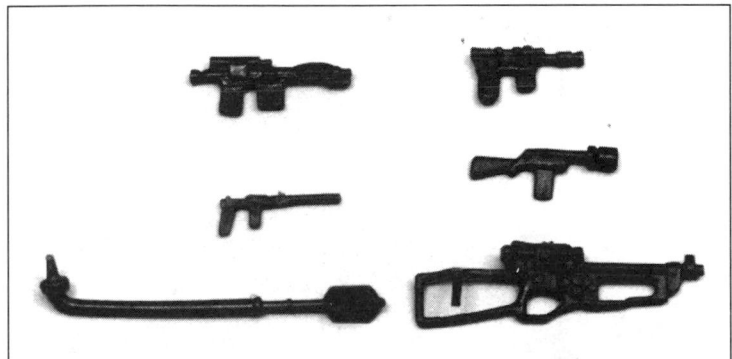

Star Wars Action Figures Weapons and Accessories. Top, left to right: 1, 2. Middle, left to right: 3, 4. Bottom, left to right: 5, 6.

The Empire Strikes Back Action Figures

ESB-A1 AT-AT Commander: 3-3/4" high, gray
  with gray hat, laser pistol (Weapon No.1), 1980 (35) 8
ESB-A2 AT-AT Driver: 3-3/4" high, light gray with
  white helmet, laser pistol (Weapon No. 7), 1980 (35) 10
ESB-A3A Bespin Security Guard: 3-7/8" high,
  black man with navy uniform, laser pistol
  (Weapon No. 1), 1981 (45) 9
ESB-A3B Bespin Security Guard: 4" high, white man
  with navy uniform, laser pistol (Weapon No. 1), 1980 (45) 9
ESB-A4 Bossk: 4" high, yellow with olive head,
  laser rifle (Weapon No.6), 1980 (65) 8
ESB-A5 C-3PO: 4" high, metallic gold with
  removable limbs, papoose (Acc. No. 13), 1980 (80) 7
ESB-A6 Cloud Car Pilot: 3-3/4" high, white with
  orange and yellow helmet, laser pistol (Weapon
  No. 9a) and walkie-talkie (Acc. No. 9b), 1981 (50) 15

Left to right: ESB-A7, ESB-A28, ESB-A9, ESB-A12, ESB-A4.

ESB-A7 Dengar: 3-5/8" high, white
  and brown with backpack and head wrap,
  laser rifle (Weapon No. 2), 1980 (35)...................... 8
ESB-A8 FX-7: 3-3/8" high with head down,
  silver with nine movable arms and
  retractable head, no accessories, 1980 (55) 8
ESB-A9 4-LOM: 3-5/8" high, tan with removable
  tan cape and brown removable backpack,
  laser pistol (Weapon No. 11), 1981 (115) 10
ESB-A10 Han Solo (Bespin outfit): 4" high,
  navy vest with brown pants, laser pistol
  (Weapon No. 3), 1980 (65) 18
ESB-A11 Han Solo (Hoth outfit): 4" high,
  blue fur-lined parka with brown boots,
  laser pistol (Weapon No. 3), 1980, (60) 13
ESB-A12 IG-88: 4-5/8" high, gray with black bandolier,
  laser guns (Weapons No. 1 & 16), 1980 (55) 11
ESB-A13 Imperial Commander: 3-7/8" high,
  black hat, laser pistol (Weapon No. 14), 1980 (30)........ 8
ESB-A14 Imperial Stormtrooper (Hoth Battle Gear):
  3-7/8" high, white with white veil and removable
  white skirt, laser rifle (Weapon No.2), 1980 (55)........... 9

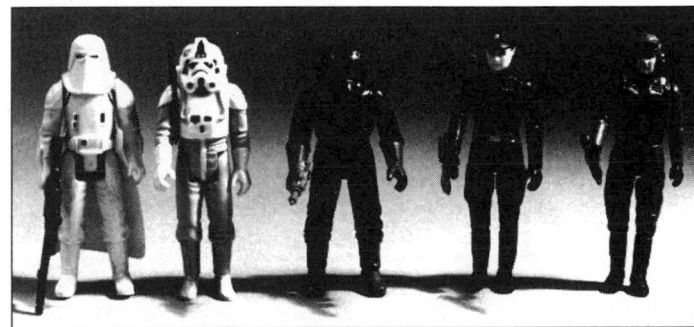

Left to right: ESB-A14, ESB-A2, ESB-A15, ESB-A13, ESB-A1.

ESB-A15 Imperial TIE Fighter Pilot:
  3-3/4" high, black with gray boots and gloves,
  laser pistol (Weapon No. 9a), 1982 (60)................. 11
ESB-A16 Lando Calrissian: 4" high, light blue
  with dark blue pants and removable cape,
  laser pistol (Weapon No. 1), 1980 (45) 10
ESB-A17 Lobot: 3-5/8" high, gray-brown
  with yellow sleeves, computerized head
  band, laser pistol (Weapon No. 1), 1980 (45)......... 8

Left to right: ESB-A17, ESB-A6, ESB-A3B, ESB-A26, ESB-A3A.

Left to right: ESB-A18, ESB-A22, ESB-A27.

Loose

ESB-A18 Luke Skywalker (Bespin Fatigues):
3-7/8" high, tan with brown boots, laser pistol,
lightsaber (Weapons No. 3 & 5), 1980 (100) 20
ESB-A19 Luke Skywalker (Hoth Battle Gear):
3-3/4" high, white with brown vest
and scarf, laser rifle (Weapon No. 17), 1981 (85) 15

Loose

ESB-A22 R2-D2 (With Sensorscope):
2-1/2" high, white with blue detail,
one head panel extends into radar,
no accessories, bottom reads "1977"
but new head was added circa 1980 (45) 8
ESB-A23 Rebel Commander: 3-7/8" high,
white with brown scarf, laser rifle
(Weapon No. 7), 1980 (30)..................................... 8
ESB-A24 Rebel Soldier: 3-7/8" high,
white with brown vest and white hat,
laser pistol (Weapon No. 1), 1980 (70) 8
ESB-A25 2-1B: 3-3/4" high, blue with transparent
middle and gas mask, medical stick
(Acc. No. 12), 1980 (60).. 8

Left to right: ESB-A19, ESB-A11, ESB-A23, ESB-A24.

ESB-A20 Princess Leia Organa (Bespin Gown):
3-1/2" high, brick red with pink cape,
laser pistol (Weapon No. 4), 1980 (95) 15
ESB-A21 Princess Leia Organa (Hoth Outfit):
3-3/4" high, white with tan vest,
laser pistol (Weapon No. 4), 1980 (50) 18

Left to right: ESB-A25, ESB-A21, ESB-A8.

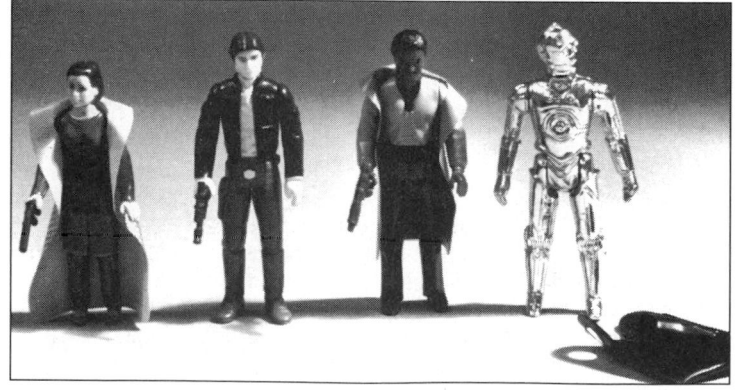

Left to right: ESB-A21, ESB-A10, ESB-A16, ESB-A5.

ESB-A26 Ugnaught: 2-3/4" high, gray with blue
apron and tool purse (Acc. No. 8), 1980 (50) 10
ESB-A27 Yoda: 2" high, brown with light
green head, cloth tan robe, removable belt,
orange snake (Acc. No. 10a), brown stick
(Acc. No. 10b), 1980 (40).. 17
ESB-A28 Zuckuss: 3-3/4" high, gray with blue
fly-like eyes, laser rifle (Weapon No. 15), 1982 (70)............ 10

The Empire Strikes Back Action Figures Weapons and Accessories. Top, left to right: 2, 1, 3, 4, 5. Second row: 6, 7, 8, 9a, 9b. Third row: 10a, 10b, 11, 12, 13. Fourth row: 14, 15, 16. Bottom: 17.

Return of the Jedi Action Figures

Loose

RJ-A1 Admiral Ackbar: 3-7/8" high, white with tan vest and rust "lobster" head, black stick (Acc. No. 1), 1983 (25) 8

RJ-A2 AT-ST Driver: 3-7/8" high, light gray with dark gray helmet, laser pistol (Weapon No. 2), 1984 (25).............................8

RJ-A3 B-Wing Pilot: 3-7/8" high, red with silver and brown helmet, laser pistol (Weapon No. 2), 1984 (20)............7

RJ-A4 Bib Fortuna: 4-1/8" high, blue with removable beige cape and removable gray chestplate, wraparound horn, staff (Acc. No. 6), 1983 (20) 8

Left to right: RJ-A5, RJ-A22, RJ-A19.

Left to right: RJ-A3, RJ-A11, RJ-A1, RJ-A17.

RJ-A5 Biker Scout: 4" high, black with white armor, laser pistol (Weapon No. 4), 1983 (30) 11

RJ-A6 Boushh: 3-5/8" high, beige and brown with silver armor, silver and orange removable helmet, laser stick (Weapon No. 7), 1983 (40)........................18

RJ-A7 Chief Chirpa: 3" high with removable brown hood, staff (Acc. No. 21), 1983 (25) 8

RJ-A8 8D8: White droid with silver and brown detail, no accessories, 1983 (25)..7

Loose

RJ-A9 Emperor's Royal Guard: Brick red and crimson cape and tunic, staff (Weapon No. 8), 1983 (30)................... 10

RJ-A10 Gamorrean Guard: 3-7/8" high, olive with brown garment, battle axe (Weapon No. 3), 1983 (35) 7

RJ-A11 General Madine: 4" high, light gray with black boots and gloves and blue sleeves, white wand (Acc. No. 16), 1983 (25) 8

RJ-A12 Han Solo (Trench Coat): 4" high, dark gray pants with light gray shirt, removable camouflage cape, laser pistol (Weapon No. 22), 1984 (30) 10

RJ-A13A Klaatu: 4" high, dark green with gray shirt and silver helmet, animal pelt skirt, skiff stick (Weapon No. 9), 1983 (30)................................... 8

RJ-A13B Klaatu (Skiff Guard Outfit): 3-7/8" high, dark green with off-white garment and brown helmet, laser stick (Weapon No. 10), 1983 (20)...................... 8

RJ-A14 Lando Calrissian (Skiff Guard Disguise): 3-7/8" high, brown vest with armor, brown helmet, skiff stick (Weapon No. 9), 1982 (25) 13

RJ-A15 Luke Skywalker (Jedi Knight Outfit): 3-7/8" high, black with removable olive cape, laser pistol and lightsaber (Weapons No. 5a and 5b), 1983 (80) 30

Left to right: RJ-A13A, RJ-A13B, RJ-A8, RJ-A18.

Left to right: RJ-A28, RJ-A7, RJ-A15, RJ-A25.

Loose

RJ-A16 Logray: 3-5/8" high, cream and brown
   striped with removable black hood,
   medicine bag and staff (Acc. No. 18), 1983 (20) 8

RJ-A17 Nien Nunb: 3-7/8" high, red with navy vest,
   dark gray helmet, laser pistol (Weapon No. 17) 1983 (20) 8

RJ-A18 Nikto: White shirt with ice-blue vest
   and gray pants, brown head wrap, laser stick
   (Weapon No. 11), 1983 (20).....................................15

RJ-A19 Princess Leia Organa (Combat Poncho): 3-5/8"
   high, gray with removable helmet and combat poncho,
   removable belt, laser pistol (Weapon No. 2), 1984 (30) 20

RJ-A20 Prune Face: 3-7/8" high, lime green pants
   with cream shirt and removable tan cape,
   eyepatch, laser rifle (Weapon No. 15), 1984 (20) 8

RJ-A21 Rancor Keeper: 4" high, olive pants,
   no shirt, removable hood, stick (Acc. No. 23), 1984 (20)........8

RJ-A22 Rebel Commando: 4" high, olive uniform
   with green helmet, brown backpack,
   laser rifle (Weapon No. 24), 1983 (20) 8

Loose

RJ-A23 Ree-Yees: 3-5/8" high, peach with three eyes,
   brick red garment, laser rifle (Weapon No. 13), 1983 (20) 8

RJ-A24 Squid Head: 4" high, white
   with white skirt, removable belt, olive
   cape, head has four tentacles,
   laser pistol (Weapon No. 14), 1983 (20) 8

RJ-A25 Teebo: 3-7/8" high, light and dark gray
   striped, removable hood and horn on sling,
   axe (Acc. No. 19), 1984 (20) 8

RJ-A26 The Emperor: 4" high,
   dark gray, staff (Acc. No. 12), 1984 (40) 9

RJ-A27 Weequay: 3-7/8" high, ice blue shirt
   with beige pants and brown vest, gray ponytail,
   skiff stick (Weapon No. 9), 1983 (20)................................... 8

RJ-A28 Wicket W. Warrick: 2" high,
   brown with creme belly, removable hood,
   spear (Weapon No. 20), 1984 (30) 11

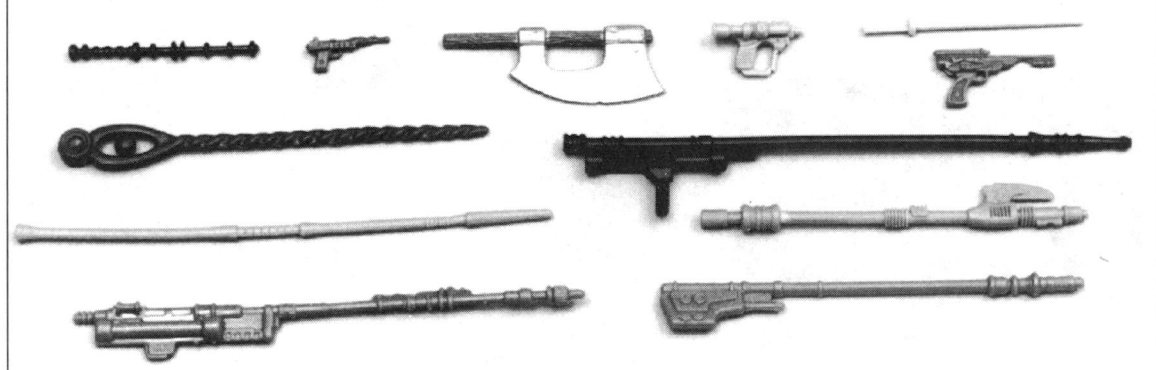

The Return of the Jedi Action Figures Weapons and Accessories.
Top, left to right: 1, 2, 3, 4, 5a, 5b.
Second row: 6, 7.
Third row: 8, 9.
Bottom row: 10, 11.

Top, left to right: 12, 13, 14, 15. Second row: 17, 18, 19, 20, 21,16. Bottom row: 22, 23, 24.

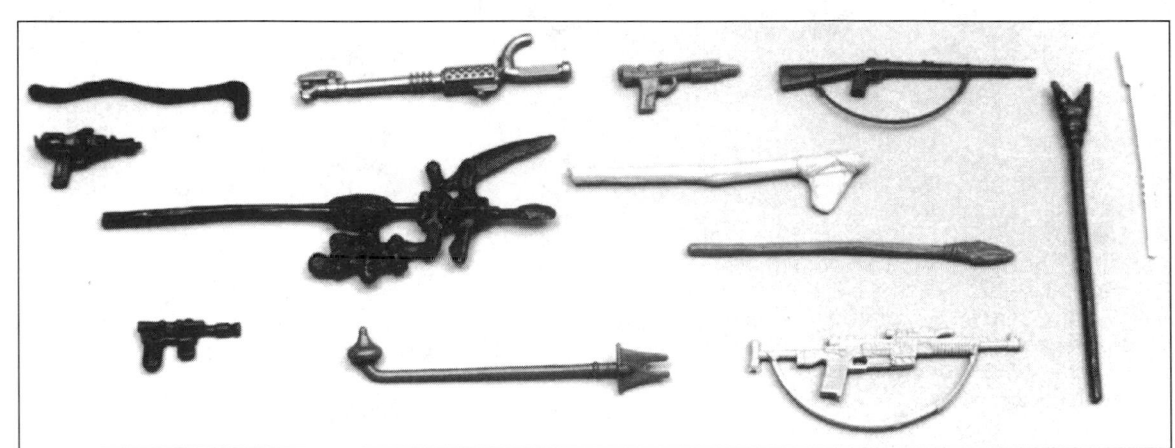

SW-V1, Darth Vader TIE-Fighter. Figure not included.

SW-V4, Landspeeder. Figure not included.

Star Wars Vehicles (SW-V). These vehicles are intended for use with the action figures and many are battery operated (B/O).

Loose

SW-V1 Darth Vader TIE Fighter: B/O, 9-3/4" long
x 11-3/4" wide, dark gray with spherical
cockpit and removable wing panels, red laser
lights up and emits a whirring sound, 1978 (110) 45

Loose

SW-V2 Imperial Troop Transport: B/O, 10-1/4" long
x 5-1/4" wide, gray with red stripes, has rear
and 6 side compartments, dual cockpit and
rotating laser cannons and radar, 2 prisoner holsters,
6 red buttons play a variety of recordings (90) 35

SW-V3 Jawa Sandcrawler: 14-1/2" long x 5-5/8" wide,
rust brown with wireless remote control, 1979 (425).......... 180

SW-V2, Imperial Troop Transport. Figures not included.

SW-V7, X-Wing Fighter. Figure not included.

*SW-V5,
Millennium
Falcon.
Figures
not
included.*

Action Figures • 435

SW-V6, Tie-Fighter. Figure not included.

ESB-V2, AT-ST (Scout Walker). Figures not included.

	Loose
SW-V4 Landspeeder: 9-1/2" long x 6" wide, brown with chrome grills, 3 jets, windshield, wheels can be lowered by shifter in cockpit, 1978 (65)	20
SW-V5 Millennium Falcon: B/O, 20-1/2" long x 16-1/2" wide, off-white with gray laser cannon, main compartment has chessboard, laser ball, floor panel and revolving laser cannon, emits whirring sound when side button is pressed, 1979 (225)	95
SW-V6 TIE Fighter: B/O, 7-1/8" long x 10-1/4" wide, white with spherical cockpit and removable black wing panels, red laser lights up and emits whirring sound, 1978 (135)	40
SW-V7 X-Wing Fighter: B/O, 13-3/4" long x 11-1/2" wide, white with red and yellow stripes, 4 laser cannons, wings open into "X" position, red laser lights up and emits whirring sound, 1978 (130)	40

The Empire Strikes Back Vehicles (ESB-V)

	Loose
ESB-V1 AT-AT: B/O, 17-1/2" high x 22" long, light gray with black detail, 4 moveable legs, swiveling cockpit, 2 laser cannons light up and pulsate, 1981 (175)	115

	Loose
ESB-V2 AT-ST (Scout Walker): 11-1/4" high, light gray, button on back moves legs, 1982 (85)	45
ESB-V3 Imperial Star Destroyer: swiveling laser cannon on bow, meditation chamber, 1981 (175)	45
ESB-V4A MCL-3: light gray with tank treads and dome top, 1981 (22)	10
ESB-V4B MTV-7: light gray with spring-loaded steamroller legs, 1981 (22)	7
ESB-V5 Slave 1: 15" long, 12-3/4" wide, gray with blue windshield, 2 swiveling wing flaps, black cargo door, gray side door, revolving laser cannons on tail, Han Solo in carbonite, 1981 (150)	40

ESB-V6, Snowspeeder. Figure not included.

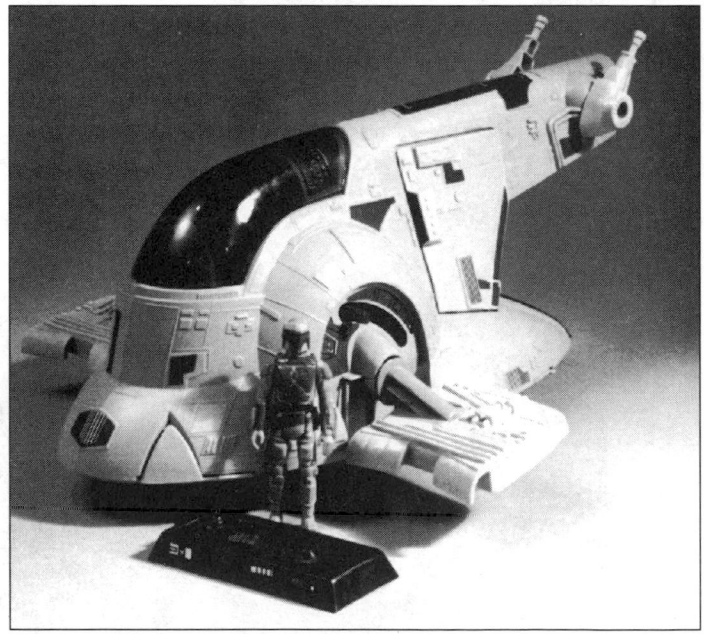

ESB-V5, Slave-1. Boba Fett not included.

ESB-V7, Twin-Pod Cloud Car. Figure not included.

Loose

ESB-V6 Snowspeeder, B/O, 12-1/4" long, 12-3/4"
    wide, light gray with 2 light-up laser cannons,
    rear harpoon gun with harpoon on string, 1980 (60) 45
ESB-V7 Twin-Pod Cloud Car: 10-1/2" wide x 8-3/4"
    long, rust orange with dual pod cockpit, 1980 (75) 25

Return of the Jedi Vehicles (RJ-V)

RJ-V1 B-Wing Fighter: light gray, cockpit on right
    side with fin-wing extending to the left, c. 1985, (125) 80
RJ-V1 A Battle-Damaged Imperial TIE Fighter (75) 45
RJ-V2 Ewok Combat Glider: brown with harness
    for one action figure and 2 stone-bombs, c.1984 (85)...........45
RJ-V3 Imperial Shuttle: light gray, stationary
    center fin and side wings that fold up, c. 1984 (225) 40
RJ-V4 Speeder Bike: 8-3/4" long, light brown
    with black engine and detail, "explodes"
    when pack is pressed, 1983 (30)......................................5
RJ-V5 Y-Wing Fighter: light gray with twin hollow
    engines, 3 retractable landing skids, c. 1984 (140) 65

Star Wars Playsets (SW-P)

SW-P1 Action Figure Display Stand: 20" long,
    5-1/2" wide, gray base with moving discs for 12
    action figures. Front has decal with the names of the
    12 original action figures. Cardboard backdrop
    depicts a spaceship dogfight. Available through
    special mail order only. 1978. (125)
SW-P2 Cardboard Cantina: 18" long, 7" high, tan base
    has 11 action figure pegs. Backdrop has scene
    from Mos Eisley city street. Available only
    with Cantina figure set, which included
    SW-A8, SW-A9, SW-19A, and SW-A21.
    1978. Sears exclusive. (400)................................195
SW-P3 Collector's Case: 2 trays hold a total of 24
    action figures. Case depicts scenes from Star Wars. (100) 25
SW-P4 Creature Cantina: 13-3/4" long, 7-3/4" wide,
    tan-orange base has bar and table, 2 action levers
    and floor button that opens the doors.
    Cardboard backdrop depicts cantina scene. 1979. (150)
SW-P5 Death Star Space Station: 22-1/4" high, gray and
    black, 3 floors and basement trash compactor.
    Compactor has foam trash and green monster. Floors
    have drawbridge, grappling hook swing, "exploding"
    laser cannon and catwalk. Main tower has
    elevator and 2nd and 3rd floors have
    cardboard surface panels. 1977. (160)...................................90

Loose

SW-P6 Droid Factory: 13" x 11", tan-orange
    base holds 38 interchangeable droid parts,
    crane with hook. 1979. (150)................................. 45
SW-P7 Land of the Jawas: 13-1/2" long, 8-1/4" wide.
    Tan base has sand cave and action lever.
    Escape pod fits into crater. Cardboard backdrop
    depicts sandcrawler and has moving elevator. 1979. (180)... 50
SW-P8 Patrol Dewback: 10-1/2" long,
    green and white lizard has 4 posable limbs
    and trap door in back. Tail and head move
    together. Brown saddle and harness. 1979. (55).................... 30

Empire Strikes Back Playsets (ESB-P)

ESB-P1 Cardboard Bespin Set: 9" high,
    11-3/4" wide, cardboard base has 6 action
    figure pegs. Backdrop depicts Cloud City
    scene and has protruding carbonite chamber.
    Available only with action figures ESB-A7,
    ESB-A10, ESB-A17, and ESB-A26.
    1980. Sears Exclusive. (350)
ESB-P2 Collector's Case: 2 trays hold a total of
    24 action figures. Case depicts scenes from
    The Empire Strikes Back. (40) 30
ESB-P3 Dagobah Playset: gray with brown
    tree stump, 3 action levers, mud puddle
    and 2 storage containers. 1981. (60)...................................... 45
ESB-P4 Darth Vader Collector Case:
    14-1/2" high, 16" wide, black with room
    for 31 action figures and accessories. C. 1980. (40).............. 10
ESB-P5 Hoth Icc Planet: 13-1/2" long, 8-1/4" wide,
    white base has snow cave and action lever.
    Tank-radar sits in crater. Cardboard backdrop
    depicts AT-AT with moving elevator. 1981. (150) 25
ESB-P6 Hoth Wampa: 6" high, white
    with 4 posable limbs. C. 1981. (30)...................................... 20
ESB-P7 Imperial Attack Base: 17-1/4" long,
    10" wide, white with revolving laser cannon
    and gray control room, 3 action levers make
    2-part snowbridge fall, control room
    "explode" and action figure fall. (55) 35

ESB-P9, Taun-taun. Figure not included.

ESB-P8 Probot and Turret: 15-1/2" long,
9-1/4" wide, white base has action lever
and post for gray probot. Turret has door
and revolving laser platform. 1979. (95) 40

ESB-P9 Tauntaun: 9-3/4" from head to tail,
gray and white with brown horns, trap door
in back and 4 posable limbs, brown saddle
and harness. 1980. Split Belly. (50) 30

ESB-P10 Tauntaun as above. 1981. Closed Belly. (50) 20

Return of the Jedi Playsets (RJ-P)

RJ-P1 C-3PO Collector Case: metallic gold with room
for 31 action figures and accessories. C. 1983. (45) 15

RJ-P2 Chewbacca Bandolier Strap: black,
holds 10 action figures and accessories. C. 1983. (20) 8

RJ-P3 Ewok Assault Catapult: brown logs
with rotating winch and 2 gray boulders. C. 1983. (20) 7

RJ-P4 Jabba the Hutt Playset: 11" long,
5-1/4" wide, grayish-brown platform
with 2 doors, with Jabba, Salacious Crumb
and a long-armed green monster. 1983. (35) 9

RJ-P5 Land of the Ewoks: 22" high, 16" long,
tan platform supported by 3 trees, spit
over the fire ring, stool, moving elevator,
net and litter for carrying action figures. 1983. (90) 50

RJ-P6 Rancor Monster: 10" high, tan
with 4 posable limbs. 1983. (50) 35

RJ-P7 Jabba The Hutt Dungeon: 13" x 11",
gray base, crane with hood and branding iron.
Complete with action figures RJ-A13B,
RJ-A18 and RJ-A8. 1983. (90) 40

RJ-P8 Sy Snootles and the Max Rebo Band:
complete with blue keyboardist and keyboard,
spotted singer and microphone,
pink clarinet player and microphone. C. 1983. (90) 40

End Star Wars

LJN "V" Action Figures (TV Series) (45) 30

Large Figures and Dolls

Ben (Obi-Wan) Kenobi, 12" high, lightsaber,
removable cape (250) 125
Boba Fett, 13-1/4" high, laser rifle, molded backpack (275) 150
C-3PO, 12" high (125) 50
Chewbacca, 18" high, stuffed (60) 40
Chewbacca, 15" high, laser crossbow (125) 60
Chewbacca, 8" high, furry (80) 15
Darth Vader, 15" high, lightsaber and removable cape (150) 85
Han Solo, 12" high, laser rifle (500) 200
IG-88, 15" high, laser weapons (600) 315
Jawa, 8-1/4" high, hooded cape and laser rifle (200) 75
Luke Skywalker, 11-3/4" high, lever-like
arm and grappling hook (225) 150
Princess Leia Organa, 11-1/2" high, combable hair (275) 90
R2-D2, 7-1/2" high, head clicks when turned (85) 50
R2-D2, radio controlled (110) 70
Stormtrooper, 12" high, laser rifle (200) 85

Die-Cast Vehicles

Kenner Series I
Darth Vader TIE Fighter (65) 30
X-Wing Fighter (65) 30
Land Speeder (65) 30
TIE Fighter (65) 30

Kenner Series II
Millennium Falcon (210) 45
Darth Vader's Star Destroyer (175) 40
Princess Leia's Command Ship (225) 75
TIE Bomber (750) 450
Y-Wing Fighter (230) 60

Kenner Series III
Snow Speeder (85) 40
Slave I Space Ship (70) 35
Twin-Pod Cloud Car (65) 30

MARX

Listing by Jim Main

---

8 to 12" Figures

	C6	C8	C10
Johnny Apollo Astronaut (135)	30	50	70
Johnny and Jane Apollo Deluxe Set w/ vehicles (450)	125	150	175
Stoney Smith (115)	35	45	55
Sir Gordon, The Golden Knight (125)	15	20	30
Bravo, The Golden Knight's Horse (90)	40	50	60
Sir Stuart, The Silver Knight (250)	60	80	100
Valor, The Silver Knight's Horse (120)	30	40	50
Mike Hazzard, Double Agent (285)	70	90	110
Girl From U.N.C.L.E. (Marx British issue) (600)	100	130	160
Erik the Viking (180)	30	50	75
Odin the Viking Chieftain (125)	25	35	65

Best of the West

	C6	C8	C10
Johnny West (90)	20	30	40
Jay West (60)	20	35	45
Janice West (75)	15	22	28
Josie West (60)	15	22	28
Jane West (85)	15	20	25
Brave Eagle (125)	25	35	75
Chief Cherokee (150)	20	30	40
Daniel Boone (235)	75	95	115
Jamie West (70)	20	30	40
Thundercolt (50)	10	15	20
Thunderbolt (125)	15	20	30
Sheriff Garrett (225)	15	25	35
Sam Cobra (85)	25	35	45

MARX Bravo, The Golden Knight's Horse (box).

MARX Valor, the Silver Knight's Horse, box.

MARX Sir Stuart, the Silver Knight (box).

MARX Erik the Viking (box).

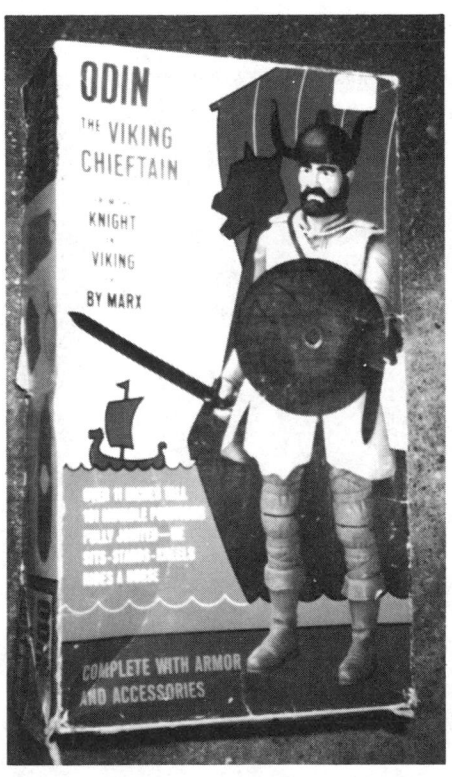

MARX Odin the Viking Chieftain (box).

	C6	C8	C10
Pancho (80)	15	22	28
Flack (65)	20	25	35
Flick (130)	25	35	50
Flame (125)	20	25	35
Flame w/ Corral set (120)	20	25	35
Jane West Set (w/ corral and horses) (140)	50	60	70

MARX Best of the West Buffalo.

MARX Best of the West Buckboard and Horse (Thunderbolt).

	C6	C8	C10
Johnny West Set w/ Horse and Jeep (300)	100	150	200
Johnny West w/ Wild Mustangs set (125)	45	60	75
Princess Wild Flower (175)	25	35	50
Buffalo (150)	55	75	90
Chief Cherokee w/ Teepee set (150)	50	65	80
Circle X Ranch Playset (230)	85	115	150
Commanche (50)	15	20	25
Buckboard and Horse (600)	60	70	80
Covered Wagon (150)	60	70	85

MARX Best of the West Daniel Boone (box).

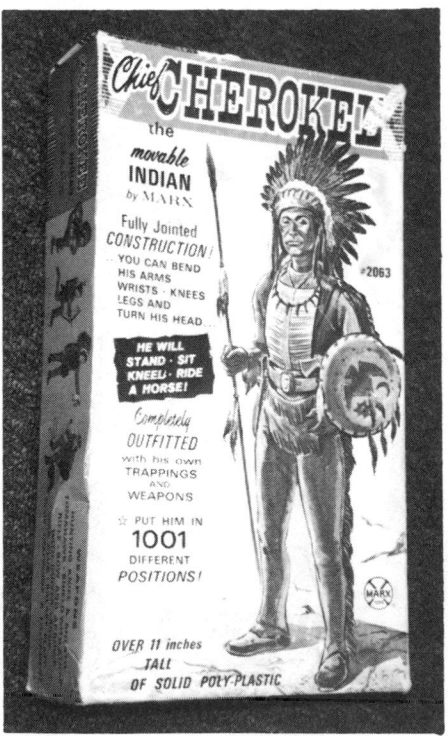

MARX Best of the West Chief Cherokee (box).

MARX Best of the West Johnny West (box).

MARX Best of the West Jane West (box).

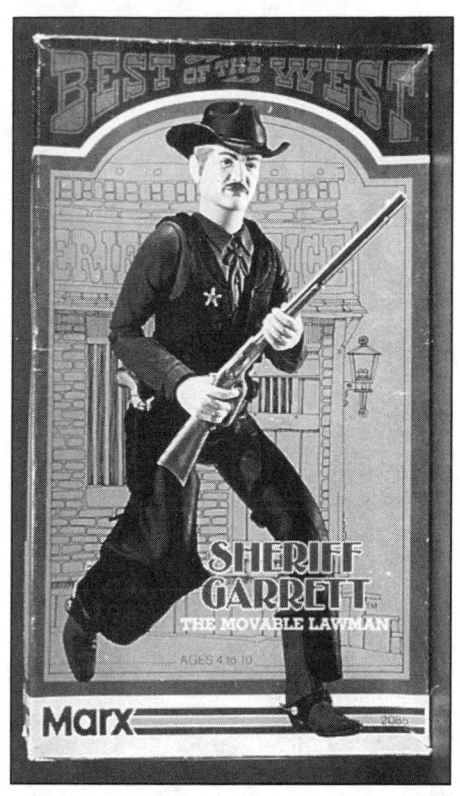

MARX Best of the West Sheriff Garrett (box). Photo by Gary Linden.

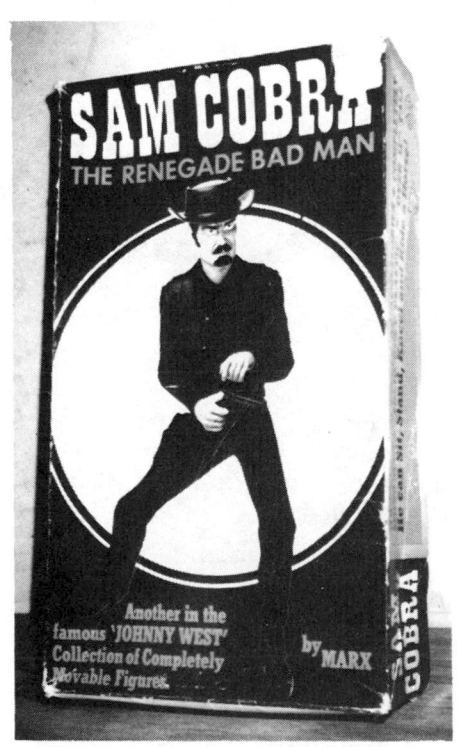

MARX Best of the West Sam Cobra (box). Courtesy Barry Goodman.

MARX Best of the West Josie West (box).

MARX Best of the West Princess Wild Flower (box). Courtesy Barry Goodman.

Fort Apache Fighters

	C6	C8	C10
Sgt. Zeb Zachary (240)	25	35	75
General Custer (140)	25	40	80
Bill Buck (450)	100	200	300
Jeb Gibson (650)	150	400	500
Capt. Maddox (145)	15	25	35
Fort Apache Playset (250)	90	175	250
Fighting Eagle			
(also Best of the West) (200)	30	60	120

MARX Fort Apache Fighters: Sgt. Zeb Zachary (box).

MARX Fort Apache Fighters: General Custer (box).

MARX Fort Apache Fighters: Capt. Maddox (box).

MARX Fort Apache Fighters: Fighting Eagle (box).

MATTEL

Listings by Jim Main

Mattel was founded in 1945 by Harold Mattson and Ruth and Elliot Handler (the "Matt" in Mattson and "El" in Elliot formed the firm's name). The business, created to make picture frames, began in a Los Angeles garage, with Mattson bowing out early due to poor health. Toys were made almost from the beginning: toy furniture was fashioned from the plastic and wood scraps left over from the frames. Mattel's most famous toy is the Barbie doll.

Battlestar Galactica

4" Figures

	Loose
Starbuck (40)	8
Cmdr. Adama (25)	8
Apollo (20)	6
Baltarr (50)	30
Cylon (35)	10
Gold Cylon (140)	50

	Loose
Boray (60)	32
Ovion (30)	7
Daggit (25)	6
Lucifer (75)	50
Imperious Leader (20)	6

MATTEL Battlestar Galactica figures. Left to right: Lt. Starbuck, Commander Adama. Courtesy Rex and Richard Gray.

12" Figures

	Loose
Cylon (70)	25
Colonial Warrior (55)	25

Big Jim's P.A.C.K.

Big Jim (60)	28
Double Trouble Big Jim (40)	30
Double Trouble Zorak (40)	30
Torpedo Fist (75)	50
Warpath (75)	50
Dr. Steel (55)	50
The Whip (60)	50

Accessories/Vehicles/Outfits

Blitz Rig (90)	60
The Howler (35)	20
P.A.C.K. Dunebuggy (30)	18
Lazervette (50)	30
The Beast (75)	40
Artic Uniform (25)	14
Construction/Machine Gunner adv. (25)	14
High Explosive Miner adv. (25)	14
Karate outfit (25)	14
Photographer/Secret Agent adv. (25)	14
Policeman/SWAT adv. (25)	14
Race Driver outfit (25)	14
Sea Spy uniform (25)	14

Clash of the Titans 4" Figures

Thallo (45)	16
Calibos (45)	16
Charon (60)	25
Perseus (50)	15
Pegasus (55)	15
Kraken (150)	75
Perseus/Pegasus set (50)	25

Flash Gordon 4" Figures

Flash Gordon (20)	5
Thun (25)	16
Ming (20)	10
Lizard Woman (25)	10

	Loose
Beastman (40)	12
Dr. Zarkov (35)	13
Captain Arak (135)	60
Vultan (135)	75

Major Matt Mason

Callisto (200)	70

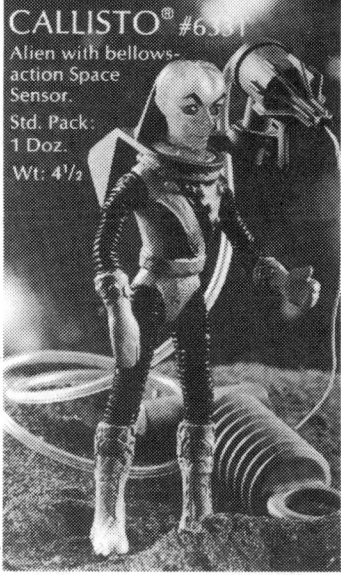

MATTEL Callisto 6331.

Captain Lazer (150)	65
Matt Mason (135)	60

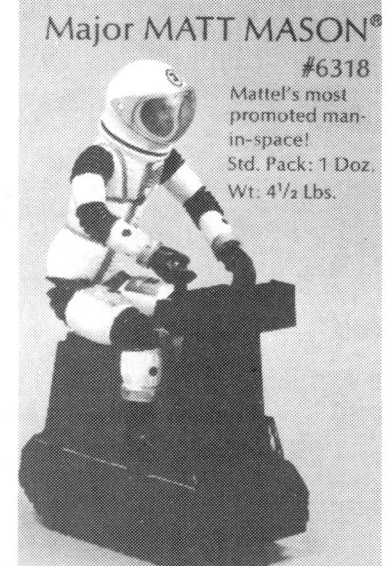

MATTEL Major Matt Mason 6318.

Sgt. Storm (350)	75
Doug Davis (400)	75
Jeff Long (450)	85
Scorpio (850)	400
XRG-1 Re-Entry Glider (275)	100
Talking Major Matt Mason (180)	100
Talking Command Console (195)	60

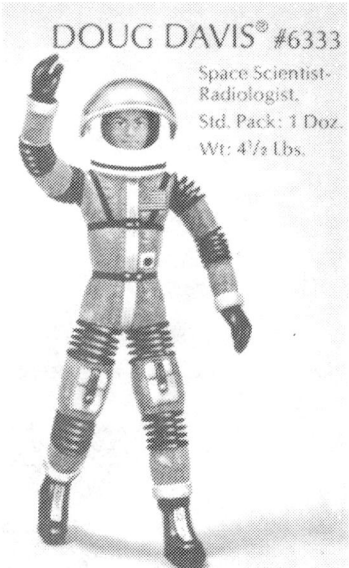

DOUG DAVIS® #6333
Space Scientist-
Radiologist.
Std. Pack: 1 Doz.
Wt: 4½ Lbs.

*MATTEL
Doug
Davis
6333.*

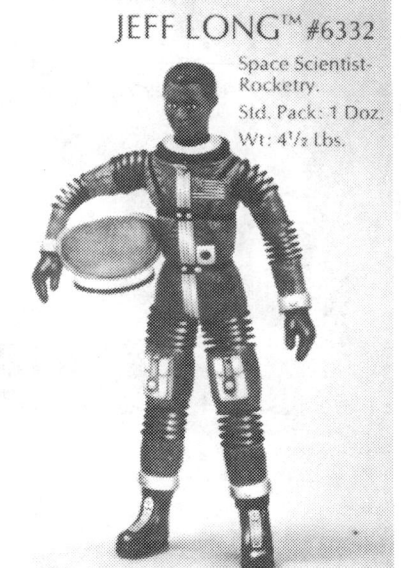

JEFF LONG™ #6332
Space Scientist-
Rocketry.
Std. Pack: 1 Doz.
Wt: 4½ Lbs.

*MATTEL
Jeff
Long
6332.*

*MATTEL
Major Matt
Mason in
flexible
space suit
with jet
propulsion
pack and
space sled.*

*MATTEL
Major
Matt
Mason
with
moon
suit.*

	Loose
Space Station (250)	90
Space Station/Space Crawler Deluxe Action Set (450)	150
Star Seeker (175)	75
Supernaut Power Limbs Pak (65)	35
Unitred (75)	30
Unitred and Space Bubble Set (225)	75
Space Bubble (35)	30
Astro Trac (130)	80
Space Shelter Pak (85)	30
Space Probe Set (85)	35
Space Power Suit Pak (65)	25
Doug Davis w/ Lunar Trac (450)	95
Galaxy 3 playset	No Price Found
Firebolt Space Cannon (100)	60
Space Mission Team w/ MMM, JL, Calisto and DD (1000)	250
Space Discovery Set w/ DD, MMM and Calisto (750)	200
Sgt. Storm w/ Cat Trac (375)	90
Sgt. Storm w/ Flight Set (400)	95
Gamma Ray Gard (75)	40
Jeff Long w/ Lunar Trac (550)	110
Lunar Base Command Set (375)	150
MMM Rocketship Case (175)	60

	Loose
Satellite Locker (120)	30
Satellite Launch Pak (50)	30

MATTEL Reentry Glider 6360.

Photo Box Accessory Paks

Space Crawler 6304.

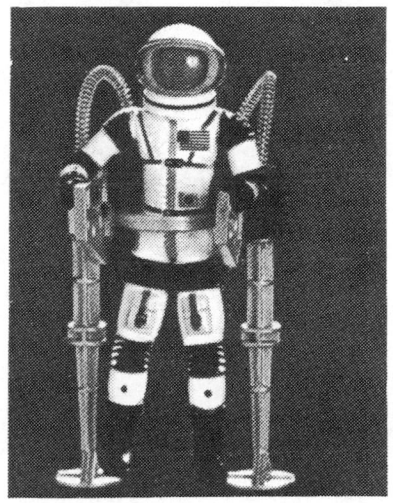

Famous spaceman with exclusive Voice Command Flight Pak. Says five things while "Flying on space cord." Removable VCF Pak may be used with all other Mattel astronauts as well.

SPACE: 1999

Marvel Super Heroes Secret Wars

4-1/4" Figures

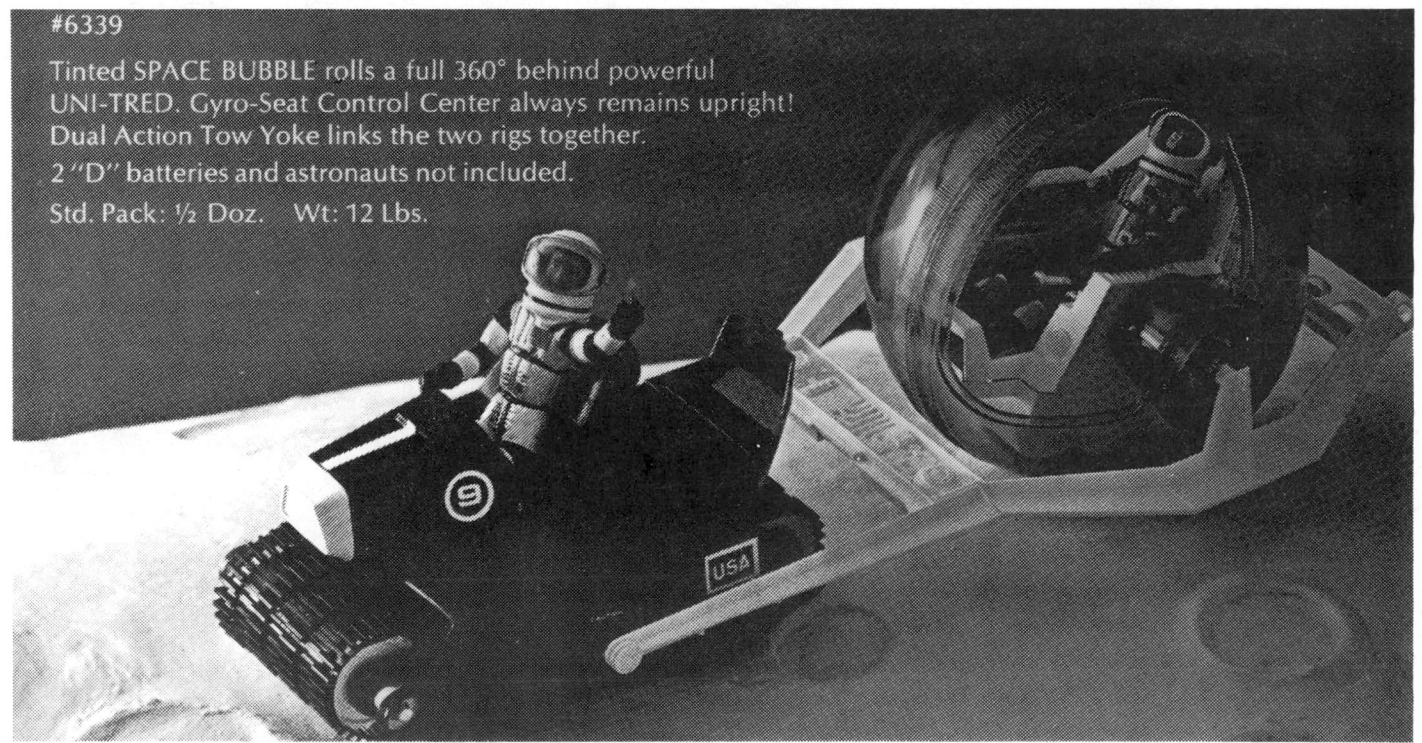

#6339
Tinted SPACE BUBBLE rolls a full 360° behind powerful UNI-TRED. Gyro-Seat Control Center always remains upright! Dual Action Tow Yoke links the two rigs together. 2 "D" batteries and astronauts not included.
Std. Pack: ½ Doz.   Wt: 12 Lbs.

MATTEL Unitred and Space Bubble set, No. 6339.

Magneto (17) 8

Baron Zemo (30) 13

Daredevil (30) 10

Falcon (60) 26

Hobgoblin (75) 18

Iceman (110) 30

Constrictor (95) 30

Electro (150) 30

Dr. Octopus (16) 10

Accessories/Vehicles

Tower of Doom (35) 20

Doom Roller (30) 16

Doom Chopper (110) 25

Turbo Copter (125) 25

Dark Star (30) 15

Star Dart (55) 30

Marvel Super Heroes Machine (125) 55

Marvel Super Villains Machine (80) 55

Turbo Cycle (28) 16

Freedom Fighter (28) 16

MEGO

Action Jackson

Action Jackson (25) 15

18 different outfits, each (10) 5

Black Hole

List by Jim Main

12" Figures

Pizer (50) 25

Dr. Durant (45) 25

Captain Holland (45) 25

Harry Booth (50) 25

Dr. Reinhardt (40) 25

Kate McCrae (45) 25

3-3/4" Figures

V.I.N. cent (50) 30

Pizer (20) 9

Capt. Holland (16) 9

Harry Booth (18) 6

Kate McCrea (18) 6

Old Bob (40) 20

Humanoid (200) 50

Dr. Durant (19) 6

Maximillian (60) 30

Starr (85) 25

Dr. Reinhardt (18) 6

Buck Rogers

List by Jim Main

12" Figures

Buck (40) 25

Wilma (75) 25

Dr. Huer (65) 20

Killer Kane (55) 16

Twiki (40) 25

Draco (57) 20

3-3/4" Figures

Buck (40) 25

Ardella (25) 12

Wilma (45) 25

Dr. Huer (25) 7

Tiger Man (28) 11

Draco (20) 12

Killer Kane (22) 12

Twiki (40) 15

Draconian Guard (20) 12

Accessories

Laser Scope Fighter (40) 30

Star Fighter (50) 25

Draconian Marauder (45) 16

Star Fighter Command Center (80) 35

Star Searcher (225) 100

Flash Gordon 10" Figures

List by Jim Main

Flash (140) 33

Dale (85) 30

Dr. Zarkov (120) 50

Ming (80) 30

KISS 12" Figures

List by Jim Main

Paul (150) 75

Gene (150) 75

Ace (180) 100

Peter (125) 60

Moonraker James Bond 12" Figures

List by Jim Main

Bond (120) 40

Holly (195) 60

Jaws (275) 100

Hugo Drax (175) 50

One Million Years B.C. 8" Figures

List by Jim Main

Mara (42) 20

Grog (40) 18

Orm (40) 18

Trag (35) 18

Dinosaurs, 3 different, per each (150) 90

Planet of the Apes 8" Figures

List by Jim Main

	Loose
Zira (45)	30
Cornelius (85)	25
Astronaut (90)	40
Burke (85)	30
Verdon (85)	25
Dr. Zaius (85)	25
Gen. Urko (50)	25
Ursus (85)	25
Soldier Ape (140)	25
Galen (90)	30

Accessories

Battering Ram (45)	20
Village Playset (90)	35
Treehouse Playset (90)	35
Fortress Playset (90)	25
Forbidden Zone Trap (70)	40
Catapult and Wagon (50)	45
Dr. Zaius' Throne (40)	16
Palamino (50)	32
Jail (40)	20

Bend N' Flex Figures

Zira (30)	10
Cornelius (30)	10
Soldier Ape (30)	15
Astronaut (40)	15
Dr. Zaius (30)	10
Galen (30)	10

Star Trek TV Series 8" Figures

List by Jim Main

Kirk (45)	25
Spock (45)	22
McCoy (100)	50
Scotty (110)	45
Klingon (50)	30
Lt. Uhura (105)	60
Andorian (475)	260
Cheron (200)	100
Mugato (370)	200
Talosian (365)	170
Romulan (550)	450
Gorn (200)	85
Neptunian (290)	105
Keeper (260)	85

Star Trek The Motion Picture

12" Figures

Kirk (60)	25
Spock (60)	35
Decker (130)	50
Illia (70)	25
Klingon (50)	25
Arcturian (95)	45

3-3/4" Figures

	Loose
Kirk (25)	7
Spock (25)	7
McCoy (25)	8
Decker (25)	7
Scotty (25)	8
Klingon (135)	70
Illia (20)	7
Arcturian (145)	65
Zaranite (140)	50
Rigellian (160)	60
Betelgeusian (195)	75
Megarite (195)	40

Superheroes 8" Figures

Lists by Jim Main

(Bx = Box, BP = Blister Pack)

Iron Man (Bx - 180)	65
Lizard (Bx - 195)	75
Kid Flash (BP - 350)	140
Speedy (BP - 400)	225
Wonder Girl (BP - 375)	160
Aqualad (BP - 300)	180
Aquaman (Bx - 150)	35
Batgirl (Bx - 250)	125
Batgirl (BP-250)	125
Batman w/ removable mask (Bx - 350)	160
Batman (Bx - 125)	30
Batman (BP - 125)	30
Joker (Bx - 125)	45
Isis (Bx - 325)	80
Isis (BP - 120)	80
Conan (BP - 325)	145
Falcon (Bx - 150)	55
Thor (Bx - 315)	135
Tarzan (Bx - 115)	45
Supergirl (Bx - 600)	125
Supergirl (BP - 350)	125
Spider-Man (Bx - 95)	20
Green Goblin (Bx - 275)	95
Shazam (Bx - 185)	40
Spider-Man (BP - 50)	22
Superman (Bx - 125)	35
Superman (BP - 95)	35
Catwoman (Bx - 275)	80
Captain America (Bx - 175)	45
Captain America (BP - 130)	45
Hulk (Bx - 70)	25
Hulk (BP - 65)	25
Mr. Fantastic (Bx - 125)	20
Mr. Fantastic (BP - 60)	20
Invisible Girl (Bx - 80)	32
Invisible Girl (BP - 110)	32
Human Torch (Bx - 125)	30
Human Torch (BP - 55)	30
Thing (Bx - 150)	45
Thing (BP - 60)	45
Riddler (Bx - 250)	70
Riddler (BP - 450)	70
Wonder Woman (Bx - 275)	100
Green Arrow (Bx - 275)	90
Penguin (Bx - 115)	40
Penguin (BP - 75)	40

Robin (Bx - 105) 35
Robin (BP - 100) 35
Robin w/ removable mask (800) 250
Mr. Mxyzptlk, open mouth (BP - 65) 22
Mr. Mxyzptlk, smirk (Bx - 105) 22

Fist Fighters 8" Figures

Robin (225) 115
Batman (350) 165
Joker (300) 80
Riddler (600) 130
Lizard (500) 250
Superman (700) 350

Alter Ego Figures

Clark Kent (500) 250
Peter Parker (500) 250
Bruce Wayne (500) 250
Dick Grayson (500) 250

Bendies

Aquaman (65)..40
Wonder Woman (125).............................30
Superman (50).......................................40
Supergirl (150).......................................90
Captain America (60)..............................25
Batgirl (225)..55
Tarzan (50)..32
Penguin (150)...50
Riddler (150)..80
Joker (150)...50
Mr. Mxyzptlk (100)................................45
Robin (60)...30
Shazam (50)...30
Spider-Man (50).....................................20
Catwoman (225)...................................100
Batman (125)...40

Accessories/Playsets for 8" Figures

Wayne Foundation Playset (1000) 750
Batcave Playset (200)..............................95
Captain Americar (130)...........................65
Green Arrowcar (150)..............................75
Jokermobile (250) 60
Batmobile (165) 40
Hall of Justice Playset (350) 175
Batcycle (165) 80
Batcopter (190).......................................65
Aquaman vs. the Great White Shark (750) ...200
Mobile Bat-Lab (300) 95
Super Action SuperVator (100) 50
Spider-Car (100) 45

Superman The Movie 12" Figures

Superman (150).......................................75

General Zod (150) 75
Jor-El (150)...50
Luthor (100) 50

Wonder Woman

Wonder Woman w/ Diana Prince outfit (150) 100
Wonder Woman w/o Lynda Carter pic (65)...... 25
Nubia (115)...50
Steve Trevor (90).....................................35
Queen Hippolite (125).............................55

The Waltons 8" Figures

List by Jim Main

John Boy (55) 32
Granpa (55)...32
Granma (55)..32
Ellen (55)..32

Comic Action/Pocket
Super Heroes 3-3/4" Figures

List by Jim Main

Captain America (60) 10
Batman (70) 17
Robin (65)... 8
Green Lantern (70) 25
Superman (55) 15
Shazam (50) 20
Green Goblin (75) 10
Joker (65)..25
Hulk (40) 15
Penguin (50) 25
General Zod (35) 12
Aquaman (50)..15
Jor-El (40)...12
Lex Luthor (35) 15
Spider-Man (40) 14
Wonder Woman (60)................................25

Accessories/Playsets

Batcave Playset (250)............................120
Fortress of Solitude Playset (275) 150
Spider-Car w/ Spider-Man and Green Goblin figures (95)........ 40
Spider-Car w/ Spider-Man and Hulk figures (80).....................55
Wonder Woman Collapsible
  Tower/Invisible Plane Playset (145)............80
Invisible Plane (60) 25
Batmachine (90) 30
Batmobile (175)..55
The Mangler (90) 30
Batman Collapsible Bridge Playset
  w/ Batman and Robin (200).....................90
Batman Collapsible Bridge Playset
  w/ Batman, Robin, Joker and Penguin (300)......................120

End Mego

Pressman Lone Ranger with His Horse Silver,
  No. 7750 new in 1967, jointed,
  40 accessories including working (cold)
  branding iron .... No Price Found

Pressman Tonto & His Horse Scout, No. 7751,
  new in 1967, jointed, 40 accessories
  including cold branding iron kit ...... No Price Found
Remco Energized Captain America, battery-operated, 9" 70

Remco Energized Green Goblin,
battery-operated, 12" (225)......................75

Remco Energized Hulk, battery-operated, 12".....................50
Remco Energized Superman, battery-operated 75

PRESSMAN Tonto No. 7751.

PRESSMAN Lone Ranger No. 7750.

TOPPER

List by Jim Main

The Tigers

Tex (42).......................................30
Sarge (60)....................................30
Big Ears (50)................................30
Bugle Ben (50).............................30

Combat Kid (50)..30
Pretty Boy (50)..30
Rock (50)..30
Machine Gun Mike (50).....................................30
The Tigers' Headquarters, Sears Exclusive (100).....................80

FIGURE KITS

(The average Mint in Box price for figure kits was $145.96 in the last edition. In this edition it is $168.63, an increase of 16%.)

CONDITION AND RELATION TO PRICE

by David Welch

In recent years plastic model kits (in particular plastic figure kits) have become associated with the world of toys. Buyers of 1960s and 1970s movie, TV and cartoon memorabilia find that figure kits fit rather nicely into their collections. The 1960s is considered the golden age for plastic kits. Aurora leads the way in diversity of product and current demand. Aurora's line-up of original and glow issue Universal Studios monsters are today's most sought-after figure kits.

Rating the condition of a figure kit can be difficult because value can be drastically affected by factors such as (1) assembled parts, (2) painted parts, (3) missing pieces, (4) missing instructions, (5) box condition, and (6) country of origin. **Mint in box [MIB] is the condition upon which the values below are based.**

MIB SEALED: Mint in box with box shrink wrap; most kits had factory wraps on boxes. Provided the boxes are *not damaged,* collectors may pay a premium over MIB price. Beware of bogus resealing by dishonest individuals.

MIB: A complete, unused kit with an excellent box and instructions and no glue or paint on pieces. Most collectors insist that plastic "trees" that held pieces be present with pieces still attached. Again, the price listed below is for a kit in this condition.

PARTIAL ASSEMBLY: A partially built kit with excellent box/instructions and no painting is worth 85% of MIB at best. The more assembly, the more price decreases. Old styrene glues actually "melted" pieces together. White glues (such as Elmers) do not decrease value as much as Styrene glues because they can be removed.

PARTIAL PAINTING: A complete, partially painted kit with excellent box/instructions and no gluing is worth 85% of MIB at best. Painting is not as serious as gluing because most experienced modelers know how to strip paint. Again, the more painting, the more price decreases because stripping takes time and is not always completely successful.

PARTIAL ASSEMBLY/PAINTING: Together, these two factors can make pricing very difficult. A general value guideline would be 70% of MIB with excellent box/instructions.

BUILT-UP: A fully assembled, complete kit with no box/instructions has a value of 15-45% of MIB. The more expensive the MIB kit, the more desirable the built-up. If a kit was issued several times, built-up value decreases. For example, Aurora's design of Frankenstein was issued four times (Aurora 1961, 1969, 1972, and Monogram 1983). Thus its value is usually only 15% of MIB. Vehicles such as Batmobiles and UFOs go toward low percentages because of low visual appeal. Further, without instructions, an inexperienced person will find it virtually impossible to determine if a built-up is complete. Except for very high-priced kits, incomplete built-ups have little value.

MISSING PIECES: One missing piece from a kit will result in a big decrease in value regardless of all other combined factors. Even a MIB kit missing one piece is worth only 80% (at best) of a truly complete MIB kit. Some collectors simply will not buy a kit missing a piece.

INSTRUCTIONS: Missing instructions reduce the MIB price by 5-10%. 1960s instructions sheets alone sell at $5-$10. Sheets for rare, expensive kits such as Aurora's Gigantic Frankenstein can bring over $35!

BOXES: The market for empty figure kit boxes is almost exclusive to Aurora boxes. Generally, an excellent condition box has no split corners, tape, paint, glue, punctures, severe creases, or scuffs. Excellent boxes alone have maximum value of 40% of MIB price. Aforementioned box defects decrease value on MIB kits by 20% or more.

FOREIGN ISSUE: Again, this factor is an issue primarily with Aurora kits. Aurora had branches in Canada, England, and Holland, which issued boxes and instructions that sometimes had wording in other languages and plastic parts in colors other than what U.S. issues had. Ninety percent of the kits you'll ever see will not be foreign issue, but just in case, some collectors (not all) devalue MIB foreign issue kits to about 75% of U.S. MIB prices.

A WORD ABOUT PRICING: If you're more confused about how to price a kit now than you were before, don't feel badly! Even experienced dealers have a difficult time pricing kits when faced with missing pieces, painted parts, box wear, etc. These guidelines are just that: guidelines.

It should be noted that kit values vary widely due to the geographic region and local collector demand. There is strong interest in American kits, for example, in Europe and Japan. American dealers have found some of these individuals willing to pay very highly relative to U.S. collectors. The values listed here are conservative, mid-range prices that are indicative of what most collectors would be willing to pay. Obviously, some collectors will pay more and some will pay less.

Special thanks to Greg Roccaro of Staten Island, New York, and to Mark Karpinski of Denver, Pennsylvania, for price information. Some kit numbers and dates were taken from *Science Fiction and Figure Kits* by John Burns of Edmond, Oklahoma. Though not a price guide, it serves as an excellent reference regarding all known kits of this genre.

David Welch is a nationally known dealer in cartoon, comic, and TV character items. He has been collecting and/or dealing since age 13. He has contributed information for various price guides including Tomart's Disneyana *(condensed edition),* Tomart's Space Adventure Collectibles, *and periodically* Overstreet's Comic Book Price Guide. *In 1991 he was the first person to pay over $3000 for a model kit: a truly mint sealed Godzilla's Go-Cart.*

AURORA

by David Welch

Regarding the Aurora monster line-up, some information may be confusing. To clarify the Frankenstein listing, for example: Frankenstein was issued first in 1961 in a long, rectangular box. The Frightening Lightning 1969 issue was the same kit with duplicate glow parts that were optional. The box was the same shape, and a lightning bolt was added to the art. In 1969 and 1972 the optional glow format continued and square boxes with altered artwork were introduced. The 1969 glow boxes are thicker and sturdier than the 1972 glows. In many cases, the color of the plastic of the original was different from the color of the glow issues. The plastic kit itself will always carry the date of its original issue. The Monster Scenes and Monsters of the Movies Frankensteins are completely different kits from the 1961, 1969, and 1972 issues.

For the Aurora line in general, dates listed may vary a year either way. It is the kit name and kit number that are most relevant. Please note, too, that different kits carried identical numbers (i.e. King Kong Glow 465 and Frankenstein's Flivver 465). The biggest movers (price and saleswise) in the Aurora line have always been the monster kits. The biggest news for vintage kit collectors lately is that many of these rare and valuable kits are being reissued in beautifully done repro boxes—a phenomenon that is sending waves of discomfort through the collecting community. Longtime model kit dealers are lamenting that they could get more for these original kits in 1990 than they can in 1997.

Collectors are asking, "Do I really want to pay hundreds of dollars for an original when I can get a virtually identical repro for under $100?" By early 1997 any market realignment will have become apparent. The hard-core collectors have always sought out the original issues, but only time will tell.

During 1994 and 1995 something of a frenzy ensued on truly mint sealed kits (primarily 1960s monster and superhero-related kits). This trend was pushed along by some collectors from the comic book hobby, in which the value of a mint condition comic book can be up to 20 times that of one in good condition. Absolutely stunning prices were realized in some auctions and private sales, leaving collectors and dealers reeling from the shock. The market during this phenomenon was thin, with only about 20 or less individuals participating at these big number levels. Several of these finicky collectors would even examine the kits under magnifying glasses. In general, only full-time, well-established dealers were able to cultivate any substantial sales with this group of collectors. Many of the high prices were never repeated. In fact, many dealers commented that sealed kits were the only "hot" commodity in Aurora, and open kits were slower than ever. The trend seems to be cooling down as a couple of the most visible individuals have stopped collecting. For now, any published model kit prices that are significantly higher than the prices listed here are most likely reports of the 1994-1995 period just discussed.

	MIB
Addams Family House, 805, 1965	675
Alfred E. Neumann, 802, 1965	200
Allosaurus, 736, 1972	125
American Astronaut, 409, 1967	80
Ankylosourus, 744, 1974	125
Apache Warrior, 401, 1961	300
Aramis, K10, 1958	100
Archie's Car, 582, 1969	85
Athos, K8, 1958	100
Babe Ruth, 862, 1965	250

	MIB
Banana Splits Buggy, 832, 1969	250
Batboat, 811	500
Batcycle, 810, 1967	500
Batman, 467, 1964	250
Batman Comic Scenes, 187, 1974	85
Batmobile, 486, 1966	300
Batplane, 487, 1966	200
Black Beauty, (Green Hornet), 489, 1967	425
Black Knight, various issues	15
Blackbeard, 463, 1965	125

AURORA Gigantic Frankenstein ("Big Frankie"). Greg Roccaro Collection. Courtesy David Welch.

AURORA Godzilla's Go-Cart. Greg Roccaro Collection. Courtesy David Welch.

Gigantic Frankenstein ("Big Frankie"),
470, 1964, with 3 bottles paint & brush 1500
Gladiator, 405, 1959, with sword.....................................175
Gladiator, 406, 1959, with trident 175
Godzilla, 469, 1964...500
Godzilla, Glow, 466, 1969/1972.......................................150
Godzilla's Go-Cart, 485, 1966...2000
Gold Knight on Horseback, K5, 1957/475, 1965...............200
Green Beret, 413, 1966..100
Gruesome Goodies, Monster Scenes, 634, 1971...............100
Guillotine, 800, 1964..500
Hanging Cage, Monster Scenes, 637, 1971 100
Hercules, 481, 1965..175
Horned Dinosaur, 741, 1972..100
Hulk, 421, 1966..250
Hulk, Comic Scenes 184, 1974 75
Hunchback, 461, 1964..250
Hunchback of Notre Dame, 481, 1969/1972 100
Illya Kuryakin, 412, 1966 200
Indian Chief, 417, 1957..75
Indian Squaw, 418, 1957..75
James Bond, 414, 1966...300
Jerry West, 865, 1965...110
Jesse James, 408, 1966...200

Jimmy Brown, 863, 1965 90
John F. Kennedy, 851, 1964..110
Johnny Unitas, 864, 1965..90
Jungle Swamp, 740, 1972...100
King Kong, 468, 1964...500
King Kong's Thronester, 484, 1966................................2000
King Kong, Glow, 465, 1969/1972...................................100
Land of the Giants, Snake Scene, 816,1968.....................400
Land of the Giants Spaceship, 830, 1968.........................400
Lone Ranger, 808, 1967 125
Lone Ranger, Comic Scenes, 188, 1974 35
Lost in Space, 419, 1966..850
Lost in Space, 420, 1966...1200
Mad Barber, 455...1000+
Mexican Caballero, 421,1957 75
Mexican Senorita, 422, 1957...75
Mod Squad Woodie, 583, 1970..100
Moon Bus, 2001: A Space Odyssey, 829, 1968................210
Mr. Hyde, Monsters of the Movies, 655, 1975 75
Mummy, 427, 1963..250
Mummy's Chariot, 459, 1965 550
Mummy, Frightening Lightning, 427/452, 1969.....................400
Mummy, Glow, 452, 1969 100
Mummy, Glow, 1972 65
Munsters Family, 804, 1965...950
Napoleon Solo, 411, 1966..175
Neanderthal Man, 729, 1972..50
Nutty Nose Nipper, 806, 1965...175
Odd Job, 415, 1966..375
Orion, 252, 1975..95
Pain Parlor, 635, 1971 125
Pan Am Space Clipper, 2001: A Space Odyssey, 148, 1968 150
Pendulum, The, Monster Scenes, 636, 1971 120
Penguin, 416, 1967...550
Phantom of the Opera, 428, 1963.....................................275
Phantom of the Opera, 451, 1969.....................................100
Phantom of the Opera, 1972...65
Phantom of the Opera, Frightening Lightning, 428/451, 1969 350
Porthos, K9, 1958...100
Pushmi-Pullyu, Dr. Doolittle, 814, 1968..........................100
Rat Patrol Diorama, 340, 1967...100
Red Knight, various issues 30
Robin, 488, 1966 100

AURORA
King Kong
No. 468
figure kit.
Photo by
Barry
Goodman.

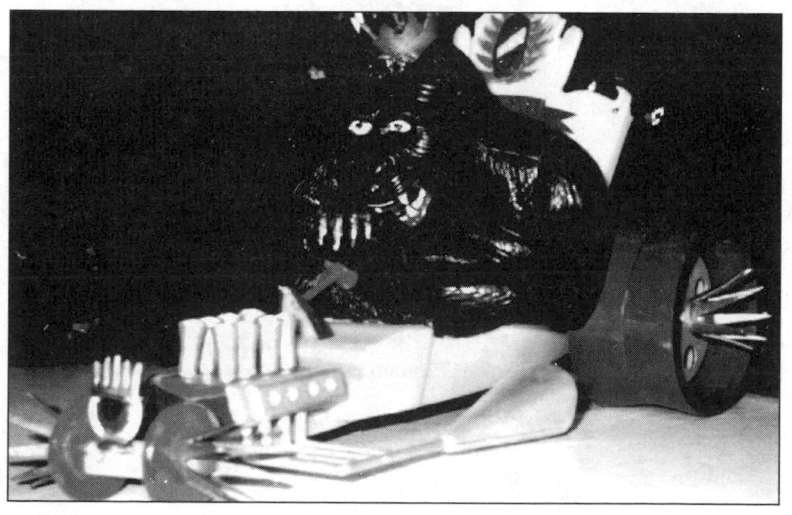

AURORA King Kong's
Thronester. Greg Roccaro
Collection. Courtesy
David Welch.

AURORA Phantom of the Opera and Napoleon Solo figure kits. Courtesy Toy Collector News. Photo by Rex Gray.

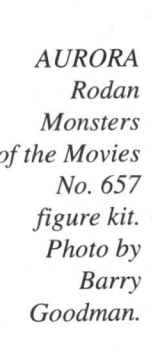

AURORA Rodan Monsters of the Movies No. 657 figure kit. Photo by Barry Goodman.

	MIB
Robin, Comic Scenes, 193, 1974	75
Robot, Lost in Space, 418, 1968	800
Rodan, Monsters of the Movies, 657, 1975	325
Sabre Tooth Tiger, 722, 1972	90
Scotch Lad, 419, 1957	40

	MIB
Scotch Lassie, 420, 1957	40
Seaview, 707, 1966	250
Seaview, 253, 1975	100
Silver Knight, various issues	15
Spartacus, 405, 1965	180
Spider-Man, 477, 1966	325
Spider-Man, Comic Scenes, 182, 1974	100
Spiked Dinosaur, 742, 1972	90
Spindrift, 255, 1975	100
Steve Canyon, 404, 1966	125
Superboy, 478, 1965	300
Superboy, Comic Scenes, 186, 1974	95
Superman, 562, 1963	300

AURORA Tarzan Figure Kit. Courtesy Toy Collector News. Photo by Rex Gray.

AURORA store display of its Monster Scenes, with Dr. Deadly, the Victim and Hanging Cage. Courtesy Toy Collector News. Photo by Rex Gray.

	MIB		MIB
Superman, Comic Scenes, 185, 1974	65	Vampirella, Monster Scenes, 638, 1971	175
Tar Pit, 735, 1971	100	Viking, K6, 1959	120
Tarzan, 820, 1967	175	Voyager, Fantastic Voyage, 831, 1969	500
Tarzan, Comic Scenes, 181, 1974	24	Wacky Back Whacker, 807, 1965	200
Tonto, 809, 1967	135	Willie Mays, 860, 1965	200
Tonto, Comic Scenes, 183, 1974	20	Witch, Glow, 470, 1969/1972	120
Tyrannosaurus Rex, 746, 1974	275	Witch, 483, 1965	350
U.S. Infantryman, 1956	75	Wolfman, 425, 1962	300
U.S. Marine, 412, 1956	75	Wolfman's Wagon, 458, 1965	550
U.S. Marshall, 408, 1959	100	Wolfman, Frightening Lightning, 425/450, 1969	400
U.S. Sailor, 410, 1958	75	Wolfman, Glow, 450, 1969	100
U.F.O., 813, 1968	200	Wolfman, Glow, 1972	65
Undertakers Dragster, 570	200	Wolfman, Monster of the Movies, 652, 1975	175
Vampire, 452, 1966	250	Wonder Woman, 479, 1965	550
		Zorro, 801, 1965	200

AURORA Store Display of its Prehistoric Scenes showing Cro-Magnon Man. Value $700 in mint. Courtesy Toy Collector News. Photo by Rex Gray.

ADDAR

Caesar, Planet of the Apes, 106, 1974	45	General Ursus, Planet of the Apes, 103, 1974	45
Cornelius, Planet of the Apes, 101, 1973	45	Jail Wagon, Super Scenes, 217, 1975	35
Cornfield Roundup, Super Scenes, 216, 1975	35	Soldier on Stallion, Planet of the Apes, 107, 1975	50
Dr. Zaius, Planet of the Apes, 102, 1973	45	Spirit in a Bottle, Super Scenes, 227, 1975	45
Dr. Zira, Planet of the Apes, 105, 1974	45	Tree House, Super Scenes, 215, 1975	45
General Aldo, Planet of the Apes, 104, 1974	45		

AMT

Bigfoot, 7701	25	Fred Flintstone's Rock Cruncher, 497, 1974	45
Dragula, Munsters TV car, 905, 1964	250	Fred Flintstone's Sports Car, 495, 1974	45
Exploration Set, 958, 1974	75	Galileo 7, 959, 1974	45
Fred Flintstone's Family Sedan, 496, 1974	45	Klingon Cruiser, 922, 1967	120

	MIB		MIB
Klingon Cruiser, 952	65	USS Enterprise with Lights, 931, 1967	175
Klingon Cruiser, 971, 1979	27.50	USS Enterprise without Lights, 951, 1976	50
Klingon Cruiser, 6682, 1985	12.50	USS Enterprise, 970, 1979	27.50
K-7 Space Station, 955, 1975	40	USS Enterprise, 6676, 1983	18
Mr. Spock with Snake, 956, 1975	60	USS Enterprise, 6675, 1985	18
Mr. Spock without Snake, 973, 1979	30	USS Enterprise Bridge, 950, 1975	27.50
Munsters Koach, Munsters TV, 1964	200	Vulcan Shuttle, 5112, 1979	24
Romulan Ship, 957, 1975	45	Vulcan Shuttle, 972, 1980	24
Spaceship Set, 953, 1975	60	Vulcan Shuttle, 6679, 1985	15
Spaceship Set, 6677, 1984	27.50		

HAWK

	MIB		MIB
Beach Bunny Catchin Rays, 542, 1964	65	Huey's Hut Rod, 538, 1963	75
Daddy the Swingin Suburbanite, 532, 1963	65	Huey's Hut Rod, Glow, 163, 1969	45
Davey the Psycho Cyclist, 531, 1963	65	Killer McBash, 539, 1963	75
Digger the Way Out Dragster, 530, 1963	65	Leaky Boat Louie, 534, 1963	75
Drag Hag, 536, 1963	65	Riding Tandem, 544, 1965	75
Endsville Eddy, 537, 1963	65	Sling Rave Curvette, 637, 1964	25
Francis the Foul, 535, 1963	30	Steel Pluckers Havin' a Bash, 547, 1965	75
Frantic Banana Punishing Skins, 548, 1965	75	Totally Fab, 550, 1965	75
Frantic Cats, 549, 1965	75	Wade A. Minit, 636, 1964	75
Freddie Flameout, 533, 1963	75	Wierdsville Customizing Kit, 301, 1964	300
Hodad Making the Scene, 543, 1964	75	Woodie on a Surfari, 540, 1964	75
Hot Dogger Hangin Ten, 541, 1964	75	Woodie on a Surfari, 165, 1970	40
Hot Dogger Hangin Ten, Glow, 164, 1970	45		

LINDBERG

	MIB		MIB
Big Wheeler, 277, 1965	100	Mad Mangler, 275, 1965	100
Blurp, 280, 1964	45	Road Hog, 276, 1965	100
Creeping Crusher, 273, 1965	100	Satan's Crate, 279, 1965	200
Glob, 281, 1964	45	Scuttle Bucket, 278, 1965	100
Green Ghoul, 274, 1965	100	Voop, 283, 1964	45
Krimson Terror, 272, 1965	150	Zopp, 282, 1964	45
Mad Maestro, 284, 1965	175		

MONOGRAM

	MIB		MIB
Dracula, 6008, 1983, reissue of Aurora kit	25	Speed Shift, Fred Flypogger, 106, 1965	200
Flip Out, Fred Flypogger, 105, 1965	200	Super Fuzz, Fred Flypogger, 104, 1965	200
Frankenstein, 6007, Aurora reissue	25	Superman, 6301, 1978, Aurora reissue	15
Godzilla, 6300, 1978, Aurora reissue	40	Wolfman, 6009, 1983, Aurora reissue	25
Mummy, 6010, 1983, Aurora reissue	25		

MPC

	MIB		MIB
Alien, 1961, movie, 1979	95	Barnabas Vampire Van, Dark Shadows, 1626, 1969	195
Barnabas Collins, Dark Shadows, 1550, 1969	250	Batman, 1702, 1984, Aurora reissue	20

MULTIPLE

PYRO

REMCO

REVELL

Many of the Ed Roth Fink kits were reissued by Revell in 1993-1995, depressing the values of the original issues.

PEZ

The average price of PEZ in C10 condition in the last edition was $142.19. In this edition it is $191.48, an increase of 35%.

History, Identification, and Condition

by David Welch

PEZ candy dispensers first became available in the U.S. around 1950. The candy itself was produced in Austria as far back as the 1930s. It wasn't until the late 1940s that the "box" or dispenser became available with the candy. The very first dispenser had no head (the aspect most of us associate with PEZ), making it resemble a Bic lighter. Soon thereafter, a Spacegun, a full-bodied Santa, a full-bodied Robot, and many more dispensers appeared. Who can forget the fun of favorite cartoon friends tilting their heads back to offer a piece of PEZ candy?

Over the years, PEZ dispensers have been manufactured in Austria, Yugoslavia, Hong Kong, and the U.S. Dispensers are usually marked with one of these five patent numbers: (a) 2,620,061; (b) 3,410,455; (c) 3,845,882; (d) 3,942,683; or (e) 4,966,305, which is shown on items from 1992 on. It is virtually impossible to date a dispenser with any certainty, although the patent number can sometimes be a vague indicator. Neither the country of origin, the patent number, nor the age are necessarily tied to value. The bottom line on value is which head is on the dispenser!

Since their introduction in the U.S., PEZ dispensers have been continuously available. As of March 1996, there are approximately 250 different PEZ dispensers known. This figure excludes color variation and other minor differences occurring on individual dispensers. Only the most valuable dispensers are currently listed here. Other companies, such as Totems, Yummies, and Smarties, copied the dispenser-with-head concept but none have approached the universal acceptance of PEZ.

Prices given are for excellent or better condition dispensers. Defects such as missing pieces, melt marks, scuffs, excessive dirt, and cracks decrease the value by a minimum of 20%. The condition of the cartridge that holds the candy does not affect value as much as the condition of the head. Exceptions to this rule apply in the cases of Regulars, Die-Cuts, Guns, Zorro A, Psychedelics, and other dispensers in which the cartridge itself is an important part of the identity or appearance. Missing head pieces and facial melt marks can render most dispensers virtually valueless. However, the heads alone are sometimes of value on the most expensive dispensers.

David Welch is certain he has spent more money on PEZ items than any other two people combined: over $300,000 since 1990. He claims the finest collection of PEZ-related advertising in the world. His first book, Pictorial Guide to Plastic Candy Dispensers featuring PEZ, *was the first book devoted to PEZ collecting. His latest book,* Collecting PEZ, *is available in bookstores. It is a 350-page encyclopedia of PEZ information.*

Photos in this section courtesy Barry Koester.

	C10
Alpine, 1972 Olympics	500
Arithmetic	250
Astronaut	
A. White helmet	90
B. Blue helmet	90
C. Clear helmet	100
D. Clear helmet with "Cocoa Marsh" on side	100
E. Small helmet (silver or white)	300

	C10
Baseball Glove with ball	135
with home plate/bat	300
Batman with cape	125
Betsy Ross	60
Bozo	110
Bozo Die-Cut ("Bozo/Butch" on side)	120
Bride with white veil	500
Brutus (from Popeye)	95

459

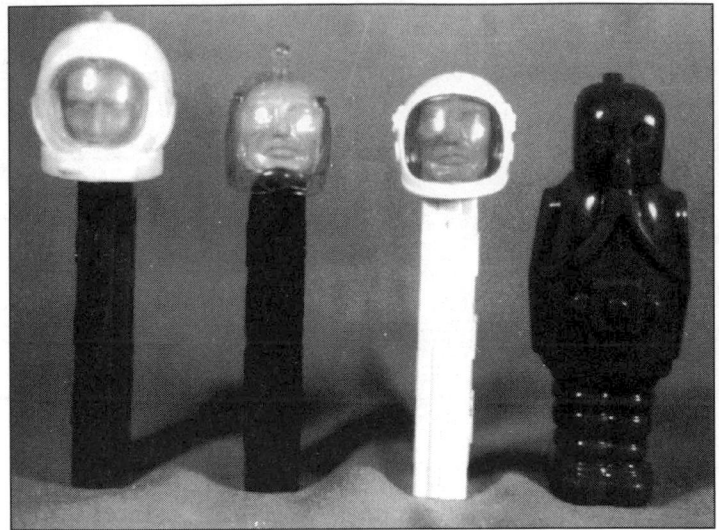

PEZ Astronauts, left to right: A, C, E, Robot, full body.

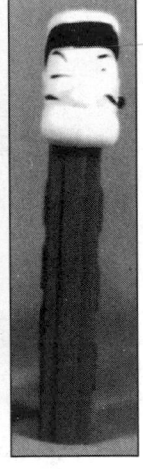

PEZ. Left to right: Brutus, Olive Oyl, Popeye.

	C10
Bullwinkle	175
Camel Whistle	25
Captain	75
Casper	80
Casper Die-Cut ("Casper" on side)	100
Chick in Egg (no hat)	85
Cow with large nose, circular ears	85
Cowboy	175
Creature from the Black Lagoon	
A. With green cartridge/head	185
B. Darker green head/orange cartridge	125
C. Black head	125
Crocodile	60
Daniel Boone with coonskin cap	100
Doctor	65
Dog	40
Donald Duck Die-Cut (three duck nephews on side)	100
Dopey	125
Easter Bunny with thin/straight ears	175
Easter Bunny Die-Cut (bunny with eggs on side)	400
Football Player	90

	C10
Frankenstein	150
Giraffe	60
Green Hornet	225
Groom with black top hat and hat band	165

PEZ. Left to right: Groom, Bride.

Gun	
A. Space 1950s	150
B. Handgun (mail-order premium)	125
C. Space 1980s	60
Indian Brave	135
Indian Chief	60
Indian Squaw	60
Joker, soft head (Batman)	75
Knight	125
Koala whistle	20
Lion's Club Lion, 1962 (stem inscribed)	800
Make-A-Face (similar to Mr. Potato Head)	
with 17 face pieces, loose	800+
Same as above, mint on card	1200+
Mary Poppins	400
Mickey Mouse Die-Cut ("Minnie" on side)	100
Monsters, soft heads, six different, each	85

PEZ. Left to right: Dopey, Snow White, Peter Pan, unlisted, Tinkerbell.

PEZ Gun, B. Handgun.

PEZ Lion's Club Lion.

PEZ Gun, A. Space 1950s.

PEZ. Left to right: Indian Squaw, Indian Chief, Indian Brave, Pilgrim (1976 Bicentennials).

	C10
Olive Oyl	150
Orange	95
Panther, blue head	60
Pear with visor	450
Penguin, soft head (from Batman)	75

PEZ Make-A-Face.

PEZ. Left to right: Mickey Mouse, Donald Duck, Easter Bunny, Casper, Bozo, all die cut.

	C10
Peter Pan	85
Pilgrim	65
Pineapple, with sunglasses	850
Pinocchio, (old version) has eyes looking up, feather is part of hat	110
Popeye, (old version) hat cannot be removed	100
Psychedelic Eye, hand holding eyeball	300
Psychedelic Flower, eyeball in flower	350
Regular (no heads)	
A. Personalized, has paper label on side	125
B. Witch, has pictures of witches on side	1000+
C. Golden Glow, with gold shiny finish	75
D. U.S. Zone Germany marking	120
E. With none of the above markings	100

PEZ Monsters, Soft Heads, left to right: Spook, Air Spirit, Vamp, Zombie, Spook, Diabolic.

PEZ. Left to right: Pear, Pineapple, Orange.

PEZ. Left to right: Psychedelic Eye, Psychedelic Flower.

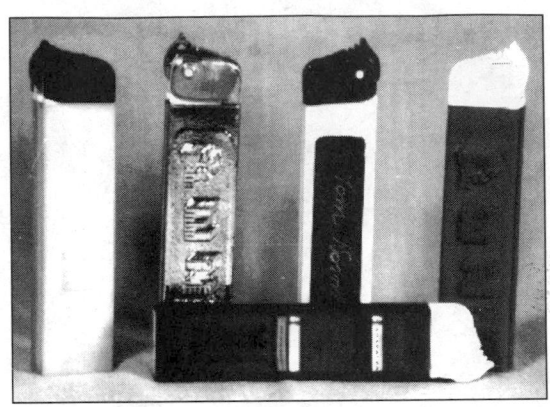

PEZ. Left to right: Regular E, C, A, E. Bottom: Arithmetic.

PEZ. Left to right: Regular B. Witch, Witch, 1 piece.

	C10
Rhino Whistle	20
Robot, full body (three colors)	200-300
Sailor, full white beard with blue hat	85
Santa, full body	100
Santa, face and beard same color	70

	C10
Santa, small head with flesh face and white beard	80
Snow White	65

PEZ. Left to right: Santa Face and beard same, full body, flesh face.

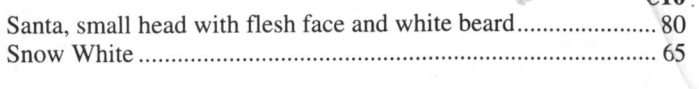

PEZ. Left to right: Uncle Sam, Wounded Soldier, Betsy Ross, Captain, Daniel Boone (1976 Bicentennials).

PEZ Wolf, 1984 Olympics, left to right: A, C, B, Snowman with Arms.

	C10
Snowman with Arms, 1976 Olympics	275
Stewardess	80
Thor (helmet with wings)	125
Tinkerbell	125
Uncle Sam	75
Witch, one-piece orange head	150

Wolf, 1984 Olympics	
A. Ski hat	450
B. Bobsled hat	450
C. No hat	450
Wolfman	160
Wounded Soldier	90
Zorro	
A. Says "Zorro" on side	65
B. Without "Zorro" on side	40

PEZ. Left to right: Wolfman, Creature from Black Lagoon, Frankenstein.

PREMIUMS

The average mint price of premiums was $109.34 in the last edition. In this edition it is $124.71, an increase of 14%. (Not included in the pricing is the Superman Comics Magazine Ring.)

TOYS FREE AS THE AIR

by Jim Harmon

Many radio premiums were nearly as free as the wonderful radio shows that advertised them.

We did have to pay the electric bill (or our folks did) to run the radio, and to get the offered toys we did have to send in a box-top from the sponsor's product.

Sometimes it was only that, a proof of purchase. Orphan Annie and Captain Midnight were particularly generous in responding with gifts for inner labels or inner seals from Ovaltine drink mix. Other times, usually only a dime was required "to handle the cost of handling and mailing." (That's really all it did do—the cost of the premium itself came from the advertising budget.)

The lure of the premium for kids then and for grown-up kids who are now collectors is difficult to explain to those who never lived through the era themselves. The ring or badge was more than the toy itself; it was our tangible link to those magical friends on the other side of the speaker cloth.

Those voices were wonderful out there: The rumbling bass of Brace Beemer as the Lone Ranger; the slightly "country" sound of Curley Bradley as Tom Mix; Bret Morrison, whom we recognized even as children was "sophisticated" as Lamont Cranston (alias The Shadow). But they were bodiless and yes, a bit remote. It was the premium they offered, the same as the one they were using in the story, that put us in touch with them.

There were historic precedents for radio premiums. There were pictures of famous actresses in cigarette packages around the turn of the century, and early radio personalities, such as bandleader Vincent Lopez, offered their autographed pictures. Such footnotes to history aside, radio premiums began with Little Orphan Annie in 1931. The plucky little waif from the Sunday comics first gave away sheet music of her theme song ("Who's that little chatterbox with the pretty auburn locks?") and her own

photo, but very shortly, she offered a drinking mug that could be used to shake up Ovaltine powder with milk to make something resembling a soda fountain milk shake. The first significant radio premium, it was the only successful one that encouraged further use of the sponsor's product.

Many different models of the shake-up mug were offered by Annie and later by Captain Midnight (on both radio and TV). So successful were the offers, shake-up mugs are not rare or high in value. (The most sought after is the orange and blue, embossed—not decaled—Midnight mug.)

It was two years after Annie came to radio that the fledgling medium developed its classic adventure heroes. In 1933 there appeared the Lone Ranger, Tom Mix, and Jack Armstrong. Unlike Annie, the two Westerners and the All-American Boy were still around until the 1950s, when television began driving out radio drama. In those nearly twenty years, the shows offered hundreds of giveaway toys, which inspired similar premiums on dozens of other shows.

Any small toy that could be manufactured inexpensively might turn up as a premium. Those concerned with the great outdoors were popular. We had compasses, pedometers, telescopes, flashlights, pocket knives, signal mirrors, and portable telegraph sets.

The secret society of childhood had its emblems and tokens. So had secret decoders and secret manuals of every size and description. It is these and other paper items that have the greatest dollar value. They were the most easily lost or used up in the rush to adulthood. A Captain Midnight Secret Manual is worth more than the metallic decoder it accompanied.

The rarest paper item is the Lone Ranger Frontier Town, offered about 1947. To complete this model of a

Western village, one had to get four different envelopes by mail, then augment this by buying several packages of Cheerios to cut out the model buildings from the packs. The complete set has been known to sell for hundreds of dollars and today might bring $1,500.00, the highest for any premium.

Perhaps the most popular single type of premium was the ring. Rings let the listener show loyalty to the fraternity of his or her favorite hero, but in a less officious and more "grown-up" way than the badge (although they were also highly popular). Besides … the rings looked neat, and many of them could **do** things—some of them pretty incredible things.

As with radio premiums in general, the Tom Mix show (and Ralston cereal's premium manufacturer, the Robbins Company) blazed the trail with ingenious ring designs. In 1937 Tom Mix Straight Shooters could get a Signet Ring with their own initial on it. (Years later, Captain Midnight would offer a ring that would ink-stamp your initial.) By 1938 Tom had a ring that let you look in a peep-hole and see a magnified picture of himself and his horse, Tony. (Technology had progressed so much that by the fifties, Straight Arrow offered a similar ring that put your own photo, if supplied, alongside radio's great Indian hero.)

After World War II and the ease in metal rationing, Tom Mix offered a Magnet Ring (good for picking up paper clips—like the one on the stolen plans to the atomic bomb, in Tom's case). His spinning siren whistle ring was neat (but admittedly borrowed in design from Jack Armstrong's 1937 Egyptian Whistle Ring). Tom's Sliding Whistle Ring, which played different musical notes (about 1948), was unique, however. His Look-Around Ring concealed an inner mirror that let you see behind you (sort of), a design rustled for a later Tennessee Jed ring.

The final Tom Mix ring looked attractive, sporting a glowing cat's-eye, but the 1949 Tiger-Eye Ring was only lightweight plastic, a far cry from the well-crafted metal rings of a decade earlier. But then, the decade was nearly over, and so was the era, fading in the light of another glowing eye in the living room.

The Shadow's own Glow-in-the-Dark Ring (1939) had a band composed of two sculpted Shadow figures holding up a jagged blue stone—a proxy lump of his sponsor's product, Blue Coal. One of the very few Shadow premiums and the best-looking, this ring has sold for $950.

The identical mold for one glowing plastic ring was used for several different radio shows. The band had two crocodiles holding a setting in their mouths. The "stone" was black when it was Jack Armstrong's Dragon Eye Ring in 1940. It was green for "Terry and the Pirates" in the mid-1940s, but it was black for Carey Salt's Shadow ring in 1947 (not the rare Blue Coal model). The setting was red for Buck Roger's Ring of Saturn in 1945. It is black again in the slightly lumpy counterfeit being manufactured today. This ring is one of the handful of premiums of simple enough design to be faked for profit. The best way to authenticate these rings is by the accompanying paper instruction sheets naming the famous character whose prize it is.

These rings are worth whatever you will pay to possess them, as are all radio premiums. A fair average price is $60, with $300 a top price for very rare, complex and fragile items. Of course, many items are priced much higher. But anybody who is not familiar with the whole field should not pay more, even though $500 or more may be easier to come by today than a dime and a box-top were in those days of yesteryear.

Since 1992 there has been a radical change in the prices of radio and early TV premiums (and associated toys). For nearly twenty years there had been no appreciable rise in premium prices. In fact, premium prices had not even kept up with inflation. You could have bought a Tom Mix Magnet Ring for $35 in 1967 and bought the Magnet Ring for the same $35 in 1987. But now there has come a radical change in premium pricing, especially for rings. The Magnet Ring generally brought $95 in 1994.

Part of the reason is the unnatural influence of "investor" types who have manipulated the market, much as they did the old comic book market. The results have been mixed. Prices have risen, but the number of premium collectors and the number of premium objects is far smaller than their counterparts in the comic book field. As a result, most premiums have virtually disappeared from the market. Now is the time to buy, if premiums can be found. They may never be cheaper, and they may never be seen again.

Despite rarity, condition is still very important. No matter how rare, a premium that is battered, defaced, or broken is virtually worthless. Premiums with missing parts can be worth something, since the missing part might be matched up eventually.

Stores of premiums newly found in attics no longer seem to be turning up, but older collectors are retiring from their occupations and, sadly, selling their collections for needed money. Some die, and survivors sell. These collectors and families know the value of collectibles and sell for top market value. The number of these "retiring" collectors is still fairly small and does not greatly affect the general state of rarity of premiums.

The items connected to once well-known characters (and those still famous) such as the Lone Ranger, Tom Mix, Buck Rogers, Buck Jones, and Gene Autry, have the highest prices. These prices are still on the rise. Even minor and nearly forgotten characters such as Scoop Ward and Speed Gibson are not being given away. Such once well-known characters will generally prevent a button from selling for less than $15, a badge for less than $25, or a ring for under $30.

Rings have a great appeal to many, and are the hottest ticket in the premium market. The rare ones are going up and up. The Shadow Blue Coal Ring, Green Hornet Seal Ring, and Captain Midnight Mystic Sun God Ring will probably go over the thousand dollar mark soon.

Cereal boxes of the sponsors who offered the premiums, especially ones with premium offers on the boxes, have become valuable. Near the top of the line are complete boxes of the nine Lone Ranger Frontier Town Cheerios packs (about $200 each; the backs off the boxes with unassembled model buildings can go for $35). Tom Mix Ralston boxes (late 1940s-1950s) go for up to $400.

A few new authentic premiums have appeared in recent years: Boraxo offered a 20 Mule Team model in 1980 (similar to the Death Valley Days original of the 1930s, 1940s, and 1950s); Cheerios offered a Lone Ranger Deputy Kit in 1981 styled after the movie of that year but similar to earlier offers with mask, badge, etc.

In 1982 Ralston began a limited Tom Mix revival with which the present author, Jim Harmon, was involved. Premiums offered included a set of four Mix Ralston cereal bowls, a wind-up wrist watch, a Straight Shooters membership kit, a Tom Mix photo, a Mix in-box miniature comic book (edited by Harmon), and a Long Play recording with old Mix radio episodes and one 1983 episode featuring Curley Bradley and produced by Harmon. In 1993-94, Ralston again showcased Tom Mix on their boxes, but offered only a chance for the customer to write in their memories of Tom.

In 1987 Ovaltine resurrected their original formula in jars and instituted new premiums of their character, Captain Midnight of the Secret Squadron. The 1987 premium was a tee-shirt, in 1988 a Midnight digital watch was offered, and in 1989 an arm patch was available (apparently the last of the current revival). Dick Tracy premiums, such as the Quaker wrist radio, came with the new movie in 1990. Superman continued his fifty-year-plus association with Kellogg's cereals in 1994, appearing on the box and inside, with a mini-comic book for Kellogg's Cinnamon Mini-Buns.

Prices on these are already comparable to older premiums, topped by the Tom Mix watch at $300. The biggest premium news of the early 1990s was the sale of a Superman comic book premium ring for a record $18,000 and its resale for $43,000. But this event was really a part of the world of incredibly-priced Golden Age comic books. In effect, the ring was treated as another rare old comic book, not as the premium ring it was. This astonishing sale only raised the value of a real radio premium, the Superman Crusaders Club ring, from $65 to a less than overwhelming $185. Real radio and TV premiums from broadcast series have broken the $1,000 barrier only rarely, with the complete Lone Ranger Frontier Town and above-catalog-value rings: Captain Midnight Mystic Sun God, Green Hornet Seal, Shadow Blue Coal, and the very overvalued Carey Salt.

Jim Harmon is a writer of nonfiction (The Great Radio Heroes) and science fiction (including the often-anthologized "The Place Where Chicago Was") and a magazine editor (Monsters of the Movies). Harmon has written in virtually every category of fiction and nonfiction, including hardcover, paperback, pulp magazines (Famous Western) and slick magazines (TV Guide). He has provided scripts and action performances for movies and television and, probably more than any other person currently active in the field, he has dramatized radio. After finding the legendary but reclusive Curley Bradley, in 1975 Harmon produced a new Western/mystery series of Curley Bradley's Trail of Mystery. In 1982-83 he went on to produce and act in a new series based on Curley Bradley's original role, Tom Mix, for Hot Ralston cereal. During this period Harmon also contributed to the design and production of a cereal box, a new comic book of Mix and a Mix dramatic LP album, as well as engineering radio and television appearances for himself and Curley Bradley. In 1992 Harmon's new book, Radio Mystery and Adventure, was well received. One reviewer described it as having "more depth than any other book on radio." In 1996 he offered a new audio production of the "lost episodes" of Carlton E. Morse's I Love a Mystery. He lives in Burbank, California, with microbiologist wife Barbara, near daughter Dawn.

	C6	C8	C10
Admiral Television Studio Giveaway, 1953 paper punch-out TV studio and characters, features Sky King, Flight to Mars, Walt Disney's Peter Pan, and Three Little Pigs, 15" x 16"	125	188	250
Amos & Andy Pepsodent Giveaway, Amos' Wedding	48	72	95
Amos & Andy Puzzle	55	83	110
Archie Comics Club Button	5	8	10
Aunt Jemima Breakfast Club Badge, metal	12	18	25
Barney Baxter Junior Birdmen of America Wings, metal, c. late 1930s	12	18	25

	C6	C8	C10
Bendix Radio, 5-1/2" WW II military figures c. 1944. Color photos with stands. a. Navy Lt. (jg); b. Marine 1st Lt. (dress uniform); c. Coast Guard Commander; d. Army Air Force officer with parachute harness; e. 2nd Lt. with modern Mae West; f. Flier with flying suit; g. Army Air Force Capt.; h. Air officer with fur-lined jacket and helmet. Price per each	4	6	9
Betty Boop Face Mask, 1931, theatre premium	27	41	55
Betty Boop Pin, "Roxy Theatre, New York," large	20	30	40

	C6	C8	C10
Blondie & Dagwood Go To Leisureland, 1940, Westinghouse	10	15	20
Bobby Benson Code Rule, 1935 cardboard decoder, Hecker H-O	48	72	95
Bobby Benson's Game Circus, 1934	37	53	75
Buck Jones Club Ring	42	63	85
Buck Jones Horseshoe Pin	42	63	85
Buck Jones Jr. Sheriff Badge	42	63	85
Buck Rogers Badge, enameled	83	125	165
Buck Rogers Birthstone and Initial Ring	250	375	500
Buck Rogers Chief Explorer Badge	70	105	140
Buck Rogers Lead Figures, solid, Cocomalt, Buck, Wilma, Killer Kane, per each	15	22	30
Buck Rogers Flight Commander Whistle Badge	83	125	165
Buck Rogers Girl's Charm Bracelet	83	125	165
Buck Rogers Helmet	193	290	385
Buck Rogers Knife	83	125	165
Buck Rogers Morton Salt Punch-O-Bag, 1930s	42	63	85
Buck Rogers Morton Salt Spaceship (came in envelope)	83	125	165
Buck Rogers Pendant	42	63	85
Buck Rogers Pinback Button, c. 1935, Whitehead and Hoag, "Buck Rogers in the 25th Century"	42	63	85
Buck Rogers Repeller Ray Ring (seal ring)	250	375	500
Buck Rogers Ring of Saturn, glows in the dark, with red stone	250	375	500

Buck Rogers Chemical Laboratory. Courtesy HAKE's Americana & Collectibles.

	C6	C8	C10
Buck Rogers items given away for Cream of Wheat green triangle (sold in stores also):			
Buck Rogers Films for Projector	10	15	20
Buck Rogers Interplanetary Game	83	125	165
Buck Rogers Lead Figures, hollow lead, Buck, Wilma, Huer, Robot, Kane, Ardala, average price per each, Britains	200	300	400
Buck Rogers Lite Blaster Flashlight	37	56	75
Buck Rogers Movie Projector	110	165	220
Buck Rogers Printing Set (12 rubber stamps)	48	72	95
Buck Rogers Super Dreadnaught, balsa wood	55	83	110
Buck Rogers Uniform	325	488	650

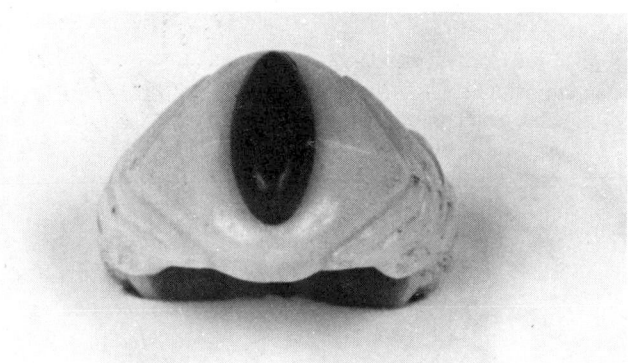

Buck Rogers Ring of Saturn. Courtesy Jim Harmon.

Buck Rogers Space Ranger Kit, Sylvania. Courtesy Toy Collector News.

	C6	C8	C10
Buck Rogers Ring of Saturn Instruction Sheet	42	63	85
Buck Rogers Solar Scouts Badge, all brass color	55	83	110
Buck Rogers Solar Scouts Spaceship Commander Badge, 1936 Cream of Wheat premium	55	83	110
Buck Rogers Solar Scout Sweater Emblem	42	63	85
Buck Rogers Space Ranger Kit, Sylvania	75	112	150
Buck Rogers Telescope	70	105	140

	C6	C8	C10
Buffalo Bill Bamby Bread Horseshoe Badge, late 1930s	12	18	25
Buffalo Bill Jr. Brass Ring, Buffalo in relief on top, TV premium	22	33	45
Buster Brown Gang (Smilin' Ed) Ring	23	48	65
Buster Brown Gang Tab Pins, assorted, price per each	10	15	20
Butter-Nut Bread Premium, "Sail-Me" glider with 4-1/2" wingspan, c. 1930	6	9	13
Captain America Sentinel of Liberty Badge	225	338	450

	C6	C8	C10
Captain Franks Air Hawks Ring	37	56	75
Captain Franks Air Hawks Wings, c. late 1930s, Post's 40% Bran Flakes premium	32	48	65
Captain Gallant Medal, c. 1950 dated 1939-1945 with an animal on it	17	26	35
Captain Gallant Medal, 1950s, this one is a cross with GRI on it	17	26	35
Captain Hawk Sky Patrol Propeller Badge, c. late 1930s	22	33	45
Captain Marvel Club Button	50	75	100
Captain Marvel's Magic Whistle, c. 1943, American Seed Co., full-color picture of Captain Marvel on both sides, American Seed Co. ad on the inside	27	41	55
Captain Midnight Aerial Torpedo Bomber (Airplane), 1941	65	98	130
Captain Midnight American Flag Loyalty Badge, 1940	42	63	85
Captain Midnight Flight Patrol Wings Badge, 1941	48	72	95
Captain Midnight Flight Patrol Wings Badge, 1942	48	72	95
Captain Midnight Code-O-Graph Decoder Pin, 1941, eagle on top	83	125	165
Captain Midnight Code-O-Graph Badge, 1942, with photo of Captain Midnight	98	138	195

Captain Midnight Code-O-Graph Badge, 1942. Courtesy Jim Harmon.

	C6	C8	C10
Captain Midnight Code-O-Graph, 1945, magnifier	83	125	165
Captain Midnight Code-O-Graph, 1946, Mirrormatic, (best looking, desirable)	110	165	220
Captain Midnight Code-O-Graph, 1947, works as a whistle	43	65	85
Captain Midnight Code-O-Graph, 1948, round, with mirror	70	105	140
Captain Midnight Code-O-Graph, 1949, Key-O-Matic (with key)	110	165	220
Captain Midnight Detect-O-Scope, 1941	55	83	110

	C6	C8	C10
Captain Midnight Flight Commander Commission, 1956	35	52	70
Captain Midnight Flight Commander Flying Cross, 1942	48	72	95
Captain Midnight Flight Commander Ring, 1941	150	225	300
Captain Midnight Flight Commander Signet Ring, 1957	175	263	350
Captain Midnight Flight Commander Ring, 1959	175	263	350
Captain Midnight Jumping Bean Target, 1939	20	30	40
Captain Midnight MJC-10 Plane Detector, 1942, distance-finder	70	105	140
Captain Midnight Magic Blackout Lite-Ups, 1942	42	63	85
Captain Midnight 1941 Manual for Decoder	82	123	165
Captain Midnight 1942 Manual for Decoder	138	205	275
Captain Midnight 1945 Manual for Code-O-Graph	55	83	110
Captain Midnight 1946 Manual for Code-O-Graph	53	80	105
Captain Midnight 1947 Manual for Code-O-Graph	52	63	105
Captain Midnight 1948 Manual for Code-O-Graph	52	63	105
Captain Midnight 1949 Manual for Code-O-Graph	52	63	105
Captain Midnight 1956 Manual for Decoder Badge	138	210	275
Captain Midnight 1957 Manual for Silver Dart Decoder	138	210	275
Captain Midnight Marine Corps Ring, 1942	100	150	200
Captain Midnight Medal, brass, pictures of cast, secret word, spinner, 1940	15	23	30

Captain Midnight Medal, 1940. Courtesy Jim Harmon.

	C6	C8	C10
Captain Midnight Mystic Eye Detector Ring, 1942	125	188	250
Captain Midnight Mystic Sun God Ring, 1946	475	715	950
Captain Midnight Printing Ring, 1948	88	132	175
Captain Midnight Secret Squadron Decoder Badge, 1955	110	165	220
Captain Midnight Secret Squadron Decoder Badge, 1956	110	165	220

	C6	C8	C10
Captain Midnight			
Secret Squadron Insignia Transfer, 1949 20	30	40
Captain Midnight Service Ribbon Pin, 1944 42	63	85
Captain Midnight			
Silver Dart Decoder Badge, 1957..............110	165	220
Captain Midnight Spy Scope, 1947 53	80	105
Captain Midnight			
Surprise Package, 1942 27	41	55
Captain Midnight			
3-Way Mystic Dog Whistle, 1942..............27	41	55
Captain Midnight Trick and Riddle Book,			
1939 Skelly Oil premium, 64 pages 17	26	35
Captain Midnight Weather Wings,			
1940, predicts weather..................42	63	85
Captain Midnight			
Whirlwind Whistling Ring, 1941 100	150	200
Capt. Tim Ivory Club Pin,			
Ivory Soap, c. 1936..................9	13	18
Captain Video Flying Saucer Ring 125	188	250
Captain Video Rite-O-Lite..................53	80	105
Captain Video Rocket Launcher			
and Ships, 1950s..................110	165	220
Captain Video Secret Seal Ring, 1950s 112	168	225
Captain Video Space Fleet Ray Gun,			
1952, TV premium, Powerhouse..............138	210	275

	C6	C8	C10
Captain Video X-9 Rocket Balloon,			
1950s..................30	45	60
Chandu the Magician Galloping			
Coin Trick, 1930s 30	45	60
Chandu the Magician Hindu Cones,			
1930s..................30	45	60
Chandu Boxed Set of Tricks 375	565	750
Charlie McCarthy Puppet Doll, 21" high,			
cardboard, Chase & Sanborn mailer...........42	63	85
Charlie McCarthy Radio Party Game,			
giveaway by Standard Brands, 1938,			
21 cardboard figures 42	63	85
Cinnamon Bear (annual Christmas show,			
c. 1940s) Silver Star..................35	52	70
Cisco Kid Badge, western hat			
on chain, 1950s..................17	26	35
Cisco Kid Cardboard Gun, 7" long,			
Harvest Bread giveaway,			
clicker sounds when handle squeezed 17	26	35
Cisco Kid and Pancho Face Masks,			
1953, price per each..................25	38	50
Cisco Kid Triple S Club Kit..................25	38	50
Cisco Kid Picture Ring, 1950s 50	75	100
Coco Wheats Radio Club Badge,			
shape of microphone..................22	33	45

CRACKER JACK

Cracker Jack was first introduced in 1893 by the Ruckheim brothers (F.W. and Louis) at the Chicago World's Columbian Exposition. Toys first appeared in the boxes of popcorn and peanuts in 1912 and were bought from various manufacturers. Over 10,000 different premiums have been produced over the years. From 1912 to 1930 they included whistles, tops, yo-yos, brooches, and puzzles. From 1930 to 1940 the accent was on miniatures, such as irons, shoes, binoculars, trolley cars, trains, and so on. From 1940 to 1950 they tended towards military items, with plastics being introduced in the late 1940s. Prices can range from $1.00 or less to $80.00. There are about thirty serious Cracker Jack collectors known in this country.

	C6	C8	C10
David Harding Counterspy,			
Junior Agent Badge 37	56	75
Davy Crockett Goldplated Ring..................10	15	20
Dick Tracy Air Detective Ring 50	75	100
Dick Tracy Badge, "Capt." 40	60	80
Dick Tracy Badge, "Crime Stoppers" 12	18	25
Dick Tracy Badge, "Detective,"			
picture of Tracy and Junior..................17	26	35
Dick Tracy Badge, "Lt." 37	55	75
Dick Tracy Badge, Republic Pictures 42	63	85
Dick Tracy Badge, "Sgt."..................30	45	60
Dick Tracy Decoder, green 1948 22	33	45
Dick Tracy Decoder, red, 1948 22	33	45
Dick Tracy Detective Club Badge,			
secret money pouch in rear..................37	53	75
Dick Tracy Glider Airplane, 1938 50	75	100
Dick Tracy Ring,			
in shape of Tracy's head..................50	75	100
Dick Tracy Secret Compartment Ring..............88	132	175
Dick Tracy Secret Service Patrol Member			
Pinback, early 1940s..................15	23	30

Dick Tracy Secret Service Patrol Member Pin. Courtesy Jim Harmon.

	C6	C8	C10
Dick Tracy Secret Service			
2nd Year Member Pin..................22	33	45
Dick Tracy's Secret Detective Methods			
& Magic Tricks, 1939 Quaker Oats,			
68 pages 30	45	60
Dionne Quints "All Aboard for Shut-Eye			
Town" Paper Dolls, Palmolive Soap 17	26	35
Don Winslow Decoder Torpedo..................45	68	90
Don Winslow Honor Badge 25	38	50

	C6	C8	C10
Don Winslow Magic Slate Secret Code Book	25	38	50
Don Winslow Ring	42	63	85
Don Winslow USN Secret Code Book, 1935, 16-page Oxydol giveaway, 7-3/4" x 4"	25	38	50
Donald Duck Punch-out Figure, c. late 1940s, Donald Duck bread	30	45	60
Donald Duck Playboard, 1946, 9" high, comics giveaway	25	38	50
Elsie The Cow, set of four figural buttons on color illustrated card, Borden, 1949	11	16	22
Fighting Devil Dogs Ring, 1938, Republic Pictures serial ring, has bulldog head on top	75	112	150
Flash Gordon Ring, 1949, Post Toasties Corn Flakes	27	41	55
Fort Apache (Rin Tin Tin) Plastic Ring, 1950s, TV premium	15	22	30
Frank Buck Explorer's Sun Watch, post-WWII (offered by Jack Armstrong)	53	80	105

Frank Buck Explorer's Sun Watch. Courtesy Jim Harmon.

	C6	C8	C10
Frank Buck Leopard Ring	175	263	350
G.E. Punch-out Circus, 65 pieces	65	98	130
G.E. Rodeo Punch-out, 65 pieces	65	98	130
G-Man Badge	10	15	20
G-Man Official Signet Ring, 1933-35, G-Man radio program premium, metal	25	38	50
Gabby Hayes Antique Cars, 1950s, price for set	37	56	75
Gabby Hayes Quaker Cannon Ring, 1950s	75	112	150
Gabby Hayes Western Gun Collection, 6 weapons, 3 pistols, 3 rifles, solid non-working, 1950s	37	56	75
Gabby Scoops Junior Press Club Card, 1945 Crackajack Comics	9	13	18
Gabby Scoops 1940-41 Press Card, Crackajack Comics	9	13	18
Gangbusters Pin	25	38	50
Goofy Playboard, 1946, 9" high, comics giveaway	17	25	35
Green Hornet Secret Compartment Ring, Hornet seal, glows in dark	475	715	950
Gun, cardboard, giveaway from Theatorium in Lykens, Pa. Pat'd Dec. 1914 by Spots Spec. Co., Lexington, Ky. Swoop downward to produce bang, "The Bang Gun For Young America"	6	9	13

	C6	C8	C10
H.C.B. Club Kit, contains badge, etc., early Cream of Wheat	22	33	45
Hop Harrigan Para-Plane, cardboard plane from Grape Nut Flakes plus two code signal blinders. Also in tail of plane is a small parachute that drops a cardboard "water" canister	162	243	325
Hop Harrigan (unmarked) Sun Dial Ring	30	45	60
Hopalong Cassidy Bar 20 Compass Ring	37	56	75
Hopalong Cassidy Face Ring	37	56	75
Hopalong Cassidy Tin Badge, Post Raisin Bran Giveaway, c. 1950s	17	26	35
Howdy Doody Climber, cardboard, with string, Welch's Premium, 1950s	37	56	75
Howdy Doody Face Flashlight Ring, 1950s	37	56	75
Howdy Doody Flicker Key Chain, 3D picture of Howdy Doody flicks to Poll Parrot (Poll Parrot Shoes), 1950s	17	26	35
Howdy Doody Flicker Ring, Poll Parrot premium, flicks from Howdy to Poll	25	38	50
Howdy Doody 8" Howdy Doody Flexible Cardboard Figure, Wonder Bread	32	48	65
Howdy Doody Puppet, Mars Candy, cardboard, 15" high, 1950s	37	56	75
Howdy Doody Princess Dancing Puppet, 13" high, joints moveable, 1950s, Snickers premium	17	26	35
Howdy Doody, Princess Spring, etc. cardboard figure, 14" high	17	26	35
I Am A Spy Smasher Button, 1940, Fawcett Comics	25	38	50
Indian Chief Tin Badge, Post Raisin Bran, c. 1950s	4	7	9
Indian Gum Chief's Head Ring, Goudey Gum card premium, 1930s, silver	10	15	20
Jack Armstrong Crocodile Ring, glows in the dark, green stone	125	188	250
Jack Armstrong Big 10 Football Game	45	68	90
Jack Armstrong Explorer's Telescope	17	25	35
Jack Armstrong Flashlight	15	23	30
Jack Armstrong Hike-O-Meter	22	33	45
Jack Armstrong Magic Answer Box	42	63	95
Jack Armstrong Ped-O-Meter (blue or silver models)	22	33	45

Jack Armstrong Ped-O-Meter. Courtesy Jim Harmon.

	C6	C8	C10
Jack Armstrong, Secret Norden Bomb Sight, c. WWII with three bombs, paper target ships	193	290	385
Jack Armstrong paper airplane models, many different, price per each	17	25	35
Reprints of above (identified as such)	5	7.50	10
Jack Armstrong Secret Whistle Code Card for Secret Egyptian Coder Siren Ring	15	23	30

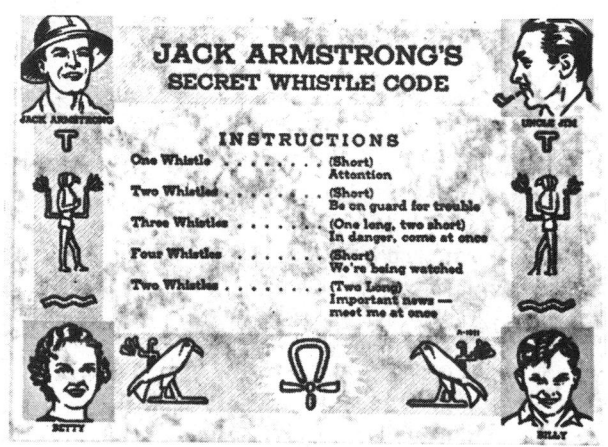

Jack Armstrong Secret Whistle Code Card. Courtesy Jim Harmon.

	C6	C8	C10
Jack Armstrong Secret Egyptian Coder Siren Ring, late 1930s, Wheaties	62	93	125
Jack Armstrong 3-D Viewer, filmstrip	37	56	75
Jeff Paper Mask, 1933, Shell Oil	10	15	20
Jimmie Allen Colonial Gasoline Flying Cadet Wings, late 1930s, bronze	17	26	35
Jimmie Allen High-Speed Gasoline Flying Cadet Wings, late 1930s, bronze	20	30	40
Jimmie Allen Richfield Hi-Octane Flying Cadet Wings, c. 1930s	20	30	40

Jimmie Allen Richfield Hi-Octane Flying Cadet wings. Courtesy Jim Harmon.

	C6	C8	C10
Jimmie Allen Richfield Hi-Octane Pilot's Identification Bracelet, late 1930s, all metal	21	32	42
Jimmie Allen Skelly Oil Die-Cut Airplane Cadet Wings, late 1930s	15	23	30
Jimmie Allen Skelly Oil Flying Cadet Wings, late 1930s, bronze	15	23	30

	C6	C8	C10
Joe E. Brown Pin	10	15	20
Junior G-Men Membership Kit, c. mid-1930s	37	56	75
Junior G-Men of America, late 1930s, gold-plated tin badge	22	33	45
Junior Texas Ranger Badge, 1936 premium	17	26	35
Kellogg's Frogmen, 1950s, add baking soda and they swim underwater	10	15	20
Kellogg's Krumbles Around-the-World Paper Dolls. Each cutout from box contains boy and girl, 10: Italy 11: Mexico 13: France 17: Czechoslovakia. Price per each	4	7	9
Kellogg's Nautilus Nuclear Submarine, 1950s	27	41	55
Kellogg's Pep Airplane Carrier, 6-1/2" x 10" cut-out sheet with airplane carrier, 5 planes with 3/4" wingspan	37	56	75
Kellogg's Pep Warplanes, c. 1945, balsa wood models, price per each	12	18	25
Kellogg's Pep Warplanes, c. 1945, balsa, with Superman ad on envelope	15	22	30
Kellogg's Pep Warplanes, c. 1944, cardboard, price per each	7	11	15
"The Liberty Gun For Young America - McGrath's Big Store," 7" cardboard with photos of Charlie Chaplin	20	30	40

"The Liberty Gun For Young America McGrath's Big Store," 7" cardboard with photos of Charlie Chaplin. Courtesy HAKE'S Americana & Collectibles.

	C6	C8	C10
Little Orphan Annie Necklace, c. 1936, metal enamel figure of LOA on metal chain	18	27	36
Little Orphan Annie Pinback Button, Little Orphan Annie, Member Funy Frosty's Club, mid-1930s	21	32	42
Lone Ranger, A Republic Serial, brass star badge	70	105	140
Lone Ranger Atom Bomb Ring (very common)	75	112	150
Lone Ranger Blackout Kit, 1942, Kix cereal glow-in-the-dark material (two pieces), glow-in-the- dark pledge to flag, glow-in-the-dark Lone Ranger Volunteers armband, plus instructions	52	78	105
Lone Ranger Bond Bread Safety Club Badge, 1938	22	33	45
Lone Ranger Chief Scout Badge, Silvercup Bread, early 1940s	75	112	150

	C6	C8	C10
Lone Ranger Clicker Pistol, black, 1939 movie giveaway, Lone Ranger on one side and ruby on other, non-moveable silver cylinder	83	125	165
Lone Ranger Deputy Shield, brass with secret compartment	37	56	75
Lone Ranger Flashlight Ring	42	63	85
Lone Ranger Frontier Town, full set	1100	1650	2200

Lone Ranger Frontier Town, complete.
Courtesy HAKE'S Americana & Collectibles.

	C6	C8	C10
Lone Ranger Glow-in-the-Dark Belt, 1941	83	125	165
Lone Ranger Hi-Yo Silver Pin, 1938	17	26	35
Lone Ranger Kix Air Base with cereal box cut-outs, precursor of Frontier Town, complete $300			
Lone Ranger Lucky Piece, advertises 17th anniversary 1933-50	25	38	50
Lone Ranger Mask, about the last radio premium, c. 1953 or 1954, back of black mask promotes a personal appearance by "The Lone Ranger and Silver!"	25	38	50
Lone Ranger Movie Film Ring, late 1940s, Cheerios	75	112	150
Lone Ranger Pedometer, 1948, Cheerios	15	23	30
Lone Ranger Rubber Band Gun and 6 different targets, 1938 Morton Salt giveaway, cardboard	37	56	75
Lone Ranger Secret Compartment Ring, with picture of Lone Ranger and Silver	125	188	250
Lone Ranger Silver Bullet, secret compartment compass	42	63	85

Lone Ranger Secret Compartment Ring.
Courtesy Jim Harmon.

	C6	C8	C10
Lone Ranger Silver Saddle Film Ring, late 1940s, Cheerios	75	112	150
Lone Ranger Safety Scout Badge, Silvercup Bread, 1935	22	33	45
Lone Ranger Silvercup Bread Safety Patrol, metal-silver and blue	22	33	45
Lone Ranger Six-Shooter Ring, gun ring with plastic and metal gun attached to top, turn wheel and flint sparks	125	188	250
Lone Ranger Victory Corps Badge, 1942, Kix Cereal	32	48	65
Lone Ranger Weather Ring, color square stone on top with litmus paper, no markings to identify as Lone Ranger	38	57	75
Magic Show Kit, 1946 General Mills	14	21	27
Magician's Book of Cigarette Tricks, 1933, Camel Cigarettes	9	13	18
Major Bowes Home Microphone	30	45	60
Maltex Health Club Pinback Button	4	7	9
Melvin Purvis Junior G-Man Corps Badge, late 1930s	22	33	45
Melvin Purvis Junior G-Man Corps Roving Operative Badge, late 1930s	22	33	45
Melvin Purvis Law and Order Ring	37	56	75
Melvin Purvis Law & Order Patrol Lieutenant's Secret Operator Badge, mid-1930s	37	56	75
Melvin Purvis Law & Order Patrol Secret Operator Badge, late 1930s	37	56	75
Melvin Purvis Secret Operator, Girl's Division	30	45	60
Mickey and Donald's Race to Treasure Island, 1939, 12" x 25" Standard Oil giveaway	98	148	195
Mickey and Donald's Race to Treasure Island, 1939, map of U.S. in full color, 20" x 27", Calco Gasoline giveaway, with stamps	330	495	660
Mickey Mouse Club Pinback Button, "Copyright 1928-30 by W.E. Disney," 1-1/4"	55	83	110
Mickey Mouse Globe Trotters Map, 28" x 20", NBC Bread, 1937	355	525	715
Mickey Mouse Globe Trotters Map, 28" x 22", NBC Bread, with all pictures pasted on	355	525	715
Mickey Mouse Globe Trotters Map, 1930s, Pevely Milk premium	355	525	715
Mickey Mouse Official Money, 1930s Mickey Mouse Cones dollar bills, denomination is "1" (each)	12	18	25
Mickey Mouse Playboard, 1946 9" high, comics giveaway	27	41	55
Morton Salt "Bat-O-Ball," 1939, features The Shadow (cartoon)	62	93	125
My-T-Fine Grocery Store, folds into an 8" x 3" full color grocery store with period products on the shelves, shoppers, workers, etc., dated 1930	37	56	75
Nabisco Finger Puppet Rings, Slim Chants, horse Humbolt, gun, hand, Prairie Mary, Tagalong Boswell, Cold Deck Charlie, Sam Spiel, price per each figure	2	3	5

	C6	C8	C10
Nabisco Santa Fe Twin Unit Diesel Train, 1956, includes engine, train, tracks, ground, background 12	18	25
Nabisco Sound-Jet Glider 10	15	20
Nabisco Trailblazers of America cards, six cards make up horse-drawn van and open van, 1956 5	8	10
Nabisco Shredded Wheat Nabisco Flying Circus, 1948, designed by Wallace Rigby, 4" x 7" cards, planes, once cut out, can glide, series of 24, price per each 5	8	10
The Nebbs - Detroit Times series No. 27544 (comic strip) 7	11	15
New York World's Fair Children's World G-Man Badge, giveaway, 3-color brass badge 25	38	50
Newsboy Brand Soups and Vegetables Official Booster Badge, late 1930s 4	7	9
Pep Pins - Dick Tracy 15	22	30
Pep Pins - Little Orphan Annie 7	11	15
Pep Pins - Flash Gordon 15	22	30
Pep Pins - Felix the Cat 5	8	10
Pep Pins - The Phantom 7	11	15
Pep Pins - Popeye and Olive Oyl - each 7	11	15
Pep Pins - Superman 20	30	40
Pep Pins - Others, includes Smitty, Inspector, Harold Teen, Skeezix, Corky, Pop Jenks, Goofy, Spud, Andy Gump, Gravel Gertie, Punjab, Hans, Kayo, Smilin' Jack, Dagwood, B.O. Plenty, Mr. Bailey, Shadow, Moon Mullins, Flattop, Rip Winkle, Uncle Willie, Emma, Inspector, Chief Brandon, Vitamin Flintheart, Sandy, Uncle Bim, Sundown, Lillums, Tilda, Uncle Walt, Perry Winkle, Judy, Min Gump, Wilmer, Smoky Stover, Daisy, Ma Winkle, Tess Trueheart, Herbie, Mamie, Breezie, Pat Patton, Maggie, Barney Google, Fat Stuff, Chief Brandon, Toots, Nina, etc., average 7	11	15
Pep Rings - Jack Kramer, Dennis O'Keefe, Burt Lancaster, Sitting Bull, Pocahontas, Pan American Clipper, Douglas F-3D Sky Knight, Republic XF91 Thundercepter, each 10	15	20
Pepsodent's Moving Picture Machine shows Mickey Mouse, Donald Duck, Snow White and Seven Dwarfs in color 325	490	650
Pillsbury-Farina Complete Tel-A-Phone Set, 1938, two holders, mouthpieces, ear phones and 50 feet of line 25	38	50
Pinocchio Playboard, 1946, Disney Comics sub. giveaway 25	38	50
Popeye The Sailor Man Button, 3/4", copyright 1935, theatre giveaway 15	22	30
Popsicle Movie Star Coins, aluminum coins, c. early 1930s, includes Irene Dunne, Clark Gable, Marion Davies, Fredric March, Marie Dressler, Gary Cooper 5	8	10
Porcelain Enamel & Mfg. Co. 6" West Point Cadet on 3" x 6" card with Pemco ad on back 2	3	5

	C6	C8	C10
Post Grape Nuts Flakes Playing-Filling Station, c. 1950s 5	8	10
Post Toasties 1939 Walt Disney cut-out figures on box, Mickey the Traffic Cop, two types of Pinocchio, etc. Price per each box 27	41	55
Post Toasties Corn Flakes Comic Rings, 1949, Fritz, Hans, Tillie the Toiler, Toots, Casper, etc. 17	26	35
Post's Cereal Junior Detective Club Sergeant Badge, late 1930s 15	22	30
Post's Explorer Ring, 1947, includes compass, sun watch, sunset predictor and star finder, plastic dome 25	38	50
Post Cereal Rings, 1948, Perry Winkle, Winnie Winkle, Harold Teen, Skeezix, Lillums, Herbie, Smoky Stover, etc. 17	26	35
Post Cereal Rings, 1948, Dick Tracy 17	26	35
Post Grape Nuts Tin Rings, Little King, Phantom, Skeezex, Lillums, Harold Teen 17	26	35
Post Raisin Bran Sheriff Badge 10	15	20
Radio Orphan Annie, Annie and Joe Corntassel button, 1931 15	22	30
Radio Orphan Annie, Associated Membership Pin, 1934 15	22	30
Radio Orphan Annie Bandanna, 1934 21	32	42
Radio Orphan Annie Birthstone Ring, 1935 125	188	250
Radio Orphan Annie Capt. Sparks Aviation Trainer 250	375	500
Radio Orphan Annie Circus Cut-Outs, 1935 150	225	300
Radio Orphan Annie Code Captain Belt and Buckle, 1940 48	72	96
Radio Orphan Annie Code Captain Pin, 1939 32	48	65
Radio Orphan Annie Manual, 1934 62	93	125
Radio Orphan Annie 1935 Decoder Manual 62	93	125
Radio Orphan Annie 1936 Decoder Manual 62	93	125
Radio Orphan Annie 1937 Decoder Manual 62	93	125

Radio Orphan Annie Decoder Badges, 1938 (left) and 1939 (right). Courtesy Jim Harmon.

	C6	C8	C10
Radio Orphan Annie 1938 Decoder Manual	62	93	125
Radio Orphan Annie 1939 Decoder Manual	62	93	125
Radio Orphan Annie 1940 Decoder Manual	83	125	165
Radio Orphan Annie 1942 Decoder Manual and Cardboard Decoder	198	300	385
Radio Orphan Annie Decoder Pin, 1935	25	38	50
Radio Orphan Annie Decoder Badge, 1936	25	38	50

Radio Orphan Annie Decoder Badge 1936. Courtesy Jim Harmon.

	C6	C8	C10
Radio Orphan Annie Decoder Badge, 1937	25	38	508
Radio Orphan Annie Decoder Badge, 1938	25	38	50
Radio Orphan Annie Decoder Badge, 1939	25	38	50
Radio Orphan Annie Decoder Badge, 1940	25	38	50
Radio Orphan Annie Foreign Coins, 1937	25	38	50
Radio Orphan Annie Goofy Circus, 1939	37	56	75
Radio Orphan Annie Identification Bracelet, 1934	37	56	75
Radio Orphan Annie Identification Bracelet, 1935	32	48	65
Radio Orphan Annie Identification Tag, 1939	32	48	65
Radio Orphan Annie Magic Transfer Pictures, 1935	32	48	65
Radio Orphan Annie Magic Transfer Picture, 1937	32	48	65
Radio Orphan Annie Mask, 1933	50	75	100
Radio Orphan Annie Mystic Eye Ring, 1939	62	93	125
Radio Orphan Annie Package, 1942, includes Whirl-O-Matic Decoder, Whistle Badge, booklet, and order blanks	193	290	385
Radio Orphan Annie Pin, 1937	17	26	35
Radio Orphan Annie Portrait Ring, 1934, ring has head of Annie embossed on top	48	72	95
Radio Orphan Annie Premium Manual, 1937	62	93	125
Radio Orphan Annie Premium Manual, 1938	62	93	125
Radio Orphan Annie Punch-Outs	120	180	240
Radio Orphan Annie Ring, 1934	48	72	95
Radio Orphan Annie Ring, 1935	48	72	95
Radio Orphan Annie Roller Skates, 1938	50	75	100

	C6	C8	C10
Radio Orphan Annie Secret Egyptian Compass and Sundial, 1938	48	72	95
Radio Orphan Annie Secret Society Pin, 1934	25	38	50
Radio Orphan Annie Signet Ring, 1937	62	93	125
Radio Orphan Annie Silver Star Pin, 1934	48	72	95
Radio Orphan Annie Silver Star Pin, 1935	48	72	95
Radio Orphan Annie Secret Society Silver Star Ring, 1936	48	72	95
Radio Orphan Annie Silver Star Ring, 1937	48	72	95
Radio Orphan Annie Silver Star Ring, 1938	48	72	95
Radio Orphan Annie School Pin, 1939	20	30	40
Radio Orphan Annie Secret Guard Clicker, 1942	25	38	50
Radio Orphan Annie Shake-Up Game, 1931	17	26	35
Radio Orphan Annie 3-Way Dog Whistle, 1940	30	45	60
Radio Orphan Annie Treasure Hunt Game, 1933	37	56	75
Radio Orphan Annie Treasure Hunt Game, 1935	37	56	75
Range Rider & Dick West Button, Peter Pan bread, 1950s	37	56	75
Red Ryder Lucky Coin	7	11	15
Renfrew of Mounted Pinback	10	15	20
Rin Tin Tin "Ball-in-the-Hole" Games (sealed coin-size games of Rinty, Rip Masters, Fort Apache, etc.), each	9	13	18
Rin Tin Tin Ring, plastic, 1950s	17	26	35
Rin Tin Tin Set of Plastic Dinosaurs (Radio-TV 1954)	62	93	125
Rin Tin Tin Wonderscope (Telescope-Microscope-Compass), radio-TV, 1954, has "Rin Tin Tin" on face (same item, without name, recently, perhaps currently, on sale in stores for under $1.00)	30	45	60
Rip Masters (Rin Tin Tin) Plastic Rings, 1950s	20	30	40
Rocky Lane's Explorer's Sun Watch, 1951, Carnation Milk	22	33	45
Roy Rogers Branding Iron Ring	62	93	125
Roy Rogers Deputy Badge	10	15	20
Roy Rogers Microscope Ring, 1947, Quaker Oats	62	93	125
Roy Rogers Paint Set, 1950s	12	18	25
Roy Rogers Signal Badge, with mirror, secret compartment and whistle	48	72	95
Roy Rogers Silver Hat Ring	30	45	60
Roy Rogers Trigger's Lucky Horseshoe, full size, black rubber	12	18	25
Roy Rogers Tuck-A-Way Gun	12	18	25
Scoop Ward News of Youth Official Reporter Badge, late 1930s, Ward's Soft Bun Bread giveaway	10	15	20
Secret Three Badge, with manual of secret codes	10	15	20
Sgt. Preston Distance Finder	42	63	85
Sgt. Preston Firefighting Set	42	63	85

	C6	C8	C10
Sgt. Preston Flashlight, signals has two filters	42	63	85
Sgt. Preston Klondike Land Pouch	25	38	50
Sgt. Preston Klondike Movie Film Viewer	52	80	105
Sgt. Preston Pedometer	25	38	50
Sgt. Preston Police Whistle, nylon cord, brass, 1950	27	41	55
Sgt. Preston Skinning Knife	35	52	70
Sgt. Preston Totem Pole Set	55	82	110
Sgt. Preston Trail Kit, rare, (probably the most complex of all premiums)	300	450	600
Sgt. Preston Yukon Village	300	450	600
Shadow Ring, Glow in Dark, "blue coal" jewel on white ring	475	715	950
Shadow "Carey Salt" Ring (same as J. Armstrong Crocodile ring with black stone; this ring has been counterfeited; original is smoothly circular with clean-cut design), requires identifying papers for C10 price	475	715	950
Shield G-Man Club Badge, 1942, Pep Comics premium, lithographed celluloid pinback	37	56	75
Skippy S.S.S.S. Captain, pinback button, all celluloid, 1930s	12	18	25
Skippy Compass, 1930s?	10	15	20
Sky Birds Propeller Ring, brass and silver, 1930s, Goudey Gum premium	12	18	25
Sky King Aztec Indian Ring	125	188	250
Sky King Detecto Microscope	53	78	105
Sky King Detecto Writer	70	105	140
Sky King Electronic Television Ring	100	150	200
Sky King Magni-Glo Ring	100	150	200
Sky King Mystery Picture Ring (picture never works)	55	83	110
Sky King Navajo Indian Ring	125	190	250
Sky King Small Plastic Statues, of Sky King, Penny, Sky King's horse, Sky King's plane The Songbird, Nabisco giveaways in Wheat Honey and Rice Honey, 1950s, each	15	22	30
Sky King Signal Scope	70	105	140
Sky King Stamp Kit	48	72	95
Sky King Teleblinker Ring	125	190	250

Sky King Teleblinker Ring. Courtesy Jim Harmon.

	C6	C8	C10
Snow White Game, Tek Toothbrush	38	57	75
Space Patrol Binoculars, c. 1950s	110	165	220
Space Patrol Diplomatic Pouch, contains money, stamps, etc.	138	210	275
Space Patrol Goggles	53	78	105
Space Patrol 1951 Jet Glow Code Belt	138	210	275
Space Patrol Ring, with secret powder compartment, c. early 1950s	138	210	275
Space Patrol Smoke Gun, 1950s	150	225	300
Space Patrol Space Helmet, c. 1950s	180	270	360
Space Patrol 1952 Space-O-Phone	98	150	195
Space Patrol Space Ship, c. 1950s	88	132	175
Speed Gibson's Flying Police Badge, Dreikorn's Bread	12	18	25
Straight Arrow Face Ring, c. early 1950s	52	80	105
Straight Arrow Magic Cave Ring, 1949 with original art	100	150	200
Straight Arrow Magic Cave Ring, reissued 1988 with new art and customer's photos (discontinued)	20	30	40
Straight Arrow Puppets and Props, 1949, Nabisco radio premium	30	45	60
Straight Arrow Target Game, lithographed tin target board, 10" x 14", National Biscuit Company copyright on the edge	37	56	75
Straight Arrow Tom-Tom, c. early 1950s	25	38	50
Straight Arrow Wrist Bracelet, with secret compartment, c. early 1950s	37	56	75
Sunbrite "Junior Nurse Corps" Brass Badge	4	7	9
Sunbrite "Junior Nurse Corps" Pinback Button, pictures of Dorothy Hart	3	5	7
Superman Comics Magazine Ring, auctioned in 1995 for 20,000			
Superman Crusader Ring	125	188	250
Superman Kellogg's Gy Rocket	48	72	95
Superman Kellogg's Silver Jet Airplane Ring, plane flies off	48	72	95
Superman Kellogg's Walkie-Talkie	37	56	75
Superman Pin, 1940s, "Read Superman Action Comics Magazine"	22	33	45
Superman Planes from Pep Cereal, set of 8, 1948	30	45	60
Superman Premium Club Set, certificate, button and decoder	125	190	250
Superman Tim Club Ring	175	263	350
Superman's Secret Code, c. 1939	24	36	48
Supermen of America Button, 1939 version, 1-3/8", pinback button	32	48	65
Tarzan Gift Statues, Foulds, 1930s, Tarzan, Jane, Kala, etc., price per set	475	700	950
Tarzan Jungle Map and Treasure Hunt Weston Biscuit, 1933	60	90	120
Tennessee Jed Lariat	37	56	75
Tennessee Jed Look Around Ring, 1940s	35	52	70
Tennessee Jed Paper Gun, c. 1940s	21	32	42
Terry And The Pirates Glow-in-the-Dark Ring, crocodiles on sides	37	56	75
Terry And The Pirates Gold Detector Ring	62	93	125
Texas Longhorn Tin Badge, Post Raisin Bran, c. 1950s	4	7	9

GIFT No. 1
TARZAN
with set of water color paints,
brush and color chart.

GIFT No. 2
KALA
the Mother Ape

GIFT No. 3
NUMA
the Lion

GIFT No. 4
JANE PORTER
the Girl

GIFT No. 5
SHEETA
the Panther

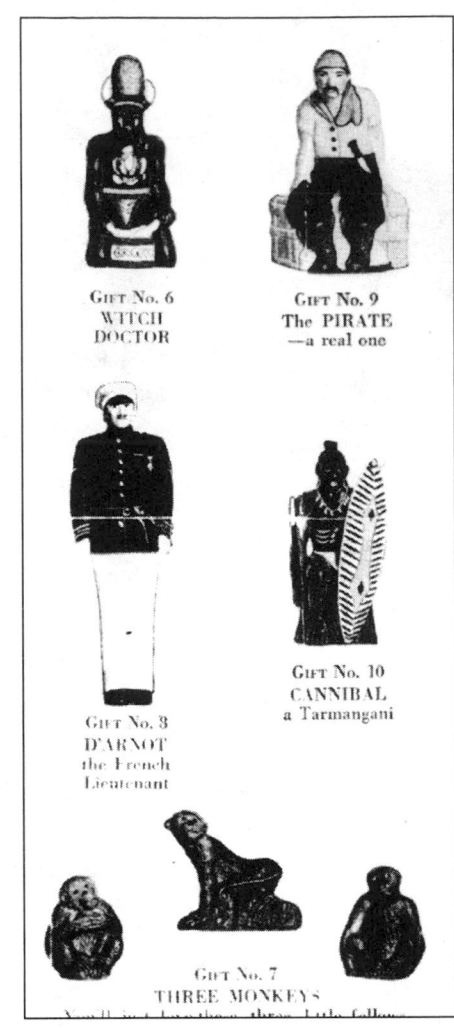

GIFT No. 6
WITCH DOCTOR

GIFT No. 9
The PIRATE
—a real one

GIFT No. 8
D'ARNOT
the French
Lieutenant

GIFT No. 10
CANNIBAL
a Tarmangani

GIFT No. 7
THREE MONKEYS

*Tarzan Gift
Statues, Foulds.*

	C6	C8	C10
Tom Corbett Space Cadet Badge, early 1950s	37	56	75
Tom Corbett Space Cadet Belt Buckle Decoder, early 1950s	83	125	165
Tom Corbett Decoder, cardboard, 1950s	35	52	70
Tom Corbett Rings, Kellogg's, 1950-55, 12 different including: Space Cruiser, Rocket Scout, Space Academy, Space Suit, Space Helmet, Corbett-Space Cadet, Cadet Dress Uniform, Girl's Space Uniform, Parallo-Ray Gun, Strate-Telescope, Sound Ray Gun, per each	17	26	35
Tom Mix Airplane and Parachute	100	150	200
Tom Mix Arm Patch (TM bar on checkerboard design) 1933 - predominantly blue; 1947 - predominantly red; 1983 - predominantly black (worth probably as much as older versions, only 1000 issued)	27	41	55
Tom Mix Badge Ranch Box	42	63	85
Tom Mix Bag of Marbles	20	30	40
Tom Mix Bandanna, has TM Brand	55	83	110
Tom Mix Baseball	25	38	50
Tom Mix Baseball Bat	25	38	50
Tom Mix Baseball Cap	27	41	55

	C6	C8	C10
Tom Mix Belt Buckle with Secret Compartment, belt glows in the dark (offered only on cereal boxes after radio show ended)	70	105	140
Tom Mix Blowdart Game	52	78	105
Tom Mix Branding Iron, TM Brand	52	78	105
Tom Mix Bullet Flashlight	52	78	105
Tom Mix Bullet Telescope, bird-call device comes with it, approx. 4" long	35	52	70
Tom Mix Catalog of Straight Shooter Premiums, 8-1/2" x 11", b/w sheet with order form on reverse and descriptions and small pictures of premiums on the front, includes sheepskin vest, rodeo rope, leather cuffs, wood gun, lucky spinner, etc.	20	30	40
Tom Mix Charm Bracelet, charm steer head, gun, horseman, TM brand	52	78	105
Tom Mix Coloring Book (Ralston, c. 1949)	20	30	40
Tom Mix Compass Magnifying Glass, 1947, silver color (Note: Originals have "Japan" written on the back. Imitations have the words "Comet-Japan" on the back)	45	68	90
Tom Mix Compass Magnifying Glass, 1939, brass	75	110	150

ANSWERS to TOM MIX mysteries!

THE TELEVISION MURDER: Photograph of Mint-more (Frame 3) shows he needed thick glasses. Why didn't he have them on if he was watching Television when shot? Window glass shows bullet was fired from inside room. Hole is always smaller on side wh... own hands to fake marks on ...eone had choked him, the little-finger ...ould have been at the bottom ... not at top.

Tom Mix Compass-Magnifying Glass, 1937. Courtesy Jim Harmon.

Tom Mix Decoder Badge. Courtesy Jim Harmon.

	C6	C8	C10
Tom Mix Identification Bracelet	42	63	85
Tom Mix Initial Ring, 1935	100	150	200
Tom Mix Look-Around Ring, c. post 1945	62	93	125

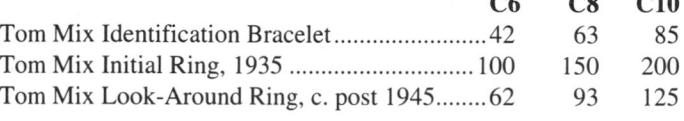

ANSWERS to TOM MIX mysteries!

THE TELEVISION MURDER: Photograph of Mint-more (Frame 3) shows he needed thick glasses. Why didn't he have them on if he was watching Television when shot? Window glass shows bullet was fired from inside room. Hole is always smaller on side wh... dore... own hands to fake marks on neck. If someone had choked him, the little-finger mark would have been at the bottom of the neck . . . not at top.

Tom Mix Compass-Magnifying Glass, 1947. Courtesy Jim Harmon.

Tom Mix Look-Around Ring. Courtesy Jim Harmon.

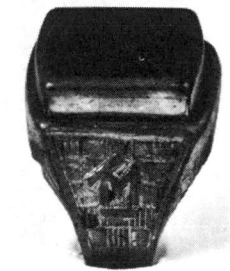

Tom Mix Brand Ring.

	C6	C8	C10
Tom Mix Compass Magnifying Glass, c. 1948, glows in the dark, plastic	75	112	150
Tom Mix Cowboy Shirt	150	225	300
Tom Mix Cowboy Vest	82	125	165
Tom Mix Cowgirl Skirt	150	225	300
Tom Mix Decoder Badge, 1940, moveable 6-shooter points to symbols	100	150	200
Tom Mix Decoder Buttons Instruction Sheet, 1946, Ralston	12	18	24
Tom Mix Decoder Pins, Tony, Jane, Sheriff, Wash, price per pin	12	18	24
Tom Mix Decoder Pin, "Curley Bradley"	18	27	36
Tom Mix Deputy Ring, 1934, chewing gum premium	225	338	450
Tom Mix Glow-in-the-Dark Arrowhead, 1946, has compass and magnifying glass	52	78	105
Tom Mix Gold Ore Badge	42	63	85
Tom Mix Ore Charm, 1940, Ralston, contains genuine gold ore under plastic dome	42	63	85
Tom Mix "Good Luck" Spinner	27	41	55
Tom Mix Horseshoe Nail Ring, 1933 (can be verified only by accompanying papers)	35	52	70
Tom Mix Lucky Wrist Band, 1936, Ralston premium, metal, TM bar brand, with leather strap and buckle	50	75	100
Tom Mix Magnet Gun and Signal Arrowhead Bracelet, gun and arrowhead glow in the dark	55	83	110
Tom Mix Magnet Ring, 1945	62	93	125
Tom Mix Makeup Kit (two grease-paint model, plus five grease-paint model)	300	450	600
Tom Mix 1941 Manual	52	78	105
Tom Mix 1944 Manual	52	78	105
Tom Mix 1946 Manual	42	63	85
Tom Mix Mask, cardboard	385	580	770
Tom Mix Mystery Picture Ring, 1939, with "look-in" picture of Tom Mix and Tony, viewed through one side of the ring	163	245	325

Tom Mix Mystery Picture Ring ad. Courtesy Jim Harmon.

	C6	C8	C10
Tom Mix Parachute, 1936 Ralston premium	53	78	105
Tom Mix Periscope	53	78	105
Tom Mix Postal Telegraph Set, blue, metal clicker, 1938	53	78	105

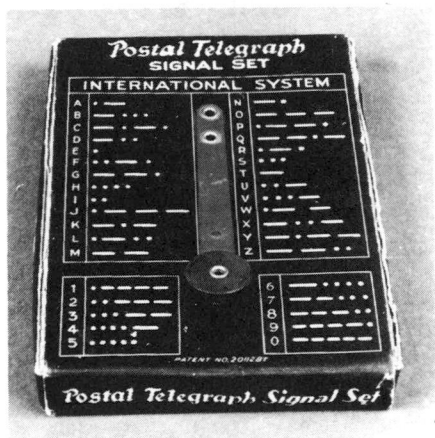

Tom Mix Postal Telegraph Set. Courtesy Jim Harmon.

Tom Mix Premium Enclosures and Correspondence, many picture postcards, letters on Straight Shooter stationery, etc. were sent out to listeners who wrote in to the radio show; these and various coupons, instruction sheets, contest entries are offered by dealers and collectors, average value	20	30	40
Tom Mix Telegraph Set, red, uses batteries, 1940	133	200	265
Tom Mix Ralston Straight Shooters Pocket Knife, 1940	53	78	105
Tom Mix RCA TV Set, shows photographs or comic strips (brown model or reddish model)	37	56	75
Tom Mix Secret Code Manual	42	63	85
Tom Mix Sharpshooters Medal, glows in the dark	83	125	165
Tom Mix Sheriff of Dobie County Siren Badge, 1946 Ralston	48	72	95

	C6	C8	C10
Tom Mix Signal Arrowhead, 1949 with magnifying glass and "whizzer" flute-type whistle, made of lucite	48	72	95

Tom Mix Straightshooters Medal. Courtesy Jim Harmon.

Tom Mix Sharpshooters Medal. Courtesy Jim Harmon.

Tom Mix Signal Flashlight	48	72	95
Tom Mix Signature Ring, pre-WWII	125	188	250
Tom Mix Siren Ring, 1945	62	93	125
Tom Mix Six-Shooter, wooden, barrel breaks and cartridge drum spins - 1933	110	165	220
Tom Mix Six-Shooter, wooden, barrel spins, 1936	110	165	220
Tom Mix Six-Shooter, wooden, no moving parts, 1939	98	150	195
Tom Mix Spinning Rope, 1936, Ralston, hemp with wood handle	53	78	105
Tom Mix Spurs, metal, with plastic glow-in-the-dark rowels, Late	70	105	140

Tom Mix Six Shooter. Courtesy Jim Harmon.

Tom Mix Western Movie Viewer. Courtesy Jim Harmon.

	C6	C8	C10
Tom Mix "Square and Fair" Spinner	37	56	75
Tom Mix Straight Shooters Campaign Medal, gold	42	63	85
Tom Mix Straight Shooters Campaign Medal, silver	42	63	85
Tom Mix Sundial Watch	55	83	110
Tom Mix Telephone Set	70	105	140
Tom Mix Telescope, TM brand on side	53	78	105
Tom Mix Tiger Eye Ring, 1949, Ralston	150	225	300
Tom Mix TM Brand Ring, c. 1933	75	112	150
Tom Mix Tri-Color Flashlight	48	72	95
Tom Mix Western Movie Viewer, shows scenes from Tom Mix films, 1935	82	125	165
Tom Mix Whistle Ring, 1945	63	95	125
Tom Mix Wrangler Badge, 1936, Ralston	53	78	105
Toonerville Trolley Cardboard Village, put out by Coca-Cola	88	132	175

	C6	C8	C10
Trigger Button, 7/8", Post Grape Nut Flakes	12	18	25
Welch's Grape Juice Train, paper engine, box car, passenger car, caboose, price for each	3	5	7
Complete set above	12	18	25

Tom Mix Brand Ring.

Welch's Grape Juice Train (part). Photo by Gary Linden.

Welch's Grape Juice Train (part). Photo by Gary Linden.

	C6	C8	C10
Wheaties Jogometer	12	18	25
Wheaties Pedometer, c. late 1940s	10	15	20
Wild Bill Hickok Bunkhouse Set (cut-out pin-ups of Bill, Jingles, guns, ropes, etc.)	15	22	30
Wild Bill Hickok Treasure Map & Guide, 1952, Kellogg's	48	72	95

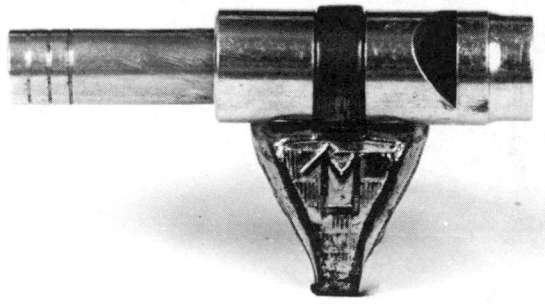

Tom Mix Whistle Ring. Courtesy Jim Harmon.

COMIC CHARACTERS

(See also Movies, Battery-Operated, Premiums, Paper, Mechanical Banks, Ramp Walkers, Vehicles - Tootsietoy)

The average mint price of these toys in the last edition was $750.09. In this edition it is $695.69, a decrease of 7%.

Comic character toys are attractive to collectors: they are often colorful and eye-catching, as well as evocative of happy childhood memories. Popeye continues to be a magnet for collectors, along with such favorites as The Yellow Kid, Buck Rogers, Flash Gordon, Tarzan, Superman, Felix the Cat, Barney Google, and Happy Hooligan.

	C6	C8	C10
Albert Alligator (Pogo) plastic, 1969, approx. 5" high ("Duz") 7	11	15
Alfred E. Neumann, Effanbee, 1960, vinyl 125	188	250
Alphonse, Hubley, in a goat-pulled cart, cast iron, 13-3/4" long, 7-1/2" high, early 1900s, from comic strip team of Alphonse and Gaston, head-nodder, movable arms and hands 300	450	600
Alphonse in horse-drawn carriage, nodder toy, c. 1910, 10-1/2" long 550	825	1100
Alphonse, Hubley, mule pulling wagon, 7" long, cast-iron nodder 300	450	600

Alphonse, 2 goats pulling wagon, Hubley. Courtesy Kruse Auctioneers.

Alphonse & Gaston animated car, cast iron. Courtesy James S. Maxwell/Virginia Caputo. Photo by Virginia Caputo.

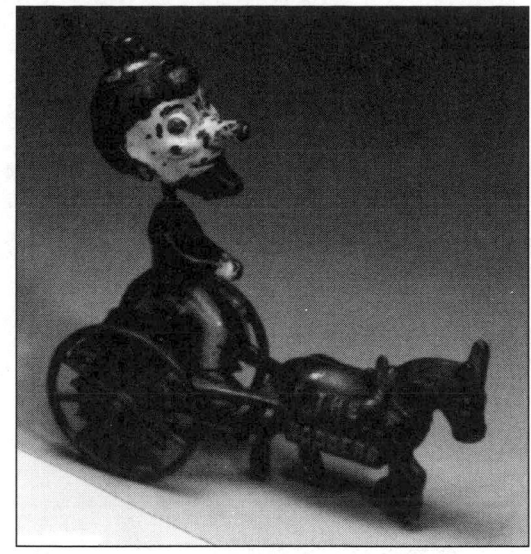

Alphonse, mule pulling wagon, Hubley. Courtesy Christie's East.

B.O. Plenty holding Sparkle Plenty. Photo by Don Hultzman.

	C6	C8	C10
Alphonse, Hubley, two goats pulling wagon, cast iron, 13-3/4" long, 7-1/2" high, early1900s, head-nodder, movable arms and hands	200	300	400
Alphonse Nodder Figure	600	900	1200
Alphonse & Gaston animated car, cast iron, auctioned in 1990 for $15,000, $7840 and $12,650			
Andy Gump Roadster, "348," Arcade, 7" long	1200	1900	2850
Same as above, deluxe version	2000	3500	6000

Andy Gump Roadster "348," Arcade. Courtesy Christie's East.

	C6	C8	C10
Andy Gump wooden dancing doll, 9", tin legs	125	188	250
Archie & Veronica Jalopy, illus. on side, 7" tin wind-up, Spanish	145	218	290
Archie Hand Puppet, 1973, Ideal, vinyl	25	38	50
B.O. Plenty holding Sparkle Plenty, c. mid-1940s, tin wind-up, Marx	180	270	360

	C6	C8	C10
Baby Snookums (The Newlyweds) fabric doll, 5-1/2" high	150	225	300
Baby Sparkle Plenty paper dolls, Saalfield No. 1510	35	52	70
Barney Google, cloth and wood, Schoenhut: See Schoenhut			

Barney Google cloth and wood doll, Schoenhut. Courtesy Sotheby's New York.

	C6	C8	C10
Barney Google Doll, 9" high, wood with composition head, movable arms and legs	200	300	400
Barney Google glass candy container	188	282	375
Barney Google Hand Puppet, Gund	48	72	95
Barney Google and Sparkplug pull toy, tin litho, Sparkplug in barn	1500	2250	3000
Barney Google and Sparkplug Scooter Race, 1920s, Nifty Toy Co., 8" long, pull toy	3000	4800	6500
Barney Google Riding Sparkplug, wooden: See Schoenhut			
Barney Google Riding Sparkplug, 3" metal paperweight	75	112	150
Barney Google tin wind-up, c. 1923	500	750	1000
Barney Google and Sparkplug, tin wind-up by Nifty	650	975	1300
Batman Bat Grenade, 1966	75	112	150
Batman Batchute, 1966	42	63	85
Batman Bat Ray, Remco, 1977	25	38	50
Batman Batmobile, Corgi No. 267	55	83	110
Batman "Batmobile-Batman Driver," 1966, Marx	65	98	130

	C6	C8	C10
Batman "Batmobile-Robin Driver," Marx, 4"long	65	98	130
Batman Bullhorn, 1966, Bayshore Ind., plastic	30	45	60
Batman candy container, PEZ: See PEZ			
Batman Escape Gun, c. 1966, Lincoln	42	63	85
Batman "Flying Batman," 1966 Ideal, 12" inflatable	10	15	20
Batman glasses, 1966	4	6	8
Batman Hand Puppet, cloth body	27	41	55
Batman Hand Puppet, vinyl, Ideal, 1965	27	41	55
Batman Helmet and cape, helmet fits over whole head, 1966, Ideal	145	218	290
Batman Hot Line Batphone, Marx	250	375	500
Batman Picture Pistol, Marx, 1966	225	338	450
Batman Playset, Ideal, 1966	900	1350	1800

	C6	C8	C10
Batman Playset, Ideal, 1973	25	38	50
Batman Soaky	26	39	52
Batman Thingmaker Set, 1960s	35	52	70
Batman Utility Belt, 1941, with belt-radio buckle	800	1300	1900
Batman Utility Belt Set, 1979, Remco	50	75	100
Beauregard (Pogo), plastic, 1969	7	11	15
Beetle Bailey Hand Puppet, Gund	45	68	90
Beetle Bailey "Pop Up Beetle Bailey," Linemar, tin litho	180	270	360
Beetle Bailey vinyl figure, 3"	8	12	16
Beetle Bailey's Camp Swampy Playset, MPC	115	172	230
Billy Batson (Capt. Marvel) Magic Box	50	75	100
Blondie "Blondie's Jalopy," 16" long	1200	2000	2800
Blondie Hingees Set, 1944	20	30	40

Blondie, "Blondie's Jalopy." Courtesy Christie's East.

Bluto (Popeye) Dippy Dumper. Courtesy Christie's East.

	C6	C8	C10
Blondie, 1940, Whitman 982, paper cut-outs	45	68	90
Blondie, 1947, Whitman 967, paper cut-outs	37	56	75
Bluto (Popeye) Dippy Dumper Truck, celluloid, tin, 9-1/2"	500	750	1000
Bluto on Horse Cart, celluloid and tin wind-up, 7-1/2"	400	600	800
Bonnie Braids (Dick Tracy), "Bonnie Braids Doll," Marx, 1950s, wind-up, 9" long	200	300	400
Bonnie Braids Paper Dolls, Dick Tracy's daughter and wife Tess, Saalfield No. 2724, 1951, cut-outs	25	38	50
Bonnie Braids Walker, Charmore Co., 1951, tin litho walker, nurse-maid pushes Bonnie, plastic: See Ramp Walkers			
Boob McNutt, 9" high: See Schoenhut			
Boob McNutt tin wind-up, Strauss	450	675	900
Boots and Her Buddies Paper Dolls, 1943, Saalfield No. 2460	27	41	55
Bringing Up Father, Hingees, 1944	17	26	35
Broom Hilda, 14" high, Knickerbocker, c. 1970	38	53	75
Brutus (Popeye) cardboard mask, 1940s	40	60	80
Brutus Soaky	22	33	44

Buck Rogers Atomic Pistol. Courtesy HAKE'S Americana & Collectibles.

	C6	C8	C10
Buck Rogers Atomic Pistol, 1946, U-235, sparks and pops, Daisy	150	225	300
Buck Rogers Battle Cruiser, Tootsietoy, 1937, two grooved wheels on top to run on string	100	150	200
Buck Rogers Casting Set, 1930s, Junior Caster, Rapaport Bros	325	488	650
Buck Rogers Chemical Laboratory, Gropper Toys, 1937	1000	1500	2000
Buck Rogers Disintegrator pistol, 1936, Daisy	223	335	445

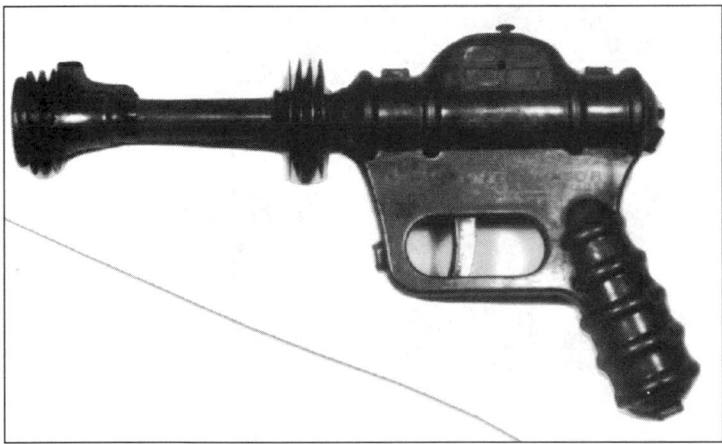

Buck Rogers Disintegrator Pistol. Courtesy James S. Maxwell/ Virginia Caputo. Photo by Virginia Caputo.

	C6	C8	C10
Buck Rogers figure, Tootsietoy, 1-3/4" high	38	56	75
Buck Rogers figures, boxed, by M.T., U.S.A., rubber, approx. 2-1/2" high, only one set known, sold in 1994 for $1300.			
Buck Rogers "Flash Blast" Attack Ship, Tootsietoy, 1937, two grooved wheels on top to run string, 4-1/2" long	225	338	450
Buck Rogers Flying Saucer, 1940s, paper	75	112	150
Buck Rogers Helmet Daisy, 1933, leather	187	290	375
Buck Rogers lead figures, these are generally new, from early casting sets, sell for $8.00 painted			

	C6	C8	C10
Buck Rogers Liquid Helium water pistol, Daisy, 1936	375	562	750
Buck Rogers "Pop" pistol, 1930s	112	168	225
Buck Rogers Rocket Pistol, XZ-31, 1934, Daisy, 9-1/2" long	132	200	265

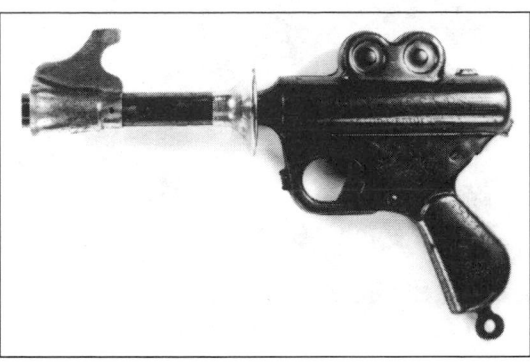

Buck Rogers Rocket Pistol. Courtesy HAKE'S Americana & Collectibles.

	C6	C8	C10
Buck Rogers Rocket Police Patrol, wind-up, Marx, 1939	800	1300	1800
Buck Rogers Rocket Ship, Marx, wind-up, 12" long, 1934	358	535	715
"Buck Rogers Rubber Band Gun," 5" x 10" punch-outs card, 1940	50	75	100
Buck Rogers Sonic Ray Gun, yellow plastic, uses bulb and battery, 1952	55	82	110
Buck Rogers Strato Kite, 1946	37	56	75
Buck Rogers Super-Scope, 1952, Norton-Honer Mfg. Co., 8-1/2" long, adjustable plastic telescope	92	138	185

Buck Rogers Rocket Police Patrol. Courtesy PB Eighty-Four, New York.

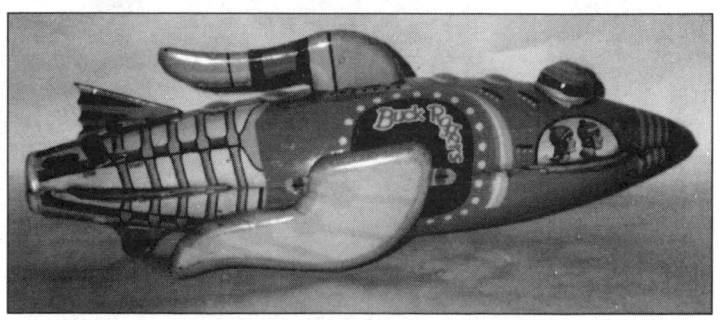

Buck Rogers Rocket Ship. Photo by Don Hultzman.

Comic Characters • 483

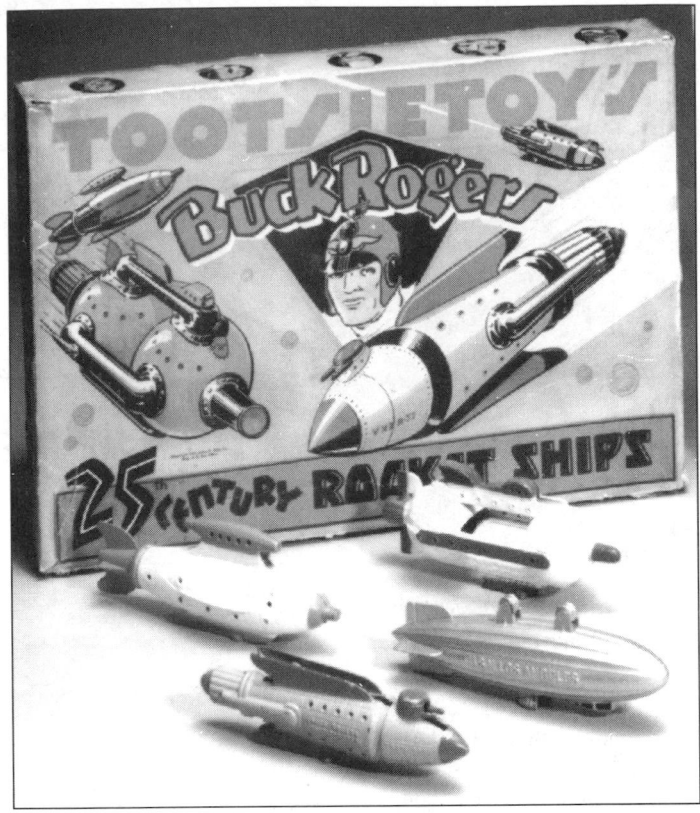

	C6	C8	C10
Buck Rogers U-238 Atomic Pistol & Holster set, with box, adventure book and coupon, 1948, Daisy 450	675	900
Buck Rogers "USN Los Angeles," Tootsietoy, 5" long, dirigible 117	175	235
Buck Rogers Venus Duo Destroyer, Tootsietoy, two grooved wheels on top to run on string, 1937......................170	255	340
Buck Rogers Walkie Talkie, 1950s..................110	165	220
Buck Rogers "Wilma" pistol and holster set, 1930s, small version of Buck Rogers "Pop" pistol.......................200	300	400
Buster Brown cast iron, painted 130	195	260
Buster Brown in cart pulled by Tige, 7-1/2" long, cast iron 413	625	825
Buster Brown & Tige paper dolls, J. Ottman Lith. Co., N.Y. Envelope, dolls, Tige, 4 suits, 4 hats, plus hat for Tige..60	90	120
Buster Brown & Tige ring, brass, 1930s.............25	38	50
Buster Brown & Tige tin wind-up, c. early 1900s, streetlamp, bell 2000	3500	5000
Buster Brown Doll, 23" high, 1920s 110	165	220

Buck Rogers Rocket Ships with box. Left to right: Battlecruiser, Venus Duo Destroyer, Flash Attack Ship, "U.S.N. Los Angeles" (the latter also listed in the Aircraft section of this book). Courtesy Christie's East.

	C6	C8	C10
Buck Rogers Super Sonic Glasses (binoculars), 1953...70	105	140
Buck Rogers Super Sonic Ray Gun 90	135	180
Buck Rogers U-238 Atomic Pistol & Holster set, 1948.....................................400	600	800

Buster Brown & Tige tin wind-up, c. early 1900s, streetlamp, bell. Courtesy Christie's East.

Buck Rogers (left to right): Sonic Ray Gun, Super Sonic Ray Gun. Photo by Charles D. Richards.

	C6	C8	C10
Buster Brown figure, lead 10	15	20
Buster Brown, Lehmann tin wind-up, drives horseless carriage 500	750	1100
Buster Brown Rolly Dolly: See Schoenhut		
Buster Brown Secret Agent Periscope, c. 1950, 20" long 13	21	27
Buster Brown Seesaw, Buster and Tige, 9-1/2", German tin wind-up.........................600	950	1400

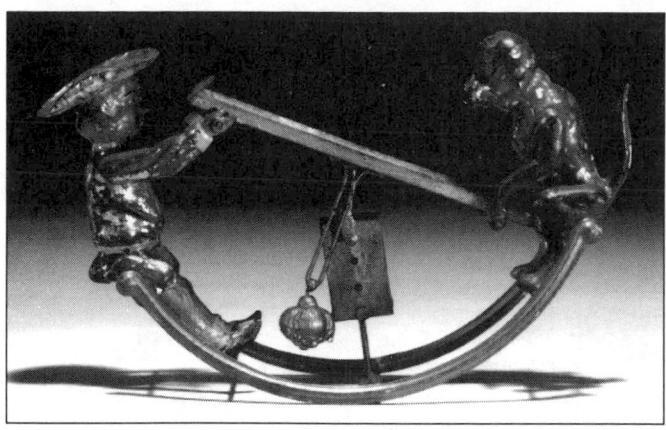

Buster Brown Seesaw, Buster and Tige. Courtesy Christie's East.

Captain Marvel Buzz Bomb. Courtesy Continental Hobby House.

	C6	C8	C10
Buttercup (Toots & Casper) stuffed cloth doll, 18" high, jointed head, arms, legs, c. 1924 250	375	500
Buttercup, 14" high cloth doll 450	700	1000
Buttercup, crawls, 4-1/4", German, tin wind-up 650	1100	1750
Buttercup & Spareribs, Nifty, Buttercup beats Spareribs with broom, 1920s, 7-1/2" long 700	1200	1600

	C6	C8	C10
Captain Marvel "Flying Captain Marvel," paper, 1944-47, Reed, 7" x 10" 25	38	50
Captain Marvel Gun, movie gun with film 175	263	350
Captain Marvel Magic Flute, copyright 1946, picture of Captain Marvel on side 70	105	140
"Captain Marvel Race Car No. 1," 1947, 4" long, tin wind-up 150	225	300
"Captain Marvel Race Car No. 2," 1947, 4" long, tin wind-up 125	188	250

Buttercup & Spareribs, NIFTY. Courtesy Christie's East.

	C6	C8	C10
Captain America Hand Puppet, 1966 30	45	60
Captain America Jailhouse Lock Set, Larami, 1974, handcuffs, etc. 10	15	20
Captain America Utility Set, Remco, 1977 16	25	33
Captain Marvel, hollow metal, c. 1947, H.B. Toys, extremely rare................... No Price Found		
Captain Marvel Buzz Bomb 15	22	30
Captain Marvel Comic Hero Punch-Outs, 1942, Samuel Lowe, has Captain Marvel (2), Capt. Marvel Jr., Bulletman, Bulletgirl, Spy Smasher, Ibis, Golden Arrow (2), Minute Man, Freddy Freeman, Mr. Scarlet, Commando Yank, Pinky, Bulletdog............. 200	300	400

Captain Marvel Comic Hero Punch-Outs. Courtesy Bruce Bergstrom-Artman Originals.

Captain Marvel Race Cars,
complete set mint in box, value $1000.
Courtesy Christie's East.

	C6	C8	C10
"Captain Marvel Race Car No. 3," 1947, 4" long, tin wind-up	125	188	250
"Captain Marvel Race Car No. 4," 1947, 4" long, tin wind-up	125	188	250
Captain Marvel Porsche Car, Corgi, 1979, No.262	37	56	75
Captain Marvel Toss Bag	40	60	80
Captain Marvel Jr. Ski Jump, 7" x 10", c. 1946, paper, Reed & Associates, Chicago	17	26	35

Captain Marvel Jr. by H.B. Toys. Left, with lightning bolt
on chest, right without. Photo by Don Patman. Courtesy
Bob Emmons.

	C6	C8	C10
Captain Marvel's Magic Picture, c. 1944, Reed	12	18	25
Captain Marvel's Magic Eyes, c. 1945, Reed	30	45	60
Captain Marvel's Rocket Raider, c. 1944-47, Reed	50	75	100
Captain Marvel Jr., hollow metal, c.1947, H.B. Toys, approx. 3-1/4" high	1000	1500	2200
Charlie Brown composition bouncing head, 1950s, possibly first Peanuts toy	20	30	40
Charlie Brown, plastic jointed, "1952"	14	21	28
Chester Gump 13" high oilcloth doll, c. 1920s, Live Long Toys	100	150	200
Chester Gump Cart, Arcade, 1920s, horse, open two-wheel cart, Chester driving	280	420	560

Chester Gump
Pony Cart.
Courtesy
PB Eighty-Four,
New York.

	C6	C8	C10
Comic Strip Rings, 1953, King Features, Phantom, Blondie, Barney Google, etc.	15	22	30
Comics Paper Doll Cut-out Book, Saalfield, 1935, page each of Popeye, Katzenjammers, Just Kids, Blondie, Dumb Dora, Annie Rooney, Polly and Her Pals	175	263	350
Churchy (Pogo) plastic, 1969, 4-1/2" high	14	21	28
Dagwood Aeroplane, 1935, Marx, "Dagwood's Solo Flight"	350	525	700
Dagwood "Dagwood the Driver" Crazy Car, 1935, Marx, 8" long	500	750	1000

"Dagwood the Driver." Courtesy Scott Smiles.

	C6	C8	C10
Dagwood Marionette, 15" wood body, plastic head, hands, feet, "Hazelle's," life-like hair, 1940s	60	90	120
Daisy Mae Dogpatch Family Doll, C. 1950s	125	188	250
Daisy Mae and Li'l Abner Paper Dolls with Mammy and Pappy Yokum, Saalfield No. 2360, 1941	45	68	90
Daisy Mae with Li'l Abner in Paper Dolls, Saalfield No. 280, 1942	45	68	90

Daisy Mae with Li'l Abner in Paper Dolls. Photo by Jonathan A. Newman. Courtesy Barbara and Jonathan Newman.

	C6	C8	C10
Daisy Mae Stringless Marionette, 1940s, National Mask & Puppet Corp	70	105	140
Dan Dunn Det. Corps Secret Operative 28 tin badge, c. 1930s	30	45	60
Dennis the Menace, 7" high, Hall, 1957	42	63	85

Dick Tracy Click Pistol. Courtesy PB Eighty-Four, New York.

	C6	C8	C10
Dennis the Menace Squirt Gun Figure, 5-1/2" high, 1954, plastic	40	60	80
Denny Dimwit (Winnie Winkle) 11" composition doll, 1940s	165	250	330
Dick Tracy, 13-1/2" high, painted composition, mouth moves	275	413	550
Dick Tracy Air Detective Wings, c. late 1930s	20	30	40
Dick Tracy and Junior Knife with Crimestopper whistle and clue detector	40	60	80
Dick Tracy Automatic, Hubley, with picture of Eagles	65	98	130
Dick Tracy Click Pistol, Marx No. 36	105	160	210
"Dick Tracy Copmobile," Ideal, 1963, plastic	35	52	70
"Dick Tracy Crime Stoppers Lab," 1940s, Porter Chem Co., 10" x 12" box	150	225	300
Dick Tracy Crimestoppers Set, badge, handcuffs, billy club, John Henry	45	68	90
Dick Tracy Detective Badge with secret compartment, late 1930s, large, metal, leather pouch on back	50	75	100
Dick Tracy Detective Fingerprint Set, 1933	62	93	125
"Dick Tracy Double Target Game," 1941, 9-1/2" square with 8" tin gun and darts	100	150	200

Dick Tracy "Police Station" with 7" long automatic siren car. Courtesy Don Hultzman. Photo by Ron Chojnacki.

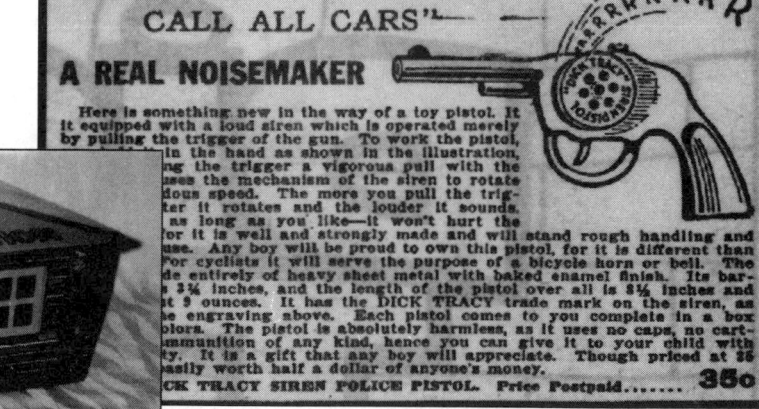

Ad for the Dick Tracy Siren Pistol by Marx, 1930s.

	C6	C8	C10
Dick Tracy Electronic Wrist Radio, Remco 35	52	70	
Dick Tracy G-Man wind-up gun, Marx 100	150	200	
Dick Tracy Hand Puppet, Ideal, 1961 37	56	75	
Dick Tracy Hingee, paper figures, 1940s, set of six 20	30	40	
Dick Tracy Inspector General badge............... 300	450	600	
Dick Tracy Pen-Lite, 1940s?............................ 30	45	60	
Dick Tracy Playset, Ideal, 1973 36	54	72	
Dick Tracy "Police Station" with 7" long automatic siren car, 1950s 175	263	350	
Dick Tracy Power Jet Squad Gun, Mattel, 28" long, 1962 72	108	145	
Dick Tracy Riot Car, c. 1946, Marx, heavy tin or sheet metal litho, 7-1/2" long, friction motor........................... 95	143	190	

Dick Tracy Squad Car No.1 Police Dept., Marx, 6-3/4" long. Courtesy Gary Linden.

Dick Tracy Riot Car. Courtesy Gary Linden.

	C6	C8	C10
Dick Tracy Shootin' Shell Snubnose .38 pistol and holster 112	168	225	
Dick Tracy Siren Pistol, red with blue siren, c. late 1930s 35	52	70	
Dick Tracy Siren Police Whistle No. 64, Marx, tin 40	60	80	
Dick Tracy Soaky... 22	33	45	
Dick Tracy Space Coupe, 1966, Aurora 375	563	750	
Dick Tracy Sparkling Pop Pistol, tin litho, Marx No. 96 100	150	200	
Dick Tracy Squad Car, convertible, heavy tin or sheet metal, 20" long, Marx, c. 1948, friction motor with siren and battery-powered flashing light, Dick Tracy and Sam Catchum in plastic 200	300	400	
Dick Tracy Squad Car No. 1, Marx, 11" long, friction 168	252	335	

	C6	C8	C10
Dick Tracy Squad Car No. 1, Marx, 6-3/4" long, friction 95	143	190	
Dick Tracy Sub-Machine Gun, 1946, "Raider" 100	150	200	
Dick Tracy Target Game, Marx, G25 100	150	200	
Dick Tracy Target Game, Marx, G34 100	150	200	
Dick Tracy Telephone, Marx, 1967 37	56	75	
Dick Tracy tin wind-up police car, 1949, 7" long 150	225	300	
Dick Tracy Viewer, 1940s, two films 80	120	160	
Dick Tracy Jr. Click Pistol No. 78, Marx, aluminum 45	68	90	
Dick Tracy's Handcuffs for Junior, c. 1946, John Henry Products No. 700 50	75	100	
Dick Tracy Walter Pistol, plastic, 1955 50	75	100	
Dr. Pimm (Little Nemo) Rolly Dolly, 11-1/2" high, Schoenhut 2000	3000	4000	

Dr. Pimm (little Nemo) Rolly Dolly. Courtesy Christie's East.

Dick Tracy Squad Car No. 1 Police, Marx, 11" long. Courtesy Gary Linden.

	C6	C8	C10
Don Winslow Flashlight Gun............................ 70	105	140	
Ella Cinders 17" high cloth and composition, 1925............................... 100	150	200	
Elmer Fudd Hand Puppet, 1950s........................ 35	52	70	

	C6	C8	C10
Elmer Fudd Soaky, 10" high, 1960s	14	21	28
Famous Komics Acme Film Viewer, 3 boxes of films, 1940	200	300	400
Favorite Funnies large size rubber print set, Dick Tracy, Orphan Annie, etc. 14 stamps, pad, booklet	45	68	90
Felix the Cat, 2" high, cast iron, 1923, Dent	180	270	360
Felix the Cat, 2" high, pot metal nodding head figure, copyright Pat Sullivan on bottom of feet	100	150	200
Felix the Cat, 2-1/2" high, lead	188	285	375
Felix the Cat, 2-1/2" high, cast iron, with tin umbrella	200	300	400
Felix the Cat, 4" high, wooden: See Schoenhut			
Felix the Cat, 6" high, wood: See Schoenhut			
Felix the Cat, 6-1/2" rubber squeeze toy, Eastern Moulded Products	60	90	120
Felix the Cat, 7-9", wood: See Schoenhut			
Felix the Cat, 9" high, 1940s, wood, jointed with rubber head	100	150	200
Felix the Cat, 12" high, wood	300	450	600
Felix the Cat, 13" high, composition, c. 1930s	275	363	550

Felix the Cat on scooter. Courtesy Phillips New York.

	C6	C8	C10
Felix the Cat Pull Toy, Felix chases mice	525	800	1150
Felix the Cat pulled by Mule, c.1920s (Spain), auctioned for $14,850 in 1993			
Felix the Cat Soaky	35	52	70
Felix the Cat "Speedy Felix" in car	1000	1600	2400
Felix the Cat Walker, German tin wind-up	325	490	650

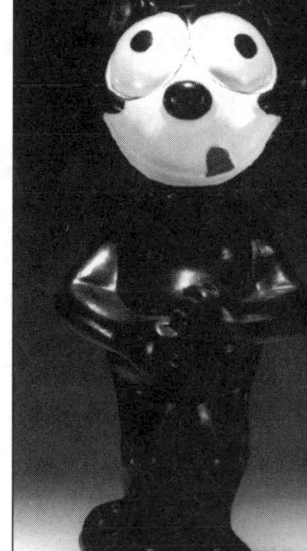

Felix the Cat, 13" high, composition. Courtesy Christie's East.

Felix the Cat "Speedy Felix" car and Felix the Cat, 2-1/2" high, cast iron, with tin umbrella. Courtesy Christie's East.

	C6	C8	C10
Felix the Cat Doll, 15" high, stuffed, Gund, hands molded rubber, the rest cloth, c. 1950	80	120	160
Felix the Cat, China Set	60	90	120
Felix the Cat on fire truck, gong bell pull toy	110	165	220
Felix the Cat on pole, Schoenhut, 9" high, wood	287	432	575
Felix the Cat on scooter, Nifty	600	950	1400
Felix the Cat on tricycle, gong bell pull toy	220	330	440
Felix the Cat Pull Car, 12" long, Borgfeldt, 1925	300	450	600

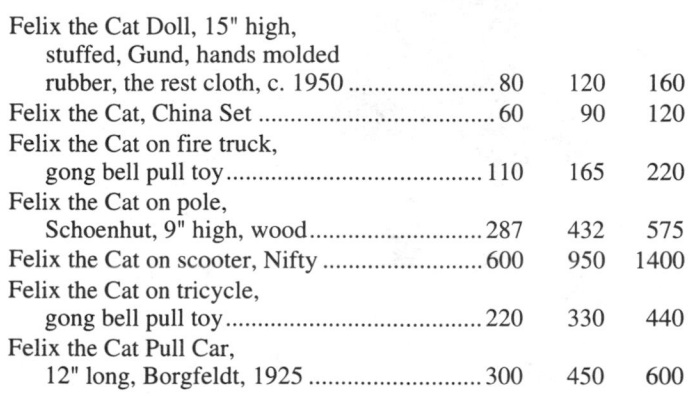

Left to right: Felix the Cat Walker, German, tin wind-up; Felix the Cat pull toy; Felix chases mice. Courtesy Sotheby's New York.

	C6	C8	C10
Flash Gordon "Air Ray" pistol, 10" long, shoots blast of air using rubber diaphragm	125	188	250
Flash Gordon Arresting Ray, Marx, 1952, picture of Flash on handle	133	200	265
Flash Gordon Automatic Disintegrator, Hubley	200	300	400
Flash Gordon Belt, many illus., large plastic buckle showing rocket ship flight, 1950s	70	105	140
Flash Gordon Casting Set, Home Foundry, 1934, boxed price	600	850	1000
Flash Gordon Click Ray Pistol, 1950s, 10" long, Marx	300	450	600
Flash Gordon Jet-Propelled Kite	27	41	55
Flash Gordon Playset, Tootsietoy, No. 1793, die-cast, 1978, w/ box	27	41	55
Flash Gordon Playset, Mego	58	87	115
Flash Gordon Radio Repeater clicker pistol, Marx No. 58, 1950s, 10" long	205	308	410
Flash Gordon Rocket Fighter, Marx wind-up, 12" long, 1939	265	400	530

Flip (little Nemo) Bell Toy. Courtesy Christie's East.

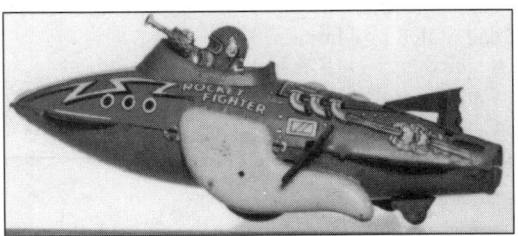

Flash Gordon Rocket Fighter. Courtesy PB Eighty-Four, New York.

	C6	C8	C10
Flash Gordon Water Gun, plastic, 1950s, Marx, 7" long	150	225	300
Flip (Little Nemo) Bell Toy, 6-1/2" long, cast iron	400	600	800
Foxy Grandpa, 17" high, cloth and composition	450	675	900
Foxy Grandpa Bell Toy, vehicle pulled by two boys, cast iron, 7" long	425	638	850
Foxy Grandpa Clockwork Figure, tin, German, 8-1/4" high	300	450	600

	C6	C8	C10
Flash Gordon Signal Pistol, tin litho, Marx No. 74, 1940s	500	750	1100

Foxy Grandpa clockwork figure. Courtesy PB Eighty-Four, New York.

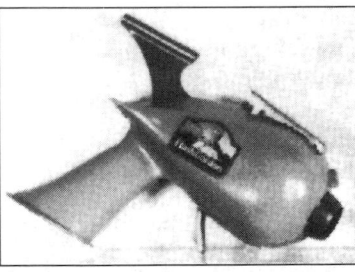

Flash Gordon Signal Pistol. Courtesy PB Eighty-Four, New York.

	C6	C8	C10
Foxy Grandpa Jack in the Box, papier mache and paper litho on wood, 1900, 4" square	160	240	320

	C6	C8	C10
Flash Gordon Solar Commando, three plastic space men and one ship, 1950s	60	90	120
Flash Gordon Space Cruiser, 1952	50	75	100
Flash Gordon Space Outfit, Esquire Novelty, 1952	90	135	180
Flash Gordon Space Target, metal, standup, Alex Raymond illustration, 12" x 14"	80	120	160
Flash Gordon Sparkling Battle Rocket, 1969	40	60	80
Flash Gordon Strat-O-Wagon, 9" long, Wyandotte	100	150	200
Flash Gordon Two-Way Telephone, Marx, c. 1940	100	150	200

Foxy Grandpa Jack in the Box. Courtesy PB Eighty-Four, New York.

	C6	C8	C10
Foxy Grandpa Nodder, papier mache, 1900, 6" tall	120	180	240
Foxy Grandpa Nodder, Hubley, c. 1910, cast iron, 6-1/2", Grandpa large-headed in cart pulled by donkey	500	750	1000
Foxy Grandpa Nodder, Harris, cast iron, in donkey cart, 7-1/4" long	225	338	450

Left to right: Foxy Grandpa nodder, Harris; Foxy Grandpa Bell Toy. Courtesy Christie's East.

	C6	C8	C10
Foxy Grandpa Composition, rides donkey, 9" long platform, pull toy	450	675	900
Foxy Grandpa Roly Dolly: See Schoenhut			
"Gasoline Alley Garage and Auto Racer," 1924, Girard, tin litho garage and "Bearcat Racer" car	400	600	800

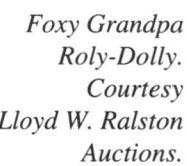

Foxy Grandpa Roly-Dolly. Courtesy Lloyd W. Ralston Auctions.

Gloomy Gus in horse cart, Harris. Courtesy Christie's East.

	C6	C8	C10
"Gloomy Gus," (Happy Hooligan's brother), 1903, Harris Toy Co., cast iron, 5" tall	150	225	300
Gloomy Gus in goat cart, cast iron, 14" long	400	600	800
Gloomy Gus in horse cart, Harris, cast iron, 14" long	1600	2400	3200
Gloomy Gus in mule cart, Harris, cast iron	300	450	600
Gremlin (Gloom) T.E. Powers, in leather clothes, 1943	20	30	40
Happy Hooligan, 9-1/2" high, bisque face, dressed as clown	550	825	1100

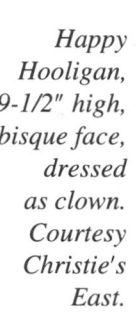

Happy Hooligan, 9-1/2" high, bisque face, dressed as clown. Courtesy Christie's East.

	C6	C8	C10
Happy Hooligan Cymbals Player	300	450	600
Happy Hooligan Donkey Cart, c. 1925, (possibly Wilkins), 10" long	240	360	480
Happy Hooligan Hand Puppet, cast iron and cloth, 9-1/4"	35	52	70
Happy Hooligan in Car, 5-3/4", c. 1903, Hill Brass, cast iron	1800	2900	4000

Happy Hooligan in car, Hill Brass. Courtesy Christie's East.

	C6	C8	C10
Happy Hooligan in Cart, Kenton, early 1900s, 10-1/4" long, 7-1/2" high, horse-pulled, head nods, cast iron	500	800	1200
"Happy Hooligan in Donkey Cart," 1930s, Ingap Co., 6-3/8" long, wind-up	500	800	1155

Comic Characters • 491

Happy Hooligan in cart, horse pulled.

	C6	C8	C10
Happy Hooligan in Goat Cart, 7-1/2" long, cast iron	200	300	400
Happy Hooligan in Horse Cart, Wilkins, cast iron, 17" long	500	750	1000
Happy Hooligan in Horse-Drawn Wagon, with Gloomy Gus, driver, Harris, c. 1905, cast iron	1750	2650	3500
"Happy Hooligan Jigger," 1920s, Kiddee Metal Toys, 10" tall, crank action	800	1200	1600

Happy Hooligan in horse-drawn wagon with Gloomy Gus, Driver. Courtesy Christie's East.

Happy Hooligan on a ladder. Courtesy PB Eighty-Four, New York.

	C6	C8	C10
Happy Hooligan Jigger, Kiddies' Metal Toys Co., tin litho, dressed as clown, tap dances on drum, wind-up, 9"	650	975	1300
Happy Hooligan on a Ladder	200	300	400
Happy Hooligan on Donkey, celluloid	212	318	425
Happy Hooligan on Rabbit, Candy Container, composition, 7-1/2"	900	1350	1800
Happy Hooligan Police Patrol, Kenton, 18" long, Happy hit by cop as Gloomy Gus Drives	1000	1800	2650
Happy Hooligan Roly Poly	50	75	100
Happy Hooligan walking toy, Chein, wind-up, 1932, 6" high	362	543	725
Happy Hooligan, wooden: See Schoenhut			

Happy Hooligan Roly-Poly. Courtesy Lloyd W. Ralston Auctions.

Happy Hooligan Police Patrol. Courtesy James S. Maxwell/ Virginia Caputo. Photo by Virginia Caputo.

Happy Hooligan walking toy, Chein. Photo by Ron Chojnacki. Courtesy Don Hultzman.

	C6	C8	C10
Harold Teen Ukulele, wood, 21", 1930s	100	150	200
Henry, 9-1/2" high rubber squeeze toy, 1950s	20	30	40
Henry and his Brother, celluloid wind-ups, Japanese, on wheels	600	1000	1460

Left to right: Henry and His Brother, Henry's Mahout on Donkey, Henry on Trapeze. Courtesy Christie's East.

	C6	C8	C10
Henry on Elephant, celluloid & tin wind-up, Japanese, Henry sits on elephant's trunk, w/Mahout	600	1000	1450

Henry on Elephant, celluloid and tin wind-up, Japanese, Henry sits on elephant's trunk. Courtesy Christie's East.

	C6	C8	C10
Henry "Henry and his Swan," celluloid mechanical	1800	3000	4300
Henry "Henry Eating Candy," 1950s, Linemar	440	660	880
Henry On Trapeze, just Henry, celluloid wind-up	330	495	660
Henry Trapeze, Japan, wind-up, part celluloid, Henry, brother and Mahout	750	1250	1700
Henry's Mahout on donkey	350	525	715
Herby, 10" oilcloth doll	20	30	40
Herman (Harvey Comics Character) "Herman Nodder," 1950s, Linemar, 4-1/2" high, rare	300	450	600
Hi-Way Henry, wind-up, 1920s, jalopy with man, woman, laundry above roof	1500	2700	3800

Henry Trapeze. Courtesy Christie's East.

Hi-Way Henry. Courtesy Phillips New York.

Hingees comic figures (listed in this book by character), c. 1944.

	C6	C8	C10
Hoppy the Flying Marvel Bunny, c. 1944-47, Reed, paper	6	9	12
Howland Owl (Pogo), 1969, plastic, 4-1/2" high ("Duz")	6	9	12
Humphrey, 14-1/2" high, Ideal, cloth and composition	175	263	350
Humphrey Mobile (Joe Palooka) tin wind-up, c. mid-1940s, Wyandotte, 7-1/2" high with smokestack	310	465	620

JAYMAR wood-jointed toys, 5" high and shorter. Left to right: Popeye, Olive Oyl, Wimpy, Moon Mullins, Kayo, Little Orphan Annie, Sandy. Photo by Blossom Abell.

Humphreymobile. Courtesy Mapes Auctioneers & Appraisers.

Jeep (Popeye) wood-jointed. Courtesy Christie's East.

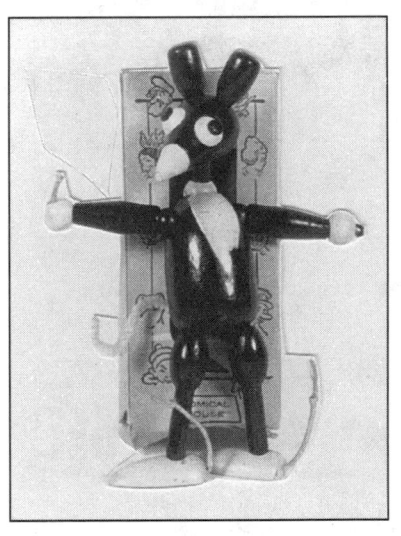

Ignatz (Krazy Kat), 6" high. Courtesy James S. Maxwell Jr./Virginia Caputo.

	C6	C8	C10
Jeff Stick Puppet, 12" high	40	60	80
Jiggs, 3" high, hard plastic, 1960s	6	9	12
Jiggs, 5" wood-jointed doll, Jaymar?	80	120	160
Jiggs, 7" high, wood-jointed doll, Schoenhut: See Schoenhut			
Jiggs Bumper Car, 1920s, German, auctioned 1993 for $11,500			
"Jiggs Jazz Car," Nifty, 1920s, wind-up, 6-1/2" long	1100	3000	5500
Jiggs Stick Puppet, 12" high	80	120	160

	C6	C8	C10
Ignatz (Krazy Kat), 6" high	115	162	230
Jane Arden, 1942, Saalfield No. 2408, paper dolls	30	45	60
Jean (Gasoline Alley), Live Long Toys	25	38	50
Jeep (Popeye) wood-jointed, 1930s, 6" (rare)	425	638	850
As above, 7-1/4"	350	525	700
As above, 8" (rare)	500	750	1000
As above, 14"	800	1400	2000
Jeff, 6" composition doll, ball joints, felt clothes	188	282	375
Jeff bendable figure, 1946	120	180	240

"Jiggs Jazz Car," Nifty. Courtesy Christie's East.

	C6	C8	C10
Joan Palooka doll, Ideal	78	117	155
Joe Palooka, 4" high, wood-jointed	35	52	70
Joe Palooka 5-1/2" high, wood-jointed doll	50	75	100
Joe Palooka Championship belt buckle, c. early 50s, heavy gold-plated brass buckle shows Palooka with hands raised in victory	50	75	100
Joe Palooka Filmatic, 12 different comic strips	30	45	60
Joe Palooka Punching Bag, c. 1950	30	45	60
Katzenjammer Kids, Hingees, 1945	16	24	32
Katzenjammer Kids, Mama spanking Kid, other Kid standing, as Sailor Drives mule cart, Kenton, 1911, 12" long	1050	1700	3250

	C6	C8	C10
Kayo, 9-3/4" oilcloth doll	60	90	120
Kayo, 10" high, Sun Rubber, c. 1937, head swivels	200	300	400
Komic Kamera, all metal viewer, c. mid-1930s, used to view 35mm filmstrips, with set of five filmstrips	80	120	160
Komic Kamera, without filmstrips	24	36	48
Krazy Kat Platform Toy, tin wind-up, Nifty, 1920s, 7-1/2" long	500	800	1300
Krazy Kat Teacup & Saucer, 1930s, Chein	20	30	40
Li'l Abner Dogpatch Family doll, c. 1950s	110	165	220
Li'l Abner Hand Puppet, Baby Barry, 1957	42	63	85
Li'l Abner and His Dogpatch Band, 1945, Unique, wind-up	350	525	700

Katzenjammer Kids, mama spanking kid, Kenton, 1911. Courtesy Ed Hyers Antique Toys.

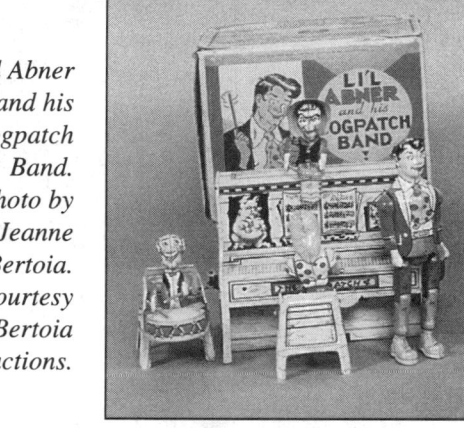

Li'l Abner and his Dogpatch Band. Photo by Jeanne Bertoia. Courtesy Bill Bertoia Auctions.

	C6	C8	C10
Katzenjammer Kids See-Saw Bell Toy, Kenton	900	1350	1800
Kayo (Moon Mullins), 5" high, Jaymar, wood jointed	56	84	112

Krazy Kat platform toy (Nifty) used Felix the Cat's head as a cost-cutting measure. It also made the Felix version. Courtesy Phillips New York.

Little Lulu doll. Courtesy Toy Collector News.

	C6	C8	C10
Li'l Abner stringless marionette, 1940s, National Mask & Puppet Corp	40	60	80
Li'l Abner's Flyin' Saucer, 1962, Brian Specialties	42	63	85
Little Beaver Archery Set, 1951	30	45	60
Little King Walker, plastic, c. 1956: See Ramp Walkers			
Little King, wooden pull toy, Jay-Mar, 1938, 4" high	70	105	140
Little Lulu, 10" high, felt doll	100	150	200
Little Lulu 14" high, Georgene Novelties, Stuffed doll	365	545	730

Little Mary Mixup and Her Friend Peggy. Photo by Jonathan Newman. Courtesy Barbara and Jonathan Newman.

Little Lulu, 14" high, Georgene Novelties. Courtesy Christie's East.

	C6	C8	C10
Little Lulu, 14" high, doll with mask face, 1944, M.H. Buell	55	83	110
Little Lulu "Shape Book," 1971, Whitman No. 1970	10	15	20
"Little Max Speshul," (Joe Palooka), SALS metal tin wind-up	3500	5250	7000
Little Mary Mixup And Her Friend Peggy, 1922, Saalfield No. 294, paper dolls	40	60	80
Little Nemo and Mr. Flip bell toy	435	650	870
Little Orphan Annie, 5" high, Jaymar, wood jointed	55	83	110
Little Orphan Annie, 9-1/2", printed fabric doll, 1930s	60	90	120
Little Orphan Annie, 16-1/4", oilcloth doll, c. 1920s	100	150	200
Little Orphan Annie Hingees, 1944, Annie, Sandy, Daddy, Punjab, price per set	20	30	40

	C6	C8	C10
Little Orphan Annie Junior Commandos, 1943, Saalfield No. 299	30	45	60
Little Orphan Annie & Sandy, celluloid	450	675	900
Little Orphan Annie & Sandy Pull Toy, wood, 1930s, 8"	130	195	260
Little Orphan Annie Skipping Rope, tin wind-up, 1930s, Marx, 5" high	425	638	850

Little Orphan Annie skipping rope. Courtesy Christie's East.

Little Orphan Annie Stove, 4-3/8" high. Courtesy James S. Maxwell/Virginia Caputo. Photo by Virginia Caputo.

	C6	C8	C10
Little Orphan Annie and Sandy, tin wind-up, Marx, 1930s, 2-piece set, 4-1/2" long 450	450	675	900
Little Orphan Annie Soaky 14	14	21	28
Little Orphan Annie Stove, 8" high, c. 1930s, Marx 80	80	120	160
Little Orphan Annie Stove, 4-3/8" high 62	62	93	125

Comic strip toys of the 1920s from Live Long Toys, of 221 W. Madison Street, Chicago, Illinois. The owners seem to have been William A. Benoliel and Eileen Benoliel. The stuffed oilcloth dolls shown here are from "Gasoline Alley." From left: Baby Skeezix, Uncle Walt, Pal, Rachel the Maid, Jean the Playmate, Auntie (Phyllis) Blossom, Skeezix as a boy. Photo by Blossom Abell.

	C6	C8	C10
Little Orphan Annie Water Pistol 70	70	105	140
Lonesome Polecat (Li'l Abner), 1950s, rubber squeak toy, Reinert............................ 50	50	75	100
Lucy, 7-3/4" high, squeeze toy, 1950s 12	12	18	24
Lucy, plastic, jointed, "1952" 14	14	21	28
Lucy, 8-3/4" high, vinyl squeeze toy, 1950s 15	15	22	30
Maggie, 3" high, hard plastic, 1960s 6	6	9	12

Maggie & Jiggs, 1920s, Nifty. Courtesy PB Eighty-Four, New York.

	C6	C8	C10
Maggie, 9" high, wood jointed doll: See Schoenhut			
Maggie & Jiggs, 1920s, Nifty, seated on 4-wheeled platform, 8" long 700	700	1050	1485
Maggie & Jiggs, tin litho squeeze toy, c. 1925, German, 8" 400	400	600	800

Maggie & Jiggs tin litho squeeze toy. Courtesy Christie's East.

	C6	C8	C10
Maggie & Jiggs wind-up, Strauss, 1924, 7-1/4" long, German............ 800	800	1200	1600
Mammy Yokum, Dogpatch Family doll, 1957, Baby Barry Co................ 30	30	45	60
Mammy Yokum Hand Puppet, 1957, Baby Barry Co. 42	42	63	85
Mandrake the Magician Magic Kit, 1949, Transogram 55	55	83	110
Mighty Mouse, rubber, 9" high, no mfr. listed 45	45	68	90
Mighty Mouse, 15" high, vinyl 300	300	450	600
Mighty Mouse Soaky 14	14	21	28
Moon Maid's Daughter (Dick Tracy) 16-1/2" doll with space helmet, Ideal, 1965 92	92	140	185
Moon Mullins, 5" high, Jaymar, wood jointed.................................... 55	55	83	110
Moon Mullins, 11-1/2" high, Famous Artists Synd., 1930s, stuffed doll....50	50	75	100

Moon Mullins and Kayo on Hand Car. Courtesy Phillips New York.

	C6	C8	C10
Moon Mullins and Kayo on Handcar, 1930s, 6" long, Marx, tin wind-up	395	600	790
Moon Mullins and Mamie Face Masks, 1933, each	20	30	40
Movie Komics, reels of film for toy viewers, c. 1940s	14	21	28
Mrs. Blossom (Gasoline Alley) 17" high, oilcloth, Live Long Toys	120	180	240
Mutt 8" high composition doll with ball joints, felt clothes	188	282	375
Mutt bendable figure, 1946	140	210	280
Mutt Wooden Dancing Doll	40	60	80
Nancy 14" high stuffed doll, Georgene Novelties	90	135	180
Olive Oyl, 2-1/2" high, cast iron	175	263	350
Olive Oyl, 11" Gund marionette	37	56	75
Olive Oyl "Ballet Dancer," Linemar, tin mechanical	250	375	500
Olive Oyl Hand Puppet, c. 1938, Gund	60	90	120
Olive Oyl Hingees No. 102, paper punch-outs, Reed & Associates	12	18	24
Olive Oyl Mask, cardboard, 1940s	20	30	40
Olive Oyl Riding Tricycle, 4", Linemar	1400	2100	2800
Olive Oyl Rubber Squeeze Toy, 1950s	90	135	180
Olive Oyl approx. 5" high, Jaymar, c. 1940s, jointed wood figure	92	137	185
Olive Oyl and Swee' Pea Handcar, Marx, 1930s	240	360	480
Pal (Gasoline Alley) oilcloth doll, cotton-stuffed, 1923, Live Long Toys	90	135	180

	C6	C8	C10
Peter Rabbit Chickmobile	312	468	625
Pogo plastic, 1969, 4" high	7	11	14
Pogo Pogomobile	200	300	400
Popeye, 3-1/2" high, cast iron, c. 1930	175	263	350
Popeye, 4" high, solid celluloid, 1930s	70	105	140
Popeye, 5" high, Jaymar, wood, jointed	68	102	135
Popeye, 6-1/2" high, Chein, tin wind-up walker	320	480	640
Popeye, 7" high, hollow rubber, dated "1935" on back	90	135	180
Popeye, 8" high, wood body, jointed, composition head	90	135	180
Popeye, 8" high, celluloid, keywind, head spins, foreign, 1930s, Japan	355	535	710

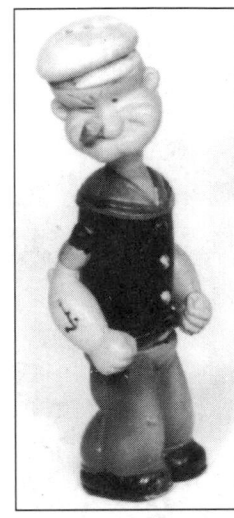

Popeye, 8" high, celluloid, key-wind, head spins, foreign. Courtesy Phillips New York.

Pal (Gasoline Alley), oilcloth, cotton stuffed.

Pete the Pup by J.L. Kallus, 10-3/4" high, strung wooden beads. Photo by Ann Spivak.

Popeye, 10-1/2" high, wood-jointed, c. 1932. Courtesy Christie's East.

Popeye, 14" high, composition. Courtesy Christie's East.

	C6	C8	C10
Pappy Yokum Doll, Dogpatch Family Doll, 1957, Baby Barry Co.	100	150	200
Pappy Yokum Hand Puppet, Baby Barry, 1957	42	63	85
Peanuts figures: Charlie Brown, Lucy, Linus, Schroeder, Snoopy, Avon, price per each	10	15	20
Pete the Pup, 1930s, composition doll, strung, from movie cartoons?	142	215	285

	C6	C8	C10
Popeye, 9" high, celluloid wind-up, neck goes up and down, c. 1930 450	675	900	
Popeye, 10" high, cast-iron doorstop, Hubley 1500	2300	3400	
Popeye, 10-1/4" high, wood-jointed, c. 1932 225	338	450	
Popeye, 11" high, wood jointed, c. 1935 300	450	600	
Popeye, 11" high, Chein, c. 1935 293	440	585	
Popeye, 14" high, "Cameo" hard rubber, jointed at neck, hips, shoulders 115	172	230	
Popeye, 14" high, composition, "Popeye 1935 King Features Syn" 300	450	600	
Popeye, 14" high, wood and composition, jointed arms and legs, "1935" 200	300	400	
Popeye 15" high, composition, rolling up sleeve 100	150	200	
Popeye 17" high, Knickerbocker, stuffed cloth, 1930s 187	230	375	
Popeye 20" high, rubber arms and head, stuffed body, Gund, c. 1950s 70	105	140	
Popeye Acrobat, Marx, tin wind-up 2700	4050	5400	
"Popeye and Mean Man" Mechanical Fighters, 1950s, Linemar Co., 6" long, rare 6000	9000	12,000	
"Popeye Basketball Player," Linemar tin wind-up 600	950	1400	

Popeye "Boom Boom Popeye." Courtesy Mapes Auctioneers & Appraisers.

Popeye the Champ, Marx 1100	1700	2565	
Popeye "Dippy Dumper" truck, Marx 550	925	1200	
Popeye Drummer, 7-1/8" high, Chein, thumb-worked 550	925	1200	

Popeye Basketball Player box. Courtesy Phillips New York.

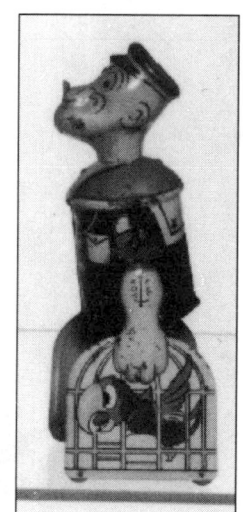

Popeye carrying parrots in cages. Courtesy PB Eighty-Four, New York.

	C6	C8	C10
Popeye "Bifbat" paddle toy, 1929 46	70	95	
Popeye "Bo Lo Paddle," 1929 20	30	40	
Popeye "Boom Boom Popeye," Fisher Price, drummer, 491: See Fisher-Price			
Popeye carrying parrots in cages, Marx wind-up, 1935, 7-3/4" high 268	405	535	

"Popeye The Champ," Marx. Courtesy Phillips New York.

Popeye Dippy Dumper. Courtesy Christie's East.

Popeye in a Barrel, celluloid wind-up walker. Courtesy Christie's East.

Popeye in a Barrel, Chein. Photo by Don Hultzman.

	C6	C8	C10
Popeye "Eccentric Plane," 1940, Marx wind-up, 8" long	375	565	750
Popeye Express, Marx, overhead airplane, 1935, flies over train	500	800	1100
Popeye Express, Marx, Popeye pushing box with parrot, wind-up, 1935	500	800	1100

"Popeye Express." Courtesy PB Eighty-Four, New York.

Popeye in a Rowboat, 1935, Hoge. Courtesy Christie's East.

	C6	C8	C10
Popeye Handcar, Marx, 1935, Popeye & Olive Oyl, composition, 6" long	700	1050	1400
Popeye Hand Puppet, Gund	20	30	40
"Popeye Heavy Hitter," Chein, tin wind-up, 11-1/2"	2500	3900	6000
Popeye Hingee paper figures, Reed No. 102, 1945	60	90	120
Popeye in a Barrel, celluloid wind-up walker, 5-1/2" high, Japan	700	1100	1500
Popeye in a Barrel, Chein, 7" high	350	525	700
Popeye in a Horsecart, Marx, celluloid and tin, c. 1935, 7-1/2"	1500	2400	3500
Popeye in a Rowboat, 1935, Hoge	2500	4000	5500
Popeye Jack-in-the-Box, Mattel Co., tin mechanical, Popeye pops out of spinach can	45	68	90

"Popeye Patrol," Hubley, 8-1/2" long. Courtesy Phillips New York.

	C6	C8	C10
Popeye Knockout Bank, 1935, Straits Mfg. Co.	800	1300	1900
"Popeye Lantern Toy," 1950s, Linemar, 7-1/2" high	325	490	650
Popeye "Popeye Jigger" (on rooftop), Marx, wind-up, 9-1/2" high	500	750	1000
Popeye Mask, cardboard, 1940s	30	45	60
Popeye Moving Van, tin friction, Linemar	400	600	800
Popeye on a Tricycle, Linemar, metal and celluloid	370	555	740
Popeye "Popeye On A Unicycle," Linemar, 1950s, wind-up	600	900	1200
Popeye One-Man Band, pole with drum and cymbals, rubber Popeye head on top, 69" high, 1950s	100	150	200
Popeye Pirate, click pistol, Marx No. 68	175	263	350
Popeye the Pilot, 1930, Marx, wind-up, early version, 8" long	500	800	1200
Popeye the Pilot, later version, 8" long	490	735	980

Popeye the Pilot. Courtesy Sotheby's New York.

Popeye the Pilot. Photo by Don Hultzman.

	C6	C8	C10
Popeye "Popeye & Olive Oyl Slinky Handcar" 1950s, pull toy, Linemar	500	750	1050
Popeye "Popeye Patrol," Hubley, 8-1/2" long	2500	4000	5400
Popeye Puncher, Chein, 1930, tin and celluloid, floor bag	800	1300	1745

Popeye Puncher. Courtesy Sotheby Parke Bernet.

Popeye Rollerskating. Courtesy PB Eighty-Four, New York.

	C6	C8	C10
Popeye Puncher, Chein, overhead bag	1600	2700	3500
Popeye Pushing wheelbarrow, plastic walker, Marx, c. 1950s	50	75	100
Popeye Rollerskating, Linemar	550	825	1200
Popeye Roly-Poly, 3-1/2" celluloid, Japan	100	150	200
Popeye Roly Poly Target Game, Knickerbocker, 1958	95	143	190
Popeye rubber squeeze toy, 1950s	20	30	40
Popeye Sand Toy teeter-totter with Popeye, Swee' Pea, Olive Oyl, Jeep, tin litho	500	750	1000
"Popeye Shadow Boxer," 1930s, Chein, 7" tall	700	1150	1600
Popeye "Smoking Popeye," battery-operated, Linemar, 8-1/2" high	1500	2250	3000
Popeye Soaky	22	33	45
Popeye "Sparkling Popeye," 1959, Chein Co., 5" long	173	260	345
Popeye on Sparkplug, 1930s: See Fisher-Price			
Popeye "Popeye Spinning Olive Oyl in a Chair," 1950s, Linemar, 9" high	800	1300	1700
Popeye "Spinach Patrol" Hubley	1400	2500	3600

Popeye Spinach Patrol. Photo by C.B.C. Lee.

	C6	C8	C10
Popeye Spinach Wagon	1000	1600	2265
Popeye Squeeze Toy, Linemar	400	600	800
Popeye Strength Tester, Holgate, 14"	65	98	130
Popeye Transit Co., Linemar, tin trailer truck	650	1050	1550
Popeye "Tumbling Popeye," Linemar, 5" high, wind-up	450	675	900
Popeye Turnover Tank, Linemar, tin wind-up, 1950s, 6" long	360	540	720

Popeye Turnover Tank, Linemar. Photo by Don Hultzman.

Popeye on a Unicycle, Linemar. Courtesy Phillips New York.

	C6	C8	C10
Popeye Yazoo Pipe, Northwestern Productions, St. Louis, Mo., 1934	80	120	160
Popeye & Olive Oyl Ball Toss, c. 1950, 19" long, Linemar, tin wind-up	600	950	1300
Popeye & Olive Oyl Jiggers (Popeye dancing on roof, Olive Oyl playing concertina), Marx	900	1450	2075
Popeye & Olive Oyl Sand Toy, tin litho, T. Cohn, 8-1/4" high	450	675	900

	C6	C8	C10
Popeye Whistle Pipe, Northwest Products of St. Louis, 3-1/2" long, cardboard bowl with illus. of Popeye characters, metal stem with whistle at base	70	105	140
"Popeye Xylophone Player," 1957, American Preschool Co., 9" long	263	395	525

"Popeye & Olive Oyl Slinky Popeye Handcar." Courtesy Christie's East.

	C6	C8	C10
Porky (Pogo) plastic, 1969	7	11	14
Porky Pig Cowboy with lariat, Marx, tin wind-up, 1949, 9" high	325	490	650

Popeye & Olive Oyl, Ball Toss. Courtesy Christie's East.

Left to right: Popeye & Olive Oyl jiggers, Popeye Express overhead airplane (Marx).

Porky Pig, tin wind-up, with original box. Courtesy Wilkinson Collection, Detroit Antique Toy Museum.

	C6	C8	C10
Porky Pig squeeze toy, Sun Rubber, approx. 6" high, hollow with squeaker, has hands behind back, c. 1940	68	100	135
Porky Pig Hand Puppet, 1950s, 8" high	30	45	60
Porky Pig Soaky, 9" high, 1960s	14	21	28
Porky Pig tin litho wind-up, 1939, 8-1/2" high, holding umbrella, Marx	250	375	500
Porky Pig tin litho wind-up, holds umbrella, raises hat, Marx, 1939, 8"	500	750	1000
Prince Valiant Castle Fort, Marx, boxed set with knights, etc.	225	340	450
Prince Valiant Crossbow Pistol Game	22	33	45
Prince Valiant Shield, tin litho	30	45	60
Prince Valiant Sword and tin Scabbard, 1950s, Mattel	29	45	58
Rachel (Gasoline Alley) oilcloth doll, cotton-stuffed, 1923, Live Long Toys	120	180	240

Rudy the Ostrich. Courtesy James S. Maxwell/Virginia Caputo. Photo by Virginia Caputo.

Rachel (Gasoline Alley), oilcloth, cotton stuffed.

	C6	C8	C10
Rudy the Ostrich (Barney Google), 1924, tin, Nifty	448	730	975
Sad Sack 15-1/2" vinyl doll, 1950	105	158	210
Sad Sack 20" high vinyl doll, cloth uniform, Sterling Doll Co., c. 1952	70	105	140
Sandy, 5" long, Jaymar, wood jointed	60	90	120

Sandy (Orphan Annie) with suitcase in mouth. Courtesy Christie's East.

	C6	C8	C10
Red Ryder BB guns: See BB Guns			
Red Ryder Molding Set, 1948	40	60	80
Red Ryder Target Game, 1939	34	51	68
Robin (Batman) Soaky	34	51	68
Robin Hand Puppet, Ideal, 1966	70	105	140
Roosevelt Bear on Bicycle, tin litho, 9" long, c. 1920	225	338	450

Roosevelt Bear on Bicycle. Courtesy Wilkinson Collection, Detroit Antique Toy Museum.

"Sandy's Dog House" (Orphan Annie). Courtesy Christie's East.

	C6	C8	C10
Sandy, 10-1/2" long, oilcloth doll, c. 1920s, Live Long Toys ... 140	140	210	280
Sandy (Orphan Annie's dog) with suitcase in mouth, tin wind-up ... 215	215	325	430
Sandy (Orphan Annie) "Sandy Dog with Magic Tail," 1930s, Marx, 7" long ... 162	162	245	325
Sandy (Orphan Annie) "Sandy's Dog House" with wheeled Sandy, Marx ... 300	300	450	600
Schroeder (Peanuts) rubber squeeze toy, c. 1960 ... 10	10	15	20
Secret Agent X-9 Gun and Billy Club ... 12	12	18	24
Sergeant Snorkel (Beetle Bailey) Hand Puppet ... 37	37	56	75
Shmoo (Li'l Abner) doll, vinyl inflatable, 15" high, 1940s ... 60	60	90	120
"Sight Seeing Auto 899," cast iron, Kenton, c. 1910, has Mama Katzenjammer, Uncle Heine, Alphonse, Gloomy Gus, Happy Hooligan, 10-1/2" long ... 2500	2500	4000	6350

"Sight Seeing Auto 899." Courtesy Christie's East.

	C6	C8	C10
Skeezix oilcloth doll, cotton-stuffed, 1924 (Baby Skeezix), Live Long Toys ... 95	95	142	190
Skeezix oilcloth doll, cotton-stuffed, 1924 (as boy) Live Long Toys ... 100	100	150	200
Skeezix Radio Toy, c. 1924, 5" high, tin litho ... 1000	1000	1500	2000
Skippy, celluloid, 5-1/2" high ... 150	150	225	300

Skeezix, oilcloth, cotton stuffed.

	C6	C8	C10
Skippy oilcloth doll, 12" high, with hat ... 50	50	75	100
Smitty 9-3/4" oilcloth doll ... 100	100	150	200
"Smitty On A Scooter," tin wind-up, Marx, c. 1930, 8" high ... 1100	1100	1700	2500

"Smitty On A Scooter." Courtesy PB Eighty-Four, New York.

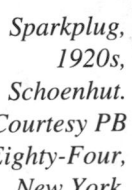

Sparkplug, 1920s, Schoenhut. Courtesy PB Eighty-Four, New York.

	C6	C8	C10
Smokey Stover, hard plastic, 3" high, 1960s ... 12	12	18	25
Smokey Stover, Hingees, 1944 ... 8	8	13	17
Snoopy Astronaut, doll, 9-1/2" high, 1969, vinyl ... 30	30	45	60
Snoopy Bus, 1960s, tin litho ... 16	16	24	32
Snoopy rubber squeeze toy, 1958 ... 25	25	38	50
Snowflakes & Swipes platform toy, 7-1/2" long, tin litho, c. 1929 ... 800	800	1350	1850
Snuffy Smith Hand Puppet, cloth, with rubber head, Gund, "King Features" ... 35	35	52	70

Snowflake & Swipes. Courtesy Christie's East.

	C6	C8	C10
Sparkle Plenty Paper Doll Set, 1948, Saalfield No. 5160	20	30	40
Sparkle Plenty Washing Machine, Kalon Radio Corp., litho tin, crank action, c. 1947, 13" tall	100	150	200
Sparkplug, 1920s, Schoenhut, jointed wood figure: See Schoenhut			
"Sparkplug" (Barney Google), on wheels, 3-1/4" high	225	338	450
Sparkplug (Barney Google) stuffed cloth	125	188	250
Sparkplug (Barney Google) Wa-Gee Walker, U.S., wind-up, cloth, felt & metal, 9" long	295	445	590
Sparkplug Candy Container	145	218	290
Spider-Man Hand Puppet, 1966, Ideal	42	63	85
Spider-Man Walker, 1966, Marx, wind-up	125	188	250
Spider-Man Webmaker, Chemtoy, 1977	16	25	33
Steve Canyon Glider Bomb Truck, Ideal	88	132	175
Steve Canyon Jet Helmet, 1959	50	75	100
Steve Canyon Space Goggles, c. 1950s, Rock Industries	25	38	50
Sunshine (Jockey) riding Sparkplug (Barney Google), platform toy, 9" long	1400	2300	3200
Superman, 5" high, Mego Bendy, 1973	22	33	45
Superman, 13" high, wood and composition, Ideal, 1940	600	1000	1400
Superman Acme Movie Viewer, 1940	333	500	665
Superman Acme Movie Viewer, 1947, with film	95	142	190
Superman Acme Movie Viewer, 1955, with film	22	33	45
Superman Acme Movie Viewer, 1965	30	45	60
Superman City of Metropolis Adventure Set, Corgi, 1979	55	83	110

	C6	C8	C10
Superman Colorforms, 1964	18	27	35
Superman Cut-Out Adventure Book	60	90	120
"Superman Cut-Outs," Saalfield No. 177, 1940	500	750	1000
Superman Flying Toy, Transogram, 1954	68	102	135
Superman Hand Puppet, Ideal, 1965	32	48	64
Superman Holding Airplane, Marx, wind-up, 1940	900	1600	2200
Superman Krypto-Ray Gun, Daisy No. 94, 1939, with seven filmstrips	255	380	510
Superman Krypton Rockets, c. 1939	150	225	300
Superman Kryptonite Rock, 1978	10	15	20
Superman Playset, Ideal, 1973	34	51	68
"Superman Rollover Airplane," 1940s, Marx Co., 6-1/2" long, blue version	1000	1500	2200
"Superman Rollover Airplane," 1940s, Marx Co., 6-1/2" long, bronze-tone version	700	1100	1650
"Superman Rollover Airplane," 1940s, Marx Co., 6-1/2" long, red version	950	1600	2100

Superman Rollover Airplanes. Left to right: Blue, Red, Bronze-tone or Gold. Courtesy Christie's East.

	C6	C8	C10
Superman Rollover Tank, 1940s, 4" long	290	435	580
"Superman Rollover Tank," silver version, Marx, 1940s, 4" long	550	850	1300
Superman Soaky	27	41	55
"Superman Tank," Linemar, 12" long: See Battery Operated			
"Superman Tank," Linemar, 4" long	325	488	650
Superman Tricky Trapeze, 1966, Kohner	15	22	30
Superman "2 in 1" Hand Puppet, one side Supe, other Clark, early 1950s	150	225	300
Superman Water Pistol, shape of Superman flying, c. 1950s	35	52	70
Swee' Pea Hingees No. 102, 1944, paper punch-outs, Reed	20	30	40
Swee' Pea Mask, cardboard, 1940s	10	15	20
Tarzan, Corgi Gift Set No. 36, figures and truck with cage trailer	40	60	80

DAISY Superman Krypto-Raygun Ad.

	C6	C8	C10
Tarzan, Mask of Akut the Ape, 1933, Northern Paper Mills	60	90	120
Tarzan, Mask of Numa the Lion, paper, 1933, Northern Paper Mills	60	90	120
Tarzan, Mask of Tarzan, 1933, Northern Paper Mills	70	105	140
Tarzan In The Jungle dart board game, 1935, large	130	195	260
Tarzan "Tarzan In The Jungle," 1935, battery-operated target game	140	210	280
Tarzan Thingmaker Kit, Mattel, 1966	44	66	88
Terry And The Pirates Hingees, 1944, set contains Terry, Flip Corkin, Pat Ryan, Burma, Taffy Tucker	22	33	45
Thimble Theatre Mystery Playhouse "Starring Popeye with Wimpy and Olive Oyl," copyright 1939, Harding Products, Philadelphia, 12" x 10" x 3", figures composition, with wooden "Shuffle" feet, individual figures sell for $325 in mint	1250	1875	2500

Toonerville Trolley, "Crackerjack" size. Courtesy Wilkinson Collection, Detroit Antique Toy Museum.

Toonerville Trolley, Dent. Photo by Don Hultzman.

Thimble Theatre Mystery Playhouse figures: Olive Oyl, Popeye, Wimpy. Courtesy Mapes Auctioneers & Appraisers.

Toonerville Trolley, tin wind-up, Nifty. Courtesy PB Eighty-Four, New York.

	C6	C8	C10
Three Flying Marvels (Captain, Jr., Mary), paper, c. 1944-47, Reed	20	30	40
Toonerville Trolley, lead, c. 1923	100	150	200
Toonerville Trolley, tin wind-up, "Copyright 1922 by Fontaine Fox," 7-1/2" high, Skipper driving, Nifty	500	750	1000
Toonerville Trolley, 1921, Strauss wind-up, rare	425	638	450

Toonerville Trolley, lead, c. 1923. Courtesy PB Eighty-Four, New York.

Left to right: Toonerville Trolley "The Powerful Katrinka," 6-1/2" long, pushing boy in wheelbarrow; "The Powerful Katrinka," raises and lowers boy in her hand. Courtesy Sotheby's New York.

	C6	C8	C10
Toonerville Trolley, 1-7/8" high, sometimes called Crackerjack size 275	410	550
Toonerville Trolley, Dent, aluminum 357	562	750
Toonerville Trolley, Dent, cast iron 450	675	900
Toonerville Glass Candy Container, 3-1/4" long 250	375	500
Toonerville Trolley, "Powerful Katrinka," 6-1/2" long, pushing boy in wheelbarrow, tin wind-up, Lehmann, 1925 1200	2200	3000
Toonerville Trolley, "The Powerful Katrinka," raises and lowers Jimmy in her hand, tin wind-up, 6-3/4" high, Nifty, 1925 900	1400	2100
Toonerville Trolley, wood, 7" long, 6 people 125	188	250
Tweety Bird rubber squeeze toy, 1950s 15	22	30
Tweety Bird Soaky 15	22	30
Uncle Walt (Gasoline Alley), oilcloth, 26" high, Live Long Toys 80	120	160
Uncle Wiggily Crazy Car, Distler (Germany), c. 1922, 9-1/2" long 2000	3700	5200

	C6	C8	C10
Willie The Worm and Sammy in Car Trouble, paper toy, Fawcett Comics characters, Reed, c. 1944-47 10	15	20
Willie The Worm and Sammy Flying Machine . 12	18	25
Willie The Worm and Sammy Fish-n Fun 10	15	20
Wimpy, 3" hard plastic figure, 1960s 12	18	24
Wimpy, 3-1/8" high, cast iron, Hubley 175	263	350
Wimpy, 4" high, wood-jointed, "by K.F.S." 100	150	200
Wimpy, 5" high, Jaymar, jointed wood figure 100	150	200
Wimpy, 8" high, rubber squeeze toy 60	90	120
Wimpy Dippy Dumper 500	800	1000
Wimpy Hand Puppet, Gund 29	44	58
Wimpy mask, cardboard, 1940s 10	15	20
Wimpy Motorcyclist, Linemar 400	600	800
Wimpy Tricyclist, Linemar 500	750	1000

Wimpy Tricyclist, Linemar. Courtesy Phillips New York.

Uncle Wiggily Crazy Car, Distler (Germany). Courtesy Wilkinson Collection, Detroit Antique Toy Museum.

Uncle Wiggily, Marx, Crazy Car 438 660 875

Uncle Wiggily, Marx, Crazy Car. Courtesy Sotheby's New York

Walter Lantz ink stamp character set, 12 different rubber stamps 12 18 24
Western Thrills with Billy The Kid, character from Funny Animals Comics, c. 1944-47, Reed, paper toy 12 18 24

	C6	C8	C10
Wonder Woman String Puppet, Madison, 1977 37	56	75
Woody Woodpecker Hand Puppet, Mattel, 1962, "W. Lantz" rubber head, cloth body 20	30	40
Woody Woodpecker, 6-1/2" high, rubber, "Walter Lantz" 10	15	20
Woody Woodpecker Soaky 13	20	27
Yellow Kid Cap Bomb, cast iron, 1-1/2" high 83	125	165
Yellow Kid 6-1/2" high, cast iron, burlap gown, movable arms 475	713	950

Left to right: Yellow Kid, 6-1/2" high, cast-iron, burlap gown; Yellow Kid in Goat Cart. Courtesy Christie's East.

	C6	C8	C10
Yellow Kid, 8" high, Arnold Printworks, "Design copyrighted 1894 and 1896"	225	338	450
Yellow Kid in Cart, Kenton, early 1900s, 10" long, 6" high, pulled by mule, cast iron	800	1200	1600
Yellow Kid in Goat Cart, Kenton, 1890, painted cast iron, 7-1/2" long	400	600	800
Yellow Kid Ladder Toy, 16-1/2" high	600	900	1200
Yellow Kid papier mache and wood, 11" high, early 1900s	400	600	800
Zero (Beetle Bailey) Hand Puppet, Gund, 1960s, vinyl & cloth	30	45	60

Yellow Kid Ladder Toy. Some figures missing in photo. Courtesy James S. Maxwell/Virginia Caputo. Photo by Virginia Caputo.

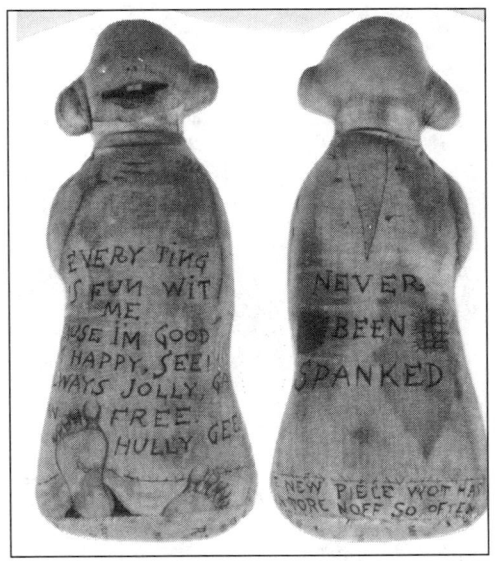

Yellow Kid Stuffed Doll, Arnold Print Works, 8" high. Courtesy James S. Maxwell/Virginia Caputo. Photo by Virginia Caputo.

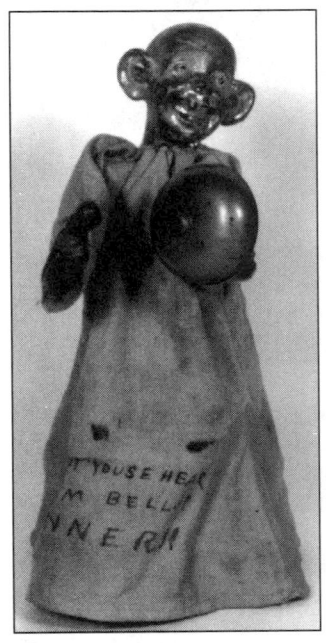

Yellow Kid Standing Bell Ringer. Courtesy James S. Maxwell/Virginia Caputo. Photo by Virginia Caputo.

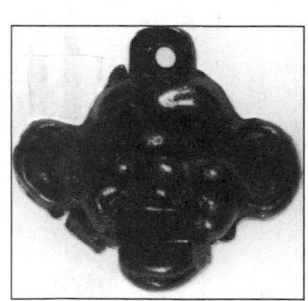

Yellow Kid Cap Bomb, 1-1/2" high. Courtesy James S. Maxwell/Virginia Caputo. Photo by Virginia Caputo.

Movies, Radio, Television

(See also Paper, Premiums, Banks, Miscellaneous, Comic Character,
Ramp Walkers, Marx Playsets, Action Figures, Figure Kits)

The average mint price in this category in the last edition was $374.16. In this edition it is $328.38, a decrease of 12%.

	C6	C8	C10
Alien doll, Kenner, 1979	125	188	250
Alvin Chipmunk Soaky	10	15	20
Amos Sparkler	500	750	1050
Amos tin wind-up, 1930, Marx, 12" high, moving eyes	493	740	985
Same as above, eyes don't move	450	675	900

Amos & Andy Fresh-Air Taxi, cast iron. Courtesy Christie's East.

Amos & Andy tin wind-ups, 12" high, eyes move. Photo by Ron Chojnacki. Courtesy Don Hultzman.

	C6	C8	C10
Amos and Andy in car, glass, 4-1/2" long, Victory Glass Co.	218	327	438
Amos and Andy wood jointed dolls, 6" high, price for pair, Jaymar	300	450	600
Amos and Andy Fresh-Air Taxi, cast iron, 6", Dent	600	950	1300

Amos & Andy Fresh-Air Taxi. Courtesy Sotheby's New York.

	C6	C8	C10
Amos and Andy Fresh-Air Taxi, tin wind-up, Marx, 8" long, 1930s	500	800	1185
Andy tin wind-up, 12" high Marx, 1930s, moving eyes	485	725	970
Same as above, eyes don't move	450	675	900
Andy Panda, 14" high, Ideal, plush, copyright 1960	60	90	120
Augie Doggie Soaky	27	41	55
Babalooie Soaky	15	22	30

	C6	C8	C10
Babalooie, 14", vinyl face, Knickerbocker	30	45	60
Baby Huey Hand Puppet, Gund, late 1950s	24	36	48
Baby Sandy Pull Toy, Gong Bell, 12-1/2" long, Sandy & Goose	150	225	300
Bat Masterson Gun & Holster set with cane and vest, 1958, Carnell	138	205	275

Box for Bat Masterson Gun & Holster set with cane and vest. Photo by Barry Goodman.

Beany & Cecil

List by Brad Krewson

	C6	C8	C10
Beany Doll (doesn't talk), 15" high, Mattel, 1960	45	68	90
Beany Doll, Talks, 17" high, Mattel, 1960	62	93	125
Beany Halloween Costume, Ben Cooper	35	52	70

Beany & Cecil Getar and Leakin' Lena, Pound 'N' Pull. Courtesy Brad Krewson.

	C6	C8	C10
Beany Hat with Two Propellers	35	52	70
Beany & Cecil Colorforms set, 1961, with box	60	90	125
Beany & Cecil Getar, Cecil's eyes move, 1961, Mattel	78	115	155
Beany & Cecil Tea Set, 6 place settings, 1960, Worcester	36	54	72
Cecil Halloween Costume, Ben Cooper	37	56	75
Cecil Disguise Kit, Mattel, 1962			
Cecil Doll (doesn't talk), Mattel, 24" high, 1960	30	45	60
Cecil Doll, talks, Mattel, 29" high, 1960	90	135	180
Cecil Hand Puppet, talks, Mattel, 1961	32	48	65
Cecil Music Box, metal, plays show's theme song, Cecil pops up, 1961, Mattel	85	128	170
Cecil Soaky, 8" high, 1950	30	45	60
Dishonest John Hand Puppet, talks, Mattel, 1961	63	95	125
Leakin' Lena plastic toy boat, Irwin Toy, 1962	75	112	150
Leakin' Lena wood toy ship, Pressman, 1960s	138	205	275
Leakin' Lena Pound & Pull, wooden, Pressman, 1961	48	72	95

Beany & Cecil Leakin' Lena, plastic toy boat. Courtesy Brad Krewson.

End Beany & Cecil

	C6	C8	C10
Beatles, Ringo, John, Paul, George, 5" vinyl figures, 1964, Remco, price per each	45	68	90
Beatles Soakies, each	62	93	125
Ben Casey Doll, 12" high, 1962	85	127	170
Ben Casey Play Hospital Set, Transogram	60	90	120
Ben Hur Sword, scabbard and shield, Marx, only produced in 1959, when movie was made	142	213	285
Betty Boop, approx. 3-3/4" high, "1931," wood-jointed, Jaymar	90	135	180
Betty Boop, 7" high, celluloid, Japanese, head shakes	600	900	1200
Betty Boop, 9-1/2" tall, 1930s jointed	240	360	480
Betty Boop, 12" high, jointed, wood and composition, c. 1930	550	800	1300
Betty Boop, Acrobat, celluloid and metal, Japanese, 1930s, wind-up	700	1100	1550
Betty Boop and Bunny mechanical toy	150	225	300

Left to right: Betty Boop, 12" high, jointed wood and composition; Betty Boop, 7" high, celluloid, Japanese. Courtesy Christie's East.

	C6	C8	C10
Bozo the Clown Bendee, 6" high, Lakeside	10	15	20
Bozo the Clown Bendem Doll, Knickerbocker, 9" high	11	16	23
Bozo the Clown Hand Puppet, Capital, 1962	15	22	30
Bozo the Clown Jumpkin, Kohner, 1960	25	38	50
Bozo the Clown Soaky	14	21	29
Bozo the Clown Squeeze Toy, 9"	60	90	120
Bozo the Clown talking doll, Mattel	45	68	90
Buck Jones Rangers chaps	90	135	180
Buffalo Bill Jr. belt and buckle (TV), 1950s	25	38	50
Bugs Bunny Hand Puppet, early 1950s	22	33	45
Bugs Bunny Soaky, 10" high	12	18	25
Bugs Bunny & Porky Pig talking toy, 1940s, has record that talks	95	143	190
"Bullet" (Roy Rogers' dog) stuffed doll, c. 1955	40	60	80
Bullwinkle, 14" high, stuffed, 1970, Gund	75	112	150
Bullwinkle, Terrytoons, 15" high, 1961	80	120	160
Bullwinkle Flexie, Wham-O	8	12	17
Bullwinkle Periscope, Lido, 1960s	8	12	16
Bullwinkle Soaky, 11" high	22	33	44
Buster Keaton Sparkler, Spanish, c. 1925, tin litho, 7" high, arms and legs move	1650	2475	3300

Beverly Hillbillies Car, Ideal. Photo by Ron Chojnacki. Courtesy Don Hultzman.

	C6	C8	C10
Beverly Hillbillies car, Ideal 1960s, wind-up	270	405	540
Bob Burns Bazooka, brass kazoo-like toy, patterned after radio-movie comic Burns' famous musical invention (the Army weapon gets its name from it) metal sliding tube, M.M. Pochapia Toys, 13" long when not extended, 1930s	20	30	40
Bob Hope Hand Puppet, c.1940	32	48	65
"Bojangles Dances Again," tin litho and wood, 1930s, tap button on base and he dances	200	300	400

Buster Keaton Sparkler, Spanish, Courtesy Christie's East.

	C6	C8	C10
Captain Gallant Foreign Legion Holster outfit	80	120	160
Captain Gallant Marx playset	400	600	800
Captain Kangaroo 20" talking doll, 1967, Mattel	21	32	42

	C6	C8	C10
Captain Kangaroo badge, tin shield, 1960s	20	30	40
Captain Kangaroo Hand Puppet, 1960s	22	33	45
Captain Video Spaceport playset, Superior	250	375	500
Casper The Friendly Ghost 11" stuffed doll, body is beanbag, 1960s	35	52	70
Casper The Friendly Ghost Hopper, 1950s, Linemar, 5" high	200	300	400
Casper The Friendly Ghost Soaky	16	24	33
Casper The Friendly Ghost Squeak toy, 8"	48	72	95
Casper The Friendly Ghost Turnover Tank, Linemar tin wind-up	150	225	300
"Casper the Talking Ghost, " Mattel, 14"	65	98	130
Cecil Sea Serpent: See Beany & Cecil			
Charlie Chaplin Bell Ringer squeeze toy, German, tin litho, metal bell, 7-1/4"	900	1350	1800
Charlie Chaplin Bell Toy, cast iron, c. 1912, 9-3/4"	300	450	600
Charlie Chaplin Bell Toy, metal, 3-wheeled, 5-1/4"	350	525	700
Charlie Chaplin Bicycle Rider String Toy, c. 1920s	350	525	700
Charlie Chaplin, celluloid, 4" high	900	1350	1800
Charlie Chaplin "Charlie's Back" doll, 1971, Milton Bradley	35	52	70
Charlie Chaplin, CKO No. 256, pre-war Germany, tips hat	150	225	300
Charlie Chaplin Cymbal-Player, tin litho, squeeze action, German-made, 6-3/4"	700	1050	1400
Charlie Chaplin "Dancing Charlie," cardboard	87	131	175
Charlie Chaplin Doll, Boucher, 7-1/2" high, steel, lead and cloth, ball-jointed, movable arms, legs and feet	250	375	500
Charlie Chaplin Doll, Louis Amberg, 14" high, c. 1915, composition and cloth	75	113	150

	C6	C8	C10
Charlie Chaplin driving 3-wheel vehicle, tin wind-up, Paya (Spain)	1100	1650	2200
Charlie Chaplin, Ferguson Novelty Co., 9" high, wind-up, composition, cloth and metal walker	1100	1650	2200
Charlie Chaplin flat tin litho, tips hat when string is pulled	110	165	220
Charlie Chaplin, Mark Hampton Company, 9" high, composition, "CHAS. CHAPLIN" on base	350	525	700
Charlie Chaplin, Martin, 1920, clockwork, 7" high, papier mache, lead, wire cane, cloth clothes	500	750	1000
Charlie Chaplin, Schuco, tin wind-up, 1920s	285	428	570
Charlie Chaplin tin litho squeeze toy, Spanish, c. 1925, 7-3/4" high	900	1350	1800
Charlie Chaplin tin litho wind-up, 7" high, walks	1300	1950	2600
Charlie Chaplin tin wind-up, 8-1/2" high, Nifty, 1920s	625	935	1250

Left to right: Charlie Chaplin Tricycle Rider, Charlie Chaplin driving 3-wheel vehicle. Courtesy Christie's East.

Charlie Chaplin. Left to right: Charlie Chaplin Cymbal-Player; Charlie Chaplin wind-up, 7" high, French; Charlie Chaplin, Mark Hampton Co.; Charlie Chaplin tin litho squeeze toy, Spanish; Charlie Chaplin Wind-up Walker; Charlie Chaplin Bell Toy, metal, 3-wheeled; Charlie Chaplin, Ferguson Novelty Co. Courtesy Christie's East.

Left to right: Charlie Chaplin tin wind-up with spinning cane; Charlie Chaplin Doll, Boucher; Charlie Chaplin wind-up, Boucher; Charlie Chaplin wooden whistler toy; Charlie Chaplin Bell Ringer squeeze toy; Charlie Chaplin doll, Louis Amberg; Charlie Chaplin bell toy, cast-iron, c. 1912, 9-3/4". Courtesy Christie's East.

	C6	C8	C10
Charlie Chaplin tin wind-up with spinning cane, 6-3/4" high (Unique Art?)	900	1350	1800
Charlie Chaplin Tricycle Rider tin wind-up, c. 1930, 3-1/2"	900	1350	1800
Charlie Chaplin wind-up, Boucher, metal, tin and cloth, 8-1/4" high	1000	1500	2000
Charlie Chaplin wind-up, 7" high, French, composition, tin and cloth walker	450	675	900
Charlie Chaplin Wind-up Walker, composition, cloth and metal, 11-1/2" high	500	750	1000

	C6	C8	C10
Charlie Chaplin wooden whistler toy, c. 1920, whistles "How Dry I Am," 13-1/4" high	1250	1875	2500
Charlie McCarthy, 7-1/2" high, celluloid	337	455	675
"Charlie McCarthy" written on top hat, standing erect, tin wind-up, c. 1938, 8" high	185	278	370
Charlie McCarthy rubber doll, Effanbee	45	68	90
Charlie McCarthy 13" high, composition mouth moves, 1930s	238	357	475

Charlie McCarthy, approx. 20" high, Effanbee, mouth moves. Courtesy Christie's East.

Charlie McCarthy, 20" high, Effanbee, mouth moves, in tweed jacket. Courtesy Christie's East.

	C6	C8	C10
Charlie McCarthy, 20" high 1950s cardboard puppet	45	68	90
Charlie McCarthy, approx. 20" high, Effanbee, mouth moves	308	462	615
Charlie McCarthy, 20" high, Effanbee, mouth moves, in tweed jacket	425	638	850
Charlie McCarthy, 20" high, Effanbee in summer suit, mouth moves	400	600	800
Charlie McCarthy in his Benzine Buggy, Marx	463	695	925

Charlie McCarthy in his Benzine Buggy. Courtesy PB Eighty-Four, New York.

Charlie McCarthy Drummer Boy. Photo by Ron Chojnacki. Courtesy Don Hultzman.

	C6	C8	C10
Charlie McCarthy Drummer Boy, 1938, Marx, tin wind-up, 8" high	500	750	1000
Charlie McCarthy Facemask, molded gauze, complete with separate monocle	50	75	100
Charlie McCarthy Hand Puppet, composition head, c. 1939	75	112	150
Charlie McCarthy paper money	3	4	5
Charlie McCarthy Tap Dancer, Marks Bros., 1938	125	188	250
Charlie McCarthy Ventriloquist Doll, composition with cloth body, ring pull in back of head to activate lower jaw, 14-1/2" tall	600	900	1200

Charlie McCarthy paper money. Courtesy Toy Collector News.

Charlie McCarthy paper money. Courtesy Rex and Richard Gray.

	C6	C8	C10
Charlie McCarthy Ventriloquist Doll, 18"	300	450	600
Charlie McCarthy Ventriloquist Doll, 33", Puppet Maker K&S	500	750	1000
Charlie McCarthy "Charlie McCarthy and Mortimer Snerd Private Car," Marx, two heads sticking out of top of car	1000	1700	2265

"Charlie McCarthy and Mortimer Snerd Private Car." Courtesy Phillips New York.

	C6	C8	C10
Charlie Weaver Nodder	112	188	225
Cheyenne Target Game, Mettoy, 1961	62	93	125
C.H.i.P.s. Motorcycle, Mego	10	15	20
C H.i.P.s Police Chase Car, Mego, 1981	18	27	35
C.H.i.P.s. Rescue Copter Fleet, 1979	20	30	40
Chitty Chitty Bang Bang, Corgi	125	188	250
Cisco Kid Broomstick Horse, 1950s, "Ride 'em Cisco Kid"	35	53	70

	C6	C8	C10
Cisco Kid Neckerchief with nickel sombrero slide	50	75	100
Cisco Kid Western Outfit, 1950s	98	145	195
Clyde Beatty Hingees Set, 1944	25	38	50
Cowardly Lion (Wizard Of Oz) molded gauze facemask	40	60	80
Creature Soaky	55	83	110
Dale Evans holster outfit	90	135	180
Daniel Boone (Fess Parker) Canoe, vinyl, 18" long	15	22	30
Daniel Boone Cannon, Remco, 1964	80	120	160
Daniel Boone Doll, Remco	40	60	80
Daniel Boone Playset, Grant exclusive, w/ box	80	120	160
Danny O'Day (Jimmy Nelson) ventriloquist doll	40	60	80
Deputy Dawg, 14" high stuffed doll, Ideal, 1961	37	56	75
Deputy Dawg Soaky	15	22	30
Dick Van Dyke doll from Chitty Chitty Bang Bang, 1967, talks, Mattel	125	188	250
Doggie Daddie, Knickerbocker, vinyl head	100	150	200
Dr. Doolittle Pushmi Pullyu, 1965	43	65	87
Dr. Doolittle Music Box, Gee-Tar, Mattel, 1967	40	60	80
Dr. Doolittle Talking Hand Puppet, 1967, Mattel	32	48	65
Dragnet Crime Lab, 1955, flashlight, signal gun, badge, handcuffs, fingerprint kit, etc.	90	135	180
Dragnet Police Set, gun, handcuffs, badge	35	52	70
Dragnet Los Angeles Police No. 714 badge	10	15	20
Dragnet Shoulder Holster & Pistol, 1950s	62	93	125
Dragnet talking police car, Ideal Toys, c. 1954	105	158	210
Dragnet Water Pistol, c. 1955, 714 badge emblazoned on handle	25	38	50
Dragnet Whistle, black plastic	6	9	12
Dukes of Hazzard, 4 vehicles, Ertl set	15	22	30
Ed Wynn Fire Chief, ax in hand, jointed wood	80	120	160
Ed Wynn Fire Chief, litho on wood, pull toy, Schoenhut, 12" long: See Schoenhut			
Fanny Brice (Baby Snooks), Ideal, composition and wire doll, 12" high	125	188	250
Farfel (Jimmy Nelson) Hand Puppet, Juro	85	127	170
Farmer Alfalfa (Terrytoons) c. 1950, 17-1/2" high, stuffed body, vinyl head, hands	30	45	60
Flintstones Bam Bam, 12-1/2" high, Ideal	39	60	78
Flintstones Bam Bam Soaky	15	22	30
Flintstones Barney Rubble, 10" high, vinyl doll, 1960	36	48	72
Flintstones "The Flintstones Bedrock Express Handcar," 1962, Marx, wind-up playset 22x26	225	338	450
Flintstones Choo Choo Train, Marx, "Bedrock Express," tin wind-up, Linemar Co., 13" long, 1950s	188	280	375

Fanny Brice (Baby Snooks), Ideal. Courtesy Christie's East.

	C6	C8	C10
Flintstones "Dino On Tricycle," 1962, Linemar, 4" high	500	750	1000
Flintstones "Dino the Dinosaur," 1961, Linemar, 9" long	188	280	375
Flintstones "Flintstone Friction Cars," (Fred, Barney, Wilma, etc.), 1962, Linemar, 4" long, price per each	123	185	245
Flintstones "Flintstone Pals" (Barney on Dino), Linemar, 1962, 8" long, wind-up	193	290	385
Flintstones "Flintstone Pals" (Fred on Dino), Linemar, 1962, 8" long, wind-up	260	390	520

Flintstone Pals on Dino, Fred and Barney riders, Marx.

	C6	C8	C10
"Flintstone Flivver," 1962, Marx, (Japan), Friction, 6-3/4" long	308	460	615
Flintstone's Fred Flintstone, 5-3/4" high, hollow vinyl figure	37	56	75
Flintstones "Hopping Barney Rubble," 1962, Marx (Japan), wind-up, 4" high	200	300	400
Flintstones "Hopping Fred Flintstone," Linemar, 4" high	200	300	400
Flintstones "Hopping Dino," 1962, Linemar, 4" high	240	360	480
Flintstones Pebbles 7" jointed doll	60	90	120
Flintstones Playset, Marx	205	308	410

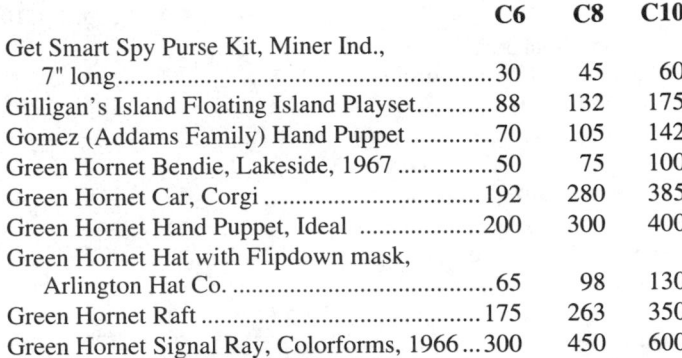

Flintstones Playset, Marx. Photo by Barry Goodman.

	C6	C8	C10
"Flintstones Mechanical Shooting Gallery," 1962, Marx, 13" long	48	72	95
Flintstones Motorized Yacht	375	562	750
Flintstones Paddy Wagon, Remco, 1961	100	150	200
Flintstones Tinykins, Marx	25	38	50
"Flintstones Tricycle," Wilma rider, Marx	240	360	480
Flintstones Turnover Tank, Linemar tin wind-up, 1950s, 4" long	310	465	620
Flip Wilson Geraldine talking doll, Shindana, 1970	25	38	50
Flying Nun, 4-3/4", Hasbro, 1960s	25	38	50
Flying Nun Flying Toy, Rayline, 1970	25	38	50
Frankenstein Soaky	55	83	110
Froggie the Gremlin hollow rubber doll, squeeze toy, 5" high, of the Buster Brown radio with TV show, squeeze and tongue sticks out, 1950s, Rempel	62	93	125
Froggie the Gremlin, 6-1/2" squeeze toy	34	51	68
Froggie the Gremlin, 9-1/4" squeeze toy	40	60	80
Froggie the Gremlin, 10-3/4" squeeze toy	170	255	340
Gabby (Gulliver's Travels), 10-1/2" high, Ideal, wood-jointed	300	450	600
Gangbusters Target Game, Marx	55	83	110
Gene Autry Marionette, 18" high, 1940s	140	210	280
Gene Autry Spurs	60	90	120

	C6	C8	C10
Get Smart Spy Purse Kit, Miner Ind., 7" long	30	45	60
Gilligan's Island Floating Island Playset	88	132	175
Gomez (Addams Family) Hand Puppet	70	105	142
Green Hornet Bendie, Lakeside, 1967	50	75	100
Green Hornet Car, Corgi	192	280	385
Green Hornet Hand Puppet, Ideal	200	300	400
Green Hornet Hat with Flipdown mask, Arlington Hat Co.	65	98	130
Green Hornet Raft	175	263	350
Green Hornet Signal Ray, Colorforms, 1966	300	450	600

Froggie the Gremlin. Courtesy Toy Collector News.

	C6	C8	C10
Green Hornet Walkie Talkies, Remco	200	300	400
Groucho Marx "Ventriloquist Play Pal," Goldberger	40	60	80
Gulliver's Travels Boat, wooden (Paramount)	110	165	220
Gulliver's Travels Drum, tin, Chein, 1939	25	38	50
Gulliver's Travels Musical Top, Chein	30	45	60
Gulliver's Travels Sandpail, tin, Chein	45	68	90
Gumby "Bendee" figure	11	16	23
Gumby "Gumby's Jeep," 12", metal, 1960s	125	188	250
Gumby Hand Puppet, 1965, Lakeside	17	26	35
Gumby vinyl wind-up, dated 1966, approx. 4" high	50	75	100
Gunsmoke Handcuffs & Badge, c.1952	42	63	85
Harold Lloyd Bell Toy, German, 6-1/2" high	300	450	600
Harold Lloyd Bumper Car, German, 1920s, auctioned 1993 for $17,600			

Harold Lloyd Bell Toy. Courtesy Sotheby's New York.

Harold Lloyd. Left to right: Harold Lloyd Bell Toy, Harold Lloyd "Funny Face," Harold Lloyd Sparkler. Courtesy Christie's East.

Harold Lloyd Donkey Cart. Courtesy Christie's East.

Hoot Gibson cowboy outfit "Wornova Clothes," apparently new in 1935 and still on sale in 1939. Courtesy Heinz Mueller, Continental Hobby House.

	C6	C8	C10
Harold Lloyd Donkey Cart, tin litho, Spanish, c. 1929, 9-1/4" long	2200	3300	4500
Harold Lloyd "Funny Face," Marx wind-up walker, 1929	400	600	800
Harold Lloyd Policeman, 12" high, tin wind-up	375	562	750
Harold Lloyd Sparkler, German tin litho	375	562	750
Henry Fonda Texas Ranger Sheriff Badge, The Deputy, 1951	17	26	35
Herman Munster Doll, Mattel	88	132	175
Herman Munster Hand Puppet, vinyl, 1960s	95	140	190
Herman Munster Talking Puppet	200	300	400
Highway Patrol "Highway Patrol Car," Broderick Crawford, litho, 8" long	75	112	150
"Highway Patrol Pistol Outfit," Halco, 1956, gun, holster, badge, handcuffs, ID, whistle, etc.	125	188	250
Hoot Gibson Cowboy Outfit, Wornova Clothes, 1935	70	105	140
Hoot Gibson Lariat	40	60	80
Hoot Gibson Wornova Clothes (Squaw style), 1930s	60	90	120

	C6	C8	C10
"Hopalong Cassidy Automatic Television Set," 1950s, Automatic Toy Co., 5" cube	150	225	300
Hopalong Cassidy Badge, tin with insert photo	27	41	55
Hopalong Cassidy Binoculars, c. 1950, plastic	78	115	155
Hopalong Cassidy compass	105	158	210
Hopalong Cassidy Cowboy outfit	200	300	400

Hopalong Cassidy Cowboy Outfit box. Photo by Barry Goodman.

	C6	C8	C10
Hopalong Cassidy Cowgirl's outfit.............. 125		188	250
Hopalong Cassidy Dart Board, 14" x 17", stagecoach holdup and target practice, 1950, Toy Ent. 110		165	220
Hopalong Cassidy Doll, 1930s-40s, 28" high 175		263	350
Hopalong Cassidy Field Glasses, 1940, metal 85		128	170
Hopalong Cassidy Flashlight Gun, plastic, 8" long, Hoppy's name on side 30		45	60
Hopalong Cassidy Hand Puppet, 1940s 200		300	400
Hopalong Cassidy "Hop-A-Long Cassidy," Marx, 9-1/2" high (on "Range Rider" rocker base) 315		472	630
Hopalong Cassidy Knife, c. mid-1940s, 3-1/2" long 80		120	160
Hopalong Cassidy Photo Ring, c. late 1940s 35		52	70
"Hopalong Cassidy Picture Gun and Theater," 1939, Stephens Co., 12" long x 8" high...... 200		300	400
Hopalong Cassidy Rocking Horse, Topper...... 188		282	375
"Hopalong Cassidy Shooting Gallery," 1950s, Automatic Toy Co., 18" long 170		255	340
Hopalong Cassidy Signet Ring, all metal, late 1940s...................................... 30		45	60
Hopalong Cassidy Spurs, leather and metal..... 110		165	220
Hopalong Cassidy Western Frontier set, with figures, stagecoach and buildings....... 300		450	600
Hopalong Cassidy Zoomerang Gun, shoots paper, Tigrett Enterprises, Chicago, 1950, 9" long 100		150	200
Howdy Doody 4" high plastic push-puppet, Kohner, has NBC mike............................... 85		128	170
Howdy Doody 6" high, wall walker doll 27		41	55
Howdy Doody 7-1/2" high, 1950s, plastic cloth clothes, eyes close, mouth opens................................ 312		468	625

	C6	C8	C10
Howdy Doody 12" high, moveable jaws, Goldberger Dolls 85		130	170
Howdy Doody, 21" high, Ideal, 1950s 225		338	450
Howdy Doody 26" ventriloquist dummy 75		112	150
Howdy Doody Acrobat, Arnold, 1950s............205		308	410
"Howdy Doody Air-O-Doodle Circus Train," Kagran, 1950s, wind-up, 16" long 90		135	180
Howdy Doody Airplane Squeeze Toy, Stahlwood 230		345	460
Howdy Doody and Bob Smith at the piano, tin wind-up, Unique 680		1020	1360
Howdy Doody "Clarabelle Clown," 1950s, Linemar, squeeze action cable, 6-1/2" high 188		280	375
Howdy Doody "Clarabelle Clown," 1950s, Linemar, 5" high, Kagran Corp., wind-up 225		338	450
Howdy Doody "Clarabelle Hurdy Gurdy," 1950s, FBA Industries, Kagran, 8" long.....200		300	400
Howdy Doody, Clarabelle's horn 1950s 50		75	100
Howdy Doody Clarabelle Marionette, Peter Puppet Playthings, 1950s...................140		210	280
Howdy Doody, Clarabelle Playsuit, Wonderland Costumes...............................145		220	290
Howdy Doody, Dilly-Dally Marionette, Peter Puppet Playthings, 1950s...................260		390	520
Howdy Doody, Flub-A-Dub Marionette, early 1950s....................................225		338	450
Howdy Doody Flub-A-Dub Push Puppet, felt, wood, 5" high 50		75	100
Howdy Doody Flub-A-Dub 3-1/2" plastic figure 65		98	130
Howdy Doody hand puppets, no date, mo. mfr., rubber heads, cloth bodies 25		38	50
Howdy Doody Jeep, Marx wind-up 200		300	400
Howdy Doody Life Preserver, plastic, 1950s, shows Howdy, Mr. Bluster, etc. 21		31	42
Howdy Doody Marionette, 17" high, wooden arms and legs, composition head...120		180	240
Howdy Doody Marionette, 16" high, composition head, hands and feet, hand-painted features, 1950s 145		220	290
Howdy Doody Mask, rubber 12		18	24
Howdy Doody Piano, Howdy plays it..............160		240	320
Howdy Doody plastic puppet toys, with levers in back of head to move mouths. Consists of Howdy, Bluster, Clarabelle, Princess, Dilly Dally, Tee-Vee Toys No. 549, price for set 70		105	140
Howdy Doody plastic ukulele, Emenee, 1950s..55		82	110
Howdy Doody Princess Summer-Fall Winter-Spring Marionette, Peter Puppet 125		188	250
Howdy Doody "Pump-Mobile," Nylint, unauthorized Howdy, rides cart, 8-1/2" long, 7" high: See Vehicles			
Howdy Doody "Put-In-Head," similar to Mr. Potato Head, but with Howdy characters: Howdy, Bluster, Clarabelle, Princess, price for set 50		75	100

Howdy Doody and Bob Smith At The Piano. Courtesy PB Eighty-Four, New York.

Howdy Doody Pumpmobile. Photo by Don Hultzman.

	C6	C8	C10
Howdy Doody Sand Forms, 1952, molds of Howdy, Bluster, Flub-A-Dub, Clarabelle, plus shovel	43	65	85
Howdy Doody Squeeze Toy, 7" high	75	112	150
Howdy Doody TV Set with paper filmstrips, Lego, 1950s	42	63	85
Howdy Doody tin wind-up, c. 1950, Marx, 5" high, Howdy plays banjo and moves head	240	360	480
Howdy Doody tin wind-up, c. 1950, Howdy does jig and Bob Smith sits at piano, Marx, 5-1/2" high	550	825	1100
Howdy Doody wood-jointed doll, 13" high	175	263	350
Howdy Doody wood-jointed doll, 5-1/2" high, holding NBC mike	200	300	400
Howdy Doody Zippy the Chimp Marionette, 1950s, Peter Puppet Playthings	550	800	1200
Huckleberry Hound, 18" stuffed doll, 1959, Knickerbocker	27	41	55
Huckleberry Hound as Fireman, rubber squeeze toy, 1960s, 9" high	100	150	200

	C6	C8	C10
Huckleberry Hound Hand Puppet, Knickerbocker, 1959	14	21	28
Huckleberry Hound with top hat, Dell, rubber squeeze toy, 1960s, 6" high	22	33	44
Huckleberry Hound "Huckleberry Hound Car," 1962, Marx (Japan), wind-up, 4" long	130	195	260
Huckleberry Hound "Huckleberry Hound Hopper" 1962, Linemar, 4-1/2" high	200	300	400
"Huckleberry Hound Tricycle," 1961, Linemar, 4" high	400	600	800
"Huckleberry Hound Yogi Bear" friction "Huckleberry Aeroplane"	425	638	850
Hugh O'Brian-Wyatt Earp, Dodge City Western Town, Marx, 1950s	450	675	900
I Spy Target Set	17	26	35
J. Fred Muggs ("Today" show) Hand Puppet, 1954	41	62	82
J. Fred Muggs pull toy, Gong Bell	90	135	180
Jackie Coogan glass candy container, 5" high	800	1200	1600
Jackie Coogan 5-1/2" high celluloid, 1920s	130	195	260
Jackie Coogan ("The Kid") tin wind-up walker, German, 7" high	800	1200	1600
Jackie Gleason "Away We Go" bus, 13"	450	675	900

Jackie Coogan ("The Kid") tin wind-up walker.

"Huckleberry Hound Yogi Bear Friction Huckleberry Aeroplane." Photo by Ron Chojnacki. Courtesy Don Hultzman.

Jackie Gleason "Away We Go" Bus. Courtesy Don Coviello.

	C6	C8	C10
Jackie Gleason Costume (Kramden), money-change, etc.	187	280	375
Jackie Gleason (Reggie Van Gleason) climbing toy	62	93	125
Jackie Gleason Doll, 30" high, 1950s	200	300	400
Jackie Gleason "Story Stage Theatre," Utopia Enterprises, copyright 1955	123	185	245
James Bond "Aston Martin" No. 271, Corgi, die-cast..............................	105	158	210
James Bond "Aston Martin" No. 270, Corgi, Die-cast..............................	98	150	195
James Bond Aston Martin: See Battery-Operated			
James Bond 007 Attache Case, 11", code book, rifle (which converts to pistol), bullets, Code-O-Matic, billfold with money, James Bond business cards and instructions, c. 1965	263	395	525
James Bond Camera, shoots............................	138	205	275
James Bond Hand Puppet, A.C. Gilbert, 1965	140	210	280
James Bond Moonraker Shuttlecraft.................	38	57	75
"James Bond 100 Shot Repeater Cap Pistol with Silencer," 1961, 9" long, from "Goldfinger," Lone Star Co.	88	132	175
Jerry Mahoney ventriloquist dummy	115	173	230
Jerry Lewis/Dean Martin two-sided Hand Puppet...............................	150	225	300
Jetsons "Astro - the Jetsons' Dog," 1963, Marx (Japan), wind-up, 5" high..................	212	318	425
Jetsons "George Jetson" 1963 Marx (Japan), squeeze action cable, 4" high	150	225	300
Jetsons George Jetson c. 1965, Marx, tin wind-up, 4" high	190	275	380
Jetsons "Jetson Express Choo Choo Train," 1960s, Marx (Japan), wind-up, 13" long	250	375	500

Joe Penner tin wind-up. Courtesy Sotheby's New York.

	C6	C8	C10
Joe Penner tin wind-up, Marx, c. 1930s, 8" high, tips hat, walks, "Wanna Buy a Duck?"	350	525	700
Jungle Jim Playset, Marx.................................	500	800	1100
King Little (Gulliver's Travels), Ideal, 12" jointed composition	325	488	650
Kukla & Ollie Puppet Theatre, cardboard, 1962	50	75	100
Lambchop Shari Lewis Hand Puppet.................	18	27	36
Little Rascals: See Our Gang			
Lone Ranger Acme Moviescope Set, 1948, includes 4 films: No. 1 Superman, No. 2 Lone Ranger, No. 3 Lone Ranger, No. 4 Lone Ranger. With pop-up box including films and viewer	72	108	145

Jetson Express Choo Choo Train. Photo by Don Hultzman.

	C6	C8	C10
Jetsons Turnover Tank, Linemar, tin wind-up	205	308	410

Jetsons Turnover Tank, Linemar. Photo by Don Hultzman.

L to R: Lone Ranger Doll, 20" high, Tonto, 20" high, both Dollcraft. Courtesy Christie's East.

	C6	C8	C10
Lone Ranger and Silver composition figure, 1938, 4-1/2" high..........88	132	175
Lone Ranger Bendy, Lakeside, No. 8705, 6" high, 1967 16	24	32
Lone Ranger Chuck Wagon Lantern.................75	112	150
Lone Ranger Deputy Badge, 1950s 9	13	18
Lone Ranger Doll, 20" high, 1938, very realistic composition head, hands, feet, Dollcraft 300	450	600
Lone Ranger Double Target Set, 1939, two-sided target, gun, 2 darts, Marx...........125	188	250

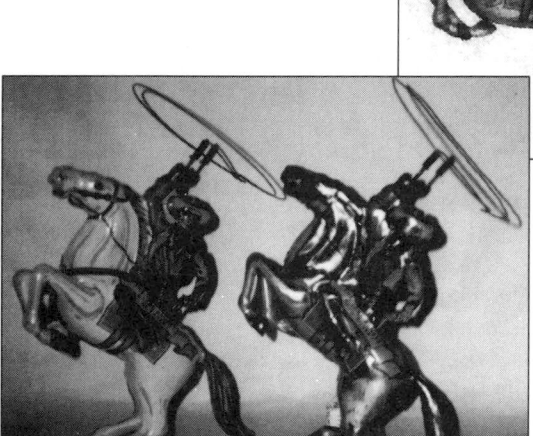

Lone Ranger, "Hiyo Silver." Courtesy PB Eighty-Four, New York.

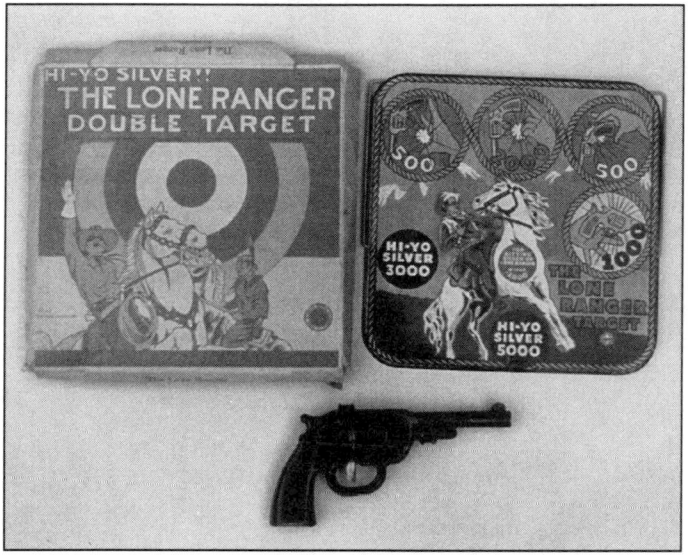

Lone Ranger Double Target set. Photo by Charles D. Richards.

Lone Ranger. Left to right: 1938 Marx wind-up, litho version; 1938 Marx wind-up, chrome version. Photo by Don Hultzman.

	C6	C8	C10
Lone Ranger Flashlight 80	120	160
Lone Ranger Hand Puppet, vinyl head, c. 1956.........................80	120	160
Lone Ranger Hand Puppet, Ideal, 1966 25	38	50
Lone Ranger Harmonica, Magnus, 1950 40	60	80
Lone Ranger Hat, 1930s, official 65	98	130
Lone Ranger Hat, cowboy hat of white felt w/ red trim. "Lone Ranger Hi! Yo! Silver!" inscribed, 1940s................22	33	45
Lone Ranger Official First-Aid Kit with contents, 1938, tin litho 105	158	210
Lone Ranger "Official Outfit," 1939, mask, jail keys, badge, silver bullet, glow belt, Lone Ranger buckle, Lee Powell and Chief Thundercloud on belt 62	93	125
Lone Ranger "Lone Ranger Official Outfit," M.A. Henry Co., 1942 (belt, holster, guns, cuffs) 70	105	140
Lone Ranger, 1938, Marx, wind-up (on "Range Rider" rocker base), 10-1/2" high 350	525	700
Lone Ranger, 1938, Marx, wind-up, chrome version, 8-1/2" high from top of lariat 180	270	360
Lone Ranger, 1938, Marx, wind-up, litho version, 8-1/2" high from top of lariat 193	290	385

	C6	C8	C10
Lone Ranger Picture Printing Set, 1939, 8 rubber stamps.................75	112	150
Lone Ranger Push Toy, Kohner, wood base, 1950s............42	63	85
Lone Ranger, Ranch Set, series 500, Marx playset 250	375	500
Lone Ranger Rides Again movie viewer, 1939 113	170	225
Lone Ranger Rodeo, Marx set with metal bldgs., plastic figures, etc., 1950s, No. 9392 200	300	400

Lone Ranger Ranch Set, series 500. Photo by Barry Goodman.

	C6	C8	C10
Lone Ranger Signal Siren, Flashlight, 1950s, with silver bullet secret code, United States Electric Mfg. Co.	65	98	130
Lone Ranger Silver Bullet Knife, 3" long closed	92	138	185
Lone Ranger "Stringless Marionette" Hand Puppet, cloth and vinyl	120	180	240
Lone Ranger Strongbox (coin bank), 1938	100	150	200
Lone Ranger Target Game, 1938, Marx	52	78	105
Lucy (Peanuts) 1950s, vinyl squeeze doll	15	22	30
Lurch (Addams Family), Remco	100	150	200
Magilla Gorilla Hand Puppet, Ideal, 1960s	24	36	48
Magilla Gorilla, Ideal, 8" high	62	93	125
Magilla Gorilla, Ideal, 1960s, 19" high	90	135	180
Mary Poppins Hand Puppet, Gund	48	72	95
Matt Dillon, U.S. Marshall badge (Gunsmoke)	19	30	38
Man from U.N.C.L.E. Secret Print Putty, c. 1965	25	38	50
Men Into Space space helmet, retractable visor, space mike, etc. From series starring William Lundigan as Col. McCaulety, made of fortiflex	65	98	130
Milton Berle Car, two large wheels, two small, Marx, 1950s, "What the Hey," etc. written on car	215	323	430

Mortimer Snerd Band, Marx. Courtesy Christie's East.

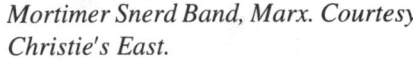

Mortimer Snerd Band, Marx. Courtesy Christie's East.

	C6	C8	C10
Mortimer Snerd Tin Wind-up, Marx, c. 1939, Mortimer's hat tips as he walks	300	450	600
"Mortimer Snerd's Tricky Auto," 1939, Marx	370	555	740

Milton Berle Car. Courtesy Mapes Auctioneers & Appraisers.

Mortimer Snerd, 13" high, Ideal. Courtesy Christie's East.

	C6	C8	C10
Morticia (Addams Family), 1964, Remco	93	140	195
Mortimer Snerd, 5" high, Celluloid	200	300	400
Mortimer Snerd, 13" high, Ideal, composition and wire	338	505	675
Mortimer Snerd Band, Marx, wind-up, 1935, "Hometown Band"	450	675	900
Mortimer Snerd Hand Puppet	75	112	150
Mortimer Snerd, Jack In The Box, c. 1930s, 8" high	100	150	200
"Mortimer Snerd Teeth," plastic teeth and dental wax, c. 1950	15	22	30

	C6	C8	C10
Mr. Ed Hand Puppet, Mattel, 1962	48	72	95
Mr. Magoo Car, battery, tin litho: See Battery Toys "MaGoo"			
Mr. Magoo Doll, Ideal, 15" high	45	68	90
Mr. Magoo Hand Puppet, 1962, vinyl	32	48	65
Mr. Magoo Soaky, 11" high	20	30	40
Mummy Soaky	60	90	120
Munsters, Grandpa hand puppet, vinyl, 1960s	93	140	185
Munsters, Herman: See Herman Munster			
Munsters, Lily Munster Hand Puppet, 1960s	95	140	190

	C6	C8	C10
My Favorite Martian "Martian Magic Tricks," Gilbert, 1964, magic set	115	175	230
Oliver Hardy Bendem Doll, 1960, Knickerbocker, 9" high	27	41	55
Oliver Hardy Doll, Dean	400	600	800
Oliver Hardy Hand Puppet, Knickerbocker	25	38	50
Oliver Hardy Roly Poly, 10-1/2" high, plastic	22	33	44
Oliver Hardy Sparkler, Isla, Spanish	1000	1500	2000
Oliver Hardy wind-up, Lakeside, 5" high, 1960s	35	52	70

Oliver Hardy Sparkler, ISLA. Courtesy Christie's East.

	C6	C8	C10
"Oswald, Universal Pictures, Irwin Prod." 18-1/2" wind-up, wood and cardboard body with cloth clothes, stuffed arms and head, character created by Disney, early	800	1300	1800
Oswald Stuffed Toy, 20-7/8" high	200	300	400
Our Gang Dolls and Clubhouse, Mego, 1975	160	240	320
Pink Panther Hand Puppet, early, cloth body, Gund	20	30	40
Pinky Lee Pull Toy, Gong Bell	100	150	200
Pinky Lee vinyl doll, squeeze and his head pops up, 1950	90	135	180
Poky (Gumby) "Bendee" figure	14	22	29
Poky Hand Puppet, 1965, Lakeside	24	36	47
Poky "Jack In The Box," Lakeside, 1965	16	24	32
Poky vinyl wind-up, dated 1966, approx. 4" high	37	56	75
Quick Draw McGraw, 17-1/2", Knickerbocker	105	158	210
Quick Draw McGraw, "Animal Airplane," 1960s, Linemar, 8-1/2" long, 9-1/2" wingspan (Yogi Bear and Huckleberry Hound's head also used)	400	600	800
Quick Draw McGraw "Quick Draw McGraw Hopper," 1962, Linemar, 4-1/2" high	200	300	400
Quick Draw McGraw Squeeze Toy, Dell, 9-1/2" high	100	150	200
Ramar of the Jungle Playset	217	325	435
Rat Patrol Giant Action Battle Set	250	375	500
Rat Patrol Jeep, Marx	200	300	400
Ricochet Rabbit, Ideal	52	78	105
Rifleman (TV) Ranch, Marx	600	1000	1500

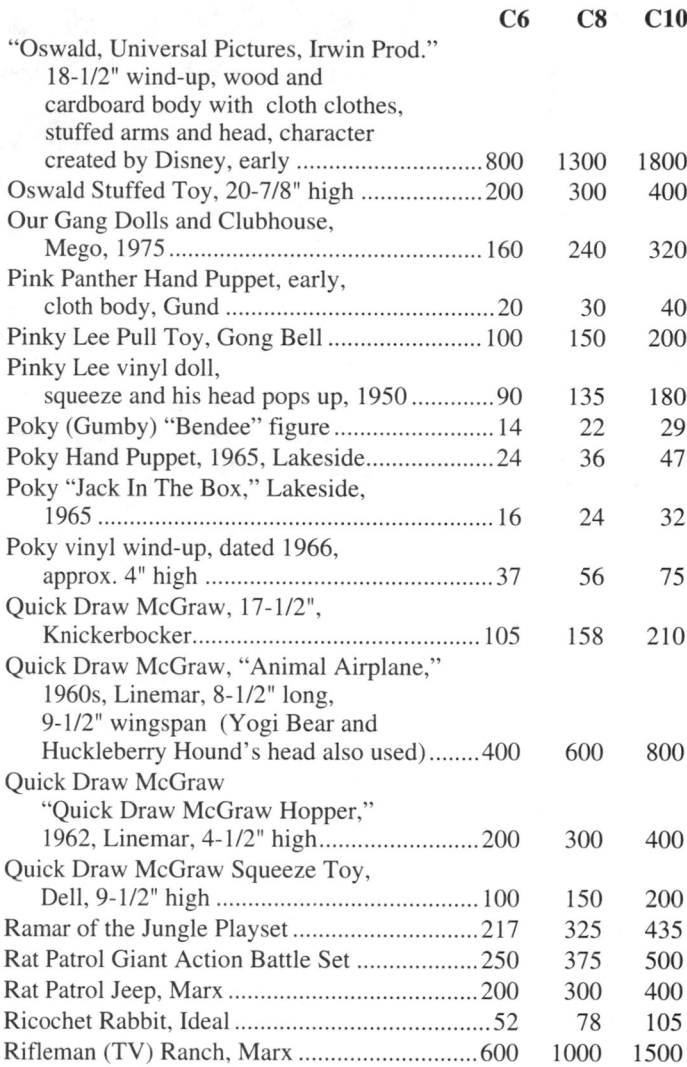

Oswald stuffed toy, 20-7/8" high. Courtesy James S. Maxwell/Virginia Caputo. Photo by Virginia Caputo.

"Oswald" wind-up, wood and cardboard body with cloth clothes (1932 ad).

Rifleman Ranch, Marx. Photo by Barry Goodman.

	C6	C8	C10
Rin Tin Tin and Rusty Knife, 1950s	60	90	120
Rin Tin Tin Bugle with Banner	37	56	75
Rin Tin Tin, Marx Fort Apache Stockade, 1950s, No. 3628	190	285	380
Rin Tin Tin stuffed dog, Ideal	37	56	75
Robin Hood Bow & Arrow Set, 1956, Richard Greene	6	9	12

Rin Tin Tin Marx Fort Apache stockade playset. Photo by Barry Goodman.

"Roy Rogers Chuckwagon," Nellie Belle Jeep. Photo by Don Hultzman.

	C6	C8	C10
Robin Hood Money Pouch, six foreign coins from Richard Greene TV series, 1953-54	20	30	40
Robin Hood Money Pouch, fifteen foreign coins, from Richard Greene TV series	20	30	40
Robin Hood Shield. Badge with embossed Robin Hood and gem stone, c. 1956	25	38	50
Rocky The Flying Squirrel Bendee Figure, 1960s, Wham-O	10	15	21
Rocky The Flying Squirrel Hand Puppet	25	38	50
Rocky The Flying Squirrel Soaky	20	30	40
Rookies (TV) Official Police Car, Fleetwood, 1975	15	22	30
Rootie Kazootie Marionette, 14" hard rubber head and hands, wooden shoes and body wearing clothes	90	135	180
Rootie Kazootie, 19", Effanbee	62	93	125
"Roy Rogers and Bullet Hobby Horse," No. 812, 1950s, N.N. Hill Brass Co., 19" long	200	300	400
Roy Rogers bandanna, large	48	72	95
Roy Rogers Bobbin' Head doll, 6" high, 1962	90	135	180
Roy Rogers Branding Iron Set	40	60	80
Roy Rogers Double R Bar Ranch, 1950s, tin litho ranch house, Marx	175	263	350
Roy Rogers Mineral City, town with hotel, music hall, cafe, bank, barber shop, trade goods, etc., tin	185	278	370
Roy Rogers Nellie Belle Jeep, metal	30	45	60
Roy Rogers Pocket Flashlight	37	56	75
Roy Rogers Quickshooter Hat with Secret Gun	90	135	180
Roy Rogers "Ranch Lantern," No. 90, metal, hurricane type with plastic chimney, 1950s, 7-3/4" tall	78	115	155
Roy Rogers Rodeo Ranch, Marx playset	125	188	250
Roy Rogers "Roy Rogers Buckboard," 1950s, Ideal, 16" long	65	98	130

	C6	C8	C10
Roy Rogers "Roy Rogers Chuck Wagon," Ideal, 1950s, 13" long	123	185	245
Roy Rogers "Roy Rogers Fix-it Stagecoach," 1950s, Ideal, 13" long	90	135	180

Roy Rogers Signal Flashlight. Photo by Gary J. Linden.

Roy Rogers "Stage Coach Wagon Train." Courtesy Continental Hobby House.

	C6	C8	C10
Roy Rogers "Roy Rogers Horse Trailer & Jeep," Ideal, 1950s, 15" long	180	270	360
Roy Rogers "Roy Rogers Stagecoach Wagon Train," wind-up, 14" long, plastic, 1950s	80	120	160
Roy Rogers Signal Flashlight	95	140	190
Roy Rogers Telescope	40	60	80
Roy Rogers and Trigger Pocket Knife	75	112	150
Roy Rogers Wagon Train, Marx	150	225	300
Roy Rogers Western Town Playset, Marx	125	188	250
Scarecrow (Wizard of Oz) molded gauze facemask	60	90	120
Scrappy (Columbia Pictures), 14-1/2" high, c. 1935, E.D. & T.C. Co., cloth and composition	320	480	640

Scrappy (Columbia Pictures), 14-1/2" high. Courtesy Christie's East.

	C6	C8	C10
Scrappy & Margie wooden pull toy, 13-1/2" long, he plays xylophone, she revolves	165	248	330
Sgt. Bilko Holster Set from CBS TV series "You'll Never Get Rich," starring Phil Silvers. Photo-illustrated box contains leather holster and belt with realistic Army .45 made of silvered die-cast metal. Sgt.'s arm patch and Sgt. Bilko hat with Badge, Halco Brand, 1956	100	150	200
Secret Squirrel Soaky	37	56	75
Shadow Crimefighter Detection Belt, with pistol, handcuffs, etc., 1978, Madison Ltd.	15	22	30
Shadow Felt Hat, early 1940s	187	280	375
Shirley Temple Playhouse	120	180	240
Simon Chipmunk Soaky	11	16	23
Small Fry Club Kit, 1949, button, etc., Dumont TV show (may be premium)	30	45	60
"Sneak" Facemask, molded gauze (Gulliver's Travels,) 1939	50	75	100
Soupy Sales doll, 1965, Sunshine Doll Co., 5" high	90	135	180
Soupy Sales Marionette, Knickerbocker, 1966	37	56	75

	C6	C8	C10
Stan Laurel Bendem Doll, 1960, Knickerbocker, 9" high	22	33	45
Stan Laurel Doll, Dean	400	600	800
Stan Laurel Hand Puppet, Knickerbocker	24	36	48
Stan Laurel wind-up, Lakeside, 5" high, 1960s	35	52	70
Star Trek, Mr. Spock Vulcan Ears, 1976	7	11	15
Sylvester Hand Puppet, early 1950s	50	75	100
Sylvester, 1971, 15" high, cloth	30	45	60
Sylvester Soaky	16	24	32
Tales of the Texas Rangers Deputy Badge	12	18	24
Tarzan Bendy, Mego, 1972	25	38	50
Tennessee Tuxedo Soaky	17	26	35
Theodore (Chipmunk) Soaky	10	15	20
Three Stooges Hand Puppet, 1959, 9-1/2" high, Moe, Curley, and Larry, price per each	90	135	180
Three Stooges as part of Jolly Theatre, 1930s	125	188	250
Tim Holt Litho Target with Dart Gun	70	105	140
Tinman Facemask (Wizard of Oz) molded gauze	60	90	120
Tom Corbett Space Academy Set, Marx No. 7000	238	355	475

Tom Corbett "Space Academy Set," Marx. Photo by Don Hultzman.

	C6	C8	C10
Tom Corbett, 7 different figures, same as above, price per set	28	42	56
Tom Corbett Cosmic Vision Space Helmet, one-way vision, plastic, early 1950s	207	310	415
Tom Corbett Space Cadet Molding and Coloring Set, Model Craft (All Tom Corbett toys 1950-55)	55	82	110
Tom Corbett Space Cadet Field Glasses, 3 power, Herald, 5-1/2" long	60	90	120
Tom Corbett Space Cadet Flashlight with built-in signal siren, 7" long, metal, U.S. Alite Corp	90	135	180

Tom Corbett Space Cadet Flashlight with built-in signal siren. Photo by Gary J. Linden.

"Tom Mix Circus Wild West" by Arcade. The wagon is wood.

	C6	C8	C10
Tom Mix Rocking Horse, wooden 1930s	175	263	350
Tom Mix Rodeo Rope, 1928, comes with box and instructions	100	150	200
Tonto (Lone Ranger) 20" high doll, 1938, very realistic, composition head, hands, feet, Dollcraft	500	750	1000
Tonto Hand Puppet, mid 1950s, vinyl head	48	72	95
Tonto Hand Puppet, Ideal, 1966	21	31	42
Topo Gigio (Ed Sullivan Show) Nodder	75	112	150
Topo Gigio Airplane, friction	75	112	150
Umbriago (Jimmy Durante) Hand Puppet, 1945, American Merchandise	45	68	90
Uncle Fester Hand Puppet, vinyl, 1960s	65	98	130
Underdog, small	40	60	80
Underdog, medium	50	75	100

	C6	C8	C10
Tom Corbett Official Outfit, Yankiboy	92	138	185
Tom Corbett "Polaris" Rocket Ship, wind-up Marx, 1952, 12" long, Tom, Astro and Rogers looking out of cockpit	300	450	600

Tom Corbett "Polaris" Rocket Ship. Photo by Don Hultzman.

Tom Corbett Space Hat, Lee	40	60	80
Tom Corbett Space Cadet Official Space Pistol, Marx No. 105	180	270	360
Tom Corbett Space Cadet Rifle, Marx No.0239	140	210	280
Tom Corbett Space Station	325	490	650
Tom Corbett Space Cadet, 2-Way Space Phone, Zimmerman	80	120	160
Tom Corbett "Tom Corbett Space Cadet Atomic Rifle," Marx, 1950s, 24" long	150	225	300
Tom Corbett "Tom Corbett Space Cadet Official Space Pistol," 1950s, Rockhill, 9-1/2" long	105	158	210
Tom Mix "Circus Wild West," Arcade circus wagon with driver, two horses, 14-1/2" long, c. 1936, wagon is wood (See Animal Drawn, Arcade "Big Six")	550	825	1100
Tom Mix metal and leather spurs, 1934 (not a premium)	150	225	300
Tom Mix on Tony, Arcor Rubber, 1930s	85	128	170

W.C. Fields, 19" high, Effanbee. Courtesy Christie's East.

	C6	C8	C10
Underdog, large	62	93	125
Untouchables Detective Set, Marx, gun, holster, etc.	112	168	225
Untouchables Tommy Gun, 1950s, Marx, 23" long	48	72	96
W.C. Fields, 19" high, Effanbee, movable mouth	425	638	850
Wagon Train Playset, Marx	213	320	425
Waterfront (TV series) "Cheryl Ann" tug, 21", 1950s	100	150	200
Wendy (Casper) Soaky, 10" high	16	24	32
Wild Bill Hickok & Jingles holster set	50	75	100
Wild Bill Hickok Marshal Star Badge with picture of Hickok and Jingles in center	42	63	85
Wile E. Coyote, Dakin, 1970s	12	18	25
Wizard of Oz Masks, set of five, Einson-Freement Co., Inc., 1939, "Par-T-Mask"	138	205	275
Wizard of Oz, Mattel, four-headed hand puppet, c. 1967, talks	105	158	210
Wizard of Oz, Mego, Dorothy & Toto	19	28	38
Wizard of Oz, Mego, General	45	68	90
Wizard of Oz, Mego, Glinda, 8", 1972	19	28	38
Wizard of Oz, Mego, Lion, 1972, 15" long	15	22	30
Wizard of Oz, Mego, Mayor Munchkin	45	68	90
Wizard of Oz, Mego, Munchkins (4), per each	48	72	95
Wizard of Oz, Mego, Scarecrow, 1972, 8" high	14	21	28
Wizard of Oz, Mego, Tinman, 8" high, 1972	15	22	30
Wizard of Oz, Mego, Wicked Witch, 8", 1972	20	30	40
Wizard of Oz, Mego, Wizard, 8"	8	12	17
Wizard of Oz, Mego, Emerald City Playset	80	120	160
Wizard of Oz Munchkinland Playset	65	98	130
Wizard of Oz, Witch's Castle, Mego	175	262	350
Wolfman Soaky	60	90	120
Wyatt Earp Playset, Marx	275	415	550
Wyatt Earp U.S. Marshall Badge, Lone Star	18	27	36
Wyatt Earp U.S. Marshall Badge, 20th century, 1950s, Hugh O'Brian photo	14	21	28
Wyatt Earp U.S. Marshall's Outfit, Pla-Master	80	120	160
Yellow Submarine (Beatles), Corgi	180	270	360
Yogi Bear, 7-1/2" high, stuffed, 1973, Knickerbocker	45	68	90
Yogi Bear Friction Car, Marx, 1962	100	150	200
Yogi Bear Go-Cart, Linemar	138	205	275
Yogi Bear Hand Puppet, 1959	12	18	24
Yogi Bear "Jellystone National Park" Marx playset	350	525	700
Yogi Bear Tricky Trapeze, 1967, 5" high	17	25	34
Yogi Bear "Yogi Bear Car," 1962, Marx (Japan), 4" long	100	150	200
Yogi Bear "Yogi Bear Hopper," 1962, Linemar, 4" high, wind-up	300	450	600
Yosemite Sam, Dakin Squeak Toy, 1970, 4" high	16	24	33

DISNEY

(See also Paper, Premiums, Fisher-Price)

The average mint price of Disney toys in the last edition was $663.41. In this edition it is $591.11, a decrease of 13%.

WALT'S WONDERFUL WORLD

Walt Disney was involved in animation as early as 1920, but his first truly notable character was Oswald the Rabbit, introduced in 1927. Disney did not own the rights to Oswald, however, and they eventually fell into the hands of another animator, Walter Lantz.

Although Mickey Mouse first appeared in the 1928 short "Plane Crazy," the third Mickey cartoon, "Steamboat Willie," seems to have been the first released (on No-

vember 18, 1928). Mickey was a success from then on. Minnie Mouse also appeared in "Steamboat Willie," and Pluto emerged in 1930 but was not known by that name until 1931. Goofy debuted in 1932 and Donald Duck came along in 1934. Mickey Mouse toys were first produced in 1930 and since then the stream of Disneyana (apparently all of it deemed collectible) has been endless.

	C6	C8	C10
Alice in Wonderland Marionette, Peter Puppet	85	128	170
Babes In Toyland, tin litho wind-up, Indian on rollerskates, Linemar, 1950s, 6-1/2" tall	100	150	200

"Babes In Toyland Soldier," 1950s, Linemar. Photo by Scott Smiles.

	C6	C8	C10
"Babes In Toyland Soldier," 1950s, Linemar, 6-1/2" tall, tin wind-up	175	263	350
Babes In Toyland Wood Officer on horseback, wheeled, Jaymar	175	263	350
Babes In Toyland Wood Soldier with cannon, Jaymar	210	315	420
Babes In Toyland Wood Soldier with rifle, Jaymar, 9" high	60	90	120
Bambi "Jumping Bambi," Linemar, 1950s, trigger action, 6" high	250	375	500
Bambi Soaky	15	22	30
Bashful 1-1/2" lead figure, Britains	40	60	80
Bashful, 5-3/4" high, Seiberling Rubber	90	135	180
Bashful, approx. 7" high, Ideal	125	188	250
Bashful, approx. 12" high, 1938, Ideal	80	120	160
Bashful Party Mask, 1937	20	30	40
Bashful Stuffed Doll	60	90	120
"Big Bad Wolf and The Three Little Pigs," 1950s, Linemar, 4-1/4" tall, 4-piece set	750	1125	1500
Big Bad Wolf Halloween costume, 4' high	60	90	120
Big Bad Wolf celluloid pinback, 1-1/4"	38	53	75
Big Bad Wolf stuffed toy in tux, with carnation, glass eyes, 20" tall	450	675	900
Captain Hook Hand Puppet, Gund, 1950	17	26	35
Captain Hook Marionette, Peter Puppet Playthings	95	143	190
"Casey Jr. Disneyland Express," loco, 3 cars, tin & plastic, Marx	73	110	145

	C6	C8	C10
Cinderella Handcar, Jaq & Gus, 8" long 383	575	775
Cinderella Hand Puppet, "1957" 22	33	45
Cinderella Soaky, 1960s, arms move 15	22	30
Cinderella, wind-up, 4-3/4" high, Irwin, umbrella, spins and dances 62	93	125
Cinderella and Prince Dancing, No. 7000, Irwin Co., 1950s, plastic wind-up, 5" high 65	98	130
Cleo Facemask, (Pinocchio), Gillette, 1939 20	30	40
Cleo The Goldfish (Pinocchio), Sun Rubber, squeeze toy 23	35	47
Davy Crockett Alamo Playset, Marx 250	375	500
Davy Crockett Auto-Magic Picture Gun 42	63	85
Davy Crockett Badge, 1950s, "Frontier Marshal" 27	41	55
Davy Crockett Coonskin Hat 22	33	45
Davy Crockett Doll, 8" high, Fortune Toy, 1950s 60	90	120
Davy Crockett Doll, 20" high, Gund, vinyl 60	90	120
Davy Crockett Flying Arrows, balsa wood figures to be made into flying arrows. Copyright 1955 25	38	50
Davy Crockett "Frontierland Davy Crockett Outfit," gun, coonskin hat, etc. 70	105	140
Davy Crockett Handgun, pop-action, tin litho, 1950s 40	60	80
Davy Crockett Play Knife, 1950s 22	33	44
Davy Crockett Playset 275	412	550
Davy Crockett Powder Horn, Daisy 20	30	40

Disneyland Ferris Wheel. Courtesy HAKE'S Americana & Collectibles.

	C6	C8	C10
"Disneyland Happy Birthday Carousel," 1950s, Ross Co., 6" high 80	120	160
"Disneyland Jeep," 1960s, Marx, 10" long, push toy 100	150	200
"Disneyland Melody Player," 1950s, Chein, 7" cubic, 4 rolls 95	142	190

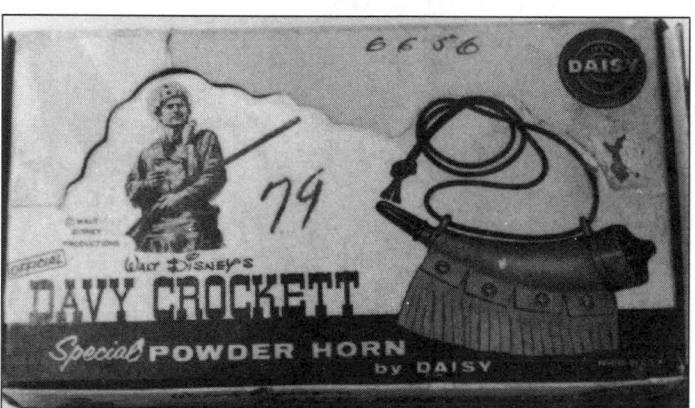

Davy Crockett Powder Horn, Daisy. Courtesy Toy Collector News.

	C6	C8	C10
Davy Crockett Prairie Wagon, 5" long 26	39	52
"Davy Crockett Wagon Train," 1950s, Marx (plastic) 14" long 150	225	300
Disney Showboat, 1960, large 62	93	125
"Disney Show Boat," 1981 Playworld Toys, plastic 4	6	8
Disneyland Concert Xylophone, Tudor, 18" long 30	45	60
Disney Ferris Wheel, c. late 1956, Chein, tin wind-up, 17" high 350	525	700
Disneykins, Marx, set 105	158	210

Disneykins Display. Photo by Ron Chojnacki. Courtesy Don Hultzman.

Disneyland Happy Birthday Carousel. Courtesy Continental Hobby House.

	C6	C8	C10
"Disneyland Melody Player," extra paper rolls, different songs, 1950s, for Melody Player, each	10	15	20
Disneyland Playset, Marx	425	638	850
Disneyland Roller Coaster, Chein, 10" high, 2 tin cars, 1950s	250	375	500

Disneyland Roller Coaster, Chein. Courtesy Continental Hobby House.

	C6	C8	C10
Doc, 1-1/2" lead figure, Britains	60	90	120
Doc (Snow White), approx. 7" high, Ideal	125	188	250
Doc, 9" composition with velvet clothes, Knickerbocker	100	150	200
Doc, 11-1/2" high, stuffed molded oilcloth face, Ideal	82	123	165
Doc Party Mask, 1937	14	21	28
Doc Seiberling Rubber, 1938	50	75	100
Donald Duck, 3-1/2" high, celluloid walker, Japan wind-up	400	600	800
Donald Duck, 4" high tin wind-up, Linemar, with umbrella	300	450	600

	C6	C8	C10
"Donald Duck," 5" high, 1930s, long-billed celluloid, Borgfeldt (Japan)	262	395	525
Donald Duck, 6" high, 1930s, long-billed, celluloid wind-up	700	1100	1500
"Donald Duck," 6" high, 1950s, Linemar squeeze action	140	210	280
"Donald Duck," 6" high, Schuco, wind-up, German, "984"	158	235	315
Donald Duck 6" high, Seiberling Rubber, long-billed, 1930s	150	225	300

Donald Duck, 6" high, Sieberling, rubber long-billed. Courtesy HAKE'S Americana & Collectibles.

	C6	C8	C10
"Donald Duck" 7" high, 1960s, Marx, wind-up, hard plastic	30	45	60
Donald Duck, 9" high, composition and cloth, long-billed, in Russian costume	1000	1500	2000
Donald Duck, 9" high, 1930s, long-billed, composition, Knickerbocker	250	375	500
Donald Duck, 10" high, Sun Rubber	21	32	42
Donald Duck, 13" high, stuffed doll, long-billed, Knickerbocker, 1930s	150	225	300
Donald Duck, 13" high, celluloid, 1940s	135	198	270
Donald Duck, 13-1/2" high, Gund, c. 1949	110	165	220
Donald Duck, 13-1/2" high, Character Novelty, 1940	110	165	220
Donald Duck, 16" high, long-billed, 1930s	75	112	150
Donald Duck Acrobat, Linemar, 1950s, 8-1/2" high	325	490	650
"Donald Duck and His Nephews," 1950s, Marx, 11" long-plastic wind-up	225	338	450
"Donald Duck and Huey With Voice," 1950s, Linemar, 7" long (string pull toy)	500	750	1000

Donald Duck, 9" high, composition and cloth, long billed, in Russian costume. Courtesy Christie's East.

Donald Duck Climbing Fireman. Photo by Don Hultzman.

	C6	C8	C10
Donald Duck Captain, Kohner push puppet, 1950s, wood and plastic	100	150	200
Donald Duck "Choo Choo" No. 450: See Fisher-Price			
"Donald Duck Climbing Fireman," 1950s, Linemar, 13-1/2", wind-up	300	450	600
"Donald Duck Convertible," 1950s, Linemar, 5" long, tin, friction	263	395	525
Donald Duck Crawler, celluloid wind-up, 9-3/4" long	650	1100	1500
Donald Duck Delivery Tricycle, tin and plastic, 5", Marx	450	675	900
"Donald Duck Dipsy Car," 1950s, 5-1/4" long, Marx, tin car, (plastic Mickey or Donald)	385	575	770
Donald Duck "Dipsy Car - Donald Duck," 1950s, Linemar, wind-up, 6" long	450	675	900

	C6	C8	C10
"Donald Duck Disney Flivver," 1950s, Linemar, 5-1/2" long, push down on head	300	450	600
Donald Duck Doctor Kit	60	90	120
Donald Duck "Donald & His Nephew" 1950s, Linemar, pull-string action, 5-1/2" high	400	600	800
Donald Duck "Donald the Driver" 1950s Linemar, friction car, 6-1/2" long	225	338	450
Donald Duck "Donald the Drummer," 1950s, Marx, wind-up, 9" tall	275	363	550
Donald Duck "Donald Race Car," celluloid wind-up, occupied Japan	225	338	450
"Donald Duck Drummer," 1950s, Linemar, wind-up, 6" high, walker	265	400	530

Donald Duck Dipsy Car. Photo by Don Hultzman.

Donald Duck and his Nephews. Photo by Don Hultzman.

Donald Duck on Rocking Horse. Courtesy James S. Maxwell/Virginia Caputo. Photo by Virginia Caputo.

	C6	C8	C10
"Donald Duck Drummer," 1950s, Linemar, wind-up, 6" high, rocker	250	375	500
Donald Duck Duet, small Donald, large Goofy, c. 1945, Marx, tin wind-up	440	660	880

Donald Duck Duet. Courtesy Mapes Auctioneers & Appraisers.

	C6	C8	C10
"Donald Duck on Trapeze," 1930s, Borgfeldt, 9" high - Donald 4-3/4" long	275	362	550
Donald Duck pulled by Pluto, celluloid, with tin cart, Japan, 1930s, long-billed	1750	2625	3500
Donald Duck pull toy, baton-twirler, No. 400: See Fisher-Price			
Donald Duck pull toy, No. 765, plastic feet, 1950s: See Fisher-Price			
Donald Duck pull toy, 6-1/2" long, long-billed, on platform: See Fisher-Price			
Donald Duck pull toy, No. 400, 1940. 10" tall, 7-1/2" long, wooden figure with moveable arms and legs, composition head: See Fisher-Price			
Donald Duck pull toy, wagon, c. 1940, No. 544: See Fisher-Price			
Donald Duck pull toy, with xylophone, c. 1938, No. 185: See Fisher-Price			
"Donald Duck Railroad Car" with Pluto, doghouse, 10" long, Lionel No. 1107, 1930s	413	625	825
Donald Duck riding Mule, long-billed celluloid wind-up, 7-3/4"	850	1275	1700
Donald Duck Roly Poly, 3-3/4", 1940s	187	280	375

	C6	C8	C10
"Donald Duck Dump Truck," 1950s, Linemar, 5" long	300	450	600
Donald Duck Fire Chief Crazy Car, Linemar, wind-up, tin litho, rubber hat, extremely rare	700	1250	1700
"Donald Duck In His Convertible," 1950s, Linemar, friction, 6" long	275	415	550
Donald Duck Jigger, 11" high, papier mache wind-up	800	1200	1600
Donald Duck Mousketeers hat	15	22	30
Donald Duck on Paddle, string-puller, long-billed: See Fisher-Price			
Donald Duck on Pluto, celluloid wind-up	1400	2200	3200
Donald Duck on Rocking Horse, Japan, celluloid tin, wind-up, 3-3/8" long	3000	4500	6000
"Donald Duck on Tractor," 1950s, Marx, friction, 3-1/2" long, plastic	120	180	240

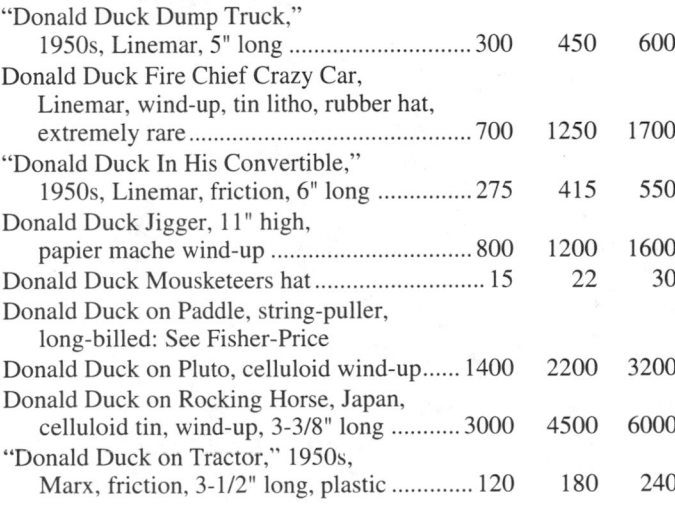

Donald Duck Railroad Car. Courtesy Christie's East.

Donald Duck Rowboat, Chad Valley. Courtesy Christie's East.

Donald Duck and Pluto in Roadster, Sun Rubber. Photo by David Leopard.

	C6	C8	C10
Donald Duck Rowboat, Chad Valley (England), wood and paper litho, 12-1/4" long	300	450	600
Donald Duck Rubber Boat, Sun Rubber Co., c. 1940s	40	60	80
Donald Duck Skier, Linemar	300	450	600
Donald Duck Skier, Marx, 1940s, plastic Donald	375	565	750
Donald Duck Soaky	11	16	23
"Donald Duck Straight Shooter," 1960s, plastic wind-up, 6-1/2" high	187	280	375
Donald Duck Swimmer, celluloid wind-up, 6-1/2"	650	1000	1500
Donald Duck Teapot, Ohio Art	30	45	60
Donald Duck Tractor, Sun Rubber	112	188	225
Donald Duck Tricycle, 3-1/2" long, Linemar, wind-up, 1950s	285	430	570
"Donald Duck Tricycle," (with twirling parasol), 1950s, MT Co., Japan, 7-1/2" high	200	300	400
"Donald Duck Waddler," 1930s, "K" Co., Japan, long-billed, tin and celluloid, 3-1/4" high	600	900	1200
"Donald Duck Waddler," 1930s, "K" Co., 3-1/2" tall	600	900	1200
"Donald Duck Washing Machine," 1950s, MT Co., Japan, 7-1/2" high	400	600	800
"Donald Duck with Whirling Tail," 1950s, Linemar, tin wind-up, 5-1/4" high	300	450	600
"Donald Duck with Whirling Tail," 1950s, Marx, plastic wind-up, 6-1/2" high	92	135	185
Donald Duck Zylophone, Tudor, 10" long	55	83	110

	C6	C8	C10
Donald Duck and Pluto in Roadster, Sun Rubber, 1930s, about 6-1/2" long	80	120	160
Donkey (Pinocchio), Knickerbocker, stuffed	95	142	190
Donkey (Pinocchio), rubber, Seiberling, 1940	70	105	140

Donkey (Pinocchio) rubber, 4" high. Courtesy HAKE'S Americana & Collectibles.

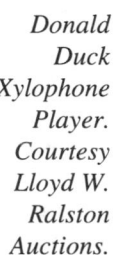

Donald Duck Xylophone Player. Courtesy Lloyd W. Ralston Auctions.

Dopey tin wind-up, Marx. Courtesy PB Eighty-Four, New York.

	C6	C8	C10
Dopey 1-1/2" lead figure, Britains	40	60	80
Dopey, approx. 7" high, Ideal	125	188	250
Dopey Doll, 9" high, composition with velvet clothes, Knickerbocker	175	263	350
Dopey, 10" high, rubber squeeze toy, 1950s	10	15	20
Dopey, approx. 12" high, Ideal, 1938	150	225	300
Dopey, Doc pull toy, 14" long	200	300	400
Dopey Doll, Madame Alexander, 1938	150	225	300
Dopey Hand Puppet, composition, 1938, Crown Toys, bell, buckling belt	90	135	180

	C6	C8	C10
Dopey Hand Puppet, Gund, 1950s	12	18	25
Dopey Marionette, c. 1952, Peter Puppet Playthings	80	120	160
Dopey Party Mask, 1937	20	30	40
Dopey Soaky	17	25	34
Dopey tin wind-up, Marx, 1938	263	395	525
Dumbo 9" vinyl squeeze doll, 1960s	22	33	45
Dumbo Hand Puppet, Gund, c. 1955, 10"	25	38	50
Dumbo tin wind-up, Marx, Dumbo flips over, 1941, 4" high	300	450	600

Ferdinand the Bull, copyright 1938, Marx. Photo by Don Hultzman.

	C6	C8	C10
Ferdinand The Bull, Linemar	130	195	260
Ferdinand The Bull, copyright 1938, Marx, tail whirls, body shakes, wind-up	212	320	425
Ferdinand The Bull, hand puppet, 1938, Crown	55	82	110
Ferdinand The Bull pull toy, Hill, 8-3/4" long	170	255	340
Ferdinand The Bull, late 1930s, Seiberling Latex Products, hard rubber, 6" long, 3-1/2" high	102	153	205
Ferdinand The Bull, jointed, wood, 9"	125	188	250
Ferdinand and Matador, 1938, Marx, tin wind-up	600	900	1200

Dumbo tin wind-up, Marx. Dumbo flips over. Photo by Don Hultzman.

	C6	C8	C10
Eeyore vinyl squeeze doll, 1960s	37	56	75
Elmer Elephant 5" celluloid and string figure, 1930s	120	180	240
Elmer Elephant pull toy, 1936: See Fisher-Price			
Elmer Elephant, rubber, Seiberling, head moves	162	243	325

Ferdinand & Matador. Photo by Don Hultzman.

Elmer Elephant, rubber, Seiberling. Head moves. Courtesy HAKE'S Americana & Collectibles.

	C6	C8	C10
"Figaro," 1950s, Linemar, tin friction toy, 3" long	70	105	140
Figaro (Pinocchio) paper mask, 1939, Gillette	25	38	50
Figaro tin wind-up, Marx, 1940, 4-3/4" long	105	158	210
"Flower," 1950s, Linemar, 3" long friction, tin	115	172	230
Frontierland Logs, No. 915, Halsam	45	68	90
Gepetto facemask (Pinocchio), Gillette, 1939	22	33	45
Gepetto 5-1/2" wood figure holding his chin, Multi Products, 1940	70	105	140
Goofy, 5 1/4" high tin wind-up, Linemar	200	300	400
Goofy "Goofy the Walking Gardener," Marx, tin wind-up	482	625	965

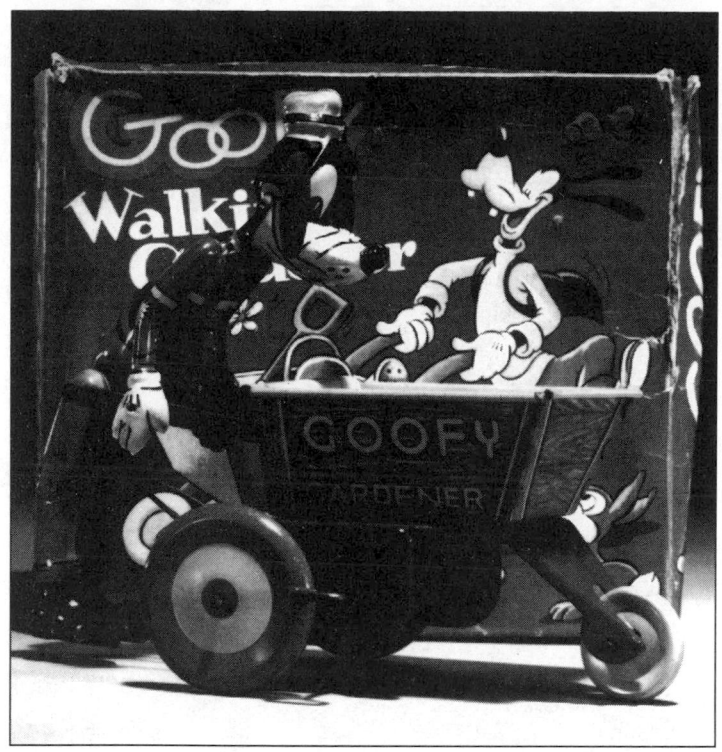

"Goofy the Walking Gardener." Courtesy Christie's East.

	C6	C8	C10
Happy Party Mask, 1937 40	60	80
Happy rubber squeeze toy, 1950s.......................10	15	20
Happy, approx. 12" high, Ideal, 1938 110	165	220
Horace Horsecollar Hand Puppet, Gund, c. 1960.....................................17	25	34
"Huey - Louie - Dewey Locomotive," 1950s, Marx, friction, 3-1/2" long, plastic....50	75	100
"Jiminy Cricket," 6" high, 1950s Linemar squeeze cable hopper....................200	300	400
Jiminy Cricket, 9" high, wood jointed, Ideal, 1940 225	368	450
Jiminy Cricket, 10" high, Knickerbocker, c. 1940..........................300	450	600
Jiminy Cricket, 12" approx. rubber head, wooden feet, cloth body, Gund.....................22	33	45
Jiminy Cricket, 13" high, latex head, hands and feet, cloth body 60	90	120
Jiminy Cricket, 14" high, Crown Toy, felt and cloth 150	225	300
Jiminy Cricket, 15-1/2" high, Crown Toy, felt and cloth 150	225	300
Jiminy Cricket Facemask (Pinocchio) 1939 from Gillette.................................25	38	50
Jiminy Cricket Hand Puppet, vinyl and cloth, Gund 32	48	65
Jiminy Cricket, Linemar, tin litho wind-up, 1950s, 5-1/2" tall............300	450	600

Jiminy Cricket, tin litho wind-up, Linemar. Photo by Don Hultzman

Ludwig Von Drake, litho tin wind-up, Linemar. Photo by Don Hultzman.

	C6	C8	C10
Goofy on a Unicycle, tin wind-up, 5-1/2" high, Linemar 500	750	1000
Goofy Soaky...20	30	40
Goofy, 1930, tin figure......................................400	600	800
"Goofy Tricycle," 1950s, Linemar, 4" tall 650	975	1300
"Goofy With Whirling Tail," 1950s, Linemar, 5" tall 300	450	600
"Goofy with Whirling Tail," 1950s Marx, plastic wind-up, 8" high 92	140	185
"Goofy's Disneyland Stock Car," 1950s, Linemar, 6" long 200	300	400
"Goofy's Stock Car," Linemar, 1950s, 6" long 200	300	400
Grumpy lead figure, 1-1/2" high, Britains 40	60	80
Grumpy, approx. 7" high, Ideal........................140	210	280
Grumpy 9" high, composition, velvet clothes, Knickerbocker 100	150	200
Grumpy Doll, stuffed, oilcloth face, velvet pants, 11" high, 1938 80	120	160
Grumpy, 11-1/2" high, stuffed, molded oilcloth face, Ideal 90	135	180
Grumpy, Ideal, approx. 12" high, 1938............125	188	250
Grumpy Par-T Mask, 1937 7	11	15
Grumpy rubber squeeze toy, 1950s....................10	15	20
"Gym Toys Acrobats," 1950s Linemar, 8-1/2" high (Mickey, Donald, Minnie, etc.), each.........200	300	400
Happy 1-1/2" lead figure, Britains 30	45	60
Happy 3-1/4" high, Seiberling Rubber, 1938..............................60	90	120
Happy, approx. 7" high Ideal 130	195	260
Happy Marionette, Madame Alexander, 9-1/2" high, 1938 110	155	220

	C6	C8	C10
Jiminy Cricket Pushing Bass Fiddle, Marx, walkie 15	22	30
Jiminy Cricket Soaky 10	15	20
Johnny Tremain Flintlock cap pistol, Marx 60	90	120
Jungle Book Dancing Bear, Marx, plastic wind-up..................................80	120	160
Ludwig Von Drake, 7" rubber squeeze toy, c. 1960, Dell.............58	90	115

	C6	C8	C10
Ludwig Von Drake, litho tin wind-up, Linemar, 1950s, 6" tall	290	435	580
Ludwig Von Drake talking doll	50	75	100
Ludwig Von Drake Go-Cart, friction, Marx, 1961	158	235	315
Mad Hatter Puppet (Alice in Wonderland)	85	130	170
Mad Hatter, Gund	200	300	400
Mad Hatter's Taxi, Linemar, 5" long, 1950s	300	450	600
Mickey Mouse, first toy made by Borgfeldt of NY, 1930, wooden Mickey with jointed hands, arms, legs and wire tail, leather ears. "Copyright 1928-1930 by Walter E. Disney"	550	825	1100
Mickey Mouse larger-size squeeze toy with clothes, 1950, Sun Rubber	30	45	60
Mickey Mouse with red shirt and yellow pants, squeeze toy, Sun Rubber, 1950	34	51	68
Mickey Mouse, 3-1/2" high, Seiberling Rubber, 1930s	90	135	180
Mickey Mouse, 3-1/2" high, 1930s, Fun-E-Flex	150	225	300
Mickey Mouse, 5" high celluloid, "fat head"	150	225	300
Mickey Mouse, 5" high, wood doll, Fun-E-Flex, leather ears	250	375	500

Mickey Mouse, 7" high, wood-jointed, early, Borgfeldt. Courtesy HAKE'S Americana & Collectibles.

	C6	C8	C10
Mickey Mouse, 9-1/2" high, "Dell," rubber	50	75	100
Mickey Mouse, 10" high, Sun Rubber, 1940s	30	45	60
Mickey Mouse, 11" high, cloth "Walt Disney Mickey Mouse Geo. E. Borgfeldt & Company New York" on bottom of one foot	337	505	675

Mickey Mouse, 5" high wood doll, Fun-E-Flex leather ears. Courtesy HAKE'S Americana & Collectibles.

Mickey Mouse, 11" high, cloth, "Walt Disney Mickey Mouse Geo. E. Borgfeldt & Company, New York" on bottom of one foot. Courtesy HAKE'S Americana & Collectibles.

	C6	C8	C10
Mickey Mouse, 5-1/2" high, vibrates, Linemar, tin wind-up, 1950s	300	450	600
Mickey Mouse, 6" high, rubber, c. 1935, Seiberling	168	250	335
Mickey Mouse, 7" high, wood jointed, early, Borgfeldt	300	450	600
"Mickey Mouse," 7" high, 1960s, Marx, wind-up, hard plastic	130	195	260
Mickey Mouse, 7-1/2" high, wood, Fun-E-Flex	325	490	650
Mickey Mouse, 8" high, Sun Rubber	65	98	130
Mickey Mouse, 8" high, wooden, jointed arms and legs, c. 1933	600	900	1200

	C6	C8	C10
Mickey Mouse, 12" high, 1930s, Knickerbocker	325	488	650
Mickey Mouse, 12" high felt doll, early 1930s, Steiff	600	950	1280
Mickey Mouse, 12" high Bandleader, Knickerbocker, 1935	650	1100	1500
Mickey Mouse, 12" high, Borgfeldt	625	938	1250
Mickey Mouse, 12" high, "Cowboy Mickey," Knickerbocker, 1936	2000	4000	6200
Mickey Mouse, 13-3/4" high, stuffed, early (Dean Rag?)	400	600	800

Mickey Mouse Felt Doll, Steiff, 12" high. Courtesy Lloyd W. Ralston Auctions.

Mickey Mouse, 13-3/4" high, stuffed. Courtesy James S. Maxwell/Virginia Caputo. Photo by Virginia Caputo.

	C6	C8	C10
Mickey Mouse 14" high, Mickey the Bandleader, stuffed, Knickerbocker	650	1000	1500
Mickey Mouse, 16" high, stuffed, 1930s	700	1100	1760
Mickey Mouse, 17", rubber, Lakeside Mfg. Co.	80	120	160
Mickey Mouse, 18" high, felt, Character Co., c. 1939-40	70	105	140

Mickey Mouse, 14" high, Mickey the Bandleader. Photo by Ron Chojnacki. Courtesy Don Hultzman.

Mickey Mouse. Left to right: 18" high, 16" high, both stuffed. Courtesy Sotheby's New York.

Mickey Mouse, 19-1/2" high, c. 1935, Knickerbocker. Courtesy Christie's East.

	C6	C8	C10
Mickey Mouse, 19-1/2" high, c. 1935, Knickerbocker, in cowboy outfit	1400	2100	2800
Mickey Mouse, 21" high, c. 1933	350	525	700
Mickey Mouse, 31" high, all felt dressed, opening in back for storing things, black jacket with yellow buttons, red pants, bells on toes of yellow shoes, 1950s	120	180	240
Mickey Mouse, 1950s, Linemar, tin friction toy, 3" long	70	105	140
Mickey Mouse, 1930s, 4" long, pie-eyed tumbler, Schuco	150	225	300
Mickey Mouse, Acrobat, clockwork trapeze, celluloid Mickey, 1930s, Japan, 9" high	243	365	485

Mickey Mouse Acrobat (1930s, Japan). Courtesy PB Eighty-Four, New York.

	C6	C8	C10
"Mickey Mouse Acrobat," 1950s, Linemar (Gym Toys), 9" high, Mickey 6" long	235	352	470
Mickey Mouse Acrobat, wood, Strombecker, 1950s	45	68	90
Mickey Mouse Airmail, rubber, "Mickey's Airmail"	77	115	155

	C6	C8	C10
Mickey Mouse and Donald on Boat, celluloid	1050	1650	2300
Mickey Mouse and Donald on Back of Alligator, Marx, 1950s, plastic walker	60	90	120
Mickey Mouse and Donald Handcar, wind-up, plastic, 1948, Marx	200	300	400

"Mickey Mouse and Donald Duck Handcar." Photo by Don Hultzman.

	C6	C8	C10
Mickey Mouse and Donald in Fire Truck, late 1930s, Sun Rubber, 6-1/2" long	75	112	150
Mickey Mouse and Minnie Mouse Tea Set, c. 1935, 13 pieces	140	210	280
Mickey Mouse and Minnie Mouse Swing Toy, celluloid with red and green flag, 11-1/2" tall	420	630	840
Mickey Mouse Bank, cast iron, 9" high, France, "Depose," auctioned for $880 and $9504 in late 1990 Same as above, aluminum, also France	550	850	1300

Mickey Mouse Bank, cast-iron, 9" high, French-made. Courtesy James S. Maxwell/ Virginia Caputo. Photo by Virginia Caputo.

	C6	C8	C10
Mickey Mouse banjo, 1930s, 17" long............ 140	210	280
Mickey Mouse beverages felt soda jerk hat, shows Mickey from shoulders up saying "have one on me," 5" x 11", c. 1930 60	90	120
Mickey Mouse Boat, 13"................................ 150	205	300

Mickey Mouse Boat. Courtesy Continental Hobby House.

	C6	C8	C10
Mickey Mouse Bubble Buster Gun, metal Mickey standing at gun sight, cast iron, Kilgore, 6" long 75	112	150
"Mickey Mouse Bus Lines - Walt Disney Stars," gong bell, c. 1960, 19-1/2" long, riding toy 150	225	300

"Mickey Mouse Bus Lines Walt Disney Stars." Courtesy Wilkinson Collection, Detroit Antique Toy Museum.

Mickey Mouse Circus Train Set. Courtesy PB Eighty-Four, New York.

Mickey Mouse, celluloid, on wood hobby horse. Courtesy Christie's East.

Mickey Mouse Circus. Courtesy PB Eighty-Four, New York.

	C6	C8	C10
Mickey Mouse Cardboard Mask, c. 1935 60	90	120
Mickey Mouse, celluloid on wood hobby horse, 4-1/2", c. 1935 1050	1700	2300
Mickey Mouse Circus, Geo. Borgfeldt 6/3785, 1931, two wood figures revolving on swinging mechanism, 11" long 500	850	1200
Mickey Mouse Circus Train Set, Lionel No. 1536, engine, tender, containing Mickey, three carriage cars, dining car, Mickey Mouse Circus, Mickey Mouse Band, composition Mickey and track 1300	2200	3500
Mickey Mouse Circus Train, Mickey shoveling tender, three Disney Circus cars, wind-up train, red, c. 1931 900	1550	2200
Mickey Mouse Clicker, tin litho, c. 1930, Mickey showing teeth while playing violin 90	135	180
Mickey Mouse, "Climbing Mickey Mouse," 1930s, Dolly Toy Co., cardboard, 8" long..................................... 325	490	650
Mickey Mouse Club Auto-Magic Picture Gun, 1946, projects films 35	52	70
Mickey Mouse Club Newsreel Projector 68	102	135

Mickey Mouse "Climbing Mickey Mouse," Dolly Toy Company. Courtesy Phillips New York.

	C6	C8	C10
"Mickey Mouse Dipsy Car," 1950s, 5-1/4" long, Marx, tin car, plastic Mickey	318	475	635
"Mickey Mouse Dipsy Car," 1950s, Linemar, 5-1/4" long, all tin	300	450	600

Mickey Mouse Express. Photo by Don Hultzman.

Mickey Mouse Dipsy Car, Marx. Photo by Don Hultzman.

	C6	C8	C10
"Mickey Mouse Express," 1950s, Marx, 9" diameter (Mickey in airplane)	425	638	850
Mickey Mouse Express, tin litho train set, 14" long, base 21" x 13", Marx, 1950s	700	1100	1700
Mickey Mouse Handcar, green base	550	850	1300
Mickey Mouse Handcar, red base	700	1350	1850
"Mickey Mouse Handcar," 1930s, Lionel Co., 7" long with Minnie, orange housing	650	1100	1700

	C6	C8	C10
Mickey Mouse Drum, Ohio Art, 6" diameter, tin	130	195	260
Mickey Mouse Drum Set, tin and cardboard, c. 1940, Minnie watching while Mickey juggles	240	360	480
Mickey Mouse Drummer, Kohner push puppet, 1950s	100	150	200
Mickey Mouse Explorer's Outfit	62	93	125

Mickey Mouse Drum, Ohio Art, 6" diameter, tin. Courtesy HAKE'S Americana & Collectibles.

Mickey Mouse Hand Car. Courtesy PB Eighty-Four, New York.

	C6	C8	C10
Mickey Mouse Hingees, 1944	25	38	50
Mickey Mouse Holding Flag, cast iron, 1930s	140	210	280
Mickey Mouse Hurdy Gurdy, auctioned in 1993 with reattached arm, possible repaint, for $18,700			
Mickey Mouse Jazz Drummer, finger-activated tin toy, Nifty, 4-3/4" high	1500	2700	4100
"Mickey Mouse Jockey," 1935, M-T Co., 4-1/2" long, celluloid Mickey on wooden hobby horse	1200	1800	2400
Mickey Mouse Kaleidoscope, 1950s	32	48	65
Mickey Mouse Knickerbocker doll, 1935, 22" high	500	750	1000
Mickey Mouse, lead, 2-1/2" high, 1933, Allied Toys	70	105	140
Mickey Mouse Marionette, c. 1930, 9-1/2" high, felt body stuffed with cotton	112	158	225
Mickey Mouse Marionette, Peter Puppet Playthings Co., 1952, 14" tall	55	83	110
"Mickey Mouse Meteor Five-Car Train, Walt Disney's" tin litho, Marx, 43" long	800	1000	1500
Mickey Mouse "Mickey-In-The-Box," 7" high jack-in-the-box	260	390	520

Mickey Mouse, "Mickey on Scooter," 1950s, Linemar. Courtesy Christie's East.

	C6	C8	C10
Mickey Mouse "Mickey on Scooter," 1950s, Linemar, 4-1/2" high, all tin, rare	350	525	700
Mickey Mouse "Mickey on Unicycle," 1950s, Linemar, 5" high	650	975	1300
Mickey Mouse "Mickey Race Car," celluloid wind-up, occupied Japan	250	375	500
Mickey Mouse "Mickey the Driver," 1950s, Marx (Japan), 6-1/2" long, friction	400	600	800
Mickey Mouse "Mickey the Magician," Linemar, 10", battery-operated	500	800	1200
Mickey Mouse "Mickey the Musician - I Play the Xylophone," 1950s, Marx, wind-up, 10" high	312	465	625

Mickey Mouse "Mickey-In-The-Box." Courtesy PB Eighty-Four, New York.

Mickey Mouse, "Mickey the Magician." Courtesy Christie's East.

Mickey Mouse, Mickey on Scooter, Linemar. Photo by Don Hultzman.

Mickey's Tractor, Sun Rubber. Photo by Dave Leopard.

Mickey Mouse Racing Car.
Courtesy PB Eighty-Four,
New York.

	C6	C8	C10
Mickey Mouse "Mickey's Delivery," Pluto on Tricycle-Cart, tin litho wind-up, celluloid head on Pluto, Linemar, 1950s, 5-1/2" long 375	375	565	750
Mickey Mouse "Mickey's Mousekemovers" moving van, 13" long, 1950s, Linemar 500	500	750	1025
Mickey Mouse "Mickey's Service Truck," 1950s Marx friction, 3-1/2" long, plastic 50	50	75	100
Mickey Mouse "Mickey's Tractor," Sun Rubber, 1930s, Mickey's head turns, 4-1/2" long 65	65	98	130
"Mickey Mouse Motorcycle," 1950s, Linemar, friction, 3" long 200	200	300	400
"Mickey Mouse Motorcycle," 1950s, Linemar, tin friction, 3-1/2" long 150	150	225	300
"Mickey Mouse Movie Fun Optical Toy," 1950s, Mastercraft, 7" x 7" x 5" 150	150	225	300
Mickey Mouse Movie-Jector, 1935 135	135	200	270
Mickey Mouse Movie Projector No. E-18, Keystone, 1930s, 10" high 125	125	188	250
"Mickey Mouse Newsreel," 1950s, Mattel, 9-1/2" high, includes 3 records and 5 films 110	110	165	225
Mickey Mouse on Handcar, Japan, 8" long, basket on back 138	138	208	275
Mickey Mouse Old Fashioned Sailing Vessel: See Mickey Mouse Pirate Ship			
Mickey Mouse Organ Grinder, Minnie Mouse dancing on organ pushed by much larger Mickey, German 1200	1200	1800	2400
Mickey Mouse Piano, wooden, grand, with decal showing Mickey playing, Minnie listening, c. 1935 200	200	300	400
Mickey Mouse Piano, Marks Bros., c. 1935, 10" 1250	1250	1875	2500
Mickey Mouse Pirate Ship, Ideal 138	138	210	275
Mickey Mouse Pocket Knife, 1935 40	40	60	80
"Mickey Mouse Projector No. E-18" 1930s, Keystone Co., 7" long, 10" high, 9" wide .. 195	195	290	390
Mickey Mouse "Puddle Jumper," No. 310, c. 1950s: See Fisher-Price			
Mickey Mouse Puppet, approx. 10" high, "Gund" 11	11	16	22
Mickey Mouse Puppet, early 40s style, very large composition head, hands and feet, the rest of the body wood, cloth costume, felt ears 175	175	263	350
Mickey Mouse Puppet, Pelham 24" high, rubber legs and arms, wood body 40	40	60	80
Mickey Mouse Push Puppet, Gabriel, 1977 10	10	15	20

	C6	C8	C10
"Mickey Mouse Race Car," 1930s, T.M. Co., 3" long 300	300	450	600
Mickey Mouse Racing Car, red lithographed tin wind-up car with Mickey at the wheel, 4" long, 1930s 400	400	600	800
Mickey Mouse, Rocking Mickey Mouse on Pluto, Linemar 800	800	1400	2000
"Mickey Mouse Rollerskater," 1950s, Linemar, 6" high 450	450	750	1130
Mickey Mouse Roly Poly, celluloid, early, 4" high 187	187	280	375
Mickey Mouse Rower, Fun-E-Flex, wooden, 10-3/4" 1700	1700	2550	3400

Mickey Mouse Rower, Fun-E-Flex. Courtesy Christie's East.

	C6	C8	C10
Mickey Mouse "Running Mickey on Pluto," 1940s, M-T Co., 5-1/2" long, celluloid, occupied Japan 2000	2000	3500	6500
Mickey Mouse "Santa Car with Mickey Mouse and His Gift Pack" handcar, Lionel No. 1105, 1935 900	900	1350	1800
Mickey Mouse Saxophone Player, 1930s 800	800	1300	2000
Mickey Mouse "Scooter Jockey," Mavco Co., 1950s, all plastic, 6" high wind-up 400	400	600	800
Mickey Mouse Slate Dancer, c. 1931, auctioned for $29,150 in 1993			
Mickey Mouse Soaky 20	20	30	40
Mickey Mouse Soldier Set, cardboard soldiers, gun 500	500	850	1200
Mickey Mouse Sparkler Toy, 1930s, 5-1/2" tall, Nifty 325	325	490	650
Mickey Mouse Tambourine, Noble & Cooley Co., 1936, 9" heavy paper head, Mickey juggling while Minnie watches 310	310	465	620

Mickey Mouse Tap Dancer, crank toy, German. Courtesy Christie's East.

	C6	C8	C10
Mickey Mouse Viewer, with film of "Brave Little Tailor," 1946	60	90	120
Mickey Mouse Walker, Borgfeldt, 1934	3000	5000	8000
Mickey Mouse Washer, 1932 or 1933, Ohio Art Co., tin litho washing machine, 7" high, two scenes with Mickey, Minnie, Pluto	100	150	200

Mickey Mouse Washer. Courtesy Phillips New York.

	C6	C8	C10
Mickey Mouse Tap Dancer, crank toy, German, sold for $17,600 in 1990			
Mickey Mouse Tea Service, 24 pieces, tin, Chein, 1930s	120	180	240
Mickey Mouse Tin Flute	40	60	80
Mickey Mouse Tin Washboard set, c. 1935, complete	80	120	160
Mickey Mouse Tool Chest, 1935, Hamilton Metal, complete	170	255	340
Mickey Mouse on Tricycle, tin litho, wind-up, celluloid Mickey, 1940s, 3-1/2" long	450	675	900
"Mickey Mouse Tricycle," 1950s, Linemar, 4" tall	500	775	1100
Mickey Mouse Trapeze, celluloid, 1930s, Borgfeldt	500	750	1000
Mickey Mouse Trapeze, wood, c. 1930s	34	51	68
Mickey Mouse Tumbler, Schuco, 4" high	200	300	400
Mickey Mouse Tumbling, 1947, Marks Bros., 8" high	42	63	85

	C6	C8	C10
"Mickey Mouse with Twirling Tail," 1950s, Linemar, 5-1/2" high	130	195	260
Mickey Mouse Xylophone, tin wind-up, 1930s	425	638	850
Mickey Mouse Xylophone Player, Linemar, tin wind-up, 1950s, 6" high	333	500	665

Mickey Mouse Xylophone Player, Linemar. Photo by Don Hultzman.

Mickey Mouse Tumbler (Schuco) atop Mickey Mouse Piano (Marks Bros.). Courtesy Christie's East.

	C6	C8	C10
Mickey Mouse Club Bow and Arrow Set, c. 1955	20	30	40
Mickey Mouse Club Snap-On Ears, plastic, 1950s	10	15	20
Mickey & Minnie Acrobats," 1934, Borgfeldt (Japan) 11" high	500	750	1000
Mickey & Minnie Barrel Organ, English	112	168	225
Mickey & Minnie Mouse Car, Gong Bell, c. 1933, wood & metal, 10-3/4" long	1050	1575	2100

Disney • 543

Mickey & Minnie on Elephant, celluloid, Japan. Courtesy Christie's East.

	C6	C8	C10
Mickey & Minnie on Elephant, celluloid, Japan, 1930s, auctioned in 1990 for $7150			
Mickey & Minnie on Motorcycle, tin litho	8000	14,000	20,000
Mickey & Minnie Mouse Playland, celluloid, Japan	3000	5500	10,000
Minnie Mouse, 3" high, wooden, jointed, 1940s	200	300	400
Minnie Mouse, 4" high, wooden, Fun-E-Flex	140	210	280
Minnie Mouse, 5" high, celluloid, 1930s, "Fat head"	225	338	450
Minnie Mouse, 5-1/2" high, wooden, 1930s	187	286	375

Mickey & Minnie Mouse Playland, 10-1/4". Courtesy Christie's East.

	C6	C8	C10
Minnie Mouse, 6" high, celluloid, 1930s, string tail	425	638	850
Minnie Mouse, 7" high, Fun-E-Flex	300	450	600
"Minnie Mouse," 7" high, 1960s, Marx, wind-up, hard plastic	70	105	140
Minnie Mouse, 10-1/2" high, Sun Rubber, 1940s	85	125	170
Minnie Mouse, 12" high, 1930, wearing dress, high heels, undies	225	338	450
Minnie Mouse 14-1/2" high, early cloth figure dressed in a red and white polka dot skirt, wearing composition heeled shoes	300	450	600

Left to right: Minnie Mouse Doll, 14-1/2" high; Mickey Mouse, 21" high. Courtesy PB Eighty-Four, New York.

Minnie Mouse, 16" high, cloth, early 1930s. Courtesy HAKE'S Americana & Collectibles.

	C6	C8	C10
Minnie Mouse 16" high, cloth, early 1930s	650	975	1300
Minnie Mouse cardboard mask, c. 1935	40	60	80
Minnie Mouse carrying two suitcases, tin wind-up, 6-1/2" high, c. 1928, Spanish, auctioned for $12,100 (with replaced ears) in 1990			
Minnie Mouse Cowgirl, Knickerbocker, 18" high, 1936	470	705	940
Minnie Mouse Hand Puppet, Peter Puppet Playthings, c. 1952	100	150	200

Minnie Mouse carrying two suitcases.
Courtesy Christie's East.

	C6	C8	C10
Minnie Mouse Puppet, Pelham, 24" high, rubber legs and arms, wood body	195	292	390
Minnie Mouse Roly Poly, celluloid, 4"	60	90	120
Minnie Mouse Tricycle, 1950s, Linemar, 4"	450	675	900
Minnie Mouse Walker, plastic	20	30	40
Minnie Mouse Washing Machine, 1950, Precision Specialties, Inc.	100	150	200
Mousketeer Ears, snap-on, early, Kohner	14	21	27
Mousketeer Electric TV Story Teller, T. Cohn, late 1950s, tin litho TV set and record player, records and film reels	160	240	320
Mousketeer Hat, 50% wool, 50% rayon, Benay-Albee, 1950s	5	8	10
Mousketeer Play Outfit	75	112	150
Mousketeer Soaky	17	26	35
Nautilus Submarine ("20,000 Leagues Under the Sea")	155	235	310
"1001 Dalmatians" set of 6 wooden nodders, 1959	125	188	250
Oswald the Rabbit, c. 1927, 6-1/2" long celluloid crib toy	250	375	500
"Parade Roadster" Marx lithographed tin wind-up, convertible car decorated with Mickey and other characters, with Donald at the wheel, Pluto, Mickey and Minnie as passengers, 1950s, 11-1/4" long	350	525	700
Pecos Bill, Marx, wind-up, plastic, 1950s	200	300	400

	C6	C8	C10
Minnie Mouse Knitter, tin litho wind-up, Linemar, 1950s, 7" high	375	562	750
Minnie Mouse Lead, 2-1/2" high, 1933, Allied Toys	70	105	140
Minnie Mouse Marionette, c. 1930, 9-1/2" high, felt body stuffed with cotton	112	168	225
Minnie Mouse Marionette, 13", wood and composition, 1950s	150	225	300

Minnie Mouse Knitter. Photo by Don Hultzman.

Pecos Bill, plastic wind-up, Marx, 1950s. Photo by Don Hultzman.

	C6	C8	C10
Peter Pan 9-3/4" high, Sun Rubber, c. 1952	30	45	60
Peter Pan Jolly Roger Pirate Ship	17	26	35
Peter Pan Marionette, c. 1952, Peter Puppet Playthings	70	105	40
Peter Pan Tea Set, c. 1953, 23 pieces	275	363	550
Peter Pan Train Car, 1977	22	33	45

	C6	C8	C10
Piglet vinyl squeeze doll, 1960s	9	14	17
Pinocchio cloth and jointed wood figure, Kreuger	160	240	320

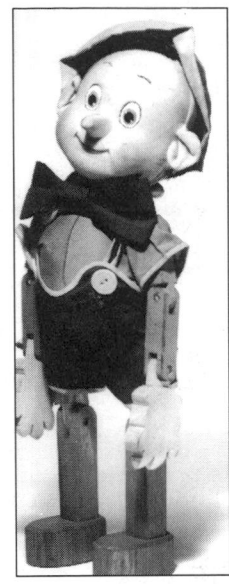

Pinocchio, cloth and jointed wood figure, Kreuger. Courtesy PB Eighty-Four, New York.

Pinocchio Doll, Ideal, 8" high. Lloyd W. Ralston Auctions.

	C6	C8	C10
Pinocchio, 2-1/2" high, molded wood fiber figure, Multi Products, 1940	100	150	200
Pinocchio, 5" high, molded wood fiber figure, Multi Products, 1940	100	150	200
Pinocchio, 5-1/2" high, rubber, Seiberling	27	41	55
Pinocchio, 7-1/2" high, jointed, circa 1940, Ideal	150	225	300
Pinocchio, 8" high, Ideal	132	198	264
Pinocchio 10-1/2" high, Ideal, wood and composition	250	375	500

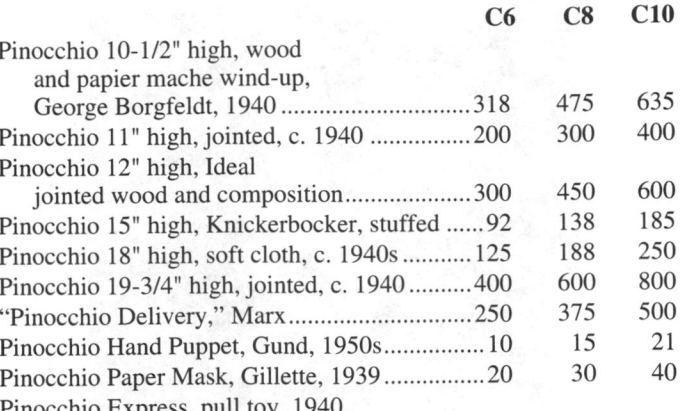

	C6	C8	C10
Pinocchio 10-1/2" high, wood and papier mache wind-up, George Borgfeldt, 1940	318	475	635
Pinocchio 11" high, jointed, c. 1940	200	300	400
Pinocchio 12" high, Ideal jointed wood and composition	300	450	600
Pinocchio 15" high, Knickerbocker, stuffed	92	138	185
Pinocchio 18" high, soft cloth, c. 1940s	125	188	250
Pinocchio 19-3/4" high, jointed, c. 1940	400	600	800
"Pinocchio Delivery," Marx	250	375	500
Pinocchio Hand Puppet, Gund, 1950s	10	15	21
Pinocchio Paper Mask, Gillette, 1939	20	30	40
Pinocchio Express, pull toy, 1940, 11" long: See Fisher-Price			
Pinocchio on Donkey, pull toy, 1940, bell-ringer: See Fisher-Price			

Pinocchio, tin wind-up, Marx, "Walking Pinocchio." Courtesy Ed Hyers Antique Toys.

Pinocchio. Free Pinocchio masks offer from 1940 (see Cleo, Figaro, Gepetto, Jiminy Cricket), Gillette. Courtesy Rex and Richard Gray.

	C6	C8	C10
Pinocchio Soaky	12	18	25
Pinocchio The Acrobat, "Watch Him Go!" tin wind-up, 1939, Marx	385	575	770
Pinocchio, tin wind-up, litho eyes, 8-1/2" high, Marx, standing erect, c. 1940	300	450	600
Pinocchio, tin wind-up, Marx, standing erect, moving eyes, 1939, 8-1/2" high.................	312	470	625
Pinocchio, tin litho wind-up, Linemar Co., 1950s, 5-1/2" tall	350	525	700

Pluto Drum Major. Photo by Don Hultzman.

Pinocchio, tin litho wind-up, Linemar. Photo by Don Hultzman.

	C6	C8	C10
Pluto Drum Major, Marx, tin wind-up, 1940s	195	295	390
Pluto "Drum Major," Linemar, 1950s, 6-1/2" tall, tin litho wind-up	225	338	450
Pluto Hand Puppet, Gund, 1950s	15	22	30
"Pluto in His Sports Car," 1950s, 4" long, friction drive, all plastic	50	75	100
Pluto, lead, 2-1/2" high, 1933 Allied toys	60	90	120
"Pluto Motorcycle," 1950s, Linemar, tin friction toy, 3-1/2" long	300	450	600
Pluto "Musical Pluto," 1960s, Marx, (Dog Race Type), 8" x 8" base with 2-1/2" Pluto, plastic	400	600	800
Pluto Mysterious Pluto, Marx	150	225	300
Pluto on Rockers, wooden, c. 1930s	150	225	300
Pluto, plastic wind-up, Marx, metal tail spins, 1950s...................................	75	112	150
Pluto "Playful Pluto & Goofy" 1950s Linemar, 2-piece set, wind-ups..................	800	1300	2000
"Pluto Pulling Cart," 1950s Linemar friction, 8-1/2" long	392	588	785
Pluto pull toy, wood, c. 1940s, unmarked, looks un-Disney	65	98	130

	C6	C8	C10
Pinocchio "Walking Pinocchio," Marx, plastic, 1950s	40	60	80
Pluto, 3", bendable legs, c. 1934, wooden...................................	140	210	280
Pluto, 4" long Seiberling Rubber, c. 1935	60	90	120
Pluto, 6" long, wood, Borgfeldt	175	263	350
Pluto, 7-1/2" long, Seiberling Rubber	65	98	130
Pluto, 9" long, wood jointed............................	250	375	500
"Pluto," 1950s, Linemar, tin friction toy, 3" long	105	158	210
"Pluto," Marx wind-up, 1960s plastic, 4-1/2" high	133	200	265
Pluto Acrobat, Gym Toys, Linemar	318	475	635
Pluto "Begging Rollover Pluto," 1950s, Linemar, 6-1/2" long	100	150	200

Pluto, plastic wind-up, Marx, metal tail spins.

Pluto Mysterious Pluto, Marx. Photo by Don Hultzman.

Pluto "Playful Pluto & Goofy." Photo by Don Hultzman.

	C6	C8	C10
Pluto, sitting position, rubber squeeze toy, 1960s	20	30	40
Pluto Soaky	11	16	22
Pluto Squeeze Toy, Sun Rubber No. 11520, 1930s	30	45	60
Pluto, tin litho squeeze-action with cable, Linemar, 1950s, 4-1/4" tall	200	300	400

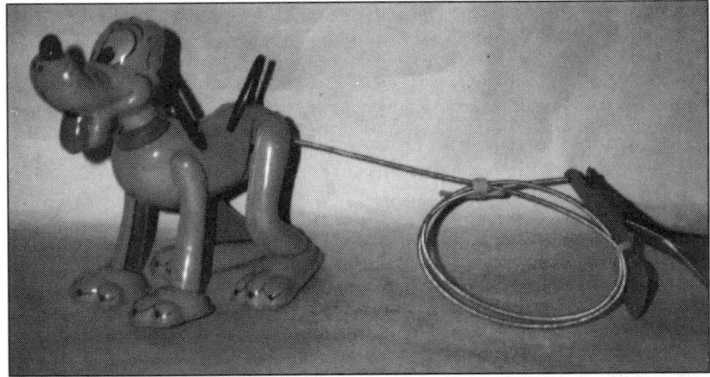

Pluto tin litho squeeze-action with cable, Linemar. Photo by Don Hultzman.

"Pluto tricycle," 1950s, Linemar, 4" tall	278	415	555
Pluto "Watch Me Roll Over," Marx, 1939	130	195	260
Pluto, "Wise Pluto," 1939, Marx, 8" long, (like "Watch Me Roll Over")	212	318	425

Pluto "Watch Me Roll Over," Marx.

"Pluto Pulling Cart," 1950s, Linemar. Courtesy Ed Hyers Antique Toys.

Pluto "Wise Pluto." Photo by Don Hultzman.

Pluto With Basket, 8" long. Courtesy Lloyd W. Ralston Auctions.

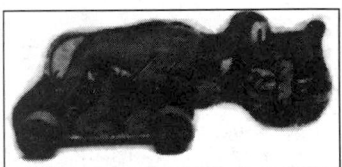

	C6	C8	C10
Pluto With Basket, paper litho on wood, 8" long: See Fisher-Price			
"Pluto with Whirling Tail," 1950s, Linemar, wind-up, 4" high	235	350	470
Pluto, wooden, hand base, string-operated, many jointed, marionette-type, 1936, No. 440: See Fisher-Price			
Practical Pig Doll, Gund	112	168	225
Practical Pig, tin litho wind-up, Linemar	260	390	520
"Professor Von Drake Go Mobile," 1950s, 6" long, Linemar, wind-up	150	225	300
Sand Pail, 1938, Ohio Art, tin litho, Mickey, Minnie and Goofy pictured	112	168	225
Seven Dwarfs, all, puppet-marionettes, Pelham	1500	2250	3000
Seven Dwarfs, all, Seiberling Rubber, 1938, 5-1/2" high	350	525	700
Seven Dwarfs, approx. 8", vinyl squeeze, 1950s, each	30	45	60

Seven Dwarfs, puppet-marionettes, Pelham.

	C6	C8	C10
Si-Am (Lady & Tramp) 16" high, stuffed, vinyl face, Gund, c. 1955 40	60	80
Sleeping Beauty Hand Puppet, Gund, 1950s 31	47	62
Sleeping Beauty Squeeze Toy, sitting with animals, 6-1/2" 44	66	88
Sleepy 1-1/2" lead figure, Britains 45	68	90
Sleepy, Ideal, approx. 7" high 125	188	250
Sleepy, Ideal, approx. 12" high, 1938 120	180	240
Sleepy Party Mask, 1937 20	30	40
Sneezy, 1-1/2" lead figure, Britains 45	68	90

	C6	C8	C10
Sneezy, 3-1/4" high, Seiberling Rubber, 1938 60	90	120
Sneezy, Ideal, approx. 7" high 125	188	250
Sneezy, Ideal, approx. 12" high, 1938 120	180	240
Sneezy Party Mask, 1937 20	30	40
Sneezy rubber squeeze toy, 1950s 10	15	20
Snow Shovel, 26" long, shows Mickey and Pluto building snowman 90	135	180
Snow White and the Seven Dwarfs, Britains No. 1654, per each 20	60	90

Snow White and the Seven Dwarfs, Ideal. Snow White approx. 15" high, the Dwarfs 7" high. Courtesy Christie's East.

Seven Dwarfs, Seiberling Rubber, 1938, 5-1/2" high. Photo by Stan Alekna.

	C6	C8	C10
Snow White and the Seven Dwarfs, lead figures by Lincoln Logs, all	500	750	1000
Snow White, 2-1/2" lead figure, Britains	45	68	90
Snow White Doll, Seiberling Rubber	250	375	500
Snow White, 12" high, Knickerbocker, 1940s	187	280	375
Snow White, 13" high, Madame Alexander, 1938	120	180	240
Snow White, Ideal, 15" high, 1938	150	225	300
Snow White Kitchen Set, Wolverine	60	90	120
Snow White Party Mask	20	30	40
Snow White Soaky	17	26	35
Snow White Washing Machine, c. 1950, Revell Plastics, 7-1/2" high with wringer	80	120	160
Snow White and the Seven Dwarfs blocks, 18 blocks, in box	175	263	350
Snow White and the Seven Dwarfs, 4-1/2" dishes, china, with cups, creamer, sugar bowl, 6" plate	210	315	420
Snow White and the Seven Dwarfs drum, tin litho, 1930s	125	188	250
Snow White and the Seven Dwarfs musical top, Chein, 6-1/2" across	110	165	220
Snow White and the Seven Dwarfs sewing set, Hasbro	20	30	40
Snow White sink and stove, Wolverine	40	60	80
Three Little Pigs Acrobats, celluloid, Japan	312	465	625
Three Little Pigs clothes washer, Chein	102	153	205
"Three Little Pigs - Drummer," 1930s, 4-1/2" tall, Schuco	175	263	350
"Three Little Pigs - Flutist," 1930s, 4-1/2" tall, Schuco	175	263	350
Three Little Pigs Mask, 1933, Par-T-Mask	40	60	80
Three Little Pigs Sand Bucket, 3" tall	30	45	60
"Three Little Pigs - Violinist," 1930s, 4-1/2" tall, Schuco	212	318	425
Three Little Pigs Walkers, Linemar, tin wind-up, per each	130	195	260

	C6	C8	C10
Three Little Pigs Wooden Pig, c. 1933, Borgfeldt, fiber arms and legs, 3-1/4" high	120	180	240
"Thumper," 1950s, Linemar, tin friction toy, 3" long	70	105	140
Thumper Soaky	11	16	22
Thumper, 6" high, friction, Marx, 1950s	100	150	200
Thumper, 7" high, squeeze toy, Sun Rubber	30	45	60
Thumper, 14" high, Gund, 1950s	38	57	76
Thumper, 17" high, Gund, early 1940s	80	120	160
Tigger, 9" squeeze doll, 1960s	9	13	18
Timothy Mouse (Dumbo), stuffed, 17" high, Character Novelty, 1942	150	225	300
Tinkerbell Hand Puppet, Gund	32	48	65
"Tramp The Dog," 1960s, Linemar friction, 4" high	90	135	180
Tramp Hand Puppet, Gund	35	52	70
Uncle Scrooge Hand Puppet, 1960s? wearing high hat	20	30	40
Uncle Scrooge Limousine, "$" on back fender	110	165	220
Uncle Scrooge vinyl squeeze toy bank, 7" high, c. 1960	40	60	80
"Walt Disney Character Carousel," 1950s, Linemar Co., 7" high with 3" characters	300	450	600
"Walt Disney Character T.V. Set," 1950s, Automatic Toy Co., 5" cubic	150	225	300
"Walt Disney Stars" bus, 19" long, Gong Bell	450	675	900
Walt Disney Television Car, Marx, 1950s, 7-1/2" long	275	365	550
"Walt Disney's Friction Delivery Wagon," 1950s, Linemar, 6" long, Mickey, Donald, Pluto, etc.	450	675	900
"Walt Disney's Friction Go-Mobile," 1960s, Marx (Japan), 6" long, Mickey, Pluto, Donald, etc.	150	225	300
"Walt Disney's Mechanical Tricycle," 1950s, Linemar, 4" high, Pluto, Mickey, Donald, etc.	200	300	400
"Walt Disney's Television Playhouse," Marx playset, 39 characters	232	348	465
Wendy (Peter Pan), hand puppet, Gund	14	21	28
Wendy Marionette, 1950s	75	112	150
Witch (Snow White) Party Mask	20	30	40
Zorro Flintlock Pistol, Marx	35	52	70
Zorro Hand Puppet, Gund	50	75	100
Zorro Hat, hideaway mask and gloves, 1950s	46	69	92
Zorro on Rearing Horse, Marx	160	240	320
Zorro Playset, Marx	400	600	800
Zorro Ring, black top with Z and "Zorro" name	22	33	44
Zorro Sword, 24" long, 1960s	5	8	10

RAMP WALKERS

MANUFACTURING HISTORY OF WALKERS

by Randy Welch

Ramp walkers date back to at least 1873, when Ives patented two versions of a cast-iron elephant walker. One version has a pivoting trunk; the other has a fixed trunk and lead feet.

Walkers made of wood, cardboard, and composites were produced in Czechoslovakia, Argentina, and the U.S. from the 1930s through the early 1950s. The most popular were made by John Wilson of Watsontown, Pennsylvania, and were sold worldwide. These became known as "Wilson Walkies." Most are two-legged and stand approximately 4-1/2" tall. An empty cardboard thread cone was used for the body. The Wilson walkers produced between 1940 and 1950 have the U.S. patent number 2140275 stamped on the bottom of one foot. Earlier versions were marked "Made in U.S.A. Pat. Pending" or "Made in U.S.A. Pat'd. 12-18-40."

Plastic ramp walkers were primarily manufactured by the Louis Marx Co. and were made from the early 1950s through the mid-1960s. By far the majority were produced in Hong Kong, although some were made in the U.S. and sold under either the Marx logo or by the Charmore Co., a subsidiary of Marx. Other manufacturers include Fun World (U.S.), Dolls Inc. (U.S.), Ohio Art (U.S.), Educational Toys, subsidiary of Topper Corp. (U.S.), and Gantoy (England).

The three common sizes are (A) Small premiums (approx. 1-1/2" x 2"), (B) the more common medium size (approx. 2-3/4" x 3"), and (C) large size (approx. 4" x 5"). Most of the smaller walkers were unpainted. The medium and larger sizes were hand-painted and/or spray painted.

Colorful tin lithographed ramps were available for some of the Marx plastic walkers but most relied on homemade ramps or a weighted string that hung over the end of a table and pulled the toy along.

There were interesting variations on the use of walkers. A few are listed below:

• The Minnesota Electronics Corp. took the generic pig made by Marx and glued a small magnet in the back end. This was boxed with a plastic children's ring, which had a small magnet glued to the top. When the ring was placed near the pig's back end, the two magnets forced the pig to walk along a flat surface. The toy was named "Maggie the Magnetic Pig."

• Ohio Art produced a plastic farm set named the "Walker Farm." This included a barn and a ramp along with seven walking people and animals pushing interchangeable parts such as a lawnmower, lawn roller, wheelbarrow and spreader.

• The "Colonial Action Target Game" by Marx included a long lithographed tin ramp, a plastic bear ramp walker, a small working plastic rifle, and five wooden bullets. The box was placed behind the ramp as a backdrop. The child would shoot at the bear as it waddled down the ramp.

• In 1971 Educational Toys (subsidiary of Topper Corp.) made a Sesame Street walking letter set named "Big Bird's Blunder Proof Walking Letter Set." This set

---

"I began collecting tin wind-up toys more than ten years ago while visiting a local auction house. I became interested in ramp walkers (for the second time) a few years later when I purchased a plastic Huckleberry Hound and Yogi Bear walker at a flea market for $5. I remember marching the walkers down the incline of my old wooden school desk top in the late 1950s.

After discovering that there was no reference material available on walkers, I began contacting dealers and collectors and have compiled a list and photos of more than 300 known walkers. My other areas of interest include tin lithographed sparklers. An updated and more detailed list of ramp walkers is available by contacting the author. Correspondence is welcomed and appreciated."

Randy Welch

Charmore. Courtesy Randy Welch.

A Charmore backing card. Courtesy Randy Welch.

included six walking letters, twelve word keys and a plastic ramp. A word key with a picture on it was inserted into the base of the ramp. The child would then attempt to spell the word for the picture on the key. The letters would march down the ramp and if the word was spelled correctly, Big Bird would pop up with a sign saying "OK!" If the word was misspelled, all the letters would fall down. Additional letters and a ramp extension were sold separately.

Because the value of walkers is significantly reduced when the paint is scratched or when there are cracks and breaks, I have decided to list only the prices for those in mint condition.

Photos in this section by Randy Welch, unless otherwise noted.

C10

Disney (Plastic)

Big Bad Wolf & mason pig, Marx	40
Big Bad Wolf & 3 Little Pigs, Marx	125
Donald pushing a wheelbarrow, Marx	25
Donald pulling 3 nephews in a wagon, Marx	35
Donald & Goofy riding a go-cart, Marx	40
Fiddler & Fifer Pigs, Marx	40
Goofy riding a hippo, Marx	45
Jiminy Cricket w/ cello, Marx	30
Mad Hatter & March Hare, Marx	50
Mickey & Minnie carrying a basket of food, Marx	40
Mickey pushing lawn roller, Marx	35
Minnie pushing baby stroller, Marx	35
Mickey & Donald riding on an alligator, Marx	40
Mickey w/ Pluto hunting, Marx	40
Pluto, Marx	20

Big Bad Wolf & 3 Little Pigs (Disney)

Donald & Goofy Riding A Go-Kart (Disney)

Mickey with Pluto Hunting (Disney)

Hanna-Barbera & King Features (Plastic)

	C10		C10
Astro, Marx	150	Fred Flintstone & Barney, Marx	40
Astro & Rosey, Marx	95	Fred & Wilma riding on dinosaur, Marx	60
Astro & George Jetson, Marx	90	Fred riding on green Dino, Marx	70
		Little King & guard	70
		Pebbles riding on purple Dino, Marx	70

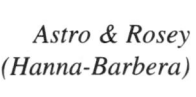

Astro & Rosey (Hanna-Barbera)

Fred Riding Dino (Hanna-Barbera)

	C10
Popeye pushing spinach can wheelbarrow, Marx	25
Top Cat & Benny, Marx	65
Yogi Bear & Huckleberry Hound, Marx	50

Fred Flintstone and Barney (Hanna-Barbera)

Little King & Guard (King Features)

*Top Cat
and Benny
(Hanna-
Barbera)*

*Yogi Bear
and
Huckleberry
Hound
(Hanna-
Barbera)*

Marx Animals with Riders Series (Plastic)

	C10
Ankylosaurus w/ clown	25
Bison w/ native	25
Brontosaurus w/ monkey	25
Hippo w/ native	25
Lion w/ clown	25
Stegosaurus w/ black caveman	25
Triceratops w/ native	25
Zebra w/ native	25

*Bunny
with
Carrot
on back
of Dog*

Other (Plastic)

	C10
Baseball player w/ bat & ball, Marx	40
Bear, Marx	15
Boy & girl dancing, Marx	40
Bull, Marx	15
Bunnies carrying large carrot, ?	30
Bunny pushing cart, Marx	45
Bunny w/ carrot on back of dog, Marx	60
Camel w/ 2 humps, head bobs up & down, ?	20
Chicks carrying large Easter egg, ?	30
Chilly Willy penguin on sled pulled by parent, Marx	25
Chinamen carrying a duck in a basket, Marx	30
Chipmunks in marching band playing drum & horn, Marx	30
Chipmunks carrying acorns, Marx	30
Dachshund dog, Marx	15
Dairy Cow, Marx	15
Duck Mama w/ 3 ducklings, Marx	25
Duck, Marx	15
Dutch boy & girl, Marx	30
Elephant, Marx	20
Farmer pushing wheelbarrow, Marx	20
Figaro the cat w/ ball, Marx	25
Firemen, Marx	30

*Left: Frontiersman with dog.
Right: Indian Woman
with baby on travois.*

Frontiersman w/ dog, Marx	95
Goat, ?	20
Hap & Hop soldiers, Marx	20
Horse circus style, Marx	15
Indian woman pulling baby on travois, Marx	95
Kangaroo w/ baby in pouch, Marx	25
Marty's Market lady pushing shopping cart, Marx	40
Monkeys carrying bananas, Marx	50
Mother Goose w/ goose, Marx	60
Nurse maid pushing baby stroller, Marx	15
Pig, Marx	15
Pigs, two carrying third in basket, Marx	40

Poodle (made by Gantoy England), Gantoy	40
Pumpkin head man & woman, faces on both sides, Fun World	45
Reindeer, Marx	35
Sailors S.S. Shoreleave, Marx	20
Santa w/ white sack, Marx	40
Santa w/ yellow sack, Marx	35
Santa w/ gold open sack, Marx	45
Santa & Mrs. Claus (faces on both sides), Fun World	40
Santa & Snowman (faces on both sides), Fun World	40
Sheriff facing outlaw, Marx	65
Spark Plug the horse, Marx	175
Tin Man robot pushing a cart, Marx	125

Figaro the Cat with Ball

Monkeys carrying bananas

Pumpkin Head Man and Woman

Tin Man Robot pushing a cart

Left: Poodle (Gantoy). Right: Baseball Player with bat and ball.

Long John Silver Premium (Plastic)

(1989 - with plastic coin weight)

	C10
Capt. Flint parrot (green), LJS	15
Flash turtle (green & yellow), LJS	15
Quinn penguin (black & white), LJS	15
Sylvia dinosaur (lavender & pink), LJS	15
Sydney dinosaur (yellow & purple), LJS	15

Funny Face Kool-Aid Premium (Plastic)

(All with plastic coin weight)

Choo-Choo Cherry, Pillsbury	60
Goofy Grape, Pillsbury	60
Jolly Ollie Orange, Pillsbury	60
Root'n Toot'n Raspberry, Pillsbury	60

Small Plastic w/ Metal Legs

Cow, head up, Marx	15
Cow, head down, Marx	15
Cowboy on horse, ?	20
Donald Duck pushing wheelbarrow, Marx	30
Dog (brown Pluto-like), Marx	15
Elephant, ?	20
Mexican cowboy on horse, ?	20
Mickey & Minnie Mouse, Marx	40
Pluto, Marx	30

Large Plastic

Baby Walk-a-Way baby, Marx	40
Baby Teeny Toddler walking girl, Dolls, Inc.	40
Baby Walking baby w/ moving eyes, cloth dress, Marx	40
Baby Walking baby in Canadian Mountie uniform, Marx	50
Baby Walking baby in Pirate clothes, Marx	50
Cow Milking cow, Marx	40
Cow Wiz Walking Milking Cow Charmore, Marx	40
Double Walking Doll (boy behind girl), Hong Kong	45

Double Walking Doll

Horse w/ English rider, Marx	40
Horse, Marx	30
Horse w/ rubber ears & string tail, Marx	30
Popeye & Wimpy w/ heads on springs, Marx	65

Popeye and Wimpy

Argentina (Plastic)

	C10
Horse cream color w/ pink legs (similar to Marx)	20
Pig blue (similar to Marx only smaller)	15
Cow blue (same size as pig)	15

Argentina (Bakelite Cone and Legs)

Penguin (very similar in size & shape to Wilson)	50

Argentina (Paper Cone and Wood Legs)

Gaucho (cowboy)	50
China (Gaucho's wife), versions red, blue grn	50
Policeman	50
Musketeer	50
School boy	50
Gaucho cowboy w/ elephant head pushing tin cart	65
Gaucho cowboy w/ pig head pushing tin cart	65
Clown pushing tin cart	65
Clown w/ elephant head pushing tin cart	65
Chinese man pushing tin cart	65

Erwin (Celluloid)

Popeye, 5-3/4" tall	60

Ives (Cast Iron)

Elephant Pat. 1873 (with iron feet & swivel trunk)	125
Elephant Pat. 1873 (with lead feet & fixed trunk)	100

IVES cast-iron Elephant. Patented 1873.

Wilson (Wood & Composite)

	C10
Black Mammy	35
Clown	30
Donald Duck	175
Elephant on 4 legs	30
Eskimo	75
Indian Chief,	45
Little Red Riding Hood	40
Nurse	30
Olive Oyl	175
Penguin	25
Pig	40
Pinocchio	175
Popeye	175
Rabbit	40
Sailor	30
Santa Claus	60
Soldier	25
Wimpy	175

Czechoslovakia (Wood & Composite)

	C10
Dog on 4 legs	20
Man with carved wooden hat	25
Monkey	30
Pig	20
Policeman	40

Ramps in Box

Circus Horse, Marx	65
Comical Action Bear w/ long ramp, including gun & bullets, Marx	125
Dick Tracy's Nursemaid takes Bonny Braids for stroll, Marx	125
Disney long ramp w/ generic street scene, Marx	200
Felix wood ramp w/ wood walker	1,400
Hap & Hop the Dauntless Doughboys, Marx	80
"I Like Ike" elephant, Marx	125
Nora the Nursemaid, Marx	75
Plank ramp (generic) for cow, pig, ducks, bear etc., Marx	50
S.S. Shoreleave sailors, Marx	75

WILSON. Left to right: Indian Chief, Black Mammy, Soldier

WILSON. Left to right: Penguin, Elephant on 4 legs, Pig

WILSON. Left to right: Little Red Riding Hood, Clown, Nurse

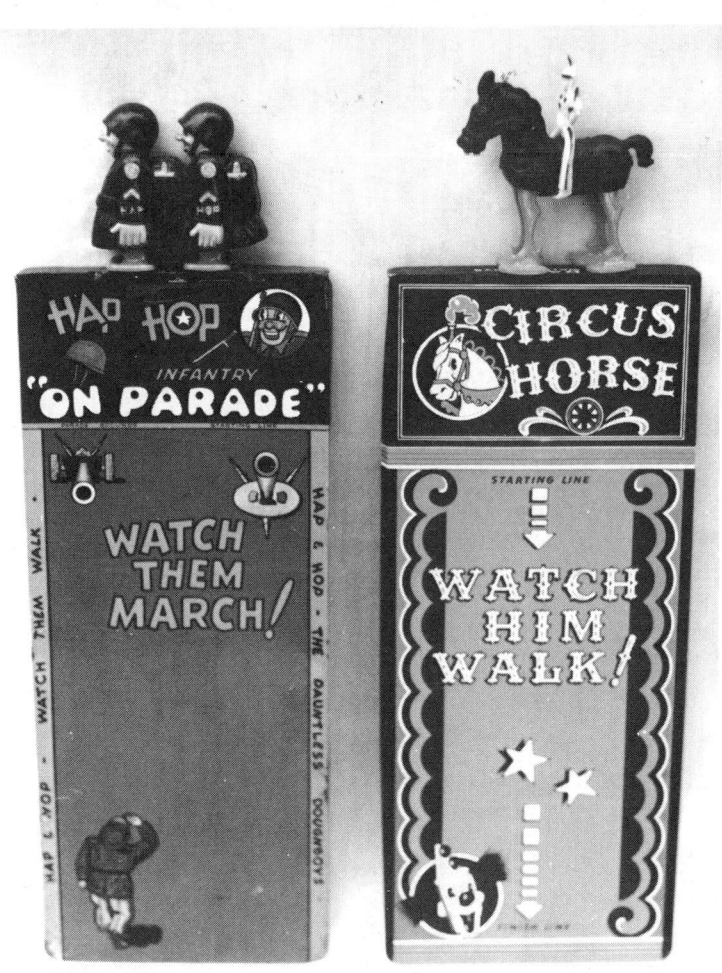

Left to right: Hap & Hop, Circus Horse (both tin litho)

A Marx flier.

A Marx flier.

WHITE KNOB WIND-UPS

MODERN MOVERS

by M. Aaron Roy

White knob wind-ups (WKW) are small, plastic mechanical toys that came on the market around the mid to late 1970s. They get their name from the little white (sometimes colored on newer toys) ridged knob at the end of a metal rod which extends from the body and winds the motor when rotated.

Most WKWs offer a single basic movement or action. "Walkers," "hoppers," "climbers," "rollers," "flip-overs," or "pop-overs" perform on a flat surface, while toys intended to be pinned on clothing may have eyes that move up and down or ears that wiggle back and forth. "Swimmers" move in water. A few of the most desirable WKWs have multiple movements occurring at the same time or in sequence. White knob wind-ups were (and are) typically sold loose or in bubble packaging. A few came boxed in sets with other figures or with accessories. Production originally was in Japan, Macao, Singapore, and Taiwan, but more recently is centered in China.

WKWs come in a variety of themes: transportation, tools and utensils, sports, space, popular culture, novelty, musical, movies and television, holidays and seasons, foods, fast-food giveaways, fairy tales, Disney, cartoon and comic characters, animals, and anatomical parts. Some white knob wind-ups have been produced by well-known companies such as Tomy™, Galoob™, Russ™, and Mattel™, while others seem to be sold by small companies or importers with no reference as to manufacturer.

The following list is only representative of the many hundreds of WKWs that have been produced. Color, structural, and decorating variations exist in many examples, and toys originally issued by one company (e.g., Tomy™) may be released later by another company (e.g., Playskool™). Prices quoted below reflect the original releases that are often marked as to manufacturer. As with other toys, WKWs in original packaging are more valuable. C10 values reflect mint, working wind-ups with all accessories.

Aaron Roy is a professor of psychology at Ashland University in Ashland, Ohio, and owner of the Lake Erie Toy Museum on Kelleys Island near Marblehead, Ohio, where his personal collection of toys from 1870 to 1980 is on display. He has collected a wide range of toys for about 30 years and is the author of numerous professional and hobby-related articles.

Photos in this section by M. Aaron Roy.

CHARACTERS

	C6	C8	C10
Barbie (Mattel, 1986 & Arco, 1988) Microwave Oven, Sewing Machine, Radio/Tape Deck, VCR, Camera, Telephone, Computer, Mantel Clock, Stereo, Mixer. Each	1	2	3

	C6	C8	C10
Cabbage Patch Kids (Tomy, 1985)			
Crawler: boy or girl, each	4	6	8
Girl in walker	4	6	8
Boy with basketball	6	9	12

TOMY White Knob Wind-up Cabbage Patch Kids.

TOMY White Knob Wind-up Cabbage Patch Kids.

TOMY White Knob Wind-up Cabbage Patch Rocking Baby.

Variations in 1977 Mickey Mouse by Durham (left) and Tomy (right).

	C6	C8	C10
Boy on stick horse	6	9	12
Girl Cheerleader	6	9	12
Girl Baton Twirler	6	9	12
Rocking Babies: Basinette, Swing, Rocking Horse, each	10	15	20
E.T. Walker (LJN, 1982)	6	9	12
Mickey Mouse			
Smile with white dots on pants (Tomy)	5	10	15
No smile or dots (Durham Ind.)	20	30	40
Muppets (Tomy, 1983)			
Pop-Ups: Animal Drummer or Great Gonzo's Shark Escape, each	8	12	16
Pop-Overs: Miss Piggy or Great Gonzo, each	8	12	16
Flip-Floppers: Animal Jalopy or Miss Piggy Swinetrek, each	8	12	16
Swimmers: Kermit the Frog, Miss Piggy, Fozzie the Bear, each	7	10	14
Pac Man rollers (Tomy, 1982)			
Mr. or Mrs., each	3	5	7
Inky Ghost (Blue)	10	15	20
Blinky Ghost (Red)	10	15	20

TOMY White Knob Wind-up Pac Man.

	C6	C8	C10
Pink Panther (Bandai-America, 1981)			
Pink Panther Walker	8	12	16
Inspector Walker	8	12	16
Popeye or Brutus Walker (Durham, 1980), each	10	15	20
Q*Bert Hopper (Kenner, 1983)	6	9	12
Smurfs Walkers (Galoob, 1982)			
Musicians: trumpet, guitar, drum	2	4	6
Figures: Jokey holding present, Smurfette, Papa Smurf, Flying Smurf, Gargomel, each	4	6	8
Plain Walker (Blue Knob)	10	15	20
Smurf on Swing	6	9	12
Smurfs on Teeter Totter	6	9	12
Smurfs Jumping Rope	6	9	12
Smurf Fun House (Mushroom)	10	15	20
Snoopy (Aviva)			
Swimmer or walker	6	9	12
Walkers: Snoopy with Top Hat, Snoopy Matador, Snoopy Tennis Player, Snoopy as Red Baron, Snoopy as Bull Fighter, Woodstock with flowers, each	3	5	7
Snorks (Tomy, 1984)			
Swimmers: 5 different, each	6	9	12
Walkers: 5 different, each	6	9	12

Snoopy as (left to right): tennis player; football player; matador (by Aviva).

	C6	C8	C10
The Chipmunks Hoppers (Imperial, 1983)			
Alvin with harmonica	6	9	12
Simon with guitar	6	9	12
Theodoor with drums	6	9	12
Tom & Jerry Walkers (Multitoys, 1989)			
Tom or Jerry	4	6	8
Spike, Tyke, Droopy, Quacker, each	5	8	10
Wizard of Oz Walkers (Multitoys, 1988)			
Scarecrow, Alice, Witch, each	4	6	8

TOMY White Knob Wind-up smurfs.

TOMY White Knob Wind-up Snorks.

NON-CHARACTERS

	C6	C8	C10
Babies (Tomy, 1977) Crawler or Walker, each	4	6	8
Bathtubbies (Tomy, 1983)			
Swimming Whale, Frog, Bear, Seal, Penguin, Turtle, Goldfish, and Duck, each	2	3	4
Box Pops (Tomy, 1981) Rolling box stops and "Wacky Clown," "Funny Face" or "Looney Bird" pops out of the top, each	10	16	22
Bumbling Boxing Game (Tomy, 1982)			
Two walking boxers on ring	15	22	30

	C6	C8	C10
Christmas (Russ)			
Santa Hopper	4	6	8
Tree Hopper	4	6	8
Snowball on Skis Roller	6	8	10
Curious Critters (Tomy, 1984) (Rollers that are directed by a magnetic wand)			
Dogs: 2 different ones, each	8	12	16
Cats: 2 different ones, each	8	12	16

TOMY White Knob Wind-up Babies.

Christmas types (left to right): Santa hopper; tree hopper; snowball on skis roller.

	C6	C8	C10
Flip Floppers (Tomy, 1983) Bus, Plane, Car, Racer, Space Ship, Helecopter, Train, Dune Buggy, each 2		3	4
Get Along Gadgets Rollers (Tomy, 1983) Toaster, Clock, Phone, Coffee Pot, Record Player, each 6		8	10
Get Along Gang Rollers (Tomy, 1984)			
Zipper Cat or Dotty Dog on a handcar, each 6		9	12
Lamb or Moose on a raft, each 6		9	12
Porcupine or Moose on a skateboard, each 6		9	12
Hamburgers			
Hopper (Russ) 8		10	12
Roller 3		5	7
Walker 2		4	6
Home Run Homer Game (Tomy, 1982)			
Baseball hopper on green playing field 15		22	30
Hop-A-Long Hoopster Game (Tomy, 1982)			
Hopping basketball on court 15		22	30
Hilarious Hats Walkers (Tomy, 1983)			
Cowboy, Football, Police, each 8		12	16

	C6	C8	C10
Inch-A-Longs (Bandai-America, 1981) Dog, Crocodile, locomotive and truck crawling rollers, each 6		9	12
Lil' Big Toppers (Tomy, 1983)			
Elephant roller, multi-actions 10		15	20
Clown in Car or Bear, each 5		8	10
Mad Balls Rollers (Spearhead, 1986)			
Screamin Meemie, Horn Head, Skull Face, Slobulus. Heads w/ moving tongues, each 2		3	4
Major League Baseballs (Russ, 1989)			
Baseball Hoppers w/ colors and logos of each team, each 4		6	8
Major League Football (Russ, 1989)			
Helmet Hoppers w/ colors and logos of each team, each 4		6	8
Mini-Appliances (Galoob, 1979) Floor Buffer, Stereo & Speakers, Sewing Machine, Blender, Mixer, Food Processor, each 3		5	7
Mini-Tools (Galoob, 1980) Circular Saw, Jigsaw, Sander, Drill, Chain Saw, each 4		6	8
Mini-Tools (Imperial, 1988) Chain Saw, Drill, Jigsaw and Circular Saw, each 2		3	4

Three types of moving hamburgers (left to right): "Hopper"; "Roller"; "Walker."

TOMY White Knob Home Run Homer Wind-up Game.

	C6	C8	C10

Minimals (Tomy, 1982) Dog, Duck,
Elephant, Hippopotomus, Horse, Giraffe
rollers about 1-1/2" long w/ exterior
wheels and back hole "hook," each 15   23   30

Mity Machines (Galoob, 1984) Pile Driver,
Pounder, Bulldozer and Backhoe, each 5   7   9

Pocket Pets Hoppers (Tomy, 1983) Goose,
Squirrel, Penguin, Turtle, Frog, Toucan,
Beetle, Rabbit, Dog, Owl, Duck,
and Chicken, each 2   3   4

Prancing Ponys (Tomy, 1983) Pinto,
Arabian Stallion, Palomino, Appaloosa
w/ accessories of a saddle, bridle,
bucket, and brush 8   12   16

Rascal Robots or Pocket 'Bots (Tomy, 1977)
Three different walkers 4   6   8

Robot Lion Force (LJN, 1984) Black, red,
green, yellow robot 5   10   15

Scurry Furries (Tomy, 1982) Rabbit, Dog,
Raccoon, Owl, and Green Dragon Hoppers
or Rollers that are "fur" covered 7   10   14

Snow Funnies Rollers (Tomy, 1981) Bear
or Rabbit on skis, each 2   4   6

	C6	C8	C10

Strolling Bowling Game (Tomy, 1982)
Hopper bowling ball knocks pins
over on lane 15   22   30

Ugh-A-Bugs Crawlers (Tomy, 1981)
Stag Beetle, Tarantula,
and Atlas Beetle, each 6   9   12

TOMY White Knob Wind-up Rascal Robots.

GUNS

(See also Premiums, Comic Characters)

The average mint price of guns in the last edition was $172.86. In this edition it is $177.72, an increase of 3%.

THOUGHTS ON TOY GUN COLLECTING

by Charles W. Best

It can be argued that guns have changed and shaped the course of history in the United States. Throughout every conflict, beginning with the Revolutionary War, guns played a major role in the outcome of battles, both here and abroad. Important in a historical context, guns are a vital and important category of toy collecting. When toys began to be mass-produced after the Civil War, toy guns were among the first to appear on the market. Their success was instantaneous, and toy guns remained among the most popular selling toys through the 1960s.

Although toy guns were patented in the 1850s, they were not manufactured in any quantity until a decade later due to the wartime shortages. These early toy guns were, for the most part, pea shooters and cork poppers and were usually made of wood with metal hardware, although iron and lead types may occasionally be found among them. These early examples are hard to find today and most are known only through their patent drawings. By 1870 inventors, trying to add realism to these toy guns, began using paper caps. This invention had been developed just prior to the Civil War and was known as the Maynard Tape Primer. The tape primer was originally intended to detonate muzzle-loading arms and closely resembled a roll of modern paper caps. For the first time, toy guns could make a loud noise yet still be relatively safe and harmless. Naturally this spurred the demand for these new toys and designers worked overtime to create new and appealing guns. Their output was prolific and today the period from 1870 to 1900 in the U.S. is regarded as the "golden age" of the toy gun and especially the toy cap pistol.

By 1880 the cast-iron cap pistol had become the most popular type of toy gun by far, and the various toy makers, primarily J. & E. Stevens and Ives, were competing among themselves to see who could produce the most unique and appealing designs. A glance at any collection of these early toy pistols will show that realism was secondary to artistic imagination. Many pistols from this period were literally covered with ornamentation and, in some cases, any resemblance to a real gun was purely coincidental. Leaf and scroll designs were the most popular, but pistols can also be found with numerous other designs, including both two-dimensional and three-dimensional figures. Those guns with moving figures are known as "animated" pistols and, though not as rare as some, are worth much more to a collector than an ordinary-looking pistol from the same period.

Another very desirable pistol from the same era is known as the "head" pistol and featured a head, either animal or human, placed at the breech end of the barrel with the mouth open to receive the cap. Over two dozen varieties of head and animated pistols are known to exist but are so much in demand that they are seldom offered for sale.

The most popular material used to make these early toy pistols was cast iron, which continued to be used heavily into the twentieth century, until the demands of WWII cut off the supply. Many varieties of old toy guns were, however, made of materials other than iron. I have seen examples made from such diverse materials as paper, wood, steel, tin, lead, rubber, zinc, glass, and even wax. During WWII toy guns were even made of molded sawdust mixed with glue. After the war a few cast-iron pistols were produced and assembled, using both new and old parts, but the cost proved to be prohibitive, and makers soon turned to less expensive metals such as steel and die-cast zinc. By 1950 most toy pistols were being made of the die-cast material and also plastic, both of which continue to be used today.

From almost the very beginning, toy gun makers have felt the need to personalize their products, and literally hundreds of different names can be found embossed on these little guns. Some examples that come to mind are

Excelsior, Victor, American Bulldog, Acorn, Sun, Boom, Darb, Ace, Daisy, Cowboy King, Polo, Triumph, Terror, etc. Many names were used only once on one particular gun and then dropped, while others have reappeared time and again on different guns over the years. This custom of naming toy guns still goes on today and a visit to any toy store will turn up names such as Cowhand, Top Gun Jr., 007, etc. Many of these names seem to reflect current events or personalities but the meanings of others have become obscure.

Collectors of toy guns can choose from a large diversity of models and styles and, because of the tremendous historical popularity of these toys, collectors have the opportunity to acquire interesting and unusual examples at an affordable price. Guns from as far back as the 1920s and 1930s can still be found at flea markets, garage sales, and second-hand stores, often at a price that is only a fraction of what other toys from these same years will sell for.

Charles W. Best is a leading authority on toy weapons and has been collecting them in earnest since 1966. His collection is regarded as one of the finest and most comprehensive in existence and has won many awards at various gun shows. In addition to writing a number of articles on the subject in such magazines as Gun Report and Antique Toy World, he is the author of Cast-Iron Toy Pistols (see bibliography).

Photos in this section by Charles W. Best, unless otherwise noted.

Note: Measurements given, in general, are from one end of the gun to the other, rather than on a diagonal from grip to muzzle. Much of the information on manufacturers, measurements, etc., comes from Charles W. Best's excellent book Cast-iron Toy Pistols (see bibliography). Dates of manufacturers can vary within five years, though most of the later dates are considerably more accurate.

	C6	C8	C10
Ace cast-iron cap pistol, Stevens, "Made in U.S.A." 5" long, 1930	27	41	55
Ace cast-iron cap pistol, Kilgore, 5" long, 1935	22	33	45

"Ace" cast iron cap pistol, Kilgore.

	C6	C8	C10
Acme steel cap automatic, repeater, c. 1930	12	18	25
Acorn cast-iron pistol	75	100	150
Admiral Dewey cast-iron cap bomb	50	75	100
Aeromatic Glider Gun, steel automatic, c. 1940, shoots balsa airplanes	50	75	100
Agitator, The, cast-iron cap and torpedo shooter, John Fox, 1908, 8-1/4"	125	188	250
Aim To Save, c. 1909	150	225	300
Air Blaster, Wham-O, shoots burst of air, plastic	40	60	80

	C6	C8	C10
Air Raid Warning Signal pistol	30	50	75
America cap pistol with shield, pat. 1873	150	225	300
America, Stevens, 1880, 8-3/4"	135	200	275

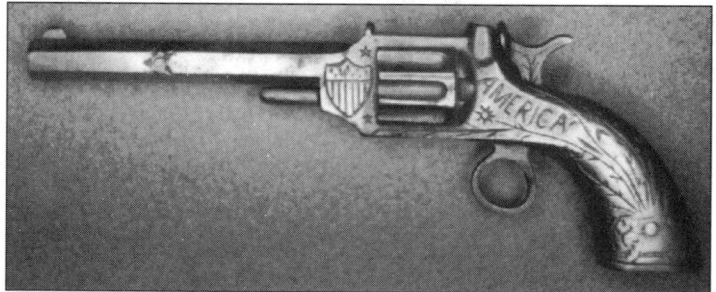

"America" by Stevens.

	C6	C8	C10
American cast-iron cap pistol, Kilgore, 1940, 9-5/8"	275	365	550

"American" by Kilgore.

"American Bulldog," 1910. Courtesy Sotheby's New York.

	C6	C8	C10
American Bulldog cast-iron .22 cal. blank shooter, Kenton, 1910, 4-1/2" long, second trigger tips barrel to load, handle projects outward	40	60	80
American Bulldog cast-iron .22 blank shooter, 1920, 4-1/2" long, Kenton, second trigger tips barrel to load, handle curves inward	45	68	90
Army cast-iron cap pistol, 1910	40	60	80
Army 45 cast-iron cap automatic, Hubley, 1940 "Made in U.S.A." 6-5/8"	80	120	160
Army 45 die-cast zinc cap automatic, Hubley, 1940, plastic grips, "Made in U.S.A." 6-1/2" long	45	68	90

Army 45.

	C6	C8	C10
Army pistol with revolving cylinder, tin litho, Marx No. 625	17	25	35
Army sparkling pop gun, Marx No. 197	17	25	35
Astro Ray Signal-Dart gun, plastic, 10", 1960s, Ohio Art	50	75	100
Atomic Disintegrator cap pistol, Hubley	175	260	350
Atomic Flash space gun, Chein	31	46	62
Auto Magic Picture Gun, projects film onto wall, 1936, comes with film and instructions, in box	75	112	150
Auto Repeating Cap Exploder	45	68	90
Automatic die-cast cap pistol, Hubley No. 290, 6-1/2"	55	83	110
Automatic Repeater Paper Pop Pistol, Marx No. 74, aluminum	15	20	25
Automatic Repeater, pressed steel, 7" long, 1920s, Wyandotte No. 40	20	25	30

	C6	C8	C10
Bang cast-iron cap pistol, Kilgore, "Made in U.S.A.," 6" long	25	38	50
Bang-O cast-iron cap pistol, Stevens, 1938, "Made in U.S.A.," 7" long	42	63	85
Banner, blank-shooting mechanical cast-iron pistol, Ives, 5"	150	175	250

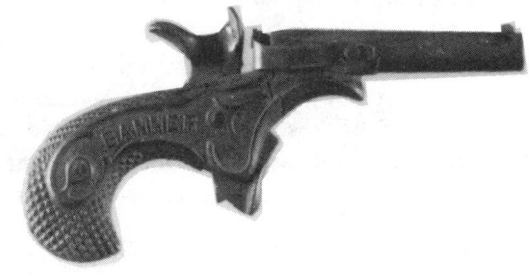

"Banner." Courtesy Sotheby's New York.

	C6	C8	C10
Bell Pistol, Wyandotte	15	23	31
Benjamin Pump early BB gun, before 1910	75	112	150
Biff cast-iron cap automatic, Kenton, 1935, "Made in U.S.A. Pat. Apld. For," 4-1/2"	42	63	85
Biff Jr. cast-iron cap automatic, Kenton, 1935, "Made in U.S.A. Pat. Apld. For," 4-1/8" long	30	45	60
Big Bang Pistol No. 6P, 7-7/8" long	150	225	300
Big Bang Rifle No. 21-60, 21-3/16" long	750	2000	3500
Big Bill cast-iron cap pistol, large hammer, "Made in U.S.A.," Kilgore, 1935, 4-7/8"	30	45	60

Left to right. Top: Big Bill, Pluck, Dick. Middle: Atomic Disintegrator, Sure Shot Safety. Bottom: Tiger, Gene Autry 44. Photo Courtesy Garth's Auctions Inc.

	C6	C8	C10
Big Bill cast-iron cap pistol, Kilgore, 1925, 5-1/2" long	30	45	60
Big Bill cast-iron cap pistol, large hammer, "Made in U.S.A.," Kilgore, 1930, 5-3/4"	50	75	100
Big Buster cast-iron cap automatic, Kilgore, 1915, "Patd Jul 2 1907, Made in U.S.A.," 5", two-piece trigger	75	112	150
Big Chief cast-iron cap pistol, Kilgore, 1935, 6" long	22	33	45
Big Chief cast-iron cap pistol, Kilgore, 1935, has star and "K," 6"	22	33	45
Big Chief cast-iron cap pistol, early-looking but made in 1930, 3-1/2", Dent, "Made in U.S.A."	22	33	45
Big Clip cast-iron cap pistol, Stevens, 1930, "Made in U.S.A.," 6-3/4"	25	38	50

	C6	C8	C10
Big Horn cast-iron cap pistol, revolving cylinder, Kilgore, 1939, 8-3/8"	182	275	365
Big Injun, hammerless	150	225	300
Big Scout, 1935	67	100	135
Big Scout, 1940 (engraved)	30	45	60
Bigger Bang large hammer cast-iron cap pistol, Kilgore, 1930, 6" long	32	48	65
Bill	35	52	70
Billy The Kid cast-iron cap pistol, Stevens, 1938, 6-3/4"	75	112	150
Black Jack cast-iron cap pistol, long barrel, Kenton, 1930, "Pat. Sept. 11-23," 11"	125	188	250
Blaze Away Dart Pistol, Marx No. G23	15	22	30
Bob cast-iron cap pistol, Kilgore, 1930, 5" long	25	38	50
Bobcat die-cast cap pistol, Kilgore, 1950s, 4-1/4"	19	28	38
Boom	150	225	300

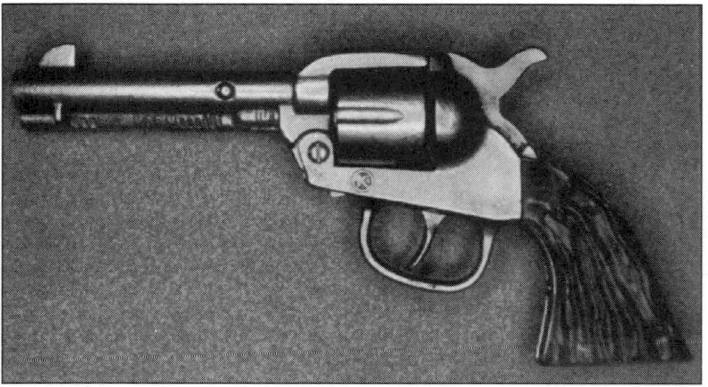

"Big Horn."

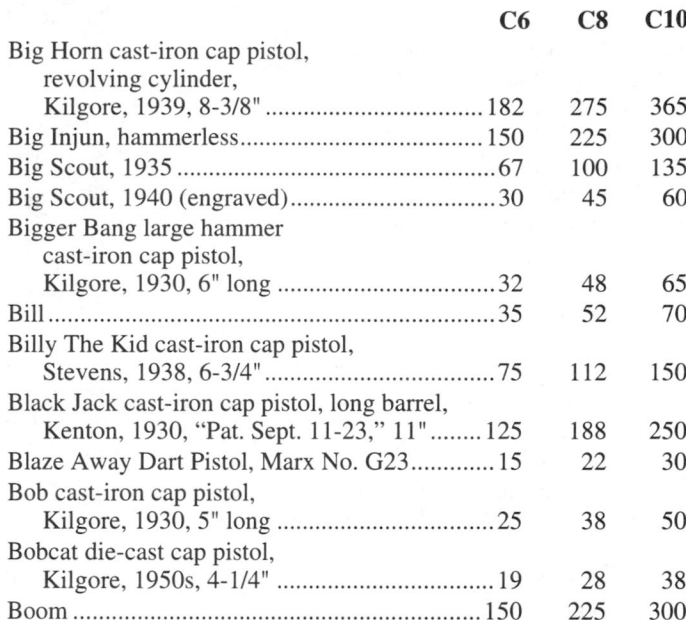

"Border Patrol," 1940. Courtesy Sotheby's New York.

"Bull's Eye Safety."

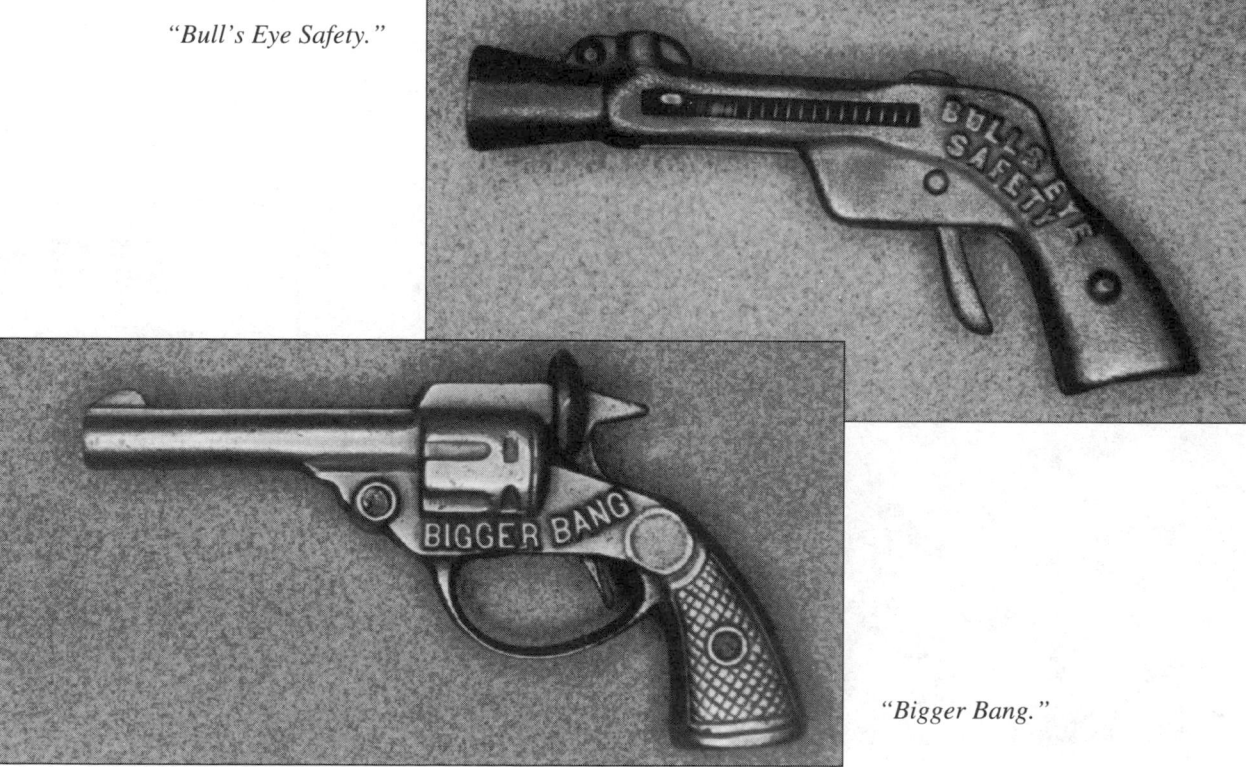

"Bigger Bang."

	C6	C8	C10
Border Patrol cast-iron cap automatic, Kilgore, 1930, 4-1/4" long	32	48	65
Border Patrol cast-iron cap automatic, Kilgore, 1935, "Pat. Apld. For, Made in U.S.A.," 4-1/2" long	50	75	100
Border Patrol, 1940	35	52	70
Boss cast-iron mammoth cap pistol, Kenton, 1925, 6-1/4"	30	45	60
Boy's Delight, pat. June 1891, cast-iron cap pistol	150	225	300
Boy's Police Automatic 8" cardboard pop gun, c. 1940s	8	12	15
Brat cast-iron cap pistol	30	45	60
Bravo	75	112	150
Brevet Depose	300	450	600
Bronc cast-iron cap pistol, Kenton, 1935, "Kenton Made in U.S.A.," 6"	30	45	60
Buc-A-Roo cast-iron cap pistol, Kilgore, 1940, 7-3/4"	50	75	100
Buccaneer flintlock pistol, fires plastic bullets, 1958, Nichols, 3-1/2"	37	56	75
Buck cast-iron pistol, Hubley, 1930, looks earlier, 3-1/4"	55	82	110
Buckle Gun, Mattel, w/ bullets	48	72	95
Buddy, 1930	25	38	50
Buddy, 1935	25	38	50
Buffalo cap rifle, Hubley	82	125	165
Buffalo Bill, 1890	200	300	400
Buffalo Bill cast-iron cap pistol, Kenton, 1925, "Pat. Sept. 11-23," 11-3/8", very long barrel	150	225	300
Buffalo Bill cast-iron cap pistol, Kenton, 1930, "Pat. Sept. 11-23," 13-1/2", perhaps the longest barreled cap pistol	150	225	300
Buffalo Bill cast-iron cap pistol, Stevens, 1940, "Made in U.S.A.," 7-3/4" long	72	110	145
Bull cast-iron cap pistol, Hubley, 1940, "Pat Appld. for Pat. Mch. 25, '24," 6-1/4"	25	38	50
Bulldog cast-iron cap pistol, Kenton, 1923, 5-1/2"	37	56	75
Bull Dog cast-iron cap pistol, Hubley, 1935, "Pat. 1,488,046," 6-1/4" long	27	41	55
Bulldozer cast-iron cap pistol, six-shooter, July 1874	150	225	300

	C6	C8	C10
Bull's Eye cast-iron cap pistol, Kenton, 1940, "Gene Autry" signature on grips, 6-1/2"	125	188	250
Bullseye Safety cast-iron pistol, flare barrel, with spring	75	112	150
Bunker Hill cast-iron cap pistol, National, 1925, 5-1/4" long	25	38	50
Burp Gun, Mattel, 1956, 13" long, aluminum, die-cast, plastic	45	68	90
"Buster," maker unknown, 1901, 6"	212	318	425
Buster cast-iron cap automatic, 1910, Kilgore 5-1/2"	45	68	90
Butting Match mechanical pistol, cast iron	250	375	500
Cadet, 1930	27	41	55
Cal, 1925	30	45	60
Cannon Animated Cap Pistol	250	375	500

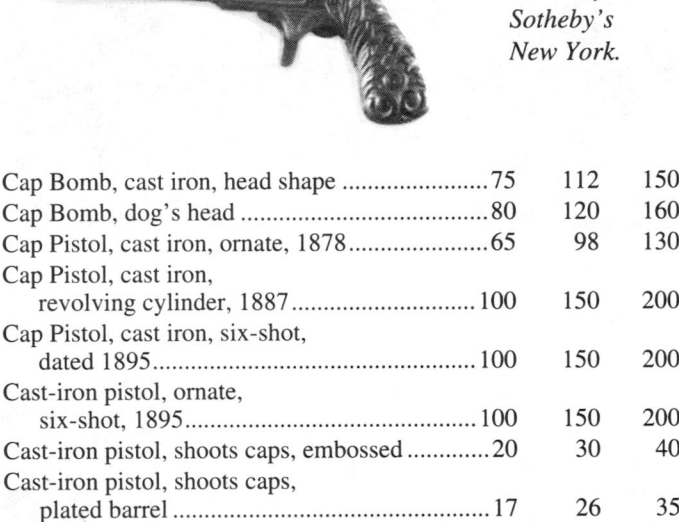

"Cannon." Courtesy Sotheby's New York.

	C6	C8	C10
Cap Bomb, cast iron, head shape	75	112	150
Cap Bomb, dog's head	80	120	160
Cap Pistol, cast iron, ornate, 1878	65	98	130
Cap Pistol, cast iron, revolving cylinder, 1887	100	150	200
Cap Pistol, cast iron, six-shot, dated 1895	100	150	200
Cast-iron pistol, ornate, six-shot, 1895	100	150	200
Cast-iron pistol, shoots caps, embossed	20	30	40
Cast-iron pistol, shoots caps, plated barrel	17	26	35

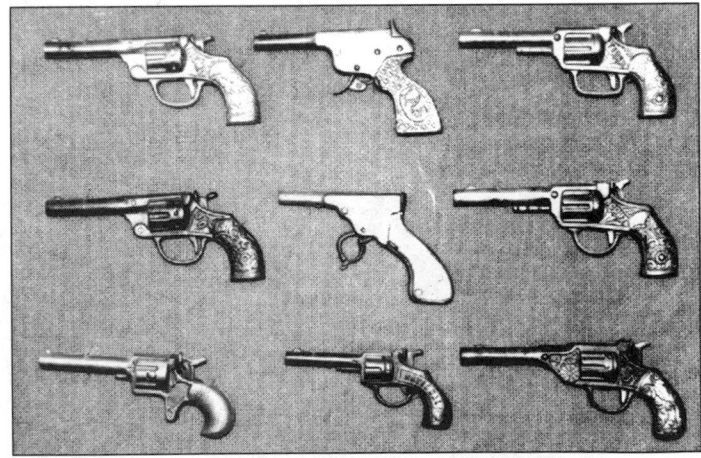

Typical cast-iron cap pistols 1900-1910. Top, left to right: Nemo, Las, Tiger 1915. Middle: Go, Buster 1910, Scout 1890. Bottom: Unmarked, National (Stevens 1920), Unmarked. Courtesy Charles W. Best.

"Buster," maker unknown, 1901, 6" long.

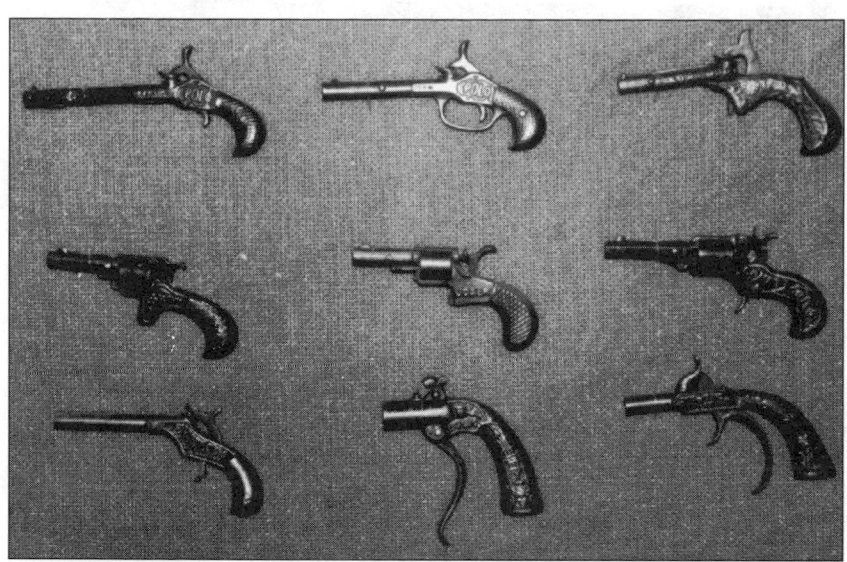

Typical cast-iron cap pistols, 1870-1880. Top, left to right: Polo, Polo, Triumph. Row 2: Bravo, Joker, Comet. Bottom: Excelsior, L.F. & C., Stephans Pat. Courtesy Charles W. Best.

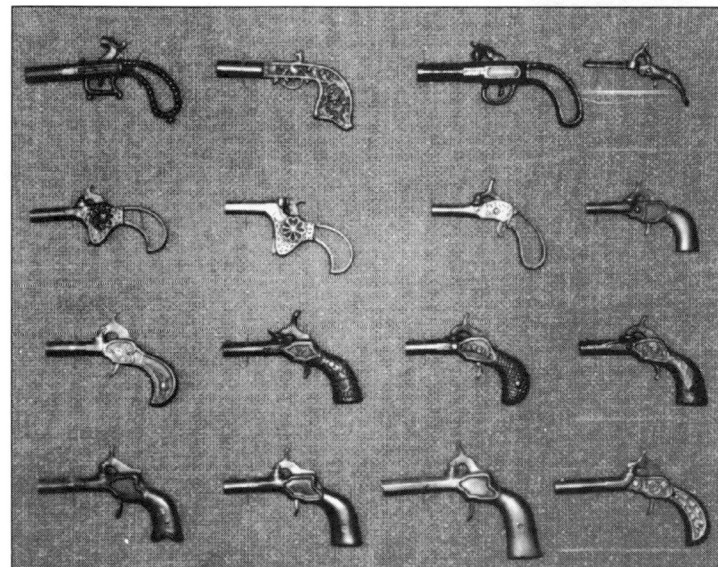

Typical cast-iron cap pistols, 1880-1890. Top, left to right: Frontier, Echo, Lion; Row 2: Terror, Brevet Depose, US Navy; Row 3: Hammerless, America; Row 4: Unmarked, Texas Jack. Photo courtesy Charles W. Best.

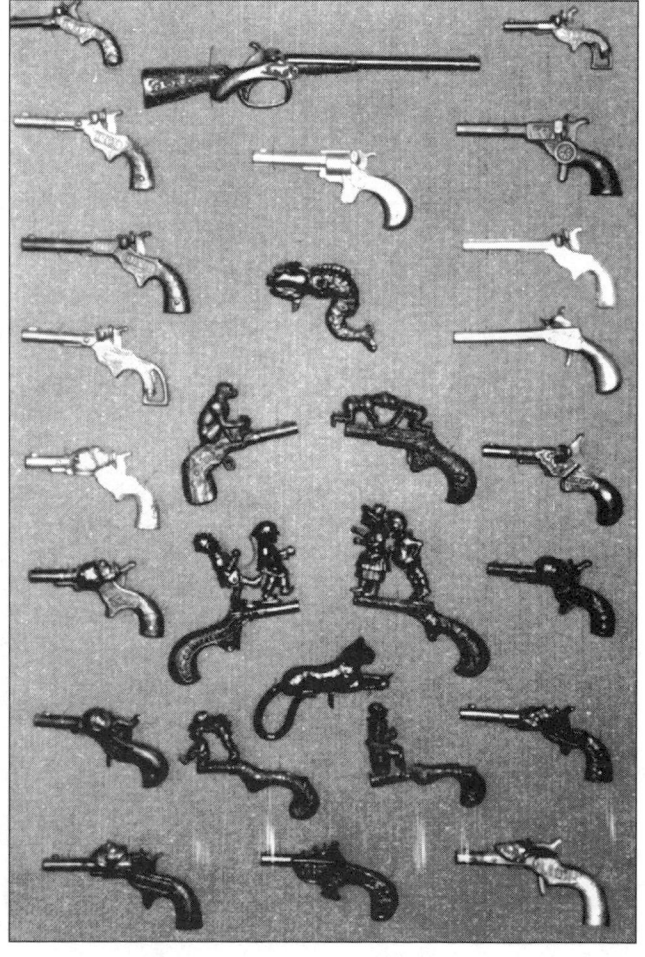

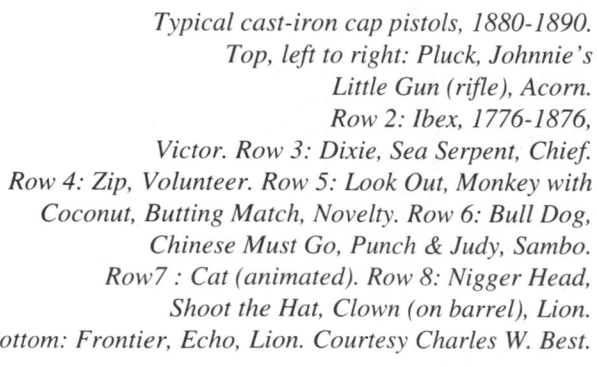

Typical cast-iron cap pistols, 1880-1890. Top, left to right: Pluck, Johnnie's Little Gun (rifle), Acorn. Row 2: Ibex, 1776-1876, Victor. Row 3: Dixie, Sea Serpent, Chief. Row 4: Zip, Volunteer. Row 5: Look Out, Monkey with Coconut, Butting Match, Novelty. Row 6: Bull Dog, Chinese Must Go, Punch & Judy, Sambo. Row7 : Cat (animated). Row 8: Nigger Head, Shoot the Hat, Clown (on barrel), Lion. Bottom: Frontier, Echo, Lion. Courtesy Charles W. Best.

Typical cast-iron cap pistols, 1890-1900. Top, left to right: Unmarked, S&S, Unmarked, Fido. Row 2: Halt, Colt, Ranger. Row 3: Cupid, Navy, Army. Bottom: 6-Shot 1895, U.S.A. Liquid Pistol, Star. Courtesy Charles W. Best.

Typical cast-iron cap pistols, 1900-1910. Top, left to right: American Bulldog 1920, Agitator, The Hanson-Lindsborg K.S. Middle: Magic 1900, Unmarked .22 blank shooter, Unmarked. Bottom: Cowboy 1890, Boss 1925, Star 1910. Courtesy Charles W. Best.

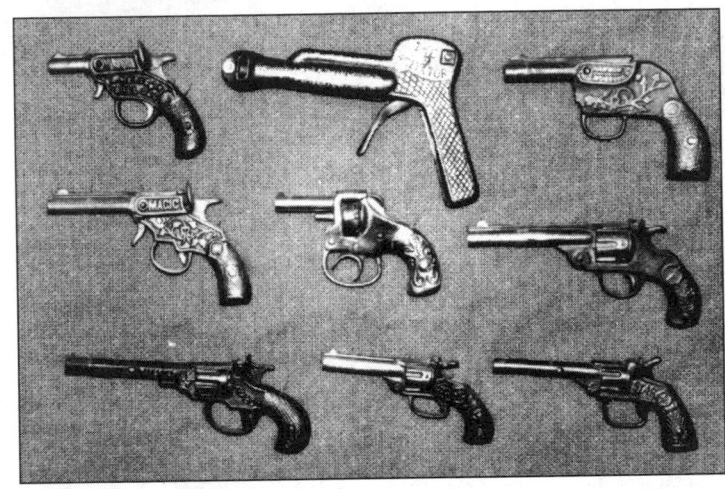

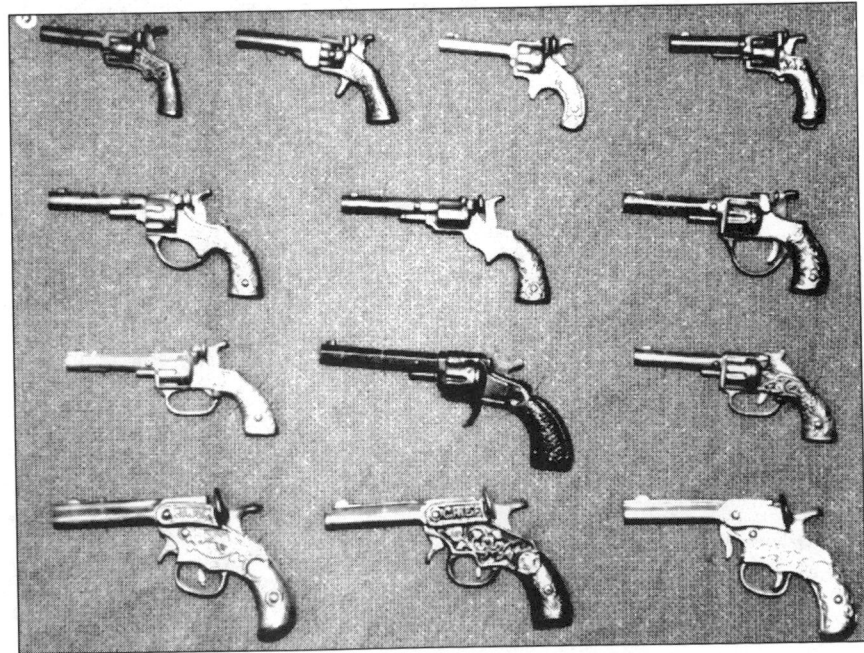

Typical cast-iron cap pistols 1900-1910. Top, left to right: Star, Unmarked, "P", Snap; Second Row: Model, Model, Unmarked; Third Row: GIP, Wildwest, Unmarked; Bottom: Major, Chief, Rival. Courtesy Charles W. Best.

Typical cast-iron cap pistols, 1910-1920. Top, left to right: Echo, Crack, Cal. Row 2: Unmarked, Unmarked, Peerless. Row 3: "730," Lion, Lion, Unmarked Automatic. Row 4: Premier Safety, Unmarked, OK, Premier Safety. Bottom (small pistols): Gem, Gem. Courtesy Charles W. Best.

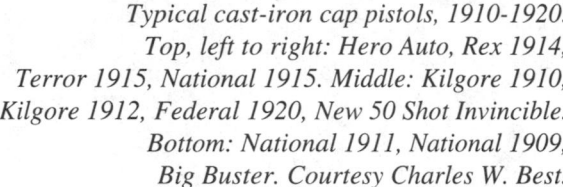

Typical cast-iron cap pistols, 1910-1920. Top, left to right: Hero Auto, Rex 1914, Terror 1915, National 1915. Middle: Kilgore 1910, Kilgore 1912, Federal 1920, New 50 Shot Invincible. Bottom: National 1911, National 1909, Big Buster. Courtesy Charles W. Best.

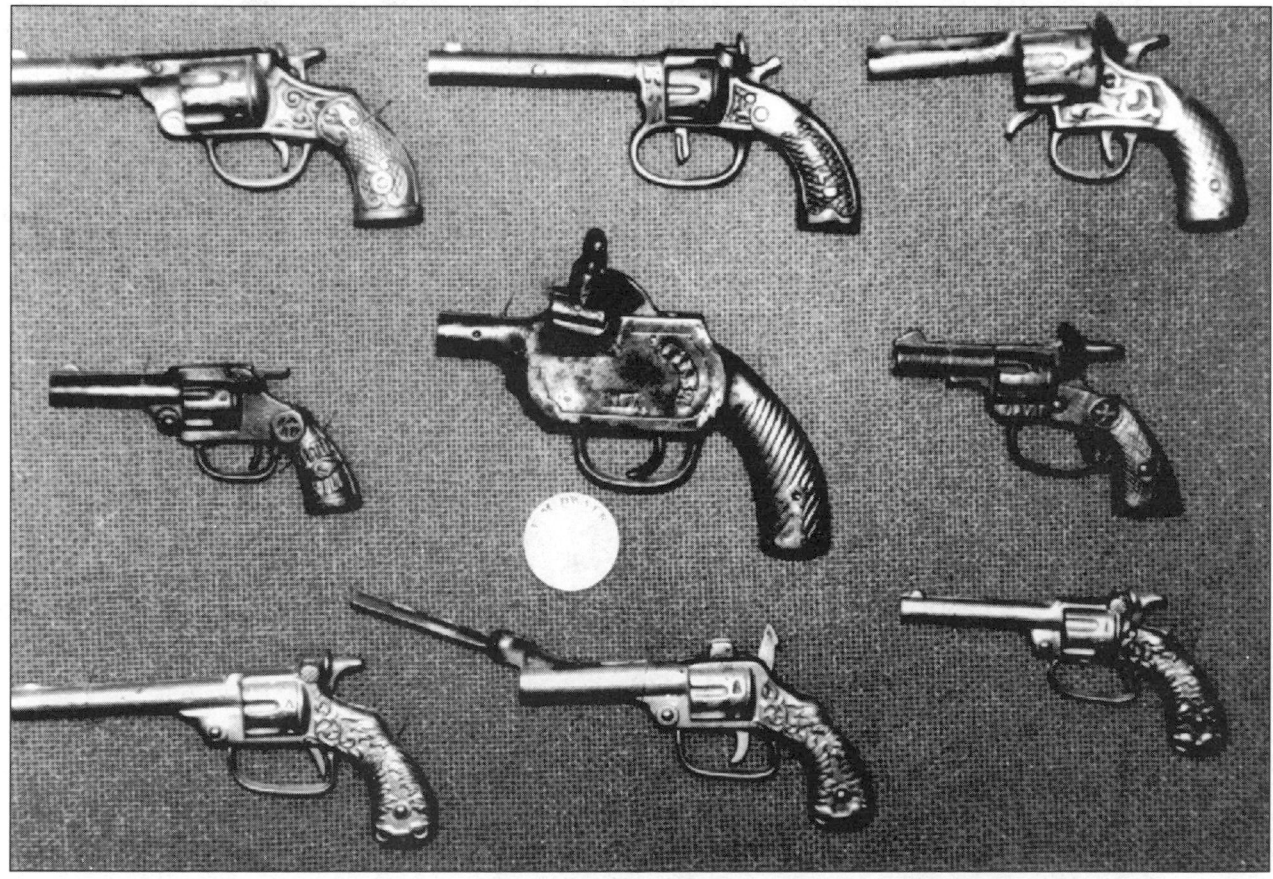

Typical cast-iron cap pistols, 1910-1920. Top, left to right: Detroit, Wild West, Unmarked. Middle: Little Bill, First No. 1, David. Bottom: all unmarked, in the middle a disk shooter. Courtesy Charles W. Best.

Typical cast-iron cap pistols, 1920-1930. Top, left to right: Oh Boy 1922, Bunker Hill, Big Bill 1925. Middle: Federal 1920, Ranger 1920, New 50 Shot Invincible. Bottom: Imperial, Master 1922, National No. 380. Courtesy Charles W. Best.

Typical cast-iron cap pistols, 1920-1930. Top, left to right: Unmarked, OK, Unmarked. Row 2: Safety First, Scout Master, Army. Row 3: Warrior, Unmarked, Two Time. Bottom: Unmarked blank shooters. Courtesy Charles W. Best.

Typical cast-iron cap pistols, 1920-1930. Top, left to right: Pluck, Buck, Gem, Unmarked, Unmarked. Row 2: Daisey, Bill, Villa. Row 3: Zip, Bill, King. Bottom: Safety, Bull, Cop. Courtesy Charles W. Best.

Typical cast-iron cap pistols, 1920-1930. Top, left to right: Dandy (Police .38), Six Shooter. Row 2: Army .45, Texas Centennial 1936, G-Man. Row 3: Bull Dog, Machine Gun, Target. Row 4: Texan Jr., Six Shooter. Row 5: Lasso 'em Bill, Lone Ranger. Row 6: Gene Autry, American. Bottom: Gene Autry, Pawnee Bill. Courtesy Charles W. Best.

	C6	C8	C10
Cap pistol, steel, repeating, red, Wyandotte, 8" long	15	22	30
Captain cast-iron cap automatic, Kilgore, 1940, 4-1/4" long	35	52	70
Cat (animated)	450	675	900
Cavalier cast-iron cap automatic, Kilgore, 1935, "Pat. Appld. For, Made in U.S.A.," 4-1/2"	35	52	70
Challenge, 1890	150	225	300
Champ Automatic, 5", die-cast, Hubley	55	82	110

"Champ."

	C6	C8	C10
Chief (1900-1910)	110	165	220
Chief cast-iron .22 cal. blank shooter, Kenton, 1915, 6" long, second trigger tips up barrel to load	50	75	100
Chief cast-iron cap pistol, Hubley, 1930, "Pat 1,488,046," 6-1/8"	25	38	50
Chief cap pistol, aluminum single shot, Hubley	30	45	60
Chieftain cast-iron cap pistol, National, 1920, 11" long	75	112	150
Chinese Must Go mechanical cap pistol	250	375	500
"Click Pistol," Marx No. 32	15	22	30
Click Pistol, Marx, approx. 7-3/4" long, pressed steel, with box	15	22	30
Click Pistol, tin litho, Marx No. 36	15	22	30
Clicker Pistol, plain black, late 1930s, early 1940s	15	22	30
Clip 50, bakelite & cast-iron, Kilgore, 1940, 4-1/4"	60	90	120

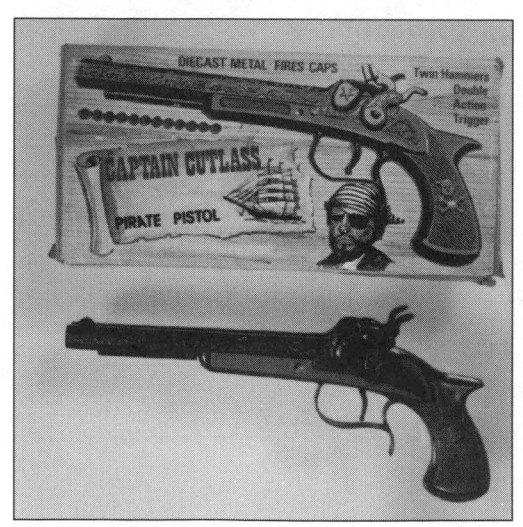

Captain Cutlass Pirate Pistol, Spanish-made, 9-1/2" long. Copy of Pirate by HUBLEY. Cast zinc. No price found.

Clown (on barrel).

	C6	C8	C10
Clip Jr. cast-iron cap pistol, Stevens, 1935, 5-1/4"	25	38	50
Clipper cast-iron cap automatic, Kilgore, 1935, 4-1/8"	48	72	95
Clown and mule animated pistol	500	750	1000
Clown (on a barrel)	350	525	700
Colt cast-iron cap pistol, Stevens, 1920, "Patented June 17, 1890, Made in U.S.A.," 5-1/2"	50	75	100
Colt cast-iron cap pistol, Stevens, 1935, 6-1/2"	27	41	55
Colt .45 die-cast Hubley	85	130	170
Columbia, 1885 cast-iron cap pistol	200	300	400
Columbia, 1890 cast-iron cap pistol, Stevens 8-3/4"	200	300	400
Columbia cast-iron cap pistol, pat. June 1891	200	300	400
Columbian Junior early BB gun	250	375	500
Comet, 1885, 5-1/2", Stevens	150	225	300
Comet, 1925, 7-1/8", Stevens	40	60	80

	C6	C8	C10
Cop cast-iron cap pistol, Hubley, 1930 "Pat 1,488,046" or "Pat. Mch. 25 '24," 5"	25	38	50
Cork-popper pistol, Wyandotte, spur trigger	7	11	15
Cork-shooting rifle, Marx No. 206	10	15	20
Corn Shooter cap pistol	55	82	110
Corporal, maker unknown, 1900, 8-7/8"	62	93	125
Cowboy cast-iron cap pistol, Ives, 1890, 7-5/8"	125	188	250
Cowboy cast-iron cap pistol, Stevens, 1935, "Made in U.S.A.," 3-1/2"	15	22	30
Cowboy cast-iron cap pistol, long barrel, Stevens, 1930, "Made in U.S.A."	175	263	350
Cowboy cast-iron cap pistol, Hubley, 1940 "Made in U.S.A.," 8"	55	83	110
Cowboy King, 1940	138	205	275
Coyote, die-cast, Hubley	27	41	55
Crack, 1925, Stevens 5"	40	60	80

"Columbia" by Stevens, 1890.

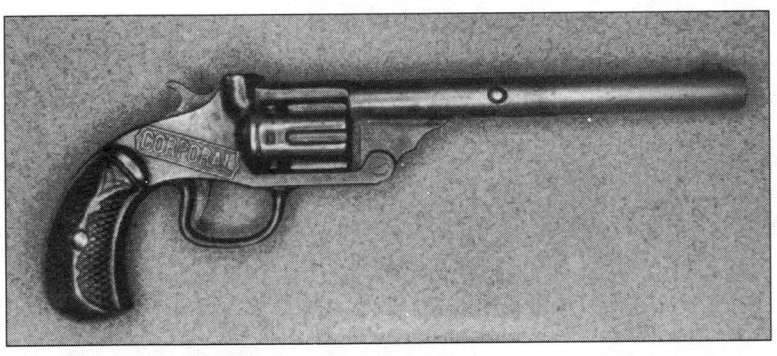

"Corporal."

"Dagger Derringer."

	C6	C8	C10
Cupid, 1900, 5-1/4"	62	93	125
Dagger Derringer, die-cast, Hubley	35	52	70
Dandy cast-iron cap pistol, Hubley, 1935, can have variety of markings, 5-3/4"	35	52	70
Daniel Boone Wilderness Scout Derringer, Marx, mint on card	25	38	50
Darb cast-iron cap pistol, Kenton, 1930, "Pat. Sept. 11-23," 5-1/2" long	30	45	60
Dart Pistol, Wyandotte, colorful, fancy lithographing	11	16	22
David	40	60	80
Dead Shot, Stevens, 8-3/4"	125	188	250
Defence, 1896	75	112	150
Derby cast-iron cap pistol, Hubley, 1930, 7"	30	45	60

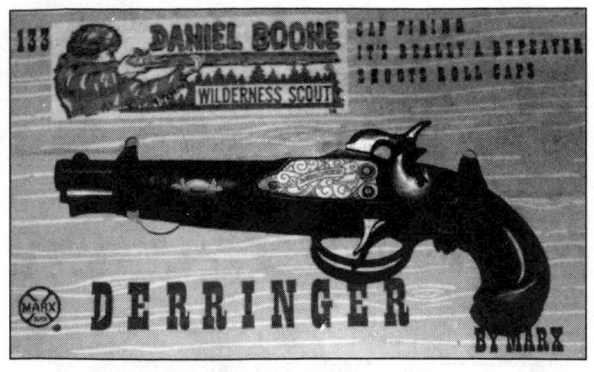

Daniel Boone Wilderness Scout Derringer. Photo by Gary J. Linden.

	C6	C8	C10
Desert Patrol Luger & Silencer, Marx, 1960s, 10"	15	22	30
Detroit cast-iron cap pistol, 1910, 6-5/8" long	65	98	130
Dick cast-iron cap pistol, Hubley, 1930, 6"	30	45	60
Dick cast-iron cap automatic, Hubley, 1940, "Made in U.S.A.," 4-1/8"	30	45	60
Dick die-cast cap automatic, 4-1/4"	21	31	42
DIK cast-iron cap pistol, Kenton, 1935, "Pat. Sept. 11-23," 4-3/4"	27	41	55
Dixie (1888-1890)	75	112	150
Dixie cast-iron cap pistol, Kenton, 1935, "Made in U.S.A. Pat. Appld. For," 6-1/4"	42	63	85
Doc cast-iron cap pistol, Kenton, 1926, "Pat. Sept. 11-23," 4-1/2"	55	82	110
Dolphin animated cap pistol (may actually be Sea Serpent)	400	600	800

Dragnet Detective Special Reporting Revolver Cap Gun, c. 1955. Courtesy HAKE'S Americana & Collectibles.

	C6	C8	C10
Dragnet Detective Special repeating revolver cap gun, c. 1955	27	41	55
Duck, animated cap pistol, cast iron, 3-3/4" long, 1884	2500	3000	5000

Dolphin. Courtesy Sotheby's New York.

Duck. Courtesy Sotheby's New York..

	C6	C8	C10
Double-barrel cast-iron cap pistol, dated 1880	125	188	250
Double-barrel pop gun-rifle, Marx No. 230	50	75	100
Double-barrel cork gun-rifle, Marx No. 232	50	75	100
Double-faced cap bomb, cast iron	60	90	120
Double-trigger cast-iron match-shooting pistol, large, Stephens PA, 1873	125	188	250
Doughboy cast-iron cap automatic, Kilgore, 1920, "Made in U.S.A.," 5"	45	68	90

	C6	C8	C10
Dude cast-iron pistol, Stevens, 1887, "Pat. Mar. 22 '87," 3-1/2"	75	112	150
Dude cast-iron cap pistol, plastic grips, Kenton, 1941, 6-1/2"	40	60	80
Eagle cast-iron cap pistol, Stevens, 1985, "Pat. June 17, 1890," 7-1/2"	82	123	165
Eagle, c. 1940	40	60	80
Echo cap pistol, six-shooter, cast iron, 1881	425	638	850

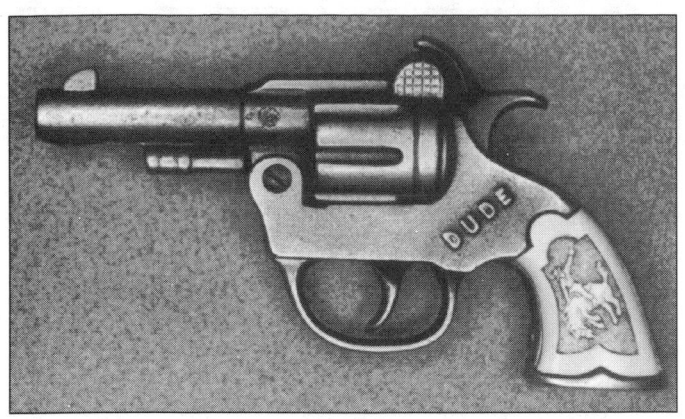

Dude cast-iron cap.

	C6	C8	C10
Echo cast-iron cap pistol, Stevens, 1920, 4-1/4"	32	48	65
Echo cast-iron cap pistol, Stevens, 1930, "Made in U.S.A.," 4-1/2"	25	38	50
Electronic Space Gun, flashlight gun, plastic, Remco	37	56	75
Excelsior cast-iron cap pistol, Stevens, 1875, "Pat'd Apr. 22, '73," 5-1/4"	125	188	250
Federal cast-iron cap pistol, Kilgore, 1920, 5-1/2"	25	38	50
Federal cast-iron cap automatic, Kilgore, 1940, has removable clip to hold caps, 4-7/8"	37	56	75

Federal-Kilgore No. 1. Courtesy Sotheby's New York.

	C6	C8	C10
Federal cast-iron cap pistol, Kilgore, 1920, "Pat. Dec. 14; Made in U.S.A."	37	56	75
Federal-Kilgore No.1, cast-iron cap pistol, Kilgore, 1925, 5-1/4"	25	38	50
Federal No. 2, cast-iron cap pistol, Kilgore, 1925, 6-3/8"	60	90	120
Fido, 1910, 4"	50	75	100
Firecracker pistol, filigree handle, cast iron	100	150	200
First No. 1, 1920, 6-3/4"	135	190	270
Five-barrel firecracker pistol, iron and brass, 1877	500	800	1200
5-Star steel dart pistol, Wyandotte	15	22	30
Flash cast-iron cap pistol, Hubley, 1934, "Pat'd," 6-1/4"	37	55	75
Flintlock, die-cast, Hubley No. 280, 9-1/4"	35	52	70
Flintlock Junior, die-cast, Hubley	17	26	35
Flintlock Midget, die-cast, Hubley	15	22	30
Flying Saucer Gun, Auburn Rubber, 1964	12	18	25
Four Way, cast-iron cap pistol, Kenton, 1930, "Pat. Appld. For," shoots pea or dart, rubber band and cap, all at same time	150	225	300
.45 Smoker, blows cap smoke, c. 1946	30	45	60
49-ER, cast-iron cap pistol, Stevens, 1940, 9"	142	215	285

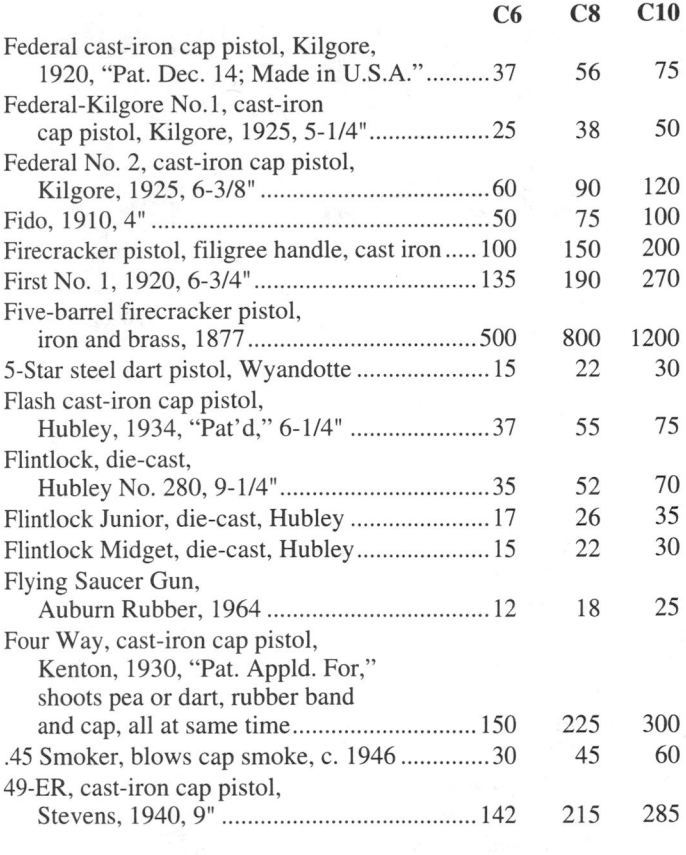

Top to bottom: Flintlock, Flintlock Jr., Flintlock Midget.

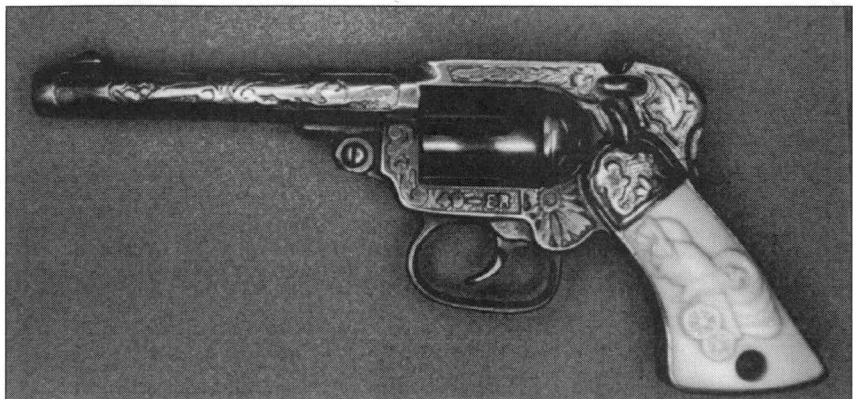

"49-ER."

	C6	C8	C10
Fox, cast-iron cap pistol, Hubley, 1935, 4-1/2"	22	33	45
Frontier, cast-iron cap pistol, Ives, 1890, "Pat. June 21, 1887 and June 17, 1890," dog's head atop the barrel facing hammer	200	300	400
G-Man, cast-iron cap automatic, Kilgore, 1935, looks like German Luger, removable magazine holds caps, 6"	100	150	200

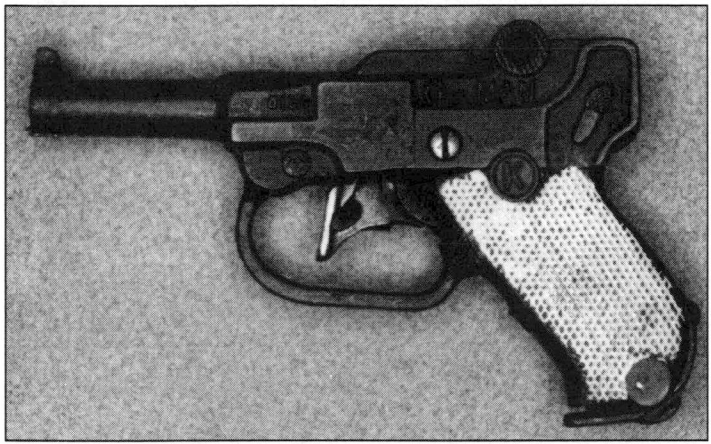

G-Man cast-iron cap automatic, Kilgore 1935.

	C6	C8	C10
G-Man, bakelite-framed cap automatic, Kilgore, 1940, 6"	50	75	100
G-Man, clicker pistol, tin, black	17	26	35
G-Man, wind-up steel spark pistol, painted finish	58	90	115
G-Man, wind-up steel spark pistol, nickel finish with jewels on grip	58	90	115
"G-Man Automatic," Marx, sparkles when wound, 1930s	58	90	115
G-Man automatic sparkling pistol, Marx No. 43, aluminum	58	90	115
G-Man automatic sparkling pistol, Marx No. 44, tin	58	90	115
G-Man automatic sparkling pistol, Marx No. 85, tin	58	90	115
G-Man Gun, Marx, tin litho w/ wood stock, machine gun	165	250	330
G-Man Gun, Marx No. 707	37	56	75
G-Man Silent Alarm Pistol, Marx No. 54, tin	17	26	35

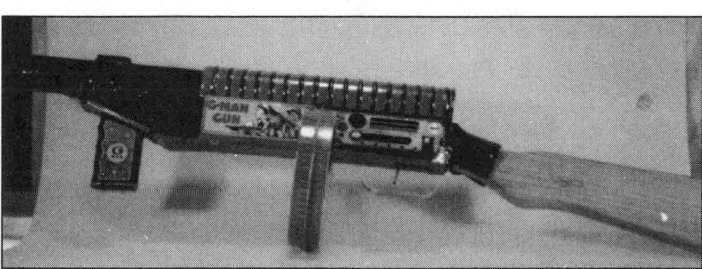

G-Man Gun, Marx, tin litho with wood stock. Courtesy Gary Linden.

	C6	C8	C10
G-Man Sparkling Sub-Machine Gun, Marx, siren, tin, 26" long	60	90	120
G-Man Tin Wind-Up Machine Gun, 1940s, miniature	20	30	40
Gang Busters full-size Marx Sub-Machine Gun	125	188	250
Gem cast-iron pistol, Stevens, 1900, 3"	27	41	55
Gem, 1925	16	24	33
Gene Autry cast-iron cap pistol, Kenton, 1939, 8-3/8"	88	130	175

Gene Autry cast-iron cap pistol, Kenton 1939, 8-3/8".

	C6	C8	C10
Gene Autry cast-iron cap pistol, Kenton, 1939, "Made in U.S.A. Pat. Appl'd For," 6-1/2"	75	112	150

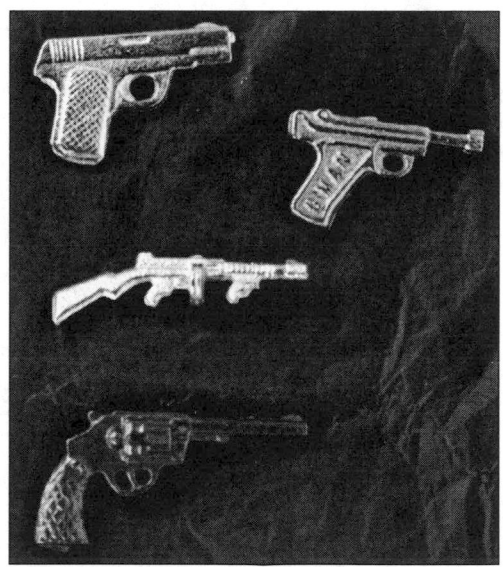

GREY IRON cast these solid cast iron weapons in the 1930s and early 1940s. John Wright casts them today. The Revolver is 2-1/2" long. Since there may be no way of telling old castings from new, the price averages about $1 each.

	C6	C8	C10
Gene Autry cast-iron cap pistol, Kenton, 1940, "Made in U.S.A." red grips, 6-1/2" 75		112	150
Gene Autry cast-iron cap pistol (doesn't fire caps), Kenton, 1940, "Made in U.S.A.," 6-1/2" 90		135	180
Gip, 1900.....................................25		38	50
Go cast-iron cap pistol, 1910, maker unknown, 6-3/4" 35		52	70
Go Bang 100		150	200
Guard cast-iron cap pistol, Kilgore, 1935, "Made in U.S.A.," 6-1/4" 30		45	60

	C6	C8	C10
Hi-Ho cast-iron cap pistol, Kilgore, 1940, 6-1/2" 37		56	75
Hi-Ho cast-iron cap pistol, Kenton, 1940, "Pat. Sept. 11-23," 5-1/8" 37		56	75
Hi-Ranger cast-iron cap pistol, Stevens, 1940, 7-3/4" 40		60	80
Hopalong Cassidy 9" Revolver, Wyandotte, "Hopalong" on both sides of handle 180		270	360
Hopalong Cassidy 10" Revolver with bust of Hopalong, Schmidt................135		200	270

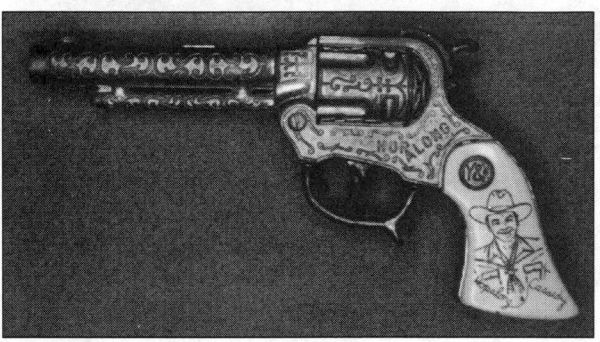

"Hopalong Cassidy."

	C6	C8	C10
Hub cast-iron cap pistol, Hubley, 1940, 6-1/4" 25		38	50
Hustler cast-iron pistol 55		82	110

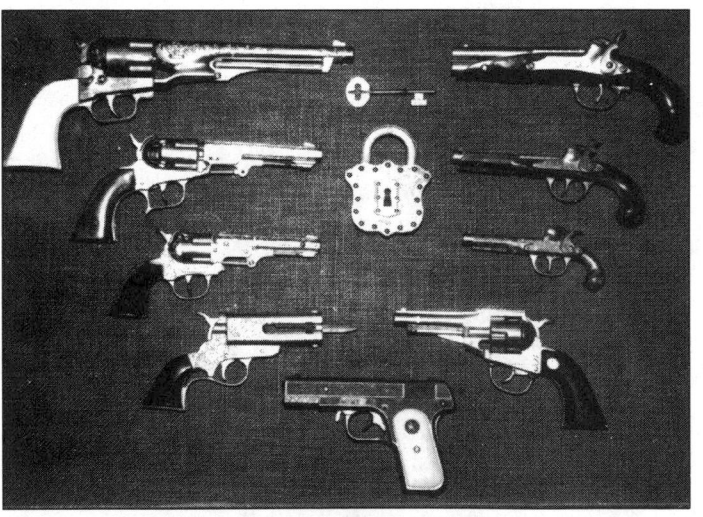

Some classic Hubley die-cast cap pistols from the 1950s. Top, left to right: Colt .45, Flintlock. Row 2: Pioneer, Padlock Pistol with key, Flintlock Jr. Row 3: Coyote, Flintlock Midget. Row 4: Dagger Derringer, Remington .36. Bottom: Army .45 (automatic). Courtesy Charles W. Best.

	C6	C8	C10
Ibex, Stevens, 1895, 4-1/2" 60		90	120
Ideal, tin dart-shooter 15		22	30
Imperial cast-iron cap pistol, Kilgore, 1935, 5-1/4" 45		68	90

This dart gun came with "The Great Family Amusement Game," manufactured by Elastic Top Co., 370 Atlantic Ave., Boston, Massachusetts. The set shows patent dates of 1889, 1890 and 1892. Value of the set in mint about $120. Photo by Al Smith.

	C6	C8	C10
H-Bar-O cast-iron cap pistol, Kilgore, 1925, "Made in U.S.A." 7-1/2" 45		68	90
Halt...40		60	80
Hammerless cast-iron cap pistol, Stevens, 1892, "Pat. Appl'd For" four revolving triggers, hammer, concealed, 7-1/4" 150		225	300
Hanson-Lindsborg K.S. cast-iron firecracker pistol, Hanson, 1905, "Pat. Appl'd For," fires firecracker, 6-3/8" 65		98	130
Hawk die-cast automatic cap pistol, Hubley No. 2343, 5-3/4" 32		48	65
Hero cast-iron cap pistol, Stevens, 1937, 5-1/4" 30		45	60
Hero, 1940...................................15		22	30
Hero Auto, cast-iron cap automatic, Stevens, 1920, 4-3/4" 37		56	75
Hi-Ho cast-iron cap pistol, Stevens, 1940, "Made in U.S.A.," 7" 37		56	75
Hi-Ho cast-iron cap pistol, can fire caps, Stevens, 1940, "Made in U.S.A.," 7" 37		56	75

	C6	C8	C10
Indian cast-iron cap pistol, Kenton, 1931, 8-1/8"	60	90	120
Invincible New 50 Shot, 1930	30	45	60
Invincible cast-iron cap pistol, Kilgore, 1935, "Pat. Dec. 14," 5-1/4"	30	45	60

Invincible. Courtesy Sotheby's New York.

	C6	C8	C10
Jack Armstrong airplane gun, Daisy, 1936	35	52	70
Jax cast-iron cap pistol, Kenton, 1930, "Pat. Sept. 11-23," 4"	22	33	45
Jet Jr. die-cast space cap gun, 1949, 6-3/8"	110	165	220
Johnnie's Little Gun	700	1100	1700
Joker	135	200	270
Jumbo cast-iron cap pistol, "Pat. June 17, 1890: Made in U.S.A.," Stevens, 1895, 9-1/2"	110	165	220
Jr. Police Chief, cast-iron cap automatic, Kenton, 1938, "Made in U.S.A.," 3-7/8"	30	45	60
Junior: Police .32 cast-iron cap pistol, Hubley, 1940, "Hubley; Pat'd. 2088891," 5-1/4"	30	45	60
Jr. Ranger .32 cal., 1925	25	38	50
Junior Six-Shooter cast-iron cap pistol, Kilgore, 1935, 5-1/2"	30	45	60
"Just Out" cast-iron animated cap pistol, 1880s	2000	3500	6200
Kid, 1930	27	41	55

	C6	C8	C10
Kido cast-iron cap pistol, Kenton, 1936, "Kenton Made in U.S.A.," 5-3/8"	25	38	50
Kilgore cast-iron cap pistol, Kilgore, 1910, 5"	42	63	85
Kilgore cast-iron cap pistol, Kilgore, 1912, 5-1/4"	42	63	85
King cast-iron cap pistol, Pat. Aug. 1879	100	150	200
King cast-iron cap pistol, Stevens, 1925, "Made in U.S.A.," 4-3/4"	72	108	115
King, 1930	22	33	45
Kit Carson cast-iron cap pistol, Kenton, 1928, "Pat. Sept.11-23," 9"	30	45	60
Korker	135	200	270
L.F. & Co.	75	112	150
Las cast-iron cap pistol	80	120	160
Lasso 'Em Bill, cast-iron cap gun, red rubies in handle, cylinder turns, 1930, 9"	145	220	290
Lawmaker cast-iron cap pistol, Kenton, 1941, 8-3/8"	100	150	200
Liberty, 1875	162	243	325
Liberty, c. 1912, tin, ornate	35	52	70
Lightning Express, mechanical cap pistol, train slides forward along barrel to explode cap at end, Arcade or Kenton, 1913, 5"	300	450	600
Lion, Ives, 1887, 3-3/4"	300	450	600
Lion, Stevens, 1890, 5-1/4"	200	300	400
Lion, 1920	37	56	75

Lightning Express. Courtesy Sotheby's New York.

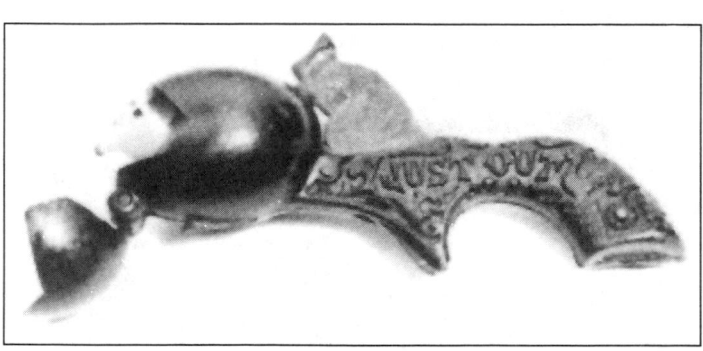

"Just Out." Courtesy Lloyd W. Ralston Auctions.

"Lion" by Ives, 1887.

	C6	C8	C10
Lion head cast-iron cap pistol, Pat. 1890, Stevens 5-1/4"	200	300	400
Little Bill cast-iron cap pistol, Kilgore, 1925, 5"	22	33	45
Little Chief Firefighter, water squirt gun	8	12	16
Lone Eagle cast-iron cap pistol, Kilgore, 1929, 5-1/4"	50	75	100

Top to bottom: "Lone Eagle," "Patrol."

	C6	C8	C10
Lone Ranger cast-iron cap pistol, Kilgore, 1938, 8-1/2"	170	255	340
Lone Ranger click pistol, Marx, 9"	55	82	110
Lone Ranger .45 Flasher Flashlight Pistol, Marx	30	45	60
Lone Ranger Smoking Click Pistol, Marx	20	30	40
Lone Ranger Sparkling Pop Pistol, tin litho, Marx No. 096	35	52	70
Lone Ranger tin pop gun, 1950s, picture of Lone Ranger on handles	30	45	60
Lone Ranger Western Gun Collection, c. 1939, six miniature guns mounted on a card w/ history of guns on back	60	90	120
Long Boy cast-iron cap pistol, Kilgore, 1922, "Made in U.S.A.," 11"	80	120	160

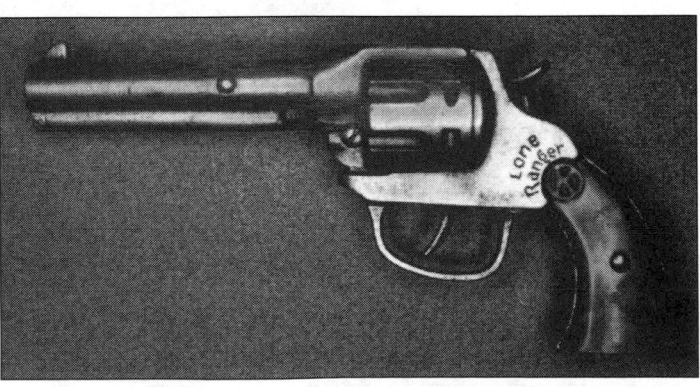

"Lone Ranger," 1940.

	C6	C8	C10
Long Tom cast-iron cap pistol, Kilgore, 1939, 10-3/8"	250	375	500
Look Out, dog's head cast-iron cap pistol	200	300	400
Luger water pistol, plastic, Park Plastics, 7", 1960s	10	15	20
M&L water pistol, die-cast, rubber ball	10	15	20
Machine Gun, cast-iron cap automatic, Kilgore, 1938, comes w/ crank, which when turned, fires the caps rapidly, "Ra-Ta-Ta-Tat," 5"	195	300	390
Magazine, 1892	100	150	200
Magic cast-iron .22 cal. blank pistol, Kenton, 1900, "Pat'd Oct. 17, '99," ornate, has second trigger to open barrel for loading, 6-1/4"	85	130	170
Major	42	63	85
Man from U.N.C.L.E. cap gun, c. 1965, Ideal	35	52	70
Mars, 1920	45	68	90
Marx miniatures of Famous Guns: Civil War Revolver, Mare's Leg, Tommy Gun, Saddle Rifle, price for mint on card	50	75	100
Mascot cast-iron cap automatic, Kilgore, 1936, 3-7/8"	27	41	55
Master cast-iron cap automatic, Kilgore, 1922, 4-5/8"	27	41	55
Master cast-iron cap automatic, Kilgore, 1930, 4-5/8"	60	90	120
Mauser, The, maker unknown (English?), 1915, 6-3/4"	250	375	500
Me and My Buddy, animated pistol w/ figure, steel, Wyandotte	55	82	110
Medrick Repeater	75	112	150
Mick, 1930	32	48	65

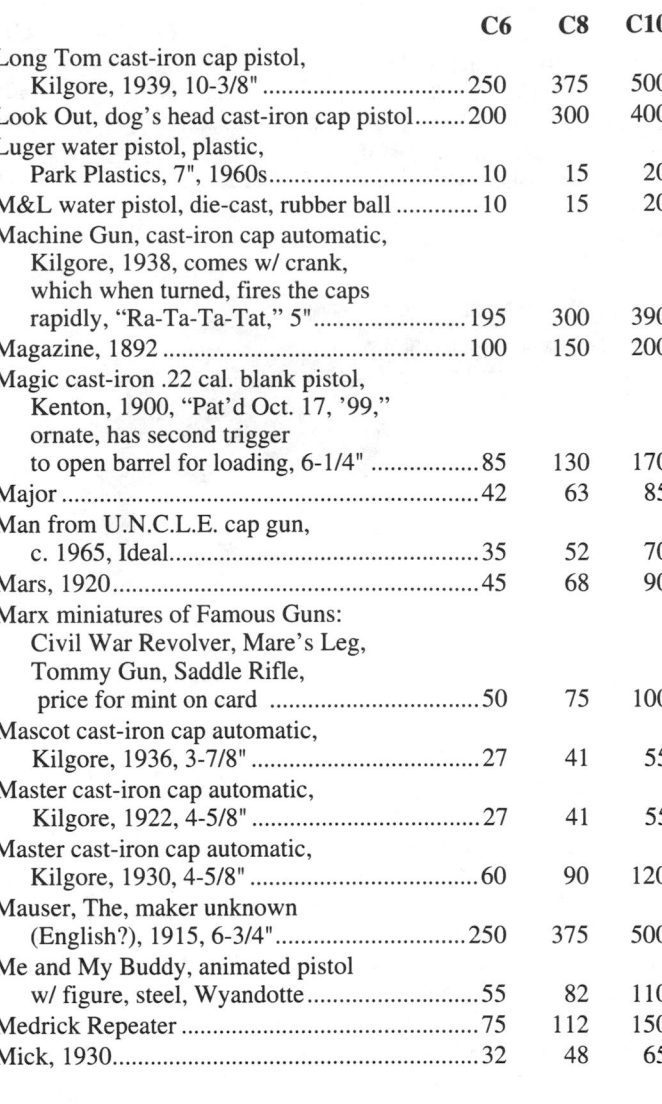

"The Mauser."

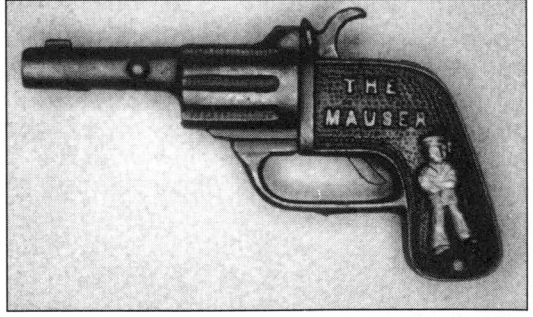

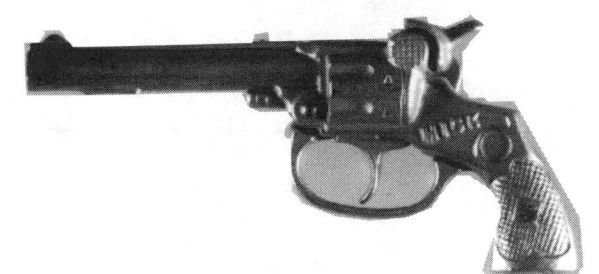

Mick. Courtesy Sotheby's New York.

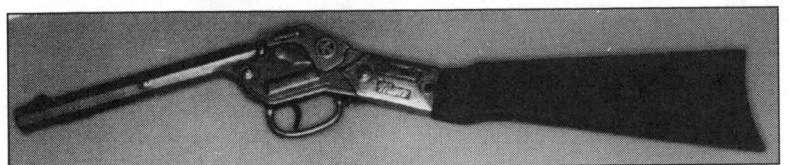

Minute Man cast-iron cap rifle, Kilgore.

	C6	C8	C10
Minute Man cast-iron cap rifle, Kilgore, 1936, "Pat. Appl'd For," "Made in U.S.A.," 20"	162	243	325
Model, Pat. 1890, cast iron , 5-3/8"	30	45	60
Model 1900	70	105	140
Monkey and Coconut animated cap pistol, 1878, 1882, 4-1/4"	No Price Found		

Monkey and Coconut.

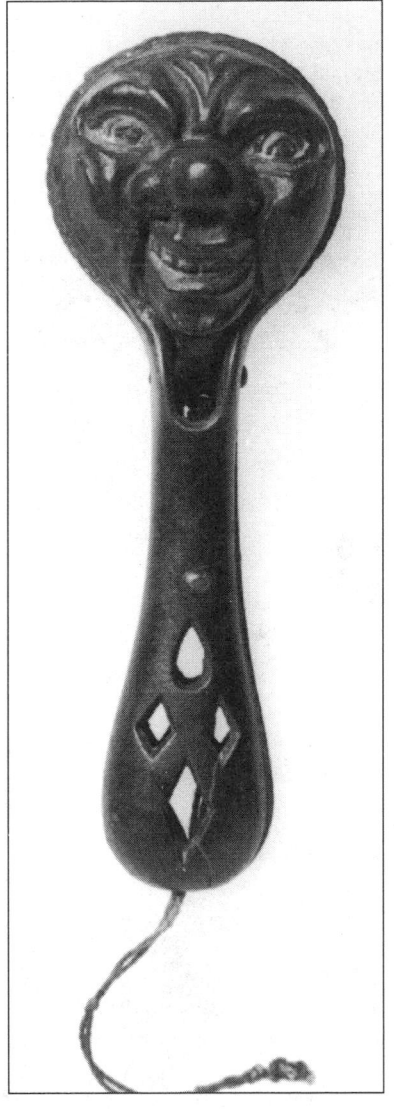

"Moonface."

	C6	C8	C10
Monkeys animated cap pistol, Lockwood, 1882, 4-1/4"	550	825	1100

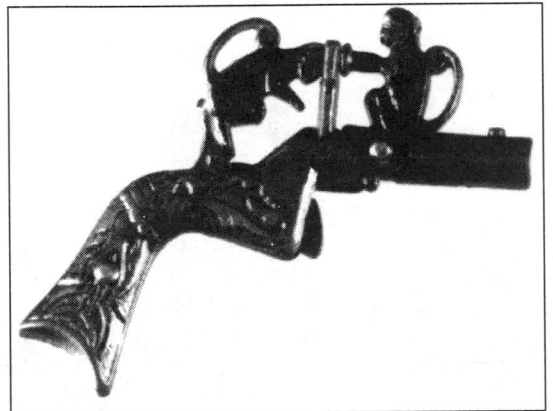

Monkey. Courtesy Sotheby's New York.

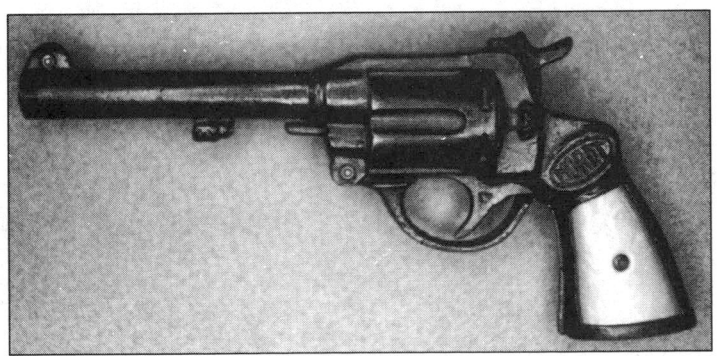

"Mordt."

	C6	C8	C10
Moonface capshooter, Stevens c. 1880	500	750	1000
Mordt cast-iron cap pistol, maker unknown, 1930, 8"	60	90	120
Mountie cap automatic, Kilgore No. 6, die-cast, 6", 1950	17	26	35
National, 1915	37	56	75

	C6	C8	C10
National cast-iron cap automatic, National, 1915, 3-3/4"	55	82	110
National cast-iron cap pistol, National, 1909, 4-7/8"	25	38	50
National cast-iron cap pistol, National, 1911, 5"	50	75	100
National cast-iron cap pistol, Stevens, 1920, 3-5/8"	42	63	85
National cast-iron cap automatic, National, 1925, "Made in U.S.A.," 5-1/4"	42	63	85
National cast-iron cap automatic, National, 1925, 4-1/4"	40	60	80

National cast-iron cap automatic, National, 1925, 4-1/4". Courtesy Sotheby's New York.

	C6	C8	C10
National No. 350, cast-iron cap automatic, National, 1928, 5-1/2"	37	56	75

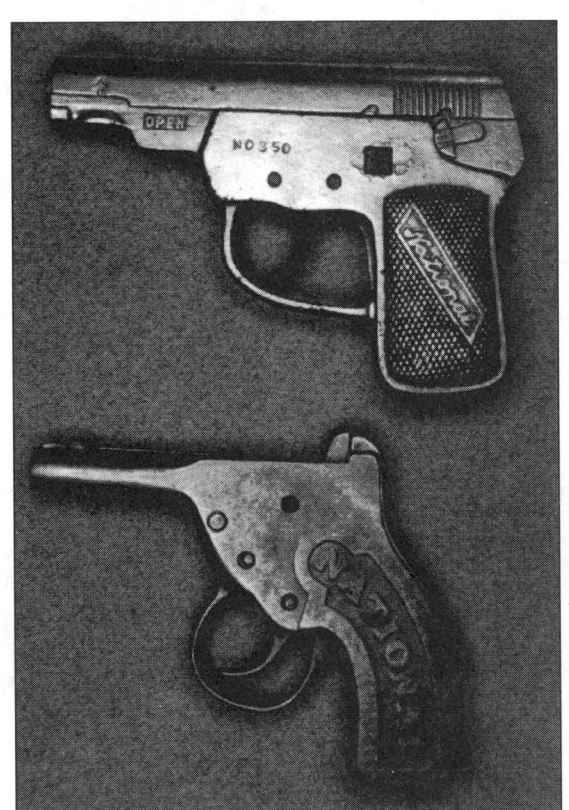

Top to bottom: "National No. 350," "National" by National, 1911.

	C6	C8	C10
National No. 380 cast-iron cap pistol, National, 1930s, 7"	35	52	70
National Liquid Pistol, Parker/Stearns, 1900, 4-7/8"	55	82	110

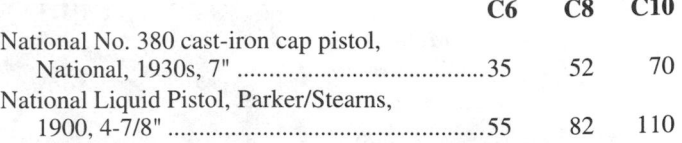

"National Liquid Pistol."

	C6	C8	C10
Navy, 1878	125	188	250
Navy, 1907	75	112	150
Navy, 1925	35	52	70
Navy cast-iron cap pistol, Kenton, 1930, "Pat. Sept. 11-23," 5-1/2"	37	56	75
Navy double barrel cap pistol	150	225	300
Nemo cast-iron cap pistol, maker unknown, 1910, 6-5/8"	45	68	90
New 50-Shot Invincible cast-iron cap pistol, Kilgore, 1930, 5-1/2"	27	41	55
Nigger Head cap pistol, cast iron, Ives, 1887, 4-1/2"	600	900	1200
No. 500 (like Luger), 1935	55	82	110
Novelty cast-iron cap pistol, Stevens, 1885, "Pat. Appl'd For," 5"	150	225	300
Nu-Matic Paper pop gun, 7"	22	33	45
Officer Pistol, cast-iron cap automatic, Kilgore, 1940, modeled after German Luger, 6"	62	93	125

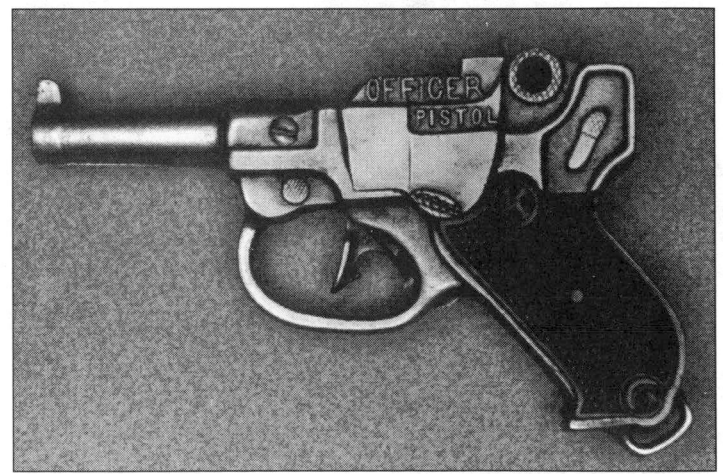

"Officer Pistol."

	C6	C8	C10
Official Detective-Type sub-machine Gun, Marx No. 2146	50	75	100
Oh Boy automatic cap, Kilgore, 1933, "Made in U.S.A.; Pat'd., Aug. 8, 1933," works both as automatic and crank-operated rapid-fire gun, 4-1/8"	85	128	170
Oh Boy cast-iron cap pistol, National, 1922, 5-1/2"	35	52	70
Oh Boy iron cap pistol, Kenton, 1930, "Pat. Sept. 11-23," 5-1/8"	25	38	50
OK cast-iron cap automatic, maker unknown, 1935, 3-3/4"	35	52	70
Old Ironsides cast-iron cap pistol, 10-3/4"	65	98	130
101 Ranch	165	250	330
Our Army Forever	175	263	350
"P"	70	105	140
P-38 steel clicker pistol, c. 1945	17	26	35
Padlock cup pistol, and key, Hubley, 4-1/4"	92	140	185
Pal cast-iron cap pistol, Kilgore, 1930, 4"	20	30	45
Pal cast-iron cap automatic, Kilgore, 1930, 4"	22	33	45
Parole	40	60	80
Pat cast-iron pistol, Kenton, 1935, "Pat. Sept. 11-23," 6-1/8"	22	33	45
Patrol cast-iron cap pistol, Hubley, 1939, "Made in U.S.A.," 6"	32	48	65
Pawnee Bill, c. 1940	100	150	200
Pea Matic pea-shooting steel repeater	15	22	30
Pea Shooter	15	22	30
Pea Shooter, pewter, highly embossed handle	35	52	70
Peacemaker cast-iron cap pistol, Stevens, 1940, "Made in U.S.A.," 8-1/2"	68	100	135
Peerless, 1905, 5-1/2"	70	105	140
Persuader cast-iron cap pistol, Kenton, 1939, "Made in U.S.A., Pat. Appld. For," 6-3/8"	70	105	140

	C6	C8	C10
Pet, Hubley, die-cast, 4-1/4"	12	18	25
Ping-Pong rifle	10	15	20
Pioneer, die-cast, Hubley	60	90	120
Pirate cap pistol, die-cast zinc w/ cast-iron hammers and trigger, Hubley, 1941, two-barrel, two hammers that cock, 9-3/8"	58	85	115
Pirate, as above, but nonfiring, 1950	60	90	120

Pirate, Hubley, with original box. Rare colored stock and blue finish, probably post-WWII.

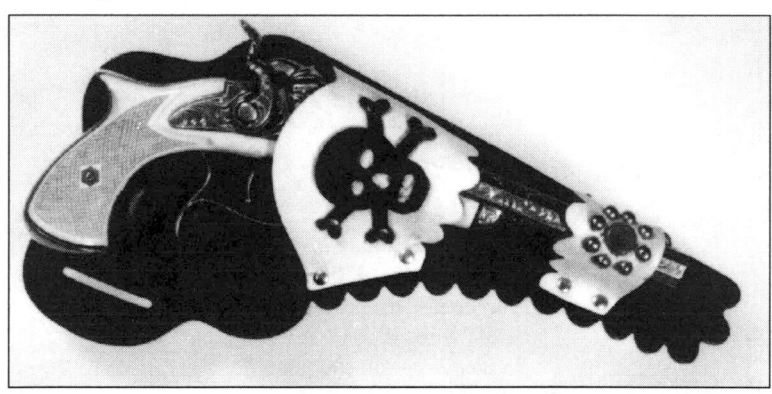

Pirate, Hubley, in rare original holster. Value $390 in mint.

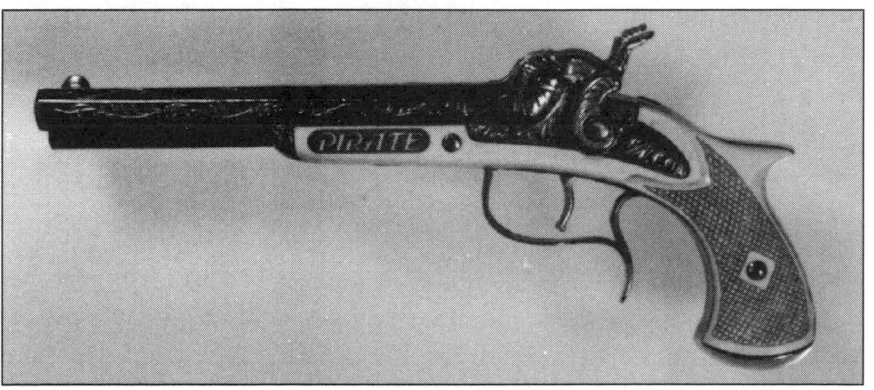

Pirate, Hubley, 1941.

	C6	C8	C10
"Pistol Packin' Mama," wood w/ cardboard sides, c. 1944, four revolving triggers, shoots wooden pegs, 8-1/2"	20	30	40
Pluck cast-iron cap pistol, at least 4 versions known, 1895 version	62	93	125
Pluck cast-iron cap pistol, Stevens, 1930, "Made in U.S.A.," early-looking, 3-1/2"	17	25	34

Presto, with original box. Courtesy James S. Maxwell/Virginia Caputo. Photo by Virginia Caputo.

Top: Pluck, Stevens, 1930. Bottom: Big Chief, 1930, Dent.

	C6	C8	C10
Presto cast-iron cap automatic, Kilgore, 1940, 5-1/8"	27	41	55
Private Eye cap pistol, Kilgore, 6-1/2"	12	18	25
Punch & Judy cast-iron animated cap pistol, Ives, 1880, "Patented," Punch explodes cap w/ nose on Judy's back, 5"	412	318	425

Punch & Judy. Courtesy Sotheby's New York.

	C6	C8	C10
Police large steel automatic cap pistol 8"	20	30	40
Police automatic, 1935	40	60	80
Police bakelite-framed cap automatic, Kilgore, 1940, 5-1/4"	55	83	110
Police Chief, 1938, Kenton, 4-5/8"	48	72	95
Police Chief gun and leather shoulder holster set, c. late 1940s, Wyandotte	25	38	50
Polo, Ives, 1878, 6"	50	75	100
Polo, later, Ives, has trigger guard	50	75	100
Pono cast-iron cap pistol, Kenton, 1936, "Pat. Sept. 11-23," 5-1/8"	30	45	60
Powder keg cast-iron cap bomb	85	128	170
Premier Safety, 1914	37	56	75
President, cast-iron cap pistol, 1925, Kilgore 8-3/4"	40	60	80

	C6	C8	C10
Pup, 1930	27	41	55
Ranger (1890-1900)	80	120	160
Ranger cast-iron cap pistol, Kilgore, 1920, 5-3/8"	50	75	100
Ranger cast-iron cap pistol, Kilgore, 1939, 8-1/2"	85	127	170

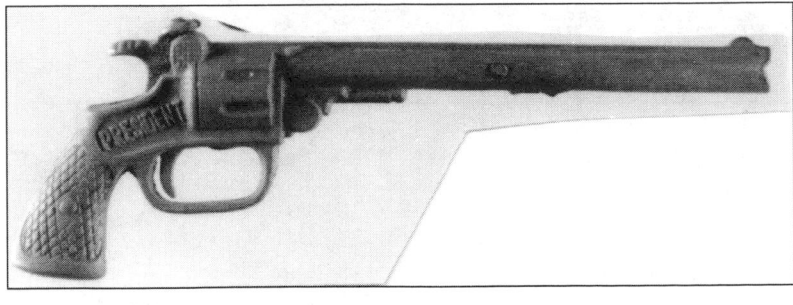

President. Courtesy Sotheby's New York.

Red Ranger Steel Clicker Pistol, Wyandotte. Courtesy Continental Hobby House.

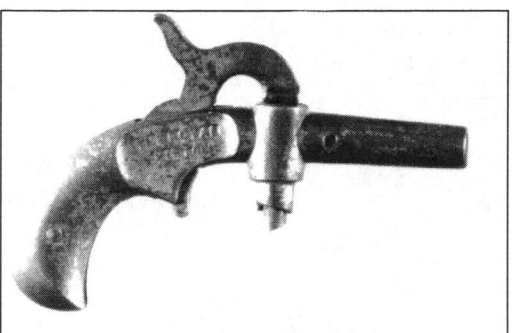

The Royal Pistol. Courtesy Sotheby's New York.

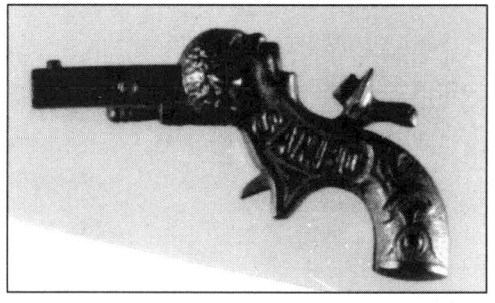

Sambo. Courtesy Sotheby's New York.

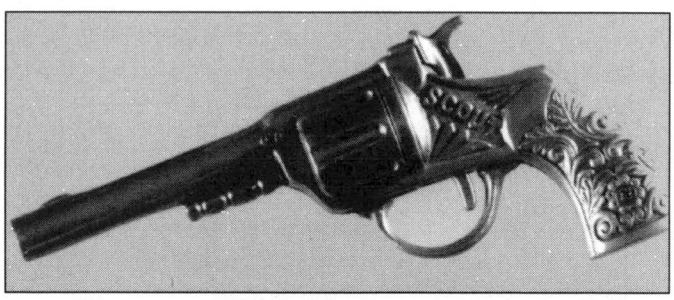

Scout cast-iron cap pistol, Stevens, 1890. Courtesy Sotheby's New York.

	C6	C8	C10
Scoutmaster, Dent, 6-3/4"	65	98	130

Sea Serpent: See Dolphin

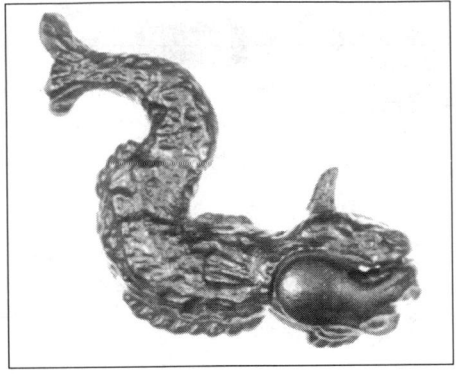

Sea Serpent.

	C6	C8	C10
Senator cast-iron cap pistol, Kilgore, 1925, marked w/ star and "K," 7"	50	75	100
1776-1876 cast-iron cap pistol, Stevens, 1876, produced for America's (100th) centennial, 5-1/4"	150	225	300
Sharpshooter cap rifle, Hubley, 37"	75	112	150
Shoo Fly cast-iron cap pistol............................	90	135	180
Shoot the Hat cast-iron mechanical cap pistol...	475	715	950
Shootin' Shell Buckle Gun, Mattel, cap derringer, 1959	42	63	85
Shotgun, double-barreled, steel, wooden stock, 28", both barrels break down, cock and shoot	35	52	70
Siren Signal Pistol, Marx, 1940s, tin..............	20	30	40
Siren Signal Pistol, Marx, 1950s, hard plastic	20	30	40
Siren Sparkling Airplane Pistol, tin litho, Marx No. 182	50	75	100
Siren Sparkling Pistol, tin litho, Marx No. 164..	45	68	90
Six Shooter cast-iron cap pistol, Kilgore, 1935, 6-1/2"	40	60	80
Six Shooter cast-iron cap pistol with plastic-type grips, Kilgore, 1935, 6-1/2"	80	120	160
Six Shooter cast-iron cap pistol, Kilgore, 1938, "Made in U.S.A." on hammer, 6-1/2"	50	75	100

	C6	C8	C10
Six Shooter cast-iron cap pistol, Kilgore, 1938, "Made in U.S.A.," on hammer, plastic type grips, 6-1/2"	90	125	180
Six Shooter cast-iron cap pistol, Kilgore, 1930, 7"	37	56	75
Six Shooter Automatic cast-iron cap pistol (not an automatic), Kilgore, 1934, 6-1/2"	72	108	145
6-Shot cast-iron cap pistol, Stevens, 1895, "Pat. U.S.A., Jan. 22, 1895," 6-3/4"	275	365	550
Sliko cast-iron cap pistol, Kenton, 1930, "Pat. Sept. 11-23," 6-1/4"	27	41	55
Snap, 1890	35	52	70
Snappy, 1930, Dent, 5".,.................................	37	56	75

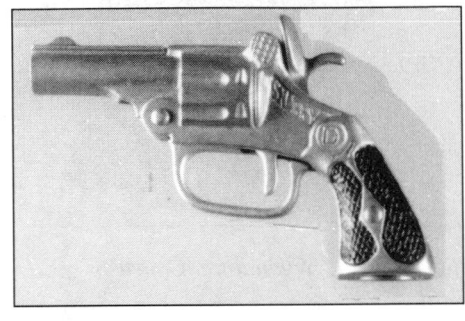

"Snappy." Courtesy Sotheby's New York.

	C6	C8	C10
Snappy Jack, c. 1935, English	37	56	75
Space Gun, Remco	25	38	50
Space Rocket Gun, plastic, fires two "Space Rocket Spheres," M&L, 9"	62	93	125
Sparkling Atom Buster, die-cast, Marx No. 46	30	45	60
Sparkling G-Man Sub-Machine Gun, Marx No 2308	62	93	125
Sparkling G-Man Sub-Machine Gun, Marx No. 2310	62	93	125
Sparkling Pop Gun, Marx No. 198	25	38	50
Sparkling Space Gun, Marx	45	68	90
Sparkling Sure Shot..	17	26	35
Spitfire cast-iron cap automatic, Stevens, 1940, "Made in U.S.A.," 4-5/8"	40	60	80
Sport, Ives, 1875, 4"	175	263	350

6 Shot cast-iron cap pistol, Stevens, 1895.

"Sport" by Ives.

	C6	C8	C10
Sport cast-iron cap pistol, Kilgore, 1930, "Made in U.S.A.," 7-1/2"	50	75	100
Spud Gun, tin automatic, c. 1940	15	22	30
Spud Gun No. 504, B.J. Cossman, Hollywood, Calif., die-cast	30	45	60
Spy cast-iron cap pistol, Kilgore, 1936, "Made in U.S.A.," 4-1/4"	30	45	60
Star pot metal cap pistol, steer on handle	5	8	10
Star, c. 1878	125	188	250
Star cast-iron cap pistol, Stevens, 1910, 6-1/4"	35	52	70
Stephans Pat., 1873, 5"	120	180	240
Stevens Repeater cast-iron cap pistol, Stevens, 1930, "Mammoth Cap; Made in U.S.A.," 6-1/4"	70	105	140
Stevens 6-Shot, 1932, Stevens 6-1/4"	35	52	70

Top, left to right: "Teddy," "Chief." Middle: "Buffalo Bill." Bottom, left to right: "25 Jr.," "Pal," "Army .45." Courtesy Mapes Auctioneers & Appraisers.

STEVENS 6 Shot. Courtesy Sotheby's New York.

	C6	C8	C10
Stevens 6-Shot Rapid Load cast-iron cap pistol, Stevens, 1932, "Made in U.S.A.," 6-1/2"	62	93	125
Streamline Siren Sparkling Pistol, tin litho, Marx No. 155	35	52	50
Sun cast-iron cap pistol	125	188	250
S & W cast-iron cap gun, 6"	27	41	55
Super cast-iron cap pistol, Kenton, 1930, "Pat. Sept. 11-23," 8-3/4"	35	52	70
Super Automatic Tom Gun, steel spark automatic	15	22	30
Super Nu-Matic Paper Buster Gun	30	45	60
Sure Shot, 1870-1880	165	250	330
Sure Shot cast-iron cap automatic, Hubley, 1940, 4-1/4"	32	48	65
Target cast-iron cap pistol, Hubley, 1935, "Pat. 1,488,046," 8"	50	75	100
Targeteer pistol, Daisy	45	68	90
Teddy cast-iron cap pistol, Hubley, 1938, 5-5/8"	25	38	50
Terror, 1888	250	375	500
Terror, cast-iron cap automatic, Dent, 1915, "Pat. Jan 16 '15," 4-1/4"	35	52	70
Terror, 1925	30	45	60
Terror, people embossed, cast-iron cap pistol, 1882	175	260	350
Texan cast-iron cap pistol, Hubley, 1940, "Made in U.S.A.," 9-1/4"	100	150	200

Texan, die-cast, gold-plated deluxe version, Hubley, c. 1950. Value mint in box $250.

	C6	C8	C10
Texan Jr. cast-iron cap pistol, Hubley, 1941, "Made in U.S.A.," 8-1/8"	88	132	175
Texas cast-iron cap pistol, Kenton, 1936, "Pat. No. 1993916," 5-3/4"	45	68	90
Texas cast-iron cap pistol, Kenton, 1930, "Pat. Sept. 11-23," 6-5/8"	45	68	90
Texas Centennial, 1936, 11"	225	338	450
Texas Jack, Ives, 1886, 9-3/8"	150	225	300
The Big Noise, c. 1922	45	68	90
The Forty Five cast-iron cap pistol, unusual shape, National, 1928, "Made in U.S.A.," 11-1/8"	110	165	220
The Sheriff cast-iron cap pistol, Stevens, 1940, 8-1/2"	75	112	150
Thunder-Burp machine gun, Mattel, 1960s	40	60	80

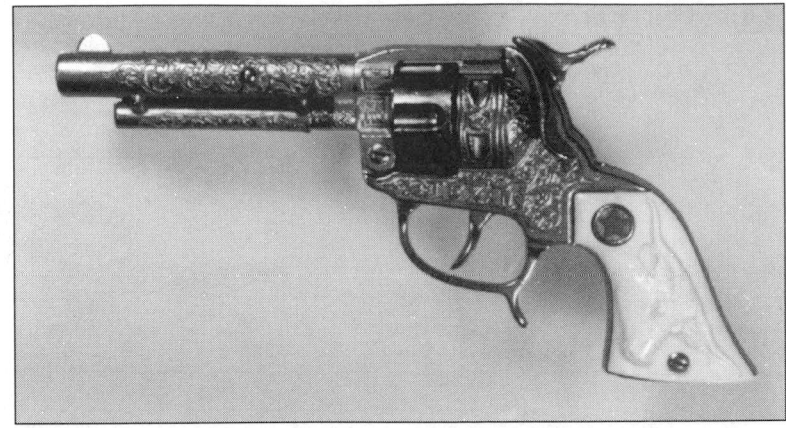

Texan, Hubley, late cast-iron model. Early models have a rampant colt instead of a star on the grips. The cylinder is die-cast, c. 1940-48.

	C6	C8	C10
Thundergun rifle, Marx, 36" long, smoke, sound	100	150	200
Tiger cast-iron cap pistol, Stevens, 1915, 6-3/4"	32	48	65
Tiger cast-iron cap pistol, Hubley, 1935, 6-7/8"	27	41	55
Tin Tin Gun, turn crank and it makes noise, Woodhaven Metal Stamping Co., 3 x 5"	15	22	30
Tip Top cast-iron cap pistol, 1880, Stevens, 3-1/2"	125	188	250

Top to bottom: "Tip Top," Unmarked, maker unknown, 1878, 3-3/4" long.

	C6	C8	C10
Tommy Gun, Marx, plastic, 24" long	36	54	72
Trainer	20	30	40
Trapper cast-iron cap automatic, Kilgore, 1935, fires only single shot, but roll of caps can be carried in the grip, 4-1/2"	45	68	90
Triumph, 1878, 5-1/8"	125	188	250
Trooper, cast-iron cap pistol, Hubley, 1938, 5-1/8"	20	30	40
Trooper die-cast, Hubley 6-1/2"	25	38	50
Trooper Safety, 1925	35	52	70

	C6	C8	C10
Trooper Safety cast-iron cap pistol, Kilgore, 1930, "Pat. Pend; Made in U.S.A.," operates either as straight cap pistol or can be fired w/ crank, 10"	85	128	170
Trooper Safety cast-iron cap pistol, Kilgore, 1925, 10-1/4"	75	112	150
25 Jr. cast-iron cap automatic, Stevens, 1930, "Made in U.S.A., Patented," 4-1/8"	30	45	60

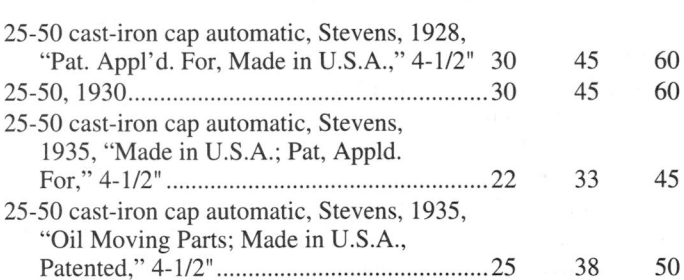

25 Jr. with original box. Courtesy James S. Maxwell/ Virginia Caputo. Photo by Virginia Caputo.

	C6	C8	C10
25-50 cast-iron cap automatic, Stevens, 1928, "Pat. Appl'd. For, Made in U.S.A.," 4-1/2"	30	45	60
25-50, 1930	30	45	60
25-50 cast-iron cap automatic, Stevens, 1935, "Made in U.S.A.; Pat, Appld. For," 4-1/2"	22	33	45
25-50 cast-iron cap automatic, Stevens, 1935, "Oil Moving Parts; Made in U.S.A., Patented," 4-1/2"	25	38	50

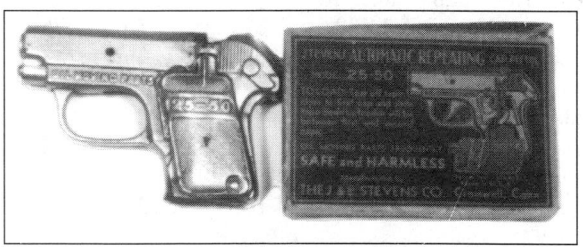

25-50 cast-iron cap automatic, Stevens, 1935, "Oil Moving Parts" with original box. Courtesy James S. Maxwell/Virginia Caputo. Photo by Virginia Caputo.

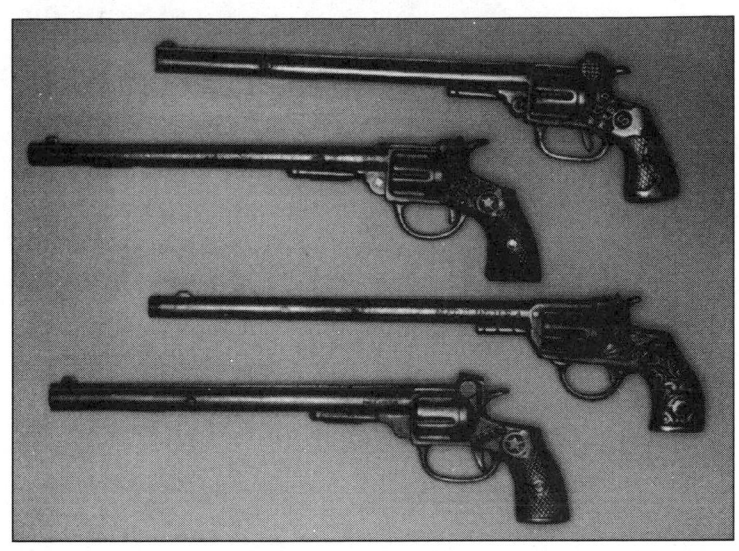

Top to bottom: "Wild West," "101 Ranch," "Victor," "Rodeo."

Wyandotte guns, as shown in a January 1925 ad.
Courtesy Playthings *Magazine.*

	C6	C8	C10
Xtra cast-iron pistol, Kenton, 1936, "Made in U.S.A.," 5"	27	41	55
Yank cast-iron cap pistol, 1880	125	188	250
Yankee cast-iron cap pistol, Stevens, 1895, 5-1/2"	125	188	250
York cast-iron cap pistol, Kenton, 1930, "Pat. Sept. 11-23," 7"	35	52	70
Young Sportsman, wood, c. 1868	75	112	150
Zip (1880-1890)	37	56	75
Zip cast-iron cap pistol, Hubley, 1930, 5"	27	41	55
Zip cast-iron cap pistol, Hubley, 1938, 6"	27	41	55
Zulu cast-iron cap pistol, maker unknown, 1890, has decoration of African warrior with spear pursuing bird, 6-5/8"	150	225	300

Wyandotte Toys,1935 ad.

BB GUNS

There has been no change in the average BB gun price since the last edition.

EVERYTHING'S COMING UP A DAISY

by Jim Buskirk

Spring Air BB guns, sometimes referred to as air rifles, are simple in design and operation. They cannot be pumped up to high pressures and their muzzle velocity is usually in the neighborhood of 400 feet per second. Operation is simple: a one-stroke cocking action compresses a spring and draws a piston back through a cylindrical air chamber. Locked in this position, the BB gun is ready to fire. Meanwhile a BB has been placed in the breach, either manually or by an automatic feed mechanism. When the trigger is pulled the piston is driven forward, forcing the air in the cylinder out through the barrel, driving the BB ahead of this blast of air.

A BB gun is not a toy in the traditional sense. If improperly handled it can be dangerous and can cause injury. Yet it was conceived, designed, manufactured, and advertised for use by children. Common sense tells us that a BB gun should not be placed in the hands of a child too young to understand its dangers or who has not been properly instructed in its safe use. When I hear the BB gun criticized because of its dangers I like to compare it to the bicycle. A recent television news report stated that during the period from 1983 to 1993 more than six hundred thousand children were seriously injured or killed in bicycle accidents. In my opinion, during that period far fewer were seriously injured or killed by BB guns.

Daisy and Markham/King both went into the BB gun business in the late 1880s. Located just across the railroad tracks from one another in Plymouth, Michigan, they were in vigorous competition for years. By the early 1930s Daisy not only owned King but the King guns were being produced in the Daisy plant. During that period of about 40 years as many as 30 companies tried their hand at the BB gun business. Few made a great success of it; none have survived. By the 1930s "Daisy" and "BB Gun" had become pretty much synonymous terms.

Daisy started life as the Iron Windmill Company in 1882. Iron windmills weren't great sellers, and when windmill designer C. J. Hamilton brought in a small prototype BB gun to be considered for manufacture the board of directors was cool toward the idea. Eventually it was decided that the little gun would be made as a premium to be given to windmill purchasers. But as Cass Hough, grandson of one of Daisy's founders, said in his 1976 book *It's A Daisy,* "It didn't take long for the tail to begin to wag the dog." A few months later production started in earnest and the first Daisy was on the market.

The people who were running the Iron Windmill company didn't realize that their BB gun was only the first of hundreds of models that would be produced over the next century. Neither that first Daisy nor the variations and new models that followed over the next few years were assigned a letter or number designation. Finally, in 1900 Daisy produced a variation with the designation "Model B." The designations such as "first model, second model," etc. are informal terms used by collectors. The BB guns are not so marked. The first Daisy was simply marked "DAISY MFD. BY IRON WIND MILL CO. PLYMOUTH MICH. PAT. APD. FOR." After that Daisy produced BB guns with names, letters, numbers, or combinations of same. Their system, or more accurately, lack of system, is confusing to the average collector, and even the advanced collector cannot answer questions about the chronology of Daisy BB guns with absolute certainty every time. Daisy didn't know they were making "collectibles," or that anyone would care a hundred years later when a particular model was manufactured. Some guns have no special marking except a name, which may be shared with several models. Some have a single letter or number designation, still others may have a combination of letters and numbers. Many of Daisy's guns from the late 1930s have a number and a model number such as "No. 111 Model 40," in addition to a name, in this case "Red Ryder." A classic case is the No. 50 Golden Eagle of 1936. This out of sequence number was used because the gun was made to commemorate Daisy's 50th anniversary.

To make it easy for the reader we have broken the Daisy listing down into several sections. Name-only guns are in the first section. Those identified by a letter (alphabet guns) are next, followed by numbered guns. Guns with a combination of letters and numbers will be listed according to whichever appears first, the letter or the number.

With a few exceptions we have limited our listing to guns made between 1888 and early 1942, at the onset of WWII. BB guns made after WWII have not yet aroused much collector interest. That is not to say that none of the post-WWII guns are collectible or that some collectors do not collect these later models, but most collector interest is focused on the pre-WWII era. This will eliminate most of the plastic-stocked guns from our list and also most of the guns from Daisy's facility at Rogers, Arkansas. Daisy switched to plastic stocks around 1950 and moved to Rogers in 1958. We have included some of the later Red Ryder guns and the Double Barrel Model 21 of 1968.

Like the prices of all collectibles, BB gun prices are somewhat subjective and actual prices paid can vary widely. Many factors have to be considered. Supply and demand, nostalgia, condition, how badly the buyer wants the item, and the thickness of the buyer's wallet are all important factors in the collectibles game. There is no infallible guide to BB gun values. The prices we have listed are based on our own experience in collecting, buying and selling BB guns over the past few years and may not reflect prices in every area. We believe they are a fair representation of the current market. One last word on the listing method used in this book: the term C10 means a piece that is in exactly the condition it was in on the day it was made. In the case of many of the early BB guns, no such piece will ever be found.

Just because it is the best example you have ever seen or heard of does not make it a C10.

My contacts with other BB gun collectors from all over the country have been an important part of my BB gun education. There have been many contributors, far too many to list here, and my thanks go out to each one of them. I must, however, mention two of them in particular. Jim E. Thomas of Tulsa, Oklahoma, has long been my mentor in learning the intricacies of Daisy BB gun chronology. Jim, whom I often refer to as "Mr. Daisy," and his wife Elouise have always made us welcome by phone or in person at their beautiful home, where Jim has shared his seemingly endless wealth of BB gun knowledge. In addition, Bill and Lynn Johnson of Rosamond, California, have been a great assistance in sorting out the very early Daisys and Kings. Much of this early information is very obscure. Daisy did not bother to keep complete records of early model changes or production. Bill, who has studied the subject for many years and has a fine collection of old Daisy/King ads and other paper, was nice enough to go over the evaluations and to give us his personal input prior to publication.

Two other important sources of information have been Arni Dunathan's 1971 book *The American BB Gun,* and *It's A Daisy,* by Cass S. Hough. Hough, grandson of one of Daisy's founders, was mainly responsible for developing the great Daisy character guns of the 1930s. The Buck Jones, Buzz Barton, and that most famous of all BB guns, the Daisy Red Ryder, were all Hough creations.

Photo, left to right: Fred Harman ("Red Ryder") look-alike Jim Buskirk next to Roy Rogers look-alike Roy Rogers.

Jim Buskirk, born in Peru, Indiana, in 1930, came to California in an aunt's Model-T Ford in 1934. He lived in Los Angeles and later Monte bello, where he completed high school in 1948. Jim enlisted in the USAF in January 1951 and upon his return from military service in 1957 received his degree in fire science from Santa Ana College. He joined the Anaheim Fire Department, where he served until retirement in 1987. He and his wife Eleanor, a registered nurse who was born and raised in San Diego, California, moved to the small town of San Marcos, California, in 1995. A casual collector for several years, Jim began serious collecting in 1985 and in 1989 began to publish the Toy Gun Collectors of America Newsletter, *a quarterly magazine for toy gun buffs. His collection of cap guns, BB guns, and related items numbers several hundred pieces. The collection consists mostly of pre-WWII items, and its main focus is the 1930s era. The Daisy Red Ryder BB guns are a special interest and his collection includes what is believed to be the first Red Ryder ever made, a factory prototype that was hand-built on a King Model 5536 frame. Another star of his collection is one of the very rare first versions of the first model Daisy, one of the few examples known of the so-called "premium" gun that was never sold but was given to windmill purchasers in 1888.*

Abbreviations Used

LA:	Lever Action	WS:	Wood Stock
BA:	Break Action	PLAS:	Plastic Stock
PA:	Pump Action	NIC:	Nickel Finish
SS:	Single Shot	BLU:	Blued Finish
RPTR:	Repeater	PNTD:	Painted Finish

DAISY

	C6	C8	C10

Daisy with Names

"Daisy" first model, 1889, marked "Daisy Pat Apd For" or "Daisy Pat Aug 13, 89," LA, SS, wire stock, NIC, cast metal grip frame . 360 / 420 / 600

"Daisy" second model, 1890, marked "Daisy Imp'd Pat May 6, 90," BA, SS, wire stock, NIC, cast metal grip frame .... 300 / 350 / 500

"Daisy" third model, 1891, marked "Daisy Pat May 6, 90," July 14, 91, BA, SS, stock may be wire or wood, NIC, cast metal grip frame may have checkering, wire stock may have wood insert .... 210 / 275 / 375

"Daisy," 1901, BA, SS, WDS, NIC, marked "Daisy" in indented rectangle on side of grip frame, also marked "Pat. Aug 13, 1889, July 14, 91, Jan. 21, 92, March 26, 1901," frame is all sheet metal, referred to by collectors as the "20th Century sheet metal," but not so marked .... 100 / 115 / 175

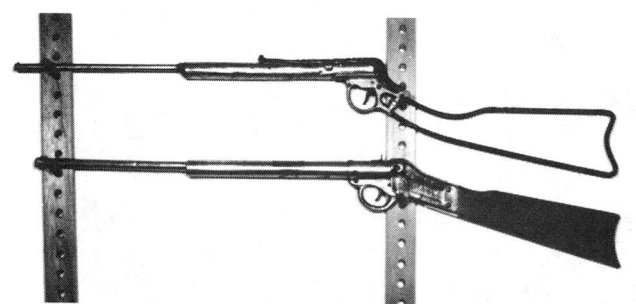

Top: A Daisy First Model, second variation of 1889. A product of the Iron Windmill Company of Plymouth, Michigan, the piece was marked "Daisy" on the cast-iron top cocking lever. It is not marked with any model number or other designation. The 20th Century Daisy, sheet metal version (seen below the Daisy First) was not so marked. It is referred to in ads as "The Daisy 20th Century" model and has a cast-iron trigger guard.

Here a collection of pre-WWII Daisy BB guns is used to decorate a bedroom wall. Each piece is identified with a magnetic plastic tag.

	C6	C8	C10
"Daisy," 1901, repeater variation of above gun	120	140	200
"20th Century," 1899, marked "20th Century" BA, SS, WDS, NIC, has cast metal grip frame	180	210	300
"1000 Shot Daisy," 1903, marked "1000 Shot Daisy" on top and/or side of frame, LA, RPTR, WDS, NIC	150	175	250
"500 Shot Daisy," 1905, marked "500 Shot Daisy" on top and/or side of frame, LA, RPTR, WDS, NIC	150	175	250

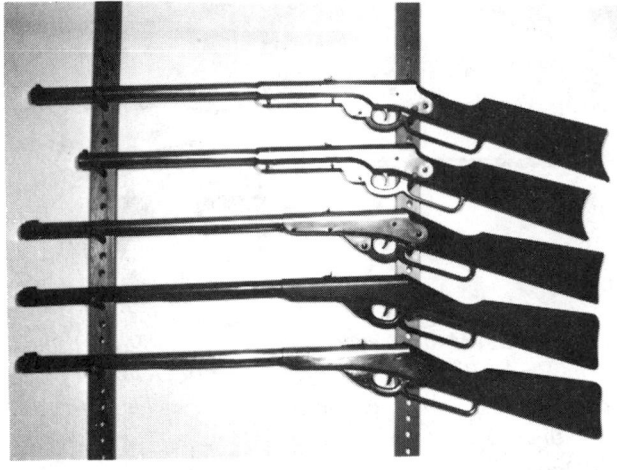

Top to bottom: the "1000 Shot Daisy," generally referred to as the "Bennett" but not so marked; the "500 Shot Daisy"; the Model B nickel plated version; the Model B blued version; the Model 27.

	C6	C8	C10
"Sentinel," 1899, marked "Sentinel," BA, SS, WDS, NIC, Daisy's first all sheet metal gun, somewhat streamlined in appearance compared to the earlier guns, semi pistol-grip stock & grip frame	100	115	175
"Sentinel," 1899, marked "Sentinel," BA, RPTR, WDS, NIC, repeater variation of the above gun	100	115	175

Daisys with Letter Designations

	C6	C8	C10
"Model A," 1907, BA, SS, WDS, NIC	120	140	200
"Model A," 1907, BA, RPTR, WDS, NIC, repeater variation of the above	90	105	150
"Model B," 1909, LA, RPTR, WDS, BLU (500 shot)	40	50	70
"Model B," 1909, LA, RPTR, WDS, NIC (500 shot)	55	65	90
"Model B," 1909, LA, RPTR, WDS, BLU (1000 shot)	35	50	75
"Model B," 1909, LA, RPTR, WDS, NIC (1000 shot)	60	75	120
"Model C," 1910, BA, SS, WDS, NIC	60	75	120
"Model C," 1912, BA, RPTR, WDS, NIC, repeater variation of the above (350 shot)	60	75	120
"Model H," 1913, LA, SS, WDS, BLU	55	65	90
"Model H," 1913, LA, SS, WDS, NIC	75	90	125
"Model H," 1914, LA, RPTR, WDS, BLU (350 or 500 shot)	55	65	90
"Model H," 1914, LA, RPTR, WDS, NIC (350 or 500 shot)	75	90	125

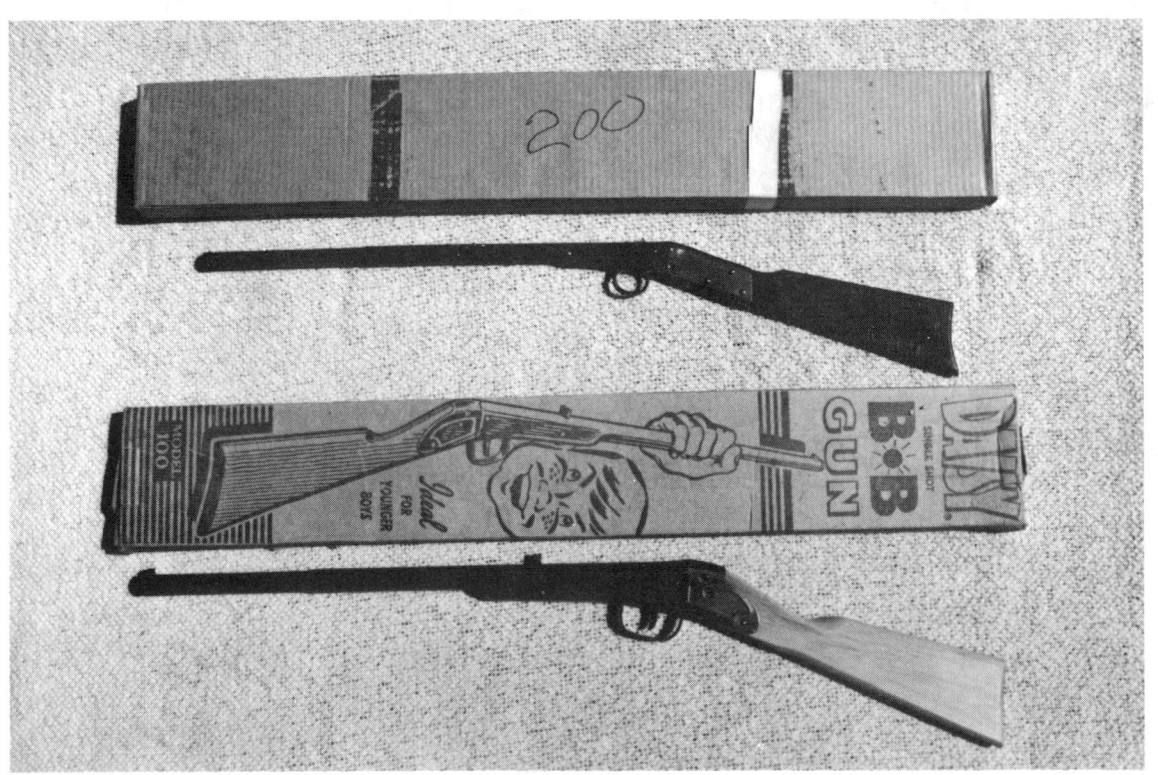

Top to bottom: a "Little Daisy No. 20" in near mint condition; a No. 100 Model 38 with original box.

Daisys with Number Designations

	C6	C8	C10
"Number 3B," 1914 (1000 shot), LA, RPTR, WDS, Black Nickel finish, came in colorful lithographed box marked "Daisy Special"	90	105	150
"Number 11," 1917 (500 shot), LA, RPTR, WDS, BLU, may also have model number	55	65	90
"Number 11," 1917 (500 shot), LA, RPTR, WDS, NIC, may also have model number	75	90	125
"Number 12," 1918, LA, SS, WDS, BLU, may also have model number	55	65	90
"Number 12," 1918, LA, SS, WDS, NIC, may also have model number	75	90	125
"Number 20 Little Daisy," 1908, BA, SS, WDS, NIC, (has no grip frame)	75	90	125
"Number 20 Little Daisy," 1912, BA, SS, WDS, NIC, (two screws in grip frame)	75	90	125
"Number 20 Little Daisy," 1915, BA, SS, WDS, BLU (has three rivets in grip frame and "ring" trigger)	55	65	90
"Number 20 Little Daisy," 1915, BA, SS, WDS, NIC, (has three rivets in grip frame and "ring" trigger)	70	80	110
"Model 21," 1968 (doubled barrel), BA, RPTR, PLAS, PNTD	180	210	300
"Number 25," 1914 (pump gun), PA, RPTR, WDS, BLU (has straight stock)	40	50	75

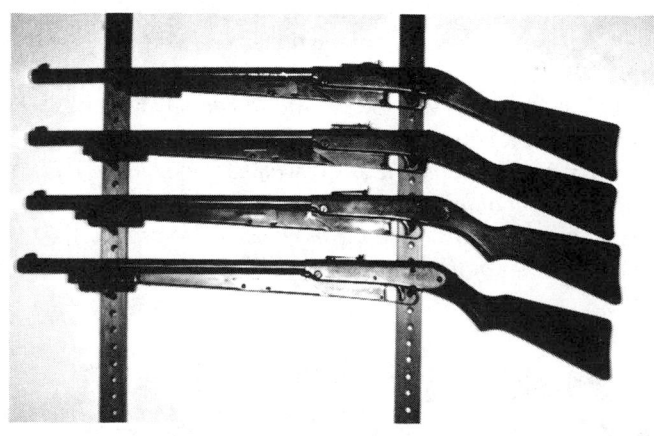

Four Daisy Number 25s (top to bottom): early version with short cocking lever and straight stock; long lever and straight stock; long lever, pistol grip stock; long lever, pistol grip stock with hunting scene stamped on frame.

	C6	C8	C10
"Number 25," 1925 (pump gun), PA, RPTR, WDS, BLU (has pistol grip stock)	40	50	75
"Number 25," 1936 (pump gun), PA, RPTR, WDS, BLU (has pistol grip stock and engraved frame)	30	35	50
"Number 25" BB Gun, 1986, Daisy's Centennial Commemorative Model, comes in colorful litho box, has medallion in stock	40	50	75

	C6	C8	C10
"Number 30," 1925 (500 shot), LA, RPTR, WDS, BLU, may also have model number	34	38	40
"Number 30," 1925 (500 shot), LA, RPTR, WDS, NIC, may also have model number	44	48	60
"Number 40," 1916, LA, RPTR, WDS, BLU, Daisy's WWII military-styled gun, has full-length wood stock, sling and bayonet, lack of bayonet has serious effect on price!	150	175	250
"Number 50 Golden Eagle," 1936, LA, RPTR, WDS, entire gun is copper plated, stock painted black and has special eagle decal, has rear tube sight, lack of rear tube sight has serious effect on price	75	90	125

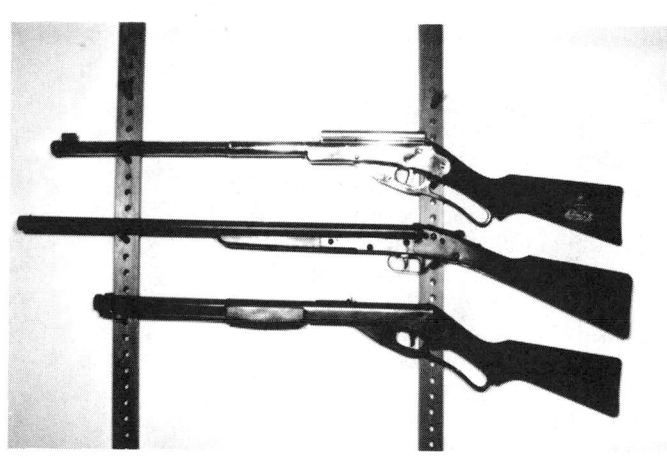

Top: the Daisy No. 50 Golden Eagle had a polished copper-plated finish and a black painted stock with a special decal marking it as Daisy's 50th Anniversary Commemorative 1886-1936. Middle: The Daisy No. 104 double barrel had a blued finish and wood stock. Bottom: The Daisy No. 108 Model 39 Carbine was a forerunner of the Red Ryder.

	C6	C8	C10
"Number 94" Red Ryder, 1955, LA, RPTR, PLAS, PNTD (1000 shot)	28	32	40
"Number 100 Model 38," 1938, BA, SS, WDS, BLU	30	35	50
"Number 101 Model 33," 1933, LA, SS, WDS, BLU	18	20	30
"Number 101 Model 36," 1936, LA, SS, WDS, BLU	18	20	30
"Number 102 Model 33," 1933, LA, RPTR, WDS, BLU (500 shot)	18	20	30
"Number 102 Model 36," 1936, LA, RPTR, WDS, BLU (500 shot)	18	20	30
"Number 102 Model 36," 1936, LA, RPTR, WDS, NIC	28	32	40
"Number 103 Model 33," 1933, LA, RPTR, WDS, NIC, has rear tube sight which must be present to realize full value	100	115	165

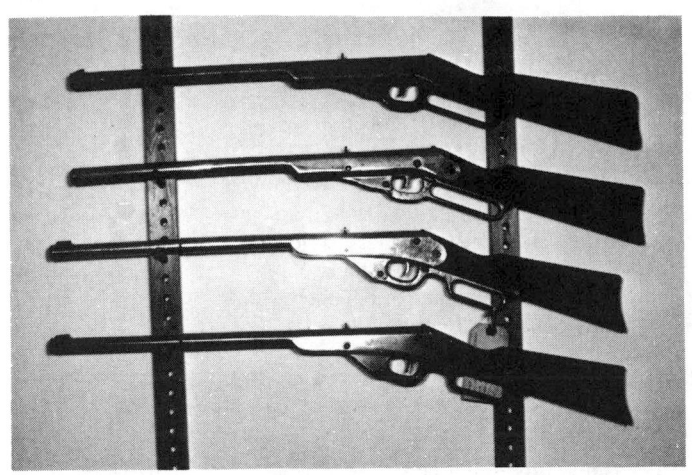

Top to bottom: No. 101 Model 33 blued finish; No. 102 Model 33 nickel finish; No. 12 Model 29 nickel finish; No. 11 Model 29 blued finish.

	C6	C8	C10
"Number 103 Model 33," 1934, LA, RPTR, WDS, NIC, "Buzz Barton" variation of the above gun, has star shaped Buzz Barton brand on stock, rear sight tube must be present to realize full value!	110	120	180
"Number 104" (double barrel), 1938, BA, RPTR, WDS, BLU	300	350	500
"Number 105 Junior Pump Gun," 1932, PA, RPTR, WDS, BLU	120	140	200
"Number 107 Buck Jones Special," 1934, PA, RPTR, WDS, BLU, engraved frame, compass and sundial stock	70	80	110
"Number 108 Model 39 Carbine," 1939, LA, RPTR, WDS, BLU	45	55	75

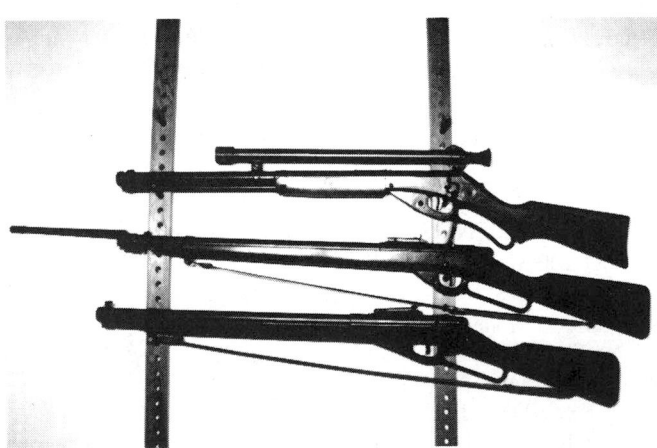

Top: A Daisy Red Ryder, No. 111 Model 40. This early version has an iron cocking lever and a Daisy No. 300 telescope sight is attached. This sight could be added to most of the Daisy Lever Action BB Guns. Middle: A Daisy No. 4 "Military" shown with the cloth sling and detachable rubber-tipped bayonet. Bottom: A Daisy No. 140 Defender shown with cloth sling.

	C6	C8	C10
"Number 111 Model 40 Red Ryder," 1940, LA, RPTR, WDS, BLU, has cast-iron cocking lever and copper plated barrel bands	75	90	125
"Number 111 Model 40 Red Ryder," 1941, LA, RPTR, WDS, BLU, has cast-iron cocking lever	50	63	90
"Number 111 Model 40 Red Ryder," 1947, LA, RPTR, WDS, BLU, has aluminum cocking lever	40	50	75
"Number 111 Model 40 Red Ryder," 1950, LA, RPTR, WDS, BLU, has plastic forestock	40	50	75

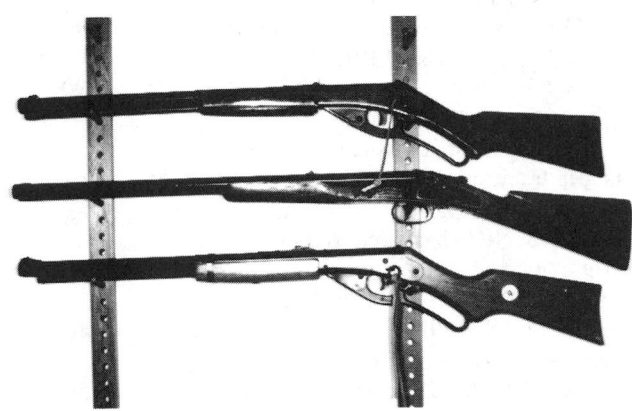

Three postwar Daisys. Top to bottom: the last version of the No. 111 Model 40 Red Ryder has a plastic stock and forestock; the Model 21 Double Barrel of 1968 had a plastic stock and forestock and a painted finish; and the "Christmas Story" Red Ryder, made to coincide with the movie A Christmas Story *in 1983. Due to the screenplay writer's error the red Ryder was described in the movie as having a compass and sundial in the stock, which it never had. Daisy, however, went along with the error and not only made a special prop gun for use in the movie but also produced a limited number of these special Red Ryders for sale.*

A near-complete collection of Daisy Red Ryders makes a nice display on this office wall. There are several models displayed, including No. 111 Model 40s, Model 94s, Models 1938, 1938A and 1938B, as well as many variations of these models.

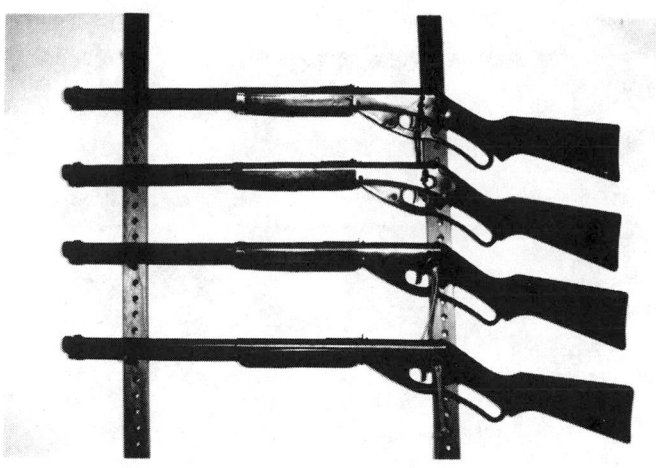

Four variations of the No. 111 Model 40 Red Ryder. Top to bottom: first two guns have iron levers, third gun has aluminum lever, fourth gun has plastic forestock.

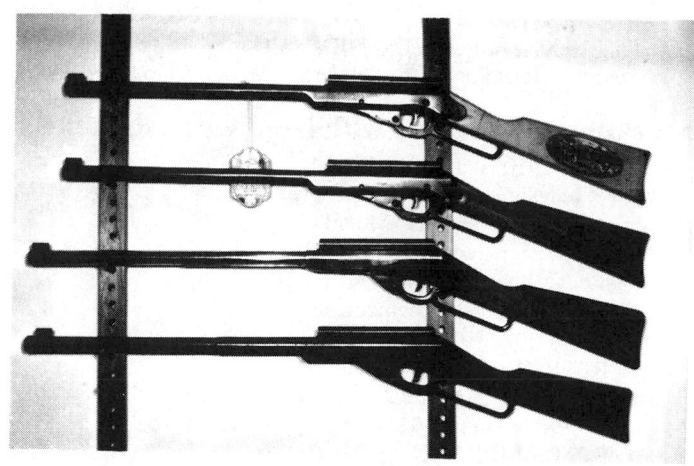

The four versions of the Buzz Barton Special. Top to bottom: No. 195 with paper Buzz Barton stock label; No. 195 with Buzz Barton brand on stock; the No. 103 Model 33 Buzz Barton Super Special was nickel-plated and had a star-shaped brand on the stock; No. 195 Model 36 was blued and had the same oval brand as the first model. All models or variations of the Buzz Barton Guns had a non-optical tube, rear peep sight.

	C6	C8	C10
"Number 111 Model 40 Red Ryder," 1951, LA, RPTR, PLAS, BLU or PNTD, both stock and forestock are plastic 38		48	60
"Number 140 Defender," 1941, LA, RPTR, WDS, BLU, has long wooden forestock, dummy bolt and bolt handle and sling 120		140	200
"Number 195 Buzz Barton Special," 1932, LA, RPTR, WDS, BLU, has oval Buzz Barton brand on stock 70		90	125
"Number 195 Model 36 Buzz Barton Special," 1936, LA, RPTR, WDS, BLU, has oval Buzz Barton brand on stock 60		70	100

	C6	C8	C10
"Model 1938 Red Ryder," 1972, LA, RPTR, WDS, PNTD, later variation, similar in appearance to the earlier variations, brand may be on left or right side of stock 25		45	80

MARKHAM/KING BB GUNS

Markham/King All Wood Guns

"Challenge," 1887, under-barrel cast-iron cocking lever, sheet metal trigger guard, single shot, may have no markings............ 225		265	375

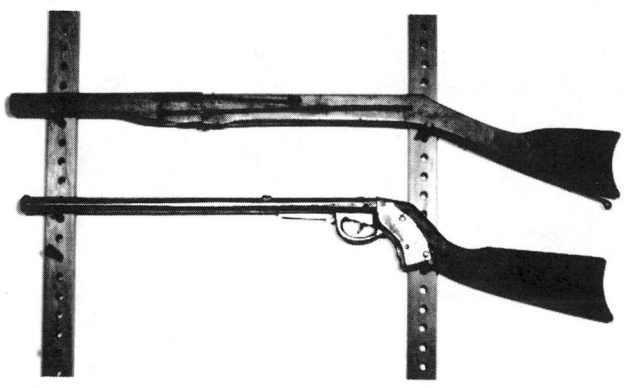

Two early Markham Guns, the all-wood "Chicago" and the "New King."

"Chicago," 1888, break action, single shot, outside cocking rods on both sides, oval Markham logo on stock 90   105   150

Markham/King Metal Guns with Names

"New King," 1895, BA, SS, WDS, NIC, stock stained red, pistol grip stock is stamped "New King Patent 483153" in oval logo 80   95   135

"New King," 1896 (repeater), BA, RPTR, WDS, NIC, repeater variation of the above gun, has small lever on muzzle cap used to allow a BB to drop into the shot tube 90   105   150

"Model D," 1905, BA, SS, WDS, NIC, grip frame wraps around wrist of stock, streamlined shape without pistol grip stock 45   55   75

"Model C," 1905, repeater variation of the above gun 45   55   75

"Prince," 1900, BA, SS, WDS, NIC, has straight stock with wraparound grip frame .... No Price Found

	C6	C8	C10

"Queen," 1900, BA, SS, WDS, NIC,
    take down variation of the Prince .... No Price Found

Markham/King Guns with Number Designations

"Number 1," 1910, same as "Model D"
    above, redesignated No. 1 in 1910 45   55   75

"Number 2," 1910, same as "Model C"
    above, redesignated No. 2 in 1910 45   55   75

"Number 4," 1908 (500 shot), LA, RPTR,
    WDS, NIC, frame has octagon shape 100   115   175

"Number 5," 1908 (1000 shot),
    LA, RPTR, WDS, NIC,
    frame has octagon shape 100   115   175

"Number 5 Pump Gun," 1931,
    PA, RPTR, WDS, BLU 75   100   150

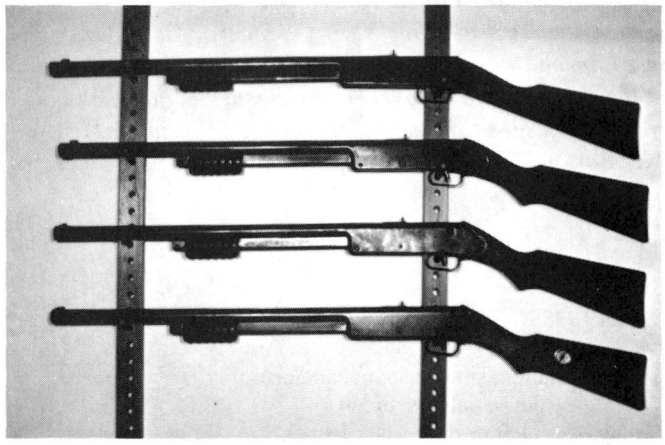

Four related guns. Top to bottom: the "Sears & Roebuck Ranger" was made by King; the King No. 5 Pump Gun; the Daisy No. 105 Junior Pump Gun; the Daisy No. 107 Buck Jones Special with compass and sundial in the stock.

"Number 5B," 1910, LA, RPTR, WDS,
    BLU, a deluxe variation of the No. 5
    (above) came in a lithographed box 120   140   200

"Junior No. 10," 1910, BA, SS, WDS, NIC 60   70   100

"Number 17," 1917, BA, SS, WDS,
    BLU, has outside cocking rods 65   80   115

"Number 21," 1916, LA, SS, WDS, NIC 60   70   100

"Number 22," 1916, LA,
    RPTR, WDS, BLU 60   70   100

"Kadet No. 23," 1916, LA, RPTR,
    WDS, BLU, had sling and bayonet .... No Price Found

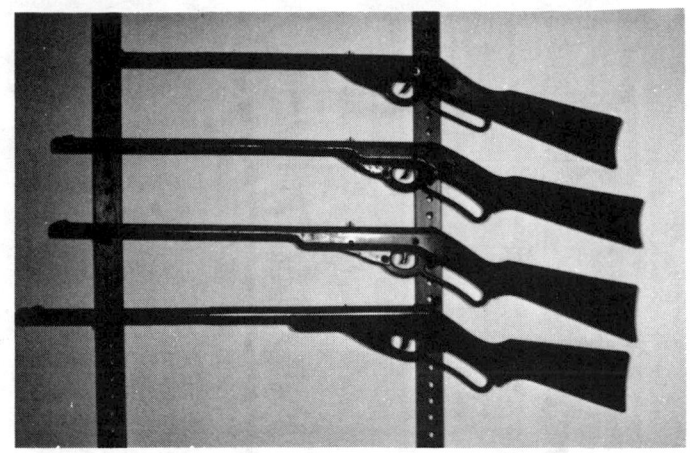

Top to bottom: King No. 21; King No. 55; King No. 5533; King No. 5536.

	C6	C8	C10

"New Chicago No. 24," 1923,
    BA, SS, WDS, BLU 75   90   125

"Number 2136," 1936, LA,
    SS, WDS, BLU 18   21   30

"Number 2236," 1936 (500 shot),
    LA, RPTR, WDS, BLU 18   21   30

"Number 55," 1921 (1000 shot),
    LA, RPTR, WDS, BLU,
    may have straight or curved lever 38   42   60

"Number 5533," 1933 (1000 shot),
    LA, RPTR, WDS, BLU 38   42   60

"Number 5536," 1936 (1000 shot),
    LA, RPTR, WDS, BLU 45   55   75

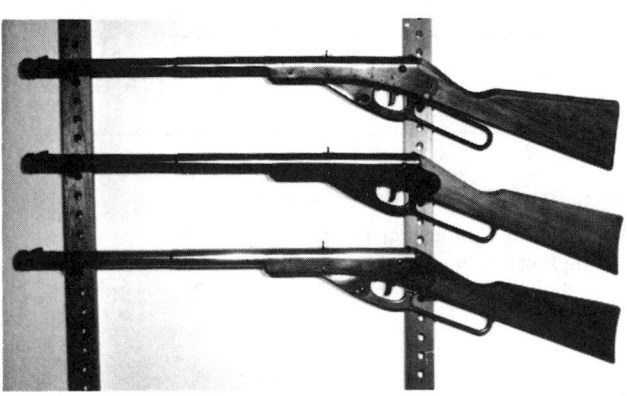

Top to bottom: a King Model 2236 is identical to the two Daisys; Daisy No. 101 Model 36; Daisy No. 102 Model 36.

AIRCRAFT

(See also Tin Wind-Ups, Comic Characters, Premiums and Paper)

The average price for mint condition aircraft in the last edition was $371.25.
In this edition it is $452.76, an increase of 22%.

A GROWING HOBBY TAKES FLIGHT

by Capt. Perry R. Eichor, USAF, Ret.

The airplane, until the last several years, was one aspect of toy collecting that attracted little interest and even less enthusiasm. Prices of toy airplanes generally reflected this lethargy.

As those of us born and raised during 1920-1940 (the golden age of aviation) acquired the time, the inclination, and the means to obtain those objects on which our fantasies were transported during childhood, the scramble began, and demand and prices have been climbing steadily ever since.

Collecting toy aircraft and memorabilia has finally come into its own. As an investment, they seem a good risk, although I find few true collectors who get any joy from acquiring only objects that are guaranteed to appreciate in value. True value lies in the ability of an object to rekindle our memories.

Those interested in collecting die-cast toy aircraft can choose from Tootsietoy, Hubley, Erie, Manoil, Barclay, Dinky, Mercury, S.R., Solido, Tekno, C.I.J., and a host of others. Cast iron was used by numerous companies before WWII, including Hubley, Arcade, Dent, and Kilgore. Pressed steel seemed to be dominated by Wyandotte and Marx for the smaller types, and Keystone, Kingsbury and Steelcraft, among others, produced the larger types. Tin toy aircraft was made by many companies. The pre-war types were made by Marx, Strauss, Chein, Kingsbury, Girard, American Flyer, and numerous European manufacturers. Japanese companies joined the fray in the 1950s. Some of the later Japanese tin types were very accurate representations of actual aircraft, while others resembled real aircraft as much as Godzilla resembles Snow White.

Some of the nicest toy aircraft ever produced were the "Gnom" series made by Lehmann in the 1930s. These ac-

curate small tin toys were based on two Heinkel aircraft and variations thereof. They are difficult to find and quite a nice display item.

In addition to the above, there are numerous examples of slush-cast items from Barclay, Kansas Toy and Novelty, Tommy Toy, Ralstoy, etc., in addition to rubber facsimiles made by the Sun and Auburn companies. Undistorted, well-preserved rubber toy aircraft are very rare.

Some excellent plastic types were produced immediately after WWII and into the 1950s. Some items, such as the P-38, B-25, B-17 and P-40 by Renwal and the B-26 by Hubley, were faithful copies, while others, such as the P-39 by Ideal, are so out of proportion that they lack even the

Capt. Perry R. Eichor, USAF (retired), was born in Oklahoma and is currently living in South Carolina. His interest in aircraft toys was reborn when he was a young officer in the Air Force and his mother sent him several toys that had been his as a boy. Twenty-one years in the Air Force only served to deepen his interest in the subject. Today, when he is not out collecting, researching or writing about aeronautical toys, he works as a criminal justice administrator as well as an appraiser and auctioneer.

symbiotic charm that often accompanies grotesqueness. Other toy manufacturers of plastic toy aircraft were Thomas, Acme, Premier, Lido, and Reliable.

If one collects toy aircraft, it follows that one wants to display toy aircraft, and they really look best on the numerous toy airports depicting structures of the same time period. In addition to airfields and hangars, there were numerous ground support personnel and vehicles.

Interest in aviation is on the rise, and the flight of the Voyager, along with numerous other record-setting craft, will have a dramatic effect on the interest in things related to flight. Consequently, prices will rise and availability will decrease in inverse proportion to interest.

However, there will always be room for those of us who were excited during our youth by the sound of a rotary engine in a biplane, doing slow rolls among cottonball clouds. Who doesn't still secretly yearn to fly with heroes and perform daring feats of aerial combat? Do you have a leather jacket in your closet? I rest my case.

A.C. GILBERT "Erector" Biplane, incomplete in photo. Photo by Bill Kaufman. Courtesy Good Old Days Store.

American Flyer No. 560 Monoplane, "A.F. Lines Air Service," 1929. Courtesy Wilkinson Collection, Detroit Antique Toy Museum.

	C6	C8	C10
A. C. Gilbert "Erector" Biplane, with electric motor	150	250	500
Adam Bomb, c. 1946, wingspan approx. 11", wood and metal (also "Atom Bomb")	50	100	150

Adam Bomb. Photo by Bill Kaufman. Courtesy Good Old Days Store.

	C6	C8	C10
Airford, small, cast iron, two-passenger, steel wheels, single engine	45	65	125

AMERICAN FLYER aircraft as advertised in the January 1929 issue of Playthings Magazine.

	C6	C8	C10
Airplane, early 1900s, single wing, prop behind tail, pilot, open fuselage 300	300	450	600
Airplane, wood, ride-on 75	75	100	150
Airport Set No. 88 T. Cohn Co., c. 1940s, mechanical tin litho airport w/ early plastic planes that fly, control tower controls for stunts, crash truck pumps water, airport bus, gasoline truck, etc. 50	50	100	200
American Flyer No. 560 Monoplane, "A.F. Lines Air Service," c. 1929, wingspan 24" 350	350	525	700
American Flyer Spirit of America, c. 1928, wingspan 18" 150	150	225	400
American Flyer Spirit of Columbia, "555," pressed tin friction, wingspan 18" 500	500	750	1000
American National air mail pedal plane, 1926.............................. 3000	3000	5000	9000
American National "Swallow" high wing monoplane, 24" wingspan 1200	1200	2000	3000
"Ancient Art Metal Co., Brooklyn, N.Y." Spirit of St. Louis, c. 1927, "Pat. No. 74042," lead, 5-1/8" wingspan 30	30	50	100

	C6	C8	C10
Arcade Airplane No. 3630, cast-iron body, twin engine, pressed steel wing, 7" wingspan 175	175	265	350
Arcade Airplane No. 3640, cast-iron body, single engine, pressed steel wing, body resembles Corsair, red and yellow, or blue and yellow, wingspan 10" 230	230	345	460
Arcade "Arcadia Airport" 600	600	950	1400
Arcade Monocoupe No. 355, cast iron, steel wing, 8-1/2" wingspan..................... 462	462	695	925
Arcade Monocoupe No. 357, cast iron, pull toy, 11" wingspan 1300	1300	2100	3200
Arcade Monocoupe, 5-1/2" long 262	262	395	525
Arcade "The Monocoupe" No. 353, 4-1/2" long 150	150	200	300
AA1 Auburn Rubber No. 1548 Boeing C-98 "Clipper," 8" wingspan 15	15	25	60
AA2 Auburn Rubber Consolidated A-11 light bomber, 4" wingspan 10	10	20	40
AA3 Auburn Rubber No. 586 Army Pursuit Plane, "US 1X2755" on wings, Curtiss P-37 10	10	15	35
AA4 Auburn Rubber Douglas DC2 Transport 20	20	40	75
AA5 Auburn "Jet 559".. 22	22	33	45
AA6 Auburn Jet "XR577," 8" 35	35	52	70
Automatic Toy Co. Futurmatic Airport............ 150	150	225	300
Automatic Toy Co. Rocket and Space Ship No. 305, friction, tin litho w/ rubber wheels, sparks, 9" long, 4-1/2" wide, 3" tall, late thirties 30	30	50	75

"Ancient Art Metal Co." Lindy-type plane. Photo by Bill Kaufman.

	C6	C8	C10
Arcade Airplane No. 361, cast iron, twin engine, "United Boeing," wingspan 4-7/8" 50	50	90	150
Arcade Airplane No. 3620, cast iron, tri-motor, pressed steel props, wingspan 4" 40	40	60	90

Left: ARCADE "Arcadia Airport," missing awnings. The two planes displayed here were included with the airport. At right is the Arcade Monocoupe No. 355.

AUBURN. Top, left to right: AA1, AA2. Bottom: AA3, AA4. Photo by Ed Poole.

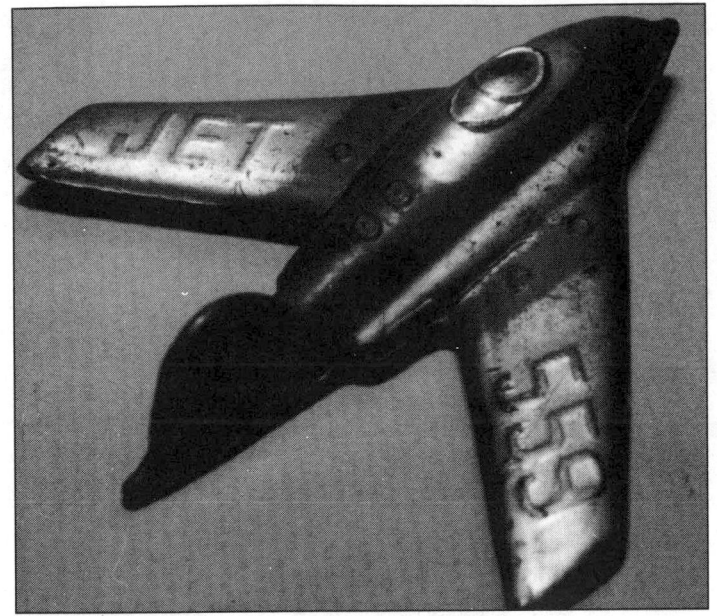

AUBURN AA5 "JET 559." Photo by Max Heiss.

	C6	C8	C10
Automatic Toy Co. Silver Eagle, aluminum plane, wooden wheels, two-engine, c. 1930s, 13" wingspan	75	125	200
Barclay, BA 1 307 Lindy-type plane, early to mid-1930s, wingspan approx. 4-3/8" long	15	20	30
Barclay, BA 1a 307 Monoplane, single engine	48	72	95

BARCLAY BA1, BA4a. Photo by Bill Kaufman. Courtesy Evelyn Besser.

	C6	C8	C10
Barclay, BA 2 The Atlantic Bremen, c. 1928	17	25	35

BARCLAY BA2. Photo by Bill Kaufman.

	C6	C8	C10
Barclay, BA 3 Monoplane, single engine, high wing, Crackerjack size, 1-piece, sold with Aeroplane Carrier and piggy-back on 195 Aeroplane	17	25	35

BARCLAY (BA3) Monoplanes atop the Barclay No. 372 Aeroplane Carrier. From the Barclay Catalog Book.

	C6	C8	C10
Barclay, BA 4 No. 57 Giant Zeppelin	17	25	35

BARCLAY (BA4) No. 57 Giant Zeppelin. From the Barclay Catalog Book.

	C6	C8	C10
Barclay, BA 4a Dirigible, early to mid-1930s, 4-3/8"	20	30	40
Barclay, BA 5 610 Rocket Ship	100	150	200

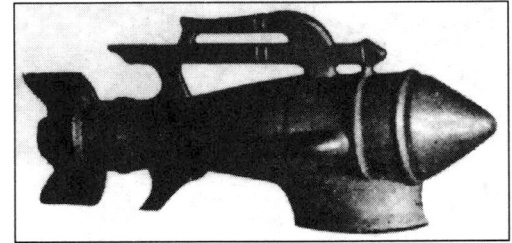

BARCLAY (BA5) No. 610 Rocket Ship. From the Barclay Catalog Book.

	C6	C8	C10
Barclay, BA 6 611 Rocket Ship	100	150	200

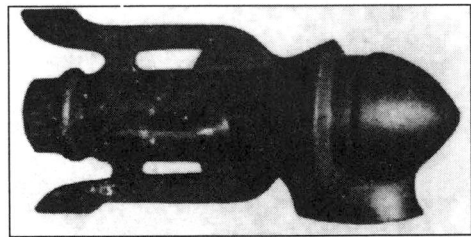

BARCLAY (BA6) No. 611 Rocket Ship. From the Barclay Catalog Book.

	C6	C8	C10
Barclay, BA 7 195 Aeroplane, "U.S. Army," single engine transport, 3-3/4" wingspan	17	25	35
Barclay, BA 7a 195 Aeroplane w/ BA3 Monoplane piggy-backed on it	45	68	90
Barclay, BA 7b 195 Aeroplane w/ clip of bombs attached to it	40	60	80
Barclay, BA 8 "Old 307"	12	18	24
Barclay, BA 9 Thick-winged monoplane, approx. 2-1/2" long w/ oversized wheels in 1935 Butler Bros. Catalog	17	25	35

BARCLAY BA7. Photo by Bill Kaufman.

BARCLAY (BA8) "Old 307." From the Barclay Catalog Book.

BARCLAY BA7b. Courtesy Hank Anton.

BARCLAY (BA10) No. 52.

BARCLAY BA9. Courtesy Perry R. Eichor.

	C6	C8	C10
Barclay BA 10 No. 52 Small Lindy-type plane 6		9	12
Best: See Kansas Toy & Novelty			

Big Bang Bombing Plane No. 11-P,
    cast iron, single barrel, die-cast propeller,
    13" long 600
		900	1500

Big Bang Bombing Plane No. 11-P,
    cast iron, double barrel,
    steel propeller, 13" long............................. 350
		600	800

	C6	C8	C10

Bing Amphibian, two overhead engines,
    hand-painted, tin wind-up,
    16" wingspan 1400
		2500	3400

Big Bang Bombing Plane No. 11-P, steel propeller. Courtesy Sotheby's New York.

	C6	C8	C10
Biplane, wooden, tin tail, aluminum propeller, pull plane, propeller spins, approx. 7-1/2" wingspan	40	70	125
Boycraft "NX-130," high wing monoplane, pressed steel, 22" wingspan	350	525	850
Buddy L. No. 603 Transport Airplane (Ford), c. 1946, 27" wingspan	300	450	600
Buddy L. No. 959 Army Tank Transport Plane, 2 detachable tanks under wings, tanks have hum motor device, pressed steel, 1941, 27" wingspan	460	690	925
Buddy L. No. 2007 Monoplane and Catapult Hanger, c. 1930-31	1200	2200	3000
Buddy L. No. 5000 single high wing monoplane, c. 1929-31	400	600	800
Buddy L. No. 5010 Triple Hangar and three planes, c. 1931, planes are monocoupes	1700	2700	3750

BUDDY L No. 959 Army Tank Transport Plane. MacNary Collection. Photo: RLM.

C.A.W. NOVELTY COMPANY

by Fred Maxwell (Slushmold Contributing Editor) and Perry Eichor (Aircraft Contributing Editor)
with the assistance of Gary Franson and The Clay Center Historical Society

Charles A. Wood was known as the "Pioneer Birdman" in Clay Center, Kansas. Master aircraft mechanic, early pilot and aviation booster, his emphasis on aircraft in his toy line reflected his life-long love. Unfortunately his toys have been largely unavailable to collectors. As a toymaker, did he fly too high?

Wood's line was heavy with miniature airplanes. It was reported he flew his toys to Eastern markets: This could have been true under special circumstances only, for in its best years (over 60 employees and two million toys) the company output would have been too large to ship by air.

In comparing his toys and others, we see that Wood didn't take any shortcuts. He manufactured a Ford Trimotor with the landing gear and outboard motors on struts; pilots' heads showing through open cockpit windows; and a most realistic model of Ben Howard's famous stunt-plane with "Mr. Mulligan" prominently embossed. Wood's early production had metal disk wheels with painted black "tires." Later toys had rubber or plastic wheels. All aircraft had cast propellers, tapered and rounded wings except C.W.A. All of his pieces are more models than toys. His replicas of famous aircraft, local airliners, and mailplanes are miniature souvenirs of history.

Because Wood was such an activist a brief biography may be of interest. He was born about 1891, and went to work for Longren Aircraft Mfg. Co. in Topeka, Kansas in 1915. He opened the toy factory in Clay Center in 1925, and was influential in establishing a local airport in a wheat field in 1929. He received a pilot's license, bought a Waco F biplane, erected a Butler hangar, and opened a repair service in 1930. He was active in persuading Midland Air Express and Western Air Express lines to make route stops in Clay Center, which put this county seat on the air map.

In 1938, during National Airmail Week, Wood flew a commemorative load (wish I had one of those First Day Covers) from Morganville to Kansas City. One mail sack was delivered to the airfield by a "Pony Express" horseman. During the war he was an instructor at a naval training center. Later, he owned a Rearwin plane, was a Piper Cub dealer, and in 1955 designed and built a monoplane dubbed "Little Monster." He continued to fly until 1976—a grand old man of early aviation.

A few years ago the author found a neat little monoplane with initials "C.A.W." under the tail plane. After putting the pressure on his Kansas friends, he finally found a mint collection of Wood's toy aircraft.

Note: A sales flyer of C&H Mfg. Co. was issued about 1940. All evidence suggests this sheet covered only toys originally from C.A.W.

	C6	C8	C10
CWA1 Small Monoplane, high wing Lindy type, 6 cyl. radial engine, negative dihedral in wings, see #41 set, 2-3/8" x 2-1/8"	15	20	30
CWA2 Small Monoplane, high wing racing type, V-8 engine, closed cockpit in front of wing, 6 windows, "C A W" & "Pat., appld. for," under tail plane, 2-5/8" x 2-1/2"	30	45	60
CWA2b ? Small Monoplane, similar to above, except no markings and stubbier wings (CAW copy?)	34	51	68
CWA3 Monoplane, high wing, Ford model 2 ?, V-12 engine, 8 window + 2 restroom, crew of 2 in open cockpit behind wing, tail wheel, 3-5/8" x 3-1/2", C.A.W.?	20	25	40

C.A.W. NOVELTY CO.
Back, left to right:
CWA1, CWA2,
CWA8, CWA6.
Front, left to right:
CWA5, CWA9, CWA7.
Photo by Perry Eichor.

C.A.W. NOVELTY CO. CWA1. Courtesy of Gary Franson.

	C6	C8	C10
CWA4 Monoplane, same as above with closed cockpit ahead of wing, no crew, C.A.W.?	10	20	35

C.A.W. NOVELTY CO. Left to right: CWA3, CWA4, CWA2. Photo by Fred Maxwell.

	C6	C8	C10
CWA5 Small Monoplane, Amphibian, Douglas Dolphin?, bimotored, see #41 set, 2-1/4" x 2-1/2"	20	30	40
CWA6 Monoplane, larger version of CWA5, 3-1/4" x 3-5/8"	20	30	45
CWA7 Monoplane, #12, Ford Trimotor model 4, 7 cyl. radial engines, outboards and landing gear on struts, tail wheel, complex molding, 3-1/8" x 4-3/8"	60	90	120
CWA8 Jr. Low Wing Monoplane #28, Lockheed or Northrop? Cowled radial engine, 6 windows, pilot in open cockpit near tail, (modern copy available, in different finish and "wire" wheels, 2-7/8" x 3")	20	40	60
CWA9 Sr. Low Wing Monoplane #29, larger version of above, tail wheel, 3-3/4" x 4"	20	40	60

C.A.W. NOVELTY CO. CWA7. Courtesy of Gary Franson.

	C6	C8	C10
CWA10 Mr. Mulligan Airplane #34, high wing, "Mr. Mulligan," "NR-273Y," cowled radial engine, 2 windows, 2 doors, c. 1936 production, 3" x 3-1/2"	40	80	120

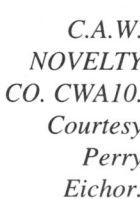

C.A.W. NOVELTY CO. CWA10. Courtesy Perry Eichor.

C.A.W. NOVELTY CO. Top, left to right: CWA13, CWA9, CWA8. Bottom, left to right: CWA11, CWA12. Photo by Perry Eichor.

	C6	C8	C10
CWA11 Boeing Bomber #36, low wing "Boeing," "NC 13361," "Made in USA," bimotored, 3 bladed props, called a "bomber" (war was in the air), it looks like a Boeing model 247 airliner, 2-5/8" x 3-1/2"	20	40	60
CWA12 Army Pursuit Plane #37, low wing "Seversky" P-37 Monoplane, under wings is Air Corps "star-in-circle," "37" and "Made in USA," cowled radial engine, 2-7/8" x 3-1/2"	30	60	80
CWA13 Monoplane, low wing cabin or pursuit plane, cowled radial engine, forward cockpit, divided windshield, open windows w/ pilot's head inside, 3-1/2" x 3-5/8"	20	40	60
CWA14 ? Large Monoplane, high wing Lindy Ryan type, but V-8 engine, oversized propeller, 5 windows and door, probably C.A.W.	No Price Found		
CWA15 Small biplane, (this from the maker's own mouth, but no description available), has not been seen	No Price Found		
CWA16 Three-Piece Airplane Set #41, apparently 2 types, see CWA1 and CWA5, above	No Price Found		
"Champion" high wing monoplane, cast iron, 5" long	90	135	180
Chein Graf Zeppelin, 9" long, push toy	450	675	900
Dayton No. 700 high wing Monoplane, open cockpit and pilot, red, yellow or blue, painted disc wheels, 13" wingspan	125	250	400
Dent "Air Express," cast iron, 12" wingspan	750	1200	1500
Dent "Air Express," cast iron, trimotor, 11-1/2" wingspan	2500	4000	7000
Dent "Airline" Monoplane, "?" on fuselage, cast aluminum, stripes on rudder, 12-1/2" wingspan	700	1050	1400
Dent "Airline" Monoplane, "X5043" cast on rudder, cast iron, 12-1/2" wingspan	500	750	1000
Dent Ford trimotor, cast iron, #1417 cast on rudder above "Ford," 12" wingspan	2000	3500	5750

DENT "Air Express." Courtesy Wilkinson Collection, Detroit Antique Toy Museum.

	C6	C8	C10
Dent "Lindy," cast iron, 12-1/2" wingspan	1000	1700	2400
Dent "Los Angeles" dirigible, cast iron, c. 1925, 13" long	1000	1500	2000

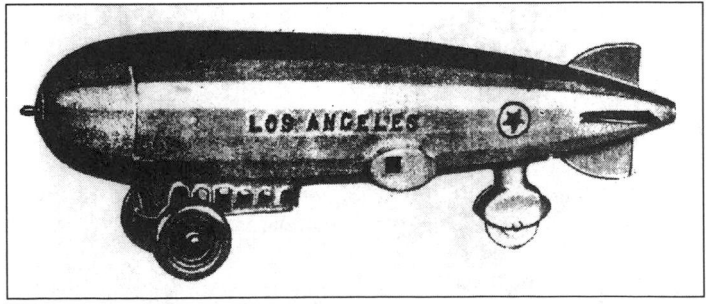

DENT "Los Angeles" Dirigible.

	C6	C8	C10
Dent "Los Angeles" dirigible, cast iron, c. 1920s, 10-3/4" long	700	1200	1700
Dent "Los Angeles" dirigible, cast iron, c. 1925, 8-1/2"	450	675	900
Dent "Los Angeles" dirigible, c. 1932, 6-3/4" long	150	225	300

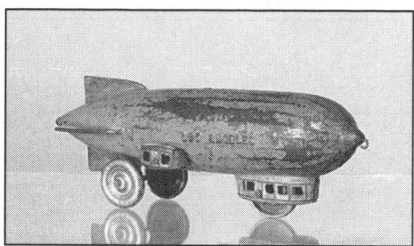

*DENT "Los Angeles"
Dirigible,
10-3/4" long.
Photo by Jeanne
Bertoia. Courtesy
Bill Bertoia Auctions.*

DENT "Lucky Boy" Glider.

	C6	C8	C10
Dent "Lucky Boy" 4" wingspan	175	263	350
Dent "Lucky Boy" cast iron, X6043 cast on rudder, 12-1/2" wingspan	600	1000	1400
Dent "Lucky Boy" trimotor, cast iron, 7" wingspan	500	750	1000
Dent "Lucky Boy Glider," cast iron, high wing, 6-1/2" wingspan	312	470	625
Dent "Question Mark" trimotor, cast iron, "?" on fuselage, 12" wingspan	3000	5500	7800
Dent "Zep" Zeppelin, cast iron, 6-1/2" long	150	280	375
Dent "Zep" Zeppelin, cast iron, 5"	100	150	200
Dent "Zep" Zeppelin, aluminum, 5" long	65	198	130
Eldon Cargo Plane, 11" long	20	30	40

	C6	C8	C10
Erie E1 Single seat open cockpit Northrup Gamma	40	75	100
Erie E2 2-place open cockpit, "U.S. Army" on wings	25	40	60
Erie E3 Northrup Delta single engine passenger airliner	30	60	125

*ERIE. Left to right:
E1, E2, E3. Photo
by Perry R. Eichor.*

ERIE. Left to right: E4, E5. Photo by Perry R. Eichor.

	C6	C8	C10
Erie E4 Boeing 247 twin engine "U.S. Army"	25	45	70
Erie E5 Boeing B-17	25	60	125
Fighter, tin, c. 1940, single engine, 4 machine guns mounted on wing	20	30	60
"Flagship America" airplane, metal Ford trimotor, pressed steel, c. 1930s, 25" wingspan	175	250	400
Girard high wing monoplane, pressed steel, 10" wingspan	125	250	470
Girard high wing monoplane, pressed steel, 18" wingspan	150	500	750
Girard Whiz Skyfighter biplane, early	85	130	170
Glass Airplane, candy container, 5" long	75	112	150
Helicopter, Army, tin litho, friction drive, spinning prop, 13" long	20	25	45
Hillclimber Biplane, c. 1917	225	338	450

HUBLEY H1.

	C6	C8	C10
H1 "America" cast iron, largest cast-iron plane made, trimotor, open cockpit, pilot, copilot, 17" wingspan	1800	3700	5800
H2 Bell Airacuda, XFM-1, die-cast, red and silver, folding landing gear, movable guns in front of twin pusher engines, 3-bladed props, new in 1940	100	150	250
H3 No. 377 "Lindy" cast iron, single engine, 3-1/2" wingspan	65	98	130

HUBLEY H2. Photo by Perry R. Eichor.

	C6	C8	C10
H5 No. 389 twin engine, cast iron, painted and nickel plate, "TAT NC 431," 5-5/8" wingspan	25	50	75
H6 Twin engine, silver and red or green, 3-3/8" wingspan	20	40	50
H7 No. 430 Jet, die-cast, single engine, folding wings, retractable landing gear, cast cockpit, red and silver or blue and silver, 6" wingspan	30	45	60
H8 "U.S.N. 3-B-4" die-cast, twin engine, twin vertical stabilizer, retractable landing gear, 5-1/8" wingspan	52	78	105
H9 "Lindy," cast iron, 10" wingspan	500	900	1200
H10 "Lindy," cast iron, prop turns via gear attached to wheel, 10" wingspan	750	1200	3000
H11 "Lindy," cast iron, w/ "Spirit of St. Louis" decals, ratchet drive action noisemaker, has wing struts	1000	1800	2500
H12 "Bremen," aluminum, 6-1/2" wingspan	250	500	1000
H13 "Bremen," cast iron, 6-1/2" wingspan	600	1000	1450

HUBLEY. Left: H3. Right: H5. Photo by Perry R. Eichor.

H4 No. 431 U.S. Army Plane, die-cast, white rubber tires, enclosed in cast fairings, single engine, low wing monoplane, 5-1/2" wingspan 15 25 40

HUBLEY. Left to right: H7, H20, H22. Photo by Perry R. Eichor.

HUBLEY H9. Photo by Perry R. Eichor.

HUBLEY H17, cockpit variations. Photo by Perry R. Eichor.

	C6	C8	C10
H18 "U.S. Army," plastic, like above, folding wheels, "U.S. Army" embossed on horizontal stabilizer, 6" wingspan	15	25	40
H19 No. 326 Attack Bomber, plastic, retractable landing gear Martin B-26 Marauder copy, 7-7/8" wingspan	20	30	60

HUBLEY H13. Photo by Jeanne Bertoia. Courtesy Bill Bertoia Auctions.

	C6	C8	C10
H13A "Bremen," cast iron, 7" wingspan	500	1000	1500
H14 "Bremen," cast iron, "Junkers Bremen" on fuselage, open cockpit w/ 2 pilots, prop turned by wheels, 10" wingspan	1000	5000	10,000
H15 "America," cast iron, single engine, wire spring drive, w/ 2 pilots in open cockpit, 17" wingspan	3000	7500	12,000
H16 "Friendship," cast-iron seaplane, "Fokker" embossed on fuselage, 13" wingspan	2500	6000	10,000

HUBLEY H19. Photo by Perry R. Eichor.

HUBLEY H16 Photo by Jeanne Bertoia. Courtesy Bill Bertoia Auctions.

	C6	C8	C10
H17 "U.S. Army" die-cast, low wing, single engine Monoplane, folding wheels, silver and red (early versions had red wood hubs w/ white rubber tires, cast cockpit may have openings or be cast or solid), introduced in 1939, 8" wingspan	62	93	125

HUBLEY H21, early and later versions. Photo by Perry R. Eichor.

HUBLEY planes, as shown in the December 1929 Butler Bros. catalog.

	C6	C8	C10
H23 P-40, die-cast, early version was silver & red w/ 3-bladed prop, later version orange & yellow w/ 2-bladed prop, 8" wingspan	68	100	135
H24 P-38, die-cast, red & silver, retractable landing gear, later versions are yellow & green camouflage, 12-5/8" wingspan	100	150	200
H25 No. 467, die-cast, folding wings, retractable landing gear, plastic cockpit, resembles Brewster Buffalo, red & silver w/ 4-bladed prop in early version, later version was green & yellow w/ 2-blade prop, 8-5/8" wingspan	52	78	105

HUBLEY. Left to right: H25, H23. Photo by Perry R. Eichor.

	C6	C8	C10
H20 P-39, die-cast and tin, "U.S. Army" imprinted on rear horizon stabilizers, tin wings are 5-1/2"	20	30	55
H21 No. 495 on wings, single engine, die-cast, folding wings, retractable landing gear, sliding plastic cockpit (numerous versions, and later packaged as "American Eagle" or "Flying Circus"), 11-1/2" wingspan:			
Early - red & silver, 4-bladed prop, no airscoop on top of engine cowl	42	63	85
Mid - two tone blue, red cowl, large airscoop atop engine cowl, 4-bladed prop	42	63	85
Late - orange & yellow, large airscoop, either 4 or 2-bladed prop	12	18	25
H22 No. 433 Piper Club, red, also in olive drab L-4 version, 7-7/8" wingspan	10	20	40

	C6	C8	C10
H26 No. 751 folding delta wing jet, die-cast, retractable landing gear, red & silver plastic cockpit, 6-1/8" wingspan	12	20	40
H27 No. 427 Crusader, die-cast, twin engine, twinboom "TAT NC-31," 5-1/8" wingspan	25	45	80

HUBLEY H27. Photo by Perry R. Eichor.

	C6	C8	C10
H28 No. 303 cast iron, low wing single engine monoplane, nickel plate wings & prop w/ various colored body, 5" wingspan	40	75	100
H29 No. 305 cast iron, low wing single engine monoplane, nickel plate wings & prop, 3-3/4" wingspan	20	40	60
H30 No. 304 Giro plane, cast iron w/ nickel plate rotor, prop & engine	50	75	100
H31 302 DO-X, cast iron, high wing seaplane, 6 engine, 4" wingspan	212	318	425
H32 DO-X cast iron, larger version of above, 5" wingspan	70	100	200
H33 Hellcat, plastic, 9-1/4" wingspan	10	15	20

HUBLEY H24, two variations. Photo by Perry R. Eichor.

HUBLEY.
Left to right:
H28, H29, H8, H4.
Photo by
Perry R. Eichor.

HUBLEY
H31, DO-X.

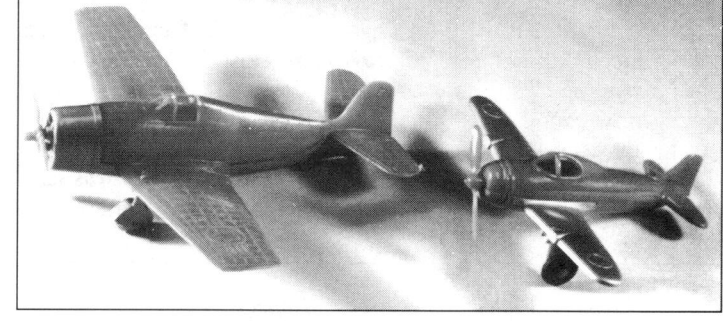

HUBLEY. Left to right: H33, H18. Photo by Perry R. Eichor.

	C6	C8	C10
H34 "Lindy" Glider, cast iron, 6-1/4" long	300	700	1200

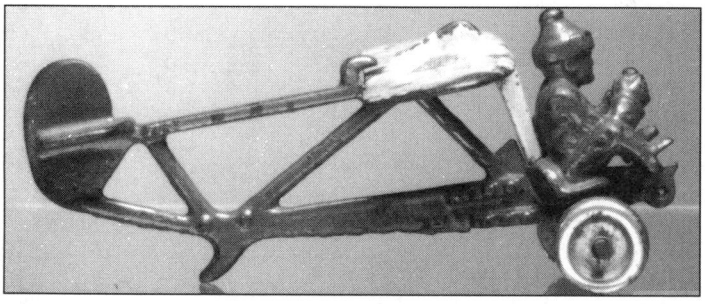

HUBLEY H34. Courtesy Sotheby's New York.

	C6	C8	C10
H35 Helicopter	45	68	90
H36 "Question Mark" trimotor, 12-1/2" wingspan	1500	2750	4250

	C6	C8	C10
H37 Lockheed Sirius, "Lindy NR-211," 9" long	3000	6200	9300
H38 "Air Ford" cast iron, 2 open cockpits, 4" long	150	225	300
H39 "Navy" Blimp, 4-1/2" long	85	125	170
H40 "Air Ford," 3-3/4" wingspan	140	210	280

HUBLEY H37.
Photo by Jeanne
Bertoia.
Courtesy
Bill Bertoia
Auctions.

I.D. PLANES

by Richard L. MacNary

Black I.D. planes, as they are popularly known, were manufactured during WWII primarily as training aids, initially for the U.S. Navy and then U.S. Army. There were also post-WWII I.D.s. The WWII airplanes covered in this section were all made in 1/72 scale (1"=6'). All were black and usually marked on the bottom in raised lettering with (1) the country of ownership/design (U.S., British, German, etc.), (2) the aircraft type (P-38, Spitfire, FW 189, etc.), and (3) the date of model issue (7-42, 8-42, 5-42, etc.).

The program reportedly started the day after Pearl Harbor, but the earliest marking on any of the known models is 5-42. (The dates so marked on the planes are dates of model issue or copyright, not the date the actual plane became operational.) Some of the early WWII attempts at manufacturing these identification aircraft used materials such as reinforced plaster (too lumpy), papier-mâché (too little detail), a hard rubber-like material (too pliable for long sections like wings), metal, and even cast iron (too heavy for shipping and perhaps needed elsewhere).

The vast majority of these I.D. aircraft were molded by the Cruver Company of Chicago. The master molds were made by either the Comet Engraving Company or H & H Specialty Company, also both of Chicago. A few models were produced (molded) by Design Center and Leominster, as noted in the listing.

These airplanes were manufactured for the U.S. Armed Forces, but Polk's Hobbies of New York did sell some domestically under the Aristo-Craft name. Most of the surviving WWII types, though, were probably "midnight requisitioned" by pilot or gunner trainees. The quantity produced during the WWII was staggering. The February 1944 issue of *Flying* magazine states that Cruver had manufactured over 2,000,000 model aircraft since the spring of 1941 (they meant spring of 1942). Not many remain today.

The following listing of WWII model planes was taken from the most complete compilation known: it may not be totally inclusive nor may all of these planes have been made in quantity. The best history of I.D. aircraft made from different materials and in different scales, as well as those of the later Korean War vintage, was written by Robert C. Mikesh in the May/June 1984 issue of *Fine Scale Modeler* magazine.

You will note in the guide that not much distinction is made between the values for similar-size models. There is just not enough buying and selling nor enough large collections to accurately determine which plane is more rare than another. They could all be equally hard to find today.

As to grading, C9 means no scuffs, no warpage, no "prune-skin," no repainting or, in other words, a brand new 45-year-old airplane. C7 covers models that are very nice: planes should be complete with wheels or floats if on originally; free of serious defects like "prune-skin" or missing parts, and not repainted (restored maybe). The C5 grade covers everything else and probably includes the majority of the models still in existence.

A special thanks is still due to master modeler Ray ".43 Magnum" Wheeler of Lilburn, Georgia, for his help in identifying some of the more obscure types listed.

Comments and especially documented corrections are always welcome.

Each model is identified by type and date marked.

United States

	C5	C7	C9
A-20 Havoc, 6-42	25	37	50
A-24 Dauntless, SBD - 3, 7-42	15	22	30
A-26 Invader, 2-44	25	37	50
A-29 Hudson (PBO-16), none	25	37	50
A-30 Baltimore, 2-43	25	37	50
A-31 Vengeance, 7-42	15	22	30
A-31 Vengeance, 7-44	15	22	30
A-35 Vengeance, 4-44	15	22	30
AT17 Bobcat*, 7-43	25	37	50
B-17 Flying Fortress, 7-42	75	100	125
B-24 Liberator, 7-42	75	100	125
B-25 Mitchell, 7-42	30	45	60
B-26 Marauder, 10-42	25	37	50

	C5	C7	C9
B-26 Marauder, none	25	37	50
B-29 Super Fortress, 3-44	50	75	100
B-29 Super Fortress, 9-44	50	75	100
B-29 Super Fortress, none	50	75	100
B-32 Dominator, 12-44	75	100	125
C-46 Commando, 3-43	40	60	80
C-47 Skytrain, 3-43	30	40	60
C-47 Skytrain**, 5-43	30	40	60
C-54 Skymaster, 3-43	50	75	100
C60A Lodestar, 3-43	25	38	50
C69 Constellation, 4-44	75	100	125
C78 Bobcat, 6-44	25	38	50
C87 Liberator, 3-44	75	100	125
CG-4A Waco Glider, 6-43	20	30	40
F4F-4 Wildcat, 5-43	15	22	30
F4U-1 Corsair, 3-43	15	22	30
F6F Hellcat, 4-43	15	22	30
GH-1 Nightingale*, 5-43	25	37	50
J2F-4 Duck, 12-42	30	45	60
JRF OA-09 Goose*, 7-43	30	45	60

ID PLANE, U.S. B-29 Super Fortress, 9/44. Courtesy RLM.

ID PLANE/JR2S1 (S44) Excalibur. Courtesy RLM.

ID PLANE, U.S. P-38 Lightning. Courtesy RLM.

	C5	C7	C9
JRS-1 (S43), 11-42	30	45	60
JR2S-1 (S44) Excalibur, 11-44	75	100	125
L-1 Vigilant, 3-43	25	37	50
L-2 Grasshopper, 7-44	25	37	50
L-4 Grasshopper, 2-43	25	37	50
L-5 Sentinel, 1-44	25	37	50
OS2U (on floats)*, 2-43	25	37	50
OS2U (on wheels)*, 2-43	25	37	50
OS2U-1 (on floats), 7-43	25	37	50
PBM-3 Mariner, 6-43	30	45	60
PBY-5 Catalina, 5-43	30	45	60
PB2Y-3 Coronado, 4-43	75	100	150
PV-1 (B-39) Ventura, 5-43	25	37	50
PV-2 Harpoon, 5-43	25	37	50
P-38 Lightning, 7-42	25	37	50
P-39 Airacobra, 6-42	15	22	30
P-40 Warhawk, 9-42	15	22	30
P-40 Warhawk, 4-44	15	22	30
P-43 Lancer, 5-43	15	22	30
P-47 Thunderbolt, 9-42	15	22	30
P-47 (D) Thunderbolt, 2-44	15	22	30
P-47 (N) Thunderbolt, 4-45	15	22	30
P-47 Thunderbolt*, none	15	22	30
P-51 Mustang, 6-42	15	22	30
P-51D Mustang, 4-45	15	22	30
P-61 Black Widow, 2-44	25	37	50
P-63 King Cobra, 5-44	15	22	30
P-80 Shooting Star, 4-45	20	30	40
SB2A-2 Buccaneer, 5-43	15	22	30
SB2C-1 Helldiver, 3-43	15	22	30
SB2C-2 Helldiver, 2-45	15	22	30
SB2C-2 Helldiver, (floats)*, 3-43	25	37	50
SB2C-2 Helldiver, (wheels)*, 3-43	25	37	50
SB2U-3 Vindicator, 6-43	15	22	30
SNJ-2 Texan, 7-42	15	22	30
SNJ-3 Texan, 7-42	15	22	30
S03C-1 Seagull (floats), 3-43	25	37	50
S03C-2 Seagull (wheels), 3-43	25	37	50
SR-10B Reliant, 10-42	25	37	50
TBD-1 Devastator, 5-43	15	22	30
TBF Avenger, 7-43	15	22	30

*molded by Design Center
**molded by Leominster
All other molded by Cruver

British

	C5	C7	C9
Albacore, 8-42	30	45	60
Albemarle, 9-44	25	37	50
Barracuda, 2-43	15	22	30
Beaufighter 1, 9-42	25	37	50
Beaufighter 2, 9-42	25	37	50
Beaufighter 6, 5-44	25	37	50
Beaufort, 9-42	25	37	50
Beaufort, none	25	37	50
Blenheim IV, 8-42	25	37	50
Boomerang (Aust.)*, none	15	22	30
Botha, 8-42	25	37	50
Defiant, 8-42	15	22	30
Firefly, 2-43	15	22	30
Fulmar, 8-42	15	22	30
Halifax, 9-42	75	100	125
Hampden, 8-42	25	37	50
Hastings, none	50	75	100
Horsa, 9-44	25	37	50
Hotspur, 6-43	15	22	30
Hurricane, 8-43	15	22	30
Lancaster, 4-43	50	75	100
Lerwick, 9-42	30	45	60
Lysander, 7-43	25	37	50
Manchester, 8-42	25	37	50
Maryland, 2-43	25	37	50
Mosquito, 3-43	25	37	50
Roc, 8-42	15	22	30
Skua, 8-42	15	22	30
Spitfire, 8-42	15	22	30
Spitfire, 1-44	15	22	30
Spitfire 9A, 10-44	15	22	30
Spitfire 9B, 10-44	15	22	30

ID PLANE, British. Left to right: Spitfire 9B (10/44), Spitfire 8/42. Courtesy RLM.

	C5	C7	C9
Spitfire 22, 7-45	15	22	30
Stirling, 5-42	50	75	100
Sunderland, 9-42	90	120	150
Swordfish, 9-42	30	45	60
Tempest 2, 3-45	15	22	30
Tempest 5, 10-44	15	22	30
Typhoon, 6-43	15	22	30
Walrus, 4-44	25	37	50
Wellington 2, 9-42	25	37	50
Wellington 3, 9-42	25	37	50

	C5	C7	C9
Whirlwind, 8-43	25	37	50
Whitley, 9-42	25	37	50
York, 9-44	50	75	100

German

	C5	C7	C9
Arado Ar196, 12-43	25	37	50
Blohm & Voss BV138, 5-44	50	75	100
Blohm & Voss HA139, 11-42	90	120	150
Blohm & Voss BV222, 2-44	90	120	150
DFS 230, 8-43	15	22	30
Dornier DO 172, 9-42	25	37	50
Dornier DO 215, 9-42	25	37	50
Dornier DO 217E, 8-42	25	37	50
Fi 156 Storch, none	30	40	60
Focke Wulf FW 187, 8-42	25	37	50
Focke Wulf FW 189, 5-42	25	37	50
Focke Wulf FW 190, 7-42	15	22	30
Focke Wulf FW 190, 12-42	15	22	30
Focke Wulf 200, 3-44	75	100	125
Focke Wulf FW 200K, 9-42	75	100	125
Gotha Go 242, 7-42	25	37	50
Heinkel He 111, 9-42	25	37	50
Heinkel He 112, 7-42	20	30	40
Heinkel He 113, 5-42	20	30	40
Heinkel He 113, 9-42	20	30	40
Heinkel He 115K, 9-42	40	60	80
Henschel Hs 126, 10-42	25	37	50
Henschel Hs 129, 8-44	25	37	50
Junkers Ju 52, 8-42	50	75	100
Junkers Ju 86K, 9-42	25	37	50
Junkers Ju 87B, 8-42	15	22	30
Junkers Ju 88, 9-42	25	37	50
Junkers Ju 90, 9-42	50	75	100
Junkers Ju 188, 7-44	25	37	50
Messers. Me 109E, 7-42	20	30	40
Messers. Me 109F, 7-42	20	30	40
Messers. Me 110, 8-42	25	38	50
Messers. Me 210, 7-43	30	45	60

*Molded by Design Center
**Molded by Leominster
All others molded by Cruver

Italy

	C5	C7	C9
Cantiere Z. 506B, 9-42	75	100	125
Cantiere Z. 1007, 9-42	30	45	60
Caproni CA. 133, 9-42	75	100	125
Fiat BR. 20, 6-42	25	38	50
Fiat CR. 42, 9-42	40	60	80
Fiat CR. 42, 1-43	40	60	80
Fiat G. 50, 8-42	20	30	40
Macchi C. 200, 8-42	20	30	40
Macchi MC. 202, 3-43	20	30	40
Piaggio P. 32 BIS, 9-42	25	38	50
Reggiane Rc. 2000, 9-42	20	30	40
Reggiane Re. 2001, 3-43	20	30	40
Savoia Marchetti 79, 9-42	40	60	80
Savoia Marchetti 81, 9-42	75	100	125
Savoia Marchetti 82, 9-42	30	45	60
Savoia Marchetti 84, 4-43	30	45	60

Japan

	C5	C7	C9
(Adam) Naka. 97, 11-42	25	37	50
(Ann) Mitsu. T-98, 7-42	25	37	50
(Babs) Mitsu. T-97, 6-42	25	37	50
Betty (G4M1), 9-43	25	37	50
Betty (G4M2), 4-45	25	37	50
(Claude) Mitsu. T-96, 6042	25	37	50
(Dave) Naka. T-95-NOB, 7-42	25	37	50
Dinah (Ki46), 8-44	25	37	50
Emily (H8K2), 3-45	25	37	50
Francis (PIY), 3-45	25	37	50
Frank (Ki84), 5-45	20	30	40
George (NIKI-J), 5-45	15	22	30
Hamp (T-00, Zeke 32), 7-43	15	22	30
Helen (Ki49), -44	30	45	60
(Ida) Mitsu. T-98 ALB, 6-42	30	45	60
Irving (J1N1), *5-45	30	45	60
Jack (J2M1), 12-44	15	22	30
Jake (E13A), 9-44	25	37	50
Jill (B6N)*, 5-45	15	22	30
Judy (D4Y), 3-45	15	22	30
(Kate) Naka. T-97, 6-42	15	22	30
Lily (Ki48), 9-43	30	45	60

ID PLANE, German, Focke Wulf FW189, with box. Courtesy RLM.

	C5	C7	C9
(Mary) T-97 ALB, 6-42	30	45	60
(Mavis) Kawa., 11-42	100	150	200
Myrt (C6N), 3-45	15	22	30
(Nate) "97" Fighter, 9-42	25	37	50
(Nell) Mitsu. T-96, 6-42	25	37	50
Nell (G3M), 1-44	25	37	50
Nick (Ki45), 8-44	25	37	50
Oscar T-01 (Ki43), 9-43	15	22	30
Paul 14, Exp*, 12-44	25	37	50
Pete (F1M2), 6-43	30	45	60
Rufe (A6M2-N), 8-43	30	45	60
(Sally) Mitsu. T-97, 6-42	25	38	50
(Sonia) Mitsu. T-99, 7-42	15	22	30
Tojo (Ki44), 6-44	15	22	30
Tojo (Ki44), 3-45	15	22	30
Tony (Ki61), 4-45	15	22	30
(Topsy) Mitsu. MC-20, 10-42	25	37	50
(Val) Aichi T-99, 6-42	30	45	60
Val T-99 MK2, 8-43	30	45	60
(Zeke) Mitsu. 00, 9-42	15	22	30
Zeke 52 (A6M5)*, 12-44	15	22	30

Note: *Japanese abbreviations used above: Kawa.=Kawanishi; Mitsu.=Mitsubishi; Naka.=Nakajima*

Netherlands

	C5	C7	C9
Fokker T8W, 11-42	30	45	60

Russia

	C5	C7	C9
DB-3F, 9-42	25	50	75
DB-3F, 4-44	25	50	75
I-16, none	15	22	30
IL-2, 9-42*	15	22	30
IL-2, 12-43	15	22	30
MiG-3, 8-42	15	22	30
I-18 (MiG-3), 2-43	15	22	30
MiG-3, 2-44	15	22	30
Pe-2, 9-42	15	22	30
SB-3, 11-43	15	22	30
TB-7*, 4-44	15	22	30

End I.D.

	C5	C7	C9
Ideal Electronic Fighter Jet, c. 1959	135	200	270
Ideal Globemaster	42	63	85
Ideal Heliport City Playset	70	105	140
Ideal "U.S. Navy" Rescue Float Plane, plastic wind-up, 10" wingspan	32	48	65
Irwin Helicopter, friction, c. 1950, 15" long	30	45	60

KANSAS TOY & NOVELTY COMPANY

*by Fred Maxwell (Slushmold Contributing Editor) and Perry Eichor (Aircraft Contributing Editor)
with the assistance of Bob Condray and Lorene Sorell*

The years 1920-1940 were decisive for aviation: it was an era of ferment and growth, and was a time of barnstorming and record-breaking. Lindbergh and Earhart made headlines.

Kansas played a large part in the development of airmail and airlines with its manufacturing centers at Topeka and Wichita (Beach, Boeing, Cessna, Laird, Stearman, and others), but the toy industry reflected only dimly the excitement of the era.

Even Lindy's Flight of the Decade was poorly represented. Tootsietoy had a recognizable replica but called it Aero Dawn. The closest Kansas Toy & Novelty (KT&N) came to it was #32, probably already in production in 1927, with the Army Air Corps insignia. Years later Best Toy reproduced it with the name "Combat Airplane."

KT&N barely got the fever, settling for a few basic designs, yet they must have been aware of diversity in cast-iron toys and Tootsietoy and other slushmolders. KT&N #6 and other versions of mailplanes are reminiscent of the Stout-Ford predecessors of the famous "Tin Goose." KT&N #45 and #47 are probably Fokkers. Although of foreign origin, these fine aircraft were more prominent in building U.S. aviation than most of us remember. These and #56 glider are not easy to rationalize; Best toy later named #47 a "Seaplane"— with its engine on its prow?

Listed below are the aircraft said to have been made by KT&N from 1924 to about 1931, using metal disc or wire wheels. Reproductions from Best Toy and Ralstoy will be found with later wheels. KTA4, below, has not been positively identified; it could have been made by others or been a sample.

KANSAS TOY Aircraft: KTA2, KTA1. Photo courtesy of Perry R. Eichor.

	C6	C8	C10

KTA1 Cabin Plane, "6", high wing
with flaring positive dihedral, Army Air Corps
star-in-circle insignia, 6 cyl. radial engine,
pilot head in open cockpit, 8 oval windows,
cast prop, lacquer finish, also unnumbered
version with large tin propeller,
3-3/4" x 3" 14   21   35

KTA2 Cabin Plane, no #, similar to above,
Air Service dot-in-circle insignia,
V-8 engine, cast propeller, 3-5/8" x 3" 14   21   35

KTA3 Large Cabin Plane, "24," high wing,
larger "U.S. Mail" version of above,
dot-in-2-circles insignia, V-8 engine,
cast propeller, white disc wheels
w/ painted black "tires," also an
unnumbered version, 5-5/8" x 4-3/8" 20   35   50

KANSAS TOY Aircraft: KTA3, unnumbered version "U.S. Mail" on both sides. Photo by Perry R. Eichor.

KTA4 ? Large Cabin Plane, no #, Lindy type,
high negative dihedral wing w/ large stars,
6 cyl. radial engine, wheels w/ black
"Tires," Kansas Toy ?, about 5" 20   35   50

KTA5 Small Cabin Plane, "32," high,
positive dihedral wing, Air Corps star
insignia, 6 cyl. radial engine, 6 oval
windows, 3 metal "wire" wheels, large tin
or cast propeller, 2-3/8" x 2-1/8" 10   20   30

KTA6 Small Cabin Plane, no #, similar
to above, w/o "windows" and diff. rudder,
or wingtip, 2-3/8" x 2-1/8" 10   20   30

KANSAS TOY Aircraft: KTA6, KTA5. Photo courtesy of Perry R. Eichor.

	C6	C8	C10

KTA7 Zeppelin, "44," front and rear cabins,
3 tail planes, mooring loop on nose,
rear axle through rear cabin
(unusual design), 4-1/4" 50   75   100

KTA8 Airliner, "45," Fokker?, high, oval,
corrugated wing and tail, 9 circular
cabin windows, 9 rectangular flightdeck
windows, 6 cyl. radial engine,
large tin propeller, 2-1/2" x 2-1/2" 20   35   45

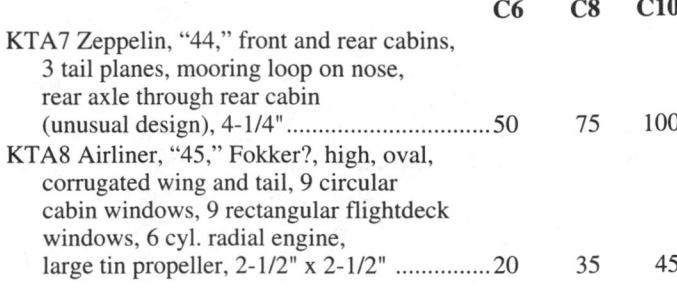

KANSAS TOY KTA8. Photo by Bill Conover.

KTA9 Airliner, "KTN 47," Fokker,
similar to #45, sometimes called a
"seaplane," Why?, 3-5/8" x 3-1/2" 20   35   45

KANSAS TOY KTA9, KTA11. Drawing by Deb Eccles.

KANSAS TOY KTA9. Photo by Al Lane.

	C6	**C8**	**C10**
KTA10 Airliner, "KTN 47," larger version of above, 4" x ?" 20	30	40
KTA11 Glider, "56," high oval wing w/ "GLIDER," pilot in front, flat lattice fuselage, 2-5/8" x 2-3/8" 15	25	40

Note: Best Toys' later reproductions will have "Made in U.S.A." embossed; and may have small white rubber wheels.

	C6	**C8**	**C10**
Jet, USAF, friction powered, tin litho, 5" wingspan 15	20	35
Katz Toys "The Pathfinder," trimotor monoplane, 22" wingspan 350	600	900
Katz Toys "The Red Arrow" No. 137 single monoplane, pull toy 300	450	750

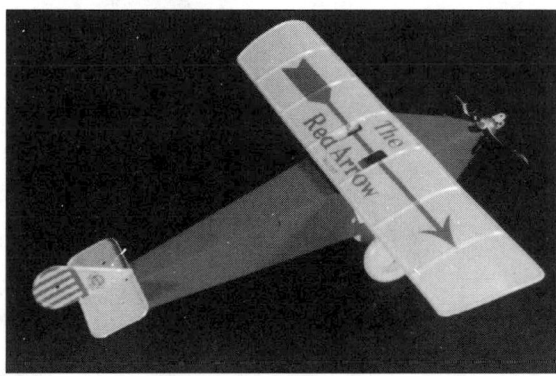

KATZ TOYS "The Red Arrow" No. 137. Photo by Perry R. Eichor.

	C6	**C8**	**C10**
KD-1 Mak-a-plane, 4" long, all metal w/ rubber wheels, mechanical, 1940s 40	50	70
Kenton "Air Mail," wingspan approx. 8" 600	1000	1450

KENTON "Air Mail," wingspan approx. 8". Courtesy Chic Gast.

	C6	**C8**	**C10**
Kenton "Los Angeles" dirigible, 8" long 500	750	1050
Kenton "Pony Blimp," cast iron, 6" long 125	200	400
Kenton "United Boeing" twin engine, cast iron 112	168	225
Keystone "Airmail" plane, pressed steel, "NX-265," 24" wingspan 800	1500	2130
Keystone "Airmail," "NC-263" 500	750	1000
Keystone Ride 'Em Mail Plane, 1930s, 23-1/2" wingspan, "NC-273" 1200	2000	3000

KEYSTONE Mail 27" wingspan. Photo by Calvin L. Chaussee.

KEYSTONE Riding plane, 28" wingspan, No. 293 "Ride 'Em" Fighter. Courtesy Bob Black, Jr.

	C6	**C8**	**C10**
Keystone riding plane, seat over tail, steering bar over cabin, single wing, high, one engine, 23-1/2" long 500	750	1000
Keystone riding plane, No. 293, "Ride 'Em" fighter, 28" wingspan 400	600	850
Keystone trimotor, 1920s 900	1400	2200
Kilgore "Bullet" open cockpit monoplane, cast iron, 4" long 100	150	225
"Kilgore Comet" cap-firing plane 25	38	50
Kilgore Ford Trimotor, cast iron, "TAT," 13-1/2" wingspan 2000	3000	6000

KILGORE "Sea Gull," approx. 9" wingspan. Courtesy Chic Gast.

	C6	C8	C10
Kilgore high wing monocoupe, 5-1/2"	125	188	250
Kilgore high wing monoplane, 3-1/2" long	50	75	100
Kilgore "N4," open cockpit monoplane, cast iron, 4" long	125	188	250
Kilgore, Seagull, high wing, pusher prop, 8-1/4" wingspan	625	938	1250
Kilgore Seagull, like above, but 4" wingspan	200	300	400
Kilgore "TAT," largest Kilgore plane	2500	4200	7700

KILGORE "TAT," largest Kilgore plane. Photo by Jeanne Bertoia. Courtesy Bill Bertoia Auctions.

	C6	C8	C10
Kilgore "TAT No. 401," twin engine passenger monoplane, 4-1/2" long	150	250	325
Kilgore "Travel Air Mystery," double open cockpits, cast iron, 6" long	250	375	500
Kingsbury Biplane, steel wind-up, cast-iron pilot, 16" long	350	525	700
Kingsbury Monoplane, high wing, trimotor, clockwork, 15" wingspan	475	715	950
Kingsbury Tin Goose, tri-engine, c. 1930s, 21" wingspan	600	900	1500
Kingsbury "Trans Atlantic" Monoplane, painted pressed steel wind-up, c. 1930, 11" long	200	300	450
Kingsbury "U.S. Airmail" biplane, steel wind-up, 15" long	200	500	900
Lehmann "Ikarus," 18" wingspan, tin & paper, early	1200	2000	3000

KINGSBURY "Trans Atlantic" Monoplane. Courtesy Lloyd W. Ralston Auctions.

	C6	C8	C10
Lehmann Shenandoah Dirigible, 7-1/2" long	225	388	450
Liberty Playthings "Flying Plane" c. early 1930s	125	188	250
Lincoln White Metal LWA1 Airplane, trimotored, Fokker F-11?, tapered high wings w/ wings symbol embossed, 7 cyl. radial engines, outboards mounted on landing gear struts, tin propellers, metal wheels, no windows, 3-1/4" x 4-1/2"	25	50	100

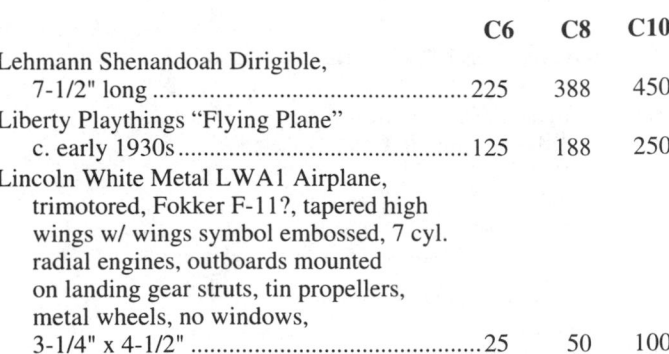

LINCOLN WHITE METAL LWA1. Photo by Fred Maxwell.

	C6	C8	C10
Lincoln White Metal LWA2 Airplane, trimotored, similar to above but outboard engines mounted in wings, unrealistic window patterns, metal wheels, 2-1/2" x 2-1/2"	20	30	40

LINCOLN WHITE METAL: LWA1, LWA2. Photo by Perry R. Eichor.

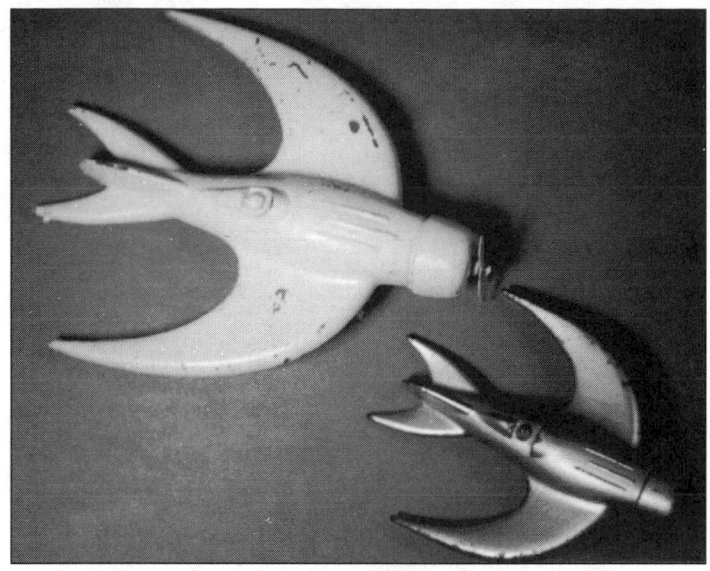

Though there is no hard evidence as yet, these two "Batplanes" have been attributed to Lincoln White Metal. Left to right: LWA3, LWA4.

	C6	C8	C10
Lincoln White Metal LWA3 Airplane, streamlined, swallow-shaped, pilot, cowled radial engine, tin propeller. It would be called "Batplane" today, c. 4-1/2" x 3"	40	60	100
Lincoln White Metal LWA4 Airplane smaller version of above, c. 3" x 2-1/2"	30	45	60
"Lindy" cast iron, nickel prop and wheels, 3-1/2" wingspan	105	158	210
Lindy type plane, lead, 2-1/4" wingspan	10	20	30
Lionel No. 55 Airplane and Pylon	300	450	1100
Luscombe Airplane, 4" long	30	45	60
Manoil No. 517, Lockheed F90	20	30	50
Manoil No. 518 Navion	20	30	50
Manoil No. 519 Bonanza B-35	20	30	50
Manoil No. 520 Ercoupe	20	30	50

MANOIL Airplanes, left to right: 517, 518, 519, 520. Courtesy Peter and Marjorie Ruben.

	C6	C8	C10
Marx American Airlines Flagship, 27-1/2" wingspan	155	230	310
Marx "Army Bomber" No. 1025, trimotor, c. 1935, 26" wingspan	75	150	250
Marx Astrojet Airport Set, planes, copter, etc.	155	230	310
Marx Bomber, 4 engines, drops wooden bombs, 14-3/4" wingspan	75	120	200

MARX Bomber, 14-3/4" wingspan, 4 engine, drops wooden bombs. Photo by Perry R. Eichor.

	C6	C8	C10
Marx Bomber, tin litho, sparkling mechanism, camouflaged, 4 engine, 18" wingspan	60	140	200

MARX Bomber, tin litho, sparkling mechanism, camouflaged, 4-engine. MacNary Collection. Photo: RLM.

	C6	C8	C10
Marx City Airport Set	300	500	750
Marx Crop Duster Plane	20	40	80

MARX Crop Duster Plane. Photo by Perry R. Eichor.

	C6	C8	C10
Marx Crop Duster Plane Set	65	98	130
Marx Curtiss Transport, khaki, pressed steel, 9-1/2" wingspan	50	75	100
Marx DC-3 Transport, pressed steel, c. 1939, 10" wingspan	50	75	100
Marx DC-4 type, 4-motor passenger, c. 1930s, pressed steel	60	125	250
Marx DC-6 Transport plane, plastic	75	120	150

MARX DC-6 Transport plane, plastic. Photo by Perry R. Eichor.

	C6	C8	C10
Marx "Electric Lighted Radio Airport," 1930s 5" x 2-1/2" x 3-1/2"	200	300	400
Marx F84 Jet Fighter, remote control	68	100	135
Marx Friction-powered 4-motor transport w/ whirling propellers, tin litho	60	90	200
Marx Futuristic Airport	212	318	425
Marx Gyroplane	40	75	100
Marx Hangar, tin litho, c.1941	50	75	100

MARX Hangar, tin litho, c. 1941. Photo by James Apthorpe.

	C6	C8	C10
Marx "Little Lindy Aeroplane," 1930s, friction, 6" wingspan	100	150	200
Marx Lockheed Prop Jet	125	188	250

	C6	C8	C10
Marx Mainstream Airport, c. 1930s	110	165	220
Marx "Municipal Airport" hangar, early, w/ plane	400	600	800
Marx P35, pressed steel, w/ and w/o wheel skirts, 13-1/2" wingspan	60	90	120

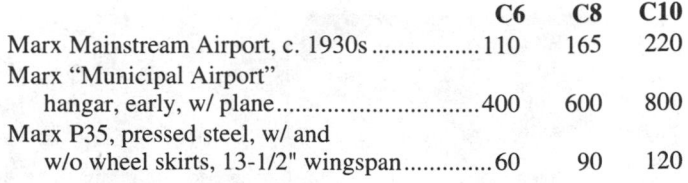

MARX P-35, 13-1/2" wingspan. Photo by Perry R. Eichor.

	C6	C8	C10
Marx P35-type, 2-engine bomber, 15-7/8" wingspan	105	158	210

MARX P-35-type 2-engine bomber. MacNary Collection. Photo: RLM.

	C6	C8	C10
Marx Pan American 4-motor, propeller-driven, also as PAA, 1940, pressed steel, 27" wingspan	175	265	350

MARX Pan American 4-motor, 1940, 27" wingspan. Courtesy Lloyd W. Ralston Auctions.

*MARX Pan American Super 7 Clipper, 17-1/2"
wingspan, also as American Airlines. Photo by
Perry R. Eichor.*

*MARX "Skycruiser Stratoliner 700," 4-engine. MacNary
Collection. Photo: RLM.*

	C6	C8	C10
Marx Pan American Super 7 clipper, also as American Airlines, 17-1/2" wingspan	150	225	300

*MARX
Piggyback
Airplane Set.
Photo by
Tim Oei.*

	C6	C8	C10
Marx Piggyback Airplane Set	75	112	150
Marx "Pioneer Air Express," tin litho, high wing monoplane, 25-1/2" wingspan	75	100	200
Marx "Sky Cruiser" 2-motored Transport Plane w/ siren and whirling propellers, Stratoliner 700, rubber wheels, c. 1940s, 18" wingspan	163	245	325
Marx "Skycruiser Stratoliner 700," 4-engine	45	75	125
Marx "Sky Cruiser Stratoline 700," 2-engine	50	75	100

*MARX
"Skycruiser
Stratoliner 700,"
2-engine.
MacNary
Collection.
Photo: RLM.*

	C6	C8	C10
Marx Sparkling Rocket Fighter, No. 1425, tin litho	37	56	75
Marx Swingtail Flying Tiger transport	300	450	600
Marx trimotor Biplane, 9-1/2" wingspan	40	75	100

*MARX. Left to right:
Trimotor Biplane with
9-1/2" wingspan,
Gyroplane.
Photo by
Perry R. Eichor.*

	C6	C8	C10
Marx TWA Mail Plane	90	135	180
Marx Universal Airport w/ 2 metal planes, c. 1940s, 12" long	55	90	200
Metal Cast No. 43 twin engine bomber, B-25?, 5-1/4" wingspan	10	15	20
Metal Cast No.66 Aeroplane, 2-engine, c. 1940s, lead (some marked "Fred Greene"), approx. 4-1/2" wingspan	5	10	20
Metal Cast No. 321, Aeroplane, "U.S. 256," Air Corps star insignia, 3-1/4" long	10	15	20
Metalcraft Build-A-Zep, builds 21 different 18" zeppelins	242	365	485

METALCRAFT Spirit of St. Louis, 9" long. Courtesy Mapes Auctioneers & Appraisers.

METAL CAST No. 66 Aeroplane. Photo by Norbert Schachter.

	C6	C8	C10
Metalcraft Ford Trimotor	112	162	225
Metalcraft Northrup Alpha Monoplane, "PURE the Pure Oil Company," wingspan approx. 17"	500	800	1200
Metalcraft Riding Rocket, 24" long	100	150	200
Metalcraft Spirit of St. Louis, came as kit, 9" long	118	175	235
Metalcraft Zeppelin	245	370	490

METALCRAFT Aircraft Construction Sets, as shown in a December 1929 Butler Bros. catalog.

MIDWEST

Listing by Fred Maxwell

MWA?1 Monoplane, 2 pilots in open cockpit (early record breakers?), Liberty V-12 engine, cast propeller, 8 oval & 2 round windows, 2 painted main gear disc wheels, 3-1/8" x 3-5/8" .... No Price Found

MWA?2 Monoplane, same as above but no crew, ailerons and tail surfaces detailed & 3 disc wheels w/ those black painted "tires," 3-3/16" x 3-5/8" .... No Price Found

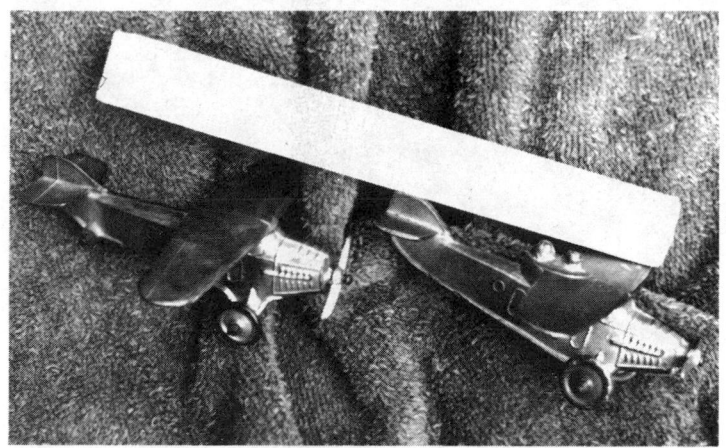

MID-WEST. Left to right: MWA?2, MWA?1. Photo by Fred Maxwell.

	C6	C8	C10
North & Judd Lindy-type plane, cast iron, 4-3/8" long	175	265	350
P-38 glass candy container	50	75	100
Passenger Plane, high wing, 4-engine, 3 wooden wheels, approx. 9" wingspan	9	13	18
Pedal Car, Biplane, 2-motor, 54" long	500	900	1800
Pedal Car, Pursuit Plane, 1941	1800	3100	4450
Pyro Jet, 6" long, plastic	4	5	7

RALSTOY AIRCRAFT

by Perry Eichor, Aircraft Contributing Editor, and Fred Maxwell, Slushmold Contributing Editor

Ralstoy issued new aircraft and reproduced popular Kansas Toy numbers issued during the 1920s. The late 1930s toy reflected the growing awareness of the war in Europe.

	C6	C8	C10
RAA1 Small Cabin Plane, "32," "Ralstoy," wings positive dihedral, (See Kansas KTA5), 2-1/2" x 2-1/4"	5	10	20
RAA2 Cabin Plane, "NC414," "Ralstoy" midwing, V-12 engine, tin propeller, 3-3/8" x 3-3/8"	20	30	40
RAA3 Cabin Plane, high wing, cowled radial engine, 2 doors, 6 windows, "Ralstoy," "Made in USA," 3-5/8" x 3-1/2"	20	30	40
RAA4 Pursuit Plane, P40," Curtiss "U.S. Army," midwing, Air Corps star-in-circle insignia, V-12 engine, 2 machine guns, 3-bladed propeller, "Made in USA," "Ralstoy" in diamond, 3" x 3-1/4"	20	30	40
RAA5 Cabin Plane, slim midwing, cowled radial engine, pilot, tin propeller, underside is "Scout," "Made in USA," 3" x 3-3/4"	20	30	40
RAA6? Large Cabin Plane, Lindy-type, high wing, 6 cyl. radial engine, metal wheels, Ralstoy?	20	30	40

RALSTOY. Left to right: RAA4, RAA2, RAA3. Photo by Perry R. Eichor.

RALSTOY? RAA5. Photo by Perry R. Eichor.

	C6	C8	C10
Remco Flying Boxcar	35	52	70
Remco Kennedy Airport	58	85	115
Remco Whirlybird Helicopter	20	30	40
Remco WWI "Air Aces" Playset, 1965	138	205	275
Renwal B-17, small	5	10	20
Renwal B-17, plastic, c. 1944, 9-1/4" wingspan	15	30	60

RENWAL DC-4. Photo by James Apthorpe.

RENWAL. Top, left to right: B-17 No. 777, P-38. Middle: B-25 No. 25, B-29 No. 29, C54 Transport. Bottom: B-17 (small) No. 17, P-40. Photo by Perry R. Eichor.

RENWAL Martin Mars No. 15. Photo by James Apthorpe.

	C6	C8	C10
Renwal B-25, plastic, c. 1944, 6-3/4" wingspan	20	30	40
Renwal B-29, No. 29	20	30	40
Renwal C54 Transport, large, plastic	20	30	40
Renwal DC-4, 7" wingspan	15	22	30
Renwal Martin Mars No. 15	20	30	40
Renwal P38, plastic	10	25	40
Renwal P40, plastic	10	15	20
Renwal P47, plastic	15	20	30
Renwal PB2Y Flying Boat	15	20	40
Savoye Blimp, "U.S.N.," 4" long	20	30	40
Savoye Monoplane, 3-1/2" wingspan	20	30	40
Schieble Biplane, c. 1920s, 15-1/2" long	300	450	600
Schieble Ford trimotor, steel, 29-1/2" long	500	900	1550
"Schoenhut's Airplane Builder" wood kit	130	195	260
"Sky Cruiser," tin litho, 2-motor transport, engines turn w/ friction mechanism, 18" wingspan	40	75	100

SAVOYE Blimp, "U.S.N." Photo by Al Lane.

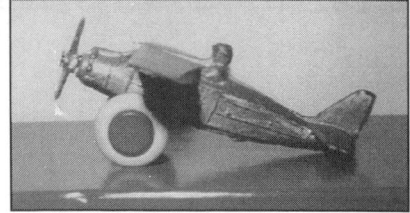

SAVOYE Monoplane. Photo by Al Lane.

SCHIEBLE Ford Trimotor, 26-1/4" wingspan, No. 30. Courtesy Wilkinson Collection, Detroit Antique Toy Museum.

	C6	C8	C10
"Spirit of America" pull toy aeroplane, steel and litho, 14" long	12	18	24
Spirit of St. Louis glass candy container, 4-3/8" long	150	225	300
Steelcraft "Akron" blimp pull toy, 25" long	75	112	150
Steelcraft "Army Scout Plane" single engine, high wing monoplane, c. 1920s, 22-1/2" wingspan	700	1100	1825

	C6	C8	C10
Steelcraft "Army Scout Plane" trimotor, single high wing, c. 1920s	200	600	1000
Steelcraft Army Scout Plane, green and orange, 23" wingspan	100	200	400
Steelcraft "Graf Zeppelin," pressed steel pull toy, 30-1/2"	250	375	500
Steelcraft Graf Zeppelin, pull toy, 32" long	300	450	600
Steelcraft Lockheed Sirius, pull toy, 21-1/2" wingspan	650	1200	1740

STEELCRAFT Lockheed Sirius. Courtesy Chrisie's East.

	C6	C8	C10
Steelcraft "Macon" Zeppelin, 25" long	350	525	700
Steelcraft Monoplane, 2 open cockpits, c. 1930s, 16" wingspan	250	375	600

STEELCRAFT "Army Scout Plane," single engine. Courtesy Continental Hobby House.

STEELCRAFT "NX 130 U.S. Mail Plane," one engine. Photo by Calvin L. Chaussee.

STEELCRAFT "Graf Zeppelin," 30" long. Restored and photographed by Tim Oei.

	C6	C8	C10
Steelcraft No. 79 Pedal Plane, high wing Monoplane, 32" wingspan, 48" long	1500	2500	4000
Steelcraft NX107, "Little Jim" 23" wingspan	550	825	1300
Steelcraft NX130, blue eagles on wings, 23" wingspan	475	700	950
Steelcraft "NX130 U.S. Mail Plane," one-engine	388	580	775
Steelcraft NX131, trimotor, U.S. Mail plane, pull toy, 26-1/2" wingspan	650	1100	1580
Steelcraft Pan Am airliner, 26"	135	200	270
Steelcraft Pedal Plane "Pursuit," 1940	1000	1700	3000
Strauss "Chicago" Dirigible, tin litho, 10"	125	188	250
Strauss "Flying Airship" (boxtop description) aluminum wind-up	275	350	550
Strauss Graf Zeppelin, 16" long	240	360	480
Sun Rubber "Pursuit Ship," "25-P75," c. 1940-41, 4-1/4" wingspan	15	20	30
Sun Rubber No. 12008 Racing Plane, c. 1947, also called "Scout," both same plane as "Pursuit Ship"	15	20	30

	C6	C8	C10
Sun Rubber No. 12009 Transport, 4" long	37	56	75
Sun Rubber No. 12010 Dual-Control Plane, 4-1/2" long	20	30	40
Theodore Hahn Aeroplane No. 187, lead alloy, 1920s	20	40	75
Thomas Toys Defiant, plastic, 4" long	20	30	40
Thomas Toys F-80 Jet Action Rocket Launcher	20	30	40
Thomas Toys Warhawk, plastic, 4" long	20	30	40
Tip Top Giant Flyer Monoplane, c. 1920s, 23" long	200	350	500
Tommy Toy Dirigible, "USN" slush lead, 1930s	25	38	50

SUN RUBBER. Left to right: No. 12009, Pursuit Ship, No. 12010. Courtesy Ed Poole.

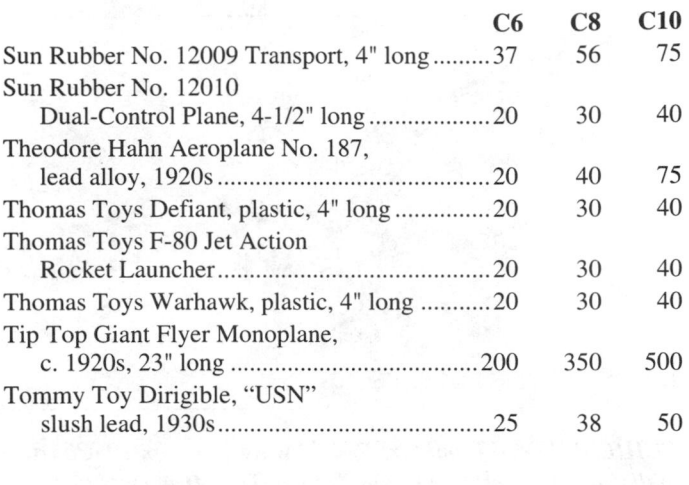

THOMAS TOYS F-80 Jet Action Rocket Launcher. Courtesy Islyn Thomas.

THEODORE HAN Aeroplane.

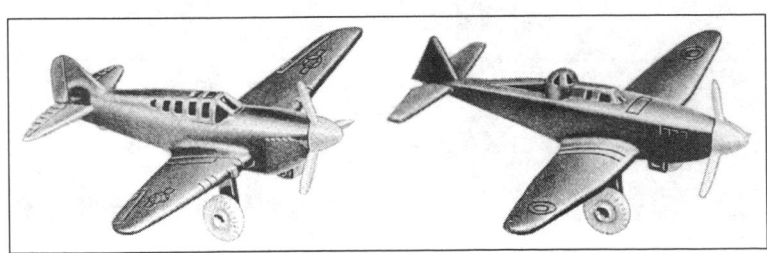

THOMAS TOYS. Left to right: Warhawk, Defiant, plastic, 4" long.

TOMMY TOY
"U.S.N."
Dirigible. Photo
by Bill Kaufman.
Courtesy Charles
W. Weldon, Jr.

Early Tootsietoy Airplanes. Left to right: No. 4482 Bleriot without loop; unnumbered "Spirit of St. Louis" (not SR of France); No. 4482 Bleriot with loop. John Gibson Collection. Photo by John Gibson.

TOOTSIETOY. Left to right: No. 106 Low Wing Monoplane (1932); No. 107 High Wing Monoplane (1932). Collection and photo by John Gibson.

	C6	C8	C10
Tootsietoy 106 Lockheed Sirius, tin low wing	36	48	60
Tootsietoy 107 Bellanca, high tin wing Monoplane	33	44	55
Tootsietoy 119 Northrup Alpha "U.S. Army" Pursuit	15	20	40
Tootsietoy 125 Lockheed Electra, twin engine	10	20	40

	C6	C8	C10
Tootsietoy 717 DC-2, "TWA"	20	40	75
Tootsietoy 718 Waco, "U.S. Navy," C model Biplane	35	50	90
Tootsietoy no #, Waco "Dive Bomber," model Biplane	240	320	400
Tootsietoy 719 Crusader, twin boom, twin engine	48	64	80
Tootsietoy 720 "Fly-N-Giro" Auto-Gyro, small version	240	320	400
Tootsietoy 721 "Curtis P-40" Pursuit, silver	100	200	400
Same as above, olive	125	250	500

TOOTSIETOY 722 Military DC-4, 1941. John Gibson Collection. Photo by John Gibson.

TOOTSIETOY P-38 Lightning Fighter Plane (1950), 5-1/4" wingspan. Collection and photo John Gibson.

TOOTSIETOY Unnumbered Waco "Dive Bomber" biplane. Collection and photo John Gibson.

	C6	C8	C10
Tootsietoy 722 Military DC-4 "Army Bomber"	30	75	120
Tootsietoy DC-4 "Super Mainliner"	39	52	65
Tootsietoy 722 Military DC-4, "Army Transport"	40	75	100
Tootsietoy 4482 Bleriot, 67mm long	39	52	65
Tootsietoy 4491 Bleriot, 25mm long	15	20	25
Tootsietoy 4649 Ford Trimotor, tin wing	90	120	150

TOOTSIETOY Unnumbered P-39 Airacobra Fighter Plane (issued postwar). Collection and photo John Gibson.

	C6	C8	C10
Tootsietoy 4650 Biplane, Jenny type	30	50	100
Tootsietoy 4659 Auto-Gyro, tin wing, large version	25	60	100
Tootsietoy 4660 AC Aero-Dawn, high wing Monoplane, tin wing	15	25	50
Tootsietoy 4660 Aero-Dawn, seaplane version	20	30	55

TOOTSIETOY Unnumbered P-39 Airacobra Fighter Plane (issued postwar), rarer color combination. Collection and photo John Gibson.

TOOTSIETOY U.S. Coast Guard Amphibian (resembles Sikorsky S-43), 1950. Collection and photo John Gibson.

TOOTSIETOY
No. 1030 Los Angeles
dirigible (1934), with box.
Collection and photo
John Gibson.

TOOTSIETOY DC4 "Super Mainliner," three versions.
Photo by Perry R. Eichor.

	C6	C8	C10
Tootsietoy 4675 Wings, Biplane, tin wing	25	35	55
Tootsietoy 4675 Wings, Seaplane version	30	40	60

	C6	C8	C10
Tootsietoy P-38	20	50	100
Tootsietoy P-39, tin wing, 2-bladed prop	150	200	250
Tootsietoy S-58, Sikorsky Helicopter	36	48	60
Tootsietoy Lockheed 749 Constellation, "PAA N88846"	30	60	120
Tootsietoy Boeing 377 Stratocruiser, "PAA N102SV"	30	50	100
Tootsietoy Corvair CV-240 twin engine	20	40	80
Tootsietoy "Piper Cub," low wing monoplane	5	10	20
Tootsietoy Navion	5	10	20
Tootsietoy Beechcraft Bonanza	5	10	20
Tootsietoy P-80 "Shooting Star" Jet	15	20	25
Tootsietoy F7V-3 "Cutlass" Jet	10	15	20
Tootsietoy "F-86 Sabre" Jet, 2-piece casting	20	35	60
Tootsietoy "F-86 Sabre" Jet, 1-piece casting	5	10	15
Tootsietoy F9F-2 Panther Jet, 2-piece casting	25	35	60
Tootsietoy F9F-2 Panther Jet, 1-piece casting	5	10	15
Tootsietoy F4D Douglas Skyray	5	10	15

TOOTSIETOY. Top, left to right: 4679 Tri-Motor Plane; 4660
Aero-Dawn; 4650 Biplane; 4675 Wings, High-Wing Floatplane.
Middle: 4659 Autogyro; 718 Waco Bomber; 719 Crusader.
Bottom: 119 Army Plane; 125 Lockheed Electra; 717 TWA
Douglas Airliner; DC4 Super Mainliner. Photo by Ed Poole.

TOOTSIETOY. Top, left to right: P-39, 720. Bottom: Sikorsky
S-43, 721, 722. Photo by Perry R. Eichor.

	C6	C8	C10
Tootsietoy "Delta," 2-piece casting	20	35	60
Tootsietoy "F-94 Starfire" Jet	10	15	20
Tootsietoy Boeing 707	10	15	20
Tootsietoy Sikorsky S-43	40	60	100
Tootsietoy "Tootsietoy Airport," hangar and two planes, boxed set	540	720	900
Tootsietoy U.S. Moon Rocket, 3 types, all have 2 wheels to run on string, mid-1960s replicas of original Buck Rogers spaceships (see Comic Character)	40	75	100
Tootsietoy "U.S.N. Los Angeles" dirigible, two grooved wheels on top to run on string (also was sold as part of Buck Rogers set)	40	60	80

Tootsietoy Miniature Airplanes

List by John Gibson

	C6	C8	C10
1353 High Wing Monoplane	8	12	16
1407 Air Defense 10-piece carded set	75	100	150
1636 DC2 TWA	6	9	12
1637 Atlantic Clipper	6	9	12
1639 P38	15	23	30
1743 Aeroplane whistle tin litho (Crackerjacks)	20	30	40
1744 High Wing Monoplane tin litho, (Crackerjacks)	20	30	40
1746 Aerodawn tin litho (Crackerjacks)	20	30	40
1747 Low Wing Monoplane tin litho (Crackerjacks)	20	30	40
1812 Sky Fleet 5-piece carded set (1946) contains 3 - #1636 TWA planes and 2 - #1637 clippers	38	56	75

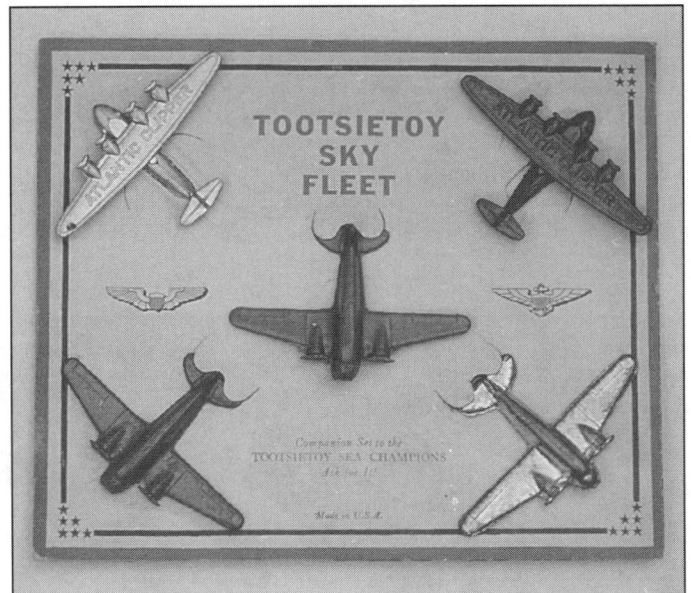

TOOTSIETOY Miniature Airplanes No. 1812 Sky Fleet. John Gibson Collection. Photo by John Gibson.

	C6	C8	C10
4550 DC4 (charm)	2	3	4
9951 Pursuit Plane	6	9	12

	C6	C8	C10
Turner High Wing Monoplane, one-engine, 1930s, 18-1/2" wingspan	260	390	520
Turner High Wing Monoplane, pressed steel, 22-1/2" wingspan	300	450	600
United Electric "Spirit of St. Louis," go around tower, 2 planes, pressed steel, electrical	800	1200	1600
"U.S." High Wing Monoplane, single engine, open ironwork body, spool wheel works, prop, 8" wingspan	200	300	400

Vindex Fokker, c. 1929, cast iron, high wing, single engine, 10" wingspan. Auctioned in mint condition in May 1994, with salesman's tags and original pullstring and ball attached for $24,000.

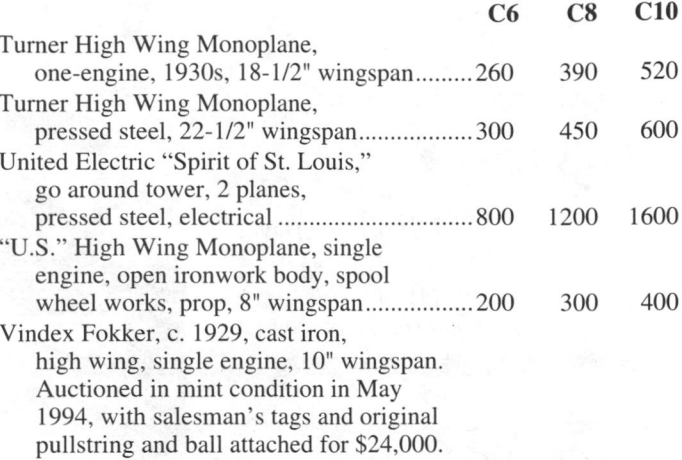

VINDEX FOKKER, cast-iron. Photo by Perry R. Eichor.

	C6	C8	C10
Watrous single engine biplane, pressed steel bell toy, c. 1915, 8-1/4" wingspan	200	300	600
Williams, A.C. UX83, cast iron, 3-1/4" wingspan	100	150	200
Williams, A.C. "UX-99," cast iron, wingspan approx. 4-1/2"	112	170	225

WYANDOTTE Airliner, 12-3/4" wingspan, 4-engine, pressed steel. Photo by Perry R. Eichor.

	C6	C8	C10
Williams, A.C. "UX-166," Lindy-type plane, cast-iron nickeled engine and wheels, wingspan approx. 5-3/4"	75	112	150
Wyandotte Airacuda, pressed steel, twin vertical stabilizers, twin pusher engines, blue or red, 8-1/2" wingspan	45	70	90

WYANDOTTE. Left to right: Airacuda; Airliner c. WWII, 2-engine. Photo by Perry R. Eichor.

	C6	C8	C10
Wyandotte Airliner, 4 engine, pressed steel, 12-3/4" wingspan	73	110	145
Wyandotte Airliner, C. WWII, two-engine, wooden wheels	75	110	150

WYANDOTTE China Clipper. Courtesy Wilkinson Collection, Detroit Antique Toy Museum.

	C6	C8	C10
Wyandotte Bomber, Army, pressed steel, two-engine	90	135	180
Wyandotte China Clipper, No. 207, 13" wingspan	123	185	245
Wyandotte City Airport, American Airlines, two hangars, control tower, etc., lights up	125	190	250
Wyandotte Crusader, 9-3/4" wingspan	32	48	65
Wyandotte Crusader, 12-window version	42	63	85
Wyandotte Gyrocopter, twin engine passenger plane, c. 1930s, 12-1/2" wingspan	60	90	120

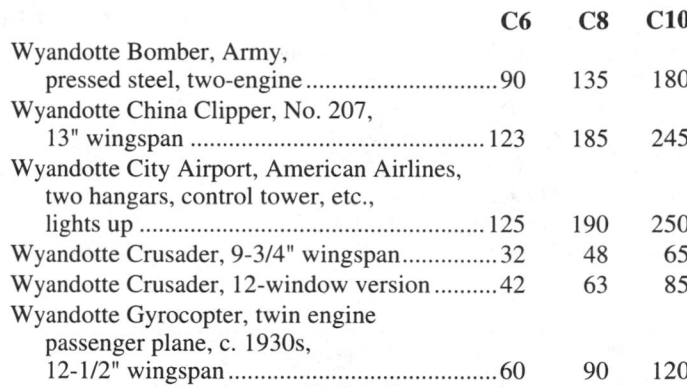

WYANDOTTE Gyrocopter, 12-1/2" wingspan. Photo by Perry R. Eichor.

WYANDOTTE High Wing Passenger Monoplane, No. 2 Lockheed Vega. Photo courtesy Dick and Nancy Dice.

WYANDOTTE Crusader, two variations. Photo by Perry R. Eichor.

	C6	C8	C10
Wyandotte High Wing Passenger Monoplane, No. 2 Lockheed Vega, single engine, bullet nose, 18" wingspan	175	265	350
Wyandotte Military Air Transport, 13" wingspan	25	40	60
Wyandotte Mystery Plane No. 101, twin engine, wings trail backward, 4-1/2" wingspan	30	50	100

WYANDOTTE Stratocruiser, 13" wingspan. Photo by Perry R. Eichor.

WYANDOTTE Mystery Plane No. 101. John Gibson Collection. Photo by John Gibson.

	C6	C8	C10
Wyandotte Rocket Racer No. 319, rocket ship sold in 1935	67	100	135

WYANDOTTE "Rocket Racer #319" Rocket Ship, from an August 1935 ad in Toys and Novelties magazine.

	C6	C8	C10
Wyandotte Stratocruiser, 13" wingspan	75	112	150
Wyandotte Super Jet	80	120	160
Wyandotte "U.S. Navy" Seaplane, 14-1/2" wingspan, c. 1941	215	322	430
Zeppelin, cast iron, approx. 3" long	40	60	80
Zeppelin, "Akron" Marx, c. 1930s, 28" long	100	140	250
Zeppelin, "EPL 1," Lehmann No. 651	300	600	1000

	C6	C8	C10
Zeppelin, "EPL 2," Lehmann No. 652, c. 1907	225	400	800
Zeppelin, "Graf Zeppelin," aluminum, Strauss, 16" long	175	250	350
Zeppelin, "Graf Zeppelin," A.C. Williams, cast iron, 8" long	75	150	250
Zeppelin, "Graf Zeppelin," A.C. Williams, cast iron, 5-1/2" long	100	150	200
Zeppelin, "Graf Zeppelin," A.C. Williams, cast iron, 5" long	50	75	125
Zeppelin, "Los Angeles," cast iron, 12" long	300	750	1500
Zeppelin, pull toy, "Little Giant"	50	100	200
Zeppelin, "Pony DE107," cast iron, 5-1/2" long	50	100	250
Zeppelin, "U.S. Akron," pot metal, c. 1932, 6" long	25	40	75
Zeppelin, "ZEP," cast iron, 4" long	80	120	160
Zeppelin, "Goodyear" decals, hatch opens, 25" long	125	190	300
Zeppelin, pull toy, silver, c. 1920-30s, cast iron, 6" long	60	90	120
Zeppelin, metal, 25" long	42	64	85
Zeppelin, metal, 26-1/2" long	45	68	90
Zeppelin, metal, 27-1/2" long	50	75	100

ZEPPELIN, "Graf Zeppelin," A.C. Williams, cast-iron, 5-1/4" long (1932 ad).

SHIPS

(See also Tin Wind-Ups, Paper)

The average mint price in this category was $995.60 in the last edition. In this edition it is $1412.96, an increase of 42%.

	C6	C8	C10
"Adirondack" Sidewheeler, cast iron, approx. 13" long	500	750	1000
Admiral Dewey's Flagship from the White Fleet, wood and paper, 6" long	100	150	200
Admiral Dewey Flagship, paper litho on wood, c. 1900, 30" long	300	450	600
Aircraft Carrier "65," tin litho, large, c. 1950s	50	75	100
Althof-Bergmann "America," painted tin sidewheeler, c. 1874, 20" long	7000	11,000	18,000
Althof-Bergmann "Pacific" Riverboat, 14" long, auctioned in 1995 for $3850			
Arcade "Showboat," cast iron, 1929, approx. 10-3/4" long	500	750	1050

ARCADE "Showboat," 1929.

Top, left to right: Arnold Ocean Liner, tin keywind, c. 1930; Falk "Bremen." Middle: Ives Merchant Marine Ship; Fleischmann Oil Tanker "Esso." Bottom: Bing Ocean Liner; Ives "New York." Courtesy Christie's East.

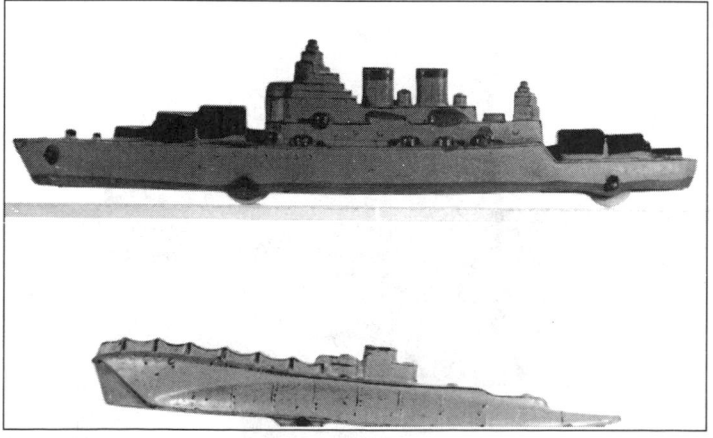

AUBURN RUBBER Battleship and Submarine. Photo by Ed Poole.

	C6	C8	C10
Argo Aircraft Carrier, steel, w/ three 6" jet planes that fire rockets, shell or drop bombs, 36" long	68	102	135
Arnold Ocean Liner, tin keywind, c. 1930, 11-1/2" long	400	650	900
"Automatic Submarine," remote-controlled, tin litho	40	60	80
Atwood Motors, California "Amazon Sidewheeler," plastic and metal, c. 1950s	125	188	250
Auburn Rubber Battleship, c. 1940, No. 1582, 8-1/4" long	22	33	45

AUBURN RUBBER freighter (damaged).

	C6	C8	C10
Auburn Rubber Dreadnaught, new in 1941, extremely rare, 9-1/8" long	30	50	70
Auburn Rubber Freighter, new in 1941, 9-1/4" long	22	33	45
Auburn Rubber Submarine, c. 1941, 6-1/2" long	20	30	40
Auburn Rubber Tugboat, plastic	37	56	75
Authenticast French Warships, incl. Richelieu, Algiers, Fantasque and others, each	17	26	35
Authenticast German Warships, scale models including Narvik, Galster and others, each	22	33	44
Authenticast Japanese Warships, incl. Fuso, Kaga, Mogani and others, each	17	26	35

	C6	C8	C10
Authenticast U.S. scale model warships, WWII including Iowa, Enterprise, Sims and Farragut and submarine Sarge, each	17	26	35
B-LO Submarine, metal, pat. no. 1318048	75	112.50	150
"Baby," cast-iron racing boat, c. 1930, wheeled, Hubley?, 4-1/2" long	60	90	120
Banner Battleship, plastic, 4" long	15	22	30
Barclay 372 Aeroplane Carrier	25	38	50
Barclay 373 Battleship	27	41	55
Battleship "Admiral," paper litho, 1890, 20" long	600	900	1200
Battleship, cast iron, 14-1/2" long	400	600	800
Battleship, glass, candy container, approx. 3" long	60	90	120
Battleship Hillclimber, pressed steel, 15" long	200	300	400
Battleship Oregon, paper litho and wood, 25" long	700	1050	1400

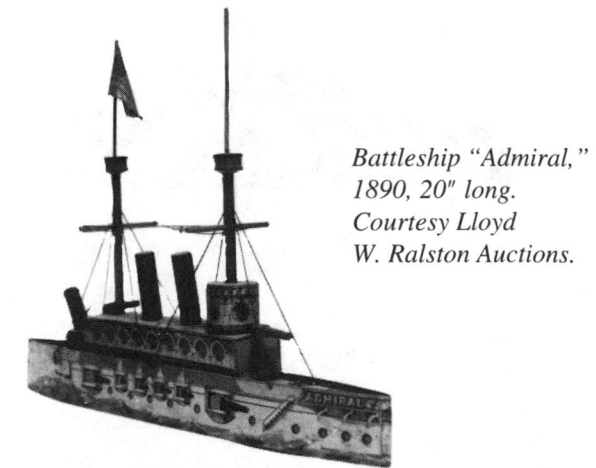

Battleship "Admiral," 1890, 20" long. Courtesy Lloyd W. Ralston Auctions.

Top: BARCLAY 372 Aeroplane Carrier. Bottom: BARCLAY 373 Battleship. Photo by Ed Poole.

	C6	C8	C10
Battleship "Rover," paper litho and wood, 20" long	600	900	1200
Battleship, tin friction, c. 1920s, 9-1/2" long	200	300	400
Big Bang Navy Gun Boat No. 9B, cast iron, 8-1/4" long	125	200	250
Bing Battleship, tin clockwork, 16"	800	1300	1800
Bing Destroyer, tin clockwork, 22-1/2" long	1500	2400	3500
Bing Ferry, clockwork, 16" long	800	1300	1800

BING Torpedo Boat, 27-1/2" long. Photo by Jeanne Bertoia. Courtesy Bill Bertoia Auctions.

BING Ferry, clockwork, 16" long. Photo by Jeanne Bertoia. Courtesy Bill Bertoia Auctions.

BING Warship, c. 1915, clockwork, 19" long. Photo by Jeanne Bertoia. Courtesy Bill Bertoia Auctions.

	C6	C8	C10
Bing Gunboat, hand-painted tin, 29" long	1800	3000	5500
Bing "Leviathan" Ocean Liner, c. 1915, tin keywind, 40" long			No Price Found

BING "Leviathan." Courtesy Christie's East.

BLISS Battleship "New York," 36" long. Courtesy Lloyd W. Ralston Auctions.

	C6	C8	C10
Bing Ocean Liner, tin keywind, c. 1925, 13-1/2" long	400	650	900
Bing Torpedo Boat, 27-1/2" long	2000	3500	6500
Bing Warship, c. 1915, clockwork, 19" long	500	800	1100
Bliss "Admiral" gunboat, 20", gun shoots	260	390	520
Bliss Battleship, litho & wood, 36"	1800	3000	4300
Bliss "Battleship New York," paper litho and stained wood, 1890, 36" x 22"	450	675	900

	C6	C8	C10
Bliss "Conqueror," paper litho on wood, 20" long	900	1400	2000
Bliss "Marguerite" Sailing Schooner, 22" long	350	525	700
Bliss "Rover" Torpedo Boat, paper litho on wood, c. 1896, 20" long	850	1375	1900
Bliss "St. Louis," litho on wood liner, c. 1895, 34-1/2" long	800	1300	1800
Bliss? "Union" ferry, sidewheel, c. 1900, 24" long	225	375	450
Bliss "Vesuvius" gunboat, paper litho on wood, 25-1/2" long	1200	2000	2800

BLISS Battleship, litho and wood, 36" long. Photo by Jeanne Bertoia. Courtesy Bill Bertoia Auctions.

Top, left to right: Bliss "Conqueror"; Bliss "Rover" torpedo boat. Middle: Reed "Ocean Queen." Bottom: Converse Battleship "Indiana." Courtesy Christie's East.

BLISS "St. Louis," litho on wood. Courtesy Christie's East.

BLISS "Union" Ferry. Photo by Jeanne Bertoia. Courtesy Bill Bertoia Auctions.

BLISS "Vesuvius" Ferry. Photo by Jeanne Bertoia. Courtesy Bill Bertoia Auctions.

Boat, tin friction, 13" long, 2 smokestacks, 4 lifeboats (probably D.P. Clark or Schieble, c. 1908-1924). Courtesy PB 84 New York.

	C6	C8	C10
Boat, Hot Air, tin with driver, 9" long	100	150	200
Boat, pull motor, metal	100	150	200
Boat, tin friction, lithographed	100	150	200
Boat, tin friction, painted, early	100	150	200
Boat, tin friction, painted, early	150	225	300
Boat, tin friction, two smokestacks, four lifeboats, 13" long	90	135	180
Boucher "Gee Whiz" speedboat, painted sheet metal, heavy clockwork motor, bronze propeller, 25" long	550	825	1000
Bradley "Columbia" side paddlewheeler, paper litho on wood, c. 1890, 24" long	400	600	800
Bramwell-Smith, tin sidewheeler, pat. 1872	2000	3500	5000
Buckman "Pike" steam launch	2500	3800	5500
Buckman Steamboat No. 55, c. 1870, 19" long	1500	2500	3500
Buckman Steamboat, c. 1872, 11" long	1300	2000	3000

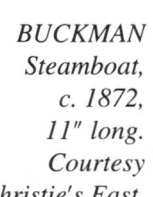

BUCKMAN Steamboat, c. 1872, 11" long. Courtesy Christie's East.

BUCKMAN twin sidewheeler steamboat, 11" long. Courtesy Wilkinson Collection, Detroit Antique Toy Museum.

	C6	C8	C10
Buckman twin sidewheeler steamboat, "Patented May 7, 1872," steam engine, 11" long	2000	3500	5000
Buddy L "49 LST," 12" long, includes tank	50	75	100
Buddy L No. 3000 Tugboat, 1929-30, 28" long	5000	8500	13,500
Buffalo Toys "Betsy" sidewheeler, 26" long	350	525	700
"C.C. JR" brass-mounted wood boat, wind-up motor concealed within the rudder, controlled from the wheel in the circular cockpit with a start-stop lever, 14-1/2" long	90	135	180

BUDDY L "49 LST." Photo by Ed Poole.

BUDDY L No. 3000 Tugboat. Photo courtesy Thomas W. Sefton.

	C6	C8	C10
Canoe, wood, 6" long	15	22	30
Cass Tugboat, wood, c. WWII?, 15" long	37	56	75
Cass Yacht, c. WWII?, wood, 15" long	37	56	75
Chein Hercules "Peggy Jane" Sailboat, 23" long	252	375	505
Chein "Peggy Jane" Speedboat, 14-1/2" long	115	175	235
Chein Sailboat, wheeled	112	168	225
Cohn Naval Base #888 Playset	180	270	360
"Columbia" Riverboat, c. 1890, paper litho, tin litho, wood, working walking beam, 2' long	700	1100	1650

"Columbia" riverboat, 1890, 2' long. Courtesy Lloyd W. Ralston Auctions.

	C6	C8	C10
Comet Navy Ship "Tirpitz," 19" long	75	112	150
Converse Battleship "Indiana," c. 1900, litho on wood, 32" long	650	1100	1600
Converse Battleship "Oregon," tin litho, wood, c. "1900"	500	750	1000
Cragstan Aircraft Carrier, friction, 8-1/2" long	60	90	120
Cruiser, glass, candy container, approx. 3" long	50	75	100

	C6	C8	C10
Dayton Battleship, friction, c. 1920, 16" long	200	300	400
Dent Adirondack, cast iron, 15" long	1000	1700	2300

DENT Adirondack. Photo by Jeanne Bertoia. Courtesy Bill Bertoia Auctions.

	C6	C8	C10
Dent Battleship "New York," c. 1900, largest cast-iron boat made, 21"	2000	3200	4350

DENT Battleship "New York." Courtesy Christie's East.

	C6	C8	C10
Destroyer, on wheels, cast iron, 12" long	1000	1500	2000
Eldon Aircraft Carrier, 22" long	55	83	110
Eldon Freighter, 20" long	40	60	80
Eldon L.C.T. Landing Craft, 10" long	17	26	35
Eldon U.S. Coast Guard Patrol Boat, 22", w/ figures	37	56	75
Falk "Bremen" tin keywind, c. 1920, 18" long	1300	2100	3000
Fallows "Columbia" Sidewheeler, auctioned in 1995 for $3300			
Fallows "Constitution" Sidewheeler, 10" long	2000	3000	4000
Fallows "Jumbo" Riverboat, sidewheel, painted tin, 1880, mechanical walking beam, 14" long	1000	1500	2000

FALLOWS "Jumbo" riverboat, 14" long. Courtesy Lloyd W. Ralston Auctions.

	C6	C8	C10
Fallows Pleasure Launch, auctioned in 1995 for $6820			
Fallows "Volunteer IXL," 16" long	1800	2700	3600
"Ferry Go" Twin Paddlewheel Ferryboat, pull toy, tin litho, 14" long	125	185	250
Fleetline "Sea Wolf" Motorboat, 16" long	112	168	225
Fleischmann Battleship	2000	3000	4000
Fleischmann Ocean Liner, 15-1/2" long	1000	1600	2250
Fleischmann Ocean Liner, 7-1/2 long	80	120	160
Fleischmann Ocean Liner, 1930, painted tin clockwork, working, 20-1/2" long	700	1350	1800

FLEISCHMAN Ocean Liner, 1930, 20-1/2" long. Courtesy Lloyd W. Ralston Auctions.

	C6	C8	C10
Fleischmann Oil Tanker, "Esso," 20" long	600	1000	1350
Freidag Boat, cast iron, c. 1920s	225	338	450
George Brown "Atlantic" Sidewheel Riverboat, painted and stenciled tin, 14" long	2250	3375	4500

GEORGE BROWN "Atlantic" sidewheel riverboat, 14" long. Courtesy Lloyd W. Ralston Auctions.

	C6	C8	C10
George Brown "New York," auctioned in 1995 for $3300			
George Brown "Victory" Sidewheeler, auctioned in 1995 with box for $9900			
Gunboat, tin friction, rocks back and forth on wheels, 10" long	250	375	500
Gunboat, friction, 19" long	400	600	800
Gunboat, two guns, 2 small stacks, 2 stories above deck, wheeled, friction, 1920s or earlier	300	450	600
Hasbro Atomic Submarine	32	48	65
Hess Voyager Tanker, 1966, price mint in box $2300			
Hill Climber, pressed steel battleship, 18" long	300	450	600

HESS Voyager Tanker, 1966. Photo by Thomas G. Nefos.

HILL-CLIMBER pressed steel battleship. Courtesy Mapes Auctioneers & Appraisers.

HUBLEY "Sea Horse." Courtesy Ed Hyers Antique Toys.

HUBLEY. Left to right: "Static," "Penn Yann." Photo by Jeanne Bertoia. Courtesy Bill Bertoia Auctions.

	C6	C8	C10
Hubley "Baby" Speedboat, cast iron	60	90	120
Hubley "Penn Yan" Motorboat, very rare, 5 people, 15" long, unauthorized by Penn Yan, which stopped Hubley's production, auctioned in 1995 in mostly very good condition for $8800			
Hubley "Sea Horse," cast-iron motorboat	1750	2625	3500
Hubley "Static" Speedboat, cast iron, auctioned in 1994 in good condition for $4200			
Ideal Destroyer, plastic, 15" long	17	28	35

IDEAL Destroyer, with original box. Courtesy Toy Collector News.

	C6	C8	C10
Ideal Harbor Police Boat	30	45	60
Ideal Houseboat, 5" long	12	18	25
Ideal Phantom Raider	60	90	120
Ideal Pirate Ship, plastic, w/ 6 pirates, new in 1953	75	112	150

IDEAL Pirate Ship (missing pirate flag).

	C6	C8	C10
Ideal PT Boat	50	75	100
Ideal Pumping Fireboat w/ siren, 1955 plastic	60	90	120
Ideal Slo Motion VI, wind-up motorboat, 13" long	60	90	120

	C6	C8	C10
Ideal Sparking Torpedo Boat, plastic, wind-up, 12" long	50	75	100
Ideal Submarine, plastic, 1950s, w/ torpedoes	20	30	40
Ideal "Treasure Hunter," plastic	75	112	150
Ideal Varsity Racing Scull, 8 rowers, coxswain, c. 1890, cast iron, oars move, 14" long	2000	3000	4000

IDEAL Varsity Racing Scull, 8 rowers, coxswain. Courtesy Wilkinson Collection, Detroit Antique Toy Museum.

	C6	C8	C10
Irwin Motorboat, wind-up	25	38	50
Ives Merchant Marine Ship, tin keywind, 13" long	450	675	900
Ives "Miss Liberty" Speedboat, steam-powered, 13-1/2" long	750	1125	1500
Ives "New York" Ocean Liner, 13" long	500	800	1100
Ives Submarine, dives, c. 1910, tin keywind, 10" long	400	600	800

IVES Merchant Marine Ship. Courtesy Christie's East.

IVES U.S. Merchant Marine, painted pressed tin clockwork.

	C6	C8	C10
Ives U.S. Merchant Marine Boat, painted pressed tin clockwork, 10-1/2" long	250	375	500
Ives "Vim" Speedboat, 10-1/2" long	650	975	1300
Ives "Vixen" Speedboat, 12" long	650	975	1300
"Johnson's Sea Horse," cast-iron speedboat w/ figure, 10-1/2" long	1750	2625	3500
"Kearsage" Gunboat, cast iron, 13-3/4" long	700	1150	1700

"Kearsage" gunboat. Courtesy PB 84 New York.

	C6	C8	C10
Kenton Speedboat, cast iron	90	135	180
Keystone Action Submarine	50	75	100
Keystone Aircraft Carrier, wooden, 12" long	50	75	100

KEYSTONE Action Submarine. Courtesy Jack Matthews.

KEYSTONE Aircraft Carrier, wooden, 12" long. Courtesy Mapes Auctioneers & Appraisers.

	C6	C8	C10
Keystone Battleship, wooden, approx. 2' long with guns, airplanes take off from a spring on deck of ship	130	195	260
Keystone Battleship, early 1940s, under 2' length	64	96	128
Keystone Ferryboat, wooden, c. 1930s, 2 wood cars, 2 wood trucks, 14" long	40	60	80
Keystone Fishing Boat, wooden, c. 1940s, 12" long	37	56	75
Keystone Racing Sailboat, wood	30	45	60
Keystone Radar Rocket Ship	75	112	150
Kilgore Chris-Craft Commuter Yacht, c. 1930, cast iron, 11" long	2000	3500	6000
Kingsbury Boat, 10" long	100	150	200
Knickerbocker Fighting Fire Boat, 1950s, 13" long, host works	40	60	80

KILGORE Chris-Craft commuter yacht. Photo by Chic Gast from his collection.

LIBERTY PLAYTHINGS

Liberty Playthings was in business in the late 1920s and early 1930s in Niagara Falls, New York. All its toys, which were made of wood and metal, seem to have borne names with some variations of the word "Liberty," and all seem to have been sea-connected. Those advertised in 1929 were No. 2 Tug and Scow, No. 5 Freighter, No. 6 Airplane Carrier, No. 7 Fireboat, No. 8 Destroyer, and No. 22 Seaplane. The Carrier, which in the ad was called "Liberator," sold for $10. The "Libertania" Aircraft Carrier seems to be the same ship, or a slight variation.

	C6	C8	C10
Liberty Playthings Cruiser or Battleship	225	338	450
Liberty Playthings Destroyer No. 8	225	338	450
Liberty Playthings Fire Boat, 23"	200	300	400
Liberty Playthings "Libertania" Aircraft Carrier, wood and tin litho with lead planes, 27-3/4" long	250	375	500

LIONEL No. 43 wind-up speedboat. Courtesy Phillips New York.

LIBERTY PLAYTHINGS Aircraft Carrier "Libertania." Courtesy Mapes Auctioneers & Appraisers.

	C6	C8	C10
Liberty Playthings Runabout, wind-up	155	233	310

End Liberty Playthings

	C6	C8	C10
Life Boat, steel, simple design, c. late 1930s, 11" long x 5-1/4" wide	20	30	40
Lionel Craft No. 43 wind-up speedboat	290	435	580
Lionel Craft No. 44 wind-up speedboat	750	1100	1700
Manoil No. 79 Submarine, lead alloy, also No. 71	15	22	30
Marklin Battleship, clockwork, 28" long	2500	4500	9000
Marklin "Columbus" liner, tin, electrified, 42" long	4000	8000	16,500

LIONEL No. 44 wind-up speedboat. Courtesy Sotheby's New York.

MANOIL Submarine. Courtesy K. Warren Mitchell.

MARKLIN "Columbus." Courtesy Christie's East.

MARKLIN "Dreadnought," 42" long, handpainted tin, 13 brass cannons. Sold for $21,000 in late 1994 in excellent condition, professionally restored. Photo by Jeanne Bertoia. Courtesy Bill Bertoia Auctions.

MARKLIN "Priscilla" Riverboat, 30" long. Photo by Jeanne Bertoia. Courtesy Bill Bertoia Auctions.

MARKLIN "H.M.S. Resolution," tin, 36" long. Offered at auction in 1994, it sold for $14,950. Courtesy Christie's East.

MARKLIN U-Boat, tin clockwork, 30" long, offered at auction in 1994 in a suggested range of $4000-6000, but it failed to sell. Courtesy Christie's East.

MARKLIN "New York" Sidewheeler. Photo by Jeanne Bertoia. Courtesy Bill Bertoia Auctions.

MARKLIN "Kronzprinz Wilhelm," tin, 37" long, offered at auction in 1994. It sold for $23,000. Courtesy Christie's East.

MARKLIN "Priscilla" Steam Yacht. Courtesy Christie's East.

MARKLIN "New York" Battleship, c. 1910, 28" long, tin. Offered at auction in 1994, it sold for $33,350. Courtesy Christie's East.

	C6	C8	C10
Marklin "New York" sidewheeler, tin & cast iron, 5 lead figures, 19-1/2" long, auctioned in 1994 in excellent condition with some restoration for $47,000			
Marklin "Priscilla" Steam Yacht, tin, 20-1/2" long	2000	3500	6000
Marklin "Priscilla" Riverboat, 30" long, auctioned in 1995 in excellent condition, some accessories gone, for $17,600			
Marklin Submarine, tin, clockwork, 9-1/2" long	288	430	575

	C6	C8	C10
Marx "Caribbean" friction Luxury Liner, sparkling, 15" long, 3-1/2" tall	42	63	85
Marx Mosquito Fleet Putt Putt Boat	55	83	110
Multiple Products Patrol Boat w/ radar mast, accessories	27	41	55
Multiple Products Pirate Ship, plastic with pirates	60	90	125
"New Orleans" Sidewheeler, cast iron, 11" long	600	950	1400
"New York" Battleship, cast iron, c. 1920s, 20"	375	565	750
"New York" Sidewheeler, cast iron, 15" long	500	750	1000
Ohio Battleship, friction, painted pressed steel, 16" long	140	210	280
"Oregon" tin warship	400	600	800

ORKIN

Orkin, of Cambridge, Massachusetts, was founded by Samuel Orkin about the end of WWI. His metal ships were modeled after the real thing. They were big, ranging from about 15" to 35", but relatively inexpensive.

	C6	C8	C10
Orkin Battleship B2, pressed steel, 36" long	3000	5000	8000
Orkin Battleship "Constitution," steel keywind, c. 1914, 25" long	500	750	1000
Orkin Battleship "Marcella," 18" long	600	900	1350
Orkin Battleship "Nevada," steel keywind, c. 1914, 22" long	550	825	1100
Orkin Battleship "New Jersey" tin and wood, c. 1920, 35" long	600	900	1400
Orkin Battleship "New Mexico," steel keywind, c. 1914, 25" long	500	750	1000

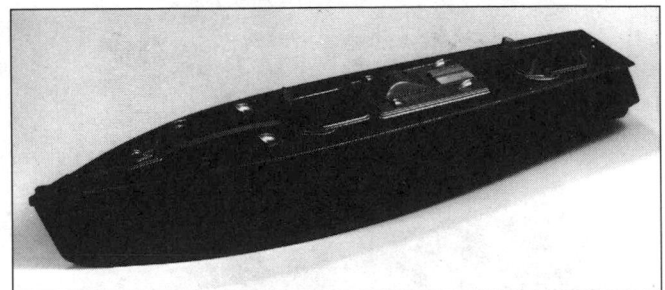

ORKIN Craft Speedboat, clockwork, 29" long. Courtesy Mapes Auctioneers & Appraisers.

Top, left to right: Orkin Battleship "New Jersey"; Orkin Battleship "Nevada." Middle: Orkin Battleship "Pennsylvania"; Orkin Battleship "New Mexico." Bottom: Orkin Battleship "Constitution." Courtesy Christie's East.

ORKIN Battleship B2. Courtesy Sotheby's New York.

	C6	C8	C10
Orkin Battleship "Pennsylvania," steel keywind, c. 1914, 30" long	700	1100	1700

	C6	C8	C10
Orkin Battleship "Texas," steel keywind, 30" long	1000	1800	3800

ORKIN CRAFT

Orkin Craft was owned by the president of the Waterman Pen Company. Manufacturing was done by Calwis Industries Ltd. of Beverly Hills, California. The pleasure boats sold by the firm were too expensive for the era (the price was in the $15-$20 range), which is probably why it failed about 1935 or 1936. All the boats were motor-driven. Some were all metal, and some had wooden decks.

	C6	C8	C10
Orkin Craft Cabin Cruiser, 30" long	700	1200	1700
Orkin Craft Speedboat, clockwork, 29" long	600	1000	1450

End Orkin Craft

	C6	C8	C10
Payton Sea Raider, 34" long	20	30	40
"Priscilla," paper litho on wood sidewheeler, 37" long	2000	3500	5800
"Priscilla" Sidewheeler, Dent or Wilkins, cast iron, approx. 10" long	500	750	1000
PT107	30	45	60

	C6	C8	C10
"Pull For The Shore," W.S. Reed, litho paper on wood	3500	8000	12,000
Pull Toy Boat by Hustilar Toy Corp., Sterling Ill., wood with some metal parts, oarsmen row in unison	75	112	150
"Puritan" Sidewheeler, cast iron, approx. 10-1/2" long	480	720	960
Pyro Ferry & Cars, plastic, 7" long	25	38	50
Reed Clipper Ship, c. 1887, wood & paper litho, 36" long	550	800	1200
Reed "Ocean Queen" Riverboat, litho on wood, 23" long	750	1300	1800

"Priscilla," paper litho on wood sidewheeler, 37" long. Photo by Jeanne Bertoia. Courtesy Bill Bertoia Auctions.

REED "River Queen." Photo by Jeanne Bertoia. Courtesy Bill Bertoia Auctions.

REED Clipper ship, c. 1887, wood and paper litho, 36" long. Photo by Jeanne Bertoia. Courtesy Bill Bertoia Auctions.

	C6	C8	C10
Reed Ocean Wave Freighter, c. 1883, with cargo, paper litho on wood, 35" long	650	1100	1500
Reed "Philadelphia" Battleship, paper litho on wood, 30" long	440	660	880

	C6	C8	C10
Reed "Pilgrim" Riverboat, paper litho, 28-1/2" long	1000	1500	2000
Reed "River Queen" Sidewheeler, litho on wood, c. 1895, 25" long	440	660	880
Remco Barracuda Sub., 23 man crew	75	112	150
Remco "Big Caesar" Roman Warship, with figures, 29" long	175	265	350
Remco "Fighting Lady" Battleship No. 710, 31" long	115	172	230
Remco Gallant Gladiator Roman Warship, plastic, 17" long	60	90	120
Remco Mighty Magee Carrier	80	120	160
Remco "Mighty Matilda" Aircraft Carrier, plastic, complete with all accessories, 35" long	83	125	165
Remco Showboat Theater	75	112	150
Renwal Cargo Ship No. 139, 4" long	4	6	8
Renwal Drawbridge Set, bridge, 12 cars and boats	50	75	100
Renwal Ferry No. 140, 4" long	4	6	8
Renwal Ocean Liner	30	45	60
Renwal "Panama Canal," c. 1957, No. 273, 29" x 11"	108	162	215

REED "Philadelphia" battleship, paper litho on wood, 30" long. Photo by Jeanne Bertoia. Courtesy Bill Bertoia Auctions.

RENWAL "Panama Canal," c. 1957. Courtesy Islyn Thomas.

Renwal Speedboat No. 141, 4" long 4   6   8
Renwal Tugboat No. 142, 4" long 4   6   8
Renwal Viking Ship No. 245,
    sold in 1955, 17" long 55   83   110

RENWAL Viking Ship No. 245, sold in 1955. Courtesy Islyn Thomas.

Rowboat with four men and oars,
    cast iron, mechanical, 9" long 1250   1875   2500
Rowboat, tin, rubber band driver,
    9" long with man rowing 40   60   80
"St. Louis" (Reed?) Passenger Liner,
    paper litho on wood, 31" long 800   1300   1800
Saunders Aircraft Carrier, plastic, 12" long 32   48   65
Schiebel Battleship, c. 1927, unpowered 1000   1500   2000
Schiebel Battleship, wood stacks
    and large wood guns and turrets,
    friction motor, c. 1920 1250   1875   2500
Schoenhut Submarine and Dreadnought
    Naval War Toy, Pat. 4/6/15,
    torpedo explodes ship 70   105   140
Scull, 9-man crew, U.S. Hardware,
    wheeled, 14" long 1600   2400   3200
Shore Patrol, battery operated,
    tin boat, 9" long 10   15   20
Showboat, cast iron, 11" long 1000   1500   2000
Sidewheeler Boat, "The Star," tin,
    height with stand, 21", length 14-1/2" 3500   5200   7000
Sidewheeler, cast iron, approx. 5-1/2" long 100   150   200
Sidewheeler, cast iron, 8" long........................ 188   275   375
Sidewheeler, cast iron, 10-1/2" long 150   225   300
Sidewheeler, tin clockwork, 11" long 90   135   180
"Sinking Battleship" Walbert Mfg.,
    rubber band torpedo strikes die
    on ship and sinks it 250   375   500
"Speed Boat," A.C. Williams,
    cast iron, 5-1/4" long 60   90   120
"Speed Boat," A.C. Williams,
    cast iron with rider, 4-3/4" long................ 120   180   240
"Speed Boat," A.C. Williams,
    cast iron, 4" long... 45   68   90

Side Wheeler Boat, tin, "The Star," 21" high with stand, 14-1/2" long.

"Speed Boat," A.C. Williams, 4" long, cast-iron (1932 ad).

	C6	C8	C10

"Speed Boat," Kansas Toy & Novelty,
    "52," lead alloy, driver, 2-3/4" long .... No Price Found
Speedboat, wood, rubber band propelled 40   60   80
SS United States, tin friction, 6-1/2" long 50   75   100
Steamboat "Memphis" Kansas Toy
    & Novelty, "53," lead alloy,
    metal disc wheels, 2-7/8" long........................ No Price Found

Steamship, alcohol burner, c. 1885, 19" long. Courtesy Mapes Auctioneers & Appraisers.

	C6	C8	C10
Steamboat, tin, self-propelled, 17" long	150	225	300
Steamer, litho paper on wood, 39" long, 22-1/2" high	450	675	900
Steamship, alcohol burner, c. 1885, 19" long	200	300	400
Sterling "56" scale model, all wood and metal Battleship Missouri, radio control, w/ three electric motors	350	525	700
Submarine, "575," tin litho, remote controlled, c. 1960	40	60	80
Submarine, glass	225	338	450
Submarine, steel, 6" long	40	60	80
Texaco Tanker	80	120	160
Thomas Toys Aircraft Carrier, plastic, 5-1/2" long	12	18	25
Thomas Toys Battleship, plastic, 5-1/2" long	12	18	25
Thomas Toys Freighter, plastic, 5-1/2" long	12	18	25
Thomas Toys Queen Mary, plastic, 5-1/2" long	15	22	30

THOMAS TOYS No. 480 Racing Hydroplane, plastic
wind-up. Courtesy Islyn Thomas.

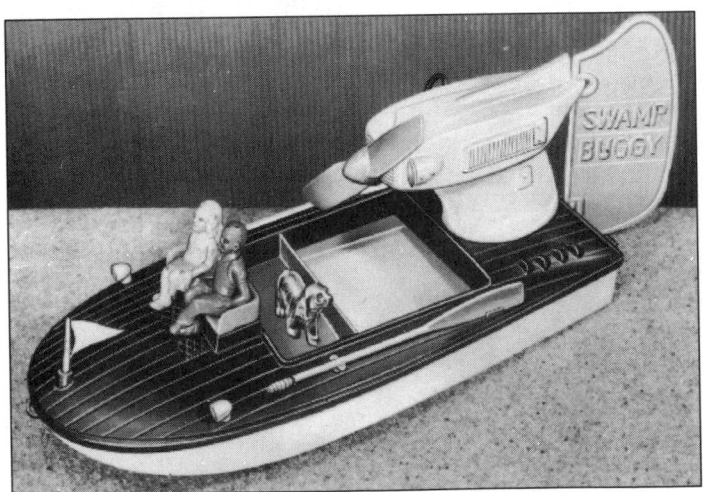

THOMAS TOYS No. 487 Swamp Buggy, motorized. Courtesy
Islyn Thomas.

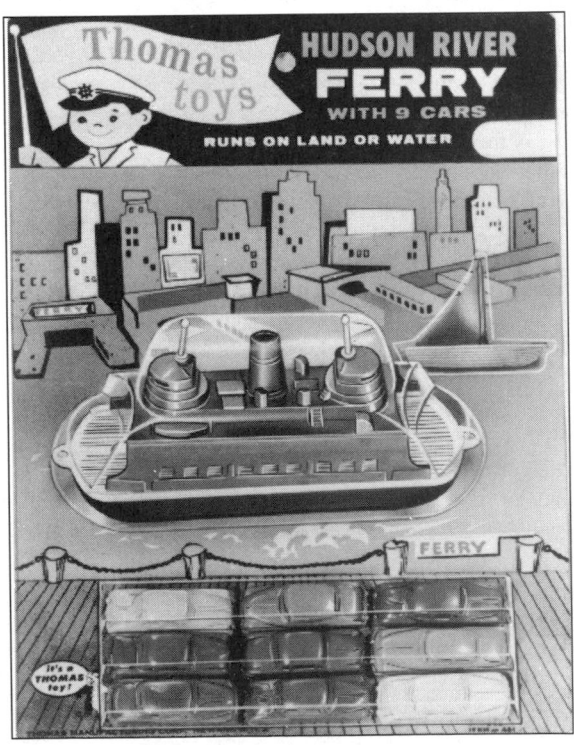

THOMAS TOYS No. 481 Ferry Boat with 9 cars and
sailboat. Courtesy Islyn Thomas.

	C6	C8	C10
Thomas Toys Submarine, 11-1/2" long, fires torpedo	12	18	25
Thomas Toys Tugboat, 8-1/4" long	15	22	30
Thomas Toys No. 339 Weekend Cruise Set, 4-1/4" car, 4-1/2" boat, boat trailer	22	33	45

	C6	C8	C10
Thomas Toys No. 480 Racing Hydroplane, plastic	12	18	25
Thomas Toys No. 481 Ferryboat with sailboat, 9 cars, plastic	12	18	25
Thomas Toys No. 487 Swamp Buggy, motorized, plastic	12	18	25

TILLICUM

In 1930 Tillicum wood toys were made in Tacoma, Washington.

	C6	C8	C10
Tillicum Battle Fleet No. 115, Milton Bradley, c. late 1920s	31	46	62
Tillicum Convoy Set, Milton Bradley, c. 1940s, 2 destroyers, 3 freight boats, 3 ocean liners, 2 patrol boats, painted wood, destroyers 5-1/2" long, others about 4-1/2" long	350	525	700
Tillicum Harbor Set, Milton Bradley	20	30	40
Tillicum National Defense Set, Milton Bradley	40	60	80

Tillicum Battle Fleet No. 115. Courtesy John D. (Jack) Matthews.

Tillicum Convoy Set, Milton Bradley. Courtesy John D. (Jack) Matthews.

Tillicum National Defense Set, Milton Bradley. Courtesy John D. (Jack) Matthews.

TOOTSIETOY

Compiled by Ed Poole and John Gibson

	C6	C8	C10
127 Destroyer, 4"	9	12	15
128 Submarine, 4"	9	12	15
129 Tender, 4"	10	15	20

	C6	C8	C10
130 Yacht, 4"	18	24	30
1034 Battleship, 6"	15	20	25
1035 Cruiser, 5-1/2"	15	20	25

TOOTSIETOY. *Top, left to right:*
1034 Battleship, 1036 Carrier.
Middle: 1035 Cruiser, 1037 Liner.
Bottom: 127 Destroyer, 128 Submarine.
Photo by Ed Poole.

	C6	C8	C10
1036 Aircraft Carrier, 6"	14	21	28
1037 Transport, 6"	15	20	25

TOOTSIETOY. *Top, left to right: 1037 Transport, 1039 Tanker.*
Bottom: 129 Tender, 130 Yacht. Photo by Ed Poole.

1038 Freighter, 5-1/2"	15	20	25
1039 Tanker, 5-1/2"	15	20	25

Tootsietoy Miniature Ships

	C6	C8	C10
196 Battleship	4	6	8
1405 Fleet, 9-piece carded battleship assortment (1941): USS Idaho, USS Indiana, USS Tennessee, USS Texas, USS New Mexico, USS Maryland, USS Arizona, USS New York, USS Pennsylvania	50	75	100
1408 Naval Defense, 14-piece carded assortment (1941)	70	105	140
1612 Cruiser	3	4	6
1613 Destroyer	3	4	6
1614 Submarine (smaller)	2	3	4
1618 Submarine	3	4	6
1619 Destroyer	3	4	6
1620 Aero Carrier	4	6	8
1638 Battleship	4	6	8
1811 Sea Champions, 5-piece carded set (1946) contains two #1638 battleships, one #1618 submarine, one #1619 destroyer, and one #1620 aero carrier	30	45	60
4519 Battleship	8	12	16
4538 Tugboat	2	3	4
4539 Speedboat	2	3	4

End Tootsietoy

Turbo Boat, pressed tin, 10-1/2" long	40	60	80
U.S. Naval Base, Superior	60	90	120

U.S. HARDWARE *Rowers, c. 1890. Courtesy Ed Hyers Antique Toys.*

	C6	C8	C10
U.S. Hardware Rowers, c. 1890, 8 man crew and coxswain, cast iron, large wheels, 14-1/2" long	1800	3000	4200
U.S. Hardware Rowers, c. 1890, 4 man crew and coxswain, cast iron, large wheels	2000	3500	5200

Top: "U.S.S. New Mexico," "U.S.S. Narwahl." *Courtesy Hank Anton.*

	C6	C8	C10		C6	C8	C10
"U.S.S. Maine" paper litho on wood, Reed?	600	900	1200	"U.S. Submarine," painted wood, fires torpedo for target set, 13" long	20	30	40
"U.S.S. Narwahl," submarine, lead, mfg. unknown, 1930s, 7-1/2" long	20	30	40	U.S. Wasp, carrier, wood storage under deck for planes, 27" long	50	75	100
"U.S.S. New Mexico," battleship, lead, manufacturer unknown, 1930s	20	30	40				

WANNATOYS

Wannatoys were manufactured by Dillon-Beck Manufacturing Company of Irvington, New Jersey, from 1941 on. They were plastic.

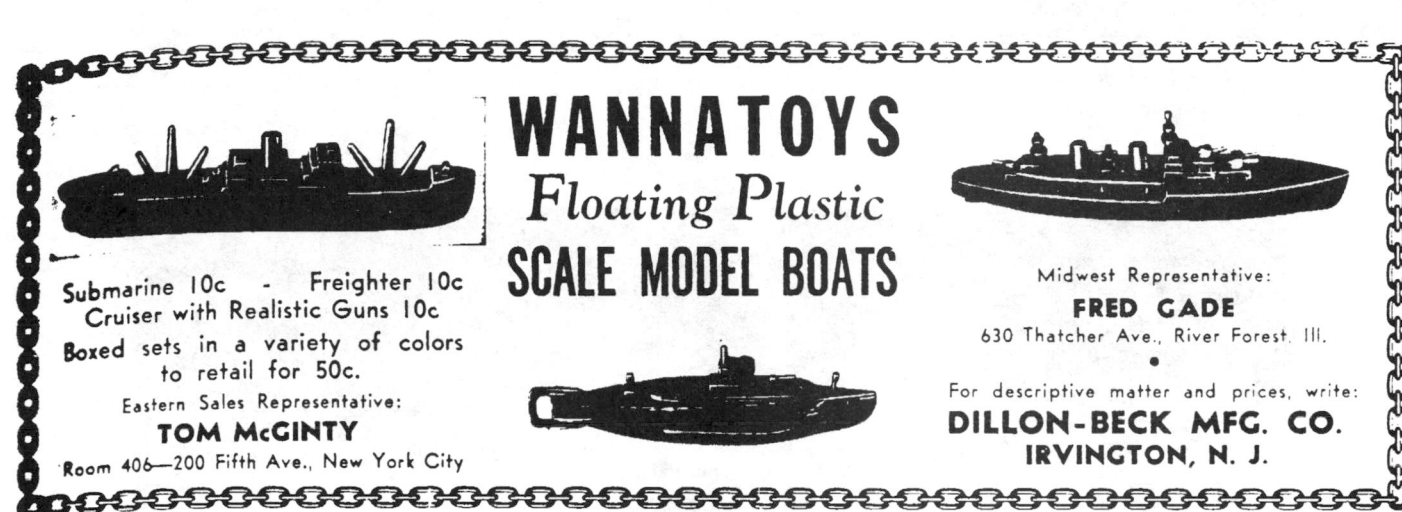

WANNATOYS (Dillion-Beck) plastic ships, advertised in the July 1941 issue of Playthings. Plastic Toys, Inc. copied the submarine a few years later.

	C6	C8	C10		C6	C8	C10
Wannatoys Cruiser	25	38	50	Wilkins Battleship, cast iron	800	1400	2000
Wannatoys Freighter	25	38	50	Wilkins "City of New York" Riverboat, 15" long	800	1400	2035
Wannatoys Submarine	25	38	50	Wilkins "Puritan" Riverboat, 10-1/2" long	600	1000	1400
End Wannatoys				Wilkins Riverboat, 5-3/4" long	135	205	270
Weeden "Dewey" Steamboat, c. 1900, 15-1/2" long	500	750	1000	Wilkins Riverboat, c. 1910, cast iron, 7-1/2" long	250	375	500
Weeden Launch, steam-driven, 18" long	350	525	700	Wilkins Riverboat, cast iron, 10-1/2" long	450	675	900
Weeden Steamboat, live steam, 15" long	300	450	600	Wilkins Rowers, c. 1890, 4 man crew and coxswain, 10" long, big-wheeled boat, cast iron	1250	1875	2500
				Williams, A.C., Blue Speed Boat, cast iron, 4-3/4" long	120	180	240
				Wolverine Diving Submarine, 13" long	105	158	210
				Wolverine Ocean Liner	125	188	250
				Wolverine "Sandy Andy Ferry," tin litho, 13-1/2" long	75	113	150
				Wolverine Sandy Andy "Ferrygo," tin and wood, 11" long	150	225	300
				Wyandotte Aircraft Carrier	55	82	110
				Wyandotte Pocket Battleship, tin litho, wheeled, 7" long	70	105	140
				Wyandotte "S.S. America," moves on metal wheels, 1930s, 7" long	50	75	100

WEEDEN Launch, steam-driven, 18" long. Courtesy Heinz Mueller, Continental Hobby House.

	C6	C8	C10
Wyandotte "Sand-O'Land," tin litho sandtoy, wood wheels, 1940s, 10" long	55	83	110
Wyandotte Submarine	112	168	225

	C6	C8	C10
Wyandotte "U.S.S. Enterprise"	80	120	160
Yacht-type ship, either Ives or Bing, spring wind motor, 28" long	2000	3000	4000

WOLVERINE Diving Submarine. Courtesy Mapes Auctioneers & Appraisers.

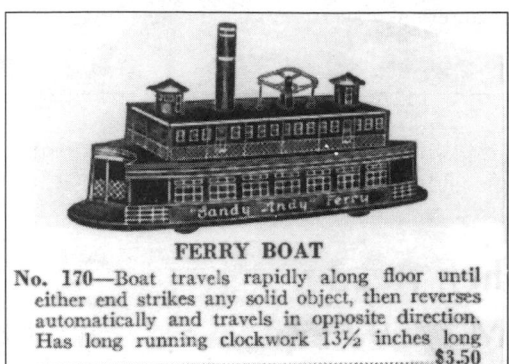

FERRY BOAT

No. 170—Boat travels rapidly along floor until either end strikes any solid object, then reverses automatically and travels in opposite direction. Has long running clockwork 13½ inches long $3.50

WOLVERINE "Sandy Andy" Ferry.

WILKINS Riverboat, 10-1/2" long. Courtesy Mapes Auctioneers & Appraisers.

SCHOENHUT

The average C8 price for Schoenhuts was $850.42 in the last edition. In this edition it is $873.42, an increase of 3%.

UNDER THE BIG TENT

by Blossom Abell with Jim and Patsy Carlson

The A. Schoenhut Company had a long history of toy manufacturing. Many items were produced, including animals, figures, moving pictures, Palmer Cox Brownies, children's musical instruments, and dolls. This section covers some of the items in the Humpty Dumpty Circus.

A brief chronological history of the A. Schoenhut Company follows:

1872	Produced the first toy pianos
1903	Began producing Humpty Dumpty Circus items
	Began producing glass-eyed animals, molded/two-part head personnel
1909/11	Produced Teddy Roosevelt figures
1910	Produced bisque head ring master, lady circus rider, lion tamer, lady/gent acrobats
1918	Produced painted-eyed animals, wooden-head personnel
1923	Began producing reduced-size circus
1927	Produced miniature set (donkey, elephant, clown)
1935	Company closed
1950	Nelson Delavan purchased manufacturing rights and produced several figures and animals

This history is not all inclusive, but should help the collector identify age for some animals/figures.

The Humpty Dumpty items covered in this section span the years of 1903 to 1935. Glass-eyed animals and two-part head personnel, along with other rare examples, are priced higher than painted-eye animals and pressed-head figures produced later. Delavan items are generally priced lower than reduced-size figures.

In the past few years, the toys' popularity among toy collectors and folk art collectors has driven prices up. Particular interest in Teddy Roosevelt's "Adventures in Africa" series (produced from 1909 to 1911) has led the price increase.

This price list should serve as a guideline for the collector. Several points deserve additional comment:

- Condition determines price (see photo of four horses for examples of condition C2 to C6)
- Mint condition Schoenhut toys are virtually nonexistent. Mint condition means the toy was never played with. Toys found in this condition demand higher prices. Boxes increase value, and mint with the box commands a sizable premium.
- Glass-eyed animals, early figures with plaster faces, and rare animals demand high prices also.
- It is acceptable to include rare figures and rare animals of lesser condition in a collection.
- Bisque-headed figures and molded/two-part head figures usually are priced higher than carved-face figures.
- Condition on the majority of animals and figures found today is between C4 and C7.
- Skillful restoration can increase value. Anyone selling an animal or figure with restored sections should indicate where restoration has occurred.
- Prices in this guide have not been established for every style of animal and figure.

Because of the importance of condition and classification for the Schoenhut category of toys, the authors felt the need to enhance the existing definitions of Schoenhut categories and therefore assist pricing.

In addition, the authors call your attention to the prices shown. These prices reflect average prices realized at numerous auctions during the past year. Other factors applied to condition to determine prices are shown for each category. Private sales often differ from the prices shown. Exceptional condition remains difficult to find.

Jim and Patsy Carlson purchased a partial Schoenhut circus in 1988 as a remembrance to a deceased parent. That "remembrance" has now grown to include several specialized Schoenhut pieces, including an almost complete "Teddy Roosevelt's Adventures in Africa" play set. The additional pieces would not have been acquired without the help of their dear friend Blossom Abell, who passed away in March 1994. She openly shared her love and vast knowlege of Schoenhut with the Carlsons. Jim and Patsy are members of the Schoenhut Collectors Club and Antique Toy Collectors of America. In addition to collecting Schoenhut, the Carlsons actively collect platform animals, American rocking horses, early squeak toys, folk art and American Primitive paintings, especially of children. They have one daughter and reside in Clarkston, Michigan.

Rating	Definition
C1	Bits and pieces of Schoenhut toys.
C2	Poor quality with no paint or with a "child's" effort to repaint, or missing a major part. Definitely needs repair.
C3	Fair with no missing major part but with little paint, moisture/moth/animal damage and soiling. Needs repair.
C4	Good with play wear, soiled/worn clothing, damaged paint/chips, missing leather and/or other attachable parts.
C5	Very good with restored paint, clothes, and/or leather. Or could be good enough not to require restoration.
C6	Fine with good paint, new or worn leather and minor restorations. Could also have some soiling/wear/color loss and missing minor attached parts.
C7	Very fine with minor wear/color loss and fractional restoration.
C8	Almost perfect with no restoration but may have slight color loss. This is a wonderful piece.
C9	Perfect, meaning no damage or color loss of any kind. Almost new.
C10	Mint, meaning never played with and stored under ideal conditions. Factory new.

Note: Restringing is not considered restoration. If the restringing effort is not done properly, however, wood damage can occur and reduce the value of the piece. Additional information on Schoenhut figures or dolls can be obtained by joining the Schoenhut Collectors Club. For a membership application, please contact Pat Girbach, 103 West Huron Street, Ann Arbor, MI 48103.

Circus Animals: Glass-Eyed and Painted-Eyed (Regular Size)

Prices below are for the animals that are most frequently seen; not all animals have been included. Glass-eyed animals are aged from 1903, when A. Schoenhut Company began to produce Circus animals and performers, to about 1918. Painted-eyed animals are aged from about 1918 to 1933, the closing of the A. Schoenhut company.

SCHOENHUT. Left to right: Buffalo (C6) GE, cloth mane, mane worn; Buffalo (C8) GE, carved mane. Collection and photo Blossom Abell.

	C2	C4	C6	C8
Alligator, GE	100	175	350	475
Alligator, PE	75	125	250	385

	C2	C4	C6	C8
Brown Bear, GE	175	325	425	600
Brown Bear, PE	75	120	250	375
Bulldog, GE	200	350	700	1000
Bulldog, PE	100	150	250	425
Buffalo, GE, cloth	100	200	325	500
Buffalo, GE, curved	200	400	750	1050
Buffalo, PE	100	200	300	450
Burro, PE	100	175	275	400
Camel, 1 hump, GE	100	150	300	425
Camel, 1 hump, PE	95	120	250	375
Camel, 2 hump, GE	200	475	950	1400
Camel, 2 hump, PE	95	135	275	400

*SCHOENHUT. Right to left: Store Display-size Donkey, 14"
tall, PE, C6; Donkey with Saddle, GE, C6 (Humpty-Dumpty
Circus). Collection and photo Jim and Patsy Carlson.*

*SCHOENHUT. Left to right: Camel (C9) reduced; Camel (C9),
GE, Arabian, 1 hump; Camel (C8) GE, Bactrian, 2 humps. Collection and photo Blossom Abell.*

	C2	C4	C6	C8
Donkey, GE	30	60	120	175
Donkey, PE	20	30	50	75
Elephant, GE	40	70	135	200
Elephant, PE	30	50	100	150
Gazelle, GE	400	1000	1600	2400
Gazelle, PE	300	400	775	1200
Giraffe, GE	100	175	350	500
Giraffe, PE	75	120	250	350

Cat, GE	500	1000	1600	2400
Cat, PE	200	360	725	1100
Cow, PE	50	125	250	385

*SCHOENHUT Cat, GE, C8, from Humpty-Dumpty
Circus. Collection and photo Jim and Patsy
Carlson.*

*SCHOENHUT. Left to right: Giraffe (C8) PE, carved head;
Giraffe closed mouth (C8) GE. Collection and photo Blossom
Abell.*

Deer, GE	200	300	575	875
Deer, PE	175	325	425	600

	C2	C4	C6	C8
Goat, GE..................................	75	200	275	350
Goat, PE...................................	50	150	225	300
Goose, PE.................................	75	150	350	475
Gorilla, molded ears	1000	1300	1600	2400
Hippopotamus, GE.......................	100	275	550	800
Hippopotamus, PE........................	75	120	250	375

SCHOENHUT. Left to right: Tiger (C9) reduced; Tiger (C6) PE; Tiger (C9) PE (early). Collection and photo Blossom Abell.

SCHOENHUT. Left to right: Hippo, Style I, early, GE, (C7); Hippo, Style II, GE, (C7). Humpty-Dumpty Circus. Collection and photo Jim and Patsy Carlson.

Horse, brown, GE..................................	75	100	160	250
Horse, brown, PE	30	50	100	150
Horse, white, GE..................................	85	120	175	275
Horse, white, PE...................................	40	75	125	190
Hyena, GE	1200	1400	1850	2600
Hyena, PE	400	500	950	1400
Kangaroo, GE.....................................	400	500	2100	3000
Kangaroo, PE	200	350	700	1000
Leopard, GE......................................	100	275	550	825
Leopard, PE.......................................	75	150	300	450
Lion, GE, curved mane	300	475	850	1275
Lion, GE, cloth mane	100	200	400	600

SCHOENHUT. Left to right: Lion, PE (C6); Lion, GE, carved ears (C6). Both from Humpty-Dumpty Circus. Collection and photo Jim and Patsy Carlson.

SCHOENHUT. Left to right: Glass-eyed Horse, missing leather belly strap, (C6); GE Horse, very worn paint and missing platform and belly strap, (C3); GE Horse, repainted, chipped wood and missing all attachable parts, (C2); (foreground) GE Horse, good paint, missing attachable parts, (C4). Photo by Blossom Abell.

*SCHOENHUT.
Left to right:
Lion (C10) GE,
cloth mane;
Monkey (C8),
white face.
Collection
and photo
Blossom Abell.*

SCHOENHUT. Left to right: Polar Bear (C8) PE; (foreground) Polar Bear (C7) PE; 12" Wild Animal Cage Wagon (C8); Polar Bear (C7) GE; Lion Tamer (C9) 1-part head. Collection and photo Blossom Abell.

	C2	C4	C6	C8
Lion, PE	95	175	375	525
Monkey, black face	100	200	400	600
Monkey, white face	120	225	500	750
Ostrich, GE	200	300	600	900
Ostrich, PE	100	225	300	425
Pig, GE	125	275	550	825
Pig, PE	100	175	300	450

	C2	C4	C6	C8
Sheep, GE	100	175	385	550
Sheep, PE	75	135	275	400
Tiger, GE	100	275	550	825
Tiger, PE	75	150	300	450
Wolf, GE	1000	1300	1600	2400
Wolf, PE	300	400	775	1200

SCHOENHUT. Left to right: Ostrich (C9) GE; Ostrich (C9) PE. Collection and photo Blossom Abell.

SCHOENHUT. Wolf, PE (C8), Humpty-Dumpty Circus. Collection and photo Jim and Patsy Carlson.

Polar Bear, GE	300	475	850	1275
Polar Bear, PE	250	350	575	875
Poodle, GE, curved mane	100	225	400	675
Poodle, PE	40	70	135	200
Rhinoceros, GE	175	375	600	950
Rhinoceros, PE	125	300	400	600
Sea Lion, GE	200	400	625	900
Sea Lion, PE	125	225	450	700

Zebra, GE	175	375	625	950
Zebra, PE	150	325	425	600
Zebu, GE	1200	1400	2100	3000
Zebu, PE	400	500	950	1400

Circus Accessories (Regular and Reduced Size)

These items are most commonly found in "play wear" condition in the C4 to C7 category. Not all accessories have been included.

Ball	10	20	40	50

SCHOENHUT Cloth Circus Tent, 34" high, with performers and animals. Courtesy Wilkinson Collection, Detroit Antique Toy Museum.

	C2	C4	C6	C8
Ball, reduced	10	15	30	40
Barrel	2	4	6	10
Chair	2	4	6	10
Flexible Cage	75	175	375	500
Goblet	3	5	8	12
Hoop	10	15	25	40
Horizontal Bar	75	175	375	500
Ladder	2	4	6	10
Pedestal, short	10	20	30	45
Pedestal, tall	15	25	40	60
Table	15	25	40	65
Tent, 24" x 16" (small)	200	400	500	750
Tent, 24" x 36" (large)	700	1100	1400	2200
Tent, litho w/ panels	2000	3000	6000	9000
Tub	10	20	35	50
Weights, 50/100/200 lbs	75	150	200	325
Whip, 4-1/2" shaft	10	20	30	45
Whip, 5-1/2" shaft	15	25	40	65
Wild Animal Cage Wagon	300	400	775	1200

Performers Wooden/Pressed One-Part Head (Regular Size)

Not all figures have been included, but where data is available, notation is made. The manufacturing sequence for figures was plaster face two-part head/faces, bisque heads, and finally wooden/pressed one-part head.

	C2	C4	C6	C8
Chinaman	100	200	325	450
Clown	20	65	100	125
Hobo	45	145	250	325
Lady Acrobat	65	150	275	375
Lady Rider	45	145	250	325

SCHOENHUT. Left to right: Clown (C7) wood hat/leather ears; Clown (C7) cloth hat over wood cone; Poodle (C7) reduced; Clown (C7) molded ears. All clowns reduced. Collection and photo Blossom Abell.

This Schoenhut Humpty-Dumpty Circus Bandwagon, 40" long, was auctioned for $15,000 in 1994 by Bill Bertoia Auctions.

SCHOENHUT. Left to right: Clown (C7) plaster face, 2-part head, sunburst suit; Clown (C7) wood head; Clown (C7) wood head. Collection and photo Blossom Abell.

SCHOENHUT bisque-headed circus performers. Left to right: Hoop, paper-covered; Lion Tamer (C6); Lady Rider (C6); Lady. Courtesy Jim and Patsy Carlson.

SCHOENHUT. Background: earliest clowns, plaster face, 2-part head with "footprint" or "snail" on front of uniform. Left to right: (C5), (C6), (C7). Front, left to right: wood head, striped suit, (C5); wood head, card suit (C6); 2-part head, sunburst suit (C7). Collection and photo Jim and Patsy Carlson.

	C2	C4	C6	C8
Lion Tamer	45	145	250	325
Negro Dude	100	200	325	450
Ring Master	65	150	275	375

SCHOENHUT. Left to right: Lady Rider, reduced (C8); Lady Rider Bisque Head (C8); Lady Rider, 2-part Head (C6), replaced skirt. Collection and photo Blossom Abell.

SCHOENHUT. Left to right: Hobo (C8) 2-part head; Chinaman Acrobat (C5) 2-part head, replaced felt on jacket. Collection and photo Blossom Abell.

SCHOENHUT Negro Dude, Style I, black coat (C6) from Humpty-Dumpty Circus. Collection and photo Jim and Patsy Carlson.

Reduced-Size Figures and Animals

Not all figures and animals have been included, but where data is available, notation is made. Reduced-size figures and animals were first produced about 1927 by the A. Schoenhut Company to appeal to another market and perhaps to save the company. Even with this action the company closed in 1933.

Circus Figures, Reduced

	C2	C4	C6	C8
Clown	15	40	65	100
Hobo	55	130	280	410
Lady Rider	30	65	125	225
Negro Dude	65	140	370	500
Ring Master	30	60	120	200

Animals, Reduced

	C2	C4	C6	C8
Brown Bear	75	120	275	400
Buffalo	65	140	225	350
Camel, 2 humps	75	120	275	375
Donkey	20	30	40	50
Elephant	25	45	95	125
Giraffe	75	120	275	400
Hippopotamus	100	240	325	500

SCHOENHUT. Left to right: Pig (C9) reduced, fancy face; Pig (C8) GE, one piece head/neck; Pig (C5) ball joint head, body restoration. Collection and photo Blossom Abell.

SCHOENHUT. Left to right: Leopard (C8) GE; Leopard (C9) reduced; Leopard (C7) PE, worn paint on face. Collection and photo Blossom Abell.

This SCHOENHUT Humpty Dumpty Circus with banners for a side show was auctioned in overall excellent condition in 1995 for $8250. The tent is 27" high. Photo by Jeanne Bertoia. Courtesy Bill Bertoia Auctions.

	C2	C4	C6	C8
Horse, brown	30	50	100	135
Horse, white	30	50	100	135
Leopard	75	120	275	375
Lion	75	120	275	375
Ostrich	85	150	300	425
Pig	100	250	400	425
Poodle	75	120	275	400
Rhinoceros	85	150	300	425
Tiger	75	120	275	375
Zebra	150	325	450	600

Teddy Roosevelt's Adventures in Africa

These figures were produced in low volume from 1909 to 1911 and represent "rare" or "scarce" toys. Some of the animals were used in circus play-toys produced with glass eyes (GE) until 1918.

Teddy Roosevelt Figures

Teddy Roosevelt	750	1000	1300	2000
Photographer (Kermit)	850	1300	1700	2450
African Native	950	1400	1800	2700
African Drummer	950	1400	1800	2700

A Schoenhut Humpty-Dumpty Circus, c. 1915. It was auctioned in 1994 for $2185. Courtesy Christie's East.

This boxed Schoenhut Humpty-Dumpty Circus No. 2036, c. 1925, with jointed figures and glass-eyed animals, was auctioned in 1994 for $3680. Courtesy Christie's East.

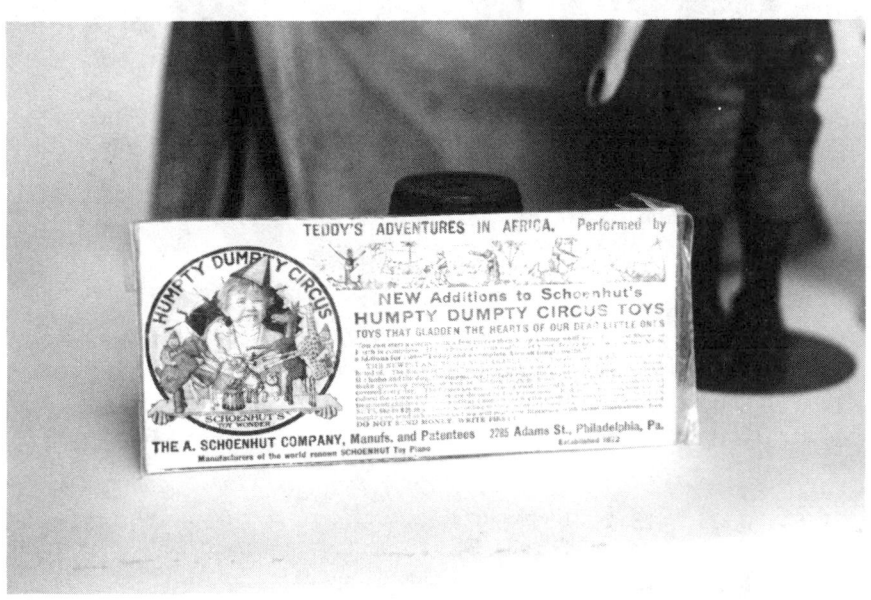

Magazine ad (1910) for "Teddy's Adventures in Africa," 2-1/2" x 5-3/4". Collection and photo Jim and Patsy Carlson.

SCHOENHUT African Chief, pouty lips and mouth (C7), from "Teddy's Adventures in Africa." Collection and photo Jim and Patsy Carlson.

SCHOENHUT Naturalist (C10) from "Teddy's Adventures in Africa" (modeled after J. Alden Loring). Collection and photo Jim and Patsy Carlson.

SCHOENHUT. Personnel from "Teddy's Adventures in Africa." Left to right: Kermit (C6); Accessories (wire frame tent, bowl, barrel and jug); Naturalist (C10); African Drummer (C6); Teddy Roosevelt with rifle (C6); African Chief (C7). Collection and photo Jim and Patsy Carlson.

SCHOENHUT Gorilla, 2-part head, leather ears (C7) from "Teddy's Adventures in Africa." Collection and photo Jim and Patsy Carlson.

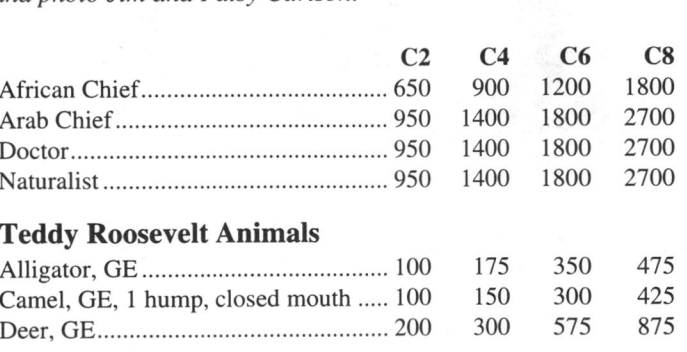

	C2	C4	C6	C8
African Chief	650	900	1200	1800
Arab Chief	950	1400	1800	2700
Doctor	950	1400	1800	2700
Naturalist	950	1400	1800	2700

Teddy Roosevelt Animals

	C2	C4	C6	C8
Alligator, GE	100	175	350	475
Camel, GE, 1 hump, closed mouth	100	150	300	425
Deer, GE	200	300	575	875

	C2	C4	C6	C8
Elephant, GE	40	70	135	200
Gazelle, GE	400	1000	1600	2400
Giraffe, GE, closed mouth	175	350	475	650

	C2	C4	C6	C8
Gorilla, leather ear	1100	1400	1700	2500
Hippopotamus, GE	100	275	550	800
Hyena, GE	1200	1400	2100	3000
Lion, GE, curved mane	300	475	850	1275
Rhinoceros, GE	175	375	600	950
Zebra, GE, closed mouth	175	375	625	950
Zebu, GE	1200	1400	2100	3000

Miscellaneous

	C2	C4	C6	C8
Doll House, small	100	150	250	375
Doll House, medium	125	175	375	425
Doll House, large	150	225	500	750
Golfer, Girl	125	200	375	475

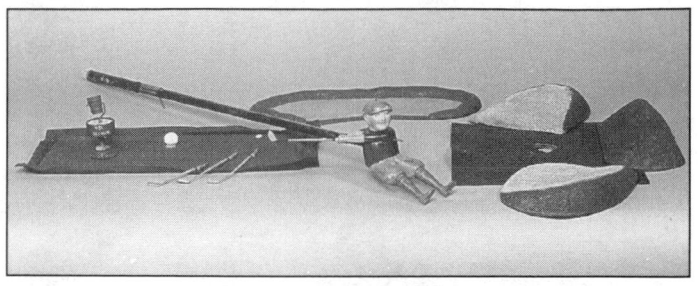

This Schoenhut Indoor Golf Game (3 feet long) with Male Golfer was auctioned in 1995 in mint condition for $2145.

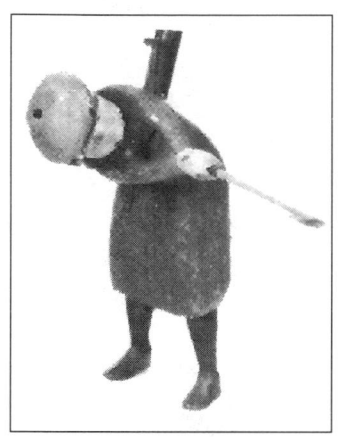

SCHOENHUT Golfer in skirt. Courtesy PB 84 New York.

SCHOENHUT Golfer Man. Courtesy Sotheby's New York.

	C2	C4	C6	C8
Golfer, Man	125	175	350	425
Milk Wagon, horses and driver	1250	2400	3000	4000
Piano, 14" x 10"	30	60	120	175
Railroad Station, large	125	175	350	475
Roly Poly, Black Clown	200	300	600	850

Comic Character

Items shown as "rare" means not enough examples have been sold to determine prices.

	C2	C4	C6	C8
Barney Google and Sparkplug	300	360	725	1100
Bonzo	300	360	725	1100
Boob McNutt	250	575	1050	1500
Felix, 4"	30	60	120	175

	C2	C4	C6	C8
Felix, 6"	100	275	550	800
Felix, 8"	95	135	275	400
Happy Hooligan	250	575	1050	1500
Koko the Clown				Rare
Maggie/Jiggs, rolling pin & bucket	200	400	775	1200
Mary and Her Lamb	325	450	600	900
Max and Moritz, pair, early model	275	675	1100	1600
Rolly Dolly				
Dutch Girl	65	150	275	375
Foxy Grandpa, large	100	275	550	800
Santa, medium	225	475	975	1350
Santa, large	500	1000	1600	2400

SCHOENHUT
Felix the Cat, 6" (C7),
4" (C7), 8" (C8).
Photo by
Blossom Abell.

SCHOENHUT.
Left to right:
Barney Google
(early), 7-3/4"
(C7); Sparkplug
(C7); Barney, 7"
(C7). Photo by
Blossom Abell.

FISHER-PRICE

The average price of mint Fisher-Price toys was $352.38 in the last edition. In this edition it is $331.49, a decrease of 6%.

THE TOYS IN ALL OUR ATTICS

by John Murray

On October 1, 1930, in East Aurora, New York, the Fisher-Price Toy Company began operation. Located on a small side street of a small town, it would eventually be considered one of the major manufacturers of toys.

Herman Fisher and Irving Price shared their names to develop a name for their new company. Herman Fisher, a past employee of the FairChild Company (a manufacturer of games), and Irving Price, who had sound experience with the Woolworth Company, formed the guidelines by which they would run their new company.

The first manufacturing facility was located on Church Street in East Aurora, New York. It still exists, but was sold by Fisher-Price in the 1970s due to lack of use. The Church Street facility would be considered small for any type of manufacturing today, but it served as the only facility for Fisher-Price toys for the company's first twenty years.

The most important factor in constructing this new company was to create a work force that could contribute their efforts towards a smooth, profitable venture. Among the most important employees were Helen M. Schelle and Margaret Evans Price.

Helen M. Schelle was the first secretary and treasurer of Fisher-Price toys. She developed her skills in the retail management field in the Walker Toy Shop in Binghamton, New York. Given the opportunity to manage the company's early activities, Helen proved to be a great asset to the advancement of Fisher-Price toys.

Margaret Evans Price was the company's first artist and designer for their new line of toys. She developed her skills as a writer and illustrator for Rand McNally and Harper & Brothers, and as a creator of children's art for Strecher Lithography Company of Rochester, New York. Much of Evans Price's artwork can still be found on early postcards, Valentines, and children's books. These early paper collectibles are most often marked "M.E.P."

Evans Price created the early artwork for the reproduction of color lithography for the toys. She was also talented in drawing, produced designs for early toys, and contributed to the development of her concepts for Fisher-Price's early line of toys. The Roycroft Printers contributed their skills to produce the sales catalogs that prospective retailers would use to choose the toys that they would market.

The company began to form the labor force that would build the new toy line, to be sold to the public in 1931. The initial work force was approximately 25 employees. Typical of any small town, most employees were neighbors, friends, and relatives, who contributed to a work force that took great pride in the product that they made, since many of the operations were done by hand. Many of the early operations, such as band sawing, drilling, nailing, and painting, were shared by these early employees. Quality control would be created by one employee checking the other and making any corrections immediately.

As Fisher-Price began toy making, numbers were assigned to each toy. This number system started at Number 5 and went up into the thousands. To add to the confusion for collectors today, many of the numbers have been used more than once on various toys.

Because pine was abundant and easy to work with, it was the main wood used in construction of Fisher-Price toys. During the 1930s another material was used, a heavy cardboard in which brass eyelets were inserted to prevent wear from spinning axles.

Creating action from child power was of great importance. The use of bellows was common to produce sound and, as time passed, the introduction of bells was added to create sound and action.

Because of the immense amount of time required to assemble various toys, cottage-type industries were set up by employees, families, and residents of East Aurora. Toys such as the Pop-up Kritter were completely hand assembled in area homes. This would prove to be a quick and efficient method of assembly.

As the demand for Fisher-Price toys consistently rose, the company began to use the skills of a freelance designer, Edward Savage. A mechanical engineer from the University of Minnesota, Savage created some of Fisher-Price's most successful toys. In his home in Rochester, New York, Savage created such toys as the Pop-Up Kritters, Snoopy Sniffer, and many of the wind-up toys. The most popular of the toys that he created was the Snoopy Sniffer, which was produced from the 1930s to the 1980s, in four different versions.

After well over a decade of positive growth in the 1930s and 1940s, Fisher-Price faced the challenge of limited production. When the U.S. entered WWII, Fisher-Price, like many companies, turned to quite a different type of manufacturing. Fisher-Price was set up to create and produce wood products, and this dictated which essential goods they produced for the war. Ship fenders, first-aid kits, cots, bomb crates, and glider ailerons were among the items Fisher-Price produced from 1943-1946.

During this time of nearly nonexistent toy manufacturing, very limited toy production continued on a material-available basis. These toys were made from scraps of wood, with bells and some metal parts painted instead of plated. Toys made during this time sometimes used parts from similar toys, resulting in odd and sometimes unusual variations.

As WWII came to an end, normal production began to resume. Well into the 1950s, Ponderosa pine, with its proven durability, was the main source of material in Fisher-Price toys. As wood became more difficult to obtain, the experimentation with plastics began. The first toy to use this new material successfully was the Busy Bee. Because of the ease of molding, durability, and bright colors, plastic was more prevalent in toys of the 1950s.

In 1951 Fisher-Price moved to its new manufacturing facility on Girard Avenue in East Aurora, New York. The Girard Avenue facility handled most operations well into the late 1950s. In 1957 Tri Mold of Kenmore, New York, a plastics manufacturer, became a subsidiary of Fisher-Price and their main molding facility. As the demand for plastics became greater and greater, a new molding facility was built in Holland, New York. This was completed in July 1962. The Holland Plant produced many of the plastic parts used in the construction of a more plastic-dominated toy line. As the 1960s advanced, plastic eventually took over as the main material used to produce toys.

In 1969 the Quaker Oats Company acquired Fisher-Price toys. Three years prior to this acquisition, Herman Fisher had resigned as president of the company. He was chairman of the board until the Quaker Oats acquisition. After Fisher-Price was taken over by Quaker Oats, a plant was built in Medina, New York, and numerous plants and facilities were created both nationally and internationally.

Considered one of the oldest and largest manufacturers of toys, Fisher-Price still has its main offices at the Girard Avenue address in East Aurora, New York. As many of you are aware, the earlier Fisher-Price toys are not the only ones that are collectible: those produced in 1963 and later are fast becoming desirable collectibles as well.

Fisher-Price has created a large following with their limited edition (under 5,000) toys manufactured for the Toyfest celebration held in East Aurora, New York, each year since 1987. This event attracts collectors of toys from all over the U.S., Canada, and Europe. The toys manufactured for this event are as follows:

#6550 Buzzy Bee, 1987
#6558 Little Snoopy, 1988
#6575 Toot Toot Engine, 1989
#6590 Prancing Horses, 1990
#6592 Teddy Bear Parade, 1991
#6599 Molly Bell, 1992
#6145 Jingle Elephant, 1993
#6464 Gran'pa Frog, 1994

The second year toy has sold for well over $500 MIB, and others are moving upwards in value because of the limited availability. In 1991 Fisher-Price also manufactured a very limited (less than 4,000) number of the traditional 1930s Snoopy Sniffer, #6588.

The Fisher-Price Collectors Club is a great opportunity for fellow collectors to advance their knowledge, buy and sell, and communicate with other collectors. I would encourage collectors to join the club, as information on new and old Fisher-Price toys is plentiful in the newsletter. For information, contact the Fisher-Price Collector's Club, Attention: Jeanne Kennedy, 1442 North Ogden, Meza, AZ 85205.

Many factors may contribute to the value of a Fisher-Price toy. The most important factor to consider is the paper lithography. Most Fisher-Price toys found have what I call "edge wear." Edge wear may be considered as wear only around the outer corners of the toy. Most toys found with edge wear may also be called normal wear toys. Toys with this type of wear most often fall in a value class of good/very good. When determining condition of a toy, other areas of importance to the litho would be the amount of soil on the litho, and the extent to which it has faded and/or lost its color. These areas may be considered less important, unless there is more than slight soiling or discoloration. When a Fisher-Price toy has advanced conditions of wear, soiling, or missing litho, the toy is considered in less than good condition and therefore, a value of less than good (poor) would be placed on it.

Another area of importance in determining a toy's value is paint. Toys with slight paint wear on wheels, bases, and handles fall into the good/very good condition category, unless there is litho damage as stated above. Any parts missing also affect the value of the toy, especially lithography parts, such as arms, legs, and heads. These are especially important since, once the litho is gone, there is no means of replacement. Missing wheels and axles also lessen the value of a toy.

A toy that is mint has absolutely no wear or damage. Litho, paint, wheels, etc. are all in mint condition. These toys are worth the highest values. Boxes for older Fisher-

Price toys may add up to 20% to the value of a mint toy, depending upon the condition of the box. Boxes from the 1930s are of the highest value because of their age and scarcity. Always consider condition of the box when calculating the value of a toy.

Higher prices can be demanded for comic character toys and toys displaying other companies' names. Most often toys of this nature have much higher values than other Fisher-Price toys, due to the fact that there are many Disney, Popeye, and other comic-area collectors. Because a toy is a Disney, Popeye, or comic figure does not necessarily mean that it is a rare toy, however. Rarity is based on the amount of toys produced over a given period of time and the amount still in existence.

Toys that had accessories or figures that were often misplaced will also bring higher values. Often these accessories and/or figures are difficult to locate separately from the toy itself. If a toy is found mint in the box with accessories, it most certainly will demand a higher price. The Fisher-Price toy prices listed in this guide were established by averaging toy prices taken from toy shows, flea markets, dealers, and collectors.

John J. Murray was born, raised, and educated in the Buffalo, New York, area. He presently resides in Eden, a suburb of Buffalo, with his wife Mary and daughter Amanda. John, known to many as Jack, began his career in the printing industry. After serving in the Armed Forces, Murray began his long career with Fisher-Price in the Research and Development Art Production Department. He is responsible for creating new color development and decoration for photo and TV models. Murray pioneered the first documentation of Fisher-Price in Collecting Toys (volumes 4 and 5), and has since completed the most extensive book on Fisher-Price, entitled Fisher-Price 1931-1963: A Historical, Rarity, Value Guide and authored by John J. Murray and Bruce R. Fox. The book is available from Murray by writing to him at Box 29, Eden, NY 14057. The cost is $24.95 plus $3.00 shipping. Murray also serves as chairman of Toyfest (held annually in East Aurora, New York), which has become one of the largest antique toy gatherings in the U.S.

Photos in this section by Ross MacKearnin and courtesy of John J. Murray.

	C6	C8	C10
7 Looky Fire Truck (see picture)	62	93	125
8 Bouncy Racer	40	60	80
10 Bunny Cart	90	135	180
11 Ducky Cart	85	125	170
16 Ducky Cart	85	125	170
28 Bunny Egg Cart	85	125	170
50 Baby Chick Tandem Cart	85	125	170
100 Musical Sweeper	120	180	240
120 Cackling Hen (white)	30	45	60
123 Cackling Hen (red)	40	65	80
123 Roller Chimes (with push stick)	78	100	155
125 Uncle Timmy Turtle (with glasses) (see picture)	75	112	150
131 Toy Wagon	225	325	450

	C6	C8	C10
132 Dr. Doodle	170	255	340
137 Pony Chime	40	60	80
138 Pony Chime	30	40	50
139 Tuggy Turtle	85	125	160
140 Katy Kackler (see picture)	120	180	240
145 Musical Elephant (with original ears) (see picture)	250	375	500
150 Timmy Turtle	40	60	80
151 Happy Hippo	85	125	170
155 Moo-oo Cow	70	105	140
156 F/P Circus Wagon (see picture)	375	562	750

7 Looky Fire Truck.

125 Uncle Timmy Turtle.

145 Musical Elephant.

166 Bucky Burro.

140 Katy Kackler.

156 Fisher-Price Circus Wagon.

	C6	C8	C10
161 Looky Chug-Chug (with tender)	90	135	180
164 Mother Goose	65	95	135
166 Bucky Burro (see picture)	115	175	230
168 F/P Chug Chug (with 2 cars)	30	45	60
168 Snorky Fire Engine (with all figures)	85	125	170
169 Snorky Fire Engine (with all figures)	85	125	170
170 American Airlines Flagship (with original propellers)	600	900	1200
175 Gold Star Stage Coach (with baggage-two)(see picture)	190	285	375
177 Donald Duck Xylophone (see picture)	180	270	360
180 Snoopy Sniffer (see picture)	70	105	140
185 Donald Duck Xylophone	400	600	800

	C6	C8	C10
190 Molly Moo-Moo	225	275	350
191 Golden Gulch Express	85	125	170
192 Playland Express	85	125	170
195 Teddy Bear Parade	600	900	1200
200 Winky Blinky Fire Truck	55	85	110
210 Pluto the Pup	350	475	600
211 Walt Disney's Elmer the Elephant	350	475	600
215 Streamliner Express	800	1200	1600
220 Looky Chug-Chug (see picture)	95	125	170
225 Musical Sweeper	85	125	170
230 Musical Sweeper	85	125	170
234 Nifty Station Wagon (with roof and four figures) (see picture)	225	325	450
237 Riding Horse (with original tail)	600	900	1200
301 Bunny Basket Cart	40	60	80
302 Chick Basket Cart	40	60	80
303 Bunny Basket Cart	95	140	190
305 Walking Duck Cart	45	60	90
307 Bouncing Bunny Cart	45	60	90
310 Mickey Mouse Puddle Jumper	80	120	160
314 Queen Buzzy Bee (see picture)	40	65	85

177 Donald Duck Xylophone.

175 Gold Star Stage Coach.

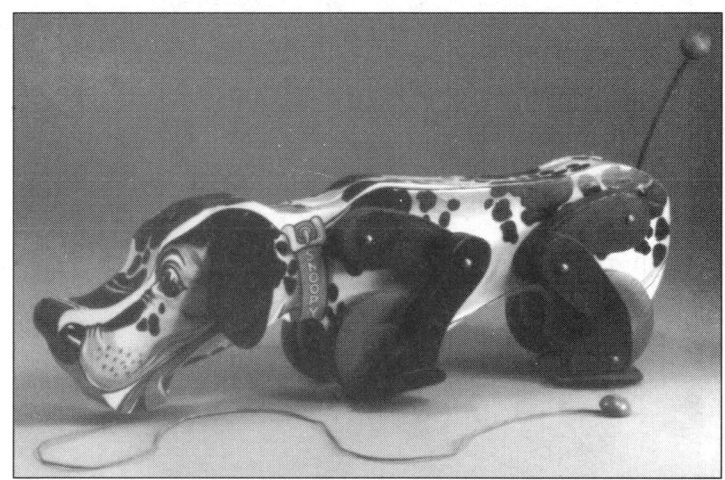

180 Snoopy Sniffer.

220 Looky Chug-Chug.

234 Nifty Station Wagon.

Fisher-Price • 671

314 Queen Buzzy Bee.

415 Super Jet.

	C6	C8	C10
325 Buzzy Bee	15	25	35
333 Butch the Pup	85	125	170
350 Go'n Back Mule (with original ears)	700	1100	1400
400 Donald Duck Drum Major	135	200	270
400 Tailspin Tabby (original pull loops) (see picture)	90	135	180

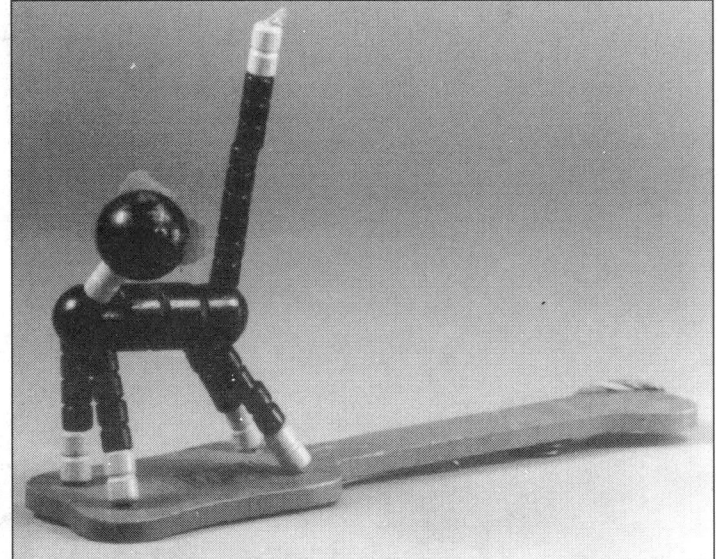

400 Tailspin Tabby.

415 Lop-Ear Looie.

	C6	C8	C10
401 Bunny Cart	200	300	400
406 Bunny & Cart	45	60	90
407 Chick & Cart	40	60	80
410 Stoopy Storky (with original cardboard feet)	275	375	550
415 Lop-Ear Looie (see picture)	225	335	450
415 Super-Jet (see picture)	110	165	220

	C6	C8	C10
432 Mickey Mouse Choo-Choo (early version)	650	975	1300
433 Dizzy Donkey (see picture)	75	115	155
434 Ferdinand the Bull (see picture)	600	900	1200
440 Goofy Gertie	300	425	575
440 Pluto Pop-Up	90	135	185
444 Puffy Engine	45	70	95
444 Fuzzy Fido (see picture)	225	325	450
445 Hot Dog Wagon (see picture)	225	300	400
445 Nosey Pup (see picture)	75	120	145
450 Donald Choo-Choo (see picture)	185	275	370
450 Jolly Jumper	85	125	170
454 Donald Duck Drummer (see picture)	225	325	450
455 Tailspin Tabby	85	125	170
462 Barky Dog	85	125	175

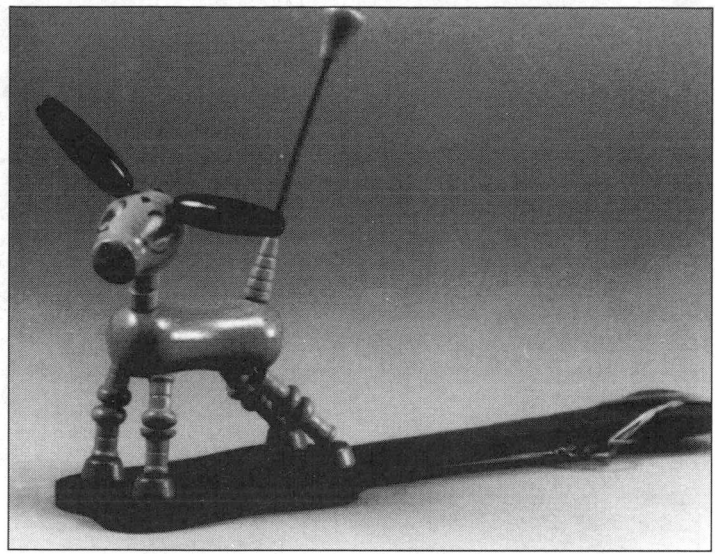

433 Dizzy Donkey.

434 Ferdinand the Bull.

444 Fuzzy Fido.

445 Hot Dog Wagon.

445 Nosey Pup.

	C6	C8	C10
472 Peter Bunny Cart (see picture)	225	275	375
472 Jingle Giraffe	175	225	275
473 Merry Mutt	85	125	170
476 Mickey Mouse Drummer	225	235	450
476 Cookie Pig	40	50	60
477 Dr. Doodle	225	350	450
478 Pudgy Pig	40	60	80
479 Donald Duck & Nephews (with 2 nephews)(see picture)	400	500	600
480 Leo The Drummer (see picture)	225	280	375
485 Mickey Mouse Choo-Choo (see picture)	80	120	160
487 Bunny Cart	225	325	450
488 Popeye Spinach Eater	500	750	1050
491 Boom-Boom Popeye (see picture)	500	750	1050
494 Plucky Pinocchio (see picture)	250	375	500
495 Sleep Sue	45	55	65
498 Happy Helicopter	175	265	350

450 Donald Duck Choo Choo.

454 Donald Duck Drummer.

472 Peter Bunny Cart.

	C6	C8	C10
508 Bunny Bell Drummer	85	125	160
533 Thumper Bunny	425	575	800
544 Donald Duck Cart	225	325	425
600 Tailspin Tabby Pop-Up	225	275	325
610 Tailspin Tabby	70	105	140
616 Chuggy Pop-Up	85	125	170
617 Whistling Engine	95	140	175
621 Suzie Seal (ball)	40	50	60
623 Suzie Seal (umbrella)	40	50	60
625 Playful Puppy	45	55	65
626 Playful Puppy	45	55	65
634 Tiny Teddy	40	65	85
635 Tiny Teddy	30	45	65
636 Tiny Teddy	60	90	120
640 Wiggily Woofer	85	120	145

479 Donald Duck & Nephews.

480 Leo the Drummer.

485 Mickey Mouse Choo Choo.

	C6	C8	C10
642 Smokie Engine 35		55	70
653 Allie Gator.. 85		120	150
654 Tawny Tiger 55		85	115
656 Bossy Bell 35		60	80
658 Lady Bug 45		60	80
662 Merry Mousewife 40		60	80
674 Sports Car... 85		125	150
678 Kriss Kricket (see picture) 100		150	200
686 Perky Pot 85		110	140
695 Pinky Pig 45		60	75
698 Talky Parrot (see picture)........................... 55		85	110
703 Popeye the Sailor (see picture).................. 600		900	1200
707 Fido Zilo.. 85		110	150
712 Teddy Tooter 135		200	270
720 Pinocchio Express 600		800	1100

491 Boom Boom Popeye.

	C6	C8	C10
721 Peter Bunny Engine.................................225		325	450
728 Buddy Bullfrog...60		90	120
730 Racing Rowboat (see picture) 140		210	280
733 Fisher-Price General Hauling (see picture) 165		250	330
733 Mickey Mouse Safety Patrol 250		375	500
735 Juggling Jumbo (see picture).....................225		300	400
738 Dumbo Circus Racer (original arms) 600		900	1200
738 Shaggy Zilo 85		120	180
739 Poodle Zilo 85		120	180
742 Dashing Dobbin.....................................275		365	550
745 Elsie's Dairy Truck with 2 milk bottles- deduct $25.00 for each missing bottle (see picture)..........475		700	900
750 Hot Dog Wagon.......................................400		600	800
750 Space Blazer..265		400	530

494 Plucky Pinocchio.

678 Kriss Kricket.

698 Talky Parrot.

703 Popeye the Sailor.

	C6	C8	C10
752 Teddy Xylophone	160	240	320
755 Jumbo Rollo	225	300	400
757 Humpty-Dumpty (see picture)	160	240	325
758 Pony Chime	165	250	335
765 Dandy Dobbin (see picture)	200	275	400
765 Talking Donald Duck (see picture)	70	105	140
770 Doc & Dopey Dwarfs (see picture)	750	1000	1500
775 Gabby Goofies	40	60	80
776 Gabby Goofies	40	60	80
777 Teddy Bear Zilo (see picture)	85	125	160
777 Squeaky the Clown (see picture)	160	250	325
785 Blackie Drummer	500	600	1000

733 Fisher Price General Hauling.

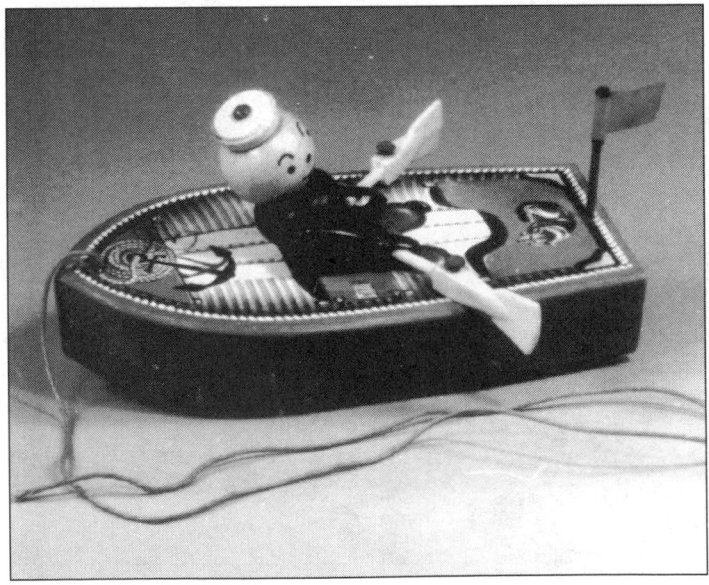

730 Racing Rowboat.

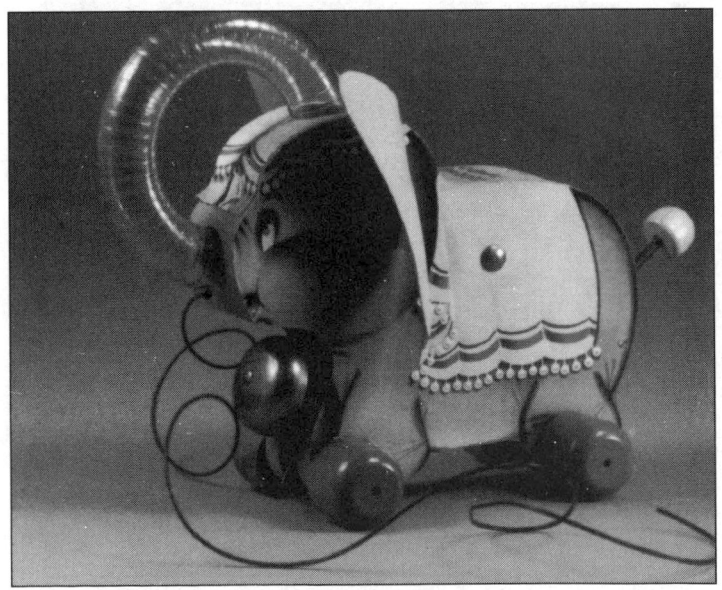

735 Juggling Jumbo.

	C6	C8	C10
794 Big Bill Pelican (with cardboard fish-add $20.00)	65	85	120
795 Musical Duck	50	75	100
798 Chatter Monk	85	125	160
799 Quacky Family	30	45	65
810 Timber Toter	85	110	150
875 Looky Push Car (w/ steering wheel push stick)	75	95	145

745 Elsie's Dairy Truck.

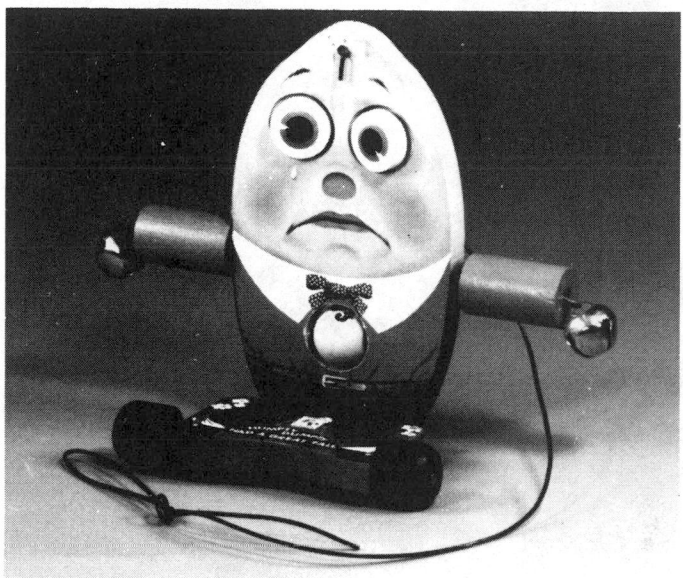

757 Humpty Dumpty.

	C6	C8	C10
900 Big Performing Circus (with all accessories)	230	345	460
926 Cement Mixer	260	325	485
983 Safety School Bus (w/ all figures)	125	275	400
984 Safety School Bus (w/ all figures)	170	275	400
999 Huffy Puffy Train (w/ 4 cars)	90	130	160

765 Dandy Dobbin.

765 Talking Donald Duck.

*770 Doc
& Dopey
Dwarfs.*

*777 Squeaky
the Clown.*

*777 Teddy Bear
Zilo.*

PLASTIC DOLLHOUSE FURNITURE

(1940s-1960s)

THE SWITCH TO PLASTIC

by Mary Brett

Baby boomers were just one side effect of WWII. Plastic toys were another. The entire continent of Europe had been devastated and U.S. imports of European toys (especially the once-so-popular German toys) ceased completely. For the first time American consumers turned solely to American toymakers. However, American toymakers had problems of their own. The war had created severe metal shortages as well as shortages of other materials previously used to create toys, such as wood, cloth and glass. A material was needed to fill the growing market demand that so many new babies were creating. It was then that these toy producers turned to a relatively new product called plastic.

Consumers were slow to respond to the new plastic toys, judging them inferior and unsafe. But the Dow Chemical Company, which produced the polystyron plastic identified by the Styron label, spearheaded a large national campaign in 1948 to make the consumer familiar with and completely confident in the Styron hallmark on toys.

Dow placed ads in national magazines and toy trade journals. They furnished window displays, counter displays, and store banners to department stores, drug stores, and dime stores featuring toys made from Styron. The campaign worked. Plastic caught on and sales soared.

Plastic proved to be everything Dow said it was: light, safe, sanitary, easy to handle, colorful and inexpensive. And even when metal and other materials were no longer scarce, plastic toys remained popular. Plastic dollhouse furniture continued as the top seller until the mid-1960s, when wood once again became the vogue.

There were several producers of plastic dollhouse furniture in the 1940s-1960s, including Marx, Superior, Jayline, Jaydon, and others. The three top quality producers were Renwal, Plastic Art Toy Corporation of America (Plasco), and Ideal. Add to these three producers the "Lit-

tle Deb/Little Hostess" line that Marx introduced in 1964 and you have the areas in which a serious collector should concentrate.

Mary Brett has literally been involved with antiques her entire life, born into a family of antique dealers. She has published over a dozen articles in leading national toy and antiques magazines on the subject of plastic dollhouse furniture and tin dollhouses and her personal collection is one of the largest and most complete in the country. Her book, A Tomart Price Guide To Tin Dollhouses and Plastic Dollhouse Furniture was recently published. She currently lives in Midlothian, Virginia, with her husband Lee and her two sons, Trey and Lee. Photo by Ellen Shuler.

When purchasing plastic furniture, accept only perfect pieces. Any piece that is broken, chipped, warped, has a burn or melt spot, or has a part missing is virtually worthless. Also, anytime you are able to locate a mint in box (MIB) piece or set, purchase it, because its value is going up daily. Today plastic dollhouse furniture is becoming more popular among antique dealers and collectors alike as baby boomers rediscover and repurchase their youth. The prices are soaring. Plastic is everything Dow promised it to be in 1948, except today it is no longer inexpensive.

Photos in this section by Mary Brett, unless otherwise noted.

RENWAL

Renwal is the most highly collectible of all the plastic dollhouse furniture. In addition, the Renwal pieces are numbered by sequence and category, making them both fun and challenging to collect.

This furniture was produced between the 1940s and the mid-1960s. The furniture was sold in room sets or by individual piece. A child could furnish an entire dollhouse for less than $7.00, and individual pieces were sold in almost every dime store, drug store, or department store for about 29¢ each. Renwal furniture caught on quickly. In 1946 Renwal introduced the Jolly Twins line of dollhouse furniture. Collier's magazine (*Toys for Tomorrow*, March 1946) reported a Renwal spokesman as saying that their company expected to sell 150,000,000 pieces that year. There is every indication Renwal did just that. In the Christmas season of 1946 over 52,000,000 pieces sold, a feat made even more spectacular when we realize that the retail holiday season in 1946 was from the day after Thanksgiving until Christmas Eve.

The Renwal Manufacturing Company was founded in 1939 by Irving Lawner (Renwal backwards), who sold it to Irving Rosenblum 14 months later. Originally it was located in New York City. Later it moved to Mineola, New York, but kept a showroom at the Toy Building on Fifth Avenue. Renwal became a division of Learning Aids Group, Inc., and on October 1, 1973, Learning Aids Group, Inc. merged into Chein Industries. Chein later merged into Revell. Renwal is also well known for their plastic cars, trucks and airplanes, which they produced in the 1940s-1960s and which are considered highly collectible. Today the great Renwal logo is no longer used.

Renwal Price Guide and Check List

These prices reflect only perfect pieces. (The exception being the Renwal dollhouse dolls.) Any piece that is broken, chipped, has a part missing, is noticeably warped, or has a burn/melt spot is virtually worthless.

MIB = Mint in Box
MP = Movable Parts
NMP = Nonmovable Parts

No.	Description		Value
5	Doll	MP	50-75
7	Tricycle	MP	20-25
8	2" Baby	MP	10-15
9	5" Baby	MP	50-75
10	Bathroom Scale (paper dial)	NMP	10-15
11	Alarm Clock (paper dial)	NMP	10-15
12	Kitchen Stool	NMP	10-15
13	Pedestal Ashtray	NMP	10-15
14	Mantel Clock (paper dial)	NMP	10-15
16	Table Radio (paper dial)	NMP	10-15
18	Radio/Phonograph (paper dial)	MP	20-25
19	Swing	MP	30-40
20	Slide	MP	10-15
21	Teeter-Totter	MP	15-20
22	Delux Sink (all parts)	MP	35-55
23	Motorcycle/Sidecar	MP	20-25
24	Delux Refrigerator (all parts)	MP	35-55
26	Delux Stove (all parts)	MP	35-55
27	Kiddie Car	MP	25-35
28	Telephone	MP	10-15
30	Highchair	MP	15-20
31	Wringer Washer	MP	25-30

No.	Description		Value
32	Ironing Board w/Iron	MP	15-20
33	School Desk	MP	15-20
34	Teacher's Desk	MP	15-20
35	Swivel Chair	MP	10-15
36	Potty Chair	MP	10-15
37	Vacuum Cleaner	MP	20-25
41	Sister	MP	25-30

RENWAL. Left to right: No. 20 Slide, No. 8 Baby in No. 19 Swing, No. 21 Teeter-Totter. The baby came in diaper only and in various color combinations of shirt and pants and with and without shoes and socks.

Examples of the stenciled Renwal furniture. All three kitchen pieces have doors that open and shut.

RENWAL. Left to right: No. 27 Kiddie Car, No. 7 Tricycle.

No.		Description	Value
42	Brother	MP	25-30
43	Mother	MP	25-30
44	Father	MP	25-30
	Any Family Doll	MIB	40-45

Left to right: Renwal Sewing Machine, Ideal Sewing Machine.

RENWAL. Left to right: Father, Mother, Brother. All mint in box (Sister not pictured). Renwal also made Doctor, Nurse, Policeman and Mechanic Dollhouse Dolls.

No.		Description	Value
44	Doctor w/Bag	MP	45-50
43	Nurse w/Cap	MP	45-50
	Any Doctor/Nurse Doll	MIB	60-75
44	Policeman	MP	50-60
44	Mechanic	MP	50-60
	Any Policeman/Mechanic	MIB	80-90
D51	Dining Table	NMP	10-15
D52	Hutch	MP	10-15
D53	Chair	NMP	5-10*
D54	Buffet	MP	10-15
	Buffet	NMP	5-10
D55	Sideboard	MP	10-15
62	Cabinet	MP	10-15
	Cabinet	NMP	5-10
K63	Chair	NMP	5-10*
64	Garbage Can	MP	15-20
65	Rocking Chair	NMP	10-15

RENWAL. Very popular accessory pieces. The broom, far right, is one of the rarest Renwals. Pictured is the flat-style broom. It also came rounded and in a "witch's broom" style.

No.	Description	Value
K66	Refrigerator..................MP	15-20
	Refrigerator..................NMP	5-10
K67	Table..........................NMP	5-10
K68	Sink...........................MP	15-20
	Sink...........................NMP	5-10
K69	Stove..........................MP	15-20
	Stove..........................NMP	5-10
L70	Floor Lamp.....................NMP	10-15
L71	Table Lamp.....................NMP	10-15
L72	Coffee Table...................NMP	5-10
L73	Round End Table................NMP	5-10
L74	Piano..........................NMP	20-25
L75	Piano Bench....................NMP	5-10
L76	Club Chair (Men's).............NMP	5-10
L77	Ladie's Chair..................NMP	5-10
L78	Couch..........................NMP	5-10
L79	Floor Radio (paper dial).......NMP	10-15
L80	Fireplace......................NMP	20-25
B81	Twin Bed.......................NMP	5-10
B82	Vanity/Mirror/Bench............MP	15-20
	Vanity/Mirror/Bench............NMP	10-15
B83	Dresser w/Mirror...............MP	15-20
	Dresser w/Mirror...............NMP	10-15

No.	Description	Value
B84	Night Stand....................NMP	5-10
B85	Chest..........................MP	15-20
	Chest..........................NMP	5-10
87	Baby Push Cart.................MP	15-20
89	Sewing Machine.................MP	40-45
T95	Tub............................NMP	10-15**
T96	Sink...........................NMP	10-15**
T97	Toilet.........................MP	10-15
T98	Hamper.........................MP	10-15**
108	Folding Card Table.............MP	20-25
109	Folding Chair..................MP	10-15
114	Baby Carriage/Spread...........MP	15-20
115	Baby Carriage w/ molded baby...MP	25-30
(117)	Mop w/cloth....................NMP	20-30
116	Carpet Sweeper.................NMP	15-20
118	Playpen........................MP	15-20
119	Cradle w/Spread................MP	15-20
120	Molded Baby....................NMP	10-15
(121)	Broom..........................NMP	45-75
122	Bathinette.....................MP	15-20
214	5 attached Hospital Cribs w/names Mary, John, Peter, Irene, Alice (set)..........NMP	30-45 set
No#	Cradle/Crib....................MP	15-20
No#	Dustpan........................NMP	10-15
No#	Mop (117)......................NMP	20-30
No#	Broom (121)....................NMP	45-75

* This piece bears two numbers
** This piece is dated

Rooms Mint in Box (MIB)

Original Room Box Sets: $135-$165, Cellophane-Topped Boxes valued lower: $95-$125

LIVING ROOM (13 pieces): Couch (L78), Club Chair (L76), Ladies Chair (L77), Fireplace (L80), 2 Round End Tables (L73), 2 Table Lamps (L71), Floor Lamp (L70), Coffee Table (72), Floor Radio (L79), Piano (L74), and Piano Bench (L75).

DINING ROOM (8 pieces): Table (D51), 4 Chairs (D53/K63), Hutch (D52), Sideboard (D55), and Buffet (D54).

KITCHEN (8 pieces): Sink (K68), Stove (K69), Refrigerator (K66), Table (K67), and 4 Chairs (D53/K63).

BEDROOM (7 pieces): 2 Twin Beds (B81), Vanity Table (82), w/ Bench (L75), Dresser (B83), Night Stand (B84), and Chest (B85).

BATHROOM (4 pieces): Tub (T95), Sink (T96), Toilet (T97), and Clothes Hamper (T98).

NURSERY (9 pieces): Night Stand (B84 pink or blue), Chest (B85 pink or blue), Bathinette (122), Cradle Crib (no No. with the Molded Baby) (120), Table Lamp (L71), Playpen (118), Carriage (115), and Highchair (30).

PLASTIC ART TOY CORPORATION OF AMERICA (PLASCO)

Overshadowed by Renwal furniture and overlooked by collectors for years, Plasco plastic dollhouse furniture is finally being appreciated for the fine quality product that it is.

The Plastic Art Toy Corporation of America was located at 1 Maple Street in East Rutherford, New Jersey, in the 1940s and later moved to East Paterson, New Jersey. They manufactured the Little Homemaker furniture line and sold it by piece or in sets. Each piece sold for about 29¢ and each set sold for about $1.00. The first sets were packaged in specially designed boxes with a lithographed interior simulating two walls of a room, complete with a pull-out floor. The later sets were packaged in boxes with no room designs and clear cellophane tops. As with the Renwal line, a mint in box (MIB) room set is valued higher because of the novelty of the box, and thus priced higher than the MIB cellophane box sets. An exception to the rule is the Plasco Nursery cellophane box, which includes the 7-inch plastic record of nursery tunes. Also note that in 1950 Plasco changed their original cellophane boxes to a new look and included the Plasco baby with each set, not just with the nursery set.

There are seven original sets: Living Room (7 pieces), Dining Room (9 pieces), Kitchen (11 pieces), Bedroom (7 pieces), Bathroom (6 pieces), Nursery (6 pieces), and Garden (8 pieces), for a total of 54 pieces. Later sets varied the number and variety of pieces offered. The furniture was designed by Eugene J. Lux and was actually a 16 to 1 scale of real furniture of that day.

Note: The prices listed reflect only perfect pieces. Any piece that is broken, chipped, has a part missing, is noticeably warped, or has a burn/melt spot is virtually worthless.

MIB = Mint in Box
MP = Movable Parts

Item	Description	Value
Living Room (7 pieces)		
Room Boxes	MIB	125-150
Other Boxes	MIB	95-75
Sofa		10-15
Club Chair		5-10
Wing Chair		5-10
Fireplace		10-15
Grandfather Clock		15-20
Coffee Table		5-10
TV	MP	30-35
Dining Room (9 pieces)		
Room Boxes	MIB	125-150
Other Boxes	MIB	75-95
Dining Table		15-20
2 Arm Chairs, per each		5-10
Breakfront		15-20
2 Console Tables, per each		10-15
Buffet		10-15
2 Straight Chairs		5-10

Item	Description	Value
Kitchen (11 pieces)		
Room Boxes	MIB	125-150
Other Boxes	MIB	75-95
Table		5-10
4 Chairs, per each		5-10
Stove		5-10
Refrigerator		5-10
Sink		5-10
Breakfast Bar		10-15
2 Cabinets, per each		5-10
Bedroom (7 pieces)		
Room Boxes	MIB	125-150
Other Boxes	MIB	75-95
2 Twin Beds, per each		5-10
Highboy	MP	15-20
Vanity with Mirror		10-15
Dresser with Mirror	MP	15-20
Night Table		5-10
Vanity Chair		2-5
Bathroom (6 pieces)		
Room Boxes	MIB	125-150
Other Boxes	MIB	75-95

PLASCO TV, Living Room Chair, Grandfather's Clock.

Item	Description	Value
Bathtub		5-10
Wash Bowl		5-10
Toilet		10-15
Hamper	MP	10-15
Vanity with Mirror		10-15
Vanity Chair		2-5

Nursery (6 pieces)

Item	Description	Value
Room Boxes	MIB	135-160
Other Boxes	MIB	75-95
w/ Plastic Record of Nursery Tunes, 7"	MIB	150-175
Crib with Mattress	MP	20-25
Doll's Bath	MP	15-20
Doll	MP	15-20

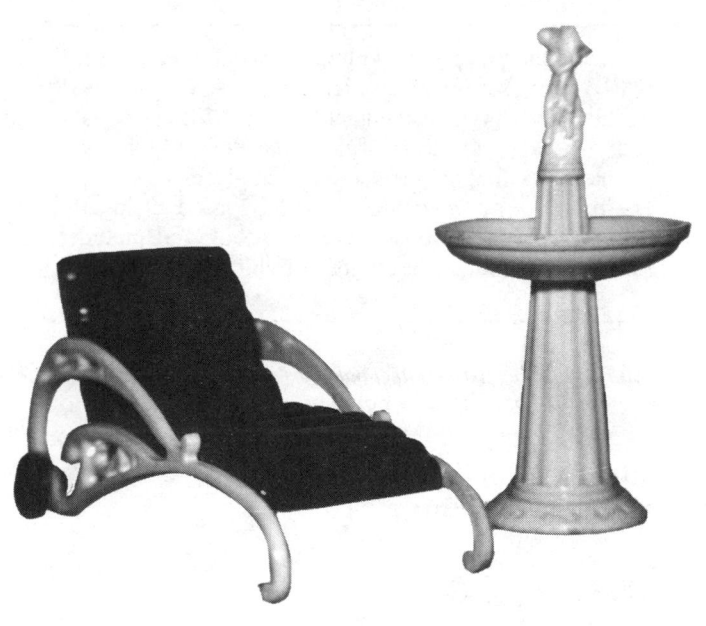

PLASCO Chaise Lounge and Fountain.

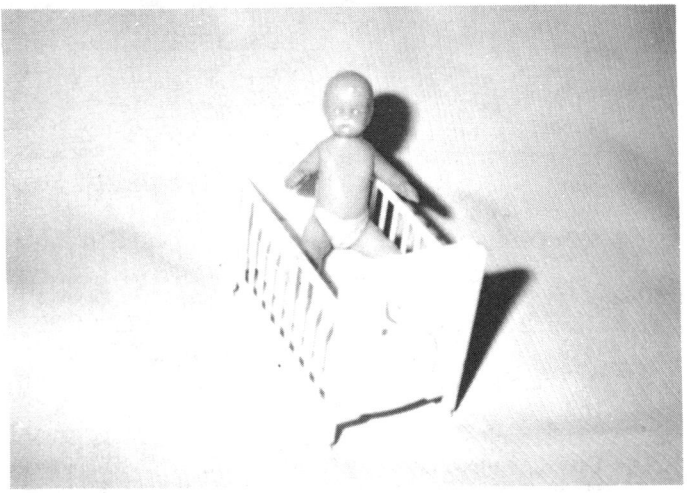

PLASCO Baby in Plasco Crib. The sides of the crib go up and down and the baby has movable joints. One version of the baby has a movable head and the others do not.

Item	Description	Value
Highboy	MP	15-20
Vanity Chair		2-5
Night Table		5-10

Garden (8 pieces)

Item	Description	Value
Room Boxes	MIB	125-150
Other Boxes	MIB	75-95
Umbrella Table		15-20
4 Chairs, per each		5-10
Sun Lounge		10-15
Refreshment Table		5-10
Fountain		5-10

IDEAL

The Ideal Novelty and Toy Company owes its start and success to the teddy bear.

In 1903 Rose and Morris Michtom owned a stationery and novelty store in Brooklyn, New York. Morris saw a politically staged newspaper picture of President Theodore (Teddy) Roosevelt with a small brown bear cub that the president had refused to shoot. Rose and Morris handmade several plush bear toys with button eyes. They placed them in their store window for sale after obtaining permission from the president to call them "Teddy Bear." The demand was so great that by 1907 the Michtoms moved to a larger store and the Ideal Novelty and Toy Company was started.

The Ideal three-quarter-inch scale furniture was sold as separate pieces and in boxed room sets. The most expensive individual piece was the combination TV/Radio/Record Player, which retailed for 75¢ in 1948. The table lamp, kitchen chair, and dog retailed for 5¢ each that same year. Boxed room sets sold for about $1.00 each.

The original boxed sets were sold in large, full-colored cardboard boxes. These boxes, when opened, represented individual rooms and could be used for play in the absence of a dollhouse. The front of the original boxes proclaimed Ideal's "tiny plastic furniture" as "an educational toy" and featured an illustration of two little girls and a little boy playing with the furniture. The original room sets were Living Room, Bedroom, Kitchen, Bath, Nursery, Dining Room, and Garden.

In the early 1950s the American post-WWII marketing trend turned towards self-service buying, requiring easy product identification. Ideal changed their dollhouse furniture packaging to cellophane-sided play cartons, which became miniature houses for the furniture when opened. When collecting dollhouse furniture, any MIB (Mint in Box) set is valuable, especially if the box as well as the furniture is in excellent condition. However, the earlier the packaging, the more valuable the product.

IDEAL. The rare and much-sought-after Dollhouse Family. The father is approximately 5" high.

MIB = Mint in Box

Item	Description	Value
Set, Original Cardboard	MIB	150-175
Set, Cellophane-sided, later	MIB	75-95

Original Room Sets

Living Room

Sofa	5-10
Chair, Ladies	5-10
Chair, Men's	5-10
Coffee Table	5-10
Tilt-Top Table	15-20
Table Lamp	10-15
Floor Lamp	10-15
Floor Radio	10-15
TV/Radio/Record Player Combo	35-45
Piano	15-20
Piano Stool	5-10

IDEAL TV Set with Stereo and Radio.

IDEAL. At left, the Hallmarked Baby in a blue collapsible high chair. At right, another style Ideal Baby in pink collapsible high chair. Ideal also made a high chair that didn't collapse. It is much rarer than the collapsible variety.

Item	Value
Secretary	20-25
Mantle with Picture	30-35
Radiator	20-25

Bedroom

2 Twin Beds, per each	5-10
Sewing Machine	20-25
Night Stand	5-10
High Chest	10-15
Dresser	15-20
Stool	5-10
Pleted Chair	5-10

Dining Room

Table	15-20
2 Armless Chairs, per each	5-15
2 Armed Chairs, per each	10-20
Buffet	15-20
China Cabinet	15-20

Bathroom

Toilet	15-25
Hamper	5-10
Medicine Chest	20-25
Tub (Regular)	5-10
Corner Tub	10-15
Sink	5-10

Kitchen (Standard)

Sink	5-10
Stove/Refrigerator	5-10
Table	5-10
4 Chairs, per each	5-10

Kitchen (Deluxe)

Table	5-10
4 Chairs, per each	5-10
Sink	20-25
Stove	20-25
Refrigerator	20-25
Mangle	15-20
Washing Machine	20-25

Item	Value
Garden	
Table with Umbrella	25-30
Doghouse with Dog	25-45
2 Benches, per each	15-20
Arbor	40-45
Birdbath	10-15
Reflecting Pool	25-35
Picnic Table	15-20
Chaise Lounge	15-20
Androck Chair	15-20

Nursery (Original)	
Crib with Mattress	20-25
Buggy	20-30
High Chair (noncollapsible)	40-45
Baby	10-15
Potty Chair with Pot	15-20

Accessory pieces, pieces added to later room sets, or pieces sold separately:

Kiddie Cart	20-25
High Chair (collapses into Kiddie Chair)	20-25
Lawn Mower	20-35
Dishwasher	20-30
Card Table with four (4) Folding Chairs	75-100
Sleeping Sofa	50-75
Vacuum Cleaner	25-30
Playpen	20-30
Bathinette	20-30

Petite Princess by Ideal

In 1964 Ideal brought out their line of plastic dollhouse furniture they termed Fantasy Furniture. This furniture was, without a doubt, the most elaborate and ornate of all the baby boomers' dollhouse furniture.

IDEAL Petite Princess Salon Drum Chair. Ideal produced the Petite Princess line only in 1964 and the Princess Patti line in 1965.

This furniture was produced in Japan. Fabric, paper, glass, and metals were used along with the plastic to create this beautiful and detailed product. You will soon be able to recognize on sight the distinctive look of the Petite Princess line with its satins, lames, brocades, and bright red velvet fabrics, its modern white antique furniture with "marble" tops and its gilded mirrors and frames.

Note: These prices reflect only Mint in Box (MIB) or perfect pieces. Any piece that is broken, chipped, has a part missing, is noticeably warped, or has a burn/melt spot is virtually worthless.

Furniture		MIB	Main piece with no Accessories
4407-3	Salon Curved Sofa	30	15
4408-1	Boudoir Chair Lounge	30	15
4409-9	Guest Chair	30	15
4410-7	Salon Wing Chair	30	15
4411-5	Salon Drum Chair	30	15
4412-3	Occasional Chair/Ottoman	30	15
4413-1	Host Dining Chairs, 12	20 set	5-8 each
4414-9	Guest Dining Chairs, 12	20 set	5-8 each
4415-6	Hostess Dining Chairs, 12	20 set	5-8 each
4416-4	Little Princess Bed	40	20
4417-2	Royal Dressing Table/stool	40	20
4418-0	Treasure Trove Cabinet	30	15
4419-8	Royal Buffet (MIB complete w/ mirror, picture plate and 2 porcelain vases)	40	20
4420-6	Palace Chest	20	10
4421-4	Dining Room Table (MIB complete with picture)	30	15
4422-2	Regency Hearthplace (MIB complete w/ 2 Andirons, 2 pieces of firewood, bucket and mirror)	40	20
4423-0	Grandfather Clock and Folding Screen	40	30
4424-8	Rolling Tea Cart (MIB complete with wine bottle and 3 wine cups)	20	10
4425-5	Royal Grand Piano (MIB complete w/ piano bench, music and metronome)	60	30
4426-3	Lyre Table Set (MIB complete with lamp & picture)	20	10
4427-1	Pedestal Table Set (MIB complete with lamp & flower vase)	20	10
4426-9	Heirloom Table Set (MIB complete with brass lamp, books & pair bookends)	20	10
4429-7	Tier Table Set (MIB complete w/ lamp & fruit bowl)	20	10
4431-3	Palace Table Set (MIB complete w/ porcelain decanter, 3 cups & leaf ashtray)	20	10

Furniture	MIB	Main piece with no Accessories
4437-0 Occasional Table Set (MIB complete w/ cig. lighter, picture frame, Buddha statue & astray)	30	20
4432-1 Fantasy Telephone Set	20	10
4433-9 Salon Coffee Table Set (MIB complete w/ flower vase, brass coffee pot, creamer and 2 bowls)	20	10
4439-6 Royal Candelabra	15	10
4438-8 Fantasia Candelabra	30	15
4440-4 Salon Planter	20	10
4450-3 Fantasy Room	40	20
9710-5 Fantasy Family, per each	20	15

Accessories

Painting	10
Mirror	10
Flower Vase	5
Lamp	10
Books, Bookends	5
Perfume Bottle	5
Ash Tray	5
Cigarette Lighter	5
Buddha Statue	5
Picture Frame	5
Wine Decanter	5
Wine Glasses (3), per each	3-5
Fruit Bowl	5
Picture Plate	5
Porcelain Base	5
Andirons (2)	3-5
Fireplace Bucket	5
Porcelain Decanter	5
Brass Coffee Pot	5
Brass Creamer	3
Brass Bowls (2)	3

Princess Patti by Ideal

In late 1965 Ideal brought out the Princess Patti line. It reproduced the Petite Princess line's look but at a more affordable production cost. The mirrors, for example, had gold strips of paper glued on instead of being contained in a gilded frame. Two additional room sets were added, the Kitchen Set and the Bathroom Set. Also added to the line was a TV, a 3-story, 5-room dollhouse, and a vinyl room carrying case. This line was scaled to match the Petite Princess line so that all pieces were interchangeable. Both lines are hallmarked only "Ideal" and are hard to differentiate. The boxes they are packaged in are very different, however. Ironically, today the Princess Patti TV, Kitchen Set, and Bathroom are valued much higher than any piece or set from the Petite Princess line.

	MIB	EX	GD
Waste Basket, Stool and Mirror	35	15	10
Hamper	15	10	5
Oval Tub with Swans	75	55	20
Sink with attached Oval Mirror	55	45	35
Toilet	55	45	15
Linen Cabinet w/ 4 Towels	85	55	25

	MIB	EX	GD
Television w/ Stand	250	175	125
Round Kitchen Table w/ Flowers	55	35	20
Kitchen Chairs (2), clear plastic	60	40	25 set
Range w/ 4 Utensils and Hood	150	100	35
Refrigerator-Freezer & Accessories	150	100	55
Sink & Dishwasher	100	65	30
Hutch with plates	55	35	20
Dollhouse	150	75	45
Vinyl Carrying Case	75	45	15

Young Decorator by Ideal

After WWII there was a tremendous building boom in America, which triggered a furniture boom. Much of our country became engrossed in "modern" decorating and many toy companies developed decorator-theme lines of toys and toy sets.

In 1950 Ideal introduced their 1-1/2" scale, detailed, high-quality plastic dollhouse furniture line called Young Decorator. The Young Decorator furniture is one of the most sought after of all the plastic furniture lines. It is also one of the most beautiful. It was produced from a high gloss hard plastic and many of the pieces were manufactured in up to two colors, with movable parts. The furniture was sold in six sets: Living Room, Dining Room, Bedroom, Bath, Kitchen, and Nursery.

	EX	GD
Living Room		
Tufted Couch, 4 pieces, 2 with arms, 2 without arms	60	40
Floor Lamp	20	15
Coffee Table	10	5
Television	55	35

IDEAL. At left, the Young Decorator 1-1/2" scale Sectional Couch and Coffee Table. At right, the Ideal 3/4" Couch.

	EX	GD
Dining Room		
Dining Table	15	10
4 Chairs, per each	8	5
Hutch	25	20
Buffet	20	15

	EX	GD
Bedroom		
Twin Bed	20	15
Night Stand	10	5
Tall Chest of Drawers	25	20
Dresser	25	20
Dresser Stool	10	5
Bath		
Corner Tub	20	15
Vanity Sink	20	15
Toilet	30	20
Diaper Pail	20	15

	EX	GD
Kitchen		
Kitchen Table	15	10
4 Chairs, per each	8	5
Refrigerator	25	20
Sink	20	15
Stove	25	20
Nursery		
Crib	25	20
Playpen	25	20
High Chair	25	20
Bathinette	25	20
Tricycle	25	20

Steam Toys

by Richard Leach

Whenever I am asked about pricing older steam toys, the thought that comes to mind is, "Whatever the seller is willing to take and the buyer is willing to pay." Obviously, this price is influenced by availability and condition of the toy and may vary greatly from place to place. However, good deals for both parties are not struck out of ignorance. I have learned a great deal about pricing in the last several years through buying, selling, or trading mostly American-made steamers in the Midwest. It is my hope that these few notes may help you strike a deal in which both parties "win."

Three major companies still sell new steam toys in the U.S. They are Jensen Mfg. in Jeannette, Pennsylvania, the British-made Mamod engines, and Wilesco from Germany. These products should not be confused with the earlier collectibles.

The more common vertical and horizontal boiler steam engines in average condition can usually be purchased between $50 and $75. These prices allow the novice to get into a very rewarding hobby with little cash outlay. The more unusual engines tend to be much higher in price. By unusual, I mean twin cylinders, double flywheels, hand rails, governors, double boilers, or other unusual features. Larger, more elaborate engines with stair steps, catwalks, embossed brick chimneys, nickel plating, or reverse levers are also more valuable. Engines with attached accessories like fire pumps, pile drivers, hoisting drums, and saws are very desirable. I cannot, in good conscience, quote reliable prices for these more valuable engines in a short article.

Live steam boats have become very popular with collectors, and will bring $500 to $1000 or more depending on the condition and completeness of the model. The tractors and steam rollers are very desirable, although there are several by Mamod and Wilesco that are still in production for around $200. I have seen these confused with antiques, so know what you are buying. Early steam tractors should bring $250 to $600, depending on their condition. Burners are often missing on tractors, so look them over closely. Very nice repro burners and other parts are available at reasonable prices.

The horse-drawn, steam-operated fire pumper is the model of all models and the epitome for steam toy enthusiasts. They are very rare and if you are lucky enough to find one for sale, you can expect to pay between $2500 and $3000.

Rarity or availability is determined by the number of engines manufactured and their survival rates. Many elaborate but fragile models never survived the Christmas season. Condition is another important factor in pricing any steam toy. An engine that will run and has a burner, whistle, pressure valve, governor, etc. all in good shape will be

Richard B. Leach has been building steam engines since 1975. He is perhaps best known for his tiny thimble steam engine with a .034 diameter cylinder and a paper clip wire piston. He enjoys building larger steam and Stirling model engines as well. Building engines quite naturally led to the repair of older toy steam engines and an extensive collection of mostly Weeden steam toys. Richard is kept busy today reprinting high quality early Weeden catalogs and other related historical information. He has consolidated much of the early information and illustrations from original Weeden advertising into his popular Pictorial Guide To Weeden Steam Toys. *Since the completion of the Weeden guide, Richard is actively collecting literature and historical data on early electric toy motors. Several repro catalogs have been finished and a toy electric motor guide is nearly complete.*

worth much more than a rusty piece with missing parts. Look closely for repairs and parts that don't appear authentic. Excessive solder on steam pipes should tip you off that there was a problem.

Once you've purchased your steam toy, you may want to run it. Remember, these toys are very old. I always run mine on compressed air, which is much safer than steam but can still be dangerous to you and your engine if too much pressure is used. Build pressure slowly using a regulator (a few pounds should suffice) and always use a safety valve.

I have found this to be a rewarding hobby in terms of building both my collection of engines and friendships. I have also met a few less scrupulous dealers, so buyer, beware! Have fun. Happy steaming.

Left: Linemar steam engine with original box, auctioned in 1995 in mint condition for $143. Right: Steam-powered log splitter, 15" long, auctioned in 1995, condition unspecified, for $302. Photo by Jeanne Bertoia. Courtesy Bill Bertoia Auctions.

BING Steam Plant, 11" long, auctioned in 1995 in excellent condition for $198. Photo by Jeanne Bertoia. Courtesy Bill Bertoia Auctions.

Steam-powered mining plant, 10" high, auctioned in 1995 in excellent condition for $880. Photo by Jeanne Bertoia. Courtesy Bill Bertoia Auctions.

Left: Marklin Steam Plant, 15-1/2" high, auctioned in mint condition in 1995 for $550. Right: Bing Steam Plant Toy, 14" high, auctioned in very good condition in 1995 for $522. Photo by Jeanne Bertoia. Courtesy Bill Bertoia Auctions.

WEEDEN No. 14, early, cast-iron, 6-leg. Value approximately $125. Photo by Richard Leach.

WEEDEN No. 43, early. Value approximately $400-$500. Photo by Richard Leach.

WEEDEN No. 42 National Playthings steam engine, c. 1940. Value $100-$125. Photo by Richard Leach.

Accessories (late). Clockwise from back center: Weeden No. 69 Stamp Mill; No. 67 Circular Saw; No. 68 Emery Wheel; Jensen Trip Hammer; Mamod Emery Wheel; Marx Power Saw; Marx Buffer; Marx Grindstone with Box. Value about $40 each. Photo by Richard Leach.

WEEDEN No. 71, early, rare, approximate value $400-$500. Photo by Richard Leach.

WEEDEN No. 138 Walking Beam (late). Approximate value $250. Photo by Richard Leach.

WEEDEN No. 702, electric, early valve weight. Value approximately $100. Photo by Richard Leach.

ERECTOR SETS

TOYS THAT BUILD IMAGINATION

by W.S. Harrison III

Erector collecting has fairly recently come to the fore as folks tire of modern toys. Very few modern toys stimulate the imagination as the toys of old. Imagine the questions posed by a chemistry set, an Erector set, or a microscope set. If you think Nintendo can supply the mental stimulation that these toys of yesteryear could, well ... you're just not in the right gear!

A.C. Gilbert, the inventor of Erector sets, was a medical doctor (1908 graduate of Yale University) as well as the winner of the gold medal for the pole vault at the 1908 World Olympics in London. In addition to his many other skills, A.C. Gilbert was an accomplished professional magician and an outgoing, gregarious individual. With this background and a taste for hard work he acquired overcoming boyhood deficiencies, there was no question of the outcome of his venture.

Erector went through three development stages. From 1913 to 1923 (Stage I) the sets featured plenty of large, strong girders. Ads showed boys sitting on the bridges built with Erector sets ... and it was no exaggeration. After the trauma of WWI and the consequent inflation in the U.S. (and worse in Europe), Erector was redesigned and

W.S. (Bill) Harrison III graduated from LaSalle Academy in New York City in 1947 as valedictorian. He then attended Rensselaer Polytechnic Institute as a student of chemical engineering. This career path resulted from his extensive work in chemistry as a teenager: he was a finalist in the Westinghouse Science Talent Search. After marriage, Harrison completed a degree in mechanical engineering at Polytechnic University of New York, where he was elected to Tau Beta Pi, the National Engineering Honor Society. Harrison's engineering background spans more than 40 years. He has engineered and designed machinery and special equipment in aerospace, executed project management assignments with Monsanto and was chief engineer in metal forging and rubber molding companies. He has retired from his position as director of technical services with Engelhard Corporation, a major processor of precious minerals and is a registered professional engineer in the states of New York and Massachusetts. His first love, after his wife Judy, is engineering, and his hobbies are woodworking and metalworking. He buys, restores, trades and sells Erector Sets and parts. Harrison has seven children and 12 grandchildren. After a nomadic engineering tour, he settled in the small town of Marion, Massachusetts, on Buzzard's Bay, where he "plays" in a well-equipped 1300 sq. ft. workshop. Says Bill, "Please come and visit."

slimmed down. Girders were smaller, narrower, and lighter, but Gilbert also introduced countless other shapes to make the Erector system more versatile and more capable of building unique and beautiful models. Thus in 1924 Stage II was born, and continued on until the advent of Stage III in 1963, which really signaled the end of the Gilbert company. Although true collectors are interested in the total history of the once great company, most are more familiar with, and desire, the products of Stage II (1924 to 1962). One may, without much word inflation, call this the shining hour of the most successful scientific toy company in the U.S.

A.C. Gilbert ceased to be a major toy producer after 1962. The decline was somewhat agonizing, ending with the purchase of the rights to the famous name "Erector" by Meccano, SA of France, which also acquired Gilbert's old competitor in England. They produce a fine construction set, but it is not the set interesting to you who are now reading this analysis.

Before launching into a discussion on how much to pay for an Erector set, consider some common sense rules. Of about 45 million Erector sets produced, 90% probably went to people who didn't take very good care of them. That leaves about 4.5 million fairly nice sets in a good state of preservation, but you should figure that about half of these were thrown out or otherwise disposed of. Now we have about 2.25 million pretty nice Erector sets left. Where are they?

Most of us are inclined toward flea markets and garage sales, but this is probably not your best source. You may get lucky, but in most cases this represents the low end of the market. Many sets from these sources are what we in the business call "mixed trash." Whether intentional or not, a set may be only fractionally complete and usually will contain a variety of parts from different years mixed together. The idea is to make you think you are getting a bargain. If you are looking for fine quality sets in the C10 category, carefully watch for estate auctions, alert high-quality dealers, or buy from established collectors who are continually refining their collections.

Estate auctions are listed in your local newspaper. All avid collectors are members of the A.C. Gilbert Heritage Society (594 Front St., Marion, MA 02738) or the Southern California Meccano and Erector Club (Box 7653, Porter Ranch Sta., Northridge, CA 91327), or both. The former is the larger of the two: together they represent 500 of the largest collections in the world. Some members have over 1000 Erector sets, and many have several hundred.

Keep in mind that unless a set was carefully preserved in a dry climate, there is little chance of acquiring a set that is truly "Mint" (meaning in the same condition as it left the factory). Standard grading categories are listed below.

C10: 100% complete, all parts pinned with the original T clips; all cardboards present, no rust or white rust, manual present, near perfect, labels near perfect, only the lightest of scratches, parts may show very light cloudy oxidation (dingy).

C8: 98 to 100% complete, some or all cardboards present but may not be all correctly pinned, manual present (may have folded corners), motor must be present and working, less than 5% of the parts may show the very slightest real rust (like in corners, the type that auto chrome polish can easily remove).

C6: 90 to 95% complete, probably no cardboard, motor there and working, acceptable manual, labels may show serious wear, considerable scratching on bottom, some on top, minor dents in metal box, some signs of rust on 5 to 10% of parts.

Anything of lesser quality is likely not a collectible of lasting value and/or will be difficult, if not impossible, to restore. Most of what you will come across in flea markets is well below C6. Unless you have the facilities for electroplating and painting, you will have a problem on your hands. Fortunately there are many small entrepreneurs making new parts for Erector sets and one of these does total restorations.

Photos in this section courtesy of Marion Designs, unless otherwise noted.

Note: "psnd" means prices not significantly different

Type I: 1913 to 1923
(the era of girders 1-1/8" wide)

Most of the more valuable sets came in oak boxes with jointed corners. Smaller sets in cardboard boxes are not often seen, but can be quite valuable if discovered. Below the #4 set, condition is everything. Sets from 1913, the first year, have a unique motor and girder and are the most valuable.

1913

	C6	C8	C10
Mysto Erector, #1, cdbd	300	500	700
Mysto #4, w/ motor, wood box	225	350	500
Mysto #8, largest, 3 layer, WB	1000	2200	5000

1914-16

	C6	C8	C10
Mysto Erector, #1, cdbd	100	175	325
Mysto #4, w/ motor, wood box	65	100	180
Mysto #8, largest, 3 layer, WB	800	1800	4000

1917-23

	C6	C8	C10
Now called Gilbert Erector, #1	100	150	275
Erector #4, w/ motor, WB	150	250	400
Erector #4, w/ motor, WB, metal cover	150	300	525
Erector #7, '23 EB, metal cover	250	400	700
Erector #8, 3 layer WB sets	500	750	2500
Erector #8, 2 layer WB sets	225	500	950
Erector #10, 3 layer WB sets	1500	2300	4600

No. 8 Erector, 1916, largest set, has "Mysto" label.

Type II: 1924 to 1962
(the era of girders 5/8" wide)

These sets have a greater variety of parts and are capable of building more complex models. Sets from #4 up continued in wooden boxes (4 w/ cdbd cover) until 1933, when metal boxes were introduced to the larger sets (except the Hudson, which went metal in 1934). Half numbers were introduced, confusing some collectors.

	C6	C8	C10
1924-26			
Erector #00 (25¢ original)	50	75	125
Erector #0 (50¢ original)	60	95	170
Erector #1	40	60	80
Erector #4, w/ motor, WB	120	160	300
Erector #8	500	1100	2500
Erector #10	1000	2000	4500
Erector #7, '26 Steam Shovel, brn box	200	350	450
Erector #7-1/2 '26 White Trk., brn box	300	500	750
1927-28			
Erector #7-1/2, White Trk., red box	150	250	475
Erector #7, Steam Shovel, red box	120	160	300
Erector "B" giant red ferris wheel	500	750	1000
Erector #10, multi drawer, WB	2000	3000	5000
1929-30			
Same as above			
except for #9 Mech. Wonders Set	600	1200	2000
1931 -32			
Erector White Trk. rec. lid w/ picture	225	300	550
Erector Hudson Loco. "A" eng. only	800	1000	1400
Erector Hudson #8 eng. only w/ 7 pts	900	1300	1700
Erector Hudson #8-1/2 Eng & Tend +ot	800	1600	3200
Erector #10 "Climax,"			
largest set ever made, 150 lbs	5000	10,000	16-20,000
Erector #9 Zeppelin Set	1000	1600	2400

	C6	C8	C10
1933			
Erector Hudson #8-1/2, in WB	1500	2600	6000
Erector Super 6, w/ P56G, 110V motor	175	275	500
Erector Sensa. 7, automotive parts	250	400	600
1934			
Erector Super 6 as above, green box	175	275	500
Erector Sensa. 7,			
no automotive parts, red box	200	350	550
Erector #7-1/2 Automotive Set	250	450	650
Erector #8 Hudson & Tend., blue met	900	1800	3400

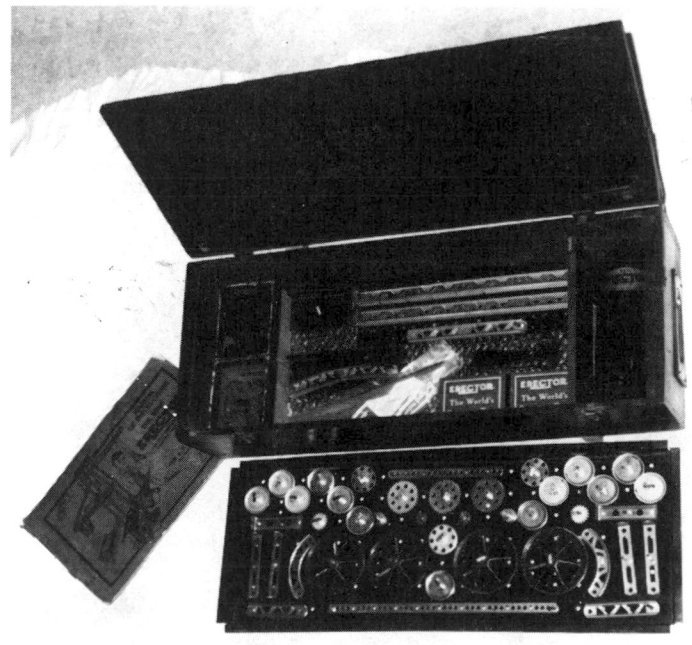

No. 7 Erector, 1929, "Steam Shovel."

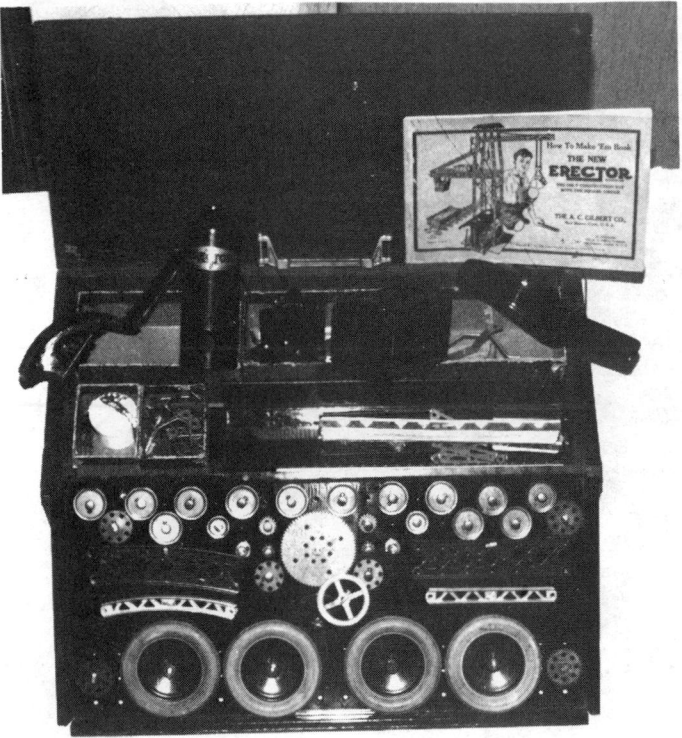

No. 7-1/2 Erector, 1929, "White Truck."

1935

Sets this year only featured architectural panels. If present, sets are more valuable. Many new parts.

	C6	C8	C10
Erector Super 6-1/2, P51 motor, boiler	225	300	550
Erector 7-1/2, Classic Ferris Wheel	275	400	600
Erector 8-1/2, Automotive Set	300	475	700
Erector 9-1/2, Hudson Set	1600	3200	6000

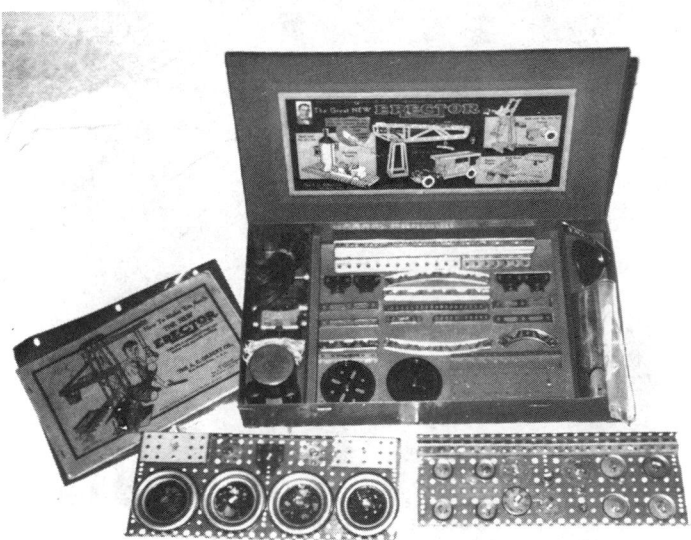

No. 6-1/2 Erector, 1935, "Super 6-1/2."

	C6	C8	C10

1936

	C6	C8	C10
Erector 5-1/2, w/ A52 110V motor	200	275	425
Erector 8-1/2, Classic Ferris Wheel	80	180	400
Erector 9-1/2, Automotive Set	335	500	675
Erector 10-1/2, Hudson Set	1500	2800	5500

1937

The last year of the Hudson Set, cdbd/metal top parts cans introduced, last year of P51 motor...... pnsd

No. 9-1/2 Erector, 1937, "Automotive" set.

1938

Famous A-49 motor w/ die-cast housing introduced; "MX" house introduced... psnd

10-1/2 becomes Electric Train Set w/ American Flyer engine and track..... 750   1500   3000

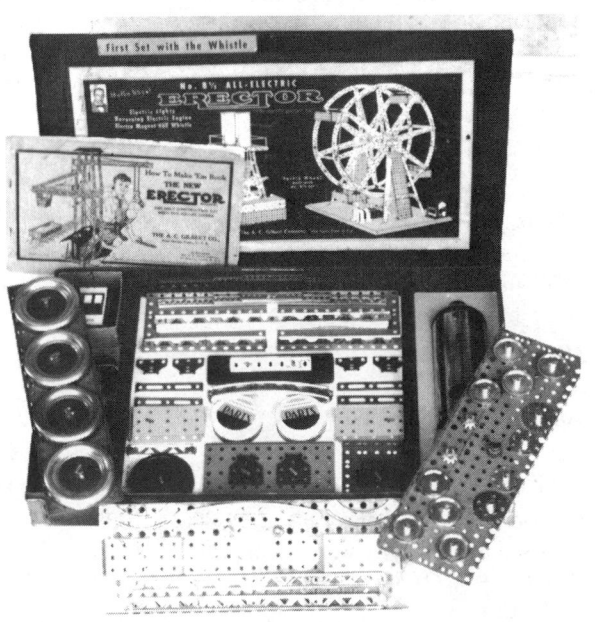

No. 8-1/2 Erector, 1939. "Ferris Wheel" set.

1939

Whistle for A-49 intro. ....pnsd

1940

Parachute Jump intro. to 9-1/2 ....pnsd

1941

Little change. Royal Blue #556 in 10-1/2

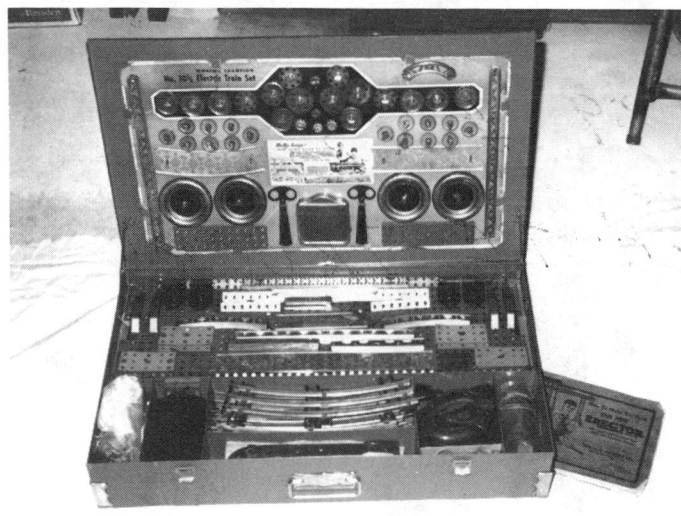

No. 10-1/2 Erector, 1941, "Electric Train" set.

1942

Sets before WW II conversion
had black rim wheels, black boiler. .....pnsd

1945-46

A confusing era. ACG brought out even numbered sets from 1933,
1934 era in a wild array of boxes.
Prices could be higher because of rarity.

*No. 7-1/2 Erector, 1948, "Engineer's" set,
with aluminum parts.*

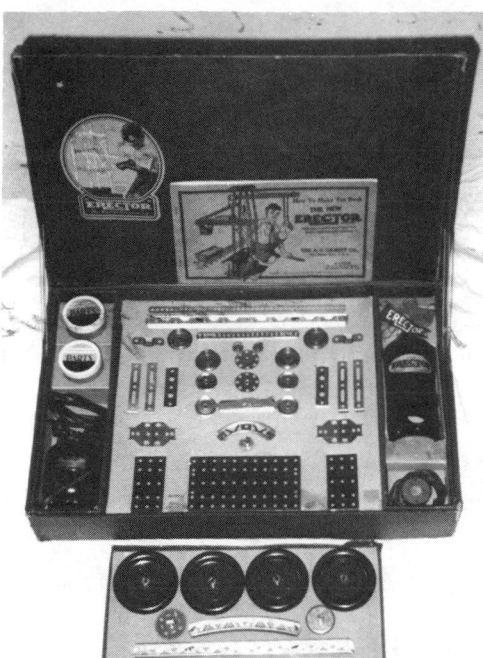

*No. 7
Erector,
1946,
"Sensational
7," a most
unusual
immediate
postwar set.*

1947-48

Except for old stock, brass metal corners
gone; half sizes back; pnsd. Late 1948
10-1/2 becomes the 12-1/2, remote
control/robot set w/ P55 motor,
A-48 and A-49 500   900   1500

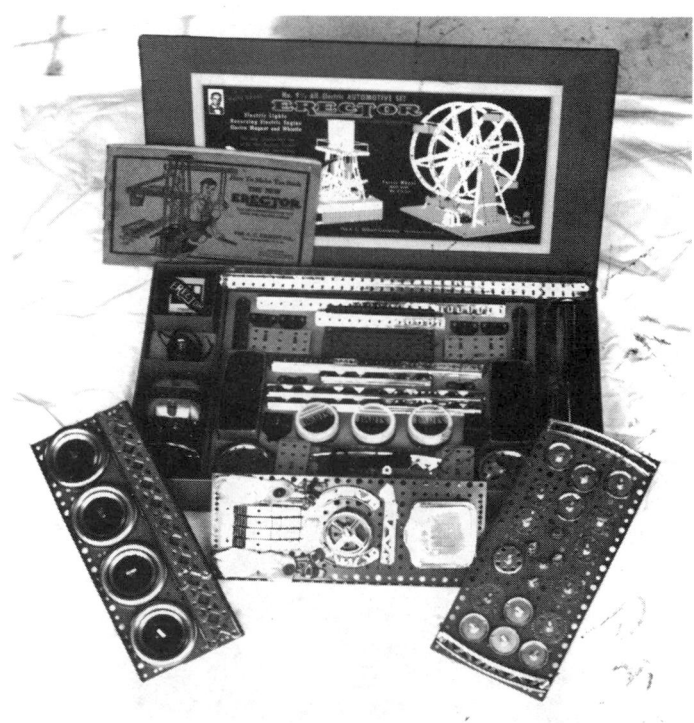

No. 9-1/2 Erector, 1948, "Automotive" set.

	C6	C8	C10

1949 Late
10-1/2 intro in 9-1/2 box
w/ Merry-Go-Round capability 200   500   800

The era 1946 through 1952 is confusing. Many sets had aluminum parts, covers, and/or boxes due to the devastating effects of a long steel strike and the Korean War. Generally sets with aluminum are not as valuable, unless a rare collector wants one of everything ever made. Aluminum work hardens and splits, a metallurgical weakness. The 12-1/2 Set disappeared in 1951 and reappeared again in 1956 as the "Master Builder" with a clamshell bucket, no P55 motor, pnsd.

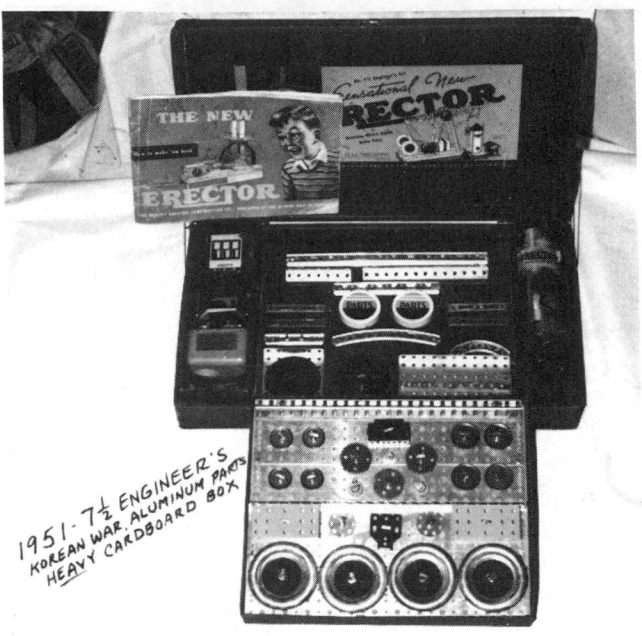

No. 7-1/2 Erector, 1951, "Engineer's" set.

No. 1-1/2 Erector, 1952 "Beginner's" set.

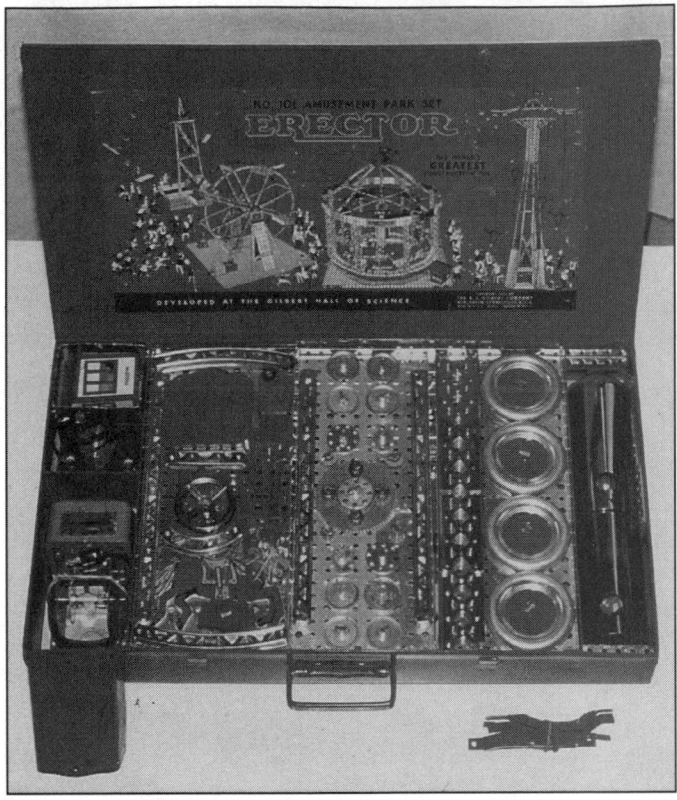

No. 10-1/2 Erector, 1951, "Amusement Park," with aluminum parts and A-47 motor. Courtesy W. S. Harrison III, Marion Designs.

	C6	C8	C10

1957
Two momentous changes occurred in 1957: metal boxes up through 8-1/2 had lithographed covers with pictures of the featured model, and the set numbers became a five-digit computer code. Unfortunately, the gauge of metal in the boxes was thinned out and these do not survive as well. The small plastic DC-3 motor of inadequate power was also a 1957 creation.

	C6	C8	C10
Erector 5-1/2 "Motorized" (DC-3) (10041) 40	75	125
Erector 6-1/2 "Electric Engine" (10051) 55	85	130
Erector 7-1/2 "Engineer's" (10061) 70	110	190
Erector 8-1/2 "All Electric" Ferris Wheel (10071) 160	275	425
Erector 10-1/2 "Amusement Park" (10080) 130	285	500
12-1/2 "Master Builder" (10091) 300	600	1000

1958
Saw the introduction of the famous "musical parts." Very fragile, hence very valuable. They are scarce! The record alone brings $100. In the same order as preceding ... note "Name" changes.

10041 "Power Model" (same as 5-1/2)
1052 "Rocket Launcher" (same as 6-1/2, additional premium of $30)
1062 "Steam Engine"

	C6	C8	C10
10072 "Musical Ferris Wheel"... 150 w/ music	225	400
10082 "Amusement Park" .... 250 w/ music	475	750
10092 "Master Builder" .... 650 w/ music	850	1300

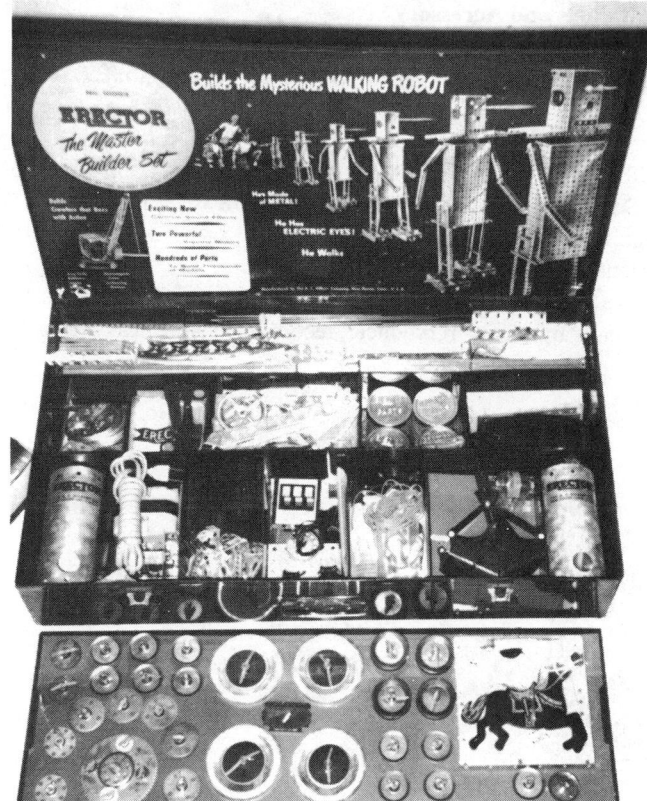

No. 12-1/2 Erector, 1958, "Master Builder" with musical parts.

1959

Saw only name changes, Rocket Launcher with 50th Anniversary label $30 premium.

	C6	C8	C10
10042 "Automatic Radar Scope" (same as 10041) ....pnsd			
10053 "Rocket Launcher" (same as 10051) $30 premium is gold label intact.			
10063 "Automatic Conveyor" (same as 10062) premium $20 if two belts present.			
10073 "Musical Ferris Wheel" (same as 10072) $20 premium if two belts present, music a must for 10072 price to apply.			
10083 "Amusement Park" (same as 10082) $20 premium if two belts present, music a must for 10082 price to apply.			
10093 "Master Builder" (same as 10092) $20 premium if two belts present, music a must for 10092 price to apply.			

1960

Musical parts were dropped and styrofoam packing introduced. A.P. & M.B. used metal boxes made by joining two smaller boxes. Sets retained earlier prices due to scarcity. Production and sales fell sharply in 1960.

10042 "Automatic Radar Scope" ....pnsd
10053 "Rocket Launcher" ....pnsd
10063 "Automatic Conveyor" ....pnsd

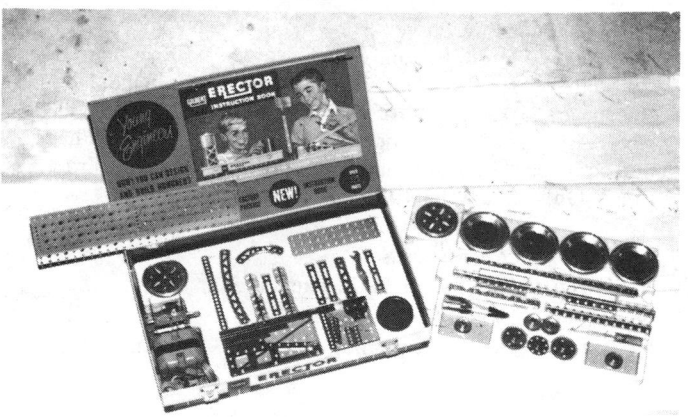

No. 10053 Erector, 1960, "Rocket Launcher."

	C6	C8	C10
10074 "Ferris Wheel"	100	150	300
10084 "Amusement Park" (same as 1959 10083) double box ...... pnsd			
10094 "Master Builder" (same as 1959 10093) double box ...... pnsd			

1961

No real changes, no name change, no number changes, pnsd.

1962

Saw the demise of the "classic" Erector set with trussed girders. In the order as in 1959:

10181 "Action Helicopter" (same as 10042) .... pnsd
10201 "Rocket Launcher" (same as 10053) .... pnsd
10211 "Cape Canaveral" (same as 10063) .... pnsd
10221 "Lunar Drilling Rig" (same as 10074) .... pnsd
10231 "Astronaut" (same as 10084) double box .... pnsd
10094 "Master Builder", double box .... pnsd

In 1962 the Gilbert Company was in receivership and production and sales continued to drop. Tooling was worn out, with little money to replace it. The system was redesigned, eliminating the truss configuration. This easily cut the cost of new tooling in half, as any tool engineer can tell you. Thus was born Type III Erector, a bit flimsier and not as true to life but still challenging to the young mind. At present, sets from this era are not much in demand compared to the classic sets of Type I and II. This could change as more collectors dry up the supply. We will deal only with the three largest sets of 1963, 1964, and 1965. Most of the smaller sets were presented in corrugated boxes, tubes, etc.: containers not given to survival.

Type III: 1963

	C6	C8	C10
10127 "Lunar Vehicle Set"	50	90	150
10128 "Planetary Probe Set"	80	150	200
10129 "Master Power Set"	100	225	300

These sets were in metal boxes with a sliding plastic cover. An overcover of cardboard was included with colorful scenes of the models in action on the moon or somewhere in space. The C10 prices include these covers, which did not survive well. If really nice, add 20% to C10 numbers. All three sizes had foam inserts to hold the parts. These are impossible to duplicate. The next two years, 1964 and 1965, saw a continuation of these three sets. After 1965 the company was sold to Gabriel Industries, hence Type 3 sets are many times referred to as Gabriel Era trash. Only time will tell!

Vital Parts and Accessory Sets   C10

	C10
P-58 Motor, 6-12 volt AC/DC, "basket case"	10
P-56G Motor, 115 volt AC, running	80
A-52 Motor, 115 volt AC, running	65

Vital Parts and Accessory Sets   C10

	C10
P-51 Motor and Gearbox, 115 volt AC, running	90
A-48 Mechanical Motor w/ Key, check for spring slip	35
A-49 Motor and Gearbox, 115 volt AC, running, EXC	40
P-55 Motor and remote control, 12 volt AC/DC, runs	125
P-58 Motor, "Joe Long" rebuild	50
1E Square Girder Kit, 20-"C," 8-"B," 14-7/8" sc & nt	60
Illumination Kit	150
Whistle Kit, 7-15 volt AC	100
Smoke and Choo-Choo Kit, 7-15 volt AC	125
Musical Parts-comp. reproducer, record, mechanism	200

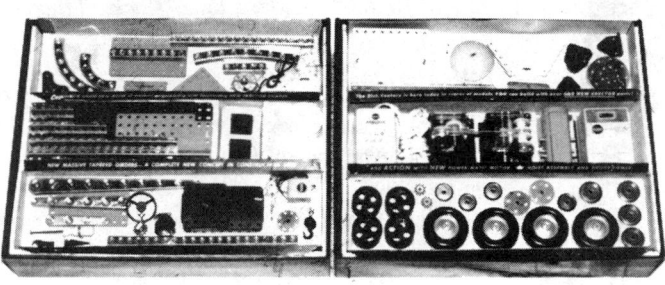

*No.10129
Erector, 1963,
"Master Power"
set (Type III).*

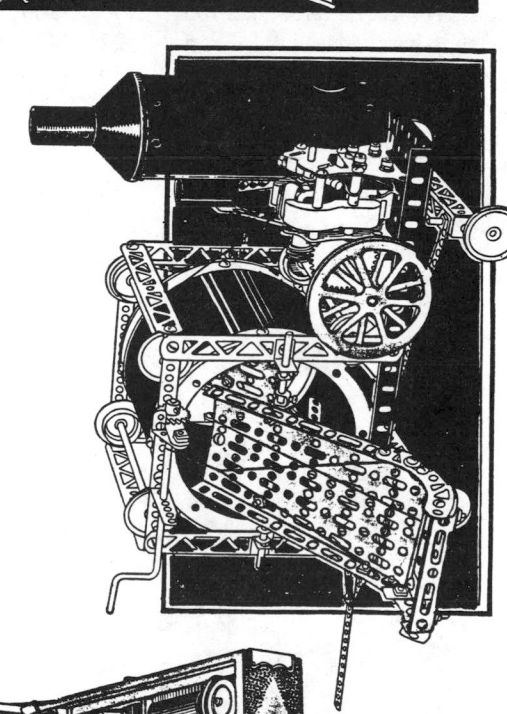

The Climax of Erector Glory

IT'S the giant DeLuxe No. 10 Erector, the set that combines all Erector thrills in one big red brass-bound chest. Think of it, boy! All the trail blazing Railroad Models! The sand-digging steam shovels and a hundred other big industrial machines. All the great ships of the sky, dirigible and airplanes. Automobiles and other fast moving vehicles of every kind and shape. The giant carnival ferris wheel and the circus Merry-Go-Round, which revolve just like the ponderous big giants of fun and pleasure. You can build everything you can think of with this Master set. It's the most gigantic, magnificent chest of sport ever offered to boys the world over. And it's so sturdy and rugged that you can hand it down to your own children when you grow up—the most treasured possession of two generations. It weighs 150 *pounds* in all and contains over 2500 engineering parts. Builds over 500 models. With the master 312-page and 72-page Locomotive "How to make 'em," books this enormous Erector set costs $69.75.

A flier for the Erector Climax set, 1931. The set weighed an extraordinary 150 pounds.

MISCELLANEOUS

The average mint price in this category was $649.33 in the last edition. In this edition it is $674.52, an increase of 4%.

	C6	C8	C10
"Acrobatic Monkey" John Henry Prod., 1950s, push toy, 10" long	60	90	120
Air Raid Warden Junior Kit, felt hat, arm band, gas mask, whistle, window sign, forms and street plan sheets, stethoscope, book of instructions, WWII era, rare	100	150	200
All-Nu Horse, not made to have rider	15	22	30
Alligator, cast iron, 9"	20	30	40
Alligator, cast iron, two-part, 9" long	30	45	60
American Badge ring, c. 1930s or 1940s, heavy metal, may have been premium	20	30	40
American Logs, similar to Lincoln Logs, c. WWII, price includes box, instructions	62	93	125

	C6	C8	C10
American Logs, 1950s	10	15	20
American Metal Toys AA Gun	27	41	55
American Metal Toys Animals, lead alloy, average price each	6	9	12
American Metal Toys Pillbox	41	63	82

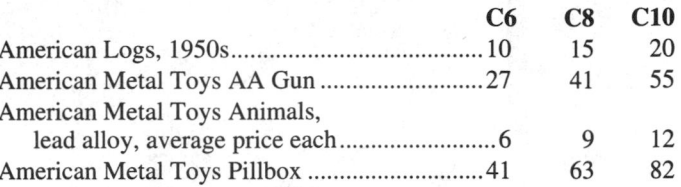

AMERICAN METAL TOYS Animals.

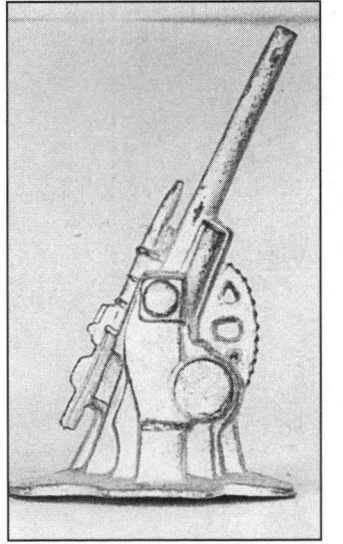

AMERICAN METAL TOYS AA Gun.

AMERICAN METAL TOYS Pillbox.

AMERICAN METAL TOYS Animals.

	C6	C8	C10
American Toy Co. Dancing Black Women, two	600	900	1200
Animate Toy Co. "Baby Haymaker," 1916, tin push toy playset	125	188	250
"Anti-Aircraft Rapid-Fire Machine Gun," cast iron, on wheels	275	363	550
Arcade Bathroom Set, 3-piece, cast-iron tub, stool, sink	425	638	850
Arcade cast-iron highway sign, "Curve"	42	63	85

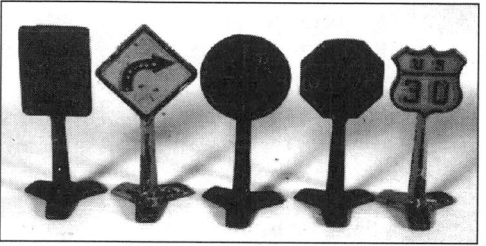

ARCADE Cast-Iron Highway Signs. Courtesy Lloyd W. Ralston Auctions.

Arcade cast-iron highway sign, "Men Working Ahead"	42	63	85

ARCADE signs and tools. "Men Working Ahead," "Road Closed," "Slow." Courtesy Continental Hobby House.

Arcade cast-iron highway sign, "Road Closed"	42	63	85
Arcade Dining Room Table, 2 chairs	245	368	490
Arcade "Don't Park Here" cast-iron sign, 4-1/2" high	42	63	85
Arcade "Don't Park Here" sign, painted cast iron, 1920, 5" tall	42	63	85

ARCADE "Don't Park Here" sign, 1920, 5" high. Courtesy Lloyd W. Ralston Auctions.

Arcade "Engine Co. No. 99" Firehouse, 12-1/2" long	450	675	900
Arcade Garage	725	1090	1450
Arcade Gas Pump, 6"	255	380	510

ARCADE Garage. Photo by Virginia Caputo. Courtesy James S. Maxwell/ Virginia Caputo.

	C6	C8	C10
Arcade Grand Piano and Bench, 3"	400	600	800
Arcade Kitchen Set, range, dinette, sink, refrigerator	500	750	1000
Arcade Pump and Tub	188	290	375
Arcade Refrigerator	212	318	425

ARCADE Pump and Tub. Courtesy Mapes Auctioneers.

"Arcade Service" gas station, No. 900, 1941	400	600	800
Arcade "Stop" sign, cast iron	42	63	85
Arcade "U.S. 30," highway sign	42	63	85
Arcade tools, cast iron, No. 779N, small, nickel finish, screwdriver, hammer, monkey wrench, pipe wrench, crescent wrench and S wrench, came in set of 6, 1938, price per each	7	11	15

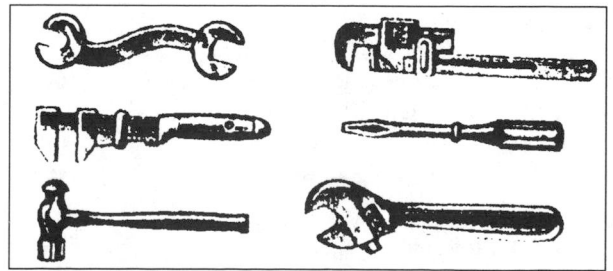

ARCADE Tools.

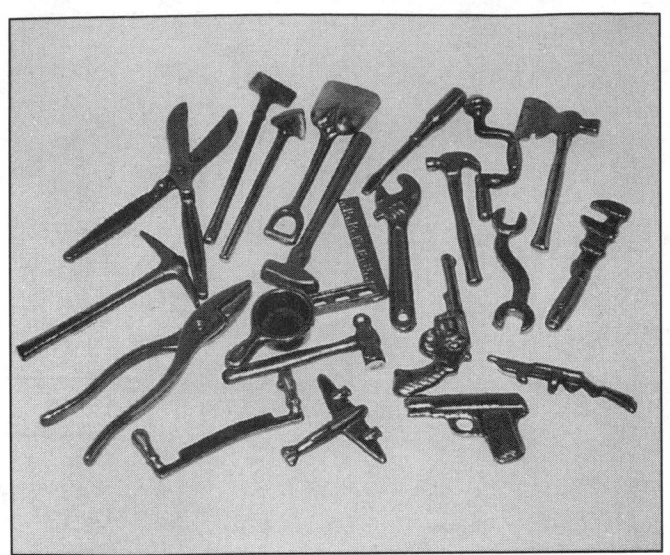

ARCADE small tools, weapons, etc. The Hedge Trimmers are said to be rare, worth $25 in mint. Photo by Stan Alekna.

	C6	C8	C10
Arcade Weapons, cast iron No. 778N, small, nickel finish, cutlass, pistol, automatic, aerial bomb, tommy gun, airplane, came in set of 6, 1938, price per each	5	8	10

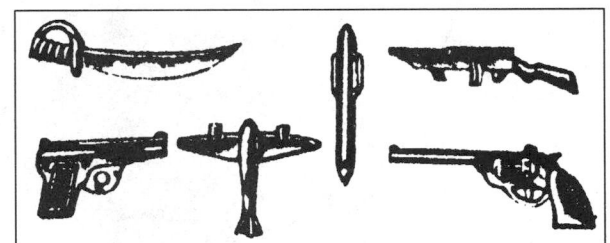

ARCADE Weapons.

	C6	C8	C10
Arcade Windmill, cast iron, 15-1/4" high	100	150	200
Arkitoy Play Lumber by G.B. Lewis Co., 1926, No. 3	20	30	40
Artascope, optical toy, c. 1920, pressed steel, spin base with multicolors, see-thru mirrors	60	90	120

	C6	C8	C10
Auburn Rubber Calf, c. 1937	6	9	12
Auburn Rubber Chicken, c. 1937	4	6	8
Auburn Rubber Collie, c. 1937	7	11	15
Auburn Rubber Colt, c. 1937	5	8	10
Auburn Rubber Cow, c. 1937	7	11	15
Auburn Rubber Duck, c. 1937	4	6	8
Auburn Rubber Farm Set, 40-plus pieces, post WWII	70	105	140
Auburn Rubber Fence Section, c. 1937	4	6	8
Auburn Rubber Firehouse Set No. 523	100	150	200
Auburn Rubber Horse, c. 1937	6	9	12
Auburn Rubber Pig, c. 1937	4	6	8
Auburn Rubber Piglet, c. 1937	4	6	8
Auburn Rubber Tomahawk	8	12	17
Automatic Toy Co., "Rocket Space Ship No. 305," 1930s, tin, friction, sparks, 8-1/2" long	80	120	160
Automatic Toy Co., "Space Rocket Ship No. 306," 1930s, tin, friction, sparks, siren, 8-1/2" long	150	225	300
Automaton Dancer, 1800s, clockwork, I & W Co., black dancer	900	1500	2200
B & R Co., "Bossy the Moo Cow," 1930s, 11" long	80	120	160
Baby Buggy, cast iron, 4-1/2" high	48	72	95
Baby Carriage, Kilgore, 4-7/8" high	250	375	500
Baby Carriage, tin, w/ folding cloth top, 7-3/4" long	40	60	80
Badge, "Dick Steel News Service"	20	30	40
Badge, G-Man, lead	5	7	10
Badge, Jet Ranger	6	9	12
Badge, Junior Counter Spy Agent w/ picture, No. 161731	10	15	20
Badge, "Junior Detective," heavy six-pointed star badge w/ copper inset, nickel badge	17	26	35
Badge, Junior G-Man, c. late 1930s, brass, shield-shaped, eagle on top	10	15	20
Badge, Junior Secret Agent, metal	12	18	24
Badge, "The Purple Mask" detective badge	10	15	20
Badge, "Sheriff," six-pointed star, black oval insert and word "Oklahoma," nickeled metal	18	27	36
Baggage Cart, cast iron, 5" high	36	54	72

BALDWIN

Baldwin was located in Brooklyn, New York, at 361 Stagg Street. Its material was pressed steel.

	C6	C8	C10
Baldwin Chicken on nest, marbles for eggs, 5" long	27	41	55
Baldwin Kingpin, spring action bowling	105	160	210
Baldwin "Little Red Hen," 1930s, crank action, 5" long	40	60	80

End Baldwin

	C6	C8	C10
Barbed Wire (Army), 8" long, for toy soldiers	7	11	14
Barbed Wire, mesh, for toy soldiers	12	18	25
Barclay Searchlight, swivels on base, 3"	20	30	40

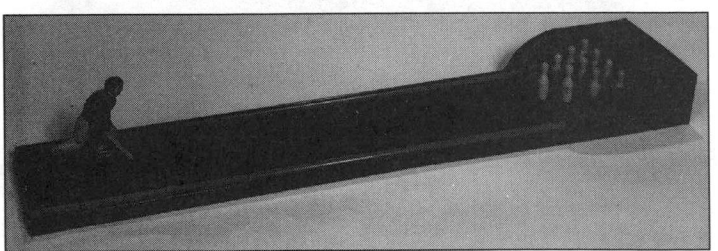

BALDWIN Kingpin, spring action. Courtesy Scott Smiles. Photo by Mike Adams.

BARCLAY. Top, left to right: 209, 210, 213, 214. Bottom: 215, 217, 218, 219, 220, 216?.

	C6	C8	C10
Barclay No. 209 Work Horse	7	10	13
Barclay No. 210 Horse	5	8	10
Barclay No. 211 Grazing Horse	5	8	10
Barclay No. 212 Standing Cow	5	8	10
Barclay No. 213 Grazing Cow	6	8	11
Barclay No. 214 Lying Cow	6	9	12
Barclay No. 215 Bull	5	8	10
Barclay No. 216? Grazing Sheep	5	8	10
Barclay No. 217 Standing Sheep	5	8	10
Barclay No. 218 Resting Sheep	6	9	12
Barclay No. 219 Ram	5	8	10
Barclay No. 220 Pig	5	8	10
Barclay Mess Table, two benches (wooden)	20	30	40
Beaut Mfg. Co., Wagon No. 50	6	9	12

BEAUT MFG. CO. Wagon. Courtesy George Buhler. Photo by Bill Kaufman.

	C6	C8	C10
Bell Toy, Acrobats holding bells, Gong Bell Co. No. 54	310	465	620
Bell Toy, Alligator ridden by Black Boy, N.N. Hill, 1910, cast iron, 5-1/2" long	1000	1700	2300
Bell Toy, Alligator snapping at teasing boy, cast iron, 9-1/4" long	1500	2400	3500
Bell Toy, Althof Bergmann, tin, "Chime & Design Patd. May 19th 1874," 3 soldiers, one w/ flag, 2 w/ rifles	1600	2400	3200
Bell Toy, "Are You a Buffalo," Gong Bell Co.	800	1200	1600
Bell Toy, bear, iron, bounces in air	800	1100	1600
Bell Toy, bear on tricycle, 4" long	150	225	300

Bell Toy, Alligator ridden by black boy. Courtesy Ed Hyers Antique Toys.

Bell Toy, "Are You a Buffalo." Courtesy James S. Maxwell/Virginia Caputo. Photo by Virginia Caputo.

	C6	C8	C10
Bell Toy, Billy Goat, Gong Bell Co., No. 51, cast iron, goat mechanically butts bell, 1900, 7-1/2" long	750	1125	1500
Bell Toy, bird and bell, tin and iron, 6" long	600	900	1200
Bell Toy, Boy and Goat, Althof Bergmann, tin, 9" long	600	900	1200
Bell Toy, Boy Scouts, iron, rest pressed steel, heart-shaped tin wheels, 13-1/2" long	750	1125	1500

Bell Toy, Billy Goat, Gong Bell Co. No. 51. Courtesy Lloyd W. Ralston Auctions.

	C6	C8	C10
Bell Toy, Boys eating Bananas, cast iron	700	1050	1400
Bell Toy, Camel with Rider, tin, Althof Bergmann, c. 1874, 9" long	1200	2000	2800
Bell Toy, Cat and Dog, Gong Bell Co.	2000	3200	4500

Bell Toy, Cat and Dog, Gong Bell Co.. Courtesy James S. Maxwell/Virginia Caputo. Photo by Virginia Caputo.

	C6	C8	C10
Bell Toy, Cinderella Chariot, 9-1/4" long	425	638	850
Bell Toy, Clown, Gong Bell Co., 5-3/4" long	262	393	525
Bell Toy, Clown bell-ringers riding back to back on a mule	1000	1500	2000
Bell Toy, Clown and Black man on see-saw, c. 1905, 6 color, Watrous, cast iron, 6-1/2" long	600	900	1200

Bell Toy, Clown and Pig, 1900. Courtesy Lloyd W. Ralston Auctions.

Bell Toy, Clown and Pig, Gong Bell Co. Courtesy Ed Hyers Antique.

	C6	C8	C10
Bell Toy, Clown and Pig, 1900	325	488	650
Bell Toy, Comic Characters, two, pressed steel and iron, 3 bells, pierced heart wheels	700	1125	1400
Bell Toy, "Daisy," Gong Bell Co., 9" long	600	1000	1400

Bell Toy, "Daisy." Courtesy Sotheby's New York.

	C6	C8	C10
Bell Toy, Darky Fishing, Stevens, 8" long	440	660	880
Bell Toy, "Ding Dong Bell, Pussy's Not In The Well," cast iron, c. 1880, Gong Bell Co., 9-1/2" long	600	925	1235

Bell Toy, "Ding Dong Bell, Pussy's Not In The Well." Courtesy Sotheby's New York.

	C6	C8	C10
Bell Toy, Dog on Platform	400	600	800
Bell Toy, Dog on Platform (Fallows)	400	650	900
Bell Toy, "Eagle," c. 1906, Gong Bell Co., cast iron, 5-1/4" long	550	850	1200
Bell Toy, Elephant & Rider in Howdah, driver on elephant's head, 4-1/2" long, cast iron	700	1100	1500
Bell Toy, Elephant on Platform, Fallows, 6-3/4" long	425	638	850
Bell Toy, Elephant w/ bell in trunk, N.N. Hill, c. 1905	700	1050	1400
Bell Toy, "Eskimo & Bear," pressed steel body, iron figures	750	1125	1500
Bell Toy, Francis, Field & Francis, Clown rotates, hits bell, 6" long	300	450	600

Bell Toy, Elephant on Platform, Fallows, 6-3/4" long. Courtesy Wilkinson Collection, Detroit Antique Toy Museum.

Bell Toy, Elephant on Platform, Fallows. Courtesy Christie's East.

Bell Toy, "Evening News Baby Quieter," Stevens. Courtesy Christie's East.

Bell Toy, Francis, Field & Francis. Clown rotates. Courtesy Sotheby's New York.

	C6	C8	C10
Bell Toy, Goat, tin, c. 1890, small woman at left leg of goat, either Althof Bergmann or Ives, 7-1/2" high	500	750	1000
Bell Toy, Goats, two, butting, Gong Bell Co.	1200	2000	3000

	C6	C8	C10
Bell Toy, Goat, Fallows, 1880, painted tin, 14" long x 14" tall	1100	1650	2200
Bell Toy, Goat, Lamb and Girl on platform, George Brown, tin, early, 11" long	550	850	1200

Bell Toy, Goat, tin, c. 1890. Photo courtesy PB Eighty-Four.

Bell Toy, Goat, Fallows. Courtesy Lloyd W. Ralston Auctions.

	C6	C8	C10
Bell Toy, "Hello Hello Telephone Chimes" w/ monkey, Gong Bell Co.	2000	3000	4000
Bell Toy, Horse, Fallows	450	675	900
Bell Toy, Horse, tin, 9-1/4" long	287	430	575
Bell Toy, Horse on Rocker	375	562	750
Bell Toy, Horse, tin, pulling heart-shaped wheel	200	300	400
Bell Toy, Ives, white horse pulling heart-shaped wheels, c. 1896, 9-1/2" long	1000	1500	2000

Bell Toy, "Hello, Hello Telephone Chimes." Courtesy James S. Maxwell/Virginia Caputo. Photo by Virginia Caputo.

Bell Toy Horse, Fallows, tin. Courtesy Lloyd W. Ralston Auctions.

Bell Toy, Hunter and Rabbit. N.N. Hill. Courtesy Lloyd W. Ralston Auctions.

	C6	C8	C10
Bell Toy, Jack and Jill on seesaw, cast iron and tin, Watrous, 7-1/2" long	440	660	880
Bell Toy, Jockey on Horse, early, 7-1/2" long	200	300	400
Bell Toy, Jonah & Whale, Hill, 5" long	800	1400	2000

	C6	C8	C10
Bell Toy, Horse and Rider, heart-shaped wheels, tin, 9" long	750	1125	1500
Bell Toy, Hunter and Rabbit, N.N. Hill, 1900, cast-iron rabbit pops out	750	1125	1500

Bell Toy, Jonah & Whale, Hill. Courtesy James S. Maxwell/Virginia Caputo. Photo by Virginia Caputo.

Bell Toy, Jack and Jill on seesaw, Watrous. Courtesy Ed Hyers Antique.

	C6	C8	C10
Bell Toy, "Landing of Columbus," 7" long	492	740	985
Bell Toy, Liberty Bell Centennial, Gong Bell Co., 8" long	800	1200	1600
Bell Toy, "Mary and Her Little Lamb," Gong Bell Co., 8" long	600	900	1250

Bell Toy, "Landing of Columbus." Courtesy Sotheby's New York.

Bell Toy, Liberty Bell Centennial. Courtesy Sotheby's New York.

Bell Toy, Monkey and Coconut, N. N. Hill. Courtesy Ed Hyers Antique.

Bell Toy, Monkey and Horse, Gong Bell Co. Courtesy James S. Maxwell/Virginia Caputo. Photo by Virginia Caputo.

	C6	C8	C10
Bell Toy, Monkey and Coconut, N.N. Hill, "Monkey Mobile," 6" long	350	525	700
Bell Toy, "Monkey and Dog," heart wheels, cast iron and tin, 7" long	500	750	1000
Bell Toy, Monkey and Horse, Gong Bell Co., cast iron and tin, "No. 23"	1500	2250	3000
Bell Toy, Monkey in wheeled chariot (Gong Bell Co.?)	2000	3000	4000
Bell Toy, Monkey on a Log, cast iron, Gong Bell Co. Mfg. Co., c. 1900	750	1125	1500
Bell Toy, "Monkey on a Velocipede," cast iron, 8" high	1500	2400	3800
Bell Toy, Monkey riding Elephant, Fallows, tin, clockwork, 10" long	1400	2100	2800
Bell Toy, Mule kicks bell, No. 42	1400	2300	3200
Bell Toy, Nursery rhymes on drums, one horse	600	900	1200

	C6	C8	C10
Bell Toy, "Oriental Clown & Poodle," No. 44, painted cast iron, 1900, cloth in hoop, poodle jumps through hoop and back, 13" long	1250	1875	2500
Bell Toy, "Pig with Clown Rider," Gong Bell Co., 6" long	418	625	835
Bell Toy, "Poodle Dog Bell Ringer" with Clown, Gong Bell Co.	1200	2800	4200
Bell Toy, Rough Rider, Watrous, early, 6-1/2" long	123	185	245
Bell Toy, "Saw the Watermelon," Gong Bell Co., 8-1/2" long	1100	1700	2800
Bell Toy, Soldier & Sailor	550	825	1100
Bell Toy, Steeplechase, 2 jockeys on horses, Hubley	600	900	1200

Miscellaneous • 709

Bell Toy, Monkey in Wheeled Chariot. Courtesy James S. Maxwell/Virginia Caputo. Photo by Virginia Caputo.

Bell Toy, Monkey Riding Elephant, Fallows.

	C6	C8	C10
Bell Toy, Stevens, "Evening News Baby Quieter," 1890s, cast iron, man reading paper to baby, 8" long	1100	1700	2450
Bell Toy, "Teddy Roosevelt"	325	490	650
Bell Toy, "Tramp," cast iron, Gong Bell Co., 6" long	438	655	875
Bell Toy, Trick Elephant, Gong Bell Co., 7-3/4" long	800	1200	1600

Bell Toy, "Oriental Clown and Poodle." Courtesy Lloyd W. Ralston Auctions.

Bell Toys. Top: "Saw the Watermelon." Bottom, left to right: Pig with Clown Rider; Monkey on a Velocipede. Courtesy Christie's East.

Bell Toy, "Poodle Dog Bell Ringer" with clown. Courtesy James S. Maxwell/Virginia Caputo. Photo by Virginia Caputo.

Bell Toys. Top, left to right: "Tramp," cast-iron, Gong Bell Co.; Acrobats holding bells, Gong Bell Co. Bottom, left to right: "Mary and Her Little Lamb," Gong Bell Co.; "Trick Pony," Gong Bell Co. Courtesy Christie's East.

Bell Toy, Trick Pony, Gong Bell Co., 1893. Photo courtesy PB Eighty-Four.

	C6	C8	C10
Bell Toy, Trick Pony, Gong Bell Co., 1893, cast iron "39," 8" long 600	1000	1350
Bell Toy, Uncle Sam and The Don, Gong Bell Co. 2250	3375	4500
Bell Toy, Victory in a shell-form Chariot, cast iron, mounted with bell and eagle 1500	2250	3000
Bell Toy, Watermelon, N.N. Hill Brass Co., c. 1905, 8-1/2" long..................600	900	1200
Bell Toy, Wild Mule Jack, cast iron 750	1125	1500
Bell Toy, "Young America," cast iron, Gong Bell Co., c. 1880, 6" long 450	675	900
Big Boy (Restaurants) vinyl doll........................27	41	55
Bill Ding Clowns, boxed.....................................50	75	100

Bell Toy, Trick Elephant, Gong Bell Co. Courtesy James S. Maxwell/Virginia Caputo. Photo by Virginia Caputo.

Bell Toy, Uncle Sam and the Don. Uncle Sam's bell is missing in photo. Courtesy James S. Maxwell/Virginia Caputo. Photo by Virginia Caputo.

	C6	C8	C10
Bilt-E-Z Skyscraper Building Blocks, Scott Mfg., Chicago, c. 1925 45	68	90
Bliss "Battle of the Toy Brigades," fort & soldiers, paper litho on wood, c. 1880....600	1000	1400
Bliss Brooklyn Bridge, 1880s, paper litho and stained wood, mechanical, 4' long x 11" tall 600	900	1200

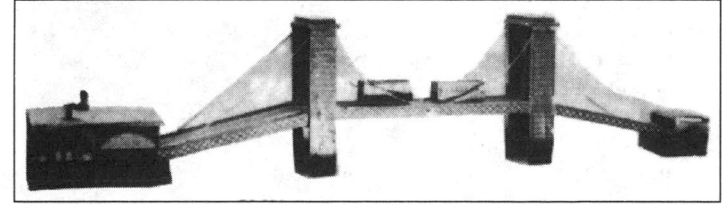

BLISS Brooklyn Bridge. Courtesy Lloyd W. Ralston Auctions.

BLISS Church building blocks, c. 1900. Courtesy Wilkinson Collection, Detroit Antique Toy Museum.

	C6	C8	C10
Bliss Church building blocks, c. 1900, litho on wood, 8-3/4" high 500		750	1000
Blocks, Auburn flexible building blocks, 1960s .. 7		10	14
Blocks, Auburn Rubber building bricks, 1940s 17		25	34
Blocks, Bill-Ding Clown, 1950s, 24 blocks 32		48	65
Blocks, The Brownie, by McLoughlin Bros., 1891, 20 litho blocks 400		600	800
Blocks, Chautauqua Architectural Building No. 510, c. 1920s 75		112	150
Blocks, Crandall's "Building Blocks" No. 3, pat. 1867 250		375	500
Blocks, Elgo American Plastic Bricks No. 705 17		26	35

	C6	C8	C10
Blocks, Elgo American Plastic Bricks No. 715 22		33	45
Blocks, Elgo American Plastic Bricks No. 725 32		48	65
Blocks, Elgo American Plastic Bricks No. 735 62		93	125
Blocks, Halsam American Blocks, wood, 1939, No. 60 27		41	55
Blocks, Halsam American Plastic Bricks No. 72 30		45	60
Blocks, Halsam Block Wagon Pull Toy 22		33	45
Blocks, Halsam Logs, Senior Size -3/4", No. 815 17		26	35
Blocks, Hill's Alphabet Blocks, c. 1870s, miniset 37		56	75
Blocks, Leecraft Circus Blocks, 12 wooden blocks, painted w/ lion, tiger, letters and numbers, contained in wooden pull-toy cage, 1930s 35		52	70
Blocks, Lincoln Bricks by Lincoln Logs 45		68	90
Blocks, Lincoln Logs, set No. 1A, John Wright, pat. 1920, complete 10		15	20
Blocks, Lincoln Logs, set 1C, post WWII 40		60	80
Blocks, Lincoln Logs, set 2-L 45		68	90
Blocks, Lincoln Logs, set 4 CF, 1950s, w/ figures 150		225	300
Blocks, Lincoln Logs, set No. 29, early 60		90	120
Blocks, Lincoln Logs, 1923 10		15	20
Blocks, Lincoln Logs, 1930 17		26	35
Blocks, Lincoln Logs, 1947 17		26	35
Blocks, Lincoln Timbers, pre-WWII, with box, complete 30		45	60
Blocks, Milton Bradley, c. 1910, six nested 262		393	525
Blocks, "Mother Goose Living Picture Blocks," c. 1890 325		487	650
Blocks, Richter's Anchor Blocks No. 2-1/2 85		128	170
Blocks, Richter's Anchor Blocks No. 7 100		150	200
Blocks, Richter's Anchor Blocks No. 11A 175		262	350
Blocks, Richter's Anchor Blocks No. 12 100		150	200
Blocks, "Stabuilt Blocks," The Embossing Co., 1916, 20" x 12" 42		63	85

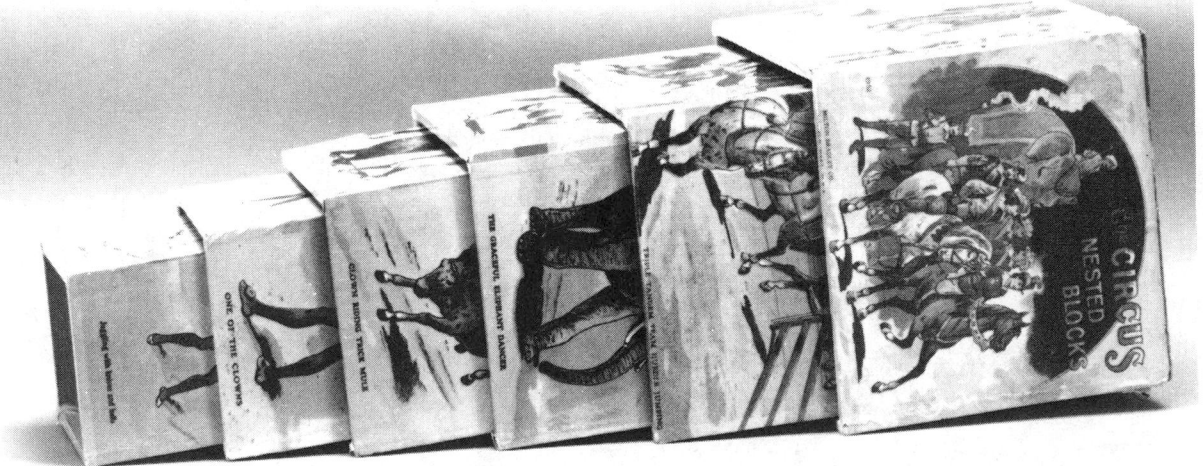

Blocks, Milton Bradley, c. 1910, six nested. Courtesy Christie's East.

Blocks, Richter's Anchor Blocks No. 7. Courtesy Continental Hobby House.

	C6	C8	C10
Blocks, "Union Building Blocks" No. 7, early 75	112	150
Blocks, set of 6 puzzle blocks depicting The Three Bears, Old Mother Hubbard, Little Bo-Peep, Puss in Boots, Jack the Giant Killer and Red Riding Hood, copyright 1892............35	52	70
Blocks, nested, 6, paper litho on cardboard, picturing children and animals, 1920, Cramer Publishing Co. 150	225	300
Blocks, 16, embossed, wooden, 1-3/4" square, red and blue, alphabet and pictures, 7-1/2" square box, Dutch scene on cover, The Embossing Company's Toy Blocks, USA, price includes box 20	30	40
Blocks, 64, wooden, 1-1/4" square, very colorful, letters and numbers on sides, box 6" square, price includes box.......22	33	45
Bobsled, cast iron, 2 riders, 5" long 135	200	270

Bones Player. Courtesy Lloyd W. Ralston Auctions.

	C6	C8	C10
Bones Player, Secor, 1880, cloth-dressed, cast iron, wood and tin figure with hair, painted pot metal head, clockwork mechanism in body.............1250	1875	2500
Boo Berry, vinyl squeeze toy 27	41	55
Boxers, Black, mechanical wind-up with Ives clockwork mechanism 1000	1500	2000
Boy climbing windmill, tin, weight driven, 1900s, 16" high 100	150	200
Boy on Sled friction toy, rear wheels have spokes, Dayton, 9" long ..262	393	525
Boy on Tricycle, boy celluloid, trike tin, wind-up 185	280	370
Boy on Velocipede, papier-mâché, cloth and cast iron, wind-up, Stevens & Brown, or Althorp & Bergmann, c. 1870-1880, 10-3/4" long 1200	2000	2625
Boy on Velocipede, same as above, black boy (rarest), auctioned in 1994 for $6820.00		
Boy Scout Five-In-One Mystery Hidden Compass...........30	45	60
Bradley's Interchangeable Combination Circus in wooden box w/ label, Pat. May 30, 1882, contains 35 3" x 5-1/4" interchangeable panels which make up a changeable 15-3/4" x 9" circus scene 400	600	800
Brownies, "Brownie Artillery," Brownies, cannon, etc., McLoughlin 650	1050	1500
Brownies, Brownie Glass Candy Container.....500	750	1000
Brownies Ten-Pin Set, early...........650	1100	1600
Buddy L Machine Gun, M101, fires caps 62	93	125
Buddy L Tool Chests, 1927-28, four different, per each, includes tools 125	188	250

Boy on Velocipede, Stevens & Brown. Courtesy Phillips New York.

Boy on Velocipede. Courtesy Sotheby's New York.

Buffalo Bill, 9" high, French? Photo by Jeanne Bertoia. Courtesy Bill Bertoia Auctions.

	C6	C8	C10
Buffalo Bill, 9" high, French?, hand-painted tin w/ lead rifle, articulated...350		525	700
Buffalo Toys "Mother Duck," 1930s wind-up (figure 8s), 9" long	60	90	120

BUFFALO TOYS "Mother Duck." Photo by Don Hultzman.

	C6	C8	C10
Bulldog, kid-covered wind-up, walks and turns head, German, rare, 7-1/2" long	200	300	400
Cackling Hen, cardboard, drum, w/ brown plaster chicken standing on top of drum, metal side handle activates cackling, dated 1936 (also Rooster), 2-1/4" x 3-1/2"	20	30	40
Campbell's Kid figure, vinyl	25	36	50
Cap'n Crunch figure	22	33	45
Candy Container, tin, shaped like cannon, candy comes out barrel when crank is turned, "West Bros. Co. Grapeville, PA.," 7-1/2" long	45	68	90
Candy Container, shaped like a desk phone, glass base with cast pewter mouthpiece and wooden receiver, paper labels "lines busy," 4-1/4" high	10	15	20

	C6	C8	C10
Cannon, "Admiral Dewey," cast iron, c. 1890s, 11" long	200	300	400
Cannon, Arcade Howitzer, c. 1941, 4" long	40	50	75
Cannon, Auburn Rubber (Aubrubr) Fieldpiece, 75mm, 7" long	17	25	34
Cannon, Auburn Rubber Howitzer, 155mm, 7" long	17	25	34
Cannon, Baldwin, "Coast Defense Gun," No. 830, wood & metal	39	60	78

Cannon, Baldwin, "Coast Defense Gun," No. 830. Photo by Bill Nutting.

	C6	C8	C10
Cannon, Baldwin, No. 890, wood and metal, 16" long	52	78	105
Cannon, Barclay, barrel elevated, 2-1/2" long	12	18	25
Cannon, Barclay, c. 1931 (may be first Barclay cannon, from 1924)	25	38	50
Cannon, Barclay Coast Guard Cannon No. 4, 5-man, 4-1/2" long	45	68	90
Cannon, Barclay, Howitzer, 4 wheels, loop hitch horizontal, 3" long	12	18	25

Cannon, Barclay, c. 1931 (may be Barclay's earliest, from 1924). Coutesy Ed Poole.

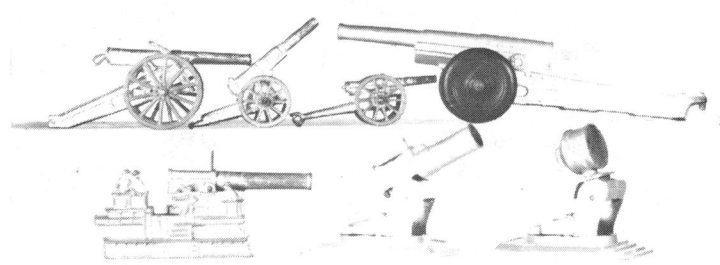

Cannons, Barclay. Top, left to right: Cannon, spring-firing, spoked wheels, 4" long; Cannon, barrel elevated; Cannon, spoked wheels, 3" long; Cannon, 7-3/4" long. Bottom: Coast Guard Cannon; Mortar, heavy; Searchlight. Photo by Ed Poole.

	C6	C8	C10
Cannon, Barclay, Howitzer, 4 wheels, loop hitch vertical, 3" long	12	18	25
Cannon, Barclay, Mortar, heavy, swivels on base, 3" long	20	30	40

	C6	C8	C10
Cannon, Barclay, post-WWII, very large wheels, 7-3/4" long	18	27	37
Cannon, Barclay, silver, black rubber wheels, 7-3/4" long	23	35	46
Cannon, Barclay, spoked wheels, 3" long	5	8	11
Cannon, Barclay, spring-firing, spoked wheels, 4" long	25	38	50

BIG BANG CANNONS

by Raymond V. Brandes

James Hunter Wily, a professor at Pennsylvania's Lehigh University, was beat out by Westinghouse by a matter of hours filing his patent for an electric refrigerator. Two years later, in 1912, the Gas Cannon Company was formed by Wily and W.S. Franklin, also a Lehigh professor. The cast-iron Gas Cannon was the first product from the tiny company. It followed closely a 1907 patent held by Franklin. In 1915 they introduced The Artillery Game, which had the outstanding feature of a cannon with a glass barrel.

About 1915 Franklin moved to the Massachusetts Institute of Technology and gave his interests in the cannon to Wily. Wily patented his own designs, which greatly simpli-

fied the toy, and trademarked Bangsite, the powered calcium carbide that was key to the toy's success. In 1916 he changed the name of the company to The Toy Cannon Works and began production of the classic breech-loading iron cannon. In 1924 the company was incorporated as The Conestoga Company, which survives today and produces six standard cannons and three reissue brass and bronze collector's editions. In the company's more than eighty- year history, no less than 25 different carbide toys have been documented, in addition to distinct variations that could add another 10 items for a very complete collection.

*Cannon still in production

Cannon, Big-Bang No. 6F, 9" long		30	60*
Cannon, Big-Bang No. 7F, 9-3/4" long	75	125	200
Cannon, Big-Bang No. 7D, 8" long	35	50	150
Cannon, Big-Bang No. 8F, 12-1/2" long	75	125	200
Cannon, Big-Bang No. 10W, 9" long	50	100	150
Cannon, Big-Bang No. 11D, 12-3/8" long	35	50	100
Cannon, Big-Bang No. 11F, 15" long	150	200	300
Cannon, Big-Bang No. 12F, 16-3/8" long	75	100	250
Cannon, Big-Bang No. 16F, 22-1/4" long	150	250	375
Cannon, Big-Bang No. 60mm, 9"		30	60*
Cannon, Big-Bang No. 10FC, 17-1/2" long		60	100*
Cannon, Big-Bang No. 15FC, 24"		50	125*
Cannon, Big-Bang No. 15AC, 16-1/4"	100	150	250
Cannon, Big-Bang No. 105mm, 17-1/2"		40	80*
Cannon, Big-Bang No. 155mm, 24"		50	100*
Cannon, Big-Bang Gas Cannon, 9"	75	250	500

Cannon, "Big-Bang," approx. 23" long. Photo by Bill Kaufman. Courtesy Good Old Days Store.

	C6	C8	C10
Cannon, Big-Bang The Artillery Game, 7" long	150	300	650

End Big Bang Cannons

	C6	C8	C10
Cannon, Big Parade, cast iron	25	38	50
Cannon, "Big Victory," tin litho, 12" long	115	172	230
Cannon, "Boy Ranger," fires marbles, cast iron, Kilgore, 17-1/2" long	180	270	360
Cannon, "Boy Scout Machine Gun," 19" with 8-1/4" wheels	250	375	500
Cannon, C.A.W. Novelty Co., with limber, 2-piece, lead, 1930s, 6"	No Price Found		
Cannon, cast iron, 5" long	45	68	90
Cannon, cast iron on wood base, 5-1/2" long	45	68	90
Cannon, cast iron, 6" long	50	75	100
Cannon, cast iron, 6-1/2" long	55	82	110
Cannon, cast iron, early, 7" long	67	100	135
Cannon, cast iron, pat. 1894, 7" long	75	112	150
Cannon, cast iron, unusual design, 8" long	75	112	150
Cannon, cast iron, pat. 1888, 9" long	90	135	180
Cannon, cast iron w/ turned barrel, "Hotchkiss," 9-1/2" long	100	150	200
Cannon, cast iron, 10" long, black	90	135	180
Cannon, cast iron, 11" long	90	135	180
Cannon, cast iron, Ives?, works on black powder, 12" long	100	150	200
Cannon, cast iron, 14" long	125	188	250
Cannon, cast iron, on 4-wheel platform, 14" long	75	112	150
Cannon, cast iron, 15-1/2" long	100	150	200
Cannon, cast iron, "Young America," "Rapid Fire Gun," 15-1/2" long	130	195	260
Cannon, Coast Defense Gun, litho tin, camouflaged, 5" long	44	66	88
Cannon, "Dainty" cast iron, on wood base, 10" long	175	263	350
Cannon, David Carlin mortar, c. WWI, cast iron, 15" long	60	90	120
Cannon, die-cast, old-type shoots, approx. 5-1/2" long	10	15	20
Cannon, "Disappearing Coast Defense Gun," Thomas & Skinner, Indianapolis, fires, 15" wood and steel	40	60	80
Cannon, field, World War I, cast iron, 15-3/4" long	32	48	65
Cannon, firecracker, cast iron, "Pat. Apr. 23, 1895," 4" long	40	60	80
Cannon, Grey Iron, 4-1/2" long	11	16	22
Cannon, Howitzer, c. 1930, double-barreled, wood-handled firing lever, 9" long	15	22	30
Cannon, howitzer type, die-cast, shoots, spring mechanism, pre-WWII, approx. 5" long	12	18	25
Cannon, Ideal Atomic Cannon	50	75	100
Cannon, Ives, muzzleloader, 1900, cast iron, 2 wheels	150	225	300
Cannon, Ives, cast iron, brass barrel	200	300	400
Cannon, Ives, red wheels, brass cannon, 7" long	150	225	300
Cannon, Jolly Roger, metal, 1950s	8	12	16
Cannon, Kansas Toy "23," lead, 3-1/4" long	10	15	20
Cannon, Kansas Toy "34," lead, 2-1/4" long	10	15	20
Cannon, Kenton, Firecracker type	40	60	80
Cannon, Kilgore, 2" cast-iron firecracker mortar, rubber cannon ball	105	158	210

	C6	C8	C10
Cannon, Kilgore, 4-1/2" cast-iron firecracker cannon, rubber cannon ball	30	45	60
Cannon, Kilgore, 17" long, cast iron	150	225	300
Cannon, Manoil 19 Metal Action Cannon, early version, "USA"	10	15	20
Cannon, Manoil 69, metal spoked wheels, early	9	14	19
Cannon, Manoil 69, metal spoked wheels, marked "M" left side, early 2nd version	9	13	18
Cannon, Manoil 69, solid wood wheels	9	13	18
Cannon, Manoil 69, solid wood wheels, variant	9	13	18
Cannon, Manoil, "Metal Action Cannon" No. 200, later version of 19, "Made is USA"	12	18	24

Cannon, Manoil, "Metal Action Cannon," No. 200, late version. Photo by Perry Eichor.

	C6	C8	C10
Cannon, Marx Anti-Aircraft Gun, No. 617	37	56	75

Cannon, Marx Anti-Aircraft Gun. Courtesy Joe and Sharon Freed.

	C6	C8	C10
Cannon, Marx "Atomic Long Range Cannon," 25" long	35	52	70
Cannon, Marx, "Big Shot Cannon"	35	52	70
Cannon, Marx Howitzer Cannon, plastic, c. 1960s, 12" long	37	56	75
Cannon, Marx, litho tin, shoots wooden balls, 21" long	100	150	200

Cannon, Marx Howitzer Cannon, plastic, c. 1960s. Photo by Bill Holt.

Cannon, Marx, litho tin, shoots wooden balls. Courtesy Charles D. Richards.

	C6	C8	C10
Cannon, Marx "Shell Shooting Long Tom Field Cannon," 1950s, plastic, 14" long	40	60	80
Cannon, Marx Twin Pom-Pom anti-aircraft cannon	50	75	100
Cannon, "Phoenix," brass barrel with touch hole, 8" long	100	150	200
Cannon, Premier, large thick barrel, large wheels, cast iron	20	30	40
Cannon, pressed steel base, 9-1/2"	15	22	30
Cannon, Ralstoy No. 23	8	12	16
Cannon, Ralstoy No. 34	8	12	16
Cannon, Ralstoy, 3-3/4" long	8	12	16
Cannon, Ranger Jr., cast iron, 10" long	125	188	250
Cannon, rapid fire, cast iron, embossed eagle	200	300	400
Cannon, "Remember The Maine," W.S. Hawkes Foundry, Dayton, Ohio, c. 1900, 13" long	250	375	500
Cannon, sheet metal, shoots small marbles, blue with red wheels, 14" long	30	45	60
Cannon, Theodore Hahn, No. 189, 1920s, lead alloy			No Price Found

	C6	C8	C10
Cannon, TootsieToy, pre-WWII, shoots, approx. 3-3/4" long	12	18	25
Cannon, TootsieToy, 40mm AA gun, pre-WWII	17	26	35
Cannon, TootsieToy, 155mm gun, pre-WWII	20	30	40
Cannon, TootsieToy, 155mm self-propelled howitzer, 1950s	20	30	40
Cannon, TootsieToy, 1930s, shoots, approx. 5-1/2" long	30	45	60
Cannon, Victory Toy Co., 1943, Sure Fire Cannon, cardboard	37	56	75
Cannon, Wyandotte, shoots marbles, 14" long	40	60	80
Canoe, Kansas Toy and Novelty, slush lead, "50," two paddling Indians "Rain-In-The-Face" and "Chief Big Foot," 4 wheels, 3-1/2" long			No Price Found
Carousel, Althof Bergmann, 1870, painted tin, wood base, cloth canopy, clockwork, bisque head doll, wood body, tin arms, turns, cranks and gives motion, 20" tall	2500	4200	6000

Cannon, Theodore Hahn No. 189.

	C6	C8	C10
Cannon, tin, camouflaged, early, 9"	45	68	90
Cannon, tin, pull lever for corks, 14" wood wheels	20	30	40
Cannon, tin, striped spring-loaded barrel with lever	20	30	40
Cannon, tin, two-wheel, c. 1915, 7-1/4", 4" high	40	60	80
Cannon, tinplate, spring action, 1950s, Japan, 7" long	20	30	40

Carousel, Althof Bergmann, 1870. Courtesy Lloyd W. Ralston Auctions.

Carousel, Marklin, c. 1909, 22" high, hand-cranked musical movement. Auctioned, with some replacements, in 1994 for $55,000

	C6	C8	C10
Carpet Sweeper, miniature Bissell 22	33	45
Cash Register, Buddy L, steel, 9" x 10-1/2" x 9" 275	363	550
Catalog: Aldens Xmas, 1946 40	60	80
Catalog: Arcade, 1889 100	150	200
Catalog: Arcade, 1899 105	158	210
Catalog: Arcade, 1900 115	172	230
Catalog: Arcade, 1901 375	562	750
Catalog: Arcade, 1902-03 85	128	170
Catalog: Arcade, 1917 500	750	1000
Catalog: Arcade, 1924 150	225	300
Catalog: Arcade, 1931 125	188	250
Catalog: Arcade, 1940 100	150	200

Catalogs, Arcade. Photo by Jeanne Bertoia. Courtesy Bill Bertoia Auctions.

	C6	C8	C10
Catalog: Auburn Rubber, pre-WWII 50	75	100
Catalog: Aurora, 1960 27	41	55
Catalog: Aurora, 1963, 1964, each 50	75	100
Catalog: Aurora, 1965, 1967, each 55	82	110
Catalog: Aurora, 1971, 1972, each 17	26	35
Catalog: Aurora, 1973 27	41	55
Catalog: Aurora, 1975 25	38	50
Catalog: Aurora, 1977 22	33	45
Catalog: Baltimore Price Reducer, 1928, illustrated w/ toys, games, etc. 15	22	30
Catalog: Barclay, pre-WWII 200	300	400
Catalog: Bilt E-Z, 1924 5	7.5	10
Catalog: Buddy L, 1926 flier 175	263	350
Catalog: Buddy L, 1929 275	352	550
Catalog: Buddy L Jr., 1930 150	225	300
Catalog: Buddy L, 1932 Robotoy flier 125	188	250
Catalog: Buddy L, 1935 175	262	350
Catalog: Buddy L, 1940 125	188	250
Catalog: Buddy L, 1941 135	202	270
Catalog: Buddy L, 1952, 1953, 1956, 1957, 1959, each 7	11	15
Catalog: Buddy L, 1961 22	33	45
Catalog: Buffalo Toy, 1939 75	112	150
Catalog: Butler Bros. 1889, tin toys, squeak toys, etc. 30	45	60
Catalog: Butler Bros. 1891, illustrated w/ mechanical banks, toys, dolls, etc. 30	45	60
Catalog: Butler Bros., Nov. 1899 40	60	80
Catalog: Butler Bros., June 1917 70	105	140

	C6	C8	C10
Catalog: Butler Bros., Xmas 1930 35	52	70
Catalog: Butler Bros., 1935, 1936, each 40	60	80
Catalog: Butler Bros., Spring, 1941 60	90	120
Catalog: Carpenter, Francis, 1880s 900	1350	1800
Catalog: Champion, 4 pages & cover 150	225	300
Catalog: Chein, 1956, 1960, each 50	75	100
Catalog: Corgi, 1966, 1967, each 10	15	20
Catalog: Daisy, 1975 22	33	45
Catalog: Dayton, 1929 150	225	300
Catalog: Dent Hardware Co., 1900, 40 pages 40	60	80
Catalog: Dent Hardware Co., 1905 37	56	75
Catalog: Dent Hardware Co., c. 1910 37	56	75
Catalog: Dent Hardware Co., Fullerton, Pa., undated 30	45	60
Catalog: Dent Hardware Co., Fullerton, Pa., iron toys, 1930 32	48	65
Catalog: Dinky, 1950s 27	41	55
Catalog: "Dunham," Buckley & Co., New York, 1895, toys, etc. 40	60	80
Catalog: Durable Toy & Novelty, c. 1920s 10	15	20
Catalog: Ehrich Bros., New York, 1892, illustrations of banks, toys, dolls, etc. 40	60	80
Catalog: Eldon, 1961, autos 6	9	12
Catalog: Eldon, 1961, boats 6	9	12
Catalog: Erector Set, 1938, 38 pp. 15	22	30
Catalog: Ertl, 1974 3	4.50	6
Catalog: Eureka Trick & Novelty Co., c. 1875, 32 pages 20	30	40
Catalog: A.J. Fisher, New York, 1877, illustrating cap pistols, etc. 18	27	36
Catalog: Fisher-Price, 1954 6	9	12
Catalog: Fisher-Price, 1966 25	38	50
Catalog: Garton pedal cars, 1940 100	150	200
Catalog: Gendron, 1927 600	900	1200
Catalog: Gilbert, 1966 27	41	55
Catalog: Gould, L., 1922, Xmas 125	188	250
Catalog: Gould, L., 1940 55	83	110
Catalog: Grey Iron, c. 1920s, No. 24 115	172	230
Catalog: Hasbro, 1975 27	41	55
Catalog: Hasbro, 1987, 1989 20	30	40
Catalog: Howdy Doody Merchandise, 1955 27	41	55
Catalog: Hubley 1914-15 55	83	110
Catalog: Hubley, 1939 60	90	120
Catalog: Hubley, 1966 16	24	32
Catalog: Hubley, 1969 11	16	22
Catalog: Hubley, 1974 22	33	45
Catalog: Ideal, 1973 12	18	25
Catalog: Ideal, 1976 12	18	25
Catalog: Ives, Blakeslee & Williams, two-sided broadside, c. 1890, 18" x 24" 70	105	140
Catalog: Ives Yachts, Ships and Shipping, c. 1915, 24 pages 50	75	100
Catalog: Illustrated brochure of cap pistols and animated cap pistols by Ives and Williams 20	30	40
Catalog: JCPenney, Xmas, 1963, 1964, 1965, each 68	102	135
Catalog: JCPenney, Xmas, 1966 through 1970, each 50	75	100

	C6	C8	C10
Catalog: JCPenney, Xmas, 1971 through 1975 each	35	52	70
Catalog: JCPenney, Xmas, 1975 through 1980, each	27	41	55
Catalog: Jones & Bixler, 1912, N-8	100	150	200
Catalog: Kenton Hardware Co., No. 16, 1920s, 112 pages	70	105	140
Catalog: Kenton Hardware Co., 1934; illus. in color	50	75	100
Catalog: Kilgore 1977-78	22	33	45
Catalog: Kingsbury, 1919	55	82	110
Catalog: Kingsbury, c. 1920, c. 1925, each	32	48	65
Catalog: Kingsbury, c. 1930s, small-size, 128 pp.	100	150	200
Catalog: Kingsbury Toys, Motor Driven, 1936, 16 pages	40	60	80
Catalog: Knapp Electric Toys No. 35	10	15	20
Catalog: Knickerbocker, 1961	8	12	17
Catalog: Manoil, c. 1935-1939	100	150	200
Catalog: Marx, 1930s, 36 pp.	225	338	450
Catalog: Marx, 1964	125	188	250
Catalog: Marx, 1966	100	150	200
Catalog: Marx, 1969	110	165	220
Catalog: Marx, 1976	12	18	25
Catalog: Matchbox, 1964	25	38	50
Catalog: Matchbox, 1965	22	33	45
Catalog: Matchbox, 1966	15	22	30
Catalog: Matchbox, 1968	7	11	15
Catalog: Matchbox, 1969	6	9	12
Catalog: Matchbox, 1970	4	6	8
Catalog: Matchbox, 1973	11	16	22
Catalog: Matchbox, 1978	13	19	26
Catalog: Mattel, 1967	150	225	300
Catalog: "McCadden & Bros." Philadelphia, illustrated iron and tin toys, banks, mechanical toys, dolls, games, etc.	50	75	100
Catalog: Mego, 1967-69, each	50	75	100
Catalog: Mickey Mouse Merchandise Catalog, 1935, by Kay Kamen Co., 80 pages, hundreds of illustrations of Mickey Mouse items	300	450	600
Catalog: Montgomery Ward, Xmas, 1934 through 1940, each	82	123	165
Catalog: Montgomery Ward, Xmas, 1941 through 1965, each	68	102	135
Catalog: Montgomery Ward, Xmas, 1966 through 1970, each	50	75	100
Catalog: Montgomery Ward, Xmas, 1971 through 1975, each	35	52	70
Catalog: Montgomery Ward, Xmas, 1976 through 1980	27	41	55
Catalog: Montgomery Ward, Xmas, 1981 through 1985	20	30	40
Catalog: Nicol & Co. 1895, illustrating banks, etc.	27	41	55
Catalog: Ohio Art, 1961	8	12	17
Catalog: Popsicle Pete Radio News and Premium catalog, early	40	60	80
Catalog: Popsicle Pete's 1949 four page gift list	10	15	20
Catalog: Pyro, 1966, 1967, each	19	28	38
Catalog: Pyro, 1970	9	13	18

	C6	C8	C10
Catalog: Rel Toy Boats foldout, 1958	20	30	40
Catalog: Revell, 1957-58	37	56	75
Catalog: Revell, 1958-59	25	38	50
Catalog: Revell, 1969	10	15	20
Catalog: Schoenhut , 1903	100	150	200
Catalog: Schoenhut, 1918, Circus	112	168	225
Catalog: Schoenhut Circus, 1928	100	150	200
Catalog: Schoenhut Humpty Dumpty Circus Toys (other toys as well), c. 1915, many illustrations	100	165	220
Catalog: Sears, 1919, Fall-Winter	30	45	60
Catalog: Sears Xmas 1926	67	100	135
Catalog: Sears Xmas 1933	60	90	120
Catalog: Sears Xmas 1936 through 1940, each	82	123	165
Catalog: Sears Xmas 1941 through 1945, each	82	123	165
Catalog: Sears Xmas 1946 through 1950, each	82	123	165
Catalog: Sears Xmas 1951 through 1955, each	82	123	165
Catalog: Sears Xmas 1956 through 1960, each	82	123	165
Catalog: Sears Xmas 1961 through 1965, each	82	123	165
Catalog: Sears Xmas 1966 through 1970, each	60	90	120
Catalog: Sears Xmas 1971 through 1975, each	45	68	90
Catalog: Sears Xmas 1976 through 1980, each	30	45	60
Catalog: Selchow & Righter, 1894-5, games and toys, illustrated trains, boats, bell toys, mechanical banks, etc.	120	180	240
Catalog: Selchow & Righter, 1908-1909, 108 pages	80	120	160
Catalog: Selchow & Righter, 1921	32	48	65
Catalog: Shure, N. 1940	85	128	170
Catalog: Smith-Miller, 1954	40	60	80

Catalog, Smith-Miller (Smitty), 1954. Photo by Bill Kaufman. Courtesy Ray Funk.

	C6	C8	C10
Catalog: Spiegel, Xmas, 1941 through 1965, each	68	102	135
Catalog: Spiegel, Xmas, 1966 through 1970, each	50	75	100
Catalog: Spiegel, Xmas, 1971 through 1975, each	35	52	70
Catalog: Spiegel, Xmas, 1976 through 1980, each	27	41	55
Catalog: Spiegel, Xmas, 1981 through 1985, each	20	30	40
Catalog: Spiegel, Xmas, 1986 through 1990, each	15	22	30
Catalog: State, Adams & Dearborn Sts., Chicago, illustrated	10	15	20

	C6	C8	C10
Catalog: Steelcraft, 1934, 44 pp. 300	450	600
Catalog: Steelcraft, 1936 350	525	700
Catalog: Carl P. Stern, illustrating cap pistols, etc. 15	22	30
Catalog: J.E. Stevens Co., 1906, illustrations of iron toys and mechanical banks 40	60	80
Catalog: J.E. Stevens Co., No. 51, Export 40	60	80
Catalog: Strauss, c. 1926, tiny, 32 pp. 37	56	75
Catalog: Structo Toys, 1931, 8 pages 10	15	20
Catalog: Supplee-Biddle of Philadelphia, 1930, 174 pages, many toys 90	135	180
Catalog: Thorsen & Cassady, 1894, guns, etc. 20	30	40
Catalog: Tinkertoy, 1926 6	9	12
Catalog: Tom Mix, 1936 Premium Catalog 30	45	60
Catalog: Toy Yearbook, 1952-53, 1956-57, 1957-58, 1958-59, each 12	18	25
Catalog: Transogram, 1949 15	22	30
Catalog: Vindex, c. 1932 275	365	550
Catalog: Walt Disney Character Merchandise, 1930s 250	375	500
Catalog: Walt Disney Character Merchandise, 1940-41 250	375	500
Catalog: Western Auto, 1960 through 1969, each 32	48	65
Catalog: A.C. Williams, 1908 220	330	440
Catalog: A.C. Williams, c. 1930, c. 1934, each 45	68	90
Catalog: A.C. Williams, c. 1934 45	68	90
Catalog: Williams, Charles, 1928 22	33	45
Catalog: Woolworth's Christmas Catalogs, pre-WWII 30	45	60
Catalog: Woolworth's Christmas, 1951 30	45	60
Catalog: Woolworth's Christmas, 1952 15	22	30
Cathedral Music Box, tin litho, of organ pipes and cherubs, plays loud or soft according to speed of cranking, no markings, German, 5" x 5" x 7" 325	488	650
Charlie Tuna rubber squeeze toy 24	36	48
Chein "Busy Mike" sand seesaw, 1940s, 7-1/2" high 90	135	180
Chein Cathedral Organ 100	150	200
Chein Drum, 6" x 3-1/2" 30	45	60
Chein Easter Egg w/ chicken on top, opens up to hold candy, c. 1938, tin, 5-1/2" 15	22	30
Chein "Sand Chute" No. 45 80	120	160
Chein Sand Pail, c. early 1940s, 7" diameter 26	39	52
Chein "Sand Loader" 75	112	150
Chein "Sand Mill," 1930s, 7" wide, 11" high 50	75	100
Chein Sand-Toy, monkey bends and twists, 7" high 20	30	40
Chein Windmill sand toy, tin litho, 8" high 15	22	30
Chemcraft No. 5 Chemistry Set, wooden box 37	56	75
Chemcraft No. 418 Master Deluxe Laboratory, wooden box 175	263	350
Chemcraft Beginners Chemistry Set No. 602 by Porter, 1956 12	18	25

CHEIN "Busy Mike" sand seesaw. Courtesy Calvin L. Chaussee.

	C6	C8	C10
Chicago Printing Press, No. 15, complete 20	30	40
Children's Telephone (set of two), 1920 10	15	20
Chimes Bell-Ringer with Elephant, 7" long 40	60	80
Climbing Monkey brings coconuts down from palm tree, tin, "Monkey Shines, Emporium Specialist," 18" high 60	90	120
Clown, balancing, copper, clown holding arched balancing pole weighted at both ends with lead balls, standing on one leg on small round platform on stationary metal ladder. Move clown in any direction and he won't fall off platform, 6-1/2" high .. 50	75	100
Clown, balancing on pedestal, painted wood, c. 1920, 15" high 100	150	200

Clown, balancing on pedestal, painted wood, c. 1920, 15" high. Courtesy Mapes Auctioneers & Appraisers.

	C6	C8	C10
Clown, clockwork, early, cloth suit, German, 9-1/2" high 300	450	600
Clown, wind-up, papier-mâché and cardboard, 43" high 90	135	180
Coffee Grinder, cast iron, 4" high 40	60	80
Cohn T. Inc. "Superior Space Port No. 75," 1950s, playset includes space drome, space cannon and plastic accessories, 17" long 350	525	700

	C6	C8	C10		C6	C8	C10

"Consul," the educated monkey, tin hand toy,
monkey automatically adds, subtracts,
multiplies and divides,
dated June 27, 1916, 5-1/2" x 6" 40   60   80

Cot, Army, canvas with steel frame,
c. early 1940s 10   15   20

Count Chocula, rubber squeeze toy 30   45   60

COURTLAND TOYS

(Numerical Order) List by Joe and Sharon Freed

800 Zylo-P-ano, 1946 retail=79¢, 1947
retail=69¢, 13-1/4" long, 5-1/2" wide 75   100   125

1000 Walt Reach Toys G-Man
Pocket Siren Signal, 3-1/2" long,
2-3/8" wide, 1-3/4" high 75   100   150

1050 Courtland Walt Reach Toys
Halloween Pocket Siren Signal,
3-1/2" long, 2-3/8" wide, 1-3/4" high 125   150   225

1060 Courtland Walt Reach Toys
New Years Pocket Siren Signal,
3-1/2" long, 2-3/8" wide, 1-3/4" high 125   150   225

9000 Mechanical 3-piece Train Set,
24" long, 2-1/4" wide, 3-1/4" high 100   150   200

9050 Fire Department w/ automatic garage
door, found to have a nonpowered fire
chief car w/ the Courtland Toy Co.,
Phila. Pa., markings, it is quite possible
that some of the 9050 garages
were also manufactured in Philadelphia,
7-3/4" x 10-1/8" x 6-3/4" 75   125   175

COURTLAND 9050 Fire Department. Courtesy Joe and Sharon Freed.

COURTLAND 9000. Locomotive and 2 gondolas. Courtesy Joe and Sharon Freed.

9075 Private Garage w/ automatic door.
Since the nonpowered car that
accompanies this garage is found
w/ Courtland Toy Co., Phila. Pa. markings,
it is quite possible that some of the
9075 garages were also manufactured
in Philadelphia, 7-3/4" x 10-1/8" x 6-3/4" 75   125   175

COZZONE

From information developed by Larry Giancola

The Cozzone Corporation was founded by John A. Cozzone during the 1930s. The company made fishing reels and, during WWII, components for incendiary bombs, etc. Located at 18 Nuttman Street in Newark, New Jersey, the firm decided to diversify after the war, and spent a great deal of money developing a construction set. Although a number of different sets were pictured in the firm's catalog, only the No. 500 was actually produced. Production seems to have been in the 1948-1950 period. A crayoned price of $12.99 on a surviving set suggests that the very high price for the time is responsible for relatively few sets being sold. John Cozzone died in 1968 and his son Tom took over, changing the name to Tomrette Corp. However, toymaking by the family seems to have begun and ended with the construction set.

	C6	C8	C10
Cozzone No. 500 Construction Set, machined metal parts, electric motor, in box	200	300	400
Crackle (Kellogg's Rice Krispies) handpuppet	16	24	32
Crackle (Kellogg's Rice Krispies) squeeze toy, 8-1/2"	19	28	38

COZZONE Construction Set No. 500. Courtesy Lawrence Giancola.

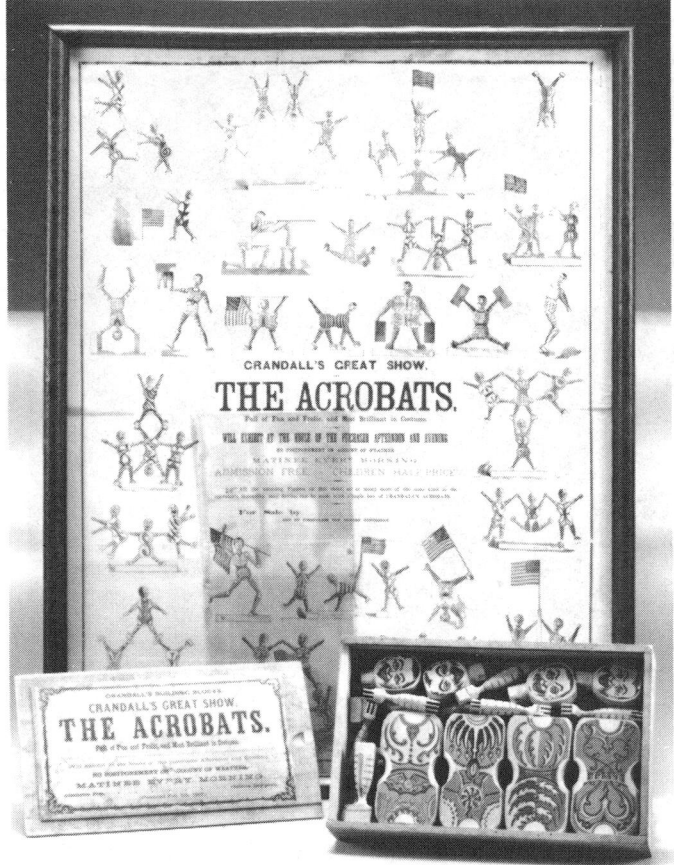

CRANDALL "Acrobats," 4 acrobats, with framed directions in background. Courtesy Christie's East.

CRANDALL "Crandall's District School." Courtesy Wilkinson Collection, Detroit Antique Toy Museum.

CRANDALL

At age 16, Charles M. Crandall took over his family's woodworking business after the death of his father in 1849. Crandall made croquet sets after the Civil War. They were packed in thin wooden boxes with tongue-and-groove corners. When his sons were ill, he took home a bag of the grooved scraps, and the buildings they made with them inspired "Crandall Building Blocks." The success of the interlocking blocks led to production of "Acrobats," with grooved parts. Crandall, who died in 1905, produced toys into the turn of the century.

	C6	C8	C10
Crandall "Acrobats," 4 acrobats	250	375	500
Crandall "Crandall's District School," c. 1875	600	950	1300
Crandall "Crandall's Expression Blocks"	288	435	575
"Crandall's Heavy Artillery," soldiers, blocks	750	1250	2000
Crandall "John Gilpin's Ride"	500	800	1200

	C6	C8	C10
Crandall, Man in Cap on Donkey, wheeled pull toy	275	413	550
Crandall Masquerade Blocks	320	528	976
Crandall Menagerie	550	900	1300

End Crandall

	C6	C8	C10
Cupboard, cast iron, open work has diamond and heart pattern, two doors and one drawer	40	60	80
Dancers, black, Automatic Toy Works, New York City, 1870, on box, clockwork, carved wood and jesso bodies, clothes, 6-1/4" w x 10-1/4" t	600	900	1200

Dancers, black, Automatic Toy Works, 1870. Courtesy Lloyd W. Ralston Auctions.

	C6	C8	C10
"Davy Crockett Alamo Express Fix-It Stage Coach," 1950s, Ideal, 13" long, push toy	62	93	125
Davy Crockett Indian Target Set by Keystone Wood Company, David Crockett rifle, all wood and hardboard litho set that pre-dates Davy popularity of the 50s, made about 1949. Wood stagecoach and horses, wood covered wagon and horses, Indians, bear, etc.	40	60	80
Doctor's Set, Transogram, 1948, Little Country Doctor, full doctor set, chest and bag	32	48	65
Do-Do Toy Co. "Do-Do Clown," 1930s, squeeze toy, 5-1/2" long	70	105	140
Doepke No. W-11 Freddie Fireplug wooden, comes apart			No Price Found
Dragon, lead alloy, Kansas Toy, c. 1920s, early 1930s, 2-5/8" long			No Price Found

Drum, Indian Motif, tin litho, 11-3/4" diameter. Courtesy James S. Maxwell/ Virginia Caputo. Photo by Virginia Caputo.

	C6	C8	C10
Drum, Indian motif, tin litho, 11-3/4" diameter	175	263	350
Drum, metal body, litho, red, white and blue design, varnished wooden hoops, leather "ears," sheepskin head and fiber bottom, w/ wooden drumsticks, c. 1910	20	30	40
Drum, about 1920, circus decor, tin, litho	40	60	80
Drum, metal w/ drumsticks, 13" diameter	10	15	20
Drum, wooden w/ harness, 13" diameter	10	15	20
Duncan Yo-Yo, 1960s	13	20	27

Elephant in Hoop, tin, Fallows?, c. 1880. Courtesy Christie's East.

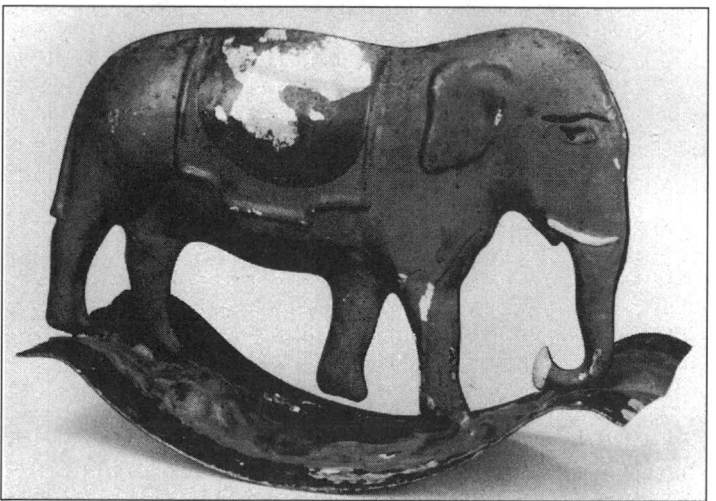

FALLOWS, Elephant on Rocker. Courtesy Wilkinson Collection, Detroit Antique Toy Museum.

	C6	C8	C10
Electric Stove, works, 1930s	42	63	85
Elephant in Hoop, tin, Fallows?, c. 1880, 12" diameter	440	660	880
Emenee Accordion	15	22	30
Fallows Buffalo Hunt, tin, c. 1886, 9"	1200	2000	2700
Fallows Elephant on Platform, tin, 9"	350	525	700
Fallows Elephant on Rocker, tin, 8"	475	712	950
Ferris Wheel, "DRGM," four figures, tin, 1895, 11-1/2" high	600	1000	1400
Flagpole, wooden, w/ flag that raises and lowers, approx. 8" high	6	9	13
Flying Propeller Ring, heavy metal, c. 1930s-40s, could have been a premium	10	15	20
Fort, Keystone No. 523, U.S. Coast Defense Fort	42	72	95
Fort, Keystone No. 525, U.S. Coast Defense Fort, with accessories, c. 1942	40	55	80

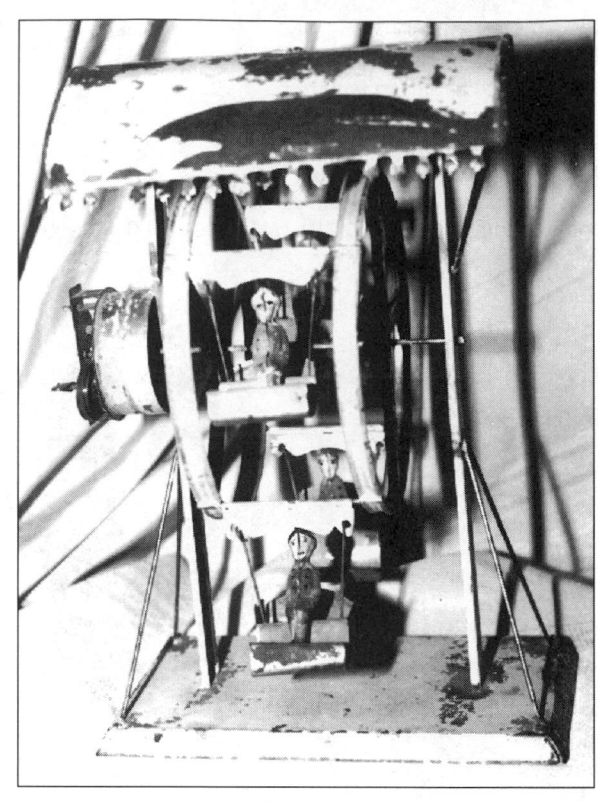

Ferris Wheel, "DRGM." First bought in 1895. Courtesy Calvin L. Chaussee.

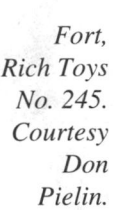

Fort, Rich Toys No. 245. Courtesy Don Pielin.

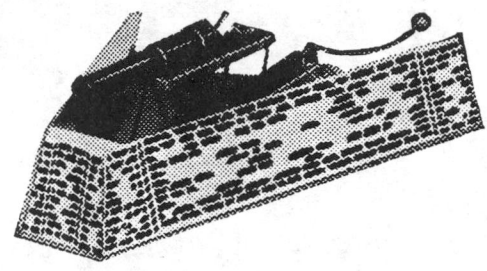

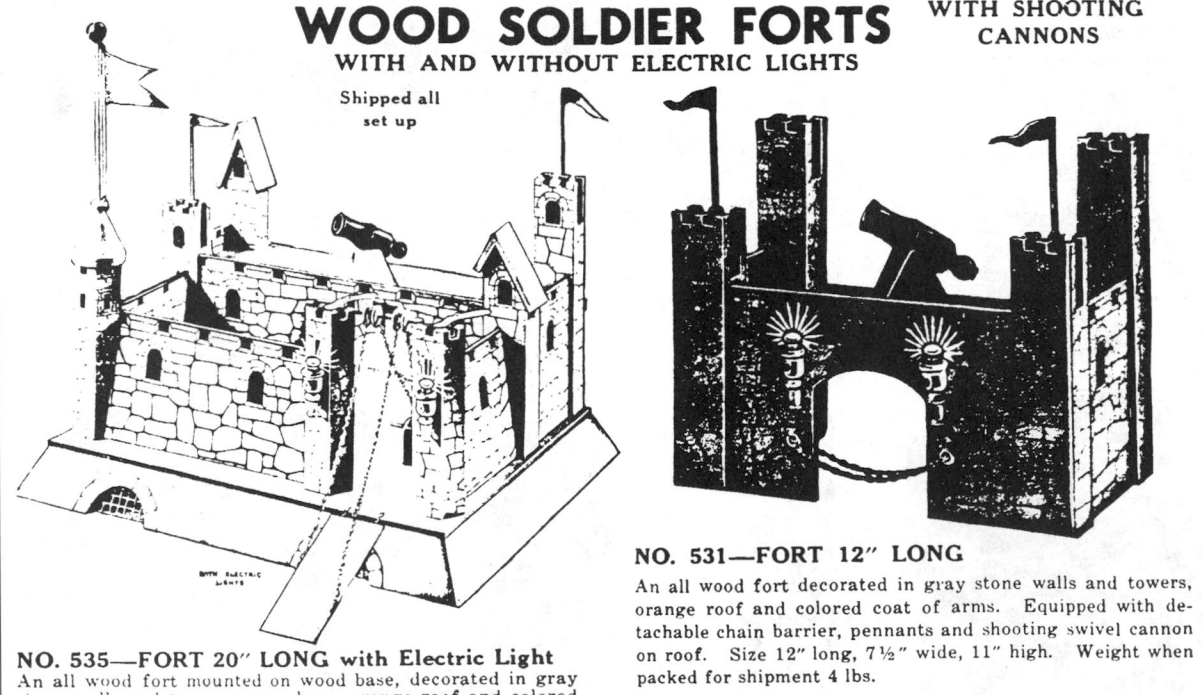

WOOD SOLDIER FORTS

WITH SHOOTING CANNONS

WITH AND WITHOUT ELECTRIC LIGHTS

Shipped all set up

NO. 535—FORT 20" LONG with Electric Light
An all wood fort mounted on wood base, decorated in gray stone walls and towers, green base, orange roof and colored turrets tops and shield. Equipped with draw-bridge, winch, swivel shooting cannon, pennants, movable flag, fire step in court yard, moat gratings and electric entrance lamps connected to batteries and operated by switch in tower tops. Size: 20" long, 17" wide and 19" high. Weight when packed in Mullen-test carton 12 lbs. No battery furnished.

NO. 531—FORT 12" LONG
An all wood fort decorated in gray stone walls and towers, orange roof and colored coat of arms. Equipped with detachable chain barrier, pennants and shooting swivel cannon on roof. Size 12" long, 7½" wide, 11" high. Weight when packed for shipment 4 lbs.

NO. 533—FORT with Electric Light
Same as No. 531 with **electric entrance lamps** connected to battery and operated by switch on the roof. Weight when packed in Mullen-test carton 5 lbs. No battery furnished.

Forts by Keystone, showing No. 535 and No. 533. Original catalog illustration courtesy Ron Fink.

KEYSTONE MFG. CO., BOSTON, MASS.   **New York Showroom, 200 Fifth Avenue**

Fort, Rich Toys No. 260. Courtesy Ron Fink.

Fort, Rich Toys No. 261. Courtesy Ron Fink.

	C6	C8	C10
Fort, Keystone No. 527, U.S. Coast Guard Defense Fort, w/ accessories, c. 1942	40	70	100
Fort, Keystone No. 531, 12" long	40	60	85
Fort, Keystone No. 533, same as 531, but 2 electric lights at entrance	50	75	100
Fort, Keystone No. 535, w/ 2 electric lights at entrance, 20" long	60	90	120
Fort, Keystone Exploding Fort with Shooting Tank	46	69	92
Fort, Rich Toys No. 245, Siege Gun with Stone Fort	25	40	75
Fort, Rich Toys No. 246, Siege Gun with Stone Fort, two guns	30	50	80
Fort, Rich Toys No. 247, Siege Gun with Stone Fort, three guns	40	60	80
Fort, Rich Toys No. 260, 26-3/4" long	35	50	75
Fort, Rich Toys No. 261, 26-1/2" long	50	75	100
Fort, Rich Toys No. 262, 27" long	100	200	300
Fort, Rich Toys No. 263, 29" long	275	363	550

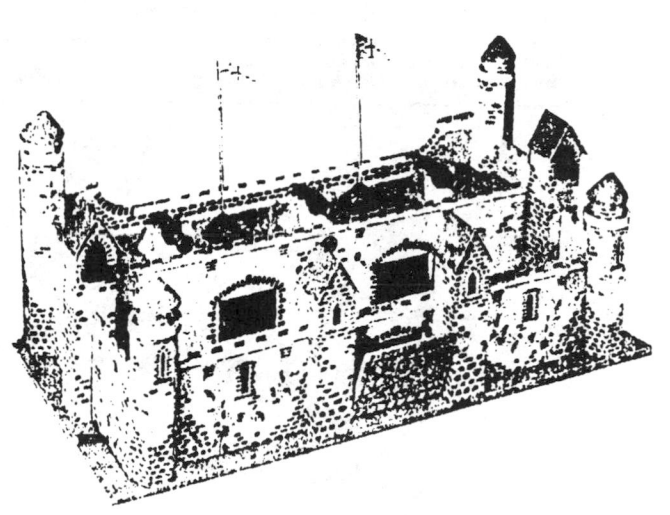

Fort, Rich Toys No. 262. Courtesy Ron Fink.

Fort, Rich Toys No. 263. Courtesy Ron Fink.

KEYSTONE U. S. COAST DEFENSE FORTS

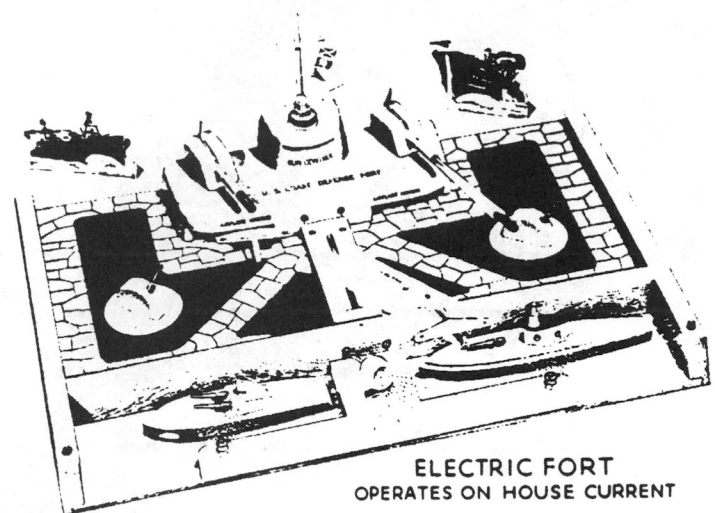

ELECTRIC FORT
OPERATES ON HOUSE CURRENT

- *Planes That Fly!*
- *Swivel Guns That Shoot!*
- *Electric Flashing Signals!*
- *Electric Searchlight!*
- *Electric Pier Lights!*
- *Turret Guns That Turn!*
- *Two Boats That Float!*
- *Two Airplane Hangars!*
- *Soldier Housing in Rear!*
- *Played From Front or Back With or Without Soldiers!*

No. 527 — U. S. COAST DEFENSE FORT

Two Flying Planes operated with catapult. *Pier and signal lights work off regular house current A.C.* Target and patrol ships and shells furnished for shooting cannons. Made of wood and fibre board. No assembling. Finished in gray, tan, green base and blue trim. Each boxed in shipping carton. Weight 175 lbs. per dozen. Size 24 x 17.

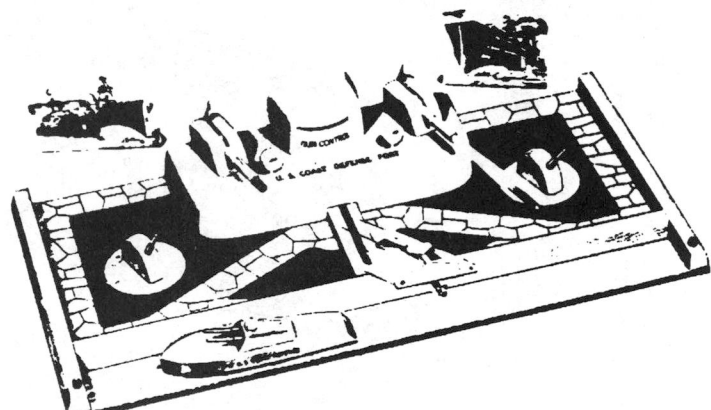

- *Plane That Flies!*
- *Swivel Guns That Shoot!*
- *Turret Guns That Turn!*
- *Boat That Floats!*
- *Soldier Housing in Rear!*
- *Battleship Target for Cannons!*
- *Play From Front or Rear With or Without Soldiers!*

No. 525 — U. S. COAST DEFENSE FORT

One Flying Plane operated with catapult. Target and scout ship and shells furnished for shooting cannons. Made of wood and fibre board. No assembling. Size 24 x 12. Finished in gray, tan, green and blue trim. Each in shipping carton. Weight 65 lbs. per dozen.

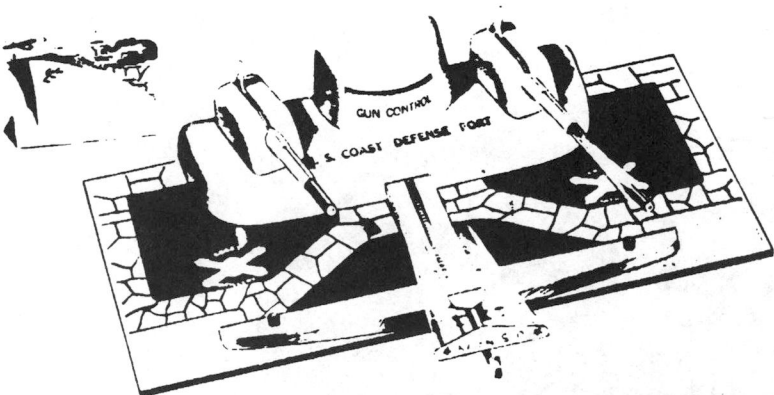

- *Plane That Flies!*
- *Swivel Guns That Shoot!*
- *Soldier Housing in Rear!*
- *Battleship Target for Cannons!*
- *Played From Front or Rear With or Without Soldiers!*

No. 523
U. S. COAST DEFENSE FORT

All wood and fibre board fort 16" x 8". Equipped with flying plane and catapult, ship target and shells for swivel shooting guns. All assembled each in a carton. Colors same as other models. Weight 30 lbs. per dozen.

KEYSTONE MFG. CO., BOSTON, MASS.
NEW YORK SHOW ROOM, 200 FIFTH AVENUE

Advertisement for Keystone forts.

	C6	C8	C10
Fort, Rich Toys, "Fort Washington" 112	168	225
Frankenberry vinyl squeeze toy 55	83	110
Fruit Brute, rubber squeeze toy 23	35	46
Gibbs Girl on Swing, c. 1910 105	158	210
Gibbs Service Station No. 81, new in 1924 250	375	500
Girard "Knife Sharpener," crank action, 1930s, 8" high 60	90	120
Glass Candy Container, shaped like Biplane ... 500	750	1000
Glass Candy Container, shaped like dog........... 15	22	30
Glass Candy Container, Dolly's milk bottle 4	6	8
Glass Candy Container, shaped like a gun 20	30	40
Glass Candy Container, shaped like a Model T 125	188	250
Glass Candy Container, shaped like rabbit, Victory Glass.................. 15	22	30
Glass Candy Container, shaped like a telephone................................ 20	30	40
Glass Candy Container, shaped like train engine, 3" long 26	39	52
Glass Candy Container, shaped like a train lantern, 3-1/2" high......... 26	39	52
Glass Candy Container, shaped like the Spirit of St. Louis airplane........................... 325	488	650
Glass Candy Container, Stop and Go, glass, etc. traffic signal 100	150	200
Glass Candy Container, shaped like a train lantern, tin top and base, "Victory Glass Inc.," 3-1/2" high 26	39	52
Glass Candy Container, shaped like a zeppelin............................... 100	150	200

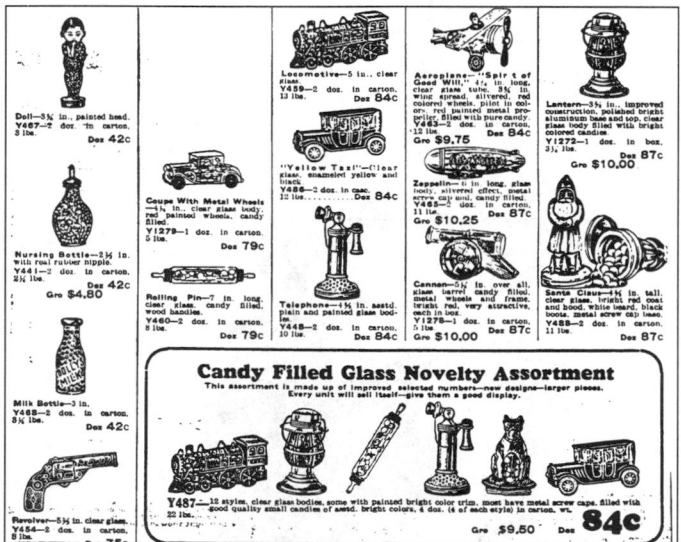

Glass Candy Containers, as seen in a December 1929 Butler Bros. catalog.

	C6	C8	C10
Grandfather's Clock, tin, has weights that make hands rotate and pendulum swing, but is not a working clock, transfer decorated, 8-3/4" high 40	60	80
Grey Iron Automatic Cap Machine Gun, 9" long 275	363	550
Grey Iron Clever Clowns Trapeze Set 275	363	550

GREY IRON Clever Clowns. Photo by Harold Haseley.

	C6	C8	C10
Grey Iron Clever Clowns large set 500	750	1000
Grocery Store, tin, scales, cash register, wrapping paper, order pad and pencil, "Little Toy Town Grocery Store," shelves with small boxes of products, 14" long 100	150	200
Grocery Store, wood, "Pet's Grocery Store" ... 400	600	800
H.K. Electric Engine, patented 1908, used DC current.................... 50	75	100
Handwashing Machine with wringer 10	15	20
Hasbro Mr. Potato Head No. 2000 19	28	38

HASBRO "Mr. Potato Head," early.

	C6	C8	C10
Hasbro "Mr. Potato Head," 1950s, plastic car and boat trailer, plus all the parts to create different faces 26	39	52
Hasbro Mr. Potato Head on the Farm................ 15	22	30
Hasbro Mr. & Mrs. Potato Head Set, No. 2004 35	52	70
Hasbro Mr. & Mrs. Potato Head Set, No. 2006 35	52	70
Hasbro Mrs. Potato Head 50	75	100
Hasbro Mrs. Potato Head w/ car 40	60	80
"Historoscope," Milton Bradley, c. 1880, rolled panorama 238	355	475

	C6	C8	C10
Hobby Horse, "Black Beauty," wooden, 34" long	25	37	50
Horse, American, painted tin, 1870, 4-1/2" long	275	415	550
Horse in Hoop, George Brown, early	550	850	1200
Horse, sheet metal, cast-iron jointed legs, full form, 10-3/4" long, 11" high	200	300	400

	C6	C8	C10
Hubley Duck, pull toy, c. 1930s, 9-3/8" long	800	1400	2000
Hubley Ferris Wheel, early, cast iron, brass and tin, clockwork, 17" high	2000	4000	6500
Hubley Grasshopper, pull toy, cast iron	258	385	515

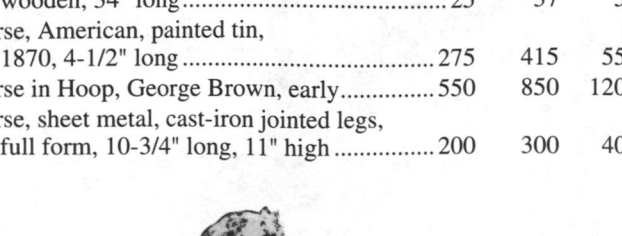

Horse, American painted tin, 1870, 4-1/2" long. Courtesy Lloyd W. Ralston Auctions.

HUBLEY Jantzen Beach Patrol. Photo by Jeanne Bertoia. Courtesy Bill Bertoia Auctions.

Horses in Hoops, Althof Bergmann. Courtesy Lloyd W. Ralston Auctions.

HUBLEY Jantzen Surf Girl. Courtesy Lloyd W. Ralston Auctions.

HUBLEY Ferris Wheel, early.

	C6	C8	C10
Horse Race, circular track within rectangular box, c. 1900, lever-activated	100	150	200
Horses in Hoops, Althof Bergmann, American painted tin, 1880, 4-1/2" diameter	800	1200	1600

HUBLEY Grasshopper, 1929.

HUBLEY Monkey Riding Tricycle. Courtesy James S. Maxwell/Virginia Caputo. Photo by Virginia Caputo.

	C6	C8	C10

Hubley Jantzen Beach Patrol,
   c. 1932, man on surfboard
   riding through waves,
   8" long, auctioned in 1994
   in near mint condition for $14,000

Hubley Jantzen Surf Girl, 1932,
   girl surfboard rider, cast iron,
   8" long, auctioned in 1995 for $9020

Hubley Jumbo the Elephant, on wheels 25   37   50

Hubley Marathon Rider
   (bicyclist) cast iron 300   450   600

Hubley Monkey Riding Tricycle,
   cast iron, aluminum, 6-1/4" long 2000   3500   5500

Hubley Old Dutch
   Cleanser Woman, cast iron 2200   3800   6000

HUBLEY Old Dutch Cleanser Woman. Photo by Jeanne Bertoia. Courtesy Bill Bertoia Auctions.

Hurdy-Gurdy, turn crank and play tune,
   shows animal playing cello 30   45   60

Ice Box, "Alaska" cast iron,
   has glass cube of ice in top, 5" high 200   300   400

Ideal Astronaut Space Helmet 37   56   75

Ideal Gas Station, 8" long,
   c. 1950s, with cars 55   82   110

Ideal "Mr. Machine," first version, can be
   taken apart and put together, 18" high 138   205   275

Ideal "Mr. Machine," 1972 version,
   whistles, 17-1/2" high 32   48   65

Ideal "Mr. Machine," 1977 version.................... 27   41   55

Iron and Trivet, cast iron 20   30   40

Iron, tin, 5" high 7.50   11.25   15

Iron, tin, 3-1/2" high 12   18   25

Irwin "Round-Up Tex the Whirling
   Cowboy," plastic wind-up,
   1950s, 10" high 40   60   80

Ives Acrobat, hand over hand,
   10-1/2" high overall 2000   3000   4000

Ives Automatic Toy Boxers,
   c. 1876, 11" high...................................... 4000   7000   12,000

Ives Automatic Dancer Circus Rider,
   standing on horse, 15" high, auctioned
   in 1991 in excellent to near mint condition for $38,500

Ives Automatic Sewing Machine and Girl,
   clockwork, auctioned in 1994 in
   excellent condition for $16,000

Ives "Autoperipateticos" walking doll 700   1050   1400

	C6	C8	C10

Ives Barrel Walkers, c. 1890, wood
   and paper litho balance toy, acrobat,
   ballerina, monkey 200   300   400

Ives Black Dancer, 1870s, clockwork 800   1300   1800

Ives Black Dancer, c. 1873 2400   3600   4800

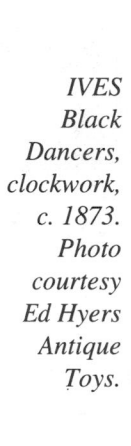

IVES Black Dancers, clockwork, c. 1873. Photo courtesy Ed Hyers Antique Toys.

Ives Black Dancer, clockwork,
   c. 1880, 11" high.. 800   1300   1800

Ives Black Mechanical Walking Man,
   c. 1875, 9-1/2" high 1000   1600   2400

Ives Boy on Rocking Horse, c. 1874, wood
   and tin, 8-1/2" high, auctioned in 1991
   in excellent condition for $57,200

Ives Boy smoking cigar
   and holding stomach, cast iron 195   263   350

Ives Chinese, "John Chinaman,"
   wind-up walker, 9-1/2" high, auctioned
   in 1994 with original box for $7200

Ives Crawling Baby, c. 1871 2000   3000   4000

IVES. Left to right: Chinese, "John Chinaman"; Automatic Sewing Machine and Girl. Photo by Jeanne Bertoia. Courtesy Bill Bertoia Auctions.

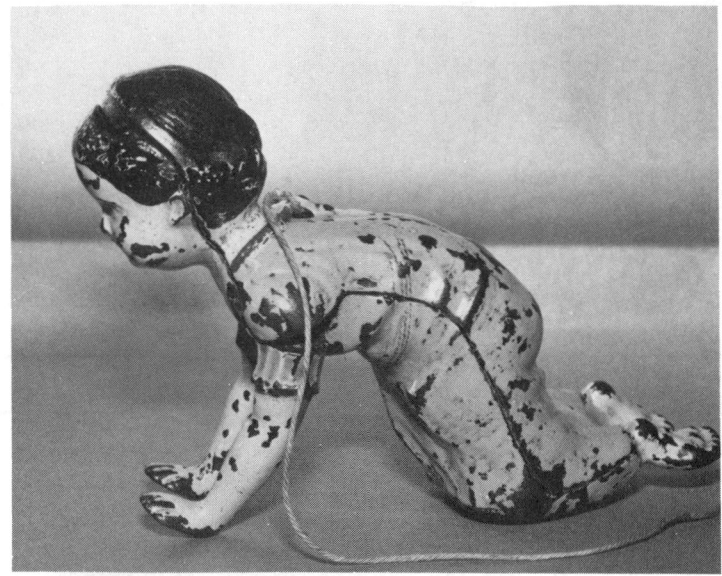

IVES "Crawling Baby," 1893. Photo courtesy Ed Hyers Antique Toys.

IVES Crawling Baby, c. 1871. Courtesy Phillips New York.

	C6	C8	C10
Ives "Crawling Baby," 1893	1500	2250	3000
Ives Elephant Ramp Walker: See Ramp Walkers			
Ives "Elephant Car," circus cage, cast iron, "serpent eggs" magic trick can be burnt in elephant's trunk, "Greatest Show on Earth	790	1125	1500
Ives Fire Engine House, c. 1890, cast iron and wood, 16" long	2000	3000	5000
Ives General Butler, wind-up walker, 9-1/2" high	2000	3500	5000
Ives General Grant, smoking, auctioned in 1991 in excellent condition with one side of wood base missing for $22,000.			

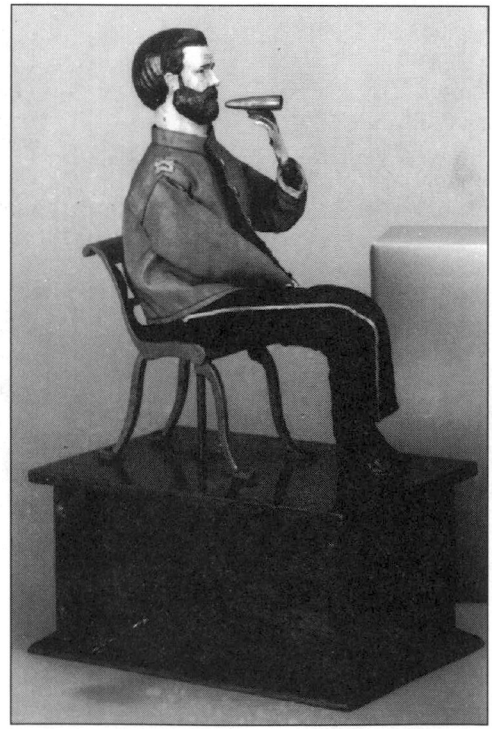

IVES General Grant, smoking. Courtesy Sotheby's New York.

	C6	C8	C10
Ives Hot Air Toy, C. 1870	250	375	500
Ives Jackass wind-up walker, 9-1/2" high, auctioned in 1994 in very good condition, missing left arm, for $12,000			

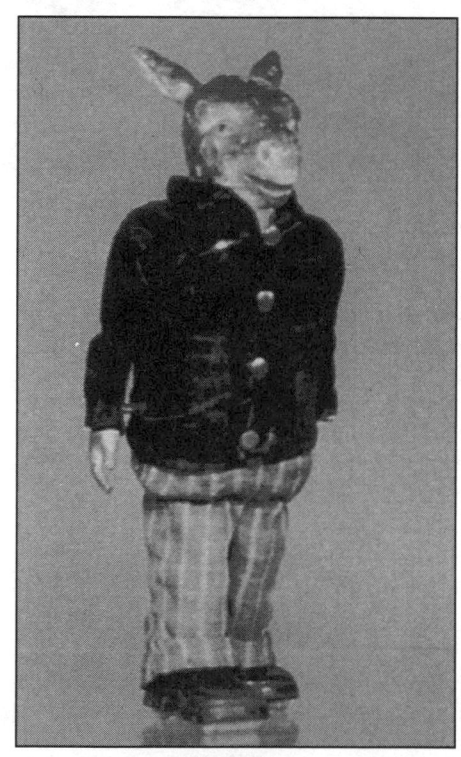

IVES Jackass. Photo by Jeanne Bertoia. Courtesy Bill Bertoia Auctions.

	C6	C8	C10
Ives Judge, clockwork, c. 1880	1500	2300	3500
Ives Juggler, clockwork early	1000	1500	2000
Ives Mechanical Bear, patent 1872	380	570	760
Ives Mechanical Performing Monkey, No. 49-10, 5-1/2" high	2250	3375	4500
Ives Mule, articulated, cast iron, pull toy, 8" long	375	565	750
Ives "Old Mammy Washing Clothes," clockwork, 11" high, auctioned in 1993 for $13,800			

IVES Mechanical Bear. Photo courtesy PB Eighty-Four, New York.

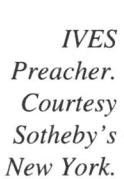

	C6	C8	C10
Ives Old Woman in a Shoe, pull toy, 9" long.	3000	4500	6000
Ives Platform Horse, pull toy, 9-1/2" long	1400	2100	2800
Ives Preacher, clockwork, 10-1/2" high	1500	2400	3800
Ives Rower, "Pat. Feb. 9," 13" long, "U.S. Grant" auctioned in 1991 in excellent condition for $7,150			

	C6	C8	C10
Ives Rower, 2-drive wheels protrude from bottom, wheel attached to rudder, 13" long	2500	5000	8000
Ives Santa Claus, clockwork, c. 1875, 10" high	1800	3000	4400
Ives See-Saw, 18" long, auctioned in 1991 in excellent condition with one upper leg replaced for $13,200			
Ives Scottish Jigger	1250	1875	2500
Ives Struktiron set, 1915	100	150	200
Ives Struktiron, 1916, nonmotorized, with box	275	363	550
Ives Vetran (sic) of '76, auctioned in 1994 for $5,175 (resembles George Washington).			
Ives Walking Horse, 6" long	375	562	750
Ives Walking Horse, c., 1890s, 10" long	1000	1600	2400
Ives Walking Santa, 9-3/4" high	1200	2200	3500

IVES "Old Mammy Washing Clothes." Courtesy Christie's East.

IVES Strukt-iron set, 1915. Courtesy Lloyd W. Ralston Auctions.

Uncle Tom Walking Toy, IVES? c. 1875. Courtesy Phillips New York.

Uncle Tom Walking Toy, IVES? Variation. Courtesy Phillips New York.

IVES Walking Horse, 10" long. Photo by Jeanne Bertoia. Courtesy Bill Bertoia Auctions.

	C6	C8	C10
Ives Zouave wind-up walker, 10-1/2" high	1500	2250	3000
Ives, Blakesley & Williams, 1890, Mule Dancers, mechanical revolving, paper litho, painted tin, wooden box, clockwork, 8" tall	1600	2400	3200

IVES Blakesley & Williams Mule Dancers. Courtesy Lloyd W. Ralston Auctions.

	C6	C8	C10
Jane Francis "Gulf Truck Service" Station	500	750	1000
"Jolly Jungleers," Milton Bradley, 1932, derringer-type pistol shoots over animal targets	40	60	80
Judy Toys Farm Set, cardboard and rubber	62	93	125
Jumping Jack, composition and wood	70	105	140
Junior Mechanic Construction Set, c. 1940	48	72	95
Junior WAC set, Hassenfeld Bros., hats, gas mask, bandages, etc.	40	60	80
Junior G-Man Whistle	20	30	40
Kaleidoscope "C. Bush, Prov. R.I., 1874," wood, brass & glass, 14" high	220	330	440
Kaleidoscope, Stevens, 1950s	10	15	20
Kangaroo, cast iron "Jumps," 6-1/4" long	125	187	250
Kenner Easy Bake oven, 1960s	20	30	40
Kenner Give A Show Projector, 112 slides	35	52	70
Kenton Baggage Cart, 6"	30	45	60
Kenton Drag Wagon, litho paper on sides, driver, 15-1/2" long	200	300	400
Kenton Egyptian Toys-Rhino, Lion, Elephant, offered at $175 each, condition unspecified			
Kenton Elephant "Land-on-Roosevelt 1936"	80	120	160
Kenton Stove, cast iron, marked "Oak" on door	30	45	60
Kenton Stove, with warming shelves and stove plates, high back for smokestack, "Royal" on door and shelves, 10" high	40	60	80

	C6	C8	C10
Keystone Bus Terminal	92	138	189
Keystone Farm	50	75	100
Keystone Firestone Station	112	168	225
"Keystone Garage," 1940s or 50s, 8" x 8" x 6"	37	56	75
Keystone "Keystone Fire Department"	90	135	180
Keystone Radiopticon, 1920s	75	112	150
Keystone Service Station	137	205	275
Keystone Warehouse	237	355	475
"Kid Flyer" boy on scooter, tin litho, string-wound, 8-1/2" long	300	450	600
Kilgore Bathroom Sink & Toilet, cast iron, per each	45	68	90
Kilgore Stroller for baby, cast iron	40	60	80
Kingsbury Fire Station, No. 8, clockwork bell and door, 9" x 10" x 13"	150	225	300
"Knockout Target Shooting Gallery," litho tin with rifle, many targets	40	60	80
Ladder for fire trucks, cast iron	15	22	30
Ladders, stamped steel, from Hubley and Arcade trucks	10	15	20
Lawnmower, Arcade, c. 1920, iron and wood, 26-1/2" long	162	243	325
Lehmann "Climbing Monkey"	90	135	180
Lehmann "Hop Hop" rabbit, tin friction	17	25	34
Lehmann "Tom Tom" spiral drive top No. 677, 1920	125	188	250
Lehmann "Toy-Kadi," 1920s friction	500	750	1000
"Lindstrom's Little Show," cardboard and wood theatre with seven show strips	250	375	500
Lion in Hoop, tin, 6-1/4" high	200	300	400

	C6	C8	C10
Lionel Science Kit, c. 1960	20	30	40
Machine Gun, Baldwin "Coast Defense Gun," wood & steel	55	82	110
Machine Gun, Grey Iron, rapid fire, cast iron, 1930s, 9" long	125	188	250
Machine Gun, McDowell, tin litho	70	105	140
Magic Lantern	55	82	110
Magic Lantern, Keystone, "Radioptocin"	40	60	80
Magic Lantern Projector, tin, embossed deer on door and side, 8" long	60	90	120
Man on Bicycle, animated, tin, high wheel bike, bell on top of bicycle, 10-1/2" high	360	540	720
Manoil Target, lead either "4-5-6" or "7-8-9." "1-2-3" doesn't appear to exist, except in a version produced by collectors Ed Poole and Ron Eccles. Manoil's order number for the targets, without specifying which, was 76	45	68	90

MANOIL Targets, "4 5 6," "7 8 9." Photo by Don Pielin.

MARBLES

Marbles are known to date back as far as ancient Rome, when they were made of clay and pottery. Marbles are divided into types, such as "Indian Swirls," "Clambroth," "Lutz Type Swirls," etc. Size numbers range from 000 (1/2-inch) to 8 (1-1/8-inch). There are estimated to be 40,000 to 50,000 current collectors of marbles in the U.S., about 1,700 of whom belong to the Marble Collectors' Society of America (see Leading Collectors and Dealers).

	Value
Sulphide, bust of Jenny Lind, size 1-7/8", near mint	$1,100
Sulphide, Standing Bear, size 1-1/2", mint	125
Handmade Swirl, size 1-1/2", mint	175
Handmade Swirl, size -3/4", mint	20
Ribbon Lutz, size 3/4", mint	400
Clambroth, size 5/8", mint	150
Indian Swirls, size, 5/8", mint	100
Mica, size 3/4", mint	25

End Marbles

	C6	C8	C10
Marky Maypo rubber squeeze toy, 1960s	25	38	50
Marx Air-Sea Power bombing set	110	165	220
Marx "Allstate Terminal & Warehouse," Sears, 1960s, 23" x 15" x 2"	150	225	300
Marx Arcade Shooting Gallery	50	75	100
Marx Army and Navy Mechanical Target No. G169	20	30	40

	C6	C8	C10
Marx Army Code Sender, Morse key and phone, pressed steel, 9-1/2	10	15	20
Marx Ballerina, operated by sawtooth bar, pulled through, 1930s, 6" high	150	225	300
Marx Bear Cyclist, metal, lever action	100	150	200
Marx "Brightelite Filling Station"	283	425	565
Marx Bust 'Em Target Game No. G38	20	30	40
Marx Cat with Ball, cable-operated, tin litho	40	60	80
Marx "Champion Skate" ballet dancer, pull spinning rod out of motor, place skater in upright position and she spins	150	225	300
Marx "Climbing Fireman," tin and plastic	105	158	210
Marx Co. A Barracks, tin litho building, 6" x 8" x 12"	20	30	40
Marx Colonial Doll House No. 4052	60	90	120
Marx "Colonial Service Station," 1960s, 27" x 15" x 4"	90	135	180

MARX Ballerina. Courtesy Scott Smiles. Photo by Mike Adams.

MARX Colonial Doll House No. 4052. Photo by Mary Brett.

MARX Cat with Ball, cable operated. Courtesy Mapes Auctioneers & Appraisers.

MARX "Climbing Fireman," tin and plastic. Courtesy Mapes Auctioneers & Appraiser.

	C6	C8	C10
Marx "Day & Nite Service Service Center"	75	112	150
Marx Deluxe Dial Typewriter, 1930s	37	56	75
Marx Dial Typewriter No. 1000A, 1930s	32	48	65
Marx Dishwasher K54, c. 1950s	60	90	120
Marx Doll House No. 4021	20	30	40
Marx Doll House No. 4030	30	45	60
Marx "Electric Lighted Filling Station," tin litho, 1930s, 10" x 13-1/2" long: See "Sunnyside Service Station"			
Marx Gas Island, 1930s	200	300	400
Marx "General Alarm Fire House," 1940s, 17" long, 11" wide, 3" high	350	525	700
Marx Gobbling Goose, plastic wind-up, 9" long	50	75	100
Marx "Gulf" Service Station	300	450	600
Marx Happitime Service Station	85	128	170
Marx Headquarters, tin litho, U.S. Army Training Center, 5" x 8" x 11"	20	30	40
Marx "Hometown Drug Store," "F.W. Woolworth," tin litho, 5" x 2" x 3-1/2"	120	180	240
Marx "Hometown Favorite Store," "F.W. Woolworth," tin litho, 5" x 2" x 3-1/2"	120	180	240
Marx "Hometown Favorite Store," "S.S. Kresge Co.," tin litho	100	150	200
Marx, "Hometown Firehouse," tin litho, 1930s, 5-1/2" x 2-1/2" x 3-1/2"	200	300	400
Marx "Hometown Grocery Store," tin litho, 1930s, 5" x 2-1/2" x 3-1/2"	60	90	120
Marx "Hometown Meat Market," tin litho, 1930s	60	90	120
Marx "Hometown Movie Theatre," tin litho, 1930s	62	93	125
Marx "Hometown Police Station"	70	105	140
Marx "Hometown Savings Bank," tin litho building, 1930s, 5" x 2-1/2" x 3-1/2"	60	90	120
Marx "Honeymoon Cottage Village," 1930s, tin litho, 17" long x 11" wide	133	200	266

MARX "Honeymoon Garage." Photo by James Apthorpe.

MARX Mechanical Gorilla, with box. Courtesy James S. Maxwell/Virginia Caputo. Photo by Virginia Caputo.

	C6	C8	C10
Marx "Honeymoon Garage," 1930s, tin litho, 6-1/2" x 7" x 3" 45		68	90
Marx "Ice Skater," 1930s, sawtooth bar operates it, 5-1/2" high 150		225	300
Marx Jumbo Climbing Monkey 100		150	200
Marx Junior Dial Typewriter No. 2109, c. 1930s 20		30	40
Marx Kitchen Sink K47, c. 1950s 10		15	20
Marx King Arthur sword and shield, tin litho 37		56	75
Marx "Knockout Champs," celluloid, 1930s ... 418		627	835
Marx "Loop the Loop," 1930s, gravity toy, track 12" long, car 1-1/2" long 50		75	100
Marx Magic Barn w/ tractor 130		195	260
Marx "Magic Garage and Car," 1950s, garage 10" long, car 7" long, wind-up 140		210	280
Marx Mechanical Gorilla 112		168	225
Marx Midtown Service Center 112		168	225
Marx Minit Car Wash 175		262	350
Marx Newlywed Library, tin litho, 1930s, 5" x 2-1/2" x 3-1/2" long 75		112	150

	C6	C8	C10
Marx Pathe News Movie Camera, tin litho 200	300	400
Marx Practice Target Ranger, 1950s, 11" long 30	45	60
Marx "Pretty Maid Washing Machine," c. 1930s, 4-1/2" high 50	75	100
Marx Refrigerator, K42, c. 1950s 15	22	30
Marx Rex Mars Planet Patrol 45 Cal. machine-gun, tin and plastic, winds up, 22" long 55	82	110
Marx "Rex Mars Space Target Game," 1950s, 14" long 150	225	300

MARX "Pretty Maid Washing Machine." Photo by Bill Kaufman. Courtesy Good Old Days Store.

MARX Roadside Rest. Courtesy Thomas G. Nefos, Federal Shipping Network.

MARX Sunny Side Service Station. Photo by Ron Chojnacki. Courtesy Don Hultzman.

	C6	C8	C10
Marx Roadside Rest, 1930	338	500	675
Marx Rock'em, Sock'em Robots	30	45	60
Marx Searchlight, tin litho, 3-1/2" high	20	30	40
Marx Son of Garloo, plastic and tin wind-up	138	205	275
Marx Stove K39, c. 1950s	20	30	40
Marx "Sunnyside Service Station," 1930s, complete	400	600	800
Marx "Super Service" Center	175	263	350
Marx Swinging Arm Target Game No. G52 and Gun	40	60	80
Marx Swinging Arm Target Game No. G55 and Gun	40	60	80
Marx Suburban Colonial Dollhouse, metal	60	90	120
Marx Trixo Monkey string climber	35	52	70
Marx Tunnel, tin litho, depicts farm scene, rolling hills, houses, 8" x 10" x 7"	10	15	20
Marx Typewriter No. 1110, metal and plastic, c. 1950s-1960s	10	15	20
Marx "Universal Gas Service Station," 1940s, 6-1/2" high, base 12" long	150	225	300

	C6	C8	C10
Mattel "Farmer In The Dell," tin, crank, 1951, 7" high	60	90	120
Mattel "Four & 20 Blackbirds," 1950s, crank action, musical toy, 9" diameter	100	150	200
Mattel Jack in the Music Box, 1961	30	45	60
Mattel Mad Scientist Dissect - An Alien	18	27	36
Mattel Mad Scientist Monster Lab	12	18	25
Mattel Mad Scientist Operating Room	10	15	20
Mattel Music Box Carousel	55	83	110
Mattel "Musical Man on the Flying Trapeze"	95	143	190

MATTEL "Musical Man on the Flying Trapeze." Courtesy Continental Hobby House.

	C6	C8	C10
Mattel Thingmaker Creeple People Kit	37	56	75
Mattel Thingmaker Creepy Crawlers Pak, 1960s	18	27	37
Mattel Thingmaker Fang 'n Claw Kit, 1967	20	30	40
Mattel Thingmaker Fighting Man, 1964	50	75	100
Mattel Thingmaker Incredible Edibles Set	45	68	90
Mattel Thingmaker People Makers Pak	35	52	70
Mattel Thingmaker Slitherees Kit, 1967	45	68	90
Mattel Vacuform with molds	35	52	70

MATTEL "Farmer In The Dell," tin, crank, 7" high. Courtesy Calvin L. Chaussee.

	C6	C8	C10
Meat Grinder with clamp, die-cast 7	11	15	
Meccano Set 0 70	105	140	
Meccano Set 00 47	70	95	
Meccano Set 1 12	18	25	
Meccano Set 1A 10	15	20	
Meccano Set 1X 75	112	150	
Meccano Set 2 600	900	1200	
Meccano Set 2A 10	15	20	
Meccano Set 3 10	15	20	
Meccano Set 3A 10	15	20	
Meccano Set 4 50	75	100	
Meccano Set 4A 25	37	50	
Meccano Set 11 600	1000	1400	
Meccano Microscope Set, 1933 10	15	20	

Mr. Peanut, wood, jointed, 9" high. Photo by Jeanne Bertoia. Courtesy Bill Bertoia Auctions.

Merry-Go-Round, wind-up, litho paper
and wood, w/ four bisque figures riding
four fur-skinned papier-mâché horses .... 600 — 900 — 1200

Merry-Go-Round, wood and litho paper,
Jenny musical wind-up
with five horse-form seats .... 200 — 300 — 400

Microphone, Ward Toy .... 40 — 60 — 80

Milton Bradley "Toy Town Post Office" .... 95 — 143 — 190

Mr. Machine: See Ideal

Mr. Peanut, wood-jointed, 9" high .... 150 — 225 — 300

Mr. Potato Head: See Hasbro

Monkey, mechanical, in red pants,
red-checked shirt, squeeze
metal lever attached to 34" spiral
wire, monkey jumps alongside
you, hitting cymbals, 10" high .... 62 — 93 — 125

Monkey Riding Tricycle, cast iron, rubber tires, articulated legs, 7" long. Photo by Jeanne Bertoia. Courtesy Bill Bertoia Auctions.

Monkey Riding Tricycle, cast iron,
rubber tires, articulated legs, 7" long .... 1500 — 2700 — 3800

Monkey, stuffed, red felt cap and jacket,
glass eyes, moveable arms and legs,
move his tail and head moves
from side to side, and up and down,
c. 1910, 9-1/2" high .... 60 — 90 — 120

Mound of Earth, tin litho,
(for toy soldiers), 4" long .... 12 — 18 — 25

	C6	C8	C10
Mound of Rocks, tin litho (for toy soldiers) 12	18	25	
Movie-Jector, hand crank 40	60	80	
Movie Projector, "Flip Movies," turn crank and flip cards from "Midgette" movies, with film, c. early 1930s 56	84	112	

Noah's Ark, German, c. 1895, 15" long. Courtesy Christie's East.

	C6	C8	C10
"Movie Projector Gun," film only, 1937, Box 1 contains Chaplin, Gasoline Alley, Babe Ruth, Buffalo Bill, Harold Teen; Box 2 contains Dick Tracy, Terry & Pirates, Smitty, Orphan Annie, Winnie Winkle; Box 3 contains Clyde Beatty, Gumps, Little Joe, Tiny Tim, Buffalo Bill; Box 4 contains Gasoline Alley, Chaplin, Tracy, Lone Ranger, Harold Teen. Price per box	10	15	20
Movie Projector, "Uncle Sam," hand cranks, c. 1920s	125	188	250
Myrioptican, optical toy, Milton Bradley	300	450	600
Mysto Erector Set No. 1	75	112	150
Mysto Erector Set No. 1A	50	75	100
Mysto Erector Set No. 2, c. 1915	50	75	100
Mysto Erector Set No. 2A	50	75	100
Mysto Erector Set No. 3A	50	75	100
Noah's Ark, wooden, 12 animals, Noah, 6-1/2" long	50	75	100
Noah's Ark, 27 animals, 11" long	115	172	230
Noah's Ark, Bliss, 10 animals, wooden, 13-1/4" long	150	225	300
Noah's Ark, cardboard, with animals, 14" long	100	150	200
Noah's Ark, Converse, carved wooden animals, 14" long	450	675	900

	C6	C8	C10
Noah's Ark, German, c. 1895, hand-carved animals, 15" long	375	562	750
Noah's Ark, Peter-Mar, wood, no animals	275	363	550
Noah's Ark, Pyro, plastic w/ animals	20	30	40
Noah's Ark w/ wooden village blocks	20	30	40
Noah's Ark, wood litho, w/ animals, 10" long	30	45	60
Noise Maker, tin, shaped like old-fashioned phone mouthpiece, 2-1/4" high	6	9	12
Nutty mads figures, Marx, 1963 issue, vinyl, each	11	16	22

Noah's Ark. Courtesy Continental Hobby House.

OHIO ART

Ohio Art was started in October 1908 by a dentist, H.S. Winzeler. Originally its intent was to make metal picture frames (thus its name), but in 1917 the firm bought C.E. Carter (Erie Toy Plant) and began producing metal toys, including a climbing monkey on a string for Ferdinand Strauss. Winzeler later sold the plant to Louis Marx, but continued making tin toys, while Marx, according to Ohio Art history, used the former Carter plant as the foundation of his own company. Ohio Art is still making toys in Bryan, Ohio.

	C6	C8	C10
Ohio Art Barrel Organ, musical, 5-1/2" tall	40	60	80
Ohio Art Beach Toy Water Pumper, c. 1939, signed "Elaine Ends Hileman," 8-1/2" high	17	26	35
Ohio Art Children's Tea Set, tin, 1950s, 14 pieces	75	112	150
Ohio Art Drum, with 2 sticks, 6" x 4"	10	15	20
Ohio Art "Fido's Musical Dog House," 1960s, 8" high	36	54	72
Ohio Art "Mini Farm Set," 1960s playset, 12" long, 5" high	80	120	160
Ohio Art "Realistic Farm Set" No. 197, 1960s playset, 16" long, 7" high	80	120	160
Ohio Art Sand Lift	50	75	100
Ohio Art Sandpail, 1940s, tin litho	42	63	85
Ohio Art Shooting Gallery, key wind, circus	48	72	95
Ohio Art Sunnyfield Farms Barn and Silo set w/ animals, tin litho, 1950s	80	120	160
Ohio Art Toyland Band, drums, bass and snare, cymbals triangle and sticks, 7-1/2" high	20	30	40

	C6	C8	C10
Ohio Art Washtub, tin litho, wood and metal scrubboard, 1940s	16	24	32
Ohio Art Watering Can, tin litho, 1940s	15	22	30

End Ohio Art

	C6	C8	C10
"Old Kentucky Home" wood litho action toy, six dancers, singer-musicians, moved by handcrank, 15-1/2" long	366	549	732
Organ Grinder, monkey, push bottom, squeaks and dances, Kohner Bros., 6" wooden	20	30	40
Paddle Wheel and Tower on base, tin, 14" high	20	30	40
"Paris Coaster," wood-wheeled cart	30	45	60
Parker Bros., 1910, Toy Town Garage, 3 litho tin penny cars, paper litho garage	1200	2000	3000
Parker Bros., "Toy Town Grocery Store"	220	330	440
Phonograph, toy, Genola, cranks with sound horn	100	150	200
Phonograph, toy, Nerona, cranks, sound comes from horn connected to needle, early	100	150	200

PARKER BROS. Toy Town Garage. Courtesy Lloyd W. Ralston Auctions.

	C6	C8	C10
Pig and Piglet in cage, wood, cloth and lithographed paper, spring-loaded squeak toy	50	75	100
Pillsbury Poppin' Fresh, 5" high	8	12	17
Pillsbury Poppin' Fresh, 6-1/2" high	8	12	17
Pillsbury Poppin' Fresh, 10" high	8	12	17
Pillsbury Poppie Fresh, 5" high	8	12	17
Plarola Corporation Organ, tin litho, with six organ rolls	300	450	600

PLASTICVILLE

From information developed by Mark Schulz

Plasticville buildings and accessories were produced by Bachmann Bros., which dates back to 1833. In its early history Bachmann produced ivory cane handles and combs. In 1907 the firm purchased the second injection molding machine ever made and began making eyeglass frames. After WWII, the growth in the toy train market led Bachmann to create plastic picket fences to enclose toy train platforms. This evolved into building kits, the first of which was the Log Cabin. Production continued into the late 1960s, with HO and N scale the main emphasis. In recent years, Bachmann has reintroduced some of the old O/S scale buildings. During its heyday the Plasticville line boasted over 100 items. C8 and C10 include box. All prices assume that no glue has been used.

	C6	C8	C10
Airport Admin Bldg	15	35	50
Airport Hangar	8	26	35
Apartment House	15	35	45
Apartment Add-a-Floor	8	18	25
Autumn Trees	15	35	50
Bank	8	21	28
Barn	8	18	25
Barbecue	1	2	2
Barnyard Animal Set (18)	15	35	45

Plasticville Birdbath, French Section, Trellis. Photo by Gary Linden.

Plasticville Barnyard Animal Set. Photo by Gary Linden.

	C6	C8	C10
Billboard	1.25	1.88	2.50
Birdbath, Fence Section, Trellis	6	10	15
Bungalow	7	15	20

Plasticville Billboard. Photo by Gary Linden.

Plasticville Cape Cod House. Photo by Gary Linden.

Plasticville Citizens. Photo by Gary Linden.

	C6	C8	C10
Cape Cod House Kit	8	26	35
Cathedral	20	48	65
Cattle Loading Pen	8	11	15
Church/Parish Church	8	22	30
Colonial Church	8	22	30
Colonial Mansion	8	26	35
Corner Store	7	18	25
Country Church	4	8	10
Covered Bridge	5	11	14
Dairy Barn	8	22	30
Diner Kit	18	42	55
Factory	25	58	75
Fence and Gate (12 pieces)	3	4.50	6

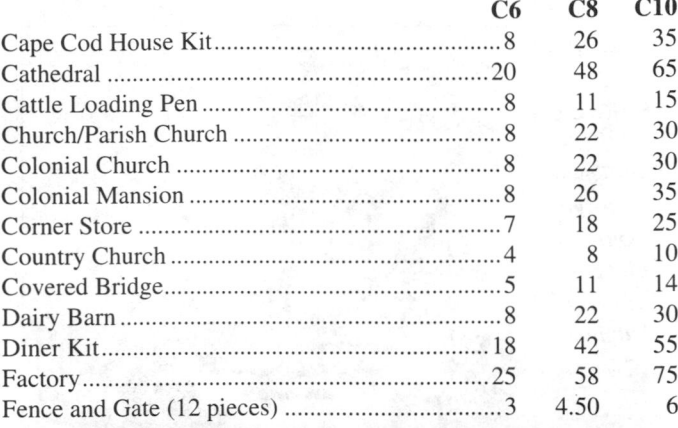

Plasticville Fence and Gate. Photo by Gary Linden.

	C6	C8	C10
Fire House Kit	6	15	20
5 & 10	11	17	36
Freight Station	12	28	38
Frosty Bar	12	30	40
Gas Station, small	9	22	30
Greenhouse	19	27	62
Hobo Shacks (two bldgs)	15	38	50
Hospital (w/ furniture)	20	48	65
House under Construction	30	75	100
Log Cabin, Rustic Fence & Tree	7	18	25
Mobile Home	15	38	50
Motel	6	15	20

Plasticville Diner Kit Box.
Photo by Gary Linden.

Plasticville Diner.
Photo by Gary Linden.

Plasticville 5 & 10. Photo by Gary Linden.

Plasticville Fire House Kit. Photo by Gary Linden.

Plasticville Frosty Bar. Photo by Gary Linden.

	C6	C8	C10
Railroad Work Car	15	38	50
Ranch House	6	12	17
Road Signs	14	33	45
Roadside Stand	6	15	20
Schoolhouse	6	15	19
Split Level House	11	25	35
Street Accessories Unit (15 pieces)	22	33	45
Suburban Station	3	7	9

Plasticville Hobo Shacks. Photo by Gary Linden.

	C6	C8	C10
New England Ranch House	10	24	32
Outhouse	4	9	12
Passenger Station	11	29	38
Pharmacy/Hardware	12	30	40
Plasticville Citizens (24 or 16)	15	25	35
Police Dept., HO scale	6	15	20
Police Dept., O scale	14	34	45
Post Office	8	21	28
Pump	2.50	3.75	5
Railroad Accessories	12	30	40
Railroad Signal Bridge	4	8	11

Plasticville House Under Construction. Photo by Gary Linden.

Plasticville Police Dept. O scale. Photo by Gary Linden.

Plasticville Log Cabin, Rustic Fence & Tree, with box. Photo by Gary Linden.

	C6	C8	C10
Supermarket, large	10	26	35
Supermarket, small	5	12	16
Switch Tower (Railroad)	5	11	15
Telephone Booth	3	8	10
Town Hall	8	18	25
Trailer	11	26	35
Turnpike Interchange	15	38	50
TV Station	5	12	16
Union Station	14	33	45
Water Tank (Railroad)	3	8	10
Well	3	8	10
Windmill	18	45	60

Plasticville Mobile Home. Photo by Gary Linden.

Plasticville Outhouse, Telephone Booth, Well, Barbecue, Pump. Photo by Gary Linden.

Plasticville Police Dept. Kit box, O scale. Photo by Gary Linden.

Plasticville Police Dept. Kit, HO scale box. Photo by Gary Linden.

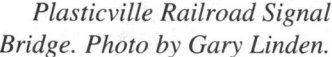

Plasticville Railroad Signal Bridge. Photo by Gary Linden.

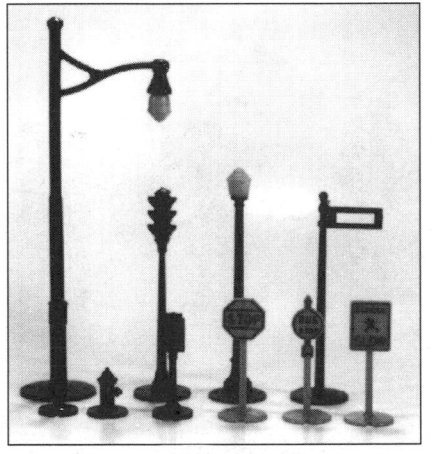

Plasticville Street Accessories Unit. Photo by Gary Linden.

Plasticville Street Accessories Unit box. Photo by Gary Linden.

Plasticville Suburban Station. Photo by Gary Linden.

Plasticville Supermarket, large. Photo by Gary Linden.

Plasticville Supermarket Box, small size. Photo by Gary Linden.

Plasticville Supermarket, small. Photo by Gary Linden.

Plasticville Switch Tower. Photo by Gary Linden.

Plasticville Trailer. Photo by Gary Linden.

Plasticville Trees and Fern. Photo by Gary Linden.

Plasticville Trees. Photo by Gary Linden.

Plasticville Water Tank. Photo by Gary Linden.

	C6	C8	C10
Roadrace Accessories			
Grandstand	12	30	40
Officials' Stand	8	18	25
Pit Stop	12	30	40
Sitting People	9	22	30
End Plasticville			
"Play Store Register," tin and brass, Durable Toy and Novelty Co., 4" high	18	27	36
Pop (Kellogg's Rice Krispies) squeeze toy, 8-1/2" high	19	28	38
Pop (Kellogg's Rice Krispies) hand puppet	16	24	32
Pull Toy, "Buffalo Bill" on horse, tin, 15" long	600	1000	1400
Pull Toy, Camel on Platform, tin, Althof-Bergmann	600	900	1200

Pull Toy, Buffalo Bill on Horse, tin (Miscellaneous). Courtesy Sotheby's New York.

	C6	C8	C10
Pull Toy, Clown on Elephant, Kenton, 1911	400	600	800
Pull Toy, Dog on Platform, animated, Fallows	1200	2000	4000
Pull Toy, Elephant, cast iron, on platform, Kenton, 5-1/2" long	210	315	420

Pull Toy, Elephant, tin, 4-1/2" long, 1870, nothing on back. Courtesy Lloyd W. Ralston Auctions.

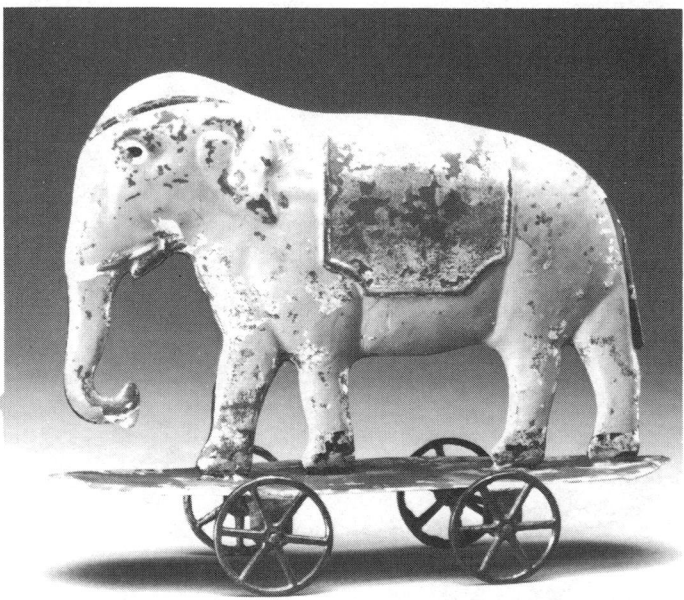

Pull Toy, Elephant, tin, 8-1/2" long, c. 1890. Courtesy Christie's East.

	C6	C8	C10
Pull Toy, Elephant, hide-covered with bisque head, native	150	225	300
Pull Toy, Elephant, tin, 1870, nothing on back, 4-1/2" long	140	210	280
Pull Toy, Elephant, tin, with blanket, iron wheels, 4-1/2" long	170	255	340
Pull Toy, Elephant with saddle, tin, iron wheels, 4-1/2" long	75	112	150
Pull Toy, Elephant, tin, c. 1890, 8-1/2" long	400	600	800
Pull Toy, Elephant, tin, early, 9" long	500	800	1100
Pull Toy, Elephant with howdah, cast iron	600	900	1200
Pull Toy, Elephants, two, on platform, tin, 12" long	300	450	600
Pull Toy, Gibbs, jockeys on horses, wood and paper litho, 10" long	750	1125	1500
Pull Toy, Goat, tin, early, 9-1/2" long	150	225	300
Pull Toy, four race horses and riders, tin w/ cast-iron wheels, 8-1/4" long	400	600	800
Pull Toy, Horse, galloping, tin, 7" long	250	375	500
Pull Toy, Horse, tin, Harwood, c. 1876, 8-1/2" long	2500	3750	5000
Pull Toy, Horse, leather reins, metal stirrups, felt saddle, c. 1880, 13-1/4" high	300	450	600
Pull Toy, Horse and Animated Figure w/ composition head and tin arms playing drum and cymbal, horse is tin, wheels, wooden platform, 13-1/2"	500	750	1000
Pull Toy, Horse and Cart w/ chicken-shaped sides, iron wheels, tin, 5-1/4" long	125	187	250
Pull Toy, Horse and Covered Delivery Wagon, tin, 5-1/4" long	150	225	300
Pull Toy, Horse and Polo Player on horse's back, tin, 4-1/4" long	75	112	150
Pull Toy, Horse and Rider, tin iron wheels, 4-1/2" long	80	120	160
Pull Toy, Horse and Rider, tin, iron wheels, 11" long	150	225	300
Pull Toy, Horse (white) and Water Wagon, tin, 6-3/4" long	250	375	500
Pull Toy, Horse (dark) and Water Wagon, tin, 7-1/4" long	150	225	300
Pull Toy, Horse and Wagon, tin, 9-1/4" long	150	225	300
Pull Toy, Horse on Platform, tin and cast iron, 10" long	435	653	870
Pull Toy, Horse on Platform, George Brown, 1880, painted tin, 6-1/2" long	250	375	500

Pull Toy, horse on platform, 6-1/2" long. Courtesy Lloyd W. Ralston Auctions.

	C6	C8	C10
Pull Toy, Horsewoman, riding side-saddle on pony, cast iron	225	337	450
Pull Toy, Jockey on Dog, tin, early, Ives, 10-1/4" long	1000	1500	2000
Pull Toy, Jockey on Goat, Ives, 9-1/2" long	3500	5200	7000
Pull Toy, Jockey on Horse, tin, c. 1875, Fallows, 7" long	500	800	1200

Pull Toy, Rider on Horse, tin, 10" long. Courtesy Sotheby's New York.

Pull Toy, Jockey on Horse, tin, Fallows, 7" long. Courtesy Christie's East.

	C6	C8	C10
Pull Toy, Jockey on Horse, early 1900s	440	660	880
Pull Toy, Jockey on Horse, tin, hair tail, 9" long	600	900	1200
Pull Toy, Jonah & Whale, cast iron	400	600	800
Pull Toy, Jumbo Elephant on wheels, Gibbs, 10" long	200	300	400

Pull Toy, Sheep, tin, c. 1890. Courtesy PB Eighty-Four.

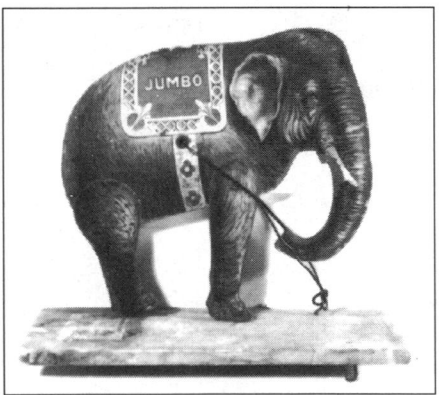

Pull Toy, Jumbo Elephant (wheels missing), Gibbs. Courtesy Continental Hobby House.

	C6	C8	C10
Pull Toy, Lion, tin, 4-1/2" long	185	280	370
Pull Toy, Mary & Lamb, tin, Fallows, c. 1890, 6-1/2" long	1000	1600	2400

Pull Toy, Rooster on platform. Courtesy Lloyd W. Ralston Auctions.

Pull Toy, Swan Chariot. Courtesy James S. Maxwell/Virginia Caputo. Photo by Virginia Caputo.

	C6	C8	C10
Pull Toy, Rider on Horse, tin, 10" long	500	750	1000
Pull Toy, Rooster, tin, 3-1/4" long	400	600	800
Pull Toy, Rooster on Platform, 1890, painted tin, 4-3/4" long	100	150	200
Pull Toy, Sheep, tin, c. 1890, 6-1/4" high	150	225	300
Pull Toy, Swan Chariot	6000	9000	12,000
Pull Toy, Three Bears by Toycraft	30	45	60
Pull Toy, Two Frogs, painted tin, Fallows, 1898, 7-1/2" long	900	1350	1800

Push Toy, Horse and Rider, Wilkins. Courtesy Wilkinson Collection, Detroit Antique Toy Museum.

Pull Toy, Two Frogs, 7-1/4" long, painted tin, Fallows, 1898. Courtesy James S. Maxwell/Virginia Caputo. Photo by Virginia Caputo.

Push Toy, large running horses, Fallows, tin. Courtesy Christie's East.

	C6	C8	C10
Pump, tin, with round trough, transfer of puppies, 7" high	15	22	30
Punch and Judy Puppet Theatre with 6 puppets: Punch, Judy, Devil, Princess, Sailor, Workman	400	600	800
Push Toy, Butterfly that flaps its wings	40	60	80
Push Toy, Clown on Log, bell toy, cast iron	500	750	1000
Push Toy, Gibbs, No. 29 Derby Rider	300	450	600
Push Toy, horse and rider, Wilkins, c. 1910, cast iron and wood, 29" long	262	395	525
Push Toy, large running horses, tin, Fallows, cast-iron wheels, 30" long	1000	1600	2300
Push Toy, horse, wooden, walks	40	60	80
Q.R.S. Playasax, uses paper rolls, Devry Corp., 12" long	175	262	350
Quake Rag Doll, 1960s, 12" high	65	98	130
Quisp Rag Doll, 1960s, 11" high	70	105	140
Quisp Space Gun	175	263	350
Rabbit, moves ears, small	110	165	220
Rabbits, two, mashing ingredients in small bowl, tin, animated by squeezing, 6" high	15	22	30

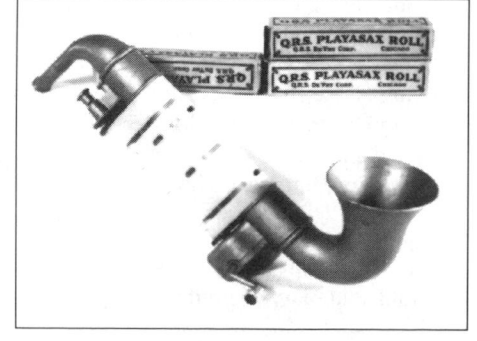

Q.R.S. Playasax, with music rolls. Courtesy Continental Hobby House.

	C6	C8	C10
Ranger Steel Bowling Alley	80	120	160
Ranger Steel "Drive Safely" set	112	168	225
Ranger Steel Co. "Gas Station-Auto Laundry," 1940s, 3" x 5" x 13" long	130	195	260
Reddy Kilowatt plastic figure, 1940s	125	188	250
Reed "Mammoth Hippodrome" circus ring, 19" diameter	600	1000	1500
Reed Military Fort Set, 8-1/2" x 18"	800	1400	2000

Rolmonica.

REED Military Fort. Photo by Jeanne Bertoia. Courtesy Bill Bertoia Auctions.

	C6	C8	C10
Refrigerator, cast iron, Hubley, "GE," 7" high	150	225	300
Remco B-52 Ball Turret	60	90	120
Remco Johnny Reb Cannon	88	132	175
Remco Movieland Drive-In Theatre	90	135	180
Remco Naval PomPom Gun	42	63	85
Remco Space Commander Walkie Talkies	35	52	70
Renwal Drawbridge, plastic, 2 plastic autos, 2 boats, cardboard river scene, early 1950s, 27" long	79	119	158
Renwal Globe Trotter Set No. 305-150, 4 boats, 3 cars, train, jet plane	19	28	38
Renwal "Visible Dog, The"	21	32	43
Renwal "Visible Horse"	14	21	27
Renwal "Visible Man, The"	16	24	33
Renwal "Visible Pigeon"	20	30	40
Renwal "Visible V-8"	19	28	38
Renwal "Visible Woman, The"	7	11	15
Ripley's Believe It or Not Disk-O-Knowledge, round piece of cardboard w/ another piece attached on top, turn to reveal questions and answers, 1932, 9-1/2" diameter	10	15	20
"Rocket Ring," with futuristic rocket on top of ring, whistles, 1930s	30	45	60
Rocking Horse, Converse, 1905	700	1200	1600
Rocking Horse, hand carved, all wood, 1890s	500	750	1000
Rocking Horse, 1930s, 24" high	112	168	225
Rocking Horse, NN Hill-Gong Bell Co.	200	300	400
Rocking Horse, "Shoo Fly"	100	150	200
Rocking Toy, tin, girl on horse, German-Penny Toy, 3-3/4" long	220	330	440
Rolmonica, harmonica that plays rolls of tunes, "Blow, crank and play," with three songs, 1930s	100	150	200

	C6	C8	C10
Roly Poly, Boy on Horse, c. 1900	140	210	280
Roly Poly Clown, c. 1900, 13" high	412	618	825
Sand Toy Set, Chick Art Co., 1942, includes tin litho frog, sailboat, shovel and round sieve	36	54	78
Sandbags, variously marked, for toy soldiers	2.50	3.75	5
Sand Pail, tin litho, c. 1940	15	22	30
Scales, cast iron, tin tray and four brass weights, 5-3/4" long	26	39	52
Scales, cast iron, "Dayton," 3-1/2" high	40	60	80
Schieble Handcar, 2 men, tin, 9" long	350	525	700

SCHIEBLE Handcar. Photo by Jeanne Bertoia. Courtesy Bill Bertoia Auctions.

Sewing Machine, c. 1920. Photo by Bill Kaufman. Courtesy Good Old Days Store.

Simplex

by Barbara and Jonathan Newman, The Paper Soldier, Clifton Park, New York

(All Simplex photos courtesy Barbara and Jonathan Newman)

The Simplex Typewriter Company of New York City (and, at their peak, of London, England) was probably the world's most prolific toy typewriter company. They produced inexpensive children's typewriters using the advertising motto, "They teach … they entertain" from about 1900 to some time in the 1930s.

Apparently Simplex toy typewriters were available in most stores, by mail order, and frequently as premiums for successfully selling seed packets, magazine subscriptions, and the like. Some models in our collection include documentation from each of these sources.

The famous Johnson Smith novelty catalog (source of such cultural icons as the whoopee cushion and those magnetic little black and white Scottie dogs) still offered several Simplex models in 1950. Whether they were remaining stock or were still being produced somewhere is not known (by us at least). What is known, however, is that somewhere between 50 and 100 different models were produced for markets all over the world. Taking into account minor variations in color, the number must be considerably higher.

All of the models used the same basic mechanism, which is much like the revolving, one-letter-at-a-time plastic label makers. The size, shape, color, material, and type were available in various permutations. The only material they seem to have missed was plastic, and perhaps there is a model of a Simplex in that material yet to be discovered out there as well.

There is very little information about the company. There was one very small monograph published around 1985 by Darryl and Roxana Matter and one or two passing references to the company in more general articles on toy typewriters.

In our own collection we have almost 30 different models, and we continue to come across models we have never seen before. We even have one model that seems to be a cheaper version of the Simplex called The Star typewriter (it still has all of the Simplex patent numbers on the dial). If anyone out there has any advertising information or catalogs and flyers from the Simplex Company we would be pleased to have copies or to purchase them.

Prices vary from about $15 up to $65. The price doesn't seem to have anything to do with specific models. We have boxes for most of the models in our collection.

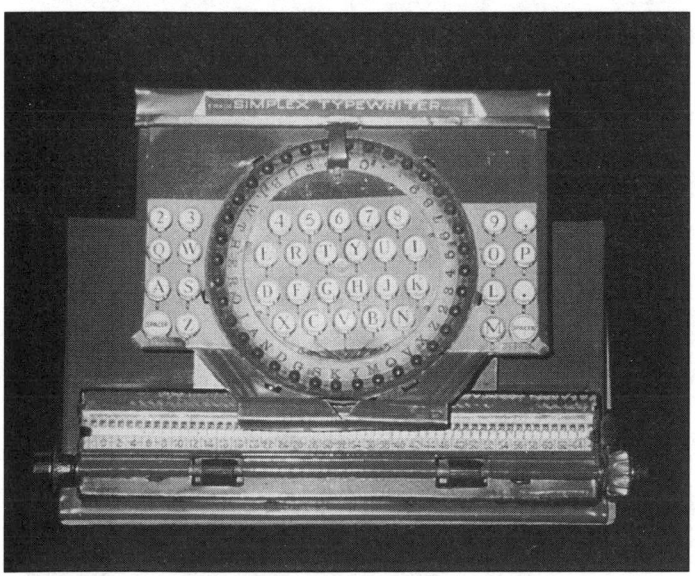

1. SIMPLEX Typewriter A35 Keyboard Model (no box).

2. SIMPLEX Typewriter D35 Special Keyboard Model (no box).

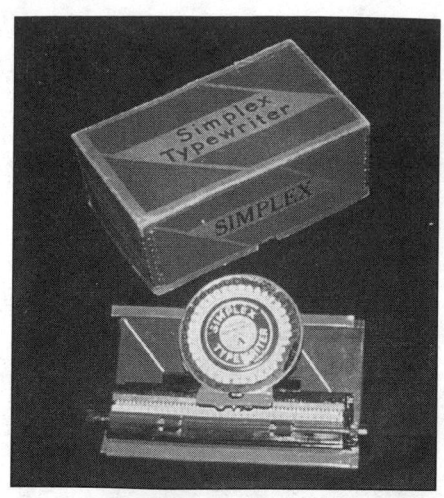

3. SIMPLEX Typewriter Special Demonstrated Model A.

4. SIMPLEX Typewriter Special Demonstrated Model C.

5. SIMPLEX Typewriter Special Demonstrated Model C.

6. SIMPLEX Portable Special Demonstrated Model.

7. Special SIMPLEX Typewriter Number 150.

8. SIMPLEX Typewriter Number 100 (seed premium).

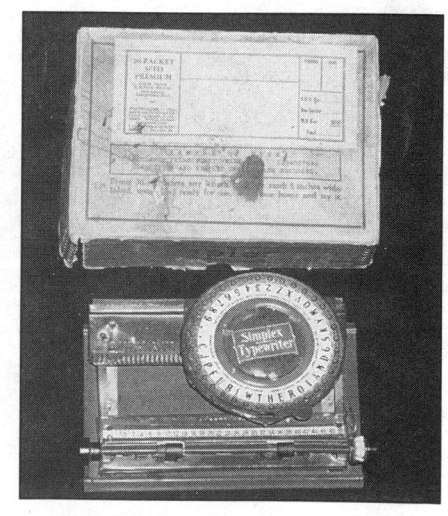

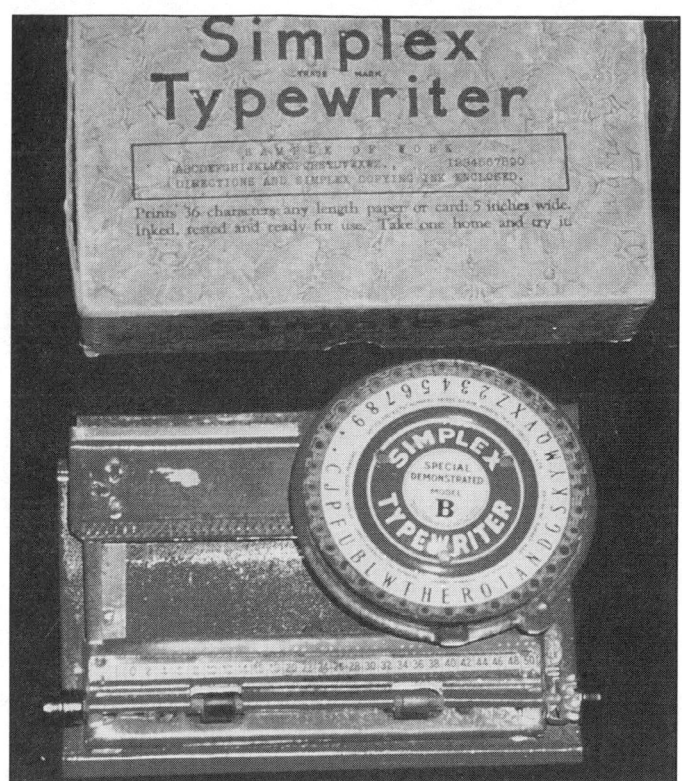

9. SIMPLEX Typewriter Special Demonstrated Model.

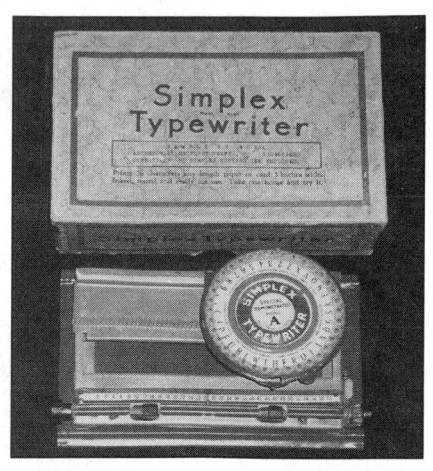

10. SIMPLEX Typewriter Special Demonstrated Model A-same as #3 but with color variations.

12. SIMPLEX Typewriter Special Demonstrated Model A-same as #3, #10 and #11, cardboard not metal base.

11. SIMPLEX Typewriter Special Demonstrated Model A-same as #3 and #10, color variation.

13. SIMPLEX Typewriter Special 1.

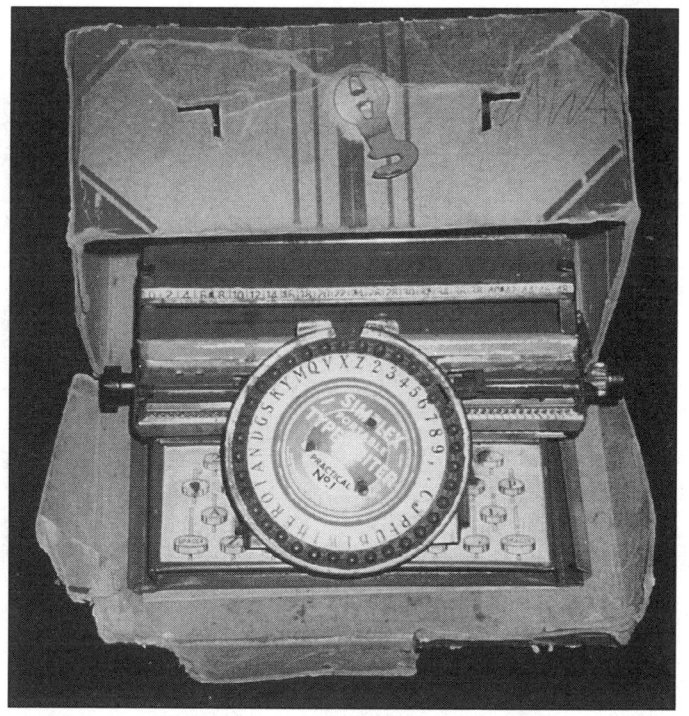

14. SIMPLEX Portable Typewriter Practical No. 1.

15. SIMPLEX
Typewriter
Practical
No. 100.

16. SIMPLEX
Typewriter
Special
Demonstrated
Model B.

17. The SIMPLEX Typewriter No. 2 (no box).

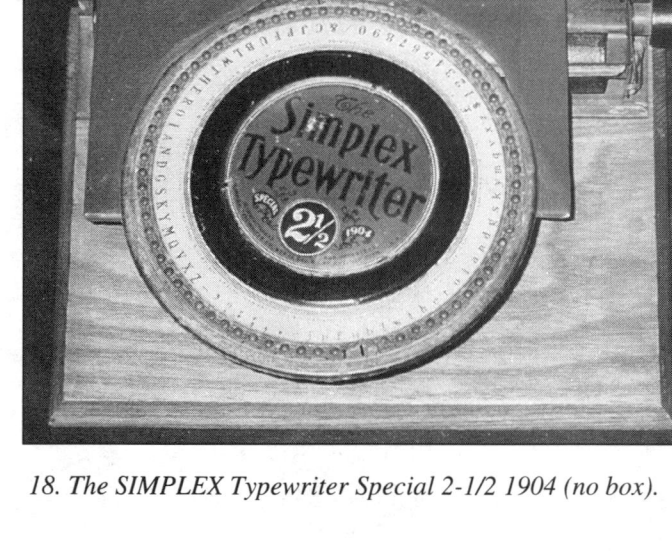

18. The SIMPLEX Typewriter Special 2-1/2 1904 (no box).

19. SIMPLEX Portable Typewriter Special Demonstrated
Model T (no box).

20. Practical
SIMPLEX
Typewriter
Number 200.

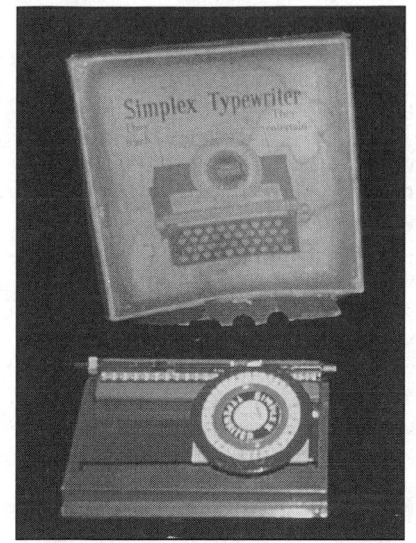

21. SIMPLEX Typewriter Model A.

22. Practical SIMPLEX Typewriter Number 300.

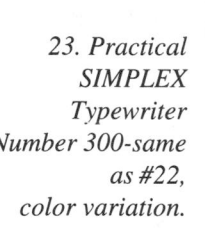

23. Practical SIMPLEX Typewriter Number 300-same as #22, color variation.

24. Practical SIMPLEX Typewriter Number 300-same as #22 and #23, color variation.

25. Special 1908 SIMPLEX Typewriter 2-1/2.

26. Special 1912 SIMPLEX Typewriter 3.

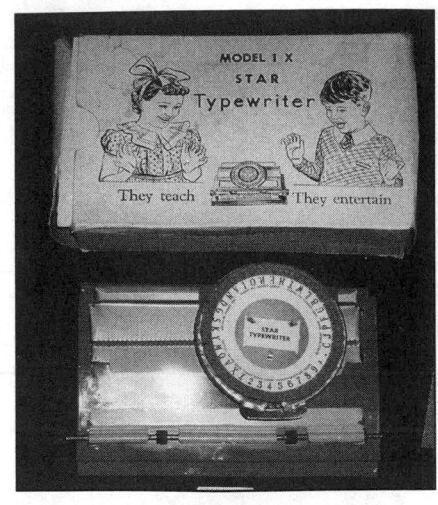

28. Not marked Simplex but Model X Star Typewriter, but patent numbers show it is a SIMPLEX.

	C6	C8	C10
Slinky, 1947, with box	12	18	25
Snap (Kellogg's Rice Krispies) squeeze toy, 8-1/2" high	21	32	42
Snap (Kellogg's Rice Krispies) hand puppet	16	24	32
Squeak Toy, Bird, c. 1884, composition, 7-1/2" long	100	150	200
Squeak Toy, Cat & Kitten, c. 1880, composition, 4"	200	300	400
Stitchwell Sewing Machine, child's floor model, c. 1920s	80	120	160
Stove, cast iron, "American"	100	150	200
Stove, "Daisy," cast white metal, 4-1/4" high	15	22	30
Stove, "Eagle," cast iron, 4-1/4" high	50	75	100
Stove, "Eagle, cast iron, 11-1/2" high	100	150	200
Stove, "Eagle," cast iron, 13-1/2" high	125	187	250
Stove, cast iron, 13" x 11-1/2" high	75	112	150
Stove, cast iron, Ark, 4" x 5"	25	37	50

	C6	C8	C10
Stove, electric, one burner, two ovens, chrome-finished steel, porcelain on oven doors, 16" wide, 14" tall	80	120	160
Stove, "Lancaster," "Eagle," on door and shelf, cast iron, 10-3/4"	120	180	240
Stove, wood-burning, cast iron, "The Queen"	45	67	90
Stove, Roper, Arcade, gas burner, cast iron, 6" high	100	150	200
Stove, "Royal," cast iron, 4-1/2"	60	90	120
Steve, Suzy Homemaker, 1968, Topper	18	27	37
Stove, wood-burning, cast iron, "The Triumph Range"	100	150	200
Stove, tin, with four plate covers, four pans and one skillet, 5" high	150	225	300
Stretcher for 3" toy soldiers, pre-WWII	6	9	12
Structo Erector Set, 1910	50	75	100
Structo No. 3	70	105	140
Superior Service Station Playset, 1950s	90	135	180
Swing, animated, cast iron and pressed steel, for doll, with eagle, wheel	600	900	1200
Swinging Clown, tin, base marked "C.D. Kenny Co.," 4-1/4" high	120	180	240
"The Symmetroscope," wood and tin type of kaleidoscope, F.P. Irving, Troy, N.Y., 6-1/4" high	60	90	120
Tea kettle, cast iron, 3-1/4" long	30	45	60
Teeter-Totter, Gibbs Toys, when inverted, two children work their way down, tin, 1910, 14-1/2" high	106	160	212
Tent, Army, two pole, two flags on top, approx. 5" long	7.50	11.25	15

Stove, "Eagle," cast iron, 11-1/2" high. Courtesy Mapes Auctioneers & Appraiser.

Teeter-Totter, GIBBS. Courtesy Garth's Auctions Inc.

	C6	C8	C10
Tent, "Bat. A," two flags	14	21	28
Tent, canvas, white, 9" long	7.50	11.25	15
Tent, Army, "Field Hangar, U.S. Aviation Corp. Squadron 1," two flags atop tent, approx. 9" long	11	16	22
Tent, Army, "U.S. Battery B. Coast Artillery," two poles, two flags on top	11	16	22
Tent "Guard Tent Co. A," 4-1/4" high	5	7.50	10
Tent, "Inf. Co. C"	9	13	18
Tent, "Medical Unit"	12	18	24
Tent, "Mess Hall," wood base	12	18	25
Tent, "Sail-Me" Co., 6 w/ box, c. 1931, paper	40	60	80

Tents, 6 with box, c. 1931, paper, Sail-Me Co. Photo by Charlie O'Brien.

	C6	C8	C10
Tent, "U.S. Infantry Co. A," two flags on top, 4-1/2" high	11	16	22
Tent, "U.S. Infantry Co. B"	6	9	12
Tent, paper, "State Camp Co. A," 5" high	1.50	2.25	3
Tent, No. 76, small pup, white with cardboard base, center support	4	6	8
Tin dog with boy rider, on wheeled platform, 13-1/2" long	600	900	1200
Tinker Toys, round box, 1940s, 12" high	12	18	24
Tinker Toys, Electric ET-1	30	45	60
Tinker Toys No. 104	12	18	25
Tinker Toys No. 136	14	21	27
Toledo Scales, cast iron, 4" x 4"	25	37	50
"Tom Thumb" cash register, metal, 6-1/2" x 7-1/2" x 8-1/4" by Western Stamping Co.	25	38	50
Tools, Grey Iron, 1933, price per set	15	22	30
Tool Set, Greycraft (Grey Iron), 1940, cast iron, steel and wood	12	18	25
Tootsietoy Bathroom set	80	120	160
Tootsietoy Bedroom set	80	120	160
Tootsietoy Dining Room set	60	90	120
Tootsietoy Kitchen set	55	82	110
Tootsietoy furniture, six chairs, moveable bar, two side tables and a dining table	100	150	200

TOOTSIETOY. Left to right: Bathroom Set, Dining Room Set. Courtesy Continental Hobby House.

	C6	C8	C10
Tootsietoy living room set, two chairs, lamp, gramophone, sofa secretaire, table	95	143	190
Tootsietoy metal kitchen and bathroom furniture, sink, bathtub, toilet, stove, table and cupboard	45	67	90
Tootsietoy Music Room set	150	225	300
Top, Carnival Whistling Top, tin litho circus decor, spring-wound, Lupor, 1930s, 4" diameter	30	45	60
Top, gyro style, 1918	16	24	32
Top, wooden, c. 1940	4	6	8
Transworld Airlines, Jr. Pilot Wings	10	15	20
Tricycle, iron, Kilgore, 2-3/4"	30	45	60
Trix Rabbit, rubber squeeze toy	19	29	39
Turner Firehouse, heavy sheet metal, 12" x 15" x 21"	200	300	400
Turner Garage, heavy sheet metal, one window on each side, divided into four panes	100	150	200
The Twister, in black cloth pants and red stripe shirt w/ porkpie hat, reminiscent of outfits worn at the Peppermint Lounge where the Twist was born. Stands on a 7" sq. platform 3-1/2" high, inscribed "Let's Twist!," which is exactly what he does, early 60s, 12" high	90	135	180
"Uncle Sam's Cash Store Register," Durable Toy and Novelty, steel 5" high	26	39	52
Waffle Iron, cast iron, Wagner	25	37	50
Wagon, Champion Express Coaster, 8" with handle	65	98	130
Wagon, "Express" wood spoke wheels	250	375	500
Wagon, Express Flyer, cast iron	125	187.50	250
Wagon, "Greyhound," full size, steel	80	120	160
Wagon, "Kiddie Kart," c. 1925, H.I. White, 20" long	50	75	100
Wagon, "Pioneer," tin, c. 1870, 25" long	312	468	625
Wagon, "Pony Express," 38" long	100	150	200
Wagon, "Radio Flyer, No. 94," 29" long	120	180	240
Wagon, wood, for child, 1900	175	263	350
Walking Horse, metal and papier mache wind-up, early, 8-1/4"	400	600	800
Washing Machine, tin, works, c. 1940, seashore scene on side	62	93	125
Water Tank Wagon, 1910, painted pressed steel, 26" long	250	375	500

4¾" HIGH

4⅝" WIDE

5⅛" DEEP

MODEL No. 150—RETAILS at $1.00

Uncle Sam's "PLAYSTORE" Cash Register

Supplied with metal "Playstore" money. Made, looks and works like a big cash register. Just press a key — the bell rings — the door shoots open, and the amount of the sale is shown. A grand toy for boys and girls. It teaches them to count . . . add . . . subtract and multiply. All steel construction.

PACKED IN A HANDSOME BOX

Lock-and-key

Uncle Sam's 2-in-1 Bank and Cash Register

For Playing — For Saving

Children will appreciate this gift. It has the same features as our No. 150 "Playstore" Cash Register, PLUS a real lock-and-key BANK. Teaches thrift. "Playstore" money supplied. Real money, and play money can be locked in the "vault" in back until ready to "open the store." An amusing toy— yet a practical savings bank. All steel construction. Finished in rich, black enamel.

No. 160

RETAILS at $1.50

4" HIGH—5⅝" WIDE—5¼" DEEP

"Uncle Sam's Cash Store Register," two varieties as shown in a c. 1940 Durable Toy & Novelty Corp. catalog. Courtesy Bill Holt.

"Uncle Sam's Cash Store Register." Courtesy James S. Maxwell/ Virginia Caputo. Photo by Virginia Caputo.

Water Tank Wagon, 1910. Courtesy Lloyd W. Ralston Auctions.

Whirligig of Life. Courtesy Lloyd W. Ralston Auctions.

	C6	C8	C10
"Western Union" telegraph key, battery powered, code printed on front......... 17		26	35
Wheelbarrow, cast iron, 1930, 4-1/2" 25		37	50
Wheelbarrow, cast iron, approx. 5-1/2" 30		40	60
Wheelbarrow, cast iron, 6-1/2" long 35		52	70
Wheelbarrow, cast iron, w/ tools, 1915, 7" long.................... 60		90	120
Wheelbarrow, steel, 9" long 31		47	62
Whirligig of Life, McLoughlin, 1870s, illusion of motion 600		1000	1400
Wilkins Fire House No. 8, tin, 18-1/2" long 600		900	1200
Wilkins Horse and Jockey, 1900, cast iron, wheeled pull toy, 10" 600		900	1200

	C6	C8	C10
Windmill, metal, with pumping apparatus 800		1300	1800

WOLVERINE

Wolverine, of Pittsburgh, Pennsylvania, was founded in 1903 by B.F. Bain. The company got its name from Bain's Michigan hometown. In later years Wolverine became a subsidiary of Spang Industries, and in 1970 moved to Boon-ville, Arkansas. The "Sandy Andy," in all its variations, was probably Wolverine's most successful and famous toy. The firm's name is now Today's Kids.

WOLVERINE Automatic Coal Loader. Photo by Don Hultzman.

	C6	C8	C10
Wolverine "Adding Machine No. 39," 1940s, 7" long 25		38	50
Wolverine Auto Magic Sand Loader, 1947, 11" high.. 87		130	175
Wolverine "Automatic Coal Loader," 1940s, 10" high 55		83	110
Woverine "Automatic Sand Crane," tin 60		90	120
Wolverine Bizzy Andy, pat. 1914, steel and tin, 11" high, sand toy 10		15	20
Wolverine Bizzy Andy Trip Hammer, 1917 100		150	200
Wolverine "Captain Sandy Andy" No. 63C sand toy, 1930s, 13" high 75		112	150
Wolverine "Corner Grocer," tin litho store 450		675	900
Wolverine "Dumping Sandy," 1916, 12" high 200		300	400
Wolverine Farm Wagon, plastic wind-up, 10" long 40		60	80

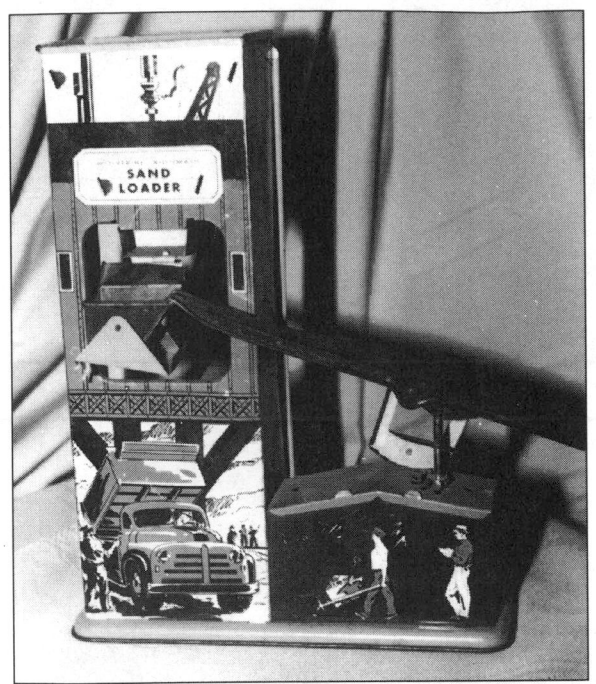

WOLVERINE Automatic Sand Loader, 1947. Courtesy Calvin L. Chaussee.

	C6	C8	C10
Wolverine "General Grocery," 1930s, includes 10-1/4" tin counter, scale, phone, paper dispenser and groceries, 20-1/4" opened and 10-1/4" closed	375	565	750

WOLVERINE "General Grocery." Photo by Ron Chojnacki. Courtesy Don Hultzman.

Wolverine Kitchen Cabinet No. 178	39	58	78
Wolverine Merry Masons sand toy, 16" high	70	105	140
Wolverine "Music Box. No. 38, 1930s, (crank action), 6" high	50	75	100
Wolverine Organ, tin, turn crank to make organ-like sounds	120	180	240

WOLVERINE Captain Sandy Andy 63C. Photo by Ron Chojnacki. Courtesy Don Hultzman.

	C6	C8	C10
Wolverine "Panama Pile Driver" No. 54	85	128	170
Wolverine "Post Office" with cardboard accessories	150	225	300
Wolverine Refrigerator No. 183	35	52	70
Wolverine "Sandy Andy No. 60 Automatic Sand Toy," patented 1909 and 1911	80	120	160

WOLVERINE Sandy Andy.

Wolverine "Sandy Andy Full Back," 1920	375	565	750
Wolverine Sandy Andy Sand Loader, 1912	65	98	130
Wolverine Sandy Andy Trick Animals, seal, polar bear pull toy	350	525	700
Wolverine Woverine "Shell" Service Station with 3 vehicles	175	263	350
Wolverine "Ski Jumper," 1940s, catapult action, 18" long	37	56	75
Wolverine "Skyscraper Elevator," 1915, 24" high with "2000 lbs" counterweight	150	225	300
Wolverine "State Capital Quiz No. 43," 1940s, 7" long	40	60	80
Wolverine "Streamline Railway No. 129," 17" long, pull toy	150	225	300
Wolverine "Sunny Andy" Cable Car Set No. 53, c. 1920-30s, 12" high	80	120	160

WOLVERINE sand and other toys, as shown in a December 1929 Butler Bros. catalog.

WOLVERINE "Sunny Andy Kiddie Kampers." Courtesy Mapes Auctioneers & Appraiser.

	C6	C8	C10
Wolverine "Sunny Andy Fun Fair No. 65," 1930s, action toy gravity activated by steel balls, 14" long	195	286	390
Wolverine Sunny Andy "Kiddie Kampers," action toy, color litho, three boy scouts and two girl scouts in backdrop camp setting, boys chop and saw wood and girls signal w/ flags, marbles drop down chute, c. 1929, 5-5/8" x 3-1/2"	250	375	500
Wolverine "Sunny Andy Rabbit Chase," 1930s, 9-1/2" diameter	150	225	300
Wolverine "Sunny Suzy" refrigerator	4	6	8

	C6	C8	C10
Wolverine "Texaco Service Station," 1960s, 25" x 15"	90	135	180
Wolverine "The Corner Grocer No. 182," 1930s, includes 16" tin counter, scale, phone, paper dispenser and groceries, 31" long opened; 15-3/4" closed	400	600	800
"Wonder Clown" No. 110, 1950s, Nesco Co., spinning top action, 5-3/4" high	80	120	160
Wood Cage with horse, when gate is opened horse pops out and whinnies	125	187	250
Wood Cage, mechanical, rooster flies out when door is open	50	75	100
Wooden Music Maker, "Auto Phone Co. H.B. Horton's, Ithaca, N.Y.," uses player rolls, 9-1/2" high	100	150	200
Wyandotte Air Raid Defense Target Game	52	78	105
Wyandotte Black Sambo target game, tin, has gun	70	105	140
Wyandotte "Carnival," with ferris wheel, carousel and airplane ride, metal	700	1300	1860
Wyandotte "Flash Strat-O-Wagon," 6" long	80	120	160
Wyandotte Hen, chubby, tin, lays egg when body pressed down, with eight eggs, 8-1/2" long	50	75	100

WOLVERINE "The Corner Grocer." Photo by Ron Chojnacki. Courtesy Don Hultzman.

WYANDOTTE "Carnival." Courtesy Joe and Sharon Freed.

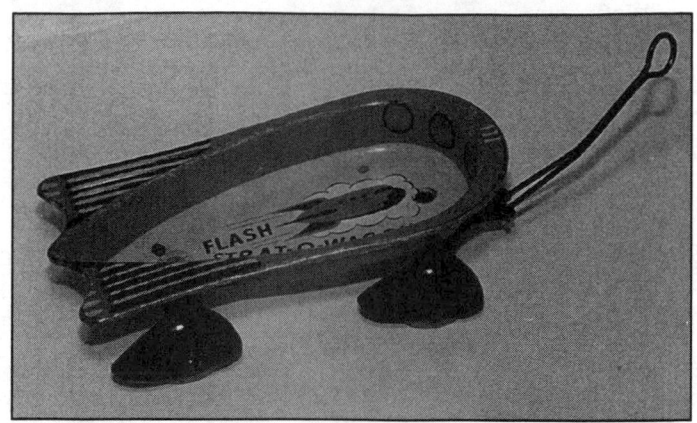

WYANDOTTE "Flash Strat-O-Wagon." Photo by Brian Seligman.

	C6	C8	C10
Wyandotte "Musical" push top, c. 1939	30	45	60
Wyandotte "Posse" Shooting Gallery, wind-up gallery, 14" wide	90	135	180
Wyandotte "Shooting Gallery," 1930s, wind-up, 14" long, 11" high	65	98	130
Wyandotte Wagon, streamlined, steel, 1930s, 8"	150	225	300
Xylophone, 1944	50	75	100
"Zoetrope," wood and cardboard, illusion of motion game, Milton Bradley	350	525	700
"Zulu Blow Gun," copyright 1925, 4 arrows, target, instructions, etc., mfd. Battle Creek, Michigan, 2' long	50	75	100
"Zulu Blow Gun" same as above, different coloring and target, no instruction sheet	45	68	90

WYANDOTTE "Musical" Push Top. Photo by Bill Kaufman. Courtesy Good Old Days Store.

WYANDOTTE "Posse" Shooting Gallery. Photo by Bill Kaufman. Courtesy Good Old Days Store.

Zoetrope. Courtesy Milton Bradley.

MUSEUMS

ANTIQUE TOY MUSEUM
Exit 230, I-44
P.O. Box 175
Stanton, MO 63079
(314) 927-5555

AUBURN-CORD-DUSENBERG
MUSEUM
Auburn, IN 46706
Auburn toys and Cord and Dusenberg
automobiles

BAUER TOY MUSEUM
(Donald A. Bauer)
233 E. Main
Fredericksburg, TX
(512) 997-9394

DAISY GUN MUSEUM
U.S. 71 South
Rogers, AR
The world's most complete collection of
air rifles, dating from the 18th century

ISLIP TOWN MUSEUM
Montauk Highway
Oakdale, NY

LAKE ERIE TOY MUSEUM
(Aaron Roy)
P.O. Box 860
Kelleys Island, OH 43438
(419) 746-2451

LAWRENCE SCRIPPS WILKINSON
COLLECTION
c/o Detroit Antique Toy Museum
6325 West Jefferson
Detroit, MI 48209
(383) 843-9775
Available only for traveling exhibitions

THE LONDON TOY & MODEL
MUSEUM
23 Craven Hill
London, England

MARGARET WOODBURY
STRONG MUSEUM
One Manhattan Square
Rochester, NY 14607

MUSEUM OF CHILDHOOD
8 Broad Street
Greensport, NY

MUSEUM OF THE CITY OF
NEW YORK
5th Avenue and 103rd Street
New York, NY

NASHVILLE TOY MUSEUM
2613 McGavok Pike
Nashville, TN
Next to Opryland USA

REMEMBER WHEN TOY MUSEUM
Box 226A
Canton, MO 63435
(314) 288-3995 or 288-3176

SAN FRANCISCO
INTERNATIONAL TOY MUSEUM
2801 Leavenworth Street
San Francisco, CA

SMITHSONIAN INSTITUTION
Public Inquiry Mail Service - MRC010
1000 Jefferson Drive SW
Washington, DC 20560
(202) 357-1300

THE STERLING COLLECTION
Stone Castle
804 North Third Street
Bardstown, KY

SULLIVAN-JOHNSON MUSEUM
223 North Main Street
Kenton, OH
Kenton Toys exhibit

THE TOY MUSEUM
42 Bridge St. Row
Chester, Cheshire
England

TOY TRAIN MUSEUM
Paradise Lane
Strasburg, PA

WASHINGTON DOLL'S HOUSE &
TOY MUSEUM
5236 44th Street NW
Washington, DC 20015

APPENDIX B

AUCTIONEERS

These are established firms experienced in disposing of large collections of toys by auction.

REX & KATHY BARRETT (mail)
P.O. Box 254
Medinah, IL 60157

BILL BERTOIA AUCTIONS
2413 Madison Ave.
Vineland, NJ 08360
(609) 692-1881
FAX: 609-692-8697

JEFF BUB
1658 Barbara Drive
Brunswick, OH 44212
(216) 225-1110

BUTTERFIELD & BUTTERFIELD
1244 Sutter Street
San Francisco, CA 94109

CHICAGO ANTIQUE TOY
AUCTION
by Just Right, Inc.
6582 RFD
Long Grove, IL 60047
(708) 949-0059

CHRISTIE'S EAST
219 East 67th Street
New York, NY 10021
(212) 606-0400

CONTINENTAL AUCTIONS (Mail)
P.O. Box 193
Sheboygan, WI 53082

DEBBIE & MARTY KRIM'S NEW
ENGLAND AUCTION GALLERY
(Mail)
Box 2273-T
West Peabody, MA 01960
(508) 535-3140
FAX: (508) 535-7522

GUERNSEY'S
108 East 73rd Street
New York, NY 10021
(212) 794-2280

HAKE'S AMERICANA &
COLLECTIBLES
P.O. Box 1444N
York, PA 17405
(717) 848-1333
Sample catalog $3.00

HENRY KURTZ, LTD.
163 Amsterdam Ave. Suite 136
New York, NY 10023
(212) 642-5904
FAX: 212-874-6018

MAPES AUCTIONEERS &
APPRAISERS
1600 Vestal Parkway West
Vestal, NY 13850
(607) 754-9193

TED MAURER
1003 Brookwood Dr.
Pottstown, PA 19646
(215) 323-1573 or 367-5024

MID-HUDSON AUCTION
GALLERIES
One Idlewild Avenue
Croton-On-Hudson, NY 12520

NOEL BARRETT ANTIQUES &
AUCTIONS
P.O. Box 300
Carversville, PA 18913

PHILIPS NEW YORK
406 E. 79th St.
New York, NY 10021

LLOYD W. RALSTON
173 Post Road
Fairfield, CT 06430
(203) 255-1233

RICHARD OPFER
AUCTIONEERING, INC.
1919 Greenspring Drive
Timonium, MD 21093

SMITH HOUSE (mail)
P.O. Box 336
Eliot, ME 03903
(207) 439-4614

SOTHEBY'S
1334 York Avenue
New York, NY 10021
(212) 606-7000

TOYSENSATIONS (Barry Goodman)
P.O. Box 218
Woodbury, NY 11797
(516) 338-2701

COLLECTORS AND DEALERS

It is suggested that, when writing to any of the following, you enclose a stamped, self-addressed envelope.

STEVE BALKIN
Burlington Antique Toys
1082 Madison Avenue
New York, NY 10028
Toy soldiers including Warren

BILL BERTOIA
1881 South Spring Road
Vineland, NJ 08360
(609) 692-1881
Mechanical banks, antique toys

CHARLES W. BEST
11523 Pine Valley Drive
Franktown, CO 80116
Old toy pistols, etc.

BOB LOWE'S TOONERVILLE
JUNCTION
7 E. Church Street
Bethlehem, PA 18018
(215) 691-6736
Classic American and European Toys

BUDDY K TOYS
Buddy L Toys, etc.
RD 9 Box 322
Bingen Road
Bethlehem, PA 18015

JIM BUSKIRK
c/o TGCA
3009 Oleander Avenue
San Marcos, CA 92069
Spring-Air BB guns, cast iron pistols

BLYSTONE'S
2132 Delaware Ave.
Pittsburg, PA 15218
(412) 371-3511
FAX (412) 244-8028
Specialists in books on toys

RAY BRANDES
2964 Brookshire Way
Duluth, GA, 30136
(404) 476-8259
Big Bang cannons collector/dealer

MARY BRETT
3607 Nuttree Woods Drive
Midlothian, VA 23112
(804) 744-9170
Plastic doll furniture, tin dollhouses

LARRY BRUCH
P.O. Box 121
Mountaintop, PA 18707
(717) 474-9202
Old toys wanted & for sale

JIM & PATSY CARLSON
7939 Caberfae Trail
Clarkston, MI 48348-3708
Schoenhut collectors

ROD CARNAHAN
541 El Paso
Jacksonville, TX 75766
Buy, sell, trade old toys

CALVIN L. CHAUSSEE
Box 22
Calhan, CO 80808
(719) 347-2000
FAX: 719-347-2780
Antique toy buyer - any quantity

CLASSIC TOYS
69 Thompson St.
New York, NY 10012
New and old toys; military, vehicles, zoo, etc.

KENT M. COMSTOCK
532 Pleasant Street
Ashland, OH 44805
(419) 289-3308
Motorcycles, all types

CONTINENTAL HOBBY HOUSE
P.O. Box 193
Sheboygan, WI 53082
Toys and trains, regular catalogs

DARROW'S FUN ANTIQUES
309 E. 61st Street
New York, NY 10021
(212) 838-0730
Old toys of all types

ROBERT A. DECENZO
P.O. Box 2266
Framingham, MA 01701
Marbles, tin wind-ups, paper litho, games, trains

DUTKINS' COLLECTABLES
1019 W. Route 70
Cherry Hill, NJ 08002
(609) 428-9559
Tin toys, soldiers, etc.

ECCLES BROTHERS
R.R. 1, Box 253-D
Burlington, IA 52601
Toy soldiers, comic figures and vehicles from original molds, catalog $3.00

PERRY R. EICHOR
703 North Almond Dr.
Simpsonville, SC 29681
Aircraft toys and literature

EXCALIBUR HOBBIES LTD
63 Exchange Street
Malden, MA 02148-5523
(617) 322-2959
Toy soldiers, all types

JOE & SHARON FREED
6209 Sandy Forks Rd.
Raleigh, NC 27615
Vehicles

JOE FREEMAN - TIN TOY WORKS
1313 North 15th Street
Allentown, PA 18102
(610) 439-8268
FAX: (610) 439-1288
Repairs, parts made for tin toys

DANNY FUCHS
209-80 18th Avenue
Bayside, NY 11360
Superman toys, games, etc.

RAY FUNK
826 East 8th St.
Upland, CA 91786
Toys, bicycles

JOHN GIBSON
P.O. Box 40054
Washington, DC 20016
(301) 527-0076
Tootsietoy restoration, parts & services

BARRY GOODMAN
P.O. Box 218
Woodbury, NY 11797
(516) 338-2701
GI Joes, Barbies, robots, PEZ, all 1950s-60s character toys

TERRY GRAHAM
3083 Crescent Street
Long Island City, NY 11102
(718) 956-3382
Dealer in toy guns

TONY AND JACKI GRECCO
P.O. Box 3490
Poughkeepsie, NY 12603
(914) 462-8829
Toy soldiers and related items

A. (GUS) HANSEN
4645 Lilac Avenue
Glenview, IL 60025
Mignot, Dimestore, Britains, etc.

RAY HARADIN
Toys of Yesteryear
1039 Lakemont Drive
Pittsburgh, PA 15243-1817
(800) 349-8009 (Call for detailed catalog)
Mechanical banks, toy soldiers

JIM HARMON
634 S. Orchard Dr.
Burbank, CA 91506
Radio premiums and tapes, comic books and strips

W.S. (BILL) HARRISON III
Marion Designs
594 Front Street
Marion, MA 02738
Erector sets, buy and sell

BILL HELLIE
All American Toy Company
P.O. Box 4266
Salem, OR 97302
American Toy Company parts and limited editions; buy sell, restore antique toys

JEFFREY L. HUBBARD
1770 4th Street South
Naples, FL 33940-7502
Doepke, Nylint collector

DON HULTZMAN
5026 Sleepy Hollow Road
Medina, OH 44256
(330) 225-2668
Tin wind-ups and battery-operated toys, also repairs, restorations

INSURANCE FOR COLLECTIBLE TOYS
Debbie Riley
Reeves & Melvin
P.O. Box 229
Millville, NJ 08332
(800) 298-4318

BRAD KREWSON
588 Lindford Drive
Bay Village, OH 44140
Beany & Cecil toys

BILL LANGO
127 74th Street
North Bergen, NJ 07047
Barclay vehicles, animals and soldiers from original and new molds; send for flyer

RICHARD LEACH
26146 Redfield Rd.
Edwardsburg, MI 49112
Old steam engine toys, literature

STEVE LEONARD
Box 127T
Albertson, LI, NY 11507
(516)742-0979
Antique mechanical toys, etc.

DAVID M. LEOPARD
2507 Feather Run Trail
West Columbia, SC 29169-4915
Old toy cars and trucks

CARL LOBEL
Box 74A
Warren, VT 05674
(802) 496-4025
Toys of all eras

LONDON BRIDGE COLLECTOR'S TOYS
East Penn Plaza
1325 Chestnut Street
Emmaus, PA 18049
(215) 967-6887
Britains soldiers, etc. and Britains replacement parts

RICHARD MacNARY
4727 Alpine Drive
Lilburn, GA 30247
Marx trains, Coca-Cola vehicles, wood, cardboard, paper toys, soldiers

MARBLE COLLECTORS SOCIETY OF AMERICA
P.O. Box 222
Trumble, CT 06611

JOHN D. (JACK) MATTHEWS
13 Bufflehead Dr.
Kiawah Island, SC 29455
World War II toys, etc.

FRED MAXWELL
4722 No. 33 Street
Arlington, VA 22207
Collector/researcher; slush mold cars, planes, novelties, literature, toys

MARK McMANUS
120 Main Street
Boonville, NY 13309
(315) 942-2185
FAX: (315) 942-5579
Matchbox, PEZ, GI Joe, Tonka, etc.

K. WARREN MITCHELL
1008 Forward Pass
Pataskala, OH 43062
Soldiers of all types, regular lists at no charge

JOHN MURRAY
Box 29
Eden, NY 14057
Fisher-Price

THOMAS G. NEFOS
779 East Merritt Island Csway
Merritt Island, FL 32952-3516
Investment quality transportation toys

NEW ERA TOYS
P.O. Box 10
Lambertville, NJ 08530
(609) 397-2113
Restorations service for pressed steel toy, pedal cars

BARBARA & JONATHAN NEWMAN
The Paper Soldier
8 McIntosh Lane
Clifton Park, NY 12065
Paper toys, old and new

TIM OEI - OEI ENTERPRISES, LTD.
241 Rowayton Ave.
Rowayton, CT 06853-1227
(203) 866-2470
Buys, sells, trades, restores old toys

DON PIELIN
1009 Kenilworth
Wheeling, IL 60090
Toy soldiers

PLYMOUTH ROCK TOY CO.
P.O. Box 1202
Plymouth, MA 02362
(508) 746-2842 or (508) 830-1180
FAX: (508) 830-0364
Toy pistols, etc., all eras

EDWARD K. POOLE
926 Terrace Mtn. Drive
Austin, TX 78746
Toy soldiers, 1/36 scale ID vehicles and
old wooden military vehicle kits

HARVEY K. RAINESS
Rustic Ridge - N13
289 Mount Hope Avenue
Dover, NJ 07801
(201) 366-4677
Dealer in vehicles, tin, soldiers

SALUNGA (Don Eckel)
P.O. Box 369
Talmage, PA 17580
(717) 656-4857
Cast-iron parts for toys

PHIL SAVINO
Rt. 2, Box 76
Micanopy, FL 32667
Mail auctions in various toy categories -
send SASE

SECOND CHILDHOOD
283 Bleecker Street
New York, NY
Antique toys

RONALD L. SIMKOFF
5171 Mayfield Rd.
Lyndhurst, OH 44124
(216) 461-2660
Holgate toys

SCOTT SMILES
848 S. Atlantic Dr., E.
Lantana, FL 33462
Tin wind-ups, etc.

BOB SMITH
62 West Ave.
Fairport, NY 14450
(716) 377-8394
Sells toys of all types, Toy Show

RON SMITH
33005 Arlesford
Solon, OH 44139
(216) 248-7006
Tin plate cars and planes, plastic
promotional cars

MARK SUOZZI
Box 102
Ashfield, MA 01330
(413) 628-3241
Antique penny banks & toys

FRED THOMPSON
Smith-Miller Inc.
P.O. Box 139
Canoga Park, CA 91305
New designs of Smitty vehicles

DAVID WELCH
P.O. Box 714
Murphysboro, IL 62966
(618) 687-2282
PEZ, Cereal boxes, model kits, TV,
Disney, premiums

RANDY WELCH
Raven' Tiques
27965 Peach Orchard Drive
Easton, MD 21601
(410) 822-5441
Ramp walkers, tin wind-ups, and
sparklers

CHARLES FRANCIS WILDING
Secretary, Capitol Miniature Auto
Collectors Club
10207 Greenacres Dr.
Silver Springs, MD 20903

FRED & MARGARET WILHELM
W & F Collectibles
Box 2054
Leucadia, CA 92024
Disney, Popeye, comic, Barclay, Manoil
soldiers

FERDINAND ZEGEL
P.O. Box 589
Ft. Belvoir, VA 22060
Antique toys, postwar, Corgi, Dinky

BIBLIOGRAPHY
& RECOMMENDED READING

A.C. Gilbert Heritage Society Newsletter. Quarterly. $6 per year; trial issue $1.50. Marion Designs, 594 Front St., Marion, MA 02738.

Antique Toy World. Monthly. $39.95 per year. Dale Kelley, P.O. Box 34509, Chicago, IL 60634.

Arcade Toys by Al Aune. 1990. Robert F. Mannella, 4441 Shari Ann Lane, Brooklyn Park, MN 55443.

The Barclay Catalog Book. Early Barclay catalogs, drawings, photos, etc. Richard O'Brien. (Sold out.)

Big Bang Cannons by Raymond V. Brandes. Ray-Vin Publishing, 2964-R Brookshire Way, Duluth, GA 30136.

Cast Iron Toy Guns and Capshooter by Samuel H. Logan and Charles W. Best. Heavily illustrated book. $55. Sam Logan, 1200 Harvard Drive, Davis, CA 95616

Collecting PEZ by David Welch. Price guide and reference book. $43.95 in U.S., 350 pages. P.O. Box 714, Murphysboro, IL 62966. (618) 687-2282, FAX (618) 684-2243.

Die Cast & Tin Toy Report. Monthly. $36 per year. Shoreline Publishing, PO Box 301, Easton, CT 06612.

Fisher-Price 1931-1963. 1991 edition. $24.95. Books Americana, 700 East State Street, Iola, WI 54990.

Marbles: Price and Identification Guide by Robert Black. $23. P.O. Box 222, Trumbull, CT 06611.

National Toy Connection. Vehicles. Bimonthly. $22.95 per year. Suite 2346, 779 East Merritt Island Csway, Merritt Island, FL 32952-3516.

Old Toy Soldier Newsletter. Bimonthly. $25 per year. Steve Sommers, 209 North Lombard, Oak Park, IL 60302.

Pictorial Guide to Weeden Steam Toys. $10. Richard B. Leach, 26146 Redfield Road, Edwardsburg, MI 49112.

Plastic Figure & Playset Collector. Bimonthly. $21 per year. Specialty Publishing Company, P.O. Box 1355, LaCrosse, WI 54602-1355.

Plastic Toys by Bill Hanlon. $72.90. All-color, 288 pages. Schiffer Publishing, 77 Lower Valley Road, Atglen, PA 19310.

Radio Mystery and Adventure by Jim Harmon. McFarland & Company, Inc., Jefferson, North Carolina & London.

Rubber Toy Vehicles by Dave Leopard. $26.95. Dave Leopard, 2507 Feather Run Trail, West Columbia, SC 29169-4915.

The Second Catalog Book. Reprints of catalogs by Manoil, Barclay, Warren, All-Nu, Authenticast, Beton, Grey Iron. $16. Richard O'Brien, 705 Greene Street, Beaufort, SC 29902.

The Story of American Toys by Richard O'Brien. 1990. $24.95. Abbeville Press.

Toy Shop. Newspaper of toy ads and articles. Biweekly. Free copy on one-time basis. Krause Publications - Sample Copy Department, 700 E. State Street, Iola, WI 54990.

Toy Gun Collectors of America Newsletter. 16-page quarterly. $15 per year. Jim Buskirk, 3009 Oleander Avenue, San Marcos, CA 92069.

The Toy Road. Old metal vehicles. Monthly. $25 per year. John Bartell, W4312 Cty. Highway C, Neillsville, WI 54456.

Toy Soldier Review. $12 for four issues. Vintage Castings Inc., 127-74th Street, North Bergen, NJ 07047.

U.S. Toy Collector. Vehicles only. Monthly. $21 per year. 231 S. Grove St., Missoula, MT 59801.

A COLLECTOR'S DREAM —
ACCURATE PRICING AT A GREAT PRICE!

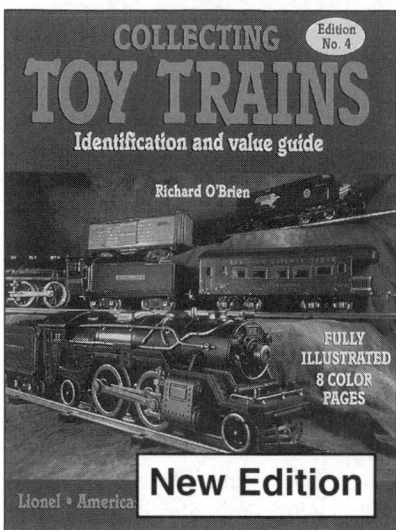

Collecting Toy Trains,

4th edition, puts you on track for accurate identification and pricing of Lionel, Marx, American Flyer, Ives, Buddy L and others. Top train collectors help author Richard O'Brien price engines, cars, accessories. New photos, listings. 8-1/2x11 SC • 432p • fully illustrated • 8p color section • **CTT4 $24.95**

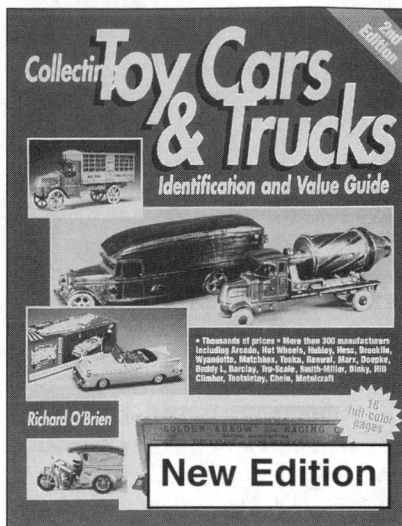

Collecting Toy Cars and Trucks

Identification and Value Guide, 2nd Edition
by Richard O'Brien This new edition surpasses the previous guide in every way. Over 600 pages of mean machines including a color section twice as big and 50 additional manufacturers for a total of 300. 8-1/2x11 SC • 632 pages • 3,400 b&w photos • 60 color photos • **TCT2 $27.95 Avail. 9/97**

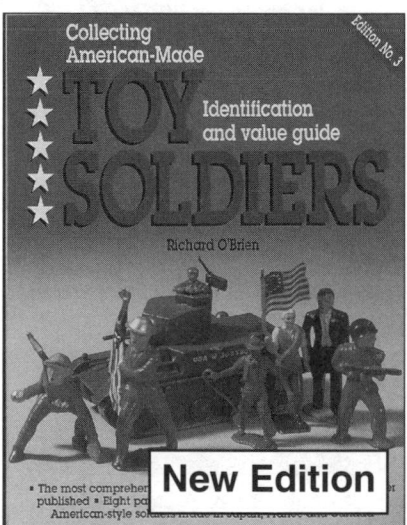

Collecting American-Made Toy Soldiers,

3rd edition, takes aim at pricing toy soldiers from a century of American manufacturing. Plus related soldiers from France, Japan, and Canada. By Richard O'Brien. 8-1/2x11 SC • 720p • fully illustrated • 8p color section • **SOLD3 $32.95**

Collecting Foreign-Made Toy Soldiers

Identification and Value Guide
by Richard O'Brien Enlist this first-ever identification and value guide on foreign toy soldiers and declare war on pricing. Take the offensive with information on more than 50 manufacturers from 12 countries, over 2,000 photos and nearly 8,000 individual prices. A 16-page full-color section identifies the most collectible allies and enemies. 8-1/2x11 SC • 496p • 2,500 photos • 16p color section • **FMTS $32.95**

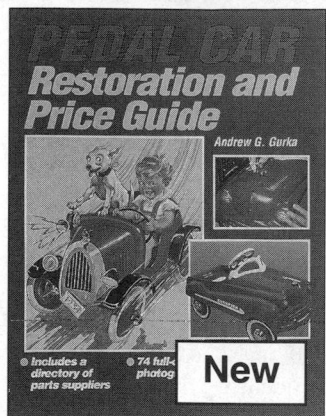